ILLINOIS CRIMINAL LAW

Student Edition

Third Edition

John F. Decker

LEXIS Publishing™

LEXIS°-NEXIS° • MARTINDALE-HUBBELL°
MATTHEW BENDER° • MICHIE°- SHEPARD'S°

QUESTIONS ABOUT THIS PUBLICATION?

For questions about the **Editorial Content** appearing in this volume or reprint permission, please call:

Judith Anderson, J.D......................................(800) 252-9257 (ext. 2244)
Jeanine Schupbach, J.D.................................(800) 252-9257 (ext. 2539)
Outside the United States and Canada please call....................(212) 448-2000

For assistance with replacement pages, shipments, billing or other customer service matters, please call:

Customer Services Department at......................................(800) 833-9844
Outside the United States and Canada, please call...................(518) 487-3000
Fax number..(518) 487-3584

For information on other Matthew Bender publications, please call
Your account manager or..(800) 223-1940
Outside the United States and Canada, please call...................(518) 487-3000

Library of Congress Catalog Card Number: 00-110691
ISBN 0-820-55018-3

Editorial Offices
2 Park Avenue, New York, NY 10016-5675 (212) 448-2000
201 Mission St., San Francisco, CA 94105-1831 (415) 908-3200
www.lexis.com

VOLUME 1

PART I

THE GENERAL PART

Chapter 1

INTRODUCTION

Chapter 2

CRIMINAL ACT AND MENTAL STATE

Chapter 3

ACCOUNTABILITY FOR THE CRIMINALITY OF OTHERS

Chapter 4

CONSPIRACY

Chapter 5

ATTEMPT AND SOLICITATION

PART 2

THE SPECIAL PART CRIMES

Chapter 6

HOMICIDE

Chapter 7

KIDNAPPING AND RELATED OFFENSES

Chapter 8

SEX OFFENSES

Chapter 9

ASSAULT, BATTERY, AND RELATED OFFENSES

Chapter 10

ELECTRONIC EAVESDROPPING

Chapter 11

THEFT AND RELATED OFFENSES

VOLUME 2

Chapter 12

ROBBERY, ARMED ROBBERY AND RELATED OFFENSES

Chapter 13

BURGLARY, ARSON, AND OTHER OFFENSES
AGAINST PROPERTY

Chapter 14

OFFENSES AFFECTING GOVERNMENTAL FUNCTIONS

Chapter 15

OFFENSES AFFECTING THE PUBLIC HEALTH, SAFETY, AND DECENCY

Chapter 16

DRUG CONTROL LAWS

PART 3

AFFIRMATIVE DEFENSES

Chapter 17

DEFENSE OF PERSON AND PROPERTY

Chapter 18

DEFENSES: LACK OF CRIMINAL RESPONSIBILITY DUE TO INSANITY, INTOXICATION, AND INFANCY

Chapter 19

DEFENSES: MISTAKE, COMPULSION, NECESSITY, ENTRAPMENT, PUBLIC AUTHORITY, AND OTHER JUSTIFICATIONS OR EXCUSES

PART I

THE GENERAL PART

The first part of this book, chapters 1 through 5, represent the general part of the essentials of the Illinois criminal code. This general part goes beyond particular offenses and examines basic considerations that cut across all the crimes discussed later in part 2. Chapter 1 (Introduction) examines the development of the current penal proscriptions, known as the Criminal Code of 1961, the scope of the present criminal laws of Illinois, the purposes of the state's penal enactments, and jurisdictional and venue concerns. In addition, there is set out in this first chapter certain classifications of offenses, related definitions, and an analysis of lesser included offense and same physical act doctrine concerns.

In chapter 2 (Criminal Act and Mental State), there appears an examination of the basic elements of criminal liability. There is an investigation of the requisite acts or omissions to act necessary to all crimes. In this connection, crimes of possession are studied. Thereafter, this chapter probes into the various mental state requirements — intent, knowledge, recklessness, and negligence — and concludes with a discussion of absolute liability strictures, which are crimes that dispense with proof of a mental state.

Chapter 3 (Accountability for the Criminality of Others) reviews the concept of accomplice liability, which explores how the criminality of one person (or more) can be imputed to another person (or persons). In addition, the unique problem of corporate criminality, where a corporate entity is held accountable for the acts of its agents, is analyzed.

The final two chapters of this general part, chapter 4 (Conspiracy) and chapter 5 (Attempt and Solicitation), examine the so-called inchoate crimes. Herein, one sees how a criminal actor can be punished for incomplete or unsuccessful criminal efforts engaged in alone or, possibly, in combination with others.

1

CHAPTER 1

INTRODUCTION

§ 1.01. Historical Background.

Prior to 1961, all Illinois criminal prohibitions were scattered throughout 148 chapters of the Illinois statutes, with various inconsistencies in penalties, overlapping provisions, and gaps of needed coverage.[1] Illinois did not have the organized, unified code that exists today.[2] In 1954, at the urging of the Supreme Court of Illinois and the governor of the state, the Illinois State Bar Association and the Chicago Bar Association established a joint committee to revise the Illinois Criminal Code.[3] Thereafter, the joint committee attempted to develop a sys-

---

[1] Joint Committee to Revise the Illinois Criminal Code, *Committee Forward to Tentative Final Draft of the Proposed Illinois Revised Criminal Code of 1961*, ILL. ANN. STAT. ch. 38, paras. 1-1 through 1-8, at xx (Smith-Hurd 1989).

[2] Joint Committee to Revise the Illinois Criminal Code, *Committee Forward to Tentative Final Draft of the Proposed Illinois Revised Criminal Code of 1961*, ILL. ANN. STAT. ch. 38, paras. 1-1 through 1-8, at xix (Smith-Hurd 1989).

[3] Joint Committee to Revise the Illinois Criminal Code, *Committee Forward to Tentative Final Draft of the Proposed Illinois Revised Criminal Code of 1961*, ILL. ANN. STAT. ch. 38, paras. 1-1 through 1-8, at xix (Smith-Hurd 1989).

tematic and unified code of substantive crimes, but did not include criminal procedure considerations.[4] The proposed code drafted by the joint committee was
completed in 1960 and was approved by the Illinois General Assembly and the
governor in 1961 taking effect on January 1, 1962.[5] Notwithstanding various
amendments[6] and additions[7] over the years, this enactment is known officially as
the Criminal Code of 1961.[8]

In 1961, the Criminal Code, which previously appeared in chapter 38 of the
Illinois Revised Statutes, initially represented the entire embodiment of the various criminal prohibitions in the state of Illinois. Subsequently, there occurred
significant developments of important criminal prescriptions *outside* the parameters of the criminal code. Most noteworthy was the creation of the Cannabis
Control Act[9] and the Controlled Substances Act[10] in Chapter 56½ of the Illinois
Revised Statutes, a chapter that encompassed food and drug regulations. Such
legislative changes in criminal law outside the Criminal Code were criticized by
some.[11] It was argued that these changes not only undermined the conceptual
integrity of maintaining a unified enactment covering all aspects of criminal
strictures within the state, but they also created confusion for courts who were
confronted with inconsistent measures reflected in the different chapters.[12]

---

[4] Joint Committee to Revise the Illinois Criminal Code, *Committee Forward to Tentative Final Draft of the Proposed Illinois Revised Criminal Code of 1961*, ILL. ANN. STAT. ch. 38, paras. 1-1 through 1-8, at xxi (Smith-Hurd 1989).

[5] Joint Committee to Revise the Illinois Criminal Code, *Committee Forward to Tentative Final Draft of the Proposed Illinois Code of Criminal Procedure*, ILL. ANN. STAT. ch. 38, paras. 1-1 through 1-8, at xxv (Smith-Hurd 1989). After completing the draft of the criminal code, the same joint committee turned its attention to developing a unified code of criminal procedure, which ultimately became part of the Illinois statutes on January 1, 1964. The current Code of Criminal Procedure appears at 725 ILCS 5/100-1 *et seq.* (1999).

[6] *See, e.g.,* P.A. 84-897 (1985) (amendment of "deceptive practices" statute to include theft from cash dispensing machines which took affect in 1985). *See also* 720 ILCS 5/17-1 (1999).

[7] *See, e.g.,* P.A. 90-787 (1998) ("residential arson" added to code in 1998). *See also* 720 ILCS 5/20-1.2 (1999).

[8] 720 ILCS 5/1-1 (1999).

[9] 720 ILCS 550/1 through 550/19 (1999) (formerly ILL. REV. STAT. ch. 56½, paras. 701 through 719 (1991)).

[10] 720 ILCS 570/100 through 570/602 (1999) (formerly ILL. REV. STAT. ch. 56½, paras. 1100 through 1602 (1991)).

[11] *See* Harry C. Fins, *Code of Criminal Law And Procedure For Illinois*, 71 ILL. B.J. 294 (1983). *See also* Harry C. Fins, *After 112 Years, Structural Revision of Illinois' Official Statutes Is Needed — The Time to Act Is Now!*, 75 ILL. B.J. 668 (1987).

[12] *See, e.g.,* People v. Taylor, 18 Ill. App. 3d 480, 481, 309 N.E.2d 595, 596 (4th Dist. 1974) (calculated cannabis conspiracy enactment in section 709 of chapter 56½ preempts and removes from chapter 38 any possible cannabis related conspiracy); *compare* People v. Caryl, 54 Ill. App. 3d 537, 539, 369 N.E.2d 926, 927 (2d Dist. 1977) (since a calculated cannabis conspiracy under section 709 of chapter 56½ cannot apply to, for example, a conspiracy to deliver less than 30 grams of cannabis, a chapter 38 conspiracy prosecution is possible).

In 1989, the Illinois General Assembly directed the Illinois Legislative Reference Bureau to submit a plan for a more comprehensive and systematic codification of the entire Illinois statutory code.[13] The last official codification of all Illinois statutes created the Illinois Revised Statutes of 1874.[14] The Illinois Complied Statutes (ILCS) became the new codification effective January 1, 1993.[15] The new codification in ILCS did not change the substance of the Revised Statutes, but merely reorganized the placement of, and renumbered the statutes.

What was previously the Criminal Code of 1961 found in chapter 38 of the Revised Statutes, consisting of the majority of the criminal proscriptions, is now included in Act 5 of chapter 720 of ILCS.[16] The drug proscriptions previously found in Chapter 56½ of the Revised Statutes are now also found in chapter 720 in a classification referred to as "offenses against the public."[17] Several other criminal proscriptions that were previously scatted throughout Illinois Revised Statutes are now also found in Chapter 720 under the classifications of either "offenses against persons," "offenses against property," or "offenses against the public."[18] Now, therefore, the Illinois criminal code once again has its proscriptions in one chapter.

§ 1.02. Scope of Illinois Criminal Law.

Any effort toward explaining the general scope of the criminal law in Illinois is fraught with difficulties. One cannot assert that the criminal prohibitions in Illinois are a reflection of the point of view that invariably there must be a close parallel between illicit behavior and conduct that is generally perceived to be immoral.[19] While this may have been the case at common law,[20] it is not true in Illinois.[21] First, the Criminal Code of Illinois clearly reflects that no behavior is

---

[13] P.A. 86-523.

[14] Timothy L. Bertschy and Robert John Kane, *The New Illinois Compiled Statutes — An Overdue Recodification of Illinois Statutory Law*, 80 ILL. B.J. 630 (1992).

[15] P.A. 87-1005.

[16] *See* 720 ILCS 5/1-1 *et seq.* (1999).

[17] *See, e.g.,* 720 ILCS 550/1 *et seq.* (1999) (Cannabis Control Act).

[18] *See, e.g.,* 720 ILCS 130/0.01 (1999) (Neglected Children Offense Act, formerly ILL. REV. STAT. ch. 23, para. 2359.9 (1991)); 720 ILCS 205/0.01 (1999) (Aircraft Crash Parts Act, formerly ch. 15½ , para. 200 (1991)); 720 ILCS 585/0.1 *et seq.* (1999) (Illinois Dangerous Animals Act, formerly ILL. REV. STAT. ch. 8, para. 240 (1991)).

[19] *See* PATRICK DEVLIN, THE ENFORCEMENT OF MORALS 1-25 (1965) (advocating that criminal law be reflective of moral imperatives).

[20] WILLIAM L. CLARK & WILLIAM L. MARSHALL, A TREATISE ON THE LAW OF CRIMES 8 (7th ed. M. Barnes 1967) ("Criminal law remains a static blend and blur of religious concepts of sin and legal notions of liability").

[21] Such behavior as lying, overcharging for goods and services, and lack of charity or patriotism is clearly not prohibited. *See* LOUIS SCHWARTZ, THE PROPOSED CRIMINAL CODE, COMPARISON OF S.

illegal in the state unless it has been explicitly codified as illegal in the Criminal Code.[22] In this connection, the general provision of the Illinois Code states: "No conduct constitutes an offense unless it is described as an offense in this Code or in another statute of this State."[23] Second, and more important, the Illinois legislature has not defined as illegal the broad range of conduct that was outlawed at common law. To illustrate, one finds no prohibition against extramarital fornication between consenting adults unless the behavior is "open and notorious,"[24] and a perusal of the code reveals no per se prohibition against homosexual conduct between consenting adults. Thus, the net effect of the Illinois legislation that limits the applicability of common law strictures in Illinois, along with the concomitant failure of the legislature to codify all common law crimes, is a rejection of the notion that the criminal code must be a reflection, to the fullest extent possible, of the jurisdiction's conventional morality.[25]

On the other hand, it is apparent that the criminal code is not based on the philosophy that a criminal code should reflect only behavior that is actually or potentially injurious to others.[26] For example, notwithstanding the fact that it may be impossible to explain how acts of prostitution or acts of patronizing prostitutes harm those who engage in such acts,[27] the code outlaws this behavior.[28] Similarly, notwithstanding significant evidence that pornographic materials are not injurious to the consumers specifically or to the public safety generally,[29] proscriptions against dissemination of obscene materials appear in the

---

1 AND THE RECOMMENDATIONS OF FEDERAL CRIMINAL LAWS 10 (Feb. 26, 1973) (statement that any criminal code will, of necessity, fall short of expressing jurisdiction's morality).

[22] 720 ILCS 5/1-3 (1999).

[23] 720 ILCS 5/1-3 (1999).

[24] 720 ILCS 5/11-8(a) (1999).

[25] This is not to say, however, that there is no correlation between the Illinois criminal law and morality concerns. Prohibitions against illicit drug usage might be viewed as one example. *See generally* TROY DUSTER, THE LEGISLATION OF MORALITY: LAW, DRUGS, AND MORAL JUDGMENT (1970).

[26] The philosopher John Stuart Mill expressed this point of view in his famous treatise "On Liberty."

> [T]he only purpose for which power can be rightfully exercised over any member of a civilized community, against his will, is to prevent harm to others. His own good, either physical or moral, is not a sufficient warrant. He cannot rightfully be compelled to do or forbear because it will make him happier, because in the opinion of others, to do so would be wise, or even right.

JOHN STUART MILL, UTILITARIANISM, ON LIBERTY, ESSAY ON BENTHAM 135 (Warnock ed. 1962). A variation of this theme is advanced by other authors, most notably H.L.A. HART. *See* H.L.A. HART, THE CONCEPT OF LAW 151-80 (1961); H.L.A. HART, LAW, LIBERTY, AND MORALITY 1-52 (1963).

[27] *See* JOHN F. DECKER, PROSTITUTION: REGULATION AND CONTROL 273-362 (1979).

[28] 720 ILCS 5/11-14 (1999) (prostitution); 720 ILCS 5/11-18 (1999) (patronizing a prostitute).

[29] THE REPORT OF THE COMMISSION ON OBSCENITY AND PORNOGRAPHY 23-27 (1970).

code.[30] On the other hand, despite the overwhelming evidence about the dangers associated with tobacco use,[31] no such proscriptions appear in the code.

Some authorities simply define criminal law as "any social harm defined and made punishable by law."[32] This seems to be a simplistic definition when considered in the context of the Illinois code, for this definition assumes that all proscribed conduct involves "social harm." In a state that funds its educational system by sponsoring lotteries and tolerates pari-mutuel betting, both of which are widely advertised[33] and exempted from the criminal code,[34] it is difficult to identify the social harm that revolves around participating in a private poker game with monetary stakes, which is considered criminal.[35] This is not to say that the Illinois legislature, in its ultimate wisdom, does not *perceive* the existence of social harm with the poker game, while simultaneously legalizing other games of chance that it presumably does not associate with social harm. Thus, in attempting to define Illinois criminal law, it may help to refer to the legislature's perception in this regard. Because of the conceptual difficulties associated with offering a useful definition of Illinois criminal law, probably the best that can be said is that *Illinois criminal law is law that defines as illegal and makes punishable by criminal sanctions behavior that involves a perceived social harm.*[36] In other words, Illinois criminal law can be best understood by referring, though implicitly, to the legislature's role; behavior only becomes criminal in Illinois when it is defined as such by the law-making body of the state.[37]

With respect to the general scope of criminal law in Illinois, one would be remiss if two important bases behind the code were overlooked: (1) the common

---

[30] 720 ILCS 5/11-20(a) (1999).

[31] U.S. DEPARTMENT OF HEALTH AND HUMAN SERVICES, SMOKING AND HEALTH IN THE AMERICAS: A 1992 REPORT OF THE SURGEON GENERAL, IN COLLABORATION WITH THE PAN AMERICAN HEALTH ORGANIZATION i, 86 (1992). Smoking tobacco alone has been determined to cause coronary heart disease, cerebrovascular disease, chronic obstructive coronary disease, and cancers of the lung, lip, oral cavity, pharynx, larynx, esophagus, pancreas, bladder and kidneys having caused an estimated 526,000 deaths annually during the 1980's. *Id.*

[32] ROLLIN M. PERKINS & RONALD N. BOYCE, CRIMINAL LAW AND PROCEDURE 12 (3d ed. 1982).

[33] For instance, the Illinois lottery is advertised on television, radio and billboards by sponsors of this state enterprise.

[34] 720 ILCS 5/28-1(b)(3), (6) (1999).

[35] 720 ILCS 5/28-1(a) (1999) (general prohibition against gambling).

[36] This definition is similar to that offered by LaFave and Scott: "The substantive criminal law is that law which, for the purpose of preventing harm to society, declares what conduct is criminal, and prescribes punishment to be imposed for such conduct." WAYNE LAFAVE & AUSTIN SCOTT, CRIMINAL LAW § 1.2 (2d ed. 1986).

[37] References to the "legislature's role" in lawmaking obviously refers to the Illinois General Assembly as the primary rulemaker. Nonetheless, one should not overlook the important role of the governor in the Illinois legislative process nor that of the various Illinois courts, which are responsible for offering judicial interpretations regarding criminal prohibitions and for reviewing the proper reach of the criminal law in view of possible legislative excesses.

law usage of terms appearing therein and (2) the Model Penal Code. First, even though the common law prohibitions not codified in the Criminal Code of 1961 were abolished, the various common law interpretations given to certain terms contained within the Illinois code cannot be safely ignored. As the revision committee responsible for drafting the code points out: "[T]he supersession of all common law definitions of particular offenses does not mean that the large mass of interpretative rules developed under the common law is superseded; these rules are a highly valuable part of our criminal law, and their effective replacement by statutory law would be exceedingly difficult."[38]

The significance of this proposition is reflected in the important case of *People v. Greer*.[39] In this case, the Illinois Supreme Court considered whether the defendant's unjustified killing of a woman who was eight and one-half months pregnant, as well as her fetus, would involve one count of murder or two. The state contended that the defendant was guilty not only of a count of murder arising from the death of the pregnant woman but also of a second count of murder arising from the death of the viable fetus.[40] The second count would make the defendant eligible for the death penalty.[41] The question revolved around what was meant by the language of the 1977 version of the Illinois murder statute that refers to the unjustified killing of "an individual."[42] Noting this was a question of first impression in Illinois,[43] the court felt compelled to turn to the common law to determine whether an unborn fetus is an "individual" within the meaning of the homicide statute.[44] After noting that the killing of a fetus was not murder at common law unless the child was born alive and then expired as a result of

---

[38] ILL. ANN. STAT. ch. 38, para. 1-3 (Smith-Hurd 1989), 1961 Committee Comments, at 16.

[39] 79 Ill. 2d 103, 402 N.E.2d 203 (1980).

[40] People v. Greer, 79 Ill. 2d 103, 111-12, 402 N.E.2d 203, 206 (1980).

[41] ILL. REV. STAT. ch. 38, para. 9-1(b)(3) (1977) ("A defendant who at the time of the commission of the offense . . . has been found guilty of murder may be sentenced to death if . . . the defendant has been convicted of killing two or more individuals. . . .").

[42] ILL. REV. STAT. ch. 38, para. 9-1(a) (1977):
A person who kills an individual without lawful justification commits murder if, in performing the acts which cause the death:

> (1) He either intends to kill or do great bodily harm to that individual or another, or knows that such acts will cause death to that individual or another; or
> (2) He knows that such acts create a strong probability of death or great bodily harm to that individual or another; or
> (3) He is attempting or committing a forcible felony other than voluntary manslaughter.

Note, however, that the current statute defines murder as killing without lawful justification while "attempting or committing a forcible felony other than *second degree murder* (emphasis added)." 720 ILCS 5/9-1(a) (1999). *See* ch. 6 for a discussion of homicide.

[43] People v. Greer, 79 Ill. 2d 103, 110, 402 N.E.2d 203, 206 (1980).

[44] People v. Greer, 79 Ill. 2d 103, 111, 402 N.E.2d 203, 207 (1980).

language

the injuries previously sustained,[45] the court concluded that the killing of the unborn fetus by the defendant could not be murder.[46] The court pointed out that while the state's General Assembly could expand the Illinois murder statute to include the unjustified killing of a fetus, they had not done so and, accordingly, the common law notion of murder would prevail.[47]

The second matter that deserves mention is the substantial reliance the revision committee placed on the American Law Institute's (ALI) Model Penal Code.[48] While the Criminal Code of 1961 is by no stretch of the imagination a carbon copy of the Model Penal Code, a thorough study and comparison of the two codes makes it abundantly clear that the revision committee patterned much of what appears in the Illinois code after what appeared in the ALI's useful model.[49]

§ 1.03. Purposes of Illinois Criminal Law.

While the Criminal Code of 1961 does not reflect a definition of criminal law that might offer guidance on the proper scope of Illinois criminal law, it does articulate the "General Purposes" the code is to serve:

(a) Forbid and prevent the commission of offenses;

(b) Define adequately the act and mental state which constitute each offense, and limit the condemnation of conduct as criminal when it is without fault;

(c) Prescribe penalties which are proportionate to the seriousness of offenses and which permit recognition of differences in rehabilitation possibilities among individual offenders;

(d) Prevent arbitrary or oppressive treatment of persons accused or convicted of offenses.[50]

It is apparent that the revision committee felt compelled to include a statement of purpose as a sort of reference point to the objectives and limitations that the code is to serve.[51] A primary focus of the statement of general purposes is

---

[45] People v. Greer, 79 Ill. 2d 103, 111, 402 N.E.2d 203, 207 (1980).

[46] People v. Greer, 79 Ill. 2d 103, 111, 402 N.E.2d 203, 207 (1980).

[47] People v. Greer, 79 Ill. 2d 103, 111, 402 N.E.2d 203, 207 (1980).

[48] *See generally* MODEL PENAL CODE (1962).

[49] *Compare*, for example, the definition of *Mental State* contained in the two codes. *Compare* 720 ILCS 5/4-3 through 5/4-7 (1999) *with* MODEL PENAL CODE § 2.02 (1962).

[50] 720 ILCS 5/1-2 (1999).

[51] ILL. ANN. STAT. ch. 38, para. 1-2 (Smith-Hurd 1989), 1961 Committee Comments, at 10 ("The object of this section is to collect certain of the generally recognized purposes of the substantive criminal law, to express the legislative purposes of the Code and to provide a convenient reference for the interpretation of its more specific provisions").

apparently the preventive and rehabilitative considerations.[52] Subparagraph (a) states an obvious, central aim of any penal code — labeling certain conduct, which is perceived as highly offensive from a social point of view, as deserving of criminal sanctions[53] with the objective of eliminating, or at least minimizing, the conduct in question.[54]

Subparagraph (b) addresses the concern that the code must clearly explain which acts and related mental states fall within the ambits of the criminal law, while simultaneously avoiding the inclusion of behavior that does not merit or allow for criminalization. The revision committee noted that such a mandate was constitutionally required.[55] Any vague criminal stricture violates federal due process[56] and Illinois caselaw[57] if it fails to extend notice to the citizenry about (1) who falls within the reach of the criminal prohibition or (2) what conduct is thereby prohibited. Similarly, if a statute, however clear concerning its content, intrudes into behavior that is innocent[58] or constitutionally protected,[59] it may be rendered invalid due to overbreadth considerations.

---

[52] ILL. ANN. STAT. ch. 38, para. 1-2 (Smith-Hurd 1989), 1961 Committee Comments, at 10.

[53] Alternative methods for controlling conduct beyond those revolving around criminal law may be equally effective — for example, civil liability, taxes, licensing, administrative rules and regulations, and cultural, religious, or other social pressures. SANFORD KADISH & STEPHEN SCHULHOFER, CRIMINAL LAW AND ITS PROCESSES: CASES AND MATERIALS 153-54 (6th ed. 1995). Perhaps reliance on criminal sanctions should be a last resort. See JOHN KLOTTER, CRIMINAL LAW § 1.2 (2d ed. 1986).

[54] See M. CHERIF BASSIOUNI, SUBSTANTIVE CRIMINAL LAW 75-76 (1978).

[55] ILL. ANN. STAT. ch. 38, para. 1-2 (Smith-Hurd 1989), 1961 Committee Comments, at 12 (citing People v. Beak, 291 Ill. 449, 452, 126 N.E.2d 201, 202 (1920)).

[56] Winters v. New York, 333 U.S. 507, 515-16 (1948) (obscenity statute was unconstitutionally vague). A wide variety of statutes have been struck down on this basis. See, e.g., Kolender v. Lawson, 461 U.S. 352 (1983) (statutes requiring persons stopped by police to provide "credible and reliable" identification was unconstitutionally vague).

[57] It is not clear whether some of the Illinois opinions, wherein statutes are struck down as "unconstitutionally vague," are based on federal due process grounds standing alone or on state grounds as well. See, e.g., People v. Monroe, 118 Ill. 2d 298, 305, 515 N.E.2d 42, 45 (1987) (Illinois Drug Paraphernalia Control Act unconstitutionally vague). The Illinois Constitution, like the federal constitution, provides a "due process" guarantee. ILL. CONST. art. I, § 2 ("No person shall be deprived of life, liberty or property without due process of law. . . .").

[58] See, e.g., City of Chicago v. Morales, 119 S. Ct. 1849, 1859 (1999) (municipal gang loitering ordinance which defines "loitering" as "remain[s] in any one place with no apparent purpose" is unconstitutionally vague for failing to distinguish between innocent conduct and conduct threatening harm); Papachristou v. City of Jacksonville, 405 U.S. 156, 164 (1972) (vagrancy statute was overly broad and unconstitutional); People v. Wick, 107 Ill. 2d 62, 65-67, 481 N.E.2d 676, 678-79 (1985) (aggravated arson statute unconstitutional since it punishes potentially innocent conduct).

[59] See, e.g., Texas v. Johnson, 491 U.S. 397 (1989) (burning American flag protected by First Amendment and, accordingly, flag desecration statute unconstitutional); Pope v. Illinois, 481 U.S. 497 (1987) (Illinois obscenity statute violates First Amendment); Roe v. Wade, 410 U.S. 113 (1973) (prohibition against abortion violated woman's right to privacy protected by due process of law).

Subparagraph (c) focuses on both the necessity of having criminal sanctions that are (1) proportionate to the nature of the offense and (2) consistent with the interests of the rehabilitation of offenders, while recognizing that the latter concern may require differential treatment of offenders who have engaged in comparable conduct. The "proportionality" principle is required from a constitutional perspective. In *Solem v. Helm*,[60] the United States Supreme Court reaffirmed that the cruel and unusual punishment clause of the Eighth Amendment requires that criminal sentences not be excessive and disproportionate.[61] The *Helm* Court provided objective criteria for determining whether a sentence is unconstitutional in this regard, which they outlined in a three-prong test.[62] First, a court must consider the severity of the penalty against the nature of the crime.[63] Second, a court must consider the harshness of the penalty in relation to the sanctions normally imposed on criminals in the same jurisdiction who have been convicted of the same or similar crimes.[64] Third, a court must compare the punishment in question to that imposed in other jurisdictions for the same offense.[65] However, in *Harmelin v. Michigan*,[66] a majority of the Court limited the significance of the second and third factors in the *Solem* proportionality analysis when it indicated "intra- and inter-jurisdictional analyses are appropriate only in the rare case in which a threshold comparison of the crime committed and the sentence imposed leads to an inference of gross proportionality."[67]

In addition to the federal protections against disproportionate penalties, persons convicted of crimes in Illinois enjoy the additional safeguards articulated in the Illinois Constitution that was ratified by the people in 1970. Specifically, the state Bill of Rights provides in section 11: "All penalties shall be determined both according to the seriousness of the offense and with the objective of restoring the offender to useful citizenship."[68] In accordance with this state protection, the Illinois appellate courts have struck down sentences as excessive[69] or dis-

---

[60] 463 U.S. 277 (1983).

[61] U.S. CONST. amend VIII ("cruel and unusual punishments [shall not] be inflicted"). *See also* Coker v. Georgia, 433 U.S. 584 (1977) (death penalty for rape was per se disproportionate and unconstitutional); Trop v. Dulles, 356 U.S. 86 (1958) (denationalization sanction for wartime desertion was unconstitutional); Weems v. United States, 217 U.S. 349 (1910) (prison sentence was unconstitutional).

[62] Solem v. Helm, 463 U.S. 277, 290-92 (1983).

[63] Solem v. Helm, 463 U.S. 277, 290-92 (1983).

[64] Solem v. Helm, 463 U.S. 277, 290-92 (1983).

[65] Solem v. Helm, 463 U.S. 277, 291-92 (1983).

[66] 501 U.S. 957 (1991).

[67] Harmelin v. Michigan, 501 U.S. 957, 960 (1991) (Kennedy, J. concurring).

[68] ILL. CONST. art. I, § 11.

[69] *See, e.g.,* People v. Brown, 243 Ill. App. 3d 170, 176, 612 N.E.2d 14, 19 (1st Dist. 1993); People v. Short, 66 Ill. App. 3d 172, 176-77, 383 N.E.2d 723, 727 (5th Dist. 1978); People v. Dandridge, 9 Ill. App. 3d 174, 176, 292 N.E.2d 51, 52 (4th Dist. 1973).

proportionate.[70] Specifically, the Illinois courts have determined certain sentences were not in accordance with the aim of "restoring the offender to useful citizenship," which cases are implicitly grounded in rehabilitative concerns.[71] This is not to say that rehabilitative goals are the sole, or even primary, concern in sentencing.[72] Indeed, the adoption of the "class X" sentencing provisions in 1978,[73] which resulted in the abolition of interdeterminate sentences and the expansion of harsher sentence possibilities as a general matter, signaled a lack of trust in the rehabilitative ideal.[74] On the other hand, this concern cannot be entirely ignored either.[75]

Subparagraph (c) does contemplate differential treatment of offenders who commit the same offense where such disparate results are warranted. Numerous cases recognize that within the realm of determinate sentencing, one offender may properly suffer a harsher sanction than another offender who is convicted

---

[70] People v. Lombardi, 184 Ill. 2d 462, 483-85, 705 N.E.2d 91, 102-03 (1998) (penalty for armed violence involving a category I weapon arising from a residential burglary is unconstitutionally disproportionate inasmuch as more serious offense of home invasion has a lesser penalty); People v. Wooley, 178 Ill. 2d 175, 204-05, 687 N.E.2d 979, 993 (1997) (penalty for armed violence committed with a category I weapon unconstitutionally disproportionate when compared to penalty for armed robbery); People v. Davis, 177 Ill. 2d 495, 501-08, 687 N.E.2d 24, 27-30 (1997) (penalty for felon's possession of firearm without proper registration unconstitutionally disproportionate when compared to penalty for unlawful use of weapon by felon); People v. Lewis, 175 Ill. 2d 412, 423, 677 N.E.2d 830, 835 (1996) (penalties for armed robbery and for armed violence predicated on a robbery committed with a category I weapon are unconstitutionally disproportionate); People v. Christy, 139 Ill. 2d 172, 181, 564 N.E.2d 770, 774 (1990) (penalties for aggravated kidnapping and armed violence predicated on kidnapping with a category I weapon unconstitutionally disproportionate); People v. Murphy, 261 Ill. App. 3d 1019, 1022, 635 N.E.2d 110, 112 (2d Dist. 1994) (conviction for armed violence predicated on unlawful restraint violated the proportionate penalties guarantee because a less serious offense, unlawful restraint committed with a dangerous weapon, would be punished more severely than a more serious offense, namely, aggravated kidnapping).

[71] See, e.g., People v. Smith, 178 Ill. App. 3d 976, 533 N.E.2d 1169 (3d Dist. 1989) ("The constitutional mandate requires the court to actually consider rehabilitation as an objective of the sentence").

[72] Cf. People v. Perruquet, 68 Ill. 2d 149, 154-156, 368 N.E.2d 882, 884-85 (1977). In this case, the court weighed the need to protect society against the defendant's rehabilitative prospects without in any way suggesting that the rehabilitation concern was paramount.

[73] See Marvin Aspen, New Class X Sentencing Law: An Analysis, 66 ILL. B.J. 344 (1978).

[74] See generally ANDREW VON HIRSCH, DOING JUSTICE: THE CHOICE OF PUNISHMENTS (1976) (rehabilitation approach to punishment has failed). This proposition is repudiated by some. See, e.g., FRANCIS CULLEN & KAREN GILBERT, REAFFIRMING REHABILITATION 89-138 (1982).

[75] People v. Margentina, 261 Ill. App. 3d 247, 249-50, 634 N.E.2d 29, 31 (3d Dist. 1994) (sentence within statutory limits may be an abuse of discretion where defendant's rehabilitation potential not properly considered as required by Ill. Const. art. I, § 1; sentence reduced); People v. Brown, 243 Ill. App. 3d 170, 176, 612 N.E.2d 14, 19 (1st Dist. 1993) (trial court gave inadequate consideration to defendant's rehabilitation potential as required by Ill. Const. art. I, § 1; sentence reduced).

of the same criminal act inasmuch as one perhaps has a more extensive past criminal record and future criminal proclivities than the other.[76] On the other hand, a few opinions have reduced sentences after consideration of data indicating a particular sentence was disproportionate when compared to sentences imposed for more serious offenses.[77]

Finally, subparagraph (d) appears to be of questionable significance when viewed in light of the general thrust of the Criminal Code and, more importantly, the earlier subsections. First, this is the only subparagraph that is not the subject of commentary by the revision committee in the Committee Comments that follow the "general purposes" statement. Second, it is not clear what this subparagraph contemplates beyond the others. The prevention of "arbitrary or oppressive treatment of persons *accused . . .* of offenses"[78] would seem to be the province of chapter 725, which reflects the Illinois Code of Criminal Procedure. Except for several procedural protections in the criminal law code labeled "Rights of Defendant,"[79] it is uncertain which of the various features of this 1961 substantive criminal law enactment serve this seemingly *procedural* objective. Furthermore, the prevention of such "treatment of persons . . . *convicted* of offenses"[80] appears to be adequately addressed by subparagraphs (b) and (c).

§ 1.04. State Criminal Jurisdiction.

The Criminal Code outlines in paragraph 5/1-5 Illinois law pertaining to subject matter jurisdiction. It provides:

> (a) A person is subject to prosecution in this State for an offense which he commits, while either within or outside the State, by his own conduct or that of another for which he is legally accountable, if:
>
> (1) The offense is committed either wholly or partly within the State; or
> (2) The conduct outside the State constitutes an attempt to commit an offense within the State; or
> (3) The conduct outside the State constitutes a conspiracy to commit an offense within the State, and an act in furtherance of the conspiracy occurs in the State; or
> (4) The conduct within the State constitutes an attempt, solicitation or conspiracy to commit in another jurisdiction an offense under the laws of both this State and such other jurisdiction.

---

[76] *See, e.g.,* People v. Bien, 277 Ill. App. 3d 744, 754-55, 661 N.E.2d 511, 518-20 (4th Dist. 1996) (rejecting "comparative sentence" analysis).

[77] *See, e.g.,* People v. Neither, 230 Ill. App. 3d 546, 552-554, 595 N.E.2d 124, 126-29 (1st Dist. 1992) (referring to Illinois Department of Corrections statistical sentencing report).

[78] 720 ILCS 5/1-2(d) (1999).

[79] 720 ILCS 5/3-1 through 5/3-8 (1999).

[80] 720 ILCS 5/1-2(d) (1999) (emphasis added).

(b) An offense is committed partly within this State, if either the conduct which is an element of the offense, or the result which is such an element of the offense, occurs within the State. In a prosecution pursuant to paragraph (3) of subsection (a) of Section [5/]9-1 [first-degree felony murder], the attempt or commission of a forcible felony other than second-degree murder within the state is conduct which is an element of the offense for which a person is subject to prosecution in this State. In homicide, the "result" is either the physical contact which causes death, or the death itself; and if the body of a homicide victim is found within the State, the death is presumed to have occurred within the State.

(c) An offense which is based on an omission to perform a duty imposed by the law of this State is committed within the State, regardless of the location of the offender at the time of the omission.[81]

The principle focus of this provision is to confer on the Illinois courts jurisdiction over crimes occurring within the territorial jurisdiction of the state of Illinois. Yet, the rapid advances in transportation and communications, facilitating interstate and international criminality, have necessitated the expansion of jurisdictional concerns where the crime has taken place only partly within the state or has had an impact on the citizens of the state.[82] The revision committee's comment makes clear that it is immaterial for jurisdictional purposes whether the defendant is present within the state or is outside the state when the offense is committed if the defendant's offense otherwise has the features described in any of the four subparagraphs of subparagraph (a).[83] Thus, where defendant, while situated in Ohio, harassed by telephone his victim in Illinois, defendant could properly be convicted in Illinois of harassment by telephone[84] because the "result" of his harassment occurred in Illinois.[85]

The "partly within the state" language of subparagraph (a)(1) is designed to cover all situations where a crime commences within the state and is consummated in another state or where the crime commences in another state and is consummated within the state.[86] Thus, if a defendant stole an automobile in Missouri and "exerted control" over the automobile in Illinois, he or she could properly be convicted of theft in Illinois.[87] Similarly, if a person or corporation situ-

---

[81] 720 ILCS 5/1-5 (1999).

[82] ILL. ANN. STAT. ch. 38, para. 1-5 (Smith-Hurd 1989), 1961 Committee Comments, at 20.

[83] ILL. ANN. STAT. ch. 38, para. 1-5 (Smith-Hurd 1989), 1961 Committee Comments, at 23.

[84] 720 ILCS 135/1-1 (1999) (harassment by telephone prohibition).

[85] People v. Baker, 268 Ill. App. 3d 16, 16, 643 N.E.2d 286, 287 (3d Dist. 1994) (quoting 720 ILCS 5/1-5(a)(1), (b) (1993)).

[86] ILL. ANN. STAT. ch. 38, para. 1-5 (Smith-Hurd 1989), 1961 Committee Comments, at 23.

[87] People v. Spicuzza, 44 Ill. App. 3d 420, 422, 358 N.E.2d 315, 317 (5th Dist. 1976). In Illinois, the theft prohibition provides in part: "A person commits theft when he knowingly: (a) Obtains or exerts unauthorized control over property of the owner. . . ." 720 ILCS 5/16-1(a) (1999).

ated outside the state obtained by deceptive means control over something of value that belonged to a person situated in Illinois, that person or corporation could be properly convicted of theft by deception.[88] Subparagraph (a)(1) also extended jurisdiction in a controlled substances trafficking situation where a defendant, acting in Florida with the intent that cocaine be delivered in Illinois, aided and abetted a transaction by which cocaine was caused to be delivered in Illinois.[89]

Subparagraph (b) of paragraph 5/1-5 seeks to clarify the "partly within the state" language of subparagraph (a). If any "element" of the offense in question or the "result which is such an element" occurs within the territorial limits of Illinois, the State of Illinois has subject matter jurisdiction over the offense.[90] In view of the importance of effective prosecution of unjustified homicides, this subsection includes a specific reference to this crime.[91] With homicide, the "result" is either the mortal contact that causes death or the death itself.[92] Accordingly, if A inflicted an unjustified mortal wound on B while in a neighboring state and thereafter brought B to Illinois where B died as a result of the wound, Illinois would have jurisdiction over the crime. Although there previously existed a significant decision to the contrary,[93] a more recent amendment to subparagraph (b) makes clear that if a defendant were to engage in a forcible felony, such as kidnapping, in Illinois and thereafter transport his victim to a neighboring state where he decides to, and does, kill his kidnap victim, the commission of the underlying forcible felony in Illinois would provide a basis for Illinois jurisdiction for felony-murder even though the intent to kill and actual killing arose only after arrival in the neighboring state.[94]

Judicial interpretation of subsection (a)(1) makes clear that it is "not enough that some part of a course of criminal conduct, some related crime, be committed in Illinois; the *particular crime charged* must be committed partly within this state."[95] Thus, where a defendant forced his victim into the trunk of his car

---

[88] *Cf.* People v. Gill, 122 Ill. App. 2d 60, 68, 257 N.E.2d 115, 119 (3d Dist. 1970). In Illinois, the theft statute reads in part: "A person commits theft when he knowingly: . . . (b) Obtains by deception control over property of the owner. . . ." 720 ILCS 5/16-1(b) (1999).

[89] People v. Govin, 213 Ill. App. 3d 928, 933-34, 572 N.E.2d 450, 454 (4th Dist. 1991) (defendant convicted of controlled substances trafficking which arises where one "causes to be brought into" Illinois a controlled substance).

[90] 720 ILCS 5/1-5(b) (1999).

[91] 720 ILCS 5/1-5(b) (1999).

[92] 720 ILCS 5/1-5(b) (1999).

[93] People v. Holt, 91 Ill. 2d 480, 484, 440 N.E.2d 102, 105 (1982) (where defendant kidnapped victim in Illinois, transported her to Wisconsin, and formulated the intent to kill his victim only after arrival in Wisconsin, his killing of the victim in Wisconsin did not provide Illinois with jurisdiction under subparagraph (b) of section 5/1-5 as then written).

[94] 720 ILCS 5/1-5(b) (1999).

[95] People v. Holt, 91 Ill. 2d 480, 484, 440 N.E.2d 102, 104 (1982) (emphasis added).

in Wisconsin, later sexually assaulted her while still in Wisconsin and, thereafter, drove the car into Illinois while the victim remained in the trunk, Illinois had no jurisdiction over the sexual assault (although jurisdiction over his aggravated kidnapping was not disputed).[96] Similarly, where a defendant sexually assaulted his victim in Indiana and then forced her into the trunk of her car, which was driven to Illinois where officials found the victim shot to death while still in the trunk, defendant's aggravated criminal sexual assault conviction was reversed for lack of jurisdiction.[97] However, this defendant's armed robbery conviction, arising out of the taking of her car, was affirmed against a jurisdictional challenge on the theory that this latter offense was a "continuing offense" as the taking was an ongoing proposition when the victim's car entered Illinois.[98]

Subparagraphs (a)(2), (a)(3), and (a)(4) are aimed at establishing jurisdiction over the inchoate offenses of attempt,[99] conspiracy,[100] and solicitation.[101] If a defendant engages in substantial conduct outside the state to facilitate the commission of crime within the state but the crime is not in fact committed, he or she is guilty of criminal attempt in Illinois.[102] Likewise, if he or she engages in conduct within the state aimed at committing a crime outside the state but the crime is not completed, he or she can be convicted of a criminal attempt in Illinois.[103] And if a defendant engages either in a conspiracy outside the state to commit a crime within the state[104] or enters into such a criminal compact within the state to commit an offense outside the state,[105] there is a criminal conspiracy

---

[96] People v. Blanck, 263 Ill. App. 3d 224, 227-230, 635 N.E.2d 1356, 1360-62 (2d Dist. 1994) (reversing aggravated criminal assault conviction while rejecting argument that extended "use of force" against victim, which continued when defendant drove victim into Illinois, was part of the criminal sexual assault).

[97] People v. Moreland, 292 Ill. App. 3d 616, 619-20, 686 N.E.2d 597, 599-600 (1st Dist. 1997) (although his first degree murder and aggravated kidnapping convictions were affirmed).

[98] People v. Moreland, 292 Ill. App. 3d 616, 620, 686 N.E.2d 597, 600 (1st Dist. 1997).

[99] 720 ILCS 5/8-4 (1999) ("A person commits an attempt when, with intent to commit a specific offense, he does any act which constitutes a substantial step toward the commission of that offense"). See ch. 5 for a discussion of criminal attempt.

[100] 720 ILCS 5/8-2 (1999) ("A person commits conspiracy when, with intent that an offense be committed, he agrees with another to the commission of that offense. No person may be convicted of conspiracy to commit an offense unless an act in furtherance of such agreement is alleged and proved to have been committed by him or by a co-conspirator.") See ch. 4 for a discussion of conspiracy.

[101] 720 ILCS 5/8-1 (1999) ("A person commits solicitation when, with intent that an offense other than first degree murder be committed he commands, encourages or requests another to commit that offense."); 720 ILCS 5/8-1.1 (1999) (solicitation of murder prohibition); 720 ILCS 5/8-1.2 (1999) (solicitation of murder for hire prohibition). See ch. 5 for a discussion of the solicitation prohibitions.

[102] 720 ILCS 5/1-5(a)(2) (1999).

[103] 720 ILCS 5/1-5(a)(4) (1999).

[104] 720 ILCS 5/1-5(a)(3) (1999).

[105] 720 ILCS 5/1-5(a)(4) (1999).

in Illinois. Finally, any solicitation by a defendant outside the state aimed at the commission of a crime by another in Illinois[106] or any solicitation by the accused inside the state designed to bring about a crime outside the state[107] could be the subject of an Illinois prosecution.

Subparagraph (c), the last subparagraph of 5/1-5, extends the Illinois courts' jurisdiction where the defendant outside the state breaches a legal duty imposed on him or her within the state. Thus, where defendant harbored his two children in Ohio and failed to return them to the custodial parent in violation of an Illinois custody order, his conduct constituted a breach of a legal duty that could make him liable in Illinois for the crime of child abduction.[108]

Jurisdiction must be demonstrated beyond a reasonable doubt.[109] Jurisdiction over the person and the offense is required to enable a court to try and to punish the accused.[110] Jurisdiction over the person of the accused is acquired when he or she personally appears before the court;[111] jurisdiction over the offense, also known as subject matter jurisdiction, is conferred by express constitutional and statutory provisions.[112]

Subject matter jurisdiction over the offense is not conferred by the charging instrument,[113] and thus, failure to charge an offense does not serve to deprive a circuit court of jurisdiction.[114] Defects in the manner or form of the charging instrument — the indictment, information, or complaint — do not impair the court's jurisdiction.[115] In other words, since subject matter jurisdiction is conferred by article VI, section 9, of the Illinois Constitution, which provides that circuit courts have "original jurisdiction in all justiciable matters,"[116] the circuit courts have jurisdiction in all matters reflected in section 5/1-5 of chapter 720 regardless of a technical defect in the charging instrument.[117] Therefore, while a

---

[106] While there is no explicit provision within paragraph 5/1-5 dealing with this subject, the language of paragraphs 5/1-5(a)(1) and 5/1-5(b) lends itself to a jurisdictional grant because the "result" of the solicitation has occurred in Illinois. *See* 720 ILCS 5/1-5(a)(1), (b) (1999).

[107] 720 ILCS 5/1-5(a)(4) (1999).

[108] People v. Caruso, 119 Ill. 2d 376, 381-383, 519 N.E.2d 440, 442-46 (1987) (trial court improperly dismissed child abduction charges for lack of jurisdiction).

[109] People v. Holt, 91 Ill. 2d 480, 492-93, 440 N.E.2d 102, 108 (1983).

[110] People v. Kleiss, 90 Ill. App. 3d 53, 55, 412 N.E.2d 39, 40-41 (3d Dist. 1980).

[111] People v. Kleiss, 90 Ill. App. 3d 53, 55, 412 N.E.2d 39, 41 (3d Dist. 1980).

[112] People v. Brooks, 75 Ill. App. 3d 109, 111, 394 N.E.2d 10, 12 (5th Dist. 1979).

[113] People v. Brooks, 75 Ill. App. 3d 109, 111, 394 N.E.2d 10, 12 (5th Dist. 1979).

[114] People v. Gilmore, 63 Ill. 2d 23, 26, 344 N.E.2d 456, 459 (1976) (failure to make timely motions to dismiss charging instrument as defective constituted waiver of irregularity; incomplete charge was not jurisdictional problem that could be attacked at any time).

[115] People v. Kleiss, 90 Ill. App. 3d 53, 55, 412 N.E.2d 39, 41 (3d Dist. 1980).

[116] ILL. CONST. art. VI, § 9.

[117] People v. Gilmore, 63 Ill. 2d 23, 26-29, 344 N.E.2d 456, 458-60 (1976). *Accord* People v. Pujoue, 61 Ill. 2d 335, 339, 335 N.E.2d 437, 440 (1975) (failure of complaint to set out nature and elements of offense did not require reversal where sufficiency of complaint was attacked first time

deficient charging instrument must be dismissed pursuant to a timely pre-trial motion to dismiss,[118] it will not be the basis of a successful attack on the state charge when raised for the first time on appeal[119] unless the deficiency is so egregious as to make it impossible for the defendant to prepare a defense or ward off successive prosecutions for the same offense.[120]

Similarly, personal jurisdiction is not impaired by the fact that the defendant was the subject of an illegal arrest,[121] or by the fact that he or she was brought within the jurisdiction by forcible abduction.[122] On the other hand, a trial court has no jurisdiction over an offense that occurred outside the state of Illinois.[123] A judgment of conviction involving a matter that occurred wholly outside the state is void and could be challenged anytime, such as by way of a post-trial collateral attack, under the state writ of habeas corpus.[124]

§ 1.05. Criminal Venue.

Because of federal[125] and state[126] constitutional considerations, a defendant's criminal trial must occur in the state and county where the crime transpired. The United States Constitution provides in article III that criminal trials "shall be held in the state where said crimes shall have been committed."[127] The Illinois Constitution states that in criminal prosecutions, the defendant shall have a "trial

---

on appeal so long as complaint appraised defendant of charge sufficient to allow preparation of defenses and bars to subsequent prosecution).

[118] 725 ILCS 5/114-1(a)(8) (1999). *See also* People v. Thingvold, 145 Ill. 2d 441, 448, 584 N.E.2d 89, 91 (1991) (if indictment is attacked before trial it must strictly comply with the requirements of the Code of Criminal Procedure or upon review the appellate court will reverse); People v. Lutz, 43 Ill. 2d 204, 210, 383 N.E.2d 171, 172-73 (1978) (stricter scrutiny of charging instrument mandated where defendant raises challenge in trial court in timely motion in arrest of judgment).

[119] People v. Gilmore, 63 Ill. 2d 23, 26-29, 344 N.E.2d 456, 458-60 (1976).

[120] *See, e.g.,* People v. Spain, 24 Ill. App. 3d 377, 379-80, 321 N.E.2d 520, 522-23 (1st Dist. 1974) (where complaint failed to specify element of offense, it was so deficient it could be challenged "at any time").

[121] People v. Rose, 22 Ill. 2d 185, 186, 174 N.E.2d 673, 673 (1961).

[122] People v. Bradford, 3 Ill. App. 3d 81, 83, 279 N.E.2d 34, 36 (1st Dist. 1971).

[123] People v. Bovinett, 73 Ill. App. 3d 833, 835, 392 N.E.2d 428, 429 (5th Dist. 1979) (alleged eavesdropping violation that occurred in Missouri).

[124] 735 ILCS 5/10-101 through 5/10-137 (1999); *See* People ex rel. St. George v. Woods, 47 Ill. 2d 261, 262-63, 265 N.E.2d 164, 165 (1970) (state habeas corpus available where trial court lacks jurisdiction over subject matter).

[125] U.S. CONST. art. III, § 2.

[126] ILL. CONST. art. I, § 8.

[127] U.S. CONST. art. III, § 2. *See* Travis v. United States, 364 U.S. 631 (1961) (discussion of venue in federal prosecution and constitutional mandate).

by an impartial jury of the county in which the offense is alleged to have been committed."[128]

In addition, Illinois legislation states criminal offenses "shall be tried in the county where the offense was committed."[129] However, the statute that pertains to venue explicitly states that venue is not a specific element of a crime, which the state is obligated to prove during the course of a criminal trial.[130]

A comprehensive legislative enactment addressing proper venue in criminal cases appears in paragraph 5/1-6 of the criminal code provisions entitled "Place of Trial." It states:

> Place of Trial. (a) Generally. Criminal actions shall be tried in the county where the offense was committed, except as otherwise provided by law. The State is not required to prove during trial that the alleged offense occurred in any particular county in this state. When a defendant contests the place of trial under this section, all proceedings regarding this issue shall be conducted under Section [5/]114-1 of the Code of Criminal Procedure of 1963. All objections of improper place of trial are waived by a defendant unless made before trial.
>
> (b) Assailant and Victim in Different Counties. If a person committing an offense upon the person of another is located in one county and his victim is located in another county at the time of the commission of the offense, trial may be had in either of said counties.
>
> (c) Death and Cause of Death in Different Places or Undetermined. If cause of death is inflicted in one county and death ensues in another county, the offender may be tried in either county. If neither the county in which the cause of death was inflicted nor the county in which death ensued are known before trial, the offender may be tried in the county where the body was found.
>
> (d) Offense Commenced Outside the State. If the commission of an offense commenced outside the State is consummated within this State, the offender shall be tried in the county where the offense is consummated.
>
> (e) Offenses Committed in Bordering Navigable Waters. If an offense is committed on any of the navigable waters bordering on this State, the offender may be tried in any county adjacent to such navigable water.
>
> (f) Offenses Committed While in Transit. If an offense is committed upon any railroad car, vehicle, watercraft or aircraft passing within this State, and it cannot readily be determined in which county the offense was com-

---

[128] ILL. CONST. art. I, § 8.

[129] 720 ILCS 5/1-6(a) (1999).

[130] 720 ILCS 5/1-6(a) (1999). *See also* People v. Gallegos, 293 Ill. App. 3d 873, 878, 689 N.E.2d 223, 225-26 (3d Dist. 1997) (defense claim that state has constitutional obligation to prove venue as element of crime rejected).

mitted, the offender may be tried in any county through which such railroad car, vehicle, watercraft or aircraft has passed.

(g) Theft. A person who commits theft of property may be tried in any county in which he exerted control over such property.

(h) Bigamy. A person who commits the offense of bigamy may be tried in any county where the bigamous marriage or bigamous cohabitation has occurred.

(i) Kidnapping. A person who commits the offense of kidnapping may be tried in any county in which his victim has traveled or has been confined during the course of the offense.

(j) Pandering. A person who commits the offense of pandering may be tried in any county in which the prostitution was practiced or in any county in which any act in furtherance of the offense shall have been committed.

(k) Treason. A person who commits the offense of treason may be tried in any county.

* * *

(m) Inchoate Offenses. A person who commits an inchoate offense may be tried in any county in which any act which is an element of the offense, including the agreement in conspiracy, is committed.

(n) Accountability for Conduct of Another. Where a person in one county solicits, aids, abets, agrees, or attempts to aid another in the planning or commission of an offense in another county, he may be tried for the offense in either county.

(o) Child Abduction. A person who commits the offense of child abduction may be tried in any county in which his victim has traveled, been detained, concealed or removed to during the course of the offense. Notwithstanding the foregoing, unless for good cause shown, the preferred place of trial shall be the county of residence of the lawful custodian.

(p) A person who commits the offense of narcotics racketeering may be tried in any county where cannabis or a controlled substance which is the basis for the charge of narcotics racketeering was used; acquired; transferred or distributed to, from or through; or any county where any act was performed to further the use; acquisition, transfer or distribution of said cannabis or controlled substance; any money, property, property interest, or any other asset generated by narcotics activities was acquired, used, sold, transferred or distributed to, from or through; or, any enterprise interest obtained as a result of narcotics racketeering was acquired, used, transferred or distributed to, from or through, or where any activity was conducted by the enterprise or any conduct to further the interests of such enterprise.

(q) A person who commits the offense of money laundering may be tried in any county where any part of a financial transaction in criminally derived property took place or in any county where any money or monetary instrument which is the basis for the offense was acquired, used, sold, transferred or distributed to, from or through.

(r) A person who commits the offense of cannabis trafficking or controlled substance trafficking may be tried in any county.[131]

The revision committee insisted that all defense motions for a change of trial be advanced prior to trial or be waived, with said policy being "designed to prevent a defendant who knows that the place of trial is improperly alleged from saying nothing until his gamble on the verdict has lost and then raising the issue for the first time."[132] Also, it is important to bear in mind that the state need not prove the existence of proper venue beyond a reasonable doubt in Illinois.[133] The State's obligations regarding venue are procedural and are satisfied so long as the county in which the offense took place is specified in the charging instrument.[134] A charging instrument that fails to properly allege the county in which the offense has occurred can be dismissed by the trial court on a timely pre-trial motion[135] or can be transferred to an appropriate county.[136] However, place of trial is not jurisdictional and, accordingly, can be waived by a failure to object before trial.[137]

With respect to the substantive venue provision, paragraph 5/1-6 "does clarify and make more specific the law which shall apply" in various situations.[138] Since the code carefully specifies proper venue requirements for many Illinois offenses, proceeding beyond the code to the caselaw is generally unnecessary. But there are several venue problems not specifically covered by the code that have been considered by the appellate courts. For instance, with respect to the crime of failure to report a bribe,[139] the place of trial shall be in that county

---

[131] 720 ILCS 5/1-6 (1999).

[132] ILL. ANN. STAT. ch. 38, para. 1-6 (Smith-Hurd 1989), 1961 Committee Comments, at 30.

[133] 720 ILCS 5/1-6(a) (1999); People v. Gallegos, 293 Ill. App. 3d 873, 878, 689 N.E.2d 223, 225-26 (3d Dist. 1987). Prior to the enactment of Public Act 89-288 (1995), which eliminated the requirement, the State was required to prove venue at trial beyond a reasonable doubt. *See, e.g.,* People v. Hagan, 145 Ill. 2d 287, 300, 583 N.E.2d 494, 500 (1991).

[134] 725 ILCS 5/111-3(a)(4) (1999).

[135] 725 ILCS 5/114-1(a)(7) (1999); People v. Wallace, 125 Ill. App. 2d 455, 457, 261 N.E.2d 214, 216 (4th Dist. 1970) (trial court properly dismissed official misconduct charge for lack of proper venue).

[136] 725 ILCS 5/114-1(f) (1999); People v. Gibson, 109 Ill. App. 3d 316, 322, 440 N.E.2d 339, 342 (4th Dist. 1982) (court transferred case to appropriate county, which was held to be proper, instead of dismissing it).

[137] People v. Dunn, 52 Ill. 2d 400, 402, 288 N.E.2d 463, 464 (1972).

[138] ILL. ANN. STAT. ch. 38, para. 1-6 (Smith-Hurd 1989), 1961 Committee Comments, at 30.

[139] 720 ILCS 5/33-2 (1999).

where the bribe offer occurred.[140] Forgery[141] charges must be tried where the forgery of the document occurred or was delivered.[142] A syndicated gambling[143] charge must be tried in the county where the defendant received a wager, not the county where an undercover officer placed a telephone call to make a bet.[144] Where a public official engages in official misconduct,[145] venue is proper in the county of his or her office or in the county wherein the actual improper activity occurred.[146] A vehicular hijacking charge can be tried in any county wherein the defendant exerted control over the stolen vehicle.[147]

Motions for change of venue can only be made by the defendant[148] "on the ground that there exists in the county in which the charge is pending such prejudice against him on the part of the inhabitants that he cannot receive a fair trial in such county."[149] Thus, a court could not on its own motion or on the motion of the state's attorney change the place of trial from the county in which the offense occurred over the objection of the defendant, regardless of the circumstances. If the defendant insisted on his right to venue in the county where the crime took place notwithstanding the existence of community and potential juror prejudice against him, he would prevail on the venue issue but would simultaneously waive his right to trial in another county where he would be free of the prejudice. In other words, he would waive the prejudice issue in these circumstances by demanding proper venue.

§ 1.06. Classifications of Offenses.

There are certain classifications of crimes that may have a direct bearing on the scope of certain offenses; for example, only crimes designated as "forcible felonies" satisfy the felony-murder rule. In addition, these classifications may relate to sentencing alternatives (addressed in the Appendix) or procedural matters (which are beyond the scope of this book). These various categories will be considered at this juncture.

---

[140] People v. Choura, 84 Ill. App. 3d 228, 230-31, 405 N.E.2d 493, 495 (5th Dist. 1980).

[141] 720 ILCS 5/17-3 (1999).

[142] People v. Smith, 91 Ill. App. 3d 242, 246, 414 N.E.2d 751, 754 (5th Dist. 1980) (no forgery or delivery of forged document occurred in county). See also People v. Hagan, 145 Ill. 2d 287, 298-302, 583 N.E.2d 494, 499-501 (1991) (where document forged in first county and sent by facsimile from that county to second county, venue proper in first county).

[143] 720 ILCS 5/28-1.1 (1999).

[144] People v. Dixon, 219 Ill. App. 3d 1, 3-5, 579 N.E.2d 405, 407-08 (2d Dist. 1991).

[145] 720 ILCS 5/33-3 (1999).

[146] People v. Clark, 71 Ill. App. 3d 381, 396-98, 389 N.E.2d 911, 922-23 (2d Dist. 1979).

[147] People v. Eggerman, 292 Ill. App. 3d 644, 650, 685 N.E.2d 948, 952 (1st Dist. 1997).

[148] 725 ILCS 5/114-6(a) (1999).

[149] 725 ILCS 5/114-6(a) (1999).

§ 1.07. — Felonies and Misdemeanors.

All criminal offenses defined in the Criminal Code of 1961 fall into the category of either a felony or a misdemeanor. The Criminal Code of 1961 defines a felony as any crime that is punishable by death or a term of imprisonment for one year or more.[150] A misdemeanor means any offense that is punishable by a term of imprisonment in other than a penitentiary for less than one year.[151] This delineation is most important with respect to determining what sanctions attach to each offense in Illinois.

§ 1.08. — Forcible Felonies.

The Criminal Code of 1961 distinguishes between forcible felonies and non-forcible felonies. A forcible felony "means treason, first degree murder, second degree murder, predatory criminal sexual assault of a child, aggravated criminal sexual assault, criminal sexual assault, robbery, burglary, aggravated arson, arson, kidnapping, aggravated kidnapping, aggravated battery resulting in great bodily harm or permanent disability or disfigurement and any other felony which involves the use or threat of physical force or violence against any individual."[152] Determining that a crime is a forcible felony is important in several respects. For instance, the felony-murder doctrine is only applicable where a person takes a life without justification while "attempting or committing a forcible felony other than second degree murder."[153] If an assailant is involved in committing a forcible felony on a person or a third party, that person may use deadly force against the assailant in self-defense or in the defense of another.[154] Illinois law states that if an assailant is about to commit a forcible felony, such as an arson, a person can use deadly force in the interest of preventing the infliction of harm on the property in question, even if the property is something other than a dwelling.[155] An Illinois statute provides that a police officer can use deadly force in order to effect the arrest of an assailant who has committed or is attempting to commit a forcible felony.[156]

---

[150] 720 ILCS 5/2-7 (1999).

[151] 720 ILCS 5/2-11 (1999).

[152] 720 ILCS 5/2-8 (1999).

[153] 720 ILCS 5/9-1(a)(3) (1999).

[154] 720 ILCS 5/7-1 (1999).

[155] *See* 720 ILCS 5/7-3 (1999).

[156] *See* 720 ILCS 5/7-5(a)(2) (1999). *But see* Tennessee v. Garner, 471 U.S. 1 (1985) (police officer may not use deadly force to effectuate arrest unless arrestee poses serious danger to officer or others).

§ 1.09. — Mala in Se and Mala Probibita.

Although the penal code of Illinois makes no direct reference to the difference between mala in se (wrong in itself) offenses and mala prohibita (wrong because prohibited) infractions, this distinction between crimes sometimes takes on significance in the Illinois caselaw. At common law, a criminal act was considered malum in se if it was considered inherently wrong by its very nature, based on common morality and natural law principles.[157] Murder would be an obvious example of a malum in se offense. On the other hand, there were mala prohibita crimes that involved behavior not wrong in and of itself, but wrong merely because it was prohibited.[158] Stemming from positive law principles, this concept was developed to describe conduct labeled criminal by certain societal exigencies.[159] Of course, whether an offense is malum in se as opposed to malum prohibitum is not easy to decipher in many instances.

In any event, this distinction has some utility in the caselaw. For instance, where a court is attempting to determine if an offense is in the nature of strict liability (an offense that has no mental-state requirement), it will be more prone to tolerate the proposition that a particular criminal act is unlawful without an accompanying mental state if the offense is malum prohibitum.[160] For example, a municipal animal control ordinance was judicially interpreted by an Illinois court as allowing for strict liability, in part, because the ordinance was considered malum prohibitum.[161] The rationale for such a conclusion is based on the theory that since mala prohibita offenses normally carry civil type penalties, such as a fine only, no real hardship will be imposed on the wrongdoer who is convicted without reference to his mental blameworthiness.

The malum in se/malum prohibitum dichotomy may have relevance regarding whether a defendant has sufficient notice of the details of a criminal charge. Thus, where an indictment charged defendant with official misconduct for acting "in excess of lawful authority" by accepting reimbursement for legal expenses incurred as a private citizen, the court held that because (1) official misconduct is a malum prohibitum offense and (2) there is no per se wrongful act in accepting reimbursement from a governmental body for legal expenses incurred as a private citizen, the indictment was fatally defective for not specifying *how* the reimbursement was in excess of defendant's authority."[162]

---

[157] M. CHERIF BASSIOUNI, SUBSTANTIVE CRIMINAL LAW 270 (1978).

[158] M. CHERIF BASSIOUNI, SUBSTANTIVE CRIMINAL LAW 270 (1978).

[159] M. CHERIF BASSIOUNI, SUBSTANTIVE CRIMINAL LAW 270 (1978).

[160] *See* Village of Northbrook v. Cannon, 61 Ill. App. 3d 315, 320-21, 377 N.E.2d 1208, 1212-13 (1st Dist. 1978). *See also* Morissette v. United States, 342 U.S. 246 (1952).

[161] Village of Northbrook v. Cannon, 61 Ill. App. 3d 315, 320-21, 377 N.E.2d 1208, 1212-13 (1st Dist. 1978).

[162] People v. Williamson, 285 Ill. App. 3d 727, 732-33, 674 N.E.2d 794, 798 (3d Dist. 1996).

Some authorities go so far as to claim that these "public welfare"[163] offenses, known as mala prohibita strictures, are really not "crimes" at all.[164] This assertion is summarily rejected by this author on the ground that if the penalties attached to a public welfare offense, albeit through strict liability concepts, allow for incarceration, conduct proscribed in a malum prohibitum statute is nothing less than a crime.

§ 1.10. — Infamous Crimes.

A further category of offenses that no longer has major significance in Illinois was the so-called "infamous" crimes. Before this statutory categorization was repealed in 1986,[165] infamous crimes were defined as "the offenses of arson, bigamy, bribery, burglary, aggravated criminal sexual assault, criminal sexual assault, subsequent conviction for criminal sexual abuse, forgery, kidnapping or aggravated kidnapping, murder, perjury, robbery, sale of narcotic drugs, subornation of perjury, and theft if the punishment imposed is imprisonment in the penitentiary."[166] Although early Illinois Supreme Court decisions indicated that whether a crime is infamous depends "not upon the common law or the court's view of its moral aspects, but upon the statute,"[167] later opinions indicated the above statutory listing was not all inclusive but rather the determination of what constituted an infamous crime was open to judicial interpretation based on whether the crime fell within the general classification of being inconsistent with commonly accepted principles of honesty and decency.[168] Under this interpretation, both felonies and misdemeanors could be classified as infamous.[169] In any event, whether a crime is infamous has ramifications on, among other things, the applicability of certain civil disabilities following conviction.[170] For example, the Illinois Constitution provides that a person who is guilty of a felony, bribery, perjury, or other infamous crime is ineligible to hold any public office created by the constitution.[171] At one time, only crimes denominated as infamous could be used during the cross-examination of a witness to impeach

---

[163] Francis Sayre, *Public Welfare Offenses*, 33 COLUM. L. REV. 55 (1933).

[164] ROLLIN M. PERKINS & RONALD N. BOYCE, CRIMINAL LAW 886 (3d ed. 1982).

[165] P.A. 84-1407 (1986).

[166] ILL. REV. STAT. ch. 38, para. 124-1 (1985) (repealed).

[167] People v. Green, 292 Ill. 351, 356, 127 N.E. 50, 52 (1920).

[168] People ex rel Keenan v. McGuane, 13 Ill. 2d 520, 532-33, 150 N.E.2d 168, 176 (1958).

[169] People ex rel Ward v. Tomek, 54 Ill. App. 2d 197, 203, 203 N.E.2d 744, 746 (1st Dist. 1964).

[170] *See* John F. Decker, *Collateral Consequences of a Felony Conviction in Illinois*, 56 CHI.-KENT L. REV. 731, 733-36 (1980).

[171] U.S. CONST. art. XIII, § 1.

the credibility of the witness.[172] However, this is no longer true, since the Illinois courts, in essence, adopted Rule 609 of the Federal Rules of Evidence.[173]

§ 1.11. — Inchoate Offenses.

Chapter 720 of the Illinois Compiled Statutes consists of four basic categories of criminal offenses: (1) "Criminal Code of 1961" prohibitions (2) other "Offenses against Persons," (3) other "Offenses Against Property" and (4) other "Offenses Against the Public." This book will concentrate primarily on the criminal proscriptions of the Criminal Code of 1961 but will briefly describe the other three categories .

The Criminal Code of 1961 places all its offenses into certain categories. First, there are the "inchoate offenses."[174] Inchoate offenses include solicitation,[175] conspiracy,[176] and attempt.[177] Inchoate crimes have in common the fact that "each is preliminary to another and more serious principal offense."[178] These will be discussed further in subsequent chapters.[179]

§ 1.12. — Offenses Directed Against the Person.

The second kind of offense listed in the Criminal Code of 1961 is "offenses directed against the person."[180] These offenses include the commission and concealment of illegal homicides,[181] kidnapping and related offenses,[182] sex offenses,[183] crimes involving bodily harm such as assault and battery,[184] and elec-

---

[172] *See, e.g.,* People v. Beard, 67 Ill. App. 2d 83, 87-88, 214 N.E.2d 577, 579 (1st Dist. 1966) (disorderly conduct not "infamous" crime and, accordingly, could not be used for impeachment of witness).

[173] People v. Montgomery, 47 Ill. 2d 510, 516, 268 N.E.2d 695, 699 (1971) (for the purpose of attacking the credibility of a witness, evidence that he has been convicted of a crime, except on a plea of nolo contendere, is admissible but only if the crime (1) was punishable by death or imprisonment in excess of one year under the law under which he was convicted or (2) involved dishonesty or false statement, regardless of the punishment, unless, (3) in either case, the judge determines that the probative value of the evidence of the crime is substantially outweighed by the danger of unfair prejudice). *See also* People v. Williams, 161 Ill. 2d 1, 41, 641 N.E. 296, 313 (1994) ("*Montgomery* rule remains the law in this state. . . .").

[174] 720 ILCS 5/8-1 through 5/8-4 (1999).

[175] 720 ILCS 5/8-1 (1999).

[176] 720 ILCS 5/8-2 (1999).

[177] 720 ILCS 5/8-4 (1999).

[178] ILL. ANN. STAT. ch. 38, art. 8 (Smith-Hurd 1989), 1961 Committee Comments, at 465.

[179] *See* ch. 4 (conspiracy) and ch. 5 (attempt and solicitation).

[180] 720 ILCS 5/9-1 through 5/14-9 (1999).

[181] 720 ILCS 5/9-1 through 5/9-3.3 (1999).

[182] 720 ILCS 5/10-1 through 5/10-8 (1999).

[183] 720 ILCS 5/11-6 through 5/11-22 (1999).

[184] 720 ILCS 5/12-1 through 5/12-34 (1999).

tronic eavesdropping strictures.[185] These will also be discussed in detail in later chapters.

§ 1.13. — Offenses Directed Against Property.

The third codified category of specific offenses in the Illinois Criminal Code is "offenses directed against property."[186] This category includes theft,[187] retail theft,[188] library theft,[189] unlawful sale of household appliances,[190] computer crime,[191] delivery container crime,[192] wireless service theft,[193] deceptive practices,[194] WIC (food stamp) fraud,[195] robbery,[196] burglary,[197] arson,[198] causing a catastrophe,[199] criminal damage or trespass to property,[200] residential picketing,[201] and interference with a public institution of higher education.[202]

§ 1.14. — Offenses Affecting Public Health, Safety, and Decency.

A fourth category of crimes listed in the Criminal Code of 1961 is "offenses affecting public health, safety and decency."[203] These offenses include prohibitions concerning the possession and use of deadly weapons,[204] mob action,[205] disorderly conduct,[206] gambling,[207] bribery in athletic contests,[208] commercial bribery,[209] money laundering[210] and international terrorism.[211]

---

[185] 720 ILCS 5/14-1 through 5/14-9 (1999).
[186] 720 ILCS 5/16 through 5/21.2-6 (1999).
[187] 720 ILCS 5/16-1 though 5/16-15 (1999).
[188] 720 ILCS 5/16A-1 through 5/16A-10 (1999).
[189] 720 ILCS 5/16B-1 though 5/16B-5 (1999).
[190] 720 ILCS 5/16C-1 through 5/16C-3 (1999).
[191] 720 ILCS 5/16D-1 though 5/16D-7 (1999).
[192] 720 ILCS 5/16E-1 through 5/16E-4 (1999).
[193] 720 ILCS 5/16F-1 through 5/16F-6 (1999).
[194] 720 ILCS 5/17-1 through 5/17-22 (1999).
[195] 720 ILCS 5/17B-1 through 5/17B-30 (1999).
[196] 720 ILCS 5/18-1 through 5/18-5 (1999).
[197] 720 ILCS 5/19-1 through 5/19-5 (1999).
[198] 720 ILCS 5/20-1 though 5/20-2 (1999).
[199] 720 ILCS 5/20.5-5 (1999).
[200] 720 ILCS 5/21-1 through 5/21-7 (1999).
[201] 720 ILCS 5/21.1 through 5/21.3 (1999).
[202] 720 ILCS 5/21.2-1 through 5/21.2-6 (1999).
[203] 720 ILCS 5/24-1 through 5/29C-15 (1999).
[204] 720 ILCS 5/24-1 through 5/24-8 (1999).
[205] 720 ILCS 5/25-1 through 5/25-2 (1999).
[206] 720 ILCS 5/26-1 through 5/26-4 (1999).
[207] 720 ILCS 5/28-1 through 5/28-9 (1999).
[208] 720 ILCS 5/29-1 through 5/29-3 (1999).
[209] 720 ILCS 5/29A-1 through 5/29A-3 (1999).
[210] 720 ILCS 5/29B-1 (1999).
[211] 720 ILCS 5/29C-5 through 5/29C-15 (1999).

§ 1.15. — Offenses Affecting Governmental Functions.

Fifth, within the Criminal Code of 1961 there are "offenses affecting govern-mental functions."[212] They include treason and related offenses,[213] crimes in-volving interference with public officers,[214] crimes involving interference with a penal institution,[215] crimes involving interference with judicial procedure[216] and official misconduct and related offenses.[217]

§ 1.16. — Certain Aggravated Offenses.

The sixth group of specific substantive crimes listed in the Illinois Criminal Code of 1961 is called "certain aggravated offenses."[218] The various "aggra-vated" crimes are, for the most part, scattered throughout the code. For example, aggravated kidnapping,[219] aggravated criminal sexual assault,[220] aggravated stalking,[221] and aggravated battery[222] appear in the section dealing with crimes "directed against the person." Aggravated arson[223] and aggravated computer tampering[224] appear in the category of "offenses directed against property." Al-though the offenses in this category of "certain aggravated offenses" might logi-cally have been placed in one of the preceding categories, the General Assem-bly, however, created this classification in a special code section, articles 5/33A through 5/33F. These articles cover the crimes of armed violence,[225] contribut-ing to the criminal delinquency of a juvenile,[226] unlawful use of body armor,[227] offenses involving deception relating to certification of disadvantaged business enterprises,[228] public contract crimes[229] and include the state's habitual-criminal

---

[212] 720 ILCS 5/30-1 through 5/33-4 (1999).
[213] 720 ILCS 5/30-1 through 5/30-3 (1999).
[214] 720 ILCS 5/31-1 through 5/31-8 (1999).
[215] 720 ILCS 5/31A-1.1 through 5/31A-1.2 (1999).
[216] 720 ILCS 5/32-1 through 5/32-13 (1999).
[217] 720 ILCS 5/33-1 through 5/33-4 (1999).
[218] 720 ILCS 5/33A-1 through 5/33F-3 (1999).
[219] 720 ILCS 5/10-2 (1999).
[220] 720 ILCS 5/12-14 (1999).
[221] 720 ILCS 5/12-7.4 (1999).
[222] 720 ILCS 5/12-4 (1999).
[223] 720 ILCS 5/20-1.1 (1999).
[224] 720 ILCS 5/16D-4 (199).
[225] 720 ILCS 5/33A-1 through 5/33A-3 (1999).
[226] 720 ILCS 5/33D-1 (1999).
[227] 720 ILCS 5/33F-1 through 5/33F-3 (1999).
[228] 720 ILCS 5/33C-1 through 5/33C-5 (1999).
[229] 720 ILCS 5/33E-1 through 5/33E-18 (1999).

legislation,[230] which provides for a mandatory life sentence for a third or subsequent conviction of certain serious offenses.[231]

§ 1.17. — Added Articles.

A seventh, and most odd, category of crimes in the Criminal Code of 1961 are the so-called "added articles."[232] While the "added article" offenses have in common the fact that they were not part of the original Criminal Code of 1961, it is curious as to why they were not treated like other additions to the penal code and placed along side other, at least somewhat, related prohibitions. For example, the section on retail theft[233] that was added in 1975 was placed alongside other theft crimes in the "offenses directed against property," while the section on criminal sexual assault[234] that was added in 1984 was placed in the "offenses directed against persons" provisions. However, the crimes of maintaining a public nuisance,[235] criminal usury,[236] looting,[237] unlawful transfer of telecommunications device to a minor (for use in a drug transaction),[238] disclosing location of domestic violence victim[239] and insurance fraud[240] enjoy their own unique category. But, again, it would seem that these prohibitions could have been placed in one of the preceding categories by the same amendment process that was used by the legislature for the additions of retail theft and criminal sexual assault. For instance, since maintaining a criminal nuisance involves use of buildings to advance a criminal purpose, it would seem it would be more logical to place this offense in the category of "offenses affecting the public health, safety and decency." Likewise, usury is a theft-type offense that could have been placed with "offenses directed against property."

§ 1.18. — Criminal Proscriptions Outside the Criminal Code of 1961.

Within Chapter 720 of Illinois Compiled Statutes are criminal proscriptions that were not part of the Criminal Code in 1961, as amended, but were moved into the "criminal offenses" chapter during the 1993 recompilation of the entire Illinois Code.[241] These added proscriptions are divided into three categories:

---

[230] 720 ILCS 5/33B-1 through 5/33B-3 (1999).
[231] 720 ILCS 5/33B-1 (1999).
[232] 720 ILCS 5/36-1 through 5/47-25 (1999).
[233] 720 ILCS 5/16A-1 (1999).
[234] 720 ILCS 5/12-13 (1999).
[235] 720 ILCS 5/37-1 (1999).
[236] 720 ILCS 5/39-1 through 5/39-3 (1999).
[237] 720 ILCS 5/42-1, 5/42-2 (1999).
[238] 720 ILCS 5/44-1, 5/44-2 (1999).
[239] 720 ILCS 5/45-1, 5/45-2 (1999).
[240] 720 ILCS 5/46-1 (1999).
[241] See § 1.01 of this chapter.

(1) "offenses against persons," (2) "offenses against property," and (3) "offenses against the public." As with the "certain aggravated offenses" and the "added articles" crimes, it is unclear why these provisions were not placed in one of the earlier categories listed above. For example, the "offenses against persons" should have been made part of "offenses directed against persons" in the Criminal Code of 1961. The net effect of this additional category is to give the code an appearance of being a patchwork structure. The "offenses against persons" articles include the Hazing Act,[242] the Neglected Children Offense Act,[243] and the Harassing and Obscene Communications Act.[244] The "offenses against property" articles include the Coin Slug Act,[245] the Illinois Credit Card and Debit Card Act,[246] the Deceptive Advertising Act,[247] the Horse Mutilation Act,[248] the Telephone Line Interference Act,[249] the Telephone Coin Box Tampering Act,[250] the Ticket Scalping Act[251] and the Video Movie Sales and Rentals Act.[252] The "offenses against the public" articles include the Abandoned Refrigerator Act,[253] the Cannabis Control Act,[254] the Illinois Controlled Substances Act,[255] the Discrimination in Sale of Real Estate Act,[256] the Draft Card Mutilation Act,[257] the Drug Paraphernalia Control Act,[258] the Flag Desecration Act,[259] the Hypodermic Syringes and Needles Act,[260] the Party Line Emergency Act[261] and the Sale of Tobacco to Minors Act.[262]

§ 1.19. Lesser Included Offenses and Same Physical Act Doctrine.

Concerns relating around lesser included offenses and related issues have been a thorn in the side of the Illinois courts. One appellate opinion observed,

---

[242] 720 ILCS 120/0.01 through 120/10 (1999).
[243] 720 ILCS 130/0.01 through 130/3 (1999).
[244] 720 ILCS 135/0.01 through 135/2 (1999).
[245] 720 ILCS 235/1, 235/1a (1999).
[246] 720 ILCS 250/1 through 250/24 (1999).
[247] 720 ILCS 295/1a through 295/1e (1999).
[248] 720 ILCS 315/0.01, 315/1 (1999).
[249] 720 ILCS 360/1, 360/1.1 (1999).
[250] 720 ILCS 370/0.01 through 370/2 (1999).
[251] 720 ILCS 375/0.01 through 375/4 (1999).
[252] 720 ILCS 395/1 through 395/4 (1999).
[253] 720 ILCS 505/0.01, 505/1 (1999).
[254] 720 ILCS 550/1 through 550/19 (1999).
[255] 720 ILCS 570/100 through 570/603 (1999).
[256] 720 ILCS 590/0.01 through 590/3 (1999).
[257] 720 ILCS 595/0.01, 590/1 (1999).
[258] 720 ILCS 600/1 through 600/7 (1999).
[259] 720 ILCS 620/0.01 through 620/5 (1999).
[260] 720 ILCS 635/0.01 through 635/6 (1999).
[261] 720 ILCS 660/0.01 through 660/4 (1999).
[262] 720 ILCS 675/0.01 through 675/2 (1999).

"Illinois courts have struggled with the issue of whether a lesser crime may be considered included in a greater offense and whether a need then may arise to instruct the jury accordingly."[263] In addition, there are few concerns that have been the subject of as many "confusing, illogical and inconsistent results" in the caselaw as those revolving around the extent to which multiple crimes can arise out of a defendant's single act or transaction.[264] However, this difficulty necessitates that these topics be fully explored and analyzed. Moreover, the importance of these issues becomes evident when one considers that they raise issues of due process,[265] double jeopardy,[266] and prejudicial sentences.[267]

There exists a "nearly universal acceptance of the rule in both state and federal courts" that a defendant is entitled to jury instructions of possible lesser included offenses.[268] Quite likely mandated by due process,[269] the "reason for this [rule] is clear: an instruction on a lesser offense provides an important third option to a jury which, believing that the defendant is guilty of something but uncertain whether the charged offense has been proven, might otherwise convict rather than acquit the defendant of the greater offense."[270] It appears a tendered lesser included offense jury instruction should be given (1) when a jury could rationally find the defendant guilty of the lesser included offense and acquit him or her of the greater offense; and (2) where the jury must find a disputed factual element necessary to convict of the greater offense but unnecessary to convict of the lesser included one.[271] If these two factors are met, a court's failure to tender a defendant's requested lesser included offense instruction can be deemed re-

---

[263] People v. Ross, 226 Ill. App. 3d 392, 394, 589 N.E.2d 854, 855 (1st Dist. 1992). *See also* Christen R. Blair, *Constitutional Limitations on the Lesser Included Offense Doctrine*, 21 AM. CRIM. L. REV. 445 (1984).

[264] People v. King, 66 Ill. 2d 551, 565-66, 363 N.E.2d 838, 844, *cert. denied*, 434 U.S. 894 (1977).

[265] Keeble v. United States, 412 U.S. 205, 213 (1973) ("[W]hile we have never explicitly held that the Due Process Clause of the Fifth Amendment guarantees the right of a defendant to have the jury instructed on a lesser included offense, it is nevertheless clear that a [failure of a trial court to do so] would raise difficult constitutional questions").

[266] Brown v. Ohio, 432 U.S. 161 (1977) (violation of double jeopardy to convict defendant of auto theft after defendant convicted of lesser included offense of joyriding).

[267] People v. King, 66 Ill. 2d 551, 566, 363 N.E.2d 838, 844, *cert. denied*, 434 U.S. 894 (1977).

[268] Beck v. Alabama, 447 U.S. 625, 636-37 (1980); *see also* People v. Bryant, 113 Ill. 2d 497, 502, 499 N.E.2d 413, 415 (1986) ("The principle is well established that a defendant may be entitled to have the jury instructed on a less serious offense that is included in the one he is charged with").

[269] Keeble v. United States, 412 U.S. 205, 213 (1973).

[270] People v. Bryant, 113 Ill. 2d 497, 507, 499 N.E.2d 413, 417-18 (1986) (citing Keeble v. United States, 412 U.S. 205, 212-13 (1973)).

[271] People v. Bryant, 113 Ill. 2d 497, 507, 499 N.E.2d 413, 416-18 (1986).

versible error.[272] For example, where a defendant, charged with possession of more than 30 grams of cocaine with intent to deliver, requested the court to tender instructions on the lesser included offenses of possession of cocaine or possession of less than 30 grams of cocaine, the court committed reversible error in not giving the instruction because of the facts surrounding the defendant's alleged possession that were in dispute.[273] Likewise, a defendant, charged with aggravated battery and resisting a police officer, was entitled to an instruction on reckless conduct where there was an issue of fact regarding whether the defendant acted "knowingly" or "recklessly."[274] However, it is not clear at this time whether a trial court can instruct a jury, sua sponte, about a possible lesser included offense over the express objection of a defendant.[275]

Just as a trial court's failure to instruct a jury about a lesser included offense can lead to reversible error, a trial court's instruction beyond the crime charged and offenses included within that crime can amount to reversible error.[276] Injecting into a case, by way of instruction, an issue about a charge not properly before the jury has much potential for confusion and is considered prejudicial.[277]

Another area where the lesser included doctrine's importance can be seen is in its protection of the constitutional prohibition against double jeopardy.[278] This prohibition protects against three possibilities: "(1) a second prosecution after acquittal; (2) a second prosecution after conviction; and (3) multiple punishments for the same offense."[279] Thus, in order to protect against double jeopardy implications, the courts must determine whether (1) the two offenses are essentially the same or (2) one offense is a lesser included of another. For example,

---

[272] People v. Bryant, 113 Ill. 2d 497, 507, 499 N.E.2d 413, 416-18 (1986) (failure to instruct on criminal damage to property where defendant charged with attempted burglary was reversible error); People v. Dace, 104 Ill. 2d 96, 102-03, 470 N.E.2d 993, 996 (1984) (failure to instruct on theft where evidence at defendant's residential burglary trial possibly established theft rather than greater crime was reversible error).

[273] People v. Castro, 190 Ill. App. 3d 227, 235, 546 N.E.2d 662, 666-67 (1st Dist. 1989).

[274] People v. Willis, 170 Ill. App. 3d 638, 641-42, 524 N.E.2d 1259, 1261-62 (3d Dist. 1988).

[275] People v. Garcia, 292 Ill. App. 3d 685, 687-90, 686 N.E.2d 700, 702-03 (1st Dist. 1997) (trial court lacked discretion to instruct jury on possession of controlled substance where defendant charged with possession with intent to distribute and defendant objected to lesser included offense instruction); *compare* People v. Sinnot, 226 Ill. App. 3d 923, 925, 590 N.E.2d 502, 503 (4th Dist. 1992) (contra).

[276] People v. English, 287 Ill. App. 3d 1043, 1047, 679 N.E.2d 494, 496-97 (3d Dist. 1997).

[277] *See, e.g.,* People v. English, 287 Ill. App. 3d 1043, 1047, 679 N.E.2d 494, 496-97 (3d Dist. 1997) (instruction on resisting arrest and attempted escape where defendant charged with burglary and aggravated battery reversible error).

[278] U.S. CONST. amend. V ("[N]or shall any person be subject for the same offense to twice put in jeopardy of life or limb."); ILL. CONST., art. I, § 10 ("No person shall be . . . twice put in jeopardy for the same offense").

[279] People v. Stefan, 146 Ill. 2d 324, 332, 586 N.E.2d 1239, 1244 (1992) (citing Illinois v. Vitale, 447 U.S. 410, 415 (1980)).

the Illinois Supreme Court ruled that it would violate double jeopardy to allow a trial court to retry or resentence the defendants for unlawful delivery of more than thirty grams of cocaine after they had already been convicted of the lesser offense of unlawful delivery of less than thirty grams of the substance where the incident involved the same delivery.[280] Here, the court relied on the double jeopardy principle that a conviction on the lesser offense operates as an acquittal of the greater offense.[281] Similarly, an Illinois appellate court ruled that where a defendant had pled guilty to the lesser included offense of possession of a stolen motor vehicle, double jeopardy prevented the state from attempting to prosecute the defendant for the greater charges of armed robbery, robbery, aggravated vehicular hijacking and vehicular hijacking.[282]

Beyond the "lesser included offense" concerns is the somewhat related but distinct concern known as the "same physical act" doctrine.[283] Recognizing that while "[m]ultiple convictions and *consecutive* sentences have been permitted against claims of double jeopardy for offenses based on a single act but requiring proof of different facts," the Illinois Supreme Court has held that these multiple convictions and sentences may nevertheless create "prejudice" to a defendant "where more than one offense is carved from the same physical act."[284] Thus, where a defendant was tried and convicted for attempted murder and three counts of aggravated battery, based on the rapid firing of six shots in a single location at the victim, the aggravated battery convictions and sentences had to be vacated because they arose out of the same physical act as the attempted murder.[285]

As mentioned earlier, these areas of the law are complex and confusing. Some of the complexity and confusion arises from the Illinois courts' inconsistent and sometimes selective analytical approach to the lesser included offense doctrine. A good illustration of this inconsistency is the courts' treatment of the charges of first degree murder[286] and second degree murder[287] after the revision of the homicide legislation in 1987.[288] During the early 1990's, the Illinois appellate

[280] People ex rel. Daley v. Limperis, 86 Ill. 2d 459, 467-68, 427 N.E.2d 1212, 1215-16 (1981).

[281] People ex rel. Daley v. Limperis, 86 Ill. 2d 459, 468, 427 N.E.2d 1212, 1215 (1981). *See also* Green v. United States, 355 U.S. 184, 190-91 (1957) (stating principle); People v. Gray, 69 Ill. 2d 44, 51, 370 N.E.2d 797, 800 (1977) (same); People v. Fisher, 259 Ill. App. 3d 445, 452, 632 N.E.2d 689, 694 (5th Dist. 1994) (same).

[282] People v. Eggerman, 292 Ill. App. 3d 644, 647-50, 685 N.E.2d 948, 950-52 (1st Dist. 1997).

[283] People v. King, 66 Ill. 2d 551, 565-66, 363 N.E.2d 838, 844-45, *cert. denied*, 434 U.S. 894 (1977).

[284] People v. King, 66 Ill. 2d 551, 565-66, 363 N.E.2d 838, 844, *cert. denied*, 434 U.S. 894 (1977) (emphasis original).

[285] People v. Guzman, 208 Ill. App. 3d 525, 535, 567 N.E.2d 500, 508 (1st Dist. 1990).

[286] 720 ILCS 5/9-1 (1999).

[287] 720 ILCS 5/9-2 (1999).

[288] P.A. 84-1450 (1987).

courts had taken three different positions on the important issue of whether second degree murder is a lesser included offense of first degree murder. Some courts held that second degree murder was a lesser included offense of first degree murder, based on the theory that second degree murder carries a less culpable mental state.[289] Another court instead used an abstract elemental composition comparison analysis and found that second degree murder was not a lesser included offense of first degree murder because it requires proof of all the elements of first degree murder, including the same mental state, *plus* an element of mitigation.[290] And, yet another appellate court took the analysis one step further, holding that second degree murder is a "lesser mitigated offense" of first degree murder, as opposed to a lesser included offense, reasoning that it is a *lesser* offense because it carries a lesser penalty than first degree murder and a *mitigated* offense since this crime "is first degree murder *plus*" mitigation.[291] Finally, the Illinois Supreme Court in 1995 endorsed the conclusion that second degree murder was a "lesser mitigated offense" of first degree murder.[292]

The Illinois courts have also shown a degree of inconsistency in determining whether a defendant is prejudiced by being charged with several offenses based on the same physical act or course of conduct. In one instance, where the defendant ran after his victim, caught her, dragged her into a park where he raped her, the court concluded that the defendant could not be convicted of both rape (which is now referred to as criminal sexual assault) and unlawful restraint because they were all part of one criminal act.[293] In another instance, a defendant choked his victim while stopped on a deserted road, then drove her to a secluded area and sexually assaulted her.[294] After the sexual assault, the woman jumped out of the car and the defendant physically prevented her from entering her grandfather's house. The court held the defendant could properly be convicted of both unlawful restraint and criminal sexual assault as the convictions were based on separate unrelated acts.[295] Meanwhile, where a defendant was found in the possession of cocaine and PCP, the court held that the defendant could only

---

[289] *See, e.g.,* People v. Timberson, 213 Ill. App. 3d 1037, 1040-43, 573 N.E.2d 374, 375-77 (5th Dist. 1991); People v. Swanson, 211 Ill. App. 3d 510, 514-16, 570 N.E.2d 503, 506-07 (1st Dist. 1991).

[290] People v. Thomas, 216 Ill. App. 3d 469, 472-73, 576 N.E.2d 1020, 1023-24 (1st Dist. 1991) ("second degree murder is first degree murder plus an element of mitigation"). *See also* Timothy O'Neill, *An Analysis of Illinois' New Offense of Second Degree Murder*, 20 J. MARSHALL L. REV. 209, 224 (1986).

[291] People v. Newbern, 219 Ill. App. 3d 333, 353, 579 N.E.2d 583, 596 (4th Dist. 1991).

[292] People v. Jeffries, 164 Ill. 2d 104, 121, 646 N.E.2d 587, 595 (1995).

[293] People v. Jones, 114 Ill. App. 3d 576, 591-92, 449 N.E.2d 547, 559-60 (1st Dist. 1983) (citing three appellate decisions adopting the same view).

[294] People v. Alvarado, 235 Ill. App. 3d 116, 117, 600 N.E.2d 1236, 1237 (3d Dist. 1992).

[295] People v. Alvarado, 235 Ill. App. 3d 116, 117, 600 N.E.2d 1236, 1237 (3d Dist. 1992).

be convicted for possession with intent to deliver cocaine.[296] Here, the appellate court reasoned that simultaneous possession of more than one controlled substance constituted only one offense because it arose from the same act.[297] On the other hand, where the defendant, an alleged drug seller, simultaneously possessed cocaine and a "look-alike" substance, which was determined not to be a controlled substance but rather a powder that looked like a controlled substance, he was convicted of possession with intent to deliver a controlled substance *and* possession with intent to deliver a look-alike substance over "same physical act" doctrine objections.[298]

Another area that has proved troublesome for the courts is whether certain forms of forced sexual misconduct add up to one or more acts of criminal sexual abuse or criminal sexual assault. In one case, where the defendant fondled his victim's vagina with his hands and fondled her breasts with his mouth, this was considered one count of aggravated criminal sexual abuse, not two.[299] The court reasoned: "[t]he acts were almost simultaneous in time; they involved the same victim; and they were different violations of the same statute."[300] Meanwhile, in another case, a defendant's convictions for two counts of aggravated criminal assault were sustained where defendant forcibly entered the victim's apartment and forced her to succumb to vaginal and oral intercourse.[301] The court, noting the sensitive nature of rape and stressing rape's difference from other sex crimes, held that a conviction for each criminal sexual assault was proper.[302]

---

[296] People v. Love, 222 Ill. App. 3d 428, 433-34, 584 N.E.2d 189, 193-94 (1st Dist. 1991).

[297] People v. Love, 222 Ill. App. 3d 428, 433-34, 584 N.E.2d 189, 193-94 (1st Dist. 1991) (citing People v. Manning, 71 Ill. 2d 132, 374 N.E.2d 200 (1978) and numerous other Illinois opinions). The legislature enacted in 1998 Public Act 90-593 which is designed to punish simultaneous possession of more than one type of controlled substance in response to decisions like *Manning* and *Love. See* ch. 16 for a discussion of drug offenses.

[298] People v. Watkins, 172 Ill. App. 3d 168, 171, 526 N.E.2d 448, 449 (1st Dist. 1988) (distinguishing *Manning*).

[299] People v. Burmeister, 147 Ill. App. 3d 218, 226, 497 N.E.2d 1212, 1217 (2d Dist. 1986).

[300] People v. Burmeister, 147 Ill. App. 3d 218, 226, 497 N.E.2d 1212, 1217 (2d Dist. 1986). However, the court ruled the defendant could be convicted of criminal sexual abuse as well as criminal sexual assault, since he had also penetrated the victim's vagina. *Id.*

[301] People v. Segara, 126 Ill. 2d 70, 78, 533 N.E.2d 802, 805 (1988).

[302] The Illinois Supreme Court stated:

> For the defendant to claim only one rape occurred, "demeans the dignity of the human personality and individuality." To the victim, each rape was "readily divisible and intensely personal; each offense is an offense against *a person*." To permit defendant to rape an individual several times over a period of time in the same place with little or no break between each act deprecates the heinous and violent nature of each act and the effect each act has upon the victim. * * * Rape is unlike other offenses: with each act, the victim's psychological constitution and most intimate part of her being have been violently invaded.

Additionally, differences and changes in philosophical approach to the subject add to the confusion and complex nature of the area. This philosophical change is evident in the context of armed robbery and theft. In the past, the Illinois courts differed as to whether theft is a lesser included offense depending on which philosophical approach they took as to lesser included offenses. Where an appellate court used an abstract elemental or statutory definition comparison approach, it would hold that theft is not a lesser included offense of armed robbery.[303] However, if the appellate court examined the language of the charging instrument and/or the evidence adduced at trial, theft might be found to be a lesser included offense of armed robbery.[304] Finally, in *People v. Jones*,[305] the Illinois Supreme Court adopted the pleadings or charging instrument approach in holding that theft may be a lesser included offense of armed robbery if the charging instrument sufficiently alleges that the defendant knowingly took property with intent to deprive the victim of the property.[306] This approach varies with the language of the charging instrument and the interpretation of that language by the judge, offering greater discretion and flexibility, but less predictability as to future results.[307]

§ 1.20. Various Approaches to Lesser Included Offenses.

Illinois has codified the included offense doctrine in section 5/2-9(a) of chapter 720, which states that an included offense is "an offense which is established by proof of the same or less than all of the facts or a less culpable mental state (or both), than that which is required to establish the commission of the offense charged. . . ."[308] However, this codified definition of an included offense has not explained "which of the following is determinative in deciding if a particular offense is an included offense of another: the abstract statutory definition of the greater crime; the greater crime as it is alleged in the indictment or other charging instrument; or the greater crime as its necessary elements are proved at trial."[309] The Illinois courts have examined these different tests over the years

---

People v. Segara, 126 Ill. 2d 70, 78, 533 N.E.2d 802, 805 (1988) (citations omitted; emphasis original).

[303] *See, e.g.*, People v. Kimble, 90 Ill. App. 3d 999, 1000-01, 414 N.E.2d 135, 136 (1st Dist. 1980).

[304] *See, e.g.*, People v. Rivers, 194 Ill. App. 3d 193, 196-98, 550 N.E.2d 1179, 1181-83 (1st Dist. 1990) (rejecting *Kimble* and similar decisions).

[305] 149 Ill. 2d 288, 595 N.E.2d 1071 (1992).

[306] People v. Jones, 149 Ill. 2d 288, 295-96, 595 N.E.2d 1071, 1074-75 (1992).

[307] For an excellent discussion and criticism of the *Jones* case, *see* Thomas A. Long, *Recent Decisions, Criminal Law/Lesser Included Offenses*, 81 Ill. B.J. 108 (1999).

[308] 720 ILCS 5/2-9 (1999).

[309] People v. Bryant, 113 Ill. 2d 497, 503, 499 N.E.2d 413, 415 (1986) (quoting People v. Mays, 91 Ill. 2d 251, 255, 437 N.E.2d 633, 635 (1982)).

and they have considered four basic approaches in determining whether an offense is a lesser included one: an abstract statutory definition or elemental composition approach, an evidentiary approach, a pleadings or charging instrument approach, and a related offense approach. Examples of each will be examined in turn.

§ 1.21. — Statutory Definition or Abstract Elemental Composition Approach.

The first approach focuses on the elemental comparison of the offenses, as codified in the Illinois statutes, by examining the language of the stricture purely in the abstract. For example, using this analysis, neither aggravated battery nor battery is a lesser included offense of home invasion.[310] Home invasion requires an unauthorized entry into the home which is not an element of either aggravated battery or battery.[311] Aggravated battery has an element of causing great bodily harm, which home invasion does not.[312] Further, under this approach, it was held that battery is not a lesser included offense of unlawful restraint.[313] Unlawful restraint does not require any element of touching whereas battery requires some physical contact, while unlawful restraint requires proof of unlawful detention of the victim which battery does not.[314]

Where a defendant, on trial for armed violence, requested a lesser included offense instruction on unlawful use of weapons, the appellate court ruled that the trial court had properly denied the request.[315] A comparison of the statutory elements of the two offenses showed that unlawful use of weapons had two elements not necessary to establish the commission of armed violence — possessing a concealed firearm and the possession occurring while the defendant is not on his land, abode, or place of business — while a person could commit armed violence without committing the offense of unlawful use of a weapon.[316] While relying on an abstract elemental comparison analysis, another appellate court determined that attempted theft is not a lesser included offense of forgery since forgery arises where a person makes, alters, issues, delivers or possesses a document with the intent to defraud, whereas attempted theft requires a substantial step toward unlawfully obtaining control over another's property.[317] Using

---

[310] People v. Donnelly, 226 Ill. App. 3d 771, 777, 589 N.E.2d 975, 979 (4th Dist. 1992).

[311] People v. Donnelly, 226 Ill. App. 3d 771, 777, 589 N.E.2d 975, 979 (4th Dist. 1992).

[312] People v. Donnelly, 226 Ill. App. 3d 771, 777, 589 N.E.2d 975, 979 (4th Dist. 1992).

[313] People v. Story, 114 Ill. App. 3d 1029, 1033, 449 N.E.2d 935, 937-38 (1st Dist. 1983).

[314] People v. Story, 114 Ill. App. 3d 1029, 1033, 449 N.E.2d 935, 937-38 (1st Dist. 1983).

[315] People v. Maldonado, 224 Ill. App. 3d 913, 917, 586 N.E.2d 788, 790-91 (2d Dist. 1992).

[316] People v. Maldonado, 224 Ill. App. 3d 913, 917, 586 N.E.2d 788, 790-91 (2d Dist. 1992).

[317] People v. Austin, 93 Ill. App. 3d 495, 496-97, 417 N.E.2d 671, 672-73 (1st Dist. 1981).

this analysis, theft is not a lesser included offense of burglary, as each offense contains an element the other does not.[318]

As stated earlier, section 5/2-9 provides that an included offense is established by finding "a less culpable mental state" than that necessary for committing the crime charged.[319] After referring to this statute, an appellate court found that theft is not a lesser included offense of armed robbery under the abstract statutory definition comparison approach because it requires the specific intent to deprive another of their property permanently while robbery only requires a general intent but does, unlike theft, require proof of force.[320]

Similarly, Illinois caselaw states that felony murder is a lesser included offense of intentional murder because it involves a less culpable mental state — intent to commit a forcible felony is less culpable than intentionally and knowingly killing another.[321] On the other hand, an appellate court held a jury verdict of guilty but mentally ill (GBMI) for murder does not require a less culpable mental state than that necessary for murder.[322] The court reasoned that GBMI required a finding of guilty of the offense charged with the additional element of mental illness.[323] Thus, one found GBMI of murder could be retried and convicted of ordinary murder following an appellate reversal of the GBMI conviction on procedural grounds since the GBMI verdict was not an implied acquittal for ordinary murder.[324]

Section 5/2-9 also states that an included offense is one which is "established by proof of the same or less than all the *facts* . . . than that which is required to establish commission of the offense charged."[325] After consideration of the statute, an appellate court ruled an unlawful restraint conviction was a lesser included offense of an aggravated criminal sexual assault where these offenses "each were an interrelated act in the same transaction."[326] So too, where a defendant pled guilty to possession of a stolen motor vehicle in Lake County, later vehicular hijacking and robbery charges arising out of the same incident that

---

[318] People v. McCreary, 123 Ill. App. 3d 880, 889, 463 N.E.2d 455, 458-59 (2d Dist. 1984).

[319] 720 ILCS 5/2-9 (1999).

[320] People v. Kimble, 90 Ill. App. 3d 999, 1000-01, 414 N.E.2d 135, 136 (1st Dist. 1980). *But see* People v. Jones, 149 Ill. 2d 288, 297-98, 595 N.E.2d 1071, 1075 (1992) (specific intent offense of theft is a lesser included offense of the general intent offense of armed robbery despite the differing mental states).

[321] People v. Cardona, 158 Ill. 2d 403, 412, 634 N.E.2d 720, 723 (1994); People v. Pitsonberger, 142 Ill. 2d 353, 377-78, 568 N.E.2d 783, 792 (1990); People v. Mack, 105 Ill. 2d 103, 137, 473 N.E.2d 880, 898 (1984).

[322] People v. Fierer, 196 Ill. App. 3d 404, 407, 553 N.E.2d 807, 809 (3d Dist. 1990).

[323] People v. Fierer, 196 Ill. App. 3d 404, 407, 553 N.E.2d 807, 809 (3d Dist. 1990).

[324] People v. Fierer, 196 Ill. App. 3d 404, 407, 553 N.E.2d 807, 809 (3d Dist. 1990).

[325] 720 ILCS 5/2-9 (1999) (emphasis added).

[326] People v. Allman, 180 Ill. App. 3d 396, 403-04, 535 N.E.2d 1097, 1102 (1st Dist. 1989) (while also relying on same physical act doctrine).

were lodged against defendant in Cook County had to be dismissed on double jeopardy grounds, which bars a successive prosecution for a greater offense where a defendant has already been prosecuted for a lesser included offense.[327] Here, the court determined that the same facts that would prove the vehicular hijacking and robbery would have proved the possession of a stolen motor vehicle charge and since "[n]o additional facts are needed to establish the possession offense," it thereby was a lesser included offense.[328]

Absent the less culpable mental state aspect, the Illinois courts' abstract elemental comparison approach is the same as the approach articulated by the United States Supreme Court in *Blockburger v. United States*.[329] *Blockburger* set out the test for determining whether multiple crimes are for double jeopardy purposes the "same offense."[330] The Court ruled: "The applicable rule is that where the same act or transaction constitutes a violation of two distinct statutory provisions, the test to be applied to determine whether there are two offenses or only one, is whether each provision requires proof of a fact which the other does not."[331] Thus, in *Brown v. Ohio*,[332] the court held that the defendant could not be tried for the offense of auto theft after he pleaded guilty to joyriding, since neither offense required proof of a fact that the other did not.[333] In other words, auto theft and joyriding were sufficiently similar in terms of their elemental composition that they could be viewed as the same offense.

In contrast, in *Illinois v. Vitale*,[334] it was held that the defendant could be prosecuted for involuntary manslaughter,[335] arising out of an automobile collision where a person was killed, even though the defendant had already been convicted of the failure to reduce speed to avoid the same collision.[336] In this case, the Court found that involuntary manslaughter required proof of the unjustified taking of a life, which the charge of failure to reduce speed did not, and the motor vehicle code infraction required proof of a failure to reduce speed, which is not a necessary ingredient of involuntary manslaughter, regardless of the circumstances.[337] In *Albernez v. United States*,[338] the defendants were con-

---

[327] People v. Eggerman, 292 Ill. App. 3d 644, 647-50, 685 N.E.2d 948, 949-51 (1st Dist. 1997) (citing Brown v. Ohio, 432 U.S. 161, 169 (1977)).

[328] People v. Eggerman, 292 Ill. App. 3d 644, 647-50, 685 N.E.2d 948, 949-51 (1st Dist. 1997).

[329] 284 U.S. 299 (1932).

[330] *See* CHARLES H. WHITEBREAD & CHRISTOPHER SLOBOGIN, CRIMINAL PROCEDURE § 30.04 (3d ed. 1993) (discussion of "same offense" test).

[331] Blockburger v. United States, 284 U.S. 299, 304 (1932).

[332] 432 U.S. 161 (1977).

[333] Brown v. Ohio, 432 U.S. 161, 168 (1977).

[334] 447 U.S. 410 (1980).

[335] *See* 720 ILCS 5/9-3 (1999) (involuntary manslaughter codified).

[336] *See* 625 ILCS 5/11-601(a) (1999) (failure to reduce speed codified).

[337] Illinois v. Vitale, 447 U.S. 410, 416-19 (1980).

[338] 450 U.S. 333 (1981).

victed in a single trial for conspiracy to import marijuana and conspiracy to distribute marijuana in violation of federal law, and they received separate sentences to run consecutively. Here, the Court rejected the argument that the consecutive punishments were barred by double jeopardy. The Court held that the two statutes at issue specified different ends of the proscribed object of the conspiracy (distribution as opposed to importation) and that each section required proof of a fact that the other did not.[339]

Although the Illinois Supreme Court has relied on the pleading/charging instrument comparison approach[340] instead of the abstract elemental comparison approach since 1992, the latter analysis has nevertheless appeared in some recent appellate cases. For example, in the 1996 decision of *People v. Miller*,[341] one Illinois appellate court relied on the *Blockburger* approach in assessing whether one offense was the lesser included of another.[342] In that case, the court's analysis led to the conclusion that all of the elements of aggravated battery were not "entirely included in the greater offense" of attempted murder.[343] Likewise, in *People v. Eggerman*,[344] another appellate court in 1997 utilized the *Blockburger* test in determining possession of a stolen motor vehicle was a lesser included offense of vehicular hijacking and robbery.[345]

§ 1.22. — Evidentiary Approach.

In some Illinois cases, the paramount concern in determining whether a lesser included offense may have been established appears to involve an examination of the evidence adduced at trial.[346] In *Keeble v. Unites States*,[347] the United States Supreme Court stated:

---

[339] Albernez v. United States, 450 U.S. 333, 339 (1981). *Compare* Rutledge v. United States, 517 U.S. 292, 297-300 (1996) (federal conspiracy to distribute controlled substances is a lesser included offense of federal continuing criminal enterprise, relying on *Blockburger* test).

[340] *See* § 1.23 of this chapter.

[341] 284 Ill. App. 3d 16, 671 N.E.2d 376 (2d Dist. 1996).

[342] People v. Miller, 284 Ill. App. 3d 16, 26-27, 671 N.E.2d 376, 384-85 (2d Dist. 1996), *citing* Blockburger v. United States, 284 U.S. 299 (1932).

[343] People v. Miller, 284 Ill. App. 3d 16, 26-27, 671 N.E.2d 376, 384-85 (2d Dist. 1996).

[344] 292 Ill. App. 3d 644, 685 N.E.2d 948 (1st Dist. 1997).

[345] People v. Eggerman, 292 Ill. App. 3d 644, 647-50, 685 N.E.2d 948, 949-51 (1st Dist. 1997).

[346] *See, e.g.,* People v. Rivers, 194 Ill. App. 3d 193, 196, 550 N.E.2d 1179, 1181-82 (1st Dist. 1990) (discussed in text this section); People v. Williams, 24 Ill. App. 3d 666, 669, 321 N.E.2d 74, 76 (3d Dist. 1974) ("With respect to the issue relating to the instruction on the lesser included offense, if there is any evidence which tends to prove the lesser rather than the greater offense, defendant is normally entitled to such an instruction").

[347] 412 U.S. 205 (1973).

it is now beyond dispute that the defendant is entitled to an instruction on a lesser included offense if the evidence would permit a jury rationally to find him guilty of the lesser offense and acquit him of the greater.[348]

This language was echoed by the Illinois Supreme Court in *People v. Bryant*,[349] where a trial court refused to give a lesser included offense instruction on criminal damage to property in a trial on a charge of attempted burglary because the indictment did not refer to the value of the damage, which is an element of criminal damage to property. The court ruled the attempted burglary indictment "set out the main outline of the lesser offense" as it referred to property damage to a building; "that the indictment did not expressly allege all the elements of the lesser offense is not, in our view, fatal under these circumstances."[350] More importantly, "[t]he evidence introduced at trial showed the defendant's presence at the service station and the occurrence of the damage there, circumstances from which the jury could infer the defendant's responsibility for the damage without also necessarily inferring his intent to commit burglary."[351]

In *People v. Rivers*,[352] a defendant was charged with robbery and aggravated battery but the jury returned a verdict of guilty of theft. The defendant appealed claiming the theft verdict was void since he was not charged with theft, and theft is not a lesser included offense of robbery.[353] The appellate court noted the Illinois Supreme Court in *Bryant* used an analysis that "particularly emphasized . . . [whether] the evidence adduced in each case might support a particular conviction."[354] The fact that the charging instrument did not allege theft or refer to the specific intent element common to theft "is not fatal here, especially where the evidence fully proves that specific intent."[355]

Thus, decisions like *Bryant* and *Rivers* seem most concerned about the evidence adduced at trial and as to whether it supports the lesser crime. While there is considerable overlap between these decisions and those that stress as more important the allegations in the pleadings or charging instrument,[356] there exists an obvious difference in emphasis that cannot be ignored.

---

[348] Keeble v. United States, 412 U.S. 205, 208 (1973).

[349] 113 Ill. 2d 497, 507, 499 N.E.2d 413, 417 (1986) (quoting *Keeble*).

[350] People v. Bryant, 113 Ill. 2d 497, 505, 499 N.E.2d 413, 416-17 (1986).

[351] People v. Bryant, 113 Ill. 2d 497, 506, 499 N.E.2d 413, 417 (1986).

[352] 194 Ill. App. 3d 193, 550 N.E.2d 1179 (1st Dist. 1990).

[353] People v. Rivers, 194 Ill. App. 3d 193, 194, 550 N.E.2d 1179, 1180 (1st Dist. 1990).

[354] People v. Rivers, 194 Ill. App. 3d 193, 196, 550 N.E.2d 1179, 1181 (1st Dist. 1990).

[355] People v. Rivers, 194 Ill. App. 3d 193, 197, 550 N.E.2d 1179, 1182 (1st Dist. 1990).

[356] *See* § 1.23 of this chapter.

§ 1.23. — Pleadings or Charging Instrument Approach.

While some decisions appear to give about equal consideration to the adequacy of evidence and the sufficiency of the charging instrument in assessing whether one crime is a lesser included offense of another,[357] certain Illinois cases have placed primary emphasis on the charging instrument and whether it explicitly or implicitly alleges a lesser included offense.[358] These decisions voice concern about the fact that "[t]he constitution and statutes of this State provide, of course, that no person shall be convicted of an offense which he has not been charged with committing."[359] Although a charging instrument may not allege a lesser crime, a charging instrument "serves as an indictment for all included offenses, even though the latter are not specifically set forth"[360] so long as the elements of the lesser *are* "implicitly set forth."[361]

In the 1992 decision of *People v. Jones*,[362] the Illinois Supreme Court adopted what might be referred to as the pleadings or charging instrument approach when they held that theft was a lesser included offense of armed robbery.[363] In *Jones*, the defendant was charged with armed robbery for taking a car and a purse from his victims, while brandishing a gun and threatening the imminent use of force. The trial court found the evidence presented at trial insufficient to convict the defendant of armed robbery but found him guilty of theft.[364] The appellate court reversed, holding that the defendant could not be convicted of an offense he was not charged with unless it was a lesser included offense of the charged offense.[365] Because it felt theft is not a lesser included offense of armed robbery, the appellate court could not allow the theft conviction to stand.[366]

In reversing the appellate court decision, the Illinois Supreme Court held that the information charging the defendant with armed robbery also set out the elements of theft.[367] The court explained that the mental states required by theft — knowingly obtaining control over another's property and intent to deprive the owner permanently of his property — were "implicitly set out" in the charging instrument.[368] The court stated that the armed robbery mental state could be sat-

---

[357] *See, e.g.*, People v. Dace, 104 Ill. 2d 96, 103, 470 N.E.2d 993, 996 (1984).

[358] *See, e.g.*, People v. Schmidt, 126 Ill. 2d 179, 183-84, 533 N.E.2d 898, 900 (1988).

[359] People v. Schmidt, 126 Ill. 2d 179, 183, 533 N.E.2d 898, 900 (1988) (quoting People v. Lewis, 83 Ill. 2d 296, 300, 415 N.E.2d 319, 320 (1980)).

[360] People v. Schmidt, 126 Ill. 2d 179, 184, 533 N.E.2d 898, 900 (1988) (quoting People v. Melmuka, 173 Ill. App. 3d 735, 736, 527 N.E.2d 982, 983 (1st Dist. 1988)).

[361] People v. Jones, 149 Ill. 2d 288, 296, 595 N.E.2d 1071, 1075 (1992).

[362] 149 Ill. 2d 288, 595 N.E.2d 1071 (1992).

[363] People v. Jones, 149 Ill. 2d 288, 300, 595 N.E.2d 1071, 1076 (1992).

[364] People v. Jones, 149 Ill. 2d 288, 291, 595 N.E.2d 1071, 1072 (1992).

[365] People v. Jones, 149 Ill. 2d 288, 291, 595 N.E.2d 1071, 1072 (1992).

[366] People v. Jones, 149 Ill. 2d 288, 291, 595 N.E.2d 1071, 1072 (1992).

[367] People v. Jones, 149 Ill. 2d 288, 300, 595 N.E.2d 1071, 1076 (1992).

[368] People v. Jones, 149 Ill. 2d 288, 296, 595 N.E.2d 1071, 1075 (1992).

isfied by either intent, knowledge, or recklessness because it was a general intent offense.[369] Further, where the information alleged that the defendant took the property of the victim, it implied that the taking of property was done with knowledge, satisfying one of the theft mental states.[370] The court used "common sense" to find that when a defendant commits or attempts to commit armed robbery he obviously intended to deprive the owner of his property, which satisfied the mental state required for theft.[371] Further, the evidence presented at defendant's trial supported a conviction for the theft.[372]

In *People v. Novak*,[373] the Illinois Supreme Court in 1994 reaffirmed its adoption of the charging instrument or pleadings approach and went on to hold that aggravated criminal abuse was not available to the defendant as a lesser included offense of aggravated criminal sexual assault as charged in the indictment where the indictment described sexual penetration but made no mention of touching or fondling of the victim's body parts for the purpose of sexual gratification or arousal.[374]

In *People v. Hamilton*,[375] in 1997 the Illinois Supreme Court again followed what it described as the "charging instrument" approach, which requires the trial court to examine both (1) the charging instrument and (2) the evidence adduced at trial.[376] As to the first aspect of this approach, a charging instrument may *implicitly* "describe" a lesser included offense even though it does not "mention all the statutory elements" of the lesser crime.[377] Second, even if the charging instrument explicitly or implicitly describes a lesser included offense, the trial judge must consider whether the evidence adduced at trial would support a conviction on the lesser offense and an acquittal on the charged offense.[378] If so, lesser included offense instruction is warranted. Here, the (1) burglary charge implicitly described theft as a possible lesser offense and (2) evidence suggested the possibility of a mere theft rather than a burglary; thus, a theft instruction should have been provided.[379]

---

[369] People v. Jones, 149 Ill. 2d 288, 296, 595 N.E.2d 1071, 1075 (1992).

[370] People v. Jones, 149 Ill. 2d 288, 296, 595 N.E.2d 1071, 1075 (1992).

[371] People v. Jones, 149 Ill. 2d 288, 296, 595 N.E.2d 1071, 1075 (1992).

[372] People v. Jones, 149 Ill. 2d 288, 296, 595 N.E.2d 1071, 1076 (1992).

[373] People v. Novak, 163 Ill. 2d 93, 643 N.E.2d 762 (1994).

[374] People v. Novak, 163 Ill. 2d 93, 112-14, 643 N.E.2d 762, 772-73 (1994); *see also* People v. Buress, 274 Ill. App. 3d 164, 165-67, 653 N.E.2d 841, 842-43 (1994) (discussion of the abstract elements, inherent relationship and charging instruments approaches and Illinois courts' preference for latter).

[375] 179 Ill. 2d 319, 688 N.E.2d 1166 (1997).

[376] People v. Hamilton, 179 Ill. 2d 319, 323-24, 688 N.E.2d 1166, 1169 (1997).

[377] People v. Hamilton, 179 Ill. 2d 319, 324, 688 N.E.2d 1166, 1169-70 (1997).

[378] People v. Hamilton, 179 Ill. 2d 319, 324, 688 N.E.2d 1166, 1169-70 (1997).

[379] People v. Hamilton, 179 Ill. 2d 319, 325-28, 688 N.E.2d 1166, 1168-70 (1997).

The ramifications of these decisions are evident. The trial courts now have greater discretion in finding an uncharged offense as lesser included if the charging instrument by implication outlines all its elements. Thus, a defendant can be convicted of an offense of which he has not been charged and which was not, in the abstract definitional comparison sense, a lesser included offense.

§ 1.24. — Inherent Relationship Approach.

In one Illinois Supreme Court opinion, the court considered an "inherent relationship" test in conjunction with two other tests in determining whether battery was a lesser included offense of rape.[380] In *People v. Mays*,[381] the court noted this test allows a court to find an offense included in another if the two offenses are inherently related and the evidence at trial will prove the lesser offense.[382] To be inherently related, multiple offenses "must relate to the protection of the same interest, and must be so related that in the general nature of these crimes, though not necessarily invariably, proof of the lesser offense is necessarily presented as part of the showing of the commission of the greater offense."[383] In *Mays*, where the defendant, charged with rape (now called criminal sexual assault), requested an instruction on battery by bodily harm as a lesser included offense, the court held that battery by bodily harm was not inherently related to rape for purposes of this included offense analysis.[384] Both offenses protected different interests because, for example, rape could occur without any apparent bodily harm.[385]

Later, the Illinois Supreme Court explicitly rejected the inherent-relationship test in *People v. Dace*.[386] In this case, the court was considering the issue of whether theft was a lesser included offense of residential burglary.[387] Although the court found that theft was included in the greater offense under the pleadings approach, they rejected the inherent relationship approach because the test would only be limited "by the ingenuity of counsel" in defining the interests protected by the multiple offenses.[388] The court went on to say that "it would be very nearly impossible to formulate general governing principles and would require decisions on an *ad hoc* basis depending on the evidence adduced."[389]

---

[380] People v. Mays, 91 Ill. 2d 251, 257, 437 N.E.2d 633, 636 (1982).

[381] 91 Ill. 2d 251, 437 N.E.2d 633 (1982).

[382] People v. Mays, 91 Ill. 2d 251, 257, 437 N.E.2d 633, 636 (1982).

[383] People v. Mays, 91 Ill. 2d 251, 258, 437 N.E.2d 633, 636 (1982) (quoting United States v. Whitaker, 447 F.2d 314, 319 (D.C. Cir. 1971)).

[384] People v. Mays, 91 Ill. 2d 251, 258, 437 N.E.2d 633, 638 (1982).

[385] People v. Mays, 91 Ill. 2d 251, 258, 437 N.E.2d 633, 638 (1982).

[386] 104 Ill. 2d 96, 102, 470 N.E.2d 993, 996 (1984).

[387] People v. Dace, 104 Ill. 2d 96, 102, 470 N.E.2d 993, 996 (1984).

[388] People v. Dace, 104 Ill. 2d 96, 102, 470 N.E.2d 993, 996 (1984).

[389] People v. Dace, 104 Ill. 2d 96, 102, 470 N.E.2d 993, 996 (1984).

The United States Supreme Court has also rejected the inherent relationship test. In *Schmuck v. United States*,[390] the defendant, charged with mail fraud, requested an instruction on odometer tampering. The Court, in denying defendant's jury instruction request, rejected the "inherent relationship" test[391] and relied instead on the elemental comparison approach to hold that odometer tampering was not a lesser included offense of mail fraud because odometer tampering has the element of knowingly and willfully causing an odometer to be altered, which is not an element of mail fraud, and mail fraud requires use of the mail which odometer fraud does not.[392]

In conclusion, four different general approaches to what constitutes a lesser included offense have appeared in the Illinois caselaw. While most of the Illinois reviewing courts' latest pronouncements suggest that they are now prepared to follow the pleadings approach[393] one can only speculate as to whether this approach will be scrupulously followed in the future. Already, post-*Jones* opinions have appeared where it is not at all clear upon which theory the appellate court relies in its judgment.[394] Moreover, in others, it is readily apparent that the court is relying on an approach other than the pleadings approach.[395]

As a final matter, an instruction on a "lesser offense" — as opposed to a lesser *included* offense — may be warranted in some circumstances. For example, in the 1998 decision of *People v. Di Vincenzo*,[396] the Illinois Supreme Court

---

[390] 489 U.S. 705 (1988).

[391] Schmuck v. United States, 489 U.S. 705, 716-17 (1988).

[392] Schmuck v. United States, 489 U.S. 705, 721-22 (1988).

[393] *See, e.g.,* People v. Hamilton, 179 Ill. 2d 319, 321-23, 688 N.E.2d 1166, 1169-71 (1997) (instruction of lesser included offense of theft was warranted in residential burglary prosecution); People v. Poulos, 303 Ill. App. 3d 818, ___, 709 N.E.2d 303, 306-07 (2d Dist. 1999) (instruction on battery not warranted as lesser included offense of criminal sexual assault); People v. Kyles, 303 Ill. App. 3d 338, 349-50, 708 N.E.2d 391, 399-400 (1st Dist. 1999) (instruction on criminal damage to property was warranted as lesser included offense of attempted aggravated arson); People v. Trotter, 299 Ill. App. 3d 535, 537-39, 701 N.E.2d 272, 274-75 (1st Dist. 1998) (instruction on battery not warranted as lesser included offense of first degree murder); People v. DeWeese, 298 Ill. App. 3d 4, 8-12, 698 N.E.2d 554, 556-59 (1st Dist. 1998) (criminal sexual abuse was lesser included offense of aggravated criminal sexual assault).

[394] *See, e.g.,* People v. Buford, 235 Ill. App. 3d 393, 404-05, 601 N.E.2d 1099, 1108 (1st Dist. 1992) where the court states "[a]ggravated battery is a lesser included offense of the attempted murder conviction" without further explanation.

[395] *See, e.g.,* People v. Moore, 301 Ill. App. 3d 728, 733, 704 N.E.2d 80, 84 (3d Dist. 1998) ("The aggravated battery charge was a lesser included offense of the armed violence charge . . . since the *elements* of the aggravated battery served as the predicate felony for armed violence. * * * By contrast, the armed violence was not a lesser included offense of second degree murder. Armed violence contains a dangerous weapon *element which is not included in the definition* of second degree murder.") (emphasis added). *See also* People v. Lynch, 241 Ill. App. 3d 986, 992-93, 609 N.E.2d 889, 893-94 (1st Dist. 1993) (possession of cannabis with intent to deliver is lesser included offense of cannabis trafficking based on abstract definition comparison).

[396] 183 Ill. 2d 239, 700 N.E.2d 981 (1998).

ruled that a defendant convicted of first degree murder was entitled to a jury instruction on the "lesser offense" of involuntary manslaughter where the circumstances indicated that the defendant was merely reckless when he killed his victim.[397] Although the court indicated that involuntary manslaughter carries a "less culpable mental state than first degree murder," it did not see fit to label the former offense as a lesser included offense of the latter.[398]

§ 1.25. Same Physical Act Doctrine.

Beyond lesser included offense concerns, the Illinois courts have discussed and applied a related concern: "the same physical act doctrine." This doctrine adds another protection for a defendant charged with multiple offenses that arise from the *same physical act*.[399] To fully understand the same physical act doctrine, one must consider the Illinois courts' *past* unwillingness to uphold multiple convictions arising out of the "same conduct" or "same transaction" where the defendant's motivation was to advance one single objective, and the courts' *current* unwillingness to affirm multiple convictions arising out of the same criminal "act." In *People v. Stewart*,[400] the Illinois Supreme Court in 1970 broadened the scope of what was known as the "same conduct" or "same transaction" doctrine[401] by holding that where the defendant engaged in multiple criminal acts that were part of the same transaction and these were motivated by a single criminal purpose, only the more serious offense would stand.[402] In *Stewart*, the defendant had been convicted of attempted robbery and aggravated battery resulting from the act of inflicting serious bodily injury on his victim while simultaneously demanding money from the victim. The court ruled that since none of the evidence suggested that "the acts which constituted the offense of aggravated battery were independently motivated or otherwise separable from the conduct which constituted the offense of attempted robbery," the lesser offense of aggravated battery had to be reversed.[403]

In *People v. King*,[404] the Illinois Supreme Court in 1977 abolished the "independent motivation" test: "The rationale of the 'independent motivation' test . . . has never been fully articulated. Rather, it has been criticized on the grounds that it lacks statutory authority, permits a defendant to escape the consequences of his acts, and, in fact, encourages the commission of lesser offenses in order to

---

[397] People v. Di Vincenzo, 183 Ill. 2d 239, 249-51, 700 N.E.2d 981, 987-88 (1998).

[398] People v. Di Vincenzo, 183 Ill. 2d 239, 249-51, 700 N.E.2d 981, 987-88 (1998).

[399] People v. King, 66 Ill. 2d 551, 566, 363 N.E.2d 838, 844, *cert. denied*, 434 U.S. 894 (1977).

[400] 45 Ill. 2d 310, 259 N.E.2d 24 (1970).

[401] *See* People v. King, 66 Ill. 2d 551, 562, 363 N.E.2d 838, 843, *cert. denied*, 434 U.S. 894 (1977).

[402] People v. Stewart, 45 Ill. 2d 310, 313, 259 N.E.2d 24, 26 (1970).

[403] People v. Stewart, 45 Ill. 2d 310, 313, 259 N.E.2d 24, 26 (1970).

[404] 66 Ill. 2d 551, 363 N.E.2d 838, *cert. denied*, 434 U.S. 894 (1977).

accomplish the greater."[405] Accordingly, the court affirmed the defendant's separate offenses of rape and burglary even though it appeared that the burglary was motivated by the defendant's interest in committing rape. The *King* court did not, however, explicitly reject the "same conduct" test — where two or more offenses arise from the same conduct, only the judgement for the most serious offense is permitted[406] — in its entirety; rather, the court approved a scaled-down version of the concept. This is evident from the language of the *King* decision: "Prejudice results to the defendant only in those instances where more than one offense is carved from the *same physical act*. . . . 'Act,' when used in this sense, is intended to mean any overt or outward manifestation which will support a different offense."[407] In other words, to the extent the term *conduct* can be equated with act, the "same conduct" concept still has vitality. But since the term *conduct* may take on broader connotations than the term *act*, it appears most advisable to now refer to the concept, by quoting from the language in *King*, as the "same physical act" test.[408]

On the other hand, the *King* court apparently rejected wholesale the notion that if multiple acts arise out of one transaction, there can be only one crime:

> Prejudice, with regard to *multiple acts*, exists only when the defendant is convicted of more than one offense, some of which are, by definition, lesser included offenses. Multiple convictions and concurrent sentences should be permitted in all other cases where a defendant has committed *several acts*, despite the interrelationship of those acts. . . . We hold, therefore, that when more than one offense arises from a series of incidental or closely related acts and the offenses are not, by definition, lesser included offenses, convictions with concurrent sentences can be entered.[409]

Only if one or more of the several criminal acts reflect "lesser included" criminality does there exist a problem with multiple convictions.

Analytically, the Illinois courts now have to hurdle two obstacles to convict a defendant of multiple offenses. First, the court must determine that the offenses arose from separate physical acts.[410] Second, they must determine that the of-

---

[405] People v. King, 66 Ill. 2d 551, 564, 363 N.E.2d 838, 843, *cert. denied*, 434 U.S. 894 (1977).

[406] *See, e.g.*, City of Chicago v. Hill, 40 Ill. 2d 130, 135-36, 238 N.E.2d 403, 406 (1968) (impermissible to punish multiple offenses arising out of the "same conduct").

[407] People v. King, 66 Ill. 2d 551, 566, 363 N.E.2d 838, 844-85 (1977) (emphasis added). *See also* People v. Rodriguez, 169 Ill. 2d 183, 188, 661 N.E.2d 305, 307 (1996) (reaffirming definition of "act," while quoting *King*).

[408] *See* People v. Pearson, 108 Ill. App. 3d 241, 243, 439 N.E.2d 31, 33 (4th Dist. 1982) (referring to "same physical act" test).

[409] People v. King, 66 Ill. 2d 551, 566, 363 N.E.2d 838, 844-45, *cert. denied*, 434 U.S. 894 (1977).

[410] People v. Rodriguez, 169 Ill. 2d 183, 186, 661 N.E.2d 305, 306 (1996).

fenses are not included in each other by definition.[411] For example, when a defendant shot at the victim in her car and continued to point his gun at her after his first shot shattered the car window, the court held the defendant could be convicted of both attempted first degree murder and unlawful restraint.[412] The court first found separate physical acts: the act of shooting supported the attempted first degree murder conviction and continuing to point the gun at the victim after the shot was a separate act supporting the unlawful restraint charge.[413] Then, the court held that unlawful restraint was not a lesser included offense of attempted murder because attempted murder could be proved without showing any type of restraint.[414] Where a defendant unlawfully entered a residence and took another's property, convictions for both burglary and looting were upheld against a same physical act doctrine challenge since the burglary was complete at the point of the unlawful entry with an unlawful purpose while the looting required the additional act of executing control over the burglary and looting the victim's property.[415] Where a defendant bent on robbery fired one shot at the victim, shattering the victim's car window but missing the victim, and then fired a second shot at the victim, killing him, convictions for attempted armed robbery and first degree murder were not barred by the same physical act doctrine since the two offenses were the result of two separate and distinct shots.[416] Where a defendant placed his penis in his minor victim's mouth knowing that he was HIV positive, thereby exposing the victim to the virus, defendant's convictions for aggravated criminal sexual assault and criminal transmission of HIV were not barred by the same physical act doctrine because the former crime occurred when defendant placed his penis into his victim's mouth and second occurred when he released ejaculatory semen or fluid into the victim.[417]

Some Illinois caselaw is difficult, if not impossible to reconcile. For example, in one case, where the defendant stabbed the victim rapidly and repeatedly four times, the court found one single physical act which did not support a finding of both attempted murder and armed violence, and accordingly, they determined the armed violence conviction had to be vacated.[418] Here, the court did not decide whether armed violence was a lesser included offense of attempted murder because they could not find separate physical acts.[419] On the other hand, in another case, where the defendant stabbed the victim five times, the court held that

---

[411] People v. Rodriguez, 169 Ill. 2d 183, 186, 661 N.E.2d 305, 306-07 (1996).

[412] People v. Wrightner, 219 Ill. App. 3d 231, 234, 579 N.E.2d 573, 575 (3d Dist. 1991).

[413] People v. Wrightner, 219 Ill. App. 3d 231, 234, 579 N.E.2d 573, 575 (3d Dist. 1991).

[414] People v. Wrightner, 219 Ill. App. 3d 231, 234, 579 N.E.2d 573, 575 (3d Dist. 1991).

[415] People v. Flores, 269 Ill. App. 3d 196, 208-10, 645 N.E.2d 1050, 1058-59 (1st Dist. 1995).

[416] People v. Harris, 182 Ill. 2d 114, 133-34, 695 N.E.2d 447, 457 (1998).

[417] People v. Dempsey, 242 Ill. App. 3d 568, 594, 610 N.E.2d 208, 224-25 (5th Dist. 1993).

[418] People v. Hope, 142 Ill. App. 3d 171, 175-76, 491 N.E.2d 785, 788-89 (3d Dist. 1986).

[419] People v. Hope, 142 Ill. App. 3d 171, 175-76, 491 N.E.2d 785, 788-89 (3d Dist. 1986).

convictions for attempted murder and armed violence were proper.[420] The court held that one stab wound would support an attempted murder charge and the other stab wounds would support the armed violence charge.[421] Similarly, where the defendant shot the victim, demanded and took his money, the court held that it was proper to convict him of both attempted murder and armed robbery.[422] The court found two separate acts: the shooting supported the attempted murder conviction and the taking of the money was a separate act supporting the armed robbery conviction.[423] This same court also held that the armed robbery was not a lesser included offense of the attempted murder.[424] Where the defendant hit the victim over the head with a bottle and then took the victim's bag, the court held that convictions for both aggravated battery and armed robbery were proper.[425] The court found two distinct acts: the hitting over the head supported the aggravated battery charge while the taking of the bag supported the armed robbery charge.[426]

Where the defendant took the victim's wallet out of her desk and then pushed her out of his way as he fled the scene, which constituted robbery, the court held that the battery and theft charges had to be vacated because they arose from the same physical act as the robbery charge.[427] Where the defendant's convictions of residential burglary and home invasion was carved out of the same physical act of entering the victim's dwelling, the residential burglary conviction had to be vacated.[428] In that same case, where the defendant's convictions for intentional murder and aggravated arson arose out of the same physical act of starting a fire, the aggravated arson had to be vacated.[429]

Some courts have delineated a number of factors which help in determining whether multiple offenses in fact arise out of a single physical act. These factors are: "(1) prosecutorial intent, as reflected in the language of the indictment; (2) the existence of an intervening act; (3) the time interval between successive parts of the defendant's conduct; (4) the victim's identity; (5) the similarity of

---

[420] People v. Pressley, 160 Ill. App. 3d 858, 866, 513 N.E.2d 921, 927 (1st Dist. 1987).

[421] People v. Pressley, 160 Ill. App. 3d 858, 866, 513 N.E.2d 921, 927 (1st Dist. 1987).

[422] People v. Agnelly, 167 Ill. App. 3d 477, 486, 521 N.E.2d 306, 312 (5th Dist. 1988).

[423] People v. Agnelly, 167 Ill. App. 3d 477, 486, 521 N.E.2d 306, 312 (5th Dist. 1988).

[424] People v. Agnelly, 167 Ill. App. 3d 477, 486, 521 N.E.2d 306, 312 (5th Dist. 1988).

[425] People v. Cobern, 236 Ill. App.3d 300, 303-04, 603 N.E.2d 693, 695-96 (1st Dist. 1992).

[426] People v. Cobern, 236 Ill. App.3d 300, 303-04, 603 N.E.2d 693, 695-96 (1st Dist. 1992).

[427] People v. Houston, 151 Ill. App. 3d 718, 723, 502 N.E.2d 1174, 1177 (5th Dist. 1986).

[428] People v. McLaurin, 184 Ill. 2d 58, 106, 703 N.E.2d 11, 34 (1998).

[429] People v. McLaurin, 184 Ill. 2d 58, 106-07, 703 N.E.2d 11, 34 (1998). However, the defendant's home invasion (entering the victim's dwelling) was not carved out of the same physical act as the intentional murder (setting the fire). Id. at 105, 703 N.E.2d at 33.

the acts; and (6) the location of the acts."[430] For example, where the defendant was charged with aggravated battery while in a public place and aggravated battery causing great bodily harm for inflicting multiple blows on his victim with his fists, the court applied these factors and held the multiple convictions could not be upheld because the blows were all part of a single physical act.[431] The court noted that the blows were all thrown rapidly and in succession, without any intervening acts, in the same location and at the same time upon the same victim.[432] All the blows were similar in nature and the indictment charged the same actions — beating the victim about the head with fists — in both counts of the indictment, indicating the prosecution's characterization of the multiple blows as resulting from the same physical act.[433]

Three additional related matters that were not explicitly addressed in the above discussion of lesser included offenses and the same physical act doctrine have not yet been explored. First, where a defendant is charged with multiple counts of the same criminality through a single "act," such as participating in a drag race that results in the death of three persons, the court will most assuredly divide the act in terms of its results and will allow three counts of reckless homicide to stand.[434]

Second, where defendant inflicts a severe blow on his victim, is then convicted of assault and battery, and thereafter the victim dies from the blow, the defendant can subsequently be tried for murder because of the later occurrence of the death.[435] The state will not be penalized for its promptness in bringing the defendant to trial for the lesser offense of assault and battery before the victim had died. For example, where a defendant was convicted of attempted murder and, thereafter, his victim died nine years later from injuries traceable to his original assault, he could later be convicted of first degree murder.[436] Of course, once the murder conviction is accomplished, the lesser included offenses have to be vacated.

Third, because of the United States Supreme Court decision of *Ohio v. Johnson*,[437] it is permissible to prosecute a defendant for an offense where he has already pleaded guilty, *over the state's objection*, to a lesser included offense. In *Johnson*, the defendant entered a plea of guilty, over the state's objection, to

---

[430] People v. Guzman, 208 Ill. App. 3d 525, 535, 567 N.E.2d 500, 507 (1st Dist. 1990). *See also* People v. Melton, 282 Ill. App. 3d 408, 421, 667 N.E.2d 1371, 1381 (1st Dist. 1996) (following six-factor test).

[431] People v. Ellis, 143 Ill. App. 3d 892, 897, 493 N.E.2d 739, 743 (3d Dist. 1986).

[432] People v. Ellis, 143 Ill. App. 3d 892, 897, 493 N.E.2d 739, 743 (3d Dist. 1986).

[433] People v. Ellis, 143 Ill. App. 3d 892, 897, 493 N.E.2d 739, 743 (3d Dist. 1986).

[434] *See* People v. Evans, 124 Ill. App. 3d 634, 464 N.E.2d 1083 (1st Dist. 1984), *cert. denied*, 469 U.S. 1211 (1985).

[435] Diaz v. United States, 223 U.S. 442, 448-49 (1912).

[436] People v. Carillo, 164 Ill. 2d 144, 148-50, 646 N.E.2d 582, 584-86 (1995).

[437] 467 U.S. 493 (1984).

involuntary manslaughter and grand theft and thereafter successfully moved to dismiss, on double jeopardy grounds, the charges of murder and aggravated robbery, which were the potentially greater crimes arising from the same incident. The Supreme Court held that the trial court's dismissal of the greater charges on this theory was error in that (1) double jeopardy could not be a barrier to the state's pursuit of the murder and aggravated robbery charge, since the state had never been given an opportunity to marshall its evidence and resources more than once or to present its case through a trial, and (2) acceptance of a guilty plea on the lesser included offenses while the charges on the greater offenses remained pending had none of the implications of an implied acquittal, which results from a guilty verdict rendered by a jury charged to consider both greater and lesser included offenses.[438]

In summary, where a crime can analytically be viewed as a lesser included offense of another, double jeopardy considerations require that the lesser convictions be set aside. Where the state has already prosecuted the lesser included offense at trial, successfully or unsuccessfully, double jeopardy implications will be a barrier to the state's interest in prosecuting the more serious, related offense. But if the related offenses are not lesser included offenses of one another, the defendant may have an alternative protection against standing convicted of multiple crimes if it is apparent that the multiple offenses arose from a solitary physical act committed by the accused.

---

[438] Ohio v. Johnson, 467 U.S. 493, 501-02 (1984).

Chapter 2

CRIMINAL ACT AND MENTAL STATE

§ 2.01. Introduction.

This chapter will explore the basic elements of a crime: the criminal act and mental state. First, there will be a review of the required components of a criminal act. This will include an examination of acts of commission, acts of omission, and crimes of possession. Second, there will be an exploration of the mental states — intent, knowledge, recklessness, and negligence — that appear in various contexts throughout the criminal code. Finally, there will be a consideration of absolute liability crimes, those offenses that require no proof of mental state. The ultimate purpose of this chapter is to lay a foundation for the understanding of the basic requirements for criminal liability that is necessary for analyzing the wide variety of crimes that will be studied in subsequent chapters.

§ 2.02. — Criminal Acts: Commissions.

Paragraph 5/4-1 of the Criminal Code of 1961 provides that "[a] material element of every offense is a voluntary act, which includes an omission to perform a duty which the law imposes on the offender and which he is physically capable of performing."[1] Demonstrating the existence of a criminal act, often referred to as the *actus reus*,[2] is absolutely essential to a finding of criminal liability. If there is no criminal act, there is no crime. While it is possible to prove the existence of some crimes without proving the existence of a particular mental state on the part of an offender,[3] this is never possible with respect to the act. Bad thoughts or wrongful intentions without any act to further them can never be the basis of criminal liability.[4]

To understand the nature of the *act*, a precise meaning must be given to this term. The revision committee responsible for drafting this legislation pointed out that although the word *act* is sometimes understood to include not only the actor's physical movement but also certain attendant circumstances and the consequences of that movement, the committee's intent was to limit the meaning of the word *act* to the relevant physical movements of the criminal actor in question.[5] The language of paragraph 5/4-1 itself makes it clear that the act must be a "voluntary act."[6] An involuntary muscular movement, such as a physical reflex or a motion not accompanied by the volition of the person making the motion, cannot give rise to criminal liability.[7] Thus, it is imperative that the defendant had some element of control over his or her conduct.

---

[1] 720 ILCS 5/4-1 (1999).

[2] A. GOLDSTEIN, THE INSANITY DEFENSE 203 (1967).

[3] 720 ILCS 5/4-9 (1999) ("Absolute Liability").

[4] WAYNE LAFAVE & AUSTIN SCOTT, CRIMINAL LAW § 3.2(b) (2d ed. 1986).

[5] ILL. ANN. STAT. ch. 38, para. 4-1 (Smith-Hurd 1989), 1961 Committee Comments, at 192.

[6] 720 ILCS 5/4-1 (1999).

[7] ILL. ANN. STAT. ch. 38, para. 4-1 (Smith-Hurd 1989), 1961 Committee Comments, at 192.

With respect to the capacity of a defendant to engage in a voluntary criminal act or to control his or her conduct for the purposes of paragraph 5/4-1, the legislature clearly intended to include in the definition of voluntary acts behavior that emanates from urges or impulses that the defendant may have some difficulty resisting.[8] Thus, if a defendant were to claim he could not overcome his sexual urge, thereby suggesting his sexual assault was involuntary, he could still be convicted of the assault, in the absence of evidence of insanity.[9]

§ 2.03. — Automatism.

On the other hand, if a defendant were to assert that because of automatism, he or she lacked "the volition to control or prevent involuntary acts — those bodily movements which are not controlled by the conscious mind,"[10] the defendant would have a defense.[11] Such involuntary acts might include those committed during convulsions, sleep, unconsciousness, hypnosis, or seizures.[12] Such an automatism defense could be based on the absence of a voluntary act, rather than on the existence of insanity.[13]

There is a significant limitation on excluding from criminal liability acts that might be committed during the course of a state of automatism. If the state can establish that a defendant could have foreseen the consequences of his or her unconscious behavior, based on prior experiences with lapses into unconsciousness, and did nothing to avoid those consequences, the defendant has no defense.[14] Thus, if a person who knows that he or she is prone to periodic epileptic seizures decides to operate a motor vehicle and loses control of the motor vehicle because of such a seizure, thereby killing an innocent pedestrian, he or she

---

[8] If it were true that such lack of control flowed from the defendant's mental illness, it is possible that he might have an affirmative defense of insanity: "A person is not criminally responsible for conduct if at the time of such conduct, as a result of mental disease or mental defect, he lacks substantial capacity to appreciate the criminality of his conduct." 720 ILCS 5/6-2(a) (1999).

[9] People v. Jones, 43 Ill. 2d 113, 120, 251 N.E.2d 195, 199 (1969).

[10] People v. Dunigan, 96 Ill. App. 3d 799, 824-25, 421 N.E.2d 1319, 1338 (1st Dist. 1981) (defense claim rejected).

[11] In *Dunigan*, the court referred to this claim as the automatism defense. People v. Dunigan, 96 Ill. App. 3d 799, 824-25, 421 N.E.2d 1319, 1338 (1st Dist. 1981). *See* Janet H. Bassitt, *Automatism: An Involuntary Act Defense*, 68 ILL. B.J. 740 (1980).

[12] People v. Grant, 71 Ill. 2d 551, 558, 377 N.E.2d 4, 8 (1978) (defense claim rejected).

[13] People v. Grant, 71 Ill. 2d 551, 558-59, 377 N.E.2d 4, 8 (1978) ("(T)he defense of involuntary conduct and the insanity defense are *alternative* theories at the disposal of a defendant whose volition to control or prevent his conduct are at issue.") (emphasis added). For example, a person who would commit a crime under an uncontrollable hypnotic trance could hardly be said to be necessarily insane. *See* Janet H. Bassitt, *Automatism: An Involuntary Act Defense*, 68 ILL. B.J. 740, 742 (1980).

[14] *See* Janet H. Bassitt, *Automatism: An Involuntary Act Defense*, 68 ILL. B.J. 740, 741 (1980), and cases from other states cited therein.

can be convicted of reckless homicide. Similarly, if a person with an apparent sleep disorder acknowledged that he had been involved in seventy-five automobile accidents as a result of his falling asleep at the wheel prior to his falling asleep and killing a bicyclist, there would be criminal liability for reckless homicide because of the element of foreseeability of loss of his consciousness prior to his collision with the bicyclist.[15]

§ 2.04.   — Character of Act.

Notwithstanding the absolute necessity of demonstrating a voluntary act on the part of an offender before criminal liability considerations come into play, it is important to note that in some contexts the act in question may not take on a complex character, particularly where the act is examined outside its context. For instance, a mere verbal utterance could be considered a criminal act where the communication involved the solicitation of another to commit a crime.[16] Similarly, mere words or gestures of encouragement could cause one to be accountable for the conduct of another under the state's accomplice liability statute.[17]

Since the heart of a criminal conspiracy[18] is the *agreement* between two or more parties to carry out a criminal act, not the offense that is the object of the

---

[15] People v. Shaffer, 49 Ill. App. 3d 207, 212, 364 N.E.2d 109, 113 (2d Dist. 1977).

[16] 720 ILCS 5/8-1 (1999) ("A person commits solicitation when, with intent that an offense be committed, . . . he commands, encourages, or requests another to commit that offense."); *see, e.g.,* People v. Barnett, 173 Ill. App. 3d 477, 484, 527 N.E.2d 1071, 1076 (2d Dist. 1988) (defendant's solicitation of another to kill her husband supported conviction for solicitation to commit murder); People v. Lewis, 84 Ill. App. 3d 556, 562, 406 N.E.2d 11, 16 (1st Dist. 1980) (solicitation may be based on words or acts designed to cause another to commit crime).

[17] 720 ILCS 5/5-2(c) (1999):

A person is legally accountable for the conduct of another when . . . (c) [e]ither before or during the commission of an offense, and with the intent to promote or facilitate such commission, he solicits, aids, abets, agrees or attempts to aid, such other person in the planning or commission of the offense.

See, e.g., People v. Cobb, 97 Ill. App. 3d 615, 617, 422 N.E.2d 1106, 1108 (1st Dist. 1981) (court relied heavily on defendant's statement, "Blow him, blow him," which was made before codefendant's shotgun slaying of victim, as supportive of defendant's liability for murder under accomplice theory).

[18] 720 ILCS 5/8-2 (1999):

A person commits conspiracy when, with intent that an offense be committed, he agrees with another to the commission of that offense. No person may be convicted of conspiracy to commit an offense unless an act in furtherance of such agreement is alleged and proved to have been committed by him or by a co-conspirator.

conspiracy,[19] a defendant's mere entry into such a criminal compact 〈
for criminal responsibility purposes.[20] The agreement can be based on words or
agreement[21] or can be drawn from circumstances surrounding the commission of
an act.[22] Although in Illinois there must be some overt act to further the conspiracy,[23] that act can be performed either by the defendant or by a coconspirator.[24]
Accordingly, the actus reus requirement essential to establishing a particular
conspirator's criminal liability could be based on his illegal agreement alone.[25]

With respect to the overt act requirement in the conspiracy context, it should
be understood that it, too, can be relatively easy to satisfy. Since often "conspiracies are hard to detect and since such combinations of criminals impose a
greater threat to the public than the criminal acting alone, the legislature obviously intended that *any* overt act in furtherance of the conspiracy, even in the
planning stage, would satisfy that element of the offense of conspiracy."[26] Thus,
it is conceivable that the mere purchase of a gun weeks in advance of a planned
agreement to commit a bank robbery would be a sufficient overt act for criminal
conspiracy purposes.

It is true that (1) certain criminal acts sufficient for criminal liability purposes
may seem relatively unsophisticated, if not trivial, in nature, and that (2) certain
omissions can give rise to criminality if there is a legal duty to act (this concern
will be addressed later in this chapter). However, inaction cannot ordinarily be

---

[19] People v. Mordick, 94 Ill. App. 3d 497, 499-500, 418 N.E.2d 1057, 1059 (2d Dist. 1981). *Cf.*
People v. Perruquet, 173 Ill. App. 3d 1054, 1064, 527 N.E.2d 1334, 1341-42 (5th Dist. 1988)
(absent evidence showing agreement to carry out the crime of burglary, the defendants could not
be convicted of conspiracy to commit burglary).

[20] People v. Jayne, 52 Ill. App. 3d 990, 1004, 368 N.E.2d 422, 432 (1st Dist. 1977) ("The essence of conspiracy is an agreement to commit a crime and the offense is complete when the
agreement is made, even though no act is done to carry it into effect").

[21] *See, e.g.,* People v. Cramer, 64 Ill. App. 3d 688, 694, 381 N.E.2d 827, 831 (4th Dist. 1978)
(defendant's conversations with another supported his conviction for conspiracy to commit murder), *cert. denied,* 444 U.S. 828 (1979).

[22] People v. Bailey, 60 Ill. 2d 37, 45, 322 N.E.2d 804, 809 (1975) (although agreement to commit murder not established in instant case); People v. Persinger, 49 Ill. App. 3d 116, 121-22, 363
N.E.2d 897, 901-02 (5th Dist. 1977) (circumstantial evidence supported conspiracy to deliver
controlled substance), *cert. denied,* 435 U.S. 917 (1978).

[23] 720 ILCS 5/8-2(a) (1999).

[24] People v. Ambrose, 28 Ill. App. 3d 627, 630, 329 N.E.2d 11, 15 (3d Dist. 1975) (conspiracy
to commit armed robbery conviction upheld).

[25] People v. Jayne, 52 Ill. App. 3d 990, 1004, 368 N.E.2d 422, 432 (1st Dist. 1977) (conspiracy
to commit murder convictions upheld).

[26] People v. Ambrose, 28 Ill. App. 3d 627, 630, 329 N.E.2d 11, 15 (3d Dist. 1975) (emphasis
added) ("If that had not been their intention there would have been no need to differentiate between the overt act necessary for attempt and the overt act necessary for conspiracy as the statute
does"). The *Ambrose* court was referring to the overt-act requirement of the criminal attempt statute, which states that the act must be a "substantial step toward . . . commission" of the target
crime. 720 ILCS 5/8-4(a) (1999).

equated with criminal action. For instance, mere presence at the scene of a crime is not sufficient for conspiracy[27] or accomplice liability purposes.[28] Similarly, mere knowledge of, acquiescence in, or approval of a criminal plan of another or association or transaction with a guilty party is not considered a proper foundation for a conviction.[29]

§ 2.05.   — Status Offenses.

A person cannot be convicted of a crime where the gist of the prohibition is aimed at an offender's personal condition[30] or status.[31] For instance, in *Robinson v. California*,[32] the United States Supreme Court ruled that a California statute that made it a crime for a person to "be addicted to the use of narcotics"[33] was cruel and unusual punishment prohibited by the Eighth Amendment[34] inasmuch as the prohibition in question was aimed at the defendant's status as opposed to his conduct.[35] The Court indicated that just as it would be impermissible to punish a person for being mentally ill, suffering leprosy, or being afflicted with venereal disease[36] — matters over which the defendant has little or no control — so, too, a state could not properly outlaw the status of addiction, which, as the court pointed out, the state had conceded is an illness.[37] In a later case, *Powell v. Texas*,[38] the Supreme Court clarified the reach of the *Robinson* holding when it upheld the conviction of a defendant, apparently a chronic alcoholic, for being found drunk in a public place in violation of a state law.[39] The *Powell* court dis-

---

[27] *See* People v. Duckworth, 180 Ill. App. 3d 792, 793, 536 N.E.2d 469, 472 (4th Dist. 1989) (since no conspiracy was established where defendant was present at the scene of another's delivery of controlled substance to undercover police officer, defendant's conviction for delivery reversed).

[28] People v. Evans, 87 Ill. 2d 77, 83, 429 N.E.2d 520, 522 (1981) (appellate court reversal of defendant's conviction for involuntary manslaughter and aggravated battery based on accomplice theory affirmed).

[29] People v. Perruquet, 173 Ill. App. 3d 1054, 1064, 527 N.E.2d 1334, 1341 (5th Dist. 1988) (burglary and conspiracy to commit burglary convictions reversed).

[30] Robinson v. California, 370 U.S. 660 (1962) (statute prohibiting being addicted to narcotics held unconstitutional).

[31] Farber v. Rochford, 407 F. Supp. 529 (N.D. Ill. 1975) (statute prohibiting "known prostitutes" from loitering held unconstitutional).

[32] 370 U.S. 660 (1962).

[33] Robinson v. California, 370 U.S. 660, 663 (1962).

[34] U.S. CONST. amend. VIII ("Excessive bail shall not be required, nor excessive fines imposed, nor cruel and unusual punishment inflicted").

[35] Robinson v. California, 370 U.S. 660, 666 (1962).

[36] Robinson v. California, 370 U.S. 660, 666 (1962).

[37] Robinson v. California, 370 U.S. 660, 667 (1962). A discussion of the implications of *Robinson* appears in JOHN F. DECKER, PROSTITUTION: REGULATION AND CONTROL 380-87 (1979).

[38] 392 U.S. 514 (1968).

[39] Powell v. Texas, 392 U.S. 514, 532 (1968).

tinguished *Robinson* on the theory that the California statute at issue in *Robinson* was directed at the defendant's status as an addict, whereas the Texas statute under consideration in *Powell* was concerned with the conduct of the defendant, something he was not powerless to control notwithstanding his disease of alcoholism.[40]

In the case of *Papachristou v. City of Jacksonville*,[41] the Supreme Court struck down a city ordinance aimed at vagrants,[42] as being unconstitutional on due process grounds.[43] The Court reasoned that the legislation was "void for vagueness"[44] because it failed to give fair notice about what conduct was forbidden and because it encouraged arbitrary arrests for seemingly innocent activities.[45] While the Court did not characterize the ordinance as one aimed at status considerations, there were clear status overtones in the decision: "Those generally implicated by the imprecise terms of the ordinance — poor people, nonconformists, dissenters, idlers — may be required to comport themselves according to the life-style deemed appropriate by the Jacksonville police and the courts."[46] This the Court would not tolerate.

In a case involving a Chicago municipal ordinance, *Farber v. Rochford*,[47] the Federal District Court for the Northern District of Illinois offered a clear illustration of how due process protections contained in the Fourteenth Amendment could be used to successfully attack the constitutionality of a stricture that made it unlawful for a person "known to be a prostitute" or previously convicted of prostitution to, among other things, loaf or loiter in or about premises where alcoholic beverages were sold.[48] The court struck down the statute as being unconstitutional in the face of due process considerations on the theory that a person's reputation was the basis for being subjected to

---

[40] Powell v. Texas, 392 U.S. 514, 531-37 (1968).

[41] 405 U.S. 156 (1972).

[42] JACKSONVILLE, FLA., ORDINANCE CODE § 26-57 (1979):

> Rogues and vagabonds, or dissolute persons who go about begging, common gamblers, persons who use juggling or unlawful games or plays, common drunkards, common night walkers, thieves, pilferers or pickpockets, traders in stolen property, lewd, wanton and lascivious persons, keepers of gambling places, common railers and brawlers, persons wandering or strolling around from place to place without any lawful purpose or object, habitual loafers, disorderly persons, persons neglecting all lawful business and habitually spending their time by frequenting houses of ill fame, gaming houses, or places where alcoholic beverages are sold or served, persons able to work but habitually living upon the earnings of their wives or minor children shall be deemed vagrants.

[43] U.S. CONST. amend. XIV ("No State shall . . . deprive any person of life, liberty or property without due process of law").

[44] Papachristou v. City of Jacksonville, 405 U.S. 156, 162 (1972).

[45] Papachristou v. City of Jacksonville, 405 U.S. 156, 165-71 (1972).

[46] Papachristou v. City of Jacksonville, 405 U.S. 156, 170 (1972).

[47] 407 F. Supp. 529 (N.D. Ill. 1975).

[48] Farber v. Rockford, 407 F. Supp. 529, 530 (N.D. Ill. 1975).

son's reputation was the basis for being subjected to criminal prosecution, rather than the person's acts.[49]

Another Chicago municipal ordinance was found to unconstitutionally focus on the status of the party. *City of Chicago v. Youkhana,*[50] decided by the Illinois Appellate Court, involved a city ordinance that prohibited street gang members from loitering in a public place.[51] The Appellate Court found the ordinance unconstitutional because, among other reasons, it punished a person due to his or her status as a member of a gang, instead of for the action of illegal loitering.[52] The Illinois Supreme Court in the consolidated decision of *City of Chicago v. Morales,*[53] agreed that the ordinance was unconstitutional although it did not reach the status issue. Likewise, the United States Supreme Court found the loitering stricture — "to remain in one place with no apparent purpose" — to be unconstitutionally vague without addressing the status claim.[54]

It is important to note that a law directed at a category of persons does not necessarily mean that the enactment is unconstitutional. For example, a "status" argument in *United States v. Jester*[55] was denied because the statute, which criminalized the possession of firearms by a convicted felon, was found to punish the conduct inherent in the act of possession instead of simply the person's status of being a convicted felon.[56]

---

[49] Farber v. Rockford, 407 F. Supp. 529, 532 (N.D. Ill. 1975).

[50] 277 Ill. App. 3d 101, 660 N.E.2d 34 (1st Dist. 1995).

[51] The ordinance provides in part:

> Whenever a police officer observes a person whom he reasonably believes to be a criminal street gang member loitering in any public place with one or more other persons, he shall order all such persons to disperse and remove themselves from the area. Any person who does not promptly obey such an order is in violation of this section.
>
> It shall be an affirmative defense to an alleged violation of this section that no person who was observed loitering was in fact a member of a criminal street gang.
>
> As used in this Section:
>
> > 'Loiter' means to remain in any one place with no apparent purpose.
> > 'Criminal street gang' means any ongoing organization, association in fact or group of three or more persons, whether formal or informal, . . . and whose members individually or collectively engage in or have engaged in a pattern of criminal gang activity.
> > 'Public place' means the public way and any other location open to the public, whether publicly or privately owned.

Chicago Municipal Code § 8-4-015

[52] City of Chicago v. Youkhana, 277 Ill. App. 3d 101, 113, 660 N.E.2d 34, 42 (1st Dist. 1995).

[53] 177 Ill. 2d 440, 687 N.E.2d 53 (1995).

[54] City of Chicago v. Morales, 527 U.S. 41 (1999).

[55] 139 F.3d 1168 (7th Cir. 1998).

[56] United States v. Jester, 139 F.3d 1168, 1170 (7th Cir. 1998).

§ 2.06. — Criminal Acts: Omissions.

As the language of paragraph 5/4-1 makes clear, criminal acts in Illinois include "an omission to perform a duty which the law imposes on the offender and which he is physically capable of performing."[57] Prerequisites to convicting a person for a failure to act are (1) the existence of a legal duty to act and (2) the breach of that legal duty. The Criminal Code of 1961 does not list the sources or bases of legal duties that give rise to criminal liability possibilities, and there is a scarcity of Illinois opinions on the subject. It is imperative, therefore, that one consider caselaw outside Illinois, as well as statements by recognized authorities in the criminal law field. For one to assume that the Illinois courts would deny the existence of various types of legal duties simply because they have not yet become an issue in the Illinois courts is simplistic and shortsighted.

§ 2.07. — Duty Based on Statute.

Legal duties that give rise to criminal liability when they are breached can be placed into two general categories: (1) explicit codified duties — omissions that are clearly defined in the code, and (2) implicit duties — omissions that are not explicitly codified but that are inherent in, or assumed to flow from, other criminal strictures in the code. The first category of duties can easily be identified by a perusal of the various criminal code provisions. To illustrate, paragraph 5/31-8 of chapter 720 provides: "Whoever upon command refuses or knowingly fails reasonably to aid a person known by him to be a peace officer in: (a) Apprehending a person whom the officer is authorized to apprehend; or (b) Preventing the commission by another of any offense, commits a petty offense."[58] Other examples that appear in the Criminal Code of 1961 include the failure of any public officer, public employee, or juror to report to the proper legal authority the receipt of a bribe offer;[59] the failure of any person participating, officiating, or connected with any professional or amateur athletic contest or sporting event to report to the proper authorities the receipt of a bribe offer;[60] and the failure of a criminal defendant admitted to bail, who incurs forfeiture of his bail, to surrender himself to proper authorities.[61] In addition to the statutes that are couched in terms of the "failure to" which create certain legal duties, there are other similar offenses that clearly command persons in certain circumstances to take certain actions that, if not taken, will create criminal liability. For instance, the "Misprision of Treason" statute reads: "A person owing allegiance to this State commits misprision of treason when he conceals or withholds his

---

[57] 720 ILCS 5/4-1 (1999).

[58] 720 ILCS 5/31-8 (1999).

[59] 720 ILCS 5/33-2 (1999).

[60] 720 ILCS 5/29-3 (1999).

[61] 720 ILCS 5/32-10 (1999).

knowledge that another has committed treason against this State."[62] These crimes of omission raise few difficulties — the statute articulates the duty to act, and breach of the duty is made a crime.[63]

§ 2.08. — Duty Not Based on Statute.

The second type of duty is more difficult to identify:

> More difficult, however, are crimes which are not specifically defined in terms of omission to act but only in terms of cause and result. Murder and manslaughter are defined so as to require the "killing" of another person. . . . Nothing in the definition of murder or manslaughter . . . affirmatively suggests that the crime may or may not be committed by omission to act. But these crimes may, in appropriate circumstances, be thus committed. So a parent who fails to call a doctor to attend his sick child may be guilty of criminal homicide if the child should die for want of medical care, though the parent does nothing of an affirmative nature to cause the child's death.[64]

Furthermore, this type of duty is more difficult, although not impossible, to justify from an analytical perspective since the illegal conduct is not explicitly codified.[65]

The existence of a moral duty to act does not invariably translate into a legal duty to act.[66] Thus, the failure to come to the aid of a stranger who is about to drown, even though one would not endanger oneself by doing so, is not a crime.[67] Similarly, the failure to call the police to report an illegal assault on an innocent victim is not a crime.[68] On the other hand, if the person has some legal relationship to the person in need of assistance, such as parent to child, or has

---

[62] 720 ILCS 5/30-2(a) (1999).

[63] WAYNE LAFAVE & AUSTIN SCOTT, CRIMINAL LAW § 3.3 (2d ed. 1986).

[64] WAYNE LAFAVE & AUSTIN SCOTT, CRIMINAL LAW § 3.3 (2d ed. 1986).

[65] This is true because of the following statement in the code: "No conduct constitutes an offense unless it is described as an offense in this Code or in another statute of this state." 720 ILCS 5/1-3 (1999).

[66] WAYNE LAFAVE & AUSTIN SCOTT, CRIMINAL LAW § 3.3(a) (2d ed. 1986); Lionel H. Frankel, *Criminal Omissions: A Legal Microcosm*, 11 WAYNE L. REV. 367, 368 (1965).

[67] ROLLIN M. PERKINS & RONALD N. BOYCE, CRIMINAL LAW 661 (3d ed. 1982).

[68] *See* Diane Kiesel, *Who Saw This Happen?*, 69 A.B.A.J. 1208 (1983), wherein this is pointed out to be the case in most states. However, Kiesel points out that some states are beginning to make non-responsive bystanders criminally responsible in such situations. *See, e.g.*, Minn. Stat. Ann. § 604A.01 (West 1998) and Vt. Stat. Ann. tit. 12, § 519 (1998) (Good Samaritan laws which punish non-responsive bystanders for failure to intervene). *But see* People v. Woodward, 45 Cal. 293 (1873) (no duty to intervene).

created the predicament in which the person in need now finds himself or herself, then there might indeed be a legal duty to act.[69]

There appear to be at least five situations beyond the range of the clear statutory duties in which legal duties with criminal prosecution possibilities may arise: (1) where a person stands in a status relationship to another; (2) where a person has contractually assumed certain legal duties; (3) where a person has voluntarily assumed the care of another, thereby isolating the person in need of care from other sources of assistance; (4) where a person has voluntarily assumed an otherwise legitimate business or activity that is fraught with possible danger to others; and (5) where a person has created the perilous situation now suffered by another through his or her prior illegitimate activity.[70] These five situations are not mutually exclusive. It is conceivable that more than one of these sources of legal duties could come into play in a particular setting. There may also be overlap from a conceptual standpoint. For instance, where there was a binding legal agreement in which one party to the compact agreed to assume certain duties of care on behalf of the other party to the compact, it could be fairly asserted that the agreement created status duties, that is, duties that flow from the status of a contractor as well as from the contract itself.

§ 2.09.   — Duty Based on Status Relationship.

The first source of a legal duty listed above, namely, that emanating from a status relationship, is best illustrated in the immediate family setting. It is generally understood that parents have a clear legal duty to care for their dependent

---

[69] WAYNE LAFAVE & AUSTIN SCOTT, CRIMINAL LAW § 3.3(a) (2d ed. 1986).
The United States Court of Appeals for the District of Columbia has ruled:

> There are at least four situations in which the failure to act may constitute breach of a legal duty. One can be held criminally liable: first, where a statute imposes a duty to care for another; second, where one stands in a status relationship to another; third, where one has assumed a contractual duty to care for another; and fourth, where one has voluntarily assumed the care of another and so secluded the helpless person as to prevent others from rendering aid.

Jones v. United States, 308 F.2d 307, 310 (D.C. Cir. 1962).
[70] *See* WAYNE LAFAVE & AUSTIN SCOTT, CRIMINAL LAW § 3.3(a) (2d ed. 1986), which sets out the following list:

   (1) Duty based upon relationship
   (2) Duty based upon statute
   (3) Duty based upon contract
   (4) Duty based upon voluntary assumption of care
   (5) Duty based upon the creation of the peril
   (6) Duty to control the conduct of another
   (7) Duty of landowner

children.[71] Assuming that a parent was derelict in his or her duty in this regard by allowing an infant to die of malnutrition or by failing to procure necessary medical assistance for a sick child, this breach of legal duty could be the basis for a criminal homicide.[72] Where the mother of a child knew of ongoing physical abuse of her child by her boyfriend, which abuse ultimately resulted in the child's death, the mother had a legal duty to intervene and prevent the abuse in a timely fashion and her failure to do so constituted first degree murder.[73] Similarly, if a spouse failed to take any action after his or her marital partner accidentally fell down a flight of stairs and was rendered helpless by the fall, and thereafter the partner died from the unattended injuries, a finding of criminal homicide would be appropriate.[74]

Just how far this conceptual framework can be carried, even within the family unit, is difficult to gauge. While the above examples and their results may not be open to dispute, the word *family* is not a talisman in whose presence a legal duty automatically appears. The failure of a parent to be concerned about a destitute adult child or the failure of a child to look after his poverty-stricken aged parent is disconcerting but is probably not criminal.[75]

---

[71] *See* People v. Stanciel, 153 Ill. 2d 218, 606 N.E.2d 1201 (1992) (mother had duty to protect her child from physical abuse inflicted by her boyfriend and failure to do so made her liable for murder).

[72] State v. Nicholson, 585 P.2d 60 (Utah 1978) (parent's neglect of child who died of malnutrition and dehydration was second degree murder); People v. Burden, 72 Cal. App. 3d 603, 140 Cal. Rptr. 282 (1977) (parent's failure to provide food to child who died of malnutrition and dehydration was second-degree murder); State v. Williams, 4 Wash. App. 908, 484 P.2d 1167 (1971) (parents' failure to supply 17-month-old child with necessary medical attention was manslaughter); Biddle v. Commonwealth, 206 Va. 14, 141 S.E.2d 710 (1965) (parent's failure to care for child could be murder or manslaughter); Commonwealth v. Hall, 322 Mass. 523, 78 N.E.2d 644 (1948) (failure to feed child who died of starvation was second-degree murder); State v. Staples, 126 Minn. 396, 148 N.W. 283 (1914) (failure to provide care, nurture, sustenance, and medical assistance to helpless child, who dies therefrom, is manslaughter); Pallis v. State, 123 Ala. 12, 26 So. 339 (1899) (exposure or neglect of infant or dependent child constituted assault with intent to murder); Lewis v. State, 72 Ga. 164 (1883) (five-year-old child's death because of lack of food, exposure to inclement weather and physical abuse supported murder conviction).

[73] People v. Stanciel, 153 Ill. 2d 218, 606 N.E.2d 1201 (1992). *Accord* People v. Abraham, 257 Ill. App. 3d 587, 629 N.E.2d 148 (1st Dist. 1993) (first degree murder). *See also* State v. Williquette, 129 Wis. 2d 239, 385 N.E.2d 145 (1986) (where defendant knew her spouse repeatedly abused her children physically and sexually but took no action to stop the abuse and instead left her children in spouse's sole physical custody for substantial periods, defendant breached legal duty to protect children and was properly convicted of child abuse); Palmer v. State, 223 Md. 341, 164 A.2d 467 (1960) (parent's failure to prevent fatal beating of child by her lover was manslaughter).

[74] *Cf.* Territory v. Manton, 8 Mont. 95, 19 P. 387 (1888) (where husband failed to remove intoxicated spouse from snow and spouse died as result, husband was guilty of manslaughter).

[75] People v. Heitzman, 9 Cal. 4th 189, 886 P.2d 1229 (1994) (adult daughter charged with elder abuse had no legal duty to protect her elderly father from abuse and neglect caused by her brothers

Outside the family unit, criminal liability based on status relationship is rare. In a significant 1982 Illinois case, the appellate court affirmed the involuntary manslaughter conviction of a "caretaker" of a child who had been immersed in water hot enough to cause death on the ground that the caretaker had a duty to protect the child under his care from harm.[76] On the other hand, whether one has a legal duty when a dependent child or spouse is not involved is doubtful. The scarcity of supportive caselaw regarding a duty to protect a person such as a mistress or servant[77] suggests the existence of a general judicial reluctance to extend the status duties beyond parental and spousal relationships.

§ 2.10.   — Duty Based on Contract.

The second ground on which one could base a legal duty that could cause criminal liability if not honored is a contractual arrangement.[78] If the owner of a nursing home for the elderly entered into a contract with an aged person to extend to that person food, shelter, medical, and other nursing care but thereafter failed to do so, with the result that the aged person died from lack of care, the infliction of criminal liability on the nursing-home owner would seem wholly appropriate.[79] Similarly, a contractual baby-sitting agreement would require the babysitter to seek emergency medical care for a child in distress and, as such, the failure to do so could amount to criminal homicide.[80] Neither the defendant nor the victim has to be one of the direct parties to the contract before this legal proposition can be used. In the above example, the failure of a nurse employed

---

that resulted in his death); Regina v. Shepherd, 9 Cox C.C. 123 (1862) (where mother failed to provide her 18-year-old daughter who was in labor with midwife and where daughter died, mother's failure was not criminal).

[76] People v. Watson, 103 Ill. App. 3d 992, 998, 431 N.E.2d 1350, 1355 (4th Dist. 1982).

[77] *Compare* People v. Beardsley, 150 Mich. 206, 113 N.W. 1128 (1907) (defendant had no duty to mistress who consumed poison on adulterous weekend rendezvous) *with* the statement by Professor Graham Hughes: "[S]tatus need not be domestic: the duty of the master, recognized by common law, to care for his servant or the captain of a ship to care for the crew might be included." Graham Hughes, *Criminal Omissions*, 67 YALE L.J. 590, 599 (1958).

[78] Jones v. United States, 308 F.2d 307, 310 (D.C. Cir. 1962) (dictum); People v. Montecino, 66 Cal. App. 2d 85, 100, 152 P.2d 5, 13 (1944) (it was involuntary manslaughter where victim, aged and infirm woman confined to bed, died as result of defendant's neglect where defendant had contracted to care for woman).

[79] *Cf.* Commonwealth v. Pestinikas, 421 Pa. Super. 371, 617 A.2d 1339 (1992) (92-year-old victim's death caused by defendants' failure to provide food and medical care, which they had contractually agreed to provide victim, was basis for finding of murder); Davis v. Commonwealth, 230 Va. 201, 335 S.E.2d 375 (1985) (where defendant shared in elderly mother's social security benefits and lived in mother's home, she breached implied contract to care for her mother when her mother died of starvation and exposure and, thus, committed involuntary manslaughter).

[80] People v. Wong, 182 A.D.2d 98, 588 N.Y.S.2d 119 (1992) (the contractual babysitting agreement created a legal duty of care "substantially coextensive with those which would be borne by a parent" making defendants liable for manslaughter).

by the nursing-home owner to extend care to the aged victim would render the nurse culpable. A lifeguard employed by a municipality who deliberately failed to come to the aid of a drowning victim he could have saved could not claim he was under no contractual duty to the victim, for third-party beneficiaries to a contract have protected rights.[81]

§ 2.11. — Duty Based on Assumption of Care.

A third basis for legal obligations that carry the potential for criminal prosecution if breached exists where a person voluntarily assumes the care of another, thereby isolating him or her from other sources of care, and then fails to follow through on the promised assistance.[82] The basis for criminal responsibility in this situation does not come from the existence of a per se duty to offer care from the outset. Rather, it emanates from the willing assumption of the care of another in conjunction with the consequential loss of other sources of care. If an individual were to suffer severe injuries in an automobile accident on a remote country road and then be encountered by a stranger, the stranger could drive on and not offer aid. However, if the stranger were to offer to drive the injured person to a hospital while simultaneously advising another "Good Samaritan" present at the accident scene that he or she would do so, with the result that the other person willing to offer aid drives off and leaves the injured person and the stranger behind, the stranger would have a legal duty to follow through on his or her promise. If the stranger were to drive off without the injured party and the car accident victim were to thereafter die from the sustained injuries, the stranger could encounter criminal liability. However, the stranger's failure would have to be deliberate under the circumstances. If the stranger made a serious effort to follow through on his volunteered assistance but failed because he or she experienced automobile difficulties — becoming stuck in the muddy road or running out of gas on the way to the hospital — criminal liability would be out of the question.[83]

---

[81] *See* BRIAN BLOOM, CONTRACTS: EXAMPLES AND EXPLANATIONS § 19.2 (1998).

[82] Stehr v. State, 92 Neb. 755, 139 N.W. 676 (1913) (man who assumed responsibility for illegitimate stepson, but failed to procure medical attention for child after child's feet were severely frozen, was liable for manslaughter); Regina v. Instan, 1 Q.B. 450, 17 Cox. C. C. 602 (1893) (niece who assumed responsibility for care of her aunt but failed to adequately care for her was liable for criminal homicide). *But see* People v. Phillips, 64 Cal. 2d 574, 414 P.2d 353, 51 Cal. Rptr. 225 (1966) (where chiropractor represented that he could treat fast-growing cancer without surgery but where cancer caused death of patient, chiropractor was not responsible for murder).

[83] *See* ROLLIN M. PERKINS & RONALD N. BOYCE, CRIMINAL LAW 668-69 (3d ed. 1982).

§ 2.12. — Duty Based on Venture Fraught with Danger Arising from Otherwise Legitimate Activity.

The fourth basis for a legal duty that takes on criminal possibilities revolves around a person's voluntary assumption of an activity, including a business venture or trade that carries serious consequences in terms of the health or safety of the public.[84] In modern society, there is a massive body of regulatory and licensing measures that governs professions, trades, and other activities. These measures invariably reflect a variety of legal duties that are shouldered by the parties involved in the activities. Since most activities that carry potential hazards in terms of public health, safety, or welfare are the subject of codified enactments, one need go no farther than the statutes or regulations themselves to identify the legal duties that exist. In other words, most of this terrain is now subsumed into the body of the clear statutory duties discussed above. Although not all of these duties are reflected in the penal code, a breach of such a duty can be the basis of criminal liability. For instance, a person who operates a motor vehicle with a willful and wanton disregard for safety[85] or who drives an automobile under the influence of intoxicants[86] is clearly in violation of the Illinois Vehicle Code.[87] But the failure of this type of driver to show due care for others who might be affected by his hazardous driving may be the basis for criminal liability: reckless conduct[88] or reckless homicide.[89] Thus, the violation of the Motor Vehicle Code traffic regulations could be used as *evidence* of criminality and, thus, be used to support a criminal prosecution.[90]

It would be inappropriate to assume that noncompliance with any licensing or regulatory measure surrounding certain activities creates criminal liability possibilities. A person who holds himself or herself out as a barber, although not properly licensed, will not be liable for criminal battery merely because he or she accidentally jabs with the scissors a person whose hair he or she is cutting. Similarly, the mere fact that a person drove through a red light or was speeding at the time of an automobile collision does not in and of itself establish criminal recklessness.[91]

---

[84] Graham Hughes, *Criminal Omissions*, 67 YALE L.J. 590, 599-600 (1958).

[85] 625 ILCS 5/11-503 (1999).

[86] 625 ILCS 5/11-501 (1999).

[87] *See generally* 625 ILCS 5/1-100 (1999).

[88] 720 ILCS 5/12-5(a) (1999).

[89] 720 ILCS 5/9-3(a) (1999).

[90] People v. Davis, 105 Ill. App. 3d 129, 133, 434 N.E.2d 13, 16 (5th Dist. 1982) (intoxication while driving was evidence of reckless homicide).

[91] *See* People v. Rowe, 9 Ill. App. 3d 460, 462, 292 N.E.2d 432, 433 (1st Dist. 1972) (although driving at speed greatly in excess of speed limit through red light in case at hand evinced recklessness sufficient for involuntary manslaughter). *See also* People v. Poter, 5 Ill. 2d 365, 125 N.E.2d 510 (1955) (Driving in excess of speed limit does not alone constitute willful and wanton miscon-

Most activities fraught with danger to the public health, safety, or welfare are strictly governed by a myriad of rules and regulations that reflect various duties that must be honored by the participants in those activities. There is, however, a permitted sphere of public activities of this nature that does not fall within the ambits of a comprehensive codified body of legal regulations and duties. These unregulated activities are the central focus of this fourth approach to finding legal duties that carry criminal liability implications. The legal duties that exist here flow not from specific duties created by a legislature or regulatory body but rather from the *nature* of the activity involved. Assume, for example, that a person goes into the business of producing for sale crushed rock or gravel. This person buys a parcel of land containing a quarry, which holds a large deposit of rock. In order to gain access to the rock deposits the person plans to crush into gravel, he or she will be compelled to discharge dynamite blasts to break the rock into manageable size. Obviously, if this person were to discharge the dynamite without concern for the safety of innocent bypassers immediately adjacent to the quarry, he or she could be potentially liable for injuries to such persons. The absence of state or local regulations governing this activity would not dispose of the question of whether criminal liability could be lodged against the operator of the business. Since this activity is fraught with danger, the operator would surely be under a duty to protect others from the dynamite blasts. A breach of such a duty under certain circumstances may be the basis of criminal liability.

There is no condition precedent that the conduct in question be illegal in and of itself before this type of duty arises. Thus, where a store owner sold canned heat containing poisonous methanol to customers known to be alcoholics and known to drink the substance as a source of alcohol, which resulted in thirty-one deaths of persons in a skid-row area, the defendant was deemed to be criminally reckless sufficient for involuntary manslaughter.[92] Although the sale of canned heat was lawful in itself, it was done in an unlawful manner.[93] It was the employment of a *reckless method* in this business that brought about the criminal liability. Similarly, although the state did not specify that any particular statutes had been violated by the overcrowding and absence of fire doors and sufficient exits in a night club where a fire occurred that killed several hundred people, the court stated "where as here there is a duty of care for the safety of business visitors invited to premises which the defendant controls, wanton and reckless conduct may consist of an intentional failure to take such care in disregard of the

---

duct for purposes of reckless homicide). *Compare* People v. Baler, 54 Ill. App. 2d 74, 203 N.E.2d 633 (1964) (Excessive speed and failure to observe stop sign was sufficient in case at hand to constitute reckless and wanton misconduct for purposes of reckless homicide).

[92] Commonwealth v. Feinberg, 433 Pa. 558, 565-71, 253 A.2d 636, 640-43 (1969).

[93] Commonwealth v. Feinberg, 433 Pa. 558, 565-71, 253 A.2d 636, 640-43 (1969).

probable harmful consequences to them or of their right to care."[94] Thus, the breach of care toward the patrons of defendant's business premises made defendant liable for manslaughter.[95]

§ 2.13. — Duty Based on Creation of Peril Arising From Illegitimate Activity.

The final basis of a legal duty in the criminal area is where a defendant has created a perilous situation now suffered by another.[96] For instance, where a defendant raped a young girl, thereby causing her such distress that she fell into a creek, the defendant's failure to rescue her, which resulted in her drowning, made him liable for murder.[97] Where a defendant inflicted an unjustified battery on a victim, thereby causing great pain and suffering to the victim, who then attempted to take her own life to end her suffering while still in the presence of the defendant, the defendant's failure to intervene in order to save the life of the victim was cause for holding the defendant responsible for criminal homicide.[98] Where a defendant assaulted and robbed a victim and then left the victim behind in a dazed condition on an isolated road in the extreme cold, and where the victim was then struck by a car while still in a dazed condition, the defendant was responsible for the victim's death because of, among other reasons, his failure to retrieve the victim from the predicament in which he placed him.[99]

Some authorities think that a person who places a victim in a perilous situation by his conduct is duty-bound to remove that person from the perilous position even if the conduct creating the victim's hazardous predicament was innocent.[100] This theory would compel a person to come to the aid of a drowning victim where the person had pushed the victim into the water, whether deliberately or innocently. However, this theory is open to question. Where A shot C in defense of B, the father of A, because C was attacking B and then failed to summon medical help for C, thereby allowing C to die of the wounds incurred in the shooting, A was held to be under no duty to C if the shooting of C was justified on defense-of-another grounds.[101] In other words, since A was without legal

---

[94] Commonwealth v. Welansky, 316 Mass. 383, 397, 55 N.E.2d 902, 909 (1944).

[95] Commonwealth v. Welansky, 316 Mass. 383, 397-401, 55 N.E.2d 902, 909-12 (1944).

[96] WAYNE LAFAVE & AUSTIN SCOTT, CRIMINAL LAW § 3.3(a)(5) (2d ed. 1986).

[97] Jones v. State, 220 Ind. 384, 43 N.E.2d 1017 (1942).

[98] Stephenson v. State, 205 Ind. 141, 179 N.E. 633 (1932).

[99] *Cf.* People v. Kibbe, 35 N.Y.2d 407, 321 N.E.2d 773, 362 N.Y.S.2d 848 (1974). *See also* People v. Fowler, 178 Cal. 657, 174 P. 892 (1918) (where defendant struck victim on head with intent to kill him and left victim lying unconscious on a road at night where he was struck by passing automobile, defendant was liable for murder).

[100] WAYNE LAFAVE & AUSTIN SCOTT, CRIMINAL LAW § 3.3(a)(5) (2d ed. 1986).

[101] King v. Commonwealth, 285 Ky. 654, 148 S.W.2d 1044 (1941).

fault when he or she shot C, A had no duty to remove C from the hazardous situation.

§ 2.14.   — Capability of Complying with Duty.

A major limitation on basing criminal liability on the breach of a legal duty exists where the defendant is incapable of performing the duty. The clear language of paragraph 5/4-1 reflects this limitation: a person is obligated to perform only those legal duties "which he is physically capable of performing."[102] A parent who does not have the means to supply food for his child or an automobile owner who does not have an opportunity to control his or her chauffeur's sudden, unexpected reckless driving would not be liable for a crime.[103] Of course, if the parent who did not have the means to nurture his or her child failed to seek relief from public welfare authorities, he or she would still be liable.[104] Similarly, if the automobile owner had the means to control his or her chauffeur's recklessness but failed to do so, he or she might be liable for injuries caused by the recklessness.

If a person has no knowledge of certain facts that, if known, would prompt a reasonable person to take action to avoid the difficulty, there is no liability.[105] Thus, the failure of a husband to seek medical assistance for his wife, who died during childbirth because of the lack of medical aid, was not a breach of a legal duty if he did not know she was pregnant or did not know she was about to give birth.[106] On the other hand, if the husband was reckless in informing himself about his wife's condition, presumably he would be criminally liable for the death of his wife.[107]

§ 2.15.   — Omissions — Other Considerations.

Beyond the general categories of duties discussed above — statutory duties, status duties, contractual duties, and so on — there are some situations where omissions may prove to be of *evidentiary* value when attempting to prove the commission of a crime. One example is reflected in the Illinois caselaw involving accomplice liability. In one case, the appellate court ruled that while mere presence at a crime scene does not make one a criminal accomplice if the proof shows that the accused was present at the scene of the crime and did not disapprove or oppose it, the trier of fact may competently consider that conduct in connection with other circumstances and thereby reach the conclusion that the

---

[102] 720 ILCS 5/4-1 (1999).

[103] ROLLIN M. PERKINS & RONALD N. BOYCE, CRIMINAL LAW 669 (3d ed. 1982).

[104] Stehr v. State, 92 Neb. 755, 760, 139 N.W. 676, 678 (1913).

[105] *See* JEROME HALL, GENERAL PRINCIPLES OF CRIMINAL LAW 203 (2d ed. 1960).

[106] *Cf.* Westrup v. Commonwealth, 123 Ky. 95, 100, 93 S.W. 646, 648 (1906).

[107] *See* JEROME HALL, GENERAL PRINCIPLES OF CRIMINAL LAW 203-04 (2d ed. 1960).

accused assented to the commission of the criminal act, lent to it his countenance and approval and was thereby aiding and abetting the crime.[108] In other situations, an omission might be one element of a crime. In the area of criminal possession (discussed in depth in the next section of this chapter), a defendant's failure "to terminate his possession"[109] of contraband of which he had inadvertently taken control made him liable for criminal possession of the contraband if the state could prove the existence of all of the other requirements for possession as well.

An omission is only a crime when a recognized legal duty is identified. It should be noted that the courts in Illinois seem to shy away from analyzing criminal liability problems by identifying defendants' legal duties toward their victims and rely instead on alternative legal theories to justify a conviction. For example, in *People v. Ryan*,[110] a woman was charged with involuntary manslaughter after she surreptitiously gave birth to a child in a bathroom, wrapped it in a towel, and placed it in an overnight case where it died.[111] While the Illinois appellate court upheld her conviction for manslaughter, it made no mention of the woman's legal duty toward her child. Rather, it asserted that the woman's "reckless and wanton disregard for the welfare, safety and life of her infant daughter" made her criminally culpable.[112] Similarly, in *People v. Banks*,[113] the defendant, who was the live-in boyfriend of the 16-month-old victim's mother and father of the victim's brother and sister, was convicted of first degree murder.[114] In this case, the victim died of hypothermia and starvation after the defendant had locked the child in an unheated room for several months and threatened to kill the mother when she attempted to feed the child.[115] The court rejected defendant's claim that he was not guilty of first degree murder because he had no legal duty to provide the victim with food, clothing and adequate shelter, pointing instead to the defendant's affirmative acts which led to the victim's death in upholding defendant's conviction.[116] In *People v. Smith*,[117] the defendant burglarized a residence, encountered a person, and attempted to strangle her.[118] Frightened by the defendant's actions, the person jumped out of the win-

---

[108] People v. Porter, 28 Ill. App. 3d 411, 414, 328 N.E.2d 618, 621 (5th Dist. 1975) (murder conviction based on accomplice theory affirmed). *See* Ch. 3 this volume for a discussion of accountability of others.

[109] 720 ILCS 5/4-2 (1999).

[110] 9 Ill. 2d 467, 138 N.E.2d 516 (1956).

[111] People v. Ryan, 9 Ill. 2d 467, 138 N.E.2d 516 (1956).

[112] People v. Ryan, 9 Ill. 2d 467, 474, 138 N.E.2d 516, 521 (1956).

[113] 161 Ill. 2d 119, 641 N.E.2d 331 (1994).

[114] People v. Banks, 161 Ill. 2d 119, 641 N.E.2d 331 (1994).

[115] People v. Banks, 161 Ill. 2d 119, 123-31, 641 N.E.2d 331, 334-37 (1994).

[116] People v. Banks, 161 Ill. 2d 119, 132-36, 641 N.E.2d 331, 337-39 (1994).

[117] 56 Ill. 2d 328, 307 N.E.2d 353 (1974).

[118] People v. Smith, 56 Ill. 2d 328, 330, 307 N.E.2d 353, 354 (1974).

dow of her apartment, sustaining serious injuries from which she died.[119] The court's opinion affirming the defendant's conviction for murder did not, given the facts, explore the possibility of a breached legal duty based on creation of peril arising from illegitimate activity. Instead, the court stated: "It is unimportant that the defendant did not anticipate the precise series of events that followed upon his entry into the apartment of [the victim] Judy Tolbert. His unlawful acts precipitated those events, and he is responsible for the consequences."[120]

The court's analysis in *Ryan, Banks,* and *Smith* suggests that Illinois courts may not be inclined to follow a "legal duty" reasoning where the nursing-home owner or nurse allows a resident to die of starvation, where the rock quarry owner kills an innocent bystander with his dynamite blasts, where the drunk driver kills an innocent pedestrian, or where the distressed rape victim jumps into the creek and drowns. In order to support the conviction, the court is more likely to assert in these situations that the defendant by his or her *affirmative* acts recklessly disregarded a grave risk to life or limb and that this disregard caused the foreseeable consequences of death. When a defendant's criminality can be easily established by focusing on the defendant's affirmative conduct, "legal duty" analysis may be not only unnecessary but inappropriate. However, the Illinois judiciary's avoidance of duty analysis may, in some difficult cases, deny the state the opportunity to demonstrate that a defendant's criminality may actually rest on *alternative* grounds and, in other cases, discourage the State from pursuing criminality which can *only* be proven by reliance on a breach of legal duty theory.

The 1982 Illinois appellate court decision of *People v. Watson* [121] is very important in this connection for it clearly does rely on a duty analysis in affirming a conviction. In this opinion (discussed above), the appellate court affirmed the involuntary manslaughter conviction of a defendant who was a caretaker of a twenty-three-month-old baby that was immersed in hot water, causing its death. In this case, there was conflicting evidence: some evidence suggested that the child had pulled a pan of boiling hot water off a stove onto herself; other evidence suggested that the defendant had deliberately immersed the child in the hot water.[122] The court obviously felt compelled to lay blame on the defendant one way or another, so it used reasoning based on the defendant's duty under the circumstances:

---

[119] People v. Smith, 56 Ill. 2d 328, 330, 307 N.E.2d 353, 354 (1974).

[120] People v. Smith, 56 Ill. 2d 328, 333-34, 307 N.E.2d 353, 355-56 (1974). *See also* People v. Parker, 90 Ill. App. 3d 1052, 414 N.E.2d 190 (1st Dist. 1980) (defendant's involuntary manslaughter conviction was affirmed where nine-year-old victim leaped from 12th floor window to death following severe beating inflicted by defendant).

[121] 103 Ill. App. 3d 992, 431 N.E.2d 1350 (4th Dist. 1982).

[122] People v. Watson, 103 Ill. App. 3d 992, 994-95, 431 N.E.2d 1350, 1352-54 (4th Dist. 1982).

> The defendant . . . complains that the counts charge him with an omission without alleging a corresponding duty. The defendant did have a duty to watch out for the well-being of the child, Shalita. He had a duty to prevent her from being immersed into water hot enough to cause great bodily harm or death. Although counts III and IV do not specifically state the nature of defendant's duty, they imply all of the elements of his duty. The counts say that Shalita was a 23-month-old baby and allege that she was immersed into water hot enough to cause death or great bodily harm. The caretaker of a child has a duty to protect the child from harm.[123]

Perhaps *Watson* is an important step in the direction of the Illinois courts being willing to express themselves in these situations in terms of a duty analysis.

§ 2.16. — Criminal Acts: Possession.

Crimes of possession involve unique analytical problems. Possession charges, particularly those based on a "constructive possession" theory, encompass a blend of concepts: access, control, exclusivity, proximity, knowledge, awareness, and opportunity to terminate connection with the item in question.

The code includes a specific reference to crimes of possession: "Possession is a voluntary act if the offender knowingly procured or received the thing possessed, or was aware of his control thereof for a sufficient time to have been able to terminate his possession."[124] Although this provision by its very terms includes mention of certain mental states — *knowledge* and *aware* — it falls in the code under the general heading of "Possession as Voluntary Act."[125] Accordingly, particular attention should be given to the interpretation of these mental-state terms as they appear in these provisions. They should not be confused with the mental-state requirements attached to many Illinois crimes (examined in the next section of this chapter). The revision committee's comment clarifies this point:

> Possession is another aspect of behavior which, while it does not necessarily involve a physical movement, is conveniently brought within the definition of "act" when it refers to the keeping of a physical object. Again, only the voluntary aspect is significant here — a consciousness of purpose, derived from knowingly procuring or receiving the thing possessed, or awareness of control thereof for a sufficient time to enable the person to terminate his possession.[126]

---

[123] People v. Watson, 103 Ill. App. 3d 992, 998, 431 N.E.2d 1350, 1355 (4th Dist. 1982).

[124] 720 ILCS 5/4-2 (1999).

[125] 720 ILCS 5/4-2 (1999).

[126] ILL. ANN. STAT. ch. 38, para. 4-2 (Smith-Hurd 1989), 1961 Committee Comments, at 195.

The basic purpose of this provision, paragraph 5/4-2, is to establish a basis for finding criminal liability where it can be proved that a defendant is in possession of items that he or she has no right to possess — items that endanger him or her personally or the public at large. An examination of the code reveals a number of items, normally referred to as contraband, that are relevant to this crime. They include possession of matter reflecting child pornography;[127] possession of keys or devices designed to illegally open or damage coin-operated machines;[128] assumption of control over property knowing it was stolen;[129] possession of stolen or fraudulently obtained checks;[130] possession of implements of check fraud;[131] illegal possession of a check guarantee card, key card, or bank identification card;[132] possession with intent to issue or deliver forged documents;[133] possession of burglary tools;[134] possession of explosive or incendiary devices with intent to commit an offense;[135] unauthorized possession of weapons;[136] unauthorized possession of gambling paraphernalia;[137] possession of cannabis;[138] possession of a controlled substance;[139] and possession of drug paraphernalia.[140]

§ 2.17.   — Actual and Constructive Possession.

There are two types of possession situations that give rise to criminal liability: *actual possession* and *constructive possession*.[141] These terms are not mutually exclusive; rather, they form a continuum based on relative immediacy of control.[142] Actual possession exists where a defendant knowingly assumes total, exclusive, immediate, physical control over an item.[143] Constructive possession is that which exists without actual personal present dominion over the item, but with an intent and capability to maintain control and dominion over the item in

---

[127] 720 ILCS 5/11-20.1(a)(6) (1999).

[128] 720 ILCS 5/16-6(a) (1999).

[129] 720 ILCS 5/16-1(a)(4) (1999).

[130] 720 ILCS 5/17-1(C)(2) (1999).

[131] 720 ILCS 5/17-1(C)(3) (1999).

[132] 720 ILCS 5/17-1(C)(4) (1999).

[133] 720 ILCS 5/17-3(a)(3) (1999).

[134] 720 ILCS 5/19-2(a) (1999).

[135] 720 ILCS 5/20-2(a) (1999).

[136] 720 ILCS 5/21-6(a); 5/24-1(a); 5/24-3.1(a) (1999).

[137] 720 ILCS 5/28-1(a)(5) (1999).

[138] 720 ILCS 550/4 (1999).

[139] 720 ILCS 570/402 (1999).

[140] 720 ILCS 600/3.5 (1999).

[141] People v. Rentsch, 167 Ill. App. 3d 368, 370, 521 N.E.2d 213, 215 (2d Dist. 1988).

[142] People v. Gore, 115 Ill. App. 3d 1054, 1057, 450 N.E.2d 1342, 1344 (3d Dist. 1983).

[143] People v. Archibald, 3 Ill. App. 3d 591, 595, 279 N.E.2d 84, 87 (3d Dist. 1972) ("Physical possession giving the defendant immediate and exclusive control is of course, sufficient").

question.[144] In the instance of actual possession, there is usually evidence that the defendant was carrying the object on his or her person. However, where a conviction is based on an actual possession theory rather than a constructive possession theory, the state is not required to show a physical touching of the object but only that the defendant had "dominion" over the object.[145] With constructive possession, the object in question is in a *place* under the defendant's control.[146] Obviously, the latter situation gives rise to much greater problems of proof than the former.[147] Regardless of which theory of possession is employed, the basic elements of criminal possession are: (1) exclusive control over the item, (2) accessibility to the item, (3) knowledge or awareness of the presence of the item, and (4) an opportunity to terminate connection with the item where the initial assumption of control over, or access to, the item was innocent. Although the code does not set out these four requirements for possession and although no particular case articulates these requirements in the exact terms set out here, the Illinois body of caselaw revolving around problems of possession seems to require no less.

§ 2.18. — Possession — Requirement of Control.

First, the defendant must have control over the object. Physical possession giving the defendant immediate and exclusive control is sufficient.[148] However, the possession need not be actual physical possession; constructive possession can be shown by establishing that the property involved was subject to the defendant's dominion and control.[149] Although Illinois caselaw states that the control must be *exclusive*,[150] this term is not construed in the narrow sense of sole control. In other words, more than one individual can have exclusive control over an item for possession purposes.[151] Courts have explained that the "rule that possession must be exclusive does not mean that possession may not be joint."[152] Thus, if more than one person had access to the contraband or to the

---

[144] People v. Valentin, 135 Ill. App. 3d 22, 31, 480 N.E.2d 1351, 1358 (1st Dist. 1985).

[145] People v. Clark, 173 Ill. App. 3d 443, 451, 526 N.E.2d 356, 362 (2d Dist. 1988).

[146] People v. Chicos, 205 Ill. App. 3d 928, 935, 563 N.E.2d 893, 898 (1st Dist. 1990) (controlled substances found in apartment where defendant lived).

[147] People v. Archibald, 3 Ill. App. 3d 591, 595, 279 N.E.2d 84, 87 (3d Dist. 1972) ("What constitutes sufficient external relationship between a defendant and contraband property to complete the concept of 'possession' is a question which is not susceptible of a short generalized answer").

[148] People v. Alexander, 202 Ill. App. 3d 20, 24, 559 N.E.2d 567, 569 (3d Dist. 1990).

[149] People v. Archibald, 3 Ill. App. 3d 591, 595, 279 N.E.2d 84, 87 (3d Dist. 1972).

[150] People v. Nettles, 23 Ill. 2d 306, 307, 178 N.E.2d 361, 362 (1961), *cert. denied*, 369 U.S. 853 (1962).

[151] People v. Scott, 152 Ill. App. 3d 868, 871, 505 N.E.2d 42, 45 (5th Dist. 1987).

[152] People v. O'Neal, 35 Ill. App. 3d 89, 92, 341 N.E.2d 36, 39 (1st Dist. 1975).

premises in which the contraband was situated, this does not overcome a finding that a defendant exercised exclusive control and dominion:[153]

> When the relationship of others to the contraband is sufficiently close to constitute possession, the result is not vindication of the defendant, but rather a situation of joint possession. To hold otherwise would enable persons to escape criminal liability for possession of contraband by the simple expediency of inviting others to participate in the criminal enterprise.[154]

Thus, exclusivity is interpreted only to negate the possession of an object that was solely in the control of another.[155]

A court can determine that a defendant had exclusive possession of an object or contraband despite the fact that another person apparently had greater access to it. Thus, where a defendant told an informant to whom he was making a delivery of cannabis that the contraband was "more or less his roommate's,"[156] his conviction for possession was sustained even though the defendant may have had a lesser degree of control than his roommate.[157]

Where there is relatively equal access to, and control over, contraband, a court will have little difficulty establishing possession. In one case, a defendant was one of three occupants of a dwelling in which a sawed-off shotgun was found and there was evidence that the defendant and at least one of the other occupants frequently handled the shotgun.[158] The court found that the requisite control needed to establish possession was present even though others had access to the contraband.[159] A person may share criminal possession with another and, thus, it is not a defense that another also had control over the contraband.[160] Where contraband was found in a defendant's home and in the trunk of his car, evidence that several other people lived on the premises and had access to the car would not defeat the conclusion of constructive possession for the defendant.[161]

---

[153] People v. Williams, 98 Ill. App. 3d 844, 848, 424 N.E.2d 1234, 1236-37 (3d Dist. 1981).

[154] People v. Williams, 98 Ill. App. 3d 844, 849, 424 N.E.2d 1234, 1237 (3d Dist. 1981).

[155] See, e.g., People v. Jump, 56 Ill. App. 3d 871, 872, 371 N.E.2d 691, 692 (3d Dist. 1978) (where driver-owner testified defendant had no control over vehicle and had not placed cannabis in vehicle in which defendant was passenger, defendant was not in constructive possession of the cannabis in the vehicle); People v. Martin, 1 Ill. App. 3d 798, 799, 274 N.E.2d 593, 594 (3d Dist. 1971) (no constructive possession of gun where item in exclusive, sole possession of another).

[156] People v. Hanson, 44 Ill. App. 3d 977, 980, 359 N.E.2d 188, 192 (3d Dist. 1977).

[157] People v. Hanson, 44 Ill. App. 3d 977, 985, 359 N.E.2d 188, 195 (3d Dist. 1977).

[158] People v. Williams, 98 Ill. App. 3d 844, 849, 424 N.E.2d 1234, 1237 (3d Dist. 1981).

[159] People v. Williams, 98 Ill. App. 3d 844, 849, 424 N.E.2d 1234, 1237 (3d Dist. 1981).

[160] People v. Birge, 137 Ill. App. 3d 781, 790, 485 N.E.2d 37, 44 (2d Dist. 1985).

[161] People v. Eiland, 217 Ill. App. 3d 250, 260-61, 576 N.E.2d 1185, 1193 (5th Dist. 1991).

Courts have found that possession may be established when a defendant has exhibited the capacity and intent to maintain control over the contraband.[162] Where a defendant did not presently live in the house or have a key to the house where cocaine was found, the evidence supported a finding that the defendant had sufficient knowledge and control over the drugs because defendant's fingerprint was found on one of the cocaine packets and the defendant previously lived in the house with his aunt, recently received mail at that address, and was able to return to the house to pick up his clothes.[163] Likewise, constructive possession of heroin and cannabis sufficient for convictions of possession with intent to deliver was based on the presence of several pieces of defendant's identification and large male clothing matching defendant's body size in the apartment where the drugs were found.[164] On the other hand, considerable doubt was cast on the control the defendant had over certain premises where it was established that drugs were found in an apartment that was accessible to others, little of defendant's personal belongings were found in the apartment, and the single letter found in the apartment that was addressed to defendant was unopened.[165] Similarly, where police found two bags of narcotics on top of an air conditioning duct in an alley from which the defendant fled, the bags were not shown to be in defendant's exclusive possession or control since the evidence did not support a finding that the defendant had the necessary intent and capability to maintain possession and control over the bags of contraband.[166]

Where a package of cocaine was carried on and hidden in an airplane restroom by the defendant, the Illinois Supreme Court found that the defendant's control over the drugs could be inferred even though the defendant neither had control over the place where they were found nor was apprehended with the drugs on his person.[167] In that case, the court held that since the defendant had not abandoned the drugs since boarding the plane, he continued to have the requisite control over the drugs necessary for criminal possession.[168] Similarly, where packets of cocaine were found under a rock in a public place a short distance from a defendant, a hiding place from which defendant's accomplices retrieved cocaine to deliver to purchasers whenever defendant signaled them to do so, the state was able to show that the defendant maintained constructive possession from evidence that he knew the location of the drugs and intended to maintain control over the contraband from his nearby vantage point.[169] Other courts

---

[162] People v. Jones, 295 Ill. App. 3d 444, 452, 692 N.E.2d 762, 768 (1st Dist. 1998).

[163] People v. Butler, 242 Ill. App. 3d 731, 733, 611 N.E.2d 603, 605 (2d Dist. 1993).

[164] People v. McCoy, 295 Ill. App. 3d 988, 994-95, 692 N.E.2d 1244, 1248-49 (1st Dist. 1998).

[165] People v. Jones, 105 Ill. App. 3d 1143, 1149, 435 N.E.2d 823, 827 (5th Dist. 1982).

[166] People v. Lawrence, 46 Ill. App. 3d 305, 309, 360 N.E.2d 990, 993 (4th Dist. 1977).

[167] People v. Adams, 161 Ill. 2d 333, 344-45, 641 N.E.2d 514, 519 (1994).

[168] People v. Adams, 161 Ill. 2d 333, 345, 641 N.E.2d 514, 520 (1994).

[169] People v. Jones, 295 Ill. App. 3d 444, 453-54, 692 N.E.2d 762, 769 (1st Dist. 1998).

have followed this reasoning and found that where contraband is not under the defendant's immediate physical control nor on premises under his control, possession can still be found by examining the defendant's "relationship to the contraband."[170] Where police observed an exchange involving defendant that they suspected to be a drug sale, whereupon defendant fled upon approach by the police, and a short time later found the defendant hidden underneath patio furniture a few feet from the location where narcotics were found by the police, the court found that the circumstantial evidence supported a finding of possession.[171] Similarly, when a defendant was pulled over in his car by the police for a traffic violation and kept his hands out of view of the officer after exiting the car, while refusing to comply with orders to stand still and walking away several times, the plastic bag of cocaine found lying on the ground at the location where defendant had walked was sufficient evidence to support a conviction of possession.[172]

Where a defendant has control over certain premises in which contraband is found, control of the article in question may be inferred.[173] This permissive inference is not defeated merely because others have had access to the area in question.[174] Where the defendant was the driver of a borrowed car where police found contraband ammunition in the glove compartment, which was situated closer to the passenger than the defendant, the court relied on this legal inference in upholding defendant's conviction for criminal possession of these items.[175] On the other hand, it should be noted that although possession may be shared, in cases involving joint control of an area, "courts generally look for corroborating evidence connecting defendant to the contraband found."[176]

Evidence regarding control over an area in which contraband is located is a two-edged sword. For instance, where the evidence showed that the defendant, who was merely a passenger in another's car, had no control over the area in which cannabis was located, the state's charge of possession was thus defeated.[177] Similarly, where the evidence revealed defendant had no control over a drug house in which he was present during a police raid in which drugs were

[170] People v. Menniweather, 301 Ill. App. 3d 574, 578, 703 N.E.2d 912, 914 (4th Dist. 1998).

[171] People v. Menniweather, 301 Ill. App. 3d 574, 578, 703 N.E.2d 912, 915 (4th Dist. 1998).

[172] People v. Beverly, 278 Ill. App. 3d 794, 797, 663 N.E.2d 1061, 1064 (4th Dist. 1996).

[173] People v. Scott, 152 Ill. App. 3d 868, 871, 505 N.E.2d 42, 44-45 (5th Dist. 1987) ("narcotics being found on premises under the control of defendant gives rise to an inference of knowledge and possession by him which alone may be sufficient to sustain a conviction for unlawful possession of controlled substances").

[174] People v. Williams, 98 Ill. App. 3d 844, 847-48, 424 N.E.2d 1234, 1236-37 (3d Dist. 1981).

[175] People v. O'Neal, 35 Ill. App. 3d 89, 91, 341 N.E.2d 36, 39 (1st Dist. 1975).

[176] People v. Fabing, 42 Ill. App. 3d 379, 384, 355 N.E.2d 719, 723 (1st Dist. 1976). Cf. People v. Wolski, 27 Ill. App. 3d 526, 528, 327 N.E.2d 308, 309 (1st Dist. 1975) (insufficient corroboration).

[177] People v. Jump, 56 Ill. App. 3d 871, 872, 371 N.E.2d 691, 692 (3d Dist. 1978).

found, no drugs were found on his person and he had been present only a few minutes prior to the raid, constructive possession was not established.[178]

It is not necessary that the defendant be the true owner of, or have title to, an object to be convicted of criminal possession of an object.[179] Thus, where a defendant accepted a bag containing heroin with the intention of protecting it from everyone except the true owners, the appellate court found he had control for the purposes of criminal possession of a controlled substance.[180]

§ 2.19. — Possession — Requirement of Access.

Implicit in a criminal possession case is the requirement that a defendant have access to the object in question. Thus, where a defendant had access to illicit drugs that he placed in the lavatory of a commercial airline on which he was a passenger, he was convicted of criminal possession even though he had no immediate control over the drugs.[181] On the other hand, where defendant had not only moved out of a house but had also relinquished his keys to the home, he could not be convicted of criminal possession of cannabis found in the home.[182] Similarly, where the defendant had knowledge of drugs in the premises where he was not actually present, did not frequently visit there, had no key to the premises, and the envelope with the narcotics was marked with another person's name, there was no finding of constructive possession.[183]

Beyond conventional criminal possession charges, it is important to note that some crimes require as an essential element true, immediate accessibility to the object in question. For example, various "unlawful use of weapons" prohibitions directed at the possession or carrying of weapons require true accessibility.[184] Accessibility in this connection requires, as a practical matter, "within one's reach" or an "arm's length" showing of accessibility.[185] For instance, a pistol located four to six inches under the front seat of a car between the defendant driver and the drive-train hump was found to be accessible to the defendant, af-

---

[178] In re K.A., 291 Ill. App. 3d 1, 6-9, 682 N.E.2d 1233, 1238-40 (2d Dist. 1997).

[179] People v. Agyei, 232 Ill. App. 3d 546, 556, 579 N.E.2d 696, 703 (1st Dist. 1992).

[180] People v. Agyei, 232 Ill. App. 3d 546, 556, 579 N.E.2d 696, 703 (1st Dist. 1992).

[181] People v. Adams, 161 Ill. 2d 333, 345, 641 N.E.2d 514, 520 (1994).

[182] People v. Tomasello, 166 Ill. App. 3d 684, 690-91, 520 N.E.2d 1134, 1138-39 (2d Dist. 1988).

[183] People v. Bedford, 78 Ill. App. 2d 308, 311-12, 223 N.E.2d 290, 292 (1st Dist. 1966).

[184] See 720 ILCS 5/24-1 (a)(4) (1999) ("Carries or possesses in any vehicle or concealed on or about his person except when on his land or in his own abode or fixed place of business any pistol, revolver, stun gun or taser or other firearm"). See also 720 ILCS 5/24-1(a)(10) (1999) ("Carries or possesses on or about his person, upon any public street, alley, or other public lands . . . except for the purpose of the display of such weapon or the lawful commerce in weapons").

[185] See 720 ILCS 5/24-2(b)(4) (1999) (person is entitled to exemption where there are "transportation of weapons that are broken down in a non-functioning state or are not immediately accessible").

ter the Illinois Supreme Court explained that a weapon might be considered immediately accessible even if it were not considered "on or about the person" of the defendant.[186] Similarly, where a defendant could not have reached a rifle that was situated behind the car's back seat on the driver's side unless he rose from his seat, turned, and grabbed it, the rifle was nevertheless found to be sufficiently accessible to convict the defendant of criminal possession of the item.[187] The court ruled that accessibility could be properly inferred because the defendant "was the owner with exclusive possession of the vehicle and the owner of the gun [and he] knew where it was placed."[188]

Other cases demonstrate how inaccessibility will destroy a claim of *actual* possession, as required by the terms of the unlawful use of weapons prohibition. Where the defendant was a stout man and could not readily reach the weapon situated under the front seat of a compact car, the appellate court held that the gun was inaccessible to the defendant.[189] Similarly, a defendant could not be convicted of unlawful possession of a weapon on an actual possession theory where the weapon was situated in the locked trunk of an automobile the defendant was driving because the weapon was inaccessible to the defendant.[190]

§ 2.20.   — Possession — Requirement of Knowledge or Awareness.

The third requirement for possession is knowledge or awareness of the article.[191] Just as mere proximity to an object, by itself, is insufficient to establish possession, so too mere knowledge of the place or location of the object is insuf-

---

[186] People v. McKnight, 39 Ill. 2d 577, 580, 237 N.E.2d 488, 490 (1968), *cert. denied*, 394 U.S. 993 (1969).

[187] People v. Clodfelder, 172 Ill. App. 3d 1030, 1033, 527 N.E.2d 632, 634 (4th Dist. 1988).

[188] People v. Clodfelder, 172 Ill. App. 3d 1030, 1034, 527 N.E.2d 632, 634 (4th Dist. 1988). *See also* People v. McIntosh, 53 Ill. App. 3d 958, 961, 369 N.E.2d 217, 219 (1st Dist. 1977) (gun was "accessible" where situated inside cushion on driver's seat, even though defendant could not have reached gun without getting out of car); People v. Smith, 71 Ill. 2d 95, 100-02, 374 N.E.2d 472, 473-74 (1978) (gun was "immediately accessible" although locked in glove compartment).

[189] People v. Adams, 73 Ill. App. 2d 1, 2-3, 220 N.E.2d 17, 18 (1st Dist. 1962), *cert. denied*, 389 U.S. 943 (1967).

[190] People v. Reed, 72 Ill. App. 3d 405, 407-08, 390 N.E.2d 962, 965 (3d Dist. 1979) (defendant entitled to inaccessibility exemption under unlawful use of weapons statute); *see also* People v. House, 29 Ill. App. 3d 994, 997, 331 N.E.2d 72, 74 (1st Dist. 1975) (gun in garbage can outside defendant's reach inaccessible for purposes of actual possession of concealed weapon); People v. McClendon, 23 Ill. App. 3d 10, 12, 161 N.E.2d 584, 586 (1st Dist. 1959) (gun under seat in auto driven by defendant and outside defendant's reach inaccessible for purposes of actual possession of concealed weapon). *Compare* People v. Hammer, 228 Ill. App. 3d 318, 322-24, 591 N.E.2d 554, 557 (2d Dist. 1992) (unlawful possession of weapon by felon can be based on constructive possession).

[191] 720 ILCS 5/4-2 (1999).

ficient for possession.[192] What is required, in the words of one court, is "knowledgeable control,"[193] regardless of whether the charge of possession of contraband depends on an actual or a constructive possession theory.[194]

Knowledge may be proved by evidence of defendant's acts, declarations, or conduct from which it can be inferred he knew the contraband existed in the place where it was found.[195] Knowledgeable control may be established by a defendant's acknowledgement that the object belongs to him or her[196] or, in the absence of such evidence of scienter, by circumstantial evidence.[197] Thus, a physical motion by a defendant towards where he or she is attempting to conceal an item of contraband, or throw it away upon police approach, suggests dominion and control over the item and raises an inference of knowledge.[198] Similarly, where a defendant acknowledged that he had opened the glove compartment of a borrowed automobile after he took custody of the automobile, it was reasonable to infer that he knew of the existence of contraband shotgun shells in the compartment that fell out immediately when it subsequently was opened in the presence of the police.[199] Where a defendant traveled from Florida with the person who brought drugs into the state, repeatedly met with this person and another person who received and in turn sold drugs situated in a box to an undercover agent, and constantly remained in the presence of the box that contained the drugs before it was delivered to the agent, the defendant was found to have sufficient knowledge of the contents of the box to justify a conviction for possession of narcotics, even though there was no direct evidence that defendant carried or saw what was in the box.[200] Contraband plainly visible to the defendant

---

[192] People v. Day, 51 Ill. App. 3d 916, 917, 366 N.E.2d 895, 896 (4th Dist. 1977); *see also* People v. Lawrence, 46 Ill. App. 3d 305, 308, 360 N.E.2d 990, 992 (4th Dist. 1977); People v. Bedford, 78 Ill. App. 2d 308, 311, 223 N.E.2d 290, 292 (1st Dist. 1966).

[193] People v. Gore, 115 Ill. App. 3d 1054, 1057, 450 N.E.2d 1342, 1345 (3d Dist. 1983).

[194] People v. Gore, 115 Ill. App. 3d 1054, 1057, 450 N.E.2d 1342, 1345 (3d Dist. 1983).

[195] People v. Beverly, 278 Ill. App. 3d 794, 797, 663 N.E.2d 1061, 1064 (4th Dist. 1996).

[196] People v. Fabing, 42 Ill. App. 3d 379, 384, 355 N.E.2d 719, 724 (1st Dist. 1976) (defendant admitted that marijuana was his); *see also* People v. Williams, 200 Ill. App. 3d 503, 518, 558 N.E.2d 261, 270 (1st Dist. 1990) (where defendant told police an apartment was "his place," he could properly be convicted of possession of cocaine located therein).

[197] People v. Morrison, 178 Ill. App. 3d 76, 90-91, 532 N.E.2d 1077, 1087 (4th Dist. 1988); People v. McKnight, 39 Ill. 2d 577, 581, 237 N.E.2d 488, 490 (1968), *cert. denied*, 394 U.S. 993 (1969).

[198] People v. Beverly, 278 Ill. App. 3d 794, 799, 663 N.E.2d 1061, 1065 (4th Dist. 1996); People v. Morrison, 178 Ill. App. 3d 76, 90, 532 N.E.2d 1077, 1087 (4th Dist. 1988).

[199] People v. O'Neal, 35 Ill. App. 3d 89, 91-92, 341 N.E.2d 36, 38-39 (1st Dist. 1975).

[200] People v. Pintos, 133 Ill. 2d 286, 292-93, 549 N.E.2d 344, 347 (1989).

and sitting on his lap gives rise to knowledge and awareness,[201] as does the fact that the volume of contraband found is very large.[202]

If a defendant enjoys control over the area where the contraband is located, there is a permissive inference that he or she has knowledge of the contraband. In *People v. Nettles*,[203] the Illinois Supreme Court stated:

> [W]here narcotics are found on the premises under the control of the defendant, this fact, in and of itself, gives rise to an inference of knowledge and possession by him which may be sufficient to sustain a conviction for unlawful possession of narcotics, absent other facts and circumstances which might leave in the mind of the jury or of the court where a jury is waived, a reasonable doubt as to his guilt.[204]

Even if others have access to an area under a defendant's control, this permissive inference may be used.[205]

On the other hand, even though a defendant has control over an area, he or she does not necessarily know of the existence of contraband in the area. Thus, a defendant does not have knowledgeable control over cannabis located in a car merely because the defendant is the driver of the car.[206] So, too, cannabis admittedly thrown from a car in which other persons were present did not prove possession by the passenger seated closest to the window.[207] Contraband located in

---

[201] People v. Rhoades, 74 Ill. App. 3d 247, 252, 392 N.E.2d 923, 926-27 (4th Dist. 1979) (state trooper observed cannabis on metal tray on lap of defendant sitting in motor vehicle).

[202] People v. Janis, 56 Ill. App. 3d 160, 164, 371 N.E.2d 1063, 1066 (1st Dist. 1977) (200 pounds of burglary tools in rear of van easily visible to defendant).

[203] 23 Ill. 2d 306, 178 N.E.2d 361 (1961), *cert. denied*, 369 U.S. 853 (1962).

[204] 23 Ill. 2d 306, 308-09, 178 N.E.2d 361, 363 (1961), *cert. denied*, 369 U.S. 853 (1962). *See also* People v. Lawton, 253 Ill. App. 3d 144, 625 N.E.2d 348 (1st Dist. 1993) (Drugs found on premises controlled by the defendant, although not occupied by the defendant as a residence, gave rise to the inference that the defendant knowingly possessed the drugs found inside the premises).

[205] *See* People v. Scott, 152 Ill. App. 3d 868, 871, 505 N.E.2d 42, 45 (5th Dist. 1987); People v. Rhoades, 74 Ill. App. 3d 247, 252, 392 N.E.2d 923, 926-27 (4th Dist. 1979).

[206] People v. Waddell, 190 Ill. App. 3d 914, 925-26, 546 N.E.2d 1068, 1075 (4th Dist. 1989); People v. Roundtree, 135 Ill. App. 3d 1075, 1080-81, 482 N.E.2d 693, 698 (1st Dist. 1985); People v. Gore, 115 Ill. App. 3d 1054, 1058-59, 450 N.E.2d 1342, 1345-46 (3d Dist. 1983); People v. Day, 51 Ill. App. 3d 916, 918, 366 N.E.2d 895, 897 (4th Dist. 1977).

[207] People v. Boswell, 19 Ill. App. 3d 619, 621-22, 312 N.E.2d 17, 19 (3d Dist. 1974). *See also* People v. Millis, 116 Ill. App. 2d 283, 287, 252 N.E.2d 395, 396-97 (4th Dist. 1969) (open beer cans in car occupied by defendant and two others constituted insufficient evidence to establish constructive or actual possession); People v. Connie, 52 Ill. App. 2d 221, 228-29, 201 N.E.2d 641, 643-44 (1st Dist. 1964) (where narcotics found in defendant's car may have been placed there without defendant's knowledge, conviction for possession reversed).

the defendant's residence did not, by itself, necessarily mean that he had knowledgeable control of the contraband.[208]

While knowledge can be inferred from control over an area, it cannot be inferred from access to an area.[209] Limited access or lack of access can defeat a criminal possession charge.[210] Thus, where the defendant was present on premises on which contraband was seized, the fact that there was no evidence that he lived there, kept any personal effects there, or was even a frequent visitor there supported the defense claim that there was no wrongful possession by the defendant.[211] Similarly, there was no constructive possession despite the defendant's knowledge of the narcotics seized where the defendant did not reside on the premises, did not visit there frequently, and had no key to the premises and where the envelope containing the narcotics was marked with another person's name.[212] In another case, evidence that the defendant had a key to a third party's apartment where narcotics were seized was alone insufficient to prove knowledge of the drugs and thus could not uphold a conviction for possession.[213]

§ 2.21. — Possession — Opportunity to Terminate Control.

The fourth requirement for possession is an opportunity to terminate connection with the contraband, where the initial assumption of control over, or access to, the contraband was innocent.[214] This requirement for criminal possession would likely arise under the following circumstances: (1) a defendant receives in the mail an unsolicited parcel containing cannabis, knowing it to be cannabis, and thereafter decides to keep the contraband for his or her own use instead of disposing of it or turning it over to the authorities; (2) a defendant arrives at a social function where, unexpectedly, he finds narcotics are openly displayed and used, and the defendant remains there indefinitely while having ready access to, control over, and use of the drugs.

§ 2.22. — Possession — Accountability Theory.

Where the state is attempting to prove a defendant guilty of criminal possession in circumstances in which there was joint possession by multiple offenders,

---

[208] People v. Wolski, 27 Ill. App. 3d 526, 528-29, 327 N.E.2d 308, 309-10 (1st Dist. 1975); People v. Bolden, 96 Ill. App. 2d 129, 131-32, 237 N.E.2d 748, 749 (1st Dist. 1968).

[209] People v. Gore, 115 Ill. App. 3d 1054, 1058, 450 N.E.2d 1342, 1345 (3d Dist. 1983); People v. Wolski, 27 Ill. App. 3d 526, 528-29, 327 N.E.2d 308, 309-10 (1st Dist. 1975).

[210] People v. Tomasello, 166 Ill. App. 3d 684, 690-91, 520 N.E.2d 1134, 1138-39 (2d Dist. 1988) (defendant moved out of house and had relinquished keys to house before cannabis found in house).

[211] People v. Pugh, 36 Ill. 2d 435, 436-38, 223 N.E.2d 115, 117 (1967).

[212] People v. Bedford, 78 Ill. App. 2d 308, 311-12, 223 N.E.2d 290, 292 (1st Dist. 1966).

[213] People v. Macias, 299 Ill. App. 3d 480, 485-86, 701 N.E.2d 212, 216-17 (1st Dist. 1998).

[214] 720 ILCS 5/4-2 (1999).

it has an option available beyond a constructive possession theory, namely, the theory of accountability.[215] In *People v. Saunders*,[216] the appellate court relied on an accomplice liability theory to affirm the defendant's conviction of possession of a controlled substance in circumstances where the defendant drove a codefendant to the crime scene, spoke to an undercover police officer regarding the price and quantity of cocaine and asked the codefendant to show the officer an ounce of the cocaine.[217] In *People v. Cannon*,[218] the court used a theory of accountability as well as constructive possession to uphold a defendant's conviction for unlawful possession of unregistered hand guns. The appellate court stated that "circumstantial evidence may prove the existence of a common design to do an unlawful act and to show that the defendant assented to the commission of a crime and therefore aided and abetted."[219]

§ 2.23.   — Possession — Evidence of Other Crimes.

It is important to note that criminal possession can give rise to an evidentiary inference of the commission of other crimes beyond possession assuming other facts and circumstances support the defendants involvement in these other crimes. For instance, in *People v. Panus*,[220] the defendant was charged with burglary after it was determined that he was in possession of a ground-tiller some three to four months following the burglary during which the ground-tiller had been removed. The court stated:

> the recent unexplained possession of property stolen in a burglary may be relied upon by the trier of fact to infer guilt. . . . Such possession is a relevant circumstance in determining, for example, whether it was defendant that entered the burglarized premises and whether he did so with intent to commit a theft therein.[221]

---

[215] *See* 720 ILCS 5/5-2(c) (1999).

[216] 206 Ill. App. 3d 1008, 565 N.E.2d 183 (1st Dist. 1990).

[217] People v. Saunders, 206 Ill. App. 3d 1008, 1014-15, 565 N.E.2d 183, 187-88 (1st Dist. 1990). *See also* People v. Wiley, 174 Ill. App. 3d 444, 452, 528 N.E.2d 26, 32 (3d Dist. 1988) (husband convicted on an accomplice theory of possession of a controlled substance and possession with intent to deliver, where evidence showed he placed a controlled substance in his wife's car, and gave her directions to the place where she was to make delivery before she was apprehended and found to be possessing the substance).

[218] 18 Ill. App. 3d 781, 310 N.E.2d 673 (1st Dist. 1974).

[219] People v. Cannon, 18 Ill. App. 3d 781, 786, 310 N.E.2d 673, 677 (1st Dist. 1974). *See also* People v. Williams, 132 Ill. App. 2d 806, 809, 270 N.E.2d 144, 147 (1st Dist. 1971) (defendants convicted of unlawful possession of handguns in an automobile on an accomplice liability theory).

[220] 76 Ill. 2d 263, 391 N.E.2d 376 (1979).

[221] People v. Panus, 76 Ill. 2d 263, 269-70, 391 N.E.2d 376, 378 (1979). *Cf.* D. Stevens, *Abolishing Permissive Inference of Guilt of Burglary: Time to Update Illinois's Common Law*, 84 ILL.

However, it is important to note this evidentiary inference only becomes operable if other facts and circumstances exist which corroborate the defendant's guilt as to these other crimes.[222] Also, the normal barriers to establishing criminal possession — lack of control, access, or knowledge — are relevant with respect to these evidentiary inferences. In *People v. Ridley*,[223] for example, the access that other people had to an apartment where stereo equipment stolen in a burglary was found undermined the assertion that the defendant, whose wallet was found in the room where the stereo equipment was located, had exclusive control of the stereo equipment. This fact defeated the charge of theft lodged against the defendant based on a constructive possession theory.[224] The court stated "if the place where the goods were found was equally accessible to others who were capable of committing the theft, an inference of defendant's guilt cannot be made from that fact alone.[225]

§ 2.24. Mental States: Generally.

There are few exercises in the area of substantive criminal law that are more difficult than mastering a complete understanding of the various mental states reflected in a penal code.[226] First, there are inevitable conceptual problems inherent in such inquiries. For instance, distinguishing specific intent from general intent or recklessness from negligence can be an arduous task.[227] Second, the problem is aggravated by the differing interpretations given the mental-state terms. Often, there is simply no meaningful judicial consensus in regard to the definitions or usage of these terms[228] or agreement about the state-of-mind requirement for a particular crime.[229] Third, there are many penal codes that on the

---

B.J. 514 (1996) (criticism of common law permissive inference of guilt of burglary based on recent, unexplained possession of proceeds of burglary).

[222] People v. Housby, 84 Ill. 2d 415, 423-24, 420 N.E.2d 151, 155, *cert. denied*, 454 U.S. 845 (1981) (criminal possession of proceeds of burglary standing alone does not support legal inference of defendant's involvement in burglary).

[223] 59 Ill. App. 3d 164, 376 N.E.2d 43 (1st Dist. 1978).

[224] People v. Ridley, 59 Ill. App. 3d 164, 167, 376 N.E.2d 43, 45 (1st Dist. 1978).

[225] People v. Ridley, 59 Ill. App. 3d 164, 167, 376 N.E.2d 43, 45 (1st Dist. 1978).

[226] Frank J. Remington & Orrin L. Helstad, *The Mental Element in Crime — A Legislative Problem*, 1952 WIS. L. REV. 644, 678.

[227] WAYNE LAFAVE & AUSTIN SCOTT, CRIMINAL LAW § 3.5(e) (2d ed. 1986).

[228] 1 CHARLES E. TORCIA, WHARTON'S CRIMINAL LAW § 27, at 136 (14th ed. 1978).

[229] In some situations, a particular court may appear to be confused in this regard. For example, in 1977, the Illinois Supreme Court ruled that robbery is a crime requiring proof of specific intent to permanently deprive an owner of his or her property. People v. White, 67 Ill. 2d 107, 117, 365 N.E.2d 337, 341-42 (1977). But in 1979, the court held that robbery only requires a general intent to deprive a victim of his or her property. People v. Banks, 75 Ill. 2d 383, 392, 388 N.E.2d 1244, 1248 (1979). This determination has significant consequences. For instance, evidence of a defendant's intoxication may be a defense to a crime requiring specific intent, but will not negate a criminal actor's general intent. 720 ILCS 5/6-3 (1999) (voluntary intoxication is only a defense if

whole reflect a myriad of mental state requirements. For instance, the current federal code includes more than seventy-five different terms used to describe the mental elements of federal criminal offenses.[230]

Although the mental state requirement, sometimes referred to as the *mens rea* requirement,[231] is an important ingredient of most crimes, it is not an essential requirement. A legislature can create offenses that do not require proof of a particular mental state. These are known as absolute liability[232] or strict liability[233] offenses and will be discussed later in this chapter.

§ 2.25. General Statutory Considerations.

When the Criminal Code of 1961 was drafted, the revision committee responsible for drafting the code wisely decided to abandon the myriad of mental states that were reflected in the code before its passage by the state's General Assembly. It was determined that the respective mental element of each of the offenses in the Criminal Code of 1961 could be described adequately by using one or more of a certain few terms — such as *intentionally, knowingly, recklessly,* and *negligently* — with uniform meaning and appropriate qualifying language attached to each term.[234] Accordingly, paragraph 5/4-3(a) of the code provides:

> Mental State. (a) A person is not guilty of an offense, other than an offense which involves absolute liability, unless, with respect to each element described by the statute defining the offense, he acts while having one of the mental states described in Sections 4-4 through 4-7.[235]

Paragraph 5/4-4 refers to "intent,"[236] 5/4-5 to "knowledge,"[237] 5/4-6 to "recklessness,"[238] and 5/4-7 to "negligence."[239] These four mental states will be the central focus of this inquiry.

---

it is "so extreme as to suspend the power of reason and render him incapable of forming a specific intent which is an element of the offense."); People v. Roesler, 195 Ill. App. 3d 1007, 1012, 552 N.E.2d 1242, 1246 (5th Dist. 1990). ("[C]ourts have consistently held [that the] defense [of intoxication] applies only to specific intent crimes. . . . Since rape is a general intent offense, the voluntary intoxication defense is not available. . . .").

[230] Kenneth R. Feinberg, *Toward a New Approach to Proving Culpability: Mens Rea and the Proposed Federal Criminal Code*, 18 AM. CRIM. L. REV. 123, 125 (1980).

[231] *See* Rollin M. Perkins, *A Rationale of Mens Rea*, 52 HARV. L. REV. 905 (1939).

[232] 720 ILCS 5/4-9 (1999) (Illinois absolute liability provisions).

[233] JOSHUA DRESSLER, UNDERSTANDING CRIMINAL LAW § 11.01 (2d ed. 1995).

[234] ILL. ANN. STAT. ch. 38, para. 4-3 (Smith-Hurd 1989), 1961 Committee Comments, at 198.

[235] 720 ILCS 5/4-3(a) (1999).

[236] 720 ILCS 5/4-4 (1999).

[237] 720 ILCS 5/4-5 (1999).

[238] 720 ILCS 5/4-6 (1999).

[239] 720 ILCS 5/4-7 (1999).

The general mental state provision contained in paragraph 5/4-3 reflects other concerns as well. Subparagraph (b) provides:

> If the statute defining an offense prescribed a particular mental state with respect to the offense as a whole, without distinguishing among the elements thereof, the prescribed mental state applies to each such element. If the statute does not prescribe a particular mental state applicable to an element of an offense (other than an offense which involves absolute liability), any mental state defined in Sections 4-4, 4-5 or 4-6 is applicable.[240]

The Committee Comments explain the reason for including this language:

> Subsection 4-3(b) offers a general rule of interpretation of statutory references to mental state in defining offenses. Often, a single mental state word, such as "knowingly," is placed in a position where grammatically it may apply to all elements of the offense. To so apply it for purposes of legal interpretation seems logical, since the intent that it shall not apply to certain elements of the offense may be expressed readily by a different sentence structure. . . . However, a provision may contain no expression of mental state, although absolute liability apparently is not intended. . . . Or a provision may be so phrased that the mental state expressed applies only to some of the elements of the offense and not to others, although no indication appears that absolute liability is intended to attach to the others. In either situation, the logical conclusion seems to be that the intended mental state to be implied is intent, knowledge, or recklessness but not negligence, which seldom is an appropriate mental state for an offense.[241]

In *People v. Whitlow*,[242] the defendants were charged in a twelve-count indictment with conspiracy, theft, and violations of the Illinois Securities Law of 1953. The securities law provisions under which the defendants were convicted provided:

> It shall be a violation of the provisions of this Act for any person. . .
>
> F.   To engage in any transaction, practice or course of business in connection with the sale or purchase of securities which works or tends to work a fraud or deceit upon the purchaser or seller thereof;
>
> G.   To obtain money or property through the sale of securities by means of untrue statement of a material fact or any omission to state a material fact necessary in order to make the statements made, in the light of the circumstances under which they were made, not misleading;

---

[240] 720 ILCS 5/4-3(b) (1999).

[241] ILL. ANN. STAT. ch. 38, para. 4-3 (Smith-Hurd 1989), 1961 Committee Comments, at 207.

[242] 89 Ill. 2d 322, 433 N.E.2d 629, *cert. denied*, 459 U.S. 830 (1982).

* * *

I.   To employ any device, scheme or artifice to defraud in connection
      with the sale or purchase of any security, directly or indirectly.[243]

The state alleged these provisions do not mention and, therefore, do not require
any proof of a mental state on the part of the individuals accused of violating
this statute.[244] The Illinois Supreme Court started from the premise that absolute
liability cannot apply to a felony statute unless the legislature clearly indicates
the intent to impose it.[245] Further, the "mere absence of express language describing a mental state does not *per se* lead to the conclusion that none is required."[246] There was no indication that the legislature intended the statute to be
in the nature of strict liability.[247] Finally, the harsh penalties attached to this felony stricture militated against such a conclusion.[248] Thus, the court read paragraph 5/4-3(b) as well as judicial constructions of a similar federal enactment as
a mandate to judicially interpret the statute as one requiring scienter.[249]

In *People v. Burmeister,*[250] the accused had been convicted of criminal sexual
assault and two counts of aggravated criminal sexual abuse arising out of his
fondling his 14-year-old stepdaughter with his hands and out of the fact that he
"used his mouth" on her breasts and on her vagina. Criminal sexual assault[251]
requires proof of "sexual penetration," which means:

> any contact, however slight, between the sex organ of one person and the
> sex organ, mouth or anus of another person, or any intrusion, however
> slight, of any part of the body of one person or of any animal or object into
> the sex organ or anus of another person, including but not limited to cunni-
> lingus, fellatio or anal penetration. Evidence of emission of semen is not
> required to prove sexual penetration.[252]

Criminal sexual abuse requires proof of "sexual conduct," which means:

---

[243] 815 ILCS 5/12(F), (G), (I) (1981).

[244] People v. Whitlow, 89 Ill. 2d 322, 332, 433 N.E.2d 629, 633, *cert. denied,* 459 U.S. 830
(1982).

[245] People v. Whitlow, 89 Ill. 2d 322, 332, 433 N.E.2d 629, 633, *cert. denied,* 459 U.S. 830
(1982).

[246] People v. Whitlow, 89 Ill. 2d 322, 332, 433 N.E.2d 629, 633 (quoting People v. Valley Steel
Prods. Co., 71 Ill. 2d 408, 424, 375 N.E.2d 1297, 1304 (1978)), *cert. denied,* 459 U.S. 830 (1982).

[247] People v. Whitlow, 89 Ill. 2d 322, 333, 433 N.E.2d 629, 633, *cert. denied,* 459 U.S. 830
(1982).

[248] People v. Whitlow, 89 Ill. 2d 322, 332, 433 N.E.2d 629, 633, *cert. denied,* 459 U.S. 830
(1982).

[249] People v. Whitlow, 89 Ill. 2d 322, 333-35, 433 N.E.2d 629, 633-34, *cert. denied,* 459 U.S.
830 (1982).

[250] 147 Ill. App. 3d 218, 497 N.E.2d 1212 (2d Dist. 1986).

[251] 720 ILCS 5/12-13 (1999).

[252] 720 ILCS 5/12-12(f) (1999).

any intentional or knowing touching or fondling by the victim or the accused, either directly or through clothing, of the sex organs, anus or breast of the victim or the accused, or any part of the body of a child under 13 years of age, for the purpose of sexual gratification or arousal of the victim or the accused.[253]

The defendant contended that since "sexual penetration" did not require proof of a mental state unlike "sexual conduct" which required proof of intent or knowledge, criminal sexual assault punished potentially "innocent conduct."[254] Further, he argued to require a culpable mental state for the less serious crime of criminal sexual abuse but none for the more serious offense of sexual assault created an unconstitutional "anomaly."[255] However, the appellate court refused to accept the proposition that criminal sexual assault was a strict liability crime in the absence of legislative intent clearly making it so.[256] The court indicated that paragraph 5/4-3(b) effectively made criminal sexual assault a general intent offense that could be proved by showing the sexual penetration was carried out with either intent, knowledge or recklessness.[257] In other words, since the "sexual penetration" necessary for criminal sexual assault requires a culpable mental state like the "sexual conduct" necessary for criminal sexual abuse, there was no "anomaly" or punishment of innocent conduct.[258]

Because of the language of paragraph 5/4-3(b), the Illinois courts have construed other criminal prohibitions as requiring the mental state of intent, knowledge, or recklessness. These prohibitions include robbery,[259] assault,[260] possession of unauthorized auto salvage certificates or auto titles,[261] failure to file retailer's occupational tax returns,[262] leaving the scene of an accident involving

---

[253] 720 ILCS 5/12-12(e) (1999).

[254] People v. Burmeister, 147 Ill. App. 3d 218, 223, 497 N.E.2d 1212, 1215 (2d Dist. 1986).

[255] People v. Burmeister, 147 Ill. App. 3d 218, 223, 497 N.E.2d 1212, 1215 (2d Dist. 1986).

[256] People v. Burmeister, 147 Ill. App. 3d 218, 223-24, 497 N.E.2d 1212, 1215 (2d Dist. 1986).

[257] People v. Burmeister, 147 Ill. App. 3d 218, 224, 497 N.E.2d 1212, 1215-16 (2d Dist. 1986). Cf. People v. Terrell, 132 Ill. 2d 178, 209, 547 N.E.2d 145, 158 (1989) ("[A] mental state of either intent or knowledge is implicitly required for sexual penetration to occur. . . .").

[258] People v. Burmeister, 147 Ill. App. 3d 218, 224, 497 N.E.2d 1212, 1216 (2d Dist. 1986).

[259] People v. Banks, 75 Ill. 2d 383, 388 N.E.2d 1244 (1979) (construing ILL. REV. STAT. ch. 38, para. 18-1 (1977)).

[260] People v. Cannes, 61 Ill. App. 3d 865, 378 N.E.2d 552 (2d Dist. 1978), cert. denied, 440 U.S. 917 (1979) (construing ILL. REV. STAT. ch. 38, para. 12-1 (1977)).

[261] People v. Gean, 143 Ill. 2d 281, 573 N.E.2d 818 (1991) (construing ILL. REV. STAT. ch. 95½, para. 4-104(a)(1) (1987)).

[262] People v. Sevilla, 132 Ill. 2d 113, 547 N.E.2d 117 (1989), cert. denied, 495 U.S. 920 (1990) (construing ILL. REV. STAT. ch. 120, para. 452 (1985)).

injury or death,[263] violations of the corrupt practices act,[264] filing false reports under the Motor Fuel Tax Law,[265] and mob action.[266]

Where there is a particular mental state in a prohibition and it is apparent that the mental state requirement applies to one, but not all, of the additional elements of the offense, usually the court will judicially modify those additional elements requiring proof of intent, knowledge, or recklessness as to each element.[267] In *People v. Frieberg*,[268] the Illinois Supreme Court analyzed the Illinois controlled substances trafficking statute that provided: "any person who *knowingly brings* or causes to be brought into this state *for the purpose of* manufacture or *delivery or with the intent to* manufacture or *deliver* a controlled or counterfeit substance is guilty of controlled substance trafficking."[269] In this case, defendant had been acquitted of possession with intent to deliver a controlled substance and convicted of controlled substances trafficking, which he alleged represented legally inconsistent verdicts. He argued that since he could not simultaneously be found not to have the specific intent to deliver for the first charge and found to have the specific intent or "purpose" to deliver for the second charge, the verdicts were barred by the legally inconsistent verdicts doctrine. In other words, he claimed each offense contained the same mental state of specific intent to deliver. The court, however, disagreed by pointing out that the possession with intent charge did require proof of defendant's intent to deliver while the trafficking charge did not.[270] Focusing on the first sentence of paragraph 5/14-3(b) and examining the context of the word "knowingly" in the trafficking statute, it was fair to conclude the trafficking statute was a "general intent" stricture that could be satisfied by proof that defendant (1) *knowingly* brought drugs into the state, and (2) did so *knowing* of someone's (his own or another's) purpose to deliver.[271] In other words, the interpretative instruction in paragraph 5/4-3(b) mandated that the word "knowingly" in the trafficking statute be understood as requiring the state to prove that defendant "have both

---

[263] People v. Nunn, 65 Ill. App. 3d 981, 382 N.E.2d 1305 (3d Dist. 1978), *aff'd*, 77 Ill. 2d 243, 396 N.E.2d 27 (1979) (construing ILL. REV. STAT. ch. 95½, para. 11-401 (1977)).

[264] People v. Clark, 71 Ill. App. 3d 381, 389 N.E.2d 911 (2d Dist. 1979) (construing ILL. REV. STAT. ch. 102, para. 3 (1975)).

[265] People v. Valley Steel Prods. Co., 71 Ill. 2d 408, 375 N.E.2d 1297 (1978) (construing ILL. REV. STAT. ch. 120, para. 417 (1975)).

[266] People v. Leach, 3 Ill. App. 3d 389, 279 N.E.2d 450 (1st Dist. 1972) (construing ILL. REV. STAT. ch. 38, para. 25-1 (1969)).

[267] 720 ILCS 5/4-3(b) (1999).

[268] 147 Ill. 2d 326, 589 N.E.2d 508 (1992).

[269] People v. Frieberg, 147 Ill. 2d 326, 344, 589 N.E.2d 508, 516 (1992) (quoting ILL. REV. STAT. ch. 56½, para. 401.1 (1987) (emphasis original)). This offense now appears at 720 ILCS 570/401.1 (1999) and is discussed in ch. 16 of this treatise.

[270] People v. Frieberg, 147 Ill. 2d 326, 347-52, 589 N.E.2d 508, 518-20 (1992).

[271] People v. Frieberg, 147 Ill. 2d 326, 347-52, 589 N.E.2d 508, 518-20 (1992).

knowledge of the 'bringing' as well as knowledge of the end or aim of that activity."[272] As such, the trafficking statute did not require the state to prove the same mental state as was required of possession with intent to deliver and, consequently, the verdicts were not legally inconsistent.

Subparagraph (c) of paragraph 5/4-3 clarifies that the inclusion of the term *knowledge* in the Illinois statutory framework should in no way be construed to mean that ignorance of the law is an excuse. It states: "Knowledge that certain conduct constitutes an offense, or knowledge of the existence, meaning, or application of the statute defining an offense, is not an element of the offense unless the statute clearly defines it as such."[273] This provision is in accordance with the generally accepted rule that in the absence of a statutory requirement to the contrary, a defendant's criminal liability is not dependent on proof that the defendant actually knew that his or her conduct was criminal or that he or she understood the meaning of the applicable statute.[274] Because ignorance-of-the-law considerations are codified in chapter 720,[275] this matter will be examined in more depth later in this treatise in connection with the defense of mistake of law.[276]

§ 2.26. Mental States: Intent.

Immediately following these general provisions on the mental state requirements in Illinois, the code defines four mens rea possibilities. The first is *intent*: "Intent. A person intends, or acts intentionally or with intent, to accomplish a result or engage in conduct described by the statute defining the offense, when his conscious objective or purpose is to accomplish that result or engage in that conduct."[277] The Committee Comments clarify the meaning of this often-used term:

> The use of the word "intent" in the 1961 Code is limited to conscious objective or purpose to accomplish a described result, as distinguished from the "general intent" which often has been used to describe also a presumption of culpability which follows from injury or awareness that certain voluntary acts will, or probably will, have wrongful or unlawful results.[278]

---

[272] People v. Frieberg, 147 Ill. 2d 326, 347, 589 N.E.2d 508, 518 (1992).

[273] 720 ILCS 5/4-3(c) (1999).

[274] People v. Allen, 276 Ill. App. 28, 39, 185 N.E. 605, 607 (1934), *rev'd on other grounds*, 360 Ill. 36, 195 N.E.2d 478 (1935); People v. Becker, 179 Ill. App. 446, 452-54 (1913); ILL. ANN. STAT. ch. 38, para. 4-3 (Smith-Hurd 1989), 1961 Committee Comments, at 207 (citing People v. Cohn, 358 Ill. 326, 193 N.E. 150 (1934)). *See also* Livingston Hall & Selig J. Seligman, *Mistake of Law and Mens Rea*, 8 U. CHI. L. REV. 641 (1941).

[275] 720 ILCS 5/4-8 (1999).

[276] *See* ch. 19.

[277] 720 ILCS 5/4-4 (1999).

[278] ILL. ANN. STAT. ch. 38, para. 4-3 (Smith-Hurd 1989), 1961 Committee Comments, at 200.

§ 2.27. — Intent: General and Specific.

Much confusion has revolved around the term *intent* over the years. One problem centers on the difference between "specific intent"[279] and "general intent"[280] offenses. Professors LaFave and Scott report:

> [T]he most common usage of "specific intent" is to designate a special mental element which is required above and beyond any mental state required with respect to the actus reus of the crime. Common law larceny, for example, requires the taking and carrying away of the property of another, and the defendant's mental state as to this act must be established, but in addition it must be shown that there was an "intent to steal" the property. Similarly, common law burglary requires a breaking and entry into the dwelling of another, but in addition to the mental state connected with these acts it must also be established that the defendant acted "with intent to commit a felony therein."[281]

Thus, *specific intent* is most generally understood to mean "some intent in addition to the intent to do the physical act that the crime requires."[282] Or, as Professors Perkins and Boyce point out in their major treatise on criminal law: "A specific intent, when an element of the mens rea of a particular offense, is some intent other than to do the actus reus thereof which is specifically required for guilt."[283]

This interpretation of the concept of specific intent[284] involves two concerns that require further clarification. First, when a crime is designated as a specific

---

[279] *See* People v. Olbrot, 106 Ill. App. 3d 367, 377, 435 N.E.2d 1242, 1250 (1st Dist. 1982) (describing the mental state for attempted murder and accountability).

[280] *See* People v. Banks, 75 Ill. 2d 383, 391, 388 N.E.2d 1244, 1248 (1979) (describing mental state for robbery).

[281] WAYNE LAFAVE & AUSTIN SCOTT, CRIMINAL LAW § 3.3(e) (2d ed. 1986).

[282] WAYNE LAFAVE & AUSTIN SCOTT, CRIMINAL LAW § 4.10(a) (2d ed. 1986). In contrast, general intent means "intent to do the physical act — or perhaps, recklessly doing the physical act — which the crime requires." *Id.*

[283] ROLLIN M. PERKINS & RONALD N. BOYCE, CRIMINAL LAW 851 (3d ed. 1982). *See also* ROLLIN M. PERKINS & RONALD N. BOYCE, CRIMINAL LAW AND PROCEDURES: CASES AND MATERIALS 472-73 (6th ed. 1984).

[284] The following authorities define specific intent in a manner consistent with that offered by professors Perkins and Boyce. GEORGE FLETCHER, RETHINKING CRIMINAL LAW § 10.4.5 at 849 (1978) ("The general intent is the intent accompanying the base offense; the specific intent goes beyond the base offense to reach further unrealized objectives"); JOHN KLOTTER, CRIMINAL LAW § 2.5 at 30 (2d ed. 1986) ("Specific intent means that the prosecution must show that the person charged purposely intended to violate the law"); 1 PAUL ROBINSON, CRIMINAL LAW DEFENSES § 65(e) at 299 (1984) (specific intent is often understood as "an intention to achieve an objective beyond the base offense"); A TREATISE ON THE LAW OF CRIMES (CLARK & MARSHALL) § 5.06 at 282, n.71 (Miriam Quinn Barnes 7th ed. 1967) (quoting with approval Wardlaw v. United States, 203 F.2d 884, 887 (5th Cir. 1953) ("The intent involved in [a specific intent offense] is not inher-

intent stricture, this means that the offense is one that *invariably requires proof of intent*, construing *intent* as requiring nothing less than a conscious objective, purpose, or aim to accomplish a particular result. This view of specific intent presupposes (1) that any mental state other than intent (for example, knowledge or recklessness) will not suffice, and (2) that any interpretation given the term *intent* that allows for proof of something less than a showing of conscious objective or purpose to achieve a particular result is insufficient.[285] In contrast, a general intent offense is one that may be proved by reference to any one of several mens rea possibilities — usually, intent, knowledge, *or* recklessness.[286] Thus,

---

ent in the act itself, but is a specific intent involving bad purpose and evil motive. . . ."); Note, *Intoxication as a Criminal Defense*, 55 COLUM. L. REV. 1210, 1212 (1955) ("A 'specific intent' crime requires something more than the mere intentional doing of an act; the act must be committed with an accompanying state of mind whereby the actor intends that certain further consequences flow from his act. Conversely, a 'general intent' crime is one which penalizes, per se, the intentional doing of a proscribed act"). *See also* 21 AM. JUR. 2d *Criminal Law* § 130 n.18 (1981) ("Specific intent is present when from the circumstances the offender must have subjectively desired the prohibited result, whereas general intent exists when from the circumstances the prohibited result may reasonably be expected to follow from the offender's voluntary act, irrespective of any subjective desire to have accomplished such result"); 22 C.J.S. *Criminal Law* § 33 (1989) (". . . a person acts with specific intent when his conscious objective is to cause the specific result proscribed by the statute defining the offense. A specific intent crime exists when the statutory definition refers to defendant's intent to do some further act or achieve some additional consequence. . . . Where, however, a specific intent is not made an ingredient of a statutory offense, it is not necessary to prove such specific intent in order to justify a conviction. In such case the commission of the act wilfully and knowingly is sufficient."); BLACK'S LAW DICTIONARY 1399 (6th ed. 1990) (original emphasis) ("The most common usage of 'specific intent' is to designate a special mental element which is required above and beyond any mental state required with respect to the *actus reus* of the crime"); Annot., *Modern Status of the Rules as to Voluntary Intoxication as Defense to Criminal Charge*, 8 A.L.R.3d 1236, 1246 (1966) ("The definitions of certain offenses include a specific intent to do certain things for a specific purpose, while as to ordinary offenses, the general intent necessary to convict is deduced from the doing of the criminal act").

The following cases define specific intent consistent with this view. People v. Hood, 1 Cal. 3d 444, 456-57, 82 Cal. Rptr. 618, 626, 462 P.2d 370, 378 (1969) (general intent means intent to do proscribed act; specific intent refers to defendant's intent to do some further act or achieve additional consequence); People v. Wirth, 77 Ill. App. 3d 253, 257, 395 N.E.2d 1106, 1109 (1st Dist. 1979) ("The crime of burglary requires the act of entering or remaining in a building or vehicle together with 'intent to commit therein a felony or theft.' In this regard, burglary differs from other crimes . . . which 'do not require specific intent.'"); People v. Agee, 205 Ill. App. 3d 146, 151, 562 N.E.2d 545, 548 (1st Dist. 1990) (attempted murder requires the "specific intent to kill"); People v. Remon, 40 Ill. App. 3d 337, 340, 352 N.E.2d 374, 376 (1st Dist. 1976) (unlawful use of weapons in violation of para. 24-1(a)(10) [which requires the mental state of knowledge] "has been construed as requiring only a general intent").

[285] *See* text accompanying notes 320-21.

[286] People v. Mitchell, 200 Ill. App. 3d 969, 981, 558 N.E.2d 559, 567 (5th Dist. 1990) ("Criminal sexual assault is a general intent offense in which the mental state of intent, knowledge, or recklessness is implied").

since every criminal attempt inevitably requires proof of "intent to commit a specific offense,"[287] attempted murder necessarily requires a "specific intent to kill."[288] Attempted murder must be understood to be a specific intent crime. On the other hand, since a consummated murder can be proved by either (1) an intent to kill, (2) an intent to do great bodily injury, (3) knowledge that one's actions could kill, or (4) knowledge that such actions could cause great bodily injury,[289] it is understood to be a general intent offense.[290]

To illustrate, if a defendant were to become involved in a heated argument with a woman, the woman attempted to drive off, and the defendant shot his gun in the general direction of her car, missing it, with the mere intent of scaring her and without any intent to kill her, he cannot be held guilty of attempted murder.[291] Similarly, if a defendant were to inflict a brutal beating on his child with the intent to merely discipline the child and the child survived, there is no attempted murder.[292] On the other hand, if either of these defendants involved in the shooting or the brutal attack on the child actually caused the death of the victim, he would be guilty of murder if he *knew* "that such acts create a strong probability of death or great bodily harm to that individual."[293] Obviously, not

---

[287] 720 ILCS 5/8-4(a) (1999).

[288] People v. Agee, 205 Ill. App. 3d 146, 151, 562 N.E.2d 545, 548 (1st Dist. 1990); People v. Brown, 199 Ill. App. 3d 860, 876, 557 N.E.2d 611, 621 (1st Dist. 1990).

[289] 720 ILCS 5/9-1(a) (1999).

[290] People v. Heffernan, 312 Ill. 66, 70, 143 N.E. 411, 413 (1924) (proof of general malice as distinguished from specific intent to kill is sufficient); *see also* People v. Smith, 26 Ill. App. 3d 1062, 1065, 325 N.E.2d 623, 625 (4th Dist. 1975) (discussion of voluntary intoxication defense in relation to "general intent" required for murder).

[291] *Cf.* People v. Harris, 72 Ill. 2d 16, 26-28, 377 N.E.2d 28, 33-34 (1978) (where shooting occurred when victim tried to escape from defendant in her automobile after prolonged argument wherein he accused her of infidelity, erroneous instruction susceptible to interpretation by jury that person could be found guilty of attempted murder even if he or she did not actually intend to cause death was reversible error). For an excellent review of *Harris, see* Nancy L. Barrett, Note, *Specific Intent Made More Specific: A Clarification of the Law of Attempted Murder in Illinois-People v. Harris,* 28 DePaul L. Rev. 157 (1978). *See also* People v. Trinkle, 68 Ill. 2d 198, 203, 369 N.E.2d 888, 890 (1977) (jury instruction allowing verdict of attempted murder where defendant knew that his act created strong probability of death or great bodily harm was reversible error); People v. Viser, 62 Ill. 2d 568, 581-82, 343 N.E.2d 903, 910 (1975) (jury instruction allowing verdict of attempted murder where defendant merely had intent to commit another forcible felony was reversible error).

[292] *Cf.* People v. Mitchell, 105 Ill. 2d 1, 8-11, 473 N.E.2d 1270, 1273-75 (1984), *cert. denied,* 470 U.S. 1089 (1985) (parent who severely beat her child to take out her anger toward its father was not guilty of attempted murder because no specific intent to kill the child existed).

[293] 720 ILCS 5/9-1(a)(2) (1999); People v. Bosworth, 160 Ill. App. 3d 714, 720, 513 N.E.2d 1173, 1177 (2d Dist. 1987) (where defendant struck his seven-week-old daughter in the head with his fist while angry with his wife and child thus killing her, defendant guilty of murder where he knew his acts created a strong possibility of death or great bodily harm); People v. Szerletich, 86 Ill. App. 3d 1121, 1124, 408 N.E.2d 1098, 1101 (4th Dist. 1980) (where defendant struck one-

only inchoate offenses like criminal attempt but also other substantive offenses are specific intent crimes. Deceptive practices clearly fall into this category. A person commits a deceptive practice when, *"with intent to defraud,"* he or she engages in some type of deceptive practice for monetary gain.[294] Similarly, intimidation is a specific intent crime. A person commits intimidation when *"with intent to cause another to perform or to omit the performance of any act,"* he communicates to a person a threat to perform an illegal act against that person or another.[295] The key language that normally triggers these specific intent characterizations is the phrase *with intent to.*

The second major feature of a specific intent crime, as this type of offense is understood by authorities such as LaFave, Scott, Perkins, and Boyce, is that the offense mandates the prosecutor to show that the offender had some criminal *result* or *goal* in mind beyond the commission of the actus reus. Thus, in the attempted murder example, merely showing that the defendant had the intent to shoot a gun in the direction of the victim he is seeking to frighten would not be sufficient. Merely showing that the defendant had the intent to scare the victim would not be adequate. His intent to accomplish a particular actus reus, namely, pulling the trigger of a gun that is aimed in the general direction of the victim, is not sufficient in and of itself. Rather, it is essential to prove that he engaged in the sequence of activities described above with a particular purpose in mind, namely, killing the victim. The defendant must have (1) intended to engage in certain acts that constitute the actus reus and (2) performed those acts with an intended criminal result.

If an offense includes a combination of mental state requirements, not all of which mandate proof of a specific intent, the offense will still be considered a specific intent offense as long as *one* of the essential mental state requirements is such. An example of this is burglary. "A person commits burglary when without authority he *knowingly* enters or without authority remains within a building, housetrailer, watercraft, aircraft, motor vehicle,... railroad car, or any part thereof, *with intent to commit therein a felony or theft.*"[296] Proof of a knowledgeable, unjustified entry would not be sufficient. For example, assume a group of young boys wrongfully entered a building with an enclosed, indoor

---

year-old child with his fist because he was mad at child for crying and as a result killed child was murder).

[294] 720 ILCS 5/17-1(B) (1999) (emphasis added); People v. Sumner, 107 Ill. App. 3d 368, 372, 437 N.E.2d 786, 788 (1st Dist. 1982) (evidence was insufficient to establish "specific intent to defraud" required by deceptive practices prohibition).

[295] 720 ILCS 5/12-6 (1999) (emphasis added); People v. Haybron, 153 Ill. App. 3d 906, 908, 506 N.E.2d 369, 371 (3d Dist. 1987) ("Intimidation is a specific intent crime").

[296] 720 ILCS 5/19-1(a) (1999) (emphasis added); People v. Loden, 27 Ill. App. 3d 761, 762, 327 N.E.2d 58, 60 (2d Dist. 1975) ("The specific intent to commit a felony or theft must exist at the time of an unauthorized entry into the building of another").

swimming pool merely to take a swim. Since they did not have an intent to commit a felony or theft in the building, there might be criminal trespass,[297] but there is no burglary. As long as the statute insists on proof of specific intent regardless of the circumstances, the offense is considered a specific intent crime even though its elemental composition includes an additional (as opposed to alternative) mental state.

Many statutes have a number of subparagraphs covering different types of conduct that will trigger criminal liability. One or more subparagraphs may require proof of specific intent while the others do not. One example in the penal code of Illinois is arson:

> A person commits arson when, by means of fire or explosive, he knowingly:
>
> (a) Damages any real property, or any personal property having a value of $150 or more, of another without his consent; or
>
> (b) *With intent to defraud an insurer*, damages any property or any personal property having a value of $150 or more.[298]

When viewed in its entirety, this statute is clearly a general intent statute in that the state is under no obligation to show a specific intent if it opts to proceed under subparagraph (a). On the other hand, if the state's attorney proceeds against an arsonist by way of a formal charging instrument, such as an information or indictment, that charges the defendant solely under subparagraph (b) of the arson statute, then the state's attorney would be obligated to prove specific intent to defraud an insurer. Thus, a state's attorney may, under some circumstances, needlessly complicate the proof requirements he or she shoulders as prosecutor by pursuing an offender under a penal subparagraph requiring evidence of a specific intent when a conviction could be achieved by simply relying on an alternative subparagraph that requires mere evidence of general intent. Obviously, not all factual circumstances will lend themselves to such a choice, but it is a point to bear in mind.

The above differentiation between specific intent crimes and general intent crimes is offered to clarify the most useful and most accepted analytic distinctions in this regard. But the practicing attorney must be exceedingly cautious when encountering problems in this area of the law. It has been said that "when it comes to attaching a precise meaning to *mens rea* [generally], courts and commentators are in hopeless disagreement."[299] Nowhere is this more evident than in connection with attaching an appropriate definition to *specific intent*. A

---

[297] 720 ILCS 5/21-3 (1999).

[298] 720 ILCS 5/20-1 (1999) (emphasis added).

[299] DONALD H.J. HERMANN, THE INSANITY DEFENSE: PHILOSOPHICAL, HISTORICAL AND LEGAL PERSPECTIVES 109 (1983).

thorough scrutiny of the legal literature and caselaw reveals no less than three different interpretations of this concept beyond the one described above–namely, that *specific intent* means an intent to bring about a particular criminal objective above and beyond the commission of the act constituting the crime. First, there is the view that *specific intent* simply means purposeful, and that *general intent* covers all other mental states.[300] This approach is distinguishable from the generally accepted view described above in that *specific intent* could conceivably be used here to describe the accused (1) who harbored a purpose or conscious objective to bring about the actus reus (without regard to a criminal objective beyond the physical act) *or* (2) who had in mind a criminal objective beyond the commission of the physical act (which standing alone constitutes the generally accepted view). In this sense, *specific intent* could be taken to refer to the highest culpability level on the spectrum of negligence, recklessness, knowledge, and intent.[301] In this view, any crime not requiring *intent* could be described as a general intent proscription. A second divergent view of *specific intent* is that it means either intent or knowledge. If the crime only requires recklessness or negligence, it is considered to be a general intent crime.[302] A third point of view is that specific intent exists whenever a "particular mental state is one of the requisite elements of a ... crime, and the charge of the crime will be insufficient unless it contains an allegation of that mental state."[303] *Specific intent* is used here to describe a crime that contains *any* mens rea. Thus, if the crime specifies any mental state — intentionally, willfully, knowingly, maliciously, wantonly,

---

[300] William Roth, *General v. Specific Intent: A Time for Terminological Understanding in California*, 7 PEPP. L. REV. 67, 71-74 (1979). *See also* HYMAN GROSS, A THEORY OF CRIMINAL JUSTICE 100 (1979) ("the actor has a purpose...."); JUSTIN MILLER, HANDBOOK OF CRIMINAL LAW 64 (1934) ("specific intent implies a condition of mind or purpose directed toward a particular objective"); Harold Edgar, *Mens Rea*, 3 ENCYCLOPEDIA OF CRIME AND JUSTICE 1028, 1036 (Sanford Kadish ed. 1983) (crime requires more than general intent if it uses term purposely); Kenneth R. Feinberg, *Toward a New Approach to Proving Culpability: Mens Rea and the Proposed Federal Code*, 18 AM. CRIM. L. REV. 123, 127 (1980) ("When [intent is] used in the context of a 'specific intent' crime, e.g., assault with intent to rape, it connotes 'purpose'").

[301] *See* 1 PAUL ROBINSON, CRIMINAL LAW DEFENSES § 65(e) (1984) (Robinson merely describes this approach without agreeing with it).

[302] M. CHERIF BASSIOUNI, SUBSTANTIVE CRIMINAL LAW 178-84 (1978); Monrad G. Paulsen, *Intoxication as a Defense to Crime*, 1961 U. ILL. L.F. 1, 9 (intoxication negates specific intent, which includes intent or knowledge). *See also* People v. Drakeford, 139 Ill. 2d 206, 215, 564 N.E.2d 792, 796 (1990) ("To commit aggravated battery causing great bodily harm, a specific intent crime, the defendant must act 'intentionally' or 'knowingly'") (citations omitted); People v. Jones, 67 Ill. App. 3d 477, 478, 384 N.E.2d 523, 525 (3d Dist. 1978) ("Battery and resisting a police officer are both specific intent crimes requiring proof that the defendant acted knowingly."); People v. Long, 30 Ill. App. 3d 815, 819, 333 N.E.2d 534, 538 (2d Dist. 1975) ("The specific intent relevant to aggravated kidnaping is knowledge").

[303] Douglas R. Young, *Rethinking the Specific-General Intent Doctrine in California Criminal Law*, 63 CAL. L. REV. 1352, 1356 (1975).

recklessly, or with premeditation — it can, within this definition, be called a specific intent stricture and only if the statute contains no mens rea requirement whatsoever is it not considered a specific intent crime.[304] This approach leads to the rather confusing semantics that a crime having *no* mental state requirement in its definition is to be considered a "general intent" crime.[305]

Given this lack of consensus on the meaning to be ascribed to the specific intent language, as well as the confusing use of the specific-general intent distinction (for example, *specific intent* can mean knowledge, recklessness, or even negligence, and *general intent* can mean no intent), various respected authorities have recommended the outright rejection of further use of these terms.[306] However, one would be remiss if one simply ignored the specific-general intent dichotomy, particularly in Illinois. As seen, certain crimes, such as all criminal attempts, require proof of a specific intent to further the target crime. The availability of certain defenses, most notably, voluntary intoxication, may turn on whether the crime is in the nature of specific intent.[307] In addition, where a crime

---

[304] *See* JAMES JAQUESS ROBINSON, CASES ON CRIMINAL LAW AND PROCEDURE 424 (1941) (proponent of this point of view). *See, e.g.,* People v. Harkey, 69 Ill. App. 3d 94, 96-97, 386 N.E.2d 1151, 1153 (5th Dist. 1979) (crime is in nature of specific intent if it has "a mental state which is an element of the crime").

[305] *See, e.g.,* People v. Harkey, 69 Ill. App. 3d 94, 96-97, 386 N.E.2d 1151, 1153 (5th Dist. 1979) ("[T]he instant offense [aggravated assault] is a general intent crime and therefore has no mental state which is an element of the offense. . . ."). The position taken in the *Harkey* case is curious. It seems to effectively ignore the 720 ILCS 5/4-3(b) (1999) interpretative presumption: "If the statute does not prescribe a particular mental state applicable to an element of an offense (other than an offense which involves absolute liability), any mental state defined in Paragraphs [5/]4-4 [intent], [5/]4-5 [knowledge] or [5/]4-6 [recklessness] is applicable." For example, in People v. Burmeister, 147 Ill. App. 3d 218, 223-24, 497 N.E.2d 1212, 1215-16 (2d Dist. 1986), it was held that criminal sexual assault is not an absolute liability crime simply because it contains no mental state in its definition, but is in the nature of general intent, requiring either intent, knowledge or recklessness. Similarly, in People v. Grant, 101 Ill. App. 3d 43, 47-48, 427 N.E.2d 810, 813-14 (1st Dist. 1981), it was held that assault, criminal trespass to land and mob action are not absolute liability offenses because they contain no express mental state requirement, but ones that must be proven with reference to paragraph 5/4-4, 5/4-5, or 5/4-6.

[306] *See* MODEL PENAL CODE § 2.02, comment at 125 (Tentative Draft No. 4, 1955); JEROME HALL, GENERAL PRINCIPLES OF CRIMINAL LAW 142 (2d ed. 1960) (specific and general adjectives should be discontinued); Gerhard O.W. Mueller, *On Common Law Mens Rea*, 42 MINN. L. REV. 1043, 1056 (1958) ("[t]he partition of mens rea into specific intent and general intent is both unworkable and meaningless").

[307] Voluntary intoxication is not a defense unless it is "so extreme as to suspend the power of reason and render [the defendant] incapable of forming a specific intent which is an element of the offense. . . ." 720 ILCS 5/6-3(a) (1999); *see, e.g.,* People v. Roesler, 195 Ill. App. 3d 1007, 1012-13, 552 N.E.2d 1242, 1256 (5th Dist. 1990) (voluntary intoxication "applies only to specific intent crimes. . . . Since rape is a general intent offense, the voluntary intoxication defense is not available to defendant."); People v. Gerrior, 155 Ill. App. 3d 949, 955, 508 N.E.2d 1119, 1123 (2d Dist. 1987) ("The defense of voluntary intoxication . . . [is] unavailable as the offense of armed robbery does not require a specific intent"); People v. Berlin, 132 Ill. App. 2d 697, 699, 270

requires a general intent, a trial court's failure to instruct the jury about a mental state that is implied in the statute will not be considered error[308] whereas if the offense requires the element of specific intent, failure to instruct the jury about that specific intent will be considered trial error.[309]

One must be alert to the court's usage of these mental state terms and how exactly it defines them, since inconsistency is not uncommon. In one Illinois appellate decision, for example, it was stated that murder "requires a specific intent,"[310] notwithstanding that murder clearly can rest on intent or knowledge[311] and that most Illinois courts emphatically state that specific intent is not essential to the crime of murder.[312] Likewise, one Illinois appellate opinion stated that where the defendant was convicted of murdering two victims on an accomplice liability theory, "his guilt did not depend upon proof that he had the specific intent to murder,"[313] even though historically most other Illinois opinions have pointed out that the Illinois accountability statute requires that the accomplice's participation must be "with the concurrent, specific intent to promote or facilitate the commission of the offense."[314] Meanwhile, in a 1992 Illinois Supreme Court opinion, *People v. Stanciel*,[315] the court stated:

> Accountability, tied as it is to the crime charged, must comport with the requirements of that crime. Thus, for example, the charge of assault with intent to rape, a specific intent crime, must require a specific intent for one

---

N.E.2d 461, 463 (1st Dist. 1971) (voluntary intoxication is no defense because no specific intent is required for robbery). *See also* ch. 19 for a discussion of how some courts have limited the "mistake" defenses to crimes requiring a specific intent.

[308] *See, e.g.*, People v. Burton, 201 Ill. App. 3d 116, 119-22, 558 N.E.2d 1369, 1371-74 (4th Dist. 1990) (no explicit mental state instruction required for aggravated criminal sexual assault). People v. Talley, 177 Ill. App. 3d 170, 173-74, 531 N.E.2d 1139, 1140-44 (4th Dist. 1988) (no explicit mental state instruction required for robbery).

[309] *See, e.g.*, People v. Jones, 81 Ill. 2d 1, 9, 405 N.E.2d 343, 346 (1979) (attempted murder requiring specific intent to kill).

[310] People v. Mocaby, 194 Ill. App. 3d 441, 447, 551 N.E.2d 673, 677 (5th Dist. 1990).

[311] People v. Jerome, 206 Ill. App. 3d 428, 435, 564 N.E.2d 221, 225 (2d Dist. 1990) ("In order to prove murder . . . the state must prove intent or knowledge").

[312] *See, e.g.*, People v. Calhoun, 4 Ill. App. 3d 683, 689, 281 N.E.2d 363, 367 (1st Dist. 1972) (proof of specific intent is not necessary for murder).

[313] People v. Reed, 104 Ill. App. 3d 331, 338, 432 N.E.2d 979, 984 (1st Dist. 1982).

[314] *See, e.g.*, People v. Johnson, 167 Ill. App. 3d 659, 666-67, 521 N.E.2d 609, 613-14 (4th Dist. 1988). *See also* People v. Mikel, 73 Ill. App. 3d 16, 19, 391 N.E.2d 558, 560 (4th Dist. 1979) ("Just as one cannot attempt murder without an intent to kill . . . it would seem that one could not intend to 'promote or facilitate' the commission of a homicide without intending that the victim be killed"). *But see* People v. Terry, 99 Ill. 2d 508, 515, 460 N.E.2d 746, 749-50 (1984) (incorporating "common-design rule" where state must only prove that defendant had the specific intent to promote or facilitate a crime, and not the actual crime for which he was charged but which was a natural consequence of crime intended).

[315] 153 Ill. 2d 218, 606 N.E.2d 1201 (1992).

who is accountable as well. Under this analysis, then, one whose guilt of murder, a general intent crime, is established through accountability, need only possess a general intent, with all the requirements that state of mind entails.[316]

This decision simply adds to the confusion as to the required mental state for accountability and is at odds with the plain language of the accountability statute which reflects a specific intent component.[317] In any event, the remainder of this book will use the specific-general intent language in a manner consistent with the generally accepted view discussed at length above.

§ 2.28.   — Intent: Its Meaning and Scope.

Beyond the specific intent versus general intent dichotomy, which takes on important consequences not only in terms of proof but also with respect to various defenses such as voluntary intoxication, there is another major area of confusion. It centers on a proper definition of *intent*.

> [T]he traditional view is that a person who acts (or omits to act) intends a result of his act (or omission) under two quite different circumstances: (1) when he consciously desires that result, whatever the likelihood of that result happening from his conduct; and (2) when he knows that the result is practically certain to follow from his conduct, whatever his desire may be as to that result.[318]

In other words,

> the word "intent" in the substantive criminal law has traditionally not been limited to the narrow, dictionary definition of purpose, aim, or design, but instead has often been viewed as encompassing much of what would ordinarily be described as knowledge.[319]

Common sense offers an explanation for why this watered-down definition of *intent* has found its way into the criminal law. The difficulties often associated with offering hard proof about what the defendant had in mind when he engaged in certain criminal acts has prompted many reviewing courts to simply assume that since the defendant presumably *knew* what he was doing, he *must have intended* the prohibited consequences. Accordingly, this analytical leap-frogging

---

[316] People v. Stanciel, 153 Ill. 2d 218, 233, 606 N.E.2d 1201, 1210 (1992) (citations omitted). A more complete discussion of *People v. Stanciel* appears in chapter 3.

[317] 720 ILCS 5/5(c) (1999) ("Either before or during the commission of an offense, and with the intent to promote or facilitate such commission," he aids and abets "such other person in the planning or commission of the offense").

[318] WAYNE LAFAVE & AUSTIN SCOTT, CRIMINAL LAW § 3.5(a)(2d ed. 1986).

[319] WAYNE LAFAVE & AUSTIN SCOTT, CRIMINAL LAW § 3-5(b)(2d ed. 1986).

will prompt some courts to conclude that the defendant who shot the victim to scare her or who brutally beat the child to discipline him had the intent to kill as well, when in fact there was no evidence on which to base such a conclusion. Beyond the question of the unjustified imposition of criminal liability, this reasoning effectively muddies the waters in terms of maintaining a clean line of demarcation between true intent and true knowledge.

To avoid this element of confusion, the General Assembly carefully defined *intent* in paragraph 5/4-4 by including only the narrow meaning of that term. The language of this provision is clear, for it states that a person intends an act or result only "when his conscious objective or purpose is to accomplish that result or engage in that conduct."[320] Additionally, the revision committee, which drafted the code, rejected the broad meaning of intent described above.[321]

Yet, many Illinois opinions that discuss the issue of intent tend to obscure the real meaning of this important mental element. Notwithstanding the obvious import of the language of paragraph 5/4-4, as well as the intended scope of the term *intent* articulated in the revision committee's comments, some state reviewing courts seem to have done their utmost to gravitate back to the broad, confused definition of *intent*. Tracing this movement seems to involve two steps: the first is legally cogent; the second, which some courts suggest logically follows from the first, raises more difficult analytical difficulties.

The first step involves demonstrating intent by way of inferences flowing from certain facts or evidence. For example, many Illinois opinions state that the requisite specific intent to kill for attempted murder can be "established by proof of surrounding circumstances, including the character of the assault, the use of a deadly weapon and other matters of which an intent to kill may be inferred."[322] Where a murder charge rests on an allegation of intent to kill, the intent could be inferred from the vicious character of the attack[323] or from proof of the defen-

---

[320] 720 ILCS 5/4-4 (1999).

[321] ILL. ANN. STAT. ch. 28, para. 4-3 (Smith-Hurd 1989), 1961 Committee Comments, at 200.

It is interesting to note that the American Law Institute decided to use the term *purposely* instead of intentionally to denote purposeful goal-oriented activity. *See* MODEL PENAL CODE § 2.02(2)(a) (1962). It can be inferred that the American Law Institute was interested in avoiding the inconsistent, confusing judicial interpretations of the term *intent*. Why the Illinois General Assembly, which patterned the mental-state requirements contained in paragraphs 5/4-4 through 5/4-7 after those of the MODEL PENAL CODE, did not follow the American Law Institute's suggestion is not clear.

[322] People v. Mitchell, 209 Ill. App. 3d 562, 569, 568 N.E.2d 292, 297 (1st Dist. 1991); *see also* People v. Cruz, 196 Ill. App. 3d 1047, 1055, 554 N.E.2d 598, 603 (1st Dist. 1990) (attempted murder); People v. Coolidge, 26 Ill. 2d 533, 536, 187 N.E.2d 694, 696 (1963) (assault with intent to commit murder).

[323] People v. Terrell, 132 Ill. 2d 178, 203-06, 547 N.E.2d 145, 156 (1989), *cert. denied*, 495 U.S. 959 (1990) (repeatedly beating and sexually assaulting 15-month-old victim); *see also* People

dant's stated intent to kill another.[324] Where a defendant is charged with conspiracy to murder, the necessary element of specific intent to kill may be inferred from his or her agreement with another co-conspirator that a murder be committed.[325] The specific intent necessary to the commission of attempted criminal sexual assault may be inferred from the defendant's expressed desire,[326] or the character of the assault, the acts done, and the time and place of the occurrence.[327] Thus, a defendant's intent to commit criminal sexual abuse necessary for attempted criminal sexual abuse could be inferred from his conduct of completely undressing in the presence of his minor victim and requesting mutual masturbation with the victim.[328] Similarly, the specific intent necessary for accomplice liability can be inferred from surrounding circumstances.[329] Where there was evidence that the defendant was shopping with her roommate and was present when her roommate purchased a diamond ring, silverware, and china on the defendant's checking account; that the defendant admitted that she was aware of her roommate's activities; and that the defendant subsequently falsely

---

v. Miles, 188 Ill. App. 3d 471, 478-79, 544 N.E.2d 986, 991 (1st Dist. 1989) (defendant repeatedly hit victim with pipe).

[324] People v. Forrest, 133 Ill. App. 2d 70, 72, 272 N.E.2d 813, 815 (1st Dist. 1971) (immediately prior to killing, defendant had announced his intention to shoot at the next car containing white persons).

[325] People v. Cart, 102 Ill. App. 3d 173, 188, 429 N.E.2d 553, 565 (2d Dist. 1981), cert. denied, 459 U.S. 942 (1982). See also People v. Cannon, 176 Ill. App. 3d 49, 57-58, 530 N.E.2d 1035, 1040-41 (1st Dist. 1988) (defendant's statement that he sought to "get even" with other parties, coupled with his acts of arming himself with a sawed-off shotgun and going to the place where those parties lived, is sufficient to demonstrate the requisite intent for conspiracy to commit murder).

[326] People v. James, 200 Ill. App. 3d 380, 390, 558 N.E.2d 732, 739 (4th Dist. 1990) (attempted aggravated criminal sexual assault established where defendant, while displaying a knife, attempted to rip clothes off victim after he had earlier stated to another with reference to the victim that "I'm going to get some of that pussy").

[327] People v. Williams, 128 Ill. App. 3d 384, 396, 470 N.E.2d 1140, 1149 (4th Dist. 1984) (murder and attempted rape established where victim found dead was nude from waist down, except for her pantyhose which were torn and pulled down to her ankles, and her legs were spread apart).

[328] People v. Jones, 175 Ill. 2d 126, 134, 676 N.E.2d 646, 650 (1997) (although aggravated criminal sexual abuse conviction reversed on other grounds). See also People v. Enoch, 122 Ill. 2d 176, 198, 522 N.E.2d 1124, 1135, cert. denied, 488 U.S. 917 (1988) ("Evidence of an assault with concomitant disrobing of the victim is sufficient to support a conviction for attempted rape."); People v. Kleba, 110 Ill. App. 3d 345, 354, 442 N.E.2d 605, 612 (1st Dist. 1982) (defendant's acts — knocking complainant to ground, repeatedly threatening to kill her, holding her neck in immobilizing armlock, dragging her to alley where he forcefully held her, ordered her to remove her jeans and underwear and bend over and clasp her ankles, and began fondling her vagina — were in furtherance of substantive crime of rape and constituted step toward commission of offense, from which trial court could infer specific intent needed to convict defendant of attempted rape).

[329] See, e.g., People v. Maxon, 35 Ill. App. 3d 670, 675, 341 N.E.2d 479, 482 (3d Dist. 1976).

reported her checkbook to have been stolen, this was sufficient to support the trial court's finding that she had intentionally aided and abetted the commission of theft.[330] The mental state of intent, which is an essential element of certain substantive crimes, can likewise be inferred in certain circumstances.[331] Where the defendant was discovered in the kitchen of another's home without the owner's consent, the screen door of the home had been pried open, the panel of the front door had been broken out, various items were stacked in the dining room and bedrooms, and a search of the defendant disclosed a watch taken from a bedroom in the home, this was sufficient to establish the defendant's felonious intent for the substantive offense of burglary.[332]

The second step that is used in many Illinois cases to establish intent is based on a questionable extension of the first step. Specifically, the language in some of these opinions seems to (1) conclusively infer intent from certain acts, (2) conclusively infer intent from lesser states of mind, or, worse yet, (3) equate intent with lesser mental states.[333] Regarding the first point, where courts casually assume the existence of intent from certain acts, one might again consider the example of crimes requiring an intent to kill.[334] In this connection, many Illinois opinions mechanically recite[335] the following:

> [S]ince every sane man is presumed to intend all the natural and probable consequences flowing from his own deliberate act, it follows that if one wilfully does an act the direct and natural tendency of which is to destroy another's life, the natural and irresistible conclusion, in the absence of qualifying facts, is that the destruction of such other person's life was intended.[336]

While this conclusion might be appropriate with respect to murder inasmuch as it can be based on the various general intent possibilities, it is doubtful that it is

---

[330] People v. Maxon, 35 Ill. App. 3d 670, 675, 341 N.E.2d 479, 482 (3d Dist. 1976).

[331] *See, e.g,* People v. Walker, 21 Ill. App. 3d 202, 206, 315 N.E.2d 244, 247 (1st Dist. 1974), *cert. denied,* 421 U.S. 919 (1975).

[332] People v. Walker, 21 Ill. App. 3d 202, 206, 315 N.E.2d 244, 247 (1st Dist. 1974), *cert. denied,* 421 U.S. 919 (1975).

[333] *See* Nancy L. Barrett, Note, *Specific Intent Made More Specific: A Clarification of the Law of Attempted Murder in Illinois-People v. Harris,* 28 DEPAUL L. REV. 157, 159 (1978).

[334] People v. Mendez, 221 Ill. App. 3d 868, 876, 582 N.E.2d 1265, 1271 (1st. Dist. 1991) ("Attempted murder requires proof of . . . specific intent to kill the victim").

[335] Nancy L. Barrett, Note, *Specific Intent Made More Specific: A Clarification of the Law of Attempted Murder in Illinois-People v. Harris,* 28 DEPAUL L. REV. 157, 159 (1978).

[336] People v. Muir, 67 Ill. 2d 86, 92, 365 N.E.2d 332, 335, *cert. denied,* 434 U.S. 986 (1977), and numerous cases cited in *Muir. See also* People v. Salazar, 126 Ill. 2d 424, 450, 535 N.E.2d 766, 776 (1988), *cert. denied,* 497 U.S. 1031 (1990); People v. Fitzgerald, 171 Ill. App. 3d 218, 223-24, 524 N.E.2d 1190, 1193 (1st Dist. 1988); People v. Coolidge, 26 Ill. 2d 533, 537, 187 N.E.2d 694, 697 (1963).

appropriate for a crime such as attempted murder, since it dilutes the proof necessary for the required specific intent formulation.[337]

In *Sandstrom v. Montana*,[338] the defendant was charged with deliberate homicide. The defendant admitted killing another but contended it was not done purposely or knowingly. The trial judge charged the jury that the "law presumes that a person intends the ordinary consequences of his acts" over objection.[339] The United States Supreme Court reversed the defendant's conviction on the ground that the jury may have interpreted the presumption reflected in the instruction as a conclusive presumption or as shifting the burden of persuasion.[340] The court pointed out that either interpretation would violate the Fourteenth Amendment's requirement that the state prove every element of a criminal offense beyond a reasonable doubt.[341] Consistent with *Sandstrom*, the Illinois appellate court struck down a similar instruction in *People v. Dodd*.[342] In that case, a jury instruction stating that the defendant's intent to permanently deprive a retailer of merchandise "shall" be presumed from the fact that an accomplice had carried that merchandise past the last payment station, amounted to a conclusive presumption violative of due process.[343] Similarly, in *People v. Watts*,[344] the Illinois Supreme Court, in an opinion that contained an excellent discussion of presumptions in a criminal case, found unconstitutional a provision criminalizing home repair fraud, which created a rebuttable presumption that a home repair contractor had no intent to perform his obligations as promised in a home repair contract based upon the state's proof of certain predicate acts involving non-completion of the repairs.[345] Here, the court found that this presumption placed an unconstitutional burden of persuasion on a defendant-contractor and the court determined that the presumption allowed "the state to avoid proving intent" by proof of the predicate acts, then required the defendant to bear the burden of rebutting the presumption and, if the defendant failed to carry this

---

[337] Nancy L. Barrett, Note, *Specific Intent Made More Specific: A Clarification of the Law of Attempted Murder in Illinois-People v. Harris*, 28 DEPAUL L. REV. 157, 159-60 (1978).

[338] 442 U.S. 510 (1979).

[339] Sandstrom v. Montana, 442 U.S. 510, 513 (1979).

[340] Sandstrom v. Montana, 442 U.S. 510, 524 (1979).

[341] Sandstrom v. Montana, 442 U.S. 510, 520-24 (1979). *See also* Francis v. Franklin, 471 U.S. 307 (1985) (it was unconstitutional to instruct jury that the acts of a person of sound mind are presumed to be the product of the person's will "but the presumption may be rebutted" for such is at odds with requiring the state to prove all elements of crime); Mullaney v. Wilbur, 421 U.S. 684 (1975) (it was unconstitutional to put burden of persuasion regarding defense on defendant's shoulders); In re Winship, 397 U.S. 358 (1970) (beyond-a-reasonable-doubt standard required as to every fact necessary to prove the existence of a crime).

[342] 173 Ill. App. 3d 460, 527 N.E.2d 1079 (2d Dist. 1988).

[343] People v. Dodd, 173 Ill. App. 3d 460, 467-70, 527 N.E.2d 1079, 1084-85 (2d Dist. 1988).

[344] 181 Ill. 2d 133, 692 N.E.2d 315 (1998).

[345] People v. Watts, 181 Ill. 2d 133, 148-51, 692 N.E.2d 315, 323-24 (1998).

burden, required the trier of fact to find criminal intent "even if the state has offered no evidence that directly shows such an intent."[346] In response to *Sandstrom*, some Illinois courts have been careful to point out that the ordinary presumption that a person intends the natural and probable consequences of his actions (1) merely shifts the burden of production, rather than the burden of persuasion, to the defendant, and (2) is a rebuttable, not a conclusive, presumption.[347] In *People v. Farrell*,[348] an appellate court recognized that this presumption had to be so interpreted and added: "Like all rebuttable presumptions, once the defendant introduced evidence contrary to the presumption, the presumption ceased to have effect. Only the evidence presented by the parties and natural inferences drawn from the evidence could be considered."[349] Thus, it seems that once the defendant offers some evidence suggesting that he or she did not have the requisite intent for the crime charged, the defendant has effectively destroyed this presumption.

However, *People v. Watts*,[350] discussed above, contains language indicating a presumption is unconstitutional to the extent that it may be interpreted as (1) giving rise to a conclusive or irrebuttable presumption of intent flowing from the defendant's actions, (2) essentially placing the ultimate burden of persuasion regarding intent on the shoulders of the defendant *or* (3) is a "production-shifting presumption [which] places a burden on the defendant to come forward with a certain quantum of evidence to overcome the presumption."[351] What this ruling means in relation to the "natural and probable consequences" doctrine is unclear at this time.

The second aspect of the problematic second step mentioned above involves conclusively inferring intent from lesser states of mind. In *People v. Olbrot*,[352] which involved charges of attempted murder, aggravated battery, and attempted armed robbery, the court offered the following language in regard to the intent for attempted murder: "Belief on the part of an actor that certain results would follow his conduct is sufficient to show a specific intent for that result to occur."[353] What the court appeared to be saying was that if the defendant was aware of, or had knowledge of, certain results that emanated from his conduct, this was conclusively sufficient for intent. This is like asserting that the law pre-

---

[346] People v. Watts, 181 Ill. 2d 133, 150, 692 N.E.2d 315, 324 (1998).

[347] People v. Farrell, 89 Ill. App. 3d 262, 265, 411 N.E.2d 927, 930 (1st Dist. 1980).

[348] 89 Ill. App. 3d 262, 411 N.E.2d 927 (1st Dist. 1980). The charge at issue in *Farrell* was aggravated battery, which the court concluded was supported by evidence of intent to cause serious bodily damage to the victim.

[349] People v. Farrell, 89 Ill. App. 3d 262, 265, 411 N.E.2d 927, 930 (1st Dist. 1980).

[350] 181 Ill. 2d 133, 692 N.E.2d 315 (1998).

[351] People v. Watts, 181 Ill. 2d 133, 147, 692 N.E.2d 315, 322-23 (1998).

[352] 106 Ill. App. 3d 367, 435 N.E.2d 1242 (1st Dist. 1982).

[353] People v. Olbrot, 106 Ill. App. 3d 367, 377, 435 N.E.2d 1242, 1250 (1st Dist. 1982).

sumes that a person intends what he or she knows, which is difficult to reconcile with the entire thrust of criminal attempt liability:

> Attempt has a connotation of purposive goal-oriented activity. To attempt something ... necessarily means to seek to do it, to make a deliberate effort in that direction. Intent is inherent in the notion of attempt; it is the essence of the crime. An attempt without intent is unthinkable; it cannot be.[354]

In addition, suggesting that one invariably intends the consequences of acts one knows one is committing is simplistic. While this may prove true in many cases, it is not true per se.

It must be recognized that one "acts intentionally if one's conscious objective or purpose is to accomplish the result ... [whereas one] acts knowingly if he is consciously aware that the conduct is practically certain to cause the result."[355] Thus, a belief, an awareness, or knowledge that a result will occur cannot be equated with an intent that it occur. In the context of attempted murder, for instance, numerous Illinois opinions insist that knowledge that an act creates a strong possibility of death or great bodily harm is not the equivalent of the requisite intent to kill.[356] *If* one can interpret the *Olbrot* language as carrying a *rebuttable presumption* of intent that does not impinge on defendants' constitutional rights identified in *Watts*, this judicial statement may be acceptable. In other words, just as one can infer intent from a defendant's conduct, it seems appropriate to infer it from his or her knowledge. However, if the *Olbrot* passage is stating a defendant is *conclusively* presumed to have *intended* certain results of his conduct based on evidence that he was merely *aware* might occur, then the state is inappropriately relieved of its burden of proof on the critical element of intent.

The third aspect of the insupportable second step referred to above involves equating intent with lesser mental states. In a 1963 Illinois Supreme Court case, the court stated that a "wanton and reckless disregard of human life" may be the equivalent of intent.[357] While more recent Illinois Supreme Court opinions[358] apparently recognize that this is not the case, various appellate court opinions

---

[354] Arnold N. Enker, *Mens Rea and Criminal Attempt*, 1977 AM. B. FOUND. RES. J. 845, 847 (1977).

[355] People v. Farrell, 89 Ill. App. 3d 262, 264-65, 411 N.E.2d 927, 930 (1st Dist. 1980).

[356] *See* People v. Page, 163 Ill. App. 3d 959, 971-72, 516 N.E.2d 1371, 1380-81 (4th Dist. 1987), and cases cited therein.

[357] People v. Coolidge, 26 Ill. 2d 533, 537, 187 N.E.2d 694, 697 (1963).

[358] *See, e.g.*, People v. Jones, 81 Ill. 2d 1, 9, 405 N.E.2d 343, 346 (1979); People v. Harris, 72 Ill. 2d 16, 27, 377 N.E.2d 28, 33 (1978); People v. Trinkle, 68 Ill. 2d 198, 201-04, 369 N.E.2d 888, 889-92 (1977).

still tend to equate knowledge and specific intent.[359] In 1979, in *People v. Morano*,[360] the Illinois Appellate Court for the First District affirmed an attempted murder conviction after stating that if the defendant had a "belief" or "knew" that his conduct would result in death, this would be sufficient to show a specific intent for that crime.[361] In passing, the *Morano* court cited with favor a hypothetical situation from a comment to the Model Penal Code:[362] "They suggest the example of a man who, with the purpose of destroying a building, intends to dynamite it. If he does so knowing and believing that persons inside the building will be killed, although not consciously desiring the inhabitants to die, there would be an attempt to kill."[363] Careful scrutiny of the *Morano* ruling and the Model Penal Code provisions regarding criminal attempt liability shows that reliance by an Illinois court on such reasoning and example is misplaced.

First, it is essential to consider the Model Penal Code language:

A person is guilty of an attempt to commit a crime if, acting with the kind of culpability otherwise required for commission of the crime, he:

(a) purposely engages in conduct which would constitute the crime if the attendant circumstances were as he believes them to be; or (b) when causing a particular result is an element of the crime, does or omits to do anything with the purpose of causing *or with the belief that it will cause such result* without further conduct on his part; or (c) purposely does or omits to do anything which, under the circumstances as he believes them to be, is an act or omission constituting a substantial step in a course of conduct planned to culminate in his commission of the crime."[364]

Next, one must compare the Illinois provision for criminal attempts: "A person commits an attempt when, with *intent to commit a specific offense*, he does any act which constitutes a substantial step toward the commission of that offense."[365] The revision committee responsible for drafting the 1961 code reaffirmed the clear scope of the attempt enactment by saying "[t]here *must* be an intent to commit a specific offense. . . ."[366] Obviously, the scope of the Model

---

[359] *See, e.g.,* People v. Brown, 199 Ill. App. 3d 860, 871, 557 N.E.2d 611, 618 (1st Dist. 1990) ("A conviction [for attempted murder] will be sustained if the defendant is actuated 'by wanton and reckless disregard of human life that denotes malice. . . .'").

[360] 69 Ill. App. 3d 580, 387 N.E.2d 816 (1st Dist. 1979).

[361] People v. Morano, 69 Ill. App. 3d 580, 586, 387 N.E.2d 816, 821 (1st Dist. 1979).

[362] People v. Morano, 69 Ill. App. 3d 580, 586, 387 N.E.2d 816, 821 (1st Dist. 1979) (citing MODEL PENAL CODE § 5.01, comments at 29 (Tentative Draft No. 10, 1960)).

[363] People v. Morano, 69 Ill. App. 3d 580, 586, 387 N.E.2d 816, 821 (1st Dist. 1979) (citing MODEL PENAL CODE § 5.01, comments at 29 (Tentative Draft No. 10, 1960)).

[364] MODEL PENAL CODE § 5.01(1) (1962) (emphasis added).

[365] 720 ILCS 5/8-4(a) (1999) (emphasis added).

[366] ILL. ANN. STAT. ch. 38, para. 8-4 (Smith-Hurd 1989), 1961 Committee Comments, at 499 (emphasis added).

Penal Code formulation of criminal attempt allows basing attempt liability on a person's "belief"; the Illinois provision bases such liability on nothing other than "intent." In a nutshell, the *Morano* court is wrong in relying on the broad Model Penal Code notion of intent in a state where the Model Penal Code definition has not been employed. *Morano* illustrates the willingness of some Illinois courts to treat a lesser mental state and intent as equivalents and the tendency of many to accept that the former satisfies the latter.

§ 2.29. — Proof of Intent.

In the absence of an admission by the defendant that he had intent, this mental state can only be proved by surrounding circumstances.[367] Reliance on circumstantial evidence is an appropriate method of proving intent in cases[368] where the defendant's state of mind is not subject to direct proof.[369] Furthermore, the consideration of such evidence presented by the state is justified where the defendant has offered evidence on his mental state, since the trier of fact need not accept the defendant's version.[370]

A court may properly infer intent in certain situations from circumstantial evidence such as the defendant's own words and actions.[371] The court can also draw certain conclusions regarding the defendant's alleged intent — supportive of his defense — from what he *failed* to do. This important consideration is reflected in *People v. Thomas*.[372] In that case, the defendant had been convicted of attempted murder, aggravated battery, robbery, and rape. The state's evidence showed that the defendant had forced his way into the victim's apartment while brandishing a knife, told the victim to shut up or be killed, banged her head against a chest of drawers, and hit her in the head. After raping and robbing the victim, he fled. The *Thomas* court ultimately reversed the attempted murder charge, leaving the other convictions intact, on the theory that since the opportunity to commit any intended murder was so great and the defendant had not availed himself of that opportunity, one could not conclude beyond a reasonable

---

[367] People v. Koshiol, 45 Ill. 2d 573, 578, 262 N.E.2d 446, 449 (1970), *cert. denied*, 401 U.S. 978 (1971) (attempted murder conviction affirmed).

[368] People v. McManus, 197 Ill. App. 3d 1085, 1096, 555 N.E.2d 391, 399 (2d Dist. 1990) (circumstantial evidence supported specific intent required for theft by deception).

[369] People v. Bryant, 79 Ill. App. 3d 501, 505, 398 N.E.2d 941, 944 (3d Dist. 1979) (circumstantial evidence supported specific intent required for burglary).

[370] People v. Bryant, 79 Ill. App. 3d 501, 505, 398 N.E.2d 941, 944 (3d Dist. 1979); People v. Henderson, 18 Ill. App. 3d 457, 461, 309 N.E.2d 242, 245 (3d Dist. 1974); People v. Konetzke, 17 Ill. App. 3d 800, 802, 308 N.E.2d 649, 650 (3d Dist. 1974).

[371] People v. Jones, 93 Ill. App. 3d 475, 479, 417 N.E.2d 647, 651 (1st Dist. 1981) (intent required for unlawful use of weapon can be inferred from surrounding circumstances including defendant's words and actions).

[372] 127 Ill. App. 2d 444, 262 N.E.2d 495 (1st Dist. 1970).

doubt that the defendant's violent acts supported any intent beyond rape.[373] In *People v. Mitchell*,[374] the defendant had been convicted of attempted murder and aggravated battery for attacks on her seventeen-month-old daughter. Notwithstanding the evidence that the defendant had struck her daughter with her fist and belt, causing serious injury to the child, the defendant's attempted murder conviction was reversed by the appellate court and the supreme court affirmed. The court stated:

> There was ample opportunity for her to complete her crime if, in fact, she intended to kill the child. Further, following the [victim's] loss of consciousness, defendant applied a cool cloth and ultimately took her to the hospital for emergency medical attention, actions which are not consistent with an intent to murder.[375]

In the discussion of possession earlier in this chapter,[376] it was pointed out that possession of an item may give rise to certain inferences that would support criminality. While mere possession will not lead to an inference of criminal intent as a matter of law,[377] it can be considered circumstantial evidence supportive of other crimes, as was the case where the unexplained possession of property stolen in a recent burglary was considered relevant in determining whether the defendant committed the burglary with the requisite intent.[378]

Although the presence of intent is a question of fact and cannot be implied as a matter of law, criminal intent may be shown by various types of circumstantial evidence.[379] For example, a defendant's intent to kill was indicated by his carrying of a loaded gun, pointing the gun at the victim, and firing the gun three times.[380] Intent to kill could also be inferred from a defendant's action of manually strangling his wife until she lost consciousness.[381] Intent to deliver controlled substances may be inferred by the amount of drug possessed, the combination of drugs and the manner in which they are kept, the presence of drug paraphernalia, and the presence of large amounts of cash and weapons.[382] In other words, criminal intent may be manifested by the circumstances connected with the perpetration of the offense without any positive evidence as to the in-

---

[373] People v. Thomas, 127 Ill. App. 2d 444, 451, 262 N.E.2d 495, 501-02 (1st Dist. 1970).

[374] 105 Ill. 2d 1, 473 N.E.2d 1270 (1984), *cert. denied*, 470 U.S. 1089 (1985).

[375] People v. Mitchell, 105 Ill. 2d 1, 10, 473 N.E.2d 1270, 1274 (1984), *cert. denied*, 470 U.S. 1089 (1985).

[376] *See* § 2.23 of this chapter.

[377] People v. Housby, 84 Ill. 2d 415, 423-24, 420 N.E.2d 151, 155, *cert. denied*, 454 U.S. 845 (1981); People v. Beacham, 358 Ill. 373, 377, 193 N.E. 205, 206 (1934).

[378] People v. Carter, 197 Ill. App. 3d 1043, 1046-47, 557 N.E.2d 299, 300 (1st Dist. 1990).

[379] People v. Murff, 29 Ill. 2d 303, 305, 194 N.E.2d 226, 227 (1963).

[380] People v. Wilks, 175 Ill. App. 3d 68, 75-76, 529 N.E.2d 690, 695 (1st Dist. 1988).

[381] People v. Petty, 160 Ill. App. 3d 207, 211, 513 N.E.2d 486, 488 (3d Dist. 1987).

[382] People v. Berry, 198 Ill. App. 3d 24, 28-29, 555 N.E.2d 434, 437 (2d Dist. 1990).

tention.[383] Thus, jury instructions that point out that proof of intent can be established by direct or circumstantial evidence are not erroneous.[384] Since questions about criminal intent are questions of fact to be determined by the trier of fact, the findings of fact will not be reversed unless they are palpably contrary to the manifest weight of the evidence.[385]

§ 2.30. — Unintended Victims and Results.

An additional problem of intent requiring review involves the unintended victim and the concept of "transferred intent." This type of problem often arises in the context of murder or attempted murder.[386] Generally, if a person without legal excuse or justification attempts to kill one individual and inadvertently kills or attempts to kill another, the person is guilty of the same degree of unlawful homicide or attempted homicide as if he or she had killed or attempted to kill the object of his or her aim,[387] but if the person acts in self-defense and, for example, accidentally kills another, he or she is guilty of no crime.[388] Of course, this rule is not absolute and may be subject to modification depending on the circumstances involved.[389] In *People v. Swaney*,[390] the defendant invaded a home in which a married couple were sleeping. After the couple awoke, they ran after the defendant. In the darkness, a struggle ensued between the couple and the defendant during which the defendant stabbed the husband twenty-seven times and the wife once. Since both victims survived, the defendant was convicted of, among other offenses, two counts of attempted murder. The defendant appealed, contending that there was no evidence of intent to kill the wife. He maintained

---

[383] People v. Kopke, 376 Ill. 171, 175, 33 N.E.2d 216, 217-18, *cert. denied*, 314 U.S. 646 (1941).

[384] People v. Stockton, 355 Ill. 405, 410-11, 189 N.E. 281, 282 (1934).

[385] People v. Starks, 190 Ill. App. 3d 503, 510, 546 N.E.2d 71, 77 (2d Dist. 1989), *cert. denied*, 498 U.S. 827 (1990).

[386] *See, e.g.,* People v. Lenius, 293 Ill. App. 3d 519, 538-39, 688 N.E.2d 705, 718-19 (1st Dist. 1997) (first degree murder and attempted murder convictions affirmed while relying on transferred intent doctrine).

[387] People v. Lenius, 293 Ill. App. 3d 519, 538-39, 688 N.E.2d 705, 718-19 (1st Dist. 1997) (where bomb designed to kill one victim exploded to kill second victim, attempted first degree murder and first degree murder convictions affirmed while relying on doctrine of transferred intent); People v. Shelton, 293 Ill. App. 3d 747, 754, 688 N.E.2d 831, 833-35, (1st Dist. 1997) (where defendant shot two victims, one of whom was killed in possible case of mistaken identity, attempted first degree murder and first degree murder conviction affirmed while relying on doctrine of transferred intent); People v. Hill, 276 Ill. App. 3d 683, 687-89, 658 N.E.2d 1294, 1297-98 (1st Dist. 1995) (attempted first degree murder conviction affirmed on transferred intent theory); People v. Franklin, 225 Ill. App. 3d 948, 949, 588 N.E.2d 398, 399-400 (3d Dist. 1992) (attempted murder conviction affirmed on transferred intent theory);

[388] People v. Adams, 9 Ill. App. 3d 61, 63, 291 N.E.2d 54, 55-56 (5th Dist. 1972).

[389] People v. Adams, 9 Ill. App. 3d 61, 64, 291 N.E.2d 54, 56 (5th Dist. 1972).

[390] 2 Ill. App. 3d 857, 276 N.E.2d 346 (3d Dist. 1971).

that where a person unintentionally injures a third person while assaulting another with intent to kill, he or she cannot be guilty of intent to injure the third person.[391] The appellate court responded that "[s]uch is not the law of Illinois."[392] Although there was evidence that the defendant did intend to kill the wife as well as the husband, the court implied that even without that evidence, the defendant's conviction would have been affirmed with respect to the count in question.[393] The court's reasoning essentially involved *transference of intent* from that directed at one victim to the second.

> For example, A's intent to kill B may suffice as to his causing the death of C. This is . . . referred to as "transferred intent." This is applicable only within the limits of the same crime, however, as for example, A's intent to kill B would not suffice as to causing the burning of C's property. That is, while a defendant can be convicted when he has both the *mens rea* and commits the *actus reus* required for a given offense, he cannot be convicted if the *mens rea* relates to one crime and the *actus reus* to another.[394]

In *People v. Hickman*,[395] the court was faced with an aggravated battery conviction where the defendant went to the home of his former wife with the intention of shooting his brother, who was living with her. When he shot at his brother, Hickman's former wife stepped into the line of fire and was wounded. The appellate court affirmed the conviction, reasoning:

> [T]he doctrine of transferred intent in criminal cases has been established for hundreds of years by the old English case of Reg. v. Sauders, 2 Plowd. 473, 75 Eng. Reprint 706 (1576), 18 A.L.R. 923, in which the court pointed out that if a man maliciously shoots an arrow at another man with intent to kill him and a person to whom he bore no malice is killed by it, this would be murder for the person who shot the arrow with intent to kill, and is the same offense as to such person as if he had killed the person he aimed at. One who does an unlawful act is liable for the consequences even though they may not have been intended. Thus where one in the commission of a wrongful act commits another wrong not meant by him, or where in the execution of an intent to do wrong, an unintended act resulting in a wrong ensued as a natural and probable consequence, the one acting with wrongful intent is responsible for the unintended wrong.[396]

---

[391] People v. Swaney, 2 Ill. App. 3d 857, 859, 276 N.E.2d 346, 347 (3d Dist. 1971).

[392] People v. Swaney, 2 Ill. App. 3d 857, 859, 276 N.E.2d 346, 347 (3d Dist. 1971).

[393] People v. Swaney, 2 Ill. App. 3d 857, 859, 276 N.E.2d 346, 347 (3d Dist. 1971).

[394] JOHN KLOTTER, CRIMINAL LAW § 2.7 at 34 (2d ed. 1986).

[395] 9 Ill. App. 3d 39, 291 N.E.2d 523 (3d Dist. 1973).

[396] People v. Hickman, 9 Ill. App. 3d 39, 44, 291 N.E.2d 523, 526-27 (3d Dist. 1973).

The court said that Hickman's "intent follow[ed] the bullet."[397] This concept has not been without its critics. Professors Perkin and Boyce claim that it "has no proper place in criminal law . . . In the field of crime this concept has the vice of being a misleading half-truth."[398] Notwithstanding the appeal of the rhetoric contained in *Hickman's* "intent follows the bullet" statement, one can understand the authorities' difficulty in accepting that a person can intend the "unintended," as *Hickman* posits.

Where the state failed to prove a defendant had the intent to kill his alleged "intended victim," it was legally impossible to convict him of the attempted murder of an unintended victim based on a transferred intent theory.[399] In other words, if the defendant had no criminal intent whatsoever, there is no intent capable of being transferred.

In *People v. Adams*,[400] the opposite side of this conceptual coin is illustrated. In that case, Adams, the defendant, and Robinson had an argument over a small amount of money. Subsequently, Adams shot Robinson, the assailant, at close range and killed him. In addition, one of the bullets that struck the assailant passed through his body and struck his companion, Mary Davis, killing her. Adams was charged with two counts of murder. At his jury trial, Adams raised the defense of self-defense. The jury returned a verdict of acquittal concerning the shooting of Robinson, apparently on self-defense grounds, but convicted the defendant of involuntary manslaughter for the death of Davis. Adams appealed his conviction. The state argued that self-defense does not necessarily protect an individual from criminal responsibility for all of his acts performed in defending his life against a felonious assault and that even though the defendant's conduct may have been justified concerning Robinson, it nevertheless constituted a reckless disregard for the life of Davis, which would be a proper basis for a finding of involuntary manslaughter.[401] The appellate court disagreed and reversed the conviction. They pointed out that since the defendant had to act immediately in response to the fact that Robinson was not just threatening him but was shooting at him, and since there was no evidence that he shot wildly or carelessly at Robinson, he could not be convicted of a criminal homicide for the death of Davis merely because her death was an incident to his justified shooting of Robinson.[402]

---

[397] People v. Hickman, 9 Ill. App. 3d 39, 44, 291 N.E.2d 523, 527 (3d Dist. 1973).

[398] ROLLIN M. PERKINS & RONALD N. BOYCE, CRIMINAL LAW 921 (3d ed. 1982).

[399] People v. Homes, 274 Ill. App. 3d 612, 623, 654 N.E.2d 662, 670 (1st Dist. 1995) (where trial court acquitted the defendant of attempted murder of intended victim but convicted him of attempted murder of unintended victim, latter conviction was vacated on appeal).

[400] 9 Ill. App. 3d 61, 291 N.E.2d 54 (5th Dist. 1972).

[401] People v. Adams, 9 Ill. App. 3d 61, 63, 291 N.E.2d 54, 55 (5th Dist. 1972).

[402] People v. Adams, 9 Ill. App. 3d 61, 64, 291 N.E.2d 54, 56 (5th Dist. 1972).

Closely related to this concern are those cases in which unanticipated results transpire. In *People v. Smith*[403] (discussed earlier in this chapter in connection with legal duties),[404] the defendant encountered a woman in premises he was burglarizing and attempted to strangle her. She jumped out of a window, killing herself in order to get away from him. The court upheld his murder conviction even though he "did not anticipate the precise series of events" that resulted in her death.[405] It is interesting to consider the question of the defendant's liability if the woman had survived the fall. Since the defendant did try to kill her by strangulation before she broke away and jumped, it is reasonable to conclude that he had the specific intent to kill necessary for attempted murder. In addition, in placing a pillow over her face, he clearly took a "substantial step"[406] toward committing murder. The fact that his conduct, supported by his intent, put into motion a sequence of events that he did not exactly anticipate but that emanated from his menacing conduct appears to be sufficient for criminal attempt liability.

§ 2.31. — Conditional Intent.

Another concern that deserves mention at this juncture is "conditional intent." In *People v. Connors*,[407] the Illinois Supreme Court upheld the conviction of a union organizer who had pointed a gun at a worker and threatened to kill him if he did not remove his overalls and quit work. The court ruled that the "specific intent to kill" necessary for an assault with intent to murder conviction could be established even though the intent was "coupled with a condition" that the defendant would not shoot if the victim complied with the demand.[408] In *Holloway v. United States*,[409] the United States Supreme Court upheld federal carjacking charges where defendant threatened to shoot the driver if he failed to hand over the car keys.[410] In this case, the defendant could not claim his intent to kill was equivocal because it was conditional: "a defendant may not negate a proscribed intent by requiring the victim to comply with a condition the defendant has no right to impose."[411]

---

[403] 56 Ill. 2d 328, 307 N.E.2d 353 (1974).

[404] *See* § 2.15 of this chapter.

[405] People v. Smith, 56 Ill. 2d 328, 333-34, 307 N.E.2d 353, 355-56 (1974).

[406] Such is the overt act requirement for criminal attempt in Illinois. 720 ILCS 5/8-4(a) (1999).

[407] 253 Ill. 266, 97 N.E. 643 (1912).

[408] People v. Connors, 253 Ill. 266, 272-73, 97 N.E. 643, 645 (1912).

[409] 526 U.S. 1, 119 S. Ct. 966 (1999).

[410] Holloway v. United States, 526 U.S. 1, 119 S. Ct. 966, 970-72 (1999) (offense requires proof of intent to cause death or serious bodily harm).

[411] Holloway v. United States, 526 U.S. 1, 119 S. Ct. 966, 971 (1999).

§ 2.32.   — Motive.

Although intent is an important aspect of the mens rea conceptual framework, it should not be confused with a defendant's motive, which is not essential for conviction of a crime.[412] Whether a defendant's possession of a controlled substance and cannabis was motivated by his interest in demonstrating to municipal officials how easy it was to procure illicit drugs in the municipality, which he claimed to be a form of "civic protest," or was motivated to possess it to consume it was irrelevant where he was charged with criminal possession.[413] Similarly, where A is charged with the unjustified killing of B, A cannot argue that since the state has failed to offer some explanation for his motivation for killing B, he cannot be convicted of the murder of B.[414] But though motive is not a necessary ingredient to proving murder (or any other crime), it may be an important circumstance in determining the defendant's guilt where the evidence is entirely circumstantial.[415] Thus, the state will be allowed to show the defendant's motive if it deems such a showing necessary to establish guilt. On the other hand, proof of motive alone is not a sufficient basis for sustaining a conviction where there is no other evidence that, in connection with the proof of motive, establishes the requisite mens rea and actus reus for the crime.[416] In addition, when the state undertakes to prove facts which the state asserts constitute motive for the crime charged, it must be shown that the accused knew of those facts.[417] Thus, it was error for a trial court to admit into evidence at defendant's trial for murder of two police officers the existence of an outstanding warrant to arrest defendant absent evidence the defendant knew he was wanted by the police.[418]

§ 2.33.   Mental States: Knowledge.

The second mental state covered by article 5/4 of the Criminal Code of 1961 is that of knowledge. Paragraph 5/4-5 sets out the definition:

> Knowledge. A person knows, or acts knowingly or with knowledge of:
>
> (a) The nature or attendant circumstances of his conduct, described by the statute defining the offense, when he is consciously aware that his conduct

---

[412] A TREATISE ON THE LAW OF CRIMES (CLARK & MARSHALL) 263 (Miriam Quinn Barnes 7th ed. 1967). Of course, motive may have importance in sentencing. GEORGE FLETCHER, RETHINKING CRIMINAL LAW § 6.5.5 at 452 (1978).

[413] See People v. Davis, 165 Ill. App. 3d 648, 651, 519 N.E.2d 103, 105 (2d Dist. 1988).

[414] See People v. Smith, 141 Ill. 2d 40, 56, 565 N.E.2d 900, 906 (1990) (murder conviction reversed on other grounds).

[415] People v. Willson, 401 Ill. 68, 74, 81 N.E.2d 485, 489 (1948).

[416] People v. Holtz, 294 Ill. 143, 155-56, 128 N.E. 341, 345 (1920).

[417] People v. Wilson, 116 Ill. 2d 29, 52, 506 N.E.2d 571, 581 (1987).

[418] People v. Wilson, 116 Ill. 2d 29, 52, 506 N.E.2d 571, 581 (1987).

is of such nature or that such circumstances exist. Knowledge of a material fact includes awareness of the substantial probability that such fact exists. (b) The result of his conduct, described by the statute defining the offense, when he is consciously aware that such result is practically certain to be caused by his conduct.

Conduct performed knowingly or with knowledge is performed wilfully, within the meaning of a statute using the latter term, unless the statute clearly requires another meaning.[419]

The revision committee's comments state that a person need not be absolutely certain of the existence of a fact or completely certain about the result of his or her conduct before it can be said he or she had "knowledge" of the fact or result.[420] Rather, proof that there was a "substantial probability" that the person was aware of a fact will suffice where knowledge of a fact is at issue. In addition, proof that it was "practically certain" that the person was aware of the result of his or her actions will be sufficient where this is in question.

The Illinois statute defining *knowledge* involves the following basic elements: (1) conscious awareness of (2) the existence of facts with a substantial certainty and of (3) the results of conduct that are practically certain to be caused by that conduct. Knowledge is similar to intent in the sense that conscious awareness is inherent in acting purposely but is distinguishable from intent in that it does not require a showing of conscious objective or aim on the part of the accused. Likewise, knowledge has in common with recklessness[421] the element of conscious awareness of the facts but is different in that the level of risk involved in knowledge is "substantial probability" or "practical certainty"; for recklessness, it is merely "substantial risk" and "gross deviation" from the norm.[422] Knowledge is clearly different from negligence[423] in that the latter involves not "con-

---

[419] 720 ILCS 5/4-5 (1999).

[420] ILL. ANN. STAT. ch. 38, para. 4-3 (Smith-Hurd 1989), 1961 Committee Comments, at 201-02.

[421] 720 ILCS 5/4-6 (1999):

A person is reckless or acts recklessly, when he consciously disregards a substantial and unjustifiable risk that circumstances exist or that a result will follow, described by the statute defining the offense; and such disregard constitutes a gross deviation from the standard of care which a reasonable person would exercise in the situation.

[422] 720 ILCS 5/4-6 (1999).

[423] 720 ILCS 5/4-7 (1999):

A person is negligent, or acts negligently, when he fails to be aware of a substantial and unjustifiable risk that circumstances exist or a result will follow, described by the statute defining the offense; and such failure constitutes a substantial deviation from the standard of care which a reasonable person would exercise in the situation.

scious awareness" but rather inadvertent risk creation; and the element of risk is only a "substantial deviation" from the normal standard of care.[424]

In some circles, usage of the term *unlawfully* connotes knowledge. This point of view is rejected in Illinois.[425] In one case, the Illinois Supreme Court reviewed a conviction for the illicit possession of policy tickets based on an indictment which alleged that the defendant had unlawfully possessed the policy tickets but which failed to mention the element of knowledge, an element reflected in the stricture in question.[426] The court reversed the defendant's conviction, since the charging instrument had not alleged knowledge as required by statute: "Inclusion of the word 'unlawfully' merely connotes that the possession was contrary to or in defiance of law, whereas 'knowingly' implies that the act was performed consciously, intelligently, and with actual knowledge of the facts."[427]

Just as *unlawful* does not connote "knowledge," the mens rea of knowledge does not satisfy a specific intent requirement contained in a statute. Thus, where a defendant is charged with conspiracy, which requires specific intent, knowledge on the part of the defendant that he or she is perpetrating an offense would be insufficient.[428] On the other hand, it would be proper to infer — as long as the inference presumption is not unconstitutional[429] — intent from the defendant's knowledge or belief.[430]

§ 2.34.   — Proof of Knowledge.

Because of the very nature of knowledge, which probes into what the accused was subjectively, consciously aware of, knowledge is ordinarily proved by circumstantial evidence rather than by direct proof.[431] For example, in a conviction for aggravated battery, a mother's knowledge that she was injuring her child was shown by the testimony of a doctor who stated that the water in which the mother had bathed her child was between 120 and 150 degrees and that the child would have immediately cried out in pain.[432] Also, in a conviction for home in-

[424] 720 ILCS 5/4-7 (1999).

[425] People v. Edge, 406 Ill. 490, 493-94, 94 N.E.2d 359, 361 (1950).

[426] People v. Edge, 406 Ill. 490, 493-94, 94 N.E.2d 359, 361 (1950).

[427] People v. Edge, 406 Ill. 490, 494, 94 N.E.2d 359, 361 (1950). *Accord* People v. Arnold, 3 Ill. App. 3d 678, 682, 279 N.E.2d 436, 439 (1st Dist. 1972).

[428] People v. Persinger, 49 Ill. App. 3d 116, 122, 363 N.E.2d 897, 902 (5th Dist. 1977), *cert. denied*, 435 U.S. 917 (1978).

[429] *See* § 2.28 of this chapter.

[430] *See* People v. Olbrot, 106 Ill. App. 3d 367, 377, 435 N.E.2d 1242, 1250 (1st Dist. 1982) (attempted murder conviction affirmed).

[431] People v. Easy Life Real Estate, 153 Ill. App. 3d 74, 80, 505 N.E.2d 1197, 1201 (1st Dist. 1987).

[432] People v. Flores, 168 Ill. App. 3d 284, 290, 52 N.E.2d 708, 711-12 (1st Dist. 1988).

vasion, circumstantial evidence that a car was parked in the driveway, several lights and a television set were on inside the home, and the homeowner moved about inside, was sufficient to show the defendant's knowledge of a person's presence in the home, which is a necessary element for conviction of that crime.[433] While scienter, which is the equivalent of knowledge,[434] must normally be proved by circumstantial evidence, it is incumbent on the state to present such evidence.[435] An inference that constitutes an element of a criminal offense, such as knowledge, should be based directly on an established fact, and not pyramided on an intervening inference.[436] For example, the knowledge or awareness required of criminal possession may be inferred from other established facts, such as ownership; it cannot be premised on the coincidental presence of a person and contraband within confines of the same motor vehicle.[437] Even where the defense presents direct evidence based on defendant's own testimony where defendant claims a lack of requisite knowledge, circumstantial evidence may be relied on by a jury in dismissing the defense evidence as untrue. Thus, where the defendant, who was charged with two counts of battery, alleged that he was not consciously aware that his conduct with two victims, which he claimed was harmless wrestling or tickling, was practically certain to cause conduct of an insulting nature, the child-victims' demonstration on an anatomically correct doll as to how they were grabbed in the crotch area belied the defendant's argument that he had no knowledge of the effect of his actions.[438]

Many offenses can be committed with either intent or knowledge. Where the evidence does not lend itself to the difficult task of providing the conscious objective or aim of the accused, it is likely it will more easily satisfy the mens rea of knowledge. For example, since either intent to kill or knowledge that one's acts create a strong probability of death or great bodily harm is sufficient for murder, evidence of specific intent to murder need not be alleged or proved.[439]

§ 2.35. — Willful: Equivalent of Knowledge.

While clarity was the hallmark of the legislative drafting effort reflected in virtually all of the mens rea definitions contained in article 5/4 of the 1961 code, a notable exception appears in the last paragraph of the paragraph 5/4-5 definition of *knowledge*. The code states that "[c]onduct performed knowingly or with

---

[433] People v. Redisi, 172 Ill. App. 3d 1003, 1011, 527 N.E.2d 684, 689-90 (2d Dist. 1988).

[434] BLACK'S LAW DICTIONARY 1345 (6th ed. 1990).

[435] People v. Quiver, 205 Ill. App. 3d 1067, 1071, 563 N.E.2d 991, 994 (1st Dist. 1990).

[436] *See, e.g.*, People v. Pinta, 210 Ill. App. 3d 1071, 1078, 569 N.E.2d 1255, 1260 (2d Dist. 1999); People v. Davis, 50 Ill. App. 3d 163, 168, 365 N.E.2d 1135, 1138 (3d Dist. 1977).

[437] *See, e.g.*, People v. Davis, 50 Ill. App. 3d 163, 168, 365 N.E.2d 1135, 1138 (3d Dist. 1977).

[438] People v. Pinta, 210 Ill. App. 3d 1071, 1077-78, 569 N.E.2d 1255, 1259-60 (2d Dist. 1991).

[439] *See, e.g.*, People v. Soteras, 295 Ill. App. 3d 610, 617-21, 693 N.E.2d 400, 404-07 (2d Dist. 1998).

knowledge is performed willfully." The Committee Comments are essentially silent about the intended thrust of this language. The comments point out that before the adoption of the 1961 code, "'Willful' was used to describe intent in some provisions . . . although more often it carries the meaning 'knowingly' — or perhaps both meanings."[440] Later, in the same comment, the revision committee reported that "in a considerable number of instances 'willfully' was used in the sense of knowledge"[441] in the prior code. It is disturbing to find nowhere in the code a definition of the term *willful*, given the inconsistent prior usage of the term.

At first glance, one might interpret the terms *intentionally* and *willfully* as synonyms[442] and use them interchangeably. Perkins and Boyce have pointed out: "The word 'willful' or 'willfully' when used in the definition of a crime, it has been said time and again, means only intentionally or purposely as distinguished from accidentally or negligently. . . ."[443] The United States Supreme Court has considered the definition of *willful*: "The word often denotes an act which is intentional, or knowing, or voluntary, as distinguished from accidental. But when used in a criminal statute it generally means an act done with a bad purpose; without justifiable excuse; stubbornly, obstinately, perversely."[444] Yet one cannot assume that the drafters of the Illinois Criminal Code of 1961 were equating the term *willfully* with *intentionally* inasmuch as they did *not* provide in paragraph 5/4-5 that "conduct performed knowingly . . . is performed willfully and (or) intentionally." As Justice John Paul Stevens of the United States Supreme Court has stated in another connection, "the structural detail of this statute precludes a reading that converts silence into thunder."[445] Moreover, because the United States Supreme Court has stated that it is unconstitutional to assert that the law conclusively presumes that a person intends the natural and probable consequences of his or her acts,[446] it may well be equally unconstitutional to declare by statute that the law conclusively presumes that a person intends the results of that which the person knows he or she is doing. Finally, it is difficult to assume that the legislature intended to equate *knowledge* with *intent*,

---

[440] ILL. ANN. STAT. ch. 38, para. 4-3 (Smith-Hurd 1989), 1961 Committee Comments, at 199.

[441] ILL. ANN. STAT. ch. 38, para. 4-3 (Smith-Hurd 1989), 1961 Committee Comments, at 201.

[442] *Roget's Thesaurus* equates the terms intentional, deliberate and premeditated with willful. ROGET'S THESAURUS 542 (New Roget's Thesaurus in Dictionary Form, updated ed. 1978).

Legal dictionaries define the term willful as "intending the result which actually comes to pass; designed; intentional; purposeful; not accidental or involuntary." BLACK'S LAW DICTIONARY 1599 (6th ed. 1990).

[443] ROLLIN M. PERKINS & RONALD N. BOYCE, CRIMINAL LAW 921 (3d ed. 1982).

[444] United States v. Murdock, 290 U.S. 389, 394 (1933) (citations omitted).

[445] Dalia v. United States, 441 U.S. 238, 263 (1979) (Stevens, J., dissenting).

[446] Sandstrom v. Montana, 442 U.S. 510, 524 (1979).

for that would eliminate the need for drawing, as they did, a careful line of demarcation between intent and knowledge in article 5/4.[447]

On the other hand, paragraph 5/4-5 clearly states that a person's knowledgeable conduct is performed *willfully*.[448] This is exactly the way Illinois courts interpret this term. For example, in *People v. Albarran*,[449] the Illinois Appellate Court for the First District stated that the Illinois "bail-jumping" statute,[450] which employs the mens rea of willfully, could be construed in that fashion: "[m]isconduct is performed willfully if it is performed knowingly."[451]

Notwithstanding the fact that a common sense, dictionary definition of *willful* carries purposive implications, it may reasonably be concluded that these implications are not contemplated in the Illinois usage of this term. The reasoning offered above supports the statement that not only does *knowledge* mean willful — as the statute and caselaw clearly articulate — but *willful* means merely performing conduct "with knowledge" — nothing more, nothing less.

§ 2.36. Mental States: Recklessness.

The third mental state used in the Criminal Code of Illinois is that of recklessness. It is defined in paragraph 5/4-6 as follows:

> Recklessness. A person is reckless or acts recklessly, when he consciously disregards a substantial and unjustifiable risk that circumstances exist or that a result will follow, described by the statute defining the offense; and such disregard constitutes a gross deviation from the standard of care which a reasonable person would exercise in the situation. An act performed recklessly is performed wantonly, within the meaning of the statute using the latter term, unless the statute clearly requires another meaning.[452]

A perusal of the "recklessness" statute and the comments of the drafters of the statute reveals two basic elements involved in this mental state: (1) a conscious awareness of the created risk and (2) a disregard of the risk, which risk creation amounts to a gross deviation from proper standards of conduct. Recklessness is similar to intent and knowledge in that conscious awareness of the risk is required. However, this mental state is distinguishable from intent in that a purposeful state of mind is not contemplated. In addition, recklessness is different than knowledge in that the former involves a lower level of risk creation. Recklessness arises where there is a "gross deviation" from the norm or a "high prob-

---

[447] *See* 720 ILCS 5/4-4, 5/4-5 (1999).

[448] 720 ILCS 5/4-5 (1999) ("Conduct performed knowingly or with knowledge is performed wilfully. . . .").

[449] 40 Ill. App. 3d 344, 352 N.E.2d 379 (1st Dist. 1976).

[450] 720 ILCS 5/32-10 (1999).

[451] People v. Albarran, 40 Ill. App. 3d 344, 347, 352 N.E.2d 379, 382 (1st Dist. 1976).

[452] 720 ILCS 5/4-6 (1999).

ability of harm," whereas knowledge is defined in terms of "practical certainty" and "substantial probability."[453] Recklessness is distinguishable from negligence in two respects: (1) recklessness requires conscious awareness of the risk, which negligence does not, and (2) recklessness involves a higher degree of risk (gross deviation) than negligence (substantial deviation). The term *wantonly* is considered synonymous with *recklessness*. In conclusion, offenses involving the mental state of recklessness require a lower degree of mental culpability than intent or knowledge.[454]

The most significant use of the mental state of recklessness arises in connection with involuntary manslaughter[455] and reckless homicide.[456] With respect to those offenses, recklessness is the sole mens rea requirement employed. While there are other offenses, such as reckless conduct[457] that include only this mental state, there are offenses such as mob action[458] that can be satisfied either by recklessness or by any of the other alternative mental states — intent, knowledge, or negligence.[459] Crimes that employ recklessness as the requisite mental state must be understood as general intent crimes.[460]

Because of the operation of paragraph 5/4-3(b)[461] (discussed above),[462] where a prohibition is facially silent as to a mens rea requirement, the mens rea of intent, knowledge, or recklessness is usually incorporated judicially into the statute in the absence of a clear indication that the legislature intended the offense to be an absolute liability crime.[463] Thus, in *People v. Burmeister*,[464] the appel-

---

[453] ILL. ANN. STAT. ch. 38, para. 4-3 (Smith-Hurd 1989), 1961 Committee Comments, at 201-02.

[454] *See, e.g.,* People v. Spears, 112 Ill. 2d 396, 408, 493 N.E.2d 1030, 1035 (1986); People v. Higgins, 86 Ill. App. 2d 202, 207, 229 N.E.2d 161, 163 (5th Dist. 1967).

[455] 720 ILCS 5/9-3(a) (1999):

> A person who unintentionally kills an individual without lawful justification commits involuntary manslaughter if his acts whether lawful or unlawful which cause the death are such as are likely to cause death or great bodily harm to some individual, and he performs them recklessly, except in cases in which the cause of death consists of the driving of a motor vehicle, in which case the person commits reckless homicide.

[456] 720 ILCS 5/9-3(a) (1999).

[457] 720 ILCS 5/12-5(a) (1999): "A person who causes bodily harm to or endangers the bodily safety of an individual by any means, commits reckless conduct if he performs recklessly the acts which cause the harm or endanger safety, whether they otherwise are lawful or unlawful."

[458] 720 ILCS 5/25-1(a) (1999).

[459] People v. Leach, 3 Ill. App. 3d 389, 393, 279 N.E.2d 450, 452 (1st Dist. 1972). *But see* People v. Montgomery, 179 Ill. App. 3d 330, 334, 534 N.E.2d 651, 653 (1st Dist. 1989) (mob action requires mental state of intent, knowledge and recklessness).

[460] People v. Cunningham, 123 Ill. App. 2d 190, 209, 260 N.E.2d 10, 19 (1st Dist. 1970).

[461] 720 ILCS 5/4-3(b) (1999).

[462] *See* § 2.25 of this chapter.

[463] 720 ILCS 5/4-9 (1999).

[464] 147 Ill. App. 3d 218, 497 N.E.2d 1212 (2d Dist. 1986).

late court ruled that criminal sexual assault could be satisfied by any one of these mental states, including recklessness.[465]

§ 2.37.   — Proof of Recklessness.

What actually amounts to a reckless state of mind is more difficult to assess. The operation of a motor vehicle driven several miles an hour over the posted speed limit does not amount to the recklessness necessary for reckless homicide.[466] On the other hand, the combination of excessive speed and other circumstances, such as the failure to observe a stop sign, could indicate conscious disregard of a substantial risk likely to cause death or great bodily injury for the purposes of this offense.[467] A defendant who was familiar with the narrow street as well as with its residential character, was aware of the posted speed limit of twenty-five miles per hour and was aware of a sharp curve ahead could be guilty of reckless homicide where he was driving between forty-five and fifty miles per hour and was therefore unable to negotiate the sharp curve because of the speed.[468] Where a defendant fell asleep while driving an automobile, which struck and killed a bicyclist, his conduct constituted reckless homicide in light of his own admission that he had already had some seventy-five accidents because of falling asleep at the wheel.[469]

The operation of a motor vehicle while intoxicated is prima facie evidence of a reckless act for purposes of proving guilt for reckless homicide.[470] Evidence of intoxication, therefore, while not an element of the charged offense, is probative on the issue of recklessness.[471] If the state introduces evidence of intoxication in a reckless homicide prosecution, "it need only present *some* evidence of intoxication from which, along with other circumstances, recklessness may be inferred."[472] Thus, where a defendant who was extremely intoxicated drove off the side of the road and then veered back across the center line, hitting an oncoming vehicle and causing a death, the court had no difficulty in finding reckless homicide.[473]

---

[465] People v. Burmeister, 147 Ill. App. 3d 218, 223-24, 497 N.E.2d 1212, 1215-16 (2d Dist. 1986).

[466] People v. Brajcki, 150 Ill. App. 3d 506, 512, 501 N.E.2d 774, 778-79 (2d Dist. 1986).

[467] People v. Brajcki, 150 Ill. App. 3d 506, 512, 501 N.E.2d 774, 778-79 (2d Dist. 1986). *See also* People v. Gittings, 136 Ill. App. 3d 655, 660, 483 N.E.2d 553, 558 (1st Dist. 1985) (driving greatly in excess of speed on hilly, curvy road while intoxicated was reckless).

[468] People v. Griffith, 56 Ill. App. 3d 747, 751, 372 N.E.2d 404, 407 (2d Dist. 1978).

[469] People v. Shaffer, 49 Ill. App. 3d 207, 212, 364 N.E.2d 109, 113 (2d Dist. 1977).

[470] 720 ILCS 5/9-3(b) (1999); People v. Giere, 192 Ill. App. 3d 520, 527, 548 N.E.2d 1104, 1108 (2d Dist. 1989).

[471] People v. Smith, 149 Ill. 2d 558, 565, 599 N.E.2d 888, 891 (1992).

[472] People v. Smith, 149 Ill. 2d 558, 565, 599 N.E.2d 888, 891 (1992) (emphasis added).

[473] People v. Russell, 31 Ill. App. 3d 178, 181-82, 334 N.E.2d 320, 320-22 (5th Dist. 1975).

The Illinois courts state that merely pointing a loaded pistol at another is such a gross deviation from the standard of care that a reasonable person would exercise that it constitutes recklessness[474] for the purposes of the crime of reckless conduct[475] or involuntary manslaughter.[476] In *People v. Bauman*,[477] where a defendant pointed a loaded gun at a friend, which he stated fired accidentally and killed his friend, the court held that his conduct was reckless and was a sufficient basis to warrant a finding of involuntary manslaughter.[478] The fact that the defendant did not know the gun was loaded when he pulled its trigger while it was aimed at the victim did not defeat a finding of recklessness.[479] In *People v. Schwartz*,[480] the defendant, after a conversation with the victim about a potential disagreement over the sale of cocaine, aimed a gun at the victim, cocked it, and pulled the trigger, shooting the victim. Immediately, the defendant dropped the gun, stepped back and said, "Oh, my God."[481] Although the defendant claimed he did not know that the gun was loaded, the court stated "we believe the trier of fact could have properly determined that defendant acted recklessly in not checking the condition of the gun prior to the incident. . . ."[482] Accordingly, the defendant's conviction for involuntary manslaughter was affirmed.[483] In *People v. Chew*,[484] the appellate court affirmed another involuntary manslaughter conviction where a defendant claimed he was not aware that the gun was loaded. In *Chew*, the defendant and his uncle were drinking intoxicating beverages. His uncle went to another room and came back with a shotgun, which he pointed at the defendant. Being afraid of the gun, defendant struggled to get the shotgun away from his uncle. The uncle then attempted to regain possession of the gun, and at this point the gun discharged, striking the uncle in the chest. Although evidence showed that the defendant and his uncle were on friendly terms, it also revealed that they were arguing at the time of the incident and that the defendant

---

[474] People v. Smith, 186 Ill. App. 3d 89, 94, 542 N.E.2d 112, 114 (1st Dist. 1989) (involuntary manslaughter conviction affirmed); People v. Bembroy, 4 Ill. App. 3d 522, 526, 281 N.E.2d 389, 393 (1st Dist. 1972) (involuntary manslaughter conviction supported by evidence). However, when a defendant *unintentionally* points a gun at the victim, it may not, of itself, give rise to a presumption of recklessness. See, e.g., People v. Smith, 208 Ill. App. 3d 538, 547, 567 N.E.2d 489, 495 (1st Dist. 1990) (involuntary manslaughter conviction reversed).

[475] People v. Thomas, 1 Ill. App. 3d 139, 143, 275 N.E.2d 253, 255-56 (4th Dist. 1971).

[476] People v. Schwartz, 64 Ill. App. 3d 989, 994-95, 382 N.E.2d 59, 64 (1st Dist. 1978); People v. Carlton, 26 Ill. App. 3d 995, 998, 326 N.E.2d 100, 103 (1st Dist. 1975).

[477] 34 Ill. App. 3d 582, 340 N.E.2d 178 (1st Dist. 1975).

[478] People v. Bauman, 34 Ill. App. 3d 582, 589, 340 N.E.2d 178, 183 (1st Dist. 1975).

[479] People v. Bauman, 34 Ill. App. 3d 582, 589, 340 N.E.2d 178, 183 (1st Dist. 1975).

[480] 64 Ill. App. 3d 989, 382 N.E.2d 59 (1st Dist. 1978).

[481] People v. Schwartz, 64 Ill. App. 3d 989, 991, 382 N.E.2d 59, 61 (1st Dist. 1978).

[482] People v. Schwartz, 64 Ill. App. 3d 989, 994, 382 N.E.2d 59, 64 (1st Dist. 1978).

[483] People v. Schwartz, 64 Ill. App. 3d 989, 994, 382 N.E.2d 59, 64 (1st Dist. 1978).

[484] 45 Ill. App. 3d 1024, 360 N.E.2d 417 (1st Dist. 1977).

had possession of the gun and had pulled the trigger when it discharged.[485] The court stated that notwithstanding the defendant's assertion that he did not know that the gun was loaded,

> [T]he jury could have inferred that the defendant's careless disregard for his uncle's safety while handling the gun and while possibly under the influence of alcohol was so reckless as to constitute a deviation from the standard of care which a reasonable person would exercise in a like situation. . . . We do not believe that the jury abandoned the domain of allowable inferences or entered the area of speculation in determining that defendant's conduct in shooting his uncle was reckless. . . .[486]

Recklessness can be established with respect to the use of guns without showing that the defendant pointed a gun at the victim. For example, in *People v. Zahner*,[487] the careless handling of a loaded gun was found to be a sufficient basis for recklessness. In *Zahner*, the defendant, his brother, and the deceased were engaged in a friendly wrestling match over a shotgun. At some point in this encounter, the defendant obtained exclusive possession over the gun. When the wrestling ended, he first loaded an empty shell, and then a live round, into the gun. It was the defendant's belief that the shells would fire in the order loaded. However, when he cocked the gun, it went off, fatally wounding the victim. Later, he stated that he did not know the gun was pointed at the victim or that he was pulling the trigger as the shell was jacked into the chamber. The appellate court ruled that this series of acts constituted recklessness for the purposes of involuntary manslaughter.[488]

The "accidental" discharge of a loaded gun does not constitute recklessness.[489] An accident is not a voluntary act. Nor can accidental conduct be equated with recklessness, which is an element of the offense of involuntary manslaughter.[490] Thus, where a defendant laid a gun on a table and the gun discharged, killing a little girl, the defendant's involuntary manslaughter conviction was reversed because the trial court had characterized the defendant's conduct as accidental.[491]

Furthermore, not all incidents involving the deliberate shooting of a gun evince recklessness. The shooting of a .22 caliber pistol toward the ground, for

---

[485] People v. Chew, 45 Ill. App. 3d 1024, 1028, 360 N.E.2d 417, 420 (1st Dist. 1977).

[486] People v. Chew, 45 Ill. App. 3d 1024, 1028, 360 N.E.2d 417, 420 (1st Dist. 1977) (citations omitted).

[487] 77 Ill. App. 3d 706, 396 N.E.2d 593 (3d Dist. 1979).

[488] People v. Zahner, 77 Ill. App. 3d 706, 707, 396 N.E.2d 593, 595 (3d Dist. 1979).

[489] People v. Smith, 208 Ill. App. 3d 538, 547, 567 N.E.2d 489, 495 (1st Dist. 1990); People v. Spani, 46 Ill. App. 3d 777, 780, 361 N.E.2d 377, 379 (3d Dist. 1977).

[490] People v. Spani, 46 Ill. App. 3d 777, 780, 361 N.E.2d 377, 379 (3d Dist. 1977).

[491] People v. Spani, 46 Ill. App. 3d 777, 780, 361 N.E.2d 377, 379 (3d Dist. 1977).

instance, is not reckless per se and is not an act that would be likely to cause death or bodily harm to a person some distance away.[492] The repeated discharge of a gun in a confined, residential area, on the other hand, could constitute the recklessness necessary for involuntary manslaughter.[493] Firing warning shots in the direction of the victim would be recklessness sufficient for involuntary manslaughter, even though the defendant did not intend to strike the victim and did not know the gun was actually pointed at the victim.[494] Finally, if a defendant goes so far as to deliberately fire a rifle into a crowd, causing a death, the defendant cannot argue that the conduct was merely reckless, for this conduct is sufficient for murder.[495]

With respect to the reckless use of guns, the courts are clearly willing to accept the notion of shared recklessness. Thus, where several defendants, all of whom are armed, together fire numerous shots in a confined area and kill someone with one of their bullets, all will be responsible for involuntary manslaughter.[496]

Handling an infant or child in such a rough manner that the child dies may constitute the recklessness necessary for involuntary manslaughter.[497] Thus, where a defendant dropped his wife's three-week-old infant on a bed and spanked it and the child subsequently died from the injuries, the defendant was convicted of involuntary manslaughter.[498] Similarly, the appellate court affirmed an involuntary manslaughter conviction where the defendant, who knew that his four-year-old victim's sore shoulder was causing the child pain and nonetheless was roughhousing with the victim and pushed him, whereupon the victim fell and, unable to break his fall with his sore shoulder, struck his head on the floor and died.[499] Finally, where a defendant shook his infant daughter, which resulted in her death, this act was sufficiently reckless to establish involuntary manslaughter.[500]

The failure to adequately care for a child may rise to the level of recklessness. Where a woman wrapped her newborn child, to whom she had surreptitiously given birth in a bathroom, in a towel and placed it in a small overnight case, in

---

[492] People v. Post, 39 Ill. 2d 101, 105, 233 N.E.2d 565, 567 (1968).

[493] People v. Bolden, 59 Ill. App. 3d 441, 448, 375 N.E.2d 898, 903 (1st Dist. 1978).

[494] People v. Kelly, 24 Ill. App. 3d 1018, 1025, 322 N.E.2d 527, 533 (2d Dist. 1975).

[495] People v. Tiller, 61 Ill. App. 3d 785, 794, 378 N.E.2d 282, 290 (5th Dist. 1978).

[496] People v. Bolden, 59 Ill. App. 3d 441, 447-48, 375 N.E.2d 898, 902-03 (1st Dist. 1978).

[497] People v. Yocum, 122 Ill. App. 2d 126, 133, 257 N.E.2d 793, 796 (2d Dist. 1970).

[498] People v. Yocum, 122 Ill. App. 2d 126, 133, 257 N.E.2d 793, 796 (2d Dist. 1970).

[499] People v. York, 57 Ill. App. 3d 243, 248-49, 373 N.E.2d 90, 93-94 (3d Dist. 1978).

[500] People v. Holmes, 246 Ill. App. 3d 179, 179-80, 616 N.E.2d 1000, 1001-02 (3d Dist. 1993). See also People v. Ripley, 291 Ill. App. 3d 565, 569, 685 N.E.2d 362, 365 (3d Dist. 1997) (Circumstantial evidence was sufficient to prove that injuries to fifteen-month-old child by shaking him were intentionally or knowingly inflicted, even where a defendant testified that he did not intend to injure the victim, and as such defendant was properly convicted of aggravated battery).

which it died before she removed the infant the following afternoon, the court held that this constituted the wanton and reckless disregard of life and would support an involuntary manslaughter conviction.[501] Where a defendant placed her child, who was two and one-half years old, on a highway alone at night, this conduct constituted recklessness sufficient for involuntary manslaughter.[502] The evidence was enough to convict a defendant of involuntary manslaughter where a twenty-three-month-old child, while under the sole care of the defendant, was immersed in hot liquid and no evidence existed to support any other theory about how the child's injury that ultimately caused death occurred.[503]

Where a defendant employs excessive force or makes an unjustifiable physical assault on another, there may be recklessness. Where the defendant, who was living with the nine-year-old victim's mother, administered severe beatings to the victim as punishment, he was convicted of involuntary manslaughter for having caused the death of the child, who leaped from a twelfth floor window to his death following one such severe beating.[504] Where a defendant struck an adult with his fists and, as a direct consequence of the blow, the recipient of the blow fell, struck his head, and died, there was a sufficient basis to affirm a conviction for involuntary manslaughter.[505] However, where the brutality and duration of a beating by repeatedly punching his victim as well as the severity of the victim's injuries belied a finding of mere recklessness, the defendant was properly denied instructions on involuntary manslaughter and convicted of first degree murder of the victim.[506]

There are certainly other offenses beyond involuntary manslaughter where recklessness has been an issue. For instance, in *People v. McMullen*,[507] a mentally handicapped rape victim was lured into a small room in which the defendant and two companions pulled down her pants. One boy held her hands while the defendant had sexual intercourse with her, even though the victim was crying and told her attackers she wanted to go home. The trial court instructed the jury that they could find the defendant guilty of rape if either (1) the sexual intercourse was by force, or (2) the victim lacked the mental capacity to consent.[508] The jury returned a verdict of guilty. Because of the nature of the general verdict, which made it impossible to determine the basis on which the jury rested its verdict, the appellate court considered the evidence as to both theories

---

[501] People v. Ryan, 9 Ill. 2d 467, 475-76, 138 N.E.2d 516, 520-21 (1956).

[502] People v. Eveland, 81 Ill. App. 3d 97, 101, 400 N.E.2d 1078, 1081 (4th Dist. 1980).

[503] People v. Watson, 103 Ill. App. 3d 992, 995, 431 N.E.2d 1350, 1353 (4th Dist. 1982).

[504] People v. Parker, 90 Ill. App. 3d 1052, 1057, 414 N.E.2d 190, 193 (1st Dist. 1980).

[505] People v. Parr, 35 Ill. App. 3d 539, 542, 341 N.E.2d 439, 441 (5th Dist. 1976).

[506] People v. Rodgers, 254 Ill. App. 3d 148, 153-54, 626 N.E.2d 260, 264 (2d Dist. 1993).

[507] 91 Ill. App. 3d 184, 414 N.E.2d 214 (4th Dist. 1980).

[508] People v. McMullen, 91 Ill. App. 3d 184, 186-87, 414 N.E.2d 214, 216 (4th Dist. 1980).

of rape.[509] First, the court concluded that there was ample evidence to support forcible rape.[510] Next, the court stated that since rape was a general intent crime that could be based on recklessness, it was proper to conclude that the defendant was at least reckless in his assessment that the victim had the mental capacity to consent even though the defendant himself had a limited mental capacity.[511]

In *People v. Better*,[512] various defendants were charged with obscenity[513] under a state statute which explicitly includes the mens rea of recklessness,[514] regarding certain nude, erotic dancing in a nightclub. The evidence was unclear as to the presence of defendant Cardamon, one of the operators of the business, on the night of the alleged obscene dance. The court concluded that, at a minimum, Cardamon recklessly failed to exercise reasonable inspection of the dancer's activities, which would have disclosed the content of the dance, and that he thereby wrongfully permitted it.[515]

The question has been raised about whether a physician can be held criminally reckless for prescribing a drug that is likely to cause death. In *People v. Munoz*,[516] the appellate court reversed, due to insufficient evidence, an involuntary manslaughter conviction of a physician whom the state had alleged had prescribed and caused to be administered to a geriatric patient at a state hospital a drug likely to cause death or great bodily harm to her.[517] It is important to note that the court was not rejecting the theory of criminal responsibility in such circumstances, only the evidence in the case before them.[518] On the other hand, where a defendant who was not a physician injected a transsexual with silicone, causing her death, the appellate court said he was reckless and affirmed his involuntary manslaughter conviction.[519]

---

[509] People v. McMullen, 91 Ill. App. 3d 184, 187, 414 N.E.2d 214, 216 (4th Dist. 1980).

[510] People v. McMullen, 91 Ill. App. 3d 184, 188, 414 N.E.2d 214, 216 (4th Dist. 1980).

[511] People v. McMullen, 91 Ill. App. 3d 184, 190, 414 N.E.2d 214, 218 (4th Dist. 1980). The crime of rape has been repealed in Illinois and replaced by criminal sexual assault, 720 ILCS 5/12-13 (1999) and aggravated criminal sexual assault. 720 ILCS 5/12-14 (1999). These offenses can also be established by recklessness. People v. Burmeister, 147 Ill. App. 3d 218, 223-23, 497 N.E.2d 1212, 1215-16 (2d Dist. 1986).

[512] 33 Ill. App. 3d 58, 337 N.E.2d 272 (1st Dist. 1975).

[513] 720 ILCS 5/11-20 (1999).

[514] 720 ILCS 5/11-20 (1999) ("recklessly failing to exercise reasonable inspection" of the content of disseminated material which proves to be obscene amounts to obscenity).

[515] People v. Better, 33 Ill. App. 3d 58, 66-67, 337 N.E.2d 272, 279 (1st Dist. 1975).

[516] 31 Ill. App. 3d 689, 335 N.E.2d 35 (2d Dist. 1975).

[517] People v. Munoz, 31 Ill. App. 3d 689, 694, 335 N.E.2d 35, 36-39 (2d Dist. 1975).

[518] *See* People v. Munoz, 31 Ill. App. 3d 689, 694, 335 N.E.2d 35, 36-39 (2d Dist. 1975).

[519] People v. Ellison, 100 Ill. App. 3d 282, 289-90, 426 N.E.2d 1058, 1064 (1st Dist. 1981).

Any effort to equate acting recklessly with acting intentionally or knowingly will fail.[520] If a defendant is charged with battery[521] which requires intent or knowledge, showing recklessness on the defendant's part will be insufficient as a matter of law.[522] On the other hand, one must be alert to the fact that some courts continue to confuse these concepts. For instance, in *People v. Forrest*,[523] the court stated that a defendant's "wanton and reckless disregard of human life" would satisfy murder.[524] However, the statute clearly requires intent or knowledge, not recklessness.[525]

As is true with respect to proving the elements of intent and knowledge, the mental state of recklessness can be demonstrated by reference to circumstantial evidence.[526] A jury is not bound to accept the defendant's self-serving version of the events.[527] The failure of the trial court to mention and define recklessness as an essential element of a particular crime is a reversible error.[528]

§ 2.38. — Mental States: Negligence.

The last of the four major mental states that is employed in article 5/4 of the Illinois code is that of negligence. It is defined in paragraph 5/4-7:

Negligence. A person is negligent, or acts negligently, when he fails to be aware of a substantial and unjustifiable risk that circumstances exist or a result will follow, described by the statute defining the offense; and such failure constitutes a substantial deviation from the standard of care which a reasonable person would exercise in the situation.[529]

The revision committee's comments state that negligence involves the least culpable mental state, both legally and morally, of the principal mental states of article 5/4, inasmuch as — unlike intent, knowledge, and recklessness — negligence does not contemplate awareness of the harm that will probably result from the person's acts.[530] Negligence merely reflects a person's failure to be aware of a risk he or she is creating by his or her conduct in circumstances in which the reasonable person should be aware of the risk of harm involved. In any event,

---

[520] People v. Barrington, 15 Ill. App. 3d 445, 447, 304 N.E.2d 525, 527 (3d Dist. 1973).

[521] 720 ILCS 5/12-3 (1999) (a person commits battery if he "intentionally or knowingly" without legal justification causes bodily harm or makes physical contact of an insulting nature).

[522] People v. Barrington, 15 Ill. App. 3d 445, 447, 304 N.E.2d 525, 527 (3d Dist. 1973).

[523] 133 Ill. App. 2d 70, 272 N.E.2d 813 (1st Dist. 1971).

[524] People v. Forrest, 133 Ill. App. 2d 70, 72-73, 272 N.E.2d 813, 815 (1st Dist. 1971).

[525] *See* 720 ILCS 5/9-1(a) (1999).

[526] *In re* Thur, 80 Ill. App. 3d 592, 596, 400 N.E.2d 564, 567 (1st Dist. 1980); People v. Zahner, 77 Ill. App. 3d 706, 707, 396 N.E.2d 593, 594 (3d Dist. 1979).

[527] People v. Carlton, 26 Ill. App. 3d 995, 999, 326 N.E.2d 100, 104 (1st Dist. 1975).

[528] People v. Bolden, 103 Ill. App. 2d 377, 382, 243 N.E.2d 687, 690 (1st Dist. 1968).

[529] 720 ILCS 5/4-7 (1999).

[530] ILL. ANN. STAT. ch. 38, para. 4-3 (Smith-Hurd 1989), 1961 Committee Comments, at 205.

the elemental composition of negligence involves the following factors: (1) the unconscious creation of a risk, (2) the breach of a duty that the reasonable person would exercise in the situation, and (3) a substantial deviation from the standard of care. An important consideration with respect to the framework of article 5/4 is that paragraph 5/4-3(b) has no operative effect with respect to negligence. That is to say, the normal judicial construction given a statute by reason of paragraph 5/4-3(b) — that one must imply in a statute that does not prescribe a mental state the elements of intent, knowledge, or recklessness — does not include the element of negligence. The net effect of paragraph 5/4-3(b), combined with the General Assembly's sparing use of *negligence* in the code, raises the conclusion that this final mental state is not only qualitatively, but also quantitatively, the least significant of the four basic mens rea requirements in chapter 720.

There are a few offenses like "mob action"[531] that have been judicially interpreted to include the requirements of intent, knowledge, recklessness, or negligence.[532] The code itself rarely makes reference to negligence. One example is the offense of "abuse and gross neglect of a long term care facility resident,"[533] which criminalizes, in certain circumstances, the mere negligent failure, by an owner or licensee of a nursing home or the like, to provide adequate medical or personal care to a resident of such a facility.[534] Moreover, the Illinois caselaw that refers to negligence as sufficient for a crime appears for the most part to be opinions rendered before the development of the Illinois Criminal Code of 1961.[535]

§ 2.39. — Mental States: Absolute Liability.

Except for paragraph 5/4-8, which involves ignorance or mistake of fact or law[536] — matters that will be explored in a subsequent chapter in connection with the discussion of the other affirmative defenses[537] — the only provision of article 5/4 not yet examined is paragraph 5/4-9:

---

[531] 720 ILCS 5/25-1(a) (1999).

[532] People v. Leach, 3 Ill. App. 3d 389, 392, 279 N.E.2d 450, 452 (1st Dist. 1972).

[533] 720 ILCS 5/12-19 (1999).

[534] 720 ILCS 5/12-19(b), (d)(3) (1999). This offense is punishable as a petty offense. 720 ILCS 12-19(b) (1999). "Gross neglect" of such a resident, which is defined as "recklessly failing" to provide appropriate care to a resident, 720 ILCS 12-19(d)(2) (1999), is treated as a more serious offense. 720 ILCS 12-19(c) (1999) (business offense). Finally, "abuse" of such a resident, which is defined as the intentional or knowing infliction of (1) physical or mental injury or (2) a sexual offense against the resident, 720 ILCS 12-19(d)(1), is punishable as a felony. 720 ILCS 12-19(a) (1999).

[535] *See, e.g.,* People v. Hansen, 378 Ill. 2d 491, 497, 38 N.E.2d 738, 741 (1941) (gist of involuntary manslaughter with motor vehicle is criminal negligence).

[536] 720 ILCS 5/4-8 (1999).

[537] *See* §§ 19.02-19.10 of this treatise.

Absolute Liability. A person may be guilty of an offense without having, as to each element thereof, one of the mental states described in Sections 4-4 through 4-7 if the offense is a misdemeanor which is not punishable by incarceration or by a fine exceeding $500, or the statute defining the offense clearly indicates a legislative purpose to impose absolute liability for the conduct described.[538]

The Committee Comments are again instructive:

> This section is intended to establish, as an expression of general legislative intent, rather strict limitations upon the interpretation that mental state is not an element of an offense, although the express language of the provision defining the offense fails to describe such an element. Most of the states have numerous provisions of this type, imposing upon the courts the responsibility of determining, as to each such provision, either that mental state is not an element, or (particularly in the more serious offenses) that the legislature intended that a particular mental state be implied, perhaps as a matter of common-law analogy. . . . Many such provisions are in legislation of a regulatory, police, or public welfare nature, involving the sale of specified kinds of property to certain classes of persons or to the public generally; the commission of nuisances, the violation of laws concerning motor vehicles, health, and safety; and game laws. . . . Only a few involve felonies, or misdemeanors carrying substantial confinement penalties — mainly those in which age or marital status is an element.[539]

After noting that the prior Illinois code and judicial interpretations of that code reflected considerable confusion about which offenses were absolute liability and which were not, the drafters of the code stated that these problems could be best alleviated by clearly designating the mental state requirement in the definition of each of the specific offenses in the Illinois code.[540] However, it was determined that a general restrictive rule of interpretation was necessary to address those offenses where it was unclear as to why the legislature failed to specify a mental state. Thus, unless (1) the stricture carries a relatively minor penalty — a mere fine of five hundred dollars or less — or (2) there exists a clearly indicated legislative intent to create an offense in the nature of absolute liability, a mental state requirement is implied as a matter of law for the offense in question.

The "abandonment of *mens rea*,"[541] that is at the heart of the development of absolute liability in the context of criminal liability has not been without its crit-

---

[538] 720 ILCS 5/4-9 (1999).

[539] ILL. ANN. STAT. ch. 38, para. 4-9 (Smith-Hurd 1989), 1961 Committee Comments, at 226.

[540] ILL. ANN. STAT. ch. 38, para. 4-9 (Smith-Hurd 1989), 1961 Committee Comments, at 228.

[541] CRIMINAL LAW AND ITS PROCESSES: CASES AND MATERIALS 296 (Sanford Kadish & Stephen Schulhofer, eds., 5th ed. 1989).

ics.[542] Professor Rollin Perkins, a principal authority in the field of substantive criminal law, staunchly opposes the concept.[543] His point of view can be summarized as follows: without a blameworthy mental state, there is no fault; without fault there is no crime; and to inflict imprisonment on one who has committed no crime is cruel and unusual punishment, in violation of the Eighth Amendment and of the due process clause of the Fourteenth Amendment.[544]

§ 2.40. — Judicial Interpretation and Approval of Strict Liability.

Notwithstanding this point of view, the United States Supreme Court has clearly approved of strict criminal liability. In *United States v. Balint*,[545] the Court approved in 1922 a federal absolute liability statute that prohibited the sale of a derivative of opium and a derivative of cocoa leaves not in pursuance of a written order on a form issued in blank for that purpose by the Internal Revenue Service.

> Its manifest purpose is to require every person dealing in drugs to ascertain at his peril whether that which he sells comes within the inhibition of the statute, and if he sells the inhibited drug in ignorance of its character, to penalize him. Congress weighed the possible injustice of subjecting an innocent seller to a penalty against the evil of exposing innocent purchasers to danger from the drug, and concluded that the latter was the result preferably to be avoided. Doubtless considerations as to the opportunity of the seller to find out the fact and the difficulty of proof of knowledge contributed to this conclusion. We think the demurrer to the indictment [granted by the trial court because there appeared therein no allegation of knowledge] should have been overruled.[546]

Later, in *Morissette v. United States*,[547] the Supreme Court declared that with respect to common law crimes that traditionally have required proof of a mens rea, congressional silence about whether abandonment of mens rea was clearly intended "may warrant quite contrary inferences than the same silence in creat-

---

[542] *See, e.g.*, Rollin M. Perkins, *Criminal Liability Without Fault: A Disquieting Trend*, 68 IOWA L. REV. 1067 (1983). *But see* Richard A. Wasserstrom, *Strict Liability in the Criminal Law*, 12 STAN. L. REV. 731 (1960); James B. Brady, *Strict Liability Offenses: A Justification*, 8 CRIM. L. BULL. 217 (1972) (defense of that principle). *See also* WALTER L. GORDON, CRIME AND CRIMINAL LAW: THE CALIFORNIA EXPERIENCE 1960-1975, at 7-14 (1981).

[543] Rollin M. Perkins, *Criminal Liability Without Fault: A Disquieting Trend*: 68 IOWA L. REV. 1067 (1983).

[544] Rollin M. Perkins, *Criminal Liability Without Fault: A Disquieting Trend*: 68 IOWA L. REV. 1067, 1081 (1983).

[545] 258 U.S. 250 (1922).

[546] United States v. Balint, 258 U.S. 250, 254 (1922).

[547] 342 U.S. 246 (1952).

ing an offense new to general law. . . ."[548] The Court stated that a court must judicially construe the codifications of common law criminality so as to read into the statute a mental state element unless Congress has made clear its intent that one is not required for the offense in question.[549] Here, the federal statute, a codification of common law theft, made it illegal to convert government property; there was no clear congressional pronouncement that the common law mental state had been abandoned for this particular crime; and accordingly, the Court interpreted the statute in question as requiring a mens rea.[550]

In 1971, in *United States v. Freed*,[551] the Supreme Court considered a federal statute in the nature of absolute liability that was not a reflection of common law criminality, which freed the Court from the constraints of the *Morissette* interpretative presumption doctrine. This federal stricture which prohibited the possession of unregistered hand grenades did not mention scienter. The Court upheld the statute as written while rejecting the argument that it contravened due process by failing to require that the accused had knowledge that the hand grenades were not registered.[552] The Court expressly stated that this proscription did not fall into the *Morissette* category, not only because it had no common law history, but also because of the nature of the proscribed conduct that was governed by the offense.

> This is a regulatory measure in the interest of the public safety, which may well be premised on the theory that one would hardly be surprised to learn that possession of hand grenades is not an innocent act. They are highly dangerous offensive weapons, no less dangerous than the narcotics involved in *United States v. Balint*. . . .[553]

In 1978, in *United States v. United States Gypsum Co.*,[554] the Court seemed to backtrack to a degree from its willingness to accept the strict liability concept while it sought to identify the appropriate reach of this doctrine. In this case, the defendant corporation and certain of its officers were convicted under the federal Sherman Antitrust Act for fixing prices in restraint of interstate trade and commerce in the manufacture and sale of gypsum board. The federal district court had instructed the jury that they could convict the defendants if they concluded that the effect of the defendant's activities was to fix prices. The Court observed that the various convictions rested on a principle of strict liability — a principle that the trial court had essentially adopted with reference to the

---

[548] Morissette v. United States, 342 U.S. 246, 262 (1952).

[549] Morissette v. United States, 342 U.S. 246, 262 (1952).

[550] Morissette v. United States, 342 U.S. 246, 261-63 (1952).

[551] 401 U.S. 601 (1971).

[552] United States v. Freed, 401 U.S. 601, 607-10 (1971).

[553] United States v. Freed, 401 U.S. 601, 609 (1971).

[554] 438 U.S. 422 (1978).

Sherman Act.[555] The Court felt compelled to review whether the Sherman Act lent itself to the strict liability concept and premised its analysis on the "familiar proposition" that the existence of a mens rea is the rule of, rather than the exception to, the principles of criminal jurisprudence in this country.[556] They stated that "[w]hile strict-liability offenses are not unknown to the criminal law and do not invariably offend constitutional requirements . . . the limited circumstances in which Congress has created and this Court has recognized such offenses . . . attest to their generally disfavored status."[557] With respect to the offense at hand, "the behavior proscribed by the Act is often difficult to distinguish from the gray zone of socially acceptable and economically justifiable business conduct."[558] To hold persons and entities responsible for crossing the borderline between salutary and impermissible competitive conduct without inquiring into their intent might cause business persons to act excessively cautious in the face of uncertainty about the criminal consequences of their conduct. Accordingly, the imposition of strict penal liability in these circumstances would be difficult to square with the accepted functions of the criminal law.[559] The severity of the sanctions attached to the Sherman Act militated in favor of the conclusion that absolute liability is unwarranted.[560] In summary, the Supreme Court's affirmance of the United States Court of Appeals' reversal of the Gypsum Company convictions suggests that where the nature of the conduct regulated by a statute does not lend itself to absolute liability considerations, the court will judicially construe the legislation as requiring a mental state in the absence of a clear congressional pronouncement to the contrary and, perhaps, in any event.

In *Liparota v. United States*,[561] the United States Supreme Court reiterated its position "that criminal offenses requiring no *mens rea* have a 'generally disfavored status.' "[562] In that case, the defendant had been convicted of the unlawful acquiring and possession of food stamps contrary to federal law.[563] The trial court instructed the jury about the offense without requiring proof of a wrongful mental state.[564] Following the defendant's unsuccessful appeal to the United States Court of Appeals, the defendant requested United States Supreme Court review.[565] He argued that he could only be convicted if (1) he knowingly ac-

---

[555] United States v. United States Gypsum Co., 438 U.S. 422, 434-36 (1978).

[556] United States v. United States Gypsum Co., 438 U.S. 422, 436 (1978) (emphasis original).

[557] United States v. United States Gypsum Co., 438 U.S. 422, 437-38 (1978).

[558] United States v. United States Gypsum Co., 438 U.S. 422, 440-41 (1978).

[559] United States v. United States Gypsum Co., 438 U.S. 422, 442 (1978).

[560] United States v. United States Gypsum Co., 438 U.S. 422, 442-43, n.18 (1978).

[561] 471 U.S. 419 (1985).

[562] Liparota v. United States, 471 U.S. 419, 426 (1985) (quoting United States v. United States Gypsum Co., 438 U.S. 422, 438 (1978)).

[563] Liparota v. United States, 471 U.S. 419, 421-23 (1985).

[564] Liparota v. United States, 471 U.S. 419, 422 (1985).

[565] Liparota v. United States, 471 U.S. 419, 423 (1985).

quired and possessed food stamps *and* (2) he knew he had done so in an unauthorized manner,[566] which latter element had not been part of the trial court's instruction and which the government insisted was not an element of the crime.[567]

The Supreme Court agreed with the defendant's assertions and reversed his conviction. While noting that the Congress had not explicitly included in the statute a wrongful mental state requirement,[568] the Court determined there existed no clear legislative determination that Congress intended to punish the activity in question without proof of such *mens rea*.[569] Since, in this case, the Congress had not "explicitly and unambiguously" clarified this point, the Court refused to depart "from this background assumption of our criminal law" that a wrongful *mens rea* is required.[570] To hold otherwise, would "criminalize a broad range of apparently innocent conduct,"[571] such as where a non-recipient of food stamps "possessed" such items because he or she was mistakenly sent them through the mails.[572] Furthermore, the Court stated that any ambiguity of such a statute should be addressed consistently with the principle in lenity, which requires that such ambiguity be resolved in favor of the defendant.[573] Finally, the Court rejected the argument that this was a "public welfare" offense in the nature of the one it had examined in *Freed*, where courts are more tolerant of the strict liability concept.[574] The Court responded that possession of "[a] food stamp can hardly be compared to a hand grenade."[575] Obviously, the latter type of possession would presumably alert the possessor that the possession is illegal whereas the former type of possession would not necessarily do so.[576]

In *United States v. Staples*,[577] the defendant was charged with possession of a machine gun. Defendant contended the government had not established the fact that the defendant knew that his gun, which was a semi-automatic rifle, had been modified giving it the characteristic of being a fully automatic "machinegun." The lower courts had concluded that the Government was not obliged to prove defendant's knowledge of the weapon's physical properties to convict.[578] The Court noted that "silence [as to mens rea] . . . by itself does not necessarily sug-

---

[566] Liparota v. United States, 471 U.S. 419, 422-23 (1985).

[567] Liparota v. United States, 471 U.S. 419, 422 (1985).

[568] Liparota v. United States, 471 U.S. 419, 424-25 (1985).

[569] Liparota v. United States, 471 U.S. 419, 424-25 (1985).

[570] Liparota v. United States, 471 U.S. 419, 426 (1985).

[571] Liparota v. United States, 471 U.S. 419, 426 (1985).

[572] Liparota v. United States, 471 U.S. 419, 426-27 (1985).

[573] Liparota v. United States, 471 U.S. 419, 427 (1985).

[574] Liparota v. United States, 471 U.S. 419, 432-33 (1985).

[575] Liparota v. United States, 471 U.S. 419, 433 (1985).

[576] Liparota v. United States, 471 U.S. 419, 433 (1985).

[577] 511 U.S. 600 (1994).

[578] United States v. Staples, 511 U.S. 600, 604 (1994).

gest that Congress intended to dispense with a conventional mens rea element, which would require that the defendant know the facts that make his conduct illegal. On the contrary, we must construe the statute in light of the background rules of the common law, in which the requirement of some mens rea for a crime is firmly embedded."[579] The Court concluded in the absence of clear legislative intent to not require mens rea, such was demanded of the statute and, as such, the defendant's conviction was reversed.[580]

§ 2.41.   — Strict Liability Based on Respondeat Superior Doctrine.

Although the *United States Gypsum Co.* and later cases reflects a rather dim view of the utilization of strict liability in certain contexts, the Supreme Court has approved an extension of this doctrine, namely, the concept of vicarious responsibility based on the respondeat superior doctrine.[581] This concept, the thrust of which allows a master or employer to be held responsible for the misdeeds of his or her subordinates,[582] was approved in 1943 by the Supreme Court in *United States v. Dotterweich*,[583] in which the defendant and the corporation of which he was general manager were convicted of the introduction into interstate commerce of a drug that was adulterated or misbranded. The wrongful act of the defendants' agent was imputed to the defendants themselves:

> The offense is committed . . . by all who do have such a responsible share in the furtherance of the transaction which the statute outlaws, namely, to put into the stream of interstate commerce adulterated or misbranded drugs. Hardship there doubtless may be under a statute which thus penalizes the transaction though consciousness of wrongdoing be totally wanting. Balancing relative hardships, Congress has preferred to place it upon those who have at least the opportunity of informing themselves of the existence of conditions imposed for the protection of consumers before sharing in illicit commerce, rather than to throw the hazard on the innocent public who are wholly helpless.[584]

---

[579] United States v. Staples, 511 U.S. 600, 605 (1994) (citations omitted).

[580] United States v. Staples, 511 U.S. 600, 618-19 (1994).

[581] *See* ROLLIN M. PERKINS & RONALD N. BOYCE, CRIMINAL LAW 661, 911-14 (3d ed. 1982). These authors consider this form of culpability as not involving true crimes inasmuch as imprisonment is not authorized as a consequence thereof and because of the absence of "true" wrongdoing on the part of the principal. *But see* In re Marley, 29 Cal. 2d 525, 175 P.2d 832 (1946) (imprisonment authorized in context of respondeat superior application).

[582] *See* Francis B. Sayre, *Criminal Responsibility for the Acts of Another*, 43 HARV. L. REV. 689 (1930).

[583] 320 U.S. 277 (1943).

[584] United States v. Dotterweich, 320 U.S. 277, 284-85 (1943).

In *United States v. Park*,[585] the Supreme Court in 1975 reaffirmed the vitality of this principle. Park was the president of a national retail chain for 36,000 employees and 874 retail outlets. He was convicted for a violation of the Federal Food, Drug, and Cosmetic Act because of the contamination of food by rodents in a warehouse in Baltimore even though his office was in Philadelphia. Park had been warned about the situation a year earlier by the Federal Drug Administration. The court held the defendant strictly responsible for what his agents had allowed to transpire in the warehouse:

> The requirements of foresight and vigilance imposed on responsible corporate agents [by the federal statute] are beyond question demanding, and perhaps onerous, but they are no more stringent than the public has a right to expect of those who voluntarily assume positions of authority in business enterprises whose services and products affect the health and well-being of the public that supports them.[586]

§ 2.42.   — Strict Liability: Its Disfavor in Illinois.

The Illinois Supreme Court upheld the concept of imposing liability without wrongful intent as long ago as 1919 in *People v. Fernow*.[587]

> Where a specific intent is not an element of the crime it is not always necessary that a criminal intent should exist. In the exercise of the police power for the protection of the public the performance of a specific act may constitute the crime regardless of either knowledge or intent, both of which are immaterial on the question of guilt. For the effective protection of the public the burden is placed upon the individual of ascertaining at his peril whether his act is prohibited by criminal statute.[588]

Although the Illinois courts have generally concluded that the clear legislative intent was lacking to treat various offenses as being in the nature of absolute liability and have therefore held that paragraph 5/4-3(b) required a mens rea as to these offenses, such as criminal sexual assault[589] and leaving the scene of an accident,[590] they have sustained convictions on strict liability grounds in other

---

[585] 421 U.S. 658 (1975).

[586] United States v. Park, 421 U.S. 658, 672 (1975).

[587] 286 Ill. 627, 122 N.E. 155 (1919) (possession of motor vehicle from which manufacturer's identification had been removed).

[588] 286 Ill. 627, 630, 122 N.E. 155, 157 (1919).

[589] People v. Burmeister, 147 Ill. App. 3d 218, 223-24, 497 N.E.2d 1212, 1215-16 (2d Dist. 1986) (construing ILL. REV. STAT. ch. 38, para. 12-13 (1985)).

[590] People v. Nunn, 77 Ill. 2d 243, 246-48, 396 N.E.2d 27, 30-31 (1979) (construing ILL. REV. STAT. ch. 95½, para. 11-1401(a) (1975)).

circumstances, including setting a motor vehicle in motion without authority,[591] driving a motor vehicle after revocation of driving privileges,[592] unlawful use of a driver's license,[593] operating a motor vehicle under a fraudulent permit,[594] unlawful entry into a motor vehicle,[595] and driving while intoxicated.[596] It is noteworthy that all of these offenses that the courts have said are usually in the nature of "absolute liability"[597] are violations of the Illinois Motor Vehicle Code.[598] Regarding chapter 720 crimes, the courts usually treat them as crimes requiring a mens rea even where the offense in question, such as criminal trespass,[599] is a relatively minor one. The court typically concludes that if the offense carries the substantial consequences of imprisonment and large fines, strict liability is not warranted.[600] Where the offense in question is malum prohibitum, such as a municipal animal control ordinance,[601] which is not true of most chapter 720 crimes, then the court may tolerate strict culpability. Thus, when one encounters a new chapter 720 offense, such as "drug induced infliction of bodily harm"[602] that reflects no mental state requirement on its face, one must consider whether the courts are prepared to accept it at face value or, instead, reject it in the context of absolute liability.

---

[591] *See, e.g., In re* J.R., 82 Ill. App. 3d 714, 716-17, 403 N.E.2d 114, 117 (5th Dist. 1980) (construing ILL. REV. STAT. ch. 95½, para. 4-102(b) (1977)).

[592] People v. Turner, 64 Ill. 2d 183, 185, 354 N.E.2d 897, 898-99 (1976) (construing ILL. REV. STAT. ch. 95½, para. 6-303(a) (1973)).

[593] People v. Van Cura, 49 Ill. App. 3d 157, 159, 364 N.E.2d 564, 565-66 (2d Dist. 1977), *cert. denied*, 434 U.S. 1034 (1978) (construing ILL. REV. STAT. ch. 95½, para. 6-301 (1973)).

[594] People v. White Bros. Equip. Co., 63 Ill. App. 3d 445, 450, 380 N.E.2d 396, 400-01 (5th Dist. 1978) (construing ILL. REV. STAT. ch. 95½, para. 15-301(i) (1975)).

[595] People v. Ruberg, 76 Ill. App. 3d 671, 672-74, 395 N.E.2d 205, 206-08 (3d Dist. 1979) (construing ILL. REV. STAT. ch. 95½, para. 4-102(b) (1975)).

[596] People v. Teschner, 76 Ill. App. 3d 124, 125-27, 394 N.E.2d 893, 894-95 (2d Dist. 1979) (construing ILL. REV. STAT. ch. 95½, para. 11-501 (1977)).

[597] *See, e.g.,* People v. Espenscheid, 109 Ill. App. 2d 107, 111, 249 N.E.2d 866, 868-69 (3d Dist. 1969) (construing ILL. REV. STAT. ch. 38, para. 6-303 (1967) (driving an automobile on suspended license)).

[598] 625 ILCS 5/1-100 et seq. (1999).

[599] People v. Ulatowski, 54 Ill. App. 3d 893, 896-97, 368 N.E.2d 174, 176 (4th Dist. 1977) (construing ILL. REV. STAT. ch. 38, para. 21-3 (1975)).

[600] People v. Clark, 71 Ill. App. 3d 381, 395, 389 N.E.2d 911, 921 (2d Dist. 1979) (construing ILL. REV. STAT. ch. 36, para. 38 (1975) (violation of county treasurer's act not absolute liability offense considering sanctions)).

[601] Village of Northbrook v. Cannon, 61 Ill. App. 3d 315, 320, 377 N.E.2d 1208, 1212 (1st Dist. 1978).

[602] 720 ILCS 5/12-4.7 (1999).

CHAPTER 3

ACCOUNTABILITY FOR THE CRIMINALITY OF OTHERS

§ 3.01. Introduction.

The commission of a crime often involves the participation of more than one person. For example, a bank robbery might include one person who masterminds the job, another who supplies weapons, a third who actually enters the bank to make an unlawful demand for cash, a fourth who acts as a getaway driver, and a fifth who provides a hideout after a crime is completed. Although the state has a strong interest in convicting the person who actually robbed the bank, an equally compelling interest lies in convicting anyone else who aided in the crime's commission. Accordingly, all persons who participate in the commission of a crime either directly or indirectly may be considered parties to the crime and may be accountable for the crime's commission. In Illinois, sections 5/5-1, 5/5-2, and 5/5-3 of chapter 720 contain the bulk of the law applicable to the identification, prosecution, conviction, and sentencing of individuals who are accountable for the criminal conduct of another.[1] In addition, article 5/5 includes prohibitions dealing with criminal responsibility of a corporation for the conduct of its agents[2] and strictures aimed at the liability of corporate agents for criminal acts engaged in on behalf of a corporation.[3] Finally, there are other crimes for which persons[4] who wrongfully lent assistance to others engaging in criminality may be convicted that do not fall within the ambits of the state's accomplice liability statute.[5]

Accountability, unlike conspiracy[6] or solicitation,[7] is not a separate and distinct offense.[8] Rather, accountability principles provide an alternative method or theory of proof whereby a defendant is held responsible for a crime that he personally did not commit, but which was actually committed by another individual.[9] Thus, a defendant who is accountable for another's criminal conduct can be charged and tried for the same offense as a perpetrator even though his participation in the crime falls short of direct personal involvement in its actual commission.[10]

§ 3.02. Common Law.

Accountability principles have a long history in criminal law. At common law, parties to a felony were separated into four categories depending on their role in the felony: (1) principal in the first degree; (2) principal in the second degree; (3) accessory before the fact; and (4) accessory after the fact.[11]

A principal in the first degree was the actual criminal perpetrator.[12] A principal in the second degree was any person actually or constructively present at the felony's commission who aided or stood ready to aid a principal in the first de-

---

[1] 720 ILCS 5/5-1 through 5/5-3 (1999).

[2] 720 ILCS 5/5-4 (1999).

[3] 720 ILCS 5/5-5 (1999).

[4] It is important to understand that the term "person" is defined in Illinois as any "individual, public or private corporation, government, partnership, or unincorporated association." 720 ILCS 5/2-15 (1999).

[5] See, e.g., 720 ILCS 5/31-4 (1999) (obstructing justice); 720 ILCS 5/31-5 (1999) (concealing or aiding fugitive); 720 ILCS 5/31-7 (1999) (aiding another's escape from penal institution); and 720 ILCS 5/32-1 (1999) (compounding crime).

[6] 720 ILCS 5/8-2 (1999).

[7] 720 ILCS 5/8-1 (1999).

[8] People v. Williams, 28 Ill. App. 3d 402, 404, 328 N.E.2d 682, 683-84 (5th Dist. 1975).

[9] People v. Brown, 197 Ill. App. 3d 907, 919, 557 N.E.2d 199, 207 (1st Dist. 1990).

[10] People v. Taylor, 164 Ill. 2d 131, 139, 646 N.E.2d 567, 571 (1995).

[11] WAYNE LAFAVE & AUSTIN SCOTT, CRIMINAL LAW § 6-6 (2d ed. 1986).

[12] WAYNE LAFAVE & AUSTIN SCOTT, CRIMINAL LAW § 6-6(a) (2d ed. 1986). There could be more than one principal in the first degree to the commission of a crime. Id.

gree.[13] An accessory before the fact was any person not present at the felony's commission who, before the felony, aided, counseled, commanded or procured a principal.[14] An accessory after the fact was any person who, after the felony's commission, knowingly aided a felon in order to hinder the apprehension, conviction, or punishment of the felon.[15] Originally, at common law an accessory after the fact was considered a party to the crime and subject to the same treatment as members of the other categories.[16] However, because his or her participation occurred after the felony's commission, the later common law recognized an accessory after the fact as an obstructor of justice and subjected him or her to different and lesser penalties than members of the other classes.[17]

Generally, principals and accessories before the fact could be prosecuted, convicted, and punished alike.[18] However, an accessory before the fact could not be convicted before a principal,[19] convicted if the principal was acquitted,[20] or convicted of a higher degree of the crime than the principal.[21] An accessory before the fact could be tried only in a jurisdiction where his or her acts as an accessory occurred.[22] Strict pleading rules precluded a conviction if one charged as an accessory was found to have been a principal or if the proof showed that one charged as a principal had actually been an accessory.[23] While these requirements may seem odd today, the rationale for them was to safeguard a party who had not been directly involved in the felony's commission, because at common law most felonies were capital offenses punishable by death.[24]

---

[13] WAYNE LAFAVE & AUSTIN SCOTT, CRIMINAL LAW § 6-6(b) (2d ed. 1986). A person was considered constructively present when he or she was physically absent from the crime scene but was in a position to aid or encourage the principal in the first degree if the need arose (for example, a lookout or someone who signaled the victim's approach was considered constructively present). Id.

[14] WAYNE LAFAVE & AUSTIN SCOTT, CRIMINAL LAW § 6-6(c) (2d ed. 1986).

[15] WAYNE LAFAVE & AUSTIN SCOTT, CRIMINAL LAW § 6-9(a) (2d ed. 1986).

[16] WAYNE LAFAVE & AUSTIN SCOTT, CRIMINAL LAW § 6-9(a) (2d ed. 1986).

[17] WAYNE LAFAVE & AUSTIN SCOTT, CRIMINAL LAW § 6-9(a) (2d ed. 1986).

[18] WAYNE LAFAVE & AUSTIN SCOTT, CRIMINAL LAW § 6-9(a) (2d ed. 1986).

[19] WAYNE LAFAVE & AUSTIN SCOTT, CRIMINAL LAW § 6-6(d)(3) (2d. ed. 1986). He or she could, however, be jointly tried with the principal. Id.

[20] WAYNE LAFAVE & AUSTIN SCOTT, CRIMINAL LAW § 6-6(d)(3) (2d. ed. 1986). The same result would follow if the principal was later pardoned or if his or her conviction was reversed on appeal. Id.

[21] WAYNE LAFAVE & AUSTIN SCOTT, CRIMINAL LAW § 6-6(d)(3), at 573 n. 61 (2d ed. 1986).

[22] WAYNE LAFAVE & AUSTIN SCOTT, CRIMINAL LAW § 6-6(d)(1) (2d ed. 1986).

[23] WAYNE LAFAVE & AUSTIN SCOTT, CRIMINAL LAW § 6-6(d)(2) (2d ed. 1986).

[24] WAYNE LAFAVE & AUSTIN SCOTT, CRIMINAL LAW § 6-6(d) (2d ed. 1986).

§ 3.03. Modern Accountability for Conduct of Another.

In 1846, Illinois abolished any legal distinction between a principal and an accessory before the fact, and all parties to a crime were deemed principals for the purposes of prosecution, conviction, and sentencing.[25] This is essentially the state of the law today. However, the Criminal Code of 1961, in accordance with the Model Penal Code, went one step further when it removed all references to the common law designations from the statutes.[26] Today, the term accomplice is generally used to describe any person who could previously have been indicted as either a principal or accessory before the fact.[27] While the common law categories have been abrogated by statute, a familiarity with the common law categories and their meanings is still helpful, since many courts continue to use the common law designations to characterize and identify the various roles played by a defendant in the crime's commission.[28]

§ 3.04. — Accomplice Liability Codified.

Paragraph 5/5-1 states the general principal that criminal liability can be based on the conduct of another person, while paragraph 5/5-2 states the circumstances in which a person is legally accountable for the conduct of another.[29] Paragraph 5/5-1 reads: "A person is responsible for conduct which is an element of an offense if the conduct is either that of the person himself, or that of another and he is legally accountable for such conduct as provided in Section 5-2, or both."[30] Paragraph 5/5-2 provides:

> A person is legally accountable for the conduct of another when: (a) Having a mental state described by the statute defining the offense, he causes another to perform the conduct, and the other person in fact or by reason of legal incapacity lacks such a mental state; or (b) The statute defining the offense makes him so accountable; or (c) Either before or during the commission of an offense, and with the intent to promote or facilitate such commission, he solicits, aids, abets, agrees or attempts to aid, such other person in the planning or commission of the offense. However, a person is not so accountable, unless the statute defining the offense provides otherwise, if: (1) He is a victim of the offense committed; or (2) The offense is so defined that his conduct was inevitably incident to its commission; or (3) Before the commission of the offense, he terminates his effort to pro-

---

[25] Baxter v. People, 8 Ill. 368, 383 (1846).

[26] See ILL. ANN. STAT. ch. 38, para. 5-2 (Smith-Hurd 1989), 1961 Committee Comments, at 235.

[27] People v. Turner, 92 Ill. App. 3d 265, 268, 415 N.E.2d 1114, 1117 (1st Dist. 1980).

[28] See, e.g., People v. Allen, 119 Ill. App. 3d 186, 193, 456 N.E.2d 336, 341 (4th Dist. 1983) (defendant was an "accessory after the fact").

[29] ILL. ANN. STAT. ch. 38, para. 5-1 (Smith-Hurd 1989), 1961 Committee Comments, at 232.

[30] 720 ILCS 5/5-1 (1999).

mote or facilitate such commission, and does one of the following: wholly deprives his prior efforts of effectiveness in such commission, or gives timely warning to the proper law enforcement authorities, or otherwise makes proper effort to prevent the commission of the offense.[31]

The revision committee responsible for drafting these provisions points out that subparagraph (a) was designed to hold a defendant criminally accountable for the conduct of another where he or she induces an "innocent agent," such as a child below the age of legal capacity or an insane person, to commit a crime on his or her behalf.[32] Meanwhile, subparagraph (b) was created to address the situation, not otherwise covered by the accountability statute, in which a particular statute imposes vicarious responsibility on a defendant for the conduct of another.[33] Such a case could arise, for instance, where a specific offense holds a tavern owner criminally responsible for an employee's sale of liquor to a minor.[34] Here, the particular provision would prevail.[35]

Subparagraph (c) represents the central provision of accomplice liability. It holds a defendant responsible for the conduct of another in circumstances where, at common law, the defendant was considered a principal in the second degree or an accessory before the fact.[36] It is necessary to prove that the defendant had the requisite intent to aid and abet the principal's wrongdoing.[37] It is noteworthy that the attempt to aid and abet, or a conspiracy with another, can give rise to accomplice liability.[38]

Subparagraphs (c)(1), (c)(2), and (c)(3) are designed to limit the reach of accomplice liability in circumstances otherwise covered by the general language of subparagraph (c). Subparagraph (c)(1) protects the victim of the principal's conduct. For instance, the victim of an extortion scheme who willingly pays ransom money or a girl under the age of consent who encourages an adult male to have sexual relations with her cannot be punished for the substantive crime of extortion or statutory rape even though each actually "aided" the principal.[39]

Subparagraph (c)(2) relieves from accomplice liability the person who, while not technically a victim, the legislature did not believe should be punished when it created the substantive crime but whose conduct is a necessary incident of the substantive crime. The person who purchases an illicit narcotic, accepts the solicitation of a prostitute, or accepts a bribe may not be wholly innocent; how-

---

[31] 720 ILCS 5/5-2 (1999).

[32] ILL. ANN. STAT. ch. 38, para. 5-1 (Smith-Hurd 1989), 1961 Committee Comments, at 232-33.

[33] ILL. ANN. STAT. ch. 38, para. 5-1 (Smith-Hurd 1989), 1961 Committee Comments, at 235.

[34] ILL. ANN. STAT. ch. 38, para. 5-1 (Smith-Hurd 1989), 1961 Committee Comments, at 235.

[35] ILL. ANN. STAT. ch. 38, para. 5-1 (Smith-Hurd 1989), 1961 Committee Comments, at 235.

[36] ILL. ANN. STAT. ch. 38, para. 5-1 (Smith-Hurd 1989), 1961 Committee Comments, at 235-36.

[37] ILL. ANN. STAT. ch. 38, para. 5-1 (Smith-Hurd 1989), 1961 Committee Comments, at 236.

[38] ILL. ANN. STAT. ch. 38, para. 5-1 (Smith-Hurd 1989), 1961 Committee Comments, at 236.

[39] ILL. ANN. STAT. ch. 38, para. 5-1 (Smith-Hurd 1989), 1961 Committee Comments, at 236.

ever, law enforcement concerns might not be advanced by prosecuting the illicit drug purchaser, prostitution patron, or bribe-taker for violation of a law designed to punish the more egregious conduct of the drug seller, the prostitute, or the bribemaker.[40] Of course, if the legislature determined, for instance, that the bribe-taker should be punished, this can be accomplished by creating a particular statute directed at his or her conduct.[41]

Subparagraph (c)(3) provides an inducement to a defendant, who has engaged in conduct that might otherwise aid and abet, to disassociate himself or herself from a criminal scheme before it occurs.[42] The defendant will be relieved of liability if he or she discontinues his or her aiding and abetting effort *and* takes some affirmative steps to stop the crime. Even where the criminal efforts by the principal reach fruition, the accomplice's *timely* attempt to stop the offense from occurring will preclude a finding of accomplice liability.[43] Thus, subparagraphs (c)(1), (c)(2) and (c)(3) relieve such persons from criminal liability if there is no specific provision to the contrary.

Paragraph 5/5-3 makes it clear that many of the common law barriers discussed above that would relieve an accomplice of criminal liability no longer exist in Illinois:

> A person who is legally accountable for the conduct of another which is an element of an offense may be convicted upon proof that the offense was committed and that he was so accountable, although the other person claimed to have committed the offense has not been prosecuted or convicted, or has been convicted of a different offense or degree of offense, or is not amenable to justice, or has been acquitted.[44]

By enacting this provision, which complements paragraph 5/5-2, the revision committee sought to accomplish a significant departure from the common law rules of accomplice liability.[45] Those criminal actors previously referred to as principals in the first degree, principals in the second degree, and accessories before the fact (but not accessories after the fact) are all treated as principals for purposes of prosecution, conviction, and sentencing.[46] Today, the Illinois accountability law does *not* require the principal to be found guilty as a prerequisite to a finding of guilty of the accountable accessory.[47] An accomplice can, as

---

[40] ILL. ANN. STAT. ch. 38, para. 5-1 (Smith-Hurd 1989), 1961 Committee Comments, at 236.

[41] ILL. ANN. STAT. ch. 38, para. 5-1 (Smith-Hurd 1989), 1961 Committee Comments, at 236.

[42] ILL. ANN. STAT. ch. 38, para. 5-1 (Smith-Hurd 1989), 1961 Committee Comments, at 236.

[43] ILL. ANN. STAT. ch. 38, para. 5-1 (Smith-Hurd 1989), 1961 Committee Comments, at 237.

[44] 720 ILCS 5/5-3 (1999).

[45] ILL. ANN. STAT. ch. 38, para. 5-2 (Smith-Hurd 1989), 1961 Committee Comments, at 287.

[46] 720 ILCS 5/5-2(c) (1999). *See also* People v. Gonzales, 77 Ill. App. 2d 124, 221 N.E.2d 674 (2d Dist. 1966) (abstract).

[47] People v. Schmitt, 131 Ill. 2d 128, 139, 545 N.E.2d 665, 669 (1989).

a general rule, be convicted even though a principal has been acquitted in a separate trial.[48] The only exception to this seems to be that inconsistent verdicts are not permitted where the evidence presented to the same fact finder in the same trial is "identical in all respects" as to each defendant.[49] An accomplice may be convicted of a different[50] or more serious offense than a principal,[51] and an accomplice may be subjected to a different punishment than a principal where each is convicted of the same offense.[52] However, when an accomplice is involved in a criminal venture with more than one principal who are common perpetrators of a particular crime, the accomplice cannot be convicted multiple times on the same charge on the theory that he or she aided and abetted different offenders' criminality.[53] For example, a defendant who aided two persons in their illegal entry into an apartment could not be convicted for aiding and abetting two counts of home invasion since both counts arose from the same physical entry into the same apartment.[54]

When the facts of a case show that two persons were involved in the commission of a crime where one party was necessarily the perpetrator and the other an accomplice, the court is not required to determine which party was in fact the criminal perpetrator as long as it is shown that the crime was indeed committed.[55] Thus, where two defendants were involved in a shooting but it was unclear which one had actually handled the gun, both could be held responsible for the illegal shooting.[56] However, in the case where an accomplice and a co-defendant

---

[48] People v. Wehmeyer, 155 Ill. App. 3d 931, 943, 509 N.E.2d 605, 613 (2d Dist. 1987).

[49] People v. Wehmeyer, 155 Ill. App. 3d 931, 943, 509 N.E.2d 605, 613 (2d Dist. 1987) ("Conversely, where codefendants are tried separately before different triers of fact, the acquittal of one codefendant does not have any bearing on the guilt of a codefendant regardless of the nature of the evidence presented. Part of the reason for this distinction is that the attitudes of each trier of fact may differ which could result in conflicting resolutions of factual disputes and credibility assessments"). See also People v. Morrow, 303 Ill. App. 3d 671, 677, 708 N.E.2d 430, 437 (1st Dist. 1999) ("The slightest difference in the evidence can be sufficient to support different verdicts").

[50] People v. Ruiz, 78 Ill. App. 3d 326, 332-34, 396 N.E.2d 1314, 1319-20 (1st Dist. 1979) (proper to prosecute principal for murder even though accomplice pled guilty to involuntary manslaughter).

[51] People v. Luigs, 96 Ill. App. 3d 700, 703-04, 421 N.E.2d 961, 964 (5th Dist. 1981) (rape conviction upheld even though principal who was actual perpetrator was convicted of attempted rape in a separate trial).

[52] People v. Colone, 56 Ill. App. 3d 1018, 1021, 372 N.E.2d 871, 874 (1st Dist. 1978).

[53] People v. Brown, 197 Ill. App. 3d 907, 918-19, 557 N.E.2d 199, 207 (1st Dist. 1990).

[54] People v. Brown, 197 Ill. App. 3d 907, 918-19, 557 N.E.2d 199, 207 (1st Dist. 1990).

[55] People v. Torres, 100 Ill. App. 3d 931, 937-38, 427 N.E.2d 329, 335-36 (1st Dist. 1981) (reckless conduct convictions arising out of shooting of gun upheld).

[56] People v. Torres, 100 Ill. App. 3d 931, 937-38, 427 N.E.2d 329, 335-36 (1st Dist. 1981); In Interest of C.L., 180 Ill. App. 3d 173, 183-84, 534 N.E.2d 1330, 1337-38 (1st Dist. 1989) (aggravated assault convictions arising out of pointing guns at victims upheld even though evidence unclear as to which defendant handled the gun).

are involved in a single offense, the accomplice cannot be held accountable for his own conduct as well as the co-defendant's conduct.[57] In other words, the accomplice can be convicted of only one crime, not two, where the parties conduct led to only one offense.[58] Modern pleading rules have been similarly relaxed from their common law counterparts, and a defendant charged as a principal may be properly convicted as an accessory.[59]

§ 3.05. — Elements of Accomplice Liability.

The basic elements of accountability for the criminal conduct of another, as provided for in paragraph 5/5-2, are: (1) either before or during the commission of an offense, and (2) with the intent to promote or facilitate the commission, (3) a person solicits, aids, abets, or agrees or attempts to aid (4) another in the planning or commission of a crime. An exploration of the basic elements of accomplice liability — the actus reus and mens rea — will reveal the scope of this theory of criminal liability.

§ 3.06. The Actus Reus of Accomplice Liability.

The key element in accountability is affirmative conduct on the part of an accomplice that in some way aids, encourages, or incites another person to commit an illegal act.[60] The "principal attribute" of this theory of criminality is a defendant's affirmative conduct in support of another's criminal wrongdoing.[61] Thus, where defendants were acting "at cross purposes, spontaneously shooting at each other" neither could be accountable for the other's actions in striking and wounding an innocent victim.[62] This conduct must occur either before or during the crime's commission.[63] Thus, it is critical to determine whether the offense is complete at the point where a defendant becomes involved in another's criminality for such defeats the possibility of convicting the defendant of the latter's crimes. Thus, where a defendant aided another in an escape from the scene of the latter's armed robbery, the defendant could not be convicted of the latter's armed robbery on an accountability theory since the defendant had not been involved in the actual planning before or commission of the armed robbery.[64] As the sections below reveal, there are numerous ways in which this

[57] People v. Hicks, 181 Ill. 2d 541, 549, 693 N.E.2d 373, 377 (1988) (defendant could be convicted of only one count of home invasion based on his own entry into home and not a second count based on accomplice's simultaneous effort).

[58] People v. Hicks, 181 Ill. 2d 541, 549, 693 N.E.2d 373, 377 (1988).

[59] People v. Cooney, 136 Ill. App. 3d 989, 1009, 484 N.E.2d 802, 815 (2d Dist. 1985), cert. denied, 476 U.S. 115 (1986).

[60] People v. Peterson, 273 Ill. App. 3d 412, 419, 652 N.E.2d 1252, 1258 (1st Dist. 1995).

[61] People v. Peterson, 273 Ill. App. 3d 412, 419, 652 N.E.2d 1252, 1258 (1st Dist. 1995).

[62] People v. Peterson, 273 Ill. App. 3d 412, 419, 652 N.E.2d 1252, 1258 (1st Dist. 1995).

[63] People v. Furby, 138 Ill. 2d 434, 456, 563 N.E.2d 421, 430 (1990).

[64] People v. Dennis, 181 Ill. 2d 87, 101, 692 N.E.2d 325, 333-36 (1998).

the sections below reveal, there are numerous ways in which this affirmative conduct on the part of the accomplice can be shown.

§ 3.07. — Active Assistance.

The easiest class of cases are those in which the accomplice has actively assisted or participated in the criminal venture. Before the crime, the accomplice might supply a gun to another bent on murder,[65] money to a person hired to commit murder,[66] gasoline to be used by an arsonist,[67] or deliver the eventual victim of a murder to the perpetrators.[68] One who holds a victim,[69] strikes a victim,[70] or ties up a victim[71] while the principal carries out his criminal effort is accountable. A defendant who prevents a third party from aiding the victim,[72] or who diverts the victim's attention[73] in order to facilitate the commission of a crime is liable. Certainly, where a defendant acts as an interpreter or translator during an illegal drug transaction, he or she facilitates the commission of a crime.[74] It makes no difference that the crime would have been committed even without the accomplice's aid.[75] Thus, a defendant who held a cigarette lighter to provide additional light while several co-defendants bent on rape repeatedly sexually assaulted their victim[76] was as guilty as the defendant who lured an eventual murder victim to the scene of the crime.[77] However, it must be understood that "active participation" in a crime is not required to make one an

---

[65] People v. Tate, 63 Ill. 2d 105, 107-08, 345 N.E.2d 480, 483-84 (1976).

[66] People v. Nelson, 33 Ill. 2d 48, 50-52, 210 N.E.2d 212, 213-14 (1965), *cert. denied*, 383 U.S. 918 (1966).

[67] In Interest of Weigler, 37 Ill. App. 3d 478, 479-80, 346 N.E.2d 171, 173 (4th Dist. 1976).

[68] People v. Taylor, 199 Ill. App. 3d 933, 941, 557 N.E.2d 917, 922-23 (4th Dist. 1990).

[69] People v. Davis, 43 Ill. App. 3d 603, 614, 357 N.E.2d 96, 104-05 (1st Dist. 1976) (during an attempted murder).

[70] People v. Lykins, 65 Ill. App. 3d 808, 811, 382 N.E.2d 1242, 1246 (4th Dist. 1978) (during robbery-murder).

[71] People v. Ellis, 93 Ill. App. 3d 981, 985, 418 N.E.2d 88, 91 (1st Dist. 1981) (during robbery-murder), *cert. denied*, 456 U.S. 907 (1982).

[72] People v. Richardson, 61 Ill. App. 3d 718, 730, 377 N.E.2d 1235, 1244 (1st Dist. 1978) (during deviant sexual assault).

[73] People v. Cole, 50 Ill. App. 3d 133, 143, 365 N.E.2d 133, 140 (5th Dist. 1977) (during murder), *cert. denied*, 435 U.S. 944 (1978).

[74] People v. Aguirre, 242 Ill. App. 3d 469, 473, 610 N.E.2d 771, 775 (3d Dist. 1993) (during unlawful delivery of a controlled substance).

[75] WAYNE LAFAVE & AUSTIN SCOTT, CRIMINAL LAW § 6-7(a) (2d ed. 1986).

[76] People v. Gray, 87 Ill. App. 3d 142, 147, 408 N.E.2d 1150, 1154-55 (1st Dist. 1980) (during rape and subsequent murder of victim), *cert. denied*, 450 U.S. 1032 (1981).

[77] People v. Taylor, 199 Ill. App. 3d 933, 941, 557 N.E.2d 917, 923 (4th Dist. 1990) (first degree murder); People v. Ruiz, 94 Ill. 2d 245, 255, 447 N.E.2d 148, 152 (1982) (murder).

accomplice.[78] While accomplice liability "need not rely on the defendant's overt act of assistance," it has been held "the fact finder can properly infer the defendant's support from his approving presence at the scene of the crime."[79]

§ 3.08. — Attempt to Aid.

In Illinois, an "attempt to aid" another in the commission of a crime is sufficient conduct to establish accountability.[80] Based on this rule, a defendant who supplied a criminal perpetrator with a weapon for use in a crime would be accountable even where a different weapon was used to commit the crime.[81] However, the question might arise as to whether a person's unsuccessful efforts toward assistance of the perpetrator that are *not* known to the perpetrator would make that person an accomplice to the perpetrator's criminality. While no Illinois cases address this issue, presumably the Illinois statute covers *all* attempts to aid, since this is the position taken by the Model Penal Code[82] from which the Illinois statute was drafted.[83]

The "attempt to aid" language would presumably provide the state with a basis for prosecuting multiple offenders where they are literally competing amongst themselves to be the principal perpetrator, such as where each wants to be sole triggerman in a shooting. Thus, where a defendant admitted that he pointed a rifle toward the street from the window of a tenth-floor apartment with the intent to kill a certain individual, whereupon another person seized the rifle from the defendant, saying "I want to do it; let me do it," and then the other person aimed the weapon and fired, missing the intended victim and striking a pedestrian, there was a sufficient effort by the defendant to convict him of murder.[84] The rationale for this type of rule seems sound since one who has the intent to commit the crime should not be vindicated by a failed purpose or a change in plans or circumstances at the crime's commission absent an effective withdrawal from the venture.[85]

---

[78] People v. Batchelor, 171 Ill. 2d 367, 374, 665 N.E.2d 777, 780 (1996); People v. Ruiz, 94 Ill. 2d 245, 254-55, 447 N.E.2d 148, 151 (1982).

[79] People v. Fuller, 91 Ill. App. 3d 922, 929, 415 N.E.2d 502, 507 (1st Dist. 1980).

[80] 720 ILCS 5/5-2(c) (1999).

[81] WAYNE LAFAVE & AUSTIN SCOTT, CRIMINAL LAW § 6-7(a) (2d ed. 1986).

[82] WAYNE LAFAVE & AUSTIN SCOTT, CRIMINAL LAW § 6-7(a), at 579 (2d ed. 1986) (citing MODEL PENAL CODE § 2.06(3)(a)(ii)).

[83] ILL. REV. STAT. ch. 38, para. 5-2 (Smith-Hurd 1989), 1961 Committee Comments, at 235.

[84] People v. Carter, 40 Ill. App. 3d 881, 884, 353 N.E.2d 260, 262 (1st Dist. 1976).

[85] People v. Gregory, 43 Ill. App. 3d 1052, 1056, 357 N.E.2d 1251, 1254 (1st Dist. 1976) (defendant whose confession established that he had formed intent to commit armed robbery before his accomplice committed murder of robbery victim during that robbery was properly held accountable for both crimes).

§ 3.09. — Solicitation or Encouragement.

One who commands, encourages, requests, or otherwise solicits another to commit a crime is accountable for the other person's criminal act.[86] Thus, a defendant was found guilty of aiding and abetting the sale of marijuana when he advised an undercover narcotics officer that the marijuana the officer was purchasing from another was of good quality and worth the selling price.[87] The solicitation can occur before or during the crime and criminal accountability can occur even in cases where the defendant is not present at the crime scene.[88] Thus, a defendant who requests another to commit a murder but is not present when the murder is committed[89] is as liable as the defendant at the scene who encouraged his companion to kill the victim by shouting "blow him, blow him, he'll trick."[90]

The encouragement can occur long before the crime is actually committed. For example, a defendant who discussed killing the victim with the actual perpetrators one month before the murder occurred could not escape liability.[91]

Standing by ready to render aid to a principal may constitute sufficient encouragement provided that the accomplice's intention to render aid is known to the principal.[92] Thus, where a defendant stood stationary for eight minutes in a restaurant during a robbery with his eyes fixed on an employee of the restaurant throughout the robbery, at no point asking for service, the fact that he may not have displayed a weapon which he had on his person and remained silent during the robbery perpetrated by another did not relieve him of accomplice liability for the robbery.[93] Here, the restaurant employees had offered no resistance during the robbery and no customers came into the restaurant and, accordingly, his failure to exhibit a more active role in the robbery was attributable to there being "no need for him to speak" or the like.[94] On the other hand, an undisclosed intention to render aid is not tantamount to "encouragement"[95] and an expression of mere enmity toward a victim is not a "solicitation."[96] In order to convict a person of a crime on the basis of his encouragement, it must be shown that the

---

[86] 720 ILCS 5/5-2(c) (1999).

[87] People v. Van Riper, 127 Ill. App. 2d 394, 397-98, 262 N.E.2d 141, 143 (2d Dist. 1970), *cert. denied*, 403 U.S. 918 (1971).

[88] People v. Tiller, 94 Ill. 2d 303, 309, 447 N.E.2d 174, 180 (1982), *cert. denied*, 461 U.S. 944 (1983).

[89] People v. Nelson, 33 Ill. 2d 48, 50-52, 210 N.E.2d 212, 213-14 (1965), *cert. denied*, 383 U.S. 918 (1966); People v. Rybka, 16 Ill. 2d 394, 405-06, 158 N.E.2d 17, 23-24 (1959).

[90] People v. Cobb, 97 Ill. App. 3d 615, 616, 422 N.E.2d 1106, 1107 (1st Dist. 1981).

[91] People v. Holmes, 67 Ill. 2d 236, 240, 367 N.E.2d 663, 665 (1977).

[92] People v. Hunter, 42 Ill. App. 3d 947, 950-51, 356 N.E.2d 822, 825 (1st Dist. 1976).

[93] People v. Hunter, 42 Ill. App. 3d 947, 950-51, 356 N.E.2d 822, 825 (1st Dist. 1976).

[94] People v. Hunter, 42 Ill. App. 3d 947, 950-51, 356 N.E.2d 822, 825 (1st Dist. 1976).

[95] Hicks v. United States, 150 U.S. 442, 450 (1893).

[96] People v. Mitchell, 12 Ill. App. 3d 960, 967-68, 299 N.E.2d 472, 478 (1st Dist. 1973).

encouragement was either addressed to or heard by the principal.[97] The encouragement need not be given verbally but may be given through writings, signs, or motion.[98] However, some type of communication between the alleged accomplice and perpetrator is a necessary ingredient of an "encouragement" or "solicitation." For example, after a fight in a tavern between the defendant and the victim, the defendant vowed to return and kill the victim.[99] However, even though the defendant's brother later killed the victim, the defendant was not held accountable because there was no evidence that he actually requested his brother to commit the murder.[100]

§ 3.10. — Agreement to Aid.

An agreement to aid another in the commission of a crime is culpable conduct under accountability principles.[101] Generally, the courts refer to any agreement to aid as a "community of purpose,"[102] "common plan or purpose"[103] or "common design."[104] The common purpose does not have to be supported by words of agreement[105] but can arise either through a preconceived plan[106] or by the spontaneous and combined participation of a group in the commission of an illegal act.[107] Thus, where defendant and another man went to the victim's apartment to complain about "bad narcotics," a venture apparently thought dangerous enough that the other man carried a gun, was met by the victim who displayed a gun, engaged the victim in an altercation outside the apartment and, finally, the defendant exhorted his partner to shoot the victim, the defendant was held accountable for his partner's shooting of the victim.[108] Where defendant accompanied shooter to and from the scene of a murder with knowledge of the shooter's intent, was present while the shooting occurred without disapproving of the shooter's actions or somehow distancing himself from the shooter, the defendant's actions exceeded mere presence and was a situation where a trier of fact could have rationally concluded the defendant "was part of a common design to

---

[97] People v. Mitchell, 12 Ill. App. 3d 960, 967-68, 299 N.E.2d 472, 478 (1st Dist. 1973).

[98] Brennan v. People, 15 Ill. 511, 516 (1854).

[99] People v. Mitchell, 12 Ill. App. 2d 960, 967-68, 299 N.E.2d 472, 478 (1st Dist. 1973).

[100] People v. Mitchell, 12 Ill. App. 2d 960, 967-68, 299 N.E.2d 472, 478 (1st Dist. 1973).

[101] 720 ILCS 5/5-2(c) (1999). *See* § 4.11 of this treatise for comments on the interrelationship between conspiracy and accountability.

[102] People v. Foster, 198 Ill. App. 3d 986, 993, 556 N.E.2d 1214, 1219 (1st Dist. 1990).

[103] People v. Furby, 138 Ill. 2d 434, 456, 563 N.E.2d 421, 431 (1990).

[104] People v. Brown, 197 Ill. App. 3d 907, 916, 557 N.E.2d 199, 205 (1st Dist. 1990).

[105] People v. Jones, 196 Ill. App. 3d 937, 965, 554 N.E.2d 516, 533 (1st Dist. 1990).

[106] People v. Furby, 138 Ill. 2d 434, 457, 563 N.E.2d 421, 431 (1990).

[107] People v. Hill, 53 Ill. App. 3d 280, 284, 368 N.E.2d 714, 717 (1st Dist. 1977).

[108] People v. Hill, 53 Ill. App. 3d 280, 286, 368 N.E.2d 714, 719 (1st Dist. 1977) (voluntary manslaughter conviction upheld).

murder the victim, to which he assented."[109] Lack of a preconceived plan is no defense where the circumstances surrounding the crime's commission indicate that a defendant voluntarily attached himself to a group bent on illegal acts with knowledge of its design.[110]

While an agreement or "conspiracy" between the primary criminal actor and an accomplice is not necessary to prove accountability, "the acts of conspiring may in many cases satisfy the particular requirements" of the Illinois accountability statute.[111] There are a plethora of factors which the courts take into consideration when evaluating the existence of a common design.

§ 3.11. — Association with Group Bent on Criminality.

One factor the courts consider in deciding if a defendant was party to the design to engage in criminality is whether he voluntarily attached himself to a group he knew was bent on criminality.[112] It has been held that criminal responsibility cannot rest on "guilt by association" even where the accused had knowledge of, and consented to, the principal's crime.[113] However, little more than this is required in order to hold a defendant accountable when he becomes attached to a group bent on criminality, the group actively engages in criminality and he does nothing to disassociate himself from the group.[114]

In *People v. Rybka*,[115] thirteen persons set out to "get a negro." They left together in two cars, but eventually became separated. Shortly after the cars separated, the occupants of one car, a Chrysler, disbanded. Meanwhile, the other group had spotted a victim at a bus stop where one of the members of the group beat him with a hammer and killed him. Occupants of the Chrysler were convicted along with the principal and the occupants of the second car. The Illinois Supreme Court upheld the conviction of the Chrysler's occupants, stating: "Evidence that a defendant voluntarily attached himself to a group bent on illegal acts with knowledge of its design supports an inference that he shared the com-

---

[109] People v. Taylor, 164 Ill. 2d 131, 142, 646 N.E.2d 567, 572 (1995) (first degree murder conviction upheld).

[110] People v. Richardson, 32 Ill. 2d 472, 476, 207 N.E.2d 478, 481 (1965).

[111] ILL. ANN. STAT. ch. 38, para. 5-2 (Smith-Hurd 1989), 1961 Committee Comments, at 236.

[112] People v. J.H., A Minor, 136 Ill. 2d 1, 17, 554 N.E.2d 961, 968, *cert. denied sub nom.*, Humphrey v. Illinois, 478 U.S. 942 (1990).

[113] People v. Walker, 44 Ill. App. 3d 494, 497, 358 N.E.2d 672, 675 (3d Dist. 1976).

[114] People v. Green, 179 Ill. App. 3d 1, 15-16, 535 N.E.2d 413, 421-23 (1st Dist. 1988) (where 16-year-old defendant was asked by principals to assist them in gaining entry into apartment on pretense that principals wanted to buy cocaine, whereupon principals shot to death four victims in apartment without disapproval or opposition from defendant, who failed to report incident to authorities, defendant liable for principals' criminality).

[115] 16 Ill. 2d 394, 158 N.E.2d 17 (1959).

mon purpose and will sustain his conviction as a principal for a crime committed in furtherance of the venture."[116]

The same rationale was used by the Illinois Supreme Court in *People v. Allen*.[117] In *Allen*, the defendant had actively participated in a plan to rob an armored car. The police learned of the plan. When they attempted to apprehend the defendant and others involved in the scheme, a gun battle resulted. Two of the defendant's companions and one police officer were killed. The defendant was convicted for the murder of the officer on the basis that he "voluntarily attached [himself] to a group bent on illegal acts," despite the fact that the state failed to prove conclusively that he had killed the officer or that he had even fired a shot.[118]

In *People v. Green*,[119] the defendant was asked by two others to go to the victim's dwelling and persuade the victim to open up his burglar bars on the pretext that the defendant wanted to buy some drugs. Since the victim knew the defendant, he readily opened the window and let the defendant enter. At this point, the two others rushed into the dwelling, placed a gun against the victim's head, demanded money, tied up the three other persons present in the dwelling, proceeded to kill all four individuals in the dwelling and, finally, set fire to the dwelling. Even though the two others never told the defendant precisely what they were planning to do, the defendant was convicted for their acts because he attached himself to a group bent on criminality, remained with them as they carried out the dangerous offense of home invasion, witnessed their dangerous threats and activities in the dwelling and had not in any way distanced himself from the other's violent activity.[120]

In *People v. Campbell*,[121] which involved an incident where several defendants threw rocks from a van, one of which killed a truck driver, the defendant Campbell was convicted of murder even though there was no evidence he actually threw the rock in question. The court noted that the defendant knew his friends were bent on throwing rocks in a fashion that might hurt someone but did not "prevent the throwing of the rocks,"[122] did not "insist that the rocks be removed from the van,"[123] and did not request [the driver] to let him out of the van.[124] Similarly, a defendant was held accountable for robbery because he was

---

[116] People v. Rybka, 16 Ill. 2d 394, 405, 158 N.E.2d 17, 22 (1959).

[117] 56 Ill. 2d 536, 309 N.E.2d 544 (1974).

[118] People v. Allen, 56 Ill. 2d 536, 541, 309 N.E.2d 544, 547 (1974).

[119] 179 Ill. App. 3d 1, 535 N.E.2d 413 (1st Dist. 1988).

[120] People v. Green, 179 Ill. App. 3d 1, 15-16, 535 N.E.2d 413, 421-23 (1st Dist. 1988).

[121] 77 Ill. App. 3d 804, 396 N.E.2d 607 (2d Dist. 1979).

[122] People v. Campbell, 77 Ill. App. 3d 804, 813, 396 N.E.2d 607, 613 (2d Dist. 1979).

[123] People v. Campbell, 77 Ill. App. 3d 804, 813, 396 N.E.2d 607, 613 (2d Dist. 1979).

[124] People v. Campbell, 77 Ill. App. 3d 804, 813, 396 N.E.2d 607, 613 (2d Dist. 1979). *Compare* People v. Taylor, 219 Ill. App. 3d 47, 48, 579 N.E.2d 383, 385-86 (3d Dist. 1991) (where evidence revealed defendant got together with other individuals with no particular plans in mind,

present at the crime scene, did not oppose the robbery or confiscation of the victim's car, did not attempt to intervene to prevent the victim's injuries and did not leave the area when other perpetrators knocked the victim unconscious.[125]

Obviously, "the issue [of accountability] is pertinent to cases involving deaths resulting from conflicts between street gangs or informal . . . groups."[126] Thus, where members of a street gang including defendant set out to do violence against members of a rival street gang and defendant was present when one armed member of his gang fatally shot a member of an opposing gang, he was held accountable for murder even though it had not been shown that he fired the fatal shot.[127] Similarly, where a group of individuals caused a 14-year-old girl to become intoxicated and ill on whiskey and marijuana, whereupon an armed second group including defendant decided to take revenge and attack the first group with the result that two persons were killed in the confrontation, defendant was held accountable for the actual perpetrator's murders.[128]

Where members of a street gang decide to attack certain innocent persons, typically each of the members of the gang was accountable for the violent actions of other gang members carried out in their presence.[129] Thus, where two armed members of a street gang bent on violence against a group of juveniles who had refused to join the street gang confronted the juveniles and one of them shot one of the juveniles, both gang members were convicted of murder.[130] In all of the preceding cases involving gangs or informal groups, there were "acts of two or more people indicating their knowledge of a hostile and potentially dangerous situation with one or more persons voluntarily taking up arms in anticipation of violence, and the actual violence resulting in death."[131]

Courts rely on gang affiliation as evidence of shared common purpose or motive.[132] For example, in *People v. Jones*,[133] the appellate court upheld the admission of gang-related evidence regarding a shooting into a motorcycle club where there was direct testimony indicating that the defendant belonged to a street

---

did not realize others would eventually drop rocks off an overpass killing victim, refused to drop rock himself, and often got together with group to engage in only legitimate activity, defendant's conviction for involuntary manslaughter reversed).

[125] People v. Lee, 243 Ill. App. 3d 29, 35-36, 611 N.E.2d 561, 566 (2d Dist. 1993).

[126] People v. Horton, 43 Ill. App. 3d 150, 155-56, 356 N.E.2d 1044, 1048 (1st Dist. 1976).

[127] People v. Hughes, 26 Ill. 2d 114, 119-20, 185 N.E.2d 834, 837 (1962).

[128] People v. Tate, 63 Ill. 2d 105, 109, 345 N.E.2d 480, 483-84 (1976).

[129] *See, e.g.,* People v. Horton, 43 Ill. App. 3d 150, 152, 356 N.E.2d 1044, 1045-48 (1st Dist. 1976).

[130] People v. Horton, 43 Ill. App. 3d 150, 152, 356 N.E.2d 1044, 1045-48 (1st Dist. 1976).

[131] People v. Tate, 63 Ill. 2d 105, 109, 345 N.E.2d 480, 482 (1976).

[132] People v. Smith, 141 Ill. 2d 40, 58, 565 N.E.2d 900, 907 (1991) (although admission in instant case reversible error). *Compare* People v. Gonzalez, 142 Ill. 2d 481, 489, 568 N.E.2d 864, 867 (1991) (properly admitted).

[133] 259 Ill. App. 3d 905, 632 N.E.2d 293 (1st Dist. 1994).

gang, plus that the defendants who were present before and during the shooting were acting together and had alerted fellow gang members to leave the club before the shooting.[134] In *People v. Gonzalez*,[135] the trial court properly admitted gang-related evidence to explain the meaning of certain gang terminology, namely that putting up "hoodies" meant a drug sale or stick up was to occur or that someone was about to die.[136] Similarly, in *People v. Spears*,[137] evidence of gang membership was properly admitted to establish motive for a shooting and to explain why the defendant carried out the orders of a gang leader.[138] In *People v. Lucas*,[139] gang-related evidence, including testimony regarding gang hierarchy, was properly admitted as relevant to the inmate defendant's murder of a correctional center superintendent where the defendant's status as a gang member was coupled with the defendant's presence at a meeting where plans to retaliate against the prison administration were discussed.[140] In *People v. Davenport*,[141] expert testimony regarding gang colors, attire and tattoos was deemed admissible to explain "false flagging," a tactic where a gang member enters rival territory posing as a member of a rival gang to draw a rival gang member into the open for an ambush."[142] Nevertheless, in *People v. Mason*,[143] the court found undue reliance on evidence of gang membership could be prejudicial to the defendant's right to receive a fair trial.[144]

§ 3.12. — Association or Affiliation with the Principal.

Obviously, the defendant's relationship with the principal or principals is an important factor in accountability analysis. Beyond determining whether the accused was voluntarily associated with a group bent on criminality, the courts

---

[134] People v. Jones, 259 Ill. App. 3d 905, 910, 632 N.E.2d 293, 297-98 (1st Dist. 1994).

[135] 265 Ill. App. 3d 315, 637 N.E.2d 1135 (1st Dist. 1994).

[136] People v. Gonzalez, 265 Ill. App. 3d 315, 326-27, 637 N.E.2d 1135, 1143-44 (1st Dist. 1994).

[137] 265 Ill. App. 3d 374, 628 N.E.2d 376 (1st Dist. 1993).

[138] People v. Spears, 265 Ill. App. 3d 374, 377, 628 N.E.2d 376, 379-80 (1st Dist. 1993); *see also* People v. Colon, 162 Ill. 2d 23, 30, 642 N.E.2d 118, 121 (1994) (fact that defendant and victim were members of rival gangs was evidence of defendant's motive for shooting victim).

[139] 151 Ill. 2d 461, 603 N.E.2d 460 (1992), *cert. denied*, 508 U.S. 916 (1993).

[140] People v. Lucas, 151 Ill. 2d 461, 478, 603 N.E.2d 460, 468-69 (1992), *cert. denied*, 508 U.S. 916 (1993).

[141] 301 Ill. App. 3d 143, 702 N.E.2d 335 (1st Dist. 1998).

[142] People v. Davenport, 301 Ill. App. 3d 143, 147, 702 N.E.2d 335, 340-41 (1st Dist. 1998).

[143] 274 Ill. App. 3d 715, 653 N.E.2d 1371 (1st Dist. 1995).

[144] People v. Mason, 274 Ill. App. 3d 715, 720-23, 653 N.E.2d 1371, 1374-77 (1st Dist. 1995) (holding gang evidence was irrelevant to prove defendant's criminal motive where defendant and victim were members of the same gang).

consider the prior association between the parties before the crime,[145] the defendant's "active association" with the perpetrator or perpetrators during the crime[146] and his "close affiliation" with the principal or principals after the crime.[147]

. Of course, the mere fact that a defendant present at the crime was acquainted with the principal before the crime is not enough to convict one as an accomplice.[148] In *People v. Ivy*,[149] the defendant was seen standing on a train platform with two companions. Several minutes later, the defendant and his two companions were seen leaving the train station together. Immediately after the victim exited the train station, he was robbed and shot by the defendant's companions. There was no evidence the defendant was present during the robbery or shooting. However, the defendant and his companions were later seen running away from the train station and entering the same automobile. The appellate court ruled that since there was no evidence of a preconceived plan to commit the robbery, that the defendant had acted as a lookout or that the defendant was even present or aware of his companions' "rapidly committed" crimes, he could not be convicted.[150] The mere fact that the defendant was seen with the actual perpetrators before the crime and that afterwards he ran, entered a car and drove off with two others was not enough to hold him accountable for his companions' robbery and attempted murder.[151] However, evidence of a prior association may be useful evidence *in conjunction with other evidence* to establish the existence of a common design. In *People v. Austin*,[152] the defendant was convicted of an attempted armed robbery which was actually carried out by his companions where the evidence revealed that the defendant and his companions had set out for a night of robbery and random victims and that the defendant had personally robbed victims on at least two occasions earlier that same evening.[153] This

---

[145] People v. Cole, 50 Ill. App. 3d 133, 134, 365 N.E.2d 133, 140 (5th Dist. 1977) (significant that "defendant spent a great deal of time" with perpetrators of double murder during the three days prior to their carrying out murders), *cert. denied*, 435 U.S. 944 (1978).

[146] People v. Grey, 14 Ill. App. 3d 310, 314, 302 N.E.2d 473, 477 (1st Dist. 1973).

[147] People v. Haynes, 223 Ill. App. 3d 147, 150, 583 N.E.2d 1177, 1179 (3d Dist. 1991).

[148] People v. Wright, 43 Ill. App. 3d 458, 460, 357 N.E.2d 224, 226-27 (4th Dist. 1976) (evidence that passengers in automobile driven by defendant committed theft in gasoline station was insufficient to convict defendant of theft).

[149] 68 Ill. App. 3d 402, 386 N.E.2d 323 (1st Dist. 1979).

[150] People v. Ivy, 68 Ill. App. 3d 402, 406, 386 N.E.2d 323, 386 (1st Dist. 1979).

[151] People v. Ivy, 68 Ill. App. 3d 402, 406, 386 N.E.2d 323, 386 (1st Dist. 1979).

[152] 264 Ill. App. 3d 976, 637 N.E.2d 585 (1st Dist. 1994).

[153] People v. Austin, 264 Ill. App. 3d 976, 981, 637 N.E.2d 585, 588 (1st Dist. 1994).

evidence revealed an obvious common plan between defendant and his companions.[154] In *People v. Sangster*,[155] the defendant was found accountable for murder, armed robbery and aggravated kidnapping. These charges arose out of an elaborate scheme to rob a bank. Since the defendant was not directly involved in these crimes and the actual perpetrators lived in another city, it was necessary to draw various links between the defendant's alleged planning of the crime and the perpetrators' commission. Any possible claim by defendant that he did not know or only casually knew the perpetrators was defeated by one evidentiary link.[156] Specifically, the prosecution was allowed to introduce into evidence a letter written by the defendant to one of the actual perpetrators in order to show that they knew each other "to a greater degree than a mere acquaintanceship."[157] Similarly, in *People v. Heflin*,[158] the Illinois Supreme Court thought it highly relevant in affirming defendant's murder conviction that there previously existed a "heated love affair" between the defendant and the perpetrator of a murder where the victim was the perpetrator's husband, the defendant and perpetrator had previously discussed the possibility of marriage once the husband was dead and the defendant was present when the victim was killed.[159]

Just as the courts may consider significant the relationship of the alleged accomplice and principal prior to the crime, the courts obviously focus on the relationship of the parties during the crime. For example, in *People v. Crutcher*,[160] the appellate court thought it significant that the defendant maintained a "close affiliation" with the perpetrators during an armed robbery.[161] The defendant who maintains his presence "without disapproving or opposing" the perpetrator's crime does not manifest the features of an innocent bystander but more often that of a guilty accomplice.[162]

The fact that the defendant continued a "close affiliation" with the principal or principals after the crime is also deemed highly relevant.[163] Not only are the courts concerned about the defendant's "supportive alliance" after the fact,[164]

---

[154] People v. Austin, 264 Ill. App. 3d 976, 981, 637 N.E.2d 585, 588 (1st Dist. 1994).

[155] 95 Ill. App. 3d 357, 420 N.E.2d 181 (4th Dist. 1981), *aff'd in relevant part, rev'd in part*, 91 Ill. 2d 260, 437 N.E.2d 625 (1982).

[156] Although the defendant did not deny knowing the perpetrators, the letter provided "some insight into the depth of their friendship." People v. Sangster, 95 Ill. App. 3d 357, 362, 420 N.E.2d 181, 185 (4th Dist. 1981).

[157] People v. Sangster, 95 Ill. App. 3d 357, 362, 420 N.E.2d 181, 185 (4th Dist. 1981).

[158] 71 Ill. 2d 525, 376 N.E.2d 1367 (1976), *cert. denied*, 439 U.S. 1074 (1979).

[159] People v. Heflin, 71 Ill. 2d 525, 534-35, 376 N.E.2d 1367, 1371 (1976), *cert. denied*, 439 U.S. 1074 (1979).

[160] 72 Ill. App. 3d 239, 390 N.E.2d 571 (5th Dist. 1979).

[161] People v. Crutcher, 72 Ill. App. 3d 239, 243, 390 N.E.2d 571, 575 (5th Dist. 1979).

[162] *See, e.g.*, People v. Washington, 26 Ill. 2d 207, 209, 186 N.E.2d 259, 261 (1962).

[163] People v. Reid, 136 Ill. 2d 27, 62, 554 N.E.2d 174, 191 (1990).

[164] People v. Banks, 138 Ill. App. 3d 994, 1008, 486 N.E.2d 953, 963 (2d Dist. 1985).

they wonder out loud how the defendant's failure to "extricate himself from participating in the crime"[165] or, at the very least, failure to "disassociate himself" from the principal[166] can be considered consistent with the alleged accomplice's claim of innocence.

The relationship between accomplices and principals takes on horizontal features, vertical features and various combinations in between. On the vertical side, courts are willing to convict whether the accomplice was the leader or the follower in a criminal scheme. Thus, where the defendant had allegedly ordered members of a street gang to attack eventual murder and attempted murder victims, the reviewing court obviously thought it significant in affirming defendant's convictions that defendant was the "chief" of the street gang.[167] On the other hand, where the defendant participated in an armed robbery where the victim was killed, the appellate court affirmed the defendant's convictions for murder and armed robbery on an accountability theory notwithstanding the fact that defendant claimed he was not involved in the planning of the robbery, had never actually taken any of the money in the robbery or received any afterwards, had not handled the gun nor fired the gun at the victim, where defendant was a 15-year-old mentally retarded person, who apparently "looked up" to the perpetrators who were older, larger and armed, and according to psychologist testimony, he was "more likely to follow the group" because of his mental disability.[168]

§ 3.13. — Presence at the Crime Scene.

A defendant's presence or activities, or lack thereof, at the scene of the crime, may also be taken into consideration when determining whether accountability exists. "Mere presence" at the commission of an offense, without any affirmative act of assisting, abetting, or encouraging the commission of the crime, is not sufficient conduct to render one legally accountable.[169] Also, a defendant's "knowledge,"[170] "negative acquiescence"[171] or "consent"[172] to a crime's commission will not make one responsible for the crime without any affirmative act of assisting or encouraging the actual perpetrator's acts.[173] In the absence of a legal duty,[174] no one will be held accountable for failing to oppose or stop a

---

[165] People v. Reid, 136 Ill. 2d 27, 62, 554 N.E.2d 174, 191 (1990).

[166] People v. Haynes, 223 Ill. App. 3d 147, 151, 583 N.E.2d 1177, 1180 (3d Dist. 1991).

[167] People v. Hairston, 46 Ill. 2d 348, 372, 263 N.E.2d 840, 854, *cert. denied*, 402 U.S. 972 (1970).

[168] People v. Reid, 136 Ill. 2d 27, 64, 554 N.E.2d 174, 190-92 (1990).

[169] People v. Evans, 87 Ill. 2d 77, 83, 429 N.E.2d 520, 522 (1981).

[170] People v. Deatherage, 122 Ill. App. 3d 620, 623-24, 461 N.E.2d 631, 634 (3d Dist. 1984).

[171] People v. Sauer, 177 Ill. App. 3d 870, 876, 532 N.E.2d 946, 950 (2d Dist. 1988).

[172] People v. Washington, 121 Ill. App. 2d 174, 181, 257 N.E.2d 190, 194 (1st Dist. 1970).

[173] People v. Peterson, 273 Ill. App. 3d 412, 419, 652 N.E.2d 1252, 1258 (1st Dist. 1995).

[174] *See* § 3.15 of this chapter for a discussion of legal duties and accountability.

crime[175] even though his or her failure to intervene may involve moral turpitude.[176] Accomplice liability does not extend to the legally "innocent bystander."[177] Also, flight from the scene of the crime is not sufficient to prove accountability[178] and, indeed, will amount to "slight proof if any" in the absence of other evidence of complicity.[179]

In *People v. Robinson*,[180] the Illinois Supreme Court held that two persons present at the murder of a cab driver were not accountable for the principal's criminal conduct. The court based its decision on the fact that the two had not aided or encouraged the principal and had no prior knowledge of the principal's illegal plan from which a common design could be established.[181] In reaching its decision, the court restated what is perhaps the best working definition of an accomplice:

> An accomplice is defined as one who knowingly, voluntarily and with common intent with the principal offender unites in the commission of a crime. [citations omitted] The generally accepted test as to whether a witness is an accomplice is whether he himself could have been indicted for the offense either as principal or accessory. If he could not then he is not an accomplice. The term "accomplice" cannot be used in a loose or popular sense so as to embrace one who has guilty knowledge or is morally delinquent or who was even an admitted participant in a related but distinct offense. To constitute one an accomplice he must take some part, perform some act or owe some duty to the person in danger that makes it incumbent on him to prevent the commission of the crime.[182]

Notwithstanding, the discussion that follows demonstrates that in many cases there exists a very fine line between the defense claim of mere presence and the government claim of accountability.

§ 3.14. — Participation in or Assent to Criminality.

Since active participation has never been a prerequisite for guilt based upon the theory of accountability[183] and, on the other hand, mere presence at the crime

---

[175] People v. Jones, 86 Ill. App. 3d 278, 282, 407 N.E.2d 1121, 1124 (4th Dist. 1980).

[176] People v. Ramirez, 93 Ill. App. 2d 404, 410, 236 N.E.2d 284, 288 (1st Dist. 1968).

[177] People v. Deatherage, 122 Ill. App. 3d 620, 624, 461 N.E.2d 631, 634 (3d Dist. 1984).

[178] People v. Ivy, 68 Ill. App. 3d 402, 405, 386 N.E.2d 323, 325 (1st Dist. 1979).

[179] In re Woods, 20 Ill. App. 3d 641, 649, 314 N.E.2d 606, 611 (1st Dist. 1974).

[180] 59 Ill. 2d 184, 319 N.E.2d 772 (1974).

[181] People v. Robinson, 59 Ill. 2d 184, 192, 319 N.E.2d 772, 776-77 (1974).

[182] People v. Robinson, 59 Ill. 2d 184, 190-91, 192, 319 N.E.2d 772, 776 (1974) (quoting People v. Hrdlicka, 344 Ill. 211, 221-22, 176 N.E. 308, 313 (1931)).

[183] People v. Ruiz, 94 Ill. 2d 245, 254-55, 447 N.E.2d 148, 151 (1982), *cert. denied*, 462 U.S. 1112 (1983).

scene or negative acquiescence in the action of another is insufficient to establish accountability,[184] courts routinely look at all the surrounding circumstances to determine if a defendant was more than an innocent bystander.[185] Accountability and common design can be proved by circumstantial evidence.[186] Many Illinois decisions repeat the following language:

> If the proof shows that a person was present at the commission of the crime without disapproving or opposing it, it is competent for the trier of fact to consider the conduct in connection with other circumstances and thereby reach a conclusion that such person assented to the commission of the crime, lent to it his countenance and approval and was therefore aiding and abetting the crime. Stated differently, circumstances may show there is a common design to an unlawful act to which all assent, and whatever is done in furtherance of the design is the act of all, making each person guilty of the crime.[187]

Thus, where a defendant claims mere presence, the court can consider his or her continued presence during the commission of the crime,[188] failure to oppose or disapprove of the crime,[189] failure to report the crime to the authorities or confide in anyone about the crime[190] and flight from the scene[191] to determine if the defendant is accountable. Similarly, the fact that the defendant did not attempt to aid the victim following the actual perpetrator's infliction of a serious injury upon the victim may support the existence of a common design.[192] Where both occupants of a car laughed immediately after one of the occupants had shot a thirteen-year-old girl standing outside the car, their reaction was interpreted as evidence of assent and participation in the shooting by both individuals in the car.[193] Where the defendant was "mindful of what was going on" before and during a co-defendant's robbery-murder as exhibited by acting as a lookout, sound-

---

[184] People v. Stevens, 98 Ill. App. 3d 158, 160, 423 N.E.2d 1340, 1342 (1st Dist. 1981).

[185] People v. Harris, 294 Ill. App. 3d 561, 565, 691 N.E.2d 80, 83 (1st Dist. 1998) ("Factors that raise an inference that the accused aided and abetted the commission of the crime include presence at the scene of the crime without disassociating oneself from the crime scene, flight from the scene, continued association with the perpetrator after the criminal act, failure to report the incident, acceptance of illegal proceeds of the crime, and concealment or destruction of evidence").

[186] People v. Stevens, 98 Ill. App. 3d 158, 161, 423 N.E.2d 1340, 1342 (1st Dist. 1981).

[187] See People v. Reid, 136 Ill. 2d 27, 62, 554 N.E.2d 174, 190 (1990) (quoting People v. Ruiz, 94 Ill. 2d 245, 257, 447 N.E.2d 148, 152 (1982) (quoting People v. Morgan, 67 Ill. 2d 1, 9, 364 N.E.2d 56, 60 (1977) (quoting People v. Washington, 26 Ill. 2d 207, 209, 186 N.E.2d 259, 261 (1962)).

[188] People v. Reid, 136 Ill. 2d 27, 64, 554 N.E.2d 174, 191 (1990).

[189] People v. Bell, 209 Ill. App. 3d 438, 444, 568 N.E.2d 238, 241 (1st Dist. 1991).

[190] People v. Jones, 196 Ill. App. 3d 937, 966, 554 N.E.2d 516, 534 (1st Dist. 1990).

[191] People v. Reid, 136 Ill. 2d 27, 64, 554 N.E.2d 174, 191 (1990).

[192] People v. Shaw, 98 Ill. App. 3d 682, 686, 424 N.E.2d 834, 838 (1st Dist. 1981).

[193] People v. Torres, 100 Ill. App. 3d 931, 938, 427 N.E.2d 329, 335-36 (1st Dist. 1981).

ing an alarm when police were in the area, seeing the victim struggle with the co-defendant, and hearing the victim's repeated and increasingly audible cries for help, defendant was properly convicted of the robbery-murder.[194]

A defendant's criminal assent and approval can be based on his words or actions. For example, in *People v. Hunter*,[195] the defendant and a companion approached a street peddler and asked him the price of a cap pistol. When he told them the price, the defendant stated, "I don't have to pay for anything I don't want to." Immediately after this, the defendant's companion took the peddler's display case. The court found the peddler's statement to be a clear indication that he was an accomplice to the robbery.[196] In *People v. Shaw*,[197] the defendant was present when his companion shot and killed the owner of a liquor store. The appellate court affirmed the defendant's conviction for murder. First, the court considered it significant that before the shooting the defendant and codefendant arrived in the store together and were "hitting on each other or tussling" with each other,[198] which the court apparently construed as evidence they were companions. Second, there was evidence the defendant placed his hands on the victim before the shooting.[199] Third, the court considered evidence that the defendant and the principal fled the scene together and that the defendant had failed to aid the victim after he was shot.[200]

Evidence that one acted as a lookout[201] or was standing by ready to aid the principal if necessary[202] will support an inference that a common design existed. Evidence tending to show that the defendant was present as a lookout can be established where "the defendant was furtively looking about the area when the offenses were being committed,"[203] or where the defendant positioned himself or herself where he or she could warn or hide the principal.[204] In *People v. Hunter*,[205] the defendant and the principal entered a restaurant at approximately the same time. The defendant entered through the front door while the principal entered through the rear. While the principal held two employees at gunpoint

---

[194] People v. Batchelor, 171 Ill. 2d 367, 377-78, 665 N.E.2d 777, 781 (1996). *See also* People v. Groves, 294 Ill. App. 3d 570, 580, 691 N.E.2d 86, 93 (1st Dist. 1998) (accountability may be established by presence at crime scene, knowledge of perpetrator's intent, flight, association with perpetrators after incident, and failure to report crime).

[195] 69 Ill. App. 3d 732, 387 N.E.2d 1018 (1st Dist. 1979).

[196] People v. Hunter, 69 Ill. App. 3d 732, 735, 387 N.E.2d 1018, 1021 (1st Dist. 1979).

[197] 98 Ill. App. 3d 682, 424 N.E.2d 834 (1st Dist. 1981).

[198] People v. Shaw, 98 Ill. App. 3d 682, 686, 424 N.E.2d 834, 838 (1st Dist. 1981).

[199] People v. Shaw, 98 Ill. App. 3d 682, 685, 424 N.E.2d 834, 837 (1st Dist. 1981).

[200] People v. Shaw, 98 Ill. App. 3d 682, 686, 424 N.E.2d 834, 838 (1st Dist. 1981).

[201] People v. Furby, 138 Ill. 2d 434, 457, 563 N.E.2d 421, 431 (1990).

[202] People v. Bell, 113 Ill. App. 3d 588, 600-01, 447 N.E.2d 909, 915 (1st 1979).

[203] People v. Ivy, 68 Ill. App. 3d 402, 405, 386 N.E.2d 323, 325 (1st Dist. 1979).

[204] People v. Nugara, 39 Ill. 2d 482, 487, 236 N.E.2d 693, 697 (1968).

[205] 42 Ill. App. 3d 947, 356 N.E.2d 822 (1st Dist. 1976).

and robbed the cash register, the defendant stood in the patrons' area with his eyes fixed on one of the employees. From where he stood, the defendant could see the principal. The defendant remained about eight minutes and left at about the same time as the principal. Both men were seen together shortly after the robbery, and both fled when a squad car approached them. The appellate court determined that the defendant's conduct inside the restaurant supported an inference of a common purpose.[206] While he had taken no action to assist the principal, his presence and failure to ask for service were not the actions of an innocent man.[207] The fact that he did not assist the principal was not conclusive, since at no time during the robbery did the need arise for him to render aid because no patrons entered and the employees offered no resistance.[208]

§ 3.15. — Breach of Legal Duty.

Although a person's mere knowledge or presence during another's commission of a crime does not make that person accountable for the other's crime even in circumstances where the person might have been able to prevent the other's crime, a different rule arises where the person has a legal duty to intervene.[209] In *People v. Peters*,[210] the defendant's boyfriend had apparently battered defendant's infant child for approximately five months and, finally, his physical abuse of the child caused the child's death. In affirming defendant's murder conviction, the appellate court pointed out that custodial parents have an affirmative duty to protect and provide for their minor children.[211] Moreover, they ruled that a "parent who knowingly fails to protect its child from abuse may be prosecuted under the accountability statute and, thereby, becomes legally accountable for the conduct of the abuser."[212] If the parent "knows that his or her child is in a dangerous situation and fails to take action to protect the child," the parent "presumably intends the consequences of the inaction."[213] Here, the defendant's babysitter had discussed with defendant the numerous bruises and injuries she observed on defendant's child that had commenced to appear when defendant

---

[206] People v. Hunter, 42 Ill. App. 3d 947, 950-51, 356 N.E.2d 822, 825 (1st Dist. 1976).

[207] People v. Hunter, 42 Ill. App. 3d 947, 950-51, 356 N.E.2d 822, 825 (1st Dist. 1976).

[208] People v. Hunter, 42 Ill. App. 3d 947, 950-51, 356 N.E.2d 822, 825 (1st Dist. 1976).

[209] *See* ch. 2 of this treatise for a discussion of legal duties.

[210] 224 Ill. App. 3d 180, 586 N.E.2d 469 (1st Dist. 1991), *aff'd sub nom.*, People v. Stanciel, 153 Ill. 2d 218, 606 N.E.2d 1201 (1992).

[211] People v. Peters, 224 Ill. App. 3d 180, 190, 586 N.E.2d 469, 476 (1st Dist. 1991), *aff'd sub nom.*, People v. Stanciel, 153 Ill. 2d 218, 606 N.E.2d 1201 (1992).

[212] People v. Peters, 224 Ill. App. 3d 180, 190, 586 N.E.2d 469, 476 (1st Dist. 1991), *aff'd sub nom.*, People v. Stanciel, 153 Ill. 2d 218, 606 N.E.2d 1201 (1992).

[213] People v. Peters, 224 Ill. App. 3d 180, 190, 586 N.E.2d 469, 476 (1st Dist. 1991), *aff'd sub nom.*, People v. Stanciel, 153 Ill. 2d 218, 606 N.E.2d 1201 (1992).

began dating and, later, living with her boyfriend.[214] Although the defendant may not have been present when these multiple instances of physical abuse of her child had occurred, the evidence demonstrated she was aware that her boyfriend beat her child on several occasions.[215] Accordingly, her failure to protect her child from her boyfriend's physical attacks constituted a breach of her parental obligations and made her accountable for her boyfriend's murder of her child.[216]

Obviously, where the defendant-parent is present during another person's assault upon her children, this will make it easier to establish accountability. Thus, where the defendant was present when her boyfriend beat her 23-month-old son and five-year-old daughter with his fists and feet, did not intervene during the beatings, failed to procure medical assistance for the injured children or otherwise report the matter to the authorities, her breach of duty to protect her children made her an accomplice to two counts of aggravated battery.[217] Moreover, if the defendant participates with another in the beating of her child and makes a concerted effort to "cover up" the manner in which her child sustained serious bodily injury, the court will have little difficulty finding a criminal common design.[218]

§ 3.16. — Significance of Subsequent Activity.

A defendant must assist in the commission of a crime either before or during its occurrence to be convicted of the crime on an accountability theory.[219] However, a defendant's conduct after the offense may be used to infer that the defendant's participation occurred before or during the crime.[220] The best example of this is driving a getaway car.[221] While driving the car from the scene obviously occurs after the crime is committed, the driver is still accountable because his or her acts play an important part in the entire criminal plan.[222] His or her participation in the crime is closely linked to the crime's success.[223] When an

---

[214] People v. Peters, 224 Ill. App. 3d 180, 191, 586 N.E.2d 469, 476 (1st Dist. 1991), aff'd sub nom., People v. Stanciel, 153 Ill. 2d 218, 606 N.E.2d 1201 (1992).

[215] People v. Peters, 224 Ill. App. 3d 180, 191, 586 N.E.2d 469, 477 (1st Dist. 1991), aff'd sub nom., People v. Stanciel, 153 Ill. 2d 218, 606 N.E.2d 1201 (1992).

[216] People v. Peters, 224 Ill. App. 3d 180, 191-92, 586 N.E.2d 469, 476-79 (1st Dist. 1991), aff'd sub nom., People v. Stanciel, 153 Ill. 2d 218, 606 N.E.2d 1201 (1992).

[217] People v. Bernard, 149 Ill. App. 3d 684, 689-92, 500 N.E.2d 1074, 1077-81 (5th Dist. 1986).

[218] People v. Ray, 80 Ill. App. 3d 151, 155-57, 399 N.E.2d 977, 982 (5th Dist. 1979) (murder).

[219] People v. Bell, 209 Ill. App. 3d 438, 445, 568 N.E.2d 238, 242 (1st Dist. 1991).

[220] People v. Bell, 209 Ill. App. 3d 438, 446, 568 N.E.2d 238, 243 (1st Dist. 1991).

[221] People v. Williams, 262 Ill. App. 3d 734, 742, 635 N.E.2d 781, 788 (1st Dist. 1994) (defendant found guilty of murder for driving actual shooter who killed victim to and from the crime scene).

[222] People v. Jones, 86 Ill. App. 3d 278, 282-83, 407 N.E.2d 1121, 1124 (4th Dist. 1978).

[223] People v. Jones, 86 Ill. App. 3d 278, 282, 407 N.E.2d 1121, 1124 (4th Dist. 1978).

express or implied plan calls for a person to wait in a getaway car and then to spirit others from the scene, the driver's participation is deemed to occur during the crime's commission, not afterward.[224] Although the getaway driver's efforts in support of a crime normally have their peak impact after the commission of the offense, it is imperative that the defendant's knowledge of a crime occurs either before[225] or during[226] the crime's commission. It seems to make no difference whether the driver attempts to elude police capture[227] or surrenders to the police immediately upon police demand.[228] Of course, the driver may be totally oblivious to the fact that his or her passenger has recently committed a crime.[229] A person with no knowledge that a crime has been committed by others in the car that he or she subsequently drives from the scene is not accountable.[230] Even a defendant who drives the principal from a crime scene after learning of its commission will not be accountable;[231] however, a failure to dissociate himself or herself once he or she learns of the crime may provide an inference that the defendant drove the car from the scene with knowledge of the crime's commission.[232] Moreover, it has been pointed out that it is "improbable" that the actual perpetrator would rely on an "unaware" getaway driver.[233]

In *People v. Holmes*,[234] the defendant waited outside a tavern in his car while his companions entered the tavern and killed the owner. The Illinois Supreme Court thought it significant that defendant stated that he had heard gunshots and was told "it's done" when the others returned to the car, whereupon the defendant drove the car from the scene.[235] On the other hand, in *People v. Owens*,[236] evidence was presented that the defendant was a passenger in a car outside a service station while her companion was inside engaged in a robbery-murder. Testimony of an eyewitness that she stared straight ahead and did not move dur-

---

[224] People v. Jones, 86 Ill. App. 3d 278, 282, 407 N.E.2d 1121, 1124-25 (4th Dist. 1978).

[225] People v. Ross, 100 Ill. App. 3d 607, 610, 426 N.E.2d 1271, 1273 (4th Dist. 1981).

[226] People v. Watson, 106 Ill. App. 3d 315, 317, 436 N.E.2d 7, 8 (1st Dist. 1982).

[227] People v. Ross, 100 Ill. App. 3d 607, 610, 426 N.E.2d 1271, 1273 (4th Dist. 1981).

[228] People v. Watson, 106 Ill. App. 3d 315, 317, 436 N.E.2d 7, 9 (1st Dist. 1982).

[229] People v. Wright, 43 Ill. App. 3d 458, 461, 357 N.E.2d 224, 226-27 (4th Dist. 1976).

[230] People v. Wright, 43 Ill. App. 3d 458, 461, 357 N.E.2d 224, 226-27 (4th Dist. 1976).

[231] People v. Taylor, 186 Ill. 2d 439, 446, 712 N.E.2d 326, 329-30 (1999) (where defendant drove passenger away after passenger fired two shots at occupants of other car, defendant not accomplice to aggravated discharge of firearm absent evidence defendant knew of intent of passenger to fire gun).

[232] People v. Harris, 96 Ill. App. 3d 970, 974-75, 422 N.E.2d 208, 211-12 (1st Dist. 1981).

[233] People v. Greene, 27 Ill. App. 3d 1080, 1092, 328 N.E.2d 176, 185 (1st Dist. 1975).

[234] 67 Ill. 2d 236, 367 N.E.2d 663 (1977).

[235] People v. Holmes, 67 Ill. 2d 236, 237-39, 367 N.E.2d 663, 664-65 (1977) (murder conviction upheld).

[236] 32 Ill. App. 3d 893, 337 N.E.2d 60 (4th Dist. 1975).

ing the robbery was sufficient to negate the state's contention that she was present as a lookout or otherwise involved in the crime.[237]

Of course, other activities of an alleged accomplice that occur subsequent to the crime may suggest involvement before or during the crime. Fleeing the crime scene with the perpetrator is obviously significant circumstantial evidence.[238] The fact that a defendant allegedly involved in a robbery changed jackets with a codefendant in order to avoid detection was suggestive of involvement in the robbery.[239] Where the defendant helped codefendants place the victim of a shooting in the trunk of an automobile, this was indicative of his involvement in a robbery and attempted murder of the robbery victim.[240] On the other hand, while an escape may be part of an on-going felony-murder effort,[241] involvement in an escape effort following the commission of a crime outside of a felony-murder situation does not alone provide a basis for accomplice liability.[242] Thus, where a defendant joined several individuals in their departure from an alleged burglary only after the burglary may have occurred, he could not be accountable for the alleged burglary.[243]

Acts by the defendant which attempt to cover up the details of a crime also go toward showing the existence of a common design. A defendant's continued presence during certain murders and his attempt to rid the scene of fingerprints was sufficient to support a common design.[244] Evidence that the defendant fabricated an alibi demonstrates consciousness of guilt.[245]

However, it must be emphasized that no matter how egregious the defendant's after-the-fact support of another's criminality, accountability cannot be established against the defendant if the state fails to show that the defendant's participation occurred before or during the commission of the crime by the principal. Thus, the fabrication of an alibi did not demonstrate a common design where it was developed after the principal's commission and where there were no other circumstances indicating the defendant's participation in the crime.[246] In a case where the state failed to prove, among other things, that a murder vic-

---

[237] People v. Owens, 32 Ill. App. 3d 893, 895-96, 337 N.E.2d 60, 62 (4th Dist. 1975).

[238] People v. Gilbert, 194 Ill. App. 3d 184, 188-89, 550 N.E.2d 1183, 1186 (1st Dist. 1990).

[239] People v. Gilbert, 194 Ill. App. 3d 184, 188-89, 550 N.E.2d 1183, 1186 (1st Dist. 1990).

[240] People v. Reynolds, 178 Ill. App. 3d 756, 765, 533 N.E.2d 932, 939 (1st Dist. 1989).

[241] People v. Lowery, 178 Ill. 2d 462, 472, 687 N.E.2d 973, 979 (1997); People v. Hickman, 59 Ill. 2d 89, 94, 319 N.E.2d 511, 513 (1974).

[242] People v. Dennis, 181 Ill. 2d 87, 101, 692 N.E.2d 325, 333-36 (1998) (defendant could not be accomplice to armed robbery based on his effort to effectuate robber's escape since robbery was complete and not a continuing offense).

[243] In re D.C., A Minor, 259 Ill. App. 3d 637, 640-45, 631 N.E.2d 883, 886-88 (2d Dist. 1994).

[244] People v. Ruiz, 94 Ill. 2d 245, 256, 447 N.E.2d 148, 152 (1982), cert. denied, 462 U.S. 1112 (1983).

[245] People v. Morrison, 53 Ill. App. 3d 843, 847, 368 N.E.2d 1325, 1328 (4th Dist. 1977).

[246] People v. Owens, 32 Ill. App. 3d 893, 896, 337 N.E.2d 60, 62 (4th Dist. 1977).

tim remained alive after the defendant arrived at the crime scene, this failure alone was sufficient to preclude a defendant's conviction for aiding and abetting the murder.[247] Where the state fails to prove that the defendant's participation occurred before or during the crime, the defendant is, at best, an accessory after the fact and can be found guilty only of an offense such as obstructing justice.[248]

§ 3.17. — Possession or Taking Share of Proceeds of Crime.

Proof that a defendant who was present at the crime possessed the fruits of the crime[249] or shared in the proceeds[250] from the crime will likely show a common design and sustain his or her conviction as an accomplice. Frequently, a defendant's continued close affiliation with the principal is used in conjunction with the defendant's possession of a crime's proceeds to support the inference of guilt.[251] However, a defendant's exclusive possession of theft proceeds alone will support the inference where the proof shows that he or she was present when the crime was committed.[252] Also, recent unexplained joint possession of stolen property supports an inference of guilt even where the defendant was not immediately present during a theft,[253] assuming there is evidence to corroborate defendant's involvement in the offense.[254] Accountability may also be inferred from driving a vehicle containing stolen property.[255]

In *People v. Lanzotti*,[256] the defendant was present when his girlfriend stole a ring from a jewelry store. Several weeks later, he was arrested when he tried to have the stones from the ring remounted. In this case, the defendant's exclusive possession of the stones together with his presence when the ring was stolen

---

[247] People v. Ramirez, 93 Ill. App. 2d 404, 410, 236 N.E.2d 284, 288 (1st Dist. 1968).

[248] People v. Jones, 86 Ill. App. 3d 278, 282, 407 N.E.2d 1121, 1124 (4th Dist. 1980). *See* 720 ILCS 5/31-4(1999) (obstructing justice defined).

[249] People v. Houston, 74 Ill. App. 3d 586, 593, 393 N.E.2d 529, 533-34 (1st Dist. 1979) (where codefendant took ring from police decoy feigning intoxication and handed ring to defendant who threw ring to ground when police approached, evidence was sufficient to show accountability for robbery and theft).

[250] People v. Furby, 138 Ill. 2d 434, 457, 563 N.E.2d 421, 431 (1990).

[251] *See, e.g.,* People v. Washington, 26 Ill. 2d 207, 209, 186 N.E.2d 259, 261 (1962).

[252] People v. Lanzotti, 61 Ill. App. 3d 451, 455, 378 N.E.2d 369, 372 (4th Dist. 1978).

[253] People v. Owens, 151 Ill. App. 3d 1043, 1046, 504 N.E.2d 186, 188-89 (3d Dist. 1987) (defendant drove perpetrators of theft to retail store, waited in his car during theft, placed theft proceeds in his trunk and drove proceeds and one perpetrator from the scene).

[254] People v. Housby, 84 Ill. 2d 415, 423-24, 420 N.E.2d 151, 155 (criminal possession of proceeds of burglary standing alone does not support legal inference of defendant's involvement in burglary), *cert. denied*, 454 U.S. 845 (1981).

[255] People v. McNeal, 120 Ill. App. 3d 625, 630, 458 N.E.2d 630, 634 (2d Dist. 1983) (defendant drove perpetrator of retail theft to gas station, was present during theft of cigarettes, and drove perpetrator and proceeds from scene).

[256] 61 Ill. App. 3d 451, 378 N.E.2d 369 (4th Dist. 1978).

were sufficient evidence to infer accountability.[257] In *People v. Washington*,[258] the defendant was convicted as an accomplice when it was established that he chased the victim from the scene of a robbery, maintained a close affiliation with the principal, and was arrested one week later with the principal in the victim's stolen car.[259] In *People v. Furby*,[260] the defendant was present when his brother and another person broke into a restaurant and stole some money. The court found the defendant guilty under accountability based upon evidence that he was present outside the restaurant during the crime, knew in advance of the plan to break into the restaurant, and shared equally in the proceeds of the crime.[261] In *People v. Morgan*,[262] proof that the defendant knew of a group's plan to rob the victim, his presence at the robbery-murder scene, and evidence that he shared in the proceeds from the robbery were sufficient to convict him of murder by accountability.[263] In *People v. McConnell*,[264] the defendant's arrest in the principal's company twelve days after the robbery of a boutique at which the defendant had been present, plus evidence that she was wearing a wig taken in the robbery, were sufficient to establish the existence of a common design.[265] Of course, these factors cut both ways. For instance, in *People v. Tillman*,[266] evidence that the defendants had not shared in the proceeds from a robbery and murder at which they were present was a primary reason for the court's determination that accountability had not been established.[267] On the other hand, in *People v. Reid*,[268] the Illinois Supreme Court determined that merely because defendant did not receive proceeds of an armed robbery did not defeat a finding of accountability since there was other evidence of defendant's participation.[269]

§ 3.18. — Incidental Crimes: Natural and Probable Consequences of Target Crime.

As shown above, a person can be held accountable for the criminal act of another which he intended to further if he either encouraged another's crime, actively participated in it, agreed to commit the crime with the principal or at-

---

[257] People v. Lanzotti, 61 Ill. App. 3d 451, 455, 378 N.E.2d 369, 372 (4th Dist. 1978).

[258] 26 Ill. 2d 207, 186 N.E.2d 259 (1962).

[259] People v. Washington, 26 Ill. 2d 207, 209, 186 N.E.2d 259, 259 (1962).

[260] 138 Ill. 2d 434, 563 N.E.2d 421 (1990).

[261] People v. Furby, 138 Ill. 2d 434, 457, 563 N.E.2d 421, 431 (1990).

[262] 67 Ill. 2d 1, 364 N.E.2d 56, *cert. denied*, 434 U.S. 927 (1977).

[263] People v. Morgan, 67 Ill. 2d 1, 9, 364 N.E.2d 56, 60 (1977).

[264] 48 Ill. App. 3d 355, 362 N.E.2d 1280 (1st Dist. 1977).

[265] People v. McConnell, 48 Ill. App. 3d 355, 361-62, 362 N.E.2d 1280, 1286 (1st Dist. 1977).

[266] 130 Ill. App. 2d 743, 265 N.E.2d 904 (4th Dist. 1971).

[267] People v. Tillman, 130 Ill. App. 2d 743, 750-51, 265 N.E.2d 904, 909-10 (4th Dist. 1971).

[268] 136 Ill. 2d 27, 554 N.E.2d 174 (1990).

[269] People v. Reid, 136 Ill. 2d 27, 63-65, 554 N.E.2d 174, 191 (1990).

tempted to aid the principal's criminality. However, accomplice liability does not end with the crime the accomplice specifically meant to aid and abet.[270] The defendant who aided and abetted a particular crime he intended to facilitate, hereinafter referred to as the "target" crime, may also be accountable for any incidental "natural and probable consequence" that arose out of his common purpose to achieve a crime.[271] For example, in *People v. Feagans*,[272] defendant, a second defendant who was his brother, and a third defendant met their victim in a tavern. The victim accompanied the trio in their round of other taverns, after which the four drove around in the third defendant's car. While they were driving, defendant demanded money from the victim while brandishing a club. Defendant then threatened the victim with rape if he did not come up with some money, whereupon the third defendant twice suggested the victim be murdered in order to cover up possible kidnapping charges that might be lodged against the trio in the future. In the meantime, defendant participated in tieing up the victim. At this point, defendant claimed he lost consciousness due to his intoxicated condition and later learned his brother and the third defendant pushed the victim over a bridge into a river where he drowned. Here, the defendant had himself engaged in an armed robbery effort and he had participated in tieing up the victim, the third defendant had twice communicated to defendant his desire to kill the victim and the defendant was undisputedly aware that the third defendant had the means to kill.[273] Accordingly, the defendant was responsible not

---

[270] People v. Terry, 99 Ill. 2d 508, 515, 460 N.E.2d 746, 749-50 (1984) (even though defendants only conspired to commit misdemeanor battery on victim, each person was responsible under "common-design rule" for conduct done by the other defendants which was in furtherance of the intended battery, including the victim's murder). This "common-design rule" discussed in *Terry* has a long history that precedes the enactment of the Illinois Criminal Code of 1961. *See, e.g.,* People v. Rybka, 16 Ill. 2d 394, 407, 158 N.E.2d 17, 24 (1959) (when defendants agree to engage in unlawful, dangerous act "or if its accomplishment will necessarily or probably require the use of force or violence, which may result in the taking of life unlawfully, each party to such agreement will be held criminally liable for whatever any of his co-conspirators may do in furtherance of the common design, whether he was present or not") (quoting Lamb v. People, 96 Ill. 73, 83-84 (1880)). *See also* Hamilton v. People, 113 Ill. 34, 37-38 (1885) (when defendants "deliberately" engaged in "hazardous" activity that "would result in violence endangering life or limb," they "were all co-conspirators in a dangerous criminal enterprise" and, as such, "whatever was done by one, in contemplation of law was done by all, and all are therefore equally responsible"); Brennan v. People, 15 Ill. 511 (1854) ("And he who advises or encourages another to do an illegal act is responsible for all natural and probable consequences that may arise from its perpetration"). This doctrine is critiqued in Audrey Rogers, *Accomplice Liability for Unintentional Crimes: Remaining Within The Constraints of Intent*, 31 LOY. L.A. L. REV. 1351 (1998).

[271] People v. Feagans, 134 Ill. App. 3d 252, 260, 480 N.E.2d 153, 159 (4th Dist. 1985).

[272] 134 Ill. App. 3d 252, 480 N.E.2d 153 (4th Dist. 1985).

[273] People v. Feagans, 134 Ill. App. 3d 252, 260-61, 480 N.E.2d 153, 159-60 (4th Dist. 1985).

only for armed robbery but also the "natural and probable consequences thereof," namely, murder.[274]

Where a defendant attached himself to a group bent on robbing an individual, whereupon one of his companions struck the victim with a two-by-four while another hit him with a hammer, it was held the murder was a "natural and probable consequence" of the group's common design to commit armed robbery and the defendant was responsible "even though he did not actively participate in the overt act itself."[275] Where defendant and other members of a street gang, one of whom was armed, set out to confront members of a rival street gang in response to an earlier confrontation where members of the rival street gang had beaten members of the first gang, whereupon a member of defendant's gang shot and killed a member of the rival gang, this was considered a "natural or probable consequence" of defendant's attaching himself to a "group bent on illegal acts which are dangerous and homicidal in character."[276] Where the defendant on the pretext of purchasing drugs convinced an eventual murder victim to open the burglar gates leading into his apartment in order to allow two codefendants to rush in and demand money from the victim, whereupon the codefendants murdered the victim and three others in the apartment, the defendant was responsible for four counts of murder as well as, among other crimes, residential burglary, home invasion and armed robbery, since the murders were a "natural and probable consequence" of the common purpose to commit the lesser crimes.[277] Where defendant's companion repeatedly beat defendant's child and defendant did nothing to prevent these beatings, whereupon the child died, the defendant was accountable for murder since the child's death was a "natural consequence" of her companion's battery.[278] Where, then, a defendant initially engages in a venture that is dangerous[279] or homicidal in nature,[280] the subsequent criminal acts are committed in furtherance of the initial plan[281] or as a natural and probable consequence thereof[282] *and a murder occurs,*[283] the defendant will be held

---

[274] People v. Feagans, 134 Ill. App. 3d 252, 260, 480 N.E.2d 153, 159 (4th Dist. 1985).

[275] People v. Morgan, 67 Ill. 2d 1, 8-9, 364 N.E.2d 56, 60 (1977) (quoting with approval People v. Morgan, 39 Ill. App. 3d 588, 597-98, 350 N.E.2d 27, 34 (1st Dist. 1976)).

[276] People v. Hughes, 26 Ill. 2d 114, 119-20, 185 N.E.2d 834, 837 (1962).

[277] People v. Green, 179 Ill. App. 3d 1, 15, 535 N.E.2d 413, 422 (1st Dist. 1988).

[278] People v. Ray, 80 Ill. App. 3d 151, 157, 399 N.E.2d 977, 982 (5th Dist. 1979).

[279] People v. Tate, 63 Ill. 2d 105, 105-12, 345 N.E.2d 480, 484 (1976).

[280] People v. Hughes, 26 Ill. 2d 114, 119-20, 185 N.E.2d 834, 837 (1962) ("dangerous or homicidal in character").

[281] *Cf.* People v. Horton, 43 Ill. App. 3d 150, 156, 356 N.E.2d 1044, 1048 (1st Dist. 1976).

[282] People v. Feagans, 134 Ill. App. 3d 252, 260, 480 N.E.2d 153, 159 (4th Dist. 1985).

[283] *See, e.g.,* People v. Patterson, 102 Ill. App. 3d 844, 851, 430 N.E.2d 574, 580 (1st Dist. 1981).

accountable for the murder.[284] Thus, "[w]hether that purpose encompassed . . . murder or was limited to a beating, all defendants are accountable for . . . murder since it was committed in furtherance of their common purpose."[285]

An extremely important question that is not answered by the cases above is whether a person is responsible for unintended, incidental crimes *other than murder* that flow from his or her unintended crimes. The answer appears to be yes. In *People v. Kessler*,[286] defendant and two companions embarked on a plan to burglarize a tavern. As the defendant waited outside the tavern, his two unarmed companions entered the tavern after its closing. While inside the tavern, the defendant's companions were surprised by the tavern owner, who had initially left the tavern to go home but had reentered the tavern through a back door after seeing what he believed to be an unoccupied car parked in front of the tavern. At this point, one of the defendant's companions shot the tavern owner with a gun he found in the tavern during the burglary. A few moments later, the defendant's companions exited the tavern, entered the vehicle wherein defendant was sitting, sped off in the vehicle and then lost control of it. As the defendant's companions fled on foot, one of the two shot at a pursuing police officer as the defendant remained seated in the vehicle.

In *Kessler*, the Illinois Supreme Court upheld the jury verdict finding defendant guilty of two counts of attempted murder and one count of burglary. First, the court interpreted the meaning of the word "conduct" in paragraph 5/5-2 of the Illinois accountability statute:

> We believe the statute, as it reads, means that where one aids another in the planning or commission of an offense, he is legally accountable for the conduct of the person he aids; and that the word "conduct" encompasses *any* criminal act done in furtherance of the planned and intended act.[287]

Next, the court reasoned defendant was not only accountable for his companions' conduct that amounted to burglary but also his companions' conduct in attempting to kill the tavern owner and the police officer in pursuit.[288]

The *Kessler* dissent was quick to point out that defendant Kessler did not have the specific intent to kill either individual who was shot at by his companion and, accordingly, could not be guilty of attempted murder.[289] Moreover, the

---

[284] *See, e.g.,* People v. Bolden, 59 Ill. App. 3d 441, 488-49, 375 N.E.2d 898, 904 (1st Dist. 1978).

[285] People v. Patterson, 102 Ill. App. 3d 844, 851, 430 N.E.2d 574, 580 (1st Dist. 1981).

[286] 57 Ill. 2d 493, 315 N.E.2d 29 (1974), *cert. denied,* 419 U.S. 1054 (1975).

[287] People v. Kessler, 57 Ill. 2d 493, 497, 315 N.E.2d 29, 32 (1974) (emphasis added), *cert. denied,* 419 U.S. 1054 (1975).

[288] People v. Kessler, 57 Ill. 2d 493, 497, 315 N.E.2d 29, 33 (1974), *cert. denied,* 419 U.S. 1054 (1975).

[289] People v. Kessler, 57 Ill. 2d 493, 503, 315 N.E.2d 29, 35 (1974), *cert. denied,* 419 U.S. 1054 (1975) (Goldenhersh, J., dissenting).

dissent noted all of the cases used by the majority to support its holding in-volved subsequent murders as opposed to attempted murders and that convic-tions that resulted in those earlier cases were in accordance with the felony-murder rule, where specific intent to kill is *not* required.[290] However, the major-ity of the court was not persuaded.

Thus, the paragraph 5/5-2 statement that a person can be "legally accountable for the conduct of another" has been interpreted as encompassing not only the criminal conduct inherent in the target crime the defendant intended to commit, but also, as the *Kessler* dissent observes, unintended criminal conduct that flows out of the target crime.[291] This concept, sometimes referred to as the "common-design rule,"[292] which holds that when two or more individuals engage in a common criminal design "*any* acts in furtherance thereof committed by one party are considered the acts of all parties,"[293] applies even if the intended crime was a misdemeanor.[294] Furthermore, this rule holds true even where the inciden-tal crime was not a homicide.[295] Thus, where defendant and another engaged in a burglary, whereupon the codefendant set fire to the premises without any direct encouragement from the defendant, defendant was guilty of both burglary and arson since the common design to commit burglary led to the arson.[296]

§ 3.19. Mens Rea: Specific Intent to Aid and Abet Target Crime.

Proof of accountability is not complete after showing that the defendant solic-ited, aided, abetted, or agreed or attempted to aid the principal before or during the commission of the target crime. The state must also establish beyond a rea-sonable doubt that the defendant participated in the criminal venture with the specific intent of promoting or facilitating the commission of the target crime.[297] "Intent," as used in the accountability statute, "is limited to a conscious objec-

---

[290] People v. Kessler, 57 Ill. 2d 493, 500-01, 315 N.E.2d 29, 34 (1974), *cert. denied*, 419 U.S. 1054 (1975) (Goldenhersh, J., dissenting).

[291] People v. Kessler, 57 Ill. 2d 493, 497, 315 N.E.2d 29, 35 (1974), *cert. denied*, 419 U.S. 1054 (1975) (Goldenhersh, J., dissenting).

[292] People v. Terry, 99 Ill. 2d 508, 515, 460 N.E.2d 746, 749-50 (1984).

[293] People v. Hicks, 286 Ill. App. 3d 588, 593-94, 676 N.E.2d 725, 728-29 (2d Dist. 1997) ("Under the common design rule, any actions that [co-defendant] Davis took in furtherance of the common design [to beat the victim] are the actions of defendant"; defendant liable for home inva-sion arising out of entry into victim's premises to accomplish beating).

[294] People v. Terry, 99 Ill. 2d 508, 515, 460 N.E.2d 746, 749 (1984) ("We agree that the rule does impose liability even though a misdemeanor [battery] was originally intended").

[295] People v. Kessler, 57 Ill. 2d 493, 497, 315 N.E.2d 29, 33 (1974), *cert. denied*, 419 U.S. 1054 (1975).

[296] People v. Cvetich, 73 Ill. App. 3d 580, 583, 391 N.E.2d 1101, 1104 (2d Dist. 1979).

[297] People v. Brown, 197 Ill. App. 3d 907, 916, 557 N.E.2d 199, 205 (1st Dist. 1990).

tive or purpose to accomplish the desired result."[298] Mere knowledge of another's criminality does not make one an accomplice to the target crime.[299]

Whether the defendant had the concurrent, specific intent to promote or facilitate the crime's commission is a question of fact for the jury.[300] However, the state is deemed to have met its burden of proving the defendant's specific intent beyond a reasonable doubt when it either establishes that the defendant shared the intent of the principal or establishes the existence of an illegal common design.[301] A common design may be shown either by prior deliberation to commit the specific offense or by the spontaneous and combined participation of a group in the perpetration of an offense.[302] While guilty knowledge is inadequate as the requisite mental state for accountability, evidence that one voluntarily attaches oneself to a group bent on illegal acts with knowledge of its design supports an inference of common purpose.[303]

In a case that represented a major deviation from precedent in regard to the interrelationship between mens rea and accountability, the Illinois Supreme Court in 1992, in *People v. Stanciel*,[304] ruled that proof of accountability need *not* be based on specific intent.[305] In a consolidated case which involved the legal responsibility of two women for separate murders arising out of each woman's failure to prevent the ongoing physical abuse of her child carried out by an abusive boyfriend, the court held that "requiring specific intent for accountability to murder would be illogical and inconsistent with the murder requirement of general intent."[306] The court continued:

> Accountability, tied as it is to the crime charged, must comport with the requirements of that crime. . . . Under this analysis, then one whose guilt of murder, a general intent crime, is established through accountability, need only possess a general intent, with all the requirements that state of mind entails.[307]

Here, the court ruled that a conviction for murder based on accountability could be established by evidence "sufficient to show that the defendants voluntarily and willfully committed an act, the natural tendency of which is to destroy an-

---

[298] People v. Kessler, 11 Ill. App. 3d 321, 326 n.2, 296 N.E.2d 631, 635 n.2 (2d Dist. 1973), *aff'd in relevant part*, 57 Ill. 2d 493, 315 N.E.2d 29 (1974), *cert. denied*, 419 U.S. 1054 (1975).

[299] People v. Taylor, 186 Ill. 2d 439, 446, 712 N.E.2d 326, 329 (1999); People v. Batchelor, 171 Ill. 2d 367, 375-76, 665 N.E.2d 777, 780 (1996).

[300] People v. Kelly, 39 Ill. App. 3d 988, 991, 351 N.E.2d 419, 421 (4th Dist. 1976).

[301] People v. Taylor, 164 Ill. 2d 131, 139, 646 N.E.2d 567, 571 (1995).

[302] People v. Brown, 197 Ill. App. 3d 907, 916, 557 N.E.2d 199, 205 (1st Dist. 1990).

[303] People v. Taylor, 164 Ill. 2d 131, 139, 646 N.E.2d 567, 571 (1995).

[304] 153 Ill. 2d 218, 606 N.E.2d 1201 (1992).

[305] People v. Stanciel, 153 Ill. 2d 218, 233, 606 N.E.2d 1201, 1210 (1992).

[306] People v. Stanciel, 153 Ill. 2d 218, 233, 606 N.E.2d 1201, 1210 (1992).

[307] People v. Stanciel, 153 Ill. 2d 218, 233, 606 N.E.2d 1201, 1210 (1992).

other's life."[308] In this case, the court held that both defendants either knew or should have known of the serious nature of the injuries which the victims were sustaining."[309]

More recent cases from the Illinois Supreme Court since *Stanciel* appear to have moved away from the position the court articulated in that case. For example, in *People v. Taylor*,[310] the court in a first degree murder case stated in 1995 that a conviction based on accountability requires a showing that "defendant shared the criminal *intent* of the principal, or if there was a common criminal *plan* or *purpose*."[311] In *People v. Shaw*,[312] the court commented in 1998 that "[u]nless the accomplice *intends* to aid the commission of a crime, no guilt will attach."[313] In *People v. Taylor*,[314] the court in a 1999 case involving aggravated discharge of a firearm, which is established by a showing of a knowing *or* intentional discharge of a firearm in the direction of another person,[315] stated that "under accountability, the State must show that the defendant, either before or during the commission of the offense, *intentionally* aided or abetted an offender in conduct that constitutes an element of the offense."[316] Other Illinois Supreme Court post-*Stanciel* comments on the subject usually involve a mere quote from the accountability statute which, of course, contains the "with the intent to promote or facilitate" the perpetrator's criminality language.[317]

§ 3.20. Mens Rea and Incidental Crimes.

Once a common design has been established, the common design rule provides that each participant is legally accountable for the criminal conduct of any member of the group done in furtherance of the planned and intended act.[318] Where subsequent incidental illegal acts arise out of an established common design, all defendants are liable for the subsequent offenses that are committed as part of their common purpose *or* that are natural or probable consequences of that purpose.[319] Known as the "common design" rule,[320] cases employing this

---

[308] People v. Stanciel, 153 Ill. 2d 218, 233, 606 N.E.2d 1201, 1210 (1992).

[309] People v. Stanciel, 153 Ill. 2d 218, 233-37, 606 N.E.2d 1201, 1210-12 (1992).

[310] 164 Ill. 2d 131, 646 N.E.2d 567 (1995).

[311] People v. Taylor, 164 Ill. 2d 131, 139, 646 N.E.2d 567, 571 (1995) (emphasis added).

[312] 186 Ill. 2d 301, 713 N.E.2d 1161 (1998).

[313] People v. Shaw, 186 Ill. 3d 301, 322, 713 N.E.2d 1161, 1173 (1998) (emphasis in original).

[314] 186 Ill. 2d 439, 712 N.E.2d 326 (1999).

[315] 720 ILCS 5/24-1.2(a)(2) (1999).

[316] People v. Taylor, 186 Ill. 2d 439, 446, 712 N.E.2d 326, 329 (1999) (emphasis added).

[317] *See, e.g.*, People v. Dennis, 181 Ill. 2d 87, 101, 692 N.E.2d 325, 330 (1998); People v. Batchelor, 171 Ill. 2d 367, 374, 665 N.E.2d 777, 780 (1996).

[318] People v. Kessler, 57 Ill. 2d 493, 497, 315 N.E.2d 29, 32 (1974), *cert. denied*, 419 U.S. 1054 (1975).

[319] People v. Green, 179 Ill. App. 3d 1, 15, 535 N.E.2d 413, 422 (1st Dist. 1989).

[320] People v. Terry, 99 Ill. 2d 508, 514, 460 N.E.2d 746, 749 (1984).

doctrine interpret the language of the accountability statute as meaning if a defendant is involved in the "planning or commission of *an* offense," he or she is responsible for any *other* criminality that may result from such target offense.[321] Thus, where a defendant subscribed to a common venture among a group of individuals to beat a victim into turning over certain money allegedly owed by the victim to another party, the court stated that this unlawful venture, which fostered a mood of violence, was of such a nature that the death of the victim was a natural or probable consequence.[322] Accordingly, the defendant was convicted for armed robbery and murder even though he had indicated he wanted no part of the money, did not wish to participate in the beating, and took no actual part in the beating.[323] The "common design" concept is applicable to all crimes and is not limited to felony-murder situations.[324] Where the defendant agreed to participate in a burglary, apparently as a lookout while two unarmed companions embarked on their unlawful entry into a tavern, he was convicted of aiding and abetting two attempted murders in circumstances where one of the companions used a gun he found in the burglarized premises and shot at the tavern owner, who had surprised them during the course of the burglary, as well as a police officer who attempted to apprehend the two companions as they were fleeing on foot.[325] In the case of the beating for money, the defendant insisted he did not have the specific intent to murder,[326] and in the case involving the burglary, the defendant denied he had the specific intent to commit attempted murder.[327] Indeed, even if a defendant's original intent is commission of misdemeanor battery, but this criminal design to commit the offense is so fraught with danger that other incidental offenses of a homicidal nature are reasonably foreseeable, then the defendant accomplice cannot claim he or she had no notion about the murder that ultimately occurred and thereby avoid criminal liability for it.[328]

---

[321] People v. Cole, 253 Ill. App. 3d 603, 609, 625 N.E.2d 816, 821 (4th Dist. 1993) (emphasis in quote original). *See* § 3.18 of this chapter for further discussion of this rule.

[322] People v. Morgan, 39 Ill. App. 3d 588, 597, 350 N.E.2d 27, 34-35 (1st Dist. 1976), *aff'd*, 67 Ill. 2d 1, 364 N.E.2d 56, *cert. denied*, 434 U.S. 927 (1977).

[323] People v. Morgan, 39 Ill. App. 3d 588, 598, 350 N.E.2d 27, 35 (1st Dist. 1976), *aff'd*, 67 Ill. 2d 1, 364 N.E.2d 56, *cert. denied*, 434 U.S. 927 (1977).

[324] *See* People v. Kessler, 57 Ill. 2d 493, 315 N.E.2d 29 (1974), *cert. denied*, 419 U.S. 1054 (1975).

[325] People v. Kessler, 57 Ill. 2d 493, 496-97, 315 N.E.2d 29, 32-33 (1974), *cert. denied*, 419 U.S. 1054 (1975).

[326] People v. Morgan, 39 Ill. App. 3d 588, 598, 350 N.E.2d 27, 35 (1st Dist. 1976), *aff'd*, 67 Ill. 2d 1, 364 N.E.2d 56, *cert. denied*, 434 U.S. 927 (1977).

[327] People v. Kessler, 57 Ill. 2d 493, 495, 315 N.E.2d 29, 31 (1974), *cert. denied*, 419 U.S. 1054 (1974).

[328] People v. Terry, 99 Ill. 2d 508, 515, 460 N.E.2d 746, 749 (1984). Although the concept stretches accomplice liability to the limits and has been the subject of criticism. *See, e.g.,* WAYNE LAFAVE & AUSTIN SCOTT, CRIMINAL LAW § 6-8 (b) (2d ed. 1986), such is accepted law in Illinois.

In one decision, the Illinois appellate court ruled that a common design to commit an unlawful act could be predicated on finding of recklessness on the part of the alleged accomplices.[329] Here, one defendant handed a gun with an empty chamber to the principal who then shot the victim.[330] The appellate court held that the principal and the two accomplices were reckless in agreeing to point a partially loaded gun at the victim, that this recklessness amounted to a common design to do an unlawful act, that no intent to shoot or kill was necessary to convict the parties and, accordingly, the accomplices could be convicted of involuntary manslaughter on an accountability theory.[331]

§ 3.21. Mens Rea and Subsequent Crimes Beyond the Initial Common Design.

Where a criminal venture strays beyond the common design originally contemplated to such an extent it cannot be said that it was a natural and probable consequence of the initial illegal common design, the accomplice will be responsible for the principal's subsequent criminality as well where he or she somehow facilitates the subsequent offense with a wrongful mental state. In *People v. Tyler*,[332] defendant and two codefendants planned to burglarize a secluded residence. At the house they encountered a woman and one of the codefendants eventually took the woman to a back room and raped her. Although the defendant did not directly participate in the rape, he was held accountable for the rape since he "knew perfectly well what was happening" in the back bedroom, did nothing to dissociate himself from the occurrence and, in fact, had warned the codefendants when a car approached the house.[333]

Where defendant and two codefendants followed through on a plan to commit home invasion and armed robbery, whereupon the two codefendants commenced to sexually assault two female victims in their apartment, the defendant was convicted of aggravated criminal sexual assault since he proceeded to remove property from the apartment during the assaults, admitted he left the apartment for a short time to watch for police and did nothing to dissociate himself from the others' sex crimes.[334] Where defendant and two codefendants decided to engage in an armed robbery of their victim, whereupon it became clear that one of the codefendants was inclined to kill their victim to cover up their crimes and possessed the means to do so, defendant was held accountable for the murder of the victim which eventually occurred — even though he was not directly in-

---

[329] People v. Cole, 253 Ill. App. 3d 603, 609, 625 N.E.2d 816, 821 (4th Dist. 1993).

[330] People v. Cole, 253 Ill. App. 3d 603, 606, 625 N.E.2d 816, 821 (4th Dist. 1993).

[331] People v. Cole, 253 Ill. App. 3d 603, 610, 625 N.E.2d 816, 821 (4th Dist. 1993).

[332] 78 Ill. 2d 193, 399 N.E.2d 975 (1980).

[333] People v. Tyler, 78 Ill. 2d 193, 197, 399 N.E.2d 975, 977 (1980).

[334] People v. Jones, 184 Ill. App. 3d 412, 431-32, 541 N.E.2d 132, 144 (1st Dist. 1989).

volved in the murder, was unconscious due to alcohol consumption during the murder and claimed he had argued against killing the victim — since he had participated in tying up the victim after the codefendant had announced his inclination to kill the victim.[335]

§ 3.22. Mens Rea and the Reluctant Accomplice.

The specific intent to promote or facilitate the target crime will be found even though the defendant claims to have been a reluctant participant who joined the criminal venture because he or she feared the principal.[336] When this explanation is offered, the courts expect some affirmative conduct by the defendant showing an attempt on his or her part to withdraw from the venture[337] or to warn others that the crime was going to be committed.[338] Even evidence that the defendant attempted to withdraw, however, will be insufficient to preclude a finding that the defendant lacked the requisite intent to commit the crime where the court finds that his or her efforts were perfunctory and totally without effect.[339] The court's intolerance of the reluctant defendant is evidenced by *People v. Gray*.[340] In *Gray*, a defendant was taken forcibly by the hand over her protestations by an individual named Williams and made to enter a vacant apartment building where a particular couple, male and female, were situated along with several others. She was told by Williams to hold a cigarette lighter so that Williams and the others could see what they were doing while they raped the woman. Immediately after the group raped the woman, Williams shot the woman to death. Thereafter, Williams took the defendant by the hand and led her and the male to a nearby creek where he shot the male to death. Williams then told the defendant Gray that he would kill her and her family should she inform the police about the incident. She was convicted of two counts of murder as well as rape on an accountability theory in part because she failed to make "any effort to leave the scene of the crimes or prevent their commission."[341] Also, the court considered the fact that Williams's threat regarding killing her and her family occurred after

---

[335] People v. Feagans, 134 Ill. App. 3d 252, 260-61, 480 N.E.2d 153, 159-60 (4th Dist. 1985).

[336] People v. Gray, 87 Ill. App. 3d 142, 149-50, 408 N.E.2d 1150, 1154-55 (1st Dist. 1980), *cert. denied*, 450 U.S. 1032 (1981).

[337] People v. Gray, 87 Ill. App. 3d 142, 150, 408 N.E.2d 1150, 1155 (1st Dist. 1980), *cert. denied*, 450 U.S. 1032 (1981).

[338] People v. Moon, 38 Ill. App. 3d 854, 863-64, 350 N.E.2d 179, 186 (1st Dist. 1980).

[339] In the Interest of Weigler, 37 Ill. App. 3d 478, 482, 346 N.E.2d 171, 174 (4th Dist. 1976).

[340] 87 Ill. App. 3d 142, 408 N.E.2d 1150 (1st Dist. 1980), *cert. denied*, 450 U.S. 1032 (1981).

[341] People v. Gray, 87 Ill. App. 3d 142, 149, 408 N.E.2d 1150, 1155 (1st Dist. 1980), *cert. denied*, 450 U.S. 1032 (1981).

the crimes, not before.[342] As such, defendant's claim that she should have the benefit of the defense of compulsion was denied.[343]

§ 3.23. Withdrawal from the Crime.

The revision committee that drafted the accountability statute found it desirable to provide an accomplice with an escape route, if for no other reason than to provide an inducement for the disclosure of crimes before they occur and to generally prevent the commission of crimes.[344] Thus, a person who has aided or encouraged another to commit a crime will not be accountable, unless the statute defining the offense provides otherwise, if the person terminates his or her efforts to promote or facilitate the crime before its commission *and* either wholly deprives his or her prior efforts of effectiveness, gives timely warning to the proper law enforcement authorities, or otherwise makes proper effort to prevent the crime's commission.[345] An effective withdrawal requires essentially two elements: (1) the defendant must terminate his or her conduct before the offense is committed *and* (2) the defendant must also neutralize the effect of his or her conduct.[346] A defendant's withdrawal after the commencement of the crime is not a timely withdrawal. Hence, where the defendant attempted a withdrawal after he had already hit an intended robbery victim and while codefendant was clubbing the victim, his claim of withdrawal was rejected since the robbery was already in progress.[347] Likewise, there was no withdrawal where defendant was informed of codefendant's plans to rob and kill an invalid victim, he accompanied the codefendant to a vacant lot where the crime occurred, he kicked the victim and threw dirt on his face, and served as a lookout while codefendant carried out the plan.[348]

As stated, the defendant can neutralize the effect of his or her earlier conduct toward aiding and abetting by wholly depriving his or her prior efforts of effectiveness, by giving timely warning to the authorities or by preventing the crime. A person who advised, encouraged or incited another to commit a crime has not deprived his or her efforts of effectiveness and, accordingly, cannot escape li-

---

[342] People v. Gray, 87 Ill. App. 3d 142, 149, 408 N.E.2d 1150, 1155 (1st Dist. 1980), *cert. denied*, 450 U.S. 1032 (1981).

[343] People v. Gray, 87 Ill. App. 3d 142, 148-50, 408 N.E.2d 1150, 1155-56 (1st Dist. 1980), *cert. denied*, 450 U.S. 1032 (1981). *See* ch. 19 for a discussion of the defense of compulsion.

[344] ILL. ANN. STAT. ch. 38, para. 5-2 (Smith-Hurd 1989), 1961 Committee Comments, at 236.

[345] 720 ILCS 5/5-2(c)(3) (1999).

[346] People v. Ellis, 93 Ill. App. 3d 981, 985, 418 N.E.2d 88, 91 (1st Dist. 1981), *cert. denied*, 456 U.S. 907 (1982).

[347] People v. Lykins, 65 Ill. App. 3d 808, 813, 382 N.E.2d 1242, 1246 (4th Dist. 1978), *aff'd*, 77 Ill. 2d 35, 394 N.E.2d 1182 (1979), *cert. denied*, 445 U.S. 952 (1980).

[348] People v. Riddle, 175 Ill. App. 3d 85, 91, 529 N.E.2d 713, 717 (1st Dist. 1988).

ability for his or her conduct by quietly leaving the scene[349] or simply walking away from the crime.[350] At a minimum, it is the communication to the principal of the intent to withdraw and not the mere fact of withdrawal that determines whether the defendant will be released from liability.[351] Moreover, the withdrawal must be effective and timely.[352] In order to constitute an effective withdrawal, some kind of disapproval or opposition must be shown to the activities that the defendant knew had either occurred or were about to occur.[353] To be considered timely, the defendant must give his or her conspirators a reasonable opportunity, if they desire, to follow defendant's example and refrain from further action before the crime is committed.[354] The trier of fact must be able to conclude that the accused had wholly and effectively detached himself or herself from the criminal enterprise before the crime with which he or she is charged reached consummation or had become so inevitable that its commission could not be reasonably stayed by the defendant's action.[355] Thus, where a defendant, a member of a street gang, initially participated in beating the victim as punishment because the victim had expressed the desire to become a member of a different street gang, his subsequent warning to the victim that the other codefendant members of the gang were going to do something worse to him and departure from the scene did amount to withdrawal from the codefendants' subsequent murder of the victim.[356] Here, while defendant may have terminated his criminal conduct before the codefendants' murder of the victim, defendant's warning did not neutralize the effect of his prior conduct and, consequently, could not be interpreted as wholly depriving his prior efforts of effectiveness.[357] Similarly, where an accomplice and the principal planned the robbery of a victim and the accomplice was aware of the fact that the principal might kill the victim, the accomplice's admonishment to the principal that he should not hurt the victim did not deprive his prior efforts of effectiveness and, thus, the accomplice was held liable for the murder of the victim even though he was not present during the robbery-murder.[358] His mere statement of disapproval toward the

---

[349] People v. Lacey, 49 Ill. App. 2d 301, 307, 200 N.E.2d 11, 14 (1st Dist. 1964); People v. Marx, 291 Ill. 40, 48, 125 N.E. 719, 722 (1920).

[350] People v. Nunn, 184 Ill. App. 3d 253, 272, 541 N.E.2d 182, 195 (1st Dist. 1989), *cert. denied*, 497 U.S. 1027 (1990).

[351] People v. Cooper, 164 Ill. App. 3d 734. 739, 518 N.E.2d 260, 263 (1st Dist. 1987); People v. Rybka, 16 Ill. 2d 394, 406, 158 N.E.2d 17, 23 (1959).

[352] People v. Lacey, 49 Ill. App. 2d 301, 307, 200 N.E.2d 11, 14 (1st Dist. 1964).

[353] People v. Lacey, 49 Ill. App. 2d 301, 307, 200 N.E.2d 11, 14 (1st Dist. 1964).

[354] People v. Lacey, 49 Ill. App. 2d 301, 307, 200 N.E.2d 11, 14 (1st Dist. 1964).

[355] People v. Lacey, 49 Ill. App. 2d 301, 307, 200 N.E.2d 11, 14 (1st Dist. 1964).

[356] People v. Stachelek, 145 Ill. App. 3d 391, 404, 495 N.E.2d 984, 992 (3d Dist. 1986).

[357] People v. Stachelek, 145 Ill. App. 3d 391, 404, 495 N.E.2d 984, 992 (3d Dist. 1986).

[358] People v. Tiller, 94 Ill. 2d 303, 4, 447 N.E.2d 174, 180 (1982).

principal's act was insufficient to constitute an effective withdrawal.[359] Similarly, where the defendant participated in tying up the victim of a robbery and removed his wallet, he did not neutralize the effect of his prior acts by leaving the victim behind with two codefendants, one of whom subsequently hit the victim on the head with a hammer, or by his after-the-fact expression of concern for the safety of the victim, who eventually died.[360]

A timely warning to law enforcement authorities could constitute a withdrawal.[361] However, when the police were summoned by defendant after he had already aided and abetted an armed robbery, during which a codefendant severely beat the victim, this in no way exonerated defendant of the armed robbery and subsequent murder.[362]

Finally, a general clause in the accountability statute states if the accused who initially incited or encouraged another to commit an offense "otherwise makes proper effort to prevent commission of the offense," this will free the accused from accomplice liability.[363] However, the effort must be more than perfunctory.[364] Where the accomplice shot the victim in the shoulder, was instructed by the principal to shoot the victim again, this time in the head, but the accomplice refused, whereupon the principal shot the victim in the head and killed him, the accomplice's refusal to shoot the victim in the head did not free him from accountability for the murder of the victim since this was less than a "proper effort" to prevent the crime.[365] A juvenile defendant's futile five-minute search for the gasoline he provided to other boys to use to burn a high school was considered a perfunctory effort on his part to prevent the arson where the court determined that he could have taken other action to prevent the crime.[366] He could have sought out the others and attempted to dissuade them, he could have conducted a more thorough search, or he could have enlisted the aid of adults other than the police.[367]

It is possible for a defendant to make an effective withdrawal from one crime and still be accountable for the commission of a prior offense. In *People v. Brown*,[368] the defendant joined two others in a plan to burglarize an auto dealership and steal a car. When they arrived at the dealership, the defendant and an-

---

[359] People v. Tiller, 94 Ill. 2d 303, 314, 447 N.E.2d 174, 180 (1982).

[360] People v. Ellis, 93 Ill. App. 3d 981, 985, 418 N.E.2d 88, 91 (1st Dist. 1981), *cert. denied*, 456 U.S. 907 (1982).

[361] ILL. ANN. STAT. ch. 38, para. 5-2 (Smith-Hurd 1989), 1961 Committee Comments, at 237.

[362] People v. Riddle, 175 Ill. App. 3d 85, 90-91, 529 N.E.2d 713, 717 (1st Dist. 1988) (withdrawal instruction properly denied).

[363] ILL. ANN. STAT. ch. 38, para. 5-2 (Smith-Hurd 1989), 1961 Committee Comments, at 237.

[364] In the Interest of Weigler, 37 Ill. App. 3d 478, 482, 346 N.E.2d 171, 174 (4th Dist. 1976).

[365] People v. Martin, 46 Ill. App. 3d 943, 956, 361 N.E.2d 595, 604 (1st Dist. 1977).

[366] In the Interest of Weigler, 37 Ill. App. 3d 478, 482, 346 N.E.2d 171, 174 (4th Dist. 1976).

[367] In the Interest of Weigler, 37 Ill. App. 3d 478, 482, 346 N.E.2d 171, 174 (4th Dist. 1976).

[368] 90 Ill. App. 3d 742, 414 N.E.2d 475 (3d Dist. 1980).

other person kicked in the back door. At that point the two defendants at the back door became scared. They did not enter the building but went to the front and told the third defendant that the burglary plan was "bullshit" and that they were leaving. The third defendant, who had been posing as a lookout, reluctantly left with the others. Moments later, the police arrested them as they were leaving the parking lot. The court recognized that the defendant, by preventing the burglary, had effectively withdrawn.[369] However, he was convicted of attempted burglary, since kicking in the door constituted a substantial step toward completion of the burglary, and that action had occurred before the defendant's withdrawal.[370]

§ 3.24. Exceptions to Accomplice Liability: Conduct of Victims and Those Involved in Crime as Incidental Matter.

While subparagraph (c)(3) of paragraph 5/5-2 limits the reach of the Illinois accountability statute where a defendant has effectively withdrawn from the criminal enterprise, subparagraph (c)(1) relieves from accomplice liability a person who is a "victim of the offense committed."[371] Also, subparagraph (c)(2) provides that an individual cannot be an accomplice where the "offense is so defined that his conduct was inevitably incident to its commission."[372] The first situation covers those persons such as the victim of a blackmail plot who willingly aids the plot by paying money to the blackmailer[373] or the young girl below the age of consent who willingly engages in sex with an adult male.[374] The second situation covers those persons such as the person who accepts a prostitute's solicitation[375] or the individual who purchases narcotics.[376] In none of these cases could the person be convicted as an accomplice notwithstanding his or her encouragement or aid in the commission of the crime. Although there are few reported cases in Illinois dealing with these exceptions to accountability, in one opinion, the Illinois Supreme Court held that one could not be convicted of aiding and abetting the defrauding of the state where the apparent thrust of the stat-

---

[369] People v. Brown, 90 Ill. App. 3d 742, 746-49, 414 N.E.2d 475, 479-81 (3d Dist. 1980).

[370] People v. Brown, 90 Ill. App. 3d 742, 746-49, 414 N.E.2d 475, 479-81 (3d Dist. 1980).

[371] 720 ILCS 5/5-2(c)(1) (1999).

[372] 720 ILCS 5/5-2(c)(2) (1999).

[373] ILL. ANN. STAT. ch. 38, para. 5-2 (Smith-Hurd 1989), 1961 Committee Comments, at 236.

[374] ILL. ANN. STAT. ch. 38, para. 5-2 (Smith-Hurd 1989), 1961 Committee Comments, at 236.

[375] ILL. ANN. STAT. ch. 38, para. 5-2 (Smith-Hurd 1989), 1961 Committee Comments, at 236. Although the patron could not be convicted of prostitution on an accomplice theory, he or she could be convicted of "patronizing a prostitute" which is a different offense. *See* 720 ILCS 5/11-18 (1999).

[376] 1 CHARLES E. TORCIA, WHARTON'S CRIMINAL LAW § 38, at 202 (14th ed. 1978). Although the purchaser could not be convicted of distribution on an accomplice theory, he or she could be convicted of possession of controlled substances. 720 ILCS 570/402 (1999).

ute was directed only at those who assumed a "primary" role in the fraudulent effort.[377] Similarly, where the defendant solicited a drug supplier to provide him with drugs for personal use, subparagraph (c)(2) barred his conviction for aiding and abetting the supplier's possession with intent to deliver.[378]

In any event subparagraph (c)(1) accomplishes the intent of the legislature to protect the "victim" of a crime, not punish the person. Meanwhile, subparagraph (c)(2) assures a person's incidental involvement in a crime is not punished where he or she falls outside the class of persons the legislature meant to punish.

§ 3.25. Responsibility of Corporation.

Although at common law a corporation was viewed as legally incapable of committing a crime on the theory that it was impossible for such an entity to formulate a wrongful mens rea,[379] the law in most jurisdictions has been changed to allow for such liability.[380] In article 5/5 of the Illinois criminal code, there is a provision that makes possible the conviction of a corporation for criminal acts.[381] Paragraph 5/5-4 provides:

(a) A corporation may be prosecuted for the commission of an offense if, but only if:
(1) The offense is a misdemeanor, or is defined by Paragraphs 11-20 [obscenity], 11-20.1 [child pornography], or 24-1 [unlawful use of weapons] of this code, or paragraph 44 of the "Environmental Protection Act," [hazardous waste prohibitions] . . . or is defined by another statute which clearly indicates a legislative purpose to impose liability on a corporation; and an agent of the corporation performs the conduct which is an element of the offense while acting within the scope of his or her office or employment and in behalf of the corporation, except that any limitation in the defining statute, concerning the corporation's accountability for certain agents or under certain circumstances, is applicable; or
(2) The commission of the offense is authorized, requested, commanded, or performed, by the board of directors or by a high managerial agent who is acting within the scope of his or her employment in behalf of the corporation.
(b) A corporation's proof, by a preponderance of the evidence, that the high managerial agent having supervisory responsibility over the conduct which is the subject matter of the offense exercised due diligence to prevent the commission of the offense, is a defense to a prosecution for any

---

[377] People v. Issacs, 37 Ill. 2d 205, 224-25, 226 N.E.2d 38, 49-50 (1967).

[378] People v. Raya, 250 Ill. App. 3d 795, 799, 621 N.E.2d 222, 226 (3d Dist. 1993).

[379] ROLLIN M. PERKINS & RONALD N. BOYCE, CRIMINAL LAW 718-21 (3d ed. 1982).

[380] WAYNE LAFAVE & AUSTIN SCOTT, CRIMINAL LAW § 3.10 (2d ed. 1986).

[381] 720 ILCS 5/5-4 (1999).

offense to which Subsection (a)(1) refers, other than an offense for which absolute liability is imposed. This Subsection is inapplicable if the legislative purpose of the statute defining the offense is inconsistent with the provisions of this Subsection.

(c) For the purpose of the Section:

(1) "Agent" means any director, officer, servant, employee, or other person who is authorized to act in behalf of the corporation.

(2) "High managerial agent" means an officer of the corporation, or any other agent who has a position of comparable authority for the formulation of corporate policy or the supervision of subordinate employees in a managerial capacity.[382]

The revision committee, which drafted this enactment, reflected on the intended scope of this provision:

Subsection 5-4(a)(1) deals with corporate liability for offenses of the misdemeanor category, such other offenses as may be expressly included, and those which clearly indicate a legislative purpose to impose corporate liability where the offense is defined by a statute not included in the Criminal Code. Here the problem relates principally to offenses that might be denominated "regulatory crimes." In dealing with offenses of this character, the broadest scope of liability is provided. The corporation is made criminally responsible for criminal conduct performed by any corporate employee acting within the scope of his office or employment and in behalf of the corporation. The chief justification for such broad liability in this class of cases is to provide an inducement for high managerial officers in the corporation to supervise the behavior of minor employees in such a way as to avoid criminal conduct on the part of corporate employees. In many of the regulatory offenses, the corporation which violates a criminal statute is not confronted by the threat of tort liability growing out of the same act. Thus, if the corporation is required to file a corporate report and fails to do so, the liability it will suffer may only be criminal liability. These provisions, of course, do not in any way relieve the individual corporate employees from criminal liability for their own acts. In many cases, criminal prosecution directed to the guilty individual will prove more effective in enforcing the regulatory policy of the statute. There may be times, however, in which, while it is clear that someone in the corporate employ has committed the criminal act, it may be impossible to identify the particular employee guilty of criminal behavior. In such case, the only sanction available is the imposing of a fine on the corporate body. There may also be cases in which the criminal act is committed by a corporate

---

[382] 720 ILCS 5/5-4 (1999).

employee of a foreign corporation residing outside the jurisdiction. In such a situation, again, the only feasible course open to the Illinois prosecutor may be a criminal indictment against the corporation. * * * *

Since, however, the major purpose of subsection (a)(1) is to induce due diligence on the part of managerial personnel to prevent criminal conduct on the part of corporate employees, it seems appropriate to permit the corporation to defend by proof that the criminal conduct occurred despite the exercise of due diligence on the part of supervisory personnel. Consequently, subsection (b) provides that proof of due diligence is a defense to the criminal charge against the corporation. The persuasive burden, in this case, is placed upon the corporate defendant. This is true because the facts relating to due diligence are peculiarly in the possession of the defendant and because an undue burden would be placed upon the prosecution in many cases if it were required affirmatively to show that the supervisory personnel *failed* to exercise due diligence. This defense is further qualified by the provision that if the statute in question clearly intends that the defense of due diligence should not be available to the corporation, the particular provision of the statute shall prevail over the language of subsection (b).

Subsection (a)(2) relates to the scope of liability of corporations for criminal offenses of the more serious character. It provides, in effect, that when a corporation is indicted for a felony such as embezzlement, involuntary manslaughter, and the like, the corporation may not be held liable unless the criminal conduct was performed or participated in by the Board of Directors or by a high managerial agent. The restriction on the scope of corporate liability in this class of cases is justified by the consideration that before the stigma of serious criminality attaches to a corporate body, the conduct should involve someone close to the center of corporate power. Moreover, in these cases, the argument for the necessity of corporate fines to stimulate diligent supervision of minor employees is considerably less persuasive. This is true because most of the serious felonies also involve the possibility of corporate tort liability and this possibility provides ordinarily sufficient inducements for the exercise of proper supervision by managerial officials. The restriction of corporate liability in the case of serious felonies to acts of participating high managerial officials is supported by the caselaw of certain American states and appears to be consistent with the English law on the same point. . . .[383]

---

[383] ILL. ANN. STAT. ch. 38, para. 5-4 (Smith-Hurd 1989), 1961 Committee Comments, at 291-92.

§ 3.26. — Elements of Corporate Criminality.

The Illinois law has essentially been patterned after the Model Penal Code provision.[384] It is at variance with the generally accepted approach, known as the *respondeat superior* concept, that is accepted in the federal system and in most states.[385] The respondeat superior doctrine holds a corporation criminally responsible where (1) an illegal act was performed by an agent of the corporation, who had the specific intent required by the governing statute,[386] (2) the act was within the scope of the agent's employment,[387] and (3) the agent's criminal act was committed with the intent to benefit the corporation.[388]

The Model Penal Code offers a complex, multifaceted approach with three distinct systems of corporate liability.[389] Although the face of paragraph 5/5-4 does not clearly reflect this three-tier scheme, a careful reading of the Committee Comments above reveals this to be the law in Illinois. The first system applies where no "legislative purpose to impose liability" on a corporation is "clearly indicated."[390] A corporation can be held liable for a crime committed by an agent only if the offense was performed or authorized by the board of directors or by a high managerial agent.[391] This tier is somewhat problematic in that the general definition of "person,"[392] a term that appears throughout the Criminal Code,[393] clearly includes within its meaning a "corporation."[394] It appears by reason of this general statutory definition that all crimes in the Illinois penal code clearly apply to a corporation, but paragraph 5/5-4 implicitly suggests that this is not the case. In any event, the first system applies where there is *no clear indication the particular crime applies to a corporation* and involves the following requirements: (1) an illegal act was performed by an agent of the corporation who had the requisite mental state required of the offense; (2) the act was within the scope of his employment; (3) the act was performed with the intent to benefit the corporation; and (4) the act was authorized, requested, commanded, or

---

[384] MODEL PENAL CODE § 2.07 (1962).

[385] Comment, *Developments in the Law — Corporate Crime: Regulating Behavior Through Criminal Sanctions*, 92 HARV. L. REV. 1227, 1247 (1979). This Comment is hereinafter referred to as "*Comment on Corporate Crime*."

[386] *Comment on Corporate Crime* at 1247.

[387] *Comment on Corporate Crime* at 1249.

[388] *Comment on Corporate Crime* at 1250.

[389] *Comment on Corporate Crime* at 1251.

[390] *Comment on Corporate Crime* at 1251. *See also* 720 ILCS 5/5-4(a)(2) (1999).

[391] *Comment on Corporate Crime* at 1251. *See also* 720 ILCS 5/5-4(a)(2) (1999).

[392] 720 ILCS 5/2-15 (1999) ("'Person' means an individual, public or private corporation . . . .").

[393] *See, e.g.*, 720 ILCS 5/9-1(a) (1999) (first-degree murder). *Compare* People v. Duncan, 363 Ill. 495, 2 N.E.2d 705 (1936) (under old law, corporation could not be indicted for violation of statute calling for imprisonment or death penalty).

[394] 720 ILCS 5/2-15 (1999).

performed by the corporation's board of directors or by a high managerial agent.[395]

Tier two of this statutory scheme arises where the statute in question *clearly indicates a legislative purpose to impose liability on a corporation.*[396] This approach is analogous to the traditional respondeat superior concept except in one respect: if the high managerial agent of the corporation has employed "due diligence to prevent commission of the offense" by his or her subordinate, then the corporation has an affirmative defense to the charge.[397] Thus, if this clear legislative purpose is apparent, the state must prove: (1) an illegal act was performed by an agent of the corporation who had the requisite mental state required of the offense; (2) the act was within the scope of the agent's employment; (3) the act was performed with the intent to benefit the corporation; and (4) the corporation failed to demonstrate by a preponderance of evidence that a high managerial agent used due diligence to prevent the crime.[398] This second approach also applies to all misdemeanors, unless the statute in question provides differently,[399] to all violations of the Illinois unlawful use of weapons statute,[400] to all violations of the obscenity[401] and child pornography[402] statutes, and to violations of prohibitions, pertaining to hazardous waste, contained in the Illinois Environmental Protection Act.[403]

The third tier applies to *strict liability* statutes, and it only requires proof of the commission of a criminal act, by a corporate agent, that is within the scope of his or her employment.[404] The agent's intent to engage in the unlawful act and intent to benefit the corporation by the act is not required;[405] the defense of due diligence is not allowed;[406] and authorization or ratification of the agent's conduct by the board of directors or by a high managerial agent is not required.[407]

Prosecution of corporations in Illinois is quite rare. One reason is probably the absence of appropriate sanctions.[408]

---

[395] *Comment on Corporate Crime* at 1251.

[396] *Comment on Corporate Crime* at 1252. *See also* 720 ILCS 5/5-4(a)(1) (1999).

[397] *Comment on Corporate Crime* at 1252. *See also* 720 ILCS 5/5-4(b) (1999).

[398] *Comment on Corporate Crime* at 1252.

[399] 720 ILCS 5/5-4(a)(1) (1999).

[400] 720 ILCS 5/5-4(a)(1) (1999) (referring to 720 ILCS 5/24-1 (1999)).

[401] 720 ILCS 5/5-4(a)(1) (1999) (referring to 720 ILCS 5/11-20 (1999)).

[402] 720 ILCS 5/5-4(a)(1) (1999) (referring to 720 ILCS 5/11-20.1 (1999)).

[403] 720 ILCS 5/5-4(a)(1) (1999) (referring to 415 ILCS 5/44 (1999)).

[404] *Comment on Corporate Crime* at 1252. *See also* 720 ILCS 5/5-4(b) (1999).

[405] *Comment on Corporate Crime* at 1252.

[406] *Comment on Corporate Crime* at 1252.

[407] *Comment on Corporate Crime* at 1252-53.

[408] ILL. ANN. STAT. ch. 38, para. 5-4 (Smith-Hurd 1989), 1961 Committee Comments, at 290.

In *People v. Chicago Magnet Wire Corporation*,[409] the Illinois Supreme Court addressed an issue that could have major implications in connection with corporate criminality and employee injury or death in the workplace. Indictments were returned against the corporation and five of its officers and agents for aggravated battery and reckless conduct.[410] The indictments alleged the defendants had knowingly and recklessly caused injury to 42 employees by failing to provide them with safety precautions in the work place designed to avoid their harmful exposure to "poisonous and stupefying substances" used by the company in its manufacturing endeavors.[411] However, the defendants successfully moved to dismiss the charges on grounds the federal Occupational Safety and Health Act of 1970 (OSHA) preempted the state from prosecuting the defendants for such conduct and the appellate court affirmed.[412] The Illinois Supreme Court reversed, finding the intent of Congress was not to preclude such state prosecutions[413] and that state criminal measures were a "valuable and forceful supplement" to civil OSHA regulations designed to protect workers in the workplace.[414]

§ 3.27. Individual Accountability for Conduct of Corporations.

Just as a corporation can be held accountable for the criminality of its agents, a person, such as a corporate officer, can also be held responsible for the commission of criminal acts carried out in the interests of a corporation. In other words, a person can be held to be accountable for the corporation's crimes. Paragraph 5/5-5 states:

Accountability for Conduct of Corporation.

(a) A person is legally accountable for conduct which is an element of an offense and which, in the name or in behalf of a corporation, he performs or causes to be performed, to the same extent as if the conduct were performed in his own name or behalf.

---

[409] 126 Ill. 2d 356, 534 N.E.2d 962, *cert. denied*, 493 U.S. 809 (1989).

[410] People v. Chicago Magnet Wire Corp., 126 Ill. 2d 356, 359, 534 N.E.2d 962, 963, *cert. denied*, 493 U.S. 809 (1989).

[411] People v. Chicago Magnet Wire Corp., 126 Ill. 2d 356, 359, 534 N.E.2d 962, 963, *cert. denied*, 493 U.S. 809 (1989).

[412] People v. Chicago Magnet Wire Corp., 126 Ill. 2d 356, 359, 534 N.E.2d 962, 963, *cert. denied*, 493 U.S. 809 (1989).

[413] People v. Chicago Magnet Wire Corp., 126 Ill. 2d 356, 374-75, 534 N.E.2d 962, 970, *cert. denied*, 493 U.S. 890 (1989).

[414] People v. Chicago Magnet Wire Corp., 126 Ill. 2d 356, 373, 534 N.E.2d 962, 969, *cert. denied*, 493 U.S. 890 (1989). It is important to note, when this case went to trial, the defendants were found not guilty. Lawrence Quinn, *Execs Acquitted in Safety Case*, 77 A.B.A.J. 24 (July 1991).

(b) An individual who has been convicted of an offense by reason of his legal accountability for the conduct of a corporation is subject to the punishment authorized by law for an individual upon conviction of such offense, although only a lesser or different punishment is authorized for the corporation.[415]

The revision committee comments state that paragraph 5/5-5 was designed to make it clear that corporate agents are fully responsible for their criminal conduct even though the conduct was carried out to achieve a corporate purpose.[416] The fact that the corporation itself is not, or cannot be, prosecuted is immaterial, for prosecution of the principal (the corporation) is no longer a condition precedent to prosecution of the accomplice (the corporate agent) in Illinois.[417] Similarly, the fact that the agent is subject to a greater sanction than the corporation is of no consequence.[418]

Consistent with this policy, the courts hold that officers, directors, or agents of a corporation may be criminally responsible for acts done by them on behalf of the corporation.[419] On the other hand, where a person is to be held accountable for the conduct of a corporation, the state must prove that person's relationship to the entity in question.[420] Thus, in one case, the appellate court ruled that an individual could not be held criminally accountable for the failure of a corporation to file a state income tax return where the charging instrument charged him individually as a defendant without naming him as an officer of the corporation or setting forth any relationship he might have had with the corporation.[421]

In a noteworthy case,[422] *People v. O'Neil*,[423] individual corporate defendants and sister corporations were charged with various offenses including murder, arising out of the cyanide poisoning of an employee of Film Recovery Systems, Incorporated, that allegedly stemmed from hazardous conditions in the corporation's plant. Following a joint bench trial, three individual defendants were convicted of murder and reckless conduct while the corporations were found guilty of involuntary manslaughter and reckless conduct.[424] However, the appellate court reversed all the convictions on inconsistent verdict grounds and remanded

---

[415] 720 ILCS 5/5-5 (1999).

[416] ILL. ANN. STAT. ch. 38, para. 5-5 (Smith-Hurd 1989), 1961 Committee Comments, at 294.

[417] ILL. ANN. STAT. ch. 38, para. 5-5 (Smith-Hurd 1989), 1961 Committee Comments, at 294.

[418] ILL. ANN. STAT. ch. 38, para. 5-5 (Smith-Hurd 1989), 1961 Committee Comments, at 294.

[419] People v. Floom, 52 Ill. App. 3d 971, 976-77, 368 N.E.2d 410, 415 (1st Dist. 1977).

[420] People v. King, 5 Ill. App. 3d 357, 283 N.E.2d 294 (2d Dist. 1972) (abstract).

[421] People v. King, 5 Ill. App. 3d 357, 283 N.E.2d 294 (2d Dist. 1972) (abstract).

[422] Note, *Corporate Criminal Liability for Workplace Hazards: A Viable Option for Enforcing Workplace Safety?*, 52 BROOK. L. REV. 183 (1986).

[423] 194 Ill. App. 3d 79, 550 N.E.2d 1090 (1st Dist. 1990).

[424] People v. O'Neil, 194 Ill. App. 3d 79, 81, 550 N.E.2d 1090, 1091 (1st Dist. 1990).

the matter to the trial court for possible retrial.[425] Here, the conduct alleged by the state to support all the charges was virtually the same.[426] Because murder, involuntary manslaughter, and reckless conduct require different mental states that are mutually exclusive, the convictions were held to be legally inconsistent and could not be sustained.[427]

---

[425] People v. O'Neil, 194 Ill. App. 3d 79, 96-97, 550 N.E.2d 1090, 1102 (1st Dist. 1990).

[426] People v. O'Neil, 194 Ill. App. 3d 79, 96, 550 N.E.2d 1090, 1101 (1st Dist. 1990).

[427] People v. O'Neil, 194 Ill. App. 3d 79, 96, 550 N.E.2d 1090, 1101 (1st Dist. 1990). Subsequently, the three principal defendants in *O'Neil* pled guilty, with each receiving imprisonment. Charles Nicodemus, *Ex-Boss Gets Two Years in Worker Death*, CHI. SUN-TIMES, Sept. 10, 1993, at 18.

CHAPTER 4

CONSPIRACY

§ 4.01. Introduction.

In the Criminal Code of 1961, the first category of "specific offenses" are the "inchoate offenses" of solicitation,[1] conspiracy,[2] and attempt.[3] Since criminal solicitation and criminal attempt law is conceptually similar, these two offenses will be analyzed together in chapter 5. The important inchoate offense of conspiracy will be examined in this chapter.

Since the early 1800s, Illinois has regarded an agreement between two or more persons to do an unlawful act, or a lawful act for an unlawful purpose, a criminal conspiracy.[4] At common law, an agreement to do an unlawful act, or a lawful act for an unlawful purpose, was a criminal conspiracy as long as the parties intended to enter into the agreement.[5] Previously, both statutory and common law conspiracies were punishable.[6] The unlawful object of the conspiracy

---

[1] 720 ILCS 5/8-1 (1999).

[2] 720 ILCS 5/8-2 (1999).

[3] 720 ILCS 5/8-4 (1999).

[4] ILL. REV. LAWS p. 144, § 101 (1827).

[5] People v. Tilton, 357 Ill. 47, 50, 191 N.E. 257, 259 (1934) (criminal conspiracy at common law could involve either doing an unlawful act by any means or doing any act by unlawful means); Franklin Union, No. 4 v. People, 220 Ill. 355, 376-77, 77 N.E. 176, 183-84 (1906) (conspiracy at common law amounts to agreement, whether written or verbal, to do unlawful act or do lawful act by unlawful means); Smith v. People, 25 Ill. 17, 21 (1860) (common law conspiracy is agreement or combination between two or more persons to do unlawful act or to do lawful act by unlawful means).

[6] ILL. ANN. STAT. ch. 38, para. 8-2 (Smith-Hurd 1989), 1961 Committee Comments, at 472 (citing Chicago W. & V. Coal Co. v. People, 214 Ill. 421, 73 N.E. 770 (1905); People v. Roth, 22 Ill.

did not have to be criminal but merely tortious or violative of public policy.[7] The threat of a common law conspiracy was the existence of an *agreement* to do any unlawful act, and no further act in pursuance of the agreement was required.[8]

The earlier Illinois decisions required a "bad design or criminal intent *between* two or more persons to accomplish an unlawful result."[9] A "common design" to achieve an unlawful purpose was essential.[10] In other words, a criminal "meeting of the minds" to effect the intended criminal purpose had to be proven.[11] Thus, if a person harbored a criminal intention without any connivance on the part of another *or* in circumstances where another was feigning connivance, there was no conspiracy. A "union of wills" was necessary to perfect the conspiracy.[12] While many common law courts insisted on proof of a "corrupt motive" on the part of the respective conspirators — which meant an "evil purpose" or knowledge that the object of the agreement was prohibited[13] — this was not an essential ingredient for a conspiracy in Illinois.[14]

The prior Illinois law on conspiracy reflected another common law notion, namely, the acquittal of all the other conspirators absolved the remaining conspirator, since theoretically there had to be at least two guilty conspirators in order to have a conspiracy.[15] Also, Wharton's Rule was followed which said that where the illegal object of a compact invariably required the complicity of two or more persons (for example, gambling or bigamy), the person's agreement would not constitute a conspiracy, since "no greater danger is presented by the plurality of actors" than that arising from their commission of the substantive crimes.[16] In addition, the prior law allowed for the conviction of a defendant for

---

App. 8, 159 N.E.2d 51 (1st Dist. 1959), *rev'd on other grounds*, 19 Ill. 2d 195, 166 N.E.2d 578 (1960)).

[7] ILL. ANN. STAT. ch. 38, para. 8-2 (Smith-Hurd 1989), 1961 Committee Comments, at 472 (citing People v. Tilton, 357 Ill. 47, 191 N.E. 257 (1934); Smith v. People, 25 Ill. 17 (1860)).

[8] ILL. ANN. STAT. ch. 38, para. 8-2 (Smith-Hurd 1989), 1961 Committee Comments, at 472 (citing People v. Drury, 335 Ill. 539, 167 N.E. 823 (1929); People v. Glassberg, 326 Ill. 379, 158 N.E. 103 (1927)).

[9] People v. Mader, 313 Ill. 277, 285, 145 N.E. 137, 140 (1924) (emphasis added).

[10] People v. Walczak, 315 Ill. 49, 53, 145 N.E. 660, 662 (1925) (common design is "essence" of conspiracy).

[11] Bergeson v. Mullinix, 399 Ill. 470, 475, 78 N.E.2d 297, 300 (1948).

[12] People v. Pouchot, 174 Ill. App. 1, 15 (1913).

[13] WAYNE LAFAVE & AUSTIN SCOTT, CRIMINAL LAW § 6.4(e)(5) (2d ed. 1986).

[14] *See* People v. Cohn, 358 Ill. 326, 193 N.E. 150 (1934).

[15] ILL. ANN. STAT. ch. 38, para. 8-2 (Smith-Hurd 1989), 1961 Committee Comments, at 473 (citing People v. Bryant, 409 Ill. 467, 100 N.E.2d 598 (1951)).

[16] ILL. ANN. STAT. ch. 38, para. 8-2 (Smith-Hurd 1989), 1961 Committee Comments, at 474 (citing People v. Purcell, 304 Ill. App. 215, 26 N.E.2d 153 (3d Dist. 1940)).

conspiracy and for all criminal acts in furtherance of the conspiracy.[17] Before the adoption of the Criminal Code of 1961, Illinois generally followed the common law rule that the conspiracy itself was only punishable as a misdemeanor.[18]

§ 4.02. Conspiracy Codified.

The current criminal code contains a number of significant changes in the law of conspiracy as compared to the common law approach. The definition of the offense of conspiracy is spelled out in paragraph 5/8-2(a) of chapter 720:

> A person commits conspiracy when, with intent that an offense be committed, he agrees with another to the commission of that offense. No person may be convicted of conspiracy to commit an offense unless an act in furtherance of such agreement is alleged and proved to have been committed by him or by a co-conspirator.[19]

The basic elements of a conspiracy are (1) a specific intent (2) to enter an agreement (3) with another, (4) with the intent to accomplish the commission of a criminal offense pursuant to the agreement, and (5) with the commission of an act in furtherance of that agreement by any party to that agreement.

There are several additional statutory provisions appearing in article 5/8 of chapter 720 that clarify, extend, or limit the reach of this crime.[20] Paragraph 5/8-2(b) provides:

> It shall not be a defense to conspiracy that the person or persons with whom the accused is alleged to have conspired:
>
> (1) Has not been prosecuted or convicted, or
> (2) Has been convicted of a different offense, or
> (3) Is not amenable to justice, or
> (4) Has been acquitted, or
> (5) Lacked the capacity to commit an offense.[21]

Paragraph 5/8-2(c) makes clear that sentences for conspiracy can be felony sentences, although normally the sentence "shall not exceed the maximum provided

---

[17] ILL. ANN. STAT. ch. 38, para. 8-2 (Smith-Hurd 1989), 1961 Committee Comments, at 474 (citing People v. Dorman, 347 Ill. App. 317, 106 N.E.2d 842 (3d Dist. 1952), aff'd, 415 Ill. 385, 114 N.E.2d 404 (1953)).

[18] Herman v. People, 131 Ill. 594, 22 N.E. 471 (1889).

[19] 720 ILCS 5/8-2(a) (1999).

[20] There do exist several other significant conspiracy provisions within the Illinois Controlled Substances Act and the Illinois Cannabis Control Act, discussed in chapter 16 of this book. They are: Calculated Criminal Drug Conspiracy, 720 ILCS 570/405 (1999), Criminal Drug Conspiracy, 720 ILCS 570/405.1 (1999), Streetgang Criminal Drug Conspiracy, 720 ILCS 570/405.2 (1999), and Calculated Criminal Conspiracy, 720 ILCS 550/9 (1999).

[21] 720 ILCS 5/8-2(b) (1999).

for the offense which is the object of the conspiracy . . . ."[22] Thus, the thrust of these provisions is to broaden the bite of the law of conspiracy as compared to what the common law allowed.

There are three additional paragraphs that limit the scope of conspiracy law in Illinois. Paragraph 5/8-3 states: "It is a defense to a charge of . . . conspiracy that if the criminal object were achieved the accused would not be guilty of an offense."[23] Paragraph 5/8-5 adds: "No person shall be convicted of both the inchoate and the principal offense."[24] Paragraph 5/8-6 provides: "For the purposes of this Article, 'offense' shall include conduct which if performed in another State would be criminal by the laws of that State and which conduct if performed in this State would be an offense under the laws of this State."[25]

This legislation enacted as part of the Criminal Code of 1961 resulted in six changes with respect to conspiracy law in Illinois. First, the common law crime of conspiracy was abolished. The legislature intended to restrict the reach of conspiracy law to agreements that had as their object the commission of codified offenses in Illinois and to remove therefrom strictly tortious wrongs as well as other conduct that was merely at odds with public policy.[26] Thus, unless the aim of the agreement is a *crime* in Illinois (or a crime in another state and the conduct is similarly prohibited in Illinois), the agreement cannot be prosecuted as a conspiracy.

Second, the 1961 statute requires an overt act in furtherance of the conspiracy to be alleged and proved on the part of *one* of the parties to the conspiracy. Given the facts that (1) prosecutors apparently found proof of an agreement without subsequent activity too difficult under the prior rule, and (2) the agreement alone was "too inconsequential" to warrant criminal prosecution, the revision committee felt compelled to require the commission of some act in furtherance of the agreement either by the accused or by a coconspirator.[27]

Third, the defense that the person or persons with whom the accused was alleged to have conspired had been acquitted or lacked the capacity to commit an offense was abolished. The Committee Comments point out:

> [T]his rationale was rejected as being too technical and overlooking the realities of trials which involve differences in juries, contingent availability of witnesses, the varying ability of different prosecutors and defense attorneys, etc. The defendant obtains a full and fair trial; what happened to an-

---

[22] 720 ILCS 5/8-2(c) (1999).

[23] 720 ILCS 5/8-3 (1999).

[24] 720 ILCS 5/8-5 (1999).

[25] 720 ILCS 5/8-6 (1999).

[26] ILL. ANN. STAT. ch. 38, para. 8-2 (Smith-Hurd 1989), 1961 Committee Comments, at 472.

[27] ILL. ANN. STAT. ch. 38, para. 8-2 (Smith-Hurd 1989), 1961 Committee Comments, at 472-73.

other defendant at another time and place in another trial before a different judge and jury should not be a bar to trial here.

Subsection 8-2(b)(5) supplements section 8-3. Section 8-3 provides a defense if the *accused* would not be guilty of an offense if the conduct which is the object of the conspiracy is performed. Subsection 8-2(b)(5) goes further and says . . . it is not a defense for the accused to say that his *co-conspirator* would not be guilty of any offense if the conduct which is the object of the conspiracy were to be performed. In other words, 8-3 is intended to prevent the prosecution of an individual for conspiracy to commit a principal offense when he lacks capacity to commit such principal offense, or, as a matter of policy, the State has given him a defense to such principal offense. However, 8-2(b)(5) is intended to deny to an accused who has no legal incapacity or immunity in relation to the principal offense, any rights, benefits, advantages, or defenses which the law may have conferred upon a co-conspirator.[28]

Fourth, Wharton's Rule, which precluded a conspiracy conviction for an act that necessarily required the complicity of two people for its commission, was eliminated. The revision committee determined that abolition of this barrier to the prosecution of a conspiracy furthered the general concept of deterrence by discouraging the increased dangers arising from a multiple-party agreement to further an unlawful purpose.[29] The fact that multiple-person involvement in the crime is inherently necessary to the completion of the crime was viewed as all the more reason to prosecute the agreement itself, for without the agreement to commit the substantive crime, there could be no substantive offense.

Fifth, the rule that allowed for the conviction of an offense as well as conspiracy to commit the same offense was changed. By reason of paragraph 5/8-5,[30] a defendant can be convicted of either the offense that was the target of the conspiracy or the conspiracy itself, but not both.[31] Although the reasons offered by the revision committee for this change do not appear forceful, the effect of the change is clear. While simultaneous prosecution of the conspiracy and the substantive crime that is the target of the conspiracy (assuming the principal offense is consummated) is permitted, guilty verdicts for both cannot stand; accordingly, the trial court is obligated to vacate one of the verdicts and refrain from sentencing the defendant on both.[32] However, this paragraph was not designed to prohibit the subsequent prosecution of the principal crime where the defendant had

---

[28] ILL. ANN. STAT. ch. 38, para. 8-2 (Smith-Hurd 1989), 1961 Committee Comments, at 473-74.

[29] ILL. ANN. STAT. ch. 38, para. 8-2 (Smith-Hurd 1989), 1961 Committee Comments, at 474.

[30] ILL. ANN. STAT. ch. 38, para. 8-2 (Smith-Hurd 1989), 1961 Committee Comments, at 472.

[31] 720 ILCS 5/8-5 (1999).

[32] ILL. ANN. STAT. ch. 38, para. 8-5 (Smith-Hurd 1989), 1961 Committee Comments, at 585; People v. Gomez, 286 Ill. App. 3d 232, 235, 675 N.E.2d 971, 973 (3d Dist. 1997).

already been convicted and sentenced for conspiracy at a time when the substantive crime had not yet occurred. In other words, if a judgment were entered on a guilty verdict of conspiracy to commit murder and thereafter the victim of the murder plot died, a prosecution for the substantive crime of murder would be permissible.[33]

Sixth, the code clearly treats conspiracy as a crime that can constitute a felony. "The penalty for conspiracy was thus made to correspond to the seriousness of the principal offense, with realistic maximums."[34]

§ 4.03. The Agreement.

To form a criminal conspiracy, at least two persons must agree to the commission of an offense.[35] This agreement, often referred to as a "combination" by scholars,[36] is the "gist,"[37] "heart,"[38] or "essence"[39] of a conspiracy. Because of the clandestine nature of a conspiratorial agreement, it is often difficult to prove that such an agreement existed between two or more parties through direct or positive evidence. Therefore, neither proof of an express agreement nor direct evidence of such an agreement is required.[40] Furthermore, "[t]he agreement element of the conspiracy offense does not require a showing of specific words or acts to intend the commission of an illegal act."[41] Thus, in order to prove that the parties entered into an agreement to commit an offense, broad inferences can be drawn from the conspirators' various acts, as well as the surrounding circumstances.[42]

---

[33] ILL. ANN. STAT. ch. 38, para. 8-5 (Smith-Hurd 1989), 1961 Committee Comments, at 585.

[34] ILL. ANN. STAT. ch. 38, para. 8-2 (Smith-Hurd 1989), 1961 Committee Comments, at 475.

[35] People v. Foster, 99 Ill. 2d 48, 53, 457 N.E.2d 405, 407-08 (1983).

[36] BISHOP, BISHOP ON CRIMINAL LAW § 173-2 (9th ed. 1923); ROLLIN M. PERKINS & RONALD N. BOYCE, CRIMINAL LAW 682 (3d ed. 1982).

[37] People v. Persinger, 49 Ill. App. 3d 116, 120, 363 N.E.2d 897, 901 (5th Dist. 1977), *cert. denied*, 435 U.S. 917 (1978).

[38] People v. Mordick, 94 Ill. App. 3d 497, 499, 418 N.E.2d 1057, 1059 (2d Dist. 1981).

[39] People v. Howard, 209 Ill. App. 3d 159, 186, 568 N.E.2d 56, 73 (1st Dist. 1991).

[40] People v. Soteras, 153 Ill. App. 3d 449, 453, 505 N.E.2d 1134, 1137 (1st Dist. 1987); People v. McChristian, 18 Ill. App. 3d 87, 91-92, 309 N.E.2d 388, 391-92 (1st Dist. 1974), *aff'd*, 60 Ill. 2d 37, 322 N.E.2d 804 (1975).

[41] People v. Vettese, 61 Ill. App. 3d 279, 282, 377 N.E.2d 1168, 1170 (1st Dist. 1978).

[42] People v. Melgoza, 231 Ill. App. 3d 510, 523-24, 595 N.E.2d 1261, 1272 (1st Dist. 1992). One way in which an agreement can be proved is by use of the coconspirator's exception to the rule against hearsay. This exception deals with the admissibility of statements made by coconspirators. In People v. Goodman, 81 Ill. 2d 278, 408 N.E.2d 215 (1980), the court stated: "such declarations are admissible against all conspirators upon an *independent, prima facie* evidentiary showing of a conspiracy or joint venture between the declarant and one of the other defendants, insofar as such declarations are made in furtherance of and during the pendency of the conspiracy, *even in the absence of a conspiracy indictment.*" *Id.* at 283, 408 N.E.2d at 216 (emphasis added). This requirement ensures that a defendant will not be convicted of conspiracy on hearsay alone.

§ 4.04. Proof of Agreement.

Circumstantial evidence may be used to prove that a conspiratorial agreement was entered into by the defendant.[43] Existence of the conspiracy agreement may be inferred from all surrounding facts and circumstances including the act and declarations of the accused.[44] The state does not have to prove that the coconspirators actually met and entered into a specific agreement; rather, the agreement may be established by words, acts, or understanding.[45] Of course, a conspiratorial agreement cannot be found where the evidence presented reveals only a mere suspicion that an agreement exits,[46] a mere relationship between the parties,[47] or mere presence at the scene of another's criminality.[48] However, circumstantial evidence is routinely relied upon to prove the existence of an agreement. For example, where B was present on numerous occasions when A sold to C certain prescription drugs belonging to A and B, and B aided A in the destruction of the drug labels and wrote a receipt for a debt arising out of the illegal sales, then B could be found guilty of agreeing with A to unlawfully deliver a controlled substance.[49] On the other hand, where the defendant was employed in a state driver's license facility where a "license-for-sale" scheme allegedly existed, the state was unable to prove that the defendant agreed to the license-for-sale scheme or was a knowing participant in it and, as a result, the defendant's conspiracy conviction was reversed.[50]

However, merely because a defendant's assistance to a codefendant in the codefendant's commission of criminality may provide a sufficient basis to convict

---

A close examination of the caselaw thus reveals that a statement of a coconspirator is admissible against the other members of a conspiracy as an exception to the hearsay rule if (1) the state makes a prima facie showing that two or more persons were engaged in a common plan to accomplish a criminal goal or to reach another end by criminal means, (2) the state makes a prima facie showing that the defendant against whom hearsay is offered was a member of this conspiracy, (3) the prima facie showing is made by evidence independent of the hearsay statement being offered into evidence, (4) the statement was in furtherance of the conspiracy, and (5) the statement was during the pendency of the conspiracy. All of these conditions for the admission of the hearsay are crucial, and the absence of any one is fatal to the state's offer of proof. People v. Melgoza, 231 Ill. App. 3d 510, 520-24, 595 N.E.2d 1261, 1269-72 (1st Dist. 1992); RALPH RUEBNER, ILLINOIS CRIMINAL TRIAL EVIDENCE 203-06 (3d ed. 1997).

[43] People v. Howard, 209 Ill. App. 3d 159, 186, 568 N.E.2d 56, 73 (1st Dist. 1991).

[44] People v. Melgoza, 231 Ill. App. 3d 510, 521, 595 N.E.2d 1261, 1270 (1st Dist. 1992).

[45] People v. Adams, 238 Ill. App. 3d 733, 739, 606 N.E.2d 579, 583 (1st Dist. 1992).

[46] People v. Mordick, 94 Ill. App. 3d 497, 500, 418 N.E.2d 1057, 1059 (2d Dist. 1981); People v. Persinger, 49 Ill. App. 3d 116, 122, 363 N.E.2d 897, 901 (5th Dist. 1977), cert. denied, 435 U.S. 917 (1978).

[47] People v. Mulford, 385 Ill. 48, 54, 52 N.E.2d 149, 153 (1943).

[48] People v. Duckworth, 180 Ill. App. 3d 792, 795, 536 N.E.2d 469, 472 (4th Dist. 1989).

[49] People v. Persinger, 49 Ill. App. 3d 116, 122, 363 N.E.2d 897, 902 (5th Dist. 1977), cert. denied, 435 U.S. 917 (1978).

[50] People v. Adams, 238 Ill. App. 3d 733, 739, 606 N.E.2d 579, 583 (1st Dist. 1992).

the defendant on accountability principles,[51] it does not follow that the defendant can be convicted of a conspiracy where no agreement existed between the defendants.[52] Thus, where A sold to C a controlled substance while B offered assistance to A to effectuate the sale, it was held that B was properly convicted of delivery of a controlled substance on an accomplice liability basis,[53] even though it had been determined in the trial court that there was no basis for a conspiracy.[54] Here, B had aided and abetted A's sale to C, but, because there was no proof of an agreement between A and B to sell controlled substances to C, there was no conspiracy.[55]

§ 4.05. Single Conspiracy Versus Multiple Conspiracies.

The scope of the conspiracy is defined by the agreement to commit an offense or offenses as opposed to the overt acts performed in furtherance of the conspiracy.[56] A conspirator can perform many acts in furtherance of a conspiratorial agreement without entering multiple conspiracies.[57] Instead of creating a new conspiracy, these many acts only continue to renew the original conspiracy.[58] However, a person could be convicted of multiple conspiracies if he or she entered into multiple agreements to commit offenses with the requisite intent to form multiple conspiracies.[59] Thus, if A and B agree to rob a bank, go to the bank with the requisite intent to commit the robbery, but abandon their objective because too many persons are present in the bank, A and B are still guilty of conspiracy to commit robbery.[60] If the same parties agree several days later to attempt to commit the robbery again, then they are guilty of an additional conspiracy to commit robbery.[61]

---

[51] *See* ch. 3.

[52] People v. Valen, 183 Ill. App. 3d 571, 578, 539 N.E.2d 261, 265 (1st Dist. 1989).

[53] People v. Valen, 183 Ill. App. 3d 571, 577-78, 539 N.E.2d 261, 264 (1st Dist. 1989).

[54] People v. Valen, 183 Ill. App. 3d 571, 578, 539 N.E.2d 261, 265 (1st Dist. 1989).

[55] People v. Valen, 183 Ill. App. 3d 571, 578, 539 N.E.2d 261, 265 (1st Dist. 1989).

[56] People v. Burleson, 50 Ill. App. 3d 629, 633, 365 N.E.2d 1162, 1166 (4th Dist. 1977).

[57] People v. Sauer, 177 Ill. App. 3d 870, 878-79, 532 N.E.2d 946, 952 (2d Dist. 1988) (four cocaine deliveries part of one ongoing conspiracy); People v. Bolla, 114 Ill. App. 3d 442, 448, 448 N.E.2d 996, 1002 (2d Dist. 1983) (kidnapping victim, making extortion demands, threatening victim and threatening victim's family members part of single conspiracy).

[58] People v. Pascarella, 92 Ill. App. 3d 413, 418, 415 N.E.2d 1285, 1289 (3d Dist.), *cert. denied*, 454 U.S. 900 (1981); *see also* Braverman v. United States, 317 U.S. 49, 53 (1942); People v. Perry, 23 Ill. 2d 147, 155-56, 177 N.E.2d 323, 328 (1961), *cert. denied*, 369 U.S. 868 (1962).

[59] People v. Burleson, 50 Ill. App. 3d 629, 634-35, 365 N.E.2d 1162, 1166-68 (4th Dist. 1977) (defendant entered two different conspiracies to commit armed robbery on different days, each of which was composed of three prerequisites of conspiracy: intent, agreement, and act in furtherance of agreement).

[60] People v. Burleson, 50 Ill. App. 3d 629, 634-35, 365 N.E.2d 1162, 1166-68 (4th Dist. 1977).

[61] People v. Burleson, 50 Ill. App. 3d 629, 634-35, 365 N.E.2d 1162, 1166-68 (4th Dist. 1977).

Whether there exists a single conspiracy as opposed to multiple conspiracies has several ramifications. The most obvious concern relates to whether the defendant has committed one crime or several, and accordingly, whether he is to suffer a single sentence for one count of conspiracy or several sentences for multiple counts of conspiracy. Second, whether there are multiple conspiracies as opposed to a single conspiracy could determine a conspirator's responsibility for the acts of his coconspirators. By a combination of the principles of accomplice liability and conspiracy law, if multiple defendants have a common design to do an unlawful act, any criminal act of any one of them in furtherance of the common design is considered the act of all.[62] For example, assume A, B, and C are all involved in the sale of illicit narcotics. Assume that A and B, by common design, make a sale of narcotics to a purchaser. The sale is consummated, but a companion of the purchaser requests the opportunity to purchase more illegal drugs for his use. Later that same day, B and C, by common design and with the encouragement of A but without A's direct participation, make a sale of additional quantities of illegal narcotics to the companion. If this situation were to be viewed as one single conspiracy with one common design, then A would be responsible not only for the initial sale that he was directly involved in but also for the second sale carried out by B and C. In effect, A would be liable for two counts of illicit sale as opposed to one. On the other hand, if this situation were to be viewed as involving two separate conspiracies — one between A and B and another between B and C — then A could not be held liable for the second sale to the second purchaser.[63]

---

[62] People v. Vettese, 61 Ill. App. 3d 279, 282, 377 N.E.2d 1168, 1170 (1st Dist. 1978).

[63] By reason of the development of the concepts of "wheel" and "chain" conspiracies in the federal courts (concepts that have not evolved in the Illinois courts), even more complicated questions exist. In Kotteakos v. United States, 328 U.S. 750 (1946), the government argued unsuccessfully that the facts reflected the existence of a "wheel" conspiracy. There was an indictment of 32 persons, 19 of whom were brought to trial, for conspiracy to violate the National Housing Act. Here, there was one common key figure, Simon Brown, who undertook to act as a broker to gain illegal loans for multiple defendants, including Kotteakos. The government alleged the existence of a single massive conspiracy that revolved around Brown, who might be considered the hub of the wheel. The aim of the government was to impute to each defendant all of the various substantive crimes carried out by each of the parties to the conspiracy. In other words, each conspirator would be held liable for each illegal loan handled by Simon, whether or not that loan was one in which they had an actual interest. On the other hand, the defendants argued that there were multiple conspiracies, with Simon common to all, which limited the extent to which one could impute the illegal loans to each of the respective defendants who had no direct connection with the various loans in question. The defense prevailed on the theory that while there may have been "separate spokes" (for example, Kotteakos) meeting "in a common center" (Brown), there was insufficient evidence of a connection between the various "spokes." Kotteakos v. United States, 328 U.S. 750, 754-55 (1946). Here, the wheel was incomplete because the government's evidence was "without the rim of the wheel to enclose the spokes." *Id.* at 755. In other words, there was no proper link between the various defendants, who constituted the various separate spokes. It is important to note that the

§ 4.06. Object of Conspiratorial Agreement: An Offense.

In Illinois, a criminal conspiracy must have as its object, focus, or purpose, the commission of an offense.[64] An *offense* is statutorily defined as "a violation of any penal statute of this State,"[65] within the general definitions of the criminal code, and includes "conduct which if performed in another State would be criminal by the laws of that State and which conduct performed in this State would be an offense under the laws of this State."[66] If the object of the conspiratorial agreement is the commission of a statutory offense within the state or a crime outside the state, then the offense requirement of the statute has been fulfilled. This legislative scheme precludes the possibility of a common law conspiracy.[67]

The Illinois judiciary has considered a plethora of principle offenses on a conspiracy theory. They include conspiracy to commit murder,[68] perjury,[69]

Kotteakos court was not rejecting the "wheel" concept per se; it was merely rejecting the evidence supporting it in this case.

The reach of a "chain" conspiracy was outlined in the federal case of United States v. Bruno, 105 F.2d 921 (2d Cir.), *rev'd on other grounds*, 308 U.S. 287 (1939). Therein, smugglers of illegal drugs, "middlemen" who paid the smugglers and distributed the drugs to "retailers," and two groups of drug "retailers" were all considered part of one massive conspiracy and, accordingly, were all considered liable for the various substantive crimes committed by each coconspirator as part of their common design. Although the Court did not express itself in terms of the "chain" analysis, the United States Supreme Court found a single conspiracy in a chain-type situation in Blumenthal v. United States, 332 U.S. 539 (1947), because by "their separate agreements, if such they were, [defendants] . . . became parties to the larger common plan, joined together by their knowledge of its essential features and broad scope, though not of its exact limits, and by their common single goal" of selling whiskey over the ceiling prices set by federal regulation. *Id.* at 558.

[64] 720 ILCS 5/8-2(a) (1999).

[65] 720 ILCS 5/2-12 (1999).

[66] 720 ILCS 5/8-6 (1999).

[67] ILL. ANN. STAT. ch. 38, para. 8-2 (Smith-Hurd 1989), 1961 Committee Comments, at 472.

[68] People v. Bailey, 60 Ill. 2d 37, 322 N.E.2d 804 (1975) (conviction reversed); People v. Atkins, 161 Ill. App. 3d 600, 515 N.E.2d 272 (1st Dist. 1987) (conspiracy conviction vacated since murder conviction affirmed); People v. Cart, 102 Ill. App. 3d 173, 429 N.E.2d 553 (2d Dist. 1981), *cert. denied*, 459 U.S. 942 (1982) (convictions affirmed); People v. Kiel, 75 Ill. App. 3d 1030, 394 N.E.2d 883 (3d Dist. 1979) (conviction reversed); People v. Kellas, 72 Ill. App. 3d 445, 389 N.E.2d 1382 (1st Dist. 1979) (conviction reversed); People v. Cramer, 64 Ill. App. 3d 688, 381 N.E.2d 827 (4th Dist. 1978), *cert. denied*, 444 U.S. 828 (1979) (conviction affirmed).

[69] People v. Smith, 22 Ill. App. 3d 377, 317 N.E.2d 300 (4th Dist. 1974) (dismissal of indictment affirmed).

robbery,[70] armed robbery,[71] theft,[72] aggravated battery,[73] delivery of controlled substances,[74] escape,[75] burglary,[76] gambling,[77] operation of a place of prostitution,[78] pimping,[79] soliciting for a prostitute,[80] pandering,[81] forgery,[82] aggravated kidnapping,[83] and arson.[84]

§ 4.07. Mental State.

The crime of conspiracy has a two-part mental state requirement. There must be (1) an intent to agree and (2) an intent to accomplish a criminal offense pursuant to the agreement.[85] Not only is evidence of an agreement, by words or ac-

---

[70] People v. Perry, 23 Ill. 2d 147, 177 N.E.2d 323 (1961), *cert. denied*, 369 U.S. 868 (1962) (conviction affirmed).

[71] People v. Del Percio, 118 Ill. App. 3d 539, 454 N.E.2d 1169 (2d Dist. 1983) (conviction affirmed); People v. Brisbon, 89 Ill. App. 3d 513, 411 N.E.2d 956 (1st Dist. 1980), *cert. denied*, 451 U.S. 990 (1981) (conspiracy conviction vacated since armed robbery conviction affirmed); People v. Burleson, 50 Ill. App. 3d 629, 365 N.E.2d 1162 (4th Dist. 1977) (conviction affirmed); People v. Ambrose, 28 Ill. App. 3d 627, 329 N.E.2d 11 (3d Dist. 1975) (conviction affirmed).

[72] People v. Mordick, 94 Ill. App. 3d 497, 418 N.E.2d 1057 (2d Dist. 1981) (conviction reversed); People v. Pascarella, 92 Ill. App. 3d 413, 415 N.E.2d 1285 (3d Dist.), *cert. denied*, 454 U.S. 900 (1981) (conviction affirmed); People v. Collins, 70 Ill. App. 3d 413, 387 N.E.2d 995 (1st Dist. 1979) (conviction affirmed); People v. Lewandowski, 43 Ill. App. 3d 800, 357 N.E.2d 647 (2d Dist. 1976) (conviction reversed); People v. Wurbs, 38 Ill. App. 3d 360, 347 N.E.2d 879 (4th Dist. 1976) (conviction affirmed); People v. Kroll, 4 Ill. App. 3d 203, 280 N.E.2d 528 (1st Dist. 1972), *cert. denied*, 410 U.S. 930 (1973) (conviction affirmed).

[73] People v. Olivier, 3 Ill. App. 3d 872, 279 N.E.2d 363 (1st Dist. 1972) (convictions affirmed).

[74] People v. Jackson, 49 Ill. App. 3d 1018, 364 N.E.2d 975 (2d Dist. 1977) (conviction affirmed).

[75] People v. McNair, 102 Ill. App. 3d 322, 429 N.E.2d 1233 (1st Dist. 1981) (conviction affirmed).

[76] People v. Hill, 108 Ill. App. 3d 716, 439 N.E.2d 549 (4th Dist. 1982) (conviction reversed).

[77] People v. Roberts, 83 Ill. App. 3d 311, 404 N.E.2d 278 (5th Dist. 1980) (conviction affirmed).

[78] People v. Laws, 224 Ill. App. 3d 167, 586 N.E.2d 453 (1st Dist. 1991) (trial court dismissal of indictment reversed with instructions to reinstate); People v. Hammond, 82 Ill. App. 3d 839, 403 N.E.2d 305 (4th Dist. 1980), *cert. denied*, 450 U.S. 966 (1981) (conviction affirmed).

[79] People v. Laws, 224 Ill. App. 3d 167, 586 N.E.2d 453 (1st Dist. 1991) (trial court dismissal of indictment reversed with instructions to reinstate).

[80] People v. Laws, 224 Ill. App. 3d 167, 586 N.E.2d 453 (1st Dist. 1991).

[81] People v. Laws, 224 Ill. App. 3d 167, 586 N.E.2d 453 (1st Dist. 1991).

[82] People v. Charleston, 46 Ill. App. 3d 141, 360 N.E.2d 822 (4th Dist. 1977) (conviction affirmed); People v. Simmons, 21 Ill. App. 3d 310, 315 N.E.2d 226 (3d Dist. 1974) (conspiracy conviction vacated since forgery conviction affirmed).

[83] People v. Love, 60 Ill. App. 3d 16, 376 N.E.2d 342 (1st Dist. 1978) (conspiracy conviction vacated since aggravated kidnapping conviction affirmed).

[84] People v. Abdennabi, 157 Ill. App. 3d 979, 511 N.E.2d 719 (1st Dist. 1987).

[85] ILL. ANN. STAT. ch. 38, para. 8-2 (Smith-Hurd 1989), 1961 Committee Comments, at 473.

tion, necessary to prove a conspiracy, but the agreement must also be entered into with the purpose of accomplishing a particular offense.[86]

This requirement makes conspiracy a specific intent crime[87] and must be satisfied regardless of the mens rea requirement of the principal offense.[88] The revision committee's comments clarify that "the very nature of the offense requires an intent *separate and distinct* from the intent required in a prosecution for the principal offense which is the object of the conspiracy."[89] It is useful to note that the drafters of the code did not employ the common law "corrupt motive" or "evil intent" mens rea,[90] as the requisite mental state for conspiracy, because the terms of the conspiracy statute make it clear that "the object of the conspiracy has been limited to *criminal* activity."[91]

§ 4.08. — Intent to Agree.

While the requirement of "intent to agree"[92] to commit a conspiracy is a matter of fact and cannot be implied as a matter of law, criminal intent may be shown by circumstantial evidence.[93] The state is not required to have direct evidence of intent to agree any more than it is required to have direct evidence of an agreement.

The "intent to agree" to the commission of an offense must be mutual between the parties.[94] If only one of two alleged conspirators intended to agree to the conspiratorial agreement and the other merely considered the possibility of entering into the agreement without formulating the specific intent required of conspiracy, then the state of mind necessary for an agreement does not exist.[95] Similarly, if A is approached by B with his conspiratorial plan to rob C and A merely feigns his approval and thereafter alerts the police about B's plans, there

---

[86] ILL. ANN. STAT. ch. 38, para. 8-2 (Smith-Hurd 1989), 1961 Committee Comments, at 473.

[87] People v. McChristian, 18 Ill. App. 3d 87, 90, 309 N.E.2d 388, 391 (1st Dist. 1974), *aff'd*, 60 Ill. 2d 37, 322 N.E.2d 804 (1975).

[88] *See generally* ch. 2 for an extensive discussion of specific intent and general intent.

[89] ILL. ANN. STAT. ch. 38, para. 8-2 (Smith-Hurd 1989), 1961 Committee Comments, at 473 (emphasis added).

[90] ILL. ANN. STAT. ch. 38, para. 8-2 (Smith-Hurd 1989), 1961 Committee Comments, at 473.

[91] ILL. ANN. STAT. ch. 38, para. 8-2 (Smith-Hurd 1989), 1961 Committee Comments, at 473.

[92] People v. Cramer, 64 Ill. App. 3d 688, 693, 381 N.E.2d 827, 830 (4th Dist. 1978), *cert. denied*, 444 U.S. 828 (1979).

[93] People v. Perry, 23 Ill. 2d 147, 154, 177 N.E.2d 323, 327 (1961), *cert. denied*, 369 U.S. 868 (1962).

[94] People v. Foster, 99 Ill. 2d 48, 55, 457 N.E.2d 405, 408 (1983); People v. Hill, 108 Ill. App. 3d 716, 719, 439 N.E.2d 549, 551 (4th Dist. 1982); People v. Ambrose, 28 Ill. App. 3d 627, 629, 329 N.E.2d 11, 14 (3d Dist. 1975).

[95] People v. Hill, 108 Ill. App. 3d 716, 720, 439 N.E.2d 549, 551-52 (4th Dist. 1982).

is no conspiracy.[96] In this situation, the defendant, B, could be convicted of criminal solicitation,[97] which does not require mutuality of intent.[98]

Although Illinois adopted the American Law Institute's formulation for prohibiting conspiracies in 1961,[99] which is reflected in the Model Penal Code,[100] the Illinois judiciary has interpreted the statute to exemplify the "bilateral theory" instead of the "unilateral theory" of conspiracy.[101] In other words, even though the Model Penal Code presents the unilateral theory of conspiracy, which requires only a wrongful mental state on behalf of one conspirator in order to sustain his conviction,[102] in *People v. Foster*,[103] the Illinois Supreme Court decided that the bilateral model should be followed.[104] The court stated that such a profound change in the law could not have been intended since the revision committee's comments failed to address the unilateral/bilateral issue.[105] The fact that criminal solicitation embraces virtually every situation contemplated by the unilateral theory of conspiracy negated the state's contention that the unilateral theory of conspiracy was warranted.[106] Moreover, since the Illinois courts had been rejecting the unilateral theory since 1975 without any legislative change from the General Assembly, the legislative "inaction is suggestive of legislative agreement."[107] The court was mindful of the rule of judicial construction in Illi-

---

[96] People v. Foster, 99 Ill. 2d 48, 50-53, 457 N.E.2d 405, 406-08 (1983).

[97] 720 ILCS 5/8-1(a) (1998): "A person commits solicitation when, with intent that an offense be committed, other than first degree murder, he commands, encourages or requests another to commit that offense." *See* People v. Hill, 108 Ill. App. 3d 716, 721, 439 N.E.2d 549, 551-52 (4th Dist. 1982) (defendant could have been convicted of solicitation to commit burglary, but not of conspiracy).

[98] People v. Foster, 99 Ill. 2d 48, 53, 457 N.E.2d 405, 408 (1983).

[99] *See* Dierdre A. Burgman, *Unilateral Conspiracy: Three Critical Perspectives*, 29 DePaul L. Rev. 75, 76 (1979).

[100] Model Penal Code § 5.03 (1962):

> A person is guilty of conspiracy with another person or persons to commit a crime if with the purpose of promoting or facilitating its commission he: (a) agrees with such person or persons that they or one or more of them will engage in conduct which constitutes such crime or an attempt or solicitation to commit such crime. . . .

[101] People v. Foster, 99 Ill. 2d 48, 55, 457 N.E.2d 405, 408 (1983); People v. Breton, 237 Ill. App. 3d 355, 359-61, 603 N.E.2d 1290, 1294-95 (2d Dist. 1992).

[102] Dierdre A. Burgman, *Unilateral Conspiracy: Three Critical Perspectives*, 29 DePaul L. Rev. 75, 76-77 (1979).

[103] 99 Ill. 2d 48, 457 N.E.2d 405 (1983).

[104] People v. Foster, 99 Ill. 2d 48, 55, 457 N.E.2d 405, 408 (1983).

[105] People v. Foster, 99 Ill. 2d 48, 53, 457 N.E.2d 405, 407 (1983).

[106] People v. Foster, 99 Ill. 2d 48, 53, 457 N.E.2d 405, 408 (1983).

[107] People v. Foster, 99 Ill. 2d 48, 55, 457 N.E.2d 405, 408 (1983) (citing People v. Hill, 108 Ill. App. 3d 716, 439 N.E.2d 549 (4th Dist. 1982); People v. Ambrose, 28 Ill. App. 3d 627, 329 N.E.2d 11 (3d Dist. 1975)).

nois that requires the courts to resolve statutory ambiguities in a light most favorable to an accused.[108]

The *Foster* interpretation, which insists on an actual meeting of the minds between the coconspirators, emphasizes the prohibition of the *relationship* between coconspirators in order to protect the public from the dangers of defendants in *combination* in pursuit of their common criminal design. The state can intercept the single party who is bent on companionship in his criminal ambitions before a principal offense is committed by using the criminal solicitation statute.

§ 4.09. — Intent to Commit an Offense.

The "intent to commit an offense" requires that each conspirator understand and agree to perpetrate a crime in furtherance of the agreement.[109] The intent to commit the offense is usually more important than the other elements for conspiracy because the state cannot proceed with a conspiracy prosecution unless it offers substantial evidence that the parties combined with a criminal objective in mind. Indeed, it is because the conspirators must have had a specific, particularized, illegal objective in mind that the mental state requirement for conspiracy has been labeled "specific intent."[110] Mere knowledge, acquiescence, approval, or attempt to commit a crime is insufficient to make one a conspirator.[111] Thus, in *People v. Mordick*,[112] the evidence was insufficient to sustain a conviction for conspiracy to commit theft, where the defendant allowed a friend to park a stolen car without license plates in his driveway.[113] The court ruled that even if the defendant's knowledge of his friend's dealings in stolen automobiles had "readily be[en] demonstrated, it is the finding of the intent to enter an agreement to commit an offense . . . rather than mere knowledge of an offense" that must be established and, thus, no conspiracy existed under the circumstances.[114]

"Intent to commit an offense" is proved in the same manner as "intent to agree" and as the agreement itself. Therefore, the intent to commit an offense can be proved by circumstantial evidence and the inferences from that evidence

---

[108] People v. Foster, 99 Ill. 2d 48, 55, 457 N.E.2d 405, 408 (1983) (citing People ex rel. Gibson v. Cannon, 65 Ill. 2d 366, 357 N.E.2d 1180 (1976)).

[109] People v. Hoffmann, 124 Ill. App. 2d 192, 196-97, 260 N.E.2d 351, 353-54 (1st Dist. 1970) ("intent that an offense be committed" is necessary ingredient of conspirator's criminal liability).

[110] People v. Adams, 238 Ill. App. 3d 773, 739-40, 606 N.E.2d 579, 583 (1st Dist. 1992); People v. McChristian, 18 Ill. App. 3d 87, 90, 309 N.E.2d 388, 391 (1st Dist. 1974), *aff'd*, 60 Ill. 2d 37, 322 N.E.2d 804 (1975).

[111] People v. Perruquet, 173 Ill. App. 3d 1054, 1064, 527 N.E.2d 1334, 1341 (5th Dist. 1988).

[112] 94 Ill. App. 3d 497, 418 N.E.2d 1057 (2d Dist. 1981).

[113] People v. Mordick, 94 Ill. App. 3d 497, 500, 418 N.E.2d 1057, 1060 (2d Dist. 1981).

[114] People v. Mordick, 94 Ill. App. 3d 497, 500, 418 N.E.2d 1057, 1060 (2d Dist. 1981).

that disclose a common criminal purpose,[115] but not by a mere relationship or transaction.[116] Thus, where evidence showed that the defendant had agreed with others to "get even" with a rival gang, armed himself with a sawed-off shotgun, and then went to the residence of a rival gang member, the court found such evidence sufficient to support the defendant's specific intent to enter a conspiracy to commit murder.[117]

Although the existence of a mere relationship between parties is not by itself proof of a common intent to commit an offense, such a relationship as group membership may be material evidence which supports a conspiracy.[118] In *People v. Ganci*,[119] evidence of the defendant's membership in a "formal group" of youngsters was material to the state's assertion that he had banded together with other formal members as a "heavily armed 'task force'" to "clear up" their "problems" with the victim and was supportive of their conspiracy to murder the victim.[120] Similarly, while insufficient per se to prove intent, a defendant's knowledge,[121] as well as his or her affirmative acts in furtherance of another's criminality, is of *evidentiary* worth to the state in proving intent to achieve an illegal purpose.[122] Thus, sufficient evidence existed to prove a conspiracy to commit forgery where the defendant drove her companions to a building, the companions stole public aid checks from a mailbox at this building, and the defendant then drove the companions to a bank with knowledge that the companions intended to commit forgery there.[123]

§ 4.10. Overt Act.

In order to convict someone of conspiracy, the conspiracy statute[124] explicitly requires that an overt act in furtherance of the conspiracy be alleged and proved.[125] This act may be any act that aided the completion of the conspir-

---

[115] People v. Bailey, 60 Ill. 2d 37, 45, 322 N.E.2d 804, 809 (1975); People v. Cart, 102 Ill. App. 3d 173, 188, 429 N.E.2d 553, 560-61 (2d Dist. 1981), *cert. denied*, 459 U.S. 942 (1982).

[116] People v. Mordick, 94 Ill. App. 3d 497, 501, 418 N.E.2d 1057, 1060 (2d Dist. 1981); People v. Gates, 29 Ill. 2d 586, 591, 195 N.E.2d 161, 163 (1963), *cert. denied*, 377 U.S. 934 (1964).

[117] People v. Cannon, 176 Ill. App. 3d 49, 58, 530 N.E.2d 1035, 1040-41 (1st Dist. 1988).

[118] People v. Ganci, 57 Ill. App. 3d 234, 242, 372 N.E.2d 1077, 1084 (1st Dist. 1978). *See also* People v. Hairston, 46 Ill. 2d 348, 371-72, 263 N.E.2d 840, 854-55 (1970) (evidence of defendant's membership and leadership position in Blackstone Rangers relevant to establishing "common design and purpose" to commit murder carried out by members of defendant's street gang).

[119] 57 Ill. App. 3d 234, 372 N.E.2d 1077 (1st Dist. 1978).

[120] People v. Ganci, 57 Ill. App. 3d 234, 242, 372 N.E.2d 1077, 1084 (1st Dist. 1978).

[121] People v. Charleston, 46 Ill. App. 3d 141, 143-44, 360 N.E.2d 822, 823 (4th Dist. 1977).

[122] People v. Charleston, 46 Ill. App. 3d 141, 143-44, 360 N.E.2d 822, 823 (4th Dist. 1977).

[123] People v. Charleston, 46 Ill. App. 3d 141, 144, 360 N.E.2d 822, 824 (4th Dist. 1977).

[124] ILL. REV. STAT. ch. 38, para. 8-2(a) (1999).

[125] People v. Burleson, 50 Ill. App. 3d 629, 632, 365 N.E.2d 1162, 1165 (4th Dist. 1977).

acy.[126] Thus, the act does not have to be an element of the offense agreed upon,[127] but may instead be an act in preparation for, or in concealment of, the commission of an offense.[128] Furthermore, only one act is necessary.[129] For example, traveling to the proposed crime scene to survey the area of a planned armed robbery would be sufficient to satisfy the act requirement.[130]

The Illinois conspiracy prohibition allows the overt act to be performed by the defendant or by any of the defendant's coconspirators.[131] Since the act of one conspirator pursuant to a common design is the act of all, if any conspirator performs an act in furtherance of the commission of a crime, that act is attributable to all conspirators for purposes of the statute.[132] Thus, if A, B, and C agreed to commit armed robbery and C bought an automobile in furtherance of the commission of the armed robbery, the act requirement of the statute has been fulfilled.[133]

The nature of the act in question is another important aspect of the overt act requirement. Defense claims often confuse the overt act requirement for attempt with that for conspiracy. This happened in *People v. Ambrose*,[134] where the court stated:

> One element of the crime of attempt is a substantial step toward the commission of the object offense. On the other hand, the conspiracy statute requires a *much lesser step* toward the completion of the object offense for the conspiracy to exist. For conspiracy, only an overt act in furtherance of the conspiracy is needed. In our opinion, an act of planning is . . . a sufficient act for conspiracy.[135]

---

[126] *See, e.g.,* People v. Charleston, 46 Ill. App. 3d 141, 143, 360 N.E.2d 822, 823 (4th Dist. 1977) (driving of companions in her automobile to bank where forgery was committed by companions).

[127] People v. Ambrose, 28 Ill. App. 3d 627, 631, 329 N.E.2d 11, 15 (3d Dist. 1975).

[128] People v. Link, 100 Ill. App. 3d 1000, 1006, 427 N.E.2d 589, 593 (2d Dist. 1981*), cert. denied,* 456 U.S. 1006 (1982) (concealment of murder part of conspiracy); People v. Vettese, 61 Ill. App. 3d 279, 282, 377 N.E.2d 1168, 1170 (1st Dist. 1978) (contacting prospective purchaser with offer to sell land was sufficient act in furtherance of illegal agreement for conspiracy to commit theft by deception).

[129] People v. Kroll, 4 Ill. App. 3d 203, 208, 280 N.E.2d 528, 532 (1st Dist. 1972), *cert. denied,* 410 U.S. 930 (1973).

[130] People v. Ambrose, 28 Ill. App. 3d 627, 631, 329 N.E.2d 11, 14 (3d Dist. 1975).

[131] People v. Burleson, 50 Ill. App. 3d 629, 631, 365 N.E.2d 1162, 1165 (4th Dist. 1977) (quoting ILL. REV. STAT. ch. 38, para. 8-2(a) (1973)).

[132] People v. Vettese, 61 Ill. App. 3d 279, 282, 377 N.E.2d 1168, 1170 (1st Dist. 1978).

[133] People v. Ambrose, 28 Ill. App. 3d 627, 630, 329 N.E.2d 11, 14 (3d Dist. 1975).

[134] 28 Ill. App. 3d 627, 329 N.E.2d 11 (3d Dist. 1975).

[135] People v. Ambrose, 28 Ill. App. 3d 627, 630-31, 329 N.E.2d 11, 15 (3d Dist. 1975) (emphasis added).

As the *Ambrose* court alluded to, mere acts of preparation for crime will not satisfy the overt act requirement for attempt,[136] whereas they will for conspiracy.[137] Furthermore, relatively small steps toward the perpetration of a crime will suffice for purposes of conspiracy.[138] This is evident not only from the code's failure to require a "substantial step toward the commission" of an offense, which is required of all criminal attempts,[139] but by policy considerations surrounding conspiracy law, namely, the essence of a conspiracy is the illegal compact, whereas the essence of attempt is the actual step in the direction of criminality.[140] *People v. Persinger*[141] expressed the bottom line with respect to the requirement of an overt act by stating: "this additional requirement rarely imposes any substantial burden on the prosecution for just about any act in furtherance of the unlawful agreement will satisfy this element and this act need not be committed by a particular defendant so long as one of the co-conspirators was involved in the act."[142]

Because paragraph 5/8-2 requires that the act be in *furtherance* of the agreement, the commission of the act must logically *follow* the agreement.[143] Thus, if A rented a room overlooking a bank and thereafter agreed with B and C to rob the bank, the renting of the room would not be an act in furtherance of the commission of the offense. However, surveillance of the bank from the room after the agreement would be an act in furtherance of the agreement.

§ 4.11. Responsibility for Crimes of Coconspirators.

Where the evidence reveals that a conspiracy has been entered into by various defendants, each conspirator becomes liable for the acts of coconspirators done in furtherance of the conspiracy, regardless of whether each participated in[144] or is present at the time the planned act is consummated.[145] In *People v. Vincent*,[146]

---

[136] *See* ch. 5.

[137] People v. Ambrose, 28 Ill. App. 3d 627, 630-31, 329 N.E.2d 11, 14 (3d Dist. 1975).

[138] People v. Burleson, 50 Ill. App. 3d 629, 636, 365 N.E.2d 1162, 1165 (4th Dist. 1977) ("a lesser step").

[139] 720 ILCS 5/8-4(a) (1999).

[140] People v. Ambrose, 28 Ill. App. 3d 627, 631, 329 N.E.2d 11, 15 (3d Dist. 1975).

[141] People v. Persinger, 49 Ill. App. 3d 116, 363 N.E.2d 897 (5th Dist. 1977), *cert. denied*, 435 U.S. 917 (1978).

[142] People v. Persinger, 49 Ill. App. 3d 116, 121-22, 363 N.E.2d 897, 901 (5th Dist. 1977), *cert. denied*, 435 U.S. 917 (1978) (emphasis added).

[143] People v. Persinger, 49 Ill. App. 3d 116, 121-22, 363 N.E.2d 897, 901 (5th Dist. 1977) ("[t]o satisfy the *actus reus* requirement, the prosecutor must show an act in furtherance of the unlawful agreement"), *cert. denied*, 435 U.S. 917 (1978).

[144] People v. Vettese, 61 Ill. App. 3d 279, 282, 377 N.E.2d 1168, 1170 (1st Dist. 1978).

[145] People v. Vincent, 92 Ill. App. 3d 446, 461, 415 N.E.2d 1147, 1159 (1st Dist. 1980); People v. Walinsky, 300 Ill. 92, 95-96, 132 N.E.2d 757, 758 (1921).

[146] 92 Ill. App. 3d 446, 415 N.E.2d 1147 (1st Dist. 1980).

three defendants were convicted of a calculated drug conspiracy and conspiracy for the sale of a controlled substance. The court rejected one of the defendants arguments that he could not be convicted of a conspiracy since he was not present when the delivery of the controlled substance occurred.[147] Even though *Vincent* mandates that a defendant can be convicted for conspiracy where some of the elements of the conspiracy were carried out by coconspirators, it does not address the issue of holding conspirators liable for *substantive* or *principal* offenses that are in furtherance of their common design and are accomplished by other coconspirators. This matter will be explored at this juncture.

In *Pinkerton v. United States*,[148] the United States Supreme Court held that "so long as the partnership in crime continues, the partners act for each other in carrying it forward. It is settled that 'an overt act of one partner may be the act of all without any new agreement specifically directed to that act.'"[149] Accordingly, the *Pinkerton* court held two bothers, Walter and Daniel Pinkerton, responsible for conspiracy and various substantive crimes in furtherance of the conspiracy even though there was "no evidence to show that Daniel participated directly in the commission of the substantive offenses on which his conviction has been sustained, although there was evidence to show that these substantive offenses were in fact committed by Walter in furtherance of the unlawful agreement or conspiracy existing between the brothers."[150] The court limited the reach of the *Pinkerton* rule by stating:

> A different case would arise if the substantive offense committed by one of the conspirators was not in fact done in furtherance of the conspiracy, did not fall within the scope of the unlawful project, or was merely a part of the ramifications of the plan which could not be reasonably foreseen as a necessary or natural consequence of the unlawful agreement.[151]

Notwithstanding the approval of the *Pinkerton* rule by the Supreme Court and its vitality in federal court, the Model Penal Code[152] and some of the states that adopted the Model Penal Code have rejected it,[153] while various other states accept it.[154]

---

[147] People v. Vincent, 92 Ill. App. 3d 446, 461, 415 N.E.2d 1147, 1159 (1st Dist. 1980).

[148] 328 U.S. 640 (1946).

[149] Pinkerton v. United States, 328 U.S. 640, 646-67 (1946) (citations omitted).

[150] Pinkerton v. United States, 328 U.S. 640, 645 (1946).

[151] Pinkerton v. United States, 328 U.S. 640, 647-68 (1946).

[152] *See* MODEL PENAL CODE § 2.06(3) (1962); MODEL PENAL CODE § 2.04(3), comment at 20-23 (Tentative Draft No. 1, 1953).

[153] Peter Buscemi, Note, *Conspiracy: Statutory Reform Since the* MODEL PENAL CODE, 75 COLUM. L. REV. 1122, 1151 (1975) (asserting most states which follow the MODEL PENAL CODE reject *Pinkerton*).

[154] State v. Walton, 630 A.2d 990, 998 (Conn. 1993) (asserting that most states which have considered *Pinkerton* accept it). It is the opinion of this author that the great majority of states hold a

Since the Illinois statute is essentially patterned after the Model Penal Code's formulation of conspiracy, it is questionable if the *Pinkerton* theory per se has any conceptual utility in Illinois. Since the *Pinkerton* rule rests solely on principles of conspiracy law and the Illinois posture regarding the reach of its conspiracy law in this connection is unclear, it is imperative to identify other Illinois law beyond paragraph 5/8-2 that can be viewed as a proper basis for imputing to conspirators the misdeeds of their coconspirators that are part of the conspiracy. A legal source for such a proposition is found in the state's accomplice liability statute.[155] It states: "[a] person is legally accountable for the conduct of another when . . . [e]ither before or during the commission of an offense, and with the intent to promote or facilitate such commission, he solicits, aids, abets, *agrees* or attempts to aid, such other person in the *planning or commission* of the offense."[156] This is reaffirmed by the revision committee's comments where it was stated that although a conspiracy between the principal actor and a defendant does not invariably make the defendant an accomplice to the principal's criminality, the "acts of conspiring *may in many cases* satisfy the particular requirements" of the accomplice liability statute.[157]

Although the Illinois opinions are somewhat nebulous about the interrelationship between Illinois conspiracy law and its accomplice liability provisions, there appears to be little question about the courts' willingness to pull accountability principles into conspiracy analysis. By blending the concepts together, the courts reach results where conspirators are held accountable for the crimes of their coconspirators. Nonetheless, the courts' respective approaches vary even though their conclusions are the same. First, there are cases such as *People v. Tate,*[158] where the court speaks of "common purpose" and "common design"[159] and analyzes the problem with reference strictly to the accountability statute. In *Tate*, the defendant was convicted of murder even though he was not guilty of the shooting that caused the victims to die.[160] His murder conviction was affirmed nonetheless without reference to a conspiracy charge or theory because there was a common design to do an unlawful act to which he assented.[161]

---

defendant responsible for the criminality of another which arises out of a "conspiracy" or "common design" between the parties, by relying on accomplice principles, conspiracy principles, or both.

[155] *See generally* ch. 3.

[156] 720 ILCS 5/5-2(c) (1999) (emphasis added).

[157] ILL. ANN. STAT. ch. 38, para. 5-2 (Smith-Hurd 1989), 1961 Committee Comments, at 236 (emphasis added).

[158] 63 Ill. 2d 105, 345 N.E.2d 480 (1976).

[159] People v. Tate, 63 Ill. 2d 105, 109, 345 N.E.2d 480, 482 (1976).

[160] People v. Tate, 63 Ill. 2d 105, 107-08, 345 N.E.2d 480, 481 (1976).

[161] People v. Tate, 63 Ill. 2d 105, 108, 345 N.E.2d 480, 482 (1976).

A second approach taken by courts in Illinois relies on conspiracy and accountability principles in tandem. In *People v. Joupperi*,[162] the defendant was convicted of attempted murder, attempted robbery and conspiracy. Here, a state undercover agent met the defendant at his residence and arranged for the delivery and purchase of controlled substances.[163] After the defendant and agent exchanged money, another defendant, Graham, struck the undercover agent and a third defendant, Roop, shot the agent.[164] The court sustained the defendant's attempted murder conviction while quoting the following language: "[C]ircumstances may show there is a common design to do an unlawful act to which all assent, and whatever is done in furtherance of the design is the act of all, making such person guilty of the crime."[165] In this case, the appellate court based its conclusion that Joupperi was responsible for Roop's shooting primarily on accountability principles since it was obligated to vacate the jury verdict on the conspiracy and attempted robbery convictions because they were subsumed into the more serious crime.[166]

In *People v. Olivier*,[167] the court also relied on both accomplice liability and conspiracy principles, but it appeared to rely more heavily on the latter. The defendants were charged with aggravated battery and conspiracy to commit aggravated battery. One victim, Connor, testified that he and one Mitchell had attempted to break up a street scuffle between some young people. The victims, Connor and Mitchell, then went into Mitchell's apartment. Later, a small boy appeared at Mitchell's apartment and said someone across the street wanted to see him. As Mitchell and Connor were about to leave the apartment building, someone shot both of them. A juvenile, Dameron, was later arrested in connection with the shooting.

Several days later, Connor again went to Mitchell's building. The defendant Olivier was standing in the building with two other men. One of the men asked Connor if he planned on pressing charges against Dameron and he replied "yes." Fifteen or twenty minutes later, while walking down the street, Connor was shot with a shotgun. Evidence later revealed that the youths involved in the initial fracas and the various shootings were members of a street gang. Further evidence revealed that Olivier, as well as the defendants Dameron, Kitchen, and Foley, were members of the gang and had an interest in protecting each other. The evidence was not clear on who shot Connor with the shotgun. Notwithstanding this fact, the trial court and jury were satisfied that there was a "common plan" to commit aggravated battery on Connor that was shared by

---

[162] 31 Ill. App. 3d 558, 334 N.E.2d 846 (2d Dist. 1975).

[163] People v. Joupperi, 31 Ill. App. 3d 558, 559, 334 N.E.2d 846, 847 (2d Dist. 1975).

[164] People v. Joupperi, 31 Ill. App. 3d 558, 559, 334 N.E.2d 846, 847-48 (2d Dist. 1975).

[165] People v. Joupperi, 31 Ill. App. 3d 558, 561, 334 N.E.2d 846, 848 (2d Dist. 1975) (quoting People v. Kessler, 57 Ill. 2d 493, 498, 315 N.E.2d 29, 32-33 (1974)).

[166] People v. Joupperi, 31 Ill. App. 3d 558, 561, 334 N.E.2d 846, 849 (2d Dist. 1975).

[167] 3 Ill. App. 3d 872, 279 N.E.2d 363 (1st Dist. 1972).

mon plan" to commit aggravated battery on Connor that was shared by various members of the gang.[168] In affirming the convictions, the appellate court remarked:

> [The defendants] contend that the State did not prove defendants Kitchen and Foley responsible or accountable for the acts of Olivier since the evidence cannot be said to show "aiding or abetting" or a "common plan." It is argued that mere presence at the scene of a crime does not amount to aiding or abetting .... We have already stated that the evidence, if believed by the jury, demonstrated that these defendants, along with Olivier, were engaged in a conspiracy to commit aggravated battery. *When a conspiracy is entered into, each conspirator then becomes liable for the acts of his co-conspirators done in furtherance of the objects of the conspiracy.*[169]

The third approach reflected in Illinois opinions to find conspirators responsible for coconspirators' crimes relies exclusively on a conspiracy analysis. In *People v. Vettese*,[170] the defendant was charged with conspiracy and attempted theft by deception arising out of an incident in which the defendant and three others attempted to sell a person's land without his authorization. Although there was evidence tying the defendant to the principal crime, the appellate court, in affirming the defendant's conviction stated: "[O]nce the conspiracy is proved, any further illegal acts committed by any one of the parties in furtherance of the common criminal purpose imposes criminal liability on all the parties, whether or not they participated in the illegal act."[171] Here the appellate court did not refer to the accountability statute. In any event, it appears that the most sound basis for holding a defendant responsible in Illinois for the substantive crimes of coconspirators in furtherance of the conspiracy is to simultaneously rely on both accountability and conspiracy theories.

Because of the apparent confusion regarding the conceptual foundation of this doctrine, a further inquiry into its analytical underpinnings is warranted. In *Pinkerton*, the United States Supreme Court indicated that holding coconspirators responsible for all conspiratorial acts in furtherance of a conspiracy rested on the same basic theory as accomplice liability but seemed to suggest that it was a doctrine that was somewhat independent thereof by stating: "[T]he rule which holds responsible one who counsels, procures, or commands another to commit a crime is founded on the same principle. That principle is recognized in the law of conspiracy when the overt act of one partner in crime is attributable

---

[168] People v. Olivier, 3 Ill. App. 3d 872, 874, 279 N.E.2d 363, 364 (1st Dist. 1972).

[169] People v. Olivier, 3 Ill. App. 3d 872, 878, 279 N.E.2d 363, 367 (1st Dist. 1972) (emphasis added) (citation ommitted).

[170] 61 Ill. App. 3d 279, 377 N.E.2d 1168 (1st Dist. 1978).

[171] People v. Vettese, 61 Ill. App. 3d 279, 282, 377 N.E.2d 1168, 1170 (1st Dist. 1978).

to all."[172] Notwithstanding, some defenders of the *Pinkerton* rule have opined that this rule is essentially an extension of accomplice liability.[173] "In other words, liability for the commission of a substantive offense does not flow from membership in a conspiracy, but rather *evidence* of one's membership in a conspiracy may establish one's role as an accessory . . . ."[174] Through such reasoning, it is claimed that *Pinkerton*'s reliance on accomplice liability theories means the *Pinkerton* doctrine "is not an aberration, but rather a reaffirmation of some basic tenets of the common law."[175] Essentially, these defenders of *Pinkerton* agree[176] with the critics[177] that *Pinkerton* confused a rule of evidence — the overt-act requirement required by federal statute — with a rule of criminal responsibility.[178] Indeed, the American Law Institute's reservations[179] about the absence of an adequate rationale supportive of this doctrine[180] prompted its rejection in the Model Penal Code.[181] Their position was that "liability for a substantive crime as an accomplice cannot be predicated on the sole fact of having been a party to a conspiracy."[182] On the other hand, the federal courts have

---

[172] Pinkerton v. United States, 328 U.S. 640, 647 (1946).

[173] *See, e.g.,* Jon May, *Pinkerton v. United States Revisited: A Defense of Accomplice Liability,* 8 NOVA L. J. 21, 32 (1983).

[174] Jon May, *Pinkerton v. United States Revisited: A Defense of Accomplice Liability,* 8 NOVA L.J. 21, 32 (1983).

[175] Jon May, *Pinkerton v. United States Revisited: A Defense of Accomplice Liability,* 8 NOVA L.J. 21, 24 (1983).

[176] Jon May, *Pinkerton v. United States Revisited: A Defense of Accomplice Liability,* 8 NOVA L.J. 21, 34-35 (1983).

[177] *See* Recent Decisions, *Criminal Law — Conspiracy and Substantive Offenses — Distinction Between Conspirators and Accomplices Conviction of Conspirator for Substantive Offenses, Although He Did Not Actually Participate in Them,* 16 FORDHAM L. REV. 275, 277-78 (1947).

[178] Jon May, *Pinkerton v. United States Revisited: A Defense of Accomplice Liability,* 8 NOVA L. J. 21, 23, 34-35 (1983); Recent Decisions, *Criminal Law — Conspiracy and Substantive Offenses — Distinction Between Conspirators and Accomplices Conviction of Conspirator for Substantive Offenses, Although He Did Not Actually Participate in Them,* 16 FORDHAM L. REV. 275, 277-78 (1947).

[179] *See* Herbert Wechsler *et al., The Treatment of Inchoate Crimes in the* MODEL PENAL CODE *of the American Law Institute: Attempt, Solicitation and Conspiracy,* 61 COLUM. L. REV. 571, 1004 (1961).

[180] *See* Note, *Developments in the Law — Criminal Conspiracy,* 72 HARV. L. REV. 920, 998 (1959).

[181] *See* MODEL PENAL CODE § 2.06(3) (1962); MODEL PENAL CODE § 2.04(3), comment at 20-23 (Tentative Draft No. 1, 1953); Peter Buscemi, Note, *Conspiracy: Statutory Reform Since the* MODEL PENAL CODE, 75 COLUM. L. REV. 1122, 1150 (1975).

[182] *See* Herbert Wechsler *et al., The Treatment of Inchoate Crimes in the* MODEL PENAL CODE *of the American Law Institute: Attempt, Solicitation and Conspiracy,* 61 COLUM. L. REV. 571, 1004 (1961).

accepted *Pinkerton* generally[183] and have not required that the acts in further-ance of the conspiracy committed by coconspirators be totally and exactly fore-seeable[184] to the conspirator who is held accountable for the acts in question.

Most courts, federal[185] and state,[186] as well as various authorities,[187] maintain that a condition precedent to holding a conspirator accountable in this connec-tion is the requirement of reasonable foreseeability as to the acts carried out by the coconspirator. Various Illinois opinions express somewhat similar terms. For example, in *People v. Hughes*,[188] the Illinois Supreme Court stated:

> [W]here one attaches himself to a group bent on illegal acts which are dan-gerous or homicidal in character, or which will probably or necessarily re-quire the use of force and violence that could result in the taking of life unlawfully, he becomes criminally liable for any wrongdoings committed by other members of the group in furtherance of the common purpose, or as a *natural or probable consequence* thereof, even though he did not ac-tively participate in the overt act itself.[189]

All of this suggests that even though it appears that Illinois conspiracy law may follow *Pinkerton*,[190] it is best, if not absolutely necessary, to rely on accountabil-ity principles in conjunction with conspiracy theories in Illinois when imputing to a coconspirator the substantive crimes carried out by a fellow conspirator. Further, it appears advisable, if not essential, from the perspective of a state's attorney to offer evidence, where such is feasible, that suggests that the substan-tive crime was either reasonably foreseeable or a natural or probable conse-quence of the conspiracy. As the Illinois legislative drafting committee's com-ments state, the mere existence of a conspiracy will not automatically make the

---

[183] *See, e.g.,* United States v. Raffone, 693 F.2d 1343 (11th Cir. 1982), *cert. denied,* 461 U.S. 931 (1983); Government of Virgin Islands v. Dowling, 633 F.2d 660 (3d Cir.), *cert. denied,* 449 U.S. 960 (1980).

[184] *See, e.g.,* United States v. Anderson, 101 F.2d 325, 332-33 (7th Cir.), *cert. denied,* 307 U.S. 625 (1939).

[185] *See, e.g.,* United States v. Iannelli, 461 F.2d 483, 487 (2d Cir.), *cert. denied,* 409 U.S. 980 (1972).

[186] *See, e.g.,* Martinez v. Florida, 413 So. 2d 429 (Fla. Dist. Ct. App. 1982).

[187] Jon May, *Pinkerton v. United States Revisited: A Defense of Accomplice Liability,* 8 Nova L.J. 21, 41-42 (1983).

[188] 26 Ill. 2d 114, 185 N.E.2d 834 (1962).

[189] People v. Hughes, 26 Ill. 2d 114, 119-20, 185 N.E.2d 834, 837 (1962). *Cf.* People v. Kolep, 29 Ill. 2d 116, 121, 193 N.E.2d 753, 756 (1963) (if group with which defendant associated had common design to rape woman, then any act of group in furtherance of original design was act of all and all were equally guilty of murder that inadvertently occurred while they perpetrated the rape).

[190] *See* Peter Buscemi, Note, *Conspiracy: Statutory Reform Since the* Model Penal Code, 75 Colum. L. Rev. 1122, 1151 n.155 (1975) (citing People v. Olivier, 3 Ill. App. 3d 872, 279 N.E.2d 363 (1st Dist. 1972)).

various members of an illegal compact responsible for any and all crimes carried out by others that have no clear nexus with the conspiracy.[191] As *Pinkerton* itself makes clear, if a person's crime is outside the scope of his or her conspiracy with others, there will be no liability suffered by the others for that person's crime.

§ 4.12. Absence of Liability of Coconspirator.

The Illinois conspiracy legislation[192] provides as long as there is a bilateral agreement to commit an illegal act (plus an overt act in furtherance of that agreement), the fact that a coconspirator has not been convicted, has been acquitted, or lacked the capacity to commit a crime is of no benefit to the accused.[193] In *People v. Rance*,[194] a codefendant's bench trial was conducted simultaneously with the defendant's jury trial on theft and conspiracy. Even though the codefendant was acquitted, the jury's verdict was not vacated in light of the fact that the jury and the trial judge operated as separate triers of fact and heard different evidence on the respective defendants.[195] However, the *Rance* court stated in dictum that if the same trier of fact considered identical evidence and convicted one party to an alleged conspiracy but not the second, the inconsistent verdict might raise a reasonable doubt about the actual existence of a bilateral meeting of the minds which is necessary for conspiracy.[196] But in *People v. Jayne*,[197] two defendants were not entitled to a reversal of their convictions for conspiracy to commit murder despite the fact that a codefendant who was convicted of murder was acquitted of conspiracy to commit murder. In *Jayne*, the court made no mention of the similarity or dissimilarity of the evidence and simply noted that recent Illinois caselaw does not require that verdicts be logical or legally consistent.[198]

Other immunity theories have been rejected in Illinois. In *People v. Martin*,[199] the Illinois Supreme Court stated that the common law fiction of unity did not immunize a husband and wife from prosecution when they entered into a con-

---

[191] ILL. ANN. STAT. ch. 38, para. 5-2 (Smith-Hurd 1989), 1961 Committee Comments, at 236.

[192] 720 ILCS 5/8-2(b) (1999).

[193] People v. Lane, 133 Ill. App. 3d 215, 219-20, 478 N.E.2d 1160, 1164 (1st Dist. 1985).

[194] 68 Ill. App. 3d 639, 386 N.E.2d 566 (1st Dist. 1979).

[195] People v. Rance, 68 Ill. App. 3d 639, 647, 386 N.E.2d 566, 572 (1st Dist. 1979).

[196] People v. Rance, 68 Ill. App. 3d 639, 647, 386 N.E.2d 566, 572 (1st Dist. 1979) (quoting People v. Stock, 56 Ill. 2d 461, 465, 309 N.E.2d 19, 21 (1974) ("For a reasonable doubt to be raised in such cases, it must be shown that the evidence given against all of the defendants is identical in all respects.")).

[197] 52 Ill. App. 3d 990, 368 N.E.2d 422 (1st Dist. 1977).

[198] People v. Jayne, 52 Ill. App. 3d 990, 1004, 368 N.E.2d 422, 432 (1st Dist. 1977).

[199] 4 Ill. 2d 105, 122 N.E.2d 245 (1954).

spiracy to sell a narcotic.[200] In *People v. Estep*,[201] the defendants could be found guilty of a conspiracy with persons whose names were unknown.[202] As long as there is a bilateral showing of wrongful intent, the subsequent death or disappearance of the coconspirator will not free the accused of liability for conspiracy.

§ 4.13. Wharton's Rule.

As noted earlier in this chapter,[203] Wharton's Rule is not a barrier under the current conspiracy statute. In *People v. Roberts*,[204] conspiracy to commit gambling was upheld even though gambling by its very nature involves the complicity of more than one criminal actor. The *Roberts* court pointed out the legislative determination to abolish Wharton's Rule and acknowledged it was supported by the rationale of preventing the greater societal threat associated with group activity.[205] Likewise, in *People v. Cooper*,[206] the Illinois appellate court found Wharton's Rule did not preclude the defendant's conviction for conspiracy to commit cannabis trafficking.[207] So too, in *People v. Laws*,[208] the Illinois Supreme Court held Wharton's Rule did not bar charges of conspiracy to commit pimping, solicitation for a prostitute, and pandering.[209]

The abolition of Wharton's Rule in the conspiracy context should not be confused with other barriers to convicting defendants that remain intact. For example, given the effect of paragraph 5/8-3, which states it "is a defense to a charge of . . . conspiracy that if the criminal object were achieved the accused would not be guilty of an offense,"[210] a minor victim could not be convicted of conspiracy to commit aggravated criminal sexual assault[211] for agreeing to have sex with an adult male, since she could never be convicted of the commission of the principal offense on herself. Also, if the state relies in whole or in part on accomplice liability principles in an effort to hold a conspirator liable for substantive crimes carried out by coconspirators in furtherance of a conspiracy, it is important to know Illinois accountability legislation explicitly states a person

---

[200] People v. Martin, 4 Ill. 2d 105, 109, 122 N.E.2d 245, 246-47 (1954).

[201] 346 Ill. App. 132, 104 N.E.2d 562 (1st Dist. 1952), *cert. denied*, 345 U.S. 970 (1953).

[202] People v. Estep, 346 Ill. App. 132, 142, 104 N.E.2d 562, 567 (1st Dist. 1952), *cert. denied*, 345 U.S. 970 (1953).

[203] *See* § 4.02 of this chapter.

[204] 83 Ill. App. 3d 311, 404 N.E.2d 278 (5th Dist. 1980).

[205] People v. Roberts, 83 Ill. App. 3d 311, 319, 404 N.E.2d 278, 284-85 (5th Dist. 1980).

[206] 239 Ill. App. 3d 336, 606 N.E.2d 705 (5th Dist. 1992).

[207] People v. Cooper, 239 Ill. App. 3d 336, 352-55, 606 N.E.2d 705, 717-19 (5th Dist. 1992).

[208] 155 Ill. 2d 208, 613 N.E.2d 747 (1993).

[209] People v. Laws, 155 Ill. 2d 208, 211-16, 613 N.E.2d 747, 749-51 (1993).

[210] 720 ILCS 5/8-3 (1999).

[211] 720 ILCS 5/12-14(b)(i) (1999) (prohibiting a person aged 17 or over from sexual penetration of a victim under the age of 9).

cannot be convicted for a principal offense under an accomplice theory if "(1) He is the victim of the offense committed; or (2) The offense is so defined that his conduct was inevitably incident to its commission . . . ."[212] Here, it would be legally impossible to convict the minor sexual abuse victim for being an accomplice to the adult male's sexual wrongdoing. Similarly, the accountability laws would not permit conviction of a purchaser of narcotics as an accomplice to a drug seller's violation of the Illinois prohibition against the illicit distribution of narcotics.

§ 4.14. Withdrawal.

Once a conspiracy is formed, a subsequent change of heart by the conspirators to carry out the criminal object of their plans will not free them from liability for the conspiracy. In *People v. Burleson,*[213] the defendants were liable for conspiracy to rob a bank even though they abandoned their plans when they discovered too many people were around the bank when they arrived.[214] As with other crimes, once a conspiracy is committed, subsequent efforts cannot undo its existence for prosecutorial purposes.[215] Withdrawal from a conspiracy after the fact is not a defense to conspiracy.[216]

With respect to substantive crimes carried out in furtherance of a conspiracy, a conspirator may have a defense of withdrawal if he effectively withdrew from the conspiracy before his coconspirators carried out the principal offenses. Because of the interplay between accomplice liability and conspiracy law in this area, it is essential to consider the "withdrawal" provision in the accomplice liability statute. The Illinois accountability statute provides that a person who initially agreed to the commission of an offense will not be accountable for others' acts in furtherance of the agreement if "[b]efore the commission of the [principal] offense, he terminates his effort to promote or facilitate such commission, and does one of the following: wholly deprives his prior efforts of effectiveness in such commission, or gives timely warning to the proper law enforcement authorities, or otherwise makes proper effort to prevent the commission of the offense."[217]

The first of these methods of withdrawal — depriving one's efforts of effectiveness — is probably the most difficult to gauge in an actual case. In *People v. Wallace,*[218] the court stated:

---

[212] 720 ILCS 5/5-2(c) (1999).

[213] 50 Ill. App. 3d 629, 365 N.E.2d 1162 (4th Dist. 1977).

[214] People v. Burleson, 50 Ill. App. 3d 629, 634, 365 N.E.2d 1162, 1166 (4th Dist. 1977).

[215] People v. Adams, 176 Ill. App. 3d 197, 202-03, 530 N.E.2d 1155, 1158 (1st Dist. 1988).

[216] People v. Adams, 176 Ill. App. 3d 197, 202-03, 530 N.E.2d 1155, 1158 (1st Dist. 1988).

[217] 720 ILCS 5/5-2(c)(3) (1999).

[218] 100 Ill. App. 3d 424, 426 N.E.2d 1017 (1st Dist. 1981).

For a withdrawal to be effective, it must be timely so that it affords one's co-conspirators a reasonable opportunity, if they desire, to follow the example and refrain from further action before the offense is committed. Therefore, it must be possible for the trier of fact to find that the accused had wholly and effectively detached himself from the criminal enterprise before the act with which he is charged was in the process of consummation or had become so inevitable it could not reasonably be stopped.[219]

In *Wallace,* the court held that by no stretch of the imagination could the defendant argue withdrawal based on a robbery victim's testimony that he fled from a robbery scene before a coconspirator took the victim's purse, considering it was the defendant's act of grabbing at the victim's purse which caused her to fall to her knees, placed the victim in a more vulnerable position to be robbed, and facilitated his coconspirator's snatching of her purse.[220] Similarly, a defendant's claim of withdrawal was ineffective where the defendant accompanied his codefendants to the scene of an eventual armed robbery in a laundromat, separated from them only moments before the crime, went into an alley behind the laundromat, did not leave the alley until the codefendants left the laundromat, fled with them, and then changed jackets with one of them after he was arrested.[221]

The second basis for finding withdrawal — notifying law enforcement authorities — is usually not difficult to assess. But again, the courts insist that the warning to the police be timely.[222]

The third possibility for withdrawing involves prevention of the coconspirator's crimes. In *People v. Richard,*[223] the defendant was charged with murder arising out of a shooting. He admitted he intended to rob someone with his companions, had carried the gun used in the shooting, and had walked along with the codefendants looking for someone to rob. He stated to the police afterward "then something changed my mind, and I went to get some cigarettes."[224] He obtained the cigarettes about a block away but then returned to a point near the crime scene where he watched his companions shoot the robbery victim to death. After being convicted of murder, the defendant claimed on appeal that his actions of leaving his companions were tantamount to a withdrawal. The appellate court affirmed the murder conviction while holding that the trial court's failure to instruct the jury regarding the withdrawal defense was proper.[225] The defendant's decision to remove himself from the immediate crime scene was "of no consequence" since he made no effort to neutralize the effect of his earlier conduct by

---

[219] People v. Wallace, 100 Ill. App. 3d 424, 431, 426 N.E.2d 1017, 1023 (1st Dist. 1981).

[220] People v. Wallace, 100 Ill. App. 3d 424, 431, 426 N.E.2d 1017, 1023 (1st Dist. 1981).

[221] People v. Gilbert, 194 Ill. App. 3d 184, 189, 550 N.E.2d 1183, 1187 (1st Dist. 1990).

[222] People v. Wallace, 100 Ill. App. 3d 424, 431, 426 N.E.2d 1017, 1024 (1st Dist. 1981).

[223] 90 Ill. App. 3d 322, 413 N.E.2d 5 (1st Dist. 1980).

[224] People v. Richard, 90 Ill. App. 3d 322, 333, 413 N.E.2d 5, 14 (1st Dist. 1980).

[225] People v. Richard, 90 Ill. App. 3d 322, 333, 413 N.E.2d 5, 14 (1st Dist. 1980).

preventing the crime.[226] The law demands some affirmative effort to prevent the coconspirator's plans; passive inaction will not suffice.

§ 4.15. Multiple Convictions: Conspiracy and Substantive Crimes.

With the enactment of the Illinois Criminal Code of 1961 came the abolition of the practice of allowing multiple convictions by allowing a person to be convicted of both an inchoate offense and the principal offense charged.[227] Since Illinois law explicitly states that "[n]o person shall be convicted of both the inchoate and the principal offense,"[228] a conspirator being prosecuted for armed robbery and conspiracy to commit armed robbery, for example, can only be convicted of one offense.[229] Normally, where the jury has found the defendant guilty of the substantive crime, the trial court will simply not enter judgment on the jury's guilty verdict on the conspiracy count.[230] If the defendant is convicted in the trial court of both the principal and inchoate crime, then the conspiracy conviction will normally be vacated on appeal.[231] The trial court's error in entering judgment of conviction on the conspiracy charge does not constitute error affecting the conviction on the principal charge so the latter conviction will stand.[232] On the other hand, where a jury was unable to reach a verdict on the substantive charge but did convict the defendant of conspiracy, whereupon the trial court entered a judgment and sentence on the conspiracy charge, a retrial on the substantive crime was barred.[233]

The principal offense will stand and the conspiracy charge will fall where the courts view conspiracy as a part of the substantive crime committed in furtherance of the conspiracy,[234] or simply as a "lesser included offense."[235] However, if a defendant entered into two separate conspiracies to rob a bank, where one led to the commission of a robbery in furtherance of the conspiracy and the

---

[226] People v. Richard, 90 Ill. App. 3d 322, 333, 413 N.E.2d 5, 14 (1st Dist. 1980).

[227] People v. Walker, 84 Ill. 2d 512, 526, 419 N.E.2d 1167, 1176 (1981), *cert. denied*, 465 U.S. 1031 (1984); People v. Love, 60 Ill. App. 3d 16, 21, 376 N.E.2d 342, 346 (1st Dist. 1978); People v. Schmidt, 25 Ill. App. 3d 1035, 1036, 324 N.E.2d 246, 247 (3d Dist. 1975); People v. Burch, 22 Ill. App. 3d 950, 958, 317 N.E.2d 136, 143 (2d Dist. 1974); People v. Casner, 20 Ill. App. 3d 107, 112, 312 N.E.2d 709, 712 (2d Dist. 1974).

[228] 720 ILCS 5/8-5 (1999).

[229] People v. Walker, 84 Ill. 2d 512, 526, 419 N.E.2d 1167, 1176 (1981), *cert. denied*, 465 U.S. 1031 (1984).

[230] *See, e.g.,* People v. Ganci, 57 Ill. App. 3d 234, 236, 372 N.E.2d 1077, 1079 (1st Dist. 1978).

[231] *See, e.g.,* People v. Henderson, 175 Ill. App. 3d 483, 490, 529 N.E.2d 1051, 1055 (1st Dist. 1988); People v. Hill, 78 Ill. 2d 465, 476, 401 N.E.2d 517, 522 (1980).

[232] People v. Schmidt, 25 Ill. App. 3d 1035, 1036, 324 N.E.2d 246, 247 (3d Dist. 1975).

[233] People v. Gomez, 286 Ill. App. 3d 232, 235, 675 N.E.2d 971, 973 (3d Dist. 1997).

[234] People v. Brisbon, 89 Ill. App. 3d 513, 527-28, 411 N.E.2d 956, 967 (1st Dist. 1980), *cert. denied*, 451 U.S. 990 (1981).

[235] People v. Burleson, 50 Ill. App. 3d 629, 635, 365 N.E.2d 1162, 1167-68 (4th Dist. 1977).

other did not, the defendant could be convicted of both the principal offense arising from the first conspiracy and conspiracy for the second illegal compact.[236] If a defendant committed several substantive crimes as part of a single conspiracy, such as murder and armed robbery, then the dismissal of the conspiracy count would not impact on the possibility of multiple *substantive* counts.[237]

Waiveable error does not arise by failure to object to a trial court's entry of judgment of conviction for both conspiracy and the substantive crime. Where a defendant was convicted of rape and conspiracy to commit rape, the appellate court viewed the situation under the plain error doctrine despite the defendant's failure to raise the error during trial.[238]

While a defendant may not be convicted of both a principal and inchoate offense, there is no bar against multiple convictions for inchoate offenses. Thus, a defendant was properly convicted of conspiracy to commit armed robbery and attempted armed robbery.[239]

---

[236] People v. Burleson, 50 Ill. App. 3d 629, 635, 365 N.E.2d 1162, 1167-68 (4th Dist. 1977).

[237] People v. Brisbon, 89 Ill. App. 3d 513, 527-28, 411 N.E.2d 956, 967 (1st Dist. 1980), *cert. denied*, 451 U.S. 990 (1981).

[238] People v. Casner, 20 Ill. App. 3d 107, 112, 312 N.E.2d 709, 712-13 (2d Dist. 1974).

[239] People v. Jones, 234 Ill. App. 3d 1082, 1094-95, 601 N.E.2d 1080, 1088 (1st Dist. 1992).

CHAPTER 5

ATTEMPT AND SOLICITATION

§ 5.01. Introduction.

Because of the close relationship between criminal attempts and criminal solicitations, these offenses will be explored in this chapter. This effort will exhaust the coverage of the three types of inchoate crimes in Illinois: conspiracy, attempt, and solicitation. Although all of these offenses have in common two essential ingredients — the specific intent to further a crime and an effort in the direction of criminality — they differ in various respects; some of these aspects were explored in the previous chapter. Although the solicitation provisions precede the attempt provision in the code, the latter crime is clearly the more important of the two and will be addressed initially.

§ 5.02. Criminal Attempt.

Illinois law defines the elements of the offense of attempt as follows: "A person commits an attempt when, with intent to commit a specific offense, he does any act which constitutes a substantial step toward commission of that offense."[1] Thus, the face of the statute reflects two essential requirements: (1) a specific intent to commit a crime, and (2) any act that involves a substantial step in the direction of that crime.

The revision committee's comments clarify one significant change from the prior law; namely, under the present code, it is no longer necessary that the at-

---

[1] 720 ILCS 5/8-4(a) (1999).

217

tempt fail.[2] The doctrine that failure of the attempt was necessary for a conviction was based on a common law merger concept.[3] Of course, if the defendant successfully commits the crime he or she has attempted to accomplish and is convicted of the principal offense, the attempt will be considered a lesser included offense and will be set aside.[4] But, if the defendant completes that crime but evidence supportive of that fact is lacking, he or she may then be convicted of the attempted commission of the crime, assuming evidence is available to support the conviction.[5]

Another important clarification in the Illinois law of attempt appears in the criminal attempt legislation: "It shall not be a defense to a charge of attempt that because of a misapprehension of the circumstances it would have been impossible for the accused to commit the offense attempted."[6] Clearly, the intent of the framers of the legislation was to reject the common law notion that legal impossibility may be a defense.[7] The "misapprehension of the circumstances" language was designed to reject not only "factual impossibility" claims (for example, the attempt to pick an empty pocket or to commit burglary in an empty building), but also "legal impossibility" arguments (for example, attempting to receive stolen goods that in reality were not stolen); however, "inherent impossibility" claims (such as attempting to murder by a witchcraft stabbing of a dummy made to represent the person intended to be murdered) remain a defense.[8]

The sentencing provisions of the criminal attempt prohibition tie the penalty for attempt to that of the principal crime.[9] Illinois law rejects the common law rule that an attempt is only a misdemeanor.[10]

---

[2] ILL. ANN. STAT. ch. 38, para. 8-4 (Smith-Hurd 1989), 1961 Committee Comments, at 498. *See, e.g.,* People v. McMillan, 239 Ill. App. 3d 467, 498-99, 607 N.E.2d 585, 607 (4th Dist. 1993) (defendant could be convicted of attempted aggravated kidnapping even though kidnapping may have been complete).

[3] ILL. ANN. STAT. ch. 38, para. 8-4 (Smith-Hurd 1989), 1961 Committee Comments, at 498.

[4] ILL. ANN. STAT. ch. 38, para. 8-4 (Smith-Hurd 1989), 1961 Committee Comments, at 498.

[5] *Cf.* People v. McMillan, 239 Ill. App. 3d 467, 498-99, 607 N.E.2d 585, 607 (4th Dist. 1993) (where evidence suggested aggravated kidnapping was complete but defendant only charged with attempt and jury only instructed on attempt, attempt conviction proper).

[6] 720 ILCS 5/8-4(b) (1999).

[7] ILL. ANN. STAT. ch. 38, § 8-4 (Smith-Hurd 1989), 1961 Committee Comments, at 500.

[8] ILL. ANN. STAT. ch. 38, § 8-4 (Smith-Hurd 1989), 1961 Committee Comments, at 499-500.

[9] ILL. ANN. STAT. ch. 38, § 8-4 (Smith-Hurd 1989), 1961 Committee Comments, at 500. *See* 720 ILCS 5/8-4(c) (1999) (sentence for attempt may not exceed sentence for crime attempted).

[10] ILL. ANN. STAT. ch. 38, para. 8-4 (Smith-Hurd 1989), 1961 Committee Comments, at 498.

The revision committee makes it clear that the criminal attempt stricture is designed to apply to all crimes designated in the code.[11] This disposes of any necessity to have special provisions for attempts elsewhere in the code.[12]

§ 5.03. Attempt: Mental State.

The Illinois courts are very clear that proof of specific intent is imperative for a conviction of criminal attempt.[13] The intent must be that a specific offense is to be committed.[14] The formulation of the intent to commit an offense cannot be merely an open-ended, vague desire to commit criminality generally; the courts make it clear that the intent must be "an intent to commit a specific offense."[15] If a defendant had the intent to engage in some wrongdoing that did not amount to a crime, he or she cannot be convicted of a criminal attempt.[16]

The importance of this intent requirement cannot be ignored, because the Illinois courts say that the gist of a criminal attempt is the specific intent charged.[17] The defendant's lack of success in accomplishing his or her criminal designs will not be viewed as undermining the formulation of the specific intent. Thus, under the former rape statute (replaced by a criminal sexual assault statute in 1984), the attempted rape victim's successful struggle to defeat the defendant's purposes and the prompt arrival of the police did not destroy the clearly manifested specific intent of the defendant to rape.[18] Similarly, where evidence established that a defendant was discovered by a police officer sitting on a ledge between the windows of a building prying at the inner shield with a table leg and surrounded by shattered glass, whereupon the defendant ran from the scene after being interrupted by the officer, this was sufficient for attempted burglary.[19]

---

[11] ILL. ANN. STAT. ch. 38, para. 8-4 (Smith-Hurd 1989), 1961 Committee Comments, at 500.

[12] ILL. ANN. STAT. ch. 38, para. 8-4 (Smith-Hurd 1989), 1961 Committee Comments, at 500.

[13] People v. Coleman, 131 Ill. App. 3d 76, 78, 475 N.E.2d 565, 567 (1st Dist. 1985).

[14] People v. Winters, 151 Ill. App. 3d 402, 405, 502 N.E.2d 841, 843 (2d Dist. 1986); People v. Sanders, 7 Ill. App. 3d 848, 849, 289 N.E.2d 110, 111 (1st Dist. 1972).

[15] People v. Dennis, 5 Ill. App. 3d 708, 711, 284 N.E.2d 67, 69 (1st Dist. 1972) (emphasis added).

[16] People v. Young, 2 Ill. App. 3d 581, 277 N.E.2d 151 (2d Dist. 1971) (abstract) (defendant could not be convicted of attempted sale of marijuana where sale of marijuana was not offense under statutes then in force).

[17] People v. Enoch, 122 Ill. 2d 176, 197, 522 N.E.2d 1124, 1135, cert. denied, 488 U.S. 917 (1988) (proof of the specific intent to commit an offense is "essential" to sustain a criminal attempt conviction); People v. Popely, 36 Ill. App. 3d 828, 834, 345 N.E.2d 125, 130 (1st Dist. 1976) ("[T]he gist of attempt rape is the specific intent charged").

[18] People v. Oetgen, 62 Ill. App. 3d 29, 33, 378 N.E.2d 1355, 1359 (3d Dist. 1978); see also People v. Fleagle, 129 Ill. App. 3d 298, 302, 472 N.E.2d 155, 158 (1st Dist. 1984) (fact that attempted rape victim successfully prevented consummation of rape did not establish a lack of intent to rape).

[19] People v. Newell, 105 Ill. App. 3d 330, 333, 434 N.E.2d 349, 352-53 (1st Dist. 1982).

The fact that the assailant's intent was not verbalized does not establish a lack of criminal intent.[20] Thus, if a defendant had opened his female victim's blouse and pulled her skirt and slip up to her waist while he kneeled between her legs in the nude, this would be indicative of intent to commit criminal sexual assault even though he may not have uttered any words consistent with such a criminal purpose.[21] Similarly, where the defendants encountered an apparent robbery victim and one of the defendants began to grab him by the neck while another tried to push him and secure his wallet, whereupon the victim broke loose, drew a revolver, and shot in the direction of the defendants, this constituted evidence of the defendants' specific intent to commit attempted robbery even though no specific demand for money was made.[22]

Anything less than a mens rea of specific intent is clearly insufficient for criminal attempt. For instance, the offense of attempted murder requires the mental state of specific intent to kill.[23] Knowledge that the consequences of an act may result in death or grave bodily injury, or intent to do bodily harm, is insufficient, and any trial court instruction stating that these lesser mental states might be sufficient for attempted murder would be in error.[24]

Notwithstanding this rigorous mens rea requirement, direct evidence of the defendant's specific intent is not mandated. Since proof of a defendant's intent to kill can rarely be based on direct evidence, the intent may be established by surrounding circumstances.[25] It may be inferred from the character of the assault, the use of a deadly weapon, and other circumstances.[26] Thus, where a defendant used a knife to cut the victim's neck, then cut another person, and then moved his knife back to the original victim's neck and gave a "pretty hefty yank" so as to possibly cause the severing of his windpipe, this was sufficient for attempted murder.[27] Where a defendant inflicted an extreme and extended

---

[20] People v. Fleagle, 129 Ill. App. 3d 298, 302, 472 N.E.2d 155, 158 (1st Dist. 1984).

[21] People v. Fleagle, 129 Ill. App. 3d 298, 302, 472 N.E.2d 155, 158 (1st Dist. 1984) (attempted rape conviction affirmed).

[22] People v. Cheatem, 35 Ill. App. 3d 414, 416, 342 N.E.2d 410, 412 (1st Dist. 1976).

[23] People v. Garrett, 216 Ill. App. 3d 348, 354, 576 N.E.2d 331, 335 (1st Dist. 1990); People v. Mitchell, 98 Ill. App. 3d 398, 402, 424 N.E.2d 658, 661 (3d Dist. 1981).

[24] People v. Jones, 81 Ill. 2d 1, 8-9, 405 N.E.2d 343, 346 (1979); People v. Harris, 72 Ill. 16, 27, 377 N.E.2d 28, 33 (1978); People v. Nuno, 206 Ill. App. 3d 160, 164, 563 N.E.2d 1165, 1168 (1st Dist. 1990); People v. Gentry, 157 Ill. App. 3d 899, 903, 510 N.E.2d 963, 966 (1st Dist. 1987).

[25] People v. Solis, 216 Ill. App. 3d 11, 17, 576 N.E.2d 120, 123-24 (1st Dist. 1991).

[26] People v. Koshiol, 45 Ill. 2d 573, 578, 262 N.E.2d 446, 449 (1970), cert. denied, 401 U.S. 978 (1971), rev'd on other grounds sub nom., People v. Nunn, 55 Ill. 2d 344, 304 N.E.2d 81 (1973); People v. Coolidge, 26 Ill. 2d 533, 536, 187 N.E.2d 694, 696 (1963); People v. Cruz, 196 Ill. App. 3d 1047, 1055-56, 554 N.E.2d 598, 603 (1st Dist. 1990).

[27] People v. Myers, 85 Ill. 2d 281, 288-89, 426 N.E.2d 535, 538-39 (1981); see also People v. Nunn, 301 Ill. App. 3d 816, 824-26, 704 N.E.2d 683, 689-90 (1st Dist. 1998) (sufficient evidence of specific intent to kill necessary for attempted murder existed where defendant and others con-

beating with his fists upon his victim, coupled with the defendant's size and strength as compared to the victim this constituted attempted murder.[28] In regards to firearms, caselaw states the very act of firing a gun at another person supports the conclusion that the person doing the shooting acted with an intent to kill.[29] For example, where a defendant fired his pistol at the face and chest of a police officer from a distance of about ten feet, this exceeded the possibility that the defendant had the mere intent to scare the officer and permitted the only conclusion that the defendant had the intent to kill the officer.[30]

A statement uttered by a defendant in which he or she admits that he or she harbored the specific intent required will normally provide the government with ample evidence of the requisite mens rea. For example, defendant's statements to police that he and an accomplice went to the victim's apartment for the purpose of robbing its occupants, corroborated by circumstances surrounding the crime, established the specific intent to commit attempted armed robbery.[31] On the other hand, a court is not required to believe the defendant's testimony where the defendant denies having had the requisite mental state, as in an attempted murder case where the defendant claimed he merely fired at the victim to warn him, but without any intent to kill.[32] Thus, when an appellate court is considering the presence of specific intent, based on either direct evidence or circumstantial evidence, it normally proclaims that the determination of the existence of the requisite intent is for the trier of fact; and that determination will not be disturbed unless there exists a reasonable doubt as to the accused's guilt.[33]

---

fronted victim, defendant said "Let's kill this punk," one of the others held victim while defendant punched victim in jaw and hit him several times in the face with 40 ounce beer bottle, whereupon victim lapsed into a coma and suffered brain damage); People v. Winters, 151 Ill. App. 3d 402, 408-09, 502 N.E.2d 841, 845 (2d Dist. 1986) (where a defendant stabbed a victim twice, then was momentarily distracted by a neighbor, and then stabbed the victim again as the victim tried to escape into the neighbor's house, this was sufficient evidence of specific intent to kill for attempted murder.

[28] People v. Scott, 271 Ill. App. 3d 307, 311-12, 648 N.E.2d 86, 88-89 (1st Dist. 1994).

[29] People v. Mitchell, 209 Ill. App. 3d 562, 569, 568 N.E.2d 292, 297 (1st Dist. 1991); People v. Thorns, 62 Ill. App. 3d 1028, 1031, 379 N.E.2d 641, 643 (1st Dist. 1978).

[30] People v. Walker, 259 Ill. App. 3d 98, 102-04, 628 N.E.2d 1111, 1114-15 (1st Dist. 1994).

[31] People v. Lee, 194 Ill. App. 3d 595, 598, 551 N.E.2d 300, 302 (1st Dist. 1990).

[32] People v. Thomas, 60 Ill. App. 3d 673, 677, 377 N.E.2d 195, 198 (1st Dist. 1978); *see also* People v. Starks, 190 Ill. App. 3d 503, 510, 546 N.E.2d 71, 77 (2d Dist. 1989) (defendant's claim that he shot at victim only to frighten her rejected), *cert. denied*, 498 U.S. 827 (1990).

[33] People v. Mitchell, 98 Ill. App. 3d 398, 402, 424 N.E.2d 658, 661 (3d Dist. 1981) (attempted murder conviction affirmed). *Compare* People v. Garrett, 216 Ill. App. 3d 348, 354, 576 N.E.2d 331, 336 (1st Dist. 1991) (attempted murder conviction reversed because evidence insufficient to establish intent to kill); People v. Jones, 184 Ill. App. 3d 412, 429-30, 541 N.E.2d 132, 143 (1st Dist. 1989) (attempted murder conviction reversed because evidence insufficient to establish intent to kill).

With respect to the intent issue, it is important to bear in mind that the Illinois courts accept the doctrine of transferred intent in connection with attempt liability.[34] Thus, where the defendant fired shots at a victim with the intent to kill him and one of the shots ricocheted and struck another, the defendant's conviction for attempted murder was sustained as to the second victim.[35] However, where the state failed to prove a defendant had the intent to kill his alleged "intended victim," it was legally impossible to convict him of the attempted murder of an unintended victim based on a transferred intent theory.[36]

§ 5.04. Attempt: Overt Act.

The language of the Illinois criminal attempt stricture demands proof of "any act which constitutes a substantial step toward the commission" of the target crime.[37] The Illinois opinions clearly hold, on the one hand, that "mere preparation" short of a substantial step to engage in criminality is an insufficient overt act for purposes of criminal attempt[38] and, on the other hand, that it is not necessary that the defendant perform the last act immediately preceding that which would render the substantive act complete.[39] While recognizing that it may prove exceedingly difficult to determine when mere preparation to commit an offense ceases and commission of the criminal attempt begins, the revision committee posited that such a determination depends on the special circumstances of each case, including how far removed in time and space the conduct in question was from the consummated crime and whether it was in "dangerous proximity to success."[40] Accordingly, it is incumbent on the fact finder at trial to determine what constitutes a substantial step toward criminality without the benefit of further definitional clarification of what is meant by the "substantial

---

[34] People v. Migliore, 170 Ill. App. 3d 581, 589, 525 N.E.2d 182, 188 (2d Dist. 1988) (discussing Illinois court acceptance of doctrine while affirming attempted murder conviction where defendant shot at one victim intending to kill another).

[35] People v. Humes, 78 Ill. App. 3d 255, 260, 397 N.E.2d 130, 133 (1st Dist. 1979); see also People v. Hill, 276 Ill. App. 3d 683, 687-89, 658 N.E.2d 1294, 1297-98 (1st Dist. 1995) (attempted first degree murder conviction affirmed while relying on transferred intent theory where defendant shot and wounded one person while intending to kill another).

[36] People v. Homes, 274 Ill. App. 3d 612, 623, 654 N.E.2d 662, 670 (1st Dist. 1995) (where the trial court acquitted the defendant of attempted murder of intended victim but convicted him of attempted murder of unintended victim, latter conviction was legally inconsistent verdict that had to be vacated on appeal).

[37] 720 ILCS 5/8-4(a) (1999).

[38] People v. Elmore, 50 Ill. 2d 10, 12, 276 N.E.2d 325, 326 (1971).

[39] People v. White, 84 Ill. App. 3d 1044, 1047, 406 N.E.2d 7, 9 (1st Dist. 1980).

[40] ILL. ANN. STAT. ch. 38, para. 8-4 (Smith-Hurd 1989), 1961 Committee Comments, at 499 (quote of Justice Holmes from Hyde v. United States, 225 U.S. 347, 387-88 (1911)).

step" language, for such was not provided by the legislature or by the revision committee.[41]

With respect to the "substantial step" standard employed in Illinois, it is useful to note that this same language appears in the Model Penal Code.[42] In addition, the Model Penal Code spells out various acts that "shall not be held insufficient as a matter of law" for purposes of the substantial step test.[43] These acts, which the American Law Institute believed should not be discounted as a matter of law, assuming they are "strongly corroborative of the actor's criminal purposes," are:

(a) lying in wait, searching for or following the contemplated victim of the crime;

(b) enticing or seeking to entice the contemplated victim of the crime to the place contemplated for its commission;

(c) reconnoitering the place contemplated for the commission of the crime;

(d) unlawful entry of a structure, vehicle or enclosure in which it is contemplated that the crime will be committed;

(e) possession of materials to be employed in the commission of the crime, which are specially designed for such unlawful use or which can serve no lawful purpose of the actor under the circumstances;

(f) possession, collection or fabrication of materials to be employed in the commission of the crime, at or near the place contemplated for its commission, where such possession, collection or fabrication serves no lawful purpose of the actor under the circumstances;

(g) soliciting an innocent agent to engage in conduct constituting an element of the crime.[44]

Although the Illinois General Assembly did not incorporate these acts into the criminal attempt legislation, the Illinois Supreme Court has used the acts enumerated in the Model Penal Code to measure whether a substantial step has taken place.[45] While the Illinois revision committee comments[46] and several Illi-

---

[41] The "substantial step" standard employed by the committee appeared in People v. Woods, 24 Ill. 2d 154, 158, 180 N.E.2d 475, 478, *cert. denied*, 371 U.S. 819 (1962).

[42] MODEL PENAL CODE § 5.01(1)(c) (1962).

[43] MODEL PENAL CODE § 5.01(2) (1962).

[44] MODEL PENAL CODE § 5.01(2) (1962).

[45] *See, e.g.*, People v. Smith, 148 Ill. 2d 454, 459-64, 593 N.E.2d 533, 536-38 (1992) (defendant's conduct fell outside acts described in MODEL PENAL CODE list); People v. Terrell, 99 Ill. 2d 427, 435-36, 459 N.E.2d 1337, 1341-42 (1984) (defendant's conduct met description of several acts on MODEL PENAL CODE list).

[46] ILL. ANN. STAT. ch. 38, para. 8-4 (Smith-Hurd 1989), 1961 Committee Comments, at 499.

nois opinions[47] refer to a "dangerous proximity" standard used in earlier common law opinions,[48] at least one Illinois court has given the Illinois substantial step test an "expanded reading" that "broaden[s] the scope of criminal [attempt] liability beyond the 'dangerous proximity' test."[49] Thus, when the overt act in question corresponds to one of the Model Penal Code acts, the trier of fact may find that the substantial step requirements have been met.[50]

As stated above, the Illinois courts adhere to the general rule that "mere preparation" does not satisfy the substantial step standard.[51] In determining which overt acts are beyond mere preparation, one authority notes the following:

> Certain tendencies may be noted. The more serious the target crime, or the stronger the showing of intent, the more inclined a court will be to treat a relatively remote act as sufficient. Similarly, the factors of time and distance may be significant. The shorter the time or distance before commission of the target crime, the more inclined a court will be to treat an otherwise remote act as sufficient.[52]

These tendencies appear in the Illinois caselaw as well.

In *People v. Burleson*,[53] the defendant and an accomplice pursuant to a plan to rob a bank approached a bank while in possession of a shotgun, suitcase and disguises which were in place. When the duo neared the front door, a man bolted the door from the inside whereupon the two scrambled from the scene. The appellate court upheld defendant's attempted armed robbery conviction after noting defendant's conduct matched behavior described on the Model Penal Code list of acts that amount to a substantial step.[54] Here, defendant was in pos-

---

[47] *See, e.g.,* People v. Pulach, 78 Ill. App. 2d 356, 360, 222 N.E.2d 508, 511 (2d Dist. 1966).

[48] *See* Hyde v. United States, 225 U.S. 347, 388 (1912) (Holmes, J., dissenting).

[49] People v. Smith, 209 Ill. App. 3d 795, 801, 569 N.E.2d 326, 329-30 (2d Dist. 1991), *aff'd in part, rev'd in part*, 148 Ill. 2d 454, 593 N.E.2d 533 (1992). In *Smith*, the appellate court noted the Illinois revision committee comments described the overt act for criminal attempt in the alternative: "a substantial step toward commission, *or as in dangerous proximity* to the principal offense." People v. Smith, 209 Ill. App. 3d 795, 801, 569 N.E.2d 326, 330 (2d Dist. 1991) (quoting ILL. ANN. STAT. ch. 38, para. 8-4 (Smith-Hurd 1989), 1961 Committee Comments, at 499 (emphasis original)), *aff'd in part, rev'd in part*, 148 Ill. 2d 454, 593 N.E.2d 533 (1992). Also, the appellate court felt the Illinois legislature's adoption of the MODEL PENAL CODE's substantial step language was a deliberate effort to broaden the reach of the overt act requirement. *Id.*

It is important to note that the revision committee did not explicitly reject the MODEL PENAL CODE listing of what conduct amounted to a "substantial step," rather, they merely said that "further definition was undesirable." ILL. ANN. STAT. ch. 38, para. 8-4 (Smith Hurd 1989), 1961 Committee Comments, at 499.

[50] *See, e.g.,* People v. Terrell, 99 Ill. 2d 427, 435-36, 459 N.E.2d 1337, 1341-42 (1984).

[51] People v. Smith, 148 Ill. 2d 454, 459, 593 N.E.2d 533, 535 (1992).

[52] 4 CHARLES TORCIA, WHARTON'S CRIMINAL LAW § 744, at 574-75 (14th ed. 1981).

[53] 50 Ill. App. 3d 629, 365 N.E.2d 1162 (4th Dist. 1977).

[54] People v. Burleson, 50 Ill. App. 3d 629, 632-33, 365 N.E.2d 1162, 1165-66 (4th Dist. 1977).

session of materials to be employed in the commission of a crime near the place contemplated for its commission where such possession served no lawful purpose.[55] In *People v. Reyes*,[56] two defendants in possession of a rifle approached a drugstore and waited outside pursuant to a plan to rob certain victims as they exited the drugstore. When several individuals exited the store, they allegedly chased after the defendants. As the defendants ran away, they fired the rifle several times. The appellate court upheld the defendants' attempted armed robbery convictions against a defense claim that their conduct of approaching the store while armed did not satisfy the substantial step test.[57] Here, as in *Burleson*, the defendants possessed the materials necessary to carry out a crime at or near the place contemplated for its commission.[58] Further, one of the defendants admitted to police the nature of their plan which clarified the criminal purpose behind their behavior.[59] In *People v. Terrell*,[60] the defendant was observed by police hiding in weeds approximately 20 to 30 feet behind a service station, carrying a fully loaded revolver and a black nylon stocking mask, and accompanied by an accomplice with an identical disguise. The Illinois Supreme Court upheld the defendant's attempted armed robbery conviction while noting the defendant's conduct — lying in wait, reconnoitering the place contemplated for the commission of a crime, possession of materials specially designed for committing a crime and possession of materials near the place contemplated for its commission — was identical to several different types of behavior on the Model Penal Code list and, accordingly, satisfied the substantial step standard.[61] The court thought it was significant that the defendant and his accomplice, like those in *Burleson* and *Reyes*, "were involved in crimes which posed a serious threat of great bodily harm to the victim."[62] In this regard, "[i]t should not be necessary to subject victims to face to face confrontation with a lethal weapon in order to make a positive finding of the essential element of a substantial threat."[63] Here, the gravity of the defendant's intended crime was an important consideration when evaluating the defendant's underlying conduct.

Meanwhile, the case of *People v. Smith*[64] illustrates how a defendant's failure to perform conduct on the Model Penal Code list may lead to a finding that no

---

[55] People v. Burleson, 50 Ill. App. 3d 629, 633, 365 N.E.2d 1162, 1166 (4th Dist. 1977) (quoting MODEL PENAL CODE § 5.01(2)(f) (1962)).

[56] 102 Ill. App. 3d 820, 429 N.E.2d 1277 (1st Dist. 1981).

[57] People v. Reyes, 102 Ill. App. 3d 820, 834-35, 429 N.E.2d 1277, 1289-90 (1st Dist. 1981).

[58] People v. Reyes, 102 Ill. App. 3d 820, 835, 429 N.E.2d 1277, 1290 (1st Dist. 1981).

[59] People v. Reyes, 102 Ill. App. 3d 820, 835, 429 N.E.2d 1277, 1289 (1st Dist. 1981).

[60] 99 Ill. 2d 427, 459 N.E.2d 1337 (1984).

[61] People v. Terrell, 99 Ill. 2d 427, 435-36, 459 N.E.2d 1337, 1342 (1984) (quoting MODEL PENAL CODE § 5.01(2)(a), (c), (e), (f) (1962)).

[62] People v. Terrell, 99 Ill. 2d 427, 435, 459 N.E.2d 1337, 1341 (1984).

[63] People v. Terrell, 99 Ill. 2d 427, 435, 459 N.E.2d 1337, 1341 (1984).

[64] 148 Ill. 2d 454, 593 N.E.2d 533 (1992).

substantial step transpired. In *Smith*, the defendant entered a taxicab and requested the driver to assist him in finding a jewelry store. After finding no jewelry store, the defendant drew a gun and robbed the taxicab driver of his vehicle. Responding to the taxicab driver's report, the police located the stolen taxicab a short time later. While surveying the area, the police saw defendant walking. When defendant saw the police, he started running and dropped his gun and a pillowcase. Subsequently, defendant was apprehended and convicted of, among other offenses, attempted armed robbery of a jewelry store. Ultimately, the Illinois Supreme Court upheld an appellate court reversal of the defendant's conviction of this offense.[65] Examining the Model Penal Code list, the court initially noted "these factors apply only if 'strongly corroborative of the actor's criminal purposes.'"[66] First, although the defendant was "searching for" a jewelry store, the "contemplated victim of the crime" was never identified.[67] Second, it would not be appropriate to conclude the defendant was "reconnoitering the place contemplated for the commission of the crime" when the defendant had not yet located and identified the jewelry store.[68] Third, it could not be said that the defendant's possession of the gun and pillowcase amounted to possession of articles "specifically designed" for a criminal purpose.[69] Finally, since the jewelry store had not been located, it would be improper to conclude the defendant was in possession of materials to be employed in the commission of a crime "at or near the place contemplated for its commission."[70] Here, then, lack of proximity in "time and space" was problematic to the state's case.[71]

In any event, it is useful to consider some other examples of where the Illinois courts have drawn the line of demarcation between acts that amount to mere preparation and overt acts that constitute the necessary substantial step. A substantial step toward the commission of a robbery occurred where one of two codefendants requested a taxi driver to stop at a place other than their original announced destination, said "this is it," and put his hands on a pistol, which the driver saw come out of his pocket as the driver jumped from the taxi and fled.[72]

---

[65] People v. Smith, 148 Ill. 2d 454, 465, 593 N.E.2d 533, 538 (1992).

[66] People v. Smith, 148 Ill. 2d 454, 463, 593 N.E.2d 533, 537 (1992) (quoting MODEL PENAL CODE § 5.01(2) (1985)).

[67] People v. Smith, 148 Ill. 2d 454, 463, 593 N.E.2d 533, 537 (1992) (quoting MODEL PENAL CODE § 5.01(2)(a) (1985)).

[68] People v. Smith, 148 Ill. 2d 454, 463, 593 N.E.2d 533, 537 (1992) (quoting MODEL PENAL CODE § 5.01(2)(c) (1985)).

[69] People v. Smith, 148 Ill. 2d 454, 464, 593 N.E.2d 533, 538 (1992) (quoting MODEL PENAL CODE § 5.01(2)(e) (1985)).

[70] People v. Smith, 148 Ill. 2d 454, 464, 593 N.E.2d 533, 538 (1992) (quoting MODEL PENAL CODE § 5.01(2)(f) (1985)).

[71] People v. Smith, 148 Ill. 2d 454, 463, 593 N.E.2d 533, 537 (1992) (quoting ILL. ANN. STAT. ch. 38, para. 8-4 (Smith-Hurd 1989), 1961 Committee Comments, at 499).

[72] People v. Turner, 108 Ill. App. 2d 132, 137, 246 N.E.2d 817, 819 (1st Dist. 1969).

An assault of an intended robbery victim as manifested by the defendant's reaching for him with his hands constituted a substantial step toward attempted robbery.[73]

In the area of attempted murder, where a defendant, on three separate occasions, gave her husband two milk shakes and an orange containing arsenic, this constituted the substantial step necessary for attempted murder.[74] Where a defendant beat a victim with his fists and kicked her, this was sufficient.[75] Where police testified that they observed a defendant attempting to lift a victim over the guardrail of a bridge over the Chicago River in order to throw the victim into the water one hundred feet below, this was sufficient for attempted murder.[76] Where the defendant, after shooting one victim, aimed his gun at two other persons, and pulled the trigger not realizing the bullets in the gun were spent, this was a substantial step for attempted first degree murder.[77]

Where testimony of nine- and ten-year-old girls revealed that as they were walking together in a residential neighborhood, the defendant approached them in his vehicle, offered them candy, indicated he would take them wherever they wanted to go if they would get in his car, continued to prowl the neighborhood after being rebuffed by the girls and, when approached by the mother of one of the girls, fled the neighborhood, there was evidence sufficient to find attempted aggravated kidnapping.[78] Testimony of a complaining witness that the defendant forced her into his car was sufficient to find attempted kidnapping.[79] Where defendant undressed and requested mutual acts of masturbation from his minor victim, this amounted to attempted aggravated criminal sexual abuse.[80] On the other hand, where a defendant inquired of a female undercover police officer posing as a prostitute how much she would charge to perform a sexual act, but did not indicate that he had the money or invite the officer into his car, this did not constitute a sufficient substantial step for attempted patronization of a prostitute.[81] Where defendant grabbed an alleged sexual assault victim in her home, threw her to the floor and told her to remove her underwear, an appellate court reasoned that this did not constitute a substantial step for purposes of attempted aggravated criminal sexual assault since defendant made no overt act toward her

---

[73] People v. Hawkins, 54 Ill. App. 2d 212, 217, 203 N.E.2d 761, 763 (1st Dist. 1964).

[74] People v. Koshiol, 45 Ill. 2d 573, 579, 262 N.E.2d 446, 449 (1970), *cert. denied*, 401 U.S. 978 (1971), *rev'd on other grounds sub nom.*, People v. Nunn, 55 Ill. 2d 344, 304 N.E.2d 81 (1973).

[75] People v. Horne, 110 Ill. App. 2d 167, 175, 249 N.E.2d 282, 286 (1st Dist. 1969).

[76] People v. Wicker, 4 Ill. App. 3d 990, 994-95, 282 N.E.2d 771, 774 (1st Dist. 1972).

[77] People v. Green, 288 Ill. App. 3d 402, 405, 680 N.E.2d 753, 756 (3d Dist. 1997).

[78] People v. Williams, 295 Ill. App. 3d 663, 665-66, 693 N.E.2d 498, 499-500 (3d Dist. 1998).

[79] People v. Sevastos, 117 Ill. App. 2d 104, 107-08, 252 N.E.2d 745, 746-47 (2d Dist. 1969).

[80] People v. Jones, 276 Ill. App. 3d 1006, 1008-09, 659 N.E.2d 415, 418 (4th Dist. 1995), *rev'd on other grounds*, 175 Ill. 2d 126, 134, 676 N.E.2d 646, 650 (1997).

[81] People v. Thoma, 171 Ill. App. 3d 313, 315, 525 N.E.2d 572, 573 (3d Dist. 1988).

genitals, did not touch, caress, or fondle any part of her body, did not force her to remove her clothing, and did not expose himself.[82]

As to attempted burglary, where a defendant ran from a small entrance door to a hardware store, out of which glass was broken, to an automobile just seconds before the police arrived, this was sufficient evidence.[83] The act of kicking a door on the premises that the defendant apparently intended to burglarize was not mere preparation but a substantial step toward attempted burglary.[84] Removal of hinge pins from the rear door of a building was also held to be a sufficient substantial step.[85] On the other hand, where a defendant was seen standing next to a car with a sounding alarm, a moved key slot emblem, which normally covers the trunk key slot, and a trunk that could not be opened with a key, the defendant's attempted burglary conviction was reversed because no burglary tools had been recovered and there was no physical damage to the lock.[86]

Where a complaining victim awoke while the defendant was going through his pockets, this was sufficient for attempted theft.[87] Where the defendant and his companions were apprehended in a bicycle storage cage where the padlock on the door of the cage had been cut, this was a proper basis for finding attempted theft.[88] Where the defendant pressed certain buttons on a cash register when no store employees were in the vicinity and the defendant was looking around furtively as she opened the cash register drawer, this was enough for attempted theft.[89] Where the defendant placed a shirt and package of underwear in his bag and passed a checkout counter in a store, this was a substantial step for the same crime.[90] Where a defendant left a store wearing certain apparel that had not been paid for, this was a proper basis to find attempted theft.[91] Where a phone caller threatened the victim and his family unless a certain sum of money that the phone caller had demanded of the victim be placed at a particular curb at a particular time, and where the defendant thereafter drove his automobile to the spot where the victim left the money, looked around carefully, and then picked up the bag of money, this was sufficient for the same offense.[92] When a

---

[82] People v. Montefolka, 287 Ill. App. 3d 199, 210, 678 N.E.2d 1049, 1056 (1st Dist. 1997).

[83] People v. Rose, 124 Ill. App. 2d 447, 450-51, 259 N.E.2d 393, 395-96 (2d Dist. 1970). *See also* People v. Nickols, 90 Ill. App. 3d 480, 483, 413 N.E.2d 212, 214 (3d Dist. 1980) (breaking of dormitory window was sufficient).

[84] People v. Brown, 90 Ill. App. 3d 742, 745, 414 N.E.2d 475, 478 (3d Dist. 1980).

[85] People v. Bean, 121 Ill. App. 2d 290, 294, 257 N.E.2d 558, 560 (1st Dist. 1970), *cert. denied*, 402 U.S. 1009 (1971).

[86] People v. Williams, 189 Ill. App. 3d 17, 24, 545 N.E.2d 173, 177 (1st Dist. 1989).

[87] People v. Richardson, 32 Ill. 2d 497, 502, 207 N.E.2d 453, 455 (1965).

[88] People v. Lonzo, 59 Ill. 2d 115, 117, 319 N.E.2d 481, 483 (1974).

[89] People v. Davis, 70 Ill. App. 3d 454, 457, 388 N.E.2d 887, 890 (1st Dist. 1979).

[90] People v. Falgares, 28 Ill. App. 3d 72, 73, 328 N.E.2d 210, 211 (1st Dist. 1975).

[91] People v. Carr, 16 Ill. App. 3d 76, 78-79, 305 N.E.2d 554, 557 (1st Dist. 1973).

[92] People v. Babic, 7 Ill. App. 3d 36, 40, 287 N.E.2d 24, 26-27 (2d Dist. 1972).

defendant presented a false claim to his insurance company alleging the loss of a stereo in a fire, this was attempted theft by deception.[93] On the other hand, when a defendant tried to obtain a lease of commercial property by delivering to the lessor documents that falsely stated his income, but the defendant and the property owner did not sign the lease, this was an insufficient substantial step toward attempted theft by deception.[94]

Where one defendant purchased gasoline, brought it into his store and transferred it into inconspicuous bottles which were hidden behind a false wall, and another defendant was at the store at the exact hour planned for setting the fire, this was sufficient for attempted arson.[95] Where a codefendant struck a match while the defendant splashed a flammable liquid on a tavern door, this was sufficient for attempted arson.[96] Where the defendant was found to be in possession of a pipe bomb in the vicinity of oil company grounds on which another pipe bomb had exploded, this was also sufficient for attempted arson.[97]

As with accomplice liability and conspiracy, the courts hold that "mere presence" at or near a crime scene is never enough for criminal attempt liability.[98] Indeed, the mere presence of the defendant in a suspicious place at a suspicious hour is not sufficient to prove an attempt *even with evidence of the defendant's improper intent.*[99] For example, a defendant's mere presence near a building on which pry marks were found without any further evidence of defendant's involvement was insufficient for an attempted burglary.[100]

Finally, it is important to remember that overt acts, though sufficient to meet the substantial step requirement, are insufficient to convict an individual for criminal attempt absent the requisite specific intent to commit a crime. In *People v. Jones*,[101] the defendants clearly met the substantial step requirement for attempted murder through the infliction of serious injuries on the victim, but the appellate court reversed their attempted murder convictions because it was not convinced that the defendants harbored the requisite mental state.[102] Although the defendants possessed both a gun and a knife, they used the gun on the victim only to hit him in a fashion that was not life-threatening and did not use the knife at all.[103] The court concluded that the character of the attack did not warrant an inference of an intent to kill.[104]

---

[93] People v. Elmore, 50 Ill. 2d 10, 13, 276 N.E.2d 325, 327 (1971).

[94] People v. Hagan, 199 Ill. App. 3d 267, 269-70, 556 N.E.2d 1224, 1236-37 (2d Dist. 1990).

[95] People v. Abdenabbi, 157 Ill. App. 3d 979, 984-85, 511 N.E.2d 719, 723 (1st Dist. 1987).

[96] People v. Stevenson, 90 Ill. App. 3d 903, 911, 413 N.E.2d 1339, 1344-45 (1st Dist. 1980).

[97] People v. Johnson, 23 Ill. App. 3d 886, 893-94, 321 N.E.2d 38, 44 (1st Dist. 1974).

[98] People v. Brown, 75 Ill. App. 3d 503, 506, 394 N.E.2d 63, 66 (3d Dist. 1979).

[99] People v. Brown, 75 Ill. App. 3d 503, 506, 394 N.E.2d 63, 66 (3d Dist. 1979).

[100] People v. Toolate, 45 Ill. App. 3d 567, 569-70, 359 N.E.2d 1062, 1064-65 (4th Dist. 1976).

[101] 184 Ill. App. 3d 412, 541 N.E.2d 132 (1st Dist. 1989).

[102] People v. Jones, 184 Ill. App. 3d 412, 430, 541 N.E.2d 132, 142-43 (1st Dist. 1989).

[103] People v. Jones, 184 Ill. App. 3d 412, 430, 541 N.E.2d 132, 143 (1st Dist. 1989).

[104] People v. Jones, 184 Ill. App. 3d 412, 430, 541 N.E.2d 132, 143 (1st Dist. 1989).

§ 5.05. Object of Attempt: An Offense.

The focus on any criminal attempt must be the commission of a criminal of-fense because of: (1) paragraph 5/8-4(a), which refers to the requirements of an "intent to commit a specific offense" and an act toward the commission of "that offense";[105] (2) paragraph 5/2-12, which defines *offense* as "a violation of any penal statute of this State";[106] and (3) paragraph 5/8-6, which states that for "purposes of this Article, 'offense' shall include conduct which if performed in another state would be criminal by the laws of that State and which conduct if performed in this State would be an offense under the laws of this State."[107] The intended wrongdoing must be a true crime and not merely at odds with the state's public policy. This statute encompasses all codified offenses appearing anywhere within the state's penal prohibitions except involuntary manslaughter and reckless homicide.

Criminal attempts have been considered by the Illinois courts with respect to a large variety of crimes including attempts to commit murder in the first de-gree,[108] criminal sexual assault,[109] armed robbery,[110] robbery,[111] aggravated bat-tery,[112] bribery,[113] theft,[114] home invasion,[115] burglary,[116] escape,[117] aggravated

---

[105] 720 ILCS 5/8-4(a) (1999).

[106] 720 ILCS 5/2-12 (1999).

[107] 720 ILCS 5/8-6 (1999).

[108] People v. Austin, 215 Ill. App. 3d 323, 574 N.E.2d 1297 (2d Dist. 1991) (attempted first de-gree murder conviction affirmed).

[109] People v. Rayfield, 171 Ill. App. 3d 297, 525 N.E.2d 253 (3d Dist. 1989) (attempted criminal sexual assault conviction reversed); People v. Traufler, 152 Ill. App. 3d 987, 505 N.E.2d 21 (4th Dist. 1987) (attempted criminal sexual assault conviction affirmed).

[110] People v. Murray, 194 Ill. App. 3d 653, 551 N.E.2d 283 (1st Dist. 1990) (attempted armed robbery conviction affirmed).

[111] People v. Robinson, 135 Ill. App. 3d 935, 565 N.E.2d 206 (1st Dist. 1990) (attempted rob-bery conviction affirmed).

[112] People v. Britz, 39 Ill. App. 3d 200, 349 N.E.2d 418 (3d Dist. 1976) (attempted aggravated battery conviction affirmed).

[113] People v. Wallace, 10 Ill. App. 3d 580, 294 N.E.2d 769 (1st Dist. 1973) (attempted bribery conviction affirmed), *aff'd*, 57 Ill. 2d 285, 312 N.E.2d 263 (1974).

[114] People v. Christiansen, 142 Ill. App. 3d 1050, 492 N.E.2d 241 (3d Dist. 1986) (attempted theft conviction affirmed).

[115] People v. Thompson, 123 Ill. App. 3d 523, 462 N.E.2d 1268 (4th Dist. 1984) (attempted home invasion conviction affirmed), *cert. denied*, 470 U.S. 1006 (1985).

[116] People v. Purnell, 154 Ill. App. 3d 220, 507 N.E.2d 195 (1st Dist. 1987) (attempted burglary conviction reversed); People v. Nickols, 90 Ill. App. 3d 480, 413 N.E.2d 212 (3d Dist. 1980) (at-tempted burglary conviction affirmed).

[117] People v. Willis, 204 Ill. App. 3d 590, 561 N.E.2d 1376 (4th Dist. 1990) (attempted escape conviction affirmed).

kidnapping,[118] sale of federal food stamps,[119] arson,[120] insurance fraud,[121] and possession of controlled substances with intent to deliver.[122] Moreover, convictions for attempted involuntary manslaughter or reckless homicide cannot lie in Illinois. There is clear logic for this position: since intent to kill is not an element of involuntary manslaughter or reckless homicide,[123] and since involuntary manslaughter or reckless homicide by its very nature could not arise where there is an intent to kill — because intent to kill brings into play murder in the first or second degree — there could be no attempted involuntary manslaughter or reckless homicide. The specific intent required of the criminal attempt — the intent to take life — clashes with the involuntary or unintentional nature of this category of manslaughter.

Prior to 1987, Illinois did not recognize the offense of attempted voluntary manslaughter.[124] Since voluntary manslaughter was predicated on (1) an unreasonable belief that the taking of life was justified or (2) a heat of passion, while criminal attempt required an intent to kill without legal justification, the courts opined that to recognize attempted voluntary manslaughter was the equivalent of asserting one can intend an "unreasonable result" or "unintended result," which they deemed impossible.[125] In any event, in 1987, the legislature repealed the voluntary manslaughter prohibition and replaced it with murder in the second degree.[126] The new statute separates the mental state element from the mitigating

---

[118] People v. Hamilton, 100 Ill. App. 3d 942, 427 N.E.2d 388 (1st Dist. 1981) (attempted aggravated kidnapping conviction affirmed).

[119] People v. White, 84 Ill. App. 3d 1044, 406 N.E.2d 7 (1st Dist. 1980) (attempted sale of federal food stamps conviction affirmed).

[120] People v. O'Dell, 84 Ill. App. 3d 359, 405 N.E.2d 809 (5th Dist. 1980) (attempted arson conviction affirmed).

[121] People v. Robinson, 120 Ill. App. 3d 644, 458 N.E.2d 206 (3d Dist. 1983) (attempted insurance fraud conviction affirmed).

[122] People v. Echols, 282 Ill. App. 3d 185, 668 N.E.2d 35 (1st Dist. 1996) (attempted possession of controlled substance with intent to deliver conviction affirmed).

[123] People v. Platter, 89 Ill. App. 3d 803, 821, 412 N.E.2d 181, 194 (2d Dist. 1980) (discussing involuntary manslaughter is based on a reckless state of mind and not on intent to kill or intent to injure).

[124] People v. Reagan, 111 Ill. App. 3d 945, 444 N.E.2d 742 (3d Dist. 1982), aff'd, 99 Ill. 2d 238, 457 N.E.2d 1260 (1983) (no attempted voluntary manslaughter can legally exist where unreasonable self-defense); People v. Weeks, 86 Ill. App. 2d 480, 230 N.E.2d 12 (2d Dist. 1967) (no attempted voluntary manslaughter can legally exist where defendant kills in heat of passion). But see Joshua Sachs, Is Attempt to Commit Voluntary Manslaughter a Possible Crime?, 71 Ill. B.J. 166, 167 (1982): "The rule of Weeks . . . is not logically or legally persuasive, and has been rejected in most other states."

[125] See discussion of pre-1987 caselaw (rejecting existence of attempted voluntary manslaughter) and appellate opinion that 1987 amendment permitted finding of attempted second degree murder in People v. Austin, 215 Ill. App. 3d 323, 331, 574 N.E.2d 1297, 1303 (2d Dist. 1991), overruled by People v. Lopez, 166 Ill. 2d 441, 655 N.E.2d 864 (1995).

[126] See 720 ILCS 5/9-2 (1999). See ch. 6 for a discussion of this offense.

factors of unreasonable belief in defense or heat of passion.[127] Under the new legislative scheme, the factfinder must first determine if the defendant had homicidal intentions and, if so, thereafter determine whether the defendant acted under either of the mitigating factors. Reliance on this "two-step process, rather than considering the defendant's intent along with the applicable statutory mitigation, as was the case with the voluntary manslaughter statute," was thought to eliminate the barrier to finding attempted second degree murder.[128] However, not all Illinois appellate courts were in accord as to whether there existed a crime of attempted second degree murder.

Finally, in *People v. Lopez*,[129] the Illinois Supreme Court held that the offense of attempted second degree murder does not exist.[130] The court explained that "the intent required for attempted second degree murder, if it existed, would be the intent to kill without lawful justification, plus the intent to have a mitigating circumstance present."[131] Thus, the court reasoned that because one can neither intend a sudden intense passion due to serious provocation nor an unreasonable belief in the need to use deadly force, the offense of attempted second degree murder cannot exist.[132]

§ 5.06. Attempt Based on Accomplice Theory.

Just as the courts are willing to base conspiracy considerations on an accomplice theory, a defendant can be held guilty of a criminal attempt on the grounds of aiding and abetting. Where a defendant was an accomplice to another's shooting of a victim without justification, he could be convicted of attempted murder.[133] Where a defendant admitted planning to rob the victim, and then turned up the music volume to enable another person to shoot the victim in the head, this was sufficient evidence to hold the defendant accountable for attempted murder, even though the other person took the defendant's gun away from him prior to the other person's shooting of the victim.[134] Where the defendant and a principal approached several unarmed members of a rival "social club," whereupon the defendant and the principal each drew a partially loaded handgun and

---

[127] People v. Austin, 215 Ill. App. 3d 323, 331, 574 N.E.2d 1297, 1303 (2d Dist. 1991), *overruled by* People v. Lopez, 166 Ill. 2d 441, 655 N.E.2d 864 (1995).

[128] People v. Austin, 215 Ill. App. 3d 323, 333, 574 N.E.2d 1297, 1303-04 (2d Dist. 1991), *overruled by* People v. Lopez, 166 Ill. 2d 441, 655 N.E.2d 864 (1995).

[129] 166 Ill. 2d 441, 655 N.E.2d 864 (1995).

[130] People v. Lopez, 166 Ill. 2d 441, 448-49, 655 N.E.2d 864, 867 (1995).

[131] People v. Lopez, 166 Ill. 2d 441, 448-49, 655 N.E.2d 864, 867 (1995).

[132] People v. Lopez, 166 Ill. 2d 441, 448-49, 655 N.E.2d 864, 867 (1995).

[133] People v. Cross, 84 Ill. App. 3d 868, 872, 406 N.E.2d 66, 69 (1st Dist. 1980) (where defendant and codefendant participated together in armed robbery during which codefendant shot victim, defendant responsible for shooting).

[134] People v. Parker, 194 Ill. App. 3d 1048, 1057, 551 N.E.2d 1012, 1018-19 (1st Dist. 1990).

pulled their respective triggers until the principal's gun discharged, striking the victim, this was sufficient evidence to convict the defendant of attempted murder.[135] Where a defendant and two companions attempted to rob a passenger on a train and, while they were waiting to leave the train at a train stop, either the defendant or one of his companions shot and killed the passenger, the defendant could be convicted of both felony-murder and attempted robbery.[136] Where a defendant kicked at a door, knowing at that time that his companion was intending to enter certain premises to commit theft, this was sufficient for the defendant to be convicted of attempted burglary under principles of accountability.[137]

The acquittal of a principal does not necessarily free the accomplice from criminal liability.[138] Thus, even if there is no prosecution or an acquittal of the person who fired the shot in an attempted armed robbery/murder situation, this would not relieve the defendant-accomplice from liability.[139]

§ 5.07. Withdrawal from Criminal Attempt.

Once specific intent and a substantial step in the direction of criminality exist, the "abandonment" or "withdrawal" of a criminal purpose will not operate as a defense to a charge of attempt, even where there was subsequently a termination of criminal activity and efforts to undo the original wrongdoing.[140] Thus, where the defendant got "scared" and decided to terminate his plans to carry out a burglary after his companion had already kicked open the door of the premises they planned on burglarizing, it was too late to claim a withdrawal from their attempted burglary.[141] Also, a defendant convicted of attempted murder could not claim abandonment of his criminal purpose to kill his victim where he had already cut the victim's throat in an effort to kill him.[142] Similarly, where the victim had been tortured for a period of three months, the defendant's attempted artificial respiration of the victim would not exonerate him from a conviction for attempted murder.[143] On the other hand, if one were to withdraw from the contemplated principal crime before its actual commission, one would be freed of liability for the *substantive* offense. Thus, in the case where the defendant got

---

[135] People v. Figures, 216 Ill. App. 3d 398, 404, 576 N.E.2d 1089, 1093 (1st Dist. 1991).

[136] People v. Green, 62 Ill. 2d 146, 147-48, 340 N.E.2d 9, 10-11 (1975), *cert. denied*, 426 U.S. 925 (1976).

[137] People v. Brown, 90 Ill. App. 3d 742, 745, 414 N.E.2d 475, 478 (3d Dist. 1980).

[138] 720 ILCS 5/5-3 (1999). *See,* § 3.04 of this treatise.

[139] People v. Smith, 53 Ill. App. 3d 395, 402, 368 N.E.2d 561, 566 (1st Dist. 1977) (dictum).

[140] *See, e.g.,* People v. Davis, 70 Ill. App. 3d 454, 456, 388 N.E.2d 887, 889-90 (1st Dist. 1979) (where defendant opened cash register and thereafter slammed it shut when a security guard approached, defendant properly convicted of attempted theft).

[141] People v. Brown, 90 Ill. App. 3d 742, 745-47, 414 N.E.2d 475, 477-80 (3d Dist. 1980).

[142] People v. Myers, 85 Ill. 2d 281, 288-89, 426 N.E.2d 535, 539 (1981).

[143] People v. Brown, 199 Ill. App. 3d 860, 869, 557 N.E.2d 611, 619 (1st Dist. 1990).

"scared" about following through on a planned burglary after his companion kicked open the door of the premises, the defendant's withdrawal operated to free him from a burglary conviction, although the attempted burglary conviction stood.[144]

§ 5.08. Impossibility: Legal and Factual.

Beyond the preceding concern of withdrawal is the situation where the defendant claims it was factually or legally impossible for him or her to consummate the offense he or she was attempting. The common law rule was to recognize the claim of legal impossibility but to reject the claim of factual impossibility.[145] Situatuions that fell under the rubric of legal impossibility included such instances as where the defendant was:

> attempting to receive stolen property when he receives property which he believes is stolen, but in fact is not stolen; he is not guilty of attempting to distribute heroin when he sells a substance which he believes is heroin, but in fact is an uncontrolled substance; he is not guilty of attempting to bribe a juror when he offers a bribe to a person he believes is a juror, but who in fact is not a juror; he is not guilty of attempted forgery when, with intent to defraud, he purportedly alters the amount on a negotiable instrument by changing the figures only, and leaving the words undisturbed; he, being a partner, is not guilty of attempted larceny or attempted embezzlement when he takes property from his own firm; he is not guilty of attempting to obtain property from another by false pretenses when, although he believes the representations are false, they are in fact true; or he, being a hunter, is not guilty of attempting to take a deer out of season when he shoots a stuffed deer, believing it to be alive.[146]

Under the heading of factual impossibility:

> a defendant is guilty of an attempt when, with intent to steal, he reaches into the pocket of another, but the pocket is empty, he reaches into a cash drawer, but the drawer is empty, he reaches into a coin box, but the box is empty, or he enters a house, but the house is empty; when, with intent to procure an abortion, he proceeds to act, but it appears that the woman is not in fact pregnant; when with intent to violate the narcotics laws, he possesses a package which, he believes contains heroin, but in fact it contains talcum powder; when, with intent to rape, he attacks a woman but, because of impotence, the offense cannot be committed; when, with intent forcibly to steal, i.e., with intent to rob, he attacks another, but the victim has no

---

[144] People v. Brown, 90 Ill. App. 3d 742, 748-49, 414 N.E.2d 475, 479 (3d Dist. 1980).
[145] 4 CHARLES TORCIA, WHARTON'S CRIMINAL LAW § 745, at 578 (14th ed. 1981).
[146] 4 CHARLES TORCIA, WHARTON'S CRIMINAL LAW § 745, at 580-81 (14th ed. 1981).

money on his person; when, with intent to obtain money or property from another, he obtains, purportedly by false pretense, such money or property, but the victim is not in fact deceived; or when with intent to kill, he fires a gun through the window of a room where he mistakenly believes the victim is sleeping.[147]

As several of the above examples illustrate — whether drug-related attempts occurred where the substance was uncontrolled or was talcum powder — the courts were often inconsistent in their assessment of whether legal, as opposed to factual, impossibility would govern the situation. A classic example of this confusion is an attempt to commit an abortion on a woman who is not pregnant: some treated the situation as a factual impossibility,[148] as noted in the above examples, but others dealt with it under the guise of a legal impossibility.[149] Many lawyers recall from their law school days the running debate that revolved around the hypothetical case of "Lady Eldon's French Lace."[150] It involved Lady Eldon's effort to bring into England from the Continent what she thought was a valuable French lace, without paying appropriate customs duty on it. The lace turned out to be an English manufactured article of little value that was not subject to duty, even though she had paid a price vastly exceeding its value when she was on the Continent. The noted authority, Wharton, opined that since Lady Eldon had the intent to smuggle valuable lace into England, she was guilty of an attempt to smuggle.[151] In other words, he treated the situation as one covered by factual impossibility. Other authorities believed that since what she intended to bring back to England was, in fact, material not subject to duty, she could not be guilty of attempt any more than she could be guilty of the substantive crime of smuggling itself.[152] Obviously, the latter conclusion is based on the theory that legal impossibility considerations apply. This was one problem with the legal impossibility/factual impossibility dichotomy.

The second problem can be illustrated by another example that is often used to show the distinction: if one were to shoot into a bed believing the intended victim to be asleep in the bed, it would be a legal impossibility if the intended victim was already dead and buried; it would be factual impossibility if the intended victim was asleep in another room or off vacationing halfway around the

---

[147] 4 CHARLES TORCIA, WHARTON'S CRIMINAL LAW § 745, at 581-83 (14th ed. 1981).

[148] People v. Cummings, 141 Cal. App. 2d 193, 296 P.2d 610 (1956); People v. Huff, 339 Ill. 328, 171 N.E. 261 (1930).

[149] State v. Stewart, 52 Iowa 284, 3 N.W. 99 (1879); State v. Sturchio, 131 N.J.L. 256, 36 A.2d 301 (1944).

[150] CRIMINAL LAW AND ITS PROCESSES: CASES AND MATERIALS 633-40 (S. Kadish & S. Schulhofer, 6th ed. 1995).

[151] 1 WHARTON, CRIMINAL LAW § 225, at 304 n.9 (12th ed. 1932).

[152] See, e.g., Edwin R. Keedy, Criminal Attempts at Common Law, 102 U. PA. L. REV. 464, 476-77 (1954).

world.[153] One might simply ask, as would the authors of the Model Penal Code,[154] what possible difference should it make where the defendant has manifested through his intention and action such an extreme indifference toward human life and the criminal law?

This was obviously the thinking of the authors of the current Illinois criminal attempt provisions in which they have explicitly rejected the defense of legal and factual impossibility.[155] Consistent with the statutory rejection of legal impossibility,[156] the courts have held that the Illinois criminal attempt provisions allow for a conviction of attempted murder of an intended victim who is already dead, provided there is evidence from which it can be found that at the time of the attempt, the defendant believed the victim was still alive.[157] Similarly, where a defendant was convicted of attempted arson, it was irrelevant that the defendant was without an ignition source, since there was evidence to conclude that he mistakenly believed he had such a source.[158]

§ 5.09. — Inherent Impossibility.

The revision committee points out that there is leeway built into the rule precluding the defense of impossibility where the rule is being stretched beyond all logic and reason: "All the authorities hold that in order to constitute an attempt the act attempted must not be impossible, but this rule has reference to inherent impossibility, and not to cases where the impossibility has been brought about by outside interference, or grows out of extraneous facts not within the knowledge and control of the accused."[159] The committee refers to the example of an attempt to kill by witchcraft by repeatedly stabbing a cloth dummy made to represent the person intended to be killed as an example of a situation in which the defense of impossibility would still be available. Other examples of what one authority refers to as "obvious" impossibility would be trying to maim a person by throwing red pepper at him or trying to steal from the pocket of a stone image.[160] On the other hand, the American Law Institute cautions:

---

[153] *See* State v. Mitchell, 170 Mo. 633, 71 S.W. 175 (1902) (factual impossibility where intended victim was not in room where defendant believed him to be when he shot through room window). *Cf.* JEROME HALL, GENERAL PRINCIPLES OF CRIMINAL LAW 589 (2d ed. 1960) (might be impossible where intended victim is dead).

[154] *See* MODEL PENAL CODE § 5.01, comment at 38 (Tentative Draft No. 10, 1960).

[155] ILL. ANN. STAT. ch. 38, para. 8-4(b) (Smith-Hurd 1989), 1961 Committee Comments, at 499.

[156] 720 ILCS 5/8-4(b) (1999).

[157] United States ex rel. Rangel v. Brierton, 437 F. Supp. 908, 909 (N.D. Ill. 1977) (interpretation of Illinois law).

[158] People v. Johnson, 102 Ill. App. 3d 122, 127, 429 N.E.2d 905, 909 (3d Dist. 1981).

[159] ILL. ANN. STAT. ch. 38, para. 8-4 (Smith-Hurd 1989), 1961 Committee Comments, at 499 (quoting Collins v. City of Radford, 134 Va. 518, 113 S.E. 735 (1922) (emphasis added)).

[160] 4 CHARLES TORCIA, WHARTON'S CRIMINAL LAW § 746, at 584 (14th ed. 1981).

The innocuous character of the particular conduct becomes relevant only if the futile endeavor itself indicates a harmless personality, so that immunizing such conduct from liability would not result in freeing a dangerous person. . . . Using impossibility as a guide to dangerousness of personality presents serious difficulties. Some cases can be imagined where it may be argued that the nature of the means selected — e.g. murder by black magic — substantially negates dangerousness of character. On the other hand, there is a good chance that one who tries to commit a crime by inadequate methods and fails will realize the futility of his conduct and seek more efficacious means.[161]

These marginal cases alluded to by the American Law Institute are best decided on a case-by-case basis.

§ 5.10. Felony-Murder Based on Criminal Attempt.

Since the Illinois felony-murder statute explicitly states that a defendant can be convicted of first degree murder where he or she "is attempting or committing a forcible felony," an *attempted forcible felony* could be the basis for finding murder.[162] Thus, in *People v. Chism*,[163] the appellate court ruled that an attempted armed robbery afforded a sufficient basis for the defendants' convictions for felony-murder.[164] Since treason, predatory criminal sexual assault of a child, aggravated criminal sexual assault, criminal sexual assault, robbery, burglary, residential burglary, aggravated arson, arson, aggravated kidnapping, kidnapping, and aggravated battery causing great bodily harm, permanent disability or disfigurement are clearly designated as forcible felonies,[165] an attempt to commit any of these offenses that brings about a death as an incidental matter would be a proper basis for finding first degree murder.

§ 5.11. Lesser Included Offenses and Attempt.

Although a successful attempt that results in the actual consummation of a crime does not rule out the possibility that a defendant will be convicted of criminal attempt,[166] normally the state will prosecute the principal offense, and the lesser included offense of attempt will be set aside.[167] A defendant cannot properly be convicted of both the principal offense and the inchoate offense of

---

[161] MODEL PENAL CODE § 5.01, Comment at 38 (Tentative Draft No. 10, 1960).
[162] 720 ILCS 5/9-1(a)(3) (1999).
[163] 65 Ill. App. 3d 33, 382 N.E.2d 377 (1st Dist. 1983).
[164] People v. Chism, 65 Ill. App. 3d 33, 37-38, 382 N.E.2d 377, 381 (1st Dist. 1978).
[165] 720 ILCS 5/2-8 (1999).
[166] *See* notes 2-5 of this chapter and accompanying text.
[167] *See* ch. 1 for a discussion of what constitutes a lesser included offense.

attempt to commit the same offense where the charges arose from the same incident.[168]

No legal problem arises where the state elects to have the defendant convicted on the lesser included offense *instead* of the greater principal crime. Thus, even where the evidence might have established completion of the offense of bribery, conviction for the lesser included offense of attempt bribery would be permissible.[169]

Where the evidence at trial warrants a conviction of attempt to commit an offense and not the consummated offense being prosecuted, the trial court may properly find the defendant guilty of the lesser included attempt.[170] Where the evidence did not sustain a conviction for burglary but was supportive of attempted burglary, the appellate court could set aside the conviction on the principal offense and reduce the degree of the offense to attempted burglary.[171]

In some cases, the criminal attempt will constitute the greater crime; accordingly, the principal stricture will be viewed as the lesser included offense that merges into the attempt. For example, where a defendant's conviction for aggravated battery arose from the same incident as that of his attempted murder, the former offense was vacated as a lesser included offense of the latter attempt conviction.[172] Similarly, one appellate court has determined reckless conduct to be a lesser included offense of attempted first degree murder.[173] On the other hand, the possession of burglary tools is not a lesser included offense of attempted burglary.[174]

One offense that is clearly not a lesser included offense of attempt is conspiracy. Conspiracy requires proof of an additional element, namely, an agreement, above and beyond attempt, while an attempt requires that substantial step that conspiracy does not require.[175] Thus, conspiracy has been determined not to be a lesser included offense of attempted murder[176] or attempted theft.[177]

---

[168] 720 ILCS 5/8-5 (1999).

[169] People v. Wallace, 57 Ill. 2d 285, 291, 312 N.E.2d 263, 267 (1974).

[170] People v. Chism, 65 Ill. App. 3d 33, 37-38, 382 N.E.2d 377, 381 (1st Dist. 1978) (although defendant charged with armed robbery/felony-murder, trial court could find defendant guilty of attempted armed robbery/felony-murder).

[171] People v. Borden, 84 Ill. App. 2d 442, 444, 228 N.E.2d 248, 248 (1st Dist. 1967).

[172] People v. Worthen, 105 Ill. App. 3d 386, 392, 434 N.E.2d 423, 428 (1st Dist. 1982).

[173] People v. Stevenson, 196 Ill. App. 3d 225, 228-30, 553 N.E.2d 441, 443-45 (2d Dist. 1990) (trial court erred in not instructing jury on lesser included offense).

[174] People v. Blakeney, 59 Ill. App. 3d 119, 124, 375 N.E.2d 1309, 1313 (1st Dist. 1978), *cert. denied*, 440 U.S. 915 (1979).

[175] People v. Jenkins, 104 Ill. App. 3d 522, 527, 432 N.E.2d 1171, 1175 (1st Dist. 1982).

[176] People v. Jenkins, 104 Ill. App. 3d 522, 527, 432 N.E.2d 1171, 1175 (1st Dist. 1982); People v. Edwards, 106 Ill. App. 3d 918, 924, 436 N.E.2d 727, 732 (4th Dist. 1982).

[177] People v. Vettese, 61 Ill. App. 3d 279, 283, 377 N.E.2d 1168, 1171 (1st Dist. 1978).

§ 5.12. Criminal Solicitation.

Beyond the prohibitions against criminal attempts (discussed above) and criminal conspiracies (reviewed in chapter 4), there is a third general inchoate offense in Illinois, namely, criminal solicitation. The criminal solicitation prohibition provides: "A person commits solicitation when, with intent that an offense be committed, other than first-degree murder, he commands, encourages or requests another to commit that offense."[178] The revision committee's comments clarify the essential elements of this offense: (1) a specific intent to commit a principal offense, and (2) the act of encouraging, commanding, or requesting another to commit that offense.[179] Solicitation to commit first degree murder is exempted in this stricture since it is covered by other solicitation prohibitions, which will be discussed below.

The various limitations on the reach of each of the Illinois inchoate crimes obviously impact on the scope of solicitation. Thus, the object of the solicitation must be a criminal offense as defined in the code.[180] Multiple convictions for the inchoate crime of solicitation and for the principal crime are precluded.[181] Additionally, Illinois law states: "It is a defense to a charge of solicitation . . . that if the criminal object were achieved the accused would not be guilty of an offense."[182] Particular note should be given to the revision committee's intent in their drafting of this latter section:

> It is a defense only if the *accused* would not be guilty of the principal offense (if committed) because of some individual capacity the *accused* might have, such as underage, victim of abortion, or any other legal defense available under Section 5-2, or otherwise. It would *not* be a defense for the accused that the person solicited would not be guilty of the principal offense (if committed) because of some legal incapacity or immunity.[183]

Thus, where defendant A solicits B, an undercover police officer, to commit murder, A could be convicted of solicitation even though B had no intent to fol-

---

[178] 720 ILCS 5/8-1(a) (1999).

[179] ILL. ANN. STAT. ch. 38, para. 8-1 (Smith-Hurd 1989), 1961 Committee Comments, at 466. *See also* People v. Schnurr, 206 Ill. App. 3d 522, 533, 564 N.E.2d 1336, 1344 (2d Dist. 1990) (citing Committee Comments).

[180] 720 ILCS 5/2-12 (1999): "'Offense' means a violation of any penal statute of this State."

[181] 720 ILCS 5/8-5 (1999): "No person shall be convicted of both the inchoate and the principal offense."

[182] 720 ILCS 5/8-3 (1999).

[183] ILL. ANN. STAT. ch. 38, para. 8-1 (Smith-Hurd 1989), 1961 Committee Comments, at 466 (original emphasis).

low through on the murder and had legal immunity because of B's legal motive in apprehending A.[184]

§ 5.13. Criminal Solicitation: Mental State.

An essential element of solicitation is proof of the defendant's specific intent to accomplish a crime.[185] This rigorous intent requirement transforms what might otherwise involve mere recitation of "loose" words, which could fall under First Amendment protections, into a criminal act.[186] In other words, insisting on proof of the defendant's specific intent of wrongdoing removes the defendant's utterance from "free speech" possibilities.[187]

Unlike conspiracy, there is no requirement that both the person who is soliciting and the person who is solicited have the specific intent to commit a crime; a specific intent is required only of the person who is soliciting.[188] Thus, where A solicited B, an undercover agent posing as a "hit-man," to commit murder, B's lack of intent was immaterial.[189] Since Illinois conspiracy law follows the bilateral theory, requiring wrongful intent on the part of two persons,[190] those solicitations to engage in criminality that have a unilateral basis, such as the "hit-man" example above, are effectively dealt with by the law against criminal solicitation.[191] Of course, while a solicitation does not require proof of conspiracy, a true conspiracy between the person who is soliciting and the person who is solicited could amount to both conspiracy and solicitation.[192]

Specific intent is often not susceptible of proof by direct evidence; thus, the courts allow evidence of the defendant's intent to be proved by circumstantial evidence. Accordingly, this intent can be demonstrated by the surrounding circumstances and by the acts of the defendant.[193]

---

[184] See People v. Pagliuca, 119 Ill. App. 3d 906, 910-11, 458 N.E.2d 908, 912 (1st Dist. 1983).

[185] People v. McCommon, 79 Ill. App. 3d 853, 862, 399 N.E.2d 224, 231 (1st Dist. 1979).

[186] People v. Lewis, 84 Ill. App. 3d 556, 561, 406 N.E.2d 11, 15 (1st Dist. 1980).

[187] People v. Lewis, 84 Ill. App. 3d 556, 562, 406 N.E.2d 11, 16 (1st Dist. 1980).

[188] See People v. Pagliuca, 119 Ill. App. 3d 906, 910-11, 458 N.E.2d 908, 912 (1st Dist. 1983).

[189] People v. Pagliuca, 119 Ill. App. 3d 906, 910-11, 458 N.E.2d 908, 912 (1st Dist. 1983).

[190] People v. Foster, 99 Ill. 2d 48, 55, 457 N.E.2d 405, 409 (1983).

[191] People v. Moorhead, 128 Ill. App. 3d 137, 142, 470 N.E.2d 531, 535 (2d Dist. 1984) ("The solicitation statute embraces virtually every situation in which one could be convicted of conspiracy under the unilateral theory."); People v. Hill, 108 Ill. App. 3d 716, 720, 439 N.E.2d 549, 551 (4th Dist. 1982) ("In most cases where conspiracy occurs under the unilateral theory, a solicitation would also take place").

[192] People v. Latham, 73 Ill. App. 3d 995, 997, 392 N.E.2d 43, 45-46 (5th Dist. 1979).

[193] People v. Barnett, 173 Ill. App. 3d 477, 483-84, 527 N.E.2d 1071, 1075 (2d Dist. 1988); People v. Lewis, 84 Ill. App. 3d 556, 561, 406 N.E.2d 11, 15 (1st Dist. 1980).

§ 5.14. Criminal Solicitation: Act.

The requisite actus reus for solicitation involves conduct where the accused "commands, encourages or requests another" to commit an offense.[194] This enactment allows the state to convict on proof of the accused's (1) command, (2) encouragement, *or* (3) request. In other words, the state has the option of prosecuting under any of these theories. Additionally, in *People v. Cole*,[195] the Illinois Supreme Court ruled that the state could prosecute a defendant's solicitation of one person to commit a single crime in more than one count, and possibly three, assuming there was evidence of his command, encouragement, and request of another to commit the crime.[196] In *Cole*, defendants were charged in the first count with requesting Haley, a special undercover agent, to murder one Jones; in the second count with encouraging Haley to murder Jones; and in the third count with conspiracy (between themselves) to murder Jones. In a jury trial, the defendants were acquitted on the first and third counts, but the jury was unable to reach a verdict on the second count; thus, a mistrial on that count was ordered. At a second jury trial on the second count, both defendants were convicted. The defendants argued on appeal that the acquittal on the first count of solicitation barred their prosecution on the second count because of the federal[197] and state[198] constitutional bars against double jeopardy, as well as the Illinois statutory bar against successive prosecutions.[199] The supreme court rejected this argument and stated:

> We agree that the State cannot charge a defendant under one theory and following an acquittal under that theory, subsequently recharge and prosecute under another theory for the *same offense*. However, that is not what occurred in the instant case. . . . [T]his case does not involve a reprosecution based upon a theory of the *same offense* that was not previously charged. Request and encouragement are two disjunctive methods by which the offense of solicitation can be committed and reflect the legislature's intent to include varying degrees of involvement on the part of the solicitor. Here, the state charged defendants with solicitation under two theories, each brought under a separate count. The jury acquitted defendants of only *solicitation by request*. Its inability to reach a verdict as to

---

[194] 720 ILCS 5/8-1(a) (1993).

[195] 91 Ill. 2d 172, 435 N.E.2d 490, *cert. denied*, 459 U.S. 863 (1982).

[196] People v. Cole, 91 Ill. 2d 172, 175-78, 435 N.E.2d 490, 491-93, *cert. denied*, 459 U.S. 863 (1982).

[197] U.S. CONST. amend. V.

[198] ILL. CONST. art. 1, para. 10.

[199] 720 ILCS 5/3-4(a) (1999).

solicitation by encouragement is not tantamount to an acquittal under such theory.[200]

It is important to add that if the state had merged the "request" and "encouragement" into one count and if the jury had acquitted the defendants on that count, the government would have been barred from reprosecuting the defendants on either theory.

Solicitation, unlike conspiracy,[201] or attempt,[202] does not require an overt act beyond the command, encouragement, or request.[203] Indeed, the verbal utterance involved in the solicitation is normally viewed as the actus reus. Solicitation can also be distinguished from accomplice liability: with accomplice liability, there must be proof that (1) the accomplice solicited or encouraged the commission of the crime by another, and (2) the person who was solicited or encouraged actually engaged in conduct normally amounting to crime.[204] With solicitation, only proof of the solicitation is needed.[205] Also, solicitation is a crime in and of itself, while accomplice liability is a theory that results in holding one accountable for another's crime.[206]

§ 5.15. Solicitation of Murder.

The Illinois General Assembly removed from the general solicitation statute solicitation to commit first degree murder and created an offense entitled "solicitation of murder,"[207] which carries class X penalties.[208] This prohibition, which took effect in 1989, reads:

---

[200] People v. Cole, 91 Ill. 2d 172, 177, 435 N.E.2d 490, 492, *cert. denied*, 459 U.S. 863 (1982) (emphasis added).

[201] 720 ILCS 5/8-2 (1999).

[202] 720 ILCS 5/8-4 (1999).

[203] People v. Harvey, 95 Ill. App. 3d 992, 1002, 420 N.E.2d 645, 653 (1st Dist. 1981).

[204] *See* 720 ILCS 5/5-2 (1993). It is important to add that the principal's conduct need only be *de facto* criminal and not *de jure* by reason of the Illinois law that allows for conviction of the accomplice where the principal has legal immunity or is unavailable for prosecution. 720 ILCS 5/5-3 (1993). To illustrate this point, if A solicits B, an undercover police officer, to engage in certain conduct that might otherwise be criminal, A cannot be a criminal accomplice to B's conduct because B has not engaged in activity that can even be considered wrongful *de facto* because of B's legitimate motivation in apprehending A. However, if A solicits B (not an officer) to do a criminal act, which B does accomplish, A can stand convicted as B's accomplice even though B has been acquitted earlier by a separate jury (and thus has immunity from possible conviction therefor by reason of double jeopardy) because at least B had engaged in activity that was *de facto* wrongful.

[205] People v. Harvey, 95 Ill. App. 3d 992, 1002-03, 420 N.E.2d 645, 653 (1st Dist. 1981).

[206] *See* generally ch. 3 of this treatise.

[207] 720 ILCS 5/8-1.1(a) (1999).

> A person commits solicitation of murder when, with the intent that the offense of first-degree murder be committed, he commands, encourages, or requests another to commit that offense.[209]

Solicitation to commit second degree murder is not contemplated by this statute.

§ 5.16. Solicitation of Murder for Hire.

In an apparent effort to punish solicitation of an illegal homicide for hire more seriously than those solicitations not for hire,[210] the Illinois legislature created the offense of "solicitation of murder for hire."[211] It provides:

> A person commits solicitation of murder for hire when, with the intent that the offense be committed, he procures another to commit that offense pursuant to any contract, agreement, understanding, command, or request for money or anything of value.[212]

A defendant may be convicted of solicitation of murder for hire and attempted murder as a result of his various efforts to effectuate an act of murder.[213] In a case where the defendant, a criminal defense attorney, hired one of his previous clients, who was an "enforcer" for the Hell's Henchmen motorcycle gang, for $10,000 to assist him in murdering his wife, with whom he was engaged in a bitter divorce, by planting a bomb in her car which ultimately led to only minor injuries to his wife, he was convicted of solicitation of murder for hire along with attempted murder on the theory of accountability.[214]

Although the statutory language provides that there must be an agreement, the term agreement is one based on a unilateral theory as opposed to a bilateral the-

---

[208] 720 ILCS 5/8-1.1(b) (1999) (imprisonment of not less than 15 years and not more than 30 years except where person solicited is under the age of 17, whereupon defendant convicted of solicitation shall receive imprisonment of not less than 20 years and not more than 60 years).

[209] 720 ILCS 5/8-1.1(a) (1999).

[210] *See* 720 ILCS 5/8-1.2(b) (1999) (solicitation of murder for hire punishable by imprisonment of not less than 20 years and not more than 40 years). 720 ILCS 5/8-1.1(b) (1999) (solicitation not for hire punishable by imprisonment of not less than 15 years).

[211] 720 ILCS 5/8-1.2(a) (1999)

[212] 720 ILCS 5/8-1.2(a) (1999).

[213] People v. Martinez, 264 Ill. App. 3d 807, 815-16, 637 N.E.2d 447, 453 (1st Dist. 1994) (defendant convicted of solicitation of murder for hire after procuring someone for $20,000, a Chevrolet Corvette, and a Chevrolet Blazer to have his girlfriend, who was four months pregnant with his child, killed because he believed that she would testify against him in the murder trial of defendant's brother-in-law).

[214] People v. Kagan, 283 Ill. App. 3d 212, 221, 669 N.E.2d 1239, 1245 (2d Dist. 1996).

ory such as that required of conspiracy.[215] Thus, where the defendant entered into an agreement with an undercover law enforcement agent for $5,000 to kill a witness who allegedly set him up on drug charges and would be testifying against him in court, he was convicted of solicitation of murder for hire even though the agreement to commit the murder was unilateral in theory in that the undercover agent did not actually intend to perform in accordance with his part of the agreement.[216] The court held that a bilateral agreement where both parties fully intend to perform the act is not a necessary requirement of solicitation of murder for hire.[217]

§ 5.17. Lesser Included Offenses and Solicitation.

Notwithstanding the fact that one cannot stand convicted of both a solicitation and the principal offense that is the focal point of the solicitation,[218] since solicitation is normally a separate and distinct offense from the crime that is the target of the solicitation, an acquittal on one would not bar a conviction on the other.[219] Thus, where the defendant, a street gang "chief," was acquitted of murder and attempted murder, he could still be convicted of the charges of solicitation to commit these crimes, since he had ordered certain members of his street gang to engage in the shootings of the victims.[220] In this case, the solicitation was not viewed as the same crime as murder, attempted murder, or a lesser included offense since the court found that each offense required different elements than the other.[221] The murder required proof of the taking of a life, which the solicitation did not; the attempted murder required proof of a substantial step toward a murder, which the solicitation did not; and the solicitation required proof of a command to murder, which the murder and the attempted murder did not.

Neither solicitation nor conspiracy is necessarily a lesser included offense of the other.[222] In solicitation cases, the state must show that the defendant commanded, encouraged, or requested another to commit a crime; in conspiracy

---

[215] People v. Breton, 237 Ill. App. 3d 355, 360, 603 N.E.2d 1290, 1294-95 (2d Dist. 1992).

[216] People v. Breton, 237 Ill. App. 3d 355, 360-63, 603 N.E.2d 1290, 1294-96 (2d Dist. 1992).

[217] People v. Breton, 237 Ill. App. 3d 355, 361, 603 N.E.2d 1290, 1295-96 (2d Dist. 1992).

[218] 720 ILCS 5/8-5 (1993); *see also* People v. Crews, 191 Ill. App. 3d 228, 234-35, 547 N.E.2d 580, 584-85 (4th Dist. 1989) (where defendant convicted of murder on accomplice basis and solicitation to commit murder, solicitation conviction had to be vacated). *See* § 1.21 of this treatise for a detailed discussion of lesser included offenses.

[219] People v. Hairston, 46 Ill. 2d 348, 358, 263 N.E.2d 840, 847 (1970), *cert. denied*, 402 U.S. 972 (1971) (no double jeopardy).

[220] People v. Hairston, 46 Ill. 2d 348, 358-59, 263 N.E.2d 840, 847-48 (1970), *cert. denied*, 402 U.S. 972 (1971).

[221] *See* People v. Hairston, 46 Ill. 2d 348, 359, 263 N.E.2d 840, 848 (1970), *cert. denied*, 402 U.S. 972 (1971)

[222] People v. Stroner, 96 Ill. 2d 204, 209-10, 449 N.E.2d 1326, 1328 (1983).

cases, the state must offer proof of a criminal agreement of two or more parties and an overt act in furtherance of that agreement.[223]

---

[223] People v. Stroner, 96 Ill. 2d 204, 209-10, 449 N.E.2d 1326, 1328 (1983); People v. Latham, 73 Ill. App. 3d 995, 997, 392 N.E.2d 43, 45-46 (5th Dist. 1979).

PART 2

THE SPECIAL PART CRIMES

In this second part of this book, there appears an examination of specific criminal strictures directed at particular forms of criminality. In chapter 6 (Homicide), there appears an examination of the various unjustified homicides, including murder and manslaughter. In chapter 7 (Kidnapping and Related Offenses) there is a review of those crimes that involve the unjustified taking of dominion and control over another's normal freedom of movement. In chapter 8 (Sex Offenses) there appears an investigation of various deviant sexual activity, including crimes of violence or the threat of violence (for example, criminal sexual assault). Chapter 9 (Assault, Battery, and Related Offenses) studies those crimes that involve nonsexual, physical attacks or the threat of such attacks directed at another's person. Chapter 10 (Electronic Eavesdropping) represents an investigation of those strictures that are aimed at a criminal actor's wrongful invasion of the conversational privacy of another through electronic means. Chapter 11 (Theft and Related Offenses) surveys the various crimes involving the wrongful appropriation of the property of another through means not involving force and violence. Chapter 12 (Robbery, Armed Robbery and Related Offenses) probes into those offenses that involve the wrongful appropriation of the property of another through means of force and violence or the threat thereof. Chapter 13 (Burglary, Arson, and Other Offenses Against Property) presents an assessment of those proscriptions directed at illicit invasions of the property interests of another not covered in chapter 11 or 12. In chapter 14 (Offenses Affecting Governmental Functions), there appears an inquiry into those offenses that undermine the integrity of governmental operations: executive, judicial, and legislative. Chapter 15 (Offenses Affecting the Public Health, Safety, and Decency) presents a review of various regulatory measures that are designed to protect various public interests. Finally, in chapter 16 (Drug Control Laws), there is an analysis of the various strictures aimed at preventing the illegitimate consumption of narcotics and other dangerous drugs.

CHAPTER 6

HOMICIDE

§ 6.01. Introduction.

This chapter reflects an examination of the most serious crimes, specifically, where a person takes the life of another without justification or excuse, thereby amounting to either first degree murder,[1] second degree murder,[2] involuntary

---

[1] 720 ILCS 5/9-1 (1999).
[2] 720 ILCS 5/9-2 (1999).

manslaughter,[3] or reckless homicide.[4] Since the homicide section of the Criminal Code of Illinois also contains provisions against intentional homicide of an unborn child,[5] voluntary manslaughter of an unborn child,[6] involuntary manslaughter and reckless homicide of an unborn child,[7] drug induced homicide,[8] and concealment of a homicidal death,[9] these will also be examined. This chapter will begin with a study of the common law evolution of laws against homicide, followed by a brief review of these laws as they exist today in other jurisdictions. Next, this chapter will explore the current Illinois laws in this regard.

§ 6.02. Homicide Generally.

Homicide is the killing of a human being by another human being.[10] If either the killer or the victim is an animal, there is no homicide unless a human being employed an animal to kill another person.[11] If a human being takes his own life, this is not homicide, but rather suicide.[12]

Homicide can be criminal[13] or innocent.[14] If the killing is not excusable or justified, it is criminal and will constitute either murder or manslaughter.[15] If the killing is either excusable or justifiable, it is innocent.[16] A homicide is excusable when committed under circumstances where the killing is not authorized by law, but a finding of criminal guilt would be inappropriate. Such is the case where a killing occurs, for instance, through accident or by the hand of one who lacks the legal capacity to commit an illegal homicide, such as where the killer is a minor or a legally insane person.[17] A homicide is justifiable when it is either commanded or authorized by law.[18] Examples of commanded justified killings would be the killing of an enemy during time of war and executing a person sentenced to the death penalty.[19] Examples of authorized justified killings would

---

[3] 720 ILCS 5/9-3 (1999).

[4] 720 ILCS 5/9-3 (1999).

[5] 720 ILCS 5/9-1.2 (1999).

[6] 720 ILCS 5/9-2.1 (1999).

[7] 720 ILCS 5/9-3.2 (1999).

[8] 720 ILCS 5/9-3.3 (1999).

[9] 720 ILCS 5/9-3.1 (1999).

[10] ROLLIN M. PERKINS & RONALD N. BOYCE, CRIMINAL LAW 46 (3d ed. 1982).

[11] ROLLIN M. PERKINS & RONALD N. BOYCE, CRIMINAL LAW 46 (3d ed. 1982).

[12] JOHN KLOTTER, CRIMINAL LAW § 3.2 (2d ed. 1990).

[13] ROLLIN M. PERKINS & RONALD N. BOYCE, CRIMINAL LAW 57 (3d ed. 1982).

[14] ROLLIN M. PERKINS & RONALD N. BOYCE, CRIMINAL LAW 56 (3d ed. 1982).

[15] ROLLIN M. PERKINS & RONALD N. BOYCE, CRIMINAL LAW 57 (3d ed. 1982).

[16] ROLLIN M. PERKINS & RONALD N. BOYCE, CRIMINAL LAW 56 (3d ed. 1982).

[17] ROLLIN M. PERKINS & RONALD N. BOYCE, CRIMINAL LAW 57 (3d ed. 1982).

[18] ROLLIN M. PERKINS & RONALD N. BOYCE, CRIMINAL LAW 57 (3d ed. 1982).

[19] ROLLIN M. PERKINS & RONALD N. BOYCE, CRIMINAL LAW 57 (3d ed. 1982).

include a civilian killing of another in self-defense or killing of a dangerous felon attempting to escape lawful custody.[20]

At common law, the law was very clear about when "life" began and when a life had ended for purposes of the prosecution of an illegal homicide. First, the killing of the unborn was not considered homicide.[21] Not even a viable fetus was considered a human being for purposes of homicide.[22] While the killing of a fetus was considered abortion,[23] the fetus was not considered a human being until it was delivered from the body of the mother and had established circulation of its own.[24] Second, one was considered legally dead when the heartbeat and breathing functions ceased.[25]

In the context of criminal prosecution of an illegal homicide, another important concept existed at common law, known as the "year and a day" rule.[26] Specifically, where an accused inflicted a blow or other harmful agent on a victim, causing injury but not death, the death of the victim would be deemed attributable to natural causes if it had not occurred within a year and a day of the injury.[27] Essentially this rule, albeit arbitrary, was designed to avoid the arduous task of determining whether a death occurring after a year and a day following the accused's injurious act was traceable to the act in question.

Today, the common law understanding of homicide still prevails with a few variations. The changes that have occurred are as follows. First, a few jurisdictions have attempted to expand through legislation the definition of homicide to include the taking of the life of a viable fetus.[28] Second, some jurisdictions have created new prohibitions designed to protect the non-viable fetus. For example, Illinois enacted the crime of "intentional homicide of an unborn child"[29] to deal with the illegal taking of the life of any fetus.[30] Third, various legislatures[31] and

---

[20] ROLLIN M. PERKINS & RONALD N. BOYCE, CRIMINAL LAW 57 (3d ed. 1982).

[21] ROLLIN M. PERKINS & RONALD N. BOYCE, CRIMINAL LAW 49 (3d ed. 1982).

[22] *See, e.g.*, People v. Greer, 79 Ill. 2d 103, 111, 402 N.E.2d 203, 207 (1980) (killing of fetus not murder unless fetus is born alive; common law view followed).

[23] 2 CHARLES E. TORCIA, WHARTON'S CRIMINAL LAW § 250 (14th ed. 1979).

[24] ROLLIN M. PERKINS & RONALD N. BOYCE, CRIMINAL LAW 50 (3d ed. 1982). Normally, this meant that the umbilical cord was severed and the child had the capacity to breathe on its own. 2 CHARLES E. TORCIA, WHARTON'S CRIMINAL LAW § 114 (14th ed. 1979).

[25] ROLLIN M. PERKINS & RONALD N. BOYCE, CRIMINAL LAW 48 (3d ed. 1982).

[26] ROLLIN M. PERKINS & RONALD N. BOYCE, CRIMINAL LAW 46-47 (3d ed. 1982).

[27] ROLLIN M. PERKINS & RONALD N. BOYCE, CRIMINAL LAW 46-47 (3d ed. 1982).

[28] ROLLIN M. PERKINS & RONALD N. BOYCE, CRIMINAL LAW 51-52 (3d ed. 1982).

[29] 720 ILCS 5/9-1.2 (1999).

[30] 720 ILCS 5/9-1.2(b) (1999) (unborn child means any individual of the human species from fertilization until birth). A legal abortion is exempted. 720 ILCS 5/9-1.2(b) (1999).

[31] *See, e.g.*, 755 ILCS 50/2(b) (1999) (under Uniform Anatomical Gift Act, *death* is defined as "the irreversible cessation of total brain function, according to usual and customary standards of medical practice"). This definition was used by the Illinois appellate court in a case not involving an organ transplant. *See* In re Haymer, 115 Ill. App. 3d 349, 354-56, 450 N.E.2d 940, 945-46 (1st

courts[32] have felt obliged to determine when death occurs and to address the medical role of maintaining life-support systems, which mechanically cause blood to circulate and respiration to continue, where a person, including the victim of crime, is otherwise dead.[33] Under the Uniform Determination of Death Act,[34] followed in a number of jurisdictions,[35] a person who has suffered "brain death" is considered legally dead even though his heartbeat and breathing activ-

---

Dist. 1983) (where child was brain dead as defined in Uniform Anatomical Gift Act, hospital was authorized to discontinue the mechanical support system connected to child's body) (citing ILL. REV. STAT. Ch. 110½, para. 302(b) (1981)); *But see* Harold L. Jacobson et al., *Towards a Statutory Definition of Death in Illinois*, 14 J. MAR. L. REV. 701 (1981) (general statutory definition of death is needed in Illinois); *See also* Marilee Clausing, *Recent Case, The Acceptance of Brain Death As A Legal Definition of Death in Illinois*: In re Haymer, 33 DEPAUL L. REV. 207 (1983) (further legislative clarification needed).

In 1988, the Illinois Living Will Act became law. This law is designed to permit a potential medical patient to execute a living will instructing his or her physician to employ no "death delaying procedure" where the patient suffers a "terminal condition," meaning "an incurable and irreversible condition which is such that death is imminent and the application of death delaying procedures serves only to prolong the dying process." 755 ILCS 35/1 *et seq.* (1999). In addition, the Health Care Surrogate Act, which became law in 1991, authorizes family members or other health care surrogates to make end-of-life treatment decisions, including withdrawal of any life support, on behalf of a patient who has no living will, has lost decision-making ability and suffers either (1) a "terminal condition," which is an illness or injury for which there is no prospect of a cure or recovery and death is imminent; (2) "permanent unconsciousness;" or (3) an "incurable or irreversible condition," which means an illness or injury for which there is no prospect of recovery, will ultimately cause the patient's death and "imposes severe pain or...an inhuman burden on the patient." 755 ILCS 40/5 *et seq.* (1999). The health care surrogate must use the substitute judgment of the patient that conforms most closely to what the patient would have wished for him or herself. *See* Robert John Kane, *The Health Care Surrogate Act: No Longer Just for Terminally, Incurably Ill Patients*, 86 ILL. B.J. 273 (1998).

[32] *See, e.g.,* In re Estate of Longeway, 133 Ill. 2d 33, 47-55, 549 N.E.2d 292, 299-302 (1989) (Illinois common law and provisions of Illinois Probate Act permit guardian of an incompetent patient, who is terminally ill and diagnosed as irreversibly comatose, to elect to refuse artificial nutrition and hydration on behalf of the patient, assuming two consulting physicians concur in diagnosis, clear and convincing evidence exists that such was intent of patient and judicial approval consistent with these standards); In re Quinlan, 70 N.J. 10, 355 A.2d 647(1976) (right to privacy exists that permits removal of life support apparatus from patient in comatose, persistently vegetative state). *Quinlan* was one of the first cases to address this issue.

[33] *See, eg.,* People v. Caldwell, 295 Ill. App. 3d 172, 180-82, 692 N.E.2d 448, 454-55 (4th Dist. 1998) (where 97-year-old victim, whose neck was broken and spinal cord severed by defendant's attack, made conscious decision to be removed from ventilator rather than live with complete paralysis, defendant was responsible for victim's death).

[34] UNIFORM DETERMINATION OF DEATH ACT, 12 U.L.A. 187 (Supp. 1981) ("An individual who has sustained either (1) irreversible cessation of circulatory or respiratory functions or (2) irreversible cessation of all functions of entire brain, including the brain stem, is dead").

[35] John M. McCabe, *The New Determination of Death Act*, 67 A.B.A.J. 1476 (1981) (29 states have adopted this or comparable enactment).

ity can be sustained.[36] Illinois recognizes dual standards for determining death: (1) irreversible cessation of total brain functions or (2) irreversible circulatory and respiratory functions, according to usual and customary standards of medical practice.[37] Thus, the failure to mechanically sustain the clinically dead individual's "life" will not be considered attributable to the omission of the medical authority, but rather to the original causal agent, such as the defendant who caused the crime victim's brain death through a vicious blow to the victim's head.[38] Finally, the "year and a day" rule has been abolished in most states.[39]

§ 6.03. Early Classifications of Illegal Homicide.

Although ancient common law recognized only one class of illegal homicide, several centuries ago homicide was divided into two crimes: murder and manslaughter.[40] As originally stated by Lord Coke, murder was said to exist "when a person, of sound memory and discretion, unlawfully killeth any reasonable creature in being and under the king's peace, with malice aforethought, either express or implied."[41] Manslaughter was apparently developed as a compromise between murder and complete exoneration.[42] Since all murders were punishable by death, manslaughter was apparently created to provide for a penalty less than death in circumstances where the killing was not excused or justified but was committed for reasons that undermined the appropriateness of the death penalty.[43] For instance, where a person killed in a heat of passion caused by the

---

[36] UNIFORM DETERMINATION OF DEATH ACT, 12 U.L.A. 187 (Supp. 1981). *See also* Report of the Ad Hoc Committee of the Harvard Medical School to Examine the Definition of Brain Death, *A Definition of Irreversible Coma*, 205 JAMA 337 (1968).

[37] People v. Lara, 289 Ill. App. 3d 675, 681, 683 N.E.2d 480, 483-84 (1st Dist. 1997) (dual definition of death accepted where victim brain dead as a result of defendant's blow to victim's head); In re Estate of Sewart, 236 Ill. App. 3d 1, 14-15, 602 N.E.2d 1277, 1286 (1st Dist. 1991) (dual definition of death accepted in dispute over decedent's estate).

[38] People v. Lara, 289 Ill. App. 3d 675, 681, 683 N.E.2d 480, 483-84 (1st Dist. 1997) (where defendant struck victim in the head with a two by four, victim's death was not the result of premature termination of life support at the hospital, but rather the defendant's blow to victim's head that caused victim's brain death). This reasoning is common in other jurisdictions. *See, e.g.*, State v. Fierro, 124 Ariz. 182, 185, 603 P.2d 74, 77 (1979) (death was attributable to defendant, not to doctors' decision to discontinue life support).

[39] ROLLIN M. PERKINS & RONALD N, BOYCE, CRIMINAL LAW 47 (3d ed. 1982); People v. Carter, 168 Ill. App. 3d 237, 246-47, 522 N.E.2d 653, 658-59 (1st Dist. 1988) ("year and a day" rule no longer exists; defendant's conviction for murder arising out of attack 23 months earlier upheld).

[40] ROLLIN M. PERKINS & RONALD N. BOYCE, CRIMINAL LAW 57 (3d ed. 1982).

[41] ILL. ANN. STAT. ch. 38, para. 9-1 (Smith-Hurd 1979), 1961 Committee Comments, at 12 (revised 1972) (citing 3 INST. 47, quoted in 4 W. BLACKSTONE, COMMENTARIES 195 (7th ed.)).

[42] ILL. ANN. STAT. ch. 38, para. 9-2 (Smith-Hurd 1979), 1961 Committee Comments, at 392 (revised 1972).

[43] ROLLIN M. PERKINS & RONALD N. BOYCE, CRIMINAL LAW 124-26 (3d ed. 1982).

provocation of the victim, it was deemed manslaughter.[44] Manslaughter was described as an unlawful homicide committed *without* malice aforethought.[45]

§ 6.04. Common Law Murder: Killing with Malice Aforethought.

At common law, murder was defined as an illegal homicide committed with
malice aforethought.[46] "Malice aforethought" was never easily defined or understood, for neither the term "malice" nor the term "aforethought" was used in its
ordinary sense.[47] In any event, malice aforethought came to be understood as
encompassing the following states of mind or mens rea:

1) An intent to kill or inflict serious bodily injury;
2) Knowledge that one's acts would result in death or the infliction of serious bodily injury;
3) A wanton (reckless) and willful (knowing) disregard of a very substantial, unreasonable human risk;
4) An intent to engage in some other felony;
5) An intent to resist a lawful arrest.[48]

The first two categories of mens rea sufficient for malice aforethought involved
actual malice as described by Lord Coke; the remaining three categories fell
within the reach of implied malice.[49]

Although intent[50] or knowledge[51] that one's action would bring about death or
great bodily injury could be more easily understood, defining a "wanton and
wilful disregard of a very substantial, unreasonable human risk" was confusing.
"Wanton" has normally been equated with recklessness,[52] while "willful" has
been seen as essentially synonymous with knowledge.[53] The "wanton and willful" nomenclature used in conjunction with common law murder denoted the
creation of a higher degree of risk than would exist with ordinary recklessness.
Some forms of recklessness might have rendered the accused liable only for
manslaughter and, accordingly, the recklessness sufficient for murder had to be
distinguished. Therefore, if ordinary recklessness involved a "conscious disre-

---

[44] JUSTIN MILLER, HANDBOOK OF CRIMINAL LAW § 91 (1934).

[45] ROLLIN M. PERKINS & RONALD N. BOYCE, CRIMINAL LAW 82 (3d ed. 1982).

[46] ROLLIN M. PERKINS & RONALD N. BOYCE, CRIMINAL LAW 57 (3d ed. 1982).

[47] ILL. ANN. STAT. ch. 38, para. 9-1 (Smith-Hurd 1979), 1961 Committee Comments, at 12 (revised 1972).

[48] ILL. ANN. STAT. ch. 38, para. 9-1 (Smith-Hurd 1979), 1961 Committee Comments, at 12 (revised 1972); *see also* ROLLIN M. PERKINS & RONALD N. BOYCE, CRIMINAL LAW 57-73 (3d 1982).

[49] ILL. ANN. STAT. ch. 38, para. 9-1 (Smith-Hurd 1979), 1961 Committee Comments, at 12 (revised 1972).

[50] *See* ch. 2 for a discussion of what constitutes "intent."

[51] *See* ch. 2 for a discussion of what constitutes "knowledge."

[52] 720 ILCS 5/4-6 (1999) (recklessness defined).

[53] 720 ILCS 5/4-5 (1999) (knowledge defined).

gard" of a "substantial risk" and a "gross deviation" from the norm expected of a reasonable person,[54] then this form of malice aforethought had to involve a conscious disregard of a *very* substantial risk and a *very* gross deviation from the norm. Hence, the mens rea of "wanton and willful" has been described as "extremely reckless."[55] Thus, for extreme recklessness to exist, the accused must "know that his acts *probably* will kill or seriously injure, but does them regardless of, though not actually intending, that result."[56] To illustrate this point with a modern example, if a driver, with no intent to kill, were to drive his or her automobile through heavy traffic on Michigan Avenue in Chicago and deliberately run a red light, while driving fifteen miles per hour above the posted speed limit of thirty-five miles per hour, with the result of killing someone, it would probably be manslaughter under common law analysis. If the driver were to deliberately drive through a series of red lights on Michigan Avenue at one hundred miles per hour, it would probably be murder. In the first case, it is not necessarily probable that someone will be killed; in the second case, a death is a strong probability. Further, the risk must be wholly unreasonable to qualify for murder. If the driver in question were driving at a great rate of speed when he or she ran the red light because he or she was taking an injured party, who was bleeding to death, to a hospital emergency room, it is doubtful that the driver's conduct could be considered unreasonable enough to constitute murder.

The fourth mental state satisfying the common law malice aforethought requirement arose through the operation of the felony-murder rule.[57] Traditionally, if a defendant was engaged in another felony, such as an armed robbery, and his or her gun discharged, even accidentally, and killed another, the defendant would have been guilty of murder notwithstanding the absence of an intent to kill.[58] Originally, under this doctrine, no consideration was given to the dangerous nature of the felony involved.[59] In the aftermath of substantial growth in the number of felonies lacking a dangerous character, the harshness of this strict early common law rule eventually made little sense.[60] Accordingly, later common law decisions limited the scope of the felony-murder rule in two ways: (1) the felony had to be dangerous in nature and (2) the death arising during the course of the felony had to be the natural and probable consequence of defendant's commission of the felony.[61] The final theory of mens rea, supportive of

---

[54] 720 ILCS 5/4-6 (1999) (recklessness defined).

[55] JOSHUA DRESSLER, UNDERSTANDING CRIMINAL LAW § 31.02(B)(2) (2d ed. 1995).

[56] ILL. ANN. STAT. ch. 38, para. 9-1 (Smith-Hurd 1979), 1961 Committee Comments, at 12 (revised 1972).

[57] ROLLIN M. PERKINS & RONALD N. BOYCE, CRIMINAL LAW 61-72 (3d ed. 1982).

[58] ROLLIN M. PERKINS & RONALD N. BOYCE, CRIMINAL LAW 61 (3d ed. 1982).

[59] WAYNE LAFAVE & AUSTIN SCOTT, CRIMINAL LAW § 7-5(a) (2d ed. 1986).

[60] WAYNE LAFAVE & AUSTIN SCOTT, CRIMINAL LAW § 7-5(a) (2d ed. 1986).

[61] WAYNE LAFAVE & AUSTIN SCOTT, CRIMINAL LAW § 7-5(a) (2d ed. 1986).

the malice aforethought necessary for common law murder, existed where the accused had the intent to resist a lawful arrest and a death occurred during that resistance.[62] However, this concept had little support as an independent approach to malice aforethought beyond the writings of various common law authorities and caselaw dictum.[63] Virtually all findings of murder in such circumstances arose through the invocation of one or more of the other mental states satisfying the malice aforethought requirement.[64]

§ 6.05. Common Law Classifications of Murder.

Although the early common law did not identify degrees of murder, murder was eventually divided into two (and sometimes three) classes through legislative enactments.[65] For the same reason that manslaughter was originally created, a lesser degree of murder was developed to limit the impact of the death penalty to only the most serious type of illegal homicide.[66] Until then the death penalty was usually the only sanction imposed for murder.[67] In 1794, the state of Pennsylvania took the first ameliorative step in this regard by creating two degrees of murder.[68] Eventually, many other states patterned their murder statutes after the Pennsylvania legislation, which read:

> All murder which shall be perpetrated by means of poison, or by lying in wait, or by another kind of wilful, deliberate and premeditated killing, or which shall be committed in the perpetration of, or attempt to perpetrate any arson, rape, robbery or burglary, shall be deemed murder of the first degree; and all other kinds of murder shall be deemed murder of the second degree.[69]

An examination of this legislation and other prohibitions modeled after it reveals that murder in the first degree was intended to apply to any murder (killing with malice aforethought) where the accused (1) harbored premeditation and deliberation, (2) carried out the murder pursuant to a certain method — poison, lying in wait, or torture — which implicitly suggested the existence of premeditation and deliberation, or (3) killed another during the course of the commission of the most life threatening felonies — arson, rape, robbery, burglary, and

---

[62] ROLLIN M. PERKINS & RONALD N. BOYCE, CRIMINAL LAW 72-73 (3d ed. 1982).

[63] ROLLIN M. PERKINS & RONALD N. BOYCE, CRIMINAL LAW 71 (3d ed. 1982).

[64] ROLLIN M. PERKINS & RONALD N. BOYCE, CRIMINAL LAW 71 (3d ed. 1982).

[65] WAYNE LAFAVE & AUSTIN SCOTT, CRIMINAL LAW § 7.7 (2d ed. 1986).

[66] WAYNE LAFAVE & AUSTIN SCOTT, CRIMINAL LAW § 7.7 (2d ed. 1986).

[67] WAYNE LAFAVE & AUSTIN SCOTT, CRIMINAL LAW § 7.7 (2d ed. 1986).

[68] ROLLIN M. PERKINS & RONALD N. BOYCE, CRIMINAL LAW 127 (3d ed. 1982).

[69] ROLLIN M. PERKINS & RONALD N. BOYCE, CRIMINAL LAW 127 (3d ed. 1982) (quoting Commonwealth v. Drum, 58 Pa. 9 (1968)).

perhaps others, such as kidnapping).[70] Premeditation connoted that the accused gave advance reflection, however brief, to the killing.[71] Deliberation suggested that the accused harbored this reflection with a "cool mind" or, perhaps, killed "in cold blood."[72] In contrast, if the defendant (1) killed with malice afore-thought but without premeditation and deliberation, (2) killed his or her victim but without poison, lying in wait, or torture, or (3) killed during the cause of some felony other than rape, robbery, arson, or burglary, such as during larceny or abortion, the crime was considered murder in the second degree.[73]

§ 6.06. Murder: Modern Law.

Today, murder continues to be defined in many jurisdictions as an unlawful homicide committed with malice aforethought.[74] However, the scope of the mens rea of malice aforethought has been narrowed, with most changes revolv-ing around the felony-murder doctrine. First, the felony-murder doctrine gener-ally operates only where the death arises during the commission of a felony that is "inherently dangerous" in nature[75] that somehow causes the death in ques-tion.[76] Second, a majority of jurisdictions (not including Illinois) refuse to apply the doctrine in situations where the death was not a result of the actions of the defendant or codefendant involved in the commission of the felony.[77] For in-stance, if a police officer were to deliberately shoot a codefendant, or acciden-tally shoot a bystander, during the course of the dangerous felony, the surviving defendant would not be held responsible for the police officer's actions.[78] Third, a few jurisdictions,[79] following the lead of the English courts,[80] have essentially abandoned the felony-murder concept.

---

[70] *See generally* WAYNE LAFAVE & AUSTIN SCOTT, CRIMINAL LAW § 7-7 (2d ed. 1986); *see also* ROLLIN M. PERKINS & RONALD N. BOYCE, CRIMINAL LAW 127-36 (3d ed. 1982).

[71] JOHN KLOTTER, CRIMINAL LAW § 3.3 (2d ed. 1990).

[72] WAYNE LAFAVE & AUSTIN SCOTT, CRIMINAL LAW § 7-7(a) (2d ed. 1986).

[73] WAYNE LAFAVE & AUSTIN SCOTT, CRIMINAL LAW § 7-7(e) (2d ed. 1986).

[74] ILL. ANN. STAT. ch. 38, para. 9-1 (Smith-Hurd 1979), 1961 Committee Comments, at 14 (re-vised 1972); *see also* ROLLIN M. PERKINS & RONALD N. BOYCE, CRIMINAL LAW 57, 82 (3d ed. 1982).

[75] WAYNE LAFAVE & AUSTIN SCOTT, CRIMINAL LAW § 7-5(a)-(b) (2d ed. 1986) (felony is inher-ently dangerous or was committed under such circumstances that there was foreseeability of dan-ger to human life).

[76] This does not necessarily mean that "proximate cause" existed, but more likely that the death was a "natural and probable consequence" of the felony. WAYNE LAFAVE & AUSTIN SCOTT, CRIMI-NAL LAW § 7-5(d) (2d ed. 1986).

[77] WAYNE LAFAVE & AUSTIN SCOTT, CRIMINAL LAW § 7-5(d) (2d ed. 1986).

[78] *See, e.g.* Commonwealth v. Redline, 391 Pa. 486, 510, 137 A.2d 472, 483 (1958) (police offi-cer shot one of two robbers to death; felony-murder conviction reversed).

[79] *See, e.g.,* People v. Aaron, 409 Mich. 672, 733, 299 N.W.2d 304, 328-29 (1980) ("[W]e exer-cise our role in the development of the common law by abrogating the common law felony-murder rule.").

[80] Homicide Act of 1957, 5 & 6 Eliz. 2, ch. 11, § 1 (1957) (felony-murder rule abolished).

The concept of malice aforethought has been narrowed in yet another way. To the extent "intent to resist a lawful arrest" had vitality at common law as an alternative basis for the finding of malice aforethought,[81] it is clearly not followed today.[82] Only if the arrestee's resistance falls into one of the other acceptable approaches to malice aforethought will his conduct qualify as murder.[83]

A significant and growing number of jurisdictions, including Illinois,[84] no longer use the "malice aforethought" nomenclature in their murder statutes.[85] Most of these jurisdictions now have statutes that simply express themselves in terms such as "intent to kill," "intent to inflict great bodily injury," "knowledgeable killing" and "intent to commit a forcible felony."[86]

A majority of the American jurisdictions, including Illinois,[87] maintain two degrees of murder,[88] while a handful have three degrees of murder[89] and some have only one.[90] However, it is important to note the differentiation between murder in the first degree and murder in the second degree in Illinois is not consistent with the traditional differentiation. Of course, the Illinois murder legislation will be studied later.[91]

§ 6.07. Common Law Manslaughter: Killing Without Malice Aforethought.

Common law manslaughter encompassed any unlawful homicide committed without malice aforethought.[92] Unknown to the early English common law,[93] it eventually became a part of the American common law by statute.[94] Essentially, it was designed to cover killings that were not egregious enough to be considered murder but were serious enough to be labeled a criminal homicide.[95] Spe-

---

[81] See § 6.04 of this chapter.

[82] WAYNE LAFAVE & AUSTIN SCOTT, CRIMINAL LAW § 7.6 (2d ed. 1986).

[83] WAYNE LAFAVE & AUSTIN SCOTT, CRIMINAL LAW § 7.6 (2d ed. 1986).

[84] 720 ILCS 5/9-1 (1993).

[85] However, in Illinois, the "malice aforethought" language continues to appear in the caselaw despite its removal from paragraph 5/9-1. See Timothy O'Neill, "With Malice Toward None": A Solution to an Illinois Homicide Quandary, 32 DEPAUL L. REV. 107, 114 (1983).

[86] See, e.g., 720 ILCS 5/9-1 (1999).

[87] 720 ILCS 5/9-1 (1999) (first degree murder); 720 ILCS 5/9-2 (1999) (second degree murder).

[88] ILL. ANN. STAT. ch. 38, para. 9-1 (Smith-Hurd 1979), 1961 Committee Comments, at 14 (revised 1972).

[89] ILL. ANN. STAT. ch. 38, para. 9-1 (Smith-Hurd 1979), 1961 Committee Comments, at 14 (revised 1972).

[90] ILL. ANN. STAT. ch. 38, para. 9-1 (Smith-Hurd 1979), 1961 Committee Comments, at 13 (revised 1972).

[91] See § 6.13-6.33 of this chapter.

[92] ROLLIN M. PERKINS & RONALD N. BOYCE, CRIMINAL LAW 82 (3d ed. 1982).

[93] ROLLIN M. PERKINS & RONALD N. BOYCE, CRIMINAL LAW 82 (3d ed. 1982).

[94] ROLLIN M. PERKINS & RONALD N. BOYCE, CRIMINAL LAW 82-83 (3d ed. 1982).

[95] WAYNE LAFAVE & AUSTIN SCOTT, CRIMINAL LAW § 7-9 (2d ed. 1986).

cifically, manslaughter was a compromise between murder, which invariably carried the death penalty, and killings involving certain circumstances not warranting the death penalty. Accordingly, manslaughter was considered a noncapital felony.[96] Thus, manslaughter was created to cover a variety of unjustified and inexcusable killings of a human being that did not comfortably fit within the murder prohibition.

§ 6.08. Common Law Classifications of Manslaughter.

At common law, manslaughter encompassed two distinct situations. First, it covered illegal killings which involved certain mitigating circumstances. Thus, if murder could be described as a killing with malice aforethought, which mens rea could be defined as "an unjustifiable, inexcusable and unmitigated person-endangering-state-of-mind,"[97] then manslaughter could be described as a killing with an unjustifiable and inexcusable person-endangering-state-of-mind, but involving particular mitigating circumstances. The recognized mitigating circumstances that transformed into manslaughter which would otherwise constitute murder arose where the accused: (1) was provoked into a heat of passion that caused him or her to kill[98] or (2) killed another in circumstances where he or she subjectively believed, although not reasonably, that he or she was justified in killing.[99] Since the taking of life in both situations was deliberate,[100] it was described as *voluntary* manslaughter.

The second category of manslaughter was designed to cover situations where the defendant killed another without justification or excuse, but his or her wrongful mental state was not as inherently life-endangering as in the case of murder. Here, the two principal situations where manslaughter arose were where the accused (1) killed another through recklessness insufficient for murder,[101] or gross negligence[102] or (2) killed another during the commission of an unlawful act which was not a felony sufficiently life threatening for application of the felony-murder doctrine.[103] Since the taking of life in neither situation was deliberate, these crimes were considered *involuntary* manslaughter.

---

[96] ROLLIN M. PERKINS & RONALD N. BOYCE, CRIMINAL LAW 83 (3d ed. 1982).

[97] ROLLIN M. PERKINS & RONALD N. BOYCE, CRIMINAL LAW 75 (3d ed. 1982).

[98] WAYNE LAFAVE & AUSTIN SCOTT, CRIMINAL LAW § 7-10 (2d ed. 1986).

[99] WAYNE LAFAVE & AUSTIN SCOTT, CRIMINAL LAW § 7-10, at 665-66 (2d ed. 1986).

[100] The use of the term "deliberate" in this context should not in any way be confused with the concept of deliberation as used in connection with common law first-degree murder, which means harboring a cold, calculating state of mind.

[101] *See* § 6.04 of this chapter.

[102] JOSHUA DRESSLER, UNDERSTANDING CRIMINAL LAW § 31-08 (2d ed. 1995).

[103] WAYNE LAFAVE & AUSTIN SCOTT, CRIMINAL LAW § 7.13 (2d ed. 1986).

§ 6.09. — Common Law Voluntary Manslaughter.

As noted above, there existed at common law two bases for a finding of voluntary manslaughter. First, there was "heat of passion" voluntary manslaughter.[104] This form of manslaughter existed where four conditions were met: (1) the defendant had suffered a reasonable, adequate provocation; (2) the defendant was in fact provoked by the act of provocation; (3) a reasonable person so provoked would not have "cooled off" between the act of provocation and the infliction of the fatal blow; and (4) the defendant had in fact not cooled off between the act of provocation and the infliction of the blow.[105]

A reasonable, adequate provocation existed where the defendant suffered a life-threatening assault or battery.[106] If the assault or battery was relatively minor, it would not be sufficient. Mere words, no matter how insulting or abusive, would not suffice unless they were uttered in connection with the serious infliction or threat of great bodily harm.[107] If the infliction of harm was directed at a third party to whom the defendant was closely related (for example, a spouse or child), this was sufficient to constitute adequate provocation.[108] Finally, where an accused discovered his or her spouse in an act of adultery, and the spouse or the spouse's lover was killed by the accused, this was considered a provocation sufficient to reduce what would otherwise be murder to voluntary manslaughter.[109]

The defendant had to have in fact been actually provoked into a heat of passion.[110] If a defendant suffered a serious blow caused by another without becoming enraged and, immediately thereafter, calmly killed his or her assailant without justification (for example, with no basis for a self-defense claim), this would be murder.[111] If a defendant, once enraged, did not cool off after a reasonable interval as would a reasonable person, and killed the assailant, it would be murder, not manslaughter.[112] If a defendant who was initially enraged, cooled off after a certain time interval and subsequently killed his or her assailant, it would also be murder.[113]

Voluntary manslaughter was established by later common law caselaw where certain other extenuating circumstances existed, namely, where the accused killed another, believing the actions to be justified, but where in fact they were

---

[104] WAYNE LAFAVE & AUSTIN SCOTT, CRIMINAL LAW § 7.10 (2d ed. 1986).

[105] WAYNE LAFAVE & AUSTIN SCOTT, CRIMINAL LAW § 7.10(a) (2d ed. 1986).

[106] WAYNE LAFAVE & AUSTIN SCOTT, CRIMINAL LAW § 7.10(b) (2d ed. 1986).

[107] WAYNE LAFAVE & AUSTIN SCOTT, CRIMINAL LAW § 7.10(b)(6) (2d ed. 1986).

[108] WAYNE LAFAVE & AUSTIN SCOTT, CRIMINAL LAW § 7.10(b)(7) (2d ed. 1986).

[109] WAYNE LAFAVE & AUSTIN SCOTT, CRIMINAL LAW § 7.10(b)(5) (2d ed. 1986).

[110] WAYNE LAFAVE & AUSTIN SCOTT, CRIMINAL LAW § 7.10(c) (2d ed. 1986).

[111] WAYNE LAFAVE & AUSTIN SCOTT, CRIMINAL LAW § 7.13(c) (2d ed. 1986).

[112] WAYNE LAFAVE & AUSTIN SCOTT, CRIMINAL LAW § 7.10(d) (2d ed. 1986).

[113] WAYNE LAFAVE & AUSTIN SCOTT, CRIMINAL LAW § 7.10(e) (2d ed. 1986).

not justified.[114] For instance, in order to kill in self-defense,[115] a defendant had to demonstrate that he or she had not provoked the attack and had reasonably believed deadly force was necessary to avert an imminent deadly attack.[116] If the defendant's defense claim was "imperfect" because, for instance, the deadly force was not necessary to thwart the attack, the defendant would be convicted of voluntary manslaughter. The same result would arise where the defendant resorted to another defense, such as defense of another, defense of necessity, or defense of duress, but failed to satisfy one or more of the essential elements of the defense.[117]

§ 6.10. — Common Law Involuntary Manslaughter.

Involuntary manslaughter existed at common law when a defendant killed another through reckless or grossly negligent actions.[118] While ordinary tort negligence would not suffice, recklessness or gross negligence satisfied involuntary manslaughter.[119] A conscious awareness of the risk, which is essential to recklessness,[120] was not required.[121] On the other hand, the negligence sufficient for involuntary manslaughter had to be extreme:[122] a gross deviation from the standard of care expected of the reasonable person when a high degree of risk of death is involved.[123] Involuntary manslaughter was found to exist in a variety of circumstances involving commissions, such as the careless handling of guns,[124] and involving omissions, such as the failure of a parent to provide medical attention for his or her sick child,[125] where that failure proximately caused a death.[126]

The other basis for establishing involuntary manslaughter arose where a defendant killed another during the commission or attempted commission of an unlawful act not sufficient for purposes of the felony-murder rule.[127] While this concept was often referred to at common law as the "misdemeanor-manslaughter rule,"[128] this characterization was not accurate given the nature of the "unlawful acts" that satisfied the rule. Specifically, the unlawful act giving rise to the op-

---

[114] WAYNE LAFAVE & AUSTIN SCOTT, CRIMINAL LAW § 7.11 (2d ed. 1986).

[115] See generally ch. 17 of this treatise for a discussion of this defense.

[116] WAYNE LAFAVE & AUSTIN SCOTT, CRIMINAL LAW § 7.11(a) (2d ed. 1986).

[117] WAYNE LAFAVE & AUSTIN SCOTT, CRIMINAL LAW § 7.11(b)-(d) (2d ed. 1986).

[118] WAYNE LAFAVE & AUSTIN SCOTT, CRIMINAL LAW § 7.12(a) (2d ed. 1986).

[119] WAYNE LAFAVE & AUSTIN SCOTT, CRIMINAL LAW § 7.12(a) (2d ed. 1986).

[120] 720 ILCS 5/4-6 (1999) (definition of term "recklessness").

[121] ROLLIN M. PERKINS & RONALD N. BOYCE, CRIMINAL LAW 107 (3d ed. 1982).

[122] ROLLIN M. PERKINS & RONALD N. BOYCE, CRIMINAL LAW 107 (3d ed. 1982).

[123] WAYNE LAFAVE & AUSTIN SCOTT, CRIMINAL LAW § 7.12(a) (2d ed. 1986).

[124] WAYNE LAFAVE & AUSTIN SCOTT, CRIMINAL LAW § 7.12(a) (2d ed. 1986).

[125] WAYNE LAFAVE & AUSTIN SCOTT, CRIMINAL LAW § 7.12(b) (2d ed. 1986).

[126] WAYNE LAFAVE & AUSTIN SCOTT, CRIMINAL LAW § 7.12(c) (2d ed. 1986).

[127] WAYNE LAFAVE & AUSTIN SCOTT, CRIMINAL LAW § 7.13 (2d ed. 1986).

[128] ROLLIN M. PERKINS & RONALD N. BOYCE, CRIMINAL LAW 108 (3d ed. 1982).

eration of this concept did not have to be a misdemeanor per se and included certain felonies that did not satisfy the felony-murder rule, as well as some local ordinance violations and civil wrongs.[129] However, these acts, which could include omissions as well as commissions,[130] had to be *malum in se*[131] to be sufficient under this rule.[132] Also, this concept, best described as the "unlawful act doctrine,"[133] required a causal connection between the unlawful act and the death in question before liability for involuntary manslaughter could attach.[134]

To illustrate the operation of the "unlawful act" doctrine at common law, the following series of hypotheticals in a more modern setting might prove helpful. Assume A had discharged a firearm without an appropriate permit in violation of law and B was killed by the discharge. Further, assume A had regularly possessed a permit to use the firearm but had inadvertently allowed the permit to expire the day before the incident. Since the failure to comply with the permit requirement could not be described as a *malum in se* omission, no liability for involuntary manslaughter could have attached. In contrast, if A had been refused a permit because of prior reckless mishandling of firearms, A's continued use of the firearm could have been viewed as *malum in se* conduct, and accordingly, A's shooting of B could constitute involuntary manslaughter unless no causal connection could be established between the mishandling of the firearm and the subsequent death. Finally, if A's mishandling of the firearm was inherently reckless at the point where B had been killed, then involuntary manslaughter could have been established under the first approach to finding involuntary manslaughter (since the conduct was reckless or grossly negligent) without regard to the "unlawful act" doctrine.

§ 6.11. Manslaughter: Modern Law.

Most jurisdictions continue to distinguish between voluntary and involuntary manslaughter, with the former generally carrying a more severe sanction than the latter.[135] Concerning voluntary manslaughter, the common law framework generally remains the law today. "Heat of passion" voluntary manslaughter exists where the defendant faced an adequate provocation that caused him or her to become enraged and kill.[136] "Other extenuating circumstances" voluntary man-

---

[129] WAYNE LAFAVE & AUSTIN SCOTT, CRIMINAL LAW § 7.13(a) (2d ed. 1986).

[130] WAYNE LAFAVE & AUSTIN SCOTT, CRIMINAL LAW § 7.13(a) (2d ed. 1986).

[131] *See* ch. 1 of this treatise for a discussion of what violations are *malum in se*.

[132] ROLLIN M. PERKINS & RONALD N. BOYCE, CRIMINAL LAW 109-11 (3d ed. 1982).

[133] WAYNE LAFAVE & AUSTIN SCOTT, CRIMINAL LAW § 7.13 (2d ed. 1986).

[134] ROLLIN M. PERKINS & RONALD N. BOYCE, CRIMINAL LAW 111-12 (3d ed. 1982).

[135] WAYNE LAFAVE & AUSTIN SCOTT, CRIMINAL LAW § 7.12 (2d ed. 1986).

[136] WAYNE LAFAVE & AUSTIN SCOTT, CRIMINAL LAW § 7.10 (2d ed. 1986); *see* § 6.09 of this chapter.

slaughter arises where the accused killed in circumstances in which he or she subjectively, but unreasonably, believed the taking of life to be justifiable.[137]

Involuntary manslaughter exists today where the defendant's reckless or grossly negligent conduct has caused the death of another.[138] Also, many jurisdictions punish a person for involuntary manslaughter if he or she engages in an unlawful act that brings about the death of another.[139] The scope of the "unlawful act" doctrine is generally limited in three ways: (1) the unlawful act must be *malum in se*[140]; (2) the death was caused by the unlawful act; and (3) the unlawful act was inherently dangerous.[141] There is a modern tendency to abandon this approach to finding involuntary manslaughter.[142] These jurisdictions, including Illinois, simply examine the nature of the act, lawful or unlawful, that has caused the death, and if it proves to have been reckless in nature, involuntary manslaughter is established.[143]

§ 6.12. Background of Illinois Homicide Prohibitions.

Before 1961, the Illinois definition of murder was consistent with the common law approach: "[t]he unlawful killing of a human being . . . with malice aforethought."[144] There was only one class of murder under this earlier Illinois law.[145] An examination of the reported pre-1961 cases reveals that the prior legislation was interpreted to cover three general classes of murder: (1) acts accompanied by an actual intent to kill or create great bodily harm; (2) actions carried out with knowledge that death or great bodily harm would result; and (3) the commission of a forcible felony during which a death occurred.[146] In the context of a felony-murder situation, it was immaterial whether the death occurred intentionally or accidentally, whether it was committed by the defendant

---

[137] WAYNE LAFAVE & AUSTIN SCOTT, CRIMINAL LAW § 7.11 (2d ed. 1986); *see* § 6.09 of this chapter.

[138] WAYNE LAFAVE & AUSTIN SCOTT, CRIMINAL LAW § 7.12(a) (2d ed. 1986); *see* § 6.09 of this chapter.

[139] WAYNE LAFAVE & AUSTIN SCOTT, CRIMINAL LAW § 7.13 (2d ed. 1986).

[140] WAYNE LAFAVE & AUSTIN SCOTT, CRIMINAL LAW § 7.13(c) (2d ed. 1986).

[141] WAYNE LAFAVE & AUSTIN SCOTT, CRIMINAL LAW § 7.13(b) (2d ed. 1986).

[142] WAYNE LAFAVE & AUSTIN SCOTT, CRIMINAL LAW § 7.13 (2d ed. 1986).

[143] 720 ILCS 5/9-3(a) (1999) ("A person who unintentionally kills an individual without lawful justification commits involuntary manslaughter if his acts whether lawful or unlawful which cause the death are such as are likely to cause death or great bodily harm to some individual, and he performs them recklessly.").

[144] ILL. ANN. STAT. ch. 38, para. 9-1 (Smith-Hurd 1979), 1961 Committee Comments, at 13 (revised 1972), citing ILL. REV. STAT. ch. 38, § 358 (1959).

[145] ILL. ANN. STAT. ch. 38, para. 9-1 (Smith-Hurd 1979), 1961 Committee Comments, at 13 (revised 1972).

[146] ILL. ANN. STAT. ch. 38, para. 9-1 (Smith-Hurd 1979), 1961 Committee Comments, at 15-16 (revised 1972).

or by a confederate without the connivance of the defendant, or even whether it was caused by an innocent third person trying to prevent the commission of the felony.[147] No cases were uncovered, however, where a successful murder prosecution was based on the common law theory of resisting arrest.[148]

Before the enactment of the Criminal Code of 1961, voluntary manslaughter covered only those homicides carried out in a heat of passion caused by an adequate provocation.[149] Meanwhile, involuntary manslaughter covered unintentional homicides that occurred (1) during the course of an unlawful act or (2) as a result of recklessness or gross negligence.[150]

The Criminal Code of 1961 retained the three principal offenses of murder, voluntary manslaughter and involuntary manslaughter. Like its earlier counterpart, murder covered those homicides where the defendant (1) had the intent to kill or inflict great bodily harm, (2) knew his conduct would kill or cause great bodily harm or (3) was attempting or committing a forcible felony.[151] Voluntary manslaughter was expanded to cover not only homicides committed in a heat of passion but also killings where the defendant had an imperfect defense.[152] Involuntary manslaughter covered any reckless killing outside the automobile context.[153] A new offense called "reckless homicide" included those killings where the cause of death consisted of the reckless driving of an automobile.[154] In addition, the unlawful act approach to involuntary manslaughter was deleted.[155] Now the focus of this offense was on whether the accused was reckless, not on whether his conduct was unlawful.[156] In addition, the pre-1985 legislation included prohibitions against feticide,[157] which outlawed the killing of a viable fetus,[158] as well as concealment of a homicidal death,[159] and concealment of the death of a bastard.[160]

---

[147] ILL. ANN. STAT. ch. 38, para. 9-1 (Smith-Hurd 1979), 1961 Committee Comments, at 16 (revised 1972).

[148] ILL. ANN. STAT. ch. 38, para. 9-1 (Smith-Hurd 1979), 1961 Committee Comments, at 16 (revised 1972).

[149] ILL. ANN. STAT. ch. 38, para. 9-2 (Smith-Hurd 1979), 1961 Committee Comments, at 393 (revised 1972), citing ILL. REV. STAT. ch. 38, §§ 361, 362 (1959).

[150] ILL. ANN. STAT. ch. 38, para. 9-3 (Smith-Hurd 1979), 1961 Committee Comments, at 476 (revised 1972).

[151] ILL. REV. STAT. ch. 38, para. 9-1 (1985).

[152] ILL. REV. STAT. ch. 38, para. 9-2 (1985).

[153] ILL. REV. STAT. ch. 38, para. 9-3(a) (1985).

[154] ILL. REV. STAT. ch. 38, para. 9-3(a) (1985).

[155] ILL. REV. STAT. ch. 38, para. 9-3(a) (1985).

[156] ILL. REV. STAT. ch. 38, para. 9-3(a) (1985).

[157] ILL. REV. STAT. ch. 38, para. 9-1.1 (1985).

[158] ILL. REV. STAT. ch. 38, para. 9-1.1(b) (1985).

[159] ILL. REV. STAT. ch. 38, para. 9-3.1 (1985).

[160] ILL. REV. STAT. ch. 38, para. 9-4 (1985).

Between 1986 and 1988, the Illinois legislature rewrote most of the state's homicide-related strictures. The net effect of this legislative effort is the development of a statutory configuration that reflects the following crimes: (1) first degree murder[161] (2) second degree murder,[162] (3) involuntary manslaughter and reckless homicide,[163] (4) concealment of homicidal death,[164] (5) intentional homicide of an unborn child,[165] (6) voluntary manslaughter of an unborn child,[166] (7) involuntary manslaughter and reckless homicide of an unborn child[167] and (8) drug induced homicide.[168] These enactments reflect several major changes. First, the type of homicide that was previously described as "murder" is now labeled "first degree murder."[169] Second, the type of conduct that was previously described as "voluntary manslaughter" is now considered "second degree murder."[170] Third, the crime of "feticide," which outlawed the killing of a viable fetus,[171] was repealed and replaced by three offenses: "intentional homicide of an unborn child,"[172] "voluntary manslaughter of an unborn child,"[173] and "involuntary manslaughter and reckless homicide of an unborn child."[174] These latter offenses define an "unborn child" as existing from the point of conception.[175] Fourth, the legislature created the offense of "drug induced homicide" to punish the person who delivers a controlled substance to an individual who dies as a result of the consumption of the controlled substance.[176] Finally, during this period the Illinois General Assembly repealed the offense of "concealment of the death of a bastard,"[177] presumably since the offense of "concealment of a homicidal death" covers the same conduct.[178]

---

[161] 720 ILCS 5/9-1 (1999).

[162] 720 ILCS 5/9-2 (1999).

[163] 720 ILCS 5/9-3 (1999).

[164] 720 ILCS 5/9-3.1 (1999).

[165] 720 ILCS 5/9-1.2 (1999).

[166] 720 ILCS 5/9-2.1 (1999).

[167] 720 ILCS 5/9-3.2 (1999).

[168] 720 ILCS 5/9-3.3 (1999).

[169] 720 ILCS 5/9-1 (1999).

[170] 720 ILCS 5/9-2 (1999).

[171] ILL. REV. STAT. ch. 38, para. 9-1.1 (1985).

[172] 720 ILCS 5/9-1.2 (1999).

[173] 720 ILCS 5/9-2.1 (1999).

[174] 720 ILCS 5/9-3.2 (1999).

[175] 720 ILCS 5/9-1.2(b) (1999) (intentional homicide of an unborn child); 720 ILCS 5/9-2.1(d) (1999) (voluntary manslaughter of an unborn child); 720 ILCS 5/9-3.2(c) (1999) (involuntary manslaughter and reckless homicide of an unborn child).

[176] 720 ILCS 5/9-3.3 (1999).

[177] P.A. 85-411 (1987).

[178] 720 ILCS 5/9-3.1 (1999).

§ 6.13. First Degree Murder.

Prior to 1987, there was only one category of murder in Illinois.[179] In 1987, the Illinois legislature created the offense of "first degree murder"[180] as well as the crime of "second degree murder."[181]

At first glance, it might appear that replacing "murder" with "first degree murder" and "second degree murder" represents a division of what previously constituted murder into two separate offenses. This did not occur. Instead the conduct that was previously described as murder has been simply relabeled "first-degree murder" and *most* of what was earlier described as "voluntary manslaughter" is now "second degree murder." On the other hand, these changes were not merely cosmetic and without any effect.

Prior to 1987, voluntary manslaughter was used to describe any unjustified killing of a person where the defendant (1) harbored a "sudden and intense passion resulting from a serious provocation" or (2) unreasonably believed his or her killing was justified.[182] However, this approach was criticized on grounds that it required the *state* to prove murder plus mitigation in order to convict an accused of voluntary manslaughter.[183] Since it was the defendant who wished to show mitigation, it would be more consistent to require the state to prove the elements of murder and, thereafter, allow the defendant an opportunity to prove mitigation.[184] The result of these criticisms led the state legislature to place the burden of proof in a murder trial on the defendant to establish by a preponderance of evidence that one of the mitigating factors existed *after* the state had proved the existence of a murder beyond a reasonable doubt.[185] Moreover, since voluntary manslaughter was "comprised of the entire offense of murder in addition to extenuating circumstances," it was thought logical to treat this conduct as a less serious form of murder.[186] In the final analysis, the consequences of this legislative change was two-fold. The first effect of this reconfiguration of the homicide laws was the obvious change in nomenclature. The second result, albeit subtle, is more significant. Under the current burden of proof scheme, what was previously voluntary manslaughter might *in a given case* amount to first

---

[179] ILL. REV. STAT. ch. 38, para. 9-1 (1985).

[180] P.A. 84-1450 (1987); 720 ILCS 5/9-1 (1999).

[181] P.A. 84-1450 (1987); 720 ILCS 5/9-2 (1999).

[182] ILL. REV. STAT. ch. 38, para. 9-2 (1985).

[183] *See, e.g.,* Timothy O'Neill, *With Malice Toward None: A Solution to an Illinois Homicide Quandary,* 32 DEPAUL L. REV. 107 (1982).

[184] Robert Steigmann, *First and Second Degree Murder in Illinois,* 75 ILL. B.J. 494 (1987); Timothy O'Neill, *"Murder Least Foul": A Proposal to Abolish Voluntary Manslaughter in Illinois,* 72 ILL. B.J. 306 (1984).

[185] 720 ILCS 5/9-2(c) (1999).

[186] Timothy O'Neill, *"Murder Least Foul": A Proposal to Abolish Voluntary Manslaughter in Illinois,* 72 ILL. B.J. 306, 307 (1984).

degree murder rather turn second degree murder where the defendant fails to meet his new-found burden of establishing by a preponderance of evidence one of the mitigating factors. Under the prior burden of proof scheme, the defendant had the burden of coming forward with only "some evidence" of mitigation before (1) the jury was instructed on voluntary manslaughter and (2) the burden shifted to the state to disprove beyond a reasonable doubt the mitigating factors.[187] Under the current burden of proof arrangement, the defendant has a *greater* burden in raising the issue of mitigation. Obviously, if he or she fails to satisfy his burden of raising the issue of mitigation by a preponderance of evidence, he or she will be convicted of first degree murder rather than second degree murder.[188]

§ 6.14. — First Degree Murder Codified.

The crime of first-degree murder[189] appears in paragraph 5/9-1 of chapter 720. It now reads:

> A person who kills an individual without lawful justification commits first degree murder if, in performing the acts which cause the death: (1) He either intends to kill or do great bodily harm to that individual or another, or knows that such acts will cause death to that individual or another; or (2) He knows that such acts create a strong probability of death or great bodily harm to that individual or another; or (3) He is attempting or committing a forcible felony other than second degree murder.[190]

When the crime of "murder," now "first degree murder," was codified in the Criminal Code of 1961, the legislature's obvious intent was to define the types of conduct previously recognized as murder but to avoid the use of the difficult "malice aforethought" language used at common law.[191] The terms intent[192] and

---

[187] *See* People v. Seaberry, 63 Ill. App. 3d 718, 722, 380 N.E.2d 511, 514 (2d Dist. 1978) (defendant failed to offer "some evidence" of mitigation requiring jury instructions on voluntary manslaughter).

[188] People v. Jeffries, 164 Ill. 2d 104, 118, 646 N.E.2d 587, 592-93 (1995).

[189] The following discussion of first degree murder will occasionally include references in the text or footnotes to cases where the defendant was prosecuted for what was previously described as "murder," as defined by paragraph 9-1(a) of the Criminal Code of 1961 — an enactment that continued in effect until July 1, 1987 when 9-1(a) became "first degree murder." These references to earlier "murder" cases will only appear in this text where the doctrine or principle from the earlier statute still maintains vitality in the new "first degree murder" configuration.

[190] 720 ILCS 5/9-1(a) (1999).

[191] ILL. ANN. STAT. ch. 38, para. 9-1, (Smith-Hurd 1979), 1961 Committee Comments, at 17 (revised 1972).

[192] *See* ch. 2 of this treatise for a discussion of the meaning of the word "intent."

knowledge,[193] as used in the statute, are to be understood by reference to the article 5/4 definitions of those terms.[194] By including the "or another" language in the statutory definition of first degree murder, the legislature sought to recognize the concept of "transferred intent," which arises where the offender has the intent to kill one person and, in fact, through his or her actions kills another whom he or she had no intent to kill.[195]

In enacting subparagraph (2), the legislature in 1961 was determined to include within the definition of murder, now first degree murder, certain killings where the accused had neither actual intent to kill or inflict great bodily harm nor knowledge that his or her conduct would kill or inflict great bodily harm with a "practical certainty."[196]

> Clearly, no sharp dividing line can be drawn, but the Committee chose "strong probability" as the plainest description of the situation which lies between the "practical certainty" of the preceding subsection, and the "likely cause" and "substantial and unjustifiable risk" of the involuntary manslaughter provision (§ 9-3, using "recklessly" as defined in § 4-6). This phrase would seem to require a minimum of further definition in jury instructions, and to permit ready comparison with the other two situations mentioned, when the evidence requires instructions thereon.[197]

Obviously, then, the Illinois first degree murder statute is designed to *not* cover killings where only ordinary recklessness was involved.

In line with the modern approach, the legislature has limited the scope of the felony-murder proscription to "forcible" felonies.[198] On the other hand, the forcible felony has been recognized to be "so inherently dangerous that a homicide occurring in the course thereof, *even though accidentally*, should be held, without further proof, to be within the 'strong probability' classification of murder."[199] Currently, the definition of *forcible felony* includes "treason, first degree murder, second degree murder, predatory criminal sexual assault of a child, aggravated criminal sexual assault, criminal sexual assault, robbery, burglary, resi-

---

[193] *See* ch. 2 of this treatise for a discussion of the meaning of the word "knowledge."

[194] 720 ILCS 5/4-4 (1999) (intent defined), 720 ILCS 5/4-5 (knowledge defined).

[195] ILL. ANN. STAT. ch. 38, para. 9-1 (Smith-Hurd 1979), 1961 Committee Comments, at 18 (revised 1972). *See* ch. 2 of this treatise for a discussion of unintended victims and results.

[196] 720 ILCS 5/4-5 (1999) ("A person knows, or acts knowingly or with knowledge of . . . [t]he result of his conduct, described by the statute defining the offense, when he is consciously aware that such result is practically certain to be caused by his conduct.").

[197] ILL. ANN. STAT. ch. 38, para. 9-1 (Smith-Hurd 1979), 1961 Committee Comments, at 18-19 (revised 1972).

[198] ILL. ANN. STAT. ch. 38, para. 9-1 (Smith-Hurd 1979), 1961 Committee Comments, at 18-19 (revised 1972).

[199] ILL. ANN. STAT. ch. 38, para. 9-1 (Smith-Hurd 1979), 1961 Committee Comments, at 18-19 (revised 1972) (emphasis added).

dential burglary, aggravated arson, arson, aggravated kidnapping, kidnapping, aggravated battery resulting in great bodily harm or permanent disability or disfigurement, and any other felony which involves the use or threat of physical force or violence against any individual."[200] Finally, it was the legislature's intent to treat certain murders as punishable by the death penalty.[201] At this time, the death penalty is available where one or more factors in aggravation appear.[202] For example, when an individual killed thirty-three victims, the court

---

[200] 720 ILCS 5/2-8 (1999).

[201] *See* ILL. ANN. STAT. ch. 38, para. 9-1 (Smith-Hurd 1979), 1961 Committee Comments, at 19-20 (revised 1972).

[202] *See* 720 ILCS 5/9-1(b) (1999):

(b) Aggravating Factors. A defendant who at the time of the commission of the offense has attained the age of 18 or more and who has been found guilty of first degree murder may be sentenced to death if:

the murdered individual was a peace officer or fireman killed in the course of performing his official duties, to prevent the performance of his official duties, or in retaliation for performing his official duties, and the defendant knew or should have known that the murdered individual was a peace officer or fireman, or;

2. the murdered individual was an employee of an institution or facility of the Department of Corrections, or any similar local correctional agency, killed in the course of performing his official duties, to prevent the performance of his official duties, or in retaliation for performing his official duties, or the murdered individual was an inmate at such institution or facility and was killed on the grounds thereof, or the murdered individual was otherwise present in such institution or facility with the knowledge and approval of the chief administrative officer thereof; or

3. the defendant has been convicted of murdering two or more individuals under subsection (a) of this Section or under any law of the United States or of any state which is substantially similar to subsection (a) of this Section regardless of whether the deaths occurred as the result of the same act or of several related or unrelated acts so long as the deaths were the result of either an intent to kill more than one person or of separate acts which the defendant knew would cause death or create a strong probability of death or great bodily harm to the murdered individual or another; or

4. the murdered individual was killed as a result of the hijacking of an airplane, train, ship, bus or other public conveyance; or

5. the defendant committed the murder pursuant to a contract, agreement or understanding by which he was to receive money or anything of value in return for committing the murder or procured another to commit the murder for money or anything of value; or

6. the murdered individual was killed in the course of another felony if:

(a) the murdered individual: (i) was actually killed by the defendant, or (ii) received physical injuries personally inflicted by the defendant substantially contemporaneously with physical injuries caused by one or more persons for whose conduct the defendant is legally accountable under Section [5/]5-2 of this Code, and the physical injuries inflicted by either the defendant or the other person or persons for whose conduct he is legally accountable caused the death of the murdered individual; and

(b) in performing the acts which caused the death of the murdered individual or which resulted in physical injuries personally inflicted by the defendant on the murdered individual under the circumstances of subdivision (ii) of subparagraph (a) of paragraph (6) of subsection (b) of this Section, the defendant acted with the intent to kill the murdered individual or with the knowledge that his acts created a strong probability of death or great bodily harm to the murdered individual or another; and

(c) the other felony was one of the following: armed robbery, armed violence, robbery, predatory criminal sexual assault of a child, aggravated criminal sexual assault, aggravated kidnapping, aggravated vehicular hijacking, forcible detention, arson, aggravated arson, aggravated stalking, burglary, residential burglary, home invasion, calculated criminal drug conspiracy . . ., streetgang criminal drug conspiracy . . ., or the attempt to commit any of the felonies listed in this subsection (c); or

7. the murdered individual was under 12 years of age and the death resulted from exceptionally brutal or heinous behavior indicative of wanton cruelty; or

8. the defendant committed the murder with intent to prevent the murdered individual from testifying in any criminal prosecution or giving material assistance to the State in any investigation or prosecution, either against the defendant or another; or the defendant committed the murder because the murdered individual was a witness in any prosecution or gave material assistance to the State in any investigation or prosecution, either against the defendant or another; or

9. the defendant, while committing an offense punishable under Sections 401, 401.1, 401.2, 405, 405.2, 407 or 407.1 or subsection (b) of Section 404 of the Illinois Controlled Substances Act, or while engaged in a conspiracy or solicitation to commit such an offense, intentionally killed an individual or counseled, commanded, induced, procured or caused the intentional killing of the murdered individual; or

10. the defendant was incarcerated in an institution or facility of the Department of Corrections at the time of the murder, and while committing an offense punishable as a felony under Illinois law, or while engaged in a conspiracy or solicitation to commit such offense, intentionally killed an individual or counseled, commanded, induced, procured or caused the intentional killing of the murdered individual; or

11. the murder was committed in a cold, calculated and premeditated manner pursuant to a preconceived plan, scheme or design to take a human life by unlawful means, and the conduct of the defendant created a reasonable expectation that the death of a human being would result therefrom; or

12. the murdered individual was an emergency medical technician — ambulance, emergency medical technician — intermediate emergency, emergency medical technician — paramedic, ambulance driver, or other medical assistance or first aid personnel, employed by a municipality or other governmental unit, killed in the course of performing his official duties, to prevent the performance of his official duties, or in retaliation for performing his official duties, and the defendant knew or should have known that the murdered individual was an emergency medical technician — ambulance, emergency medical technician — paramedic, ambulance driver, or other medical assistance or first aid personnel; or

13. the defendant was a principal . . . organizer . . . of a calculated criminal drug conspiracy . . .; or

14. the murder was intentional and involved the infliction of torture . . .; or

15. the murder was committed as a result of the intentional discharge of a firearm by the defendant from a motor vehicle and the victim was not present within the motor vehicle; or

found the aggravating factor of murdering two or more individuals as provided in subsection (b)(3) and pronounced the death penalty sentence.[203]

§ 6.15. — Elements of First Degree Murder.

First degree murder exists in Illinois where a defendant (1) kills an individual (2) without lawful justification and (3) does so with either (a) the intent to kill, (b) the intent to do great bodily harm, (c) knowledge that his or her acts will kill, (d) knowledge that his or her acts will do great bodily harm, or (e) knowledge that his or her acts create a strong probability of death or great bodily harm, *or* where the defendant (4) kills an individual during the course of attempting or committing a forcible felony. These elements require further examination.

---

16. the murdered individual was 60 years of age or older and the death resulted from exceptionally brutal or heinous behavior indicative of wanton cruelty; or

17. the murdered individual was a disabled person and the defendant knew or should have known that the murdered individual was disabled. For purposes of this paragraph (17), "disabled person" means a person who suffers from a permanent physical or mental impairment resulting from disease, an injury, a functional disorder, or a congenital condition that renders the person incapable of adequately providing for his or her own health or personal care; or

18. the murder was committed by reason of any person's activity as a community policing volunteer or to prevent any person from engaging in activity as a community policing volunteer.

19. the murdered individual was subject to an order of protection and the murder was committed by a person against whom the same order of protection was issued under the Illinois Domestic Violence Act of 1986.

If certain mitigating factors (*see* 720 ILCS 5/9-1(c) (1999)) outweigh the aggravating factors, the death penalty will not be imposed. Such a determination is to be made at a sentencing hearing by a judge or jury. 720 ILCS 5/9-1(d) (1999).

The Illinois death penalty was struck down as unconstitutional in United States v. Silagy, 713 F. Supp. 1246 (C.D. Ill. 1989) on Eighth Amendment cruel and unusual punishment grounds, on the basis that the State's Attorney had too much discretion in deciding to pursue the death penalty. The following year, however, the Seventh Circuit reversed, holding that a prosecutor's decision to pursue a death penalty sentencing hearing amounted only to a decision to initiate the proceeding, and not a decision to impose a death sentence. Silagy v. Peters, 905 F.2d 986 (7th Cir. 1990). The appellate court rejected, therefore, the defendant's Eighth Amendment challenge. Meanwhile, the Illinois Supreme Court upheld the death penalty when faced with a similar challenge. People ex rel. Carey v. Cousins, 77 Ill. 2d 531, 397 N.E.2d 809 (1979). *See also* People v. Enoch, 146 Ill. 2d 44, 585 N.E.2d 115 (1991) (death penalty statute does not unconstitutionally remove sentencing discretion to not impose death penalty).

[203] People v. Gacy, 103 Ill. 2d 1, 104-07, 468 N.E.2d 1171, 1217-18 (1984), *cert. denied*, 470 U.S. 1037 (1985).

§ 6.16. ── ── Kills an Individual.

There is no first degree murder unless the accused kills an "individual."[204] In *People v. Greer*,[205] the Illinois Supreme Court defined "individual" as one who is "born alive."[206] In *Greer*, the state sought to prosecute as murder the killing of a fetus, of the gestational age of eight and one-half months, carried by its mother at the time of the defendant's shooting. However, the court stated:

> After considering the status of the unborn in the common law, the uniform decisions of the courts of last resort in our sister states, and the attitude toward the unborn reflected in our abortion statute, we conclude that taking the life of a fetus is not murder under our current statute unless the fetus is born alive and subsequently expires as a result of the injuries inflicted.[207]

In *People v. Ehlert*,[208] a mother was convicted of murdering her newborn infant where there was conflicting evidence whether the child had been born alive. The appellate court reversed inasmuch as the evidence offered by the state and instructions given to the jury suggested the mother's failure to seek prenatal care and medical care contributed to causing her baby to fail to survive the birth process.[209] Inasmuch as the jury may have surmised a murder conviction could be based on a mother's intended effort to kill her fetus or a mother's failure to seek medical care for her fetus before it was stillborn, the appellate court concluded her conviction was contrary to the principles established in *Greer*.[210]

In addition to addressing the question of when life begins for purposes of homicide, the Illinois Supreme Court has also considered the issue of when life ends. Although it is well settled that life ends when there is no heartbeat, no respiration or brain death, Illinois courts had not until recently faced the question of whether life has essentially ended when an individual, although still breathing and not clinically brain dead, is irreversibly comatose or in a persistent vegetative state.[211] Could a physician who discontinued life-sustaining measures, such as food and water, be held criminally responsible for the taking of a life in this type of situation?[212] Could a defendant succeed with a claim that where his 97-

---

[204] 720 ILCS 5/9-1(a) (1999).

[205] 79 Ill. 2d 103, 402 N.E.2d 203 (1980) (convicted of murder under the 1961 murder statute).

[206] People v. Greer, 79 Ill. 2d 103, 116, 402 N.E.2d 203, 209 (1980).

[207] People v. Greer, 79 Ill. 2d 103, 116, 402 N.E.2d 203, 209 (1980).

[208] 274 Ill. App. 3d 1026, 654 N.E.2d 705 (1st Dist. 1995).

[209] People v. Ehlert, 274 Ill. App. 3d 1026, 1034-35, 654 N.E.2d 705, 711-12 (1st Dist. 1995).

[210] People v. Ehlert, 274 Ill. App. 3d 1026, 1034-35, 654 N.E.2d 705, 711-12 (1st Dist. 1995).

[211] *See* People v. Caldwell, 295 Ill. App. 3d 172, 179-82, 692 N.E.2d 448, 453-55 (4th Dist. 1998).

[212] Barber v. Superior Court, 147 Cal. App. 3d 1006, 116-17, 195 Cal. Rptr. 484, 490 (1983) (indictment charging physician with murder and conspiracy to commit murder for disconnection of life support dismissed).

year-old beating victim made a conscious decision to be removed from a ventilator, rather than live with complete paralysis, the victim's decision to die and not his beating of her was the cause of death?[213]

In 1989, in *In re Estate of Longeway*,[214] the Illinois Supreme Court, in effect, answered "no," as long as certain specific guidelines were met. The court held the guardian of an incompetent patient could refuse or withdraw artificially administered food and water if: (1) the patient was terminally ill and in an irreversible coma or persistent vegetative state;[215] (2) the right of the patient to terminate life-sustaining measures outweighed any state interests;[216] (3) there was clear and convincing evidence that the patient would have made the decision to terminate the measures if he had been competent to do so;[217] and (4) there was judicial supervision to protect the rights of the involved parties.[218]

Meanwhile, the United States Supreme Court was confronted with a case similar to the facts in *Longeway*. In *Cruzan v. Director, Missouri Department of Health*,[219] the issue was limited to the question of whether the federal Constitution prohibited a Missouri court from requiring clear and convincing evidence of the patient's desire to withdraw life-sustaining treatment.[220] While holding that Missouri had the right to select this rule of law,[221] the Court stated the state did

---

[213] *See* People v. Caldwell, 295 Ill. App. 3d 172, 179-82, 692 N.E.2d 448, 453-55 (4th Dist. 1998).

[214] 133 Ill. 2d 33, 549 N.E.2d 292 (1989).

[215] In re Estate of Longeway, 133 Ill. 2d 33, 47, 549 N.E.2d 292, 298 (1989).

[216] In re Estate of Longeway, 133 Ill. 2d 33, 549 N.E.2d 292, 299 (1989).

[217] In re Estate of Longeway, 133 Ill. 2d 33, 49-51, 549 N.E.2d 292, 299-300 (1989).

[218] In re Estate of Longeway, 133 Ill. 2d 33, 51, 549 N.E.2d 292, 299-300 (1989). The *Longeway* criteria were applied in In re Estate of Greenspan, 137 Ill. 2d 1, 16, 558 N.E.2d 1194, 1201 (1990).

In 1988, the Illinois Living Will Act became law. 755 ILCS 35/1 *et seq.* (1999). This law allows an individual the authority to execute a will instructing his or her physician not to employ death delaying treatments if he or she in the future suffers from a "terminal condition," which is defined as "an incurable and irreversible condition which is such that death is imminent and the application of death delaying procedures serves only to prolong the dying process." *Id.*

In 1991, the Health Care Surrogate Act was enacted and amended in 1998. 755 ILCS 40/5 *et seq.* (1999). This statute was designed to establish a private non-judicial decision-making process under which a surrogate is chosen from a hierarchical list of possible surrogates to make life-sustaining medical treatment decisions for those who lack decision-making capacity and have not executed a living will or power of attorney for health care. *Id.* Obviously, a so-called "mercy-killing" by a family member remains illegal. *See* People v. Williams, 265 Ill. App. 3d 283, 638 N.E. 2d 345 (1st Dist. 1994) (defendant's fatal shooting of his wife, who had been suffering from multiple sclerosis for many years, constituted second degree murder).

[219] 497 U.S. 261 (1990).

[220] Cruzan v. Director, Missouri Department of Health, 497 U.S. 261, 268 (1990).

[221] Cruzan v. Director, Missouri Department of Health, 497 U.S. 261, 284 (1990).

not have to accept the "substituted judgment" of close family members where the wishes of the patient were unclear.[222]

In the context of criminal prosecution, there are notable Illinois appellate court rulings. First, the caselaw recognizes the existence of dual standards for determining death: (1) irreversible cessation of circulatory and respiratory functions and (2) irreversible cessation of total brain functions.[223] Thus, where defendant struck his victim in the head with a two by four, which resulted in a diagnosis of brain death, the victim's death was considered the result of the blunt force injuries to the victim's head caused by defendant and not the premature termination of life support measures at the hospital.[224] Second, even where the victim is not clinically dead, the discontinuance of futile life support is not considered the cause of death where a competent person has exercised his or her right to refuse all types of medical treatment, including life-saving or life-sustaining procedures, after this person has been placed on a ventilator or respirator as a result of a defendant's criminality.[225] Thus, where a defendant struck his 97-year-old victim with a skillet that broke her neck and severed her spinal cord, her conscious decision that she be taken off life support, rather than live with complete paralysis, was a natural and foreseeable result of defendant's criminal act and not a superseding cause that would preclude defendant's conviction.[226]

Obviously, a person is an "individual" within the meaning of the statute even though he or she was not the individual that the defendant intended to kill or thought he or she was killing.[227] Since the legislature was determined to recognize the doctrine of "transferred intent"[228] if a person without legal justification or excuse shoots at one individual and inadvertently kills another, that person is guilty of the same degree of unlawful homicide as if he or she had killed the person who was the object of his or her aim.[229]

---

[222] Cruzan v. Director, Missouri Department of Health, 497 U.S. 261, 286 (1990).

[223] People v. Lara, 289 Ill. App. 3d 675, 681, 683 N.E.2d 480, 483-84 (1st Dist. 1997).

[224] People v. Lara, 289 Ill. App. 3d 675, 681, 683 N.E.2d 480, 483-84 (1st Dist. 1997) (second degree murder conviction affirmed).

[225] People v. Caldwell, 295 Ill. App. 3d 172, 181, 692 N.E.2d 448, 455 (4th Dist. 1998).

[226] People v. Caldwell, 295 Ill. App. 3d 172, 181, 692 N.E.2d 448, 455 (4th Dist. 1998) (involuntary manslaughter conviction affirmed).

[227] People v. Marshall, 398 Ill. 256, 263, 75 N.E.2d 310, 313 (1947).

[228] ILL. ANN. STAT. ch. 38, para. 9-1 (Smith-Hurd 1979), 1961 Committee Comments, at 18 (revised 1972). See ch. 2 for a discussion of this concept.

[229] People v. Johnson, 66 Ill. App. 3d 84, 92, 383 N.E.2d 648, 655 (5th Dist. 1978) (the defendant was convicted of murder where he shot toward one person but killed another). Compare People v. Adams, 9 Ill. App. 3d 61, 63-64, 291 N.E.2d 54, 55-56 (5th Dist. 1972) (defendant was exonerated of the shooting of a woman whom he killed while attempting to kill another individual in self-defense).

§ 6.17. —— Without Lawful Justification.

The terms of paragraph 5/9-1 require that the killing of another be "without lawful justification."[230] For example, if a defendant justifiably killed another in self-defense, he or she could not be convicted of first degree murder.[231] However, this language merely refers to affirmative defenses the defendant could interpose once charged; accordingly, the state is under no obligation to affirmatively prove in each first degree murder prosecution that the killing was without lawful justification unless the accused offers some evidence that his or her killing was justified.[232] Thus, the state's failure to allege that the killing occurred without lawful justification in its charging instrument or to offer evidence at trial in this respect where no defense claim is advanced was not reversible error.[233] In order to raise the issue of lawful justification, the accused is required to offer evidence in support of a defense.[234]

§ 6.18. —— Without Mitigating Factors.

The presence of certain mitigating factors can reduce what would otherwise be first degree murder to second degree murder.[235] Specifically, if a defendant kills another while acting under a sudden and intense passion resulting from a serious provocation, he will be convicted of second degree murder.[236] Similarly, if a defendant kills another while subjectively believing it is justifiable, such as where he believes his killing is in self defense, but his killing is not objectively reasonable, he will be convicted of second degree murder.[237] However, the burden of proof is *on the defendant* to prove either mitigating factor by a prepon-

---

[230] 720 ILCS 5/9-1(a) (1999).

[231] *See* ch. 17 for a discussion of self-defense.

[232] People v. Williams, 80 Ill. App. 3d 963, 969, 400 N.E.2d 532, 536 (5th Dist. 1980) (murder conviction affirmed).

[233] People v. Williams, 80 Ill. App. 3d 963, 969, 400 N.E.2d 532, 536-37 (5th Dist. 1980) (the failure to allege "without lawful justification" in the charging instrument is a "formal defect," and the failure of the state to prove at trial where no evidence of justification is presented is not error). However, where evidence of justification exists, a "without lawful justification" instruction must be given. People v. Thruman, 104 Ill. 2d 326, 331, 472 N.E.2d 414, 417 (1984) (failure to provide jury instruction was reversible error).

[234] People v. Williams, 80 Ill. App. 3d 963, 969, 400 N.E.2d 532, 537 (5th Dist. 1980). *See also* 720 ILCS 5/3-2(a) (1999) ("[U]nless the state's evidence raises the issue involving the alleged defense, the defendant, to raise the issue, must present some evidence thereon").

[235] *See, e.g.,* People v. Mitchell, 221 Ill. App. 3d 926, 931-32, 583 N.E.2d 78, 81 (1st Dist. 1991) (imperfect defense second degree murder conviction affirmed), *cert. denied*, 505 U.S. 208 (1992).

[236] 720 ILCS 5/9-2(a)(1) (1999).

[237] 720 ILCS 5/9-2(a)(2) (1999).

derance of evidence before he can be found guilty of second degree murder.[238] Thus, the mitigating factors set forth in the second degree murder statute are *not* elements of first degree murder to be disproved beyond a reasonable doubt by the state.[239] In other words, it is not incumbent on the state in proving the elements of first degree murder to prove the non-existence of the mitigating factors of second degree murder.[240] Obviously, the mitigating factors which lead to a second degree murder conviction will be examined in depth later in this chapter.

§ 6.19. — Mens Rea: Intent or Knowledge.

Although the defendant can be convicted of first degree murder where he or she had the intent to kill[241] or intent to inflict great bodily harm,[242] mere knowledge that his or her actions create a strong probability of death or great bodily injury is sufficient.[243] Moreover, because of the operation of subparagraph (a)(2) of the first degree murder statute, it is not necessary to directly prove that the defendant had a conscious intent to murder; all that need be proven is that he or she voluntarily and willfully committed an act, the natural tendency of which was to terminate another's life[244] or to inflict great bodily harm.[245] Thus, where a

---

[238] 720 ILCS 5/9-2(c) (1999). This statutory arrangement has survived various constitutional challenges. *See* People v. Jeffries, 164 Ill. 2d 104, 114-24, 646 N.E.2d 587, 592-96 (1995) (not violative of federal or state due process); People v. Wright, 218 Ill. App. 3d 764, 776-78, 578 N.E.2d 1090, 1098-100 (1st Dist. 1991) (placing burden on defendant to show mitigating factors does not violate due process, equal protection or separation of powers). *See also* § 6.23 of this chapter for additional decisions.

[239] People v. Willis, 217 Ill. App. 3d 909, 925, 577 N.E.2d 1215, 1225 (1st Dist. 1991).

[240] People v. Willis, 217 Ill. App. 3d 909, 925, 577 N.E.2d 1215, 1225 (1st Dist. 1991).

[241] People v. Salazar, 126 Ill. 2d 424, 454, 535 N.E.2d 766, 778 (1988) (intent to kill police officer sufficient for murder supported by defendant's shooting of officer five times at close range), *cert. denied*, 515 U.S. 1116 (1989).

[242] People v. Summers, 202 Ill. App. 3d 1, 10-11, 559 N.E.2d 1133, 1139 (4th Dist. 1990) (where defendant "wanted to hurt" his child "badly" and did so by administering a 70 foot-pound blow to the victim's head, this was sufficient for first degree murder). In most instances where it appears the defendant's mental state reflected the intent to inflict great bodily injury, the appellate court actually analyzes the charge by inquiring as to whether the defendant *knew* his acts created a strong probability of death or great bodily injury; (*see, e.g., id.* at 10-11; 599 N.E.2d at 1138-39); or does not clearly specify which mental state existed (*see, e.g,* People v. Johnson, 206 Ill. App. 3d 875, 880, 564 N.E.2d 1310, 1313 (1st Dist. 1990) ("Intent to commit the offense of murder" established where defendant threw a full milk bottle at a 17-month-old child and beat her in the stomach)).

[243] People v. King, 109 Ill. 2d 514, 542, 488 N.E.2d 949, 963 (defendant shooting loaded gun at victim's head at close range satisfies knowledge requirement), *cert. denied*, 479 U.S. 872, *rehearing denied*, 479 U.S. 956 (1986).

[244] People v. Colclasure, 200 Ill. App. 3d 1038, 1043, 558 N.E.2d 705, 709 (5th Dist. 1990) (first degree murder conviction affirmed).

[245] People v. Steffens, 131 Ill. App. 3d 141, 148, 475 N.E.2d 606, 613 (1st Dist. 1985) (murder conviction affirmed).

defendant threw a full milk bottle at a seventeen-month-old infant and struck her in the stomach, the jury could properly infer that defendant knew that his conduct would create a strong probability of death or great bodily harm.[246] Similarly, a mental state sufficient for first degree murder could be inferred where the accused handcuffed and buried a victim underground in a wooden box where the victim suffocated and died;[247] where a defendant shook a six-month-old baby so violently that it caused internal bleeding and broke two ribs, and then threw the baby across a room;[248] where a defendant repeatedly struck a fifteen-month-old infant with his fist and brutally sexually assaulted her;[249] where a defendant beat and starved his two infant daughters for a period of four or five days;[250] where an accused beat a twenty-three-month old child with a blunt instrument at least a dozen times;[251] where an eighteen-year-old male defendant, approximately six feet tall and weighing 180 pounds, struck a twenty-three-month old child who died of multiple injuries, causing a blunt trauma of type seen in automobile accident or in a child who had fallen out of third story window;[252] where a defendant inflicted three stab wounds, including two deep wounds, on his victim;[253] where a defendant shot a shotgun toward one person, apparently trying to scare him, and fatally injured another person nearby;[254] where the accused picked up and cocked a rifle intending to scare his live-in girlfriend and, when a struggle ensued with his finger on the trigger, she was shot and killed;[255] where an accused placed a pillow over the face of the victim, who was tied up, while attempting to "hypnotize" him, with the result of suffocating him;[256] and where a

---

[246] People v. Johnson, 206 Ill. App. 3d 875, 880, 564 N.E.2d 1310, 1313 (1st Dist. 1990) (murder conviction affirmed).

[247] People v. Edwards, 144 Ill. 2d 108, 172-74, 579 N.E.2d 336, 363-64 (1991) (first degree murder sufficient to warrant death penalty affirmed).

[248] People v. Myrick, 274 Ill. App. 3d 983, 986, 651 N.E. 2d 637, 640 (1st Dist. 1995) (first degree murder conviction affirmed).

[249] People v. Terrell, 132 Ill. 2d 178, 205, 547 N.E.2d 145, 156 (murder conviction affirmed), cert. denied, 495 U.S. 959 (1989).

[250] People v. Battles, 93 Ill. App. 3d 1093, 1098, 418 N.E.2d 22, 25 (1st Dist. 1981) (conviction of two counts of murder affirmed).

[251] People v. Palmer, 76 Ill. App. 3d 1014, 1026, 395 N.E.2d 713, 721-22 (5th Dist. 1979) (murder conviction affirmed).

[252] People v. Reed, 298 Ill. App. 3d 285, 304-05, 698 N.E.2d 620, 634-35 (1st Dist. 1998) (first degree murder conviction affirmed).

[253] People v. Dunnigan, 89 Ill. App. 3d 763, 765-66, 412 N.E. 37, 38-39 (3d Dist. 1980) (murder conviction affirmed).

[254] People v. Johnson, 66 Ill. App. 3d 84, 92, 383 N.E.2d 648, 655 (5th Dist. 1978) (murder conviction affirmed).

[255] People v. Colclasure, 200 Ill. App. 3d 1038, 1044, 558 N.E.2d 705, 709 (5th Dist. 1990) (first degree murder conviction affirmed).

[256] People v. Johnson, 33 Ill. App. 3d 168, 174, 337 N.E.2d 240, 244-45 (4th Dist. 1975) (murder conviction affirmed).

defendant attempted to strangle a woman he encountered during the course of a burglary of her premises and the woman jumped out of a window to her death in an effort to escape.[257]

It is a well accepted principle that intent or knowledge can be implied or inferred from other attendant circumstances.[258] For example, when a defendant intentionally uses a deadly weapon upon his victim, it can be inferred he intended to cause the death of the victim.[259] Similarly, a blow with a bare fist where there is great disparity in size and strength between the accused and the victim may evince the existence of the mental state necessary for murder.[260] Where a defendant went through a red light at 70 miles per hour, striking a car that was in the cross traffic, killing the victims, the court concluded that the defendant knew his actions created a strong probability of death or great bodily harm sufficient for murder.[261] Where defendant's vehicle during a traffic dispute chased down the victim's vehicle, swerved toward the victim's vehicle and bumped or pushed the victim's vehicle off the road while traveling 65 to 70 miles per hour, causing the victim's vehicle to roll over and kill the victim, defendant's conduct had created a strong probability of death or great bodily harm making him liable for first degree murder.[262] Where defendant started two fires late at night on the lower floors of a house, one of which was beneath the only set of stairs that led to the upper level, while realizing unattended children slept on the upper level, the defendant knew with a reasonable certainty that his actions would cause death or great bodily harm sufficient for first degree murder.[263] Whether the defendant has the requisite mental state is a question for the trier of fact.[264]

---

[257] People v. Smith, 56 Ill. 2d 328, 333-34, 307 N.E.2d 353, 355-56 (1974) (murder conviction affirmed).

[258] People v. Colclasure, 200 Ill. App. 3d 1038, 1043-44, 558 N.E.2d 705, 709 (5th Dist. 1990) (first degree murder affirmed).

[259] People v. Salazar, 126 Ill. 2d 424, 449, 535 N.E.2d 766, 776 (1988) (murder conviction affirmed), *cert. denied*, 515 U.S. 1116 (1990).

[260] People v. Terrell, 132 Ill. 2d 178, 204, 547 N.E.2d 145, 156 (murder conviction affirmed), *cert. denied*, 495 U.S. 959 (1989).

[261] People v. Thomas, 266 Ill. App. 3d 914, 926-27, 641 N.E.2d 867, 876-77 (1st Dist. 1994) (first degree murder conviction affirmed).

[262] People v. Soteras, 295 Ill. App. 3d 610, 620-21, 693 N.E.2d 400, 407 (2d Dist. 1998) (first degree murder conviction affirmed).

[263] People v. Howery, 178 Ill. 2d 1, 39-45, 687 N.E.2d 836, 854-57 (1997) (first degree murder convictions affirmed).

[264] People v. Colclasure, 200 Ill. App. 3d 1038, 1044, 558 N.E.2d 705, 709 (5th Dist. 1990) (first degree murder affirmed).

§ 6.20. — Actus Reus.

Obviously, first degree murder can arise from a wide variety of circumstances. The most typical murder involves the use of a deadly weapon, such as a gun,[265] knife,[266] baseball bat,[267] hatchet,[268] or scissors.[269] Even a weed cutter,[270] a pool cue,[271] or a piece of asphalt[272] has been used. When a deadly weapon has been intentionally used by a defendant in his or her attack on the victim, there is a presumption that the defendant knew that his or her acts would create a strong probability of death or great bodily harm.[273] Although an automobile is not commonly thought of as a deadly weapon, where the accused swerved his car toward his victim, ran over his victim, and dragged his victim underneath his car for almost a block, this conduct created a strong probability of death or great bodily injury for a charge of murder.[274]

Of course, the crime of first degree murder can also arise where no deadly weapon is used, as where the accused suffocates,[275] drowns,[276] or hangs[277] the

---

[265] *See, e.g.,* People v. Hartzol, 222 Ill. App. 3d 631, 645, 584 N.E.2d 291, 302 (1st Dist. 1991) (murder conviction affirmed).

[266] *See, e.g.,* People v. Kyse, 220 Ill. App. 3d 971, 972-73, 581 N.E.2d 285, 286 (4th Dist. 1991) (first degree murder conviction affirmed).

[267] *See, e.g.,* People v. Nitz, 143 Ill. 2d 82, 97, 572 N.E.2d 895, 904 (first degree murder conviction affirmed), *cert. denied,* 502 U.S. 1139 (1991).

[268] *See, e.g.,* People v. Reddock, 13 Ill. App. 3d 296, 301-02, 300 N.E.2d 31, 36 (2d Dist. 1973) (murder conviction affirmed).

[269] *See, e.g.,* People v. Doss, 214 Ill. App. 3d 1051, 1053-54, 574 N.E.2d 806, 808 (1st Dist. 1991) (first degree murder conviction affirmed).

[270] People v. Bryant, 212 Ill. App. 3d 452, 453, 570 N.E.2d 1270, 1271 (5th Dist. 1991) (first degree murder conviction affirmed).

[271] People v. Spagnola, 123 Ill. App. 2d 171, 181-82, 260 N.E.2d 20, 24-25 (1st Dist. 1970) (murder conviction affirmed), *cert. denied,* 402 U.S. 911 (1971).

[272] People v. Balfour, 148 Ill. App. 3d 215, 218-20, 498 N.E.2d 547, 550-52 (1st Dist. 1986) (murder conviction affirmed).

[273] People v. Colley, 83 Ill. App. 3d 834, 837-38, 404 N.E.2d 378, 380-81 (1st Dist. 1980) (murder conviction affirmed where defendant fired six shots through tavern door, knew tavern was occupied, and knew destructive power of his .38 caliber weapon). *Compare* People v. Gresham, 78 Ill. App. 3d 1003, 1007, 398 N.E.2d 398, 401-02 (3d Dist. 1979) (no presumption of death or great bodily injury where accused uses "non-lethal weapon;" murder conviction later reversed due to trial court's failure to instruct on involuntary manslaughter.

[274] People v. Steffens, 131 Ill. App. 3d 141, 148, 475 N.E.2d 606, 613 (1st Dist. 1985). *See also* People v. Batson, 144 Ill. App. 3d 1027, 1035-36, 495 N.E.2d 154, 160-61 (5th Dist. 1986) (where defendant backed up her car in direction of victim at high rate of speed while knowing victim was within close proximity to her car, this could amount to murder).

[275] People v. Fickett, 204 Ill. App. 3d 220, 232-33, 562 N.E.2d 238, 245-46 (1st Dist. 1990) (murder conviction affirmed).

[276] People v. Feagans, 134 Ill. App. 3d 252, 254, 480 N.E.2d 153, 155 (4th Dist. 1985) (murder conviction affirmed).

[277] People v. Gangestad, 105 Ill. App. 3d 774, 776-78, 434 N.E.2d 841, 845-46 (2d Dist. 1982) (murder conviction affirmed).

victim. More difficult is the situation in which the accused uses his or her bare fist to kill the victim. In some earlier cases, killing another with one's fist was not considered murder but rather involuntary manslaughter, since it was said that death was not a reasonable or probable consequence of a blow with a bare fist.[278] On the other had, repeatedly beating a victim with fists has resulted in a finding of murder.[279] Striking a 15-month-old infant with a bare fist can constitute murder.[280] So too, a great disparity between the size and strength of a victim and an attacker can warrant a conviction for first degree murder where bare fists are employed.[281] For instance, where an accused allegedly inflicted upon the head of his nineteen-month-old step-son a single 70 foot-pound blow with his fist, which caused the child's death, the defendant's conviction for first degree murder was upheld since the defendant should have known that striking the infant with such force would result in death.[282] Similarly, where the defendant, a twenty-one-year-old male, who was six feet, three inches tall and weighed 170 pounds, beat with his fists an eighty-five-year-old woman, who later died from her injuries, this conduct created a strong probability of death or great bodily injury and, accordingly, the defendant was properly convicted of murder.[283]

Actions that do not create an *imminent* threat of death may satisfy the actus reus of a first degree murder charge. For example, in *People v. Banks*,[284] the court upheld a first degree murder conviction against the defendant for the death of his live-in girlfriend's sixteen-month-old daughter who died of profound hypothermia and starvation.[285] The court found 1) controlling the amount of formula given to the victim by snatching the bottle from the infant's mouth while the mother was feeding her, 2) keeping the victim in an unheated room wearing only a diaper and a thin t-shirt during the months of November and December

---

[278] People v. Gresham, 78 Ill. App. 3d 1003, 1007, 398 N.E.2d 398, 401-02 (3d Dist. 1979) ("death is not a reasonable or probable consequence of a blow with a bare fist"); People v. Crenshaw, 298 Ill. 412, 416-17, 131 N.E. 576, 577-78 (1921) (not murder). *But see* People v. Freeman, 78 Ill. App. 2d 242, 246, 223 N.E.2d 444, 446-47 (1st Dist. 1966) (causing death by punching victim in stomach constituted murder).

[279] People v. Terrell, 132 Ill. 2d 178, 205, 547 N.E.2d 145, 156 (murder conviction affirmed where defendant repeatedly beat in stomach and sexually assaulted a 15-month-old child), *cert. denied*, 495 U.S. 959 (1989).

[280] People v. Terrell, 132 Ill. 2d 178, 205, 547 N.E.2d 145, 156, *cert. denied*, 495 U.S. 959 (1989); *see also* People v. Szerletich, 86 Ill. App. 3d 1121, 1124, 408 N.E.2d 1098, 1101 (4th Dist. 1980) (striking one-year-old child with bare fist constituted murder).

[281] People v. Drumheller, 15 Ill. App. 3d 418, 421, 304 N.E.2d 455, 458 (2d Dist. 1973) (murder conviction affirmed).

[282] People v. Summers, 202 Ill. App. 3d 1, 10-11, 559 N.E.2d 1133, 1138-39 (4th Dist. 1990) (first degree murder conviction affirmed).

[283] People v. Brackett, 117 Ill. 2d 170, 180, 510 N.E.2d 877, 882 (1987) (murder conviction affirmed).

[284] 161 Ill. 2d 119, 641 N.E.2d 331 (1994).

[285] People v. Banks, 161 Ill. 2d 119, 133-36, 641 N.E.2d 331, 338-39 (1994).

and 3) intentionally preventing the mother from coming to the aid of the child to be sufficiently life-threatening to support a first degree murder conviction.[286]

§ 6.21. — Corpus Delecti and Causation.

The corpus delecti in a criminal homicide consists of two elements: (1) the fact of death and (2) the fact that the death was produced by the criminal agency of some person.[287] Proof of the fact of death does not require the production of the body or direct proof of death.[288] Where the state is unable to present such direct evidence of death, circumstantial evidence will be sufficient.[289] For example, where the death of a baby could not be directly proven in circumstances in which it was believed that the infant's body was dumped into a trash compactor, but where other evidence linked the defendant to the murder of her baby, the defendant was properly convicted of murder.[290]

Where cause of death cannot be determined positively from the remains of a victim, the corpus delecti may still be proven.[291] Where a body found in a cornfield was reduced to skeletal remains before being discovered, thereby making a cause-of-death determination impossible, the corpus delecti was established beyond a reasonable doubt based on (1) testimony that the boy had been seen alive at a place where, according to the defendant's statement, the boy had entered the defendant's automobile; (2) the location of the boy's body where the defendant claimed to have abandoned it; and (3) the flight of the defendant following questioning by the police.[292]

---

[286] People v. Banks, 161 Ill. 2d 119, 133-36, 641 N.E.2d 331, 338-39 (1994).

[287] People v. Avery, 88 Ill. App. 3d 771, 777, 410 N.E.2d 1093, 1098 (1st Dist. 1980); People v. Banks, 287 Ill. App. 3d 273, 286-87, 678 N.E.2d 348, 357 (2d Dist. 1997):

> Proof of guilt for a criminal offense may be divided conceptually into proof that an injury or loss occurred, that the cause of the loss was criminal in nature, and that the accused was the offender. * * * The first two components — the occurrence of the injury or loss and its causation by criminal conduct — are termed the *corpus delecti*; the identity of the accused as the offender, the ultimate issue, is not considered part of the *corpus delecti*.

[288] People v. Avery, 88 Ill. App. 3d 771, 777, 410 N.E.2d 1093, 1098 (1st Dist. 1980) (murder conviction affirmed).

[289] People v. Avery, 88 Ill. App. 3d 771, 777, 410 N.E.2d 1093, 1098 (1st Dist. 1980).

[290] People v. Avery, 88 Ill. App. 3d 771, 777, 410 N.E.2d 1093, 1098 (1st Dist. 1980) (murder conviction affirmed). *Cf.* People v. Martin, 26 Ill. 2d 547, 548-50, 188 N.E.2d 4, 5-6 (1963) (murder conviction reversed where serious doubt existed both as to criminal agency and causation).

[291] People v. Milner, 123 Ill. App. 3d 656, 662-63, 463 N.E.2d 148, 153-54 (3d Dist. 1984) (although no medical expert testimony positively showed defendant killed child by shaking child, corpus delecti necessary for involuntary manslaughter conviction established through other evidence).

[292] People v. Jones, 26 Ill. 2d 381, 385-87, 186 N.E.2d 246, 249-50 (1962) (murder conviction affirmed).

The corpus delecti cannot be based solely on the defendant's extrajudicial confession or admission.[293] However, if there is evidence outside the confession that corroborates the confession to the crime, then the corpus delecti and murder can be established.[294] In addition, the corpus delecti may be proven by the defendant's own testimony, even in defense, given at trial.[295]

Related to this concern are the problems of *causation*. Where the state shows the existence of an act committed by the accused that is sufficient to cause death, the subsequent death of the victim is presumed to have resulted from the act unless it appears that the death was caused by a supervening act disconnected from the acts of the accused.[296] Thus, where defendants failed to point to any evidence suggesting the victim of their beating did not die as a consequence of their blows, the trier of fact properly attributed the victim's death to the defendants' beating of the victim.[297] In a case such as this where there is no intervening act or phenomena to which the death could be attributable, the cause is usually described as the "direct cause."[298]

The injuries inflicted by the accused need not be the sole or immediate cause of death to legally constitute a cause of death.[299] Unless some intervening act or phenomenon is a "supervening"[300] or an "independent"[301] act disconnected from the acts of the accused, the defendant's acts will be considered the cause of death.[302] A reasonable doubt regarding causation does not exist merely because other factors may have contributed to the death or because a person without the

---

[293] People v. Holmes, 67 Ill. 2d 236, 239-40, 367 N.E.2d 663, 665 (1977) (quoting People v. Norcutt, 44 Ill. 2d 256, 263, 255 N.E.2d 442, 446 (1970)). *See, e.g.,* People v. Lueder, 3 Ill. 2d 487, 489, 121 N.E.2d 743, 744 (1954) (defendant's confession alone insufficient to prove crime of burning a building).

[294] People v. Dodds, 190 Ill. App. 3d 1083, 1096, 547 N.E.2d 523, 533 (1st Dist. 1989) (murder conviction affirmed); People v. Pena, 174 Ill. App. 3d 281, 286, 528 N.E.2d 325, 329 (1st Dist. 1988) (murder conviction affirmed).

[295] People v. Neal, 98 Ill. App. 2d 454, 458, 240 N.E.2d 784, 786 (1st Dist. 1968) (murder conviction affirmed).

[296] People v. Dixon, 78 Ill. App. 3d 73, 78-79, 397 N.E.2d 45, 49 (1st Dist. 1979) (murder conviction affirmed).

[297] People v. Dillon, 28 Ill. App. 3d 11, 19-20, 327 N.E.2d 225, 232 (1st Dist. 1975) (voluntary manslaughter convictions affirmed).

[298] WAYNE LAFAVE & AUSTIN SCOTT, CRIMINAL LAW § 3.12(f)(1) (2d ed. 1986).

[299] People v. Gant, 202 Ill. App. 3d 218, 222, 559 N.E.2d 923, 926 (1st Dist. 1990) (conviction for two counts of murder affirmed).

[300] People v. Dixon, 78 Ill. App. 3d 73, 78-79, 397 N.E.2d 45, 49 (1st Dist. 1979) (murder conviction affirmed).

[301] People v. Brown, 9 Ill. App. 3d 730, 735, 293 N.E.2d 1, 4 (2d Dist. 1973) (involuntary manslaughter conviction affirmed).

[302] People v. Brown, 9 Ill. App. 3d 730, 735, 293 N.E.2d 1, 4 (2d Dist. 1973).

victim's medical history might not have died from the trauma.[303] Where a pathologist's uncontradicted testimony attributed the death of a person to a severe beating inflicted by the accused in combination with other factors, namely, the victim's high alcohol level and asphyxiation caused by the fact that the victim's blood did not properly coagulate, this intervening phenomenon did not break the chain of causation between the defendant's acts and the death.[304] A homicide conviction also stood where the defendant's criminal agency triggered a death, even though the defendant's blow would not have killed a man who was in good health.[305] The fact that there was an interval of perhaps twenty-four to thirty-six hours between a fight in which the victim was severely injured and his death did not undermine the finding that the defendant's acts were the cause of death.[306] Where the defendant beat and raped an eighty-five-year old, who died five weeks later of asphyxiation while being fed in a nursing home, this circumstance did not relieve the defendant of a felony-murder given the weak condition of the victim.[307] Where the immediate cause of the victim's death, such as meningitis,[308] pneumonia,[309] or a heart attack,[310] was traceable to defendant's felonious injury to his victim, he will be responsible for a homicide. So too, where the victim of a shooting died as an immediate result of pulmonary thromboembolism, which is a common complication or result of a severe injury and the type of surgery the victim had experienced after the shooting, the defendant was held to have caused the victim's death.[311]

---

[303] People v. Gant, 202 Ill. App. 3d 218, 223, 559 N.E.2d 923, 926 (1st Dist. 1990) (conviction for murder affirmed notwithstanding victim's high blood pressure which may have contributed to her death).

[304] People v. Brown, 9 Ill. App. 3d 730, 735, 293 N.E.2d 1, 4 (2d Dist. 1973) (involuntary manslaughter conviction affirmed).

[305] People v. Humble, 18 Ill. App. 3d 446, 451, 310 N.E.2d 51, 55 (5th Dist. 1974) (voluntary manslaughter conviction affirmed).

[306] People v. Dillon, 28 Ill. App. 3d 11, 20, 327 N.E.2d 225, 232 (1st Dist. 1975) (voluntary manslaughter convictions affirmed).

[307] People v. Brackett, 117 Ill. 2d 170, 175-79, 510 N.E.2d 877, 880-82 (1987) (murder conviction affirmed).

[308] People v. Paulson, 80 Ill. App. 2d 44, 47-49, 225 N.E.2d 424, 426-27 (1st Dist. 1967) (murder conviction affirmed).

[309] People v. Gulliford, 86 Ill. App. 3d 237, 240, 407 N.E.2d 1094, 1098 (3d Dist. 1980) (murder conviction affirmed). *See also* People v. Love, 71 Ill. 2d 74, 84, 373 N.E.2d 1312, 1318 (1978) (victim's death from pneumonia and mild peronitis caused by exploratory laparatomy and splenectomy that victim underwent as result of defendant's kicks of her abdomen; voluntary manslaughter conviction affirmed).

[310] People v. Fuller, 141 Ill. App. 3d 737, 745-50, 490 N.E.2d 977, 984-87 (3d Dist. 1986) (murder conviction affirmed).

[311] People v. Gacho, 122 Ill. 2d 221, 244-45, 522 N.E.2d 1146, 1156-57 (murder conviction affirmed), *cert. denied*, 488 U.S. 910 (1988).

In terms of intervening acts, the courts are often faced with arguments that the negligent treatment of a wound suffered by a victim was a supervening or independent act that broke the chain of causation.[312] However,

> it is the generally recognized principle that where a person inflicts upon another a wound which is dangerous, that is, calculated to endanger or destroy life, it is no defense to a charge of homicide that the alleged victim's death was contributed to by, or immediately resulted from, unskillful or improper treatment of the wound or injury by attending physicians or surgeons.[313]

Where, for example, the victim sustained multiple severe injuries after being struck by an intoxicated defendant's automobile, the fact that a defective Ambu bag (a manual device used to artificially ventilate the victim) may have been used on the victim did not constitute a supervening or independent intervening act.[314] As a related matter, once a mortally wounded victim's brainwave activity ceases to exist, the cause of the victim's death will be attributed to the defendant who inflicted the wound on the victim, not to the removal of the victim from a respirator.[315] Thus, where the victim's death was the result of being hit on the head by a two by four by the defendant, the cause of death was not the result of premature termination of life support measures at the hospital where there existed "irreversible cessation of total brain function" or brain death.[316] Similarly, a conscious decision by a ninety-seven-year old assault victim, executed in a living will, to be removed from life support rather than live with complete paralysis, was a natural and foreseeable result of defendant's criminal conduct, rather than a superseding cause of the victim's death.[317]

In some cases, it might be claimed that the victim's own actions were a supervening, intervening cause. However, where the victim's acts are attributable to the defendant's actions, murder will still lie. Where a defendant attempted to strangle a victim in her home when he encountered her during the course of a burglary and, in order to escape his efforts, she jumped out of a window to her

---

[312] *See, e.g.,* People v. Stamps, 8 Ill. App. 3d 896, 901-02, 291 N.E.2d 274, 279-80 (1st Dist. 1972) (murder conviction affirmed).

[313] People v. Dixon, 78 Ill. App. 3d 73, 79, 397 N.E.2d 45, 49 (1st Dist. 1979) (murder conviction affirmed); People v. Stamps, 8 Ill. App. 3d 896, 901-02, 291 N.E.2d 274, 279-80 (1st Dist. 1972) (murder conviction affirmed).

[314] People v. Robinson, 199 Ill. App. 3d 494, 503, 557 N.E.2d 396, 402 (1st Dist. 1990) (reckless homicide conviction affirmed).

[315] People v. Driver, 62 Ill. App. 3d 847, 851, 379 N.E.2d 840, 844-45 (4th Dist. 1978) (murder conviction affirmed).

[316] People v. Lara, 289 Ill. App. 3d 675, 680-82, 683 N.E.2d 480, 483-84 (1st Dist. 1997) (second degree murder conviction affirmed).

[317] People v. Caldwell, 295 Ill. App. 3d 172, 179-82, 692 N.E.2d 448, 453-55 (4th Dist. 1998) (involuntary manslaughter conviction affirmed).

death, the defendant was still liable for murder.[318] Thus, although the victim's actions might be described as a contributing cause of her death, they were *dependent* intervening acts that did not sever the chain of causation.

Finally, in some cases, a death may be attributable to more than one defendant, such as where two criminal perpetrators beat the same victim.[319] In a non-homicide case, where defendant picked up a child and held the child in front of himself to shield himself from bullets being shot at him by an assailant, defendant's conduct was a *contributing* cause of the child's injuries.[320]

In summary, where there is no intervening force between the infliction of injury upon a victim and the victim's resultant death, the force will be deemed the *direct* cause of death. If there is an intervening act or contributing cause, it must be a *supervening* or *independent* intervening cause to break the chain of causation. If the intervening act is a *dependent* intervening cause that naturally and foreseeably flows from the defendant's original act, it will not break the chain of causation. If there is another *contributing* cause that accounts in part for the death, this does not sever liability. In the final analysis, if the defendant's actions are considered the cause or one of the causes of death, they are described as the *proximate* cause.

§ 6.22. — Felony-Murder Rule.

A person may be convicted under the Illinois felony-murder rule, by reason of subparagraph (a)(3) of paragraph 5/9-1, if a death occurs when a defendant is committing or attempting to commit a forcible felony other than second degree murder.[321] The felony-murder rule is operative in Illinois even though the under-

---

[318] People v. Smith, 56 Ill. 2d 328, 333-34, 307 N.E.2d 353, 355-56 (1974) (murder conviction affirmed).

[319] People v. Wieland, 123 Ill. App. 3d 576, 583, 462 N.E.2d 1256, 1261 (4th Dist. 1984) (defendant's beating of victim, along with codefendant's beating, was at minimum illegal contributing cause of death; murder conviction affirmed).

[320] People v. Hall, 273 Ill. App. 3d 838, 841-42, 652 N.E.2d 1266, 1269 (1st Dist. 1995) (defendant's conviction for aggravated battery of a child affirmed).

[321] 720 ILCS 5/9-1(a)(3) (1999). A "forcible felony" is defined as including "treason, first degree murder, second degree murder, predatory criminal sexual assault of a child, aggravated criminal sexual assault, criminal sexual assault, robbery, burglary, residential burglary, aggravated arson, arson, aggravated kidnapping, kidnapping, aggravated battery resulting in great bodily harm or permanent disability or disfigurement and any other felony which involves the use or threat of physical force or violence against any individual." 720 ILCS 5/2-8 (1999). This represents a change from the common law, where an unlawful killing that occurred in the commission of *any* felony was considered murder. People v. Viser, 62 Ill. 2d 568, 580, 343 N.E.2d 903, 908 (1975).

lying felony is not independent of the homicide.[322] For example, the predicate offense for felony-murder could be aggravated battery.[323]

The felony-murder doctrine is a recognition that forcible felonies are so inherently dangerous that a resulting homicide, even an accidental one, is strongly probable.[324] However, whether the felony-murder statute is applicable is dependent not on whether the felony is normally or inherently violent, but whether, under the facts of the particular case, it was contemplated that violence may be necessary to enable the defendant or defendants to carry out their criminal purpose.[325] Thus, where the defendant conspires with another to commit a felony that is normally nonviolent, the defendant will nevertheless be liable for felony-murder where a death actually occurs if it was foreseeable that violence might prove necessary to achieve their common criminal purpose.[326] For instance, where the evidence showed that the defendant intended to participate only in a burglary or theft with a companion, the defendant was liable for a murder arising out of his companion's actual killing of the victim, since it was contemplated that violence might actually occur.[327]

The corpus delecti in a felony-murder case is similar to other cases in that the fact of death and that the death was a result of another person's criminal conduct must be proven.[328] However, proof that the killing was accompanied by intent to

---

[322] People v. Szerletich, 86 Ill. App. 3d 1121, 1123, 408 N.E.2d 1098, 1101 (4th Dist. 1980) (aggravated battery was predicate offense).

[323] See, e.g., People v. Mounson, 185 Ill. App. 3d 31, 34-35, 540 N.E.2d 834, 836-37 (3d Dist. 1989) (application of felony-murder statute to defendant whose only predicate offense was aggravated battery is not violative of due process); People v. Hall, 291 Ill. App. 3d 411, 418, 683 N.E.2d 1274, 1278-79 (1st Dist. 1998) (aggravated battery could serve as predicate offense for felony-murder conviction).

[324] People v. Jenkins, 190 Ill. App. 3d 115, 126, 545 N.E.2d 986, 994 (1st Dist. 1989), citing ILL. ANN. STAT. ch. 38, para. 9-1 (Smith-Hurd 1979), 1961 Committee Comments, at 19 (revised 1972).

[325] People v. Golson, 32 Ill. 2d 398, 407-08, 207 N.E.2d 68, 73 (1965) (sufficient evidence for jury to determine defendant's anticipated use of weapons in conspiracy to steal from mails case), cert. denied, 384 U.S. 1023, reh'g denied, 385 U.S. 892 (1966). See also People v. Banks, 287 Ill. App. 3d 273, 283-84, 678 N.E.2d 348, 354-55 (2d Dist. 1997) (mob action held to be predicate offense for purpose of felony-murder conviction)

[326] People v. Golson, 32 Ill. 2d 398, 407-08, 207 N.E.2d 68, 73 (1965), cert. denied, 384 U.S. 1023, reh'g denied, 385 U.S. 892 (1966).

[327] People v. Auilar, 59 Ill. 2d 95, 101, 319 N.E.2d 514, 517 (1974).

[328] People v. Banks, 287 Ill. App. 3d 273, 286-87, 678 N.E.2d 348, 357 (2d Dist. 1997). In People v. Viser, 62 Ill. 2d 568, 343 N.E.2d 903 (1975), the defendant was convicted of murder of one person, which was affirmed on appeal, and of attempted murder of another person, which was reversed on appeal. As to the latter count, the trial court had instructed the jury that they could find attempted murder if they believed that the defendant had the intent to commit a forcible felony, in this case, an aggravated battery on the victim. The court held:

kill or inflict great bodily injury or knowledge thereof is not required.[329] A forcible felony is deemed so inherently dangerous that a homicide occurring in the course of the felony can be held to be murder without further proof that there was a strong probability of death.[330] In other words, an attempt to commit a crime which is likely to get out of control and cause death or great bodily injury demonstrates a "willingness" to cause that result.[331] Thus, the requisite intent for a felony-murder conviction is the defendant's intent to commit the underlying forcible felony.[332] However, a conviction under felony-murder cannot be predicated upon a mere reckless state of mind.[333] The predicate felony for felony-murder must be an intended felony.[334] Thus, where defendant pulled a gun in a crowded tavern to force the bartender to return his correct change after allegedly being shortchanged by the bartender, whereupon a struggle ensued during which a person was shot and killed, there was no felony-murder since there was no evidence that the defendant had the intent to commit a robbery or other forcible felony.[335]

Normal rules of causation and foreseeability are not demanded in felony-murder analysis. "[U]nder the felony-murder doctrine it is immaterial whether the killing of the [innocent party] is intentional, accidental or committed by a

---

There can be no felony murder where there has been no death, and the felony murder ingredient of the offense of murder cannot be made the basis of an indictment charging attempt murder. Moreover, the offense of attempt requires an "intent to commit a specific offense" . . . while the distinctive characteristic of felony murder is that it does not involve an intention to kill. There is no such criminal offense as an attempt to achieve an unintended result.

People v. Viser, 62 Ill. 2d 568, 581, 343 N.E.2d 903, 910 (1975).

[329] People v. Moore, 95 Ill. 2d 404, 411, 447 N.E.2d 1327, 1330 (1983) (intent to kill not necessary for felony-murder conviction); People v. Danner, 105 Ill. App. 2d 126, 130, 245 N.E.2d 106, 108 (1st Dist. 1969) (where evidence establishes defendant was attempting to commit forcible felony and victim's death was a result of that attempt, it is immaterial who fired particular shot that killed victim or whether killing was intentional or accidental).

[330] People v. Nelson, 73 Ill. App. 3d 593, 595, 392 N.E.2d 602, 604 (1st Dist. 1979) (murder conviction affirmed).

[331] People v. Nelson, 73 Ill. App. 3d 593, 595, 392 N.E.2d 602, 604 (1st Dist. 1979).

[332] People v. Jeffrey, 94 Ill. App. 3d 455, 460, 418 N.E.2d 880, 885-86 (5th Dist. 1981) (murder conviction affirmed).

[333] People v. Land, 169 Ill. App. 3d 342, 355-57, 523 N.E.2d 711, 718-20 (4th Dist. 1988) (reckless cruelty to children cannot be predicate offense for felony-murder).

[334] People v. Land, 169 Ill. App. 3d 342, 356, 523 N.E.2d 711, 719 (4th Dist. 1988) ("An examination of the legislative policy underlying the offense of felony murder provides . . . support to the concept that the predicate felony must be an intentional felony").

[335] People v. Falkner, 61 Ill. App. 3d 84, 89-90, 377 N.E.2d 824, 828-29 (2d Dist. 1978) (defendant's conduct was reckless and, accordingly, he was liable for involuntary manslaughter).

co-felon without connivance of the defendant."[336] Where a defendant was engaged in an armed robbery of a bar and the owner of the bar said "you've got to be kidding" and started toward the defendant, the defendant's claim that the discharge of his firearm, which killed a bystander, was only a result of a struggle caused by the bar owner's grabbing him was considered immaterial, and his conviction of felony-murder was sustained.[337] Where a robbery victim died of a heart attack during the course of a robbery, the robber was convicted of murder under the felony-murder doctrine.[338] Where a home invasion and armed robbery victim jumped from his apartment window to his death, the court convicted the defendant of felony-murder while rejecting the argument that the state is required to prove as an essential element of felony-murder that the victim's actions were a "direct and foreseeable" result of the defendant's felonious action.[339] Similarly, where a burglary victim jumped from a third-story apartment window to her death during the defendant's commission of a burglary, defendant was guilty of felony-murder.[340] In this case, the Illinois Supreme Court stated:

> It is unimportant that the defendant did not anticipate the precise sequence of events that followed his entry into the apartment of [the deceased]. His unlawful acts precipitated those events and he is responsible for the consequences.[341]

Where defendant beat and raped an elderly woman who later died of asphyxiation in a nursing home while being fed by nursing home staff and it was demonstrated her injuries that were inflicted by defendant contributed to her difficulty in consuming food without choking, the Illinois Supreme Court reiterated that a defendant is not relieved from responsibility for felony-murder because "the precise manner of death" was not "foreseeable to the defendant" while he was committing his felonies.[342]

---

[336] People v. Burke, 85 Ill. App. 3d 939, 941, 407 N.E.2d 728, 730 (1st Dist. 1980); People v. Morris, 1 Ill. App. 3d 566, 569, 274 N.E.2d 898, 900 (1st Dist. 1971); People v. Danner, 105 Ill. App. 2d 126, 130, 245 N.E.2d 106, 108 (1st Dist. 1969).

[337] People v. Nelson, 73 Ill. App. 3d 593, 596, 392 N.E.2d 602, 605 (1st Dist. 1979) (murder conviction affirmed).

[338] People v. Woods, 2 Ill. 2d 240, 242, 118 N.E.2d 248, 249 (where robbery is committed with felonious intent and death occurs, offense may be adjudged murder), cert. denied, 347 U.S. 993 (1954).

[339] People v. Davis, 173 Ill. App. 3d 300, 308-09, 527 N.E.2d 552, 558 (1st Dist. 1988) (murder conviction affirmed).

[340] People v. Smith, 56 Ill. 2d 328, 333-34, 307 N.E.2d 353, 355-56 (1974) (murder conviction affirmed).

[341] People v. Smith, 56 Ill. 2d 328, 333-34, N.E.2d 353, 355-56 (1974).

[342] People v. Brackett, 117 Ill. 2d 170, 180-81, 510 N.E.2d 877, 882 (1987) (murder conviction affirmed), cert. denied, 511 U.S. 1072 (1994).

The actus reus in a felony-murder case is proven by the defendant's "participation" in the forcible felony.[343] A defendant may be convicted of felony-murder even though he did not personally kill the victim.[344] "Factual details such as who, if anyone, pulled the trigger [are], therefore, irrelevant."[345] Also, proof of the defendant's physical presence at the scene is not required where confederates or accomplices actually engage in the killing at issue.[346] However, mere presence at the scene is insufficient, without more, to prove participation in a felony-murder, even though active participation in the overt act is not required.[347]

Participation in a forcible felony may be established by the accused's own affirmative commission of a forcible felony, his or her aiding and abetting the felonious acts of another, or by a combination thereof. In addition, various circumstantial evidence might point to an accused's involvement in a felony-murder. Thus, felony-murder was established where the evidence established a defendant was handing a gun to a confederate with a statement that the victims of a robbery-murder be shot if they offered resistance;[348] present at the scene of a robbery and later found in possession of the robbery-murder victim's automobile;[349] driving an automobile in which the murder weapon was found, only a few minutes after the murder victim was killed;[350] beating a robbery victim and found in possession of robbery proceeds immediately after the robbery-murder victim was killed by a confederate;[351] holding the robbery victim's attention while a codefendant left to get a brick used to hit the robbery-murder victim on

[343] People v. Tillman, 70 Ill. App. 3d 922, 925-26, 388 N.E.2d 1253, 1256 (1st Dist. 1979) (murder conviction affirmed).

[344] People v. Miner, 46 Ill. App. 3d 273, 281, 360 N.E.2d 1141, 1148 (5th Dist. 1977) (murder conviction affirmed). See also People v. Rhoden, 299 Ill. App.3d 951, 955, 702 N.E.2d 209, 212 (1st Dist. 1998) ("The law in Illinois has long been established that the identity of the killer is not relevant for the purposes of felony murder").

[345] People v. Miner, 46 Ill. App. 3d 273, 281, 360 N.E.2d 1141, 1148 (5th Dist. 1977) (murder conviction affirmed).

[346] People v. Fuller, 91 Ill. App. 3d 922, 929-30, 415 N.E.2d 502, 507 (1st Dist. 1980) (murder conviction affirmed).

[347] People v. Stevens, 98 Ill. App. 3d 158, 160-61, 423 N.E.2d 1340, 1342 (1st Dist. 1981) (murder on felony-murder theory affirmed even though defendant did not shoot robbery-murder victim).

[348] People v. Addison, 56 Ill. App. 3d 92, 100, 371 N.E.2d 1025, 1031 (1st Dist. 1977) (murder conviction affirmed).

[349] People v. Guthrie, 7 Ill. App. 3d 243, 247-48, 286 N.E.2d 627, 630 (4th Dist. 1972) (conviction reversed on other grounds).

[350] People v. Greene, 27 Ill. App. 3d 1080, 1091-92, 328 N.E.2d 176, 183 (1st Dist. 1975) (murder conviction affirmed).

[351] People v. Goss, 10 Ill. App. 3d 543, 545-46, 294 N.E.2d 744, 746 (1st Dist. 1973) (murder conviction affirmed).

the head;[352] and handing a confederate an open knife, demanded money of an eventual robbery-murder victim, and punching the victim.[353] In some cases, the failure to act may be viewed as evidence of participation in the forcible felony. Such was the case where an accused failed to request the return of his gun that he knew his companion intended to use in a robbery,[354] did nothing to disassociate himself from his companion once he knew of his companion's plan to rob his victim,[355] and did not disassociate himself from his companion after the companion had robbed and killed the victim.[356] Similarly, where a defendant came upon a robbery-murder in progress and did not in any way oppose it, it could be inferred that she consented to those acts and aided and abetted the felony-murder.[357]

An escape from the commission of a forcible felony is considered part of the crime and can be the basis of a felony-murder finding.[358] Where two defendants, who had engaged in an armed robbery minutes before, attempted to escape from police pursuit by automobile, drove through a red light in excess of eighty miles per hour, struck an automobile in the intersection where the red light was situated, and killed the driver of the automobile, they were convicted of murder under the felony-murder doctrine.[359] However, the Illinois Supreme Court ruled in 1999 that the "felony-murder escape rule" is not applicable in prosecutions grounded in an accountability theory of liability.[360]

Even though "foreseeability" is not an element of felony-murder,[361] Illinois follows the so-called "proximate cause" theory of felony-murder, rather than the

---

[352] People v. Auilar, 59 Ill. 2d 95, 101, 319 N.E.2d 514, 517 (1974) (murder conviction affirmed).

[353] People v. Wieland, 123 Ill. App. 3d 576, 584, 462 N.E.2d 1256, 1261-62 (4th Dist. 1984) (murder conviction affirmed).

[354] People v. Stevens, 98 Ill. App. 3d 158, 160-62, 423 N.E.2d 1340, 1342-43 (1st Dist. 1981) (murder conviction affirmed).

[355] People v. Stevens, 98 Ill. App. 3d 158, 161, 423 N.E.2d 1340, 1343 (1st Dist. 1981).

[356] People v. Stevens, 98 Ill. App. 3d 158, 161, 423 N.E.2d 1340, 1343 (1st Dist. 1981).

[357] People v. Fuller, 91 Ill. App. 3d 922, 929, 415 N.E.2d 502, 508 (1st Dist. 1980) (murder conviction affirmed).

[358] People v. Lowery, 178 Ill. 2d 462, 472, 687 N.E.2d 973, 979 (1997) (killing during course of escape from an armed robbery is within felony-murder rule).

[359] People v. Burke, 85 Ill. App. 3d 939, 941, 407 N.E.2d 728, 730-31 (1st Dist. 1980) (murder conviction affirmed); see also People v. Tillman, 70 Ill. App. 3d 922, 925-26, 388 N.E.2d 1253, 1256-57 (1st Dist. 1979) (felony-murder conviction affirmed where predicate criminal act was escape from armed robbery).

[360] People v. Shaw, 186 Ill. 2d 301, ___, 713 N.E.2d 1161, 1172 (1999). Compare People v. Dennis, 181 Ill. 2d 87, 101, 692 N.E.2d 325, 333 (1998) (where alleged accomplice to armed robbery only aided perpetrator's escape from crime scene, accountability did not attach because armed robbery had ended).

[361] People v. Brackett, 117 Ill. 2d 170, 180-81, 510 N.E.2d 877, 882 (1987) (murder conviction affirmed), cert. denied, 511 U.S. 1072 (1994).

"agency theory," which is followed in the majority of American jurisdictions, when the issue arises whether a felony-murder encompasses a death that was not directly attributable to the act of a defendant or a confederate of the defendant.[362] Under the "proximate cause" theory, felony-murder liability attaches for any death that arises out of the underlying felony, including *any* killing that was carried out by one resisting the crime, whereas the "agency theory" does not extend to a killing, although growing out of the commission of the felony, if directly attributable to the actions of one other than the defendant or those associated with him or her in the unlawful enterprise.[363] For example, where the death of an innocent person is not actually caused by the hand of a forcible felon or one of his confederates but rather by a police officer, the death is within the contemplation of the Illinois felony-murder rule.[364] Thus, where a police officer mistakenly shot and killed another officer during an effort to halt the escape of robbers from the scene of the robbery, the surviving robbers' convictions were upheld under the felony-murder concept.[365] Similarly, where an intended victim of an armed robbery fired the shot that killed an innocent bystander, the perpetrator of the underlying felony was liable for first degree murder on a felony-murder theory.[366]

Where a confederate of a forcible felon dies during the forcible felony, the surviving forcible felon is liable under the Illinois felony-murder doctrine. Thus, where several defendants engaged in the forcible felony of aggravated discharge of a firearm by shooting at another group of individuals, whereupon one of the latter group returned fire and struck the confederate of the surviving forcible felons, the survivors were chargeable with felony-murder.[367] Likewise, where the intended victim of a robbery shot and killed a co-felon of the defendant, the defendant was liable for the death of the co-felon under the felony-murder rule principles.[368] In addition, where the defendant struck the victim of attempted armed robbery with his gun, which discharged and killed his co-felon, defendant was convicted for felony-murder.[369]

---

[362] People v. Dekens, 182 Ill. 2d 247, 249-50, 695 N.E.2d 474, 475-76 (1998) (first degree murder convictions affirmed where intended victim of robbery killed co-felon); People v. Lowery, 178 Ill. 2d 462, 465, 687 N.E.2d 973, 975-76 (1997) (first degree murder conviction affirmed where intended robbery victim killed innocent bystander).

[363] People v. Dekens, 182 Ill. 2d 247, 249, 695 N.E.2d 474, 475 (1998); People v. Lowery, 178 Ill. 2d 462, 466, 687 N.E.2d 973, 975-76 (1997).

[364] People v. Hickman, 59 Ill. 2d 89, 94-95, 319 N.E.2d 511, 513-14 (1974) (murder conviction affirmed), *cert. denied*, 421 U.S. 913 (1975).

[365] People v. Hickman, 59 Ill. 2d 89, 94-95, 319 N.E.2d 511, 513-14 (1974), *cert. denied*, 421 U.S. 913 (1975).

[366] People v. Lowery, 178 Ill. 2d 462, 467-72, 687 N.E.2d 973, 976-79 (1997).

[367] People v. Pugh, 261 Ill. App. 3d 75, 77-78, 634 N.E.2d 34, 35-36 (5th Dist. 1994).

[368] People v. Dekens, 182 Ill. 2d 247, 249, 695 N.E.2d 474, 474, 477 (1998).

[369] People v. Rhoden, 299 Ill. App.3d 951, 955, 702 N.E.2d 209, 212-213 (1st Dist. 1998).

The preceding cases illustrate that the death does not have to be immediately contemporaneous with the commission of the forcible felony.[370] In one case, a defendant and codefendant engaged in an armed robbery of several persons in a restaurant.[371] After the robberies were complete and as the two robbers were leaving the restaurant, the codefendant suddenly — much to the defendant's apparent surprise — shot the five persons in the restaurant to death. The appellate court refused to reverse the defendant's conviction on grounds that the killings were outside the scope of the forcible felony of armed robbery.[372] Even if the victim is beaten and killed as an "afterthought" of the robbery,[373] or the robbery is committed as an "afterthought" of the fatal beating,[374] liability under the felony-murder rule will still attach.

§ 6.23. Second Degree Murder.

The offense of voluntary manslaughter (now called "second degree murder" in Illinois) appears to have been developed as "a legal compromise between murder and exoneration, recognizing but not excusing the human weakness consisting of an intense (or irresistible) passion caused by serious provocation, resulting in homicide."[375] At common law, this heat of passion negated the "malice aforethought" necessary for murder if (1) the provocation was serious enough to excite intense passion in a reasonable person; (2) the killing occurred immediately following the provocation; and (3) there was a reasonable proportion between the provocation and the homicide.[376] The categories of "serious provocation" recognized were "substantial physical injury or assault, mutual quarrel or combat, illegal arrest, and adultery with the offender's spouse; but not mere words or gestures or trespass to property."[377]

---

[370] People v. Pugh, 261 Ill. App. 3d 75, 77, 634 N.E.2d 34, 36 (5th Dist. 1994).

[371] People v. Piche, 44 Ill. App. 3d 993, 358 N.E.2d 1260 (2d Dist. 1976).

[372] People v. Piche, 44 Ill. App. 3d 993, 994, 358 N.E.2d 1260, 1262-63 (2d Dist. 1976) (murder convictions affirmed).

[373] People v. Stout, 122 Ill. App. 3d 254, 258, 460 N.E.2d 1205, 1209 (4th Dist. 1984) (murder conviction affirmed).

[374] People v. Wieland, 123 Ill. App. 3d 576, 583-84, 462 N.E.2d 1256, 1261-62 (4th Dist. 1984) (murder conviction affirmed).

[375] ILL. ANN. STAT. ch. 38, para. 9-2 (Smith-Hurd 1979), 1961 Committee Comments, at 392 (revised 1972).

[376] ILL. ANN. STAT. ch. 38, para. 9-2 (Smith-Hurd 1979), 1961 Committee Comments, at 392 (revised 1972).

[377] ILL. ANN. STAT. ch. 38, para. 9-2 (Smith-Hurd 1979), 1961 Committee Comments, at 393 (revised 1972).

The earlier Illinois statute[378] and caselaw[379] were consistent with the common law approach to voluntary manslaughter.[380] In enacting paragraph 5/9-2 in 1961, it was the legislature's intent to continue to adhere to this theory of voluntary manslaughter.[381] Prior to 1987, voluntary manslaughter was used to describe an unjustified killing where the defendant (1) harbored a "sudden and intense passion resulting from a serious provocation" or (2) unreasonably believed his or her killing was justified.[382] However, this approach was criticized on grounds that it required the state to prove murder plus mitigation to convict the individual of voluntary manslaughter.[383] Because it was the defendant who wanted to

---

[378] ILL. REV. STAT. ch. 38, para. 361 (1959) ("Manslaughter is the unlawful killing of a human being without malice, express or implied, and without any mixture of deliberation whatever. It must be voluntary, upon a sudden heat of passion caused by a provocation apparently sufficient to make the passion irresistible . . . ."); ILL. REV. STAT. ch. 38, para. 362 (1959) ("In cases of voluntary manslaughter, there must be a serious and highly provoking injury inflicted upon the person killing, sufficient to excite an irresistible passion in a reasonable person, or an attempt by the person killed to commit a serious personal injury on the person killing. The killing must be the result of that sudden, violent impulse of passion supposed to be irresistible; for if there should appear to have been an interval between the assault or provocation given, and the killing, sufficient for the voice of reason and humanity to be heard, the killing shall be attributable to deliberate revenge, and punished as murder.").

[379] ILL. ANN. STAT. ch. 38, para. 9-2 (Smith-Hurd 1979), 1961 Committee Comments, at 393-94 (revised 1972) (citing as examples various cases, including People v. Harris, 8 Ill. 2d 431, 437, 134 N.E.2d 315, 319 (1956) (severe beating with nightstick, fracturing defendant's jaw; voluntary manslaughter conviction affirmed); People v. Sain, 384 Ill. 394, 400, 51 N.E.2d 557, 560 (1943) (throwing hot water into defendant's face, partially blinding him; voluntary manslaughter conviction affirmed); People v. Rice, 351 Ill. 604, 184 N.E. 894 (1933) (slapping defendant's child and causing quarrel; voluntary manslaughter conviction affirmed); People v. Ortiz, 320 Ill. 205, 150 N.E. 708 (1926) (verbal utterance not sufficient; murder conviction reversed); People v. Bissett, 246 Ill. 516, 92 N.E. 949 (1910) (seizing defendant and demanding contents of his pocket; murder conviction reversed); Davis v. People, 114 Ill. 86, 29 N.E. 192 (1885) (quarrel and prolonged physical struggle; voluntary manslaughter conviction affirmed)).

[380] See § 6.09 of this chapter.

[381] ILL. ANN. STAT. ch. 38, para. 9-2 (Smith-Hurd 1979), 1961 Committee Comments, at 394 (revised 1972). For whatever reason, the drafting committee had essentially nothing to report regarding the "imperfect defense" approach to this crime in the committee comments cited above.

[382] ILL. REV. STAT. ch. 38, para. 9-2 (1985).

[383] See, e.g., Timothy P. O'Neill, With Malice Toward None: A Solution to an Illinois Homicide Quandary, 32 DEPAUL L. REV. 107, 113 (1982).
Eventually, the criticisms voiced by Professor Timothy O'Neill were heeded by the courts. In People v. Reddick, 123 Ill. 2d 184, 526 N.E.2d 141 (1988) (consolidated opinion: two murder convictions, one was affirmed and the other was reversed), the Illinois Supreme Court held it was reversible error for a trial court to instruct a jury that it could find a defendant guilty of voluntary manslaughter only if the state proved one of the two mitigating mental states on the part of the defendant. Similarly, in Falconer v. Lane, 905 F.2d 1129 (7th Cir. 1990), the United States Court of Appeals ruled such instructions violated due process and could not be deemed harmless error. Also, in Taylor v. Gilmore, 954 F.2d 441 (7th Cir. 1992) the court ruled a federal habeas corpus petitioner was entitled to retroactive application of the *Falconer* ruling.

show the necessary mitigation, it appeared more logical to require the state to prove the elements of murder and, thereafter, require the defendant to prove mitigation.[384] In 1987, the result of these criticisms led to the enactment of second degree murder as a substitute for voluntary manslaughter and the placement of the burden of proof to demonstrate mitigating circumstances necessary to reduce the first degree murder to second degree murder on the shoulders of the defendant.[385]

§ 6.24. — Second Degree Murder Codified.

Paragraph 5/9-2 now prohibits second degree murder.[386] This statute provides:

Second Degree Murder: (a) A person commits the offense of second degree murder when he commits the offense of first degree murder as defined in paragraphs (1) or (2) of subsection (a) of Section 9-1 of this Code and either of the following mitigating factors are present:

---

[384] Robert J. Steigmann, *First and Second Degree Murder in Illinois*, 75 ILL. B.J. 494, 495 (1987); Timothy P. O'Neill, *Murder Least Foul: A Proposal to Abolish Voluntary Manslaughter in Illinois*, 72 ILL. B.J. 306 (1984).

[385] *See* § 6.13 of this chapter for a more complete discussion of this change.

Placement of the burden of proof, regarding the mitigation necessary to reduce a homicide to second degree murder, upon the defendant has survived various constitutional challenges. People v. Jeffries, 164 Ill. 2d 104, 646 N.E.2d 587 (1995) (not violative of due process); People v. Horton, 233 Ill. App. 3d 22, 598 N.E.2d 452 (3d Dist. 1992) (not violative of due process); People v. Mitchell, 221 Ill. App. 3d 926, 583 N.E.2d 78 (1st Dist. 1991) (not violative of separation of powers); People v. Davis, 221 Ill. App. 3d 1023, 583 N.E.2d 64 (1st Dist. 1991) (not violative of due process or equal protection); People v. Wright, 218 Ill. App. 3d 764, 578 N.E.2d 1090 (1st Dist. 1991) (not violative of due process, equal protection or separation of powers); People v. Newbern, 219 Ill. App. 3d 333, 579 N.E.2d 583 (4th Dist. 1991) (not violative of due process); People v. Willis, 217 Ill. App. 3d 909, 577 N.E.2d 1215 (1st Dist. 1991) (not violative of due process); People v. Cook, 217 Ill. App. 3d 299, 576 N.E.2d 1242 (5th Dist. 1991) (not violative of due process); People v. Thomas, 216 Ill. App. 3d 469, 576 N.E.2d 1020 (1st Dist. 1991) (not violative of due process or equal protection); People v. Hrobowski, 216 Ill. App. 3d 711, 575 N.E.2d 1306 (2d Dist. 1991) (not violative of due process). *But see* Larry R. Wells, *Presumed Guilty: Curing the Defects in the Second Degree Murder Statute*, 80 ILL. B.J. 230 (1992) (arguing burden of proof arrangement is unconstitutional); James B. Haddad, *Second Degree Murder Replaces Voluntary Manslaughter in Illinois: Problems Solved, Problems Created*, 19 LOYOLA L.J. 995 (1988) (suggesting current legislative arrangement has not entirely solved doctrinal problems in Illinois homicide legislation).

[386] The following discussion of second degree murder will occasionally include references in the text or footnotes to cases where the defendant was prosecuted for what was previously described as "voluntary manslaughter," as defined by paragraph 5/9-2 of the Criminal Code of 1961 — an enactment that continued in effect until July 1, 1987 when paragraph 5/9-2 became "second degree murder." These references to earlier "voluntary manslaughter" cases will only appear in the text where the doctrine or principle from the earlier statute still maintains vitality in the new "second degree murder" configuration.

(1) At the time of the killing he is acting under a sudden and intense passion resulting from serious provocation by the individual killed or another whom the offender endeavors to kill, but he negligently or accidentally causes the death of the individual killed; or

(2) At the time of the killing he believes the circumstances to be such that, if they existed, would justify or exonerate the killing under the principles stated in Article 7 of this Code, but his belief is unreasonable.

(b) Serious provocation is conduct sufficient to excite an intense passion in a reasonable person.

(c) When a defendant is on trial for first degree murder and evidence of either of the mitigating factors defined in subsection (a) of this Section has been presented, the burden of proof is on the defendant to prove either mitigating factor by a preponderance of the evidence before the defendant can be found guilty of second degree murder. However, the burden of proof remains on the State to prove beyond a reasonable doubt each of the elements of first degree murder and, when appropriately raised, the absence of circumstances at the time of the killing that would justify or exonerate the killing under the principles stated in Article 7 of this Code. In a jury trial for first degree murder in which evidence of either of the mitigating factors defined in subsection (a) of this Section has been presented and the defendant has requested that the jury be given the option of finding the defendant guilty of second degree murder, the jury must be instructed that it may not consider whether the defendant has met his burden of proof with regard to second degree murder until and unless it has first determined that the State has proven beyond a reasonable doubt each of the elements of first degree murder.[387]

Excepting the significant changes regarding the burden or proof to show mitigating circumstances that reduce first degree murder to second degree murder, the balance of the changes involve little more than relabeling. The offense of voluntary manslaughter under the 1961 statute, and the crime of second degree murder under the current statute are substantially the same.[388] Further, the Illinois definition of second degree murder is radically different than second degree murder as it existed at common law[389] and more closely resembles voluntary manslaughter as it was understood at common law.[390]

---

[387] 720 ILCS 5/9-2 (1999).

[388] People v. Timberson, 188 Ill. App. 3d 172, 177, 544 N.E.2d 64, 66 (1989) ("with the major exception of placing the burden on the defendant to prove the factor in mitigation, the offense of voluntary manslaughter under the old statute, and second degree murder under the new statute are substantially the same"; second degree murder conviction reversed for failure to give the jury self defense instructions).

[389] *See* § 6.05 of this chapter.

[390] *See* § 6.09 of this chapter.

Although the crime of second degree murder now requires proof of murder by the state and proof by a preponderance of evidence of one of the two mitigating factors by the defendant, the question arises whether the state can initially charge a person with second degree murder, or if the state must charge a defendant with first degree murder and permit the defendant to show mitigating circumstances to reduce the charge to second degree murder. In *People v. Burks,*[391] the Illinois appellate court indicated that it is indeed proper for the state to charge a defendant with second degree murder; however, when the state charges second degree murder, it is conceding the presence of one of the mitigating factors.[392]

In any event, second degree murder covers two different situations. First, this crime arises where a defendant kills another while laboring under a "sudden and intense passion."[393] The committee that originally drafted the substance of what now can be described as "sudden and intense passion" second degree murder stated (1) the "sudden and intense passion" language was meant to have the same meaning as the pre-1961 language expressed in terms of a "sudden, violent impulse supposed to be irresistible" that had not been negated during a subsequent "cooling off" period; (2) the "serious provocation" would be recognized where the defendant endeavors to kill the provoker but instead accidentally or negligently kills an innocent person; (3) a "serious provocation" would *not* be recognized where a revengeful defendant deliberately directs his or her attack on an innocent person, such as a friend or relative of the provoker, instead of the provoker (whereupon the defendant would be liable for first degree murder); and (4) the "serious provocation" could be caused by the same stimuli normally recognized in the various jurisdictions, such as by observing a spouse's act of adultery.[394]

Second, the terms of the second degree murder prohibition governs where a person kills another under the unreasonable belief that his or her actions are justified.[395] For example, second degree murder exists if a killing occurs when the defendant is acting under an unreasonable belief that deadly force is necessary

---

[391] 189 Ill. App. 3d 782, 784, 545 N.E.2d 782, 784 (3d Dist. 1989).

[392] People v. Burks, 189 Ill. App. 3d 782, 785, 545 N.E.2d 782, 784 (3d Dist. 1989) (reversed and remanded trial court's grant of motion to dismiss based on state's initial charge of second degree murder, stating: "[t]he statute does not, however, prohibit the state from initially charging a defendant with second degree murder. By charging a defendant with second degree murder, the state is alleging it can prove the elements of first degree murder, but is conceding the presence of mitigating factors.").

[393] 720 ILCS 5/9-2(a)(1) (1999).

[394] ILL. ANN. STAT. ch. 38, para. 9-2 (Smith-Hurd 1979), 1961 Committee Comments, at 394-95 (revised 1972).

[395] 720 ILCS 5/9-2(a)(2) (1999).

to protect himself, herself or another from death or great bodily harm.[396] Accordingly, this type of homicide can be described as "imperfect defense" second degree murder. While the circumstances surrounding a homicide often involve both types of mitigating factors that lead to second degree murder, they will be discussed separately below.

§ 6.25. — Elements of "Sudden and Intense Passion" Second Degree Murder.

In Illinois, a defendant commits second degree murder by killing another when acting under a "sudden and intense passion" resulting from "serious provocation."[397] The burden is on the defendant to prove by a preponderance of evidence that these circumstances existed which warranted mitigation of the charge to second degree murder.[398] If there is nothing in the record suggesting that the defendant was provoked into a heat of passion and the resulting murder, then the fact finder must find the defendant guilty of first degree murder.[399]

The state of mind in "provocation" second degree murder could be best described as a mind filled with "passion" or "sudden revenge."[400] Second degree murder, like first degree murder, requires the intent to kill or inflict great bodily injury or knowledge that one's acts are creating a strong probability of death or great bodily injury.[401] However, "provocation" second degree murder also requires proof that the accused's mental state was clouded by a "sudden and intense passion."[402] The "sudden and intense passion" must result from a "serious provocation," which is conduct sufficient to excite intense passion in a reasonable person.[403] The test is objective, not subjective, and the inquiry is not whether the defendant was angry at someone or at something when he or she killed, but whether there existed such provocation as would have caused the malignant state of mind in the ordinary person under the same circumstances.[404] A "slight" provocation will not be adequate.[405] The defendant's retaliation must be

---

[396] People v. Rogers, 286 Ill. App. 3d 825, 829-30, 677 N.E.2d 13, 17 (1st Dist. 1997); People v. Mitchell, 221 Ill. App. 3d 926, 932-33, 583 N.E.2d 78, 82 (1st Dist. 1991).

[397] 720 ILCS 5/9-2(a)(1) (1999).

[398] 720 ILCS 5/9-2(c) (1999).

[399] People v. Vargas, 224 Ill. App. 3d 832, 835-36, 587 N.E.2d 1217, 1219-20 (5th Dist. 1992) (trial court did not err in failing to instruct jury on second degree murder where no evidence existed that victim provoked defendant and, accordingly, first degree murder conviction affirmed).

[400] People v. Slaughter, 84 Ill. App. 3d 1103, 1110, 405 N.E.2d 1295, 1301 (1st Dist. 1980).

[401] 720 ILCS 5/9-2(a) (1999).

[402] 720 ILCS 5/9-2(a)(1) (1999).

[403] 720 ILCS 5/9-2(b) (1999).

[404] People v. Matthews, 21 Ill. App. 3d 249, 252, 314 N.E.2d 15, 18 (3d Dist. 1974) (murder conviction affirmed).

[405] People v. Austin, 133 Ill. 2d 118, 126-27, 549 N.E.2d 331, 335 (1989) (murder conviction affirmed).

_, ι.ιuⅰⅰate to the degree of provocation.[406] Therefore, if the accused in response to a slight provocation attacked the deceased with "violence out of proportion to the provocation" and killed him, the provocation will be considered inadequate.[407] This is especially true if the homicide was committed with a deadly weapon.[408] Thus, where the defendant shot and killed an unarmed female bus driver who at most insisted the defendant pay a full fare, spoke gruffly to her, struck her on the hand with a transfer punch, briefly exchanged punches with the defendant, and attempted to remove the defendant from the bus, the defendant's shooting "was an act completely out of proportion to the provocation."[409] Where the victim accidentally collided with defendant's car, the defendant tried to force the victim to stop, and the victim "flipped the defendant the finger," this was not a sufficient provocation to reduce the defendant's shotgun slaying of the victim to second degree murder.[410] Where an elderly and extremely intoxicated victim repeatedly requested sex with the defendant, hit the defendant on her shoulder with a broom, and grabbed her from behind by putting his hand on her shoulder, defendant's multiple stabbing of the victim was out of proportion to his actions.[411] Where the seven-year-old victim had broken branches from the defendant's tree, this was hardly a serious provocation sufficient to reduce the homicide to second degree murder.[412]

Passion on the part of the slayer, no matter how violent, will not relieve a defendant from liability for first degree murder unless it is engendered by a provocation which the law recognizes as being reasonable and adequate.[413] The only categories of provocation that Illinois law considers reasonable and adequate are

---

[406] People v. Arnett, 217 Ill. App. 3d 626, 632, 577 N.E.2d 773, 776 (5th Dist. 1991) (first degree murder conviction affirmed); *see also* People v. Nunn, 184 Ill. App. 3d 253, 275, 541 N.E.2d 182, 197 (1st Dist. 1989) (after defendant punched in jaw by victim, defendant and seven others beat victim to death, a response that was "out of all proportion to the alleged provocation;" voluntary manslaughter instructions properly refused).

[407] People v. Austin, 133 Ill. 2d 118, 127, 549 N.E.2d 331, 335 (1989) (murder conviction affirmed).

[408] People v. Austin, 133 Ill. 2d 118, 127, 549 N.E.2d 331, 335 (1989).

[409] People v. Austin, 133 Ill. 2d 118, 127, 549 N.E.2d 331, 335 (1989).

[410] People v. Arnett, 217 Ill. App. 3d 626, 633, 577 N.E.2d 773, 776-77 (5th Dist. 1991) (first degree murder conviction affirmed).

[411] People v. Hood, 191 Ill. App. 3d 129, 134, 547 N.E.2d 637, 641 (1st Dist. 1989) (murder conviction affirmed).

[412] People v. Epps, 197 Ill. App. 3d 376, 383, 554 N.E.2d 637, 642 (5th Dist. 1990) (first degree murder conviction affirmed).

[413] People v. Garcia, 165 Ill. 2d 409, 429-30, 651 N.E.2d 100, 110 (1995) (first degree murder conviction affirmed); People v. Austin, 133 Ill. 2d 118, 125, ⁵49 N.E.2d 331, 334 (1989) (murder conviction affirmed).

(1) substantial physical injury or assault, (2) mutual quarrel or combat, (3) adultery with the offender's spouse and (4) illegal arrest.[414]

Concerning substantial physical assaults, if several persons armed with knives physically assaulted a defendant, this may be an adequate provocation sufficient to reduce an intentional killing from first degree murder to second degree murder.[415] Similarly, if a defendant was pushed and hit in the head with a beer can by the deceased, the same result would follow.[416] Where the deceased unlawfully assaulted the defendant's friend, whereupon the defendant and the deceased, who was a bigger man than the defendant, pushed and wrestled with one another, the defendant was adequately provoked.[417] However, if the battery suffered by the defendant or another is slight in nature, such as where the deceased scratched the defendant with her fingernails, this will not suffice.[418] Where the deceased tried to seduce defendant into having sex with her, hit him with a paint brush and, somewhat later, brandished a steak knife at him, which defendant immediately grabbed from the deceased's hands, this did not amount to adequate provocation.[419] Where the deceased threw a pot of beans at defendant, her husband, this was not an adequate provocation and, accordingly, this homicide was first degree murder.[420]

A "mutual quarrel or combat" may supply adequate provocation.[421] Mutual quarrel or combat is defined as a fight or struggle into which both parties enter willingly, or in which two persons, under a sudden quarrel and in hot blood, mutually fight on equal terms.[422] If the defendant alone instigated the fight or if the

---

[414] People v. Garcia, 165 Ill. 2d 409, 429-30, 651 N.E.2d 100, 110 (1995); People v. Chevalier, 131 Ill. 2d 66, 71, 544 N.E.2d 942, 944 (1989) (quoting ILL. ANN. STAT. ch. 38, para. 9-2 (Smith-Hurd 1979), 1961 Committee Comments, at 393 (revised 1972)).

[415] People v. Dortch, 20 Ill. App. 3d 911, 914, 314 N.E.2d 324, 326 (1st Dist. 1974) (murder conviction reversed for failure to give jury voluntary manslaughter instructions).

[416] People v. Stowers, 133 Ill. App. 2d 627, 631, 273 N.E.2d 493, 496-97 (1st Dist. 1971) (voluntary manslaughter conviction affirmed).

[417] People v. Johnson, 4 Ill. App. 3d 249, 251, 280 N.E.2d 764, 766 (1st Dist. 1972) (murder conviction reversed).

[418] People v. Simpson, 74 Ill. 2d 497, 502-03, 384 N.E.2d 373, 375-76 (1978) (murder conviction affirmed).

[419] People v. Toth, 106 Ill. App. 3d 27, 32, 435 N.E.2d 748, 752 (5th Dist. 1982) (murder conviction affirmed).

[420] People v. McVay, 170 Ill. App. 3d 443, 451, 524 N.E.2d 635, 640 (4th Dist. 1988) (first degree murder conviction affirmed).

[421] See, e.g., People v. Wesley, 65 Ill. App. 3d 25, 30-31, 382 N.E.2d 358, 362-63 (1st Dist. 1978) (arguing, pushing and shoving leading to defendant pushing victim into a wall is sufficient mutual quarrel or combat to meet provocation standard; voluntary manslaughter conviction affirmed).

[422] People v. Austin, 133 Ill. 2d 118, 125, 549 N.E.2d 331, 334 (1989) (murder conviction affirmed); People v. Flores, 282 Ill. App. 3d 861, 867-68, 668 N.E.2d 1171, 1175 (1st Dist. 1996)

defendant's retaliation was disproportionate to the provocation, this is not a "mutual combat" and, thus, there will be no mitigation of the charge to second degree murder.[423] Also, if the parties' fight is no longer on equal terms at the point where the defendant kills the deceased, this is not mutual combat.[424] Where a defendant finds himself the unwilling participant in a fight and acts only to defend himself from an attack, he is not entitled to a provocation instruction based on "mutual combat."[425] A mere argument between the parties is not "mutual quarrel or combat," since mere words have never been held to be sufficient provocation to establish second degree murder.[426] Even if there is physical confrontation between the parties, if the exchange creates only "slight provocation," it will not suffice.[427] Such would be the case where the defendant received only scratches from the decedent.[428] Where the dispute involved only a "limited degree of shoving and pushing" between the parties, there would not be adequate provocation.[429] Where the defendant's husband pushed and slapped her once without serious injury, "mutual combat" did not exist.[430] Disparity in size and strength between the defendant and his victim may be considered such as where the victim, a five foot, five inch female, struck the defendant, a six foot, two inch male, with a belt buckle, the defendant's strangulation of the victim with the belt was not the result of a mutual quarrel or combat.[431] In contrast, where the victim and defendant engaged in a fist fight for five to ten minutes

---

(first degree murder conviction affirmed); People v. Delgado, 282 Ill. App. 3d 851, 857, 668 N.E.2d 173, 178 (1st Dist. 1996) (first degree murder conviction affirmed).

[423] United States ex rel. Bacon v. DeRobertis, 551 F. Supp. 269, 272 (N.D. Ill. 1982) (murder conviction affirmed), cert. denied, 469 U.S. 840 (1984); see also People v. Crum, 183 Ill. App. 3d 473, 483, 539 N.E.2d 196, 202-03 (1st Dist. 1989) (defendant was "aggressor" when she confronted her husband with a gun and ordered him to leave).

[424] People v. McVay, 170 Ill. App. 3d 443, 451, 524 N.E.2d 635, 640 (4th Dist. 1988) (where deceased approached defendant with a knife, defendant disarmed deceased, and defendant repeatedly stabbed deceased, there was no mutual combat since the two were on "unequal terms" at the point where defendant stabbed deceased; first degree murder conviction affirmed).

[425] People v. Perry, 292 Ill. App. 3d 705, 713-14, 686 N.E.2d 677, 683 (1st Dist. 1997) (first degree murder conviction affirmed).

[426] People v. Garcia, 165 Ill. 2d 409, 429-30, 651 N.E.2d 100, 110 (1995) (first degree murder conviction affirmed); People v. Simpson, 74 Ill. 2d 497, 502, 384 N.E.2d 373, 375 (1978) (murder conviction affirmed).

[427] People v. Austin, 133 Ill. 2d 118, 126, 549 N.E.2d 331, 335 (1989) (murder conviction affirmed).

[428] People v. Simpson, 74 Ill. 2d 497, 502, 384 N.E.2d 373, 375 (1978) (murder conviction affirmed).

[429] People v. Miller, 96 Ill. App. 3d 212, 215, 421 N.E.2d 406, 409 (3d Dist. 1981) (murder conviction affirmed).

[430] People v. Falconer, 168 Ill. App. 3d 618, 622, 522 N.E.2d 903, 906 (2d Dist. 1988) (murder conviction affirmed).

[431] People v. Fickett, 204 Ill. App. 3d 220, 230, 562 N.E.2d 238, 244 (1st Dist. 1990) (murder conviction affirmed).

prior to the defendant's stabbing of the victim, this was considered mutual combat.[432] Similarly, where the victim and defendant in a dispute over money engaged in a violent struggle where multiple blows were exchanged, including the victim's hitting the defendant with a five pound lead paper weight, mutual combat existed at the point where the defendant picked up a knife and stabbed the victim as the two were wrestling with each other.[433] Where the defendant and the victim, who were roommates, came home intoxicated and engaged in a struggle over a gun, during which the victim was shot, this conduct manifested a mental state in accord with second degree murder rather than first degree murder.[434] Finally, where the parties to an alleged mutual combat exhibit lacerations on their face, arms or hands indicative of a violent fight, this may be indicative of the existence of a true mutual combat.[435]

Adultery involving one's spouse is viewed as a serious provocation sufficient to enrage the reasonable person into killing.[436] However, this approach to adequate provocation has quite literally been limited to instances where the parties were discovered in the act of adultery, or immediately before or after its commission, and the killing immediately followed upon detection.[437] Where the decedent was out with the defendant's estranged wife on the night the decedent was killed by the defendant, this would not, in the absence of evidence of the commission of an adulterous act, provide such serious provocation as to reduce the homicide to second degree murder.[438] A defendant's belief, held for a substantial period of time, that his wife committed adultery, and his wife's silence when defendant asked her to give him custody of their children, were not such

---

[432] People v. Hudson, 71 Ill. App. 3d 504, 511, 390 N.E.2d 5, 9 (1st Dist. 1979) (murder conviction reversed; however, evidence warranted voluntary manslaughter conviction).

[433] People v. Goolsby, 45 Ill. App. 3d 441, 449, 359 N.E.2d 871, 877 (1st Dist. 1977) (murder conviction reversed; however, evidence warranted voluntary manslaughter conviction), *cert. denied*, 445 U.S. 952 (1980).

[434] People v. Collins, 213 Ill. App. 3d 818, 826, 572 N.E.2d 1005, 1010-11 (1st Dist. 1991) (first degree murder conviction reduced to second degree murder).

[435] People v. Leonard, 83 Ill. 2d 411, 416, 415 N.E.2d 358, 363-64 (1980) (appellate court reversal of murder conviction affirmed given evidence of mutual combat); People v. Craven, 54 Ill. 2d 419, 425, 299 N.E.2d 1, 3 (1973) (murder conviction reversed and remanded given evidence of mutual combat); People v. Johnson, 215 Ill. App. 3d 713, 728, 575 N.E.2d 1247, 1256-57 (1st Dist. 1991) (murder conviction reversed and remanded given evidence of mutual combat).

[436] ILL. ANN. STAT. ch. 38, para. 9-2 (Smith-Hurd 1979), 1961 Committee Comments, at 395 (revised 1972).

[437] People v. Chevalier, 131 Ill. 2d 66, 72, 544 N.E.2d 942, 944 (1989) (murder conviction affirmed); People v. Harris, 123 Ill. App. 3d 899, 904, 463 N.E.2d 1030, 1034 (1st Dist. 1984) (murder conviction affirmed); People v. Wax, 75 Ill. App. 2d 163, 182, 220 N.E.2d 600, 610 (4th Dist. 1966) (murder conviction affirmed), *cert. denied*, 387 U.S. 930 (1967).

[438] People v. Jenkins, 30 Ill. App. 3d 1034, 1038, 333 N.E.2d 497, 501 (4th Dist. 1975) (murder conviction reversed because involuntary manslaughter instructions were not given to the jury; however, failure to instruct on voluntary manslaughter not error).

provocations as would support reduction of the charge.[439] A victim's admission to her husband that she committed an adulterous act, even when she admitted that she enjoyed it and was smiling during the admission, did not constitute adequate provocation.[440] In a consolidated opinion, the Illinois Supreme Court held that there was insufficient provocation to establish voluntary manslaughter (now second degree murder) where the defendants suspected their respective wives of marital infidelity and, just prior to the shooting, the victims had admitted to adultery and, in one case, the victim disparaged the defendant's sexual abilities while, in the other case, the victim flaunted the fact that she had slept with her lover in the marital bed, and each victim was shot and killed during the argument.[441] The court distinguished these situations from those where the defendant discovers the victim in the act of adultery or immediately before or after, while stating a "verbal communication that adultery has occurred or will occur falls within the rule that mere words are insufficient provocation."[442]

The question of whether the defendant and victim must be in a legally recognized mutual relationship in order to invoke the "sudden and intense passion" defense in an adultery context has been raised but not explicitly answered. In *People v. McCarthy*,[443] the defendant and the victim had a long standing marriage-like relationship that ended two months prior to the victim's death. On the date of the homicide, the defendant claimed he was provoked into killing the victim when he found her in bed with another man.[444] The Illinois Supreme Court declined to grant voluntary manslaughter (now second degree murder) instructions, however, reasoning that these instructions would not even be available to divorced people whose relationship had previously ended.[445] Although the court did not explicitly decide whether spousal adultery should be enlarged as a mitigating factor to include a "marital-type relationship" because this couple had separated, the court noted that because common law marriages have not been recognized for many years, permitting a heat of passion argument in this type of case would be inconsistent with established public policy.[446] Thus, merely because there previously existed a "special relation" between the defen-

---

[439] People v. Arnold, 17 Ill. App. 3d 1043, 1048, 309 N.E.2d 89, 1046-48 (3d Dist. 1974) (murder conviction affirmed).

[440] People v. Schorle, 206 Ill. App. 3d 748, 758, 565 N.E.2d 84, 90 (1st Dist. 1990) (murder conviction affirmed).

[441] People v. Chevalier, 131 Ill. 2d 66, 70, 544 N.E.2d 942, 944-46 (1989) (murder convictions affirmed).

[442] People v. Chevalier, 131 Ill. 2d 66, 72, 544 N.E.2d 942, 944 (1989).

[443] 132 Ill. 2d 331, 547 N.E.2d 459 (1989) (murder conviction affirmed).

[444] People v. McCarthy, 132 Ill. 2d 331, 338, 547 N.E.2d 459, 461 (1989).

[445] People v. McCarthy, 132 Ill. 2d 331, 342, 547 N.E.2d 459, 463 (1989).

[446] People v. McCarthy, 132 Ill. 2d 331, 341, 547 N.E.2d 459, 463 (1989).

dant and his girlfriend (or her boyfriend) will not reduce a resultant homicide from first degree murder to second degree murder.[447]

In a few early Illinois cases, it was held that where a defendant was illegally arrested, his killing of the arresting officer might be deemed to have been in response to an adequate provocation.[448] However, Illinois law now explicitly states that a person has no right to resist arrest, whether lawful or unlawful.[449] Therefore, it is doubtful that the Illinois courts would be receptive to the adequate provocation argument if an arrestee took an officer's life. Moreover, it is significant that those statements in Illinois opinions that indicate an illegal arrest could constitute adequate provocation invariably prove to be dicta.[450]

While substantial physical injury, mutual quarrel or combat, adultery and, perhaps, illegal arrest may provide serious provocation in certain circumstances, it is clear that mere words, gestures, or trespass to property will not be sufficient.[451] The Illinois Supreme Court has unequivocally stated: "[t]the rule that mere words are insufficient provocation applies no matter how aggravated, abusive, opprobrious, or indecent the language."[452] However, this rule does not apply where, as a result of insulting or opprobrious words, "the parties suddenly become heated and engage in mutual combat, fighting on equal terms, and death results from the combat."[453] An insulting gesture, such as "flipping defendant the finger," is insufficient.[454] Trespass to property will also not satisfy the adequate provocation requirement. Where a bar owner fired his pistol, fatally wounding a patron, to protect two bottles of whiskey, serious provocation did

---

[447] People v. Elder, 219 Ill. App. 3d 223, 228, 579 N.E.2d 420, 423-24 (3d Dist. 1991) (first degree murder conviction affirmed).

[448] Rafferty v. People, 72 Ill. 37 (1874); Rafferty v. People, 69 Ill. 111 (1873).

[449] 720 ILCS 5/7-7 (1999).

[450] *See, e.g.*, People v. Elder, 219 Ill. App. 3d 223, 228, 579 N.E.2d 420, 423-24 (3d Dist. 1991) (no adequate provocation where defendant stalked former girlfriend and her fiancè):

> In Illinois, only four categories of provocation have been recognized as sufficiently serious to reduce the crime of first degree murder to second degree murder. They are: (1) substantial physical injury or assault; (2) mutual quarrel or combat; (3) illegal arrest; and (4) adultery with the offender's spouse.

[451] People v. Strong, 79 Ill. App. 3d 17, 24, 398 N.E.2d 216, 222 (1st Dist. 1979) (murder conviction affirmed).

[452] People v. Chevalier, 131 Ill. 2d 66, 71-72, 544 N.E.2d 942, 944 (1989) (murder conviction affirmed).

[453] People v. Matthews, 21 Ill. App. 3d 249, 253, 314 N.E.2d 15, 18 (3d Dist. 1974) (murder conviction affirmed).

[454] People v. Arnett, 217 Ill. App. 3d 626, 633, 577 N.E.2d 773, 776-77 (5th Dist. 1991) (first degree murder conviction affirmed).

not exist that would reduce the crime to a lesser homicide.[455] Finally, the defendant's shock and fear of family disgrace caused by the birth of her illegitimate child in no way constituted adequate provocation that mitigated her stabbing of her newborn child to the crime of second degree murder.[456]

Whenever a defendant makes a claim of adequate provocation, this claim cannot be based on a combination of theories, none of which is supported by its own weight. Thus, where a defendant, raised a "hybrid" claim based on some parts of mutual combat and some parts of spousal adultery, this was rejected as a possible basis for a finding of adequate provocation.[457]

Illinois caselaw has consistently held that there can be no significant "cooling off" period between the provocation and the defendant's killing.[458] The courts have reasoned that if there was a significant time period between the two events, time enough for the "boiling blood to have cooled, passion to have subsided," the killing could not be deemed a product of the heat of passion.[459] In other words, no successful claim of mitigation should succeed if, at the time of the killing, the defendant was "motivated not by a sudden and intense passion but by cold-blooded revenge."[460] By incorporating the "sudden and intense passion" language into the statute, the legislature intended to impose a "no cooling off period" requirement.[461] Thus, where a defendant was allegedly provoked, the passage of fifteen minutes between the provocation and the killing of the victim, during which time the defendant sat down and talked with the victim, belied any suggestion that the killing was a result of a sudden and intense passion.[462] So too, where the victim broke branches off the defendant's tree and the victim's father later beat the defendant, after which the defendant went into his house, tried to wash blood from his face, got a gun and returned to shoot the victim in the head four times, the court found that sufficient time had passed to undermine

---

[455] People v. Fausz, 107 Ill. App. 3d 558, 561, 437 N.E.2d 702, 705 (5th Dist. 1982) (voluntary manslaughter conviction reversed where jury's verdict not supported by evidence), aff'd, 95 Ill. 2d 535, 449 N.E.2d 78 (1983).

[456] People v. Doss, 214 Ill. App. 3d 1051, 1055, 574 N.E.2d 806, 809 (1st Dist. 1991) (first degree murder conviction affirmed).

[457] People v. Burts, 256 Ill. App. 3d 972, 977, 628 N.E.2d 515, 519 (1st Dist. 1993).

[458] See, e.g., People v. Harris, 8 Ill. 2d 431, 434, 134 N.E.2d 315, 317 (1956) (voluntary manslaughter conviction affirmed).

[459] People v. Epps, 197 Ill. App. 3d 376, 383-84, 554 N.E.2d 637, 642 (5th Dist. 1990) (first degree murder conviction affirmed).

[460] People v. Yates, 65 Ill. App. 3d 319, 325, 382 N.E.2d 505, 510 (1st Dist. 1978) (murder conviction affirmed).

[461] See ILL. ANN. STAT. ch. 38, para. 9-2 (Smith-Hurd 1979), 1961 Committee Comments, at 394 (revised 1972).

[462] People v. Causey, 66 Ill. App. 3d 12, 16, 383 N.E.2d 234, 237 (3d Dist. 1979) (murder conviction affirmed).

any suggestion that the killing was a result of a sudden and intense passion.[463] What constitutes a sufficient cooling-off period necessary to raise an offense from second degree murder to first degree murder depends on the magnitude of the provoking act and the degree to which passions have been aroused in the defendant.[464] No specific "yardstick of time" can govern all cases.[465]

Finally, if the defendant suffering from a sudden and intense passion negligently or accidentally causes the death of one other than the provocateur, he will be liable for second degree murder rather than first degree murder.[466] However, the law does not allow the defendant to *deliberately* transfer the result of his provocation from the provocateur to an innocent party.[467] Thus, where the victim's father severely beat the defendant, whereupon the victim's father drove off, the defendant's subsequent shooting of the victim who had earlier only broke branches off the defendant's tree was first degree murder since the defendant's killing of the victim was intentional, not negligent or accidental.[468] Here, the defendant's wrath was directed nowhere near the provocateur. This, said the court, was akin to saying "Joe made me angry, so I killed Bill."[469]

§ 6.26. — Elements of "Imperfect Defense" Second Degree Murder.

Subparagraph (a)(2) of paragraph 5/9-2 reflects what can be described as "imperfect defense" second degree murder.[470] Where an accused intentionally or knowingly kills another while believing the circumstances to be such that, if they existed, the action would be justified or excused under the defense principles of article 5/7, but in actuality this belief in justification is unreasonable, the accused has committed second degree murder.[471] The mens rea of imperfect defense second degree murder exists where the accused intentionally or knowingly kills another while acting under an unreasonable belief that the killing is justi-

---

[463] People v. Epps, 197 Ill. App. 3d 376, 383-84, 554 N.E.2d 637, 642 (5th Dist. 1990) (first degree murder conviction affirmed).

[464] People v. Hudson, 71 Ill. App. 3d 504, 511, 390 N.E.2d 5, 10 (1st Dist. 1979) (murder conviction reversed and charge reduced to voluntary manslaughter).

[465] People v. Harris, 8 Ill. 2d 431, 435, 134 N.E.2d 315, 317 (1956) (murder conviction affirmed).

[466] 720 ILCS 5/9-2(a)(1) (1999).

[467] People v. Epps, 197 Ill. App. 3d 376, 383-84, 554 N.E.2d 637, 642-43 (5th Dist. 1990).

[468] People v. Epps, 197 Ill. App. 3d 376, 383-84, 554 N.E.2d 637, 642-43 (5th Dist. 1990).

[469] People v. Epps, 197 Ill. App. 3d 376, 384, 554 N.E.2d 637, 643 (5th Dist. 1990) (first degree murder conviction affirmed).

[470] *See* People v. Monigan, 97 Ill. App. 3d 885, 889, 423 N.E.2d 546, 549 (5th Dist. 1981) ("Voluntary manslaughter [now second degree murder] may . . . be viewed as an imperfect claim of self-defense").

[471] 720 ILCS 5/9-2(a)(2) (1999).

fied.[472] Where the defendant is merely *reckless* in an imperfect defense situation, he or she will be convicted of involuntary manslaughter.[473]

The difference between a justified killing, for example in self-defense, and an unjustified killing amounting to second degree murder is that in the former instance, the belief that the use of force to defend oneself is reasonable under the circumstances, but in the latter, that belief is unreasonable.[474] In other words, the difference between first degree murder and second degree murder is that with second degree murder there exists sufficient evidence that the defendant had a *subjective* belief that his or her use of force was justified although that belief was unreasonable.[475] If the defendant did *not* actually believe his or her killing was justified, the crime is first degree murder.[476] Merely because a defendant claims that he or she thought he or she was killing with justification does not invariably require reduction of the charge from first degree murder to second degree murder.[477] The defendant's state of mind at the time of the incident is critical; and if the trier of fact believes the crime was first degree murder, its finding will normally be affirmed on appeal.[478] Where the evidence showed defendant and his three companions were the aggressors, were armed with a gun and a baseball bat, attacked victims who were sitting in a car unable to move because they were stuck in traffic, physically attacked the victims who made no move to retaliate and appeared to have no weapons and, at the time of the shooting, defendant was standing at the rear of the victims' car, with victims facing forward, and the now-deceased was shot in the back, this was "a cold and sense-

---

[472] People v. Parker, 194 Ill. App. 3d 1048, 1055, 551 N.E.2d 1012, 1017 (1st Dist. 1990) (murder conviction affirmed).

[473] People v. Woods, 80 Ill. App. 3d 56, 61-62, 398 N.E.2d 1086, 1091 (1st Dist. 1979) (action of defendant in striking deceased four times and defendant's readiness to continue beating deceased after he fell and held his head evidenced recklessness supporting involuntary manslaughter; self-defense claim rejected), *aff'd*, 81 Ill. 2d 537, 410 N.E.2d 866 (1980).

[474] *See* People v. Parker, 194 Ill. App. 3d 1048, 1055, 551 N.E.2d 1012, 1017 (1st Dist. 1990) for a discussion of the requirements for exoneration by way of self-defense, mitigation of the charge to voluntary manslaughter (now second degree murder), and conviction of the greater charge of murder (now first degree murder).

[475] People v. Hawkins, 296 Ill. App. 3d 830, 838, 696 N.E.2d 16, 22 (1st Dist. 1998) (first degree murder conviction reduced to second degree murder).

[476] People v. Horton, 233 Ill. App. 3d 22, 26, 598 N.E.2d 452, 455 (3d Dist. 1992) (first degree murder conviction affirmed).

[477] People v. Yates, 195 Ill. App. 3d 66, 69, 551 N.E.2d 999, 1001 (3d Dist. 1990) (first degree murder conviction affirmed).

[478] *See, e.g.*, People v. Parker, 194 Ill. App. 3d 1048, 1055, 551 N.E.2d 1012, 1017 (1st Dist. 1990) (trial court's verdict that defendant guilty of murder affirmed); People v. Hansen, 90 Ill. App. 3d 407, 409-10, 413 N.E.2d 103, 105 (1st Dist. 1980) (jury verdict that defendant guilty of murder affirmed), *cert. denied*, 454 U.S. 848 (1981). *Compare* People v. Dowaliby, 221 Ill. App. 3d 788, 800-01, 582 N.E.2d 1243, 1251 (1st Dist. 1991) (jury verdict that defendant guilty of first degree murder reversed due to insufficient evidence).

less killing" that belied defendant's contention that he was entitled to imperfect defense second degree murder instructions.[479] Similarly, the trial court properly refused second degree murder jury instructions where, believing the victim was carrying a gun during a confrontation with his victim, defendant left the scene of the confrontation to return with a gun, which he used to shoot the victim.[480]

> The reasonableness of an individual's belief that it was necessary to use deadly force to prevent death or great bodily harm raises a question of fact, and a reviewing court will not disturb the determination of the trier of fact . . . unless the evidence is so unsatisfactory to justify a reasonable doubt of guilt. In this regard, the trier of fact need not accept as true the testimony presented by defendant concerning the [alleged justification]; rather, in weighing such evidence, it must consider the probability or improbability of the testimony, the circumstances surrounding the killing, and the testimony of other witnesses.[481]

The jury normally determines whether a killing was entirely justified (for example, self-defense), whether the killing was totally unjustified (no evidence supportive of even an "unreasonable" defense claim) — in which case the crime is first degree murder — or whether the killing involved an imperfect defense claim — in which case the crime is second degree murder. For example, where a defendant, whose current wife informed him that she wished to marry the victim, claimed to have been threatened with violence by the victim prior to confrontation and at the point of confrontation, the victim made an effort to take a gun out of the hatchback of his car, at which point the defendant shot the victim three times, the jury was correct in determining that defendant had committed imperfect self defense second degree murder (rejecting exoneration due to self-defense).[482]

Virtually all of the cases involving imperfect defense second degree murder involve unsuccessful claims of self-defense where the assailant is killed;[483] self-defense where the defendant intends to kill the assailant, but an innocent bystander is killed;[484] or defense of another where the assailant of another is killed

---

[479] People v. Salgado, 287 Ill. App. 3d 432, 445-48, 678 N.E.2d 648, 658-59 (1st Dist. 1997) (first degree murder conviction affirmed).

[480] People v. Harper, 264 Ill. App. 3d 318, 322, 636 N.E.2d 977, 980 (1st Dist. 1994) (first degree murder conviction affirmed).

[481] People v. Hill, 53 Ill. App. 3d 280, 285, 368 N.E.2d 714, 718 (1st Dist. 1977) (voluntary manslaughter conviction affirmed).

[482] People v. Bosek, 210 Ill. App. 3d 573, 597, 569 N.E.2d 551, 566-67 (2d Dist. 1991) (second degree murder conviction affirmed), *cert. denied*, 502 U.S. 1098 (1992).

[483] *See, e.g.*, People v. Bosek, 210 Ill. App. 3d 573, 597, 569 N.E.2d 551, 566-67 (2d Dist. 1991), *cert. denied*, 502 U.S. 1098 (1992). *See* ch. 17 for a discussion of this defense.

[484] *See, e.g.*, People v. White, 8 Ill. App. 3d 574, 579, 290 N.E.2d 337, 340-41 (3d Dist. 1972) (voluntary manslaughter conviction affirmed).

by the defendant.[485] Since the second degree murder statute implies that all imperfect article 5/7 defenses could give rise to this crime, it might be arguable that other article 5/7 defenses — namely, "use of force in defense of dwelling,"[486] "use of force in defense of other property,"[487] "peace officer's use of force in making an arrest,"[488] "private person's use of force in making an arrest,"[489] "use of force to prevent escape,"[490] "compulsion,"[491] "entrapment"[492] and "necessity"[493] — could be the basis of a second degree murder finding where one or more of the elements of the respective defense is not satisfied. However, there is little caselaw dealing with these defenses. One important exception is *People v. Gleckler*,[494] where the Illinois Supreme Court explicitly ruled out the possibility that an imperfect defense claim of compulsion created the possibility of second degree murder, since the compulsion statute's "own terms, history and purpose" made clear that a taking of life was never permissible under compulsion.[495] Further, in *People v. Doss*,[496] the Illinois appellate court held the defense of necessity could not be employed to reduce a first degree murder conviction to second degree murder in circumstances where the defendant killed her infant child.[497] Here, a defense claim that her killing of the infant immediately after childbirth was somehow mitigated by her interest in avoiding the "family disgrace" associated with having a child out of wedlock had to be dismissed since the killing of the infant was "a far greater injury than any disgrace defendant might suffer as a result of giving birth."[498] In addition, in *People v. Aliwoli*,[499] the Illinois appellate court held an unproved insanity defense was not intended to be a mitigating factor for purposes of second degree murder.[500]

---

[485] *See, e.g.*, People v. Johnson, 4 Ill. App. 3d 249, 251, 280 N.E.2d 764, 766-67 (1st Dist. 1972) (murder conviction reversed and reduced to voluntary manslaughter). *See* ch. 17 for a discussion of this defense.

[486] 720 ILCS 5/7-2 (1999). *See* ch. 17 for a discussion of this defense.

[487] 720 ILCS 5/7-3 (1999). *See* ch. 17 for a discussion of this defense.

[488] 720 ILCS 5/7-5 (1999). *See* ch. 19 for a discussion of this defense.

[489] 720 ILCS 5/7-6 (1999). *See* ch. 19 for a discussion of this defense.

[490] 720 ILCS 5/7-9 (1999). *See* ch. 19 for a discussion of this defense.

[491] 720 ILCS 5/7-11 (1999). *See* ch. 19 for a discussion of this defense.

[492] 720 ILCS 5/7-12 (1999). *See* ch. 19 for a discussion of this defense.

[493] 720 ILCS 5/7-13 (1999). *See* ch. 19 for a discussion of this defense.

[494] 82 Ill. 2d 145, 411 N.E.2d 849 (1980) (murder conviction affirmed).

[495] People v. Gleckler, 82 Ill. 2d 145, 158, 411 N.E.2d 849, 855 (1980).

[496] 214 Ill. App. 3d 1051, 574 N.E.2d 806 (1st Dist. 1991) (first degree murder conviction affirmed).

[497] People v. Doss, 214 Ill. App. 3d 1051, 1055, 574 N.E.2d 806, 809 (1st. Dist. 1991).

[498] People v. Doss, 214 Ill. App. 3d 1051, 1055, 574 N.E.2d 806, 809 (1st. Dist. 1991).

[499] 238 Ill. App. 3d 602, 606 N.E.2d 347 (1st Dist. 1992).

[500] People v. Aliwoli, 238 Ill. App. 3d 602, 619-20, 606 N.E.2d 347, 359 (1st Dist. 1992).

Aside from the concerns addressed above, proving second degree murder involves most of the conceptual issues involved in the prosecution of first degree murder. The corpus delecti — the fact of death and the fact that the death was produced by a criminal agency — must be proven[501] and normal rules of causation are followed.[502]

§ 6.27. Involuntary Manslaughter and Reckless Homicide.

The offense of involuntary manslaughter appears to have had a much slower development at common law than murder and voluntary manslaughter.[503] However, the courts were determined to punish as an unlawful homicide those killings that arose during the course of a crime other than a felony (which would require treatment under the felony-murder rule), regardless of the degree of danger involved in the unlawful act and the offender's mental state.[504] Thus, the so-called "misdemeanor-manslaughter rule" was born.[505] The other branch of this offense was designed to cover those killings where the individual possessed no "malice aforethought" but killed with a criminally negligent or reckless state of mind.[506]

In reviewing the involuntary manslaughter provisions in various jurisdictions, the legislative committee responsible for drafting the Illinois Criminal Code of 1961 noted that most of the laws governing involuntary manslaughter were based on the concept of misdemeanor-manslaughter and negligence.[507] Careful examination of these laws revealed that in almost every case in which a conviction was upheld on the basis of the misdemeanor-manslaughter or "unlawful-act approach," a "dangerous act" had been involved.[508] Furthermore, under the sec-

---

[501] *See, e.g.*, People v. Bailey, 56 Ill. App. 2d 261, 272-73, 205 N.E.2d 756, 763 (1st Dist. 1965) (voluntary manslaughter conviction reversed).

[502] *See, e.g.*, People v. Love, 71 Ill. 2d 74, 84, 373 N.E.2d 1312, 1318 (1978) (defendant was liable for wife's death from pneumonia and mild peritonitis caused by exploratory laparotomy and splenectomy that she underwent as result of series of kicks administered to her abdomen by defendant, even though his acts were not sole and immediate cause of death; accordingly, state sufficiently proved that defendant's conduct contributed to wife's death; voluntary manslaughter affirmed).

[503] ILL. ANN. STAT. ch. 38, para. 9-3 (Smith-Hurd 1979), 1961 Committee Comments, at 473 (revised 1972).

[504] ILL. ANN. STAT. ch. 38, para. 9-3 (Smith-Hurd 1979), 1961 Committee Comments, at 473 (revised 1972).

[505] *See* § 6.10 of this chapter.

[506] ILL. ANN. STAT. ch. 38, para. 9-3 (Smith-Hurd 1979), 1961 Committee Comments, at 474 (revised 1972).

[507] ILL. ANN. STAT. ch. 38, para. 9-3 (Smith-Hurd 1979), 1961 Committee Comments, at 474 (revised 1972).

[508] ILL. ANN. STAT. ch. 38, para. 9-3 (Smith-Hurd 1979), 1961 Committee Comments, at 474 (revised 1972).

ond branch of involuntary manslaughter — relying on a negligence theory — it
was found that most of the courts had "narrowed the scope of the statutory provision by requiring proof of more than ordinary negligence — either recklessness or some high degree of negligence, variously designated as gross, wanton,
willful, clear or criminal — usually without further definition of these terms."[509]

The pre-1961 Illinois involuntary manslaughter statute was essentially patterned after the early common law approach articulated by Blackstone.[510]

> The literal application of these provisions would authorize conviction upon
> proof either that (1) the defendant at the time of the killing was performing
> any kind of unlawful act other than a felony — a mere trespass would suf-
> fice — and need have no causal relation to the death; or (2) the defendant
> displayed only ordinary negligence in performing an otherwise lawful act
> in a manner that "probably might" cause death"[511]

However, the judicial interpretations of the earlier involuntary manslaughter
statute resulted in a finding of criminal liability only where "the act, whether
lawful or unlawful, was . . . being done in a reckless or grossly negligent manner."[512] In some of the cases, the court concentrated on the defendant's mental
state, ignoring or merely mentioning the unlawfulness of the act.[513] In one case,
the Illinois Supreme Court held that a non-reckless unlawful act could not provide a foundation for involuntary manslaughter, since it was not the proximate
cause of the subsequent death.[514] Finally, these earlier caselaw definitions of the

---

[509] ILL. ANN. STAT. ch. 38, para. 9-3 (Smith-Hurd 1979), 1961 Committee Comments, at 475 (revised 1972).

[510] ILL. ANN. STAT. ch. 38, para. 9-3 (Smith-Hurd 1979), 1961 Committee Comments, at 476 (revised 1972). According to Blackstone:

> [I]n general, when an involuntary killing happens in consequence of an unlawful act, it will
> be either murder or manslaughter according to the nature of the act which occasioned it. If it
> be in the prosecution of a felonious intent, or in its consequence naturally tend to blood-
> shed, it will be murder; but if no more was intended than a mere civil trespass, it will
> amount only to manslaughter.

Id. at 477 (quoting 4 BLACKSTONE (7th ed.) 192-93). However, the Illinois statute added a qualification beyond Blackstone's definition: the act "probably might produce such a consequence" —
that is, death. *Id.* at 476 (citing ILL. REV. STAT. ch. 38, paras. 361, 363 (1959)).

[511] ILL. ANN. STAT. ch. 38, para. 9-3 (Smith-Hurd 1979), 1961 Committee Comments, at 476.

[512] ILL. ANN. STAT. ch. 38, para. 9-3 (Smith-Hurd 1979), 1961 Committee Comments, at 476.

[513] ILL. ANN. STAT. ch. 38, para. 9-3 (Smith-Hurd 1979), 1961 Committee Comments, at 476.
(citing as one example People v. Allen, 368 Ill. 368, 14 N.E.2d 397 (1938) (motorist sped on
wrong side of street and struck pedestrians; court's affirmance was based on finding of "wilful and
wanton negligence")).

[514] ILL. ANN. STAT. ch. 38, para. 9-3 (Smith-Hurd 1979), 1961 Committee Comments, at 476-77
(revised 1972) (citing People v. Mulcahy, 318 Ill. 332, 149 N.E. 266 (1925) (defendant-
policeman's failure to arrest gamblers and drunken persons in his presence and, perhaps, his drink-

term *negligence* actually described recklessness by insisting on conscious awareness of a life-threatening risk rather than negligent failure to be aware of the risk.[515]

§ 6.28. — Involuntary Manslaughter and Reckless Homicide Codified.

The crime of "Involuntary Manslaughter and Reckless Homicide" was enacted as part of the Criminal Code of 1961 and later amended in 1986. Paragraph 5/9-3 currently reads:

> Involuntary Manslaughter and Reckless Homicide. (a) A person who unintentionally kills an individual without lawful justification commits involuntary manslaughter if his acts whether lawful or unlawful which cause the death are such as are likely to cause death or great bodily harm to some individual, and he performs them recklessly, except in cases in which the cause of the death consists of the driving of a motor vehicle, in which case the person commits reckless homicide.
>
> (b) In cases involving reckless homicide, being under the influence of alcohol or any other drug or drugs at the time of the alleged violation shall be presumed to be evidence of a reckless act unless disproved by evidence to the contrary.
>
> (c) For the purposes of this Section, a person shall be considered to be under the influence of alcohol or other drugs while: 1. The alcohol concentration in such person's blood or breath is 0.08 or more based on the definition of blood and breath units in [625 ILCS] Section [5/]11-501.2 of the Illinois Vehicle Code; 2. Under the influence of alcohol to a degree which renders such person incapable of safely driving; 3. Under the influence of any other drug or combination of drugs to a degree that renders the person incapable of safely driving; or 4. Under the combined influence of alcohol

---

ing while on duty and carrying concealed firearm was not proximate cause of death; conviction reversed)).

[515] ILL. ANN. STAT. ch. 38, para. 9-3 (Smith-Hurd 1979), 1961 Committee Comments, at 477 (revised 1972) (citing as example People v. Sikes, 328 Ill. 64, 74, 159 N.E. 293, 297 (1927) ("The gist of the offense in a case of this character is criminal negligence. Negligence, to be criminal, must be gross or wanton negligence. Gross negligence is that which has in it the element of recklessness. Wanton negligence as applied to the running of motor vehicles, implies disregard of the rules of diligence and reckless heedlessness of consequences. Ordinary negligence connotes a negative quality in the attention and discharge of a duty. Criminal liability cannot be predicated upon every act carelessly performed merely because such carelessness results in the death of another. Negligence, to become criminal, must necessarily be reckless or wanton and of such a character as to show an utter disregard of the safety of others under circumstances likely to cause injury.")).

and any other drug or drugs to a degree which renders the person incapable of safely driving.[516]

In defining involuntary manslaughter for use in the Criminal Code of 1961, the Illinois legislature was determined to limit the scope of the prohibition to the judicial construction given the earlier legislation. The revision committee comments state that involuntary manslaughter (1) could only arise where the accused engaged in conduct that was likely to cause death or grievous bodily harm and he or she was consciously aware of the risk, in other words, that he or she was "reckless"; (2) could *not* be based on the failure to be aware of a risk (in other words, negligence would never suffice for involuntary manslaughter); and (3) could be predicated on a finding of *any* reckless conduct, whether the conduct was itself lawful or unlawful.[517] By limiting the acts sufficient for involuntary manslaughter to those involving recklessness, the drafting committee found that a "proximate cause" requirement between the wrongful act and the subsequent death was unnecessary.[518]

The legislative committee responsible for drafting paragraph 5/9-3 believed that the problem of the reckless motorist should fall within a stricture other than involuntary manslaughter.[519] Because of the opprobrium that attached to the term *manslaughter* and the penalties attached to that offense, juries in earlier prosecutions often hesitated to convict.[520] Thus, the legislative drafting committee determined that the reckless automobile driver's killing of another should be designated "reckless homicide" and that the sanction for this offense would be less than that for involuntary manslaughter.[521] However, because of the similarity between the two crimes, it was determined that no purpose would be served by placing the two offenses in separate statutory paragraphs.[522]

Significant legislative amendments were directed at what is now paragraph 5/9-3 in 1986. While the crime of involuntary manslaughter was not changed, the offense of reckless homicide was strengthened. First, if the defendant is under the influence of alcohol or drugs, this is prima facie evidence of reckless-

---

[516] 720 ILCS 5/9-3 (1999).

[517] ILL. ANN. STAT. ch. 38, para. 9-3 (Smith-Hurd 1979), 1961 Committee Comments, at 477 (revised 1972); *see also* People v. Smith, 186 Ill. App. 3d 89, 94, 542 N.E.2d 112, 114 (1st Dist. 1989) (involuntary manslaughter elemental composition discussed).

[518] ILL. ANN. STAT. ch. 38, para. 9-3 (Smith-Hurd 1979), 1961 Committee Comments, at 476-77.

[519] ILL. ANN. STAT. ch. 38, para. 9-3 (Smith-Hurd 1979), 1961 Committee Comments, at 477-78.

[520] ILL. ANN. STAT. ch. 38, para. 9-3 (Smith-Hurd 1979), 1961 Committee Comments, at 477.

[521] ILL. ANN. STAT. ch. 38, para. 9-3 (Smith-Hurd 1979), 1961 Committee Comments, at 477-78. Originally involuntary manslaughter was considered a class 3 felony (ILL. REV. STAT. ch. 38, para. 9-3(b)(1) (1983)), while reckless homicide was only a class 4 felony. (ILL. REV. STAT. ch. 38, para. 9-3(b)(2) (1983)).

[522] ILL. ANN. STAT. ch. 38, para. 9-3 (Smith-Hurd 1979), 1961 Committee Comments, at 478 (revised 1972).

ness.[523] Second, both involuntary manslaughter and reckless homicide are now generally treated as the same class of felony with identical sanctions.[524] However, effective in 1991, in cases of reckless homicide where the defendant is found to have been under the influence of drugs or alcohol, the penalty is a class 2 felony rather than a class 3 felony while, effective in 1998, involuntary manslaughter in which the victim is a family or household member is a class 2 felony rather than a class 3 felony.[525] Since the previous distinction between involuntary manslaughter and reckless homicide was based on the notion that the latter offense was less serious than the former, which is no longer the case, it is curious that the legislature when revising the sanctions did not decide to categorize all reckless killings as "voluntary manslaughter."

§ 6.29. — Elements of Involuntary Manslaughter and Reckless Homicide.

Involuntary manslaughter and reckless homicide require proof that an unjustified killing of another was caused by recklessness. If the defendant demonstrates that the killing was justified, there is no crime.[526] It should be noted that where the defendant intentionally kills another and claims self-defense, the courts are not inclined to instruct the jury on the crime of involuntary manslaughter when requested by the accused, since by definition, involuntary manslaughter (and reckless homicide) is evidenced by recklessness, not intent.[527] Similarly, where the circumstances surrounding the unjustified homicide clearly demonstrate that the crime was the result of an intentional killing rather than a reckless act, a trial court's refusal to give an involuntary manslaughter instruction will be upheld.[528]

---

[523] 720 ILCS 5/9-3(b) (1999).

[524] 720 ILCS 5/9-3(d) (1999) (both are class 3 felonies).

[525] 720 ILCS 5/9-3(e) (1999).

[526] *See, e.g.,* People v. Singleton, 41 Ill. App. 3d 665, 669, 354 N.E.2d 464, 467 (3d Dist. 1976) (involuntary manslaughter conviction reversed on self-defense grounds). *See also* People v. Thomas, 277 Ill. App. 3d 214, 218-19, 660 N.E.2d 184, 187-88 (1st Dist. 1995) (where victim, while brandishing a knife, jumped on hood of defendant's car during heated argument with defendant and defendant's escape effort resulted in death to victim, defendant's reckless homicide conviction reversed).

[527] People v. DeMumbree, 98 Ill. App. 3d 22, 25, 424 N.E.2d 73, 75 (1st Dist. 1981) (voluntary manslaughter conviction affirmed after denial of involuntary manslaughter instructions where defendant deliberately aimed and fired a shotgun at a group of men surrounding his car, which was in no way indicative of recklessness).

[528] People v. Castillo, 298 Ill. App. 3d 839, 843-45, 698 N.E.2d 604, 607-08 (1st Dist. 1998) (where defendant grabbed loaded gun in victim's hand, which resulted in a shot being fired and wrestled the gun away from the victim, and then continued to struggle with the victim over the loaded gun, resulting in a second shot being fired which killed the victim, trial court properly refused to give an involuntary manslaughter instruction inasmuch as it determined defendant's mental state was not one of mere recklessness, rather one sufficient for murder); People v. Tainter, 294 Ill. App. 3d 634, 640-43, 691 N.E.2d 55, 60-61 (1st Dist. 1998) (murder conviction affirmed after denial of involuntary manslaughter instructions; the disparity in size between the defendant and the

The "gist" of the crime of involuntary manslaughter[529] or reckless homicide[530] is recklessness. If the crime involves an intentional or knowledgeable killing, it is murder; if it involves a reckless taking of life, it is punishable as involuntary manslaughter or reckless homicide.[531] On the other hand, if the taking of life arises out of a mere accident, this is no crime, for by definition, an accident does not involve recklessness, or any other culpable mental state.[532] Unless the evidence reveals a "conscious disregard of a substantial and unjustifiable risk,"[533] there is no involuntary manslaughter[534] or reckless homicide.[535] The mere fact that an act was not totally volitional, however, will not sustain a defendant's argument that the act was an accident. For example, where the accused picked up a gun while intoxicated, stumbled, and fell backward, causing the gun to discharge and kill the victim, the appellate court held that handling a gun while intoxicated was in itself reckless, and the defendant took the risk that he would trip or stumble and cause the gun to discharge.[536] In addition, merely because a defendant *claims* a lack of conscious awareness of a life-threatening risk does not defeat a finding of recklessness. Thus, where defendant left her three-month-old infant in a parked car for four hours on a summer day, which resulted in the death of the child from heat stroke, her claim that she forgot about the child, was unaware of the danger of leaving an unattended child in a car and did not know how high the temperature could get in the car did not undermine a jury's finding of recklessness and involuntary manslaughter.[537]

The mere fact that defendant was engaged in an unlawful act when a death occurred does not mean he or she harbored a reckless mental state. For example,

---

victim, the brutality and duration of the beating, the severity of the victim's injuries and the victim's defenselessness belied any claim that the killing was reckless).

[529] People v. Frank, 98 Ill. App. 3d 388, 396, 424 N.E.2d 799, 805 (2d Dist. 1981) (murder conviction affirmed after denial of involuntary manslaughter instructions), *cert. denied*, 456 U.S. 927 (1982).

[530] People v. Luttmer, 48 Ill. App. 3d 303, 305, 362 N.E.2d 1093, 1094 (2d Dist. 1977) (reckless homicide conviction affirmed).

[531] People v. Farmer, 91 Ill. App. 3d 262, 266, 414 N.E.2d 779, 783 (5th Dist. 1980) (murder conviction affirmed).

[532] People v. Spani, 46 Ill. App. 3d 777, 780, 361 N.E.2d 377, 379 (3d Dist. 1977) (involuntary manslaughter conviction reversed because death was caused by accident).

[533] People v. Smith, 186 Ill. App. 3d 89, 94, 542 N.E.2d 112, 114 (1st Dist. 1989) (involuntary manslaughter conviction affirmed).

[534] People v. Spani, 46 Ill. App. 3d 777, 780, 361 N.E.2d 377, 379 (3d Dist. 1977) (involuntary manslaughter conviction reversed).

[535] People v. Frary, 36 Ill. App. 3d 111, 114-15, 343 N.E.2d 233, 236 (5th Dist. 1976) (reckless homicide conviction reversed).

[536] People v. Franklin, 189 Ill. App. 3d 425, 430, 545 N.E.2d 346, 350 (1st Dist. 1990) (involuntary manslaughter conviction affirmed).

[537] People v. Kolzow, 301 Ill. App. 3d 1, 6, 703 N.E.2d 424, 428-29 (1st Dist. 1998) (involuntary manslaughter conviction affirmed).

the fact that defendant was speeding approximately 10 to 15 m.p.h. over the speed limit in his automobile when a motorcycle he was following lost control did not evince recklessness toward the motorcyclist he struck and killed.[538] However, where the defendant's unlawful act involves operating a motor vehicle while intoxicated, a finding of a reckless mental state necessary for reckless homicide is presumed as a matter of law.[539] On the other hand, intoxication is not an element of reckless homicide or involuntary manslaughter that must be proved in each and every case.[540]

The Illinois courts have considered a wide range of conduct and whether the conduct in question satisfies the involuntary manslaughter or reckless homicide requirements. For a further understanding of these crimes, see chapter 2 (Criminal Act and Mental State) in which there is a review of a variety of situations where recklessness has been, or has not been, found to exist.[541] As with first degree murder and second degree murder, the corpus delecti — the fact of death plus the fact that the death was caused by the criminal agency of another[542] — must be proven. A causal relationship between the reckless act and subsequent death is required by the judiciary.[543]

---

[538] People v. Frary, 36 Ill. App. 3d 111, 114-15, 343 N.E.2d 233, 236 (5th Dist. 1976) (reckless homicide conviction reversed).

[539] 720 ILCS 5/9-3(b) (1993) (formerly ILL. REV. STAT. ch. 38, para. 9-3(b) (1991)). *See also* People v. Hester, 131 Ill. 2d 91, 101, 544 N.E.2d 797, 802 (1989) (instructions that the jury may, but is not required to, presume that a defendant is under the influence of alcohol if the defendant's blood alcohol level is 0.10% or more do not violate due process; reckless homicide affirmed); People v. Robinson, 199 Ill. App. 3d 494, 501-02, 557 N.E.2d 396, 401 (1st Dist. 1990) (although proof that defendant operated his motor vehicle at an excessive speed is not, by itself recklessness, evidence that defendant was under influence of alcohol is prima facie evidence of a reckless act; reckless homicide conviction affirmed); People v. Giere, 192 Ill. App. 3d 520, 526-27, 548 N.E.2d 1104, 1108-09 (2d Dist. 1989) (while neither intoxication nor driving at excessive speed establishes recklessness per se, driving 15 to 20 miles per hour over the speed limit while having a blood alcohol level of 0.21% constituted recklessness likely to cause death or great harm to another; reckless homicide conviction affirmed).

[540] People v. Smith, 149 Ill. 2d 558, 565, 599 N.E.2d 888, 891 (1992) (defendant's handling of loaded gun which shot his wife could be deemed recklessness under circumstances even if defendant not intoxicated; involuntary manslaughter conviction affirmed).

[541] *See* ch. 2 of this treatise.

[542] *See, e.g.,* In re Thur, 80 Ill. App. 3d 592, 596, 400 N.E.2d 564, 567 (1st Dist. 1980) (involuntary manslaughter conviction affirmed).

[543] *See, e.g.,* People v. Ellison, 100 Ill. App. 3d 282, 289, 426 N.E.2d 1058, 1063 (1st Dist. 1981) (reckless injection of victim, an alleged transsexual, with silicone was cause of death, notwithstanding defendant's claim to the contrary; involuntary manslaughter and concealment of a homicidal death convictions affirmed).

§ 6.30. Intentional Homicide of Unborn Child.

In 1986, the offense of feticide[544] was repealed and replaced by three offenses: intentional homicide of an unborn child,[545] voluntary manslaughter of an unborn child,[546] and involuntary manslaughter and reckless homicide of an unborn child.[547] Paragraph 5/9-1.2 covers the first of these offenses:

(a) A person commits the offense of intentional homicide of an unborn child if, in performing acts which cause the death of an unborn child, he without lawful justification: (1) either intended to cause the death of or do great bodily harm to the pregnant woman or her unborn child or knew that such acts would cause death or great bodily harm to the pregnant woman or her unborn child; or (2) he knew that his acts created a strong probability of death or great bodily harm to the pregnant woman or her unborn child; and (3) he knew that the woman was pregnant.

(b) For the purposes of this Section, (1) "unborn child" shall mean any individual of the human species from fertilization until birth, and (2) "person" shall not include the pregnant woman whose unborn child is killed.

(c) This Section shall not apply to acts which cause the death of an unborn child if those acts were committed during any abortion, as defined in section 2 of the Illinois Abortion Law of 1975, as amended, to which the pregnant woman has consented. This Section shall not apply to acts which were committed pursuant to usual and customary standards of medical practice during diagnostic testing or therapeutic treatment.

(d) Penalty. The sentence for intentional homicide of an unborn child shall be the same as for first degree murder, except that the death penalty shall not be imposed.

(e) The provisions of this Act shall not be construed to prohibit the prosecution of any person under any other provision of law.[548]

---

[544] ILL. REV. STAT. ch. 38, para. 9-1.1 (1985) (repealed) ("(a) A person commits the offense of feticide who causes the death of a fetus if, in performing the acts which caused the death, he, without lawful justification: (1) Either intended to kill or do great bodily harm to the mother carrying the fetus or knew that such acts would cause death or great bodily harm to the mother; or (2) he knew his act created a strong probability of death or great bodily harm to the mother; or (3) he was attempting or committing a forcible felony against the mother, other than voluntary manslaughter; and (4) he knew, or reasonably should have known under all the circumstances, that the mother was pregnant. (b) For purposes of this Section, "fetus" means a fetus which the physician or pathologist performing the fetal autopsy determines ... to have been capable, at the time of its death, of sustained life outside the mother's womb with or without equipment...").

[545] 720 ILCS 5/9-1.2 (1999).

[546] 720 ILCS 5/9-2.1 (1999).

[547] 720 ILCS 5/9-3.2 (1999).

[548] 720 ILCS 5/9-1.2 (1999); see also People v. Shoultz, 289 Ill. App. 3d 392, 394, 682 N.E.2d 446, 448 (4th Dist. 1997) (finding sanction for intentional homicide of unborn child does not vio-

This offense is significantly more broad than feticide. Feticide was committed if the fetus was viable outside the womb of its mother.[549] An "unborn child" exists from the point of conception.[550] As with the earlier offense of feticide,[551] the murder of a pregnant woman could constitute both murder and intentional homicide of the unborn child.[552]

The defendant's knowledge of the pregnancy of the mother is an essential element of the offense of intentional homicide of an unborn child.[553] Thus, where the state failed to prove the defendant was aware of the woman's pregnancy when he kicked her in the stomach and inflicted various other blows to her body, thereby killing her seven-month-old fetus, his conviction was reversed on appeal.[554]

§ 6.31. Voluntary Manslaughter of Unborn Child.

A companion enactment of intentional homicide of an unborn child is voluntary manslaughter of an unborn child[555] It reads:

> (a) A person who kills an unborn child without lawful justification commits voluntary manslaughter of an unborn child if at the time of the killing he is acting under a sudden and intense passion resulting from serious provocation by another whom the offender endeavors to kill, but he negligently or accidentally causes the death of the unborn child. Serious provocation is conduct sufficient to excite an intense passion in a reasonable person.
>
> (b) A person who intentionally or knowingly kills an unborn child commits voluntary manslaughter of an unborn child if at the time of the killing he believes the circumstances to be such that, if they existed, would justify or

---

late Illinois constitutional proportionate penalties clause by imposing greater penalties than those attached to the offense of illegal abortion); People v. Ford, 221 Ill. App. 3d 354, 366-73, 581 N.E.2d 1189, 1198-1202 (4th Dist. 1991) (finding intentional homicide of an unborn child statute did not violate equal protection and due process clauses of federal constitution).

[549] *See* ILL. REV. STAT. ch. 38, para. 9-1.1(b) (1985) (repealed).

[550] 720 ILCS 5/9-1.2(b) (1999).

[551] People v. Shum, 117 Ill. 2d 317, 363, 512 N.E.2d 1183, 1201 (1987) (defendant properly convicted for both murder and feticide based on single act of killing mother), *cert. denied*, 484 U.S. 1079 (1988).

[552] 720 ILCS 5/9-1.2(e) (1999). *See, e.g.*, People v. Compos, 227 Ill. App. 3d 434, 592 N.E.2d 85 (1st Dist. 1992) (first degree murder and intentional homicide of an unborn child convictions affirmed), *cert. denied*, 514 U.S. 1024 (1995); People v. Kuchan, 219 Ill. App. 3d 739, 579 N.E.2d 1054 (1st Dist. 1991) (murder and intentional homicide of an unborn child convictions affirmed).

[553] People v. Gillespie, 276 Ill. App. 3d 495, 499, 659 N.E.2d 12, 15 (1st. Dist. 1995).

[554] People v. Gillespie, 276 Ill. App. 3d 495, 499, 659 N.E.2d 12, 15 (1st. Dist. 1995).

[555] 720 ILCS 5/9-2.1 (1999).

exonerate the killing under the principles stated in Article 7 of this Code, but his belief is unreasonable.

(c) Sentence. Voluntary Manslaughter of an unborn child is a . . . felony.[556]

Like intentional homicide of an unborn child, this prohibition defines "unborn child" as any individual of the human species from fertilization until birth and defines "person" as excluding the pregnant woman whose unborn child is killed.[557] It also contains an exemption for a pregnant woman's legal abortion.[558]

Voluntary manslaughter of an unborn child also exceeds the reach of the prior feticide statute. As with intentional homicide of an unborn child, the fetus need not be viable.[559] On the other hand, feticide arose where the defendant intentionally or knowingly engaged in conduct that had the tendency to kill or inflict great bodily injury on the fetus without regard to possible mitigating circumstances.[560] In other words if a defendant killed a fetus in a sudden heat of passion aroused by a serious provocation or killed a fetus while, for example, harboring an unreasonable belief that it was necessary to kill a pregnant woman in self-defense, he or she would have been liable for feticide and murder-type sanctions.[561] Now, such mitigating circumstances are taken into account, which lessens the possible penalties.[562]

It is unclear why the legislature characterized this offense as a form of "voluntary manslaughter." If the killing of a person born alive is "second degree murder" where the defendant (1) killed in a heat of passion or (2) unreasonably believed his or her killing was justified, it would have been more consistent with existing nomenclature to describe that prohibited by paragraph 5/9-2.1 as second degree murder (or as lesser degree of intentional homicide) of an unborn child.

§ 6.32. Involuntary Manslaughter and Reckless Homicide of an Unborn Child.

The third of a trilogy of offenses designed to punish those who unjustifiably kill unborn children is involuntary manslaughter and reckless homicide of an unborn child.[563] Specifically, paragraph 5/9-3.2 states:

(a) A person who unintentionally kills an unborn child without lawful justification commits involuntary manslaughter of an unborn child if his acts whether lawful or unlawful which cause the death are such as are likely to

---

[556] 720 ILCS 5/9-2.1 (1999).

[557] 720 ILCS 5/9-2.1(d) (1999).

[558] 720 ILCS 5/9-2.1(e) (1999).

[559] 720 ILCS 5/9-2.1(d) (1999).

[560] ILL. REV. STAT. ch. 38, para. 9-1.1(a) (1985) (repealed).

[561] ILL. REV. STAT. ch. 38, para. 9-1.1 (1985) (death penalty excluded) (repealed).

[562] 720 ILCS 5/9-2.1 (1999).

[563] 720 ILCS 5/9-3.2 (1999).

cause death or great bodily harm to some individual, and he performs them recklessly, except in cases in which the cause of death consists of the driving of a motor vehicle, in which case the persons commits reckless homicide of an unborn child.

(b) Sentence. (1) Involuntary manslaughter of an unborn child is a . . . felony. (2) Reckless homicide of an unborn child is a . . . felony.[564]

Identical to the other prohibitions against taking the life of an unborn child, this offense states: "(1) 'unborn child' shall mean any individual of the human species from fertilization until birth, and (2) 'person' shall not include the pregnant woman whose unborn child is killed."[565] It also exempts legal abortions.[566] Finally, this prohibition states that it "shall not be construed to prohibit the prosecution of any person under any other provision of law, nor shall it be construed to preclude any civil cause of action."[567]

This law clearly goes beyond feticide, which did not prohibit reckless killing of the unborn.[568] As with the reckless killing of a person born alive, both involuntary manslaughter of an unborn child and reckless homicide of an unborn child involve the same felony sanction.[569]

§ 6.33. Drug-Induced Homicide.

In 1989, the Illinois legislature created the new offense of "drug-induced homicide."[570] It reads:

(a) A person who violates subsection (a) or subsection (b) of Section 401 of the Illinois Controlled Substances Act by unlawfully delivering a controlled substance to another, and any person dies as a result of the injection, inhalation, or ingestion of any amount of that controlled substance, commits the offense of drug-induced homicide.

(b) Sentence. Drug-induced homicide is a . . . felony.[571]

This law significantly expands criminal homicide legislation in Illinois. Under the Illinois felony-murder rule, the underlying felony must be "forcible" in nature,[572] which means it must involve the use or threat of physical force or violence toward an individual.[573] Obviously, distribution of a controlled substance

---

[564] 720 ILCS 5/9-3.2 (1999).

[565] 720 ILCS 5/9-3.2(c) (1999).

[566] 720 ILCS 5/9-3.2(d) (1999).

[567] 720 ILCS 5/9-3.2(e) (1999).

[568] ILL. REV. STAT. ch. 38, para. 9-1.1 (1985) (repealed).

[569] 720 ILCS 5/9-3.2(b) (1999).

[570] 720 ILCS 5/9-3.3 (1999).

[571] 720 ILCS 5/9-3.3 (1999) (referring to 720 ILCS 570/401 (1999)).

[572] 720 ILCS 5/9-1(a)(3) (1999). *See* § 6.22 of this chapter.

[573] 720 ILCS 5/2-8 (1999).

could not be classified as a forcible felony. However, the creation of the offense of drug-induced homicide now makes the drug "pusher" responsible for a death arising out of his or her felony distribution of narcotics in much the same fashion as the felony-murder rule makes the forcible felon responsible for the death of victims of his or her forcible felony.[574]

§ 6.34. Concealment of Homicidal Death.

The final stricture aimed at preventing criminal involvement in a homicide is the offense of concealment of homicidal death.[575] It provides:

> (a) A person commits the offense of concealment of homicidal death when he conceals the death of any other person with knowledge that such other person has died by homicidal means. (b) Nothing in this Section prevents the defendant from also being charged with and tried for the first degree murder, second degree murder or involuntary manslaughter of the person whose death is concealed. If a person convicted under this Section is also convicted of first degree murder, second degree murder or involuntary manslaughter, the penalty under this Section shall be imposed separately and in addition to the penalty for first degree murder, second degree murder or involuntary manslaughter. (c) Sentence. Concealment of homicidal death is a . . . . felony.[576]

The offense of concealment of homicidal death is composed of two elements: (1) proof of an affirmative act of *concealment* of the homicidal death, and (2) knowledge on the part of the defendant that the person died by *homicidal means*.[577] The fact that defendant was not held criminally responsible for the homicide is not a defense to concealment because the elements of concealment differ from those involving commission of a criminal homicide.[578]

Concealment involves some affirmative act on the part of defendant.[579] Mere silence or nondisclosure of information relevant to the homicidal death is insuf-

---

[574] However, a person who commits drug-induced homicide is not eligible for the death penalty. 720 ILCS 5/9-3.3 (1999).

[575] 720 ILCS 5/9-3.1 (1999).

[576] 720 ILCS 5/9-3.1 (1999).

[577] People v. Franklin, 130 Ill. App. 3d 514, 519, 474 N.E.2d 776, 780 (5th Dist. 1985) (concealment of a homicidal death affirmed); People v. Mahon, 77 Ill. App. 3d 413, 423, 395 N.E.2d 950, 958 (1st Dist. 1979) (murder and concealment of a homicidal death conviction affirmed).

[578] People v. Mueller, 109 Ill. 2d 378, 388, 488 N.E.2d 523, 528 (1985) (concealment of homicidal death convictions upheld notwithstanding earlier acquittals for murder of same victims); People v. Dyer, 28 Ill. App. 3d 436, 439-40, 328 N.E.2d 716, 719-20 (5th Dist. 1975) (concealment of homicidal death conviction upheld notwithstanding acquittal for murder in same trial).

[579] People v. Stiles, 46 Ill. App. 3d 359, 363, 360 N.E.2d 1217, 1220 (3d Dist. 1977) (concealment of a homicidal death affirmed).

ficient.[580] The defendant must perform some act to prevent or delay the discovery of a homicidal death. Acts such as defendant's wiping fingerprints from the scene of a homicide and disposing of the weapon;[581] hiding a body in a drainage ditch;[582] placing his wife's body in the trunk of her car, driving it to another section of town and failing to notify police;[583] or dismembering the body, putting it in several trash bags and throwing it in a dumpster[584] have been deemed sufficient acts of concealment.

Although the concealment prohibition does not explicitly refer to concealment of the cause of death, it has been held that the statute includes "situations where the body itself is concealed or where the homicidal nature of death is actively concealed, as in making a homicide appear an accident."[585] Thus, where defendant recklessly injected a transsexual's breast with silicone and she consequently died shortly thereafter from the injections, whereupon the defendant dressed the victim and instructed another person who was present to make no mention of his injections of the victim, this constituted a concealment of the nature of the victim's death from the authorities which was the basis for affirmance of his conviction for concealment.[586]

A defendant who initially engages in an affirmative act of concealment but later takes action designed to undo his or her cover-up efforts has no defense to concealment. For example, where a defendant strangled his victim to death, concealed the victim's body in a laundry bag and hid it from view, concealment was found even though he later moved the body to a location where it could be discovered.[587]

While one Illinois appellate court stated in dictum that a defendant may have a defense to concealment of a homicidal death where (1) he attempts to conceal or destroy a body he erroneously believes is dead as a result of potentially justified conduct or (2) where he attempts to conceal or destroy a body he errone-

---

[580] People v. Vath, 38 Ill. App. 3d 389, 391-95, 347 N.E.2d 813, 815-18 (5th Dist. 1976) (concealment of homicidal death conviction reversed).

[581] People v. Dyer, 28 Ill. App. 3d 436, 438, 328 N.E.2d 716, 719 (5th Dist. 1975) (concealment of a homicidal death conviction affirmed).

[582] People v. Stiles, 46 Ill. App. 3d 359, 363, 360 N.E.2d 1217, 1220 (3d Dist. 1977) (concealment of a homicidal death affirmed).

[583] People v. Viano, 139 Ill. App. 3d 560, 563, 487 N.E.2d 623, 625-26 (3d Dist. 1985) (murder and concealment of homicidal death convictions affirmed).

[584] People v. Eyler, 133 Ill. 2d 173, 192-93, 549 N.E.2d 268, 276-77 (1989) (murder and concealment of homicidal death convictions affirmed), cert. denied, 498 U.S. 881, reh'g denied, 498 U.S. 993 (1990).

[585] People v. Vath, 38 Ill. App. 3d 389, 395, 347 N.E.2d 813, 817 (5th Dist. 1976).

[586] People v. Ellison, 100 Ill. App. 3d 282, 291-92, 426 N.E.2d 1058, 1065 (1st Dist. 1981) (involuntary manslaughter and concealment of homicidal death convictions affirmed).

[587] People v. Kirkman, 170 Ill. App. 3d 106, 110-11, 522 N.E.2d 588, 591-92 (1st Dist. 1988) (voluntary manslaughter and concealment of homicidal death convictions affirmed).

ously believes to be dead as a result of someone else's criminal conduct, the same court explicitly ruled that a defendant has no defense of mistake of fact if the attempt to destroy or conceal involves a body he erroneously believes is already dead as a result of his own conduct.[588] Thus, if a defendant "inflicts unjustified wounds to the extent that he reasonably believes he has killed someone, misapprehension of his crime's effects does not license incineration, drowning or dismemberment to destroy evidence of what happened."[589]

Notwithstanding the dictum referred to above, it should be pointed out the plain language of the concealment statute merely states that the defendant must knowingly conceal a death caused by *homicidal means*. Homicidal means refers to "the act of a human being in taking away the life of another human being."[590] It does not "necessarily import a crime, but includes those cases in which the law justifies or excuses the taking of human life."[591] Attempts in Illinois by a defendant to limit "homicidal means" to merely felonious killings have proved unsuccessful.[592] This offense, therefore, proscribes the performance of any affirmative acts designed to prevent or delay the discovery of a lawful *or* unlawful killing of any person.

Subparagraph (b) of the concealment statute directs in relevant part that if "a person convicted under this Section is also convicted of first degree murder, second degree murder or involuntary manslaughter, the penalty under this section shall be imposed separately and in addition to the penalty for first degree murder, second degree murder or involuntary manslaughter."[593] An initial reading of this paragraph would seem to indicate that where there is a conviction both for concealment of a homicidal death and for murder or manslaughter, consecutive sentences would be required, thus preempting the concurrent imprisonment provisions of the code.[594] However, it has been held that this language does *not* require the imposition of consecutive sentences on multiple convictions of concealment of homicidal death and first degree murder or manslaughter.[595]

---

[588] People v. Rollins, 295 Ill. App. 3d 412, 418, 695 N.E.2d 61, 64-65 (5th Dist. 1998) (first degree murder and concealment of a homicidal death convictions affirmed).

[589] People v. Rollins, 295 Ill. App. 3d 412, 418, 695 N.E.2d 61, 64-65 (5th Dist. 1998).

[590] People v. Coslet, 39 Ill. App. 3d 302, 304, 349 N.E.2d 496, 498 (4th Dist. 1976) (quoting approved jury instruction).

[591] People v. Mahon, 77 Ill. App. 3d 413, 424, 395 N.E.2d 950, 958 (1st Dist. 1979) (quoting approved jury instruction).

[592] *See, e.g.,* People v. Coslet, 39 Ill. App. 3d 302, 304, 349 N.E.2d 496, 498 (4th Dist. 1976).

[593] 720 ILCS 5/9-3.1(b) (1999).

[594] 730 ILCS 5/5-8-4 (1999), which requires the imposition of consecutive sentences only on an adequate showing that it is necessary for the protection of the public.

[595] People v. Gil, 125 Ill. App. 3d 892, 896, 466 N.E.2d 1205, 1208-09 (1st Dist. 1984) (voluntary manslaughter and concealment of homicidal death convictions affirmed).

§ 6.35. Lesser Included Offenses.

While the subject of lesser included offenses was analyzed in depth in an earlier chapter,[596] it is important to note at this juncture the posture of courts regarding whether certain crimes are lesser included offenses of criminal homicides or whether specific homicides are lesser included of other criminal homicides. Where a defendant commences an attack upon his victim which ultimately results in the victim's death, a criminal conviction for homicide will preclude the defendant from being convicted of lesser included offenses of battery or aggravated battery.[597] One the other hand, convictions have been sustained for home invasion,[598] attempted armed robbery,[599] burglary,[600] and concealment of homicidal death[601] in conjunction with a criminal homicide because of their differing elements.[602] In a felony-murder prosecution, it has been held that armed robbery[603] and aggravated arson is a lesser included offense of felony murder.[604] So, too, armed robbery has been ruled a lesser included offense of a felony-murder.[605]

Where a jury returns verdicts of intentional murder and felony-murder arising out of a single homicide, obviously only one murder conviction may stand.[606] It would appear that since an intentional murder involves a more culpable mental state, the felony-murder conviction should be vacated.[607]

Finally, the Illinois Supreme Court has determined that second degree murder is not a lesser included offense of first degree murder.[608] In *People v. Jeffries*, the court held that since second degree murder required proof of mitigating circumstances, elements above and beyond those required of first degree murder, it

---

[596] *See* ch. 1 for a discussion of lesser included offenses.

[597] People v. Lyons, 26 Ill. App. 3d 193, 198-99, 324 N.E.2d 677, 681 (5th Dist. 1974), *cert. denied*, 423 U.S. 1036 (1975).

[598] People v. Amos, 204 Ill. App. 3d 75, 83, 561 N.E.2d 1107, 1113-14 (1st Dist. 1990).

[599] People v. Amos, 204 Ill. App. 3d 75, 83, 561 N.E.2d 1107, 1113-14 (1st Dist. 1990).

[600] People v. Dixon, 122 Ill. App 3d 141, 149, 460 N.E.2d 858, 863 (1st Dist. 1984).

[601] People v. Mueller, 109 Ill. 2d 378, 388-90, 488 N.E.2d 523, 528 (1985).

[602] People v. Mueller, 109 Ill. 2d 378, 388-90, 488 N.E.2d 523, 528 (1985).

[603] People v. Smith, 183 Ill. 2d 425, 429-34, 701 N.E.2d 1097, 1099-1101 (1998) (armed robbery vacated as lesser included offense of felony murder).

[604] People v. Washington, 272 Ill. App. 3d 913, 919-20, 651 N.E.2d 625, 630 (1st Dist. 1995).

[605] People v. Prince, 288 Ill. App. 3d 265, 278, 681 N.E.2d 521, 530 (1st Dist. 1997).

[606] People v. Mack, 105 Ill. 2d 103, 136-37, 473 N.E.2d 880, 898 (1984).

[607] *See, e.g.*, People v. Cardona, 158 Ill. 2d 403, 412, 634 N.E.2d 720, 723-4 (1994) (where charges of intentional, knowing and felony-murder have been established, intentional murder is the most serious and convictions on other murder theories are vacated); People v. Waldron, 219 Ill. App. 3d 1017, 1039, 580 N.E.2d 549, 564 (2d Dist. 1991) (intentional murder not a lesser included offense of felony-murder).

[608] People v. Jeffries, 164 Ill. 2d 104, 121, 646 N.E.2d 587, 595 (1995).

was most appropriate to describe second degree murder as a "lesser mitigated offense" of first degree murder.[609]

---

[609] People v. Jeffries, 164 Ill. 2d 104, 121, 646 N.E.2d 587, 595 (1995).

CHAPTER 7

KIDNAPPING AND RELATED OFFENSES

§ 7.01. Introduction.

Article 5/10 covers "kidnapping and related offenses."[1] These offenses are kidnapping,[2] aggravated kidnapping,[3] unlawful restraint,[4] aggravated unlawful restraint,[5] forcible detention,[6] child abduction,[7] unlawful visitation interference,[8]

---

[1] *See* 720 ILCS 5/10-1 through 5/10-8 (1999).

[2] 720 ILCS 5/10-1 (1999).

[3] 720 ILCS 5/10-2 (1999).

[4] 720 ILCS 5/10-3 (1999).

[5] 720 ILCS 5/10-3.1 (1999).

[6] 720 ILCS 5/10-4 (1999).

[7] 720 ILCS 5/10-5 (1999).

[8] 720 ILCS 5/10-5.5 (1998).

harboring a runaway,[9] aiding and abetting child abduction,[10] and unlawful sale of a public conveyance travel ticket to a minor.[11] All of these offenses, except the last, involve the wrongful abduction of a person who is, because of the abduction, deprived of the basic liberty to which he or she is entitled in this society.

§ 7.02. Kidnapping.

Over the last century, the basic definition of kidnapping has remained largely unchanged in Illinois.[12] While the former statute on the subject was not as clear as the current provision,[13] the courts had enunciated the elements of this earlier offense as being (1) unlawful seizure and (2) secret confinement,[14] and this remains true of the present prohibition. The courts have construed kidnapping rather narrowly to avoid including the whole field of false imprisonment in this offense.[15]

§ 7.03. — Kidnapping Codified.

In paragraph 5/10-1 of the Criminal Code, the crime of kidnapping is defined in the following terms:

Kidnapping, (a) Kidnapping occurs when a person knowingly:

---

[9] 720 ILCS 5/10-6 (1999).

[10] 720 ILCS 5/10-7 (1999).

[11] 720 ILCS 5/10-8 (1999).

[12] See ILL. REV. STAT. ch. 38, para. 166 (1901):

Whoever willfully and without lawful authority forcibly or secretly confines or imprisons any other person within this state against his will, or forcibly carries or sends such person out of the state, or forcibly seizes or confines, or inveigles or kidnaps any such other person, with the intent to cause such person to be secretly confined or imprisoned in this state against his will, or to cause such a person to be sent out of the state against his will, shall be imprisoned.

See also id. ch. 38, para. 384 (1961).

[13] ILL. ANN. STAT. ch. 38, para. 10-1 (Smith-Hurd 1979), 1961 Committee Comments, at 552 (revised 1972).

[14] ILL. ANN. STAT. ch. 38, para. 10-1 (Smith-Hurd 1979), 1961 Committee Comments, at 552 (revised 1972) (citing People v. Bishop, 1 Ill. 2d 60, 114 N.E.2d 566, cert. denied, 346 U.S. 916 (1953)).

[15] ROLLIN M. PERKINS & RONALD N. BOYCE, CRIMINAL LAW 232 (3d ed. 1982). These authors stress that false imprisonment is a much broader concept: "False imprisonment, sometimes called false arrest, is the unlawful confinement of a person. It results from any unlawful exercise or show of force by which a person is compelled to remain where he does not wish to remain or go where he does not wish to go." Id. at 224 (emphasis added). Thus, even a detention on a public street would qualify. However, if the confinement is secretive, it is more properly understood as kidnapping. Id. at 228.

(1) And secretly confines another against his will, or

(2) By force or threat of imminent force carries another from one place to another with intent to secretly confine him against his will, or

(3) By deceit or enticement induces another to go from one place to another with intent to secretly confine him against his will.

(b) Confinement of a child under the age of 13 years is against his will within the meaning of this Section if confinement is without the consent of his parent or legal guardian.

(c) Sentence. Kidnapping is a . . . felony.[16]

The revision committee points out:

> [t]he three subsections of 10-1(a) are designed to cover the three methods usually employed in kidnapping. Both (2) and (3) involve the carrying from one place to another, or inducing to go from one place or another, which is sufficient to cover the common-law aspect of conveying out of the country, or, under the former Illinois statute (§ 384), carrying or causing the victim to be conveyed out of the State. . . . The word "knowingly" in the first sentence of section 10-1(a) qualifies each of the three methods enumerated in subsections (1), (2) and (3).

Subsection (b) eliminates the defense of consent of the victim when the victim is under thirteen years of age.[17]

§ 7.04. — Elements of Kidnapping.

Basically, kidnapping exists where there occurs (1) knowledge and (2) secretive confinement of another (3) against his or her will. First, the confinement must have been done "knowingly."[18] If a person unwittingly locked a person in a building without any knowledge of this person's presence in the building, this would not be viewed as a kidnapping. The next element requires further discussion.

§ 7.05. — Secret Confinement.

In order to prove kidnapping in Illinois, the defendant must "secretly confine" his or her victim. Without secret confinement, there is no kidnapping because the courts insist that secret confinement is the "gist" of the crime of kidnapping.[19] The secret confinement contemplated by the statute may be shown by

---

[16] 720 ILCS 5/10-1 (1999).

[17] ILL. REV. STAT. ch. 38, para. 10-1 (Smith-Hurd 1982), 1961 Committee Comments, at 552 (revised 1972).

[18] See ch. 2 for a discussion of mental states.

[19] People v. Sykes, 161 Ill. App. 3d 623, 628, 515 N.E.2d 253, 256 (1st Dist. 1987).

proof of the secrecy of the confinement or the place of confinement.[20] The most common scenario in which this occurs is where the victim is abducted from his or her home[21] or off the street[22] and the victim's whereabouts are unknown to all but the abductor. Where no one beyond the victim is aware of the fact of the abduction, as was the case where a teenage girl was abducted from a home where she was babysitting at 2:30 a.m. and was repeatedly raped by her abductor in a soccer field a short distance away before she was released several hours later, the proof of secret confinement was easily proven.[23] However, Illinois caselaw clearly states that the nature of the detention need not be this extreme to satisfy the secret confinement criteria.

In *People v. Mulcahey*,[24] the defendant taped his victim to a chair in her own home before leaving to pick up ransom money. The fact that the victim was concealed in her own home was not fatal to the state's charge.[25] The Illinois Supreme Court commented that the "victim in this case was 'secretly confined' as effectively in her own home as if the defendant had asported her to some remote isolated place of confinement."[26] In *People v. Bishop*,[27] the Illinois Supreme Court rejected the argument that there could be no secret confinement of a victim who was abducted in an automobile in motion on a highway.[28] These cases clarify that the proof of " secret confinement" is not defeated because, in some respects, the victim was in a "public domain," such as where a kidnap victim is confined in an automobile on a public way.[29] Secret confinement as an element of kidnapping or aggravated kidnapping has been defined as "concealed; hidden; not made public; kept from knowledge or notice of persons liable to be affected by the act."[30]

---

[20] People v. Enoch, 122 Ill. 2d 176, 195, 522 N.E.2d 1124, 1134, *cert. denied*, 488 U.S. 917 (1988); People v. Jackson, 281 Ill. App. 3d 759, 769, 666 N.E.2d 854, 862 (1st Dist. 1996).

[21] People v. Cole, 172 Ill. 2d 85, 102-04, 665 N.E.2d 1275, 1283-84, *cert. denied*, 519 U.S. 1030 (1996).

[22] People v. Lloyd, 277 Ill. App. 3d 154, 159-60, 660 N.E.2d 43, 48 (1st Dist. 1991).

[23] People v. Tate, 94 Ill. App. 3d 192, 200, 418 N.E.2d 1048, 1054 (5th Dist. 1981).

[24] 72 Ill. 2d 282, 381 N.E.2d 254 (1978).

[25] People v. Mulcahey, 72 Ill. 2d 282, 285, 381 N.E.2d 254, 256 (1978).

[26] People v. Mulcahey, 72 Ill. 2d 282, 285, 381 N.E.2d 254, 256 (1978).

[27] 1 Ill. 2d 60, 63, 114 N.E.2d 566, 568, *cert. denied*, 346 U.S. 916 (1953) (citing prior statute).

[28] People v. Bishop, 1 Ill. 2d 60, 63, 114 N.E.2d 566, 568, *cert. denied*, 346 U.S. 916 (1953). *Accord* People v. Masterson, 79 Ill. App. 2d 117, 130, 223 N.E.2d 252, 258 (3d Dist. 1967) (citing current statute).

[29] People v. Cassell, 283 Ill. App. 3d 112, 121-22, 669 N.E.2d 655, 662 (1st Dist. 1996) (defendant's claim that aggravated kidnap victim in defendant's automobile was not secretly confined because automobile was in "public domain" rejected).

[30] People v. Franzen, 251 Ill. App. 3d 813, 823-24, 622 N.E.2d 877, 887 (2nd Dist. 1993) (quoting People v. Mulcahey, 72 Ill. 2d 282, 285, 381 N.E.2d 254, 255 (1978)) (aggravated kidnapping conviction reversed).

In addition, the confinement does not need to be secret in the sense that no one but the abducted victim is aware of the confinement. In *People v. Mulcahey*,[31] although the facts suggest that the victim's husband was unclear about his wife's whereabouts at the time of her confinement, there was secret confinement even though he had been informed that she was being held hostage as part of the ransom demand.[32] In *People v. Williams*,[33] there was secret confinement when the person walking with the victim, at the time she was forced into an automobile by her captors, was aware of her abduction.[34]

Where there is no secrecy about the confinement itself or about the place of confinement, there is no kidnapping.[35] Thus, where the defendant took a victim hostage in the victim's apartment after he shot another person, the fact that many people knew about the defendant's hostage-taking and that the defendant had discussions with the police during his holding of the victim, belied any showing of secrecy necessary for kidnapping.[36] Where the defendant jumped out of a doorway and pulled his victim into the vestibule of a building located only a few steps away from a busy city thoroughfare, where he sexually assaulted her, made no attempt to move the victim into a more concealed location in the building and remained within public view in the vestibule area clearly visible to anyone walking or driving down the street, there was no secret confinement.[37] Where another defendant grabbed a ten-year-old alleged kidnap victim by the arm and walked with her for several blocks, until she yelled for help, whereupon he ran off, this was "unlawful restraint," but it was not kidnapping due to the absence of "secret confinement."[38]

While the preceding discussion focused on the secrecy of the abduction, some attention must be given to the confinement itself. Although confinement usually means enclosure within something such as a house or car, it is not strictly limited to those types of places.[39] Confinement has occurred in one's own home,[40]

---

[31] 72 Ill. 2d 282, 381 N.E.2d 254 (1978).

[32] People v. Mulcahey, 72 Ill. 2d 282, 283, 381 N.E.2d 254, 255 (1978).

[33] 99 Ill. App. 3d 919, 425 N.E.2d 1321 (1st Dist. 1981).

[34] *See* People v. Williams, 99 Ill. App. 3d 919, 920-21, 425 N.E.2d 1321, 1322 (1st Dist. 1981).

[35] People v. Sykes, 161 Ill. App. 3d 623, 627-29, 515 N.E.2d 253, 256-57 (1st Dist. 1987) (aggravated kidnapping conviction reversed where element not proved).

[36] People v. Pasch, 152 Ill. 2d 133, 186-88, 604 N.E.2d 294, 316 (1992) (reversing aggravated kidnapping conviction), *cert. granted*, 508 U.S. 959, *cert. vacated*, 510 U.S. 910 (1993).

[37] People v. Lamkey, 240 Ill. App. 3d 435, 438-39, 608 N.E.2d 406, 409 (1st Dist. 1992) (aggravated kidnapping conviction reversed although aggravated criminal sexual assault conviction affirmed).

[38] People v. Sykes, 161 Ill. App. 3d 623, 627-29, 515 N.E.2d 253, 256-57 (1st Dist. 1987) (aggravated kidnapping conviction reversed; unlawful restraint conviction affirmed); *See* § 7.21 and § 7.22 of this chapter for a discussion of the crime of unlawful restraint.

[39] People v. Jackson, 281 Ill. App. 3d 759, 769, 666 N.E.2d 854, 862 (1st Dist. 1996).

[40] People v. Mulcahey, 72 Ill. 2d 282, 285, 381 N.E.2d 254, 256 (1978).

in a moving car,[41] in a parked car,[42] down a dark alley into a secluded yard,[43] in a dark field,[44] on a secluded bridge,[45] in an auto shop after hours,[46] and in the basement of the defendant's home when the defendant's unsuspecting parents were upstairs.[47]

Just as the courts are not particularly concerned about where the confinement occurs, they are not overly strict about the length of the confinement. The courts have found the confinement to be sufficient where it lasted for twelve hours,[48] for approximately one and one-half hours,[49] and for only a few minutes.[50]

Finally, the kidnapping must involve a detention *of another against his or her will.* Although it may appear elementary at first glance that *any* secret confinement against his or her will is kidnapping, this is a simplistic assumption. For instance, if a parent were to lock a child in his or her bedroom for the night as punishment for the child's mischief, this is clearly not kidnapping. Thus, one must address the concerns involving (1) legal authority, (2) consent by the victim or the victim's legal guardian, (3) the type of force or threats that will render the victim's detention involuntary, and (4) the type of enticement or deceit that will render the victim's detention involuntary.

§ 7.06. — Legal Authority.

When a person restrains another or forces a person to go from one place to another, this is not kidnapping if the action is within his or her legal authority. Thus, a legitimate arrest by a police officer of a person who has engaged in criminality could not be kidnapping.[51]

Where a child abduction is perpetrated by a biological parent, who had never been given legal custody of the child, the Illinois appellate court held this was not a kidnapping because a parent retained at least some limited authority over his child, consistent with that which has historically exempted parents from kid-

---

[41] People v. Canale, 52 Ill. 2d 107, 119, 285 N.E.2d 133, 139 (1972); People v. Bishop, 1 Ill. 2d 60, 63, 114 N.E.2d 566, 568, *cert. denied*, 346 U.S. 916 (1953); People v. Harris, 68 Ill. App. 3d 12, 14, 385 N.E.2d 789, 791 (5th Dist. 1979); People v. Hamil, 20 Ill. App. 3d 901, 908, 314 N.E.2d 251, 256 (1st Dist. 1974); People v. Masterson, 79 Ill. App. 2d 117, 122, 223 N.E.2d 252, 255 (3d Dist. 1967).

[42] People v. Landis, 66 Ill. App. 2d 458, 461-62, 214 N.E.2d 343, 345 (1st Dist. 1966).

[43] People v. Kleba, 110 Ill. App. 3d 345, 356-58, 442 N.E.2d 605, 613-14 (1st Dist. 1982).

[44] People v. Frazen, 251 Ill. App. 3d 813, 823-24, 622 N.E.2d 877, 887 (2d Dist. 1993).

[45] People v. Jackson, 281 Ill. App. 3d 759, 769, 666 N.E.2d 854, 862 (1st Dist. 1996).

[46] *See* People v. Utinans, 55 Ill. App. 3d 306, 310-11, 370 N.E.2d 1080, 1083-84 (1st Dist. 1977).

[47] People v. McNight, 72 Ill. App. 3d 136, 142-43, 390 N.E.2d 379, 385 (1st Dist. 1979).

[48] People v. Savage, 5 Ill. 2d 296, 298-99, 125 N.E. 2d 449, 450-51 (1955).

[49] *See* People v. Tate, 94 Ill. App. 3d 192, 193-94, 418 N.E.2d 1048, 1049-50 (5th Dist. 1981).

[50] *See* People v. Lloyd, 277 Ill. App. 3d 154, 164-65, 660 N.E.2d 43, 51 (1st Dist. 1995).

[51] JOHN KLOTTER, CRIMINAL LAW § 3.7 (2d ed. 1986).

napping prohibitions.[52] However, this same court acknowledges that the Illinois child abduction statute[53] was designed to prevent this type of parental abduction of a non-custodial child that the kidnapping statute was not intended to reach.[54]

§ 7.07. — Consent.

Kidnapping arises under subsection (a)(1) where the victim has somehow been confined *against his or her will*. Thus, a kidnapping occurred where a defendant, armed with a gun and making repeated threats, had detained his 14-year-old victim, and her failure to attempt an escape did not establish that she had voluntarily accompanied her assailant.[55] Where the victims drove the defendant, a recent prison escapee who was armed with a pistol, from a rural town to East St. Louis, after defendant had pointed a gun at one of the victims, the victims' confinement was against their will.[56] Where the body of a fifteen-year-old male prostitute showed signs of binding of his wrists and puncture wounds before he was brutally murdered by the defendant, the defendant's claim that the victim had consented to the bondage as well as the infliction of the puncture wounds, which he asserted was not uncommon in the homosexual community, was rejected because the victim had no history of the sort of bondage or sadistic sex inflicted upon him and, as such, the evidence supported "a finding that the victim was confined against his will." [57]

If the person being confined had no legal capacity to consent, then this person's confinement could amount to kidnapping.[58] For example, inasmuch as a three-year-old child does not have the legal ability to consent, an abduction of such a child would be kidnapping if it occurred without either parent's permission.[59] However, this would not be a crime if there was parental consent.[60]

---

[52] People v. Algarin, 200 Ill. App. 3d 740, 746-51, 558 N.E.2d 457, 461-64 (1st Dist. 1990) (aggravated kidnapping conviction reversed while reinstating aggravated unlawful restraint conviction).

[53] 720 ILCS 5/10-5 (1999). *See* § 7.25 of this chapter.

[54] People v. Algarin, 200 Ill. App. 3d 740, 746-51, 558 N.E.2d 457, 461-64 (1st Dist. 1990).

[55] People v. Owens, 133 Ill. App. 2d 44, 47, 272 N.E.2d 858, 860 (1st Dist. 1971) (aggravated kidnapping and rape convictions affirmed).

[56] People v. Harris, 68 Ill. App. 3d 12, 14, 385 N.E.2d 789, 791 (5th Dist. 1979) (aggravated kidnapping conviction affirmed).

[57] People v. Eyler, 133 Ill. 2d 173, 196-99, 549 N.E.2d 268, 278-79 (1989), *cert. denied*, 499 U.S. 881, *reh'g denied*, 498 U.S. 993 (1990).

[58] People v. Davis, 105 Ill. App. 3d 549, 559, 433 N.E.2d 1376, 1384 (4th Dist. 1982).

[59] People v. Davis, 105 Ill. App. 3d 549, 559, 433 N.E.2d 1376, 1384 (4th Dist. 1982) (evidence sufficient to establish aggravated kidnapping but felony-murder conviction reversed on other grounds).

[60] *See* People v. Marin, 48 Ill. 2d 205, 210, 269 N.E.2d 303, 305 (1971).

· Illinois cases which involve the alleged kidnapping of children necessarily reflect an issue of consent.[61] The kidnapping statute explicitly addresses this concern in section 5/10-1(b), which states that the confinement of a child under the age of thirteen is "against his will" if that confinement is without the consent of the child's parent or legal guardian.[62] The landmark case in Illinois regarding this subject is *People v. Marin*.[63] In that case, a seven-year-old child, on his way home from school, was told by the driver of an automobile that his mother was in the hospital. At the driver's request, the child entered the automobile and was driven to defendant's home. Once they arrived at the defendant's home, the boy was told to get into a laundry bag that was on the floor of the car and he was then carried into the home in the bag. The boy was then held pursuant to a ransom demand designed to extort money from the boy's wealthy grandfather. The defendants' primary defense advanced at trial was that the boy's father had consented to the boy's abduction as part of the ransom scheme. After being convicted, the defendants appealed on the ground that the trial court's jury instructions were insufficient because the court omitted all reference to the effect of consent by the parent or legal guardian when the victim was a child under thirteen.[64] Ultimately, the Illinois Supreme Court reversed and remanded for a new trial, holding that (1) there can be no kidnapping if the victim consented or, in the case of a child less than thirteen years old, if the parents consented and, accordingly, (2) it was reversible error to fail to instruct the jury on the legal consequences of parental consent.[65]

Thus, where lack of consent becomes an issue in a kidnapping case, the failure to instruct a jury on the legal consequences of consent is reversible error.[66] However, it should be recognized that some Illinois caselaw indicates that the failure to allege absence of consent does not render a charging instrument, such as an indictment, fatally defective.[67]

§ 7.08. — Force or Threat of Force.

Subsection (a)(2) of the kidnapping statute states that kidnapping arises when force or threat of force is used to secretly confine another.[68] What type of force, or threat of force, the kidnapper must use to secretly confine his or her victim

---

[61] *See, e.g.,* People v. Algarin, 200 Ill. App. 3d 740, 746-51, 558 N.E.2d 457, 461-64 (1st Dist. 1990).

[62] 720 ILCS 5/10-1(b) (1999).

[63] 48 Ill. 2d 205, 269 N.E.2d 303 (1971).

[64] People v. Marin, 48 Ill. 2d 205, 207-08, 269 N.E.2d 303, 304 (1971).

[65] People v. Marin, 48 Ill. 2d 205, 210, 269 N.E.2d 303, 305-06 (1971).

[66] People v. Marin, 48 Ill. 2d 205, 210, 269 N.E.2d 303, 305 (1971).

[67] People v. Williams, 131 Ill. App. 2d 280, 283-84, 268 N.E.2d 730, 732-33 (1st Dist. 1971), *aff'd*, 52 Ill. 2d 455, 288 N.E.2d 280 (1972).

[68] 720 ILCS 5/10-1(a)(2) (1999).

for the purposes of kidnapping will now be addressed. In the 1858 case of *Moody v. People*,[69] the defendant was convicted of kidnapping a fourteen-year-old child in Illinois and bringing her to Ontario, Canada. The defendant appealed on the grounds that she did not actually force the child to accompany her.[70] The Illinois Supreme Court refused to accept the defendant's argument and affirmed the conviction.[71] The court ruled that it was not necessary that actual physical force be used.[72] Furthermore, the court found that it was sufficient to show that the victim's mind "was operated upon by the defendants, by falsely exciting the fears, by [use of] threats, fraud, or other unlawful or undue influence, amounting substantially to a coercion of the will."[73]

As a result of the adoption of the *Moody* principle into the express language of subsection (a)(2), kidnapping may be performed with either actual force or with the threat of imminent force.[74] The courts have found imminent force or threat of force where two victims entered the kidnappers' car because one of the kidnappers displayed a gun;[75] where a defendant entered his victim's car at gun point;[76] where the victim complied with defendant's demands after he drew a bayonet;[77] where the severely beaten victim was placed in the trunk of her car;[78] and where the victim was told that if she did not remain quiet while she accompanied the defendant, who took her from a house to a field to rape her, she would be killed.[79]

Finally, the fact that the victim failed to make an escape attempt does not mean the threat of force was insufficient. Where a 14-year-old victim did not attempt an escape from her captor, this did not defeat the defendant's kidnapping conviction because the defendant had been armed with a gun, had made repeated threats to the victim, and had not made any showing at trial of how the victim had a reasonable opportunity to escape.[80]

---

[69] 20 Ill. 315 (1858).

[70] Moody v. People, 20 Ill. 315, 317 (1958).

[71] Moody v. People, 20 Ill. 315, 318 (1958).

[72] Moody v. People, 20 Ill. 315, 318-319 (1958).

[73] Moody v. People, 20 Ill. 315, 318 (1958).

[74] 720 ILCS 5/10-1(a)(2) (1999)

[75] People v. Masterson, 79 Ill. App. 2d 117, 130, 223 N.E.2d 252, 259 (3d Dist. 1967) (aggravated kidnapping conviction affirmed).

[76] People v. Landis, 66 Ill. App. 3d 458, 464, 214 N.E.2d 343, 346 (1st Dist. 1966) (aggravated kidnapping conviction affirmed).

[77] *See* People v. Miller, 58 Ill. App. 3d 1019, 1020, 374 N.E.2d 1118, 1119 (4th Dist. 1978) (aggravated kidnapping conviction affirmed).

[78] People v. Moreland, 292 Ill. App. 3d 616, 620-22, 686 N.E.2d 343, 597, 600-01 (1st Dist. 1997) (aggravated kidnapping conviction affirmed).

[79] *See* People v. Tate, 94 Ill. App. 3d 192, 193-94, 418 N.E.2d 1048, 1049-50 (5th Dist. 1981) (aggravated kidnapping conviction affirmed).

[80] People v. Owens, 133 Ill. App. 2d 44, 47, 272 N.E.2d 858, 860 (1st Dist. 1971).

When the defendant uses "force or [the] threat of imminent force" as prohibited by subsection (a)(2),[81] this subsection contains additional language stating that the defendant must have used such force or made such threat against the victim "with intent secretly to confine him against his will."[82] This phrase requires, then, proof of no less than a "specific intent"[83] on the part of the accused. In other words, where the defendant is charged under this subsection of kidnapping, it must be shown that the force or threat was utilized by the defendant while he or she had the "specific intent to secretly confine the victim."[84]

§ 7.09. — Deceit or Enticement.

While most kidnappings are performed by detentions *against the will* of the victim, as proscribed by subsection (a)(1), or through the use of force or the threat of imminent force, as outlawed under subsection (a)(2), there is another way in which kidnapping can occur. Subsection (a)(3) provides that if a person uses "deceit or enticement" in order to induce his or her victim "to go from one place to another," there is kidnapping as long as the defendant's employment of the deceit or enticement was with the specific "intent secretly to confine him against his will."[85] In *People v. Siegal*,[86] the defendant sent letters to his victim, a clothing retailer, representing that the defendant had on hand a supply of clothing for sale, urging the victim to come to Chicago to purchase it. When the victim arrived in Chicago, he was ushered into a basement that he believed contained the clothing. Instead of finding clothing, the victim encountered two men who bound and gagged him and demanded ransom from him. The Illinois Supreme Court ruled that this was the type of deceit that kidnapping was designed to cover.[87]

In *People v. Eyler*,[88] the defendant deceived or enticed the victim to his apartment by falsely representing that he would pay his victim, a male prostitute, money for sexual service. Once in the apartment, defendant bound and tortured the victim, and ultimately stabbed him to death. Here, there was inducement by

---

[81] 720 ILCS 5/10-1(a)(2) (1999).

[82] 720 ILCS 5/10-1(a)(2) (1999).

[83] *See* ch. 2 for a discussion of specific intent.

[84] People v. Miller, 58 Ill. App. 3d 1019, 1024, 374 N.E.2d 1118, 1122 (4th Dist. 1978) (aggravated kidnapping conviction affirmed).

[85] 720 ILCS 5/10-1(a)(3) (1999); People v. Brown, 214 Ill. App. 3d 836, 847, 574 N.E.2d 190, 197 (1st Dist. 1991) (aggravated kidnapping established where defendant deceived or enticed victim into hotel room on pretense of assisting her in gaining employment, whereupon he sexually assaulted her).

[86] 362 Ill. 389, 200 N.E. 72 (1936).

[87] People v. Siegal, 362 Ill. 389, 392, 200 N.E. 72, 73 (1936).

[88] 133 Ill. 2d 173, 549 N.E.2d 268 (1989), *cert. denied*, 498 U.S. 881, *reh'g denied*, 498 U.S. 993 (1990).

enticement or deceit leading to secret confinement which amounted to aggravated kidnapping.[89]

§ 7.10. — Specific Intent to Secretly Confine.

If the state formally charges the accused of kidnapping under subsection (a)(2) (use of force or threat) or subsection (a)(3) (use of deceit or enticement), it will be obligated to show that the accused had the "specific intent to secretly confine the victim."[90] That is not to say that kidnapping invariably requires proof of a "specific intent to secretly confine," because where the state proceeds under subsection (a)(1), it is only required to prove that the defendant "knowingly . . . and secretly confine[d] another against his will."[91] In some instances, the appellate courts confuse this issue by making simplistic statements such as "[t]he specific intent relevant to kidnapping is knowledge" while citing subsection (a)(1),[92] as though "intent" and "knowledge" were the same mental states which, of course, they are not.[93]

The evidence of specific intent that the state is required to offer to satisfy subsection (a)(2) or subsection (a)(3) can be established by "words of intention" or "may be inferred from the circumstances surrounding the commission of an act by the defendant."[94] For example, where a defendant approached the victim's automobile, drew a bayonet, drove her vehicle to a particular location, ordered her to remove her clothing, and raped her, this was sufficient circumstantial evidence from which one could infer his "specific intent to secretly confine" her.[95]

§ 7.11. — Asportation.

Asportation is the removal of people or things from one place to another.[96] At common law, asportation of the person was an essential ingredient of kidnapping, since the victim had to be taken by his or her abductor from this country to another.[97] If the abduction involved a victim's secret confinement within his or

---

[89] People v. Eyler, 133 Ill. 2d 173, 195-98, 549 N.E.2d 268, 277-78 (1989) (murder and aggravated kidnapping convictions affirmed), cert. denied, 498 U.S. 881, reh'g denied, 498 U.S. 993 (1990).

[90] People v. Miller, 58 Ill. App. 3d 1019, 1024, 374 N.E.2d 1118, 1122 (4th Dist. 1978) (aggravated kidnapping conviction affirmed).

[91] 720 ILCS 5/10-1(a)(1) (1999).

[92] See, e.g., People v. Long, 30 Ill. App. 3d 815, 819, 333 N.E.2d 534, 538 (2d Dist. 1975).

[93] See ch. 2 for a discussion of other examples of such mislabeling.

[94] People v. Long, 30 Ill. App. 3d 815, 819, 333 N.E.2d 534, 538 (2d Dist. 1975).

[95] People v. Long, 30 Ill. App. 3d 815, 819, 333 N.E.2d 534, 538 (2d Dist. 1975) (aggravated kidnapping and rape conviction affirmed).

[96] BLACK'S LAW DICTIONARY 75 (6th ed. 1991).

[97] People v. Casiano, 212 Ill. App. 3d 680, 686-87, 571 N.E.2d 742, 746 (1st Dist. 1991). See also ROLLIN M. PERKINS & RONALD N. BOYCE, CRIMINAL LAW 230 (3d ed. 1982).

her own country, then the crime was "false imprisonment."[98] Later, the courts abandoned the notion that asportation to another country was required, but insisted on some type of movement of the victim from one point to another.[99] Today, in Illinois, the "plain language" of the statute clarifies that "asportation of the victim is not an element under section 5/10-1(a)(1)."[100] On the other hand, asportation is an element under both subsection (a)(2), addressing kidnappings where the defendant "by force or threat of imminent force *carries another from one place to another*;"[101] and under subsection (a)(3), covering kidnappings where the defendant "by deceit or enticement *induces another to go from one place to another*."[102] Thus, in *Mulcahey*,[103] discussed above,[104] proof of asportation was not required under subsection (a)(1), where the victim was confined in her own home.[105] In *People v. Casiano*,[106] the Illinois appellate court rejected the argument that asportation was not an "essential element" that had to be proved under subsection (a)(2).[107] And in *Siegal*,[108] also discussed above,[109] the Illinois Supreme Court was satisfied that the element of asportation was proved as required under the statutory language that was the predecessor to subsection (a)(3).[110]

Beyond the "general legal concept of asportation" that is required, for example, by the subsection (a)(2) language that demands proof that the victim was *carried* from one place to another is the often litigated question of whether a detention or asportation is "merely incidental" to another crime.[111] For example, in *People v. Casiano*,[112] the Illinois appellate court first addressed the question as to whether a criminal sexual assault "victim was carried 'from one place to another,'" as required by subsection (a)(2), when he forced his victim at knife

---

[98] M. CHERIF BASSIOUNI, SUBSTANTIVE CRIMINAL LAW 289 (1978).

[99] ROLLIN M. PERKINS & RONALD N. BOYCE, CRIMINAL LAW 230 (3d ed. 1982).

[100] People v. Mulcahey, 50 Ill. App. 3d 421, 425, 365 N.E.2d 1013, 1016 (4th Dist. 1977), *aff'd*, 72 Ill. 2d 282, 381 N.E.2d 254 (1978).

[101] 720 ILCS 5/10-1(a)(2) (1999) (emphasis added).

[102] 720 ILCS 5/10-1(a)(3) (1993) (emphasis added).

[103] 50 Ill. App. 3d 421, 365 N.E.2d 1013 (4th Dist. 1977), *aff'd*, 72 Ill. 2d 282, 381 N.E.2d 254 (1978).

[104] *See* § 7.05 of this chapter.

[105] People v. Mulcahey, 50 Ill. App. 3d 421, 425, 365 N.E.2d 1013, 1016 (4th Dist. 1977), *aff'd*, 72 Ill. 2d 282, 381 N.E.2d 254 (1978).

[106] 212 Ill. App. 3d 680, 571 N.E.2d 742 (1st Dist. 1991).

[107] People v. Casiano, 212 Ill. App. 3d 680, 686-87, 571 N.E.2d 742, 746 (1st Dist. 1991) (In affirming defendant's kidnapping conviction, "[w]e hold that the State proved beyond a reasonable doubt that an asportation occurred as provided by the Criminal Code section 10(a)(2).").

[108] 362 Ill. 369, 200 N.E. 72 (1936).

[109] *See* § 7.09 of this chapter.

[110] People v. Siegel, 362 Ill. 389, 392, 200 N.E. 72, 73 (1936).

[111] People v. Casiano, 212 Ill. App. 3d 680, 686-89, 571 N.E.2d 742, 746-47 (1st Dist. 1991).

[112] 212 Ill. App. 3d 680, 571 N.E.2d 742 (1st Dist. 1991)

point to walk one and one-half blocks to his apartment.[113] After concluding the movement of the victim satisfied the general asportation requirement of section (a)(2), the court next addressed defendant's claim "that even if an asportation occurred, such movement was merely incidental to the 'principal' offense of criminal sexual assault."[114] Beginning its analysis of the second question by acknowledging that "[i]t is true that not every asportation rises to the level of kidnapping," the court indicated whether the *asportation* rises to the level of kidnapping depends on (1) its duration; (2) whether it occurred during a separate offense; (3) whether it is inherent in the separate offense; and (4) whether the asportation created a significant danger independent of that posed by the separate offense.[115] Here, (1) the movement, albeit a "short distance," made the assault easier to commit and harder to detect; (2) the asportation occurred prior to, rather than during, the sexual assault; (3) the one and one-half hour block walk was not inherent in the sexual assault; and (4) a significant danger to the victim independent of the sexual assault occurred when the victim became vulnerable to additional criminality while hidden in the victim's apartment.[116] Thus, the detention and asportation was not merely "incidental" to the sexual assault, but instead a separate offense.[117]

As stated, the issue as to whether an asportation is part of another offense or amounts to a separate kidnapping-related offense is a common one where kidnapping is prosecuted. Because this concern spills into the discussion of lesser included offenses, it will be more fully addressed later in this chapter.[118]

§ 7.12. — Ransom Demand — Not an Element of Kidnapping.

Just as asportation is not an element of kidnapping per se, holding the victim for ransom or making a ransom demand of another is not required of ordinary kidnapping.[119] Similarly, although the kidnapping may be motivated by a defendant's ambition of sexually assaulting or injuring his or her victim,[120] the absence of such additional wrongdoing does not defeat the kidnapping charge.[121] Obviously, the "secret confinement" of another "against his will" is sufficiently

---

[113] People v. Casiano, 212 Ill. App. 3d 680, 686-87, 571 N.E.2d 742, 746 (1st Dist. 1991).

[114] People v. Casiano, 212 Ill. App. 3d 680, 686-89, 571 N.E.2d 742, 746-47 (1st Dist. 1991).

[115] People v. Casiano, 212 Ill. App. 3d 680, 686-89, 571 N.E.2d 742, 747 (1st Dist. 1991).

[116] People v. Casiano, 212 Ill. App. 3d 680, 686-89, 571 N.E.2d 742, 747 (1st Dist. 1991).

[117] People v. Casiano, 212 Ill. App. 3d 680, 686-89, 571 N.E.2d 742, 747 (1st Dist. 1991) (aggravated kidnapping conviction affirmed).

[118] *See* § 7.30 of this chapter.

[119] People v. Masterson, 79 Ill. App. 2d 117, 130, 223 N.E.2d 252, 259 (3d Dist. 1967).

[120] *See, e.g.*, People v. Eyler, 133 Ill. 2d 173, 195-99, 549 N.E.2d 268, 277-80 (1989) (sexual assault, torture, and murder), *cert. denied*, 498 U.S. 881, *reh'g denied*, 498 U.S. 993 (1990).

[121] *See, e.g.*, People v. Harris, 68 Ill. App. 3d 12, 14, 385 N.E.2d 789, 791 (5th Dist. 1979) (defendant forced victims to transport him to another location).

injurious of a person's personal dignity and autonomy and counter to the interests of public safety to merit a criminal sanction in and of itself.

§ 7.13. — Withdrawal.

As is true of other Illinois crimes, once the defendant has engaged in conduct that satisfies the various elements of kidnapping, there is a crime. Thus, not following through on the ultimate objective behind the kidnapping will not be a defense to kidnapping. For example, where a defendant kidnaps his or her victim for the purpose of making a ransom demand, the defendant's subsequent decision to forego the ransom demand will not be a defense to the kidnapping itself, for the crime of kidnapping is complete when the victim is seized and carried off.[122] Likewise, whether a victim of a kidnapping for ransom is released and free of detention before the ransom is paid is immaterial where the kidnapping already occurred.[123]

§ 7.14. Aggravated Kidnapping.

Beyond simple kidnapping, there is the more serious offense of aggravated kidnapping.[124] This crime, which carries a greater penalty than ordinary kidnapping, was conceived as a deterrent to, amongst other things, the commission of subsequent felonies against the victim of the kidnapping.[125]

§ 7.15. — Aggravated Kidnapping Codified.

The crime of aggravated kidnapping reflects the following language:

(a) A kidnapper within the definition of paragraph (a) of Section [5]10-1 is guilty of the offense of aggravated kidnapping when he:
(1) Kidnaps for the purpose of obtaining ransom from the person kidnapped or from any other person, or
(2) Takes as his victim a child under the age of 13 years, or an institutionalized severely or profoundly mentally retarded person, or
(3) Inflicts great bodily harm or commits another felony upon his victim, or
(4) Wears a hood, robe or mask or conceals his identity, or
(5) Commits the offense of kidnapping while armed with a dangerous weapon, as defined in Section 33A-1 of the "Criminal Code of 1961."

---

[122] People v. Harrison, 261 Ill. 517, 527, 104 N.E. 259, 263 (1914) (kidnapping conviction reversed on other grounds).

[123] People v. Bolla, 114 Ill. App. 3d 442, 446, 448 N.E.2d 996, 1000 (2d Dist. 1983) (aggravated kidnapping conviction affirmed).

[124] 720 ILCS 5/10-2 (1999).

[125] People v. Scott, 45 Ill. App. 3d 487, 491, 359 N.E.2d 878, 881 (1st Dist. 1977), *aff'd*, 69 Ill. 2d 85, 370 N.E.2d 540 (1977).

As used in this Section, "ransom" includes money, benefit or other valuable thing or concession.[126]

Since kidnapping is a prerequisite to the offense of aggravated kidnapping,[127] the elements of this more serious form of kidnapping are (1) the commission of kidnapping with (2) some element of aggravation — ransom demand, infliction of injury, and so on.

§ 7.16. — Ransom.

Section 5/10-2(a)(1) states that an accused will be guilty of aggravated kidnapping if he "kidnaps for the purpose of obtaining ransom from the person kidnapped or from any other person."[128] The courts hold that one who secretly confines another for the purpose of extorting money is guilty of aggravated kidnapping even if the victim is released or the culprit is captured before the ransom is paid.[129] It is clear that the kidnapping need only occur with the intent and purpose of making a ransom demand; it is not necessary for the state to prove that some act was done toward obtaining the ransom as long as the defendant's purpose was apparent.[130]

§ 7.17. — Abduction of Children under Thirteen.

Section 5/10-2(a)(2) states that one who is guilty of kidnapping is guilty of aggravated kidnapping if his victim is under thirteen years of age.[131] In this connection, the courts have upheld a defendant's conviction in a variety of circumstances where the child abducted was less than thirteen.[132] One interesting question about this stricture is whether the defendant would have a defense to *aggravated* kidnapping if he or she kidnapped a person with the reasonable belief that the victim was over thirteen, but the child later proved to be less than that age. Although there are no cases on this subject in Illinois, there is authority on this question in other states that answers the question in the negative.[133]

---

[126] 720 ILCS 5/10-2 (1999).

[127] People v. Marin, 48 Ill. 2d 205, 210, 269 N.E.2d 303, 305 (1971).

[128] 720 ILCS 5/10-2(a)(1) (1999).

[129] People v. Bolla, 114 Ill. App. 3d 442, 446, 448 N.E.2d 996, 1000 (2d Dist. 1983); People v. Masterson, 79 Ill. App. 2d 117, 130, 223 N.E.2d 252, 259 (3d Dist. 1967).

[130] People v. Harrison, 261 Ill. 517, 527-28, 104 N.E. 259, 263 (1914).

[131] 720 ILCS 5/10-2(a)(2) (1999).

[132] *See, e.g.,* People v. Warmack, 44 Ill. App. 3d 243, 247-48, 358 N.E.2d 76, 79 (1st Dist. 1976) (conviction of aggravated kidnapping of 9-year-old victim affirmed); People v. Williams, 52 Ill. 2d 455, 460-61, 288 N.E.2d 406, 409 (1972) (conviction of aggravated kidnapping of nine-year-old victim affirmed; indictment sufficient).

[133] *See, e.g.,* Smiley v. State, 34 Ga. Ct. App. 513, 130 S.E. 359 (1925) (no defense).

Because the kidnapping statute states that confinement of a child under the age of thirteen is kidnapping "if such confinement is without the consent of his parent,"[134] Section 5/10-2(a)(2) has been interpreted as not applying to a defendant who is a natural parent of the victim.[135] In *People v. Algarin*,[136] the Illinois appellate court held that despite the fact that the defendant had never married the victim's mother, lived with the victim, or had a court determination of paternity, the offense of aggravated kidnapping could not be sustained where the defendant was the victim's biological father.[137] Because the term "parent," in the kidnapping statute, is to be given its ordinary meaning of a father and mother related by blood, an essential element of the offense, that the kidnapping occurred *without the consent of the victim's parents*, could not be met.[138]

§ 7.18. — Infliction of Great Bodily Harm or Commission of Another Felony on Victim.

Another aggravating factor that converts simple kidnapping to aggravated kidnapping is reflected in subsection (a)(3) and arises where the kidnapper inflicts "great bodily harm" or another "felony" on his or her victim.[139] In Illinois, the courts have found great bodily harm sufficient for aggravated kidnapping in a variety of cases, including where the kidnap victim was tortured,[140] where the victim was severely beaten with a crowbar,[141] and where the victim was stabbed.[142] The courts have rejected the argument that there can be no aggravated kidnapping simply because the great bodily harm preceded the completion of the offense of kidnapping.[143] "[T]he key issue [is] . . . whether the infliction if the great bodily harm . . . results from the same continuing state of mind as the kidnapping."[144]

If the predicate element of aggravated kidnapping is the commission of a felony, the appellate court must examine if the detention or asportation is merely

---

[134] 720 ILCS 5/10-1(b) (1999).

[135] People v. Algarin, 200 Ill. App. 3d 740, 750, 558 N.E.2d 457, 463 (1st Dist. 1990).

[136] 200 Ill. App. 3d 740, 558 N.E.2d 457 (1st Dist. 1990).

[137] People v. Algarin, 200 Ill. App. 3d 740, 750, 558 N.E.2d 457, 463 (1st Dist. 1990).

[138] People v. Algarin, 200 Ill. App. 3d 740, 746, 558 N.E.2d 457, 461 (1st Dist. 1990).

[139] 720 ILCS 5/10-2(a)(3) (1999).

[140] People v. Eyler, 133 Ill. 2d 173, 195-99, 549 N.E.2d 268, 277-79 (1989), *cert. denied*, 498 U.S. 881, *reh'g denied*, 498 U.S. 993 (1990).

[141] People v. Earl, 104 Ill. App. 3d 846, 848, 433 N.E.2d 722, 724-25 (2d Dist. 1982).

[142] People v. Owens, 109 Ill. App. 3d 1150, 1153, 441 N.E.2d 908, 914 (2d Dist. 1982) (kidnapping was aggravated by infliction of great bodily harm, although conviction for aggravated kidnapping vacated and conviction for armed violence affirmed where both crimes arose out of same physical act).

[143] People v. Earl, 104 Ill. App. 3d 846, 849, 433 N.E.2d 722, 725 (2d Dist. 1982).

[144] People v. Earl, 104 Ill. App. 3d 846, 850, 433 N.E.2d 722, 725 (2d Dist. 1982).

incidental to the felony or independent of it.[145] For instance, in *People v. Gully*,[146] the victim was asported and detained for forty-five minutes, then robbed and sexually assaulted. The appellate court found that the defendant's acts warranted convictions for armed robbery, criminal sexual assault and aggravated kidnapping because "the detention and asportation created significant danger to the victim independent of that posed by the criminal sexual assault and robbery."[147] In any event, the commission of first-degree murder,[148] armed robbery,[149] and aggravated criminal sexual assault[150] are felony crimes that have transformed a related kidnapping into aggravated kidnapping.

§ 7.19. — Defendant's Concealment of His or Her Identity.

Under subsection (a)(4), if the kidnapper "wears a hood, robe or mask or conceals his identity during the course of the kidnapping," the kidnapping is elevated to the more serious crime of aggravated kidnapping.[151] Although there are seldom prosecutions of aggravated kidnapping under this approach, simply because there is usually some other theory of aggravated kidnapping that the state can rely on to achieve the same result,[152] it is interesting to consider whether the "concealment of identity" language would apply where, for example, the *victim* was blindfolded. In *People v. Tate*,[153] the defendant kidnapped a teen-age girl from a house in which she was babysitting. As defendant led her to a nearby field where he raped her, he continuously covered the girl's face by draping a blanket over her head. The appellate court ultimately affirmed his conviction for aggravated kidnapping on the theory, to be discussed in the next section,[154] that he had been armed with a dangerous weapon.[155] But one can visualize a situation involving a variation of the *Tate* facts where the defendant attempts to conceal his or her identity in a manner like the defendant Tate, but is not armed and ultimately does not commit another felony on the victim. It would seem that the fair import of the subsection (a)(4) language would create a basis to hold a defendant liable in such circumstances for aggravated kidnapping, since the defendant's action would have been designed to "conceal his identity."

---

[145] *See* § 7.11 and § 7.30 of this chapter.

[146] 151 Ill. App. 3d 795, 502 N.E.2d 1091 (5th Dist. 1986).

[147] People v. Gully, 151 Ill. App. 3d 795, 800-01, 502 N.E.2d 1091, 1095 (5th Dist. 1986).

[148] People v. Cole, 172 Ill. 2d 85, 102-04, 665 N.E.2d 1275, 1283-84, *cert. denied*, 519 U.S. 1030 (1996).

[149] People v. Thomas, 163 Ill. App. 3d 670, 677-79, 516 N.E.2d 901, 906-07 (1st Dist. 1987).

[150] People v. Brown, 214 Ill. App. 3d 836, 840, 574 N.E.2d 190, 197 (1st Dist. 1991).

[151] 720 ILCS 5/10-2(a)(4) (1999).

[152] *See, e.g.*, People v. Tate, 94 Ill. App. 3d 192, 418 N.E.2d 1048 (5th Dist. 1981).

[153] 94 Ill. App. 3d 192, 418 N.E.2d 1048 (5th Dist. 1981).

[154] *See* § 7.20 of this chapter.

[155] People v. Tate, 94 Ill. App. 3d 192, 198, 418 N.E.2d 1048, 1053 (5th Dist. 1981).

§ 7.20. — Armed with a Dangerous Weapon.

The last of the bases for convicting a person of aggravated kidnapping exists where, in the language of subsection (a)(5), the defendant is "armed with a dangerous weapon."[156] It is important to emphasize that this subsection requires merely that the defendant be *armed* with such a weapon, not that he or she *use* the weapon to advance his or her criminal ambitions. In addition, subsection (a)(5) makes explicit reference to section 5/33A-1 ("armed violence" prohibition)[157] of the code for a definition of what constitutes a "dangerous weapon."[158] In *Tate*, discussed above,[159] the state successfully relied on subsection (a)(5) in establishing aggravated kidnapping, since the defendant was armed with a knife.[160]

§ 7.21. Unlawful Restraint.

Not all unlawful detentions of others without lawful authority will qualify as kidnapping or aggravated kidnapping. In Illinois, the chief barrier in the way of treating as kidnapping the broad range of confinements that fall beneath the umbrella of "false imprisonment,"[161] as it was known at common law, is the "secret confinement" requirement.[162] The asportation requirement can prove problematic as well, depending on which theory of kidnapping the state advances in its charging instrument.[163] In other words, kidnapping is best understood as an aggravated form of false imprisonment.[164] A necessary complement to kidnapping, then, would be a lesser offense that would outlaw wrongful detention of a person but without any requirement of secret confinement or asportation.

When the Criminal Code of 1961 was developed, the General Assembly codified what was previously called false imprisonment[165] and gave it the new label

---

[156] 720 ILCS 5/10-2(a)(5) (1999).

[157] 720 ILCS 5/33A-1 (1999). *See* ch. 9 for a discussion of this offense.

[158] 720 ILCS 5/33A-1 (1999) (Under this enactment, a "dangerous weapon" includes: a handgun, rifle, shotgun, spring gun, a stun gun or taser, knife with a blade of at least 3 inches in length, dagger, dirk, switch-blade knife, stiletto, axe, hatchet, bludgeon, blackjack, slingshot, sand bag, metal knuckles, billy or "other dangerous weapon of like character").

[159] *See* § 7.19 of this chapter.

[160] People v. Tate, 94 Ill. App. 3d 192, 199, 418 N.E.2d 1048, 1053-54 (5th Dist. 1981).

[161] *See* 2 CHARLES E. TORCIA, WHARTON'S CRIMINAL LAW § 209 (14th ed. 1979).

[162] *See* § 7.05 of this chapter.

[163] *See* § 7.11 of this chapter.

[164] 2 CHARLES E. TORCIA, WHARTON'S CRIMINAL LAW § 210 (14th ed. 1979).

[165] ILL. REV. STAT. ch. 38, para. 252 (1961) (repealed).

"unlawful restraint."[166] They believed that the new label more accurately described this type of criminality.[167]

§ 7.22. — Unlawful Restraint Codified.

The crime of unlawful restraint is set out in simple, but broad terms: "Unlawful Restraint. (a) A person commits the offense of unlawful restrain when he knowingly without legal authority detains another. (b) Sentence. Unlawful restraint is a . . . felony."[168] Thus, the requirements for this crime are the (1) knowledgeable (2) detention of another (3) without lawful authority.[169]

The mental state required for unlawful restraint is "knowledge."[170] Thus, where the defense tendered to the trial court an instruction requiring the jury to find the defendant "knowingly and without authority detained [victim] with an overriding intent and motivation to detain her," the appellate court ruled that the trial court properly refused the instruction because unlawful restraint simply requires that defendant knowingly without legal authority detain another.[171]

Unlawful restraint requires a willful detention against the victim's consent, which prevents the victim's movement from one place to another.[172] A perusal of the plain language describing unlawful restraint indicates the key concern is a wrongful *detention*, with no requirement of secret confinement or asportation. The nature of the required detention for unlawful restraint is not as rigorous as that for kidnapping, in that unlawful restraint exists anytime "an individual's freedom of locomotion is impaired."[173] In *People v. Satterthwaite*,[174] the defendant approached a woman on a street and grabbed her by her arm, then her leg, holding her for about two minutes as he asked her to take a ride with him. The defendant then asked the woman what her husband would think if she was raped, but the woman did not respond. Acting disgusted, the defendant released her and departed. The appellate court ruled that since the woman's "free locomotion was impaired," there was a wrongful detention within the meaning of the statute.[175]

---

[166] ILL. ANN. STAT. ch 38, para. 10-3 (Smith-Hurd 1979), 1961 Committee Comments, at 586 (revised 1972).

[167] ILL. ANN. STAT. ch 38, para. 10-3 (Smith-Hurd 1979), 1961 Committee Comments, at 586-87 (revised 1972).

[168] 720 ILCS 5/10-3 (1999). *See* People v. Wisslead, 108 Ill. 2d 389, 400, 484 N.E.2d 1081, 1086 (1983) (not unconstitutionally vague).

[169] ILL. ANN. STAT. ch. 38, para. 10-3 (Smith-Hurd 1979), 1961 Committee Comments, at 587 (revised 1972).

[170] 720 ILCS 5/10-3(a) (1999). *See* ch. 2 for a discussion of "knowledge."

[171] People v. Bergin, 227 Ill. App. 3d 32, 46-47, 590 N.E.2d 939, 947-48 (2d Dist 1992).

[172] People v. Leonhardt, 173 Ill. App. 3d 314, 322, 527 N.E.2d 562, 567 (1st Dist. 1988).

[173] People v. Warner, 98 Ill. App. 3d 433, 436, 424 N.E.2d 747, 749 (4th Dist. 1981).

[174] 72 Ill. App. 3d 483, 391 N.E.2d 162 (4th Dist. 1979).

[175] People v. Satterthwaite, 72 Ill. App. 3d 483, 485, 391 N.E.2d 162, 164 (4th Dist. 1979).

The length of the detention need not be significant to satisfy unlawful restraint. In *People v. Jones*,[176] the defendant approached a woman on the street, pulled a knife, told her not to scream or he would kill her, grabbed her and began pulling her in the direction of an abandoned building when she broke lose and ran to a nearby tavern for help. Later, the woman testified that approximately three to four seconds had elapsed from the time the defendant pulled the knife until the time she escaped his grasp. After being convicted of unlawful restraint and battery in the trial court, the defendant appealed claiming that there could be no unlawful restraint as a matter of law because his detention of the woman was so brief.[177] The appellate court rejected the defendant's argument and affirmed his conviction explaining that, "[i]f a party is actually restrained without legal authority, the duration of the restraint, however short, is inconsequential."[178]

Physical force is *not* required for unlawful restraint.[179] Neither is the threatening presence of a weapon an element of unlawful restraint.[180] Indeed, it is not even necessary that the accused touch the victim in order to sustain a conviction of unlawful restraint.[181] Thus, locking or otherwise confining the victim in a room would be sufficient.[182]

The detention must be *without consent* to be unlawful restraint. Where the defendant confined his wife in their house by tying her with chains while he went to town for provisions, there was no offense of this nature because she had not only consented to her detention, but had suggested it and had assisted her husband in his actions.[183] Meanwhile, where another defendant met his victim at a picnic, invited her to ride on his motorcycle, to which she agreed, took her to a forest preserve, where he demanded to have sex with her while she insisted on leaving to go to work, this was clearly a nonconsensual encounter amounting to unlawful restraint.[184]

The detention must be *without legal authority* to be considered unlawful restraint. If the defendant is acting under color of legal authority, such as where police officers arrested a person on the basis of a warrant between 6:00 P.M.

---

[176] 93 Ill. App. 3d 475, 417 N.E.2d 647 (1st Dist. 1981).

[177] People v. Jones, 93 Ill. App. 3d 475, 479, 417 N.E.2d 647, 651 (1st Dist. 1981).

[178] People v. Jones, 93 Ill. App. 3d 475, 479, 417 N.E.2d 647, 651 (1st Dist. 1981).

[179] People v. Bowen, 241 Ill. App. 3d 608, 627-28, 609 N.E.2d 346, 361 (4th Dist.), *cert. denied*, 510 U.S. 946 (1993); People v. Warner, 98 Ill. App. 3d 433, 436, 424 N.E.2d 747, 749 (4th Dist. 1981).

[180] People v. Wisslead, 94 Ill. 2d 190, 193, 446 N.E.2d 512, 513 (1983).

[181] People v. Story, 114 Ill. App. 3d 1029, 1033, 449 N.E.2d 935, 938 (1st Dist. 1983).

[182] People v. Warner, 98 Ill. App. 3d 433, 436, 424 N.E.2d 747, 749 (4th Dist. 1981).

[183] People v. Cohoon, 315 Ill. App. 259, 262-63, 42 N.E.2d 969, 970-71 (4th Dist. 1942) (finding no false imprisonment).

[184] People v. Leonhardt, 173 Ill. App. 3d 314, 320, 527 N.E.2d 562, 565 (1st Dist. 1988) (unlawful restraint and rape convictions affirmed).

and 6:30 P.M., extracted a confession from him later that night, and took him before a magistrate the following morning, there could be no crime of unlawful restraint.[185] On the other hand, where the defendant threatened suicide and then detained his minor son as a hostage, this detention was unreasonable and without legal authority.[186]

An interesting application of the false imprisonment-unlawful restraint prohibition that has been made in Illinois revolves around the detention of one's own children. In *Fletcher v. People*,[187] the Illinois Supreme Court stated in 1869 that although:

> the law gives parents a large discretion in the exercise of authority over their children .... this authority must be exercised within the bounds of reason and humanity. If the parent commits wanton and needless cruelty upon his child, either by imprisonment ... or by inhuman beating, the law will punish him.[188]

In the circumstances before it, where the father had shut his blind and helpless son in a cellar for several days without heat during winter and anointed the boy's body with kerosene in an attempt to remove vermin, the court upheld the defendant parent's conviction for false imprisonment.[189]

More recently, in *People v. Warner*,[190] the appellate court affirmed two counts of unlawful restraint (and four counts of contributing to the neglect of a child) where the defendant confined one child who resided in his home to a bedroom for approximately thirty days, and another child who lived there to her bedroom for one week, for "stealing" food from the family kitchen.[191] Proof of the existence of the unauthorized detention was not defeated, merely because the children were allowed periodically to leave their bedroom to go shopping and to a cemetery.[192] Also, this confinement could not be justified from a disciplinary perspective, because that concern is governed by its "reasonableness."[193]

It is essential to make explicit reference to another legal doctrine in the context of unlawful restraint. As was previously noted in the context of kidnapping,[194] if a detention or forcible asportation is a *mere incident* in the commission of another offense, such as robbery, the detention or asportation is not kid-

---

[185] People v. Scott, 401 Ill. 80, 84-85, 81 N.E.2d 426, 429 (1948) (no false imprisonment).

[186] People v. Walker, 130 Ill. App. 3d 58, 60-61, 473 N.E.2d 995, 997 (2d Dist. 1985) (unlawful restraint conviction affirmed).

[187] 52 Ill. 395 (1869).

[188] Fletcher v. People, 52 Ill. 395, 397 (1969).

[189] Fletcher v. People, 52 Ill. 395, 397 (1969).

[190] 98 Ill. App. 3d 433, 424 N.E.2d 747 (4th Dist. 1981).

[191] People v. Warner, 98 Ill. App. 3d 433, 435, 424 N.E.2d 747, 749 (4th Dist. 1981).

[192] People v. Warner, 98 Ill. App. 3d 433, 435, 424 N.E.2d 747, 749 (4th Dist. 1981).

[193] People v. Warner, 98 Ill. App. 3d 433, 435, 424 N.E.2d 747, 749 (4th Dist. 1981).

[194] *See* § 7.11 of this chapter.

napping. In *People v. Smith,*[195] where a robbery victim was transported by his captors for a period of about twenty minutes, the appellate court concluded that the detention was part of the robbery, and was not a separate crime.[196] However, the appellate court explicitly stated it "would envision the charge of unlawful restraint as an *acceptable alternative* to aggravated kidnapping where, as here, asportation is merely incidental to commission of a felony."[197] Thus, the *Smith* dictum suggests that some detentions that occur incidental to other crimes might give rise to unlawful restraint, though not kidnapping.

On the other hand, where a defendant, after entering his victim's bedroom, instructed his armed robbery victim to not move and grabbed her hand while ordering her to turn out the light in her bedroom that she had just turned on, an appellate court ruled that defendant had not committed the offense of unlawful restraint because defendant's "conduct was merely derivative of and circumstantially related to the [defendant's] armed robbery and home invasion."[198] In another case, the appellate court ruled there was no unlawful restraint where a defendant sexually abused his victim by holding her down on a couch, where she had been sleeping, and fondled her breasts, because "the conduct alleged [in this case] to constitute unlawful restraint was only that inherent in every case of sexual abuse by force."[199]

Meanwhile, other cases have found unlawful restraint where the detention was separate from the other offense. For example, a defendant was found guilty of both unlawful restraint and criminal sexual assault where the convictions were based on separate acts; the sexual assault occurred during defendant's sexual penetration of the victim, while the unlawful restraint occurred when defendant detained the victim as she struggled to get away and attempted to leave defendant's apartment after the act of penetration.[200] Likewise, a defendant was found guilty of unlawful restraint and criminal sexual assault where he stopped his car and choked his female passenger, then drove to a secluded area and sexually assaulted her, and thereafter drove her to her grandfather's house where he temporarily prevented her from entering the house; the detentions before and after the sexual assault were separate from the assault.[201] Where defendant

---

[195] 91 Ill. App. 3d 523, 414 N.E.2d 1117 (1st Dist. 1980).

[196] People v. Smith, 91 Ill. App. 3d 523, 527, 414 N.E.2d 1117, 1120 (1st Dist. 1980).

[197] People v. Smith, 91 Ill. App. 3d 523, 529, 414 N.E.2d 1117, 1122 (1st Dist. 1980) (emphasis added).

[198] People v. Haybron, 153 Ill. App. 3d 906, 908, 506 N.E.2d 369, 371 (3d Dist. 1987).

[199] People v. Yeast, 236 Ill. App. 3d 84, 91, 601 N.E.2d 1367, 1371 (4th Dist. 1992). *See also* People v. Paulick, 174 Ill. App. 3d 868, 870, 529 N.E.2d 28, 29 (2d Dist. 1988) (unlawful restraint and criminal sexual abuse arose out of same act).

[200] People v. Defyn, 222 Ill. App. 3d 504, 517, 584 N.E.2d 220, 229 (1st Dist. 1991).

[201] People v. Alvarado, 235 Ill. App. 3d 116, 117, 600 N.E.2d 1236, 1237 (3d Dist. 1992). *See also* People v. Leonhardt, 173 Ill. App. 3d 314, 322, 527 N.E.2d 562, 567 (1st Dist. 1988) (detention for purposes of unlawful restraint was separate from rape; convictions for both affirmed).

committed two separate acts: residential burglary, by entering a house with intent to commit unlawful restraint, and unlawful restraint, by forcibly detaining his estranged wife, he could be convicted of both offenses.[202]

§ 7.23. Aggravated Unlawful Restraint.

Section 5/10-3.1 states that "(a) A person commits the offense of aggravated unlawful restraint when he knowingly without legal authority detains another while using a deadly weapon. (b) Sentence. Aggravated unlawful restrain is a . . . felony."[203]

It was determined that a more serious penalty was justified if the defendant was armed during the unlawful restraint encounter.[204]

§ 7.24. Forcible Detention.

Another offense that outlaws an illegal detention of a person is the crime of "forcible detention," which is defined as follows:

(a) A person commits the offense of forcible detention when he holds an individual hostage without lawful authority for the purpose of obtaining performance by a third person of demands made by the person holding the hostage, and

(1) the person holding the hostage is armed with a dangerous weapon as defined in Section 5/33A-1 of this Code, or

(2) the hostage is known to the person holding him to be a peace officer or a correctional employee engaged in the performance of his official duties.

(b) Forcible detention is a . . . felony.[205]

This crime is obviously designed to deter persons from taking another as a hostage in order to force a third person to comply with their wishes, where either (1) the defendant is armed with a dangerous weapon or (2) the victim is a law enforcement officer. In *People v. Kavinsky*,[206] the appellate court clarified the scope of this enactment by insisting that it would be error to charge a person with forcible abduction and fail to allege that "he either intended or did seek to influence the conduct of a third party" by holding a victim hostage.[207] It appears this charge requires a form of specific intent on the abductor's part: the taking of the hostage with the intent to obtain performance by a third person of certain

---

[202] People v. Williams, 222 Ill. App. 3d 129, 137, 582 N.E.2d 1158, 1163 (1st Dist. 1991).

[203] 720 ILCS 5/10-3.1 (1999).

[204] *See, e.g.,* People v. Algarin, 200 Ill. App. 3d 740, 751, 558 N.E.2d 457, 464 (1st Dist. 1990) (aggravated unlawful restraint was justified where defendant detained victim and utilized a knife).

[205] 720 ILCS 5/10-4 (1999).

[206] 98 Ill. App. 3d 579, 424 N.E.2d 340 (2d Dist. 1981).

[207] People v. Kavinsky, 98 Ill. App. 3d 579, 583, 424 N.E.2d 340, 344 (2d Dist. 1981).

demands made by the abductor. Thus, forcible abduction requires proof that the defendant (1) held another person hostage (2) without legal authority and (3) with the intent to obtain performance of his demands by a third party, (4) where either the defendant is armed or the hostage is a law enforcement officer.

§ 7.25. Child Abduction.

The state legislature created the crime of "child abduction" to punish as criminal the abduction and concealment of a child from another who has legal custody of that child.[208] A person commits child abduction when he or she:

(1) Intentionally violates any terms of a valid court order granting sole or joint custody, care or possession to another, by concealing or detaining the child or removing the child from the jurisdiction of the court; or

(2) Intentionally violates a court order prohibiting the person from concealing or detaining the child or removing the child from the jurisdiction of the court; or

(3) Intentionally conceals, detains or removes the child without the consent of the mother or lawful custodian of the child if the person is a putative father and either: (A) the paternity of the child has not been legally established or (B) the paternity of the child has been legally established but no orders relating to custody have been entered. However, notwithstanding the presumption created by paragraph (3) of subsection (a), a mother commits child abduction when she intentionally conceals or removes a child, whom she has abandoned or relinquished custody of, from an unadjudicated father who has provided sole ongoing care and custody of the child in her absence; or

(4) Intentionally conceals or removes the child from a parent after filing a petition or being served with process in an action affecting marriage or paternity but prior to the issuance of a temporary or final order determining custody; or

(5) At the expiration of visitation rights outside the State, intentionally fails or refuses to return or impedes the return of the child to the lawful custodian in Illinois; or

(6) Being a parent of the child, and where the parents of such child are or have been married and there has been no court order of custody, conceals the child for 15 days, and fails to make reasonable attempts within the 15 day period to notify the other parent as to the specific whereabouts of the child, including a means by which to contact such child, or to arrange reasonable visitation or contact with the child. It is not a violation of this Sec-

---

[208] 720 ILCS 5/10-5 (1999).

tion for a person fleeing domestic violence to take the child with him or her to housing provided by a domestic violence program; or

(7) Being a parent of the child, and where the parents of the child are or have been married and there has been no court order of custody, conceals, detains, or removes the child with physical force or threat of physical force; or

(8) Conceals, detains, or removes the child for payment or promise of payment at the instruction of a person who has no legal right to custody; or

(9) Retains in this State for 30 days a child removed from another state without the consent of the lawful custodian or in violation of a valid court order of custody; or

(10) Intentionally lures or attempts to lure a child under the age of 16 into a motor vehicle, building, housetrailer, or dwelling place without the consent of the parent or lawful custodian of the child for other than a lawful purpose.

For purposes of this subsection (b), paragraph (10), the luring or attempted luring of a child under the age of 16 into a motor vehicle, building, housetrailer, or dwelling place without the consent of the parent or lawful custodian of the child shall be prima facie evidence of other than a lawful purpose.[209]

The scope of this offense, punishable as a felony,[210] is clarified by several definitions and "affirmative defenses." A *child* is defined as any person under the age of eighteen or an institutionalized severely or profoundly mentally retarded person at the time of the commission of the offense.[211] Likewise, *detains* is defined as any taking or retaining physical custody whether or not the child resists or objects.[212] A *lawful custodian* means any person who has legal custody of the child.[213] It is presumed, where the parties have not married, that the mother is the legal custodian unless a court order directs otherwise.[214]

---

[209] 720 ILCS 5/10-5(b) (1999). This statute was upheld as constitutional in People v. Williams, 133 Ill. 2d 449, 453-56, 551 N.E.2d 631, 632-34 (1990). The defendant challenged the statute on vagueness grounds claiming that the phrase *other than a lawful purpose* in subsection (10) was not defined anywhere in the Criminal Code and, therefore, violated due process. *Id.* at 452-53, 551 N.E.2d at 632. The Illinois Supreme Court rejected this argument and held that the phrase was to be given its ordinary meaning of any purpose that was unlawful. *Id.* at 454-55, 551 N.E.2d at 633.

[210] 720 ILCS 5/10-5(d)(1999).

[211] 720 ILCS 5/10-5(a)(1) (1999).

[212] 720 ILCS 5/10-5(a)(2) (1999).

[213] 720 ILCS 5/10-5(a)(3) (1999).

[214] 720 ILCS 5/10-5(a)(3) (1999).

A person accused of child abduction may enjoy an affirmative defense if (1) the person's custody of the child is consistent with a court order,[215] (2) the person had joint custody or joint visitation rights and, because of uncontrollable circumstances, did not return the child to the custodian in a timely fashion,[216] (3) the person was fleeing an incidence or pattern of domestic violence,[217] or (4) the person lured or attempted to lure a child under the age of sixteen into his or her motor vehicle, building, housetrailer, or dwelling place for a lawful purpose.[218]

The courts have upheld convictions of child abductions where a child was either wrongfully removed from or held in Illinois. In *People v. Harrison,*[219] the defendant's conviction was upheld where he moved his children to Mississippi in defiance of a court order.[220] Similarly, in *People v. Williams,*[221] the court upheld the child abduction conviction where the child was concealed within Illinois, where the defendant-mother was aware of a court order relieving her of custody of a child, took the child from his school, kept the child for several days, and concealed the child by taking him to a neighbor's house at night.[222]

A breach of a court order, giving rise to the crime of child abduction, can occur where the parent-defendant shares joint custody with his or her former spouse.[223] In *Harrison,* the defendant had joint custody of his child with his former wife.[224] Since neither parent could remove the child to another state without infringing on the joint custody rights of the other, the defendant stood convicted of child abduction for his breach of the court's award of joint custody.[225]

In a case not involving parental abduction, the appellate court, in *People v. Wenger,*[226] held the evidence insufficient to find either unlawful intent or that the defendant was "attempting to lure" the victim into his vehicle, notwithstanding that the defendant repeatedly encountered the victim with his vehicle, the defendant repeatedly motioned to the victim to approach his vehicle, and numerous sex toys were subsequently discovered in the defendant's vehicle.[227]

---

[215] 720 ILCS 5/10-5(c)(1) (1999). People v. Olsewski, 257 Ill. App. 3d 1018, 1024-25, 630 N.E.2d 131, 136 (2d Dist. 1994) (where defendant had sole legal custody of children at time in which she violated court order not to remove children from state, she could not be convicted of child abduction).

[216] 720 ILCS 5/10-5(c)(2) (1999).

[217] 720 ILCS 5/10-5(c)(3) (1999).

[218] 720 ILCS 5/10-5(c)(4) (1999).

[219] 82 Ill. App. 3d 530, 402 N.E.2d 822 (4th Dist. 1980).

[220] People v. Harrison, 82 Ill. App. 3d 530, 531-33, 402 N.E.2d 822, 823-24 (4th Dist. 1980).

[221] 105 Ill. App. 3d 372, 434 N.E.2d 412 (1st Dist. 1982).

[222] People v. Williams, 105 Ill. App. 3d 372, 373-74, 434 N.E.2d 412, 414 (1st Dist. 1982

[223] People v. Harrison, 82 Ill. App. 3d 530, 531-33, 402 N.E.2d 822, 823-24 (4th Dist. 1980).

[224] People v. Harrison, 82 Ill. App. 3d 530, 531, 402 N.E.2d 822, 823 (4th Dist. 1980).

[225] People v. Harrison, 82 Ill. App. 3d 530, 531-33, 402 N.E.2d 822, 823-24 (4th Dist. 1980).

[226] 258 Ill. App. 3d 561, 631 N.E.2d 277 (1st Dist. 1994).

[227] People v. Wenger, 258 Ill. App. 3d 561, 566, 631 N.E.2d 277, 281 (1st Dist. 1994).

In contrast, in *People v. Tirado*,[228] the appellate court found that the defendant had an unlawful purpose for luring the child victim where the defendant was a stranger to the nine-year-old victim and her mother, had chased the victim when she refused his request to get into his car, had been involved in similar prior encounters with the victim, had attempted to entice the victim with offers of money and candy, and had made threatening remarks to the victim.[229] Furthermore, the court found that the child abduction statute did not create a mandatory presumption of guilt nor improperly shift the burden of proof to the defendant; thus, the court found that the statute created only a permissible inference and was not unconstitutional.[230]

§ 7.26. Unlawful Visitation Interference.

In 1993, the legislature created the offense of "unlawful visitation interference."[231] This offense states:

> Every person who, in violation of the visitation provisions of a court order relating to child custody, detains or conceals a child with the intent to deprive another person of his or her rights to visitation shall be guilty of unlawful visitation interference.[232]

This offense is a petty offense, while a third or subsequent conviction of this offense is a misdemeanor.[233] The terms "child," "detain," and "lawful custodian" carry the same meaning as the definitions in the "child abduction" prohibition.[234]

It is an affirmative defense to unlawful visitation interference that: (1) the person committed the act based on a reasonable belief that such was necessary to protect the child from imminent physical harm; (2) the act was committed with the mutual consent of all parties having custodial or visitation rights; or (3) "the act was otherwise authorized by law."[235] Where a law enforcement officer has probable cause to believe a person has committed this offense, he or she "shall issue to that person a notice to appear" and, upon the person's failure to appear, "a warrant of arrest may be issued."[236]

---

[228] 254 Ill. App. 3d 497, 626 N.E.2d 1114 (1st Dist. 1993).

[229] People v. Tirado, 254 Ill. App. 3d 497, 510, 626 N.E.2d 1114, 1124 (1st Dist. 1993).

[230] People v. Tirado, 254 Ill. App. 3d 497, 510, 626 N.E.2d 1114, 1124 (1st Dist. 1993).

[231] 720 ILCS 5/10-5.5 (1999). *See* People v. Warren, 173 Ill. 2d 348, 356-67, 671 N.E.2d 700, 705-10 (1996) (offense of unlawful visitation interference as a whole not unconstitutionally vague in violation of due process nor violative of equal protection; however, provision of statute that previously barred contempt citation for same criminal conduct held unconstitutional on separation of powers grounds).

[232] 720 ILCS 5/10-5.5(b) (1999).

[233] 720 ILCS 5/10-5.5(c) (1999).

[234] 720 ILCS 5/10-5.5(a) (1999), *referring to* 720 ILCS 5/10-5 (1999).

[235] 720 ILCS 5/10-5.5(g) (1999).

[236] 720 ILCS 5/10-5.5(d) through 5/10-5.5(f) (1999).

§ 7.27. Harboring a Runaway.

The offense of "harboring a runaway" states that it is a misdemeanor[237] for any person, other than an agency or association providing crisis intervention services (as defined in the Juvenile Court Act),[238] or an operator of a youth emergency shelter (as defined in the Child Care Act),[239] "who, without the knowledge and consent of the minor's parent or guardian, knowingly gives shelter to a minor, other than a mature minor who has been emancipated under the Emancipation of Mature Minors Act, for more than 48 hours without the consent of the minor's parent or guardian, and without notifying the local law enforcement authorities of the minor's name and the fact that the minor is being provided shelter. . . ."[240]

§ 7.28. Aiding and Abetting Child Abduction.

In article 5/10 is the offense of "aiding and abetting child abduction." The statute states a person commits this offense when:

> (i) Before or during the commission of a child abduction as defined in Section [5]10-5 and with the intent to promote or facilitate such offense, he or she intentionally aids or abets another in the planning or commission of child abduction, unless before the commission of the offense he or she makes proper effort to prevent the commission of the offense; or
> (ii) With the intent to prevent the apprehension of a person known to have committed the offense of child abduction, or with the intent to obstruct or prevent efforts to locate the child victim of a child abduction, he or she knowingly destroys, alters, conceals, or disguises physical evidence or furnishes false information.[241]

This offense is a felony.[242]

In *People v. Dworzanski*,[243] the Illinois appellate court held that a conviction for aiding and abetting child abduction would not stand without a finding that the defendant possessed the knowledge that a court order existed giving the co-defendant's ex-husband custody of the child.[244] Since the trial judge did not specifically find that the defendant knew of the court order when defendant actively

---

[237] 720 ILCS 5/10-6(b) (1999).

[238] 705 ILCS 405/3-5 (1999).

[239] 225 ILCS 10/2.21 (1999).

[240] 720 ILCS 5/10-6 (1999) (referring to 750 ILCS 30/1 *et seq.* (1999) (Emancipation of Mature Minors Act)).

[241] 720 ILCS 5/10-7(a) (1999).

[242] 720 ILCS 5/10-7(b) (1999).

[243] 220 Ill. App. 3d 185, 580 N.E.2d 1263 (1st Dist. 1991).

[244] People v. Dworzanski, 220 Ill. App. 3d 185, 200, 580 N.E.2d 1263, 1273 (1st Dist. 1991).

assisted the co-defendant in abducting her child from her ex-husband, the defendant's conviction was reversed.[245]

§ 7.29. Unlawful Sale of a Public Conveyance Travel Ticket to a Minor.

The offense of "unlawful sale of a public conveyance travel ticket to a minor" was added to the criminal code in 1990. This offense is committed when:

> the person sells a ticket for travel on any public conveyance to an unemancipated minor under 17 years of age without the consent of the minor's parents or guardian for passage to a destination outside this state and knows the minor's age or fails to take reasonable measures to ascertain the minor's age.[246]

The scope of this offense is further clarified by statutory language. Evidence that the defendant demanded, was shown and reasonably relied on written evidence of the person's age in the sale of the ticket will be considered competent evidence in a criminal prosecution.[247] Moreover, *public conveyance* is defined as "an airplane, boat, bus, railroad, train, taxicab, or other vehicle used for the transportation of passengers for hire."[248] This offense is punishable as a misdemeanor.[249]

§ 7.30. Lesser Included Offenses and Kidnapping-Related Crimes.

Although the subject of lesser included offenses generally involves problematic analytical exercises,[250] there are few issues more complex in this regard than those dealing with kidnapping, aggravated kidnapping, unlawful restraint, aggravated unlawful restraint, forcible detention, child abduction, harboring a runaway, aiding and abetting child abduction, and other offenses that occur during the illegal abduction situation. Most troubling is the question of whether, for example, an alleged kidnapping is a "mere incident" of the commission of other crimes.[251] For example, if a defendant robber approached a victim in a dark alley, and ordered the victim not to move while the robber relieved the victim of his or her valuables, the question raised is whether there was a kidnapping due to the victim's secret confinement in the dark alley against his or her will. In *People v. Smith*,[252] the victim was sitting in an automobile waiting for his girl-

---

[245] People v. Dworzanski, 220 Ill. App. 3d 185, 200-01, 580 N.E.2d 1263, 1273 (1st Dist. 1991).

[246] 720 ILCS 5/10-8(a) (1999).

[247] 720 ILCS 5/10-8(b) (1999).

[248] 720 ILCS 5/10-8(c) (1999).

[249] 720 ILCS 5/10-8(d) (1999).

[250] *See* ch. 1 for a discussion of lesser included offenses.

[251] *See* § 7.11 and § 7.22 for additional cases discussing this issue.

[252] 91 Ill. App. 3d 523, 414 N.E.2d 1117 (1st Dist. 1980).

friend, who owned a car, when two defendants pulled the car door open, entered the car and told the victim to be quiet or he would be killed. One of the defendants drove the car for a short distance with the victim still inside and then, after a lapse of about twenty minutes, dropped the victim off at another location. The appellate court held that the detention and asportation of a robbery victim for a period of approximately twenty minutes was not kidnapping.[253] The court reasoned that there was no kidnapping, and only robbery of the automobile, because the detention and asportation were "merely incidental" to the robbery.[254]

In finding that no kidnapping took place,[255] the court relied on what has become known as the *Levy-Lombardi* rule, originally developed in the State of New York.[256] The *Smith* court cited with approval a case from the Virgin Islands,[257] which followed the general principles of the *Levy-Lombardi* rule, wherein the court set out four factors that should be addressed in the determination of whether there was a separate crime of kidnapping, or whether the kidnapping was merely incidental to another offense.[258] These four factors are: "(1) the duration of the detention or asportation; (2) whether the detention or asportation occurred during the commission of a separate offense; (3) whether the [detention] or asportation which occurred [was] inherent in the separate offense; and (4) whether the asportation or detention created a significant danger to the victim independent of that posed by the separate offense."[259]

Application of the factors, in some other cases, has led to a finding of kidnapping as well as other offenses. For example, an aggravated kidnapping was not inherent in a sexual assault where the asportation involved a one block walk, it occurred prior to the assault, the forced movement was not inherent in the sexual assault and the asportation into an abandoned building and out of a public area increased the vulnerability of the victim.[260]

---

[253] People v. Smith, 91 Ill. App. 3d 523, 529, 414 N.E.2d 1117, 1122 (1st Dist. 1980).

[254] People v. Smith, 91 Ill. App. 3d 523, 529, 414 N.E.2d 1117, 1122 (1st Dist. 1980).

[255] People v. Smith, 91 Ill. App. 3d 523, 527-29, 414 N.E.2d 1117, 1120-22 (1st Dist. 1980).

[256] People v. Smith, 91 Ill. App. 3d 523, 527-29, 414 N.E.2d 1117, 1120-22 (1st Dist. 1980), citing People v. Lombardi, 20 N.Y.2d 266, 282 N.Y.S.2d 519, 229 N.E.2d 206, (1967), *cert. denied*, 416 U.S. 906 (1974); People v. Levy, 15 N.Y.2d 159, 256 N.Y.S.2d 793, 204 N.E.2d 842, *cert. denied*, 381 U.S. 938 (1965).

[257] People v. Smith, 91 Ill. App. 3d 523, 529, 414 N.E.2d 1117, 1122 (1st Dist. 1980) (citing Government of the Virgin Islands v. Berry, 604 F.2d 221 (3d Cir. 1979)).

[258] People v. Smith, 91 Ill. App. 3d 523, 529, 414 N.E.2d 1117, 1122 (1st Dist. 1980) (citing Government of the Virgin Islands v. Berry, 604 F.2d 221 (3d Cir. 1979)).

[259] People v. Smith, 91 Ill. App. 3d 523, 529, 414 N.E.2d 1117, 1122 (1st Dist. 1980) (citing Government of the Virgin Islands v. Berry, 604 F.2d 221 (3d Cir. 1979)).

[260] People v. Lloyd, 277 Ill. App. 3d 154, 164-65, 660 N.E.2d 43, 51 (1st Dist. 1995) (kidnapping was not merely incidental to sexual assault conviction warranting reduced sentence for sexual assault).

An aggravated kidnapping conviction cannot be sustained where the asportation or confinement constitutes "only a technical compliance with the statutory definition but is, in reality, incidental to another offense."[261] Thus, where a defendant pulled his sexual assault victim off the street into a hallway where he assaulted her, all of which occurred within a few minutes, the court determined the detention of the victim had occurred in the course of the sexual assault.[262] However, where the asportation of an eventual murder victim created "significant dangers independent of murder," namely, provided the perpetrator with "yet another opportunity for battery and sexual assault," the aggravated kidnapping was not incidental to the murder.[263] Where another defendant bound and gagged his victim before his attempted rape and murder of her, which occurred while her boyfriend waited outside her apartment for forty-five minutes attempting to gain entry, the Illinois Supreme Court ruled that this was "more than a simple detainment incidental to the murder or rape," inasmuch as the defendant had successfully thwarted attempts by the victim's boyfriend to contact her.[264] Where another defendant induced his victim, a male prostitute, to go to defendant's apartment and then, when there, bound and tortured the victim before murdering him, the Illinois Supreme Court refused to view the aggravated kidnapping as "merely incidental" to the murder.[265] Where another defendant ordered both the victim's sister and the victim to "go for a ride" with him, with the victim's sister driving and the victim sitting in the front passenger seat while defendant sat in the back seat holding a gun, whereupon defendant eventually directed the sister to drive to an isolated area where he shot and killed the victim, the confinement was not incidental to the murder.[266]

As was pointed out in the discussion of unlawful restraint, the courts must ponder whether an unlawful restraint is "inherent" in, or separate from, another

---

[261] People v. Eyler, 133 Ill. 2d 173, 199-200, 549 N.E.2d 268, 280 (1989) (quoting People v. Enoch, 122 Ill. 2d 176, 197, 522 N.E.2d 1124, 1135, *cert. denied*, 488 U.S. 917 (1988)), *cert. denied*, 498 U.S. 881 (1990).

[262] People v. Lamkey, 240 Ill. App. 3d 435, 440, 608 N.E.2d 406, 409-10 (1st Dist. 1992) (aggravated kidnapping conviction reversed).

[263] People v. Moreland, 292 Ill. App. 3d 616, 620-22, 686 N.E.2d 597, 600-01 (1st Dist. 1997) (first degree murder, armed robbery and aggravated kidnapping convictions affirmed).

[264] People v. Enoch, 122 Ill. 2d 176, 197, 522 N.E.2d 1124, 1135 (aggravated kidnapping, rape and murder convictions affirmed), *cert. denied*, 488 U.S. 917 (1988).

[265] People v. Eyler, 133 Ill. 2d 173, 199-201, 549 N.E.2d 268, 279-80 (1989) (aggravated kidnapping and murder convictions affirmed), *cert. denied*, 498 U.S. 881, *reh'g denied*, 498 U.S. 993 (1990).

[266] People v. Cole, 172 Ill. 2d 85, 102-04, 665 N.E.2d 1275, 1283-84 (aggravated kidnapping and first-degree murder convictions affirmed), *cert. denied*, 519 U.S. 1030 (1996). *See also* People v. Jackson, 281 Ill. App. 3d 759, 768-69, 666 N.E.2d 854, 861-62 (1st Dist. 1996) (aggravated kidnapping was distinct from first degree murder); People v. Brown, 214 Ill. App. 3d 836, 847, 574 N.E.2d 190, 197 (1st Dist. 1991) (aggravated kidnapping distinct from aggravated criminal sexual assault).

355

offense committed by the defendant.[267] It is noteworthy, however, that these decisions involving unlawful restraint charges do *not* routinely use the four-factor *Levy-Lombardi* test in their analysis.

Beyond the questions concerning whether certain crimes are merely incidental to kidnapping, there are further conventional, lesser-included offense problems that need to be addressed. For example, kidnapping will normally be considered a lesser included offense of aggravated kidnapping.[268] Similarly, unlawful restraint will usually be viewed as a lesser included offense of kidnapping.[269] On the other hand, where the defendant had bound his victim's wrists with wire and had prevented the victim from responding to her boyfriend's telephone calls and her doorbell, a trail of the victim's blood disclosed that she went from room to room while she was severely wounded in an attempt to escape, and defendant then murdered her by splitting her body open from her sternum to her pubic bone, the Illinois Supreme Court stated that this defendant, who was convicted of aggravated kidnapping, was not entitled to an unlawful restraint instruction because "[u]nder the evidence in this case, the jury could not have rationally convicted the defendant of unlawful restraint and could not have acquitted him of aggravated kidnapping."[270]

Beyond the above, where a defendant threatened a kidnap victim with a dangerous weapon, the charge of aggravated assault is not necessarily a lesser included offense of an aggravated kidnapping.[271] Meanwhile, where a forcible detention and armed violence arose from the "same physical conduct," both convictions could not stand.[272] On the other hand, where the defendant asported his victim from the street to a parking lot with intent to secretly confine her against her will, and later sexually assaulted her, his aggravated kidnapping and aggravated criminal sexual assault convictions were not barred by the same physical act doctrine.[273]

---

[267] *See* § 7.22 of this chapter.

[268] *See, e.g.*, People v. Phillips, 186 Ill. App. 3d 54, 68, 541 N.E.2d 1298, 1308 (1st Dist. 1989) (kidnapping conviction vacated).

[269] *See, e.g.*, People v. Kittle, 140 Ill. App. 3d 951, 954-56, 489 N.E.2d 481, 484-85 (2d Dist. 1986) (unlawful restraint conviction vacated).

[270] People v. Enoch, 122 Ill. 2d 176, 199-201, 533 N.E.2d 1124, 1136-37 (aggravated kidnapping, murder and rape convictions affirmed), *cert. denied*, 506 U.S. 816 (1988). *See also* People v. Frampton, 248 Ill. App. 3d 238, 247, 618 N.E.2d 541, 548 (1st Dist. 1993) (where evidence was such that defendant either guilty of aggravated kidnapping or nothing, lesser included offense instruction for unlawful restraint not required).

[271] People v. Hobson, 77 Ill. App. 3d 22, 29, 396 N.E.2d 53, 59 (3d Dist. 1979). *But see* People v. Roberts, 71 Ill. App. 3d 124, 129, 389 N.E.2d 596, 600 (5th Dist. 1979) (contra).

[272] People v. Kavinsky, 98 Ill. App. 3d 579, 584, 424 N.E.2d 340, 344 (2d Dist. 1981) (referring to "same physical act" doctrine, forcible detention conviction vacated).

[273] People v. Gaines, 220 Ill. App. 3d 310, 322-23, 581 N.E.2d 214, 223 (1st Dist. 1991).

Finally, double jeopardy principles could constitute a barrier to penalizing a defendant in more than one way for his wrongful abduction.[274] Where a defendant, previously prosecuted for child abduction, was found in indirect criminal contempt for absconding and concealing his son contrary to a child custody order, the contempt citation was violative of double jeopardy.[275]

---

[274] U.S. CONST. amend. V.

[275] In re Marriage of D'Attomo, 211 Ill. App. 3d 914, 922-23, 570 N.E.2d 769, 801-02 (1st Dist. 1991).

CHAPTER 8

SEX OFFENSES

§ 8.01. Introduction.

Sexual activities affect personal, family, community, social and religious aspects of our society.[1] These activities become criminal when they significantly impact societal interests in a dire fashion. The Illinois legislature has determined that sexual activity warrants criminal sanctions when it intrudes on any one of four interests: (1) protection of the individual against forcible acts; (2) protection of the young and the immature from the sexual advances of older and more mature individuals; (3) protection of the public from open and notorious conduct which disturbs the peace, tends to promote breaches of the peace openly or openly flouts accepted standards of morality in the community; and (4) protection of the institution of marriage and normal family relationships from sexual conduct which tends to destroy them.[2] The various sex offenses are "not intended to proscribe any conduct between consenting adults unless such conduct adversely affects one of the key interests sought to be protected."[3]

The Illinois Criminal Code outlaws a broad range of nonconsensual sexual activity in the crimes of criminal sexual assault,[4] aggravated criminal sexual assault,[5] predatory criminal sexual assault of a child,[6] criminal sexual abuse,[7] and aggravated criminal sexual abuse.[8] Solicitations to engage in sexual activities

---

[1] ILL. ANN. STAT. ch. 38, para. 11-1 (Smith-Hurd 1979), 1961 Committee Comments, at 8-9 (revised 1972). Although ILL. REV. STAT. ch. 38, para. 11-1 (1983) (rape) is now repealed, the committee comments that accompanied that section stated the purposes that the legislature had in mind in criminalizing certain sexual behavior in the Criminal Code of 1961.

[2] ILL. ANN. STAT. ch. 38, para. 11-1 (Smith-Hurd 1979), 1961 Committee Comments, at 9 (revised 1972).

[3] ILL. ANN. STAT. ch. 38, para. 11-1 (Smith-Hurd 1979), 1961 Committee Comments, at 9 (revised 1972).

[4] 720 ILCS 5/12-13 (1999).

[5] 720 ILCS 5/12-14 (1999).

[6] 720 ILCS 5/12-14.1 (1999).

[7] 720 ILCS 5/12-15 (1999).

[8] 720 ILCS 5/12-16 (1999).

with children are covered by indecent solicitation of a child[9] and indecent solicitation of an adult.[10] Extramarital sexual intercourse is prohibited by the offenses of adultery[11] and fornication.[12] Sexual activity in public is addressed by the prohibition against public indecency,[13] while such activity in the presence of a minor is covered by sexual exploitation of a child.[14] Penal system employee sex with inmates is proscribed by custodial sexual misconduct.[15] A child sex offender must avoid the locale of a school or violate presence within school zone by child sex offender.[16] Incest is barred by sexual relations within families.[17] Bigamous relationships are outlawed by bigamy[18] and marrying a bigamist.[19] Prostitution-related activity is proscribed by the offenses of prostitution,[20] solicitation of a sexual act,[21] soliciting for a prostitute,[22] soliciting for a juvenile prostitute,[23] pandering,[24] keeping a place of prostitution,[25] keeping a place of juvenile prostitution,[26] patronizing a prostitute,[27] patronizing a juvenile prostitute,[28] pimping,[29] juvenile pimping,[30] and exploitation of a child.[31] Dissemination of an obscene material is prohibited by the crime of obscenity.[32] Possession or dissemination of obscene material involving minors is outlawed by the crime of child pornography.[33] Distribution of sexually explicit material to minors is covered by the offense of harmful material.[34] Finally, improper promotion of obscene materials by publication wholesalers is proscribed by the stricture called

---

[9] 720 ILCS 5/11-6 (1999).

[10] 720 ILCS 5/11-6.5 (1999).

[11] 720 ILCS 5/11-7 (1999).

[12] 720 ILCS 5/11-8 (1999).

[13] 720 ILCS 5/11-9 (1999).

[14] 720 ILCS 5/11-9.1 (1999).

[15] 720 ILCS 5/11-9.2 (1999).

[16] 720 ILCS 5/11-9.3 (1999).

[17] 720 ILCS 5/11-11 (1999).

[18] 720 ILCS 5/11-12 (1999).

[19] 720 ILCS 5/11-13 (1999).

[20] 720 ILCS 5/11-14 (1999).

[21] 720 ILCS 5/11-14.1 (1999).

[22] 720 ILCS 5/11-15 (1999).

[23] 720 ILCS 5/11-15.1 (1999).

[24] 720 ILCS 5/11-16 (1999).

[25] 720 ILCS 5/11-17 (1999).

[26] 720 ILCS 5/11-17.1 (1999).

[27] 720 ILCS 5/11-18 (1999).

[28] 720 ILCS 5/11-18.1 (1999).

[29] 720 ILCS 5/11-19 (1999).

[30] 720 ILCS 5/11-19.1 (1999).

[31] 720 ILCS 5/11-19.2 (1999).

[32] 720 ILCS 5/11-20 (1999).

[33] 720 ILCS 5/11-20.1 (1999).

[34] 720 ILCS 5/11-21 (1999).

tie-in sales of obscene publications to distributors.[35] This chapter will explore the scope of these offenses.

§ 8.02. — The Criminal Sexual Assault Act of 1984.

Central to the legislative scheme directed at sexual misconduct in Illinois are the provisions of the Criminal Sexual Assault Act of 1984.[36] This legislation addresses nonconsensual sexual activity, which includes not only assaultive conduct but also that conduct involving minors and mentally handicapped persons who are legally incapable of reasoned and intelligent choices. While many of the other prohibitions outside this legislative package may complement or reinforce the prohibitions within, the Act assumes a key role in defining what sexual activity is criminal in Illinois. First, the Act sets out the very important strictures of criminal sexual assault,[37] aggravated criminal sexual assault,[38] predatory criminal sexual assault of a child,[39] criminal sexual abuse,[40] and aggravated criminal sexual abuse.[41] Second, the Act sets out various definitions, including "sexual penetration," "sexual conduct" and "consent," which are applicable not only to the prohibitions that are part of the Act but also the other sex offenses throughout the Illinois penal code.[42] Third, the Act relabeled certain criminality, such as incest, and redefined various others, such as prostitution. While the effect of the change created by this law is reflected throughout this chapter, the most pivotal changes occurred in relation to nonconsensual sex. The net effect of this latter change is best appreciated by a review of the law before the advent of the Criminal Sexual Assault Act of 1984.

§ 8.03. — Background to Criminal Sexual Assault Act.

Prior to the Criminal Sexual Assault Act of 1984, the Illinois Legislature protected the interests identified in the introductory section through the use of article 5/11, which is labeled "sex offenses."[43] Article 5/11 included the crimes

---

[35] 720 ILCS 5/11-22 (1999).
[36] 720 ILCS 5/12-12 through 5/12-18 (1999).
[37] 720 ILCS 5/12-13 (1999).
[38] 720 ILCS 5/12-14 (1999).
[39] 720 ILCS 5/12-14.1 (1999).
[40] 720 ILCS 5/12-15 (1999).
[41] 720 ILCS 5/12-16 (1999).
[42] 720 ILCS 5/12-12, 5/12-17 (1999).
[43] 720 ILCS art. 5/11 (1999).

of rape,[44] deviate sexual assault[45] (which encompassed "deviate sexual conduct"),[46] indecent liberties with a child,[47] aggravated indecent liberties with a child,[48] contributing to the sexual delinquency of a child,[49] incest,[50] aggravated incest,[51] and sexual abuse of a child by a family member.[52]

Although this legislation's purpose was to protect victims from unwanted or inappropriate sex, it included many restrictive requirements before the state was able to gain a conviction. For example, the rape statute contained gender requirements. The rape statute explicitly stated that only males were capable of being accused of rape and that the victim of rape could only be female.[53] Therefore, a sexual assault by a female or a sexual attack against a male victim by either a male or female perpetrator was the subject of another stricture called deviate sexual assault.[54] In addition, the rape legislation also restricted the kinds of acts that could be punishable under the statute by allowing only nonconsensual acts of "sexual intercourse" to constitute rape, with sexual intercourse being narrowly defined as "any penetration of the female sex organ by the male sex or-

---

[44] ILL. REV. STAT. ch. 38, para. 11-1 (1983) (repealed) ("(a) A male person of the age of 14 years and upwards who has sexual intercourse with a female, not his wife, by force and against her will, commits rape. Intercourse by force and against her will includes, but is not limited to, any intercourse that occurs in the following situations: (1) Where the female is unconscious; or (2) Where the female is so mentally deranged or deficient that she cannot give effective consent to intercourse. (b) Sexual intercourse occurs where there is any penetration of the female sex organ by the male sex organ.").

[45] ILL. REV. STAT. ch. 38, para. 11-3 (1983) (repealed) ("Any person of the age of 14 years and upwards who, by force or threat of force, compels any person to perform or submit to any act of deviate sexual conduct commits deviate sexual assault.").

[46] ILL. REV. STAT. ch. 38, para. 11-2 (1983) (repealed) ("any act of sexual gratification involving the sex organs of one person and the mouth or anus of another").

[47] ILL. REV. STAT. ch. 38, para. 11-4 (1983) (repealed) (where person, 17 years old and upwards, with a child under the age of 16, engages in sexual intercourse, deviate sexual conduct or any lewd fondling intended to arouse or satisfy the person's or child's sexual desires; or where person, regardless of age, photographs or the like a minor under the age of 16 in a sexual context).

[48] ILL. REV. STAT. ch. 38, para. 11-4.1 (1983) (repealed) (where person, 17 years and upwards, with a child under the age of 12, engages in sexual intercourse, deviate sexual conduct, or penetration of any part of the person's or child's genital or anal opening *and* inflicts great bodily harm upon the child, except if child is under 9 years of age, in which case no great bodily harm required).

[49] ILL. REV. STAT. ch. 38, para. 11-5 (1983) (repealed) (where person, 14 years old and upward, with a person under the age of 18, engages in sexual intercourse, deviate sexual conduct, lewd fondling intended to arouse or satisfy the person's or child's sexual desires, or lewd act in the presence of the child intended to arouse or satisfy the person's or child's sexual desire).

[50] ILL. REV. STAT. ch. 38, para. 11-11 (1983) (repealed). *See* § 8.33 of this chapter for definition.

[51] ILL. REV. STAT. ch. 38, para. 11-10 (1983) (repealed). *See* § 8.33 of this chapter for definition.

[52] ILL. REV. STAT. ch. 38, para. 11-11.1 (1983) (repealed). *See* § 8.33 of this chapter for definition.

[53] ILL. REV. STAT. ch. 38, para. 11-1 (1983) (repealed). *Compare* People v. Trumbley, 252 Ill. 29, 35, 96 N.E. 573, 575 (1911) (woman could be convicted for aiding and abetting a rape).

[54] ILL. REV. STAT. ch. 38, para. 11-3 (1983) (repealed).

gan."[55] Because the definition of the element of sexual intercourse was so precise, it in effect excluded sexual attacks of women that may have fallen short of actual penetration.[56] Also, where a woman was forced to perform fellatio or was subjected to forcible anal penetration, these acts were insufficient to sustain a charge of rape.[57]

In addition to meeting the statute's requirements for gender and sexual intercourse, the state also had to show that the defendant employed a use of force that overcame the victim's will.[58] There was no set standard as to what was considered force, leaving each case to be decided on its own facts.[59] In addition, where the female victim had "the use of her faculties and physical powers the evidence must show such resistance as will demonstrate that the act was against her will."[60] Resistance was only excused if "it would be futile and would endanger the victim's life."[61] Where a victim was overcome by superior strength or was paralyzed by fear, her "acquiescence to threats of violence" excused the failure to resist.[62] Where the victim was tricked by the defendant into having intercourse,[63] was not of the mental ability to appreciate the situation,[64] or was a child,[65] then force would be implied and resistance excused.[66] Otherwise, when an alleged rape victim faced with a defendant's sexual advance "became aware

---

[55] ILL. REV. STAT. ch. 38, para. 11-1 (1983) (repealed).

[56] *See, e.g.,* People v. O'Neal, 50 Ill. App. 3d 900, 906-07, 365 N.E.2d 1333, 1338 (4th Dist. 1977) (where mentally retarded victim testified defendant put his "thing" between her legs and pushed and that his "thing" was *in* her "bottom" and defendant had told witnesses that because he had been caught, he "had not been able to finish the job," defendant's rape conviction vacated and reduced to attempted rape because evidence unclear "how far he had progressed before being interrupted.").

[57] People v. Vilt, 139 Ill. App. 3d 868, 874, 488 N.E.2d 580, 585 (3d Dist. 1985) (nonconsensual anal sex supports deviant sexual assault conviction).

[58] People v. Celmars, 332 Ill. 113, 119, 163 N.E.2d 421, 424 (1928) ("Force is an essential element where the female is of the age of consent and physically and mentally able to offer resistance.").

[59] People v. Thomas, 96 Ill. App. 3d 443, 450, 421 N.E.2d 357, 362 (1st Dist. 1981). Force was also a material element of deviant sexual assault. People v. Walsh, 80 Ill. App. 3d 754, 764, 400 N.E.2d 587, 594 (1st Dist. 1980).

[60] People v. Scott, 407 Ill. 301, 305, 95 N.E.2d 315, 317 (1950).

[61] People v. Schmitt, 99 Ill. App. 3d 184, 188, 424 N.E.2d 1267, 1270 (5th Dist. 1981).

[62] People v. Schmitt, 99 Ill. App. 3d 184, 188, 424 N.E.2d 1267, 1270 (5th Dist. 1981) (rape conviction affirmed).

[63] *Cf.* People v. Borak, 13 Ill. App. 3d 815, 820-21, 301 N.E.2d 1, 5 (2d Dist. 1973) (where defendant, a doctor performing gynecological examination, suddenly and by surprise performed oral sex on victim, defendant's conviction of deviate sexual assault affirmed).

[64] People v. Farrokhi, 91 Ill. App. 3d 421, 423-27, 414 N.E.2d 921, 923-26 (2d Dist. 1980) (rape conviction affirmed).

[65] People v. Riley, 84 Ill. App. 2d 296, 299-300, 228 N.E.2d 190, 192 (1st Dist. 1967) (where 31-year-old male had sexual intercourse with a 7-year-old child, rape conviction affirmed).

[66] People v. Riley, 84 Ill. App. 2d 296, 299-300, 228 N.E.2d 190, 192 (1st Dist. 1967).

of his intentions . . ., [i]t then became her duty . . . to use resistance to prevent further acts."[67] If the victim retained the power to resist, "her voluntary submission, no matter how reluctantly yielded, constitute[d] consent."[68] Thus, where a defendant, a medical doctor, while performing a gynecological examination of an eighteen-year-old patient, placed his tongue on her vaginal area, then told her in a commanding voice to lay back down and close her eyes after she got up on her elbows on the examination table and, about thirty seconds later, inserted his penis into her vagina, the victim's failure to satisfy her "duty" to resist defendant's vaginal penetration with his penis prompted a reversal of defendant's rape conviction.[69] Where an alleged rape victim, who evidently had no place to live, reluctantly went to defendant's apartment, was beaten, then at defendant's insistence, removed her clothing and was given a bath and, thereafter, at defendant's direction reluctantly went into the bedroom and got into bed, whereupon for the first time defendant insisted on having sexual intercourse with her, the Illinois Supreme Court ruled that from the victim's "description of the occurrence, and the five hours of sexual excesses which she claims then transpired, it is clear that, however reluctantly begun, the sexual acts were engaged in without any resistance whatsoever on the part of the prosecutrix."[70] In another case where a victim claimed that her failure to resist or cry out was attributable to her being paralyzed by fear, the Illinois Supreme Court stated "it is difficult to conceive that such a fear would have consumed her for the entire two hours that was spent in the bedroom [with defendant] before she allegedly perpetrated a ruse to escape."[71]

Where a rape victim failed to attempt an escape from her rapist, or summon assistance, when an opportunity to do so existed, this undermined the victim's claim that the sexual intercourse was against her will.[72] In another case, where an alleged rape victim claimed that she was neither able to escape the unarmed defendant nor able to enlist help as her abductor escorted her in various public

---

[67] People v. Borak, 13 Ill. App. 3d 815, 821, 301 N.E.2d 1, 6 (2d Dist. 1973).

[68] People v. Wilcox, 33 Ill. App. 3d 432, 436, 337 N.E.2d 211, 215 (2d Dist. 1975).

[69] People v. Borak, 13 Ill. App. 3d 815, 821, 301 N.E.2d 1, 6 (2d Dist. 1973) (although defendant's conviction for deviate sexual assault affirmed where victim had no opportunity to resist defendant's surprise sexual advance by suddenly performing oral sex on victim).

[70] People v. Scott, 407 Ill. 301, 305, 95 N.E.2d 315, 317 (1950) (rape conviction reversed). *See also* People v. Serrielle, 354 Ill. 182, 186, 188 N.E.2d 375, 377 (1933) (where defendant entered victim's apartment unit, conversed with her for a while, then picked victim up, threw her onto bed, turned out light, and had sex with her, rape conviction reversed because "evidence does not show...she made any resistance or unsuccessful effort to get away from him, nor that she screamed until, as she testified, she felt as though she had been torn apart" after his penetration).

[71] People v. DeFrates, 33 Ill. 2d 190, 195, 210 N.E.2d 467, 469 (1965) (rape conviction reversed).

[72] People v. Rosario, 110 Ill. App. 3d 1020, 1023-25, 443 N.E.2d 273, 276-77 (1st Dist. 1982) (rape conviction reversed).

places, and was not seen crying or distraught, either before or after the alleged assault, by witnesses who had an opportunity to observe her demeanor during this period, the appellate court concluded that the victim's claim of forced intercourse was "farfetched and improbable."[73] Obviously, then, when a defendant admitted to intercourse but claimed it was consensual, "resistance became the gist of the offense charged."[74]

Prosecutors seeking to achieve a rape conviction were faced with evidentiary barriers as well. The Illinois Supreme Court explained that, because as "Lord Hale once aptly observed[,] . . . an accusation of rape is easily made, hard to be proved and still harder to be defended by one ever so innocent," it was necessary that the courts be "especially charged with the duty to carefully examine the evidence in a rape case."[75] Specifically, this charge translated into a requirement that a rape complainant's testimony either had to be clear and convincing or be corroborated by other evidence.[76] Thus, where the victim suffered a painful and significant laceration in the vaginal area that a physician described as not seen in any woman except those giving birth, this would amount to sufficient corroborative evidence.[77] Likewise, a prompt complaint of rape would provide the necessary corroboration.[78] Meanwhile, a victim's testimony was considered clear and convincing where the victim was able to detail the events that preceded the attack and that occurred during the rape and the actions taken afterward by the defendant and herself.[79]

In conclusion, under the prior law, if a victim was of age to consent to sexual acts and was physically and mentally capable of consent, it was up to the state to prove force or threat of force was directed at the victim *and* that the victim somehow resisted that force.[80] If the victim did not actively resist the attack, then consent by the victim would be found. In effect, this legislation that required proof that the sexual intercourse was "against her will" put the burden on the *victim* to prove that she *did not* consent to the defendant's advances. In other words, a verbal or physical resistance was necessary in order to show a lack of consent, and a lack of verbal or physical resistance could in and of itself constitute consent. Resistance was a crucial element to prove because there was an assumption that if there was no resistance, there was then also no force or threat

---

[73] People v. Wright, 147 Ill. App. 3d 302, 318, 497 N.E.2d 1261, 1271 (1st Dist. 1986) (rape conviction reversed).

[74] People v. Serrielle, 354 Ill. 182, 186, 188 N.E.2d 375, 377 (1933).

[75] People v. Scott, 407 Ill. 301, 304, 95 N.E.2d 315, 316 (1950) (rape conviction reversed).

[76] People v. Reed, 57 Ill. App. 3d 533, 538, 373 N.E.2d 538, 542 (1st Dist. 1978).

[77] People v. Reed, 57 Ill. App. 3d 533, 538, 373 N.E.2d 538, 542 (1st Dist. 1978) (rape conviction affirmed).

[78] People v. Reed, 57 Ill. App. 3d 533, 538, 373 N.E.2d 538, 542 (1st Dist. 1978).

[79] People v. McKendrick, 138 Ill. App. 3d 1018, 1024, 486 N.E.2d 1297, 1302 (1st Dist. 1985).

[80] People v. Celmars, 332 Ill. 113, 119, 163 N.E.2d 421, 424 (1928).

of force. Unless the defendant was faced with a serious threat to her personal safety by her objection to the sexual advance, it was up to the victim to show that she *actively* resisted the advances of the defendant either verbally or physically. Indeed, considering the fact that the victim's claim of nonconsensual sexual intercourse had to be clear and convincing or somehow corroborated, as a practical matter, a victim would have had to say "no" *and* attempt to physically fight off her attacker or face the defense of consent.

A final barrier to victims of rape was reflected in the marital exemption.[81] The "not his wife" language in the rape statute created what was described as marital exemption, which disqualified a husband from being charged with rape when the victim was his wife.[82] In other words, the common law assumed per se that all sexual encounters within the marriage were necessarily consensual.

Of course, the offense of deviate sexual assault, which included nonconsensual anal and oral sex and contained no gender requirements,[83] addressed *some* nonconsensual sexual encounters that fell outside the scope of the rape prohibition. Nevertheless, the resistance requirement defeated many claims of unwanted sex here as well. Furthermore, egregious conduct such as the forcible penetration of an adult woman's vagina or a person's anus with one's hand, finger or object was prosecuted under less serious strictures such as battery. The fondling of a woman's breast against her will was likewise addressed by less serious prohibitions. Because of the shortcomings of these and other laws designed to protect the citizenry from unwanted or inappropriate sexual assaults, the Illinois legislature decided to significantly reshape the state's prohibitions against sex offenses.

§ 8.04. — Criminal Sexual Assault Act Codified.

Following the lead of the majority of states that instituted penal code reform of their sexual strictures,[84] the Illinois General Assembly put into effect the Criminal Sexual Assault Act of 1984.[85] These changes received both praise[86] and criticism[87] after their enactment. The net effect of this legislative effort was to repeal the crimes of rape,[88] deviate sexual assault[89] (which encompassed "de-

---

[81] ILL. REV. STAT. ch. 38, para. 11-1 (1983) (repealed).

[82] ILL. REV. STAT. ch. 38, para. 11-1 (1983) (repealed).

[83] ILL. REV. STAT. ch. 38, para. 11-3 (1983) (repealed).

[84] Katherine Lawson, *Sex Crimes Revisited*, ILL. ISSUES, Feb. 1984, at 6.

[85] Pub. Act 83-1067 (1984); 720 ILCS 5/12-12 to 5/12-18 (1999).

[86] *See* Aaron Jaffe & Reynold Becker, *Four New Basic Sex Offenses: A Fundamental Shift in Emphasis*, 72 ILL. B.J. 400 (April, 1984).

[87] *See* Arthur Inman & Melvin Lewis, *HB 606: New Problems of Policy and Enforcement*, 72 ILL. B.J. 404 (April, 1984).

[88] ILL. REV. STAT. ch. 38, para. 11-1 (1983) (repealed).

[89] ILL. REV. STAT. ch. 38, para. 11-3 (1983) (repealed).

viate sexual conduct"),[90] indecent liberties with a child,[91] aggravated indecent liberties with a child,[92] and contributing to the sexual delinquency of a child.[93] These crimes were replaced by criminal sexual assault,[94] aggravated criminal sexual assault,[95] predatory criminal sexual assault of a child,[96] criminal sexual abuse,[97] and aggravated criminal sexual abuse.[98]

These provisions removed several obstacles to the prosecution of sex offenses by eliminating gender stipulations, abrogating age limitations of crimes against adults, and repealing, in some instances, the defense of marriage.[99] The defense of consent that existed in relation to rape was narrowed significantly,[100] while definitions of certain relevant terms, such as *sexual conduct*[101] and *sexual penetration*,[102] were added. Beyond these changes, this comprehensive legislative package redefined certain crimes, such as indecent solicitation of a child[103] and public indecency,[104] and relabeled what was formerly called "incest,"[105] "aggravated incest,"[106] and "sexual abuse of a child by a family member"[107] as "criminal sexual assault,"[108] "aggravated criminal sexual abuse,"[109] and "sexual relations within families."[110] A number of other offenses, including adultery[111] and fornication,[112] were left intact.

The principal changes in the 1984 sex offense legislation appear in article 5/12, which deals with "bodily harm" concerns.[113] Because of their similarity to other forms of assault and battery, the new offenses, criminal sexual assault and

---

[90] ILL. REV. STAT. ch. 38, para. 11-2 (1983) (repealed).

[91] ILL. REV. STAT. ch. 38, para. 11-4 (1983) (repealed).

[92] ILL. REV. STAT. ch. 38, para. 11-4.1 (1983) (repealed).

[93] ILL. REV. STAT. ch. 38, para. 11-5 (1983) (repealed).

[94] 720 ILCS 5/12-13 (1999).

[95] 720 ILCS 5/12-14 (1999).

[96] 720 ILCS 5/12-14.1 (1999).

[97] 720 ILCS 5/12-15 (1999).

[98] 720 ILCS 5/12-16 (1999).

[99] Katherine Lawson, *Sex Crimes Revisited*, ILL. ISSUES, Feb. 1984, at 6. *But See* § 8.25 of this chapter.

[100] 720 ILCS 5/12-17(a) (1999) (narrowing definition of consent).

[101] 720 ILCS 5/12-12(e) (1999).

[102] 720 ILCS 5/12-12(f) (1999).

[103] 720 ILCS 5/11-6 (1999).

[104] 720 ILCS 5/11-9 (1999).

[105] ILL. REV. STAT. ch. 38, para. 11-11 (1983) (repealed).

[106] ILL. REV. STAT. ch. 38, para. 11-10 (1983) (repealed).

[107] ILL. REV. STAT. ch. 38, para. 11-11.1 (1983) (repealed).

[108] 720 ILCS 5/12-13 (1999).

[109] 720 ILCS 5/12-16 (1999).

[110] 720 ILCS 5/11-11 (1999).

[111] 720 ILCS 5/11-7 (1999).

[112] 720 ILCS 5/11-8 (1999).

[113] 720 ILCS art. 5/12 (1999).

criminal sexual abuse, were more logically placed in this article as opposed to article 5/11, which is labeled "sex offenses."[114] Article 5/11 is where the offenses such as rape — now repealed — previously appeared and where other sex crimes that were not abolished by the 1984 Act remain today.

§ 8.05. Definitions.

Section 5/12-12 reflects certain definitions that are relevant to the article 5/12 sex crimes. For the purpose of Sections 12-13 through 12-18 of this Code, the terms defined in these sections shall have the same meanings ascribed to them. Also, other offenses, such as prostitution, incorporate by reference the definition of certain terms in section 5/12-12.[115] This provision reads as follows:

(a) "Accused" means a person accused of an offense prohibited by Sections 12-13, 12-14, 12-15 or 12-16 of this Code or a person for whose conduct the accused is legally responsible under Article 5 of this Code.

(b) "Bodily harm" means physical harm, and includes but is not limited to, sexually transmitted disease, pregnancy and impotence.

(c) "Family member" means a parent, grandparent, or child, whether by whole blood, half-blood or adoption and includes a step-grandparent, step-parent or stepchild. "Family member" also means, where the victim is a child under 18 years of age, an accused who has resided in the household with such child continuously for at least one year.

(d) "Force or threat of force" means the use of force or violence, or the threat of force or violence, including but not limited to the following situations:

(1) when the accused threatens to use force or violence on the victim or on any other person, and the victim under the circumstances reasonably believed that the accused had the ability to execute that threat; or

(2) when the accused has overcome the victim by use of superior strength or size, physical restraint or physical confinement.

(e) "Sexual conduct" means any intentional or knowing touching or fondling by the victim or the accused, either directly or through clothing, of the sex organs, anus or breast of the victim or the accused, or any part of the body of a child under 13 years of age, for the purpose of sexual gratification or arousal of the victim or the accused.

(f) "Sexual penetration" means any contact, however slight, between the sex organ or anus of one person by an object, the sex organ, mouth or anus of another person, or any intrusion, however slight, of any part of the body

---

[114] 720 ILCS art. 5/11 (1999).

[115] *See* 720 ILCS 5/11-14(a) (1999) (prohibition of prostitution outlaws "any act of sexual penetration as defined in section [5/]12-12 of this code. . . .").

of one person or of any animal or object into the sex organ or anus of another person, including but not limited to cunnilingus, fellatio, or anal penetration. Evidence of emission of semen is not required to prove sexual penetration.

(g) "Victim" means a person alleging to have been subjected to an offense prohibited by Sections 12-13, 12-14, 12-15 or 12-16 of this Code.[116]

In addition, Section 5/12-17 contains a definition of "consent." It reads:

"Consent" means a freely given agreement to the act of sexual penetration or sexual conduct in question. Lack of verbal or physical resistance or submission by the victim resulting from the use of force or threat of force by the accused shall not constitute consent. The manner of dress of the victim at the time of the offense shall not constitute consent.[117]

§ 8.06. — Person Capable of Being Accused.

Any "person" can commit any of the sex offenses in article 5/12, as the definition of *accused* reflects.[118] This shows a significant departure from the prior rape statute, which was limited to "male persons."[119] Also, section 5/12-18 states that no person shall be presumed incapable of committing any article 5/12 offense because of age, physical condition, or relationship to the victim.[120] Thus, when a medical doctor performing gynecological examinations intentionally exceeds the scope of reasonable medical standards, this could constitute criminal sexual assault.[121]

§ 8.07. — Bodily Harm.

Bodily harm means any physical harm and includes the infliction of a sexually transmitted disease, pregnancy or impotency on the victim.[122] The Illinois Supreme Court commented that the words "bodily harm" have a "well-known legal

---

[116] 720 ILCS 5/12-12 (1999).

[117] 720 ILCS 5/12-17(a) (1999).

[118] 720 ILCS 5/12-12(a) (1999).

[119] ILL. REV. STAT. ch. 38, para. 11-1(a) (1983) (repealed).

[120] 720 ILCS 5/12-18(a) (1999).

[121] People v. Burpo, 164 Ill. 2d 261, 263-65, 647 N.E.2d 996, 998 (1995) (trial court dismissal of indictment of gynecologist reversed). *Compare* 720 ILCS 5/12-18(b) (1999) ("Any medical examination or procedure which is conducted by a physician, nurse, medical or hospital personnel, parent or caretaker for purposes and in a manner consistent with reasonable medical standards is not an offense. . . .").

[122] 720 ILCS 5/12-12(b) (1999).

meaning," given their use in the context of the statute defining battery.[123] The court noted it had earlier observed in relation to battery that "[a]lthough it may be difficult to pinpoint exactly what constitutes bodily harm for purposes of the statute, some sort of physical pain or damage to the body, like lacerations, bruises or abrasions, whether temporary or permanent, is required."[124] Thus, the court deemed it proper to give bodily harm the "same meaning" in the context of aggravated criminal sexual assault.[125] Thus, where a victim's face was bruised and swollen, and where she suffered blurred vision for about two months after the beating she incurred during defendant's sexual assault of her, the defendant had inflicted bodily harm for purposes of aggravated criminal sexual assault.[126] In another case, the appellate court rejected a defendant's claim that vaginal injuries, including abrasions, bruises, and a ruptured hymen suffered by the victim were the "normal incident of a criminal sexual assault" because criminal sexual assault can occur by *mere contact* between the sexual organs of the defendant and the victim's vagina and *without sexual penetration* of the vagina.[127] Bodily harm can be shown by evidence of actual injury or can be inferred by the trier of fact based on common knowledge, such that where evidence existed that defendant's penis entered his ten-year-old victim's vagina, the victim testified that it hurt when defendant's penis touched her vagina, and medical evidence indicated a perforated hymen and "ecchymotic or dark purple" coloring in two vaginal areas; thus, this was bodily harm sufficient to convict defendant of aggravated criminal sexual assault.[128]

§ 8.08. — Force or Threat of Force.

Force or threat of force involves the use or threat of force or violence and includes (1) threats to the victim or another where the victim reasonably believes the defendant has the capacity to execute that threat and (2) when the defendant has overcome the victim by use of superior strength or size, physical restraint or physical confinement.[129] The Illinois Supreme Court stated the term "force"

---

[123] People v. Haywood, 118 Ill. 2d 263, 275-76, 515 N.E.2d 45, 51 (1987) (referring to "battery" prohibition). Battery appears at 720 ILCS 5/12-3 (1999) and is discussed in ch. 9 of this treatise.

[124] People v. Haywood, 118 Ill. 2d 263, 276, 515 N.E.2d 45, 51 (1987) (quoting People v. Mays, 91 Ill. 2d 251, 256, 437 N.E.2d 633, 635-36 (1982)).

[125] People v. Haywood, 118 Ill. 2d 263, 275-76, 515 N.E.2d 45, 51 (1987) (phrase "bodily harm" not vague in violation of due process).

[126] People v. Rodarte, 190 Ill. App. 3d 992, 998-1000, 547 N.E.2d 1256, 1260-61 (1st Dist. 1989) (conviction affirmed).

[127] People v. Lauderdale, 228 Ill. App. 3d 830, 834, 593 N.E.2d 757, 760 (1st Dist. 1992) (aggravated criminal assault conviction affirmed).

[128] People v. Robinson, 267 Ill. App. 3d 900, 903-04, 642 N.E.2d 1317, 1320-21 (1st Dist. 1994).

[129] 720 ILCS 5/12-12(d) (1999).

should carry the same meaning as it did in the context of rape and deviate sexual assault.[130] As with rape, there is no definite amount of force or threat of force that the state is required to prove.[131]

Where the victim testified that she was slapped and beaten by her assailants, was heard screaming, and police and medical doctors who examined the victim reported numerous bruises and injuries about her face, this was sufficient evidence of force to establish criminal sexual assault.[132] Where another victim was sprayed with mace, was threatened with death, and was unsuccessful in verbal efforts to dissuade defendant from committing his sexual assault, there was sufficient force to establish aggravated criminal sexual assault.[133] Likewise, where the victim repeatedly told the defendant "no," "stop" and "to please leave" and attempted to push him away as he insisted on sexual intercourse with her, there was sufficient evidence of force to sustain a conviction of criminal sexual assault, even though she did not cry out for help or try to escape because she may have been overcome by the defendant's superior strength, or paralyzed by fear, and the lack of medical evidence of physical injury to her did not undermine that conclusion because physical injury and resistance are not necessary to prove nonconsensual intercourse.[134] In another case, the force element of criminal sexual abuse was sufficiently supported by proof that defendant virtually pinned his victim in a seat of a car, leaving her with nowhere that she could move to in order that she might avoid his sexual advances of poking at her breast; here, she was *physically confined* within the meaning of the statute.[135]

On the other hand, evidence of force was unsatisfactory where the complainant told a detective that defendant made no verbal threats of bodily harm before their sexual intercourse, admitted to scant or no resistance when defendant pulled down her pants and "indirectly" pushed her into the back seat, allowed a towel to be placed beneath her because she was menstruating, removed her underwear herself while defendant was outside the car, and made no attempt to escape or cry out for help, even though she knew another person was close by.[136] In another case, the evidence did not establish the defendant "forced" his victim to engage in acts of oral sex, for purposes of criminal sexual assault, though the

---

[130] People v. Haywood, 118 Ill. 2d 263, 271, 515 N.E.2d 45, 49 (1987). *See* § 8.03 of this chapter for a discussion of rape and deviate sexual assault, now repealed.

[131] People v. Bolton, 207 Ill. App. 3d 681, 686, 566 N.E.2d 348, 351 (1st Dist. 1990).

[132] People v. Bolton, 207 Ill. App. 3d 681, 686, 566 N.E.2d 348, 351 (1st Dist. 1990).

[133] People v. Fryer, 247 Ill. App. 3d 1051, 1058-60, 618 N.E.2d 377, 382-83 (1st Dist. 1993).

[134] People v. Bowen, 241 Ill. App. 3d 608, 619, 609 N.E.2d 346, 356 (4th Dist.), *cert. denied*, 510 U.S. 946 (1993). *See also* People v. Carlson, 278 Ill. App. 3d 515, 520-21, 663 N.E.2d 32, 36 (1st Dist. 1996) (where victim was "paralyzed by fear," defendant's conviction for criminal sexual assault was affirmed).

[135] People v. Satterfield, 195 Ill. App. 3d 1087, 1097, 552 N.E.2d 1382, 1388 (2d Dist. 1990).

[136] People v. Walker, 154 Ill. App. 3d 616, 621-25, 506 N.E.2d 1004, 1007-10 (2d Dist. 1987) (aggravated criminal sexual assault conviction reversed).

victim claimed the defendant placed his hand on the back of the victim's head and "forced" it down, where he also admitted defendant did not threaten him and he did not believe the defendant intended to hurt him.[137]

The phrase *force or threat of force* has been subjected to a constitutional challenge on the grounds of vagueness and overbreadth. However, in *People v. Haywood,*[138] the Illinois Supreme Court ruled that the statute, including the term force, was not vague or overbroad as to what conduct was proscribed.[139]

§ 8.09. — Sexual Conduct.

The definition of *sexual conduct,*[140] introduced into the Illinois penal code in 1984, is very significant. Under the prior code provisions, in addition to "sexual intercourse," which was required for rape,[141] "deviate sexual conduct"[142] was prohibited in certain circumstances.[143] *Deviate sexual conduct* meant "any act of sexual gratification involving the sex organs of one person and the mouth or anus of another."[144] However, the definition of *sexual conduct* under the Criminal Sexual Assault Act includes any "touching or fondling" of either the victim's or the accused's "sex organs, anus or breast," including through the victim's clothing, so long as it is done intentionally or with knowledge and "for the purpose of sexual gratification or arousal of the victim or the accused."[145] In addition, *sexual conduct* includes any such touching or fondling of "any part of the body of a child under 13 years of age" for the same purpose.[146] In other words, the concept of sexual conduct that appears in various article 5/12 strictures has broadened the range of sexual activities that now falls within the reach of criminal sanction. Thus, where a defendant deliberately touched the female victim's breasts, this was sexual conduct for purposes of criminal sexual abuse.[147] Where

---

[137] People v. Vasquez, 233 Ill. App. 3d 517, 528, 599 N.E.2d 523, 529-30 (2d Dist. 1992); *see also* Commonwealth v. Berkowitz, 641 A.2d 1161 (Pa. 1994) (holding where evidence that victim stated "no" throughout her encounter with defendant and defendant pushed her on the bed prior to having sexual intercourse with her, was insufficient to establish "forcible compulsion" necessary to support rape conviction since the victim was not restrained by defendant and she could have attempted to leave the room but did not).

[138] 118 Ill. 2d 263, 515 N.E.2d 45 (1987).

[139] People v. Haywood, 118 Ill. 2d 263, 264, 515 N.E.2d 45, 50 (1987).

[140] 720 ILCS 5/12-12(e) (1999)

[141] ILL. REV. STAT. ch. 38, para. 11-1 (1983) (repealed).

[142] ILL. REV. STAT. ch. 38, para. 11-2 (1983) (repealed).

[143] *See, e.g.,* ILL. REV. STAT. ch. 38, para. 11-3 (1983) (repealed) (deviate sexual assault); para. 11-4 (repealed) (indecent liberties with a child); para. 11-4.1 (repealed) (aggravated indecent liberties with a child).

[144] ILL. REV. STAT. ch. 38, para. 11-2 (1983).

[145] 720 ILCS 5/12-12(e) (1999).

[146] 720 ILCS 5/12-12(e) (1999).

[147] People v. Westpfahl, 295 Ill. App. 3d 327, 334, 692 N.E.2d 831, 837 (3d Dist. 1998).

a defendant massaged her minor son's penis and testicles to the point that he had an erection, and told him not to tell anyone, it was proper to conclude that this was for the purpose of sexual gratification or arousal of the victim and, as such, constituted sexual conduct.[148] However, the touching or fondling must be *of another* and does not include self-stimulation in the presence of another.[149]

§ 8.10. — Sexual Penetration.

The definition of *sexual penetration*[150] has evolved significantly in Illinois. Previously, rape required "sexual intercourse," which occurred when there was "any penetration of the female *sex organ* by the male *sex organ*."[151] The concept of sexual penetration for purposes of any of the Illinois sex crimes is now a much broader concept, as the above definition reflects. It includes "any contact, however slight, between the sex organ of one person by an object, the sex organ, mouth, or anus of another person."[152] It also includes "any intrusion, however slight, of any part of the body of one person or of any animal or object into the sex organ or anus of another person, including but not limited to cunnilingus, fellatio or anal penetration."[153] Where there is no penetration of the sex organ or anus *of another*, such as where the defendant forced his victim to penetrate her own vagina with her finger, this was not "sexual penetration."[154]

When the term "sexual penetration" was challenged on the grounds that it exceeded the ordinary definition of the term, namely, "an act of passing into or through," the appellate court ruled that the legislature had the power to broaden the meaning beyond the dictionary definition or narrow the meaning ordinarily given certain terms.[155] Where it was argued that the definitions of sexual penetration and sexual conduct are so similar in regard to the conduct proscribed that they are indistinguishable and vague, the appellate court rejected these arguments and held that it is not a denial of due process that a defendant can be

---

[148] People v. Smith, 236 Ill. App. 3d 35, 39-40, 603 N.E.2d 562, 564-65 (1st Dist. 1992) (aggravated criminal sexual abuse conviction affirmed).

[149] People v. Gann, 141 Ill. App. 3d 34, 35, 489 N.E.2d 924, 925 (3d Dist. 1986) (noting that this conduct could constitute public indecency but reversing aggravated criminal sexual abuse conviction).

[150] 720 ILCS 5/12-12(f) (1999).

[151] ILL. REV. STAT. ch. 38, para. 11-1 (1983) (repealed) (emphasis added).

[152] 720 ILCS 5/12-12(f) (1999). *See* People v. Bofman, 283 Ill. App. 3d 546, 550-52, 670 N.E.2d 796, 800 (1st Dist. 1996) (where defendant's penis made contact with the victim's penis, this was "sexual penetration" for purposes of aggravated criminal sexual assault); People v. Back, 239 Ill. App. 3d 44, 78-79, 605 N.E.2d 689, 712 (4th Dist. 1992) (holding where defendant's penis made contact with his victim's vagina, this was sexual penetration for purposes of aggravated criminal sexual assault).

[153] 720 ILCS 5/12-12(f) (1999).

[154] People v. Scott, 271 Ill. App. 3d 307, 313-14, 648 N.E.2d 86, 89-90 (1st Dist. 1994).

[155] People v. Burmeister, 147 Ill. App. 3d 218, 222, 497 N.E.2d 1212, 1214 (2d Dist. 1986).

prosecuted for separate offenses that carry different penalties even though the offenses are based on the same conduct.[156] More importantly, the appellate courts find sexual conduct and sexual penetration to be distinguishable in those cases where they find neither contact with the sex organ or anus of one person by an object, the sex organ, mouth or anus of another, nor any type of requisite intrusion within the definition of "sexual penetration" but find the "touching and fondling" that is included in the term "sexual conduct."[157]

Sexual penetration has been found where a defendant engaged in sexual intercourse,[158] anal sex,[159] fellatio,[160] or cunnilingus,[161] inserted a finger into the victim's vagina,[162] made contact with the victim's vagina with his penis,[163] or made contact with the victim's penis with his penis.[164] However, notwithstanding the broad definition of "sexual penetration," which includes both "contact" and "intrusion," "however slight," some courts have refused to accept the state's claims that other types of conduct amounted to "penetration." For example, one alleged child victim's statement that the defendant had "touched" her private area with his finger and another victim's testimony that the defendant had "touched" her with his finger in her "naughty place" were held insufficient to establish sexual penetration.[165] Finally, notwithstanding another defendant's admission that he may have accidentally touched the minor victim's vagina through her clothing, the redness around the alleged victim's vagina and the pain she experienced while urinating did not alone establish sexual penetration.[166]

---

[156] People v. Server, 148 Ill. App. 3d 888, 901-02, 499 N.E.2d 1019, 1028-29 (4th Dist. 1986), *cert. denied*, 484 U.S. 842 (1987).

[157] *See, e.g.*, People v. DeWeese, 298 Ill. App. 3d 4, 10-12, 698 N.E.2d 554, 558-59 (1st Dist. 1998) (evidence supported trial court acquittal of aggravated criminal sexual assault and conviction of aggravated criminal sexual abuse).

[158] People v. Bowen, 241 Ill. App. 3d 608, 619, 609 N.E.2d 346, 356 (4th Dist.), *cert. denied*, 510 U.S. 946 (1993).

[159] People v. Wheeler, 200 Ill. App. 3d 301, 306, 558 N.E.2d 758, 761 (4th Dist. 1990).

[160] People v. Glass, 239 Ill. App. 3d 916, 928, 606 N.E.2d 655, 664-65 (4th Dist. 1992).

[161] People v. Glass, 239 Ill. App. 3d 916, 928, 606 N.E.2d 655, 664-65 (4th Dist. 1992).

[162] People v. Wittenmeyer, 216 Ill. App. 3d 1042, 1045-46, 576 N.E.2d 528, 530-31 (3d Dist. 1991), *rev'd in part, aff'd in pertinent part*, 151 Ill. 2d 175, 601 N.E.2d 735 (1992).

[163] People v. Back, 239 Ill. App. 3d 44, 78-79, 605 N.E.2d 689, 712 (4th Dist. 1992).

[164] People v. Bofman, 283 Ill. App. 3d 546, 550-52, 670 N.E.2d 796, 800 (1st Dist. 1996).

[165] People v. Kelly, 185 Ill. App. 3d 43, 52, 540 N.E.2d 1125, 1131 (3d Dist. 1989) (although convictions for aggravated criminal sexual abuse upheld).

[166] People v. Bell, 252 Ill. App. 3d 739, 741-43, 625 N.E.2d 188, 190-91 (1st Dist. 1993) (conviction reversed).

§ 8.11. Consent.

As was pointed out earlier,[167] prior to the enactment of the Criminal Sexual Assault Act of 1984, consent in the context of rape did not have defined elements itself but was intertwined with the terms "force," "resistance" and "against her will." If there was no showing of force, or at least a threat of force, and sexual intercourse occurred, consent was implied. Even if there was force, if the victim failed to resist, again the consent of the victim was inferred. Failure to resist might have been excused where futile and life threatening, but resistance was described as the "gist" of the offense charged when defendant admitted to a sexual advance but claimed it was consensual.[168] Finally, because the state was required to establish the complainant's testimony was clear and convincing or that it was corroborated by other evidence, the state might fail to establish the unwanted sexual activity was "against her will." In effect, then, the burden was on the state and, in fact, on the victim at the time of her assailant's advance to communicate that her answer was *no* with an exclamation mark.

With the passage of the 1984 act, the General Assembly made a deliberate effort to change the rules. *Consent* now meant the alleged victim entered into "a freely given agreement" to the act of sexual penetration or sexual conduct.[169] Furthermore, the enactment clarified that "[l]ack of verbal or physical resistance or submission by the victim resulting from the use of force or the threat of force shall not constitute consent."[170] In addition, the manner of dress of the victim would not be interpreted as raising the specter of implied consent.[171] Thus, the centerpiece of a defense consent claim, namely resistance, was removed from the calculus of whether or not a sexual act was consensual. Now, in effect, the burden was placed on the shoulders of the person making the sexual advance to show that the other person *freely agreed* to respond in word or action with an affirmative response amounting to *yes.*

Thus, the mere fact that a criminal sexual assault victim does not cry out for help or try to escape "is not determinative on the issues of whether she was being forced to have sexual intercourse, or whether she consented to having sexual intercourse . . . ."[172] Lack of physical injury to the victim does not establish consent inasmuch as "[p]hysical injury or resistance is not necessary to prove a victim was forced to have sexual intercourse."[173]

---

[167] *See* § 8.03 of this chapter.

[168] People v. Serrielle, 354 Ill. 182, 186, 188 N.E.2d 375, 377 (1933).

[169] 720 ILCS 5/12-17(a) (1999).

[170] 720 ILCS 5/12-17(a) (1999).

[171] 720 ILCS 5/12-17(a) (1999).

[172] People v. Bowen, 241 Ill. App. 3d 608, 619, 609 N.E.2d 346, 356 (4th Dist.) (conviction affirmed), *cert. denied*, 510 U.S. 946 (1993).

[173] People v. Bowen, 241 Ill. App. 3d 608, 619, 609 N.E.2d 346, 356 (4th Dist.), *cert. denied*, 510 U.S. 946 (1993).

§ 8.12. Criminal Sexual Assault.

Section 5/12-13 sets out "criminal sexual assault," the first of the article 5/12 sex offenses. It is defined below:

> (a) The accused commits criminal sexual assault if he or she: (1) commits an act of sexual penetration by the use of force or threat of force; or (2) commits an act of sexual penetration and the accused knew that the victim was unable to understand the nature of the act or was unable to give knowing consent; or (3) commits an act of sexual penetration with a victim who was under 18 years of age when the act was committed and the accused was a family member; or (4) commits an act of sexual penetration with a victim who was at least 13 years of age but under 18 years of age when the act was committed and the accused was 17 years of age or over and held a position of trust, authority or supervision in relation to the victim. (b) Sentence. Criminal sexual assault is a . . . felony.[174]

Thus, criminal sexual assault exists where there is sexual penetration: (1) through force or the threat of force; (2) with the defendant knowing that the victim does not understand the nature of the act or is incapable of consenting; (3) where the victim is under eighteen years of age and the accused is a family member; or (4) where the victim is between the ages of thirteen and seventeen and the accused is at least seventeen years of age *and* the accused held a position of trust, authority or supervision in relation to the victim. Sexual penetration, as defined above, must occur for criminal sexual assault. Sexual conduct, as defined above, is not included in this prohibition.

§ 8.13. — Elements.

In regards to conduct, where a defendant forcibly engaged in sexual intercourse with his victim, he committed this offense in violation of subsection (a)(1).[175] Where a respiratory therapist tricked a patient into consenting to what she thought was a legitimate medical examination involving digital penetration of her rectum and vagina, this constituted criminal sexual assault under subsection (a)(2).[176] Where defendant sexually assaulted his minor daughter, this constituted aggravated criminal sexual assault.[177] And, where a defendant took ad-

---

[174] 720 ILCS 5/12-13 (1999)

[175] People v. Bowen, 241 Ill. App. 3d 608, 619, 609 N.E.2d 346, 356 (4th Dist.), *cert. denied*, 510 U.S. 946 (1993).

[176] People v. Quinlan, 231 Ill. App. 3d 21, 25, 596 N.E.2d 28, 31 (1st Dist. 1993). This would clearly be a violation of subsection (a)(3).

[177] People v. Wheeler, 216 Ill. App. 3d 609, 616-20, 575 N.E.2d 1326, 1332-36 (3d Dist. 1991), *rev'd on other grounds*, 151 Ill. 2d 298, 602 N.E.2d 826 (1992).

vantage of his position of trust and supervision with his victim, he was properly convicted of criminal sexual assault under (a)(4).[178]

Previously, under the Illinois statute, rape was understood to be a general intent crime, requiring either intent, knowledge, or recklessness on the part of an accused,[179] even though the statute was facially silent regarding a mental state.[180] In other words, the courts judicially construed rape as a crime that required per se proof of a mental state. On its face, the crime of criminal sexual assault does not require per se proof of a mental state on the part of the accused. However, in *People v. Burmeister*,[181] the court held that for crimes involving "sexual penetration" a mental state of intent, knowledge, or recklessness would be implied.[182] This interpretation was based on section 5/4-3(b) of the criminal code, which indicates that when a statute is silent as to a mental state, proof of intent, knowledge, *or* recklessness is required.[183] Later, in *People v. Terrell*,[184] the Illinois Supreme Court interpreted the "sexual penetration" language in criminal sexual assault to implicitly require a mental state of intent or knowledge.[185] Because

---

[178] *See* People v. Reynolds, 294 Ill. App. 3d 58, 64-66, 689 N.E.2d 335, 339-41 (1st Dist. 1997) ("position of trust, authority and supervision" not limited to relationships that are in loco parentis and included relationships where minor victim volunteered in defendant's political campaign, received from defendant various forms of financial support, including that used to attend a private school, and was often receiving counseling and mentoring from the defendant; conviction affirmed); People v. Secor, 279 Ill. App. 3d 389, 392-94, 664 N.E.2d 1054, 1056-57 (3d Dist. 1996) (discussing what constitutes a "position of trust and supervision while affirming conviction); People v. Kaminski, 246 Ill. App. 3d 77, 80-82, 615 N.E.2d 808, 810-12 (2d Dist. 1993) (discussing what constitutes a "positions of supervision" while affirming conviction).

[179] People v. Farrokhi, 91 Ill. App. 3d 421, 423, 414 N.E.2d 921, 923 (2d Dist. 1980).

[180] ILL. REV. STAT. ch. 38, para. 11-1 (1983) (repealed) ("A male person of the age of 14 years and upwards who has sexual intercourse with a female, not his wife, by force and against her will, commits rape. Intercourse by force and against her will includes, but is not limited to, any intercourse which occurs in the following situations: (1) where the female is unconscious; or (2) where the female is so mentally deranged or deficient that she cannot give effective consent to intercourse. (b) Sexual intercourse occurs where there is any penetration of the female sex organ by the male sex organ.").

[181] 147 Ill. App. 3d 218, 497 N.E.2d 1212 (2d Dist. 1986).

[182] People v. Burmeister, 147 Ill. App. 3d 218, 223-214, 497 N.E.2d 1212, 1215-16 (2d Dist. 1986).

[183] 720 ILCS 5/4-3(b) (1999).

[184] 132 Ill. 2d 178, 547 N.E.2d 145 (1989), *cert. denied*, 495 U.S. 959 (1990).

[185] People v. Terrell, 132 Ill. 2d 178, 209-105, 547 N.E.2d 145, 158-59 (1989), *cert. denied*, 495 U.S. 959 (1990):

[A] mental state of either intent or knowledge is implicitly required for sexual penetration to occur . . . [B]oth aggravated criminal sexual assault and the lesser offense of aggravated criminal sexual abuse require an intentional or knowing act by the accused.

After making the pronouncements, the court stated:

When a statute fails to prescribe a mental state applicable to an element of an offense . . . a mental state of intent, knowledge or recklessness is implied. [ILL. REV. STAT. ch. 38 paras.

this opinion is slightly nebulous as to whether a "reckless" mental state would satisfy criminal sexual assault, it is unclear whether criminal sexual abuse, which requires a mental state of intent or knowledge, is considered a lesser included offense of criminal sexual assault or rather separate offenses. Some Illinois appellate courts' rulings hold that a "reckless" mental state is irrelevant to criminal sexual assault because it would be impossible to accomplish penetration unknowingly or unintentionally.[186] In these cases, criminal sexual abuse is construed as a lesser included offense of criminal sexual assault.[187] It is significant, however, that the Illinois Supreme Court, in *Terrell*, described criminal sexual abuse as a "lesser offense" of aggravated criminal sexual assault rather than a lesser *included* offense.[188] Theoretically, this leaves the door open to concluding criminal sexual assault could be based on recklessness, such as where a defendant recklessly assumed his mentally deficient sex partner had the capacity to consent, even though criminal sexual abuse can not be based on recklessness.

In *People v. Burt,*[189] the appellate court demonstrated its unwillingness to convict a defendant where he lacked the requisite mental state for criminal sexual assault. In that case, the defendant was functioning at a mental level of a seven or eight-year-old and was determined to be unable to harbor the requisite mental state that he knew (1) that the child complainants did not understand the nature of the sex act and (2) that they were unable to give effective consent for purposes of criminal sexual assault.[190]

The Illinois appellate courts have ruled that proof of specific intent is imperative for a conviction of attempted criminal sexual assault.[191] In order to prove attempted criminal sexual assault, it is incumbent upon the state to prove beyond a reasonable doubt that the defendant intended to forcibly commit an act of penetration or take advantage of the victim.[192] To determine whether the defendant intended to commit this act of penetration, an examination should be made of the utterances and acts of the defendant at the time of the incident.[193] For in-

---

4-3, 4-4, 4-5, 4-6 (1985).] This court will not presume that the legislature intended to limit the definition of "sexual penetration" only to those acts done for the purpose of sexual gratification or arousal of the accused or the victim.

[186] People v. Finley, 178 Ill. App. 3d 301, 305-06, 533 N.E.2d 94, 96 (1st Dist. 1988); People v. Smith, 152 Ill. App. 3d 589, 594, 504 N.E.2d 850, 853 (1st Dist. 1987).

[187] People v. Finley, 178 Ill. App. 3d 301, 306, 533 N.E.2d 94, 96 (1st Dist. 1988); People v. Smith, 152 Ill. App. 3d 589, 594, 504 N.E.2d 850, 853 (1st Dist. 1987).

[188] People v. Terrell, 132 Ill. 2d 178, 209, 547 N.E.2d 145, 158 (1989), *cert. denied*, 495 U.S. 959 (1990).

[189] 142 Ill. App. 3d 833, 492 N.E.2d 233 (2d Dist. 1986).

[190] People v. Burt, 142 Ill. App. 3d 833, 837, 492 N.E.2d 233, 236 (2d Dist. 1986).

[191] *See, e.g.,* People v. Rayfield, 171 Ill. App. 3d 297, 299, 525 N.E.2d 253, 255 (3d Dist. 1988).

[192] People v. Rayfield, 171 Ill. App. 3d 297, 299, 525 N.E.2d 253, 255 (3d Dist. 1988).

[193] People v. Rayfield, 171 Ill. App. 3d 297, 299, 525 N.E.2d 253, 255 (3d Dist. 1988).

stance, in *People v. Rayfield*,[194] the appellate court held that the defendant's acts did not establish defendant's specific intent to commit sexual assault, although the defendant asked the victim if he could see her vagina and threatened to harm the victim if she continued to scream. The evidence established, however, that the defendant never ordered the victim to disrobe, nor did his statements in any way refer to the act of sexual intercourse.[195] The defendant did not make any overt act toward the victim's genitals, nor did he disrobe or expose himself.[196] Additionally, when the victim refused to expose herself to the defendant, the defendant left the premises of the victim. Thus, the appellate court concluded that the utterances and acts of the defendant in this case did not establish the defendant's specific intent to commit criminal sexual assault.[197]

Where the defendant is charged with criminal sexual assault or aggravated criminal sexual assault, the Illinois appellate court ruled that it is not necessary for the trial court to instruct the jury about the mental requirement of intent or knowledge.[198] In *People v. Burton*,[199] the court ruled that a mental state requirement, implied in a statute by reason of section 5/4-3(b), does not have to be reflected in the jury instructions.[200] In the case at hand, the court stated it was "extremely unlikely" that the defendant inserted his penis into the mouths of two girls without intending to do so and without knowing he did.[201] While this "general intent" crime did not require such an instruction, the court indicated that an instruction would be necessary where the offense in question required proof of a "specific mental state".[202]

§ 8.14. Aggravated Criminal Sexual Assault.

Section 5/12-14 defines the offense of "aggravated criminal sexual assault":

(a) The accused commits aggravated criminal sexual assault if he or she commits criminal sexual assault and any of the following aggravating circumstances existed during, or for the purposes of paragraph (7) of this subsection (a) as part of the same course of conduct as, the commission of the offense: (1) the accused displayed, threatened to use, or used a dangerous weapon or any object fashioned or utilized in such a manner as to lead the victim under the circumstances reasonably to believe it to be a dangerous

---

[194] 171 Ill. App. 3d 297, 525 N.E.2d 253 (3d Dist. 1988).

[195] People v. Rayfield, 171 Ill. App. 3d 297, 299, 525 N.E.2d 253, 255 (3d Dist. 1988).

[196] People v. Rayfield, 171 Ill. App. 3d 297, 299, 525 N.E.2d 253, 255 (3d Dist. 1988).

[197] People v. Rayfield, 171 Ill. App. 3d 297, 299, 525 N.E.2d 253, 255 (3d Dist. 1988).

[198] People v. Burton, 201 Ill. App. 3d 116, 122, 558 N.E.2d 1369, 1374 (4th Dist. 1990).

[199] 201 Ill. App. 3d 116, 558 N.E.2d 1369 (4th Dist. 1990).

[200] People v. Burton, 201 Ill. App. 3d 116, 122, 558 N.E.2d 1369, 1374 (4th Dist. 1990).

[201] People v. Burton, 201 Ill. App. 3d 116, 121, 558 N.E.2d 1369, 1373 (4th Dist. 1990).

[202] People v. Burton, 201 Ill. App. 3d 116, 119, 558 N.E.2d 1369, 1372 (4th Dist. 1990).

weapon; or (2) the accused caused bodily harm to the victim; or (3) the accused acted in such a manner as to threaten or endanger the life of the victim or any other person; or (4) the criminal sexual assault was perpetrated during the course of the commission or attempted commission of any other felony by the accused; or (5) the victim was 60 years of age or over when the offense was committed; or (6) the victim was a physically handicapped person; or (7) the accused delivered (by injection, inhalation, ingestion, transfer or possession, or any other means) to the victim without his or her consent, or by threat or deception, and for other than medical purposes, any controlled substance. (b) The accused commits aggravated criminal sexual if the accused was under 17 years of age and (i) commits an act of sexual penetration with a victim who was under 9 years of age when the act was committed; or (ii) commits an act of sexual penetration with a victim who was at least 9 years of age but under 13 years of age when the act was committed and the accused used force or threat of force to commit the act. (c) The accused commits aggravated criminal sexual assault if he or she commits an act of sexual penetration with a victim who was an institutionalized severely or profoundly mentally retarded person at the time the act was committed. (d) Sentence. Aggravated criminal sexual assault is a . . . felony.[203]

A perusal of this statute reveals that the offense of aggravated criminal sexual assault arises in several types of circumstances. First, the offense exists when the defendant commits what would otherwise constitute criminal sexual assault, but there exists one or more aggravating circumstances: (1) use of a dangerous weapon or what reasonably appears to be a dangerous weapon; (2) infliction of bodily harm on the victim; (3) the victim's life or another's life is threatened; (4) the offense occurs during the course of another felony or attempted felony by the accused; (5) the victim is sixty years of age or older; (6) the victim is physically handicapped; or (7) the defendant caused the victim to receive a controlled substance without consent or through threat or deception. Second, the offense has been committed when the defendant, who is sixteen years of age or younger, engages in sexual penetration: (1) with a victim who is eight years of age or younger; or (2) the victim is between nine and twelve years old and the defendant uses force or threat of force. Third, the offense arises when the defendant engages in sexual penetration with a victim who was an institutionalized severely or profoundly mentally retarded person.

---

[203] 720 ILCS 5/12-14 (1999).

§ 8.15. — Elements.

Since the display, use or threatened use of a "dangerous weapon" is an aggravating circumstance which elevates criminal sexual assault to aggravated criminal sexual assault, a defendant's threatened use of a gun during his assault will satisfy aggravated criminal sexual assault.[204] A measuring stick of what constitutes a "dangerous weapon" is found in the "armed violence" prohibition in section 5/33A-1 of the Criminal Code.[205] For example, the term *dangerous weapon* is defined as including handguns, rifles, shotguns, spring guns, stun guns or tasers, knives with blades at least three inches in length, daggers, dirks, switchblades, stilettos, axes, hatchets, bludgeons, blackjacks, metal knuckles, "or any other dangerous weapon of like character."[206] However, a weapon that is not listed may be considered a "dangerous weapon" if it is used in a manner that is dangerous to the well-being of the victim.[207] For example, in one case, the appellate court found that a knife with a partially broken blade of about one and one-half inches that was used to scare the victim constituted a "dangerous weapon" sufficient for the conviction of aggravated criminal sexual assault.[208] Similarly, in another case, a tree branch approximately three feet long and three inches in diameter constituted a "dangerous weapon" for purposes of aggravated criminal sexual assault.[209]

The infliction of bodily harm is another aggravating circumstance. *Bodily harm* is defined as "physical harm" including "sexually transmitted diseases, pregnancy and impotence."[210] The "bodily harm" element of aggravated criminal sexual assault means some sort of physical pain or damage to the body, like lacerations, bruises, or abrasions, whether temporary or permanent.[211] For example, the bruised and swollen face of the victim, resulting from the defendant's blows, was sufficient to satisfy the "bodily harm" requirement for aggravated criminal sexual assault.[212] In a different case, the defendant argued that causing bodily

---

[204] People v. Ramsey, 147 Ill. App. 3d 1084, 1089-90, 496 N.E.2d 1054, 1058-59 (4th Dist. 1986) (referring to subsection (a)(1) and (a)(3)).

[205] 720 ILCS 5/33A-1 (1999); People v. Charles, 217 Ill. App. 3d 509, 512, 577 N.E.2d 534, 536 (2d Dist. 1991) (referring to § 33A-1).

[206] 720 ILCS 5/33A-1 (1999).

[207] People v. Charles, 217 Ill. App. 3d 509, 512, 577 N.E.2d 534, 536 (2d Dist. 1991).

[208] People v. Charles, 217 Ill. App. 3d 509, 512, 577 N.E.2d 534, 536 (2d Dist. 1991).

[209] People v. Guzman, 276 Ill. App. 3d 750, 757, 650 N.E.2d 1268, 1274 (1st Dist. 1995).

[210] 720 ILCS 5/12-12(b) (1999). *See* § 8.07 of this chapter for additional discussion of what constitutes "bodily harm."

[211] People v. Haywood, 118 Ill. 2d 263, 276, 515 N.E.2d 45, 51 (1987) (citing People v. Mays, 91 Ill. 2d 251, 256, 437 N.E.2d 633, 635-36 (1982)); People v. Boyer, 138 Ill. App. 3d 16, 18-19, 485 N.E.2d 460, 462 (3d Dist. 1985) (same).

[212] People v. Rodarte, 190 Ill. App. 3d 992, 999, 547 N.E.2d 1256, 1261 (1st Dist. 1989). *See also* People v. Wallace, 145 Ill. App. 3d 247, 252, 495 N.E.2d 665, 667 (2d Dist. 1986) (bruises on back and arms supported aggravated criminal sexual assault conviction).

harm is an inherent factor of sexual penetration through the use of force and, accordingly, criminal sexual assault and aggravated criminal sexual assault state the same offense, which he claimed was a violation of due process.[213] The appellate court, however, disagreed on the grounds that bodily harm is not necessarily inherent in criminal sexual assault, apparently recognizing that it was quite conceivable that a sexual assault victim might experience a slight sexual penetration without suffering any injury or pain.[214] Consistent therewith, in another case, bruises and abrasions to the victim's vaginal wall were found to be sufficient to constitute bodily harm.[215] In so ruling, the appellate court determined that this type of injury to the vagina was not the normal incident of criminal sexual assault[216] because criminal sexual assault does not require actual penetration of the vagina.[217] Criminal sexual assault, this court observed, can be based on mere contact between the sexual organs of the defendant and the victim's vagina.[218] However, in another case, the appellate court ruled that decreased anal sphincter muscle tone, alone, could not constitute bodily harm since a factor implicit in an offense cannot be used as an element in aggravation for purposes of that offense.[219]

Inasmuch as threatening the life of the sexual assault victim is an aggravating factor, this crime was established where it was proved that the defendant threatened to "blow [the victim's] head off."[220] However, as shown in *People v. Singleton*,[221] the defendant's threatening acts must occur at the time of the commission of the crime or so close to it that it is an inseparable part of the offense.[222] The appellate court in *Singleton* found that because the defendant's acts of domestic violence against the victim and her family, which occurred over several years, and his verbal threats to kill the victim if she did not participate in sexual intercourse with him, did not occur *at the time* of the defendant's sexual penetra-

---

[213] People v. Hengl, 144 Ill. App. 3d 405, 407-08, 494 N.E.2d 937, 939 (3d Dist. 1986).

[214] People v. Hengl, 144 Ill. App. 3d 405, 408, 494 N.E.2d 937, 939 (3d Dist. 1986).

[215] People v. Lauderdale, 228 Ill. App. 3d 830, 834, 593 N.E.2d 757, 759 (1st Dist. 1992).

[216] People v. Lauderdale, 228 Ill. App. 3d 830, 834, 593 N.E.2d 757, 759 (1st Dist. 1992).

[217] See 720 ILCS 5/12-12(f) (1999) ("'Sexual penetration' means *any contact, however slight,* between the sex organ or anus of one person by any object, the sex organ, mouth, or anus of another person, or *any intrusion, however slight,* of any part of the body of one person or of any animal or object into the sex organ or anus of another person, including but not limited to cunnilingus, fellatio, or anal penetration.") (emphasis added).

[218] People v. Lauderdale, 228 Ill. App. 3d 830, 834, 593 N.E.2d 757, 760 (1st Dist. 1992).

[219] People v. Lopez, 222 Ill. App. 3d 872, 879, 584 N.E.2d 462, 467 (1st Dist. 1991) (aggravated criminal sexual assault based on bodily harm vacated).

[220] People v. Ramsey, 147 Ill. App. 3d 1084, 1089-90, 496 N.E.2d 1054, 1058-59 (4th Dist. 1986) (referring to subsection (a)(1) and (a)(3)).

[221] 217 Ill. App. 3d 675, 577 N.E.2d 838 (5th Dist. 1991).

[222] People v. Singleton, 217 Ill. App. 3d 675, 687, 577 N.E.2d 838, 845 (5th Dist. 1991).

tion of the victim, the defendant's conviction for aggravated criminal sexual assault could not stand.[223]

Because sexual assault of a minor is an element of aggravation, the fact that the defendant's criminal sexual assault victim was a child caused an aggravated criminal sexual assault finding.[224] Inasmuch as sexual assault of a physically handicapped person is an element of aggravation, the fact that the victim suffered from spina bifida, making it difficult for her to walk, elevated this offense to aggravated criminal sexual assault.[225]

Commission of this offense during another felony or attempted felony is an aggravation factor. What constitutes a *felony* is clearly defined in the code,[226] as is criminal *attempt*.[227] What amounts to a *controlled substance* for purposes of this prohibition is also defined elsewhere in the code.[228] It should be noted that the crime of aggravated criminal sexual assault with victims of tender years, or who are elderly, does not include a defense for reasonable mistake about the victim's age, even though such a defense is available for criminal sexual abuse and aggravated criminal sexual abuse.[229]

Aggravated criminal sexual assault has been determined to be a general intent crime.[230] The Illinois appellate court rejected the argument that this offense did not require a particular mental state and, thus, was unconstitutional because it was punished more severely than criminal sexual abuse that contained a wrongful mental state.[231] The court invoked the normal judicial presumptions that where no *mens rea* is reflected in the statute, it is presumed that either intent, knowledge or recklessness must be proved.[232]

---

[223] People v. Singleton, 217 Ill. App. 3d 675, 687, 577 N.E.2d 838, 845 (5th Dist. 1991). The evidence sustained defendant's conviction for aggravated criminal sexual assault, however, because defendant was a family member who committed an act of sexual penetration with a victim under the age of 18. *Id.*

[224] People v. Boastick, 140 Ill. App. 3d 78, 488 N.E.2d 326 (4th Dist. 1986) (12 year-old); People v. Server, 148 Ill. App. 3d 888, 499 N.E.2d 1019 (4th Dist. 1986), *cert. denied*, 408 U.S. 482 (1987) (9 year-old); In re A.M.C., 148 Ill. App. 3d 775, 500 N.E.2d 104 (2d Dist. 1986) (5-year-old).

[225] People v. Sutton, 252 Ill. App. 3d 172, 624 N.E.2d 1189 (1st Dist. 1993).

[226] 720 ILCS 5/2-7 (1999). *See* § 1.07 of this treatise for a definition of "felony."

[227] 720 ILCS 5/8-4(a) (1999). *See* ch. 5 of this treatise for a discussion of criminal attempt.

[228] 720 ILCS 570/201–/216 (1999) (lists of controlled substances prohibited by the Illinois Controlled Substances Act). *See* ch. 16 of this treatise for a discussion of controlled substances prohibitions.

[229] *See* 720 ILCS 5/12-17(b) (1999).

[230] People v. Wilder, 219 Ill. App. 3d 437, 439, 579 N.E.2d 948, 950 (1st Dist. 1991).

[231] People v. Ortiz, 155 Ill. App. 3d 786, 791, 508 N.E.2d 490, 494 (2d Dist. 1987) (citing People v. Burmeister, 147 Ill. App. 3d 218, 223-24, 497 N.E.2d 1212, 1215-16 (2d Dist. 1986)).

[232] People v. Ortiz, 155 Ill. App. 3d 786, 791, 508 N.E.2d 490, 494 (2d Dist. 1987); *but see* People v. Terrell, 132 Ill. 2d 178, 209, 547 N.E.2d 145, 158 (1989) (aggravated criminal sexual assault requires proof of intent or knowledge), *cert. denied*, 495 U.S. 959 (1990).

The offense of aggravated criminal sexual assault has withstood various constitutional challenges.[233] The Illinois appellate court has also ruled that it was permissible to convict the defendant of either aggravated criminal sexual assault or aggravated criminal sexual abuse if the defendant's single act could lend itself to either finding.[234]

§ 8.16. Predatory Criminal Sexual Assault of a Child.

In 1996, the Illinois legislature enacted the offense of "predatory criminal sexual assault of a child."[235] First, this offense occurs if an act of sexual penetration is perpetrated by a defendant who is seventeen years of age or over upon a victim who is under thirteen years of age when the act occurs.[236] Second, this offense occurs if an act of sexual penetration, which causes great bodily harm that results in permanent disability or is life threatening, is committed by a defendant who is seventeen years of age or over against a victim who is under thirteen years of age when the act occurs.[237] Commission of this offense is a class X felony.[238]

§ 8.17. Criminal Sexual Abuse.

The next crime appearing in article 5/12 is "criminal sexual abuse." It provides:

(a) The accused commits criminal sexual abuse if he or she: (1) commits an act of sexual conduct by the use of force or threat of force; or (2) commits an act of sexual conduct and the accused knew that the victim was unable to understand the nature of the act or was unable to give knowing consent. (b) The accused commits criminal sexual abuse if the accused was under 17 years of age and commits an act of sexual penetration or sexual conduct with a victim who was at least 9 years of age but under 17 years of age when the act was committed. (c) The accused commits criminal sexual abuse if he or she commits an act of sexual penetration or sexual conduct

---

[233] People v. Server, 148 Ill. App. 3d 888, 901-02, 499 N.E.2d 1019, 1028-29 (4th Dist. 1986) (not unconstitutionally vague), *cert. denied*, 408 U.S. 482 (1987); *see also* People v. Williams, 263 Ill. App. 3d 1098, 1102, 638 N.E.2d 207, 210-11 (1st Dist. 1994) (statute also upheld against constitutional challenges with respect to the equal protection clause, due process clause and proportionate penalties clause); People v. Ortiz, 155 Ill. App. 3d 786, 790-91, 508 N.E.2d 490, 493-94 (2d Dist. 1987) (not violative of due process); People v. Hope, 142 Ill. App. 3d 171, 173-75, 491 N.E.2d 785, 787-88 (3d Dist. 1986) (not violative of due process).

[234] People v. Server, 148 Ill. App. 3d 888, 902, 499 N.E.2d 1019, 1029 (4th Dist. 1986), *cert. denied*, 408 U.S. 482 (1987).

[235] 720 ILCS 5/12-14.1 (1999).

[236] 720 ILCS 5/12-14.1(a)(1) (1999).

[237] 720 ILCS 5/12-14.1(a)(2) (1999).

[238] 720 ILCS 5/12-14.1(b)(1) (1999).

with a victim who was at least 13 years of age but under 17 years of age and the accused was less than 5 years older than the victim. (d) Sentence . . . [is a misdemeanor, unless subsequent offense, whereupon felony].[239]

Much of the behavior circumscribed by this law was new to the criminal code by virtue of the enactment of the Criminal Sexual Assault Act of 1984. Under the prior rape statute only forcible sexual penetration of the female sex organ by the male sex organ was covered.[240] Under the crime of "deviate sexual assault,"[241] now repealed, only "deviate sexual conduct" — meaning "any act of sexual gratification involving the sex organs of one person and the mouth or anus of another"[242] — was prohibited. "Lewd fondling" of *children*, but not adults, was circumscribed in the indecent liberties with a child strictures.[243] Following the Criminal Sexual Act of 1984, conduct that previously constituted rape and deviant sexual assault were merged into the crimes of criminal sexual assault,[244] aggravated criminal sexual assault,[245] and predatory criminal sexual assault of a child,[246] given the expanded definition of "sexual penetration."[247] In addition to these changes, certain forms of sexual misconduct *not* involving "sexual penetration" were deemed criminal offenses by the introduction of prohibitions against "sexual conduct" into the sexual abuse provisions of the statute.[248]

§ 8.18. — Elements.

The crime of criminal sexual abuse arises under subsection (a) where there is: (1) forcible sexual conduct or (2) sexual conduct where the defendant knows the victim is incapable of understanding or unable to give effective consent. *Sexual conduct* arises when there is any purposeful or knowledgeable "touching or fondling, either directly or through clothing, of the sex organs, anus or breast of the victim or the accused, or any part of the body of a child under 13 years of age, for the purposes of sexual gratification or arousal of the victim or the ac-

---

[239] 720 ILCS 5/12-15 (1999).

[240] ILL. REV. STAT. ch. 38, para. 11-11 (1983) (repealed).

[241] ILL. REV. STAT. ch. 38, para. 11-3 (1983) (repealed) ("Any person of the age of 14 years and upward who, by force or threat of force, compels any other person to perform or submit to any act of deviate sexual conduct commits deviate sexual assault.").

[242] ILL. REV. STAT. ch. 38, para. 11-2 (1983) (repealed).

[243] ILL. REV. STAT. ch. 38, para. 11-4 (1983) (repealed); para. 11-4.1 (repealed) (aggravated indecent liberties with a child).

[244] 720 ILCS 5/12-13 (1999).

[245] 720 ILCS 5/12-14 (1999).

[246] 720 ILCS 5/12-14.1 (1999).

[247] 720 ILCS 5/12-12(f) (1999).

[248] 720 ILCS 5/12-12(e) (1999). *See* § 8.09 of this chapter for a discussion of what constitutes "sexual conduct."

cused."[249] This "touching or fondling" of the victim may be done with the hands or any other part of the accused and still satisfy the meaning of "sexual conduct."[250]

Where the victim touches a body part of the defendant other than the defendant's sex organ, anus, or breasts, this is not sexual conduct.[251] Thus, where a child under the age of thirteen placed her hand on the defendant's stomach, allegedly for the purpose of sexually arousing the defendant, without any further contact between the child and the defendant, this was not sexual conduct.[252]

The statute requires that when the victim is thirteen years or older, the touching must be of the sex organ, anus, or breast of the victim.[253] In one case, the appellate court found that the fondling of a fifteen-year-old boy's buttocks was not sexual conduct because his buttocks could not be deemed either "sex organs" or the "anus."[254] In another case, the appellate court held that the labia majora is a sex organ for purposes of criminal sexual abuse.[255]

Subsection (b) covers sexual penetration or sexual conduct between an accused sixteen years old or younger and a victim aged between nine and sixteen. This raises the possibility of consensual sexual activity between minors of the same age or essentially the same age being treated as criminal sexual abuse. In *In re T.W., a Minor*,[256] a sixteen-year-old juvenile was found to be delinquent based on two counts of criminal sexual abuse with a fifteen-year-old victim. The appellate court held that where "two minors engage in a consensual sexual act, the statute may validly be applied to prosecute both minors on the basis that each is the victim of the other."[257] Meanwhile, subsection (c) covers sexual penetration or sexual conduct perpetrated against or upon a victim who is between the ages of thirteen and sixteen by an accused who is less than five years older than the victim.

As seen in the language quoted above, the offense of sexual abuse based on sexual conduct can only occur if the sexual conduct is intentional or with

---

[249] 720 ILCS 5/12-12(e) (1999).

[250] People v. Burmeister, 147 Ill. App. 3d 218, 223, 497 N.E.2d 1212, 1215 (2d Dist. 1986).

[251] People v. Higginbotham, 292 Ill. App. 3d 725, 727-28, 686 N.E.2d 720, 721-22 (2d Dist. 1997).

[252] People v. Higginbotham, 292 Ill. App. 3d 725, 727-28, 686 N.E.2d 720, 721-22 (2d Dist. 1997).

[253] 720 ILCS 5/12-15 (1999).

[254] People v. Nibbio, 180 Ill. App. 3d 513, 517, 536 N.E.2d 113, 116-17 (5th Dist. 1989).

[255] People v. Ipkoh, 242 Ill. App. 3d 365, 382, 609 N.E.2d 1025, 1038 (2d Dist. 1993), *cert. denied*, 511 U.S. 1089 (1994).

[256] 291 Ill. App. 3d 955, 685 N.E.2d 631 (1st Dist. 1997).

[257] In re T.W., a Minor, 291 Ill. App. 3d 955, 960, 685 N.E.2d 631, 635 (1st Dist. 1997) (rejecting claims of unconstitutionality on grounds of vagueness, due process, and equal protection).

knowledge.[258] In addition, the sexual conduct must be performed for "the purpose of sexual gratification or arousal."[259] The inclusion of this latter mens rea element forces the state to prove the existence of a specific intent on the part of the accused whenever it charges the accused under subsection (a).[260] If there is sexual penetration of a minor described in subsection (b) or subsection (c), there is no specific intent requirement in that no particular criminal objective on the part of the accused needs to be proved.

§ 8.19. Aggravated Criminal Sexual Abuse.

The last of the article 5/12 sex crimes is aggravated criminal sexual abuse, which is found in section 5/12-16.

> (a) The accused commits aggravated criminal sexual abuse if he or she commits criminal sexual abuse . . . and any of the following aggravating circumstances existed during, or for the purpose of paragraph (7) of this subsection (a) as part of the same course of conduct, the commission of the offense: (1) the accused displayed, threatened to use, or used a dangerous weapon or any object fashioned or utilized in such a manner as to lead the victim under the circumstances reasonably to believe it to be a dangerous weapon; or (2) the accused caused bodily harm to the victim; or (3) the victim was 60 years of age or over when the offense was committed; or (4) the victim was a physically handicapped person; or (5) the accused acted in such a manner as to threaten or endanger the life or the victim or any other person; or (6) the criminal sexual abuse was perpetrated during the course of the commission or attempted commission of any other felony by the accused; or (7) the accused delivered (by injection, inhalation, ingestion, transfer or possession, or by any other means) to the victim without his or her consent, or by threat or deception, and for other than medical purposes, any controlled substance. (b) The accused commits aggravated criminal sexual abuse if he or she commits an act of sexual conduct with a victim who was under 18 years of age when the act was committed and the accused was a family member. (c) The accused commits aggravated criminal sexual abuse if: (1) the accused was 17 years of age or over and (i) commits an act of sexual conduct with a victim who was under 13 years of age when the act was committed; or (ii) commits an act of sexual conduct with a victim who was at least 13 years of age but under 17 years of age when the act was committed and the accused used force or threat of force to commit the act; or (2) the accused was under 17 years of age and (i) com-

---

[258] 720 ILCS 5/12-12(e) (1999); People v. Finley, 178 Ill. App. 3d 301, 305, 533 N.E.2d 94, 96 (1st Dist. 1988).

[259] People v. Satterfield, 195 Ill. App. 3d 1087, 1097, 552 N.E.2d 1382, 1388 (2d Dist. 1990).

[260] *See* ch. 2 of this treatise for a discussion of "specific intent."

mits an act of sexual conduct with a victim who was under 9 years of age when the act was committed; or (ii) commits an act of sexual conduct with a victim who was at least 9 years of age but under 17 years of age when the act was committed and the accused used force or threat of force to commit the act. (d) The accused commits aggravated criminal sexual abuse if he or she commits an act of sexual penetration or sexual conduct with a victim who was at least 13 years of age but under 17 years of age and the accused was at least 5 years older than the victim. (e) The accused commits aggravated criminal sexual abuse if he or she commits an act of sexual conduct with a victim who was an institutionalized severely or profoundly mentally retarded person at the time the act was committed. (f) The accused commits aggravated criminal sexual abuse if he or she commits an act of sexual conduct with a victim who was at least 13 years of age but under 18 years of age when the act was committed and the accused was 17 years or over and held a position of trust, authority or supervision in relation to the victim. (g) Sentence . . . is a felony.[261]

A reading of the aggravated criminal sexual abuse statute reveals that the offense arises in several different types of circumstances. First, aggravated criminal sexual abuse exists if the defendant commits what would otherwise constitute ordinary criminal sexual abuse but the accused (1) employs a dangerous weapon or what reasonably appears to be a dangerous weapon; (2) causes bodily harm to the victim; (3) threatens or endangers the life of the victim or another person; (4) is committing or attempting to commit any other felony; or (5) transfers to an unwilling victim a controlled substance. Second, the offense has been committed if the defendant engages in sexual conduct with a victim who: (1) is 60 years or older; (2) is physically handicapped; (3) is under eighteen years of age, and the accused is a family member; (4) is under thirteen years of age and accused is more than sixteen years old; (5) is thirteen years through sixteen and the accused who is more than sixteen years old uses force or threat of force; (6) is under nine years of age and the accused is sixteen or younger; (7) is aged nine through sixteen and the accused who is sixteen or younger uses force or threat of force; (8) is an institutionalized severely or profoundly mentally retarded person; (9) is aged thirteen years through seventeen and the accused is over sixteen years of age and held a position of trust, authority, or supervision. Third, the crime has occurred if the accused achieves sexual penetration of or engages in sexual conduct with a victim who is at least five years younger than the accused and is between the ages of thirteen and sixteen.

---

[261] 720 ILCS 5/12-16 (1999).

The offense of aggravated criminal sexual abuse has withstood both due process[262] and equal protection[263] attacks. This crime has been upheld against claims based on vagueness grounds[264] and against claims of unreasonable classification of offenders.[265]

§ 8.20. Permitting Sexual Abuse of a Child.

In 1989, the Illinois legislature enacted a felony offense, called "permitting sexual abuse of a child," that requires the parent, step-parent, legal guardian, or other person having legal custody of a child to prevent anyone from engaging in acts of sexual abuse or sexual assault upon that child.[266] Specifically, it is a violation if a parent or other legal guardian knowingly allows or permits an act of criminal sexual assault or criminal sexual abuse on such child, or the child's involvement in prostitution, and fails to take reasonable steps to prevent its commission or future occurrence.[267]

§ 8.21. Single or Multiple Convictions of Sexual Assault or Abuse.

The Fifth Amendment of the United States Constitution provides that no person shall be put in jeopardy twice for the same offense.[268] This double jeopardy clause protects against multiple punishment for the same offense.[269] In sex offense cases, the number of crimes committed depends on the number of sexual activities the defendant engaged in with his or her victim. In *People v. Segara,*[270] the Illinois Supreme Court held that the defendant's two convictions of aggravated criminal sexual assault did not offend the defendant's constitutional right against double jeopardy because the defendant committed two separate acts of sexual assault in the same episode or transaction when he vaginally raped the victim and then turned her around and performed fellatio, ejaculating in her face.[271] The court reasoned that when several acts have been committed, al-

---

[262] People v. Sephus, 150 Ill. App. 3d 272, 278, 501 N.E.2d 175, 178-79 (4th Dist. 1986); People v. Server, 148 Ill. App. 3d 888, 902, 499 N.E.2d 1019, 1029 (4th Dist. 1986), *cert. denied,* 484 U.S. 842 (1987).

[263] People v. Chitwood, 148 Ill. App. 3d 730, 737, 499 N.E.2d 992, 997 (4th Dist. 1986).

[264] People v. Burmeister, 147 Ill. App. 3d 218, 222, 497 N.E.2d 1212, 1214 (2d Dist. 1986).

[265] People v. Chitwood, 148 Ill. App. 3d 730, 737, 499 N.E.2d 992, 997 (4th Dist. 1986).

[266] 720 ILCS 150/5.1 (1999).

[267] 720 ILCS 150/5.1 (1999).

[268] U.S. CONST. amend. V.

[269] People v. McDade, 219 Ill. App. 3d 317, 329-30, 579 N.E.2d 1173, 1182 (4th Dist. 1991). The double jeopardy clause also protects against a second prosecution of the defendant for the same offense after acquittal or after conviction.

[270] 126 Ill. 2d 70, 533 N.E.2d 802 (1988).

[271] People v. Segara, 126 Ill. 2d 70, 73, 533 N.E.2d 802, 803 (1988).

though the acts are interrelated, multiple convictions may be permitted.[272] However, the court observed that when the same physical act forms the basis for more than one offense, only one conviction may be imposed[273] because of the legal barrier sometimes referred to as the "one-act-one-crime rule" or "same physical act doctrine."[274] For example, in one case, the appellate court held that the defendant committed two acts of aggravated criminal sexual assault when he placed his penis into the mouth of the victim and then engaged in vaginal intercourse with the victim.[275] Another appellate court held that a defendant could be convicted of two counts of criminal sexual abuse for fondling the victim's vagina outside her clothes and then immediately fondling her breasts under her shirt.[276] Parenthetically, where the defendant's single contact with his victim could be viewed as either "sexual conduct" or "sexual penetration," a conviction for aggravated criminal sexual assault *or* aggravated criminal sexual abuse would be appropriate and would not somehow constitute a denial of due process.[277] Thus, when physical acts are distinct and do not involve precisely the same physical act, the defendant can be convicted of more than one offense.[278] For example, where a defendant first inserted his finger into the victim's vagina, then penetrated her vagina with his penis, then had her perform fellatio and, in addition, fondled her breasts, he could be convicted of three counts of criminal sexual assault and one count of criminal sexual abuse.[279]

§ 8.22. Defenses.

The various defenses to sex offenses will be discussed in the sections that follow.

§ 8.23. — Consent as Defense: General Considerations.

According to section 5/12-17 of the Criminal Sexual Assault Act, consent shall be a defense to any offense under section 5/12-13 through 5/12-16 "where

---

[272] People v. Segara, 126 Ill. 2d 70, 76-78, 533 N.E.2d 802, 805-06 (1988).

[273] People v. Segara, 126 Ill. 2d 70, 76-78, 533 N.E.2d 802, 805-06 (1988).

[274] *See* ch. 1 of this treatise for a discussion of the same physical act doctrine.

[275] People v. Riley, 219 Ill. App. 3d 482, 493, 579 N.E.2d 1008, 1017 (1st Dist. 1991).

[276] People v. Grimes, 215 Ill. App. 3d 182, 185, 574 N.E.2d 840, 842 (4th Dist. 1991).

[277] *See* People v. Server, 148 Ill. App. 3d 888, 902, 499 N.E.2d 1019, 1029 (4th Dist. 1986) (judgment entered on only one count), *cert. denied*, 484 U.S. 842 (1987).

[278] People v. Foley, 206 Ill. App. 3d 709, 717, 565 N.E.2d 39, 44-45 (1st Dist. 1990). Moreover, where the defendant commits another offense in pursuit of his sexual assault, he can be convicted of both where each offense involves different acts. People v. Rodriguez, 169 Ill. 2d 183, 190, 661 N.E.2d 305, 308 (1996) (home invasion and aggravated criminal sexual assault convictions affirmed).

[279] People v. Foley, 206 Ill. App. 3d 709, 717, 565 N.E.2d 39, 44-45 (1st Dist. 1990).

force or threat of force is an element of the offense that the victim consented."[280] *Consent*, which was discussed earlier,[281] is defined as "a freely given agreement to the act of sexual penetration or sexual conduct in question" and the [l]ack of verbal or physical resistance or submission by the victim resulting from the use of force or threat of force by the accused shall not constitute consent."[282] Moreover, the consent definition states: "The manner of dress of the victim at the time of offense shall not constitute consent."[283]

Where defendant took sexual advantage of his victim, who was intoxicated to the point of losing consciousness, there was no "freely given agreement" to sexual activity and, consequently, the defendant was properly convicted of criminal sexual assault.[284] Similarly, where defendant engaged in sexual intercourse with a developmentally disabled person, this could not be considered an encounter where there existed a "reasoned or intelligent choice" on the part of the victim and, thus, the defendant's conviction for criminal sexual assault was affirmed.[285]

The statute requires there to be "force or threat of force"[286] but omits the language common to the definition of rape that the force actually overcome the victim's will.[287] In essence, where there is evidence of coercion, there apparently is an assumption that the victim's sexual activity is a product of the coercion and nonconsensual. Even if the victim has the opportunity to resist the advances of the assailant, the failure to resist — either verbally or physically — cannot be interpreted as consent.[288] Where a person submits to sexual activity, there is no legal presumption that he or she did so voluntarily. Thus, the onus is on the per-

---

[280] 720 ILCS 5/12-17(a) (1999).

[281] *See* § 8.11 of this chapter.

[282] 720 ILCS 5/12-17(a) (1999).

[283] 720 ILCS 5/12-17(a) (1999).

[284] People v. Fisher, 281 Ill. App. 3d 395, 404, 667 N.E.2d 142, 148 (2d Dist. 1996).

[285] People v. Whitten, 269 Ill. App. 3d 1037, 1044, 647 N.E.2d 1062, 1067 (5th Dist. 1995) (quoting Black's Law Dictionary 377 (4th Ed. 1968)); *see also* People v. Blake, 287 Ill. App. 3d 487, 492-93, 678 N.E.2d 761, 765 (1st Dist. 1997) (where 30-year-old defendant had sexual intercourse with a 13-year-old educationally mentally handicapped victim, who was enrolled in special education classes and sometimes had difficulty articulating her feelings, "mere evidence that the victim understood the physical nature of sexual relations is not sufficient to establish the victim comprehended the social and personal costs involved").

[286] 720 ILCS 5/12-12(d) (1999).

[287] Under the earlier Illinois rape statute, the sexual intercourse with the victim had to be by force and against her will. ILL. REV. STAT. ch. 38, para. 11-1(a) (1983) (repealed). The scope of the current defense is somewhat narrower than that which previously existed in connection to the defense of rape. Under the earlier statute, in a rape prosecution, as long as the adult female had the use of her mental faculties and physical powers, the state had to present evidence showing that the victim resisted the sexual act in order to establish that it was against her will. People v. Smith, 32 Ill. 2d 88, 92, 203 N.E.2d 879, 881 (1965).

[288] People v. Bowen, 241 Ill. App. 3d 608, 619, 609 N.E.2d 346, 356 (4th Dist.), *cert. denied*, 510 U.S. 946 (1993).

son making the sexual advances to ascertain if the other party is willing to participate.

Merely because a person consents to one form of sexual activity does not mean that he or she has consented to other sexual activity. Thus, where the defendant had consensual vaginal intercourse with his victim, the subsequent anal intercourse over her objection could not be deemed consensual.[289]

In *People v. Haywood*,[290] the Illinois Supreme Court held that where the state offers proof of sexual activity by force, this implicitly demonstrates that the act was nonconsensual.[291] If the defendant does offer rebuttal evidence that raises a question about consent, the state has to prove beyond a reasonable doubt that the forceful sexual activity was without consent.[292] Of course, merely because a victim claims a lack of consent does not mean the sexual activity necessarily was nonconsensual. For example, in *People v. Yeargan*,[293] the appellate court reversed the defendant's conviction due to insufficient evidence to support a criminal sexual assault.[294] The court found that the alleged victim's testimony was improbable, unsatisfactory and contrary to the laws of human nature and experience.[295] Furthermore, no physical evidence supported the alleged victim's claim that she was physically restrained, that her clothing was forcibly removed, or that she was sexually assaulted numerous times.[296] Thus, the court concluded that the evidence was remarkably consistent with the defendants' testimony that the sexual acts were consensual.[297]

Under prior Illinois law, violations of the Criminal Sexual Assault Act required support by clear and convincing testimony of the complainant or substantial corroboration by other evidence.[298] Where the victim's testimony was not clear and convincing, the evidence must have revealed other independent facts or circumstances, such as other eyewitness accounts, a confession or admission by the defendant, the prompt reporting of the incident by the victim, or medical

---

[289] People v. Wheeler, 200 Ill. App. 3d 301, 306, 558 N.E.2d 758, 761 (4th Dist. 1990).

[290] 118 Ill. 2d 263, 515 N.E.2d 45 (1987).

[291] People v. Haywood, 118 Ill. 2d 263, 274, 515 N.E.2d 45, 50 (1987).

[292] People v. Haywood, 118 Ill. 2d 263, 274, 515 N.E.2d 45, 50 (1987).

[293] 229 Ill. App. 3d 219, 593 N.E.2d 699 (1st Dist. 1992).

[294] People v. Yeargan, 229 Ill. App. 3d 219, 229, 593 N.E.2d 699, 705 (1st Dist. 1992).

[295] People v. Yeargan, 229 Ill. App. 3d 219, 231-32, 593 N.E.2d 699, 706-07 (1st Dist. 1992) (including claim that one perpetrator ejaculated 5 times and another 3 or 4 times in the span of 15-20 minutes).

[296] People v. Yeargan, 229 Ill. App. 3d 219, 233, 593 N.E.2d 699, 707 (1st Dist. 1992).

[297] People v. Yeargan, 229 Ill. App. 3d 219, 233, 593 N.E.2d 699, 707 (1st Dist. 1992).

[298] People v. Morgan, 149 Ill. App. 3d 733, 737, 500 N.E.2d 1121, 1125 (4th Dist. 1986) (affirming conviction of criminal sexual assault).

testimony supportive of the victim's allegations.[299] However, in *People v. Schott,*[300] the Illinois Supreme Court recognized that:

> the testimony of no other crime victim has the added requirement that it be clear and convincing to sustain conviction on appeal. Even the uncorroborated testimony of an accomplice may be sufficient to support a conviction. We find it incongruous for an appellate court to view a sex-offense victim's testimony with skepticism by employing this special standard of review, when a fact finder has previously considered the testimony of the victim, together with any other evidence presented at trial, and found the defendant guilty beyond a reasonable doubt.[301]

Unless there exists some evidence of consent, the defendant is not entitled to jury instructions on this defense.[302] Thus, where defendant merely offered evidence that (1) an aggravated sexual assault victim rolled down the window of her car before defendant entered her car and (2) the police found no gun where the defendant was apprehended following defendant's assault, the trial court's refusal to instruct the jury on consent was proper.[303]

§ 8.24. — Consent as Defense: Rape Shield Law.

Defendants who are charged with forcible sex crimes often try to buttress their claims that the victim consented by introducing evidence of the victim's unchaste nature. Illinois followed the traditional rule until 1978, namely, that where the defense to a charge of rape was consent, testimony about the victim's reputation for chastity was admissible.[304] The underlying rationale for this rule was that an unchaste woman is more likely to consent to intercourse than a chaste woman.[305] The immoral character of the complainant could only be shown by proof of her general reputation; specific acts of misconduct were inadmissible.[306]

This traditional rule was highly criticized not only because it was overly prejudicial and humiliating to the victim, but also because it was based on the erroneous premise that a woman who periodically engages in extramarital sexual intercourse is more likely to consent to such intercourse on any given occa-

---

[299] People v. Morgan, 149 Ill. App. 3d 733, 738, 500 N.E.2d 1121, 1125 (4th Dist. 1986).

[300] 145 Ill. 2d 188, 582 N.E.2d 690 (1991).

[301] People v. Schott, 145 Ill. 2d 188, 202, 582 N.E.2d 690, 696 (1991) (citations omitted).

[302] People v. Barnwell, 285 Ill. App. 3d 981, 990-92, 675 N.E.2d 148, 155-56 (1st Dist. 1996).

[303] People v. Barnwell, 285 Ill. App. 3d 981, 990-92, 675 N.E.2d 148, 155-56 (1st Dist. 1996).

[304] People v. Cieslak, 319 Ill. 221, 225, 149 N.E.2d 815, 816 (1925).

[305] People v. Cieslak, 319 Ill. 221, 225, 149 N.E.2d 815, 816 (1925).

[306] People v. Fryman, 4 Ill. 2d 224, 229, 122 N.E.2d 573, 576 (1954).

sion.[307] In response to this type of criticism, the Illinois General Assembly enacted the "rape shield law" which took effect in 1978.[308] The Illinois rape shield law was designed to prohibit the use of evidence regarding the chastity of the victim of rape or deviate sexual assault. Because the victim's history of past sexual conduct was not a defense to rape or sexual deviate assault, evidence of prior unchaste acts by the victim was deemed irrelevant and inadmissible.[309]

With the passage of the Criminal Sexual Assault Act of 1984, the "rape shield" statute, as it continues to be called,[310] was amended to comport with the nomenclature employed in the present forcible sex crimes. The Illinois Code of Criminal Procedure now provides that in a prosecution, for example of criminal sexual assault or criminal sexual abuse, the prior sexual activity or reputation of the victim is not admissible as evidence unless it is evidence of past sexual conduct between the victim and the accused.[311] However, no evidence regarding the victim's prior sexual activity or reputation is admissible unless it is first ruled admissible by the trial judge after an *in camera* hearing in which the defendant has made an offer of proof that he or she has evidence to impeach the victim if the victim denies having had prior sexual activity with the defendant.[312] If the defendant cannot produce such impeaching evidence, the judge cannot allow the defendant to inquire at trial into the prior sexual activity between the alleged victim and the defendant.[313]

In *People v. Sandoval,*[314] the Illinois Supreme Court held that the defendant in a rape trial was not entitled to present evidence of the victim's prior sexual activity with another man notwithstanding that it was in rebuttal to the victim's direct testimony.[315] In *Sandoval,* the victim testified that she had anal sex with the defendant on two prior occasions but never with any other person.[316] Defendant sought to impeach the victim, concerning her testimony that she never had sex with another, by having a third person testify that the victim had anal sex with him.[317] The court held that the language of the statute is clear and unambi-

---

[307] Abraham P. Ordover, *Admissibility of Patterns of Similar Sexual Conduct: The Unlamented Death of Character for Chastity,* 63 CORNELL L. REV. 90, 98 (1977).

[308] Pub. Act 80-1159 (1978). The law, as amended, now appears at 725 ILCS 5/115-7 (1999).

[309] 725 ILCS 5/115-7(a) (1999).

[310] *See, e.g.,* People v. Hill, 289 Ill. App. 3d 859, 860, 683 N.E.2d 188, 189 (5th Dist. 1997).

[311] 725 ILCS 5/115-7(a) (1999).

[312] 725 ILCS 5/115-7(b) (1999).

[313] 725 ILCS 5/115-7(b) (1999).

[314] 135 Ill. 2d 159, 552 N.E.2d 726, *cert. denied,* 498 U.S. 938 (1990).

[315] People v. Sandoval, 135 Ill. 2d 159, 170, 552 N.E.2d 726, 731, *cert. denied,* 498 U.S. 938 (1990).

[316] People v. Sandoval, 135 Ill. 2d 159, 165, 552 N.E.2d 726, 728, *cert. denied,* 498 U.S. 938 (1990).

[317] People v. Sandoval, 135 Ill. 2d 159, 165-66, 552 N.E.2d 726, 728-29, *cert. denied,* 498 U.S. 938 (1990).

guous and leaves no room for the introduction of prior sexual activity with anyone other than the defendant.[318]

In *People v. Cornes,*[319] the Illinois appellate court held that the Illinois rape
shield law does not violate a defendant's right to due process or his or her right
to confront his or her accuser.[320] The court stated that these rights do not extend
to irrelevant matters that have little or no probative value, such as the victim's
chastity.[321] However, the Illinois Supreme Court in *Sandoval* recognized the
possibility that in some situations the defendant's constitutional right may over-
ride the victim's rights under the rape shield law.[322] The *Cornes* court also indicated that the rape shield law does not prevent the defendant from otherwise
attacking the victim's credibility or veracity or from using cross-examination as
an effective tool for impeachment.[323]

The state is likewise barred from raising these matters. In *People v. Kemblowski,*[324] the court ruled the state was barred in an aggravated criminal sexual
assault prosecution from raising the fact that the victim was a lesbian, that her
marriage had not been consummated, and that her husband was a homosexual.[325]

§ 8.25. — Other Defenses.

Prior to 1992, the marital exemption, a defense common to rape,[326] was a defense to criminal sexual abuse and aggravated criminal sexual abuse but not
criminal sexual assault or aggravated criminal sexual assault.[327] However, in
People v. M.D.,[328] the Appellate Court for the Second District found that the
marital exemptions to criminal sexual abuse charges violated equal protection
and due process clauses of the United States and Illinois Constitutions because
they were completely contrary to the general statutory objective of protecting

---

[318] People v. Sandoval, 135 Ill. 2d 159, 170, 552 N.E.2d 726, 731, *cert. denied*, 498 U.S. 938
(1990).

[319] 80 Ill. App. 3d 166, 399 N.E.2d 1346 (5th Dist. 1980).

[320] People v. Cornes, 80 Ill. App. 3d 166, 175, 399 N.E.2d 1346, 1352-53 (5th Dist. 1980).

[321] People v. Cornes, 80 Ill. App. 3d 166, 175, 399 N.E.2d 1346, 1352 (5th Dist. 1980).

[322] People v. Sandoval, 135 Ill. 2d 159, 191-92, 552 N.E.2d 726, 740, *cert. denied*, 498 U.S.
938 (1990). *See also* People v. Hill, 289 Ill. App. 3d 859, 862, 683 N.E.2d 188, 190 (5th Dist.
1997) (rape shield statute's "preclusion of prior sexual conduct is not absolute.").

[323] People v. Cornes, 80 Ill. App. 3d 166, 175, 399 N.E.2d 1346, 1352-53 (5th Dist. 1980).

[324] 201 Ill. App. 3d 824, 559 N.E.2d 247 (1st Dist. 1990).

[325] People v. Kemblowski, 201 Ill. App. 3d 824, 828-29, 559 N.E.2d 247, 250 (1st Dist. 1990).

[326] ILL. REV. STAT. ch. 38, para. 11-1 (1983) (repealed) (stating "not his wife").

[327] People v. M.D., 231 Ill. App. 3d 176, 185-86, 595 N.E.2d 702, 708 (2d Dist. 1992) (citing
ILL. REV. STAT. ch. 38, para. 12-18(c) (1991)).

[328] 231 Ill. App. 3d 176, 595 N.E.2d 702 (2d Dist. 1992).

people from physical and emotional harm resulting from forced sexual exploitation.[329]

In 1994, the Illinois Legislature amended subsection (c) of section 5/12-18, which now eliminates the differential treatment of the prohibitions but reinstates the marital exemption. It reads as follows:

> Prosecution of a spouse of a victim under this subsection for any violation by the victim's spouse of Section 12-13, 12-14, 12-15 or 12-16 of this Code is barred unless the victim reported such offense to a law enforcement agency or the State's Attorney's office within 30 days after the offense was committed, except when the court finds good cause for the delay.[330]

The reporting requirement is apparently designed to prevent assault and abuse charges from becoming factors in later divorce proceedings.[331]

There is another defense that pertains only to the sexual abuse offenses. According to subsection (b) of section 5/12-17: "It shall be a defense under subsection (b) and subsection (c) of Section 12-15 and subsection (d) of Section 12-16 of this Code that the accused reasonably believed the person to be seventeen years of age or over."[332] Thus, where defendant may have believed his attempted sexual abuse victim had attained the age of seventeen, the trial court's failure to instruct on this affirmative defense amounted to reversible error.[333]

§ 8.26. — Credibility of a Child Victim.

Although a defense claim of victim consent will never pose a problem where the sexual assault or sexual abuse victim is a child, since children do not have the legal capacity to consent to such activity, there may be a challenge to the credibility of a child victim's testimony, given the child's relative lack of competence and maturity. In Illinois, prior to 1989, a child was not presumed competent to testify until he or she reached the age of fourteen.[334] When the child was under fourteen, his or her competence was ascertained by means of an in-court examination of his or her intelligence, understanding, and moral sense.[335] In

---

[329] People v. M.D., 231 Ill. App. 3d 176, 192-93, 595 N.E.2d 702, 712-13 (2d Dist. 1992). *See also* People v. Printy, 232 Ill. App. 3d 735, 741-43, 598 N.E.2d 346, 351-53 (2d Dist. 1992) (holding defendant-spouse not denied equal protection because marital exemption not extended to crime of aggravated criminal sexual assault).

[330] 720 ILCS 5/12-18(c) (1999).

[331] Katherine Larson, *Sex Crimes Revisited*, ILL. ISSUES, Feb. 1994, at 11.

[332] 720 ILCS 5/12-17(b) (1999).

[333] People v. Jones, 175 Ill. 2d 126, 134, 676 N.E.2d 646, 650 (1997).

[334] *See* People v. Hall, 1 Ill. App. 3d 949, 959, 275 N.E.2d 196, 202 (1st Dist. 1971) (discussing rule).

[335] People v. Hall, 1 Ill. App. 3d 949, 959, 275 N.E.2d 196, 202 (1st Dist. 1971).

ILLINOIS CRIMINAL LAW

1998, the presumption that competency hearings be required for witnesses under fourteen years of age was abolished.[336] Today, all persons "irrespective of age" are presumed competent to testify.[337] Where a competency inquiry must occur because the presumption has been effectively challenged, the failure of a child to offer perfect answers during the competency determination does not mean that the child is incompetent to testify.[338] When considering the credibility of a child witness, the court must consider the age of the child, his or her degree of competence, the time lapse between the alleged offense and the trial, the child's lack of sexual experience, and his or her confusion during the alleged acts.[339]

By reason of certain legislation, corroborative hearsay testimony is permitted in certain cases during the prosecution of a sexual act perpetrated on a child under thirteen.[340] This law states in part that in a prosecution of a defendant for a sexual act perpetrated upon a child under the age of thirteen, or against an institutionalized, severely or profoundly mentally retarded individual,

> the following evidence shall be admitted as an exception to the hearsay rule: (1) testimony by the victim that he or she complained of such act to another; and (2) testimony of an out of court statement made by the victim describing any complaint of such act or matter or detail pertaining to any

---

[336] 725 ILCS 5/115-14 (1999); People v. Westpfahl, 295 Ill. App. 3d 327, 330-31, 692 N.E.2d 831, 834 (3d Dist. 1998) (13-year-old minor competent to testify; criminal sexual abuse conviction affirmed).

[337] 725 ILCS 5/115-14 (1999) ("(a) Every person, irrespective of age, is qualified to be a witness and no person is disqualified to testify to any matter, except as provided in section (b). (b) A person is disqualified to be a witness if he or she is: (1) Incapable of expressing himself or herself concerning the matter so as to be understood, either directly or through interpretation by one who can understand him or her; or (2) Incapable of understanding the duty of a witness to tell the truth."). A competency hearing is never to be initiated sua sponte by the trial judge, but rather only by motion of a party objecting to the witness' competency and "shall" be conducted outside the presence of the jury. People v. Westpfahl, 295 Ill. App. 3d 327, 330-31, 692 N.E.2d 831, 834 (3d Dist. 1998) (quoting 5/115-14). Also, the burden to show lack of competency is on the moving party. 725 ILCS 5/115-14 (1999). Since the trial judge has the opportunity to evaluate in person the demeanor, appearance and conduct of the witness at trial, a competency determination will be overturned only when it appears that the court abused its discretion. People v. Dempsey, 242 Ill. App. 3d 568, 582-83, 610 N.E.2d 208, 217-18 (5th Dist. 1993).

[338] People v. Dempsey, 242 Ill. App. 3d 568, 582-83, 610 N.E.2d 208, 217-18 (5th Dist. 1993) (where 9-year-old sexual abuse victim testified that he did not know the difference between the truth and a lie but did testify that if he told a lie he would "go to the devil" and might be spanked by his mother, victim was competent to testify).

[339] People v. Stephenson, 12 Ill. App. 3d 201, 204, 298 N.E.2d 218, 220 (1st Dist. 1973).

[340] 725 ILCS 5/115-10 (1999). This statute has been interpreted as permitting the admission of a videotape of a corroborative out-of-court statement of the complaining witness in a child sex abuse case. People v. Bowen, 183 Ill. 2d 103, 110-20, 699 N.E.2d 577, 582-86 (1998) (not violative of right to confrontation because statute requires the child, unless he or she is unavailable, to testify and be subject to cross examination).

act which is an element of an offense which is the subject of a prosecution for a sexual or physical act against that victim.[341]

Illinois courts allow into evidence in prosecutions of sex crimes against children evidence supported by the concept of child sexual abuse accommodation syndrome.[342] In an effort to explain why reports of sexual assault or abuse made by child victims may not have been promptly reported, been concrete and, possibly, recanted, the jury is enlightened about the five characteristics of the syndrome: (1) defendant's insistence on secrecy, (2) helplessness of the victim, (3) entrapment and accommodation of the victim, (4) delayed and unconvincing disclosure, and (5) retraction by the victim to protect the defendant.[343]

Prior Illinois law permitted testimony of a child victim in a criminal assault or abuse prosecution to be taken outside a courtroom and shown in the courtroom by means of closed circuit television.[344] In *People v. Fitzpatrick*,[345] the Illinois Supreme Court held this enactment, known as the Child Shield Act, unconstitutional on grounds that it violated the Illinois constitutional right to confront one's accusers.[346] However, the earlier Illinois constitutional provision that required "face-to-face" confrontation[347] was amended to remove the "face-to-face" requirement.[348] The Child Shield Act was then reenacted to allow testimony of a child victim to be shown by closed circuit television.[349] The current act has withstood constitutional challenge based on right to confrontation grounds.[350]

---

[341] 725 ILCS 5/115-10 (1999). People v. Brink, 294 Ill. App. 3d 295, 300-02, 690 N.E.2d 136, 140-41 (4th Dist. 1998) (aggravated criminal assault conviction upheld while relying on 5/115-10); People v. Shanklin, 250 Ill. App. 3d 689, 696-97, 620 N.E.2d 557, 562-63 (5th Dist. 1993) (same).

[342] People v. Leggans, 253 Ill. App. 3d 724, 733, 625 N.E.2d 1133, 1141 (5th Dist. 1993) (aggravated criminal sexual assault conviction affirmed while relying on 725 ILCS 5/115-7.2); People v. Pollard, 225 Ill. App. 3d 970, 975-79, 589 N.E.2d 175, 179-81 (3d Dist. 1992) (same); People v. Wasson, 211 Ill. App. 3d 264, 270-72, 569 N.E.2d 1321, 1325-27 (4th Dist. 1991) (same).

[343] People v. Dempsey, 242 Ill. App. 3d 568, 577-80, 610 N.E.2d 208, 214-15 (5th Dist. 1993) (aggravated criminal sexual assault conviction affirmed).

[344] 725 ILCS 5/106B-1 (1993) (repealed).

[345] 158 Ill. 2d 360, 633 N.E.2d 685 (1994).

[346] People v. Fitzpatrick, 158 Ill. 2d 360, 363-68, 633 N.E.2d 685, 687-89 (1994).

[347] See ILL. CONST. 1970, art. I, § 8 ("In criminal prosecutions, the accused shall have the right to . . . meet the witness face to face.").

[348] ILL. CONST. 1970, art. I, § 8, as amended, ("In criminal prosecutions, the accused shall have the right . . . to be confronted with the witness against him or her . . . .").

[349] 725 ILCS 5/106B-5 (1999).

[350] People v. Van Brocklin, 293 Ill. App. 3d 156, 166-69, 687 N.E.2d 1119, 1125-27 (2d Dist. 1997). See also Maryland v. Craig, 497 U.S. 836 (1990) (allowing child sex offense victim to testify via closed circuit television does not violate Sixth Amendment right to confrontation where necessary to protect children from trauma).

§ 8.27. — Rape Trauma Syndrome.

The concept of "rape trauma syndrome"[351] was introduced into the jurisprudence of Illinois criminal law in 1986.[352] This phenomenon is a form of post-traumatic stress disorder that may occur as a consequence of a sexual assault.[353] It is a psychological "hangover" type condition often suffered by rape victims that is a result of the fright and stress associated with the rape incident.[354] The testimony of a person who has expertise in rape trauma syndrome may be useful to the state in explaining to a jury why behavior of sexual assault victims may differ from popular perceptions of how persons respond to such crimes and may tend to explain why, for example, inconsistencies existed between the victim's trial testimony and earlier out-of-court statements of the victim.[355] Also, rape trauma syndrome testimony could, for instance, account for why a rape victim did not promptly report a sexual assault experience — due to fear, embarrassment, guilt, or the like — in a case where defense counsel is likely to attack the victim's credibility for failing to bring the matter to the authorities in a timely fashion.[356]

In *People v. Server,*[357] a defendant was convicted of the offense of aggravated criminal sexual assault on his nine-year-old stepdaughter. At trial, the victim testified about the defendant's various sexual assaults on her, which had not been immediately reported to the police. An array of evidence revealed that the defendant and the victim's mother had been separated and that the assaults had occurred during various visitations scheduled between the separated parents. In addition, the victim's mother testified about (1) the drastic change in the victim's attitude and behavior, (2) how the victim became a greater discipline prob-

---

[351] David McCord, *The Admissibility of Expert Testimony Regarding Trauma Syndrome in Rape Prosecutions*, 26 B.C.L. REV. 1143 (1985) (supporting admissibility of evidence based on behavioral science research and evidentiary principles and discusses judicial inconsistency in admitting such evidence); Pamela A. Wilk, Comment, *Expert Testimony on Rape Trauma Syndrome: Admissibility and Effective Use in Criminal Rape Prosecution*, 33 AM. U. L. REV. 417 (1984) (discussing symptomatology associated with rape trauma syndrome and evidentiary issues regarding expert testimony and promotes admissibility of such testimony in forcible rape situations where consent is raised as a defense).

[352] *See* People v. Server, 148 Ill. App. 3d 888, 895-99, 499 N.E.2d 1019, 1024-27 (4th Dist. 1986), *cert. denied*, 408 U.S. 482 (1987).

[353] People v. Server, 148 Ill. App. 3d 888, 897, 499 N.E.2d 1019, 1026 (4th Dist. 1986*), cert. denied*, 408 U.S. 482 (1987).

[354] People v. Server, 148 Ill. App. 3d 888, 897, 499 N.E.2d 1019, 1026 (4th Dist. 1986*), cert. denied*, 408 U.S. 482 (1987).

[355] People v. Server, 148 Ill. App. 3d 888, 898, 499 N.E.2d 1019, 1026 (4th Dist. 1986), *cert. denied*, 408 U.S. 482 (1987).

[356] *See* David McCord, *The Admissibility of Expert Testimony Regarding Rape Trauma Syndrome in Rape Prosecutions*, 26 B.C.L. REV. 1143, 1153-55 (1985).

[357] 148 Ill. App. 3d 888, 499 N.E.2d 1019 (4th Dist. 1986), *cert. denied*, 408 U.S. 482 (1987).

lem, (3) how the victim's relationship with her friends had deteriorated, and (4) how the victim started calling defendant "Richard" instead of "Daddy" during this period. The victim's mother further testified about how her daughter finally reported the assaults to her after they had occurred. Some of the testimony of the mother of the victim was corroborated in part by the observations and testimony of the victim's fourth-grade teacher. Finally, a clinical psychologist, who had studied rape trauma syndrome, testified over defense objection about this concept generally and that the victim's behavior was "not inconsistent" with the reactions of a child victim who had experienced sexual assault.[358]

The appellate court ruled, in a case of first impression in Illinois, that the expert testimony regarding rape trauma syndrome was properly admitted and not an abuse of the trial court's discretion.[359] The court reasoned that expert testimony is properly admitted where the subject matter is beyond the common knowledge and experience of persons and where it will aid the trier of fact.[360]

Later, the Illinois legislature approved of this type of expert testimony. In legislation that took effect in 1988, the following appears:

> In a prosecution for an illegal sexual act perpetrated upon a victim, including but not limited to prosecutions for violations of [criminal sexual assault, aggravated criminal sexual assault, criminal sexual abuse or aggravated criminal sexual abuse], or ritualized abuse of a child . . ., testimony by an expert, qualified by the court relating to any recognized and accepted form of post-traumatic stress syndrome shall be admissible as evidence.[361]

Relying on this statute and caselaw precedent, courts continue to admit evidence of rape trauma syndrome,[362] which the Illinois Supreme Court has described as a "subcategory of post-traumatic stress syndrome that is common to victims of sexual assaults."[363] While Illinois law bars the prior defense practice of intimidating sexual offense victims through ordering psychological examina-

---

[358] People v. Server, 148 Ill. App. 3d 888, 893-94, 499 N.E.2d 1019, 1023-25 (4th Dist. 1986), *cert. denied*, 408 U.S. 482 (1987).

[359] People v. Server 148 Ill. App. 3d 888, 895-98, 499 N.E.2d 1019, 1024-26 (4th Dist. 1986), *cert. denied*, 408 U.S. 482 (1987).

[360] People v. Server 148 Ill. App. 3d 888, 897, 499 N.E.2d 1019, 1025-26 (4th Dist. 1986*), cert. denied*, 408 U.S. 482 (1987).

[361] 725 ILCS 5/115-7.2 (1999).

[362] People v. Harp, 197 Ill. App. 3d 838, 844-45, 550 N.E.2d 1163, 1167-68 (4th Dist. 1990) (criminal sexual assault conviction affirmed while relying on evidence of rape trauma syndrome); People v. Douglas, 183 Ill. App. 3d 241, 255-57, 538 N.E.2d 1335, 1344-45 (4th Dist. 1989) (aggravated criminal sexual assault conviction affirmed while relying on evidence of rape trauma syndrome).

[363] People v. Wheeler, 151 Ill. 2d 298, 307-08, 602 N.E.2d 826, 831 (1992).

tions focusing on their competency and credibility as witnesses,[364] the Illinois Supreme Court has ruled it is a violation of a defendant's right to due process to allow the state to present testimony of an examining expert that the defendant suffered from rape trauma syndrome while denying the defendant's request to have his own expert examine the victim for evidence of such post-traumatic stress disorder.[365] It is important to note that the court only ruled that the defendant has a right to a second opinion as to whether the victim suffered from rape trauma syndrome when the state offers such evidence and its holding in no way undercut the bar against ordering a psychological examination for the purpose of assessing the victim's *competency and credibility* as a witness.[366] The defense expert examination of the witness shall be *"strictly limited to whether the victim has symptoms consistent with"* the syndrome.[367] In addition, if a victim chooses not to consent to such a defense expert evaluation, the state is precluded from offering evidence of the syndrome.[368]

§ 8.28. Indecent Solicitation of a Child.

The following crimes are the remaining article 5/11 offenses that were not abolished by the legislative changes effectuated by the Criminal Sexual Assault Act of 1984. The first of these is "indecent solicitation of a child," which reads: "A person of the age of 17 years and upwards who solicits a child under the age of 13 to do any act, or solicits a person to arrange an act with a child under the age of 13, which if done would be aggravated criminal sexual assault, predatory criminal sexual assault of a child, criminal sexual assault, aggravated criminal sexual abuse or criminal sexual abuse, commits indecent solicitation of a child."[369] It is not a defense that the defendant reasonably believed the child was of the age of thirteen or more.[370] The offense is a misdemeanor if the solicitation would involve criminal sexual abuse;[371] otherwise it is a felony.[372]

---

[364] 725 ILCS 5/115-7.1 (1999) ("Except where explicitly authorized [by law], no court may require or order a witness who is the victim of an alleged sex offense to submit to or undergo either a psychiatric or psychological examination.").

[365] People v. Wheeler, 151 Ill. 2d 298, 305-11, 602 N.E.2d 826, 830-33 (1992) (reversible error).

[366] People v. Wheeler, 151 Ill. 2d 298, 305-11, 602 N.E.2d 826, 830-33 (1992) (respecting integrity of 725 ILCS 5/115-7.1 prohibition).

[367] People v. Wheeler, 151 Ill. 2d 298, 311-12, 602 N.E.2d 826, 833 (1992) (emphasis in original).

[368] People v. Wheeler, 151 Ill. 2d 298, 311-12, 602 N.E.2d 826, 833 (1992).

[369] 720 ILCS 5/11-6(a) (1999).

[370] 720 ILCS 5/11-6(b) (1999).

[371] 720 ILCS 5/11-6(c)(1) (1999).

[372] 720 ILCS 5/11-6(c)(2) (1999).

The language of the statute clearly focuses on the nature of the act itself and not on the roles of the perpetrator and victim.[373] The statute setting forth the offense of "indecent solicitation of a child" was enacted (1) to prevent any adult-child sex crimes and (2) to stop children from being enticed into or encouraged to perform illicit sexual acts.[374] Therefore, it is inconsequential whether the child is solicited to assume the role of perpetrator or the victim.[375]

§ 8.29. Indecent Solicitation of an Adult.

In 1993, the legislature created the offense of "indecent solicitation of an adult."[376] Section 5/11-6.5 of the Criminal Code defines indecent solicitation of an adult as follows:

> A person commits indecent solicitation of an adult if the person: (1) Arranges for a person 17 years of age or over to commit an act of sexual penetration as defined in Section [5/]12-12 with a person: (i) Under the age of 13 years; or (ii) Thirteen years of age or over but under the age of 17 years; or (2) Arranges for a person 17 years of age or over to commit an act of sexual conduct as defined in Section [5/]12-12 with a person: (i) Under the age of 13 years; or (ii) Thirteen years of age or older but under the age or 17 years.[377]

This crime is a felony unless the sexual conduct between a seventeen-year-old or older perpetrator and a thirteen- to sixteen-year-old victim is contemplated, in which case it is a misdemeanor.[378]

§ 8.30. Adultery.

An offense that had its origins in the common law is "adultery."[379] If the adulterous activity is "open and notorious," it is prohibited in Illinois. Section 5/11-7 provides in relevant part:

> Any person who has sexual intercourse with another not his spouse commits adultery, if the behavior is open and notorious, and (1) The person is married and the other person involved in such intercourse is not his spouse;

---

[373] People v. Nash, 183 Ill. App. 3d 924, 929, 539 N.E.2d 822, 824-25 (4th Dist. 1989) (rejecting defendant's claim that term "solicitation" contained in statute meant solicitation of another to "commit an offense" and not solicitation of person as a victim).

[374] People v. Nash, 183 Ill. App. 3d 924, 929, 539 N.E.2d 822, 824-25 (4th Dist. 1989).

[375] People v. Nash, 183 Ill. App. 3d 924, 929, 539 N.E.2d 822, 825 (4th Dist. 1989).

[376] 720 ILCS 5/11-6.5 (1999).

[377] 720 ILCS 5/11-6.5(a) (1999).

[378] 720 ILCS 5/11-6.5(b) (1999).

[379] ROLLIN M. PERKINS & RONALD N. BOYCE, CRIMINAL LAW 454-55 (3d ed. 1982).

or (2) The person is not married and knows that the other person involved in such intercourse is married.[380]

This misdemeanor[381] contains an exemption[382] for any person who is required to reveal his or her adulterous cohabitation with another in order to comply with the requirements of the Public Aid Code.[383] This exemption is presumably designed to avoid Fifth Amendment self-incrimination problems.[384]

The scope of this legislation may be gleaned from the thoughts of the committee that drafted this legislation. Their comments are also relevant to the crime of "fornication," which will be reviewed below. First, "only the open and notorious participation in adultery and fornication" is criminal.[385] This position is consistent with the "general policy of Article [5/]11 as a whole to avoid projecting criminal penalties into matters of principally private moral concern."[386] Second, sexual intercourse does not require direct proof but can be inferred from surrounding facts, including evidence of regularly occupying the same bed.[387]

"Open and notorious" should not be confused with sexual activity in "a public place," which amounts to the crime of "public indecency."[388] Adultery is "open and notorious" if it is scandalous and an affront to public decency and the institution of marriage.[389] The notoriety must extend not only to the sexual intercourse but also to the fact of the absence of the marital relationship between the parties engaging in such behavior.[390] Thus, if a man and woman lived together under the pretense of marriage, this would not be criminal.[391]

---

[380] 720 ILCS 5/11-7(a) (1999).

[381] 720 ILCS 5/11-7(b) (1999).

[382] 720 ILCS 5/11-7(a) (1999).

[383] 305 ILCS 5/4-1.7 (1999).

[384] *Cf.* Grosso v. United States, 390 U.S. 62 (1968); Marchetti v. United States, 390 U.S. 39 (1968). In these cases, it was held that prohibitions against failure to register and pay federal tax on gambling activities clashed with the Fifth Amendment because there was reasonable fear that such information would be used in state gambling prosecutions.

[385] ILL. ANN. STAT. ch. 38, para. 11-7 (Smith-Hurd 1979), 1961 Committee Comments, at 294-95 (revised 1972).

[386] ILL. ANN. STAT. ch. 38, para. 11-7 (Smith-Hurd 1979), 1961 Committee Comments, at 294-95 (revised 1972).

[387] ILL. ANN. STAT. ch. 38, para. 11-7 (Smith-Hurd 1979), 1961 Committee Comments, at 294-95 (revised 1972).

[388] ILL. ANN. STAT. ch. 38, para. 11-7 (Smith-Hurd 1979), 1961 Committee Comments, at 294-95 (revised 1972). *See* 720 ILCS 5/11-9 (1999) (public indecency defined).

[389] ILL. ANN. STAT. ch. 38, para. 11-7 (Smith-Hurd 1979), 1961 Committee Comments, at 295 (revised 1972) (citing and discussing with approval People v. Potter, 319 ill. App. 409, 49 N.E.2d 307 (4th Dist. 1943)).

[390] ILL. ANN. STAT. ch. 38, para. 11-7 (Smith-Hurd 1979), 1961 Committee Comments, at 295 (revised 1972).

[391] ILL. ANN. STAT. ch. 38, para. 11-7 (Smith-Hurd 1979), 1961 Committee Comments, at 295 (revised 1972) (citing with approval People v. Salmon, 149 Cal. 303, 83 P. 42 (1905)).

The difference between adultery and fornication is that, with the former, there must be a "knowing interference with an existing marital bond."[392] Thus, vicarious guilt for adultery is avoided where the single person is unaware of his or her paramour's contrary marital obligation.[393] Along the same lines, where a person makes an honest mistake about his or her own marital status, he or she cannot be convicted of adultery.[394] "Thus, if A thought he was divorced from B and cohabitated notoriously with C, an unmarried person, A would be guilty only of fornication, even though his divorce were [sic] in fact void."[395]

Finally, it was the intent of the legislature not to recognize a defense of *subsequent* marriage: "The offense occurs when the marriage institution is flagrantly and publicly abused. Subsequent marriage by the offending parties does not undo that abuse, nor does compelling marriage under threat of criminal penalties do much to enhance public esteem for that institution."[396]

The present adultery statute was the subject of a criminal prosecution in the case of *People v. Cessna.*[397] In that case, the defendant, who had left his wife in Indiana, lived at his mother's house in Illinois, wherein he had sexual intercourse with a young woman on several occasions. The appellate court reversed the defendant's conviction for adultery and noted that the Illinois adultery statute does not proscribe adulterous conduct "which is essentially private or discreet."[398] The court stated that although the evidence revealed that the woman's family was seriously concerned about the woman's relationship with the defendant, the evidence did not show that the defendant's conduct had even captured public attention, much less engendered public scandal.[399] Since the record was barren of evidence of publicity that could have tended to debase and demoralize the defendant's community, it failed to satisfy the "open and notorious" requirement.[400] Except for periodic references to the adultery statute in several

---

[392] ILL. ANN. STAT. ch. 38, para. 11-7 (Smith-Hurd 1979), 1961 Committee Comments, at 295 (revised 1972).

[393] ILL. ANN. STAT. ch. 38, para. 11-7 (Smith-Hurd 1979), 1961 Committee Comments, at 295 (revised 1972).

[394] ILL. ANN. STAT. ch. 38, para. 11-7 (Smith-Hurd 1979), 1961 Committee Comments, at 295 (revised 1972).

[395] ILL. ANN. STAT. ch. 38, para. 11-7 (Smith-Hurd 1979), 1961 Committee Comments, at 295 (revised 1972).

[396] ILL. ANN. STAT. ch. 38, para. 11-7 (Smith-Hurd 1979), 1961 Committee Comments, at 295 (revised 1972).

[397] 42 Ill. App. 3d 746, 356 N.E.2d 621 (5th Dist. 1976).

[398] People v. Cessna, 42 Ill. App. 3d 746, 749, 356 N.E.2d 621, 623 (5th Dist. 1976).

[399] People v. Cessna, 42 Ill. App. 3d 746, 750, 356 N.E.2d 621, 624 (5th Dist. 1976).

[400] People v. Cessna, 42 Ill. App. 3d 746, 750, 356 N.E.2d 621, 624 (5th Dist. 1976).

civil proceeding contexts,[401] there are no reported opinions in which the present adultery statute has been successfully enforced.

§ 8.31. Fornication.

The next article 5/11 sex offense is "fornication." It reads in part: "Any person who has sexual intercourse with another not his spouse commits fornication if the behavior is open and notorious."[402] This misdemeanor[403] statute is virtually identical to adultery except for one major difference: with adultery, one or both parties must be married; with fornication, neither needs to be married. Like adultery, fornication (1) arises where there is sexual intercourse; (2) is limited to such behavior that is "open and notorious"; and (3) provides an exemption to those who reveal such activity in order to comply with public aid regulations.

The crime of fornication, like adultery, is rarely prosecuted. In the only reported opinion, *People v. Garcia,*[404] the defendant was seen with a man in her home, who may have stayed overnight, and was later seen with him in his car with her skirt raised. The court found that the state failed to establish the requisite "open and notorious" activity required by the statute and, accordingly, her conviction was reversed.[405]

§ 8.32. Public Indecency.

The crime of "public indecency" was designed by the legislature to complement the crimes of adultery and fornication. Unlike the article 5/12 sex prohibitions, which involve actual assault or a victim's incapacity to consent, the offenses of adultery, fornication and public indecency are public nuisances that are punished because of the "manner and locale" of the activity in question.[406]

---

[401] *See, e.g.,* In re R.E., 290 F. Supp. 281 (N.D. Ill. 1968) (holding previous adulterous relationship between parties now married was not basis for precluding parties from obtaining citizenship on grounds that they were not persons of good moral character); Hewitt v. Hewitt, 77 Ill. 2d 49, 66, 394 N.E.2d 1204, 1211 (1979) (holding woman's claim for recovery of equal share of profits and property, accumulated by party with whom she lived in unmarried family-like relationship to which three children had been born, was unenforceable because of public policy against knowing unmarried cohabitation).

[402] 720 ILCS 5/11-8(a) (1999).

[403] 720 ILCS 5/11-8(b) (1999).

[404] 37 Ill. App. 2d 90, 185 N.E.2d 1 (4th Dist. 1962).

[405] People v. Garcia, 37 Ill. App. 2d 90, 94, 185 N.E.2d 1, 3 (4th Dist. 1962). *See also* Mister v. A.R.K. Partnership, 197 Ill. App. 3d 105, 114-15, 553 N.E.2d 1152, 1158 (2d Dist. 1990) (holding in civil rights case that an unmarried couple seeking to rent an apartment was sufficient to satisfy the open and notorious requirement of fornication).

[406] ILL. ANN. STAT. ch. 38, para. 11-9 (Smith-Hurd 1979), 1961 Committee Comments, at 301 (revised 1972).

Adultery and fornication represent a public affront to the marriage institution whereas public indecency reflects an affront to the public in general.[407]

The public indecency statute provides:

> (a) Any person of the age of 17 years and upwards who performs any of the following acts in a public place commits a public indecency: (1) An act of sexual penetration or sexual conduct as defined in Section [5/]12-12 of this Code; or (2) A lewd exposure of the body done with intent to arouse or to satisfy the sexual desire of the person. Breast-feeding of infants is not an act of public indecency. (b) "Public place" for purposes of this Section means any place where the conduct may reasonably be expected to be viewed by others. (c) Sentence. Public indecency is a . . . misdemeanor.[408]

This statute applies to any person seventeen years of age or older. Thus, a thirteen year-old who allegedly exposed his penis in public could not be convicted of public indecency.[409] The marital status of the parties is of no consequence.[410]

The type of sexual behavior covered by the statute is not entirely clear. The revision committee's comments state that this offense is designed for the "protection of the public from shocking and embarrassing displays of sexual activities."[411] The committee explicitly stated that although this statute clearly covers sexual intercourse, deviate sexual conduct (contact between the sex organs of one person and the mouth or anus of another), and lewd exposure of the body,[412] it "does not extend to preliminary acts of 'petting' and the like."[413] However, the 1984 amendment to the public indecency statute[414] included *sexual conduct,* which is defined to encompass any "touching or fondling . . . through clothing . . . of the sex organs, anus or breast . . ." of another.[415]

The following activities have been interpreted as *indecent* for purposes of this offense: a man exposing his penis to a woman;[416] a woman disrobing in the

---

[407] ILL. ANN. STAT. ch. 38, para. 11-9 (Smith-Hurd 1979), 1961 Committee Comments, at 301 (revised 1972).

[408] 720 ILCS 5/11-9 (1999).

[409] In re Tucker, 45 Ill. App. 3d 728, 732-33, 359 N.E.2d 1067, 1070 (3d Dist. 1976).

[410] ILL. ANN. STAT. ch. 38, para. 11-9 (Smith-Hurd 1979), 1961 Committee Comments, at 302 (revised 1972).

[411] ILL. ANN. STAT. ch. 38, para. 11-9 (Smith-Hurd 1979), 1961 Committee Comments, at 304 (revised 1972).

[412] ILL. ANN. STAT. ch. 38, para. 11-9 (Smith-Hurd 1979), 1961 Committee Comments, at 302-03 (revised 1972).

[413] ILL. ANN. STAT. ch. 38, para. 11-9 (Smith-Hurd 1979), 1961 Committee Comments, at 303 (revised 1972).

[414] P.A. 83-1069 (1984); ILL. REV. STAT. ch. 38, para. 11-9(a)(1) (1984).

[415] 720 ILCS 5/12-12(e) (1999).

[416] People v. Tadla, 110 Ill. App. 2d 119, 121, 249 N.E.2d 155, 156 (1st Dist. 1969).

presence of two undercover police officers after having agreed to perform oral sex on one of them;[417] a male and nude female simulating sexual intercourse and oral sex;[418] a woman fondling a man's genital organs through his pants;[419] and a nude man masturbating while being observed by two girls.[420]

Although most of the cases involving "indecent" activity revolve around the sufficiency of the actus reus, it is important to also consider the mental state requirement. If there is sexual penetration, the act speaks for itself, and proof of mens rea is not required.[421] If the alleged indecent activity involves "sexual conduct," it must be done intentionally or knowingly.[422] If the alleged indecent behavior arises from exposure of oneself, the exposure must be "lewd" and "with intent to arouse or to satisfy the sexual desire of the person."[423] If the exposure is inadvertent or accidental, it is not criminal.[424]

An act of *public indecency,* by definition, requires proof that the behavior occurred in a public place. A *public place* for purposes of this offense means "any place where the conduct may reasonably be expected to be viewed by others."[425] For example, indecent sexual behavior in a park,[426] outside a building,[427] in a moving automobile,[428] or in a nightclub open to the public[429] would be activity in public, since it could be reasonably anticipated that the activity might be viewed by others.[430] However, commercial erotic displays by nude dancers did not amount to public indecency where patrons were required to pay an admission fee of two dollars to be admitted into a booth and then purchase coins in order to observe the dance performance through a window overlooking the stage.[431]

---

[417] S. & F. Corp. v. Bilandic, 62 Ill. App. 3d 193, 196, 378 N.E.2d 1137, 1139 (1st Dist. 1978) (upholding license revocation based in part on public indecency in business premises).

[418] City of Chicago v. Hanson, 105 Ill. App. 3d 1017, 1020, 435 N.E.2d 120, 123 (1st Dist. 1981).

[419] Cabaret, Inc. v. Daley, 66 Ill. App. 3d 326, 329, 384 N.E.2d 10, 13 (1st Dist. 1978) (upholding license revocation based in part on public indecency in business premises).

[420] People v. Stoehr, 82 Ill. App. 3d 827, 831, 403 N.E.2d 291, 294 (2d Dist. 1980).

[421] See § 8.10 of this chapter for the definition of the term "sexual penetration."

[422] See § 8.09 of this chapter for the definition of the term "sexual conduct."

[423] 720 ILCS 5/11-9(a)(2) (1999).

[424] People v. Garrison, 82 Ill. 2d 444, 457, 412 N.E.2d 483, 490 (1980), *appeal dismissed,* 450 U.S. 961 (1981).

[425] 720 ILCS 5/11-9(b) (1999).

[426] People v. Baus, 16 Ill. App. 3d 136, 137, 305 N.E.2d 592, 593 (1st Dist. 1973).

[427] People v. Mikota, 1 Ill. App. 3d 114, 119, 273 N.E.2d 618, 622 (1st Dist. 1971).

[428] People v. Grear, 98 Ill. App. 2d 372, 379, 240 N.E.2d 329, 333 (1st Dist. 1968), *rev'd on other grounds,* 42 Ill. 2d 578, 248 N.E.2d 661 (1969).

[429] Cabaret, Inc. v. Daley, 66 Ill. App. 3d 326, 329, 384 N.E.2d 10, 13 (1st Dist. 1978).

[430] See, e.g., People v. Baus, 16 Ill. App. 3d 136, 138, 305 N.E.2d 592, 593 (1st Dist. 1973).

[431] People v. Haven, 247 Ill. App. 3d 1040, 1041-43, 618 N.E.2d 260, 261-62 (1st Dist. 1992).

The "indecent" activity need not transpire, however, in an area open to the general public. Where a person performed fellatio on the defendant in a prison cell, there was public indecency, since other prisoners could observe this activity.[432] Even if the indecent activity occurs within the defendant's own residence, it may amount to public indecency if the activity could be viewed by others from a vantage point outside the home.[433] Thus, the court found public indecency where the defendant, at different times on the same evening, stood in his dining room before unveiled glass doors with a light over his head and performed masturbating motions while exposing his nude crotch area.[434] Similarly, another defendant was found guilty of public indecency when he stood nude in front of his brightly lit apartment window with his penis erect.[435]

§ 8.33. Sexual Relations Within Families.

Before 1984, the Illinois incest-related proscriptions were "incest,"[436] "aggravated incest,"[437] and "sexual abuse of a child by a family member."[438] Now "sexual penetration" of a minor by a family member of the victim is considered criminal sexual assault[439] or aggravated criminal sexual assault,[440] and "sexual conduct" between a minor victim and a family member will constitute aggravated criminal sexual abuse.[441] Any other sexual activity between members of the same family constitutes the offense of "sexual relations within families." The statute provides:

---

[432] People v. Giacinti, 44 Ill. App. 3d 699, 702, 358 N.E.2d 934, 937 (3d Dist. 1976) (upholding probation revocation because of commission of public indecency).

[433] People v. Legel, 24 Ill. App. 3d 554, 558, 321 N.E.2d 164, 167-68 (2d Dist. 1974).

[434] People v. Legel, 24 Ill. App. 3d 554, 558, 321 N.E.2d 164, 167-68 (2d Dist. 1974).

[435] People v. Christ, 32 Ill. App. 3d 1014, 1017, 337 N.E.2d 53, 56 (4th Dist. 1975).

[436] ILL. REV. STAT. ch. 38, para. 11-11 (1983) (repealed) ("Any person who has sexual intercourse or performs an act of deviate sexual conduct with another to whom he knows he is related as follows commits incest: Brother or sister, either of the whole blood or the half blood.").

[437] ILL. REV. STAT. ch. 38, para. 11-10 (1983) (repealed) ("Any male or female person who shall perform any of the following acts with a person [under 18 years of age and whom] he or she knows is his or her daughter or son commits aggravated incest: (1) Has sexual intercourse; or (2) An act of deviate sexual conduct.").

[438] ILL. REV. STAT. ch. 38, para. 11-11.1 (1983) (repealed) ("Any male or female person who performs any of the following acts with a person [under the age of 18] he or she knows is his or her daughter or son or brother or sister commits sexual abuse of a child by a family member: (1) Any lewd fondling or touching of either the victim's or actor's sex organs or anus done or submitted to with the intent to arouse or satisfy the sexual desires of the victim or the actor or both; or (2) Any act or acts of penetration or other intrusion, however slight, of any object into the sex organs or anus of the victim or actor done or submitted to with the intent to arouse or to satisfy the sexual desires of either the victim or the actor or both.").

[439] 720 ILCS 5/12-13(a)(3) (1999).

[440] 720 ILCS 5/12-14(a) (1999).

[441] 720 ILCS 5/12-16(b) (1999).

(a) Any person commits sexual relations within families if he or she: (1) Commits an act of sexual penetration as defined in Section [5/]12-12 of this Code; and (2) The person knows that he or she is related to the other person as follows: (i) Brother or sister, either of the whole blood or the half blood; or (ii) Father or mother, when the child, regardless of legitimacy and regardless of whether the child was of the whole blood or half-blood or was adopted, was 18 years of age or over when the act was committed; or (iii) Stepfather or stepmother, when the stepchild was 18 years of age or over when the act was committed.

(b) Sexual relations within families is a . . . felony.[442]

The two most important limitations regarding the reach of this statute are that (1) the sexual activity involve "sexual penetration," and (2) the accused "knows" of the relationship that exists with the victim.[443] Where defendant's eighteen-year-old stepson performed oral sex on defendant, this amounted to the commission of sexual relations within families.[444]

§ 8.34. Bigamy.

The next article 5/11 sex crime is "bigamy." It is defined in the statute as follows:

(a) Any person having a husband or wife who subsequently marries another or cohabits in this State after such marriage commits bigamy.

(b) It shall be an affirmative defense to bigamy that: (1) The prior marriage was dissolved or declared invalid; or (2) The accused reasonably believed the prior spouse to be dead; or (3) The prior spouse had been continually absent for a period of 5 years during which time the accused did not know the prior spouse to be alive; or (4) The accused reasonably believed that he was legally eligible to remarry.

(c) Bigamy is a . . . felony.[445]

The revision committee's comments show that this enactment is aimed at a subsequent marriage or cohabitation activity in the state even where the subsequent marriage took place outside the state; however, the subsequent marriage must be bigamous according to Illinois law.[446] In other words, the defendant cannot be convicted of bigamy if Illinois recognizes a defense to the alleged bigamous activity that is not recognized in the state in which the subsequent

---

[442] 720 ILCS 5/11-11 (1999).

[443] 720 ILCS 5/11-11 (1999).

[444] People v. Parker, 123 Ill. 2d 204, 208-13, 526 N.E.2d 135, 137-39 (1988).

[445] 720 ILCS 5/11-12 (1999).

[446] ILL. ANN. STAT. ch. 38, para. 11-12 (Smith-Hurd 1979), 1961 Committee Comments, at 325 (revised 1972).

marriage was consummated. The committee also decided to make the defenses "affirmative defenses," which means the defendant is required to offer "some evidence" supportive of the defenses before the state is required to disprove them, since evidence regarding such a bar to a bigamy conviction is "peculiarly available to the defense and substantially impossible for the prosecution to obtain."[447] For this reason, an annulment or divorce from a prior marriage, which might be more appropriately viewed as an "exception" to bigamy, has been codified as a "defense."[448] The second affirmative defense — a reasonable belief that the prior spouse was dead — was considered desirable inasmuch as bigamy is an affront to the institution of marriage; therefore, a person who reasonably believes his or her mate to be dead exhibits no such evil intention when he or she remarries.[449] The third defense requires that (1) the prior spouse was continually absent for five years and (2) the accused lacked knowledge that the spouse was alive.[450] This defense is not available to the accused if the accused had abandoned his or her prior marital obligations.[451] However, it is available if the accused had no affirmative knowledge that his or her absent spouse was alive; and the accused need not prove that he or she had information indicating the absent spouse was dead.[452] The fourth defense — a reasonable mistake of eligibility to remarry — covers mistakes of fact, such as where the accused mistakenly thought his or her prior spouse had procured a divorce, and mistakes of law, such as where the accused mistakenly believed that his or her divorce in a foreign jurisdiction relieved him or her of the bonds of matrimony.[453]

§ 8.35. Marrying a Bigamist.

Not only is it a crime to engage in bigamy, it is also a misdemeanor to marry a bigamist.[454] Section 5/11-13 sets out the elements of this "marrying a bigamist." It provides:

---

[447] ILL. ANN. STAT. ch. 38, para. 11-12 (Smith-Hurd 1979), 1961 Committee Comments, at 327-28 (revised 1972).

[448] ILL. ANN. STAT. ch. 38, para. 11-12 (Smith-Hurd 1979), 1961 Committee Comments, at 325 (revised 1972).

[449] ILL. ANN. STAT. ch. 38, para. 11-12 (Smith-Hurd 1979), 1961 Committee Comments, at 326 (revised 1972).

[450] ILL. ANN. STAT. ch. 38, para. 11-12 (Smith-Hurd 1979), 1961 Committee Comments, at 326-27 (revised 1972).

[451] ILL. ANN. STAT. ch. 38, para. 11-12 (Smith-Hurd 1979), 1961 Committee Comments, at 327 (revised 1972).

[452] ILL. ANN. STAT. ch. 38, para. 11-12 (Smith-Hurd 1979), 1961 Committee Comments, at 327 (revised 1972).

[453] ILL. ANN. STAT. ch. 38, para. 11-12 (Smith-Hurd 1979), 1961 Committee Comments, at 327 (revised 1972).

[454] 720 ILCS 5/11-13(b) (1999).

Any unmarried person who knowingly marries another under circumstances known to him which would render the other person guilty of bigamy under the laws of this State, or who cohabits in this State after such a marriage, commits the offense of marrying a bigamist.[455]

A single person who knowingly marries a bigamist cannot be held accountable on principles of accomplice liability, since his or her conduct is "inevitably incident to its commission."[456] This separate crime is therefore necessary if marrying a bigamist is to be punished.[457] Each of the defenses available to the bigamist would also be available to a person accused of marrying a bigamist, provided the defendant believes one of the circumstances to be true.[458]

§ 8.36. Prostitution.

The common law,[459] most other countries,[460] and at least one other state[461] do not specifically prohibit prostitution per se, but rather prohibit the nuisances that result from the activity. Nonetheless, prostitution is prohibited per se in most American jurisdictions,[462] including Illinois.[463] In 1986, the Illinois definition of prostitution was expanded to include conduct beyond sexual penetration.[464] It prohibits anyone from performing, offering, or agreeing to perform "sexual penetration . . . for any money, property, token, object, or article or anything of value, or any touching or fondling of the sex organs of one person by another person, for any money, property, token, object, or article or anything of value, for the purpose of sexual arousal or gratification . . . ."[465] Commission of prostitution is a misdemeanor unless the defendant was previously convicted of two or more prostitution-related offenses, in which case it is a felony.[466]

---

[455] 720 ILCS 5/11-13(a) (1999).

[456] 720 ILCS 5/5-2(c)(2) (1999). *See* ch. 3 of this treatise for a discussion of accomplice liability.

[457] ILL. ANN. STAT. ch. 38, para. 11-13 (Smith-Hurd 1979) 1961 Committee Comments, at 332 (revised 1972).

[458] ILL. ANN. STAT. ch. 38, para. 11-13 (Smith-Hurd 1979) 1961 Committee Comments, at 332 (revised 1972).

[459] ILL. ANN. STAT. ch. 38, para. 11-14 (Smith-Hurd 1979), 1961 Committee Comments, at 333 (revised 1972).

[460] *See* JOHN F. DECKER, PROSTITUTION: REGULATION AND CONTROL 115-44 (1979).

[461] JOHN F. DECKER, PROSTITUTION: REGULATION AND CONTROL 89-92 (1979).

[462] ROLLIN M. PERKINS & RONALD N. BOYCE, CRIMINAL LAW 470 (3d ed. 1982).

[463] 720 ILCS 5/11-14 (1999).

[464] *See* ILL. REV. STAT. ch. 38, para. 11-14 (1985) (prohibited only performing, offering or agreeing to perform "sexual penetration").

[465] 720 ILCS 5/11-14(a) (1999).

[466] 720 ILCS 5/11-14(b) (1999).

§ 8.37. — Elements of Prostitution.

To convict a person of prostitution, the state must adequately prove each of the following elements: that (1) a person (2) performed, offered, or agreed to perform (3) sexual penetration or any touching or fondling of the sex organs of one person by another person for purposes of sexual arousal or gratification in exchange (4) for money or anything of value.[467] These elements will be discussed independently.

First, it is important to note that any person can commit prostitution. Accordingly, this crime encompasses commercial homosexual conduct.[468] Obviously, it applies equally to any heterosexual penetration for monetary gain, including the sale of such sexual services by a male to a female.

Second, it is significant that no sexual activity actually need occur.[469] If the defendant "performs," "offers," *or* "agrees" to perform the proscribed sexual activity, this amounts to prostitution under Illinois law.[470] In order to prohibit not only "solicitations" but also "less urging . . . invitation[s] on the part of the prostitute," the legislature added "offering" to the statute.[471] The word *agrees* was designed by the legislature "to cover the situation where the female simply makes it a practice of accepting properly endowed propositions and permits her reputation or availability to do her soliciting for her."[472]

Third, the contemplated sexual activity must be "sexual penetration" as defined in section 5/12-12, or the "touching or fondling" of the sex organs of one party by a second party.[473] The purpose of the contemplated touching or fondling must be sexual gratification.[474]

Fourth, money or any other thing of value can be the remuneration.[475] However, an offer to engage in sexual intercourse without a mention of remuneration

---

[467] 720 ILCS 5/11-14(a) (1999).

[468] ILL. ANN. STAT. ch. 38, para. 11-14 (Smith-Hurd 1979), 1961 Committee Comments, at 333 (revised 1972).

[469] *See* People v. Young, 86 Ill. App. 3d 306, 309, 408 N.E.2d 104, 106 (3d Dist. 1980) (holding that an agreement to engage in deviant sexual conduct for money amounted to prostitution).

[470] People v. Johnson, 65 Ill. 2d 332, 336, 357 N.E.2d 1166, 1167 (1976) (stating that the offense sets out three separate and distinct methods to commit prostitution: performs, offers or agrees). *See also* People v. Martin, 240 Ill. App. 3d 260, 260-62, 606 N.E.2d 1265, 1266-67 (3d Dist. 1992) (where defendant approached undercover police officer, got into his car and offered to perform oral sex for going rate of twenty-five dollars, this amounted to prostitution).

[471] ILL. ANN. STAT. ch. 38, para. 11-14 (Smith-Hurd 1979), Committee Comments, at 333 (revised 1972).

[472] ILL. ANN. STAT. ch. 38, para. 11-14 (Smith-Hurd 1979), Committee Comments, at 333 (revised 1972).

[473] 720 ILCS 5/11-14(a) (1999).

[474] 720 ILCS 5/11-14(a) (1999).

[475] 720 ILCS 5/11-14(a) (1999).

does not constitute prostitution.[476] This does not mean, however, that "criminal liability [can] be escaped by schemes which would avoid the direct payment of cash to the prostitute."[477] For example, if a patron pays for colored-water "champagne" in a prostitution lounge, or if an agent of the prostitute receives the money from the patron, this still constitutes prostitution.[478]

Finally, the crime of prostitution is facially silent regarding a mental state element. Prostitution is presumably a general intent offense by virtue of the section 5/4-3(b) interpretive presumption.[479]

§ 8.38. Solicitation of a Sexual Act.

In 1993, the legislature created the offense of "solicitation of a sexual act."[480] The Criminal Code defines solicitation of a sexual act as follows:

> Any person who offers a person not his or her spouse any money, property, token, object, or article or anything of value to perform any act of sexual penetration as defined in Section [5/]12-12 of this Code, or any touching or fondling of the sex organs of one person by another person for the purpose of sexual arousal or gratification, commits the offense of solicitation of a sexual act.[481]

This prohibition is a misdemeanor.[482]

§ 8.39. Soliciting for a Prostitute.

A person unlawfully solicits for a prostitute when he or she (1) solicits another for the purpose of prostitution; or (2) arranges or offers to arrange a meeting of persons for the purposes of prostitution; or (3) directs someone to a place with knowledge that the direction is for the purpose of prostitution.[483] "Soliciting for a prostitute" is a misdemeanor unless the defendant was previously con-

---

[476] Daley v. License Appeal Commission, 54 Ill. App. 2d 265, 267, 204 N.E.2d 36, 38 (1st Dist. 1964) (involving the revocation of business operator's license for knowingly permitting use of his premises for prostitution).

[477] ILL. ANN. STAT. ch. 38, para. 11-14 (Smith-Hurd 1979), 1961 Committee Comments, at 334 (revised 1972).

[478] ILL. ANN. STAT. ch. 38, para. 11-14 (Smith-Hurd 1979), 1961 Committee Comments, at 334 (revised 1972).

[479] See ch. 2 of this treatise for a complete discussion of mental state requirements and the section 5/4-3(b) interpretive presumption. See also Wes Ward Entertainment, Ltd. v. Andrews, 42 Ill. App. 3d 458, 470, 355 N.E.2d 131, 140 (3d Dist. 1976) (intent will be implied when not specifically included in the criminal enactment).

[480] 720 ILCS 5/11-14.1 (1999).

[481] 720 ILCS 5/11-14.1(a) (1999).

[482] 720 ILCS 5/11-14.1(b) (1999).

[483] 720 ILCS 5/11-15(a) (1999).

victed of two or more prostitution-related offenses, in which case it is a felony.[484]

Since the mere offer by a prostitute to engage in sexual penetration for money amounts to prostitution,[485] there is no need for a separate stricture for solicitation *by* a prostitute. However, when another person solicits *for* a prostitute, this is not prostitution. Therefore, the General Assembly developed "soliciting for a prostitute" to cover all acts of those persons, such as "runners" or "middlemen," who actively seek out customers and suggest prostitution to prospective patrons.[486] If a *prospective patron* of a prostitute solicits a prostitute on his or her own behalf, this is not solicitation for a prostitute.[487] The Illinois appellate court has ruled that this solicitation crime was directed at those persons who assist another person in establishing contact with a prostitute, not at the patrons.[488]

A *solicitation,* for purposes of subsection (a)(1), requires only an invitation, made either privately or in a public place.[489] Subsections (a)(2) and (a)(3) expand the concept of solicitation to include liaisons with persons who might not have initiated the suggestion, but who participated in arranging the activity in a vital way.[490] Thus, "the elevator operator or bellhop in a hotel who establishes contact between a patron and a prostitute" is covered by subsection (a)(2).[491] Subsection (a)(3) "deals with directing the prospective patron to a prostitute or place of prostitution" and covers, for example, a taxicab driver who takes a rider to a place of prostitution after the rider asks the driver to do so.[492]

In each instance, the person must aid the prostitution activity for "the purpose of prostitution."[493] A taxicab driver will not be liable merely because he or she drives to a requested address even if he or she knows the address to be a house of prostitution.[494] In such a case, the driver may only be concerned with fulfilling his or her duty as an employee to respond to certain directions given by the

---

[484] 720 ILCS 5/11-15(b) (1999).

[485] *See* § 8.37 of this chapter.

[486] ILL. ANN. STAT. ch. 38, para. 11-15 (Smith-Hurd 1979), 1961 Committee Comments, at 341 (revised 1972).

[487] People v. Thoma, 152 Ill. App. 3d 374, 377, 504 N.E.2d 539, 541 (3d Dist. 1987).

[488] People v. Holloway, 143 Ill. App. 3d 735, 739, 493 N.E.2d 89, 93 (1st Dist. 1986).

[489] ILL. ANN. STAT. ch. 38, para. 11-15 (Smith-Hurd 1979), 1961 Committee Comments, at 341 (revised 1972).

[490] ILL. ANN. STAT. ch. 38, para. 11-15 (Smith-Hurd 1979), 1961 Committee Comments, at 341 (revised 1972).

[491] ILL. ANN. STAT. ch. 38, para. 11-15 (Smith-Hurd 1979), 1961 Committee Comments, at 341 (revised 1972).

[492] ILL. ANN. STAT. ch. 38, para. 11-15 (Smith-Hurd 1979), 1961 Committee Comments, at 341-42 (revised 1972).

[493] ILL. ANN. STAT. ch. 38, para. 11-15 (Smith-Hurd 1979), 1961 Committee Comments, at 342 (revised 1972).

[494] ILL. ANN. STAT. ch. 38, para. 11-15 (Smith-Hurd 1979), 1961 Committee Comments, at 342 (revised 1972).

passenger.[495] Only if the driver "adds some measure of essential information or direction to the pre-existing intent of the prospective customer" will his or her acts be deemed criminal.[496]

The defendant's soliciting, making arrangements, or providing direction is the essence of the crime. It is not necessary that the assistance actually lead to an act of prostitution.[497] Also, the solicitor is not relieved of liability merely because he or she did not receive some financial reward for his or her efforts.[498] For example, a bar owner whose bartender introduced a customer to a woman for purposes of prostitution was punished under this enactment.[499] Likewise, a bartender's vouching for a prostitute who offered sexual intercourse for a fee to a plainclothes police officer was sufficient to establish a violation of law.[500]

It has been argued that solicitation for purposes of prostitution is a lesser included offense of other prostitution-related strictures. Regardless, it has been held that solicitation is not a lesser included offense of pandering since it is possible to pander without committing the offense of soliciting for a prostitute.[501]

§ 8.40. Soliciting for a Juvenile Prostitute.

Although soliciting for an adult prostitute usually constitutes a misdemeanor (although it is a felony if the defendant has been previously convicted of two or more prostitution related offenses),[502] "soliciting for a juvenile prostitute" is a felony offense.[503] This crime appears as follows:

> Any person who violates any of the provisions of Section [5/]11-15(a) of this Act [soliciting for a prostitute] commits soliciting for a juvenile prostitute where the prostitute for whom such person is soliciting is under 16 years of age or is an institutionalized severely or profoundly mentally retarded person.[504]

---

[495] ILL. ANN. STAT. ch. 38, para. 11-15 (Smith-Hurd 1979), 1961 Committee Comments, at 342 (revised 1972).

[496] ILL. ANN. STAT. ch. 38, para. 11-15 (Smith-Hurd 1979), 1961 Committee Comments, at 342 (revised 1972).

[497] ILL. ANN. STAT. ch. 38, para. 11-15 (Smith-Hurd 1979), 1961 Committee Comments, at 342 (revised 1972).

[498] ILL. ANN. STAT. ch. 38, para. 11-15 (Smith-Hurd 1979), 1961 Committee Comments, at 342 (revised 1972).

[499] Daley v. Rifkin, 84 Ill. App. 2d 467, 471, 228 N.E.2d 224, 226 (1st Dist. 1967).

[500] Daley v. Jack's Tivoli Liquor Lounge, Inc., 118 Ill. App. 2d 264, 275, 254 N.E.2d 814, 819 (1st Dist. 1969) (finding criminal solicitation within establishment to be basis for revocation of liquor license).

[501] People v. Matthews, 89 Ill. App. 3d 749, 750-51, 412 N.E.2d 31, 32 (3d Dist. 1980).

[502] 720 ILCS 5/11-15(b) (1999).

[503] 720 ILCS 5/11-15.1(c) (1999).

[504] 720 ILCS 5/11-15.1(a) (1999).

It is an affirmative defense to a charge of soliciting for a juvenile prostitute that the accused reasonably believed the person was of the age of sixteen or over or was not an institutionalized severely or profoundly mentally retarded person.[505] This offense of soliciting for a juvenile prostitute does not cover the solicitation or recruitment of a child into prostitution.[506] For example, in one case, a defendant provided a thirteen-year-old child with instruction, clothing and cosmetics to assist her in soliciting customers.[507] In addition, the defendant positioned the child in a popular location, waited nearby as the child solicited customers, and then took all of the money that the child received.[508] The appellate court held that these were not among the activities proscribed as soliciting for a juvenile prostitute.[509] The offense of soliciting for a juvenile prostitute only applies to "middlemen" who solicit customers for a prostitute, and not to the prostitute or prospective customer.[510]

§ 8.41. Pandering.

"Pandering" is an activity that is often confused with "pimping."[511] The crime of pimping applies to the person who profits from the earnings of a prostitute, even if he or she does not entice a person into prostitution, solicit patrons on behalf of the prostitute, or make arrangements to aid the prostitute's activities.[512] Pandering applies to the person who profits from prostitution by *recruiting* persons into prostitution *or* by *setting up arrangements* whereby a person can ply the trade of prostitution.[513] Both the pimp and panderer are distinguishable from the solicitor in that the pimp and panderer must profit from their activities,[514] while the solicitor need not do so.[515]

Section 5/11-16 defines the felony crime of pandering: "Any person who performs any of the following acts for any money, property, token, object, or article or anything of value commits pandering: (1) Compels a person to become a prostitute; or (2) Arranges or offers to arrange a situation in which a person may

---

[505] 720 ILCS 5/11-15.1(b) (1999).

[506] People v. Harris, 157 Ill. App. 3d 70, 73, 510 N.E.2d 107, 110 (1st Dist. 1987).

[507] People v. Harris, 157 Ill. App. 3d 70, 72, 510 N.E.2d 107, 110 (1st Dist. 1987).

[508] People v. Harris, 157 Ill. App. 3d 70, 72-73, 510 N.E.2d 107, 110 (1st Dist. 1987).

[509] People v. Harris, 157 Ill. App. 3d 70, 73, 510 N.E.2d 107, 110 (1st Dist. 1987).

[510] People v. Jones, 245 Ill. App. 3d 810, 812-14, 615 N.E.2d 391, 394-95 (4th Dist. 1993).

[511] JOHN F. DECKER, PROSTITUTION: REGULATION AND CONTROL 259 (1979). *See also* ILL. ANN. STAT. ch. 38, para. 11-16 (Smith-Hurd 1979), 1961 Committee Comments, at 345 (revised 1972).

[512] *See* 720 ILCS 5/11-16 (1999). *See also* JOHN F. DECKER, PROSTITUTION: REGULATION AND CONTROL 238-59 (1979) (describing a pimp).

[513] JOHN F. DECKER, PROSTITUTION: REGULATION AND CONTROL 259-63 (1979) (describing a panderer).

[514] 720 ILCS 5/11-16, 5/11-19 (1999).

[515] 720 ILCS 5/11-15, 5/11-15.1 (1999).

practice prostitution."[516] The statute is primarily directed at "the recruiting of persons into the practice of prostitution and . . . keeping [of] practicing prostitutes in that line of endeavor."[517] Subsection (a)(1) requires "some kind of coercion," whether by taking advantage of physical force, financial destitution, or drug addiction.[518] Subsection (a)(2) requires only that "the accused arrange or offer to arrange for another to become a prostitute."[519] A mere "solicitation" of a person to enter prostitution, even if without success, is punishable by this law.[520] The state must prove the panderer was motivated to engage in the proscribed acts for money or anything of value even if none were collected.[521]

For example, a defendant committed the offense of pandering when he initiated contact with an undercover police officer, introduced him to an apparent prostitute, and then determined the price for the services, received money and made other necessary arrangements.[522] Likewise, where a defendant offered a woman a hotel room wherein she could perform acts of prostitution for twenty-five dollars in exchange for his receipt of a five-dollar fee per customer, this was sufficient for a pandering conviction.[523]

Pandering and pimping are separate and distinct crimes and are not lesser included offenses of one another.[524] Living off a prostitute's earnings is not a necessary part of pandering, although it is an element of pimping.[525] Furthermore, pandering, but not pimping, requires some type of recruitment or making of arrangements to enter prostitution.[526] Solicitation for a prostitute is not a lesser included offense of pandering.[527]

[516] 720 ILCS 5/11-16 (1999).

[517] ILL. ANN. STAT. ch. 38, para. 11-16 (Smith-Hurd 1979), 1961 Committee Comments, at 345 (revised 1972).

[518] ILL. ANN. STAT. ch. 38, para. 11-16 (Smith-Hurd 1979), 1961 Committee Comments, at 346 (revised 1972).

[519] ILL. ANN. STAT. ch. 38, para. 11-16 (Smith-Hurd 1979), 1961 Committee Comments, at 346 (revised 1972).

[520] ILL. ANN. STAT. ch. 38, para. 11-16 (Smith-Hurd 1979), 1961 Committee Comments, at 346 (revised 1972). See also People v. Russell, 69 Ill. App. 3d 59, 62, 386 N.E.2d 1369, 1371 (3d Dist. 1979) (recruiting and management activity, not success thereof, is activity sought to be prohibited under pandering statute)

[521] People v. Taylor, 64 Ill. App. 3d 279, 281, 381 N.E.2d 303, 305 (4th Dist. 1978). Compare People v. Hammond, 82 Ill. App. 3d 839, 842-43, 403 N.E.2d 305, 308 (4th Dist. 1980) (where there was no evidence defendant acted for remuneration, pandering conviction reversed).

[522] People v. Wiler, 190 Ill. App. 3d 47, 47-50, 545 N.E.2d 1014, 1014-15 (1st Dist. 1989).

[523] People v. Guzzardo, 69 Ill. App. 3d 252, 255, 387 N.E.2d 896, 897 (2d Dist. 1979).

[524] People v. Russell, 69 Ill. App. 3d 59, 63, 386 N.E.2d 1369, 1372 (3d Dist. 1979).

[525] See 720 ILCS 5/11-19(a) (1999).

[526] People v. Russell, 69 Ill. App. 3d 59, 62-63, 386 N.E.2d 1369, 1371-72 (3d Dist. 1979).

[527] People v. Matthews, 89 Ill. App. 3d 749, 750-51, 412 N.E.2d 31, 32 (3d Dist. 1980).

§ 8.42. Keeping a Place of Prostitution.

"Keeping a place of prostitution" is codified in section 5/11-17:

> Any person who has or exercises control over the use of any place which could offer seclusion or shelter for the practice of prostitution who performs any of the following acts keeps a place of prostitution: (1) Knowingly grants or permits the use of such place for the purpose of prostitution; or (2) Grants or permits the use of such place under circumstances from which he could reasonably know that the place is used or is to be used for purposes of prostitution; or (3) Permits the continued use of a place after becoming aware of facts or circumstances from which he should reasonably know that the place is being used for purposes of prostitution.[528]

Keeping a place of prostitution is a misdemeanor unless the defendant has been previously convicted of two or more prostitution-related crimes, in which case the activity is punished as a felony.[529]

It is important to note that the General Assembly carefully avoided characterizing this offense as keeping a "house" of prostitution because not only a building, but also boats, house trailers, or "even a fenced space around a swimming pool" can be used for such a purpose.[530] The enactment employs a broad, generalized description of the type of facility used, but focuses more detailed attention on the knowledge of the alleged keeper of a place of prostitution and his or her relationship to the place in question.[531] A defendant can be held liable if he or she exercises control over the place in question regardless of whether he or she is the owner, a lessor, an employee on the premises, or even a trespasser.[532] What the defendant knows or should know about the use of the facility in question is most important. If he or she "knowingly grants or permits" a place under his or her dominion to be used for prostitution, he or she is guilty.[533] A person has committed this crime even if he or she "passively ignores facts which should reasonably justify the conclusion that the place is being used for purposes of

---

[528] 720 ILCS 5/11-17(a) (1999).

[529] 720 ILCS 5/11-17(b) (1999).

[530] ILL. ANN. STAT. ch. 38, para. 11-17 (Smith-Hurd 1979), 1961 Committee Comments, at 355 (revised 1972).

[531] ILL. ANN. STAT. ch. 38, para. 11-17 (Smith-Hurd 1979), 1961 Committee Comments, at 355 (revised 1972).

[532] ILL. ANN. STAT. ch. 38, para. 11-17 (Smith-Hurd 1979), 1961 Committee Comments, at 355 (revised 1972).

[533] ILL. ANN. STAT. ch. 38, para. 11-17 (Smith-Hurd 1979), 1961 Committee Comments, at 355 (revised 1972). *See also* People ex rel. Difanis v. Futia, 65 Ill. App. 3d 1027, 1032, 383 N.E.2d 763, 767 (4th Dist. 1978) (massage parlor owner knew of nature and quality of massage parlor business and did not make good faith effort to abate; nuisance enjoined through injunction).

prostitution."[534] Thus, a resident apartment house manager who became aware but ignored the fact that certain female occupants were receiving numerous, successive male guests during evening hours could be convicted of keeping a place of prostitution.[535]

§ 8.43. Keeping a Place of Juvenile Prostitution.

Any person who knowingly violates the section 5/11-17 prohibition against "keeping a place of prostitution" commits instead "keeping a place of juvenile prostitution" when any prostitute in the place is under the age of sixteen years or is an institutionalized severely or profoundly mentally retarded person.[536] The accused has an affirmative defense to this offense where he or she "reasonably believed the person was of the age of 16 years or over or was not an institutionalized severely or profoundly mentally retarded person at the time of the act giving rise to the charge."[537] Keeping a place of juvenile prostitution is a felony.[538]

§ 8.44. Patronizing a Prostitute.

Most states do not have statutes directly aimed at customers of a prostitute,[539] but Illinois does penalize persons for "patronizing a prostitute." Section 5/11-18 provides:

> Any person who performs any of the following acts with a person not his or her spouse commits the offense of patronizing a prostitute: (1) Engaging in an act of sexual penetration as defined in Section [5]/12-12 of this Code with a prostitute; or (2) Enters or remains in a place of prostitution with intent to engage in an act of sexual penetration as defined in Section [5]/12-12 of this Code.[540]

Patronizing a prostitute is a misdemeanor but involves felony sanctions where a defendant has two or more previous convictions for prostitution-related crimes.[541]

---

[534] ILL. ANN. STAT. ch. 38, para. 11-17 (Smith-Hurd 1979), 1961 Committee Comments, at 355 (revised 1972).

[535] ILL. ANN. STAT. ch. 38, para. 11-17 (Smith-Hurd 1979), 1961 Committee Comments, at 355-56 (revised 1972).

[536] 720 ILCS 5/11-17.1(a) (1999).

[537] 720 ILCS 5/11-17.1(b) (1999).

[538] 720 ILCS 5/11-17(c) (1999).

[539] JOHN F. DECKER, PROSTITUTION: REGULATION AND CONTROL 82 (1979).

[540] 720 ILCS 5/11-18(a) (1999).

[541] 720 ILCS 5/11-18(b) (1999).

The privacy of the place, consent, and the absence of open and notorious conduct are all immaterial.[542] In addition, a person has crossed the threshold of criminality regardless of whether he or she has actually engaged in sexual penetration with a prostitute. Mere presence in a place of prostitution with the intent to engage in that activity is sufficient.[543]

A defendant is guilty of attempted patronization of a prostitute where he or she has the specific intent to patronize a prostitute and takes a substantial step toward its completion.[544] The Illinois appellate court ruled that a defendant did not take a "substantial step" toward the commission of the offense attempted patronization of a prostitute where he asked a female undercover officer posing as a prostitute how much she would charge to perform a sexual act, but neither indicated he had money nor invited the undercover officer to enter his vehicle.[545]

§ 8.45. Patronizing a Juvenile Prostitute.

Any person who engages in an act of sexual penetration with a prostitute under the age of sixteen years or with a prostitute who is mentally retarded commits the offense of "patronizing a juvenile prostitute."[546] It is an affirmative defense to this offense, if, at the time of the act giving rise to the charge, the accused "reasonably believed that the person was of the age of 16 or over or was not an institutionalized severely or profoundly mentally retarded person . . . ."[547] A person who violates this prohibition commits a felony.[548]

§ 8.46. Pimping.

The pimp is often stereotyped as a male who attracts or forces a woman into prostitution. It is commonly thought that the pimp assumes the role of boyfriend or lover, satisfies her emotional and true sexual yearnings, supplies her with illicit drugs, inflicts a dependency relationship on her through any means from promises of marriage to narcotics addiction to physical force, locates customers for her, protects her from sadistic patrons and thieves bent on stealing her evening's income, bails her out of jail, pays her fines, and often, manages to juggle simultaneously a number of relationships of this nature with the various women

---

[542] See ILL. ANN. STAT. ch. 38, para. 11-18 (Smith-Hurd 1979), 1961 Committee Comments, at 364 (revised 1972).

[543] See 720 ILCS 5/11-18(a)(2) (1999). See also People v. Anderson, 143 Ill. App. 3d 567, 571, 493 N.E.2d 410, 413 (5th Dist. 1986) (discussing distinction between soliciting for a prostitute and patronizing a prostitute).

[544] People v. Thoma, 171 Ill. App. 3d 313, 315, 525 N.E.2d 572, 573 (3d Dist. 1988).

[545] People v. Thoma, 171 Ill. App. 3d 313, 315, 525 N.E.2d 572, 573 (3d Dist. 1988).

[546] 720 ILCS 5/11-18.1(a) (1999).

[547] 720 ILCS 5/11-18.1(b) (1999).

[548] 720 ILCS 5/11-18.1(c) (1999).

who make up his "stable."[549] Legally, however, a person need not engage in any of this conduct to be considered a pimp in Illinois. The state "pimping" statute only requires the state to prove that a person has enriched himself or herself, without lawful consideration, from the earnings of a prostitute.[550] Section 5/11-19 sets out the following language: "Any person who receives any money, token, object, or article or anything of value from a prostitute, not for a lawful consideration, knowing it was earned in whole or in part from the practice of prostitution, commits pimping."[551] Pimping is a misdemeanor unless the defendant has been previously convicted of two or more prostitution-related offenses, in which case it is punishable as a felony.[552]

Pimping, then, can be committed by a person of either sex.[553] The person must receive money or "anything of value," which can include gifts of automobiles, clothing, or living accommodations.[554] The money or items of value must be received "not for lawful consideration."[555] Thus, if someone sells a legal item or service to a person who he or she suspects or knows to be a prostitute, he or she cannot be considered a pimp merely because he or she received some part of the prostitute's earnings as part of his or her normal business transactions.[556] The pimp must "know" that the person from whom he or she is receiving valuable consideration is a prostitute, and the consideration must not be gained through a legitimate business exchange.[557]

The pimp must receive the valuable consideration in question "from a prostitute."[558] This penal concern is directed at "the entrepreneur class in the 'business' complex of prostitution."[559] The pimp who actually engages in other criminal prostitution-related activities such as "solicitation for a prostitute" or

---

[549] JOHN F. DECKER, PROSTITUTION: REGULATION AND CONTROL 238-41 (1979).

[550] 720 ILCS 5/11-19(a) (1999).

[551] 720 ILCS 5/11-19(a) (1999).

[552] 720 ILCS 5/11-19(b) (1999).

[553] ILL. ANN. STAT. ch. 38, para. 11-19 (Smith-Hurd 1979), 1961 Committee Comments, at 365 (revised 1972).

[554] ILL. ANN. STAT. ch. 38, para. 11-19 (Smith-Hurd 1979), 1961 Committee Comments, at 365 (revised 1972).

[555] ILL. ANN. STAT. ch. 38, para. 11-19 (Smith-Hurd 1979), 1961 Committee Comments, at 365 (revised 1972).

[556] ILL. ANN. STAT. ch. 38, para. 11-19 (Smith-Hurd 1979), 1961 Committee Comments, at 365-66 (revised 1972).

[557] ILL. ANN. STAT. ch. 38, para. 11-19 (Smith-Hurd 1979), 1961 Committee Comments, at 365-66 (revised 1972).

[558] 720 ILCS 5/11-19(a) (1999).

[559] ILL. REV. STAT. ch. 38, para. 11-19 (Smith-Hurd 1979), 1961 Committee Comments, at 366 (revised 1972).

"pandering," or other crimes such as battery or delivery of narcotics, can be punished for these crimes as well.[560]

§ 8.47. Juvenile Pimping.

Although ordinary pimping is a misdemeanor in most cases, receiving money or property not for lawful consideration from a juvenile prostitute is always a felony.[561] The "juvenile pimping" stricture reads: "Any person who receives any money, property, token, object, or article or any thing of value from a prostitute under 16 years of age or from a prostitute who is an institutionalized severely or profoundly mentally retarded person, not for a lawful consideration, knowing it was earned in whole or in part from the practice of prostitution, commits juvenile pimping."[562] Subsection (b) of this enactment provides an affirmative defense to this charge if a defendant reasonably believes that the prostitute was sixteen years of age or older or was not an institutionalized severely or profoundly mentally retarded person at the time of the offense.[563]

For example, a defendant was found guilty of juvenile pimping where he provided a thirteen-year-old child with instruction, clothing and cosmetics to assist the child in soliciting customers for prostitution, and then positioned the child in a good location for the business of prostitution and took all of the money that she received.[564]

§ 8.48. Exploitation of a Child.

A person, such as a pimp or panderer, who confines a child against his or her will, and who uses alcohol, illicit drugs, or a threat of substantial physical harm against a child of less than sixteen or an institutionalized severely or profoundly mentally retarded person in order to compel the child or retarded person to become a prostitute; arranges a situation where the child or retarded person can practice prostitution; or receives money from the child or retarded prostitute's illicit earnings commits the class X felony of "exploitation of a child."[565] This enactment reads as follows:

> A person commits exploitation of a child when he or she confines a child under the age of 16 or institutionalized severely or profoundly mentally retarded person against his or her will by the infliction or threat of imminent

---

[560] ILL. REV. STAT. ch. 38, para. 11-19 (Smith-Hurd 1979), 1961 Committee Comments, at 366 (revised 1972).

[561] 720 ILCS 5/11-19.1(c) (1999).

[562] 720 ILCS 5/11-19.1(a) (1999).

[563] 720 ILCS 5/11-19.1(b) (1999).

[564] People v. Harris, 157 Ill. App. 3d 70, 73, 510 N.E.2d 107, 110 (1st Dist. 1987). However, these same actions did not constitute "soliciting for a juvenile prostitute." *Id.*

[565] 720 ILCS 5/11-19.2 (1999).

infliction of great bodily harm, permanent disability or disfigurement or by administering to the child or an institutionalized severely or profoundly mentally retarded person without his or her consent or by threat or deception and for other than medical purposes, any alcoholic intoxicant or a drug as defined in the Controlled Substances Act or the Cannabis Control Act and: (1) Compels the child or an institutionalized severely or profoundly mentally retarded person to become a prostitute; or (2) Arranges a situation in which the child or an institutionalized severely or profoundly mentally retarded person may practice prostitution; or (3) Receives any money, property, token, object, or article or anything of value from the child or an institutionalized severely or profoundly mentally retarded person knowing it was obtained in whole or in part from the practice of prostitution.[566]

With respect to the statute's confinement requirement, the victim's free locomotion need not be absolutely restricted.[567] In order to constitute confinement, the state must show that the child submitted, against his or her will or inclination, to the control of the accused so that the accused was able to accomplish any of the prohibited activities described in the statute.[568]

§ 8.49. Sexual Exploitation of a Child.

In 1992, the legislature created the offense of "sexual exploitation of a child."[569] Section 5/11-9.1 of the Criminal Code of 1961 prohibits any person from (1) engaging in a sexual act or (2) exposing his or her sex organs, anus, or breast for the purpose of sexual arousal or gratification of such person or the child within the presence of a child and with intent or knowledge that a child would view his or her acts.[570] This section defines "sexual act" as masturbation, sexual conduct, or sexual penetration as defined in section 5/12-12 of the Criminal Code.[571] Sexual exploitation of a child is a misdemeanor and a subsequent violation is a felony.[572]

§ 8.50. Custodial Sexual Misconduct.

In 1997, the legislature created the offense of "custodial sexual misconduct."[573] This offense is codified in Section 5/11-9.2 and prohibits an employee of a penal system from engaging in sexual conduct or sexual penetration with

---

[566] 720 ILCS 5/11-19.2(A) (1999).

[567] People v. Goodson, 131 Ill. App. 3d 734, 739, 475 N.E.2d 1356, 1359-60 (5th Dist. 1985).

[568] People v. Goodson, 131 Ill. App. 3d 734, 739, 475 N.E.2d 1356, 1359-60 (5th Dist. 1985).

[569] 720 ILCS 5/11-9.1 (1999).

[570] 720 ILCS 5/11-9.1(a) (1999).

[571] 720 ILCS 5/11-9.1(b) (1999).

[572] 720 ILCS 5/11-9.1(c) (1999).

[573] 720 ILCS 5/11-9.2 (1999).

any person who is in the custody of a penal system.[574] This stricture also prohibits a probation or supervising officer from engaging in sexual conduct or sexual penetration with a probationer, parolee, or releasee who is under the supervisory, disciplinary, or custodial authority of the officer.[575] Custodial sexual misconduct is a felony.[576] Consent is not a defense to this charge because probationers, parolees, releasees, and inmates are deemed incapable of consent as a matter of law for the purposes of this offense.[577]

§ 8.51. Presence within School Zone By Child Sex Offenders.

In 1998, the Illinois legislature enacted the offense of "presence within school zone by child sex offenders."[578] This offense can occur in two ways. First, a child sex offender commits this offense when he or she is knowingly present in any school building, on any real property comprising the school, or in any property used for transportation of students to or from school when persons under the age of eighteen are present on the school property.[579] Second, a child sex offender commits this offense when he or she knowingly loiters on a public way within 500 feet of a school building or real property comprising the school when persons under the age of eighteen are present on the school property.[580] In both situations, the offense is not committed if the child sex offender is a parent or guardian of a child on the school property or has permission from the school principal, administrator, or board to be on the school property or on the public way.[581] Commission of this offense is a felony.[582]

A "child sex offender" is any person who has been charged with a sex offense and been either convicted, found not guilty by reason of insanity or is "the subject of a finding not resulting in an acquittal."[583] A "sex offense" includes any sex-related offense involving children, any kidnapping-related offense involving children, or any attempt to commit such offense, whether the offense is a violation of Illinois law or a breach of federal or another state's law, where such fed-

---

[574] 720 ILCS 5/11-9.2(a) (1999).

[575] 720 ILCS 5/11-9.2(b) (1999).

[576] 720 ILCS 5/11-9.2(c) (1999).

[577] 720 ILCS 5/11-9.2(e) (1999).

[578] 720 ILCS 5/11-9.3 (1999). *See* People v. Stork, 305 Ill. App. 3d 714, 719-26, 713 N.E.2d 187, 190-96 (2d Dist. 1999) (statute upheld as constitutional against claims that it was violative of procedural due process and substantive due process, was vague, constituted cruel and unusual punishment, and imposed disproportionate penalties).

[579] 720 ILCS 5/11-9.3(a) (1999).

[580] 720 ILCS 5/11-9.3(b) (1999).

[581] 720 ILCS 5/11-9.3(a)(1), (a)(2), 5/11-9.2(b)(1), (b)(2) (1999).

[582] 720 ILCS 5/11-9.2(d) (1999).

[583] 720 ILCS 5/11-9.3(c)(1) (1999).

eral or other state's law is the "substantial equivalent" of any Illinois law contemplated by this statute.[584]

§ 8.52. Obscenity.

The commercial dissemination of obscenity is proscribed by section 5/11-20. The prohibition of "obscenity" reads:

> A person commits obscenity when, with knowledge of the nature or content thereof, or recklessly failing to exercise reasonable inspection which would have disclosed the nature or content thereof, he: (1) Sells, delivers or provides, or offers or agrees to sell, deliver or provide any obscene writing, picture, record or other representation or embodiment of the obscene; or (2) Presents or directs an obscene play, dance or other performance or participates directly in that portion thereof which makes it obscene; or (3) Publishes, exhibits or otherwise makes available anything obscene; or (4) Performs an obscene act or otherwise presents an obscene exhibition of his body for gain; or (5) Creates, buys, procures or possesses obscene matter or material with intent to disseminate it in violation of this Section, or of the penal laws or regulations of any other jurisdiction; or (6) Advertises or otherwise promotes the sale of material represented or held out by him to be obscene, whether or not it is obscene.[585]

The term *obscene* is defined as follows:

> Any material or performance is obscene if: (1) the average person, applying contemporary adult community standards, would find that, taken as a whole, it appeals to the prurient interest; and (2) the average person, applying contemporary adult community standards, would find that it depicts or describes, in a patently offensive way, ultimate sexual acts or sadomasochistic sexual acts, whether normal or perverted, actual or simulated, or masturbation, excretory functions or lewd exhibition of the genitals; and (3) taken as a whole, it lacks serious literary, artistic, political or scientific value.[586]

Subsection (c) of the prohibition sets forth various directives regarding interpretation of evidence in an obscenity prosecution.[587] It states that obscenity "shall be judged with reference to ordinary adults," although it should be considered with reference to children if it may be directed to such an audience.[588] If

---

[584] 720 ILCS 5/11-9.3(c)(2), (c)(3) (1999).

[585] 720 ILCS 5/11-20(a) (1999).

[586] 720 ILCS 5/11-20(b) (1999).

[587] 720 ILCS 5/11-20(c) (1999).

[588] 720 ILCS 5/11-20(c) (1999).

the dissemination of the material "is being commercially exploited for the sake of its prurient appeal," this evidence can be used to "justify the conclusion that the matter is lacking in serious literary, artistic, political or scientific value" and, hence, is obscene.[589] In a prosecution of obscenity, evidence shall be admitted to show (1) the character of the audience to whom the material was directed; (2) the predominant appeal of the material to ordinary people and the type of effect, if any, it might have on them; (3) the material's artistic, literary, scientific, educational, or other merits, or the absence of such merits; (4) the degree of public acceptance of the material; (5) possible appeal to the prurient interest; and (6) the purpose of the author, creator, publisher, or disseminator.[590]

It is an affirmative defense to an obscenity charge that the dissemination (1) was "not for gain and was made to personal associates other than children under 18 years of age" or (2) was to institutions that had a "scientific or other special justification for possession of such material."[591] Private noncommercial dissemination of such material between adults is not a crime even if it might indicate impaired personal morals or mental health of the parties involved.[592]

Notwithstanding various attacks on grounds of unconstitutional vagueness or overbreadth, this statute has been upheld.[593] Furthermore, obscenity is not within the protection of the First Amendment.[594] In *Pope v. Illinois*,[595] the United States Supreme Court clarified the definition of *obscenity*. Although it held that the first two prongs of obscenity — appeal to the prurient interest and patent offensiveness — are to be measured against contemporary standards, the literary, artistic, political or scientific *value* of the materials is *not* to be gauged in terms of community standards.[596] The Court stated that this value judgment is not dependent on whether the government or a majority of the people approve of the ideas these works represent.[597] Obscenity determinations cannot rest solely on the lack of local community acceptance of the material.[598] Thus, the "proper inquiry is not whether an ordinary member of any given community would find

---

[589] 720 ILCS 5/11-20(c) (1999).

[590] 720 ILCS 5/11-20(c) (1999).

[591] 720 ILCS 5/11-20(f) (1999); *see* People v. Capital News, Inc., 137 Ill. 2d 162, 173, 560 N.E.2d 303, 308 (1990) (holding that the second affirmative defense to obscenity is not constitutionally vague), *cert. denied*, 498 U.S. 1120 (1991).

[592] ILL. ANN. STAT. ch. 38, para. 11-20 (Smith-Hurd 1979), 1961 Committee Comments, at 371 (revised 1972).

[593] *See, e.g.,* Ward v. Illinois, 431 U.S. 767, 773 (1977) (finding statute not overbroad or vague).

[594] Roth v. United States, 354 U.S. 476, 485 (1957).

[595] 481 U.S. 497 (1987).

[596] Pope v. Illinois, 481 U.S. 497, 500-01 (1987).

[597] Pope v. Illinois, 481 U.S. 497, 501 (1987) (quoting Miller v. California, 419 U.S. 15, 34 (1973)).

[598] Pope v. Illinois, 481 U.S. 497, 501 (1987) (quoting Miller v. California, 419 U.S. 15, 34 (1973)).

serious literary, artistic, political or scientific value in allegedly obscene material, but whether a reasonable person would find such value in the material, taken as a whole."[599] The Court pointed out that merely because only a minority of the population may believe a work has serious value does not mean the "reasonable person" standard has not been satisfied.[600]

Regarding the material itself, nudity alone does not make material obscene.[601] Even material that depicts two nude people of the same sex with their limbs and bodies intertwined is not obscene where there is no suggestion of sexual activities between the persons.[602] Nor are materials deemed obscene merely because the depiction focuses on human genitals.[603] However, if the material focuses repeatedly on the genital area and suggests imminent sexual activity, then it may be obscene.[604] On the other hand, if the depicted sexual conduct is a subplot to a main story line or is a subsidiary to a discernible plot that has some type of serious literary or artistic value, it is not obscene.[605]

Certain materials that graphically depict sexual intercourse, fellatio, and group sex with particular emphasis on the participants' genitals have been found to be obscene.[606] A novel that was no more than a chronicle of sexual encounters between its characters and that included vivid, intimately detailed accounts of sexual activity — including sodomy, flagellation, masturbation, anal intercourse, oral-genital contact, lesbianism, sadism, and masochism — was found to be obscene.[607] Where photographs in a magazine portrayed lesbianism, rape, whippings, beatings, bondage, axing, and other sexual behavior as its dominant theme, this was obscene.[608] It was also considered obscene that certain women danced nude in a nightclub and fondled their breasts and vaginal areas.[609] Finally, even though no one else was present in a place of business when a naked

---

[599] Pope v. Illinois, 481 U.S. 497, 501 (1987) (quoting Miller v. California, 419 U.S. 15, 34 (1973)).

[600] Pope v. Illinois, 481 U.S. 497, 501 n.3 (1987).

[601] City of Belleville v. Morgan, 60 Ill. App. 3d 434, 438-39, 376 N.E.2d 704, 708 (5th Dist. 1978).

[602] City of Chicago v. Geraci, 10 Ill. App. 3d 688, 692, 294 N.E.2d 725, 728 (1st Dist. 1973).

[603] City of Chicago v. Geraci, 10 Ill. App. 3d 688, 692, 294 N.E.2d 725, 728 (1st Dist. 1973).

[604] People v. Melander, 10 Ill. App. 3d 879, 881, 295 N.E.2d 20, 22 (2d Dist. 1973).

[605] People v. Correa, 191 Ill. App. 3d 823, 827, 548 N.E.2d 351, 353 (1st Dist. 1989) (comic books).

[606] People v. Speer, 52 Ill. App. 3d 203, 212, 367 N.E.2d 372, 378 (1st Dist. 1977).

[607] City of Chicago v. Geraci, 46 Ill. 2d 576, 582-83, 264 N.E.2d 153, 157 (1970). *Compare* People v. Romaine, 38 Ill. 2d 325, 327-29, 231 N.E.2d 413, 413-15 (1967) (The book "Fannie Hill" not obscene since it had literary and historical importance).

[608] City of Chicago v. Geraci, 46 Ill. 2d 576, 581-82, 264 N.E.2d 153, 156-57 (1970).

[609] People v. Better, 33 Ill. App. 3d 58, 65, 337 N.E.2d 272, 277-78 (1st Dist. 1975).

woman fondled the penis of a policeman for ten dollars, this was considered an "obscene" act.[610]

Material depicting sexual activity may not be obscene where it has literary, scientific, artistic or some other form of social importance.[611] On the other hand, merely because it reflects innocuous educational, literary, historical, or sociological text does not mean that the subject matter is not obscene if it otherwise depicts patently offensive sexual activity and, on the whole, lacks any socially redeeming value.[612]

The mens rea of knowledge or recklessness is a critical element of obscenity and can be proved by circumstantial evidence.[613] Direct evidence that a defendant has seen or read the obscene materials he or she sells is not required; it is sufficient that he or she is aware of the general obscene nature of the publication.[614] In addition, a defendant can be convicted if he or she recklessly fails to inspect obscenity over which he or she has control.[615] For example, a nightclub operator was convicted of obscenity where he failed to inspect a dancer's activities and where an inspection would have alerted him to the obscene content of those activities.[616] On the other hand, a bookstore employee could not be convicted where the state failed to prove either that she made three allegedly obscene films available for viewing by the general public while knowing their nature and content or that she recklessly refused to exercise reasonable inspection of the films.[617]

If the state prosecutes a defendant for possession of obscene material, the possession must be "with intent to disseminate" obscene material in violation of the law.[618] Nevertheless, a defendant charged under this subsection will not be exonerated where he or she purposely avoided learning about the contents of that which he or she intended to sell.[619]

In 1989, the Illinois Supreme Court addressed the issue of whether it is constitutional for the state, pursuant to sections 5/37-1 and 5/37-4 of the Criminal Code, to enjoin one who has distributed obscene material from a particular building from using that building for any purpose during a specified period of time, unless the distributor posts a bond that is forfeitable upon further sales of

---

[610] People v. Taylor, 35 Ill. App. 3d 418, 421, 342 N.E.2d 96, 98 (1st Dist. 1976).

[611] People v. Sikora, 32 Ill. 2d 260, 264, 204 N.E.2d 768, 770 (1965).

[612] City of Chicago v. Allen, 26 Ill. App. 3d 502, 504, 327 N.E.2d 414, 415-16 (1st Dist. 1975).

[613] People v. Rode, 57 Ill. App. 3d 645, 648, 373 N.E.2d 605, 608 (1st Dist. 1978) (knowledge).

[614] People v. Glass, 41 Ill. App. 3d 43, 47-48, 353 N.E.2d 214, 217-18 (1st Dist. 1976).

[615] People v. Better, 33 Ill. App. 3d 58, 67, 337 N.E.2d 272, 279 (1st Dist. 1975).

[616] People v. Better, 33 Ill. App. 3d 58, 67, 337 N.E.2d 272, 279 (1st Dist. 1975). See also People v. Vavrys, 47 Ill. App. 2d 258, 261, 198 N.E.2d 187, 188 (1st Dist. 1964) (holding it was no excuse that nightclub owner did not present or direct obscene performance).

[617] People v. Hart, 101 Ill. App. 3d 343, 350, 427 N.E.2d 1352, 1358-59 (2d Dist. 1981).

[618] 720 ILCS 5/11-20(a)(5) (1999).

[619] People v. Tannahill, 38 Ill. App. 3d 767, 772-73, 348 N.E.2d 847, 851-52 (4th Dist. 1976).

obscenity from the premises.[620] In *People v. Sequoia Books, Inc.,*[621] the court found that the incidental restriction on protected speech resulting from this statute was greater than that which is essential to further the important government interest the statute was designed to promote.[622] The court determined section 5/37-1 merely stated that a building used in the commission of obscenity offenses is to be considered a public nuisance, and that a person who knowingly maintains such a nuisance commits a misdemeanor.[623] The court explicitly refused to determine whether section 5/37-1 is unconstitutional as applied to obscenity.[624] The court held, however, that section 5/37-4 is unconstitutional as applied to properties that have been adjudicated or asserted to be nuisances solely on account of their use in the commission of the offense of obscenity under section 5/11-20.[625]

§ 8.53. Child Pornography.

A felony prohibition against "child pornography" appears in section 5/11-20.1.[626] Subsection (a)(1) makes it an offense to film, videotape, photograph, or otherwise depict by a similar visual medium or computer any child the person "knows or reasonably should know to be under the age of 18 or any institutionalized severely or profoundly mentally retarded person," in which the child or retarded person actually or by simulation is (1) engaged in any act of sexual intercourse with a person or animal; (2) engaged in any sexual activity involving contact between the child's or retarded person's mouth, anus, or sex organs and another person or animal, or vice versa; (3) engaged in an act of masturbation; (4) portrayed in any act of lewd fondling or touching with another person or animal; (5) engaged in any act of excretion or urination within a sexual context; (6) portrayed as bound, fettered, or subject to sadistic, masochistic, or sadomasochistic abuse in any sexual context; or (7) portrayed in any pose involving a lewd exhibition of the unclothed genitals, pubic area, buttocks or breasts (if

---

[620] *See* People v. Sequoia Books, Inc., 127 Ill. 2d 271, 537 N.E.2d 302, *cert. denied*, 490 U.S. 1097 (1989).

[621] 127 Ill. 2d 271, 537 N.E.2d 302, *cert. denied*, 490 U.S. 1097 (1989).

[622] People v. Sequoia Books, Inc., 127 Ill. 2d 271, 288, 537 N.E.2d 302, 310, *cert. denied*, 490 U.S. 1097 (1989).

[623] People v. Sequoia Books, Inc., 127 Ill. 2d 271, 291, 537 N.E.2d 302, 312, *cert. denied*, 490 U.S. 1097 (1989).

[624] People v. Sequoia Books, Inc., 127 Ill. 2d 271, 291, 537 N.E.2d 302, 312, *cert. denied*, 490 U.S. 1097 (1989).

[625] People v. Sequoia Books, Inc., 127 Ill. 2d 271, 291, 537 N.E.2d 302, 312, *cert. denied*, 490 U.S. 1097 (1989). *See also* People v. Eagle Books, Inc., 151 Ill. 2d 235, 246-55, 602 N.E.2d 798, 803-07 (1992) (seizure of over 700 magazines constitutes prior restraint violative of First Amendment).

[626] 720 ILCS 5/11-20.1 (1999).

female) of the child, retarded person, or any other person.[627] Subsection (a)(2) makes it criminal, knowing the content thereof, to disseminate, or to possess with intent to disseminate such visual media reflecting the activities described in subsection (a)(1).[628] Subsection (a)(3) proscribes as illegal the production of any stage play, live performance, or other visual media portrayal that includes the activities described in subsection (a)(1) with knowledge of the subject matter.[629] Subsection (a)(4) labels as criminal the solicitation of any child or retarded person described in subsection (a)(1) to appear in any live performance or other visual medium that includes the activities described in subsection (a)(1).[630] Subsection (a)(5) prohibits a parent, legal guardian, or other person having control over a child or retarded person, as described in subsection (a)(1), from knowingly permitting or arranging the child's or retarded person's involvement in any live performance or visual medium while engaged in the activities described in subsection (a)(1).[631] Subsection (a)(6) prohibits a person from knowingly possessing any film, videotape, photograph, or the like, as described in subsection (a)(1), of any child whom the person knows or reasonably should know to be under eighteen or to be institutionalized or severely mentally retarded.[632] Subsection (a)(7) prohibits a person from soliciting, inducing or coercing another person to provide a child or retarded person to appear in a videotape or any other depiction engaged in the activities described in subsection (a)(1).[633] Whenever a defendant possesses more than one copy of the same film, videotape or visual reproduction or depiction by computer, containing child pornography, such possession creates a rebuttable presumption that the defendant had the intent to disseminate them.[634]

There are two affirmative defenses to charges of child pornography. First, the defendant has a defense if he or she reasonably believed the child was eighteen or older or that the person was not an institutionalized severely or profoundly mentally retarded person and "took some affirmative action or made a bonafide inquiry" regarding the age of the child or the status of the individual who was retarded on which he reasonably relied.[635] Second, the defendant has a defense if he or she was performing official law enforcement duties or was a licensed phy-

---

[627] 720 ILCS 5/11-20.1(a)(1) (1999).
[628] 720 ILCS 5/11-20.1(a)(2) (1999).
[629] 720 ILCS 5/11-20.1(a)(3) (1999).
[630] 720 ILCS 5/11-20.1(a)(4) (1999).
[631] 720 ILCS 5/11-20.1(a)(5) (1999).
[632] 720 ILCS 5/11-20.1(a)(6) (1999).
[633] 720 ILCS 5/11-20.1(a)(7) (1999).
[634] 720 ILCS 5/11-20.1(b)(4) (1999).
[635] 720 ILCS 5/11-20.1(b)(1) (1999).

sician, psychologist or social worker engaged in bona fide treatment or professional programs.[636]

In *New York v. Ferber*,[637] the United States Supreme Court ruled that the First Amendment did not protect depictions of minors engaged in actual or simulated sexual activity and, accordingly, upheld a state child pornography statute. The court allowed punishment for the depictions not because they were obscene but because they were obtained by sexually abusing and exploiting children.[638]

While *Ferber* dealt with a statute directed at the promotion and distribution of child pornography, in *Osborne v. Ohio*,[639] the Court upheld the constitutionality of a state statute that outlawed any possession or viewing of child pornography. The Court upheld the legislative judgment of the state that child pornography is harmful to the psychological, emotional, and mental health of children depicted in child pornography.[640] Since child pornography is largely an underground activity, the state could properly attempt to dry up the market for this material by prohibiting its possession and viewing as well as its distribution.[641] Thus, there was a compelling state interest that outweighed any possible First Amendment interest in possession or viewing such material.[642] In *People v. Geever*,[643] the Illinois Supreme Court found the Illinois child pornography statute constitutional after determining the purpose of the statute was to prevent the sexual abuse of children by "drying up" the market for such material rather than to limit the individual's freedom of thought and mind in his own home and, thus, not an infringement of constitutional rights.[644]

Illinois courts have interpreted the word "lewd," which is found in the Illinois child pornography statute, by examination of various factors. Whether a visual depiction constitutes the lascivious or lewd exhibition of the genitals involves consideration of (1) whether the focal point of the visual depiction is on the child's genitals; (2) whether the setting of the visual depiction is sexually aggressive, that is, in a place or pose generally associated with sexual activity; (3) whether the child is depicted in an unnatural pose, or in inappropriate attire considering the child's age; (4) whether the child is partially or totally nude; (5) whether the visual depiction suggests sexual coyness or a willingness to engage in sexual activity; and (6) whether the visual depiction is intended to elicit a

---

[636] 720 ILCS 5/11-20.1(b)(3) (1999).

[637] 458 U.S. 747 (1982).

[638] *See* Joan S. Colen, Note, *Child Pornography: Ban the Speech and Spare the Child? — New York v. Ferber*, 32 DEPAUL L. REV. 685 (1983) (excellent critique of court's reasoning in *Ferber*).

[639] 495 U.S. 103 (1990).

[640] Osborne v. Ohio, 495 U.S. 103, 109 (1990).

[641] Osborne v. Ohio, 495 U.S. 103, 110 (1990).

[642] Osborne v. Ohio, 495 U.S. 103, 110 (1990).

[643] 122 Ill. 2d 313, 522 N.E.2d 1200 (1988).

[644] People v. Geever, 122 Ill. 2d 313, 326-27, 522 N.E.2d 1200, 1206-07 (1988).

sexual response in the viewer.[645] The visual depiction need not involve all of these factors to be considered lewd.[646] In one case, the Illinois appellate court held that the pictures the defendant had in his possession were "lewd" since they were photographs depicting prepubescent girls who were adroitly and dexterously posed and were focused on the breasts, vaginas, and buttocks of the young girls.[647] Where photographs depicted a 61-year-old male defendant posing completely naked with a partial erection and with his arm around two different thirteen-year-old topless girls, the Illinois Supreme Court found these photographs to be lewd.[648] However, photographs of the same two thirteen-year-old girls standing together baring their unclothed breasts were not lewd.[649] Meanwhile, in another case, there was no "lewd" exhibition where the photograph in question depicted a sexually mature girl's breasts and pubic hair but did not show her genitals.[650] And, where another defendant directed sexual acts that minor and adult men were to perform on each other and then joined in the activity himself, this did not contribute "a live presentation or performance" as contemplated by the child pornography statute, inasmuch as the activity occurred in the privacy of defendant's office.[651]

In order to establish that the persons portrayed in child pornography material are actually under the age of eighteen, the state is not required to offer proof of the subject's age through evidence independent of the materials in question or through expert testimony.[652] Thus, a trier of fact could properly determine that persons in a videotape were below the age of eighteen based on his "own everyday observations and common experiences."[653]

§ 8.54. Commercial Processing of Films Depicting Child Sexual Activity.

In 1986, the offense falling under the heading "commercial film and photographic print processor — reports" was created.[654] It requires any commercial film and photographic print processor "who has knowledge of or observes" any film, negatives or the like that "depicts a child whom the processor knows or

[645] People v. Lamborn, 185 Ill. 2d 585, 592, 708 N.E.2d 350, 354 (1999).

[646] People v. Lamborn, 185 Ill. 2d 585, 592-93, 708 N.E.2d 350, 355 (1999).

[647] People v. Johnson, 186 Ill. App. 3d 116, 121-22, 542 N.E.2d 143, 146-47 (1st Dist. 1989).

[648] People v. Lamborn, 185 Ill. 2d 585, 595-96, 708 N.E.2d 350, 356-57 (1999).

[649] People v. Lamborn, 185 Ill. 2d 585, 594-95, 708 N.E.2d 350, 355-56 (1999).

[650] People v. Dailey, 196 Ill. App. 3d 807, 811-12, 554 N.E.2d 1051, 1054 (1st Dist. 1990).

[651] People v. Davis, 260 Ill. App. 3d 176, 192-94, 631 N.E.2d 392, 404-05 (2d Dist. 1994), cert. denied, 513 U.S. 1191 (1995).

[652] People v. Thomann, 197 Ill. App. 3d 488, 497-98, 554 N.E.2d 748, 754 (4th Dist. 1990), cert. denied, 499 U.S. 960 (1991).

[653] People v. Thomann, 197 Ill. App. 3d 488, 499, 554 N.E.2d 748, 755 (4th Dist. 1990), cert. denied, 499 U.S. 960 (1991) (expert testimony was offered in the case, but it was not necessary to judge's findings, in bench trial, that subjects portrayed in videotape were minors).

[654] 720 ILCS 5/11-20.2 (1999).

reasonably should know to be under the age of 18" involved in various types of sexual activity, or simulations thereof, to report such knowledge or observation to the police.[655] In effect, this statute creates a legal duty for the commercial film processor, the breach of which constitutes an offense.[656] The statute lists the type of activity that must alert the film processor, including activity or simulations involving (1) sexual intercourse with another person or animal, (2) fellatio, cunnilingus, or anal sex with another person or animal, (3) masturbation, (4) lewd fondling with another person or animal, (5) excretion or urination within a sexual context, or (6) binding, fettering or subjecting to sadistic, masochistic, or sadomasochistic abuse in a sexual context.[657]

§ 8.55. Harmful Material.

Section 5/11-21 punishes the dissemination of "harmful material" to persons under the age of eighteen as a misdemeanor.[658] The definition of *harmful material* overlaps significantly with the definition of *obscene material:*

> Material is harmful if, to the average person, applying contemporary standards, its predominant appeal, taken as a whole, is to prurient interest, that is a shameful or morbid interest in nudity, sex, or excretion, which goes substantially beyond customary limits of candor in description or representation of such matters, and is material the redeeming social importance of which is substantially less than its prurient appeal.[659]

It is an affirmative defense to this charge that (1) the circulation of the harmful material transpired in a library, provided that the dissemination was "in aid of a legitimate scientific or educational purpose;"[660] (2) a parent distributed such material to his child;[661] (3) a defendant distributed such material to a minor who presented false documentation of his age and the defendant relied on the documentation;[662] or (4) the defendant distributed the material to a minor (a) "where there was no personal confrontation of the child by the defendant" or his agents, such as where the harmful material was distributed to a minor by mail; (b) where the defendant's advertisement required the purchaser to certify he was eighteen or more; *and* (c) where the purchaser falsely represented his age.[663] It is a sepa-

---

[655] 720 ILCS 5/11-20.2 (1999).
[656] 720 ILCS 5/11-20.2 (1999). Failure to report constitutes a "business offense" punishable by a fine of $1000.
[657] 720 ILCS 5/11-20.2 (1999).
[658] 720 ILCS 5/11-21 (1999).
[659] 720 ILCS 5/11-21(b)(1) (1999).
[660] 720 ILCS 5/11-21(e)(1) (1999).
[661] 720 ILCS 5/11-21(e)(2) (1999).
[662] 720 ILCS 5/11-21(e)(3) (1999).
[663] 720 ILCS 5/11-21(e)(4) (1999).

rate misdemeanor offense for a minor to falsify his age in order to gain access to harmful material.[664]

§ 8.56. Tie-In Sales of Obscene Publications to Distributors.

A person, entity, or agent who is engaged in the business of distributing publications and who refuses to furnish any retail dealer certain legitimate publications because the dealer refuses to sell or distribute the distributor's publications that are "obscene, lewd, lascivious, filthy or indecent" commits a petty offense.[665] This offense, known as "tie-in sales of obscene publications to distributors," obviously protects the retailer who is pressured by his or her distributor to sell the distributor's illegal material.

---

[664] 720 ILCS 5/11-21(f) (1999).
[665] 720 ILCS 5/11-22 (1999).

CHAPTER 9

ASSAULT, BATTERY, AND RELATED OFFENSES

§ 9.01. Introduction.

Contained within the parameters of 720 ILCS article 5/12 are the offenses involving "bodily harm."[1] They include assault,[2] aggravated assault,[3] vehicular endangerment,[4] battery,[5] battery of an unborn child,[6] domestic battery,[7] aggravated battery,[8] heinous battery,[9] aggravated battery with a firearm,[10] aggravated battery of a child,[11] aggravated battery of an unborn child,[12] tampering with food, drugs or cosmetics,[13] aggravated battery of a senior citizen,[14] drug induced infliction of great bodily harm,[15] drug induced infliction of aggravated battery to

---

[1] 720 ILCS 5/12 (1999).
[2] 720 ILCS 5/12-1 (1999).
[3] 720 ILCS 5/12-2 (1999).
[4] 720 ILCS 5/12-2.5 (1999).
[5] 720 ILCS 5/12-3 (1999).
[6] 720 ILCS 5/12-3.1 (1999).
[7] 720 ILCS 5/12-3.2 (1999).
[8] 720 ILCS 5/12-4 (1999).
[9] 720 ILCS 5/12-4.1 (1999).
[10] 720 ILCS 5/12-4.2 (1999).
[11] 720 ILCS 5/12-4.3 (1999).
[12] 720 ILCS 5/12-4.4 (1999).
[13] 720 ILCS 5/12-4.5 (1999).
[14] 720 ILCS 5/12-4.6 (1999).
[15] 720 ILCS 5/12-4.7 (1999).

a child athlete,[16] reckless conduct,[17] criminal housing management,[18] intimidation,[19] compelling organization membership of persons,[20] aggravated intimidation,[21] interfering with the reporting of domestic violence,[22] compelling confession or information by force or threat,[23] hate crime,[24] educational intimidation,[25] stalking,[26] aggravated stalking,[27] threatening public officials,[28] tattooing body of minor,[29] home invasion,[30] vehicular invasion,[31] criminal transmission of HIV,[32] abuse and gross neglect of a long term care facility resident,[33] sale of body parts,[34] criminal neglect of an elderly or disabled person,[35] child abandonment,[36] endangering the life or health of a child,[37] violation of order of protection,[38] inducement to commit suicide,[39] ritual mutilation,[40] ritualized abuse of a child,[41] and female genital mutilation.[42] Article 5/12 also includes sex offenses,[43] which are explored in chapter 8. Armed violence,[44] which is not a part of article 5/12, is also discussed in this chapter.

---

[16] 720 ILCS 5/12-4.9 (1999).
[17] 720 ILCS 5/12-5 (1999).
[18] 720 ILCS 5/12-5.1 (1999).
[19] 720 ILCS 5/12-6 (1999).
[20] 720 ILCS 5/12-6.1 (1999).
[21] 720 ILCS 5/12-6.2 (1999).
[22] 720 ILCS 5/12-6.3 (1999).
[23] 720 ILCS 5/12-7 (1999).
[24] 720 ILCS 5/12-7.1 (1999).
[25] 720 ILCS 5/12-7.2 (1999).
[26] 720 ILCS 5/12-7.3 (1999).
[27] 720 ILCS 5/12-7.4 (1999).
[28] 720 ILCS 5/12-9 (1999).
[29] 720 ILCS 5/12-10 (1999).
[30] 720 ILCS 5/12-11 (1999).
[31] 720 ILCS 5/12-11.1 (1999).
[32] 720 ILCS 5/12-16.2 (1999).
[33] 720 ILCS 5/12-19 (1999).
[34] 720 ILCS 5/12-20 (1999).
[35] 720 ILCS 5/12-21 (1999).
[36] 720 ILCS 5/12-21.5 (1999).
[37] 720 ILCS 5/12-21.6 (1999).
[38] 720 ILCS 5/12-30 (1999).
[39] 720 ILCS 5/12-31 (1999).
[40] 720 ILCS 5/12-32 (1999).
[41] 720 ILCS 5/12-33 (1999).
[42] 720 ILCS 5/12-34 (1999).
[43] 720 ILCS 5/12-13 through 5/12-18 (1999).
[44] 720 ILCS 5/33A-1 through 5/33A-3 (1999).

§ 9.02. Assault.

Under former Illinois law,[45] criminal assault was an attempt to commit a battery, consistent with the early common law concept.[46] Today, in most jurisdictions, assault also encompasses the intent to frighten[47] and other unlawful conduct that places another in reasonable apprehension of receiving a battery.[48] This change in definition reflects an abandonment of the common law approach in favor of the current tort concept of intentional frightening that previously served only as the basis of civil assault.[49] In Illinois, the scope of the offense has been both narrowed by having the former type of assault that focused on the attempt to commit a battery now be encompassed by the general attempt statute, and broadened by including the tort concept of assault.[50] If there is any wrongful touching of the victim, the crime is battery and not assault.[51]

---

[45] Under ILL. REV. STAT. ch. 38 § 55 (1961) (repealed), assault was an unlawful attempt coupled with the present ability to violently injure another. Assault and battery was a single offense defined as the unlawful beating of another. ILL. REV. STAT. ch. 38 § 56 (1961) (repealed). The provisions that previously covered assault and battery were repealed in January of 1962.

[46] ROLLIN M. PERKINS & RONALD N. BOYCE, CRIMINAL LAW 159-60 (3d ed. 1982). The authors point out the early common-law distinction between the criminal offense of assault (an attempt to commit a battery) and assault as the basis of a civil action (intentionally placing another in apprehension of receiving an immediate battery). It is this latter tort concept of assault which Illinois had not included in the scope of the prior criminal assault definition.

[47] The elements of the "intent to frighten" type of assault as (a) resort to some threatening conduct, (b) intent either to injure or to frighten, and (c) success in placing the victim in reasonable apprehension of immediate bodily harm. WAYNE LAFAVE & AUSTIN SCOTT, CRIMINAL LAW § 7.16(b) (2d ed. 1986).

[48] WAYNE LAFAVE & AUSTIN SCOTT, CRIMINAL LAW § 7.16(b) (2d ed. 1986) (noting that the majority of jurisdictions have expanded the scope of simple assault to include the tort concept of civil assault in addition to the attempted battery type of assault). Illinois is in the minority in narrowing the scope to the tort concept without reference to the attempted battery. 720 ILCS 5/12-1 (1999).

[49] RESTATEMENT (SECOND) OF TORTS § 21 (1965) (actor must intend to arouse apprehension in victim). See People v. Kettler, 121 Ill. App. 3d 1, 4-5, 459 N.E.2d 7, 9-10 (4th Dist. 1984) (discussing redefinition of assault in Illinois).

[50] ILL. ANN. STAT. ch. 38, para. 12-1 (Smith-Hurd 1979), 1961 Committee Comments, at 406 (revised 1972). See People v. Kettler, 121 Ill. App. 3d 1, 4-5, 459 N.E.2d 7, 9-10 (4th Dist. 1984) (discussing legislative change).

[51] See, e.g., People v. Stuller, 71 Ill. App. 3d 118, 123, 389 N.E.2d 593, 596 (5th Dist. 1979):

> [T]o commit an assault there must be conduct which places another in a reasonable apprehension of receiving a battery and that if there has been any touching or other form of physical contact with the victim, a battery has been committed and not an assault, assuming the presence of the other requirements of battery.

§ 9.03. — Assault Codified.

The current Illinois statute on assault, found in section 5/12-1, reads as follows: "A person commits an assault when, without lawful authority, he engages in conduct which places another in reasonable apprehension of receiving a battery."[52] This statute, which makes assault a misdemeanor, was designed to change the Illinois law of assault, as it previously existed, in three important respects: (1) the prior law was defined in terms of an "unlawful attempt" to batter, but the current law requires no proof of "attempt," which in turn does away with the need to address the requirement of "specific intent" (which is always necessary to prove an "attempt"); (2) the earlier statute required proof of the defendant's "present ability" to commit a battery, whereas the present law contains no such requirement; and (3) the prior law required no reasonable apprehension of a battery by the victim, which is now an essential element of the crime.[53]

The above changes accomplished several important goals. First, removal of the "attempt" language from the assault statute returns the concern regarding attempted battery to the substantive criminal attempt statute, which addresses the attempt to commit any crime. Second, the troublesome problem of presenting evidence of the defendant's specific intent is avoided. Third, by focusing on the victim's apprehension of a felony, the assault statute expands the prosecutorial possibilities. Where evidence of the defendant's wrongful mental state is strong and evidence of the victim's fear is weak or non-existent, prosecution for an attempted battery remains an option. And where there exists strong evidence regarding the victim's apprehension, but evidence of the accused's specific intent is weak or absent, the defendant can be prosecuted for assault.

§ 9.04. — Elements of Assault.

The elements of simple assault include: (1) engaging in conduct that succeeds (2) in placing another in reasonable apprehension of receiving a battery. The element "placing another" is self explanatory. What constitutes a battery is discussed at length later in this chapter.[54] The remaining elements, conduct and reasonable apprehension, are discussed at length below.

§ 9.05. — The Meaning of "Conduct."

The conduct constituting an assault need create only the fear of actual, imminent bodily contact. If there has been any touching or any other form of physical

---

[52] 720 ILCS 5/12-1 (1999).

[53] ILL. ANN. STAT. ch. 38, para. 12-1 (Smith-Hurd 1979), 1961 Committee Comments, at 406 (revised 1972); People v. Kettler, 121 Ill. App. 3d 1, 5, 459 N.E.2d 7, 10 (4th Dist. 1984).

[54] *See* §§ 9.13-9.19 of this chapter.

contact with the victim, battery rather than assault has been committed.[55] The perpetration of a battery on the victim does not, however, preclude the commission of an assault if the battered victim is placed in apprehension of receiving a further battery.[56] Thus, where A was wounded by a shot fired by B and was thereafter apprehensive about additional shots that were being fired after he was wounded, A was assaulted and battered.[57] Similarly, where C testified that she was in reasonable apprehension of receiving a battery before she was shot by D, an assault conviction would be warranted.[58]

The apprehension-creating conduct may, but need not, include the use of a weapon or a threatening instrumentality.[59] Conduct involving a weapon may range from (1) a threat made by a display of a weapon, as where A pointed a loaded revolver at B, who was within shooting distance, in a menacing manner;[60] to (2) a purposeful suggestion of a weapon without the actual display of it, as where A thrust his hand, which he held hidden in his overcoat pocket, into B's side and said "Stick 'em up";[61] to (3) only the possibility of a weapon inadvertently suggested by the actor, as where A, an allegedly armed arrestee, suddenly dropped his hands toward his sides in disobeyance of a hands-over-head request by B, a police officer.[62]

The assaultive conduct usually consists of gestures coupled with verbal threats. Mere words alone, regardless of how threatening they might be, that are unaccompanied by some menacing act or gesture will not constitute an assault.[63] In conjunction with the use of words, the courts will look to the conduct of the defendant including the temperament and proximity of the defendant to the vic-

---

[55] People v. Abrams, 48 Ill. 2d 446, 459-60, 271 N.E.2d 37, 45 (1971); People v. Tiller, 61 Ill. App. 3d 785, 795, 378 N.E.2d 282, 290 (5th Dist. 1978).

[56] People v. Stuller, 71 Ill. App. 3d 118, 123, 389 N.E.2d 593, 596 (5th Dist. 1979). This also suggests that a battery could precede an assault where it is possible that the conduct will resume.

[57] People v. Stuller, 71 Ill. App. 3d 118, 123, 389 N.E.2d 593, 596 (5th Dist. 1979) (evidence established armed violence based on assault where victim, after he was shot, took evasive action to avoid being hit by subsequent shots).

[58] People v. Stuller, 71 Ill. App. 3d 118, 123, 389 N.E.2d 593, 596 (5th Dist. 1979) (evidence established armed violence based on assault where victim, before being shot, was in reasonable apprehension of a battery).

[59] People v. Rockwood, 358 Ill. 422, 425, 193 N.E. 449, 450 (1934).

[60] People v. Rockwood, 358 Ill. 422, 425, 193 N.E. 449, 450 (1934) (assault with intent to rob conviction affirmed).

[61] People v. Preis, 27 Ill. 2d 315, 319, 189 N.E.2d 254, 256 (1963).

[62] Anton v. Lehpamer, 534 F. Supp. 239, 242 (N.D. Ill. 1982) (decided on basis of Illinois law).

[63] People v. Ferguson, 181 Ill. App. 3d 950, 953, 537 N.E.2d 880, 882 (1st Dist. 1989). *But see* ROLLIN M. PERKINS & RONALD N. BOYCE, CRIMINAL LAW 178 (3d ed. 1982) (informational words might take place of threatening gesture and constitute assault); WAYNE LAFAVE & AUSTIN SCOTT, CRIMINAL LAW § 7.16 (2d ed. 1986) (informational words without overt acts might constitute assault).

tim.[64] Accordingly, a perpetrator was properly convicted of assault where he verbally threatened to kick the victim and the threats where made at close range with anger and hostility.[65] Assault was found where A held up a piece of cable in the manner of a club toward B, a driver of another vehicle, whose head A had just threatened to "blow off";[66] where A visited B's office and concluded the visit by stating, "I am going to shoot you," stood up while placing her hand in her bulging coat pocket, and made a hidden gesture;[67] and where A walked over to B's car and, while holding a pocket knife at his side, told B to "dim [his] damn lights."[68] The mere act of physically approaching or advancing toward another unarmed person may supply a gesture that, coupled with verbal threats, is sufficiently menacing to constitute an assault. Such was found to be the case where A, a six-foot 240-pound man, approached B, a small woman confined to a wheel chair, and verbally threatened her with physical harm,[69] and where A entered C's office, advanced to within inches of him, and demanded rent payments while threatening C with physical harm.[70]

§9.06. — The Meaning of Reasonable Apprehension.

To constitute an assault, the actor's conduct must succeed in placing another person in *reasonable apprehension* of receiving a battery. If the other person fails to notice the threatened use of force, there is no assault.[71] Thus, where A fired a shot at B that knocked B's hat from his head, there was no assault, for B was not aware that A might fire at him before the actual occurrence.[72]

When the conduct succeeds at creating apprehension, the apprehension must be reasonable under the circumstances. The standard employed in determining whether a reasonable apprehension existed is an objective standard, "the apprehension must be one which would normally be aroused in the mind of a reasonable person."[73] Thus, idiosyncratic characteristics of a particular victim, such as extreme timidity or frightfulness, are not admissible for determining apprehension.[74] However, facts known to the victim at the time of the assault are admis-

---

[64] People v. Ferguson, 181 Ill. App. 3d 950, 954, 537 N.E.2d 880, 882 (1st Dist. 1989).

[65] People v. Ferguson, 181 Ill. App. 3d 950, 954, 537 N.E.2d 880, 882 (1st Dist. 1989).

[66] People v. Holverson, 32 Ill. App. 3d 459, 460, 336 N.E.2d 88, 89 (2d Dist. 1975).

[67] People v. Preis, 27 Ill. 2d 315, 317, 189 N.E.2d 254, 256 (1963).

[68] People v. Smith, 132 Ill. App. 2d 1028, 1029, 271 N.E.2d 61, 62 (3d Dist. 1971).

[69] People v. Rynberk, 92 Ill. App. 3d 112, 116-17, 415 N.E.2d 1087, 1091 (1st Dist. 1980).

[70] People v. Rynberk, 92 Ill. App. 3d 112, 114-15, 415 N.E.2d 1087, 1092 (1st Dist. 1980). This case involved two separate assault incidents.

[71] People v. Tiller, 61 Ill. App. 3d 785, 795, 378 N.E.2d 282, 290 (5th Dist. 1978).

[72] People v. Tiller, 61 Ill. App. 3d 785, 795, 378 N.E.2d 282, 290 (5th Dist. 1978).

[73] In re C.L., 180 Ill. App. 3d 173, 177-78, 534 N.E.2d 1330, 1334-1335 (1st Dist. 1989) (quoting W. KEETON, PROSSER & KEETON ON TORTS § 10, at 44 (5th ed. 1984)).

[74] In re C.L., 180 Ill. App. 3d 173, 178, 534 N.E.2d 1330, 1334 (1st Dist. 1989).

sible in determining the reasonableness of the apprehension.[75] Therefore, where the perpetrator wore the colors black and yellow, knowledge by the victim that black and yellow were the colors of a street gang was properly considered in determining if the apprehension of receiving a battery was reasonable.[76]

The reasonableness of the apprehension is a question of fact.[77] The victim need not expressly testify about his or her apprehension if it can be inferred from the facts and circumstances that the apprehension was reasonable.[78] Where A pointed a gun at B while shouting that he was going to shoot out the spotlight on B's car, the facts supported an inference of reasonable apprehension by B.[79] Where A pulled his car into a parking lot at an angle to B's car and, after addressing profane words to the occupants of B's vehicle, threatened to shoot out B's tires, proceeded to walk to the trunk of his car, opened the trunk, and made a sound like a gun being loaded, B's apprehension was reasonable.[80] However, where defendant caused fear in his victim by riding a bicycle toward her and uttering the words "come here you," this did not amount to a reasonable apprehension required for an assault conviction.[81]

The apprehensive must be one of receiving an "imminent" or "immediate" battery.[82] The concept of immediate bodily harm, as routinely included in statutory definitions of tortious assault, refers to the actor's ability to convey to the victim that there will be no significant delay between the apprehension-creating conduct and the actual contact.[83] An examination of Illinois caselaw reveals that the judiciary has explicitly interpreted criminal assault to include the element of immediate harm.[84] Where a defendant threatened to kill two police officers while strapped in a hospital bed, the court held that no assault occurred because no reasonable person would have felt apprehension of receiving an "immediate battery" from a person who was strapped down to a hospital bed and about to have his stomach pumped.[85]

---

[75] In re C.L., 180 Ill. App. 3d 173, 178, 534 N.E.2d 1330, 1335 (1st Dist. 1989).

[76] In re C.L., 180 Ill. App. 3d 173, 178, 534 N.E.2d 1330, 1335 (1st Dist. 1989).

[77] People v. Enerson, 202 Ill. App. 3d 748, 749, 559 N.E.2d 801, 803 (3d Dist. 1990); People v. Ferguson, 181 Ill. App. 3d 950, 953, 537 N.E.2d 880, 882 (1st Dist. 1989); People v. Rynberk, 92 Ill. App. 3d 112, 116, 415 N.E.2d 1087, 1091 (1st Dist. 1980).

[78] People v. Enerson, 202 Ill. App. 3d 748, 749, 559 N.E.2d 801, 803 (3d Dist. 1990) (where defendant took a step toward victim while brandishing a knife and defendant was only one and one-half feet away, aggravated assault existed).

[79] People v. Harkey, 69 Ill. App. 3d 94, 96, 386 N.E.2d 1151, 1152 (5th Dist. 1979).

[80] People v. Chrisopulos, 82 Ill. App. 3d 581, 585, 402 N.E.2d 912, 915 (2d Dist. 1980).

[81] People v. Floyd, 278 Ill. App. 3d 568, 570-72, 663 N.E.2d 74, 76-77 (1st Dist. 1996).

[82] People v. Kettler, 121 Ill. App. 3d 1, 6, 459 N.E.2d 7, 10 (4th Dist. 1984).

[83] RESTATEMENT (SECOND) OF TORTS § 29(1) comment (1965).

[84] People v. Kettler, 121 Ill. App. 3d 1, 6, 459 N.E.2d 7, 10 (4th Dist. 1984) (assault does not encompass "some threat of harm at an unspecified future date . . . .").

[85] People v. Kettler, 121 Ill. App. 3d 1, 6, 459 N.E.2d 7, 11 (4th Dist. 1984).

In our view, the only way defendant's conviction for aggravated assault could stand is if we read the statute as making criminal a threat of a future battery, as distinguished from a threat of an immediate battery; that is, if the officers believed that there was a possibility defendant would carry out the threat after he was released from the hospital. We have discovered no authority holding that a threat of future violence is sufficient to constitute an assault and, in fact, we find the weight of authority to the contrary.[86]

Likewise, where a person is victimized by some type of forcible felony, this will not necessarily constitute the specific apprehension of receiving a battery necessary for a finding of assault. For example, where a victim is kidnapped at gunpoint, he or she may not necessarily be placed in reasonable apprehension of receiving a battery, although he or she may possibly be frightened of the captor's future actions.[87]

The requirement that the threatened harm be perceived as immediate exists even where the assault is conditional.[88] In conditional assault, the actor engages in conduct that places another in apprehension of receiving an immediate battery if the victim fails to comply with an unlawful demand or condition.[89] If the condition is not met, the threatened force will be received by the victim immediately. Even where the victim complies with the condition, thereby avoiding the battery, he or she has still been placed in apprehension of imminent contact and was therefore assaulted.[90] Thus, where A pointed a gun at B and threatened to shoot B unless B handed over money, whereupon B complied and A did not shoot, A had nevertheless assaulted B.[91]

The legislative drafting committee explicitly eliminated from the assault prohibition the requirement that the defendant have the present ability to employ actual force.[92] However, a defendant's present ability may impact on the reason-

---

[86] People v. Kettler, 121 Ill. App. 3d 1, 6, 459 N.E.2d 7, 10 (4th Dist. 1984) (quoting ROLLIN M. PERKINS, CRIMINAL LAW 132 (2d ed. 1969) and 2 CHARLES TORCIA, WHARTON'S CRIMINAL LAW § 180 at 302 (14th ed. 1979)).

The offense of aggravated assault was at issue in *Kettler* because any assault on a police officer in Illinois is an aggravated assault by reason of the officer's police status. 720 ILCS 5/12-2(a)(6) (1999).

[87] People v. Hobson, 77 Ill. App. 3d 22, 29, 396 N.E.2d 53, 59 (3d Dist. 1979).

[88] In conditional assault, the fear of being immediately battered is present despite a condition accompanying the apprehension-creating conduct that would enable the victim to avoid injury. *See* People v. Henry, 356 Ill. 141, 143, 190 N.E. 361, 362 (1934).

[89] WAYNE LAFAVE & AUSTIN SCOTT, CRIMINAL LAW § 7.16 (c) (2d ed. 1986).

[90] People v. Henry, 356 Ill. 141, 143, 190 N.E. 361, 362 (1934).

[91] People v. Henry, 356 Ill. 141, 143, 190 N.E. 361, 362 (1934).

[92] ILL. ANN. STAT. ch. 38, § 12-1 (Smith-Hurd 1979), 1961 Committee Comments, at 406 (revised 1972).

ableness of the victim's apprehensions.[93] Thus, while there may be no element of "present ability" as such, the lack of present ability may render the apprehension of battery less than "reasonable," which is an element of assault. Thus, where a defendant was placed in restraints in a hospital bed, where he threatened to kill police officers, conduct he was physically incapable of accomplishing, there was no assault.[94]

§ 9.07. — Mental State.

Proof of a mental state for assault is not explicitly required in the statutory definition.[95] Although it is clear that assault is not a specific intent crime,[96] the absence of a mental state in the statute has led courts to differing conclusions in regard to the element of mens rea. One court interpreted this to mean that no mental state is required,[97] while others have interpreted assault as requiring any one of three mental states: intent, knowledge or recklessness.[98] Those courts that have answered the issue in the affirmative have uniformly looked to section 5/4-3 of the criminal code,[99] which provides that if a statute does not prescribe a particular mental state as an element of an offense, other than an offense that involves strict liability,[100] a person is not guilty of an offense unless he or she acted with either intent,[101] knowledge,[102] or recklessness.[103]

---

[93] *See, e.g.,* People v. Kettler, 121 Ill. App. 3d 1, 5, 459 N.E.2d 7, 9 (4th Dist. 1984) (where the court observed that the defendant's physical restraint prevented any conclusion that the apprehension was reasonable).

[94] People v. Kettler, 121 Ill. App. 3d 1, 5, 459 N.E.2d 7, 9 (4th Dist. 1984).

[95] *See* 720 ILCS 5/12-1(a) (1999).

[96] People v. Cannes, 61 Ill. App. 3d 865, 870, 378 N.E.2d 552, 556-57 (2d Dist. 1978) (assault is not a specific intent crime, so either intent, knowledge or recklessness is sufficient to support a conviction for aggravated assault), *cert. denied,* 440 U.S. 917 (1979); *accord,* Daley v. Thaxton, 92 Ill. App. 2d 277, 280, 236 N.E.2d 433, 436 (1st Dist. 1968). *See also* 720 ILCS 5/4-3(b) (1999).

[97] People v. Harkey, 69 Ill. App. 3d 94, 96-97, 386 N.E.2d 1151, 1153 (5th Dist. 1979).

[98] People v. Grant, 101 Ill. App. 3d 43, 47, 427 N.E.2d 810, 813 (1st Dist. 1981); People v. Cannes, 61 Ill. App. 3d 865, 870, 378 N.E.2d 552, 556-57 (2d Dist. 1978), *cert. denied,* 440 U.S. 917 (1979). *See also* Daley v. Thaxton, 92 Ill. App. 2d 277, 281, 236 N.E.2d 433, 436 (1st Dist. 1968) (revocation of liquor license improper in absence of showing that alleged assault committed in licensed premises was willful, citing ILL. REV. STAT. ch. 38, § 4-3 (1967)).

[99] 720 ILCS 5/4-3(b) (1999).

[100] 720 ILCS 5/4-9 (1999) ("Absolute Liability. A person may be guilty of an offense without having, as to each element thereof, one of the mental states described in Sections 4-4 through 4-7 if the offense is a misdemeanor which is not punishable by incarceration or by a fine exceeding $500.00 or the statute defining the offense clearly indicates a legislative purpose to impose liability for the conduct described.").

[101] 720 ILCS 5/4-4 (1999) (intent defined).

[102] 720 ILCS 5/4-5 (1999) (knowledge defined).

[103] 720 ILCS 5/4-6 (1999) (recklessness defined).

The statutory presumption that a mens rea is included in an offense that is silent as to mens rea is applicable to all crimes except those in the nature of strict liability. The issue, then, becomes one of whether simple assault under section 5/12-1 is a strict-liability crime. While one court has held that assault is in the category of offenses for which absolute liability is imposed and that, accordingly, no mental state is required to be proved,[104] more recent decisions have correctly held that assault is not a crime of absolute liability and have consequently found that section 5/4-3(b) incorporates a mental state requirement into the definition of the offense.[105]

This latter view has been adopted by the Illinois Pattern Jury Instructions on criminal assault, as prepared by the Illinois Supreme Court Jury Instructions Committee, which state that a jury must find that the defendant intentionally or knowingly engaged in conduct that placed the victim in reasonable apprehension of bodily harm or physical contact of an insulting or provoking nature.[106] The Committee cites *People v. Grant*[107] which insists on the use of a mental state that conforms with the allegation in the charging instrument.[108]

---

[104] People v. Litch, 4 Ill. App. 3d 788, 790, 281 N.E.2d 745, 747 (2d Dist. 1972).

[105] People v. Grant, 101 Ill. App. 3d 43, 47, 427 N.E.2d 810, 813 (1st Dist. 1981) (reversing assault conviction where jury instruction that did not include instruction on mental state lacked essential element of assault).

Assault is a class C misdemeanor (720 ILCS 5/12-1(b)). A class C misdemeanor is punishable by incarceration not to exceed thirty days (730 ILCS 5/5-8-3 (1999)) and by a fine not to exceed $1500. (720 ILCS 5/5-9-1 (1999)). Therefore, assault would not appear to satisfy the first criterion for absolute liability (a misdemeanor not punishable by incarceration) or the second criterion for absolute liability (a fine not exceeding $500). Also, it is unlikely that assault may be interpreted to satisfy the third criterion (legislative intent to impose strict liability on the face of the statute) in the absence of such a legislative pronouncement in the language or legislative history of section 5/12-1.

[106] ILLINOIS PATTERNED INSTRUCTION — CRIMINAL 3d § 11.02 at 337 (3d ed. 1992) reads as follows:

11.02 Issues in Assault

To sustain the charge of assault, the State must prove the following proposition:

that the defendant [(knowingly) (intentionally)] engaged in conduct which placed _____ in reasonable apprehension of receiving [(bodily harm) (physical contact of an insulting or provoking nature)].

If you find from your consideration of all the evidence that this proposition has been proved beyond a reasonable doubt, you should find the defendant guilty.

If you find from your consideration of all the evidence that this proposition has not been proven beyond a reasonable doubt, you should find the defendant not guilty.

[107] 101 Ill. App. 3d 43, 427 N.E.2d 810 (1st Dist. 1981).

[108] People v. Grant, 101 Ill. App. 3d 43, 427 N.E.2d 810 (1st Dist. 1981).

A question exists whether the phrase *without lawful authority,* which appears in section 5/12-1,[109] is an essential element of this offense that must invariably be included in jury instructions and proved by the state. The Illinois assault statute explicitly provides that a person commits assault when he or she engages in apprehension-creating conduct "without lawful authority." Illinois appellate caselaw has held that "without lawful authority" (1) is a necessary element of the offense and (2) must be included in a valid indictment or information.[110] The Illinois Pattern Jury Instructions only requires a "without lawful authority" instruction if defendant claims his conduct was *with* lawful authority.[111] Also, inasmuch as the "without legal justification" language of *battery* is treated as an affirmative defense that has to be raised by the defendant rather than as an essential element to be proved in each and every case by the state, the "without lawful authority" language in the definition of assault more likely provides an affirmative defense rather than an element of assault.[112]

§ 9.08. Aggravated Assault.

Closely related to assault is the crime of "aggravated assault," codified in section 5/12-2 of the code.[113] This section covers those assaults committed under circumstances of aggravation.[114] The elements of assault, as discussed above, must be present and, furthermore, one of the specified elements of aggravation must be proved.[115] If there is any physical contact, the crime will be battery, attempted battery, or some other form thereof, not aggravated assault.[116]

§ 9.09. — Aggravated Assault Codified.

Aggravated assault is defined as follows:

> (a) A person commits an aggravated assault, when, in committing an assault, he:
>
> (1) Uses a deadly weapon or any device manufactured and designed to be substantially similar in appearance to a firearm, other than by discharging a

---

[109] 720 ILCS 5/12-1(a) (1999) (definition of assault).

[110] People v. McCaughan, 3 Ill. App. 3d 720, 279 N.E.2d 139 (5th Dist. 1971) (abstract) ("without legal authority" is necessary element of assault and is required in valid information); People v. Whelan, 132 Ill. App. 2d 2, 4, 267 N.E.2d 364, 366 (2d Dist. 1971) ("without legal authority" is necessary element of assault and must be included in the indictment).

[111] *See* ILLINOIS PATTERNED JURY INSTRUCTIONS — CRIMINAL 3d § 11.02 at 337 (3d ed. 1992).

[112] *See* § 9.19 of this chapter.

[113] 720 ILCS 5/12-2 (1999).

[114] ILL. ANN. STAT. ch. 38, para. 12-2 (Smith-Hurd 1979), 1961 Committee Comments, at 413 (revised 1972).

[115] ILL. ANN. STAT. ch. 38, para. 12-2 (Smith-Hurd 1979), 1961 Committee Comments, at 413 (revised 1972).

[116] ILL. ANN. STAT. ch. 38, para. 12-2 (Smith-Hurd 1979), 1961 Committee Comments, at 413 (revised 1972).

firearm in the direction of another person, a peace officer, a person summoned or directed by a peace officer, a correctional officer or fireman or in the direction of a vehicle occupied by another person, a peace officer, a person summoned or directed by a peace officer, a correctional officer or a fireman while the officer or fireman is engaged in the execution of any of his official duties, or to prevent the officer or fireman from performing his official duties, or in retaliation for the officer or fireman performing his official duties;

(2) Is hooded, robed or masked in such manner as to conceal his identity or any device manufactured and designed to be substantially similar in appearance to a firearm;

(3) Knows the individual assaulted to be a teacher or other person employed in any school and such teacher or other employee is upon the grounds of a school or grounds adjacent thereto, or is in any part of a building used for school purposes;

(4) Knows the individual assaulted to be a supervisor, director, instructor or other person employed in any park district and such supervisor, director, instructor or other employee is upon the grounds of the park or grounds adjacent thereto, or is in any part of a building used for park purposes;

(5) Knows the individual assaulted to be a caseworker, investigator, or other person employed by the State Department of Public Aid, a County Department of Public Aid, or the Department of Human Resources . . . and such caseworker, investigator, or other person is upon the grounds of a public aid office or grounds adjacent thereto, or is an any part of a building used for public aid purposes, or upon the grounds of a home of a public aid applicant, recipient or any other person being interviewed or investigated in the employees' discharge of his duties, or on grounds adjacent thereto, or is in any part of a building in which the applicant, recipient, or other such person resides or is located;

(6) Knows the individual assaulted to be a peace officer, or a community policing volunteer, or a fireman while the officer or fireman is engaged in the execution of any of his official duties, or to prevent the officer, community policing volunteer, or fireman from performing his official duties, or in retaliation for the officer, community policing volunteer, or fireman performing his official duties, and the assault is committed other than by the discharge of a firearm in the direction of the officer or fireman or in the direction of a vehicle occupied by the officer or fireman (see § 9.25 for aggravated battery with a firearm);

(7) Knows the individual assaulted to be an emergency medical technician ambulance, emergency medical technician-intermediate, emergency medical technician-paramedic, ambulance driver or other medical assistance or

first aid personnel employed by a municipality or other governmental unit engaged in the execution of any of his official duties, or to prevent the emergency medical technician-ambulance, emergency medical technician-intermediate, emergency medical technician-paramedic, ambulance driver, or other medical assistance or first aid personnel from performing his official duties, or in retaliation for the emergency medical technician-ambulance, emergency medical technician-intermediate, emergency medical technician-paramedic, ambulance driver, or other medical assistance or first aid personnel performing his official duties;

(8) Knows the individual assaulted to be the driver, operator, employee or passenger of any transportation facility or system engaged in the business of transportation of the public for hire and the individual assaulted is then performing in such capacity or then using such public transportation as a passenger or using any area of any description designed by the transportation facility or system as a vehicle boarding, departure, or transfer location;

(9) Or the individual assaulted is on or about a public way, public property, or public place of accommodation or amusement;

(10) Knows the individual assaulted to be an employee of the State of Illinois, a municipal corporation therein or a political subdivision thereof, engaged in the performance of his authorized duties as such employee;

(11) Knowingly and without legal justification, commits an assault on a physically handicapped person;

(12) Knowingly and without legal justification, commits an assault on a person 60 years of age or older; or

(13) Discharges a firearm.

(14) Knows the individual assaulted to be a correctional officer, while the officer is engaged in the execution of any of his or her official duties, or to prevent the officer from performing his or her official duties, or in retaliation for the officer performing his or her official duties; or

(15) Knows the individual assaulted to be a correctional employee, while the employee is engaged in the execution of any or his or her official duties, or to prevent the employee from performing his or her official duties, or in retaliation for the employee performing his or her official duties, and the assault is committed other than by the discharge of a firearm in the direction of the employee or in the direction of a vehicle occupied by the employee.

(b) Sentence . . . .[117]

---

[117] 720 ILCS 5/12-2 (1999).

§ 9.10. — Elements of Aggravated Assault.

The statutory definition of aggravated assault must be read together with the definition of assault.[118] Before a defendant can be convicted of aggravated assault, there must be sufficient proof of (1) conduct on his or her part in placing another in reasonable apprehension of receiving a battery,[119] (2) an element of aggravation, such as where the defendant used a deadly weapon[120] or knew the individual assaulted was a peace officer engaged in his or her official duties,[121] and (3) the requisite mental state for assault.[122] Most, but not all, aggravated assaults also have another mental state requirement, namely, *knowledge* of the capacity — teacher, police officer or the like — of the person assaulted.[123] If the assault is with a deadly weapon,[124] if the defendant is masked in such a manner as to conceal his or her identity,[125] or if the defendant assaults the victim in or about public property,[126] this particular mens rea is not required by the terms of the statute.[127]

Regarding those assaults that are considered aggravated assault because of the defendant's use of a deadly weapon,[128] a shotgun or revolver is per se a deadly weapon.[129] The instrument in question does not have to be one that was designed solely for the purpose of inflicting harm to a human or animal or be of any certain size or description.[130] In other words, a deadly weapon does not have to be deadly *per se*; the crucial question revolves around how the instrument was in fact used.[131] Thus, a small pocket knife,[132] a straight razor[133] or a garden hoe[134]

---

[118] People v. Latham, 13 Ill. App. 3d 371, 372, 299 N.E.2d 808, 809 (5th Dist. 1973).

[119] People v. Malone, 37 Ill. App. 3d 185, 193, 345 N.E.2d 801, 807 (1st Dist. 1976).

[120] People v. Enerson, 202 Ill. App. 3d 748, 750, 559 N.E.2d 801, 803 (3d Dist. 1990).

[121] People v. Malone, 37 Ill. App. 3d 185, 193, 345 N.E.2d 801, 807 (1st Dist. 1976).

[122] *See* § 9.07 of this chapter.

[123] *See, e.g.,* 720 ILCS 5/12-2(a)(3) (1999) (knowledge that a person assaulted is a teacher); People v. Infelise, 32 Ill. App. 3d 224, 227, 336 N.E.2d 559, 561-62 (1st Dist. 1975) (discussing "[k]nows the individual assaulted to be a peace officer" language of (a)(6)).

[124] 720 ILCS 5/12(a)(1) (1999).

[125] 720 ILCS 5/12-2(a)(2) (1999).

[126] 720 ILCS 5/12-2(a)(9) (1999).

[127] However, caselaw interpretation may require such proof. *See, e.g.,* People v. Sedlacko, 65 Ill. App. 3d 659, 663, 382 N.E.2d 363, 367 (1st Dist. 1978) (stating knowledge is required to convict for assault with a deadly weapon under (a)(1)).

[128] 720 ILCS 5/12-2(a)(1) (1999).

[129] People v. Estes, 37 Ill. App. 3d 889, 894, 346 N.E.2d 469, 474 (4th Dist. 1976).

[130] People v. Carter, 410 Ill. 462, 465, 102 N.E.2d 312, 313 (1951).

[131] People v. Wethington, 122 Ill. App. 3d 54, 55, 460 N.E.2d 856, 857 (3d Dist. 1984) (knunchuckus or karate sticks used as a deadly weapon); People v. Lee, 46 Ill. App. 3d 343, 347-48, 360 N.E.2d 1173, 1176 (3d Dist. 1977) (walking cane used as deadly weapon).

[132] People v. Carter, 410 Ill. 462, 465, 102 N.E.2d 312, 313 (1951).

[133] People v. Hasty, 127 Ill. App. 2d 330, 335, 262 N.E.2d 292, 295 (1st Dist. 1970).

[134] Hamilton v. People, 113 Ill. 34, 38 (1885).

may qualify. Whether an instrument is a deadly weapon is normally a question for the jury.[135]

With respect to firearms, the mere pointing of a pistol at another will normally constitute aggravated assault.[136] Where a defendant shoots at someone, this clearly will suffice for aggravated assault,[137] if not for the greater crime of attempted murder.[138] There is no requirement that the victim actually see the firearm in order to suffer reasonable apprehension.[139] For example, aggravated assault was found where a defendant placed her hand in a bulging coat pocket and said "I'm going to shoot you."[140] Similarly, defendants were found guilty of this offense where they placed a gun in a nylon bag, which was zipped, threatened to "blow [the victims] out of the house," and the victims could ascertain that the object inside the bag was heavy and metal because they had heard it "klink" against a bedframe.[141]

Aggravated assault is committed where the defendant during an assault uses any device that is "substantially similar in appearance to a firearm."[142] Thus, even though the device is not a deadly weapon, its use elevates an assault to aggravated assault.

The requisite knowledge regarding the capacity of the person assaulted — teacher, peace officer, firefighter or the like — that is necessary for certain types of aggravated assault can be proved by circumstantial evidence.[143] Adequate instructions regarding this requirement of knowledge must be provided to the jury.[144]

§ 9.11. — Assault and Aggravated Assault as Lesser Included Offense.

Simple assault is normally a lesser included offense of aggravated assault.[145] However, assault is not a lesser included offense of battery; rather, assault is

---

[135] *See* People v. Enerson, 202 Ill. App. 3d 748, 750-51, 559 N.E.2d 801, 803 (3d Dist. 1990) (knife); People v. Chrisopulos, 82 Ill. App. 3d 581, 585, 402 N.E.2d 912, 915 (2d Dist. 1980) (gun).

[136] People v. Preis, 27 Ill. 2d 315, 318-19, 189 N.E.2d 254, 256 (1963); People v. Ivy, 133 Ill. App. 3d 647, 655, 479 N.E.2d 399, 405 (5th Dist. 1985).

[137] People v. Mikel, 73 Ill. App. 3d 21, 24, 391 N.E.2d 550, 552 (4th Dist. 1979).

[138] *See* ch. 5 of this treatise for a discussion of criminal attempt.

[139] People v. Ivy, 133 Ill. App. 3d 647, 655, 479 N.E.2d 399, 405 (5th Dist. 1985); People v. Chrisopulos, 82 Ill. App. 3d 581, 585, 402 N.E.2d 912, 914-15 (2d Dist. 1980).

[140] People v. Preis, 27 Ill. 2d 315, 319, 189 N.E.2d 254, 256 (1963).

[141] People v. Ivy, 133 Ill. App. 3d 647, 655, 479 N.E.2d 399, 405 (5th Dist. 1985).

[142] 720 ILCS 5/12-2(a)(1) (1999).

[143] People v. Sedlacko, 65 Ill. App. 3d 659, 663, 382 N.E.2d 363, 367-68 (1st Dist. 1978).

[144] People v. Litch, 4 Ill. App. 3d 788, 792, 281 N.E.2d 745, 747 (2d Dist. 1972) (discussing "[k]nows the individual assaulted to be a peace officer" language of (a)(6)).

[145] People v. Alexander, 39 Ill. App. 3d 443, 448, 350 N.E.2d 144, 148-49 (1st Dist. 1976). *See* ch. 1 of this treatise for a complete discussion of lesser included offenses.

distinct from battery for if there was a wrongful touching, a battery has occurred, whereas if there was no contact with the victim, an assault may have occurred.[146] One question about aggravated assault is whether it is a lesser included offense of crimes such as attempted murder or attempted robbery. It has been held that because attempted murder requires a specific intent to kill, which aggravated assault does not, and because aggravated assault requires proof of apprehension of a battery, which attempted murder does not, these are distinct crimes.[147] Similarly, because attempted robbery requires a specific intent to rob while aggravated assault mandates evidence of the victim's apprehension of the battery, there is caselaw that indicates the latter is not a lesser included offense of the former.[148]

§ 9.12. Vehicular Endangerment.

In section 5/12-2.5 of the Criminal Code is the stricture called "vehicle endangerment."[149] It reads:

> Any person who with the intent to strike a motor vehicle causes by any means an object to fall from an overpass in the direction of a moving motor vehicle traveling upon a highway in this State, if that object strikes a motor vehicle, is guilty of vehicle endangerment.[150]

Punishable as a felony,[151] this prohibition defines an *object* as "any object or substance that by its size, weight, or consistency is likely to cause great bodily harm to any occupant of a motor vehicle" and an *overpass* as "any structure that passes over a highway."[152]

§ 9.13. Battery.

Assault and *battery* are terms frequently and incorrectly interchanged. Generally, battery is committed when a person intentionally or knowingly causes bodily harm to another or makes physical contact of an insulting or provoking nature.[153] An assault is consummated when a person places another in reasonable apprehension of receiving a battery.[154]

---

[146] People v. Abrams, 48 Ill. 2d 446, 459, 271 N.E.2d 37, 45 (1971).

[147] People v. Tiller, 61 Ill. App. 3d 785, 795, 378 N.E.2d 282, 290 (5th Dist. 1978). *See also* People v. Hill, 190 Ill. App. 3d 20, 22, 545 N.E.2d 977, 979 (1st Dist. 1989) ("It is undisputed that aggravated assault is not a lesser included offense of attempt murder.").

[148] People v. Robinson, 68 Ill. App. 3d 687, 691, 386 N.E.2d 165, 169 (4th Dist. 1980).

[149] 720 ILCS 5/12-2.5 (1999).

[150] 720 ILCS 5/12-2.5(a) (1999).

[151] 720 ILCS 5/12-2.5(b) (1999).

[152] 720 ILCS 5/12-2.5(c) (1999).

[153] 720 ILCS 5/12-3 (1999).

[154] 720 ILCS 5/12-1 (1999).

§ 9.14. — Assault and Battery Distinguished.

The key distinction between the two crimes involves physical contact or touching. If any amount of touching has occurred, a battery has been committed, not an assault.[155] Since an assault by definition involves only a reasonable *apprehension* of receiving a battery, an assault can never be a battery, although one can be assaulted and battered in the same incident.[156] If a perpetrator points a gun at the victim without touching the victim and says, "Give me your money or I'll shoot," beyond the robbery or attempted robbery, an assault has been committed, since the victim is undoubtedly apprehensive about the situation.[157] However, if in the same incident the perpetrator poked the gun against the victim's chest, a battery arises, since actual physical contact has occurred.[158]

It is sometimes said that every battery necessarily includes an assault. Such a statement is clearly wrong. A perpetrator who strikes a victim with a club from behind, where the victim neither sees nor expects the blow, has not committed an assault. Since the victim did not observe the blow, he or she could not have been placed in reasonable apprehension of receiving it. In this situation, a battery has obviously occurred, yet an assault has not.

Although the concepts of criminal battery and civil battery are strikingly similar, a caveat should be directed to the practicing attorney that stresses the two are not exactly parallel and that one should not cite a civil battery case in a criminal battery setting. Reasons for this are several. First, civil battery has different mental state requirements, depending on whether the contact caused bodily harm or caused offensive touching. Since freedom from bodily harm is traditionally given the greatest protection, the civil law protects against intentional acts as well as unintentional acts, such as negligence. But if the contact is merely offensive contact, although it is protected, it is protected to a lesser degree in that only intentional acts of battery will satisfy the mental state requirement for a tort claim.[159] Criminal battery in Illinois specifically restricts battery to intentional or knowing contacts.[160] Accordingly, negligence or recklessness will not suffice.[161]

---

[155] People v. Abrams, 48 Ill. 2d 446, 459-60, 271 N.E.2d 37, 46 (1971).

[156] *See* People v. Stuller, 71 Ill. App. 3d 118, 123, 389 N.E.2d 593, 596 (5th Dist. 1978) (individual was both battered and assaulted in same incident).

[157] *Cf.* People v. Robinson, 68 Ill. App. 3d 687, 689-91, 386 N.E.2d 165, 167-69 (4th Dist. 1980) (where defendant "pulled a gun" and demanded money from armed robbery victim, defendant properly convicted of aggravated assault).

[158] *Cf.* People v. Dunker, 217 Ill. App. 3d 410, 414, 577 N.E.2d 499, 502 (4th Dist. 1991) (where defendant poked teacher in the chest, aggravated battery established).

[159] RESTATEMENT (SECOND) OF TORTS ch. 2 (1965) (introductory notes).

[160] 720 ILCS 5/12-3 (1999).

[161] *Cf.* ROLLIN M. PERKINS & RONALD N. BOYCE, CRIMINAL LAW 157-58 (3d ed. 1982). These authorities note that it is error to think that battery requires intentional application of force to the

Second, civil battery is one of the so-called dignitary torts to which courts routinely allow recovery for any amount of touching, even though the touching is slight in nature.[162] The intent of the Illinois legislature is not to accept the civil, common law "slightest touching" concept in connection with criminal battery.[163] In other words, what may constitute a civil battery may not give rise to a criminal battery.

§ 9.15. — Battery Codified.

Section 5/12-3 defines *battery* as follows: "A person commits battery if he intentionally or knowingly without legal justification and by any means, (1) causes bodily harm to an individual or (2) makes physical contact of an insulting or provoking nature with an individual."[164]

Under the prior Illinois statute, battery was defined as an unlawful beating of another.[165] The word *beating* was somewhat of a misnomer, since courts freely held that even the "slightest touching" of another was a battery.[166] Presumably, the courts did not wish to get into a battle of degrees in drawing a line between the statutory unlawful-beating language and the common law meaning of battery. Because the courts could not differentiate between degrees of violence, they completely prohibited it at its lowest level.[167]

Under the current Illinois statute, the former phrase *unlawful beating* is replaced by "*causes bodily harm or makes physical contact of an insulting or provoking nature.*"[168] With this replacement, the common law interpretation of *unlawful beating* — that is, the "slightest touching" standard — has been deleted from the law. The law now allows for one person to intentionally touch

---

person of another. They point out that this error is due to failure to distinguish between criminal law and torts in the use of the word *battery*. In tort law, intentional application of force on the person of another was termed *trespass for battery*. Force applied to the person of another via negligence was called *trespass on the case*. On the other hand, in criminal law, absent a statute, there is no counterpart for the distinction between *trespass for battery* and *trespass on the case*; hence, the word *battery* is applied to every punishable application of force to the person of another. However, the Illinois statute, which requires an intentional or knowledgeable act, specifically limits the scope of battery to exclude the tort concept of *trespass on the case*, which requires mere negligence.

[162] *See* ROLLIN M. PERKINS & RONALD N. BOYCE, CRIMINAL LAW 157-58 (3d ed. 1982).

[163] ILL. ANN. STAT. ch. 38, para. 12-3 (Smith-Hurd 1979), 1961 Committee Comments, at 439 (revised 1972).

[164] 720 ILCS 5/12-3(a) (1999).

[165] ILL. REV. STAT. § 56 (1961).

[166] ILL. ANN. STAT. ch. 38, para. 12-3 (Smith-Hurd 1979), 1961 Committee Comments, at 439 (revised 1972) (citing Hunt v. People, 53 Ill. App. 111, 112 (1894)).

[167] *See* ILL. ANN. STAT. ch. 38, para. 12-3 (Smith-Hurd 1979), 1961 Committee Comments at 439-40 (revised 1972).

[168] 720 ILCS 5/12-3 (1999).

another in a manner that does not result in the person being insulted or provoked, such as a friendly slap on the back. The legislature sought, with this replacement, to eliminate cases involving unlawful touching that are so slight in nature that they neither result in tangible harm nor are insulting or provoking.[169]

§ 9.16. — Elements of Battery.

The basic elements of battery under the current statute are: the defendant (1) intentionally or knowingly (2) without legal justification (3) engages in conduct by any means which (4) causes bodily harm to another *or* makes physical contact of an insulting or provoking nature. For purposes of analysis, the Illinois criminal battery statute may be divided into three fundamental elements: (1) the conduct which constitutes battery, (2) the mental state and (3) the harmful result. These essential elements will be discussed independently.

§ 9.17. — Conduct Which Constitutes Battery.

In terms of *conduct* prohibited, the Illinois battery statute is worded very broadly. The statute provides that any person who "by any means" causes bodily harm or makes insulting or provoking physical contact is liable for battery. Furthermore, the statute incorporates acts that result in direct or indirect contact to the person of another.

A broad reading of the "by any means" clause has certainly been supported by caselaw. Battery includes such blatant, direct conduct as striking a victim with an extension cord,[170] a tray,[171] fist,[172] or a broomstick,[173] assuming all other necessary elements are present. Similarly, kicking,[174] choking,[175] poking,[176]

---

[169] ILL. ANN. STAT. ch. 38, para. 12-3 (Smith-Hurd 1979), 1961 Committee Comments, at 440 (revised 1972). The committee points out that the intent of the new battery statute is to limit the traditional "barest touching" that does not cause bodily harm to one of "an insulting or provoking nature."

[170] People v. Lee, 84 Ill. App. 3d 441, 444-45, 405 N.E.2d 860, 863-64 (3d Dist. 1980).

[171] People v. Neeley, 79 Ill. App. 3d 528, 530, 398 N.E.2d 988, 990 (3d Dist. 1979), *cert. denied*, 449 U.S. 865 (1980).

[172] People v. Grieco, 44 Ill. 2d 407, 408, 255 N.E.2d 897, 898, *cert. denied*, 400 U.S. 825 (1970).

[173] People v. Gant, 121 Ill. App. 2d 222, 225, 257 N.E.2d 181, 182 (1st Dist. 1970).

[174] People v. Nesbitt, 216 Ill. App. 3d 1023, 1025, 576 N.E.2d 503, 505 (4th Dist. 1991).

[175] People v. Lowe, 12 Ill. App. 3d 959, 299 N.E.2d 341 (1st Dist. 1973) (abstract).

[176] People v. Dunker, 217 Ill. App. 3d 410, 414, 577 N.E.2d 499, 502 (4th Dist. 1991) (aggravated battery conviction affirmed).

pushing,[177] or whipping[178] another person will support a conviction for battery, as will grabbing another's arm[179] or spitting in another's face.[180]

Battery may also be consummated by use of force that indirectly causes bodily harm or contact of an insulting or provoking nature. If a perpetrator sets in motion events that lead to a victim's being harmed or offensively touched, the perpetrator will be liable for battery.[181] The theory that a person is deemed to intend the natural and probable consequences of his or her deliberate acts supports the "set-in-motion" type of battery.[182] For example, where a defendant threw a dinner plate in the general direction of the victim and the plate bounced off the wall and struck the victim, the defendant was found guilty of battery.[183] Where a defendant threw a food tray at the victim and struck her in the forehead, this amounted to battery.[184]

Where there is no touching of some sort, there is no battery. Where a defendant ran away from a police officer, he may have committed the offense of resisting arrest, but not battery.[185]

§ 9.18. — Mental State.

Although battery has been referred by some courts as a specific intent offense,[186] it is actually a general intent offense because it can be established by proving the perpetrator either intentionally *or* knowingly caused bodily harm or made contact of an insulting or provoking nature.[187]

---

[177] People v. Brown, 163 Ill. App. 3d 976, 980, 516 N.E.2d 1349, 1352 (4th Dist. 1987) (conduct sufficient to prove battery but reversed on other grounds).

[178] People v. Virgin, 60 Ill. App. 3d 964, 968, 377 N.E.2d 846, 849 (3d Dist. 1978) (battery charge vacated as lesser included offense of cruelty to child).

[179] People v. Vodicka, 1 Ill. App. 3d 1062, 1066, 275 N.E.2d 731, 734 (1st Dist. 1971).

[180] ILL. ANN. STAT. ch. 38, para. 12-3 (Smith-Hurd 1979), 1961 Committee Comments at 440 (revised 1972); People v. Santana, 121 Ill. App. 3d 265, 270, 459 N.E.2d 655, 659 (2d Dist. 1984) (provided probable cause to arrest defendant for battery).

[181] People v. McEvoy, 33 Ill. App. 3d 409, 411, 337 N.E.2d 437, 439 (1st Dist. 1975) (battery is "willful touching" of person of another by aggressor or "with some substance being put in motion" by aggressor in commission of assault).

[182] People v. Hartzol, 43 Ill. App. 3d 924, 926, 357 N.E.2d 729, 731 (3d Dist. 1976) (citing People v. Coolidge, 26 Ill. 2d 533, 537, 187 N.E.2d 694, 697 (1963)).

[183] People v. Hartzol, 43 Ill. App. 3d 924, 926, 357 N.E.2d 729, 731 (3d Dist. 1976).

[184] People v. Neeley, 79 Ill. App. 3d 528, 530, 398 N.E.2d 988, 990-91 (3d Dist. 1979), *cert. denied*, 449 U.S. 865 (1980).

[185] City of Chicago v. Brown, 61 Ill. App. 3d 266, 277, 377 N.E.2d 1031, 1039 (1st Dist. 1978).

[186] *See, e.g.,* People v. Renehan, 226 Ill. App. 3d 453, 461, 589 N.E.2d 866, 871 (1st Dist. 1992) (battery is a specific intent crime). *Compare* ch. 2 of this treatise for a more narrow definition of what constitutes "specific intent."

[187] 720 ILCS 5/12-3(a) (1999).

While it has always been possible to commit a battery without a specific intent (i.e., through recklessness or gross negligence), the Committee felt it desirable to eliminate this unorthodox aspect of bodily harm from the intentional or knowing offenses, and put it into a separate category where it could be handled more easily on proof and instructions, especially in view of the increasing number of vehicular situations which cause bodily harm or endanger safety through reckless conduct. Therefore, battery is restricted to intentional or knowing . . . conduct which is without legal justification, and a separate offense of "[r]eckless [c]onduct" is prescribed in section [5/]12-5.[188]

Accordingly, under Illinois law today, criminal negligence and recklessness do not satisfy the intent requirement for battery.[189]

As with other criminal statutes, either direct evidence or circumstantial proof of intent satisfies the mental state requirement.[190] Circumstances surrounding an event evidencing an intent to commit a battery include, but are not limited to, the motivation of the defendant and the proximity of the defendant to his or her victim.[191] Anger and aggression are the common factors inducing a defendant to commit battery and, therefore, they represent, absent direct proof, evidence of intent.[192] For example, where there was conflicting evidence about whether the defendant, a dormitory resident, aimlessly threw a dinner plate in the general direction of the victim or whether she threw the plate with the intent to hit the victim (the plate bounced of a wall, hitting and cutting the victim), evidence that the defendant was incensed because she did not receive her just portion of food was crucial in upholding her conviction for battery.[193] Where a defendant threw a tray at her co-worker, even though the victim could not see the defendant, the surrounding circumstances supported the conclusion that the defendant had the required intent to commit a battery.[194] Here, the fact that the victim had rebuked

---

[188] ILL. ANN. STAT. ch. 38, para. 12-3 (Smith-Hurd 1979), 1961 Committee Comments, at 439-40 (revised 1972).

[189] See, e.g., People v. Barrington, 15 Ill. App. 3d 445, 447, 304 N.E.2d 525, 526-27 (3d Dist. 1973) (where defendant's conduct was, at best, reckless, defendant's battery conviction reversed).

[190] People v. Brown, 163 Ill. App. 3d 976, 980, 516 N.E.2d 1349, 1352 (4th Dist. 1987).

[191] See, e.g., People v. Neeley, 79 Ill. App. 3d 528, 530-31, 398 N.E.2d 988, 990-91 (3d Dist. 1979), cert. denied, 449 U.S. 865 (1980).

[192] See, e.g., People v. Hartzol, 43 Ill. App. 3d 924, 926, 357 N.E.2d 729, 731 (3d Dist. 1976). Compare People v. Allen, 153 Ill. 2d 145, 149-52, 606 N.E.2d 1149, 1151-53 (1992) (sudden and intense passion is not a mitigating circumstance where charge is battery and is irrelevant outside the homicide context.).

[193] People v. Hartzol, 43 Ill. App. 3d 924, 926, 357 N.E.2d 729, 731 (3d Dist. 1976).

[194] People v. Neeley, 79 Ill. App. 3d 528, 530-31, 398 N.E.2d 988, 990-91 (3d Dist. 1979), cert. denied, 449 U.S. 865 (1980).

the defendant for being out of her proper working place provided evidence of defendant's intent to commit a battery.[195]

Circumstantial evidence may help to prove that a defendant had the intent to make contact of an insulting or provoking nature. For example, where the defendant lifted up the victim's dress, the fact that the defendant did so "was highly probative of his intent to make physical contact" of a sexual nature.[196]

Another important circumstance crucial to the determination of constructive intent is the proximity of the defendant to the victim, especially where the defendant throws an object at his or her victim. Obviously, the closer the defendant to the victim, the more likely it is that the court will find that the defendant had the required intent or knowledge. Thus, where a defendant hurled a light tray at his victim positioned three to four feet away and directly in front of the defendant, the defendant's intent was property shown.[197] Where a defendant was standing only a few feet away from the victim when she threw a plate toward the victim, the mens rea requirement was properly found.[198]

Just as surrounding circumstances may evidence the required mental state for battery, the surrounding circumstances may vindicate the defendant from a charge of battery. For example, where a hospital security guard contemporaneously informed a hospital patient that hospital rules prohibited cameras as he grabbed a camera from the patient, the guard could not stand convicted of battery.[199] The circumstances indicated that the defendant's conscious objective was to enforce hospital rules, not to insult or provoke the patient.[200] The court held the "slight touching was unavoidable in connection with the discharge of defendant's duty" in his place of employ and, thus, his actions did not amount to battery.[201]

A doctrine that supports constructive intent cases, but which can be rebutted, is that a person is deemed to know the nature and probable consequences of his or her deliberate act.[202] One who throws an object in the direction of another person can be presumed to have intended to strike that person with that object.[203] Where a defendant who pushed a wheelchair-bound robbery victim's wheelchair out of his path in order to escape a robbery could be presumed to know his conduct could cause the wheelchair to move uncontrollably, overturn, and injure the

---

[195] People v. Neeley, 79 Ill. App. 3d 528, 530-531, 398 N.E.2d 988, 990-91 (3d Dist. 1979), cert. denied, 449 U.S. 865 (1980).

[196] People v. Siler, 85 Ill. App. 3d 304, 309, 406 N.E.2d 891, 895 (4th Dist. 1980).

[197] People v. Neeley, 79 Ill. App. 3d 528, 530-531, 398 N.E.2d 988, 990-91 (3d Dist. 1979), cert. denied, 449 U.S. 865 (1980).

[198] People v. Hartzol, 43 Ill. App. 3d 924, 926, 357 N.E.2d 729, 731 (3d Dist. 1976).

[199] People v. Craig, 46 Ill. App. 3d 1058, 1060, 361 N.E.2d 696, 697 (1st Dist. 1977).

[200] People v. Craig, 46 Ill. App. 3d 1058, 1060, 361 N.E.2d 696, 697 (1st Dist. 1977).

[201] People v. Craig, 46 Ill. App. 3d 1058, 1060, 361 N.E.2d 696, 697 (1st Dist. 1977).

[202] People v. Houston, 151 Ill. App. 3d 718, 722, 502 N.E.2d 1174, 1176-77 (5th Dist. 1986).

[203] People v. Hartzol, 43 Ill. App. 3d 924, 926, 357 N.E.2d 729, 731 (3d Dist. 1976).

victim.[204] A person involved in a scuffle is deemed to know that someone may be injured as a result.[205]

Where defendant's conduct evinces, at most, recklessness when his conduct contributes to the injury of another, he cannot be convicted of battery. In one case, high school cheerleaders were riding on a coat-rack, returning it to a hallway in which they were practicing, when the wheels on the rack became locked, which caused the rack to stop in front of a door way.[206] At this point, the defendant came out of the room yelling, "what the hell is going on?" and pushed the rack out of the doorway. Since the wheels were locked, the rack fell over, causing injury to the girls. The appellate court ruled that the defendant did not know that pushing the coat-rack would cause harm to the girls.[207] The natural and probable consequence of the defendant pushing the coat-rack was that the coat-rack would roll in the direction it was pushed, not that the rack would fall over and injure the girls.[208] The mere fact that defendant was angry or irritated did not alone establish the requisite mental state.[209] Consequently, because there was no knowledge or intent, the defendant's conviction for battery was reversed.[210]

§ 9.19. — The Harmful Result.

The third major element of battery involves the *harmful result.* Although some states limit their battery statute to include only acts resulting in actual, physical bodily harm, many states expand the scope of their battery statutes to include both bodily harm and physical conduct of an insulting or provoking nature.[211] In Illinois, battery consists of two alternative and disjunctive elements: (1) physical contact causing bodily harm *or* (2) physical contact of an insulting or provoking nature.[212] One of these must be pleaded as an essential element of

---

[204] People v. Houston, 151 Ill. App. 3d 718, 722, 502 N.E.2d 1174, 1177 (5th Dist. 1986).

[205] People v. Rickman, 73 Ill. App. 3d 755, 759-60, 391 N.E.2d 1114, 1119 (3d Dist. 1979).

[206] People v. Barrington, 15 Ill. App. 3d 445, 445-47, 304 N.E.2d 525, 525-27 (3d Dist. 1973).

[207] People v. Barrington, 15 Ill. App. 3d 445, 446-47, 304 N.E.2d 525, 526 (3d Dist. 1973).

[208] People v. Barrington, 15 Ill. App. 3d 445, 447, 304 N.E.2d 525, 526 (3d Dist. 1973).

[209] People v. Barrington, 15 Ill. App. 3d 445, 447, 304 N.E.2d 525, 526 (3d Dist. 1973).

[210] People v. Barrington, 15 Ill. App. 3d 445, 447, 304 N.E.2d 525, 527 (3d Dist. 1973).

[211] WAYNE LAFAVE & AUSTIN SCOTT, CRIMINAL LAW § 7.15(a) (2d ed. 1986). *Compare* MODEL PENAL CODE § 211.1 (1962). The MODEL PENAL CODE encompasses only the bodily injury type of battery on the grounds that the offensive touching type is not sufficiently serious to be made criminal "except in the case of sexual assaults as provided elsewhere in the Code." MODEL PENAL CODE § 211.1, comment (Tentative Draft No. 9, 1959).

[212] People v. Bissaillon, 55 Ill. App. 3d 893, 894, 371 N.E.2d 362, 364 (3d Dist. 1977).

battery.[213] Obviously, then, it is not necessary to allege that defendant's contact was both insulting or provoking *and* caused bodily harm.[214]

Whether a perpetrator's conduct results in sufficient contact to constitute a battery is determined on a case-by-case basis.[215] Because what constitutes *bodily harm* and *insulting conduct* are not susceptible to precise legal definition, whether an act constitutes a violation of the terms of the battery statute is a question of fact.[216] Since the bodily harm and insulting or provoking physical contact are disjunctive elements of battery, they will be discussed separately, and in that order.

Although the existence of bodily harm is to be determined on a case-by-case analysis, one thing is certain: there must be actual harm causing some sort of pain or damage to the body, like lacerations, bruising or abrasions, whether temporary or permanent.[217] Thus, no battery occurred where a defendant punched a police officer in the face who was wearing a face shield and no actual injury resulted.[218] A victim who was sprayed with mace and felt a tingling sensation on his forehead and arm did not suffer bodily harm within the meaning of the battery statute.[219] However, if the victim suffers "some physical pain," this is sufficient.[220]

The requirement of actual bodily harm, however, does not mandate a showing of actual, visible injury.[221] Certainly, the existence of visible injury, such as welts, bruises,[222] or cuts,[223] is helpful in gaining a conviction; and the absence of

---

[213] People v. Abrams, 48 Ill. 2d 446, 460-61, 271 N.E.2d 37, 45-46 (1971) (where alleged conduct was striking an officer, which is battery, but defendant charged with aggravated assault and not battery, charging instrument was fatally defective).

[214] People v. Bissaillon, 55 Ill. App. 3d 893, 894, 371 N.E.2d 362, 364 (3d Dist. 1977).

[215] *See, e.g.*, People v. Gaither, 221 Ill. App. 3d 629, 635, 582 N.E.2d 735, 739-40 (5th Dist. 1991); People v. Dunker, 217 Ill. App. 3d 410, 415, 577 N.E.2d 499, 502 (4th Dist. 1991); People v. Allen, 117 Ill. App. 2d 20, 28, 254 N.E.2d 103, 107 (1st Dist. 1969).

[216] People v. Allen, 117 Ill. App. 2d 20, 28, 254 N.E.2d 103, 107 (1st Dist. 1969).

[217] People v. Mays, 91 Ill. 2d 251, 256, 437 N.E.2d 633, 635-36 (1982); People v. Gaither, 221 Ill. App. 3d 629, 635, 582 N.E.2d 735, 739 (5th Dist. 1991); People v. Fuller, 159 Ill. App. 3d 441, 444, 512 N.E.2d 832, 834-35 (3d Dist. 1987).

[218] People v. Fuller, 159 Ill. App. 3d 441, 445, 512 N.E.2d 832, 834-35 (3d Dist. 1987).

[219] People v. McBrien, 144 Ill. App. 3d 489, 497, 494 N.E.2d 732, 738 (4th Dist. 1986).

[220] People v. Gaither, 221 Ill. App. 3d 629, 635, 582 N.E.2d 735, 739-40 (5th Dist. 1991); People v. Rotuno, 156 Ill. App. 3d 989, 992-93, 510 N.E.2d 463, 465-66 (5th Dist. 1987).

[221] People v. Rotuno, 156 Ill. App. 3d 989, 992-93, 510 N.E.2d 463, 465-66 (5th Dist. 1987) (police officer kicked in leg and mid-section); People v. Taylor, 53 Ill. App. 3d 810, 815, 368 N.E.2d 950, 954 (5th Dist. 1977) (officer kicked in groin); People v. McEvoy, 33 Ill. App. 3d 409, 411, 337 N.E.2d 437, 439-40 (1st Dist. 1975) (pushing officer in chest which caused him to fall against metal lockers).

[222] People v. Jenkins, 190 Ill. App. 3d 115, 127, 545 N.E.2d 986, 1001 (1st Dist. 1989) (bruises); People v. Virgin, 60 Ill. App. 3d 964, 967, 377 N.E.2d 846, 849 (3d Dist. 1978) (welts and bruises).

[223] People v. Gant, 121 Ill. App. 2d 222, 225, 257 N.E.2d 181, 182 (1st Dist. 1970).

visible injury may undermine a charge of battery.[224] Where the resultant injuries are "relatively minor," they will still support a finding of battery.[225] Accordingly, where the defendant choked and dragged his victim for a considerable distance but no visible injury resulted, a conviction for battery was properly sustained.[226] A battery was sustained where a victim was kicked in the head and groin area although no visible signs of injury were present.[227] Where the defendant shoved a peace officer into a row of metal lockers, the defendant was convicted, since visible injury, such as bruising, scratching, or bleeding, was not required.[228] Finally, a defendant was found guilty of battery where he picked up a child by the right ankle, suspended the child in the air and jerked the child at least four times causing the child to cry.[229]

Conduct falling short of bodily harm is covered by the second element of the Illinois battery statute: where a perpetrator makes contact of an "insulting or provoking nature," he or she will be liable for battery.[230] This type of harm, although it does not cause physical injury, hurt, or pain to the victim, is nevertheless considered an invasion into a person's privacy and dignity.[231]

As with bodily harm, a precise definition of *insulting or provoking contact* does not exist. Rather, the conduct is objectively determined on a case-by-case analysis. Insulting or provoking contact covers overt acts such as the following: where a defendant poked his index finger into the chest of the female victim;[232] where the defendant grabbed the victim's arms, shoulder, and left breast;[233] where the defendant entered the victim's automobile while attempting a burglary, placed his hand over the victim's mouth, and lifted up her dress;[234] and where the defendant grabbed the arm of a female train passenger and attempted to pull her onto his lap.[235] In addition, a particular physical contact may be deemed insulting or provoking based upon the factual context in which it oc-

---

[224] People v. Fuller, 159 Ill. App. 3d 441, 445, 512 N.E.2d 832, 834-35 (3d Dist. 1987) (conviction reversed where proof failed to establish victim was "harmed" when punched).

[225] People v. Tripp, 61 Ill. App. 3d 507, 510, 378 N.E.2d 273, 274 (5th Dist. 1978) (defendant struck victim in face with fist and in the side with a stapler).

[226] People v. Lowe, 12 Ill. App. 3d 959, 299 N.E.2d 341 (1st Dist. 1973) (abstract).

[227] People v. Taylor, 53 Ill. App. 3d 810, 816, 368 N.E.2d 950, 954 (5th Dist. 1977).

[228] People v. McEvoy, 33 Ill. App. 3d 409, 411, 337 N.E.2d 437, 439-40 (1st Dist. 1975).

[229] People v. Gaither, 221 Ill. App. 3d 629, 634-35, 582 N.E.2d 735, 740 (5th Dist. 1991) (described as a "shriek" or "an alarming cry" that continued for some time afterward).

[230] 720 ILCS 5/12-3(a) (1999). *See also* People v. Dunker, 217 Ill. App. 3d 410, 415, 577 N.E.2d 499, 502 (4th Dist. 1991) (poking female teacher in the chest).

[231] Illinois' protection against insulting or provoking conduct that does not result in physical harm is parallel to the common law tort concept of battery. RESTATEMENT (SECOND) OF TORTS, ch. 2 (1965) (introductory notes).

[232] People v. Dunker, 217 Ill. App. 3d 410, 415, 577 N.E.2d 499, 502 (4th Dist. 1991).

[233] People v. Hayes, 37 Ill. App. 3d 772, 775, 347 N.E.2d 327, 329 (1st Dist. 1976).

[234] People v. Siler, 85 Ill. App. 3d 304, 309, 406 N.E.2d 891, 895 (4th Dist. 1980).

[235] People v. Vodicka, 1 Ill. App. 3d 1062, 1066, 275 N.E.2d 731, 734 (1st Dist. 1971).

curs.[236] For example, a defendant, a medical doctor, was convicted of battery of an insulting or provoking nature for masturbating while performing a rectal exam on a patient because this non-insulting act (consensual rectal exam) became an insulting act when viewed in context (the concurrent masturbation).[237]

Evidently, there is no need to show that the defendant made *actual*, direct physical contact with his victim; such as by touching the victim, to qualify as insulting or provoking. Spitting upon the victim could constitute battery.[238]

The last concern to be addressed revolves around the phrase *without legal justification*.[239] In *People v. Harvey*,[240] the Illinois Supreme Court, in deciding that an indictment was not fatally defective because it did not allege "without legal justification," held that "[t]he statute defining battery contains all the elements necessary to constitute this offense, including the lack of lawful justification."[241] As such, a defendant cannot complain that he was not explicitly informed that the offense charged was committed without lawful justification to be proved at each and every trial.[242] In addition, the appellate districts have held that *without legal justification* is not an essential element of battery to be proved at each and every trial.[243] Instead, *without legal justification* is an affirmative defense which must be raised by the defendant.[244]

In a case involving a charge of battery by a parent based on corporeal punishment of a child, a trial judge is *not* obligated to provide an instruction *sua sponte* concerning parental justification.[245] Like any other battery case, where the accused offers no evidence of legal justification, no instruction is required.[246] Thus, where two parents hit their child with their hands, a plastic baseball bat, and a belt, kicked her, threw liquor in her face, and pulled her hair

---

[236] People v. d'Avis, 250 Ill. App. 3d 649, 651, 621 N.E.2d 206, 207 (1st Dist. 1993).

[237] People v. d'Avis, 250 Ill. App. 3d 649, 651, 621 N.E.2d 206, 208 (1st Dist. 1993).

[238] ILL. ANN. STAT. ch. 38, para. 12-3 (Smith-Hurd 1979), 1961 Committee Comments, at 440 (revised 1972); People v. Peck, 260 Ill. App. 3d 812, 813-15, 633 N.E.2d 222, 223-24 (4th Dist. 1994) (spitting on police officer is aggravated battery); People v. Wys, 103 Ill. App. 3d 273, 277-78, 431 N.E.2d 38, 41-42 (3d Dist. 1982) (same).

[239] 720 ILCS 5/12-3 (1999).

[240] 53 Ill. 2d 585, 294 N.E.2d 269 (1973).

[241] People v. Harvey, 53 Ill. 2d 585, 589, 294 N.E.2d 269, 271 (1973).

[242] People v. Harvey, 53 Ill. 2d 585, 589, 294 N.E.2d 269, 271 (1973).

[243] People v. Sambo, 197 Ill. App. 3d 574, 582, 554 N.E.2d 1080, 1085 (2d Dist. 1990); People v. Graves, 107 Ill. App. 3d 449, 454, 437 N.E.2d 866, 870 (1st Dist. 1982); People v. Bitner, 89 Ill. App. 3d 1106, 1112, 412 N.E.2d 721, 726 (3d Dist. 1980); People v. Voda, 70 Ill. App. 3d 430, 437, 388 N.E.2d 206, 212 (1st Dist. 1979); People v. Worsham, 26 Ill. App. 3d 767, 771, 326 N.E.2d 134, 137 (1st Dist. 1975).

[244] People v. Sambo, 197 Ill. App. 3d 574, 582, 554 N.E.2d 1080, 1085 (2d Dist. 1990); People v. Worsham, 26 Ill. App. 3d 767, 771, 326 N.E.2d 134, 137 (1st Dist. 1975).

[245] People v. Lee, 84 Ill. App. 3d 441, 445, 405 N.E.2d 860, 863 (3d Dist. 1980).

[246] People v. Sambo, 197 Ill. App. 3d 574, 581-82, 554 N.E.2d 1080, 1084-85 (2d Dist. 1990) (no "without legal justification" instruction required).

and teeth, the parents, without any showing of legal justification, were found guilty of committing battery.[247] Paranthetically, such convictions do not violate public policy or infringe on the right to privacy with respect to family and child rearing.[248]

Likewise, where the defendant, a school teacher, struck a sixth grade, eleven-year-old student with a wooden paddle ten times, his claim that this was a disciplinary measure that was legally justified was rejected and, consequently, he was guilty of battery.[249] Here, the Illinois Supreme Court ruled the trial judge in a bench trial was correct in concluding the corporeal punishment inflicted was in reality a "beating" and more severe than the child's parents could have inflicted and, as such, was unreasonable and without legal justification.[250]

§ 9.20. Aggravated Battery.

A more serious offense than simple battery is aggravated battery, codified in section 5/12-4. While battery is a misdemeanor,[251] aggravated battery is a felony.[252] As the name of this offense implies, there must be proof of (1) a battery and (2) certain aggravating circumstances,[253] each of which involves an additional social evil and merits a more serious sanction.[254]

§ 9.21. — Aggravated Battery Codified.

Aggravated battery is defined as follows:

(a) A person who, in committing a battery, intentionally or knowingly causes great bodily harm, or permanent disability or disfigurement commits aggravated battery.

(b) In committing a battery, a person commits aggravated battery if he or she:

(1) Uses a deadly weapon other than by the discharge of a firearm;

(2) Is hooded, robed or masked, in such manner as to conceal his identity;

(3) Knows the individual harmed to be a teacher or other person employed in any school and such teacher or other employee is upon the

---

[247] People v. Sambo, 197 Ill. App. 3d 574, 581-82, 554 N.E.2d 1080, 1084-85 (2d Dist. 1990).

[248] People v. Sambo, 197 Ill. App. 3d 574, 588, 554 N.E.2d 1080, 1088-89 (2d Dist. 1990).

[249] People v. Ball, 58 Ill. 2d 36, 36-40, 317 N.E.2d 54, 55-57 (1974).

[250] People v. Ball, 58 Ill. 2d 36, 38-40, 317 N.E.2d 54, 55-57 (1974).

[251] 720 ILCS 5/12-3(b) (1999).

[252] 720 ILCS 5/12-4(e) (1999).

[253] 720 ILCS 5/12-4 (1999).

[254] People v. Hanson, 53 Ill. 2d 79, 82, 289 N.E.2d 611, 613 (1972), *cert. denied,* 411 U.S. 937 (1973).

grounds of a school or grounds adjacent thereto, or is in any part of a building used for school purposes;

(4) Knows the individual harmed to be a supervisor, director, instructor or other person employed in any park district and such supervisor, director, or instructor or other employee is upon the grounds of the park or grounds adjacent thereto, or is in any part of a building used for park purposes;

(5) Knows the individual harmed to be a caseworker, investigator, or other person employed by the State Department of Public Aid, a County Department of Public Aid, or the Department of Human Services ... and such caseworker, investigator, or other person is upon the grounds of a public aid office or grounds adjacent thereto, or is in any part of a building used for public aid purposes, or upon the grounds of a home of a public aid applicant, recipient, or any other person being interviewed or investigated in the employee's discharge of his duties, or on grounds adjacent thereto, or is in any part of a building in which the applicant, recipient, or other such person resides or is located;

(6) Knows the individual harmed to be a peace officer, a community policing volunteer, or a correctional institutional employee, or a fireman while such officer, volunteer, employee or fireman is engaged in the execution of any official duties including arrest or attempted arrest, or to prevent the officer, volunteer, employee or fireman from performing official duties, or in retaliation for the officer, volunteer, employee or fireman performing his official duties, and the battery is committed other than by the discharge of a firearm;

(7) Knows the individual harmed to be an emergency medical technician-ambulance, emergency medical technician-intermediate, emergency medical technician-paramedic, ambulance driver or other medical assistance or first aid personnel engaged in the performance of any of his or her official duties, or to prevent the emergency medical technician-ambulance, emergency medical technician-intermediate, emergency medical technician-paramedic, ambulance driver, or other medical assistance or first aid personnel from performing official duties, or in retaliation for performing official duties;

(8) Is, or the person battered is, on or about a public way, public property or public place of accommodation or amusement;

(9) Knows the individual harmed to be the driver, operator, employee or passenger of any transportation facility or system engaged in the business of transportation of the public for hire and the individual assaulted is then performing in such capacity or then using such public transportation as a passenger or using any area of any description designated by

the transportation facility or system as a vehicle boarding, departure, or transfer location;

(10) Knowingly and without legal justification and by any means causes bodily harm to an individual of 60 years of age or older;

(11) Knows the individual harmed is pregnant;

(12) Knows the individual harmed to be a judge whom the person intended to harm as a result of the judge's performance of his or her official duties as a judge;

(13) Knows the individual harmed to be an employee of the Illinois Department of Children and Family Services engaged in the performance of his authorized duties as such employee;

(14) Knows the individual harmed to be a person who is physically handicapped; or

(15) Knowingly and without legal justification and by any means causes bodily harm to a merchant who detains the person for an alleged commission of retail theft under Section 16A-5 of this Code. In this item (15), "merchant" has the meaning ascribed to it in Section 16A-2.4 of this Code.

For the purpose of paragraph (14) of subsection (b) of this Section, a physically handicapped person is a person who suffers from a permanent and disabling physical characteristic, resulting from disease, injury, functional disorder or congenital condition.

(c) A person who administers to an individual or causes him to take, without his consent or by threat or deception, and for other than medical purposes, any intoxicating, poisonous, stupefying, narcotic, anesthetic, or controlled substance commits aggravated battery.

(d) A person who knowingly gives to another person any food that contains any substance or object that is intended to cause physical injury if eaten, commits aggravated battery.

(e) Sentence . . . .[255]

The 1961 revision committee's comments, which reflect on the scope of the offense, reveal that it was the legislature's intent that the current aggravated battery statute encompass three distinct categories of battery — all of which involve some extraordinary potential for harm from a societal perspective: (1) subsection (a) was designed to cover what was previously considered "mayhem" in circumstances where, for instance, attempted murder is unavailable because the defendant lacked the requisite specific intent to kill; (2) subsection (b) was created to address batteries not covered by subsection (a) where the facts surrounding the battery evidence circumstances from which great societal harm not

---

[255] 720 ILCS 5/12-4 (1999).

common to a simple battery might and usually does result; and subsection (c) was enacted to punish those "unusual type[s] of battery which usually precedes a more serious offense such as rape, robbery or even murder."[256] Subsection (d) was added later but is supported by much of the same policy considerations as the other subsections.

§ 9.22. — Elements of Aggravated Battery.

Aggravated battery most often occurs in two forms. The first encompasses those batteries which are aggravated because of the seriousness of the harm inflicted.[257] The basic elements of this form are the (1) commission of a battery (2) while intentionally or knowingly causing great bodily harm or permanent disability. The second type of aggravated battery that occurs frequently involves those batteries which are aggravated based on certain enumerated factors of aggravation, such as the status of the victim, which is not related to the harm inflicted.[258] The elements of this form of aggravated battery are (1) the commission of a battery (2) which additionally encompasses one of the enumerated factors of aggravation. Additionally, although less common, a defendant may be convicted of aggravated battery where, through threat or deception, the defendant causes a person to consume an intoxicating or poisonous substance[259] or gives a person any food that is intended to harm him or her.[260]

Factors of aggravation include the use of a deadly weapon other than the discharge of a firearm,[261] concealment of identity during the course of a battery,[262] commission of the battery in a public place,[263] and committing a battery against a member of a protected group of which the defendant knows the victim to be a member of that group. Members of protected groups include teachers,[264] employees of any park district,[265] employees of the State Department of Public Aid, a County Department of Public Aid, or Department of Human Services,[266] peace officers or persons summoned by a peace officer,[267] firemen,[268] paramedics,[269]

---

[256] ILL. ANN. STAT. ch. 38, para. 12-4 (Smith-Hurd 1979), 1961 Committee Comments, at 465-66 (revised 1972). Subsection 5/12-4(d) was added in 1979, and no comment on its import was provided.

[257] 720 ILCS 5/12-4(a) (1999).

[258] See 720 ILCS 5/12-4(b) (1999).

[259] 720 ILCS 5/12-4(c) (1999).

[260] 720 ILCS 5/12-4(d) (1999).

[261] 720 ILCS 5/12-4(b)(1) (1999).

[262] 720 ILCS 5/12-4(b)(2) (1999).

[263] 720 ILCS 5/12-4(b)(8) (1999).

[264] 720 ILCS 5/12-4(b)(3) (1999).

[265] 720 ILCS 5/12-4(b)(4) (1999).

[266] 720 ILCS 5/12-4(b)(5) (1999).

[267] 720 ILCS 5/12-4(b)(6) (1999).

[268] 720 ILCS 5/12-4(b)(6) (1999).

[269] 720 ILCS 5/12-4(b)(7) (1999).

ambulance drivers or other governmentally employed medical assistants,[270] drivers, operators, employees or passengers of a public or private transportation system,[271] persons of sixty years of age or older,[272] women who are pregnant,[273] judges,[274] persons employed by the Illinois Department of Children and Family Services,[275] persons physically handicapped,[276] and merchants.[277] Where the member is protected by virtue of their type of employment, the member must be acting in their capacity of that employment. For example, in order for an aggravated battery to occur based on the fact that the victim is a peace officer, the peace officer must be acting in his capacity as a peace officer at the time the battery takes place.[278] Where a perpetrator commits a battery upon a peace officer who is off duty, it is still aggravated battery if the battery occurred while the officer was *acting* in his or her capacity as a peace officer since (1) an officer has a duty to maintain public order wherever he or she may be and (2) his or her duties are not confined to a specific time and place.[279]

Prior to 1979, with respect to those aggravated batteries involving harm to the class of persons protected, a conflict existed among the appellate courts whether the word *harmed* included, for aggravated battery purposes, physical contact of an insulting or provoking nature or whether the term only encompassed actual physical harm.[280] In *People v. Hale*,[281] the Illinois Supreme Court adopted the rationale of the fourth appellate district noting that the legislature had intended to protect members of designated groups from harassment and interference that they may encounter because of their status or duties.[282] Accordingly, members of the protected groups are provided additional protection from both actual physi-

---

[270] 720 ILCS 5/12-4(b)(7) (1999).

[271] 720 ILCS 5/12-4(b)(9) (1999).

[272] 720 ILCS 5/12-4(b)(10) (1999).

[273] 720 ILCS 5/12-4(b)(11) (1999).

[274] 720 ILCS 5/12-4(b)(12) (1999).

[275] 720 ILCS 5/12-4(b)(13) (1999).

[276] 720 ILCS 5/12-4(b)(14) (1999).

[277] 720 ILCS 5/12-4(b)(15) (1999).

[278] 720 ILCS 5/12-4(b)(6) (1999). *See also* People v. Jenkins, 190 Ill. App. 3d 115, 127, 545 N.E.2d 986, 1001 (1st Dist. 1989).

[279] People v. Weaver, 100 Ill. App. 3d 512, 514, 426 N.E.2d 1227, 1228 (4th Dist. 1981), *cert. denied*, 459 U.S. 843 (1982).

[280] *See* People v. Haltom, 37 Ill. App. 3d 1059, 1061-62, 347 N.E.2d 502, 503-04 (1st Dist. 1976) (convictions for aggravated battery reversed on grounds that there was no showing of actual physical harm to police officer); People v. Nance, 26 Ill. App. 3d 182, 185, 324 N.E.2d 652, 655 (5th Dist. 1975) (mere physical contact of provoking nature directed at police officer was insufficient to constitute harm required for aggravated battery). *But see* People v. Meints, 41 Ill. App. 3d 215, 218-20, 355 N.E.2d 125, 128-29 (4th Dist. 1976) (insulting or provoking conduct against member of protected group sufficient to sustain aggravated battery charge).

[281] 77 Ill. 2d 114, 395 N.E.2d 929 (1979).

[282] People v. Hale, 77 Ill. 2d 114, 118-19, 395 N.E.2d 929, 931-32 (1979).

cal bodily harm and physical contact of an insulting or provoking nature.[283] For instance, in *People v. Peck*,[284] the defendant committed aggravated battery by spitting in a police officer's face. Here, the court rejected the defendant's claims that spitting was an accident and did not constitute physical contact or insulting or provoking behavior.[285] Similarly, where defendant, a prison inmate, threw liquid at a correctional officer, this was aggravated battery of an insulting or provoking nature.[286]

With respect to aggravated battery premised on great bodily harm, there is no precise definition of the term "great bodily harm."[287] Whether the victim suffered great bodily injury is determined by the trier of fact.[288] The Illinois Supreme Court has found that bodily harm for *ordinary battery* must consist of "some sort of physical pain or damage to the body, like lacerations, bruises or abrasions, whether temporary or permanent."[289] It is clear, however, that "great bodily harm" for aggravated battery involves a type of injury of a greater and more serious character than ordinary battery.[290] Whether the victim received medical attention is not determinative that the injury incurred constitutes great bodily harm.[291] The fact that the injury is not permanent does not mean it was less than great bodily harm.[292] Where a victim was shot in the foot, piercing the shoe but not the skin, the victim was not found to have suffered great bodily injury even though he limped after the shot.[293] Where the victim suffered a "graze wound" to his chest when a bullet struck him, this was insufficient evidence of great bodily harm.[294] On the other hand, great bodily harm was incurred where a victim, a child, was punched twice by an adult male in the face causing the child's nose to bleed and a bruise to develop that lasted a week, and there was

---

[283] People v. Hale, 77 Ill. 2d 114, 118-19, 395 N.E.2d 929, 931-32 (1979).

[284] 260 Ill. App. 3d 812, 633 N.E.2d 222 (4th Dist. 1994).

[285] People v. Peck, 260 Ill. App. 3d 812, 814-15, 633 N.E.2d 222, 224 (4th Dist. 1994).

[286] People v. Walker, 291 Ill. App. 3d 597, 603-04, 683 N.E.2d 1296, 1301 (4th Dist. 1997) (liquid was either water or urine).

[287] People v. Psichalinos, 229 Ill. App. 3d 1058, 1068, 594 N.E.2d 1374, 1381 (2d Dist. 1992); People v. Figures, 216 Ill. App. 3d 398, 401, 576 N.E.2d 1089, 1091 (1st Dist. 1991).

[288] People v. Psichalinos, 229 Ill. App. 3d 1058, 1068, 594 N.E.2d 1374, 1382 (2d Dist. 1992).

[289] People v. Mays, 91 Ill. 2d 251, 256, 437 N.E.2d 633, 635-36 (1982).

[290] People v. Figures, 216 Ill. App. 3d 398, 401, 576 N.E.2d 1089, 1091 (1st Dist. 1991); People v. Costello, 95 Ill. App. 3d 680, 684, 420 N.E.2d 592, 595 (2d Dist. 1982).

[291] People v. Psichalinos, 229 Ill. App. 3d 1058, 1068, 594 N.E.2d 1374, 1382 (2d Dist. 1992).

[292] People v. Smith, 6 Ill. App. 3d 259, 264, 285 N.E.2d 460, 464 (1st Dist. 1972) ("[M]any serious bodily injuries leave no lasting effect on the health, strength, and comfort of the injured person.").

[293] People v. Figures, 216 Ill. App. 3d 398, 401, 576 N.E.2d 1089, 1092 (1st Dist. 1991) (although it did support an aggravated battery conviction based on causing bodily harm through the use of a deadly weapon as outlawed by 5/12-4(b)(1)).

[294] People v. Watkins, 243 Ill. App. 3d 271, 277-78, 611 N.E.2d 1121, 1125-26 (1st Dist. 1993).

medical evidence that the child suffered a fractured nose.[295] Also, great bodily harm was inflicted on a victim where the victim was burned with a hot iron, resulting in a painful and obvious physical injury.[296]

Regarding the "permanent disability" concern in 5/12-4(a), the term disability means that "the victim is no longer whole such that the injured bodily portion or part no longer serves the body in the manner as it did before the injury."[297] Thus, where a battery victim suffered a permanent partial numbness in one lip and lost a tooth, this constituted a permanent disability for aggravated battery.[298]

§ 9.23. — Battery and Aggravated Battery — Lesser Included Offenses.

Obviously, battery is a lesser included offense of aggravated battery.[299] Reckless conduct has been ruled to be a lesser included offense of aggravated battery.[300]

Aggravated battery can be construed as a lesser included offense of more serious crimes under certain circumstances. For example, it may be a lesser included offense of attempted murder,[301] murder,[302] or armed violence.[303] But aggravated battery is not necessarily a lesser included offense of a robbery or attempted armed robbery inasmuch as a robbery effort does not invariably require proof of physical contact with the victim.[304]

§ 9.24. Heinous Battery.

In an obvious response to the rather hideous criminal proclivities of some, as exhibited by those who might throw caustic acid in one's face, the General Assembly enacted the "heinous battery" statute. This offense is found in section 5/12-4.1 and is defined in the following terms: "(a) A person who, in committing a battery, knowingly causes severe and permanent disability or disfigurement by

---

[295] People v. Psichalinos, 229 Ill. App. 3d 1058, 1069, 594 N.E.2d 1374, 1382 (2d Dist. 1992).

[296] People v. Curry, 296 Ill. App. 3d 559, 567, 694 N.E.2d 630, 637 (1st Dist. 1998).

[297] People v. Conley, 187 Ill. App. 3d 234, 240, 543 N.E.2d 138, 142 (1st Dist. 1989).

[298] People v. Conley, 187 Ill. App. 3d 234, 240-41, 543 N.E.2d 138, 142 (1st Dist. 1989).

[299] People v. Cole, 47 Ill. App. 3d 775, 780, 362 N.E.2d 432, 436 (4th Dist. 1977); People v. Foster, 32 Ill. App. 3d 1009, 1011, 337 N.E.2d 90, 92 (4th Dist. 1975).

[300] People v. Harris, 104 Ill. App. 3d 833, 840-41, 433 N.E.2d 343, 349 (2d Dist. 1982).

[301] People v. Brock, 64 Ill. App. 3d 64, 68, 380 N.E.2d 1102, 1105 (1st Dist. 1978); People v. Childs, 62 Ill. App. 3d 924, 926, 379 N.E.2d 721, 723 (1st Dist. 1978). *But see* People v. Miller, 284 Ill. App. 3d 16, 26-27, 671 N.E.2d 376, 384-85 (2d Dist. 1996) (finding aggravated battery not lesser included offense of attempt murder), *cert. denied*, 521 U.S. 1107 (1997).

[302] People v. Lyons, 26 Ill. App. 3d 193, 198, 324 N.E.2d 677, 681 (5th Dist.), *cert. denied*, 423 U.S. 1036 (1975).

[303] People v. Bolden, 210 Ill. App. 3d 940, 946, 569 N.E.2d 597, 602 (2d Dist. 1991).

[304] *See, e.g.*, People v. Davis, 50 Ill. App. 3d 506, 515, 365 N.E.2d 628, 635 (1st Dist. 1977).

means of a caustic or flammable substance commits heinous battery. (b) Sentence . . . ."[305]

The difference between heinous battery and aggravated battery is that heinous battery requires the "severe and permanent disability or disfigurement" to be the result of a "caustic substance." In *People v. Hicks*,[306] the Illinois Supreme Court explored the meaning of "caustic substance" as used in the heinous battery statute. In *Hicks*, a defendant threw boiling water on a woman he had sexually assaulted. The victim was severely burned by the boiling water, which caused permanent skin discoloration, scarring, and disfigurement. Although the appellate court ruled as a matter of law that there was no heinous battery because boiling water is not a "caustic substance,"[307] the Illinois Supreme Court disagreed and reinstated the heinous battery conviction.[308] After examining a common dictionary definition of the term *caustic*[309] and noting that it includes any substance capable of destroying tissue, the court concluded that boiling water is a caustic substance.[310] The court noted that no distinction can be made between burns caused by chemical action and those caused by thermal action.[311] Relying on *Hicks*, the first appellate district has held that grain alcohol, when ignited, is a caustic substance.[312]

On the other hand, in *People v. O'Neal*,[313] the appellate court did not find severe and permanent disfigurement required for heinous battery notwithstanding the existence of second-degree burns to the legs of a two-year-old child victim, and the fact that the child remained in the hospital for three weeks, had scar tissue on both legs, tired easily, remained sensitive to temperature changes, and had a mild discoloration of his skin.[314]

---

[305] 720 ILCS 5/12-4.1 (1999).

[306] 101 Ill. 2d 366, 462 N.E.2d 473 (1984).

[307] People v. Hicks, 101 Ill. 2d 366, 370, 462 N.E.2d 473, 474-75 (1984).

[308] People v. Hicks, 101 Ill. 2d 366, 376, 462 N.E.2d 473, 477 (1984).

[309] People v. Hicks, 101 Ill. 2d 366, 372, 462 N.E.2d 473, 475 (1984) (citing WEBSTER'S THIRD NEW INTERNATIONAL DICTIONARY 356 (1971) ("[C]apable of destroying the texture of anything or eating away its substance by chemical action; corrosive: as (a) capable of destroying animal or other organic tissue . . . (b): strongly alkaline")).

[310] People v. Hicks, 101 Ill. 2d 366, 373, 462 N.E.2d 473, 475 (1984).

[311] People v. Hicks, 101 Ill. 2d 366, 373, 462 N.E.2d 473, 475 (1984) (citing BLACKISTON'S GOULD MEDICAL DICTIONARY 257 (4th ed. 1979), the court noted that chemical action as used in the definition of caustic is defined as the "molecular change produced in any substance through the action of *heat*, light, electricity, or another chemical."). *See also* People v. Cooper, 283 Ill. App. 3d 86, 92-93, 669 N.E.2d 637, 642 (1st Dist. 1996) (evidence sufficient to support heinous battery conviction where child victim suffered second degree burns over 10 percent of his body as a result of defendant submerging the child victim in a bathtub of hot water).

[312] People v. Rogers, 222 Ill. App. 3d 774, 777, 584 N.E.2d 397, 399 (1st Dist. 1991).

[313] 257 Ill. App. 3d 490, 628 N.E.2d 1077 (1st Dist. 1993).

[314] People v. O'Neal, 257 Ill. App. 3d 490, 495, 628 N.E.2d 1077, 1081 (1st Dist. 1993).

§ 9.25. Aggravated Battery with a Firearm.

In 5/12-4.2 appears the offense of "aggravated battery with a firearm." This felony offense reads:

> (a) A person commits aggravated battery with a firearm when he, in committing a battery, knowingly or intentionally by means of the discharging of a firearm (1) causes any injury to another person, or (2) causes any injury to a person he knows to be a peace officer, a community policing volunteer, a correctional institution employee or a fireman while the officer, volunteer, employee or fireman is engaged in the execution of any of his official duties, or to prevent the officer, volunteer, employee or fireman from performing his official duties, or in retaliation for the officer, employee or fireman performing his official duties, or (3) causes any injury to a person he knows to be an emergency medical technician-ambulance, emergency medical technician-intermediate, emergency medical technician-paramedic, ambulance driver, or other medical assistance or first aid personnel, employed by a municipality or other governmental unit, while the emergency medical technician-ambulance, emergency medical technician-intermediate, emergency medical technician-paramedic, ambulance driver, or other medical assistance or first aid personnel is engaged in the execution of any of his official duties, or to prevent the emergency medical technician-ambulance, emergency medical technician-intermediate, emergency medical technician-paramedic, ambulance driver, or other medical assistance or first aid personnel from performing his official duties, or in retaliation for the emergency medical technician-ambulance, emergency medical technician-intermediate, emergency medical technician-paramedic, ambulance driver, or other medical assistance or first aid personnel performing his official duties.[315]

The elements of aggravated battery with a firearm are that a defendant (1) while committing a battery, (2) intentionally or knowingly (3) by means of discharging a firearm (4) causes injury to a person. First, it must be established that defendant's conduct constituted a *battery*, which involves causing bodily harm or making contact of an insulting or provoking nature.[316] Thus, where defendant's bullet caused a "small nick or cut" on the victim's arm, this satisfied the "causes bodily harm" element of battery that was necessary to convict defendant of aggravated battery with a firearm.[317]

---

[315] 720 ILCS 5/12-4.2 (1999). *See also* People v. Lee, 167 Ill. 2d 140, 144-47, 656 N.E.2d 1065, 1067-68 (1995) (aggravated battery with a firearm statute not violative of due process or proportionality penalties clause).

[316] People v. Durham, 303 Ill. App. 3d 763, 769, 708 N.E.2d 1249, 1253 (2d Dist. 1999).

[317] People v. Durham, 303 Ill. App. 3d 763, 769, 708 N.E.2d 1249, 1253 (2d Dist. 1999).

The defendant's discharge of a firearm must be *intentional* or *knowing*. Where there was evidence that defendant's discharge of a firearm and resultant injury was a product of his recklessness, this could be reckless conduct[318] but not aggravated battery with a firearm.[319]

The defendant must discharge a *firearm* which causes injury. "Firearm" is defined as "any device . . . which is designed to expel a projectile or projectiles by the action of an explosion, expansion of gas or escape of gas . . . ."[320]

The discharge of the firearm must cause *injury to a person*.[321] If a defendant discharges a firearm but without injuring anyone, he commits the offense of aggravated discharge of a firearm, which is a separate offense.[322]

§ 9.26. Domestic Battery.

In 1990, the Illinois General Assembly enacted the offense of "domestic battery."[323] The statute provides:

> A person commits Domestic Battery if he intentionally or knowingly without legal justification by any means: (1) Causes bodily harm to any family member or household member . . . ; [or] (2) Makes physical contact of an insulting or provoking nature with any family or household member . . . .[324]

Domestic battery is a misdemeanor unless defendant has been previously convicted of domestic battery or the offense of violation of order of protection, in which case it is a felony.[325]

Where defendant committed home invasion and domestic battery against a victim who had an order of protection against the defendant, the defendant was

---

[318] 720 ILCS 5/12-5(a) (1999).

[319] People v. Roberts, 265 Ill. App. 3d 400, 402-04, 638 N.E.2d 359, 361-62 (1st Dist. 1994) (where evidence warranted instruction on reckless conduct, aggravated battery with a firearm conviction reversed); People v. Smith, 261 Ill. App. 3d 117, 118-20, 633 N.E.2d 69, 71-72 (4th Dist. 1994) (same).

[320] 720 ILCS 5/12-4/2(c) (1999) (incorporates definition of "firearm" from Firearm Owners Identification Card Act, 430 ILCS 65/1.1 (1999)).

[321] People v. Durham, 303 Ill. App. 3d 763, 768, 708 N.E.2d 1249, 1253 (2d Dist. 1999) (aggravated battery with a firearm conviction affirmed); People v. White, 293 Ill. App. 3d 335, 338, 687 N.E.2d 1179, 1181 (4th Dist. 1997).

[322] 720 ILCS 5/24-1.2(a)(2) (1999); People v. Peterson, 273 Ill. App. 3d 412, 423, 652 N.E.2d 1252, 1261 (1st Dist. 1995) (aggravated battery with a firearm reversed and aggravated discharge of a firearm affirmed). *See* chapter 15 for a discussion of aggravated discharge of a firearm.

[323] 720 ILCS 5/12-3.2 (1999).

[324] 720 ILCS 5/12-3.2(a) (1999).

[325] 720 ILCS 5/12-3.2(b) (1999). Violation of order of protection is found at 720 ILCS 5/12-30 (1999).

convicted of home invasion, domestic battery and violation of order of protection over same physical act doctrine objections.[326]

§ 9.27. Battery of an Unborn Child.

In 1986, the offense of "battery of an unborn child" became law.[327] Section 5/12-3.1 provides in part:

> A person commits battery of an unborn child if he intentionally or knowingly without legal justification and by any means causes bodily harm to an unborn child.[328]

This offense, which is punishable as a misdemeanor,[329] defines unborn child as "any individual of the human species from fertilization until birth" and does not include the pregnant mother.[330] The offense does not apply to legal abortions or acts committed "pursuant to usual and customary standards of medical practice during diagnostic testing or therapeutic treatment."[331]

§ 9.28. Aggravated Battery of an Unborn Child.

An aggravated form of the offense of battery of an unborn child exists in Illinois.[332] A person commits "aggravated battery of an unborn child" if "in committing battery of an unborn child, [he or she] intentionally or knowingly causes great bodily harm, or permanent disability or disfigurement" to the unborn child.[333] Aggravated battery of an unborn child is punishable as a felony.[334]

§ 9.29. Aggravated Battery of a Child.

Although there is no criminal offense entitled "battery of a child," the offense of "aggravated battery of a child" has been enacted.[335] The current statute reads:

> Any person of the age 18 years and upwards who intentionally or knowingly, and without legal justification and by any means, causes great bodily harm or permanent disability or disfigurement to any child under the age of

---

[326] People v. Priest, 297 Ill. App. 3d 797, 800-07, 698 N.E.2d 223, 225-29 (4th Dist. 1998).
[327] 720 ILCS 5/12-3.1 (1999).
[328] 720 ILCS 5/12-3.1(a) (1999).
[329] 720 ILCS 5/12-3.1(c) (1999).
[330] 720 ILCS 5/12-3.1(b) (1999).
[331] 720 ILCS 5/12-3.1(d) (1999).
[332] 720 ILCS 5/12-4.4 (1999).
[333] 720 ILCS 5/12-4.4(a) (1999).
[334] 720 ILCS 5/12-4.4(b) (1999).
[335] 720 ILCS 5/12-4.3 (1999).

13 years or to any institutionalized severely or profoundly mentally re-tarded person, commits the offense of aggravated battery of a child.[336]

Aggravated battery of a child occurred where a mother placed her infant in water between 120 and 150 degrees which was likely to cause significant pain to the infant;[337] where a defendant punched his three-year-old child in the face causing the child's nose to bleed;[338] where a defendant shook a two and one-half month old baby with such force as to cause brain damage to the child;[339] where a defendant shook a fifteen-month-old child in a violent and repetitive manner, causing severe and permanent injuries of a type consistent with shaken baby syndrome,[340] where a defendant picked up a two-year-old child and held the child's body in front of his face and chest to shield himself from bullets being fired at him, which bullets struck the child,[341] and where a mother and father grabbed their six-year-old and eight-year-old daughters by the arms and legs and threw them off their third floor porch.[342]

§ 9.30. Aggravated Battery of a Senior Citizen.

An offense designed for the protection of senior citizens is "aggravated bat-tery of a senior citizen."[343] A person commits aggravated battery of a senior citi-zen when, in committing battery, he or she "intentionally or knowingly causes great bodily harm or permanent disability or disfigurement to an individual of 60 years of age or older."[344] Where the battery inflicted upon the elderly victim does *not* involve "great bodily harm or permanent disability or disfigurement," then it would be prosecuted under the general aggravated battery statute.[345] Ag-gravated battery of a senior citizen is currently punishable as a more serious fel-ony than aggravated battery.[346]

§ 9.31. Tampering with Food, Drugs or Cosmetics.

The offense of "tampering with food, drugs or cosmetics"[347] is obviously in-tended to address the problem of the malicious placement of poisons or the like

---

[336] 720 ILCS 5/12-4.3(a) (1999).

[337] People v. Flores, 168 Ill. App. 3d 284, 290, 522 N.E.2d 708, 711-12 (1st Dist. 1988).

[338] People v. Psichalinos, 229 Ill. App. 3d 1058, 1069, 594 N.E.2d 1374, 1382 (2d Dist. 1992).

[339] People v. Reneria, 232 Ill. App. 3d 409, 416, 597 N.E.2d 714, 719 (1st Dist. 1992).

[340] People v. Ripley, 291 Ill. App. 3d 565, 568-69, 685 N.E.2d 362, 365 (3d Dist. 1997).

[341] People v. Hall, 273 Ill. App. 3d 838, 841-42, 652 N.E.2d 1266, 1269 (1st Dist. 1995).

[342] People v. Moore, 208 Ill. App. 3d 515, 524, 567 N.E.2d 466, 473 (1st Dist. 1990).

[343] 720 ILCS 5/12-4.6 (1999).

[344] 720 ILCS 5/12-4.6(a) (1999).

[345] 720 ILCS 5/12-4(a)(10) (1999).

[346] 720 ILCS 5/12-4.6(b) (1999) (Class 2 felony). Aggravated battery is a Class 3 felony. 720 ILCS 5/12-4(e) (1999).

[347] 720 ILCS 5/12-4.5 (1999).

in substances where innocent consumers might be killed or seriously harmed as a consequence thereof. Section 5/12-4.5 makes it a felony[348] to violate the following measure:

> Any person who knowingly puts any substance capable of causing death or great bodily harm to a human being into any food, drug or cosmetic offered for sale or consumption commits the offense of tampering with food, drugs or cosmetics.[349]

§ 9.32. Drug Induced Infliction of Great Bodily Harm.

One of several criminal offenses enacted in an attempt to assist the "war on drugs" is the "drug induced infliction of great bodily harm" statute.[350] A person is guilty of this felony[351] if he or she violates the following provision:

> Any person who . . . deliver[s] a controlled substance to another commits the offense of drug induced infliction of great bodily harm if any person experiences great bodily harm or permanent disability as a result of the injection, inhalation or ingestion of any amount of that controlled substance.[352]

§ 9.33. Drug Induced Infliction of Aggravated Battery to a Child Athlete.

In 1997, the legislature enacted a prohibition against "drug induced infliction of aggravated battery to a child athlete."[353] This offense is committed by any person who distributes to or encourages the ingestion of a drug by a person who is seventeen years of age or younger with the intent that the person who is seventeen or younger "will ingest the drug for the purpose of quick weight gain or loss in connection with participation in athletics. . . ."[354] This prohibition does not apply to care provided by a licensed physician under usual and customary standards of medical practice or to the sale of drugs or products by a retail merchant.[355] This offense is a misdemeanor, but a second or subsequent offense is a felony.[356]

---

[348] 720 ILCS 5/12-4.5(b) (1999).
[349] 720 ILCS 5/12-4(a) (1999).
[350] 720 ILCS 5/12-4.7 (1999).
[351] 720 ILCS 5/12-4.7(b) (1999).
[352] 720 ILCS 5/12-4.7(a) (1999).
[353] 720 ILCS 5/12-4.9 (1999).
[354] 720 ILCS 5/12-4.9(a) (1999).
[355] 720 ILCS 5/12-4.9(a) (1999).
[356] 720 ILCS 5/12-4.9(b) (1999).

§ 9.34. Reckless Conduct.

Because of the fact that (1) assault and aggravated assault are limited to situations in which a defendant places another in apprehension of an imminent battery and (2) battery and aggravated forms thereof are restricted to those actual infliction of injury on another where the defendant has acted with intent or knowledge, the General Assembly created the misdemeanor offense of "reckless conduct"[357] to cover those acts deserving of criminal sanction that do not rise to the level of assault or battery, or an aggravated form thereof, and that have been performed recklessly.[358] Appearing in section 5/12-5, this offense is defined in the following language:

> A person who causes bodily harm to or endangers the bodily safety of an individual by any means, commits reckless conduct if he performs recklessly the acts which cause the harm or endanger safety, whether they otherwise are lawful or unlawful.[359]

In their drafting of this statute, the revision committee stated this enactment was "aimed primarily at the reckless homicide type of conduct where no homicide results."[360] It is important to note that no bodily injury need be suffered by the victim, for if his or her "bodily safety" is threatened, this is sufficient.[361] In addition, as long as the defendant's conduct is reckless, there is a violation regardless of whether the conduct was lawful or unlawful.[362] The crime can be carried out "by any means," which gives rise to a myriad of possibilities.[363] Finally, the courts have concluded that "an individual" as used in this statute means someone other than the person charged with the offense of reckless conduct.[364] Thus, a person who shot himself in the foot without injuring or endangering others was not guilty of reckless conduct.[365]

Although the legislative drafting committee comments states that this statute is aimed *primarily* at the situation in which reckless homicide could have occurred, the Illinois courts point out that this crime cannot be construed as limit-

---

[357] 720 ILCS 5/12-5 (1999).

[358] *See* People v. Peters, 180 Ill. App. 3d 850, 853, 536 N.E.2d 465, 467 (2d Dist. 1989).

[359] 720 ILCS 5/12-5 (1999).

[360] ILL. ANN. STAT. ch. 38, para. 12-5 (Smith-Hurd 1979), 1961 Committee Comments, at 573 (revised 1972); *see* People v. Peters, 180 Ill. App. 3d 850, 853, 536 N.E.2d 465, 467-68 (2d Dist. 1989).

[361] ILL. ANN. STAT. ch. 38, para. 12-5 (Smith-Hurd 1979), 1961 Committee Comments, at 573 (revised 1972).

[362] ILL. ANN. STAT. ch. 38, para. 12-5 (Smith-Hurd 1979), 1961 Committee Comments, at 573 (revised 1972).

[363] ILL. ANN. STAT. ch. 38, para. 12-5 (Smith-Hurd 1979), 1961 Committee Comments, at 573 (revised 1972).

[364] People v. Peters, 180 Ill. App. 3d 850, 853-55, 536 N.E.2d 465, 467 (2d Dist. 1989).

[365] People v. Peters, 180 Ill. App. 3d 850, 855, 536 N.E.2d 465, 468 (2d Dist. 1989).

ing its applicability to situations in which death was likely or plausible.[366] Where a defendant's conduct endangered the "bodily safety" of others by his reckless handling of his motor vehicle, he was convicted of reckless conduct.[367] On the other hand, because reckless conduct is "a broad and all inclusive offense," it is incumbent on the state to include in the charging instrument more specific details of the alleged criminal conduct than those contained in the statute itself.[368]

While the concept of recklessness as a mental state was explored in an earlier chapter,[369] the permissible reach of the reckless conduct prohibition is best understood by reference to some of the situations in which it has been employed. The following acts have been viewed as amounting to reckless conduct: pointing a loaded pistol at another;[370] the firing of a gun into a toilet during a domestic disturbance;[371] shooting a gun at a police squad car;[372] shooting a gun in a tavern after hours, with others present, causing a fire that required the services of the fire department;[373] shooting a gun into the ground, whereupon one of the bullets ricocheted into the chest and arm of one of the persons the defendant was attempting to scare off his property;[374] throwing rocks at passing motor vehicles;[375] throwing rocks at police officers during a civil disturbance;[376] and striking another for no apparent reason with a fist and a glass.[377] Reckless conduct can be based on a *failure to act*, such as where defendant, a building manager, allowed a dwelling to become so deteriorated that it endangered the safety of the tenants.[378]

Obviously, where the conduct of the defendant is intentional, there will not be a finding of reckless conduct.[379] Thus, where the evidence demonstrated that a defendant intentionally stabbed the victim, it was proper not to instruct the jury on the crime of reckless conduct.[380] In determining whether or not this defen-

---

[366] People v. Burton, 100 Ill. App. 3d 1021, 1025, 427 N.E.2d 625, 629 (4th Dist. 1981).

[367] People v. Burton, 100 Ill. App. 3d 1021, 1025, 427 N.E.2d 625, 629 (4th Dist. 1981).

[368] People v. Smith, 90 Ill. App. 3d 83, 86, 412 N.E.2d 1102, 1104 (5th Dist. 1980).

[369] *See* ch. 2 of this treatise for a discussion of what constitutes "recklessness."

[370] People v. Thomas, 1 Ill. App. 3d 139, 143, 275 N.E.2d 253, 256 (4th Dist. 1971).

[371] Carrigan v. Bd. of Fire & Police Comm'rs, 121 Ill. App. 3d 303, 310, 459 N.E.2d 659, 665-66 (2d Dist. 1984) (administrative employee discharge hearing).

[372] People v. Brownlee, 17 Ill. App. 3d 535, 540, 308 N.E.2d 377, 380 (1st Dist. 1974).

[373] H.B. Inv. & Dev., Inc. v. License Appeal Comm'n, 47 Ill. App. 3d 750, 754, 365 N.E.2d 457, 460 (1st Dist. 1977) (suspension of retail liquor license for tavern president's reckless conduct in discharging firearm in tavern).

[374] People v. Johnson, 20 Ill. App. 3d 1085, 1087, 314 N.E.2d 197, 198-99 (4th Dist. 1974).

[375] People v. Dekosta, 132 Ill. App. 2d 691, 695, 270 N.E.2d 475, 477 (1st Dist. 1971).

[376] People v. Mines, 132 Ill. App. 2d 628, 630, 270 N.E.2d 265, 266 (1st Dist. 1971).

[377] People v. Vasser, 62 Ill. App. 3d 523, 526, 379 N.E.2d 94, 96-97 (1st Dist. 1978).

[378] People v. Khan, 136 Ill. App. 3d 754, 758-59, 483 N.E.2d 1030, 1034 (1st Dist. 1985).

[379] People v. Solis, 216 Ill. App. 3d 11, 18, 576 N.E.2d 120, 124 (1st Dist. 1991).

[380] People v. Solis, 216 Ill. App. 3d 11, 18, 576 N.E.2d 120, 124 (1st Dist. 1991).

dant's conduct was reckless or intentional, it was appropriate to examine the manner in which the defendant used the weapon and the severity of the victim's injuries.[381]

The reckless operation of a motor vehicle can give rise to this crime, as where a defendant sharply turned his steering wheel to the right several times while overtaking another car so that the vehicles almost collided.[382] On the other hand, where a defendant drove his jeep around a gravel pit at an excessive speed and flipped over his vehicle while undertaking a right-hand turn on loose gravel, which caused fatal injuries to one of his passengers, the court characterized his conduct as negligence, not recklessness, since there was no evidence that the defendant acted in conscious disregard of the existing danger.[383]

Because of similar reasoning, where a defendant took her child from its play-pen, allowed it to play on the floor and, thereafter, left the basement door open while she went to the basement to load the washing machine with laundry, whereupon the child fell down the basement steps, the court refused to view her conduct, though negligent, as reckless in nature.[384] For good or ill, the Illinois General Assembly has not developed legislation to treat negligent behavior as criminal and the courts, accordingly, refuse to treat those acts that amount to negligence, at best, as illegal.

§ 9.35. Criminal Housing Management.

In an apparent effort to deal with egregious housing conditions tolerated by those, often referred to as "slum-lords," who own, manage, or control dilapidated residential units, the Illinois General Assembly enacted the prohibition against "criminal housing management."

> A person commits the offense of criminal housing management when, having personal management or control of residential real estate, whether as a legal or equitable owner or as a managing agent or otherwise, he recklessly permits the physical condition or facilities of the residential real estate to become or remain in any condition which endangers the health or safety of any person.[385]

---

[381] People v. Solis, 216 Ill. App. 3d 11, 18, 576 N.E.2d 120, 124 (1st Dist. 1991) (attempted murder conviction affirmed).

[382] People v. Burton, 100 Ill. App. 3d 1021, 1025, 427 N.E.2d 625, 629 (4th Dist. 1981).

[383] People v. Gosse, 119 Ill. App. 3d 733, 739, 457 N.E.2d 129, 134 (2d Dist. 1983) (reckless conduct conviction reversed).

[384] People v. Gibbs, 119 Ill. App. 2d 222, 231, 255 N.E.2d 486, 491 (2d Dist. 1970).

[385] 720 ILCS 5/12-5.1 (1999). When challenged on vagueness grounds, this statute was upheld as constitutional in People v. Kahn, 136 Ill. App. 3d 754, 757, 483 N.E.2d 1030, 1033 (1st Dist. 1985).

The obvious impact of this legislation is aimed at (1) owners or managers who (2) have knowledge of and (3) permit, by their recklessness, (4) physical conditions of residential real estate to become so deteriorated that the health or safety of any person is endangered.[386]

In addition to the sentence available under section 5/12-5.1,[387] the legislature enacted a statute granting the court the ability to use injunctions for violations of section 5/12-5.1.[388] Thus, any person who owns, manages, or has an equitable interest in such "slum" housing can be prevented from benefiting through the collection of rent or other monies.[389]

§ 9.36. Intimidation.

The crime of "intimidation" is designed to deal with that criminality that is often referred to as "extortion" or "blackmail," as well as with other socially unacceptable threats.[390] It is defined in these terms.

> (a) A person commits intimidation when, with intent to cause another to perform or to omit the performance of any act, he communicates to another, whether in person, by telephone or by mail, a threat to perform without lawful authority any of the following acts:
>
> > (1) Inflict physical harm on the person threatened or any other person or on property; or
> > (2) Subject any person to physical confinement or restraint; or
> > (3) Commit any criminal offense; or
> > (4) Accuse any person of an offense; or
> > (5) Expose any person to hatred, contempt or ridicule; or
> > (6) Take action as a public official against anyone or anything, or withhold official action, or cause such action or withholding; or
> > (7) Bring about or continue a strike, boycott or other collective action.
>
> (b) Sentence. Intimidation is a . . . felony[391]

The committee responsible for drafting this legislation stated that although the intended scope of this stricture was not designed to encompass the use of force or threat of force to extract a confession or other information from a person who may have committed, or who may have knowledge about, a crime — a separate

---

[386] See generally Douglas N. Norris, Comment, Criminal Sanctions Against Landlords? The Criminal Housing Management Statute In Illinois, 1980 S. ILL. U.L.J. 319, 323-25.

[387] 720 ILCS 5/12-5.1(b) (1999) (constitutes misdemeanor unless subsequent conviction, which constitutes felony).

[388] 720 ILCS 5/12-5.2 (1999).

[389] 720 ILCS 5/12-5.2 (1999).

[390] See People v. Tennin, 162 Ill. App. 3d 520, 525, 515 N.E.2d 1056, 1059 (2d Dist. 1987).

[391] 720 ILCS 5/12-6 (1999).

offense in section 5/12-7 is directed at this activity — the crime of intimidation is directed at "a wide range of acts or conduct" where an accused communicates a threat to another person with the specific intent to cause that person to perform or fail to perform an act that if performed, or not performed, would be "without lawful authority."[392]

§ 9.37. — Elements of Intimidation.

The basic elemental composition of the proscription against intimidation involves (1) a defendant's communication to another person, (2) made with the specific intent to cause the other person to perform or omit to perform an act against his or her will, (3) which constitutes a threat (4) to perform without lawful authority (5) certain designated acts carrying dire consequences to the other person.

With respect to the essential element of "communication to another,"[393] this could seemingly be accomplished by any reasonable means. Clearly, a threat could be made verbally,[394] pictorially,[395] by sending a letter through the mail[396] or through a telephone call.[397]

The next element of intimidation, namely, the mental state of "intent to cause another to perform or to omit the performance of any act," makes this offense a specific intent crime.[398] This essential element must be alleged in the charging instrument and the failure to do so renders the instrument fatally defective.[399] It should be understood that "intent to harm another" is *not* an element of intimidation.[400] Also, threats made as part of a "practical joke" do not constitute intimidation.[401] Conduct that merely causes a generalized sense of fear or nervousness, such as a stranger walking down the street raving and gesturing violently, or yearly predictions by psychics of catastrophic events, are not the type of threats contemplated by the intimidation statute.[402]

---

[392] ILL. ANN. STAT. ch. 38, para. 12-6 (Smith-Hurd 1979), 1961 Committee Comments, at 578 (revised 1972).

[393] *See* People v. Smalley, 43 Ill. App. 3d 600, 602, 357 N.E.2d 93, 95 (1st Dist. 1976).

[394] *See* People v. Smalley, 43 Ill. App. 3d 600, 602, 357 N.E.2d 93, 95 (1st Dist. 1976).

[395] People v. Libbra, 268 Ill. App. 3d 194, 197, 643 N.E.2d 845, 847 (5th Dist. 1994).

[396] *See* People v. Peterson, 306 Ill. App. 3d 1091, 1100, 715 N.E.2d 1221, 1228 (2d Dist. 1999).

[397] *See* People v. Annerino, 182 Ill. App. 3d 920, 923, 538 N.E.2d 770, 771 (1st Dist. 1989).

[398] People v. Smith, 78 Ill. 2d 298, 306, 399 N.E.2d 1289, 1294 (1980); People v. Verkruysse, 261 Ill. App. 3d 972, 975, 639 N.E.2d 881, 883 (3d Dist. 1994); People v. Haybron, 153 Ill. App. 3d 906, 908, 506 N.E.2d 369, 371 (3d Dist. 1987);

[399] People v. White, 29 Ill. App. 3d 438, 330 N.E.2d 521 (5th Dist. 1975) (abstract).

[400] People v. Peterson, 306 Ill. App. 3d 1091, 1100, 715 N.E.2d 1221, 1228 (2d Dist. 1999).

[401] U.S. *ex rel.* Smith v. Cadagin, 707 F. Supp. 387, 390 (1989), *rev'd on other grounds*, 902 F. 2d 553, *cert. denied,* 498 U.S. 865 (1990).

[402] People v. Peterson, 306 Ill. App. 3d 1091, 1100, 715 N.E.2d 1221, 1228 (2d Dist. 1999).

The heart of the crime of intimidation is the "threat." If there is no threat within the meaning of the statute, there can be no intimidation.[403] In this context, the word "threat" implicitly requires that "the expression, in its context, has a reasonable tendency to create apprehension that its originator will act according to its tenor."[404] A wide variety of threats that are obviously wrongful have been upheld as falling within the ambits of this stricture. The following situations were sufficient to constitute criminal intimidation: where a defendant told his former wife that unless she gave him $2,500, he would "blow her brains out";[405] where a defendant kidnapped a victim and made a ransom demand of the victim's wife while communicating his threat to her of subjecting her kidnapped husband to physical confinement;[406] where a defendant threatened to kill a woman if she appeared in court against him;[407] where a defendant threatened to harm a woman or her children in order to prevent her son from testifying against the defendant's friend;[408] where a defendant stated to a borrower of some money that he would break the borrower's legs in several places and send the "west side boys" over to see the borrower unless the borrower paid back the money;[409] where a defendant phoned the victim and threatened harm to him and his family if he failed to leave a certain sum of money at a specific location;[410] where a defendant threatened a rape victim with physical harm if she did not submit to having sexual intercourse;[411] where a defendant threatened a sexual abuse victim by telling him "something would happen" to him and his mother if he told anyone about the abuse;[412] where the defendant kidnapped a victim and later threatened to "get her" if she reported the kidnapping to the authorities;[413] where defendants sent letters to various recipients involved in court litigation against them, including three circuit court judges, a village administrator, and a newspaper reporter, indicating that God would kill them immediately if they took action adverse to the defendants' legal claims;[414] and where a defendant and another

---

[403] People v. Verkruysse, 261 Ill. App. 3d 972, 976-77, 639 N.E.2d 881, 884 (3d Dist. 1994) (holding an invitation to fight does not constitute a threat to support intimidation conviction).

[404] People v. Peterson, 306 Ill. App. 3d 1091, 1098-99, 715 N.E.2d 1221, 1227 (2d Dist. 1999); People v. Byrd, 285 Ill. App. 3d 641, 647, 673 N.E.2d 1071, 1075 (1st Dist. 1996); People v. Maldonado, 247 Ill. App. 3d 149, 153-54, 617 N.E.2d 236, 239 (1st Dist. 1993).

[405] People v. Cole, 57 Ill. App. 3d 396, 397, 373 N.E.2d 106, 106 (3d Dist. 1978).

[406] People v. Turner, 35 Ill. App. 3d 550, 555, 342 N.E.2d 158, 161 (1st Dist. 1976).

[407] People v. Annerino, 182 Ill. App. 3d 920, 923, 538 N.E.2d 770, 771 (1st Dist. 1989).

[408] People v. Houston, 21 Ill. App. 3d 209, 210, 315 N.E.2d 192, 194 (1st Dist. 1974), cert. denied, 420 U.S. 936 (1975).

[409] People v. Gallo, 54 Ill. 2d 343, 352, 297 N.E.2d 569, 571 (1973).

[410] People v. Babic, 7 Ill. App. 3d 36, 38, 287 N.E.2d 24, 25 (2d Dist. 1972).

[411] People v. Smalley, 43 Ill. App. 3d 600, 601, 357 N.E.2d 93, 94 (1st Dist. 1976).

[412] People v. Valko, 201 Ill. App. 3d 462, 473, 559 N.E.2d 104, 111-12 (1st Dist. 1990).

[413] People v. Anthony, 38 Ill. App. 3d 190, 194, 347 N.E.2d 179, 182 (4th Dist. 1976).

[414] People v. Peterson, 306 Ill. App. 3d 1091, 1100-01, 715 N.E.2d 1221, 1228-29 (2d Dist. 1999).

refused to allow the victim to leave a third party's apartment and threatened to assault her with a baseball bat unless she took pictures of herself while nude.[415]

Although the fair import of the term *threat* is relatively obvious, the next statutory element, which states that the defendant must have made the threat to perform certain acts "without lawful authority" would free the reach of the prohibitions from the vagaries of potential *legal* threats made by someone. For example, it would appear that if A threatened to charge B with criminal trespass unless B left A's land, A's threat would not amount to intimidation, since his threat was not "without lawful authority." Similarly, if X, a police officer, threatened to take legal action against Y — namely, arrest Y for theft — unless Y promptly returned certain property currently in his possession but owned by another, it would seem impossible to hold X for intimidation, since presumably his threat against Y was within his lawful authority.

However, with respect to the clause "without lawful authority," there is no requirement that these words be contained within the charging instrument.[416] Also, the courts have held that "without lawful authority" is not an element of intimidation that always needs to be proved at trial.[417] However, this does not preclude a defense against intimidation based on the fact that the threat was supported by lawful authority.[418] Thus, the burden of proof has been placed on the defendant to successfully raise an affirmative defense of "lawful authority" rather than requiring the state to prove in every case the element "without lawful authority" beyond a reasonable doubt. For example, the phrase "without lawful authority" may become important under certain circumstances, for example, where a parent or teacher addresses a child with a proper threat of discipline.[419]

The final element of the intimidation statute involves the types of threatened acts that are prohibited. They are (1) inflicting harm on the person threatened, another person, or property; (2) subjecting any person to physical confinement; (3) committing any offense; (4) accusing any person of having committed a crime; (5) exposing any person to hatred, contempt, or ridicule; (6) taking or failing to take, as a public official, certain action; *or* (7) bringing about or continuing a strike, boycott, or other collective action.[420]

Not surprisingly, this offense has been attacked as being unconstitutional in violation of federal due process and the First Amendment on grounds of over-

---

[415] People v. White, 92 Ill. App. 3d 513, 514-15, 414 N.E.2d 1347, 1348-49 (3d Dist. 1980).

[416] People v. Gallo, 54 Ill. 2d 343, 352, 297 N.E.2d 569, 574 (1973) (citing People v. Harvey, 53 Ill. 2d 585, 294 N.E.2d 269 (1973)); People v. Bradley, 12 Ill. App. 3d 783, 786-87, 299 N.E.2d 99, 102 (1st Dist. 1973).

[417] People v. Blake, 130 Ill. App. 3d 948, 956, 474 N.E.2d 892, 898 (2d Dist. 1985); People v. Hubble, 81 Ill. App. 3d 560, 564, 401 N.E.2d 1282, 1285 (2d Dist. 1980).

[418] People v. Hubble, 81 Ill. App. 3d 560, 564-65, 401 N.E.2d 1282, 1285 (2d Dist. 1980).

[419] People v. Hubble, 81 Ill. App. 3d 560, 564-65, 401 N.E.2d 1282, 1285 (2d Dist. 1980).

[420] 720 ILCS 5/12-6(a)(1)-(7) (1999).

breadth and vagueness.[421] In *People v. Holder*,[422] the Illinois appellate court held that subsection (a)(3) was unconstitutionally overbroad in the face of due process and the First Amendment where a defendant and other truck drivers who were dissatisfied with their wages and working conditions were convicted of intimidation for threatening criminal damage to certain ready-mix cement trucks unless their employer agreed to accept a union contract.[423] However, the Illinois Supreme Court reversed the appellate court, holding that subsection (a)(3) was not substantially overbroad and, accordingly, not facially invalid, since any "conceivable impermissible applications are dwarfed by the statute's legitimate reach in prohibiting threatened criminal activity."[424] Thus, the Illinois Supreme Court felt that if a court believed the statute to be unconstitutional as *applied*, then the legitimate threat could be protected. On remand, the Illinois appellate court concluded that the threats of defendant Holder and other truck drivers were not protected speech but constituted a mere edict to sign a contract or face consequence of destruction of property.[425] Finally, a federal district court ruled that subsection (a)(3) was unconstitutional since it prohibited any threat to commit any crime no matter how minor or insubstantial.[426]

§ 9.38. Compelling Organization Membership of Person.

The Illinois Criminal Code includes a prohibition against "compelling organization membership of persons" through the use of a threat of bodily harm.[427] The legislature's primary concern was apparently the "strong arm" tactics of street gangs, although it did not distinguish between the type of organizations that fall within the ambits of the statute. A person commits this felony where he or she threatens or commits bodily harm to an individual or that individual's family or

---

[421] People v. Peterson, 306 Ill. App. 3d 1091, 1101-02, 715 N.E.2d 1221, 1229 (2d Dist. 1999); People v. Holder, 103 Ill. App. 3d 353, 431 N.E.2d 427, *re'd*, 96 Ill. 2d 444, 451 N.E.2d 831 (1983), *cert. denied*, 467 U.S. 1241 (1984), *rev'd sub nom.*, U.S. *ex rel* Holder v. Circuit Court of the 17th Judicial Circuit, 624 F. Supp. 68 (N.D. Ill. 1985); Landry v. Daley, 280 F. Supp. 938 (N.D. Ill. 1968), *prob. juris. noted*, 393 U.S. 974, *rev'd sub nom. on other grounds*, Boyle v. Landry, 401 U.S. 77 (1971).

[422] 103 Ill. App. 3d 353, 431 N.E.2d 427, *rev'd*, 96 Ill. 2d 444, 451 N.E.2d 831 (1983), *cert. denied*, 467 U.S. 1241 (1984), *rev'd sub nom.*, United States ex rel. Holder v. Circuit Court of the 17th Judicial Circuit, 624 F.Supp. 68 (N.D. Ill. 1985).

[423] People v. Holder, 103 Ill. App. 3d 353, 355, 431 N.E.2d 427, 428-429, *rev'd*, 96 Ill. 2d 444, 451 N.E.2d 831 (1983), *cert. denied*, 467 U.S. 1241 (1984), *rev'd sub nom.*, U.S. *ex rel* Holder v. Circuit Court of the 17th Judicial Circuit, 624 F.Supp. 68 (N.D. Ill. 1985).

[424] People v. Holder, 96 Ill. 2d 444, 454, 451 N.E.2d 831, 835 (1983) (citing Broadrick v. Oklahoma, 413 U.S. 601, 615-16 (1973)), *cert. denied*, 467 U.S. 1241 (1984).

[425] People v. Holder, 119 Ill. App. 3d 366, 370, 456 N.E.2d 628, 631 (2d Dist. 1983).

[426] U.S. ex rel Holder v. Circuit Court of the 17th Judicial Circuit, 624 F. Supp. 68, 70 (N.D. Ill. 1985).

[427] 720 ILCS 5/12-6.1 (1999).

employs other criminal means "to solicit or cause any person to join or deter any person from leaving, any organization or association regardless of the nature" of such group.[428] When a person eighteen years of age or older commits the offense against a person under eighteen years of age, the offense is a more serious felony.[429]

§ 9.39. Aggravated Intimidation.

"Aggravated intimidation," which constitutes a felony, is committed by any person who commits intimidation and (1) commits the offense in furtherance of the activities of an organized gang; (2) commits the offense with the intent to prevent any person from becoming a community policing volunteer; or (3) commits the offense against a victim he knows to be a peace officer, correctional institution employee, fireman, or community policing volunteer engaged in the execution of official duties or in retaliation for execution of such official duties.[430] For this offense, "streetgang," "streetgang member," and "organized gang" have the meanings given to them in the Illinois Streetgang Terrorism Omnibus Prevention Act, which is designed to curtail the criminal activity of streetgangs.[431]

§ 9.40. Interfering with the Reporting of Domestic Violence.

A person violates the offense of "interfering with the reporting of domestic violence" when, after having committed an act of domestic violence, he or she prevents or attempts to prevent his or her victim or a witness to the act of domestic violence from obtaining emergency or medical assistance or making a report to law enforcement officials.[432] This offense is a misdemeanor.[433]

§ 9.41. Compelling Confession or Information by Force or Threat.

Part of the original 1961 legislative package involving Illinois criminality is an offense prohibiting "compelling [a] confession or information by force or threat."[434] This provision is violated where an individual, with intent to obtain a confession, statement or information regarding any offense, inflicts or threatens to inflict physical harm upon the person threatened or upon any other person.[435]

---

[428] 720 ILCS 5/12-6.1 (1999).

[429] 720 ILCS 5/12-6.1 (1999).

[430] 720 ILCS 5/12-6.2 (1999).

[431] 720 ILCS 5/12-6.2(c) (1999); 740 ILCS 147/10 (1999) (definitions). *See generally* 740 ILCS 147/1 *et seq.* (1999) (provisions of Streetgang Prevention Act).

[432] 720 ILCS 5/12-6.3(a) (1999).

[433] 720 ILCS 5/12-6.3(c) (1999).

[434] 720 ILCS 5/12-7 (1999).

[435] 720 ILCS 5/12-7 (1999).

The legislature was determined to treat this form of wrongful threat as a separate crime from that of intimidation. The committee's comments state that this crime (1) requires proof of the defendant's specific intent to obtain information from another person about a crime; (2) can arise whether the information sought from the person implicates himself or herself or another suspect in a crime; (3) mandates proof of the infliction, or threat of infliction of *physical harm* (as opposed to the other forms of harm that serve as a basis for finding intimidation); and (4) covers threats of physical harm whether the harm threatened is directed toward the person who has the information or a third party, such as a friend or relative of the person who has the information.[436]

Notwithstanding (1) the fact that this stricture has been on the book for over thirty-five years and (2) various reported instances or situations in which courts have felt compelled to suppress confessions because of evidence or police coercion of a physical character,[437] there are no reported opinions dealing with prosecution of this offense.

§ 9.42. Hate Crime.

In 1991, the offense "hate crime"[438] replaced its predecessor "ethnic intimidation."[439]

> (a) A person commits hate crime when, by reason of the actual or perceived race, color, creed, religion, ancestry, gender, sexual orientation, physical or mental disability, or national origin of another individual or group of individuals, he commits assault, battery, aggravated assault, misdemeanor theft, criminal trespass to residence, misdemeanor criminal damage to property, criminal trespass to vehicle, criminal trespass to real property, mob action, or disorderly conduct as these crimes are defined in . . . this Code, . . . or harassment by telephone . . . against a victim who is (i)

---

[436] ILL. ANN. STAT. ch. 38. para. 12-7 (Smith-Hurd 1979), 1961 Committee Comments, at 587 (revised 1972).

[437] *See, e.g.,* People v. O'Leary, 45 Ill. 2d 122, 125, 257 N.E.2d 112, 114 (1970) (confession and physical evidence found after defendant shot in face with tear gas were inadmissible); People v. Harper, 36 Ill. 2d 398, 401, 223 N.E.2d 841, 842-43 (1967) (confession was involuntary where defendant was held for 21 days before any hearing and where state failed to explain defendant's internal bleeding, which occurred while he was in custody); People v. Davis, 35 Ill. 2d 202, 205, 220 N.E.2d 222, 224-25 (1966) (confession was involuntary where defendant was held in custody for week without hearing and suffered injuries while in custody not explained by the state).

[438] 720 ILCS 5/12-7.1 (1999). *See* People v. Nitz, 285 Ill. App. 3d 364, 368-69, 674 N.E.2d 802, 805-06 (3d Dist. 1996) (offense of hate crime not violative of free speech clause of First Amendment). *See also* Wisconsin v. Mitchell, 508 U.S. 476 (1993) (Wisconsin statute that penalizes selection of victim of crime on basis of race, religion or other protected status does not punish thought or speech in violation of First Amendment).

[439] ILL. REV. STAT. ch. 38, para. 12-7.1 (1991) (repealed).

the other individual; (ii) a member of the group of individuals; (iii) a person who has an association with, is married to, or has a friendship with the other individual or a member of the group of individuals; or (iv) a relative (by blood or marriage) of a person described in clause (i), (ii), or (iii). (b) Hate crime is a . . . felony.[440]

An allegation that a defendant committed one or more of the enumerated predicate offenses is an essential element of hate crime.[441] However, in one case where the government established the commission of hate crime based on defendant's commission of disorderly conduct, the defendant's disorderly conduct conviction had to be vacated because of the "one-act-one-crime principle."[442]

In order to convict a defendant of hate crime, it is not necessary to prove the victim of the offense was a member or perceived to be a member of the protected classifications.[443] Thus, where defendant's depiction reflected a derogatory statement about African-Americans toward a victim who was not African-American, this constituted the offense of hate crime because the key concern of the statute is based on the motive of the perpetrator and not the status of the individual harmed.[444]

Where defendant physically attacked and seriously injured his victim while uttering a racial slur, this amounted to hate crime.[445]

§ 9.43. Educational Intimidation.

In an effort to prevent persons from engaging in activity designed to prevent a child who might be carrying the AIDS virus from attending school, the legislature has created the offense of "educational intimidation."[446] The statute provides:

> A person commits educational intimidation when he knowingly interferes with the right of any child who is or is believed to be afflicted with a chronic infectious disease to attend or participate in the activities of an elementary or secondary school in this State:
> (1) by actual or threatened physical harm to the person or property of the child or the child's family; or
> (2) by impeding or obstructing the child's right of ingress to, egress from, or freedom of movement at school facilities or activities; or

---

[440] 720 ILCS 5/12-7.1 (1999). What constitutes harassment by telephone is defined in 720 ILCS 135/1-1 (1999).

[441] People v. Kelly, 299 Ill. App. 3d 222, 227, 701 N.E.2d 114, 117 (3d Dist. 1998).

[442] People v. Kelly, 299 Ill. App. 3d 222, 227, 701 N.E.2d 114, 118 (3d Dist. 1998).

[443] In re B.C., 176 Ill. 2d 536, 551, 680 N.E.2d 1355, 1363 (1997).

[444] In re B.C., 176 Ill. 2d 536, 551, 680 N.E.2d 1355, 1363 (1997).

[445] People v. Davis, 285 Ill. App. 3d 875, 880, 674 N.E.2d 895, 898 (1st Dist. 1996).

[446] 720 ILCS 5/12-7.2 (1999).

(3) by exposing or threatening to expose the child, or the family or friends of the child, to public hatred, contempt or ridicule.[447]

The statute, however, does not confine itself only to HIV victims, but includes any "chronic infectious disease." Exempted from prosecution under this statute are school officials or a school's "infectious disease review team" acting within the course of their professional duties.[448] Educational intimidation is a misdemeanor.[449]

§ 9.44. Stalking.

A "stalking" prohibition was designed to protect persons from physical harm or intimidation by former suitors or others attracted toward such person for some nefarious purpose.[450] The "stalking" measure reads:

> (a) A person commits stalking when he or she, knowingly and without lawful justification, on at least 2 separate occasions follows another person or places the person under surveillance or any combination thereof and:
> (1) at any time transmits a threat to that person of immediate or future bodily harm, sexual assault, confinement or restraint; or
> (2) places that person in reasonable apprehension of immediate or future bodily harm, sexual assault, confinement or restraint.
> (b) Sentence . . . . Stalking is a . . . felony.[451]

The statute focuses primarily on the defendant's actions rather than the defendant's motivation. Thus, the statute is applicable to a wide variety of circumstances. However, exempted from this statute is otherwise lawful workplace picketing arising out of a bona fide labor dispute or any exercise of the right of free speech or assembly that is otherwise lawful.[452]

A defendant "places a person under surveillance" by remaining present outside the person's school, place of employment, vehicle, other place occupied by the person, or residence other than the residence of the defendant.[453] However, in one case, the appellate court held that the language of the statute "by remain-

---

[447] 720 ILCS 5/12-7.2(a) (1999).

[448] 720 ILCS 5/12-7.3(b) (1999).

[449] 720 ILCS 5/12-7.2(c) (1999).

[450] 720 ILCS 5/12-7.3 (1999). *See* People v. Rand, 291 Ill. App. 3d 431, 438, 683 N.E.2d 1243, 1247-48 (1st Dist. 1997) (offense of stalking not unconstitutionally overbroad or vague); People v. Zamudio, 293 Ill. App. 3d 976, 980-82, 689 N.E.2d 254, 256-58 (1st Dist. 1997) (stalking statute not violative of due process); People v. Cortez, 286 Ill. App. 3d 478, 479-84, 676 N.E.2d 195, 196-200 (1st Dist. 1996) (stalking statute not violative of due process, First Amendment or ex post facto prohibition).

[451] 720 ILCS 5/12-7.3 (1999).

[452] 720 ILCS 5/12-7.3(c) (1999).

[453] 720 ILCS 5/12-7.3(d) (1994).

ing present outside the . . . other place occupied by the person" does not require that the defendant remain physically outside the building occupied by the victim.[454] The court further noted that "[c]ommon sense dictates that a victim may be subjected to as much, or more, harassment by being placed under surveillance from within a separate portion of a large structure, such as a shopping mall or ice skating facility, as from outside such a structure."[455] Also, in another case, the court ruled that the State is not required to establish a minimum amount of time defendant must remain in the vicinity of the victim's building before defendant's presence amounts to surveillance.[456]

The "follows another person" language means (1) "to move in relative proximity to a person as that person moves from place to place" or (2) "to remain in relative proximity to a person who is stationary or whose movements are confined to a small area."[457] In addition, "follows another person" does not include following within the residence of the defendant.[458]

The conduct of following or surveilling must be accompanied by evidence of a threat of harm *or* of placing the victim in reasonable apprehension of harm.[459] In the case of threats under (a)(1), the statute does not require that the instances of threat precede the "following"; rather, the state must prove that the "following" and "threat" are part of the "same course of conduct."[460] Under (a)(2), the stalking statute has been interpreted as requiring two separate instances where (1) the defendant is following or surveilling the victim and (2) the victim is placed in reasonable apprehension of bodily harm, sexual assault, or confinement.[461] However, the reasonable apprehension does not have to stem from the defendant's acts of following or surveillance but could arise from a showing that the victim's fears arose apart and separate from the requisite acts of following and surveillance.[462] Also, the victim is not required to expressly testify about the apprehension felt; rather, such apprehension can be based inferentially on the conduct of the defendant and the victim.[463]

---

[454] People v. Holt, 271 Ill. App. 3d 1016, 1022, 649 N.E.2d 571, 577 (3d Dist. 1995).

[455] People v. Holt, 271 Ill. App. 3d 1016, 1022, 649 N.E.2d 571, 577 (3d Dist. 1995).

[456] People v. Daniel, 283 Ill. App. 3d 1003, 1008, 670 N.E.2d 861, 865 (1st Dist. 1996).

[457] 720 ILCS 5/12-7.3(e) (1999).

[458] 720 ILCS 5/12-7.3(e) (1999).

[459] People v. Zamudio, 293 Ill. App. 3d 976, 980, 689 N.E.2d 254, 257 (1st Dist. 1997).

[460] People v. Zamudio, 293 Ill. App. 3d 976, 980-81, 689 N.E.2d 254, 257 (1st Dist. 1997).

[461] People v. Nakajima, 294 Ill. App. 3d 809, 819, 691 N.E.2d 153, 159 (4th Dist. 1998).

[462] People v. Nakajima, 294 Ill. App. 3d 809, 819-20, 691 N.E.2d 153, 159-60 (4th Dist. 1998).

[463] People v. Nakajima, 294 Ill. App. 3d 809, 820, 691 N.E.2d 153, 160 (4th Dist. 1998).

§ 9.45. Aggravated Stalking.

An aggravated form of the stalking statute has been enacted, as well.[464] The "aggravated stalking" statute reads:

(a) A person commits aggravated stalking when he or she, in conjunction with committing the offense of stalking, also does any of the following:

(1) causes bodily harm to the victim;

(2) confines or restrains the victim; or

(3) violates a temporary restraining order, an order of protection, or an injunction prohibiting the behavior described in . . . the Illinois Domestic Violence Act . . . .

(b) Sentence . . . . Aggravated stalking is a . . . felony.[465]

Aggravated stalking has the same labor picketing exemption found in the stalking statute.[466]

§ 9.46. Threatening Public Officials.

The General Assembly has enacted a crime against "threatening public officials."[467] If any person "knowingly and willfully" conveys to any public official by "telephone communication" or by some type of "document" a threat to take the life of, or to inflict great bodily harm on the official or a member of his or her immediate family, which threat is conveyed because of "some . . . factor related to the official's public existence,"[468] that person has committed a felony.[469] "*Immediate family*" means a public official's spouse or children.[470]

§ 9.47. Tattooing Body of Minor.

In the interest of protecting minors from the disfigurement known as tattooing, the state makes it a misdemeanor for any person, except those licensed to practice medicine in all its branches, from tattooing or offering to tattoo a person under the age of twenty-one.[471] Tattooing is defined as any insertion of "pigment

---

[464] 720 ILCS 5/12-7.4 (1999).

[465] 720 ILCS 5/12-7.4 (1999). Paragraph (a)(3) refers to 750 ILCS 60/214 (1999) (Illinois Domestic Violence Act of 1986).

[466] 720 ILCS 5/12-7.4(c) (1999).

[467] 720 ILCS 5/12-9 (1999).

[468] 720 ILCS 5/12-9(a) (1999).

[469] 720 ILCS 5/12-9(c) (1999).

[470] 720 ILCS 5/12-9(b) (1999).

[471] 720 ILCS 5/12-10 (1999).

under the surface of the skin of a human being, by pricking with a needle or otherwise, so as to produce an indelible mark or figure visible through the skin."[472]

§ 9.48. Home Invasion.

The "home invasion" statute[473] was enacted to protect the personal safety of persons in their homes.[474] This felony[475] stricture reads:

> A person who is not a peace officer acting in the line of duty commits home invasion when without authority he or she knowingly enters the dwelling place of another when he or she knows or has reason to know that one or more persons is present or he or she knowingly enters the dwelling place of another and remains in such dwelling place until he or she knows or has reason to know that one or more persons is present and (1) While armed with a dangerous weapon uses force or threatens the imminent use of force upon any person or persons within such dwelling place whether or not injury occurs, or (2) Intentionally causes any injury to any person or persons within such dwelling place.[476]

§ 9.49. — Elements of Home Invasion.

The elements of home invasion include (1) the entry of a dwelling place of another without lawful authority, (2) by a person who is not a police officer acting in the line of duty, (3) where he or she knows or should know that one or more persons are present, and (4) he or she, while armed with a dangerous weapon, threatens the imminent use of force *or* intentionally injures any person within the dwelling. In effect, the offense of home invasion consists of two parts: the knowing unauthorized entry of an occupied dwelling *and* the use or threat of force by an invader armed with a dangerous weapon or an intentional injury by the invader upon an occupant.[477] It is an affirmative defense to this offense that the accused, upon gaining knowledge of the presence of one or more person present in the dwelling, "either immediately leaves such premises or surrenders to the person or persons lawfully present therein without either attempting to cause or causing serious bodily injury to any person present therein."[478]

---

[472] 720 ILCS 5/12-10 (1999).

[473] 720 ILCS 5/12-11 (1999).

[474] People v. Kolls, 179 Ill. App. 3d 652, 655, 534 N.E.2d 673, 674 (2d Dist. 1989).

[475] 720 ILCS 5/12-11(c) (1999) (Class X).

[476] 720 ILCS 5/12-11(a) (1999).

[477] People v. Ellison, 123 Ill. App. 3d 615, 621, 463 N.E.2d 175, 180 (2d Dist. 1984).

[478] 720 ILCS 5/12-11(b) (1999).

The gravamen of the offense of home invasion is the *unauthorized entry* into the dwelling of another.[479] As such, a charging instrument is defective when it fails to allege an entry "without authority."[480] An entry is "without authority" if it is not authorized by the property holder and, as such, the mere fact that one has not locked or even closed the outside door is not "an invitation to a perfect stranger to enter for any reason whatsoever."[481]

In regard to whether the entry was without authority, in *People v. Bush*,[482] the Illinois Supreme Court ruled that if a defendant gains access to his victim's residence through trickery or deceit and with the intent to commit a criminal act, his entry is unauthorized and consent is vitiated because the true purpose of the entry exceeded the limited authorization granted; however, if the defendant entered with an innocent intent, his entry is authorized and his criminal actions thereafter do not change the status of his entry.[483] In *Bush*, the court held that a trial court instruction to the effect that an unauthorized entry can occur even where the defendant had no wrongful intent when he gained entry was error.[484] Here, the court *rejected* the reasoning held that the "limited authority" doctrine extended to situations where the defendant may have entered a residence with an innocent state of mind and with the resident's consent, but his later formulation of criminal intent while in the residence exceeded the scope of the resident's consent and, thereby, rendered his continued presence unauthorized.[485]

Regarding the statute's use of the term "enter," apparently there is no requirement that the defendant completely enter the dwelling of another.[486] A conviction for home invasion was upheld where a defendant stuck his arm through a window which he had broken.[487] There is no requirement that the injury or threat occur *after* entry.[488] A conviction for home invasion was upheld where a defendant repeatedly struck the front door of the victim's home and shouted "I'll kill you" prior to his entry.[489] Similarly, there is no requirement that the injury[490] or

---

[479] People v. Peeples, 155 Ill. 2d 422, 487, 616 N.E.2d 294, 325 (1993); People v. Priest, 297 Ill. App. 3d 797, 805, 698 N.E.2d 223, 229 (4th Dist. 1998); People v. Ader, 176 Ill. App. 3d 613, 616, 531 N.E.2d 407, 410 (2d. Dist. 1988).

[480] People v. Ellison, 123 Ill. App. 3d 615, 621-22, 463 N.E.2d 175, 180-81 (2d Dist. 1984); People v. Medreno, 99 Ill. App. 3d 449, 455, 425 N.E.2d 588, 592 (3d Dist. 1981).

[481] People v. Simpson, 178 Ill. App. 3d 1091, 1096, 534 N.E.2d 217, 219 (3d Dist. 1989).

[482] 157 Ill. 2d 248, 623 N.E.2d 1361 (1993).

[483] People v. Bush, 157 Ill. 2d 248, 255, 623 N.E.2d 1361, 1364 (1993).

[484] People v. Bush, 157 Ill. 2d 248, 255, 623 N.E.2d 1361, 1364 (1993).

[485] People v. Bush, 157 Ill. 2d 248, 255, 623 N.E.2d 1361, 1364 (1993). *See also* People v. Peeples, 155 Ill. 2d 422, 487, 616 N.E.2d 294, 325 (1993) (applying limited authority doctrine); People v. Hill, 294 Ill. App. 3d 962, 973, 691 N.E.2d 797, 805 (1st Dist. 1998) (same).

[486] *See* People v. Troutt, 172 Ill. App. 3d 668, 670-73, 526 N.E.2d 910, 913 (5th Dist. 1988).

[487] People v. Troutt, 172 Ill. App. 3d 668, 670-73, 526 N.E.2d 910, 913 (5th Dist. 1988).

[488] People v. Troutt, 172 Ill. App. 3d 668, 672-73, 526 N.E.2d 910, 913 (5th Dist. 1988).

[489] People v. Troutt, 172 Ill. App. 3d 668, 670, 526 N.E.2d 910, 911 (5th Dist. 1988).

[490] People v. Kolls, 179 Ill. App. 3d 652, 655, 534 N.E.2d 673, 675 (2d Dist. 1989).

threat of injury[491] occur within the dwelling. Thus, a home invasion occurred where the defendant unlawfully entered the home of the victim, followed the victim out of the home, and proceeded to punch and kick the victim.[492] A home invasion was found where a defendant cut through the screen of the front door with a knife, broke a window, and made threats from the porch prior to entry.[493]

The language "not a peace officer acting in the line of duty" reflects a material element that must be proved by the state.[494] One case held that where a defendant entered the house of a woman, demanded money and jewelry from her, ordered her to take off her clothes, raped her, and left with her television, these actions were completely inconsistent with the claim that the defendant, even if a police officer, was acting in the line of duty.[495]

The home invasion statute requires that the defendant without authority entered an *occupied dwelling*.[496] The language which states the defendant must know "that one or more persons is present" means that it is essential that "another" person or persons be physically "present" within the dwelling at the time of the defendant's unauthorized entry.[497] The Illinois Supreme Court has rejected the proposition that one could be constructively present within a dwelling.[498] Thus, an unauthorized entry into the second floor apartment of a building by a defendant when the victim was in the first floor apartment of the building did not constitute presence within the meaning of the statute.[499] In addition, the Illinois Supreme Court has ruled that where more than one individual is present in the dwelling in question, this amounts to only one count of home invasion.[500]

The purpose for which a structure is used by the victim, rather than the nature and quality of the structure, is determinative as to whether there is a 'dwelling" for purposes of this offense. Thus, where the victim's apartment lacked electricity, gas, a bed, a refrigerator or a stove, it remained the victim's dwelling since the victim lived there.[501]

---

[491] People v. Kovacs, 135 Ill. App. 3d 448, 451, 481 N.E.2d 1071, 1073 (2d Dist. 1985).

[492] People v. Kolls, 179 Ill. App. 3d 652, 654-56, 534 N.E.2d 673, 674 (2d Dist. 1989).

[493] People v. Kovacs, 135 Ill. App. 3d 448, 451, 481 N.E.2d 1071, 1073 (2d Dist. 1985).

[494] People v. Davis, 106 Ill. App. 3d 260, 266, 435 N.E.2d 838, 844 (2d Dist. 1982).

[495] People v. Jones, 157 Ill. App. 3d 106, 110-11, 510 N.E.2d 116, 119-20 (1st Dist. 1987); People v. Davis, 106 Ill. App. 3d 260, 266, 435 N.E.2d 838, 844 (2d Dist. 1982).

[496] People v. Ellison, 123 Ill. App. 3d 615, 621, 463 N.E.2d 175, 180 (2d Dist. 1984).

[497] People v. Pettit, 101 Ill. 2d 309, 313, 461 N.E.2d 991, 993 (1984).

[498] People v. Pettit, 101 Ill. 2d 309, 313, 461 N.E.2d 991, 993 (1984).

[499] People v. Pettit, 101 Ill. 2d 309, 313, 461 N.E.2d 991, 993 (1984).

[500] People v. Cole, 172 Ill. 2d 85, 102, 665 N.E.2d 1275, 1283, *cert. denied*, 519 U.S. 1030 (1996); *see also* People v. Hicks, 181 Ill. 2d 541, 549, 693 N.E.2d 373, 377 (1998) (defendant could only be convicted of one count of home invasion based on his own entry into home and not a second count based on accomplice's simultaneous entry).

[501] People v. Stokes, 293 Ill. App. 3d 643, 650, 689 N.E.2d 625, 630 (1st Dist. 1997).

The dwelling must be that *of another*. The language "dwelling place of another" includes the situation where a defendant has a tenancy interest in the victim's property, but he or she no longer has a possessory interest due to a divorce from the victim, an order of protection, or other court order.[502] Thus, where a defendant entered his former marital residence, the court found the home a "dwelling place of another" for purposes of home invasion.[503] Although the defendant's name still appeared on the mortgage and title of the residence, the dissolution of marriage judgment entered six months prior to the incident extinguished any ownership interest defendant possessed by granting the ex-wife exclusive possession of the marital home.[504]

Beyond establishing an unauthorized entry of an occupied dwelling of another, to procure a conviction for home invasion, the use or threat of force while armed with a dangerous weapon *or* the intentional infliction of any injury against an occupant must be shown.[505] Thus, a conviction for home invasion was properly found where the defendant shot and stabbed the victims.[506] A sufficient amount of injury to warrant a conviction was found where a defendant pushed the victim into a chair and placed his hand around her throat while she struggled with him.[507] Similarly, holding a pillow over the victim's face making it difficult for the victim to breathe constituted an injury within the meaning of the home invasion statute.[508] Where a defendant engages in any act that "hurts, i.e., that causes bodily pain" to his victim, such as where defendant's victim experienced a painful reaction while he sexually penetrated her vagina with his penis, this amounted to "injury" for purposes of home invasion.[509] However, a slap to the face was not an injury within the meaning of the home invasion statute.[510] Threat of force was found where the defendant kicked in the front door and entered the dwelling with a raised knife.[511] Finally, emotional trauma or psychological injury may satisfy the injury requirement for home invasion.[512] Where a

---

[502] 720 ILCS 5/12-11(d) (1999).

[503] People v. Oakley, 299 Ill. App. 3d 684, 689, 701 N.E.2d 1197, 1201 (2d Dist. 1998).

[504] People v. Oakley, 299 Ill. App. 3d 684, 686, 701 N.E.2d 1197, 1199 (2d Dist. 1998) (decided prior to incorporation of subsection (d) into 5/12-11).

[505] 720 ILCS 5/12-11(a) (1999).

[506] People v. Bruce, 185 Ill. App. 3d 356, 373, 541 N.E.2d 708, 719 (5th Dist. 1989).

[507] People v. Foster, 103 Ill. App. 3d 372, 377, 431 N.E.2d 430, 435 (2d Dist. 1982).

[508] People v. Rachel, 123 Ill. App. 3d 600, 603-04, 462 N.E.2d 959, 963 (2d Dist. 1984).

[509] People v. Garrett, 281 Ill. App. 3d 535, 541-43, 667 N.E.2d 130, 134-35 (5th Dist 1996) ("Injury" does not require "physical evidence of bodily harm, such as bruises, lacerations, etc." for purposes of home invasion).

[510] People v. Boyer, 138 Ill. App. 3d 16, 19-20, 485 N.E.2d 460, 462 (3d Dist. 1985).

[511] People v. Ader, 176 Ill. App. 3d 613, 616, 531 N.E.2d 407, 410 (2d Dist. 1988). *See also* People v. Kovacs, 135 Ill. App. 3d 448, 451, 481 N.E.2d 1071, 1073 (2d Dist. 1985) (where the defendant verbally threatened and gestured with a knife).

[512] People v. Ehrich, 165 Ill. App. 3d 1060, 1072-73, 519 N.E.2d 1137, 1144 (4th Dist. 1988).

defendant entered the home and crept into the room of a seven-year-old girl at approximately 3:00 a.m., placed her in his lap and covered her mouth with his hand, the girl suffered sufficient emotional trauma and psychological injury to warrant a finding of home invasion.[513]

The *mental state* requirement for home invasion requires careful attention. Unlike burglary,[514] home invasion does not require that the accused have a felonious intent at the time he or she enters the dwelling without lawful authority.[515] Rather, this crime merely requires that the defendant "knows or has reason to know" that one or more persons is present at the time of the unauthorized entry.[516] One has "reason to know that one or more persons [are] present" in a dwelling where one's entry is made at a time, such as after midnight and before daylight, when it is likely that the occupants of a residence would be home;[517] where one hears a noise, such as from a television set that is turned on, from within the dwelling;[518] where one can see lights on within the residence;[519] where automobiles are parked in the driveway;[520] and where the defendants entered carrying firearms in anticipation of encountering someone within.[521]

After establishing defendant's knowledge that the dwelling was occupied, the state has the additional hurdle of showing the defendant "*intentionally* caused any injury to any person" *if* the state has charged defendant with home invasion under section (a)(2).[522] The alternative approach to prosecuting home invasion, to-wit, where defendant "while armed with a dangerous weapon uses force or threatens the imminent use of force" in violation of section (a)(1) requires no additional element of intent.[523] In any event, the unauthorized entry does *not* have to be accompanied by intent to cause injury at the time of defendant's en-

---

[513] People v. Ehrich, 165 Ill. App. 3d 1060, 1072-73, 519 N.E.2d 1137, 1144 (4th Dist. 1988).

[514] 720 ILCS 5/19-1(a) (1999) ("A person commits burglary when without authority he knowingly enters or without authority remains within a building . . . with intent to commit therein a felony or theft."). *See* ch. 13 for a discussion of burglary.

[515] People v. Gilyard, 237 Ill. App. 3d 8, 22, 602 N.E.2d 1335, 1345 (2d Dist. 1992).

[516] People v. Hickey, 178 Ill. 2d 256, 292, 687 N.E.2d 910, 927 (1997), *cert. denied,* 118 S. Ct. 2375 (1998); People v. Rodriguez, 227 Ill. App. 3d 397, 407, 592 N.E.2d 18, 25 (1st Dist. 1991).

[517] People v. Frisby, 160 Ill. App. 3d 19, 30-31, 512 N.E.2d 1337, 1344 (1st Dist. 1987) (4:00 a.m.); People v. Austin, 123 Ill. App. 3d 788, 794, 463 N.E.2d 444, 450 (2d Dist. 1984) (between midnight and 1:30 a.m.); People v. Davis, 106 Ill. App. 3d 260, 267, 435 N.E.2d 838, 844 (2d Dist. 1982) (between 3:00 and 4:00 a.m.).

[518] People v. Davis, 106 Ill. App. 3d 260, 267, 435 N.E.2d 838, 844 (2d Dist. 1982).

[519] People v. Austin, 123 Ill. App. 3d 788, 794, 463 N.E.2d 444, 450 (2d Dist. 1984).

[520] People v. Hickey, 178 Ill. 2d 256, 292-93, 687 N.E.2d 910, 927 (1997), *cert. denied,* 118 S. Ct. 2375 (1998).

[521] People v. Hickey, 178 Ill. 2d 256, 293, 687 N.E.2d 910, 927 (1997), *cert. denied,* 118 S. Ct. 2375 (1998); People v. Austin, 123 Ill. App. 3d 788, 794, 463 N.E.2d 444, 450 (2d Dist. 1984).

[522] 720 ILCS 5/12-11(a)(2) (1999) (emphasis added); People v. Gilyard, 237 Ill. App. 3d 8, 22, 602 N.E.2d 1335, 1345 (2d Dist. 1992).

[523] 720 ILCS 5/12-11(a)(1) (1999).

try.[524] In other words, if the defendant has no intent to injure when he or she makes entry but *later* forms such a mental state, this will satisfy the terms of section (a)(2).[525]

§ 9.50. Vehicular Invasion.

A person commits the felony of "vehicular invasion" when he or she "knowingly, by force and without lawful justification, enters or reaches into the interior of a motor vehicle . . . while such motor vehicle is occupied by another person or persons, with the intent to commit therein a theft or felony."[526]

§ 9.51. Criminal Transmission of HIV.

In response to growing numbers of individuals infected by the AIDS virus and the irresponsibility of some, the General Assembly has enacted the offense of "criminal transmission of HIV."[527] This felony[528] is defined as follows:

> A person commits criminal transmission of HIV when he or she, knowing that he or she is infected with HIV: (1) engages in intimate contact with another; (2) transfers, donates, or provides his or her blood, tissue, semen, organs, or other potentially infectious body fluids for transfusion, transplantation, insemination, or other administration to another; or (3) dispenses, delivers, exchanges, sells, or in any other way transfers to another any nonsterile intravenous or intramuscular drug paraphernalia.[529]

There is no requirement that the HIV virus be transmitted to the person exposed in order to procure a conviction under this statute.[530] It is a defense to this offense that the person exposed knew that the infected person was infected with HIV, knew that transmission of the HIV virus could result and consented to the action.[531] The statute defines "HIV" as "human immunodeficiency virus or any other identified causative agent of acquired immunodeficiency syndrome."[532] "Intimate contact with another" is defined as "exposure of the body of one per-

---

[524] People v. Gilyard, 237 Ill. App. 3d 8, 22, 602 N.E.2d 1335, 1345 (2d Dist. 1992).

[525] People v. Gilyard, 237 Ill. App. 3d 8, 22, 602 N.E.2d 1335, 1345 (2d Dist. 1992).

[526] 720 ILCS 5/12-11.1 (1999).

[527] 720 ILCS 5/12-16.2 (1999). People v. Russell, 158 Ill. 2d 23, 26-27, 630 N.E.2d 794, 796 (1994) (holding criminal transmission of HIV prohibition, which outlaws engaging in consensual sexual intercourse knowing oneself to be infected without informing one's sex partner, not unconstitutional on grounds of infringement on state and federal constitutional protections for free association and vagueness).

[528] 720 ILCS 5/12-16.2(e) (1999).

[529] 720 ILCS 5/12-16.2(a) (1999).

[530] 720 ILCS 5/12-16.2(c) (1999).

[531] 720 ILCS 5/16-2(d) (1999).

[532] 720 ILCS 5/12-16.2(b) (1999).

son to a bodily fluid of another person in a manner that could result in the transmission of HIV."[533] "Intravenous or intramuscular drug paraphernalia" is defined as "any equipment, product or material of any kind which is peculiar to and marketed for use in injecting a substance into the human body."[534] Thus, where an HIV-infected defendant placed his penis in the mouth of his nine-year-old victim, this constituted criminal transmission of HIV.[535] In addition, a conviction for aggravated criminal sexual assault and criminal transmission of HIV withstood same physical act doctrine objections on the theory that the sexual penetration of the victim was one act, and the release of his semen into the victim was a second act.[536]

§ 9.52. Abuse and Gross Neglect of Long-Term Care Facility Resident.

Any owner or licensee of a long-term care facility who abuses or grossly neglects a resident of the facility commits a felony violation of the crime called "abuse and gross neglect of a long term care facility resident."[537] However, if the violation is a product of the owner or licensee's failure to exercise reasonable care in the hiring, training, or supervision of staff in the facility, then the violation is (1) a petty offense if the failure merely involves "neglect"[538] or (2) a business offense if the failure only amounts to "gross neglect."[539]

"Abuse" of a resident, which carries felony sanctions, arises where the owner or licensee of the facility *intentionally* or *knowingly* causes any physical or mental injury to the resident or commits on the resident any sexual offense prohibited by the Illinois Criminal Code.[540] Physical injury, as a form of "abuse," does not require an actual, visible injury to the victim.[541] Thus, a defendant was properly convicted of abuse and gross neglect of long-term care facility resident where the defendant slapped the victim in the face even though there were no visible signs of injury.[542]

"Gross neglect" of a resident, which may be punished as a felony or business offense, depending on the circumstances, occurs where the owner or licensee *recklessly* fails to provide adequate medical or personal care, which failure results in the physical or mental injury or deterioration of the resident.[543] "Ne-

---

[533] 720 ILCS 5/12-16.2(b) (1999).

[534] 720 ILCS 5/12-16.2(b) (1999).

[535] People v. Dempsey, 242 Ill. App. 3d 568, 593-94, 610 N.E.2d 208, 224-25 (5th Dist. 1993).

[536] People v. Dempsey, 242 Ill. App. 3d 568, 594, 610 N.E.2d 208, 224-25 (5th Dist. 1993).

[537] 720 ILCS 5/12-19(a) (1999).

[538] 720 ILCS 5/12-19(b) (1999).

[539] 720 ILCS 5/12-19(c) (1999).

[540] 720 ILCS 5/12-19(d)(1) (1999).

[541] People v. Johnson, 231 Ill. App. 3d 412, 421-23, 595 N.E.2d 1381, 1387-90 (2d Dist. 1992).

[542] People v. Johnson, 231 Ill. App. 3d 412, 421-23, 595 N.E.2d 1381, 1387-90 (2d Dist. 1992).

[543] 720 ILCS 5/12-19(d)(2) (1999).

glect" of a resident, which is a petty offense, exists if the owner or licensee *negligently* fails to provide adequate medical or personal care, which failure results in physical or mental deterioration or injury.[544]

§ 9.53. Criminal Neglect of an Elderly or Disabled Person.

The Illinois legislature has proscribed the offense of "criminal neglect of an elderly or disabled person" in the criminal code.[545] A person commits this offense where he or she is a "caregiver" and *knowingly* acts or fails to act, causing "the elderly or disabled person's life to be endangered, health to be injured, or preexisting physical or mental condition to deteriorate" or abandons the elderly or disabled person.[546] By definition, an elderly or disabled person is someone who is, among other things, "incapable of adequately providing for his own health and personal care."[547] An elderly person is also someone at least sixty years of age suffering from a disease or infirmity associated with advanced age.[548] By definition, a "caregiver" is a "person who has a duty to provide for an elderly or disabled person's health and personal care, at such person's place of residence"[549] and includes live-in relatives by blood or marriage,[550] persons employed by the elderly or disabled person to provide care,[551] persons who have assumed such a duty for consideration,[552] or persons appointed by an agency or court to undertake such a duty.[553] "Caregiver" does not include a duly certified or licensed long-term care facility or its personnel.[554] "Abandon" is defined as deserting or knowingly forsaking an elderly or disabled person under circumstance in which a reasonable person would continue to provide care and custody.[555] The statute exempts from criminal liability any person who undertook to provide care for an elderly or disabled person through a "good faith effort" but through no fault of his or her own had been unable to provide such care.[556] Interestingly, the statute further exempts from criminal liability persons who pro-

---

[544] 720 ILCS 5/12-19(d)(3) (1999).

[545] 720 ILCS 5/12-21 (1999). *See* People v. Simester, 287 Ill. App. 3d 420, 426-29, 678 N.E.2d 710, 713-15 (1st Dist. 1997) (offense of criminal neglect of an elderly or disabled person upheld against claims of unconstitutional violation of due process and equal protection).

[546] 720 ILCS 5/12-21(a) (1999).

[547] 720 ILCS 5/12-21(b) (1999).

[548] 720 ILCS 5/12-21(b)(1) (1999).

[549] 720 ILCS 5/12-21(b)(3) (1999).

[550] 720 ILCS 5/12-21(b)(3)(A) (1999) (as well as a relative who "resides in the same building and regularly visits the elderly or disabled person").

[551] 720 ILCS 5/12-21(b)(3)(B) (1999).

[552] 720 ILCS 5/12-21(b)(3)(C) (1999).

[553] 720 ILCS 5/12-21(b)(3)(D) (1999).

[554] 720 ILCS 5/12-21(b)(3) (1999).

[555] 720 ILCS 5/12-21(b)(4) (1999).

[556] 720 ILCS 5/12-21(d) (1999).

vided "treatment by spiritual means through prayer alone and care consistent therewith in lieu of medical care and treatment in accordance with the tenets and practices of any church or religious denomination of which the elderly or disabled person is a member."[557] Finally, the violation of this section is a felony[558] and it is not a defense "that the accused reasonably believed that the victim was not an elderly or disabled person."[559]

§ 9.54. Child Abandonment.

In 1993, the legislature created the offense of "child abandonment."[560] This offense provides:

> (a) A person commits the offense of child abandonment when he or she, as a parent, guardian, or other person having physical custody or control of a child, without regard for the mental or physical health, safety, or welfare of that child, knowingly leaves that child who is under the age of 13 without supervision by a responsible person over the age of 14 for a period of 24 hours or more.
>
> (b) For the purposes of determining whether the child was left without regard for the mental or physical health, safety, or welfare of that child, the trier of fact shall consider the following factors: (1) the age of the child; (2) the number of children left at the location; (3) special needs of the child, including whether the child is physically or mentally handicapped, or otherwise in need of ongoing prescribed medical treatment such as periodic doses of insulin or other medications; (4) the duration of time in which the child was left without supervision; (5) the condition and location of the place where the child was left without supervision; (6) the time of day or night when the child was left without supervision; (7) the weather conditions, including whether the child was left in a location with adequate protection from the natural elements such as adequate heat or light; (8) the location of the parent, guardian, or other person having physical custody or control of the child at the time the child was left without supervision, the physical distance the child was from the parent, guardian, or other person having physical custody or control of the child at the time the child was without supervision; (9) whether the child's movement was restricted, or the child was otherwise locked within a room or other structure; (10) whether the child was given a phone number of a person or location to call in the event of an emergency and whether the child was capable of making an emergency call; (11) whether there was food and other provision left for

---

[557] 720 ILCS 5/12-21(e) (1999).
[558] 720 ILCS 5/12-21(a) (1999).
[559] 720 ILCS 5/12-21(f) (1999).
[560] 720 ILCS 5/12-21.5 (1999).

the child; (12) whether any of the conduct is attributable to economic hardship or illness and the parent, guardian or other person having physical custody or control of the child made a good faith effort to provide for the health and safety of the child; (13) the age and physical and mental capabilities of the person or persons who provided supervision for the child; (14) any other factor that would endanger the health or safety of that particular child; (15) whether the child was left under the supervision of another person.

Child abandonment is a . . . felony.[561]

§ 9.55. Endangering the Life or Health of a Child.

A person commits the offense of "endangering the life or health of a child" when he or she willfully causes or permits (1) the life or health of a child who is 17 or younger to be endangered or (2) a child to be placed in circumstances that endanger his or her life or health.[562] A violation of this prohibition is a misdemeanor, while a second or subsequent violation is a felony.[563]

§ 9.56. Sale of Body Parts.

Under the article 5/12 offenses involving "bodily harm" is an offense called "sale of body parts."[564] Any person who "knowingly buys or sells, or offers to buy or sell, a human body or any part of a human body" commits this offense.[565] A first offense is punishable as a misdemeanor while subsequent offenses are punishable as felonies.[566] This prohibition contains various exemptions for purchases or sales arising from endeavors revolving around organ transplants, blood donations, scientific research, or the like.[567]

§ 9.57. Inducement to Commit Suicide.

In order to discourage a person from influencing another to commit suicide, the crime of "inducement to commit suicide" has been created.[568] Inducement to commit suicide occurs when a person "coerces another to commit suicide and the other person commits or attempts to commit suicide as a direct result of the coercion, and he or she exercises substantial control over the person through (i) control of the other person's physical location or circumstances; (ii) use of psy-

---

[561] 720 ILCS 5/12-21.5 (1999) (there exists no subsection (c) in enrolled bill).

[562] 720 ILCS 5/12-21.6(a) (1999).

[563] 720 ILCS 5/12-21.6(b) (1999).

[564] 720 ILCS 5/12-20 (1999).

[565] 720 ILCS 5/12-20(a) (1999).

[566] 720 ILCS 5/12-20(a) (1999).

[567] 720 ILCS 5/12-20(b) (1999).

[568] 720 ILCS 5/12-31 (1999).

chological pressure; or (iii) use of actual or ostensible religious, political, social, philosophical or other principles."[569] Inducement to commit suicide also occurs when an individual, "with knowledge that another person intends to commit or attempts to commit suicide, intentionally (i) offers and provides the physical means by which another person commits or attempts to commit suicide, or (ii) participates in a physical act by which another person commits or attempts to commit suicide."[570] Furthermore, the statute indicates that the "lawful compliance or a good-faith attempt at lawful compliance" with the Illinois Living Will Act,[571] the Health Care Surrogate Act,[572] or the Powers of Attorney for Health Care Law,[573] is not inducement to commit suicide.[574] This offense is generally a felony.[575]

§ 9.58. Ritual Mutilation.

The state legislature has added "ritual mutilation" to the Illinois penal code.[576] A person commits ritual mutilation when he or she "mutilates, dismembers or tortures another person as part of a ceremony, rite, initiation, observance, performance or practice, and the victim does not consent or under such circumstances that the defendant knew or should have known that the victim was unable to render effective consent."[577] Traditional circumcision rites are exempted.[578] The offense is a felony.[579]

§ 9.59. Ritualized Abuse of a Child.

Another member of article 5/12 is "ritualized abuse of a child."[580] A person commits this felony[581] if he or she commits certain acts "with, upon or in the presence of a child as part of a ceremony, rite or similar observance."[582] The prohibited acts include: torture, mutilation or sacrifice of any warm-blooded animal or human being;[583] forcing the taking or application of any narcotic,

---

[569] 720 ILCS 5/12-31(a)(1) (1999).
[570] 720 ILCS 5/12-31(a)(2) (1999).
[571] 755 ILCS 35/1 et seq. (1999).
[572] 755 ILCS 40/1 et seq. (1999).
[573] 755 ILCS 45/4-1 et seq. (1999).
[574] 720 ILCS 5/12-31(c) (1999).
[575] 720 ILCS 5/12-31(b) (1999).
[576] 720 ILCS 5/12-32 (1999).
[577] 720 ILCS 5/12-32(a) (1999).
[578] 720 ILCS 5/12-32(c) (1999).
[579] 720 ILCS 5/12-32(b) (1999).
[580] 720 ILCS 5/12-33 (1999).
[581] 720 ILCS 5/12-33(c) (1999).
[582] 720 ILCS 5/12-33(a) (1999).
[583] 720 ILCS 5/12-33(a)(1) (1999).

drug, hallucinogen or anaesthetic for the purpose of dulling sensitivity, cognition, recollection of, or resistance to, any criminal activity;[584] forcing ingestion or external application of human or animal urine, feces, flesh, bones, body secretions, nonprescribed drugs or chemical compounds;[585] involves the child in a mock, unauthorized or unlawful marriage ceremony with another person or representation of any force or deity, followed by sexual contact with the child;[586] places a living child into a coffin or open grave containing a human corpse or remains;[587] threatens a child or child's parents, family, pets or friends with death or serious harm that instills a well-founded fear in the child that the threat will be carried out;[588] or unlawfully dissects, mutilates or incinerates a human corpse.[589] This offense does not apply to lawful circumcision rites,[590] the ingestion of animal flesh or blood in performance of a religious service ceremony,[591] state or federally approved, licensed or funded research projects,[592] lawful agriculture, animal husbandry, food preparation, wild game hunting and fishing practices or the branding or identification of livestock.[593] For purposes of this offense, "child" means any person under eighteen years of age.[594]

§ 9.60. Female Genital Mutilation.

"Female genital mutilation" is committed by any person who "knowingly circumcises, excises, or infibulates, in whole or in part, the labia majora, labia minora, or clitoris of another."[595] Consent by the minor on whom the procedure is performed or by the minor's parent or guardian is not a defense to this offense.[596] A surgical procedure is not a violation of this prohibition if it is performed by a physician licensed to practice medicine in all its branches and it: (1) is necessary to the health of the person on whom it is performed; or (2) is performed on a person who is in labor or who has just given birth for medical purposes connected to that labor or birth.[597] This offense is a Class X felony.[598]

---

[584] 720 ILCS 5/12-33(a)(2) (1999).
[585] 720 ILCS 5/12-33(a)(3) (1999).
[586] 720 ILCS 5/12-33(a)(4) (1999).
[587] 720 ILCS 5/12-33(a)(5) (1999).
[588] 720 ILCS 5/12-33(a)(6) (1999).
[589] 720 ILCS 5/12-33(a)(7) (1999).
[590] 720 ILCS 5/12-33(b)(2) (1999).
[591] 720 ILCS 5/12-33(b)(4) (1999).
[592] 720 ILCS 5/12-33(b)(3) (1999).
[593] 720 ILCS 5/12-33(b)(1) (1999).
[594] 720 ILCS 5/12-33(d) (1999).
[595] 720 ILCS 5/12-34(a) (1999).
[596] 720 ILCS 5/12-34(a) (1999).
[597] 720 ILCS 5/12-34(b) (1999).
[598] 720 ILCS 5/12-34(c) (1999).

§ 9.61. Armed Violence.

The purpose of the "armed violence" statute[599] was to enact a strong deterrent against carrying a dangerous or deadly weapon during the commission of a felony.[600] The presence of a weapon significantly increases the danger that a victim who resists may be seriously injured or killed during a felony.[601] It is this risk that the statute seeks to address by making the carrying of a weapon while committing a felony an aggravating factor which enhances the severity of the predicate felony.[602]

Since the purpose of the armed violence statute is to enhance the penalty for a felony involving the use of a weapon, that deterrent purpose cannot be satisfied where, even without the use of a weapon, the predicate felony involving the use of a weapon is punishable by a more severe sentence than is available for armed violence.[603] Thus, since first degree murder carries a stiffer penalty than armed violence, first degree murder cannot serve as the predicate offense for armed violence.[604] The same holds true for various other offenses including second degree murder[605] and involuntary manslaughter.[606] In addition, in some instances, the Illinois courts have had occasion to find an armed violence conviction predicated on another felony violated the Illinois Constitution's proportionate penalties clause.[607]

---

[599] 720 ILCS 5/33A-1 through 5/33A-3 (1999).

[600] People v. Robinson, 229 Ill. App. 3d 627, 630, 593 N.E.2d 148, 150 (3d Dist. 1992); People v. Eure, 140 Ill. App. 3d 387, 392-94, 488 N.E.2d 1267, 1272 (1st Dist. 1986).

[601] People v. Condon, 148 Ill. 2d 96, 109, 592 N.E. 2d 951, 957 (1992); People v. Shelato, 228 Ill. App. 3d 622, 626, 592 N.E.2d 585, 589 (4th Dist. 1992).

[602] People v. Shelato, 228 Ill. App. 3d 622, 626, 592 N.E.2d 585, 589 (4th Dist. 1992).

[603] People v. Hobbs, 249 Ill. App. 3d 679, 683, 619 N.E.2d 258, 261 (5th Dist. 1993).

[604] People v. Hobbs, 249 Ill. App. 3d 679, 683, 619 N.E.2d 258, 261 (5th Dist. 1993).

[605] People v. Drakeford, 139 Ill. 2d 206, 213, 564 N.E.2d 792, 795 (1990). *See also* People v. Alejos, 97 Ill. 2d 502, 513, 455 N.E.2d 48, 53 (1983) (armed violence cannot be predicated on voluntary manslaughter).

[606] People v. Fernetti, 104 Ill. 2d 19, 24-25, 470 N.E.2d 501, 503 (1984). *Compare* People v. Allen, 153 Ill. 2d 145, 149-53, 606 N.E.2d 1149, 1151-53 (1992) (aggravated battery was proper predicate felony for armed violence).

[607] *See* People v. Lewis, 175 Ill. 2d 412, 423, 677 N.E.2d 830, 835 (1996) (armed violence sanctions predicated on robbery committed with category I weapon and armed robbery sanctions are unconstitutionally disproportionate); People v. Christy, 139 Ill. 2d 172, 181, 564 N.E.2d 770, 774 (1990) (penalties for aggravated kidnapping and armed violence predicated on kidnapping with a category I weapon unconstitutionally disproportionate); People v. Murphy, 261 Ill. App. 3d 1019, 1022, 635 N.E.2d 110, 112 (2d Dist. 1994) (conviction for armed violence predicated on unlawful restraint violated the proportionate penalties guarantee because a less serious offense, unlawful restraint committed with a dangerous weapon, would be punished more severely than a more serious offense, namely, aggravated kidnapping) *See* § 1.03 of this treatise for a discussion of the proportionality principle.

§ 9.62. — Elements of Armed Violence.

The offense of armed violence is set forth in the following terms: "a person commits armed violence when, while armed with a dangerous weapon, he commits any felony defined by Illinois Law."[608] Thus, the face of the statute presents two essential requirements: (1) possession of a dangerous weapon, and (2) committing a felony defined by Illinois law.

§ 9.63. — The Meaning of "Dangerous Weapon."

Certain objects have been statutorily defined as dangerous weapons. Under section 5/33A-1:

> "(a) "Armed with a dangerous weapon." A person is considered armed with a dangerous weapon for purposes of this Article, when he or she carries on or about his or her person or is otherwise armed with a Category I, Category II, or Category III weapon.
> (b) A Category I weapon is a handgun, sawed-off shotgun, sawed-off rifle, any other firearm small enough to be concealed upon the person, semiautomatic firearm, or machine gun. A Category II weapon is any other rifle, shotgun, spring gun, other firearm, stun gun or taser . . ., knife with a blade of at least 3 inches in length, dagger, dirk, switchblade knife, stiletto, axe, hatchet, or other deadly or dangerous weapon or instrument of like character. As used in this subsection (b) "semiautomatic firearm" means a repeating firearm that utilizes a portion of the energy of a firing cartridge to extract the fired cartridge case and chamber the next round and that requires a separate pull of the trigger to fire each cartridge.
> (c) A Category III weapon is a bludgeon, black-jack, slungshot, sand-bag, sand-club, metal knuckles, billy or other dangerous weapon of like character."[609]

Any weapon specifically listed in the definition under 5/33A-1 is per se a dangerous weapon.[610] Thus, for example, a "sawed-off shotgun" is per se a dangerous weapon.[611] A handgun, even if not loaded, is a dangerous weapon.[612] There are two other types of weapons which qualify under the armed violence

---

[608] 720 ILCS 5/33A-2 (1999).

[609] 720 ILCS 5/33A-1 (1999).

[610] People v. Charles, 217 Ill. App. 3d 509, 512, 577 N.E.2d 534, 536 (2d Dist. 1991); People v. Ptak, 193 Ill. App. 3d 782, 785, 550 N.E.2d 711, 713 (2d Dist. 1990); People v. Weger, 154 Ill. App. 3d 706, 712, 506 N.E.2d 1072, 1076 (4th Dist. 1987).

[611] 720 ILCS 5/33A-1(b) (1999). *See also* People v. Stamos, 214 Ill. App. 3d 895, 904, 574 N.E.2d 184, 189 (1st Dist. 1991) (mere possession of a sawed-off shotgun is criminal; it needed not be actually used in the commission of a felony).

[612] People v. Orsby, 286 Ill. App. 3d 142, 149-50, 675 N.E.2d 237, 241-42 (2d Dist. 1996).

statute:[613] (1) objects of "like character" which are not per se dangerous but considered dangerous weapons because of the manner in which they are used,[614] and (2) objects which are per se dangerous because they are of "like character" to those weapons listed under 5/33A-1.[615] Under the first type of weapon, the use of the weapon has already demonstrated its dangerousness, while under the second type of weapon, the object must be inherently dangerous in order to sustain an armed violence conviction.[616]

An object not specifically listed as a category I or II weapon may become a dangerous weapon if it used in a dangerous manner and is also of "like character."[617] Objects of "like character" that are not dangerous per se but found to be dangerous because of the manner in which they were used include a broken glass bottle,[618] non-broken glass bottle,[619] two-inch piece of glass,[620] knives with blades smaller than three inches,[621] knives of indeterminate length,[622] and a walking cane.[623] The case involving the walking cane is often cited. In *People v. Lee*,[624] the court when confronted with whether an object not listed under 5/33A-1 is a dangerous weapon stated:

---

[613] *See* People v. Weger, 154 Ill. App. 3d 706, 712, 506 N.E.2d 1072, 1077 (4th Dist. 1987).

[614] People v. Charles, 217 Ill. App. 3d 509, 512, 577 N.E.2d 534, 536 (2d Dist. 1991); People v. Samier, 129 Ill. App. 3d 966, 968, 473 N.E.2d 601, 603 (3d Dist. 1984); People v. Hall, 117 Ill. App. 3d 788, 804, 453 N.E.2d 1327, 1339-40 (1st Dist. 1983), *cert. denied*, 467 U.S. 1228 (1984); People v. Lee, 46 Ill. App. 3d 343, 348, 360 N.E.2d 1173, 1176 (3d Dist. 1977).

[615] People v. Weger, 154 Ill. App. 3d 706, 712, 506 N.E.2d 1072, 1076 (4th Dist. 1987) (straight blade razor not a weapon "of like character").

[616] A person who commits a felony while carrying a walking cane has not necessarily committed armed violence. But if that person uses that walking cane in a deadly manner during the commission of the felony, the defendant is guilty of armed violence. *See* People v. Lee, 46 Ill. App. 3d 343, 347, 360 N.E.2d 1173, 1176 (3d Dist. 1977). Thus, if a weapon is not used in a deadly manner during the commission of a felony, it must be inherently dangerous in order to procure an armed violence conviction. In other words, the object must be of sufficient "like character" to those items listed under category I and II. Where this is the case, the mere presence of the object, regardless of its use, is sufficient to sustain an armed violence conviction.

[617] People v. Ptak, 193 Ill. App. 3d 782, 785, 550 N.E.2d 711, 713 (2d Dist. 1990) (broken beer bottle); People v. Samier, 129 Ill. App. 3d 966, 968, 473 N.E.2d 601, 603 (3d Dist. 1984) (knife with two-inch blade); People v. Hall, 117 Ill. App. 3d 788, 804, 453 N.E.2d 1327, 1340 (1st Dist. 1983) (knife of indeterminate length); People v. Lee, 46 Ill. App. 3d 343, 347, 360 N.E.2d 1173, 1176 (3d Dist. 1977) (walking cane).

[618] People v. Ptak, 193 Ill. App. 3d 782, 785, 550 N.E.2d 711, 713 (2d Dist. 1990); People v. Thornton, 145 Ill. App. 3d 669, 771, 496 N.E.2d 6, 7 (1st Dist. 1986).

[619] People v. Varela, 194 Ill. App. 3d 364, 368, 551 N.E.2d 323, 325 (3d Dist. 1990).

[620] People v. Chrisos, 142 Ill. App. 3d 747, 751, 492 N.E.2d 216, 218 (5th Dist. 1986).

[621] People v. Samier, 129 Ill. App. 3d 966, 969, 473 N.E.2d 601, 603 (3d Dist. 1984).

[622] People v. Hall, 117 Ill. App. 3d 788, 804-05, 453 N.E.2d 1327, 1340 (1st Dist. 1983).

[623] People v. Lee, 46 Ill. App. 3d 343, 347, 360 N.E.2d 1173, 1176 (3d Dist. 1977).

[624] 46 Ill. App. 3d 343, 360 N.E.2d 1173 (3d Dist. 1977).

A deadly weapon is not necessarily one manufactured for the special purpose of taking animal life, nor need it be of any certain size or description. This court has defined a deadly weapon as "an instrument that is used or may be used for the purpose of offense or defense and capable of producing death. Some weapons are deadly *per se*, others, owing to the manner in which they are used, become deadly. A gun, pistol or dirkknife is itself deadly, while a *small pocket knife*, a *cane*, a riding whip, . . . may be so used to be a deadly weapon."[625]

An object used in a dangerous manner may also still be dangerous as a matter of law.[626]

An object not specifically listed under 5/33A-1, nor used as a dangerous weapon, may still be considered a per se dangerous weapon if the object is of sufficient "like character" to a dangerous weapon listed under 5/33A-1.[627] In assessing the likeness of character, the courts have looked to whether an object has an "ascertainable legitimate use"[628] Thus, a straight-blade razor which is still used by some for shaving is not dangerous per se even though it contained a blade longer than three inches.[629]

§ 9.64. — The Meaning of "Carries on or About His Person or is Otherwise Armed."

There is no requirement that the weapon be used in the predicate offense.[630] The mere presence of a weapon during the commission of a felony is sufficient to sustain an armed violence conviction.[631] However, the defendant must have *immediate access* to or *timely control* over the weapon.[632] The Illinois Supreme

---

[625] People v. Lee, 46 Ill. App. 3d 343, 347-48, 360 N.E.2d 1173, 1177 (3d Dist. 1977) (citing People v. Dwyer, 324 Ill. 363, 364, 155 N.E. 316 (1927)).

[626] People v. Ptak, 193 Ill. App. 3d 782, 785, 550 N.E.2d 711, 713 (2d Dist. 1990) (broken beer bottle used to slice victim's ear and neck).

[627] People v. Ptak, 193 Ill. App. 3d 782, 785, 550 N.E.2d 711, 713 (2d Dist. 1990) (broken beer bottle had no legitimate use); People v. Weger, 154 Ill. App. 3d 706, 712, 506 N.E.2d 1072, 1077 (4th Dist. 1987) (straight blade razor has legitimate use).

[628] People v. Ptak, 193 Ill. App. 3d 782, 785, 550 N.E.2d 711, 713 (2d Dist. 1990); People v. Weger, 154 Ill. App. 3d 706, 712, 506 N.E.2d 1072, 1077 (4th Dist. 1987).

[629] People v. Weger, 154 Ill. App. 3d 706, 714, 506 N.E.2d 1072, 1077 (4th Dist. 1987) (the court noted, however, that a straight-blade razor may still be a dangerous weapon if it is used in a dangerous manner).

[630] People v. Melgoza, 231 Ill. App. 3d 510, 531, 595 N.E.2d 1261, 1277 (1st Dist. 1992); People v. Shelato, 228 Ill. App. 3d 622, 626, 592 N.E.2d 585, 589 (4th Dist. 1992); People v. Alejos, 97 Ill. 2d 502, 508, 455 N.E.2d 48, 50 (1983).

[631] People v. Shelato, 228 Ill. App. 3d 622, 626, 592 N.E.2d 585, 588 (4th Dist. 1992).

[632] People v. Condon, 148 Ill. 2d 96, 110, 592 N.E.2d 951, 958 (1992), *cert. denied*, 507 U.S. 948 (1993).

Court in *People v. Condon*[633] has discussed the meaning of "otherwise armed." In *Condon*, the defendant had been arrested in the kitchen of his home. Although a number of guns, including two loaded pistols, where discovered throughout the house, no guns were in the kitchen where the defendant was found.[634] In holding that the defendant was not "otherwise armed," the court stated:

> A felon with a weapon at his or her disposal is forced to make a spontaneous and often instantaneous decision to kill without time to reflect on the use of such deadly force. [Citation.] Without a weapon at hand, the felon is not faced with such a deadly decision. Hence, we have the deterrent purpose of armed violence statute. Thus, for this purpose to be served, it would be necessary that the defendant have some type of *immediate access* to or timely *control over* the weapon.[635]

Thus, a weapon wrapped in a rag inside a duffel bag which was located more than ten feet away from the defendant was not in the immediate access of the defendant and, accordingly, the defendant was not "otherwise armed" within the meaning of the statute.[636] No armed violence occurred where a defendant was arrested in her apartment on drug charges and a gun was found on a coffee table in another room where a guest was found lying on a bed.[637] In another case, a gun recovered from the back seat of the defendant's car was found not to be accessible.[638] However, a gun situated in a shoulder holster in an unlocked glove compartment was found accessible to the driver of that car and, thus, defendant was found to be armed.[639] A defendant was found to be "otherwise armed" with a gun which was located underneath the cushions of a sofa located in the same room as the defendant.[640] Similarly, a felon was found to be armed where a gun was located under the mattress six to eight inches in from the side in which the defendant was lying.[641] Where weapons on the front seat of the car were within

---

[633] 148 Ill. 2d 96, 592 N.E.2d 951 (1992), *cert. denied*, 507 U.S. 948 (1993).

[634] People v. Condon, 148 Ill. 2d 96, 110, 592 N.E.2d 951, 958 (1992) (the only guns located on first floor were an unloaded rifle and an unloaded shotgun), *cert. denied*, 507 U.S. 948 (1993).

[635] People v. Condon, 148 Ill. 2d 96, 109-10, 592 N.E.2d 951, 958 (1992), *cert. denied*, 507 U.S. 948 (1993).

[636] People v. Shelato, 228 Ill. App. 3d 622, 627, 592 N.E.2d 585, 589 (4th Dist. 1992).

[637] People v. King, 155 Ill. App. 3d 363, 370, 507 N.E.2d 1285, 1289 (3d Dist. 1987). *See also* People v. Rivera, 260 Ill. App. 3d 984, 993-94, 636 N.E.2d 753, 760 (1st Dist. 1994) (reversing armed violence conviction where a gun lay on the kitchen table while defendant, who was being apprehended for possession of a controlled substance, had ran past the gun while being chased by police).

[638] People v. Melgoza, 231 Ill. App. 3d 510, 532, 595 N.E.2d 1261, 1277 (1st Dist. 1992).

[639] People v. Zambetta, 132 Ill. App. 3d 740, 750-51, 477 N.E.2d 821, 829 (2d Dist. 1985).

[640] People v. Bond, 178 Ill. App. 3d 1020, 1023, 534 N.E.2d 156, 158 (4th Dist. 1989) (the defendant was seated on the floor when police officers entered and was ordered to sit on the sofa where the gun was hidden).

[641] People v. Hernandez, 229 Ill. App. 3d 546, 550, 593 N.E.2d 1123, 1128 (3d Dist. 1992).

the defendant's immediate reach as the defendant stood next to the car door and partially opened car window, removing any possible remaining obstruction to the defendant's unfettered access to and unrestricted control over his weapons, he was "otherwise armed" for purposes of armed violence.[642]

There is no requirement that the defendant be armed at the inception of the commission of the predicate felony.[643] Thus, armed violence occurred where a defendant engaged in a fight without a weapon, and after kicking the victim in the head, picked up a bottle and struck the victim.[644] Similarly, where evidence showed that defendant did not drop his pistol until after he punched and kicked the victim, the defendant was found to have been armed during the beating.[645]

§ 9.65. — Impermissible Double Enhancement.

The same weapon may not be used to enhance the predicate offense and raise the predicate offense to armed violence.[646] This constitutes impermissible "double enhancement."[647] For example, the presence or use of a gun may not raise the misdemeanor of battery to the felony of aggravated battery and also raise aggravated battery to armed violence.[648] In other words, the use or presence of a dangerous weapon may not be an element of the predicate felony and armed violence.[649] Similarly, basing armed robbery on an attempted armed robbery would constitute double enhancement because the presence of the weapon would elevate the robbery to armed robbery while simultaneously transforming the attempted armed robbery into armed violence.[650]

§ 9.66. — Lesser Included Offenses, the Same Physical Act Doctrine and Armed Violence.

A single physical act may not result in multiple convictions of armed violence.[651] Accordingly, a defendant who shot a victim in the hand while on a public way may not be convicted for armed violence based on aggravated battery premised on great bodily harm[652] and armed violence for committing aggravated

---

[642] People v. Harre, 155 Ill. 2d 392, 396-401, 614 N.E.2d 1235, 1237-40 (1993).

[643] People v. Varela, 194 Ill. App. 3d 364, 367, 551 N.E.2d 323, 324 (3d Dist. 1990).

[644] People v. Varela, 194 Ill. App. 3d 364, 367, 551 N.E.2d 323, 324 (3d Dist. 1990).

[645] People v. Garza, 298 Ill. App. 3d 452, 460, 699 N.E.2d 181, 187 (2d Dist. 1998).

[646] People v. Haron, 85 Ill. 2d 261, 278, 422 N.E.2d 627, 634 (1981); People v. Munson, 171 Ill. App. 3d 274, 276, 525 N.E.2d 250, 252 (3d Dist. 1988); People v. Hanson, 138 Ill. App. 3d 530, 535, 485 N.E.2d 1144, 1148 (5th Dist. 1985).

[647] People v. Del Percio, 105 Ill. 2d 372, 375-78, 475 N.E.2d 528, 529-31 (1985).

[648] People v. Haron, 85 Ill. 2d 261, 278, 422 N.E.2d 627, 634 (1981).

[649] People v. Haron, 85 Ill. 2d 261, 278, 422 N.E.2d 627, 634 (1981).

[650] People v. Del Percio, 105 Ill. 2d 372, 375-78, 475 N.E.2d 528, 529-31 (1985).

[651] People v. Nix, 133 Ill. App. 3d 1054, 1058, 479 N.E.2d 1147, 1150 (3d Dist. 1985).

[652] People v. Nix, 133 Ill. App. 3d 1054, 1058, 479 N.E.2d 1147, 1150 (3d Dist. 1985).

battery premised on committing a battery on a public way.[653] Similarly, a defendant cannot be convicted and sentenced for both armed violence and the underlying felony where a single physical act is the basis for both charges.[654] Thus, a conviction for armed violence was improper where the defendant was convicted of the underlying offense of murder.[655] However, a defendant who stabbed a victim five times was properly convicted of armed violence and attempted

---

[653] People v. Nix, 133 Ill. App. 3d 1054, 1058, 479 N.E.2d 1147, 1150 (3d Dist. 1985).

[654] People v. Edwards, 304 Ill. App. 3d 250, 254, 710 N.E.2d 507, 510 (2d Dist. 1999) (vacating aggravated battery with firearm and aggravated discharge of a firearm where based on same act as armed violence); People v. Williams, 302 Ill. App. 3d 975, 976-78, 707 N.E.2d 980, 981-82 (2d Dist. 1999) (vacating possession of controlled substance and unlawful use of weapon where based on same act as armed violence); People v. Zarate, 264 Ill. App. 3d 667, 679, 637 N.E.2d 1044, 1053 (1st Dist. 1994) (vacating armed violence conviction based on home invasion due to same physical act doctrine where defendant broke into victim's home and stabbed her in the leg); People v. Camden, 219 Ill. App. 3d 124, 141, 578 N.E.2d 1211, 1223 (5th Dist. 1991) (vacating aggravated battery conviction which was used as the predicate offense for armed violence where defendant shot the victim only once); People v. Donaldson, 91 Ill. 2d 164, 170, 435 N.E.2d 477, 479 (1982) (vacating aggravated battery based on great bodily harm conviction while upholding armed violence conviction due to same physical act doctrine).

[655] People v. Burnett, 257 Ill. App. 3d 383, 388, 628 N.E.2d 1002, 1006 (1st Dist. 1993); People v. Gill, 264 Ill. App. 3d 451, 463, 637 N.E.2d 1030, 1039 (1st Dist. 1992) (vacating armed violence conviction based on murder where defendant only stabbed the victim once)

murder.[656] Where a defendant committed second degree murder against one victim and armed violence against another, the dual convictions were upheld against a same physical act doctrine challenge.[657] Where four defendants gang-raped a sexual assault victim at gun point by repeated sexual penetration of her vagina and mouth, resulting in dozens of counts of criminal sexual assault as well as armed violence against each offender either as principal or accomplice, the Illinois Supreme Court ruled that it was necessary to order a remand for the lower court to dissect which of these counts were barred by the same physical act doctrine.[658] Also, aggravated battery premised on great bodily harm is a lesser included offense of armed violence.[659]

---

[656] People v. Pressley, 160 Ill. App. 3d 858, 866, 513 N.E.2d 921, 927 (1st Dist. 1987) (the court noted that one stab wound was sufficient to establish attempted murder while the other four stab wounds clearly constituted armed violence). *But see* People v. Burrage, 269 Ill. App. 3d 67, 72-73, 645 N.E.2d 455, 459-60 (1st Dist. 1994) (holding that attempted first degree murder is not a lesser included offense of armed violence, however, vacating the armed violence conviction due to the same physical act doctrine where defendant fired three shots at victim).

[657] People v. Floyd, 262 Ill. App. 3d 49, 59-61, 634 N.E.2d 328, 335-36 (2d Dist. 1999).

[658] People v. Garcia, 179 Ill. 2d 55, 71-72, 688 N.E.2d 57, 64-65 (1997).

[659] People v. Bolden, 210 Ill. App. 3d 940, 946, 569 N.E.2d 597, 602 (2d Dist. 1991).

CHAPTER 10

ELECTRONIC EAVESDROPPING

§ 10.01. Introduction.

At common law, the practice of eavesdropping was condemned as a nuisance.[1] The offense consisted of "listening under walls or windows, or the *eaves* of a house, to hearken after discourse, and thereupon to frame slanderous and mischievous tales."[2] While listening to and/or recording a conversation is no longer illegal per se and is approved in instances where law enforcement officials eavesdrop on criminal suspects without any electronic aid,[3] the use of an electronic device to monitor a person's conversations may constitute an illegal[4] invasion of that person's expectation of privacy.[5] In the past, the penal code of Illinois provided relatively restrictive prohibitions against all forms of electronic

---

[1] 4 W. BLACKSTONE, COMMENTARIES ON THE LAW OF ENGLAND 168.

[2] BLACK'S LAW DICTIONARY 511 (6th ed. 1990).

[3] United States v. Llanes, 398 F.2d 880, 882 (2nd Cir. 1968) (officer's permitted eavesdropping of defendant's conversations while standing next to an "apartment door, which, though locked, was hanging imperfectly, leaving a small opening."); People v. Wright, 41 Ill. 2d 170, 176, 242 N.E.2d 180, 184 (1968) (officer stationed on public right-of-way while eavesdropping on criminal activity within building held proper).

[4] 18 U.S.C. §§ 2510-22 (federal provisions governing electronic eavesdropping); 720 ILCS 5/14-1 through 5/14-9 (1999).

[5] Katz v. United States, 389 U.S. 347 (1967) (government electronic eavesdropping of defendant's conversations made in a public telephone booth was violative of the fourth amendment); People v. Sylvester, 86 Ill. App. 3d 186, 191, 407 N.E.2d 1002, 1007 (1st Dist. 1980) (Both Federal Title III, 18 U.S.C. § 2510 *et seq.*, and Illinois eavesdropping statutes "where enacted to protect the right to privacy. . . .").

eavesdropping.[6] The prior policy against eavesdropping has been modified somewhat but still significantly influences the Illinois law today. The evolution of these state strictures will be examined in this chapter.

§ 10.02.   Federal Constitutional and Statutory Considerations.

Although a complete examination of federal penal considerations is outside the scope of this book, an understanding and appreciation of the Illinois law on eavesdropping will best be accomplished by a review of federal protections in this regard. The federal regulations are reflected in the federal Constitution,[7] various judicial interpretations of it,[8] and federal statutes.[9]

§ 10.03.   Federal Constitutional Limitations: Evolution of a Person's Expectation of Privacy.

The United States Supreme Court's initial consideration of electronic eavesdropping produced the remarkable conclusion that it was not at all governed by the federal Constitution. In *Olmstead v. United States*,[10] the Supreme Court ruled that since the defendants' telephone conversations, monitored through a warrantless wiretap of the defendants' telephone, were intangible, and not "things" — "person, houses, papers, and effects" within the language on the Fourth Amendment[11] and since the wiretapping was done without any "trespass" on the defendants' premises, the defendants' Fourth Amendment right to be free of unreasonable searches and seizures was not violated.[12] Thus, by a narrow, literal reading of the Fourth Amendment, in conjunction with reliance on a "trespass" analysis, the Court in cases decided after *Olmstead* upheld any elec-

---

[6] Prior to 1989, Illinois was one of the very few states to prohibit all forms of non-consensual electronic eavesdropping. ILL. ANN. STAT. ch. 38, § 14-1 (Smith-Hurd 1979), 1961 Committee Comments, at 606 (revised 1972). Today, non-consensual eavesdropping is permissible in investigations of solicitation of murder, solicitation of murder for hire, first degree murder, money laundering, certain violations of the Illinois Controlled Substances Act, certain unlawful weapons violations, in kidnapping-hostage situations and certain streetgang-related criminality. Eavesdropping in pursuance of evidence of other criminality is prohibited. *See* 720 ILCS 5/14-2 (1999) (general prohibition); 725 ILCS 5/108B-3 (1999) (defining criminality that may be subject to non-consensual eavesdropping).

[7] U.S. CONST. amend. IV.

[8] *See* John Decker & Joel Handler, *Electronic Surveillance: Standards, Restrictions and Remedies*, 12 CAL. W.L. REV. 60, 65-78 (1975).

[9] 18 U.S.C. §§ 2510-22.

[10] 277 U.S. 438 (1928).

[11] *See* U.S. CONST. amend. IV ("The right of the people to be secure in their persons, houses, papers, and effects, against unreasonable searches and seizures, shall not be violated, and no warrants shall issue, but upon probable cause, supported by oath or affirmation, and particularly describing the place to be searched, and the persons or things to be seized.")

[12] Olmstead v. United States, 277 U.S. 438, 466 (1928).

tronic eavesdropping that was accomplished without a concomitant physical trespass on the defendant's property.[13]

Later, in 1967, the Supreme Court in *Katz v. United States*[14] reversed the *Olmstead* doctrine. *Katz* involved a situation where government agents engaged in the warrantless monitoring of a public telephone booth that the defendant was using to further his criminal gambling activities. The government claimed that since the eavesdropping was done without trespassing on an area over which Katz had some proprietary control, he had no basis to complain about a breach of constitutional rights. In a major shift in its analytical focus, the Supreme Court made its now famous pronouncement that the Fourth Amendment was designed to "protect people, not places."[15]

> What a person knowingly exposes to the public, even in his own home or office, is not a subject of Fourth Amendment protection. . . . But what he seeks to preserve as private, even in an area accessible to the public, may be constitutionally protected. . . . [W]hat [Katz] sought to exclude when he entered the booth was not the intruding eye — it was the uninvited ear.[16]

Thus, the Court concluded that the only way the government could justify its invasion of the reasonable "expectation of privacy"[17] that revolved around Katz's conversations was to procure a court order authorizing the eavesdropping.[18]

§ 10.04.   Consensual Eavesdropping — The Assumption-of-Risk Doctrine.

The *Katz* court, by focusing on the fact that neither party to the conversation had consented to the monitoring, did *not* state that all conversations would be protected by the Fourth Amendment from all types of eavesdropping. At the time *Katz* was decided, the Court had already held that where an electronic interception was sanctioned by one of the parties to the conversations, there was no Fourth Amendment protections. In *Rathburn v. United States,*[19] decided in 1957, the defendant was convicted for making a threatening interstate phone call based on a police officer's testimony derived from a wiretap consented to by the

---

[13] *See* Silverman v. United States, 365 U.S. 505 (1961) ("spike mike" which penetrated common wall until it made contact with heating duct that ran through defendant's home and permitted warrantless eavesdropping violative of Fourth Amendment); Goldman v. United States, 316 U.S. 129 (1942) (warrantless use of detectaphone placed against common wall that allowed for eavesdropping in next room not violative of Fourth Amendment since no "trespass" into next room).

[14] 389 U.S. 347 (1967).

[15] Katz v. United States, 389 U.S. 347, 351 (1967).

[16] Katz v. United States, 389 U.S. 347, 351-52 (1967).

[17] Katz v. United States, 389 U.S. 347, 361 (1967) (Harlan, J., concurring).

[18] Katz v. United States, 389 U.S. 347, 356 (1967).

[19] 355 U.S. 107 (1957), *reh'g denied*, 355 U.S. 925 (1958).

victim. In affirming the defendant's conviction, the Court stated: "Each party to a telephone conversation takes a risk that the other party may have an extension telephone and may allow another to overhear the conversation."[20] The Court held that the victim's consent to the wiretap by the officer was no different than permitting an outsider to use an extension telephone.[21] Thus, the net effect of the *Rathburn* ruling was that one assumes the risk that the person, with whom one is conversing, will consent to third-party monitoring, electronic or otherwise, of the conversation.[22]

The principle at the heart of *Rathburn* was extended to "participant monitoring" in a case in which eavesdropping devices were used in face-to-face conversation.[23] In the 1963 case of *Lopez v. United States,*[24] a federal Internal Revenue Service agent engaged in a conversation with the defendant and, without a warrant, used a wireless pocket tape recorder to tape the defendant's offer to bribe the agent. The Court said, "we think the risk that petitioner took in offering a bribe to Davis [the IRS agent] fairly included the risk that the offer would be accurately reproduced in court, whether by faultless memory or mechanical recording."[25] The Court clarified that its stance regarding the assumption-of-risk doctrine in the context of consensual eavesdropping had not changed because of *Katz,* in a post-*Katz* opinion entitled *United States v. White.*[26] In that case, a law enforcement official instantaneously transmitted electronically his conversation with the defendant to other agents equipped with radio receivers. While approving the government's actions the Court stated:

> for constitutional purposes, no different result is required if the agent instead of immediately reporting and transcribing his conversations with defendant, either (1) simultaneously records them with electronic equipment which he is carrying on his person, *Lopez*; (2) or carries radio equipment which simultaneously transmits the conversations either to recording equipment located elsewhere or to other agents monitoring the transmitting frequency.[27]

Conceptually, then, when one party consents to the revelation of his or her conversation to others who are not parties to the conversations, he or she in effect waives normal Fourth Amendment privacy protections that normally attend

---

[20] Rathburn v. United States, 355 U.S. 107, 111 (1957), *reh'g denied,* 355 U.S. 925 (1958).

[21] Rathburn v. United States, 355 U.S. 107, 110-11 (1957), *reh'g denied,* 355 U.S. 925 (1958).

[22] John Decker & Joel Handler, *Electronic Surveillance: Standards, Restrictions and Remedies,* 12 CAL. W.L. REV. 60, 70 (1975).

[23] John Decker & Joel Handler, *Electronic Surveillance: Standards, Restrictions and Remedies,* 12 CAL. W.L. REV. 60, 70 (1975).

[24] 373 U.S. 427 (1963).

[25] Lopez v. United States, 373 U.S. 427, 439 (1963).

[26] 401 U.S. 745 (1971).

[27] United States v. White, 401 U.S. 745, 751 (1971).

a conversation, including the privacy interests of those others who are party to the same conversation. In this context, one party to a conversation can effectively take away another person's constitutional claim that his or her verbal utterances were private. The Fourth Amendment only protects a subjective expectation of privacy that is objectively reasonable.[28] A defendant's subjective belief that the conversation with another will remain private may be unreasonable, and is therefore unqualified for protection.

§ 10.05.   Nonconsensual Eavesdropping — Federal Constitutional Restrictions.

When neither party to a particular conversation consents to the revelation or recording of that conversation, then there is generally a zone of privacy surrounding the conversation that can only be invaded electronically by way of a court order.[29] Thus, if two parties are conversing in the privacy of their residence or over the telephone and neither party has consented to the electronic monitoring of their conversation, then the assumption-of-risk doctrine does not apply and the conversation will be protected by the Fourth Amendment.[30]

The principle decision involving non-consensual eavesdropping decided by the United States Supreme Court is *Berger v. New York*.[31] At issue in that case was a New York court order that authorized the eavesdropping of a particular defendant under the authority of a state statute. The Court ruled that the statute and, accordingly, the court order was violative of the Fourth Amendment. The Court identified several constitutional problems with the statute: (1) it did not require a showing of probable cause supportive of commission of an offense, (2) it did not require a particularized description of the conversations to be seized, (3) it allowed for continuous eavesdropping for a period of two months, (4) it did not require a termination order mandating cessation of the eavesdropping once the conversation sought was seized, (5) it did not require notice of the seizure, at least after the fact, as do conventional warrants, and (6) it did not require the officer engaged in the monitoring to return the tapes to the court which issued the order.[32] Thus, the *Berger* court clarified the major considerations that electronic eavesdropping legislation and court orders must address.

---

[28] Katz v. United States, 389 U.S. 347, 361 (1967) (Harlan, J., concurring).

[29] Katz v. United States, 389 U.S. 347, 361 (1967) (Harlan, J., concurring).

[30] There are various exceptions or exemptions, *see, e.g.*, 18 U.S.C. § 2511(2) (various exceptions stated), including provision for warrantless eavesdropping in certain emergency situations. 18 U.S.C. § 2518 (7).

[31] 388 U.S. 41 (1967).

[32] Berger v. New York, 388 U.S. 41, 58-60 (1967).

§ 10.06.   Federal Statutory Restrictions — Title III.

As part of the Federal Omnibus Crime Control and Safe Streets Act of 1968, Congress enacted Title III,[33] which deals with wiretapping and other forms of electronic surveillance. This statute, as amended, proscribes as a federal crime all (1) electronic eavesdropping or wiretapping and (2) the willful use of the fruits of such eavesdropping by anyone, including federal and state officials.[34] Carefully delineated exceptions to this include eavesdropping by a switchboard operator in the normal course of business,[35] foreign intelligence surveillance,[36] consensual eavesdropping,[37] and eavesdropping pursuant to a court order.[38]

Beyond these clearly designated exceptions, there may be others. For instance, it has been held that the routine police department recording of phone conversations over its investigative lines is implicitly allowed[39] by certain statutory language.[40] On the other hand, it is not clear whether there exists, for example, a "prison exemption" allowing for eavesdropping of inmate conversations[41] or "interspousal exemption" allowing for eavesdropping on one spouse by another[42] inasmuch as there is no language in Title III that either explicitly makes reference to such an exception.

---

[33] 18 U.S.C. §§ 2510-20. Scattered sections were amended to a significant degree in the Electronic Communications Privacy Act of 1986, Pub. L. No. 99-508, 100 Stat. 1848, and the Communications Assistance for Law Enforcement Act of 1984, Pub. L. 103-414, 108 Stat. 4279.

[34] 18 U.S.C. § 2511(1).

[35] 18 U.S.C. § 2511(2)(a)(i).

[36] 18 U.S.C. §§ 2511(2)(a)(ii), (e), (f). *Compare* United States v. United States District Court, 407 U.S. 297 (1972) (court order required for electronic eavesdropping of domestic subversives).

[37] 18 U.S.C. §§ 2511(2)(c), (d). *See also* United States v. Caceres, 440 U.S. 741 (1979) (warrantless consensual eavesdropping upheld as consistent with *Lopez* and *White* doctrine).

[38] 18 U.S.C. §§ 2516-18.

[39] Jandack v. Village of Brookfield, 520 F. Supp. 815 (N.D. Ill. 1981) ("police chief's decision to listen to tape was justified by proper law enforcement purpose . . . police officer making telephone call had notice that call would be recorded . . . and recipient of call was barred from bringing action under the statute.").

[40] 18 U.S.C. § 2510(5)(a)(ii).

[41] Campiti v. Walonis, 611 F.2d 387 (1st Cir. 1979) (there is no "prison exemption" under Title III and § 2510(5)(a)(ii) creates no exception); United States v. Paul, 614 F.2d 115 (5th Cir.), *cert. denied*, 446 U.S. 941 (1980) (there is no general "prison exemption" under Title III but eavesdropping permissible under § 2510(5)(a)(ii). *But see* United States v. Van Poyck, 77 F.3d 285 (9th 1996) (pretrial detainee given sufficient notice of potential eavesdropping of inmate phone calls to have expressly or impliedly consented within § 2511(2)(c); alternatively, § 2510(5)(a)(ii) provides exception to general prohibition); United States v. Daniels, 902 F.2d 1238 (7th Cir. 1990) (wiretapping permissible under § 2510(5)(a)(ii)).

[42] United States v. Murdock, 63 F.3d 1391 (6th Cir. 1995) (rejecting interspousal exemption); Schieb v. Grant, 22 F.3d 149 (7th Cir.) (rejecting interspousal exemption), *cert. denied*, 513 U.S. 929 (1984); Heggy v. Heggy, 944 F.2d 1537 (10th Cir. 1991) (rejecting interspousal exemption), *cert. denied*, 503 U.S. 951 (1992). *But see* Simpson v. Simpson, 490 F.2d 803 (5th Cir.) (recogniz-

In an obvious effort to address the Supreme Court's concerns reflected in *Berger*, Congress included in Title III very sophisticated barriers in the way of gaining a court order authorizing non-consensual electronic surveillance. First, only the United States Attorney General or an assistant specially designated by him or her may authorize an application for such a court order.[43] Second, the eavesdropping order may be pursued only if it relates to a certain designated serious crime or crimes.[44] Third, the application for the court order must reflect a full and complete statement on the identity of the law enforcement officer making the application and the officer authorizing the application;[45] the particular details of the offense;[46] a particular description of the facilities from which or the place where the communication is to be intercepted;[47] a particular description of the communications sought;[48] the identity, if known, of the person whose communications will be intercepted;[49] a statement whether other investigative procedures have failed or are unlikely to succeed;[50] a statement of the period of time required to accomplish the goals of the interception;[51] and information regarding all previous applications for court orders involving eavesdropping of any of the same persons, facilities or places.[52] Fourth, the judge may require the applicant to provide any additional testimony or documentary evidence in support of the application.[53] Fifth, the court receiving the application may issue such a court order only if there is probable cause to believe that a crime has been or is about to be committed, that information about the offense will be obtained through such surveillance, that normal investigative procedures will not succeed, and that the facilities monitored are being used in connection with the offense.[54] Sixth, the court order itself must identify (a) the person whose communications are to be intercepted, (b) the location of the facilities to be monitored, (c) the type of conversations sought, (d) the agency that is authorized to engage in the eavesdropping, and (e) the period of time during which the interception is authorized, along with an indication about whether the interception must cease

---

ing interspousal exemption), *cert. denied*, 419 U.S. 897 (1974); Anonymous v. Anonymous, 558 F.2d 677 (2d Cir. 1977) (recognizing spousal exemption).

[43] 18 U.S.C. § 2516(1). *See* United States v. Giordano, 416 U.S. 505 (1974) (reversal of conviction because of noncompliance with § 2516).

[44] 18 U.S.C. §§ 2516(1)(a)-(p).

[45] 18 U.S.C. § 2518(1)(a).

[46] 18 U.S.C. § 2518(b)(i).

[47] 18 U.S.C. § 2518(b)(ii).

[48] 18 U.S.C. § 2518(b)(iii).

[49] 18 U.S.C. § 2518(b)(iv).

[50] 18 U.S.C. § 2518(c).

[51] 18 U.S.C. § 2518(d).

[52] 18 U.S.C. § 2518(e).

[53] 18 U.S.C. § 2518(2).

[54] 18 U.S.C. § 2518(3).

automatically after the described communication is first obtained.[55] Seventh, the court order cannot be authorized for a period of time longer than is necessary to achieve the objective of the authorization and, in any event, no longer than thirty days.[56] Eighth, the judge issuing the court order may require progress reports regarding the success of the interception effort.[57] Ninth, the judge must promptly receive the recorded communication, and it may be ordered sealed by him.[58] Tenth, all persons named in the application must be notified within a reasonable time after the termination of the interception order or after the filing of a denied application.[59] Eleventh, any aggrieved person whose rights were not protected may move to suppress evidence gained[60] and to recover civil damages.[61] Finally, the United States Attorney General may seek an injunction to prevent illegal felony eavesdropping.[62]

§ 10.07.   The Crime of Eavesdropping in Illinois.

Prior to 1989, Illinois did not have the necessary state enabling legislation that Title III required in order to legitimize state government non-consensual eavesdropping.[63] Consequently, any "interception" or "use" of conversations gained by state officials through non-consensual electronic eavesdropping could not be used by state officials in state court because of federal law.[64]

Beyond the absence of enabling legislation mandated by federal law in Title III, enactments in Illinois before 1989 contained strictures prohibiting electronic eavesdropping that far exceeded those in the federal constitution and Title III. Specifically, Illinois proscribed as criminal (1) all forms of non-consensual eavesdropping and (2) all consensual eavesdropping except where there had

---

[55] 18 U.S.C. § 2518(4).

[56] 18 U.S.C. § 2518(5).

[57] 18 U.S.C. § 2518(6).

[58] 18 U.S.C. § 2518(8)(a).

[59] 18 U.S.C. § 2518(8)(d).

[60] 18 U.S.C. §§ 2515, 2518(10). *See* Gelbard v. United States, 408 U.S. 41 (1972) (evidence derived from illegal eavesdropping was inadmissible in grand jury proceeding by reason of § 2515). *See also* Alderman v. United States, 394 U.S. 165 (1969) (party to conversation illegally seized and party on whose premises illegal eavesdropping occurred, whether latter party was party to conversation or not, has standing to object under Fourth Amendment). *Compare* United States v. Donovan, 429 U.S. 413 (1979) (noncompliance with Title III warrants exclusion of evidence under § 2518 only if Title III breach involves provision that plays substantive role in title III); United States v. Chavez, 416 U.S. 562 (1974) (noncompliance with Title III warrants exclusion of evidence under § 2518 only if Title III breach involves provision that plays substantive role in Title III).

[61] 18 U.S.C. § 2520.

[62] 18 U.S.C. § 2521.

[63] *See* 18 U.S.C. § 2516(2).

[64] 18 U.S.C. § 2511(1).

been (a) consent of "all of the parties to the conversation," or (b) consent of one party plus a court order permitting the participant monitoring.[65] These laws implicitly recognized that a state could impose stricter laws against eavesdropping than Title III requires and that Title III does not preempt these stricter state laws.[66]

By reason of actions of the General Assembly in 1988, effective January 1, 1989, and amended in 1993 and 1994, Illinois law now permits court-authorized non-consensual eavesdropping (1) that may assist in the apprehension of a person who has committed, is committing, or is about to commit solicitation of murder; solicitation of murder for hire; first degree murder; money laundering; certain violations of the Illinois Controlled Substances Act; certain violations of unlawful use of weapons laws; and conspiracy to commit first degree murder or money laundering; (2) in response to an immediate threat of death or great bodily injury arising out of a kidnapping, hostage taking, or forced occupation of any carrier or premises; and (3) to aid in the investigation or prosecution under the Illinois Streetgang Terrorism and Omnibus Prevention Act; or upon information and belief that a streetgang has committed, is committing, or is about to commit a felony.[67] In addition, warrantless non-consensual eavesdropping in pursuit of the above enumerated criminality is permitted in emergency situations.[68] Meanwhile, consensual eavesdropping is permitted, but is restricted to those situations where the participant monitoring has been approved in advance by judicial authority and the interception involves the commission of a felony.[69] Furthermore, consensual electronic surveillance is permitted in emergency situations without court approval where there exists a "clear and present danger of imminent death or great bodily injury to persons resulting from (1) a kidnapping or holding of a hostage . . .; or (2) the occupation . . . of premises, places, vehicles, vessels, or aircraft."[70] Finally, except for certain other very narrow exceptions, all other instances of non-consensual and consensual eavesdropping are felony offenses in Illinois.[71]

The general eavesdropping restrictions include a number of exceptions. The "exemptions" provided for in paragraph 5/14-3 of Chapter 720 include: listening to publicly made radio, wireless, and television communications; employees of common carriers overhearing conversations incidental to the normal course of business; listening to any broadcast of any function where the public is in attendance and conversations are overheard incidental to the main purpose of the

---

[65] ILL. REV. STAT. ch. 38, para. 14-2 (1983).
[66] United States v. Hall, 543 F.2d 1229 (9th Cir. 1976), *cert. denied,* 429 U.S. 1075 (1977).
[67] 725 ILCS 5/108B-3 (1999).
[68] 725 ILCS 5/108B-8 (1999).
[69] 725 ILCS 5/108A-4 (1999).
[70] 725 ILCS 5/108A-6 (1999).
[71] 720 ILCS 5/14-2 (1999).

broadcast; law enforcement or institutions dealing in emergency services in the normal course of operations recording or listening with any device to emergency communications; recording the proceedings of any meeting required to be open by the Illinois Open Meetings Act; recording or listening with any device to incoming calls of publicly listed "consumer" hotlines by manufacturers or retailers of food or drug products; recording or listening with any device to any conversation where a law enforcement officer, or person acting at their direction, is a party to the conversation and has consented to it being intercepted or recorded, under circumstances where it is necessary for the officer's or his agent's protection in investigations involving certain felony offenses, provided there has been notification to the State's Attorney of the county where it is to occur; simultaneous video and audio recording of an oral conversation between an identified peace officer and a person stopped for a traffic violation; recording of a conversation by a non-law enforcement officer or agent who is a party to the conversation and reasonably suspects that another party to the conversation is about to commit or has committed a criminal offense against the person or an immediate member of his or her household and the person reasonably believes evidence may be obtained by the recording; and recording or listening to telephone conversations of employees by a marketing, opinion research, or telephone solicitation business for the purpose of quality control, education or training of employees, or internal research related to marketing, opinion research, or telephone solicitation.[72]

§ 10.08.   State Eavesdropping Codified.

The purpose of the Illinois eavesdropping statute, as it was adopted into the Illinois Criminal Code of 1961, like its predecessors that date back to 1895, was to protect the privacy of the individual,[73] and it clearly applies to eavesdropping by both private persons and government officials.[74] The primary function of paragraphs 5/14-1 to 5/14-9 of chapter 720 of the Criminal Code is to define eavesdropping devices and eavesdroppers, state the requisite elements of the offense, and provide statutory exemptions to the act. A necessary adjunct to the eavesdropping statute is chapter 725, article 5/108A-1 to 108A-11, of the Code of Criminal Procedure, which sets forth the rules and guidelines concerning judicial supervision of the use of eavesdropping devices in *consensual* eavesdropping situations. Similarly, chapter 725 article 5/108B-1 to 108B-14, sets out the standards for permissible *non-consensual* eavesdropping. Included in these pro-

---

[72] 720 ILCS 5/14-3 (1999).

[73] ILL. ANN. STAT. ch. 38, para. 14-1 (Smith-Hurd), 1961 Committee Comments, at 606 (revised 1972).

[74] ILL. ANN. STAT. ch. 38, para. 14-1 (Smith-Hurd), 1961 Committee Comments, at 606-07 (revised 1972).

visions are the procedures required for obtaining judicial approval for the use of eavesdropping devices, the grounds for that approval, emergency exceptions to these procedures, and technical requirements concerning the handling of any recordings once they are made.

The general proscription against eavesdropping in Illinois reads as follows:

> A person commits eavesdropping when he (a) Uses an eavesdropping device to hear or record all or any part of any conversation unless he does so (1) with the consent of all of the parties to such conversation or (2) in accordance with Article 108A or 108B of the "Code of Criminal Procedure of 1963," . . .; or (b) Uses or divulges, except as authorized by this Article or by Article 108A or 108B of the "Code of Criminal Procedure," . . . any information which he knows or reasonably should know was obtained through the use of an eavesdropping device.[75]

This general stricture includes a paragraph which sets forth one significant "affirmative defense" to the charge.[76] Where a person intercepts a "privileged" conversation, it is an affirmative defense that the person charged (1) was a law enforcement officer acting in accordance with a court order; (2) did not realize that the communication was privileged; (3) stopped the interception within a reasonable time after discovering the conversation was privileged; and (4) did not disclose the contents of the privileged communication.[77] "Privileged" communications are defined as those private oral communications between a physician and a patient, a psychologist and patient, a lawyer and client, a clergyman and confider, a journalist and informer, a social worker and client, or a husband and wife.[78]

§ 10.09.   Elements of Eavesdropping.

First, article 5/14 of chapter 720 outlaws all forms of *non-consensual* eavesdropping except that permitted in accordance with the provisions of article 5/108B of chapter 725.[79] Article 5/108B authorizes state officials to engage in court-ordered electronic monitoring of conversations (1) where the interception "may provide evidence of, or may assist in the apprehension of a person who has committed, is committing, or is about to commit" first degree murder, solicitation of murder, solicitation of murder for hire, money laundering, certain violations of the Illinois Controlled Substances Act, certain violations of unlawful use of weapons laws; or conspiracy to commit money laundering or first degree

---

[75] 720 ILCS 5/14-2 (1999).

[76] 720 ILCS 5/14-2(c) (1999).

[77] 720 ILCS 5/14-2(c) (1999).

[78] 725 ILCS 5/108B-1(q) (1999).

[79] 720 ILCS 5/14-2 (1999).

murder; (2) in response to an immediate threat of death or great bodily injury arising out of a kidnapping, hostage taking, or forced occupation of any carrier or premises; or (3) to aid in the investigation or prosecution under the Illinois Streetgang Terrorism Omnibus Prevention Act, or upon information and belief that a streetgang has committed, is committing, or is about to commit a felony.[80] The specific controlled substances violations that are delineated in article 5/108B are the manufacture, delivery, or possession with intent to deliver a controlled substance,[81] controlled substance trafficking,[82] calculated criminal drug conspiracy,[83] criminal drug conspiracy,[84] and delivery of a controlled substance to a minor or on school property.[85] Next, article 5/14 forbids all *consensual* eavesdropping except where (1) all parties to the conversation consent or (2) one party to the conversation consents and this party is engaging in electronic eavesdropping that is designed to gain evidence of the commission of a felony and it is done pursuant to judicial authorization that is in accordance with the procedures set out in section 5/108A.[86]

Subsection (a) of section 5/14-2 makes it illegal to "use an eavesdropping device to hear or record all or any part of any conversation" unless it falls into one of the exceptions.[87] Subsection (b) of section 5/14-2 makes it illegal for a person to "use or divulge" such "information he knows or should reasonably know was obtained through the use of an eavesdropping device," unless it falls into one of the exceptions.[88]

Inasmuch as the difference between consensual eavesdropping and non-consensual eavesdropping was discussed above in connection with federal law, it is assumed that the difference between these two methods of eavesdropping is understood. However, a complete comprehension of the Illinois law necessitates (1) a review of the law that revolves around consensual eavesdropping, (2) a study of the provisions that permit non-consensual eavesdropping, (3) an examination of the special exceptions for emergency situations, and (4) an analysis of the scope of the term "eavesdropping." These concerns will now be examined.

---

[80] 725 ILCS 5/108B-3 (1999).

[81] 720 ILCS 570/401 (1999).

[82] 720 ILCS 570/401.1 (1999).

[83] 720 ILCS 570/405 (1999).

[84] 720 ILCS 570/405.1 (1999).

[85] 720 ILCS 570/407 (1999).

[86] 720 ILCS 5/14-2 (1999). This area of the Illinois statute has been drastically modified by judicial decisions. *See* § 10.15 of this chapter.

[87] 720 ILCS 5/14-2(a) (1999).

[88] 720 ILCS 5/14-2(b) (1999).

§10.10. Permissible Consensual Eavesdropping: Consent of All or Court Authorization.

Although non-consensual eavesdropping is absolutely prohibited in Illinois except in court-authorized investigations of certain violations of the Illinois Controlled Substances Act, first degree murder, money laundering, solicitation of murder or money laundering, certain unlawful use of weapon offenses, kidnap or hostage situations, certain streetgang offenses, and specific emergency situations, consensual eavesdropping is permissible in the investigation of any felony if it is with the consent of all the parties to the conversation or if it is with the consent of one party and that party has a court order authorizing the surreptitious electronic eavesdropping.

Although the first exception — "consent of all of the parties to such conversation" — is relatively simple to understand, the second exception is operable where there is consent of one party and the eavesdropping is "in accordance with Article 108A" of chapter 725.[89] Article 5/108A sets out the requirements for court approval. First, the state attorney must authorize the application for the court-ordered consensual eavesdropping.[90] Second, the authorization for the application is appropriate only where the offense under investigation is a felony.[91] Third, the application, which must be in writing, must include (a) details of the felony offense, (b) a description of the conversation sought, (c) the identity of the party consenting to the use of the eavesdropping device, (d) the identity of the person, if known, whose conversations will be intercepted, (e) a statement of the period of time for which the eavesdropping is to be allowed, including whether the authority to eavesdrop shall automatically terminate once the sought conversation is overheard or recorded, and (f) a statement regarding all previous applications to eavesdrop on the subject.[92] Fourth, the court may approve the application and grant a court order if it determines that (a) one party to the conversation has consented or will consent, (b) there is reasonable cause to believe the subject of the offense is involved in a felony, and (c) there is reasonable cause to believe particular conversations concerning the felony will be obtained.[93] Finally, the court order itself must contain (a) the identity of the consenting party, (b) an order that the consenting party be a party to the intercepted conversation, (c) the identity of the other persons, if known, who will participate in the conversation, and (d) the period of time for which the eavesdropping is authorized, along with a statement about whether the eavesdropping shall auto-

---

[89] 720 ILCS 5/14-2(a)(2) (1999).
[90] 725 ILCS 5/108A-1 (1999).
[91] 725 ILCS 5/108A-1 (1999).
[92] 725 ILCS 5/108A-3(a)(1)-(4) (1999).
[93] 725 ILCS 5/108A-4(a)-(d) (1999).

matically cease once the described conversations have been first obtained.[94] In any event, the consensual eavesdropping authorized cannot exceed ten days without a later court-ordered extension.[95]

Once the eavesdropping has occurred, the electronic recording shall be returned to the judge who authorized the eavesdropping and shall be reviewed by the judge to determine whether there was compliance with the article 5/108A procedures and then sealed to avoid tampering.[96] Timely notice shall be given to the subject of the eavesdropping concerning the fact of the eavesdropping.[97] If there was compliance with the article 5/108A procedures, then further disclosure to or use by other law enforcement officials, such as the prosecuting attorney, will be permissible.[98]

§ 10.11. Permissible Non-Consensual Eavesdropping.

Non-consensual eavesdropping is impermissible unless it is in accordance with the procedures mandated in article 5/108B of chapter 725.[99] Any party, whether a private person or state official, who engages in non-consensual eavesdropping that falls short of the procedural requirements specified in article 5/108B could be prosecuted for a violation of section 5/14-2 of chapter 720, which generally imposes felony sanctions for non-consensual electronic eavesdropping.[100]

Article 5/108B authorizes a State's Attorney on his own, or the head of any law enforcement agency within the state to request a State's Attorney, to apply for an order of interception.[101] If the State's Attorney sees fit, he or she may authorize an *ex parte* application to the chief judge of a court of competent jurisdiction for an order of interception.[102] As opposed to consensual eavesdropping, which may be judicially sanctioned under 5/108A in investigations of any felony, an application for a court order for non-consensual eavesdropping under 5/108B can be made only in connection with (1) investigations involving: first degree murder or conspiracy to commit first degree murder; solicitation of murder; solicitation of murder for hire; money laundering or conspiracy to commit money laundering; violations of anti-narcotic laws prohibiting (a) manufacture, delivery, or possession with intent to deliver a controlled substance, (b) controlled substance trafficking, (c) a calculated criminal drug conspiracy, (d) a

---

[94] 725 ILCS 5/108A-5(a) (1999).
[95] 725 ILCS 5/108A-5(b) (1999).
[96] 725 ILCS 5/108A-7 (1999).
[97] 725 ILCS 5/108A-8 (1999).
[98] 725 ILCS 5/108A-2 (1999).
[99] 720 ILCS 5/14-2 (1999).
[100] 720 ILCS 5/14-4 (1999).
[101] 725 ILCS 5/108B-2 (1999).
[102] 725 ILCS 5/108B-3 (1999).

criminal drug conspiracy, or (e) delivery of a controlled substance to a minor or on school property; and violations of certain unlawful use of weapons laws; (2) investigations of violations of the Illinois Streetgang Terrorism Omnibus Prevention Act, upon information and belief that a streetgang has committed, is committing, or is about to commit a felony; or (3) "in response to a clear and present danger of imminent death or great bodily harm to persons resulting from . . . a kidnapping or the holding of a hostage by force or the threat of imminent use of force . . . or . . . the occupation by force or the threat of imminent use of force of any premises, place, vehicle, vessel, or aircraft."[103]

The application must be upon oath or affirmation and in writing.[104] It must specify the authority of the applicant[105] and identify the officers who will engage in the eavesdropping.[106] Each application must include the following: (1) identification of the individual who will be the object of the eavesdropping,[107] (2) details about his or her involvement in the alleged criminality,[108] (3) a description of the type of communication sought,[109] (4) a showing of probable cause that the communication sought will transpire at the place where the interception will occur,[110] (5) a description of the place where the interception will occur,[111] (6) a statement of the objectives behind the interception,[112] (7) a statement regarding the contemplated period of time during which the eavesdropping will occur,[113] and (8) a particular assertion as to why conventional investigation techniques have not worked or will not work.[114] Any application for an "extension" of a previously authorized interception must reflect a "reasonable explanation of the failure to obtain results" during the earlier electronic surveillance.[115] If the applicant had previously applied for an order to intercept, or knows of other applications to intercept that involve the same matter, full disclosure must be made to the court receiving the instant application for an order to intercept.[116]

After the chief judge of the judicial circuit has received the application for an order to intercept, the judge must determine whether there exists probable cause to believe (1) the intended focus of the non-consensual eavesdropping effort

---

[103] 725 ILCS 5/108B-3 (1999).
[104] 725 ILCS 5/108B-4(a) (1999).
[105] 725 ILCS 5/108B-4(a)(1) (1999).
[106] 725 ILCS 5/108B-4(a)(2) (1999).
[107] 725 ILCS 5/108B-4(a)(3)(i) (1999).
[108] 725 ILCS 5/108B-4(a)(3)(ii) (1999).
[109] 725 ILCS 5/108B-4(a)(3)(iii) (1999).
[110] 725 ILCS 5/108B-4(a)(3)(iv) (1999).
[111] 725 ILCS 5/108B-4(a)(3)(v) (1999).
[112] 725 ILCS 5/108B-4(a)(3)(vi) (1999).
[113] 725 ILCS 5/108B-4(a)(3)(vii) (1999).
[114] 725 ILCS 5/108B-4(a)(3)(viii) (1999).
[115] 725 ILCS 5/108B-4(a)(4) (1999).
[116] 725 ILCS 5/108B-4(a)(5) (1999).

was, is, or will be involved in one of the designated violations of Illinois law and (2) the communication sought will occur at the place where the eavesdropping is to occur.[117] The judge must determine whether normal investigative procedures will be inadequate in gaining the evidence necessary to establish the alleged criminality.[118] If the application involves "privileged" communications (e.g. physician-patient, psychologist-patient, attorney-client, clergyman-confider, journalist-informant, or spouse-spouse), no interception can be authorized.[119]

Assuming the judge is convinced that there exists probable cause, that conventional investigatory efforts will be fruitless, and that the communications sought are not privileged, he or she may grant an order to intercept. The order must (1) identify the issuing judge, (2) identify the party whose conversations may be intercepted, (3) identify the place where the interception can occur, (4) describe the type of communications that may be intercepted, (5) identify the officers who will be authorized to carry out the interception, and (6) specify the period of time during which the authorization may occur.[120] The order of interception may authorize a period of interception no longer than that which is "necessary to achieve the objective of the authorization" and in no case longer than 30 days.[121] The order shall require that the interception "terminate as soon as practicable and be conducted in such a manner as to minimize the interception of communications not otherwise subject to interception."[122] Orders authorizing an extension shall only be made where necessary and, in any event, for periods not exceeding 30 days.[123]

All intercepted communications must normally be recorded.[124] Specific records regarding date, time, place, and identities of parties subjected to the surveillance must be kept.[125] These recordings must be promptly delivered to the chief judge and sealed for possible later evidentiary use.[126] Similarly, all applications made and orders granted must be ordered sealed by the judge.[127]

Within 90 days of the denial of a request for non-consensual interception *or* after completion of the non-consensual electronic eavesdropping, an "inventory" notice of the eavesdropping effort must be given to the parties who were the

---

[117] 725 ILCS 5/108B-5(a)(1)-(2) (1999).

[118] 725 ILCS 5/108B-5(a)(3) (1999).

[119] 725 ILCS 5/108B-6 (1999). *But see* In re Granger, 197 Ill. App. 3d 363, 374, 554 N.E.2d 586, 593 (5th Dist. 1990) (conversation between attorney and client in furtherance of criminal activity is not privileged).

[120] 725 ILCS 5/108B-7(a) (1999).

[121] 725 ILCS 5/108B-7(b) (1999).

[122] 725 ILCS 5/108B-7(b) (1999).

[123] 725 ILCS 5/108B-7(b) (1999).

[124] 725 ILCS 5/108B-9(a) (1999).

[125] 725 ILCS 5/108B-9(a) (1999).

[126] 725 ILCS 5/108B-9(b) (1999).

[127] 725 ILCS 5/108B-10 (1999).

subject of the eavesdropping effort or were charged with an offense as a result of the interception.[128] The inventory shall include the fact that an interception occurred and when it occurred.[129] The court has the discretion to make available to affected persons those portions of the recordings that it feels should be made available in the "interest of justice."[130] Where warranted, the court may delay the inventory process for up to 12 months.[131]

If an order to intercept a communication involving a violation of one of the specific sections contemplated by Article 5/108B results in an inadvertent interception of a communication involving another offense not contemplated by Article 5/108B, the State's Attorney may make a motion with the chief judge "for an order approving the interception."[132] If the chief judge determines that there existed at the time of the original application probable cause to believe that the person, whose communication was inadvertently seized, was committing or had committed an offense beyond the designed violations of Article 5/108B, the judge may approve the interception, and the communication inadvertently seized will be usable as evidence by the State.[133]

§ 10.12.   Permissible Emergency Eavesdropping.

In addition to the consensual and non-consensual eavesdropping authorized by articles 5/108A and 5/108B, which provisions primarily focus on court-authorized interceptions, the legislature also created an "emergency exception"[134] to the general barriers against consensual and non-consensual eavesdropping apparently in order to protect a police officer involved in dangerous investigations or to address "kidnapping or terrorist situations."[135] In emergency situations, where "substantial danger to life or limb" exists during the investigation of one of the enumerated offenses where court-ordered non-consensual eavesdropping is allowed, "informal" applications for court-authorized non-consensual eavesdropping may be permitted.[136] These emergency procedures require, at a minimum, "oral" authorizations by the judge, assuming the other

---

[128] 725 ILCS 5/108B-11(a) (1999).

[129] 725 ILCS 5/108B-11(b) (1999).

[130] 725 ILCS 5/108B-11(a), (c) (1999).

[131] 725 ILCS 5/108B-11(d) (1999).

[132] 725 ILCS 5/108B-12(a) (1999).

[133] 725 ILCS 5/108B-12(a) (1999).

[134] 725 ILCS 5/108A-6(a) (1999) (emergency consensual eavesdropping); 725 ILCS 5/108B-8 (1999) (emergency non-consensual eavesdropping).

[135] Richard Daley, *Fighting Organized Crime in Illinois: Tough Sentencing is Not Enough*, 77 ILL. B.J. 638, 639 (1989).

[136] 725 ILCS 5/108B-8 (1999).

requirements for an order of non-consensual eavesdropping are met by the state.[137]

In addition, emergency consensual eavesdropping conducted by law enforcement officials may occur without advance judicial approval if a reasonable effort has been made to contact the appropriate State's Attorney, the officer reasonably believes that an order permitting the use would have been granted, the conversation will occur in a short period of time, and it is "necessary for the protection of the law enforcement officer or there is a clear and present danger of imminent death or great bodily harm" to individuals resulting from (1) a kidnapping or the taking of a hostage or (2) the "occupation by force or the threat of the imminent use of force of any premises, place, vehicle, vessel, or aircraft."[138] A subsequent judicial order approving the previous or continuing eavesdropping must be made within 48 hours.[139] For the judge to approve an emergency eavesdropping, he or she must find that he or she would have granted an order for eavesdropping prior to the use[140] and that there was an emergency.[141] If subsequent judicial approval is denied, then the eavesdropping will be a violation.[142]

§ 10.13.   Subsequent Challenges of Court Authorization.

As in cases involving traditional search warrants, questions are invariably raised with respect to the sufficiency of authorization requests and the standards to be used by the judiciary in evaluating the authorization request. In *People v. Wrestler*,[143] the court discussed the standards used in determining approval of an application for consensual eavesdropping. The expression "reasonable cause" (to believe the defendant has committed a felony) contained in section 5/108A-4 was equated with "probable cause" as used in the search warrant context.[144] According to the *Wrestler* court, a reasonable cause analysis is to be based on the "totality of the circumstances"[145] test as mandated by the United States Supreme Court decision in *Illinois v. Gates*, where the Court explained the meaning of "probable cause."[146]

---

[137] 725 ILCS 5/108B-8 (1999).

[138] 725 ILCS 5/108A-6(a) (1999).

[139] 725 ILCS 5/108A-6(b) (1999).

[140] 725 ILCS 5/108A-6(b)(1) (1999).

[141] 725 ILCS 5/108A-6(b)(2) (1999).

[142] 725 ILCS 5/108A-6(c) (1999).

[143] 121 Ill. App. 3d 147, 458 N.E.2d 1348 (3d Dist. 1984).

[144] People v. Wrestler, 121 Ill. App. 3d 147, 154, 458 N.E.2d 1348, 1353 (3d Dist. 1984).

[145] People v. Wrestler, 121 Ill. App. 3d 147, 154, 458 N.E.2d 1348, 1353 (3d Dist. 1984). *See also* People v. Meyer, 197 Ill. App. 3d 687, 691, 555 N.E.2d 98, 99-100 (3d Dist. 1990).

[146] 462 U.S. 213 (1983).

The application for an order to intercept does not have to be self-sufficient because oral testimony is allowed.[147] If hearsay appears in the application for an eavesdropping device, the judge must credit (make credible) that hearsay in one of two ways: (1) either from the face of an application itself or (2) through the use of additional evidence.[148]

In opposition to an order authorizing the use of an eavesdropping device, a defendant may be found complaining of "technical or procedural" defects in the eavesdropping application. The defendant would in all likelihood rely on a "strict construction" standard for reviewing eavesdropping orders — a doctrine that had been applied to such orders in some earlier decisions.[149] Notwithstanding, later decisions in which technical or procedural defects in eavesdropping applications have been considered by reviewing courts indicate that the rule of "strict construction" will not require suppression where the legislative intent of the eavesdropping act is not impaired and where no possibility of prejudice to the defendant appears.[150] Thus, where defendant claimed that the authorizing judge illegally authorized the use of an eavesdropping device for eleven days, one day in excess of the statutory maximum, the appellate court, in upholding the authorization order for consensual eavesdropping, noted that this was a mere technical defect, not the product of intentional misconduct by law enforcement officials, and did not defeat the legislative intent of protecting the citizenry from unnecessary and prolonged governmental intrusion into their private lives.[151]

Likewise, in *People v. Nieves*,[152] police officers obtained a court order to use an eavesdropping device but failed to turn over the recorded conversations until sixteen days after the order had expired. The defendant sought to suppress the recordings for the state's failure to comply with the immediacy requirement of section 5/108A-7(b), providing that "[i]mmediately after the expiration period of the order . . ., all such recordings shall be made available to the judge issuing the order. . . ."[153] The Illinois Supreme Court held that the state's technical violation of the consensual eavesdropping statute did not warrant the suppression of the evidence. The court used the following three prong test with respect to violation of statutory requirements following interception: (1) whether the particular safeguard is a central or functional safeguard in the legislative schemes to prevent

---

[147] 725 ILCS 5/108A-3 (b) (1999); 725 ILCS 5/108B-4(b) (1999); People v. Wassell, 119 Ill. App. 3d 15, 19, 455 N.E.2d 1100, 1103-04 (4th Dist. 1983) (citing People v. Moore, 90 Ill. App. 3d 760, 413 N.E.2d 516 (4th Dist. 1980) (discussing 5/108A-3(b)).

[148] People v. Wassell, 119 Ill. App. 3d 15, 20, 455 N.E.2d 1100, 1104 (4th Dist. 1983) (quoting People v. Sylvester, 86 Ill. App. 3d 186, 193-94, 407 N.E.2d 1002, 1009 (1st Dist. 1980)).

[149] *See, e.g.,* People v. Monoson, 75 Ill. App. 3d 1, 6, 393 N.E.2d 1239, 1243 (1st Dist. 1979).

[150] People v. Sylvester, 86 Ill. App. 3d 186, 192, 407 N.E.2d 1002, 1008 (1st Dist. 1980).

[151] People v. Wrestler, 121 Ill. App. 3d 147, 154, 458 N.E.2d 1348, 1352 (3d Dist. 1984).

[152] 92 Ill. 2d 452, 442 N.E.2d 228 (1982).

[153] *See* 725 ILCS 5/108A-7(b) (1999).

abuses; (2) whether the purpose the particular safeguard was intended to accomplish had been satisfied in spite of the error, and (3) whether the statutory requirement was deliberately ignored, and if so, whether the state obtained any tactical advantages therefrom.[154] Here, the court based its ruling on its determination that the legislative purpose of the safeguard (maintaining the integrity of the recordings) had been accomplished in that the tapes were in the officer's custody until given to the judge, and the defendant had not alleged that they were tampered with, edited, or altered or that they inaccurately represented the conversation.[155]

An appellate case following the three prong test is *People v. O'Toole*.[156] In that case, the two defendants, Brenda Haney and John O'Toole, repeatedly asked their friend, Johnson, to kill Brenda's husband. Johnson contacted the police, who obtained authorization for consensual eavesdropping. Johnson then arranged a meeting between the defendants and an undercover police officer posing as a hit man. At the meeting, both defendants repeatedly insisted they wanted Brenda's husband murdered. Following the defendants' convictions of solicitation of murder for hire, defendants challenged the admissibility of the video and audio tape recording of their hiring of the "hit man" to kill Brenda's husband. They argued that the application for eavesdropping was defective because "(1) it failed to name Brenda as a party to the conversation, and (2) the consenting party named in the application, Johnson, [was not present and] did not participate in the recorded conversation."[157] The appellate court ruled that suppression was not necessary because it did "not regard the inclusion of *all*, as opposed to *some*, of the names of the parties to the conversation as central to the legislative scheme of preventing abuses . . .," the State did not deliberately ignore inclusion of the names of Brenda or the undercover agent, nor did it gain any tactical advantage by omitting those names.[158]

There have been other challenges on grounds of non-compliance with the exact terms of the eavesdropping statute that have not succeeded on appeal. Illinois courts have accepted (1) an authorization request made by an *assistant* state's attorney rather than the State's Attorney;[159] (2) an eavesdropping order not identifying the specific individuals or agency who initially requested the eavesdropping and the person actually using the eavesdropping equipment;[160] (3) less than timely after-the-fact notice to a defendant who was subjected to eavesdropping

---

[154] People v. Nieves, 92 Ill. 2d 452, 458-59, 442 N.E.2d 228, 232 (1982).

[155] People v. Nieves, 92 Ill. 2d 452, 462, 442 N.E.2d 228, 233-34 (1982).

[156] 226 Ill. App. 3d 974, 590 N.E.2d 950 (4th Dist. 1992).

[157] People v. O'Toole, 226 Ill. App. 3d 974, 979, 590 N.E.2d 950, 955 (4th Dist. 1992).

[158] People v. O'Toole, 226 Ill. App. 3d 974, 982, 590 N.E.2d 950, 956 (4th Dist. 1992).

[159] People v. George, 67 Ill. App. 3d 102, 106, 384 N.E.2d 377, 380 (2d Dist. 1978); People v. Holliman, 22 Ill. App. 3d 95, 101, 316 N.E.2d 812, 817 (2d Dist 1974).

[160] People v. Kezerian, 77 Ill. 2d 121, 127, 395 N.E.2d 551, 553-54 (1979).

that he had been monitored,[161] and (4) the failure to gain after-the-fact judicial approval of emergency, consensual eavesdropping within the 48 hour time frame.[162]

§ 10.14. Statutory Exclusionary Rule.

There are various provisions and remedies built into the eavesdropping prohibition that are obviously designed to curb violations of the state eavesdropping enactment. Besides punishing violators of the Illinois eavesdropping proscription with felony sanctions,[163] this legislative package provides for civil remedies to injured parties[164] and requires any individual, common carrier, private investigative agency, or nongovernment corporation who discovers evidence of eavesdropping to report it to the state's attorney.[165] Additionally it includes a statutory exclusionary rule that reads:

> Evidence Inadmissable. Any evidence obtained in violation of this Article is not admissible in any civil or criminal trial, or any administrative or legislative inquiry or proceeding, nor in any grand jury proceedings; provided, however, that so much of the contents of an alleged unlawfully intercepted, overheard or recorded conversation as is clearly relevant, as determined as a matter of law by the court in chambers, to the proof of such allegation may be admitted into evidence in any criminal trial or grand jury proceeding brought against any person charged with violating any provision of this Article.[166]

Generally speaking, where the government's eavesdropping efforts follow the provisions of the authorizing statute, interception of the communication is not unreasonable, and the recorded conversation can properly be admitted in a prosecution of the individual so targeted.[167] Also, the mere fact that there was illegal eavesdropping of a conversation does not mean that the information within the conversation will be deemed inadmissible. In a prosecution for bribery and solicitation, the testimony of police officers concerning the contents of certain telephone conversations that were illegally monitored by a court reporter on an extension phone were improperly suppressed, because the officers were

---

[161] People v. Ellis, 122 Ill. App. 3d 900, 904-05, 461 N.E.2d 646, 650-51 (2d Dist. 1984).

[162] People v. Rogers, 141 Ill. App. 3d 374, 379-80, 490 N.E.2d 133, 137-38 (2d Dist. 1986).

[163] 720 ILCS 5/14-4 (1999).

[164] 720 ILCS 5/14-6 (1999) (injunction, civil damages, and punitive damages provisions).

[165] 720 ILCS 5/14-8 (1999).

[166] 720 ILCS 5/14-5 (1999).

[167] See, e.g., People v. Sylvester, 86 Ill. App. 3d 186, 190-91, 407 N.E.2d 1002, 1007 (1st Dist. 1980) ("Both [federal Title III and the Illinois] statutes were enacted to protect the right of privacy and to provide for *authorization* of communication interception," which occurred in instant case.) (emphasis added).

actual participants in the various conversations and, thus, their knowledge of what was said was not derived from the court reporter's illegal eavesdropping activities.[168] Evidence, however, that is tainted by prior illegal eavesdropping activity should be suppressed unless the party's testimony can be sufficiently distinguished as to be purged of the taint.[169]

It is important to note that this Illinois statutory exclusionary rule is distinguishable from the federal constitutional exclusionary rule in a number of respects. First, the federal exclusionary rule has no effect where the illegal evidence-gathering was performed by "private persons," since there is no "state action" for due process purposes in such circumstances.[170] Because of the broad language of the Illinois statutory exclusionary rule of article 5/14, proof of official involvement in the illegal eavesdropping is not required to warrant the suppression of such evidence.[171] Second, the federal constitutional exclusionary rule does not apply to non-trial criminal proceedings[172] or civil proceedings.[173] The Illinois eavesdropping exclusionary rule normally applies in both types of proceedings.[174] Third, one can gain a suppression of evidence under the federal Constitution only if one has "standing" to complain about the government violation of *one's own personal* rights.[175] The Illinois courts do not require this under

---

[168] People v. Gervasi, 89 Ill. 2d 522, 530, 434 N.E.2d 1112, 1116 (1982) (However, the court reporter's testimony and transcript were suppressed).

[169] People v. Satek, 78 Ill. App. 3d 543, 550, 396 N.E.2d 1133, 1138 (1st Dist. 1979) (fruits of illegal eavesdropping suppressed).

[170] United States v. Jacobson, 466 U.S. 109 (1984).

[171] People v. Maslowsky, 34 Ill. 2d 456, 216 N.E.2d 669, *appeal dismissed,* 385 U.S. 11, *reh'g denied,* 385 U.S. 924 (1966).

[172] *See, e.g.,* United States v. Calandra, 414 U.S. 338 (1974) (grand jury proceeding).

[173] *See, e.g.,* Immigration & Naturalization Service v. Lopez-Mendoza, 468 U.S. 1032 (1984) (deportation hearing).

[174] People v. Maslowsky, 34 Ill. 2d 456, 463, 216 N.E.2d 669, 674, *appeal dismissed,* 385 U.S. 11, *reh'g denied,* 385 U.S. 924 (1966) (grand jury proceeding); Fears v. Fears, 5 Ill. App. 3d 610, 613-14, 283 N.E.2d 709, 711 (5th Dist. 1972) (child custody dispute). *Compare In re* Ettinger, 128 Ill. 2d 351, 363-66, 538 N.E.2d 1152, 1158-59 (1989) (exclusionary rule does not apply in attorney disciplinary hearings since the Illinois Supreme Court rules and not the General Assembly rules govern attorney disciplinary procedures; prohibiting eavesdropping evidence in a disciplinary proceeding regulated exclusively by the Supreme Court would violate separation of powers principles).

[175] Rakas v. Illinois, 439 U.S. 128 (1978) (one has standing only if one has expectation of privacy in area searched); Alderman v. United States, 394 U.S. 165 (1969) (one has standing to object to illegal eavesdropping only if one was party to conversation seized or if illegal surveillance occurred on one's premises).

the article 14 rule.[176] Anyone can exclude such evidence even if he or she is not a party to the conversation and it did not occur on his or her premises.[177]

§ 10.15.   Scope of Eavesdropping.

The discussion in this section will reveal that there has been significant conflict between the legislative intent of the statute and the Illinois Supreme Court's application of it regarding whether the statute requires that the conversation be of a "private" nature.[178] The Illinois legislature amended the statute in 1994 to clarify its intent on this issue stating that a person's intent that the conversation be of a private nature is irrelevant.[179] However, there have been no cases before the Illinois Supreme Court since the amendment was enacted to indicate how the Court will interpret and apply the amendment.[180] Thus, the discussion which follows will survey the article 14 caselaw decided over the years, some of which may have been modified by the 1994 amendment.

Article 14 was intended to protect individuals from surreptitious monitoring of their conversations by use of eavesdropping devices.[181] Consequently, the Illinois Supreme Court has held that the term *eavesdropper* in this article encompasses not only a person who participates in the use of an eavesdropping device but also one who uses or divulges the information thus obtained.[182] Prior to the 1994 amendment, the Illinois judiciary had held that this statute was enacted to protect individuals from interception of communications intended by the declarant to be of a *private* nature,[183] and refused to prohibit the warrantless recording of *all* communications.[184] A person must have had a subjective and

---

[176] People v. Satek, 78 Ill. App. 3d 543, 547-55, 396 N.E.2d 1133, 1136-38 (1st Dist. 1979) (non-party to conversation had standing to object to statement made by accomplice in police station).

[177] People v. Satek, 78 Ill. App. 3d 543, 547-55, 396 N.E.2d 1133, 1136-38 (1st Dist. 1979).

[178] *See* Robert Loeb, *Eavesdropping in Illinois: The Conflict Between Statutory and Case Law,* 81 ILL. B.J. 16 (1993).

[179] 720 ILCS 5/14-1(d) (1998) (The amendment became effective on December 15, 1994, and defined "Conversation" as "any oral communication between 2 or more persons regardless of whether one or more of the parties intended their communication to be of a private nature under circumstances justifying that expectation.").

[180] *But see* People v. Siwek, 284 Ill. App. 3d 7, 13-14, 671 N.E.2d 358, 362-64 (1996) (indicating that the amendment was subsequently amended to extend coverage to all conversations regardless of an expectation of privacy). *See also* Talanda v. KFC National Management Co., 1997 WL 160695, *6 n.6 (N.D. Ill. 1997) (containing a footnote that the Illinois legislature amended the statute to make illegal warrantless recording of conversations without the consent of all the parties to the conversation).

[181] People v. Myles, 62 Ill. App. 3d 931, 935-36, 379 N.E.2d 897, 900 (2d Dist. 1978).

[182] People v. Maslowsky, 34 Ill. 2d 456, 464, 216 N.E.2d 669, 674 *appeal dismissed,* 385 U.S. 11, *reh'g denied,* 385 U.S. 924 (1966).

[183] People v. Klingenberg, 34 Ill. App. 3d 705, 708, 339 N.E.2d 456, 459 (2d Dist. 1975).

[184] People v. Klingenberg, 34 Ill. App. 3d 705, 708, 339 N.E.2d 456, 459 (2d Dist. 1975).

objective expectation of privacy in the conversation in order to claim protection.[185] Thus, where police arrested a defendant for driving under the influence of an intoxicating liquor, requested the defendant to perform various coordination tasks, and then *recorded* these movements, as well as an interview of him by means of an audio-video recorder, this was not eavesdropping in violation of the Illinois law, because the defendant could not have had a reasonable expectation of privacy concerning this communication.[186] In another case, where the police monitored a defendant's jail telephone conversation with his wife on a telephone that was located under a large sign reading "all calls monitored," the defendant could not claim that the police monitoring was illegal, because there could be no reasonable expectation of privacy.[187]

---

[185] People v. Smith, 152 Ill. 2d 229, 235-36, 604 N.E.2d 858, 864 (1992) (where police overheard defendant's conversation from common area of apartment building without using a listening device, no reasonable expectation of privacy attached to defendant's incriminating statements).

[186] People v. Klingenberg, 34 Ill. App. 3d 705, 708, 339 N.E.2d 456, 459 (2d Dist. 1975).

[187] People v. Myles, 62 Ill. App. 3d 931, 936, 379 N.E.2d 897, 900 (2d Dist. 1978). Other obvious "exemptions" from the reach of the eavesdropping statute are codified in 720 ILCS 5/14-3 (1999):

Exemptions:

The following activities shall be exempt from the provisions of this Article:

(a) Listening to radio, wireless and television communications of any sort where the same are publicly made.

(b) Hearing conversations when heard by employees of any common carrier by wire incidental to the normal course of their employment in the operation, maintenance or repair of the equipment of such common carrier by wire so long as no information obtained thereby is used or divulged by the hearer;

(c) Any broadcast by radio, television or otherwise whether it be a broadcast or recorded for purposes of later broadcasts of any function where the public is in attendance and the conversations are overheard incidental to the main purpose for which such broadcasts are then being made;

(d) Recording or listening with the aid of any device to any emergency communication made in the normal course of operations by any federal, state or local law enforcement agency or institutions dealing in emergency services including but not limited, to hospitals, clinics, ambulance services, fire fighting agencies, any public utility, emergency repair facility, civilian defense establishment or military facilities;

(e) Recording the proceedings of any meeting required to be open by . . . [reason of the state's Open Meetings Act].

(f) Recording or listening with the aid of any device to incoming telephone calls of phone lines publicly listed or advertised as consumer "hotlines" by manufacturers or retailers of food and drug products. * * *

(g) With prior notification to the State's Attorney of the county in which it is to occur, recording or listening with the aid of any device to any conversation where a law enforcement officer, or any party to the conversation acting at the direction of law enforcement, is a party to the conversation and has consented to it being intercepted or recorded under circumstances where the use of the device is necessary for [their] protection . . . in the course of an

A very important decision which attempted to clarify[188] the scope of illegal eavesdropping, and which apparently limited the reach of the statutory prohibition, was *People v. Beardsley*,[189] decided by the Illinois Supreme Court in 1986. In that case, the defendant was stopped for speeding with his automobile and after the arresting officer requested the defendant's driver license, the defendant refused to identify himself or turn over his license until he had an opportunity to consult with counsel.[190] During this time, the officer noticed that the defendant was attempting to tape-record his conversation with the defendant and objected thereto.[191] The defendant was then placed in the officer's squad car and another officer was summoned to the scene.[192] After the second officer arrived, they conversed with one another in the squad car with the defendant present in the rear seat, allegedly unaware that their conversation was being recorded by the

---

investigation of a forcible felony, a felony violation of the Illinois Controlled Substance Act, a felony violation of the Cannabis Control Act, or any "streetgang related" or "gang-related" felony . . . . Any Recording or evidence derived as the result of this exemption shall be inadmissible in any proceeding, criminal, civil or administrative, except (i) where a party to the conversation suffers great bodily injury or is killed during such conversation, or (ii) when used as direct impeachment of a witness concerning matters contained in the interception or recording.* * *

(h) Recordings made simultaneously with a video recording of an oral conversation between a peace officer, who has identified his or her office, and a person stopped for an investigation of an offense under the Illinois Vehicle Code.

(i) Recording of a conversation made by or at the request of a person, not a law enforcement officer or agent of a law enforcement officer, who is a party to the conversation, under reasonable suspicion that another party to the conversation is committing, is about to commit, or has committed a criminal offense against the person or member of his or her immediate household, and there is reason to believe that evidence of the criminal offense may be obtained by the recording.

(j) The use of a telephone monitoring device by either ... a corporation or other business entity engaged in [marketing, opinion research, or telephone solicitation,] to record or listen to oral telephone solicitation conversations or marketing or opinion research conversations by an employee ... for the purpose of service quality control ..., the education or training of employees ..., or internal research ..., and the monitoring is used with the consent of at least one person who is an active party to the [telephone conversation]. No communication or conversation ... acquired ... under this exemption ... may be, directly or indirectly, furnished to any law enforcement agency ..., used in any inquiry or investigation, used ... in any administrative, judicial, or other proceeding, or divulged to any third party.

[188] *But see* Robert Loeb, *Eavesdropping in Illinois: The Conflict Between Statutory and Case Law,* 81 ILL. B.J. 16 (1993).

[189] 115 Ill. 2d 47, 503 N.E.2d 346 (1986).

[190] People v. Beardsley, 115 Ill. 2d 47, 48, 503 N.E.2d 346, 347 (1986).

[191] People v. Beardsley, 115 Ill. 2d 47, 48-49, 503 N.E.2d 346, 347 (1986). Although the tape recorder appeared to be functioning, at this point the microphone had not been activated.

[192] People v. Beardsley, 115 Ill. 2d 47, 49, 503 N.E.2d 346, 347 (1986).

defendant.[193] When it was determined that he had recorded their conversation, the defendant was arrested, and later convicted, for eavesdropping.[194]

On appeal, the defendant claimed his conduct was not violative of the statute, since the officers could not entertain an expectation of privacy in their conversations given his presence during the conversation.[195] The appellate court held that the plain and clear language of the statute had been violated.[196] In effect, the state successfully argued before the appellate court that there is no language in the statute that the conversations must be intended to be private. Inasmuch as all of the parties to the conversation had not consented to the recording, and the defendant's recording was not conducted pursuant to a court order, the appellate court concluded that a violation had occurred.[197]

On review, the Illinois Supreme Court reversed the defendant's conviction.[198] The court reasoned that the eavesdropping statute had been designed to protect the *privacy* of conversations.[199] While conceding that the section 5/14-2 Illinois eavesdropping protections were not "coextensive with those imposed on governmental action by the fourth amendment," the court stated that the reasoning of United States Supreme Court in *Lopez v. United States*,[200] was "helpful" to a resolution of defendant's claim.[201]

> Under the rational of *Lopez*, clearly our eavesdropping statute should not prohibit the recording of a conversation by a party to that conversation or one known by the parties to be present.[202]

Since the defendant, like the government agent in *Lopez*, was in a position to hear the conversation with the non-consenting parties and repeat the gist of the conversation in a court of law, the preservation of a more accurate account of the conversation through the use of a recording device was permissible.[203] As to any privacy claim surrounding the conversation, the court stated:

> [I]t seems logical that if the officers intended their conversation to be entirely private, then they would have left the squad car instead of carrying on their conversation in the defendant's presence. Thus, under the circum-

---

[193] People v. Beardsley, 115 Ill. 2d 47, 49, 503 N.E.2d 346, 348 (1986).

[194] People v. Beardsley, 115 Ill. 2d 47, 50, 503 N.E.2d 346, 348 (1986).

[195] People v. Beardsley, 115 Ill. 2d 47, 50, 503 N.E.2d 346, 348 (1986).

[196] People v. Beardsley, 115 Ill. 2d 47, 50, 503 N.E.2d 346, 348 (1986).

[197] People v. Beardsley, 115 Ill. 2d 47, 50, 503 N.E.2d 346, 348 (1986).

[198] People v. Beardsley, 115 Ill. 2d 47, 59, 503 N.E.2d 346, 352 (1986).

[199] People v. Beardsley, 115 Ill. 2d 47, 52-53, 503 N.E.2d 346, 349-50 (1986) (citing ILL. ANN. STAT. ch. 38, para. 14-1 (1961), 1961 Committee Comments, at 581 (Smith-Hurd 1972)).

[200] 373 U.S. 427 (1963).

[201] People v. Beardsley, 155 Ill. 2d 47, 56, 503 N.E.2d 346, 351 (1986).

[202] People v. Beardsley, 115 Ill. 2d 47, 56, 503 N.E.2d 346, 351 (1986).

[203] People v. Beardsley, 115 Ill. 2d 47, 58-59, 503 N.E.2d 346, 352 (1986).

stances, the officers cannot be heard to allege that they intended their conversation to be private.[204]

In a special concurring opinion, Justice Simon determined that the majority ruling has "rendered portions of the statute superfluous and has frustrated the intention of our General Assembly as expressed in the language of the statute."[205] His review of the legislative intent behind the statute convinced him eavesdropping was illegal under this law unless committed with consent of all parties or committed with consent of one, plus a court order.[206] In this case, however, he felt no violation had occurred simply because the officers were aware, as they conversed, that the defendant had a tape recorder, was intent on using it and, accordingly, the officers impliedly consented to being recorded by speaking in defendant's presence.[207] In any event, Simon implied he would see a major difference between a defendant's recording performed with the other conversational participant's knowledge, which impliedly creates consent of all parties, and a defendant's secretive recording of his conversations with another. In the latter situation, because there is no implied consent of all parties, a court order would be essential.[208]

The *Beardsley* majority ruling seemingly defeated the plain language and the legislative purpose of paragraph 5/14-2(a) of the Criminal Code.[209] If a participant in a conversation must assume the risk, as *Beardsley* made clear, that his conversations with another may be secretly recorded as he speaks, it would make little sense for a law enforcement officer, for instance, to ever feel compelled to procure a court order authorizing his surreptitious interception of his conversation with another. This rendered the consent "of any one party" plus a court order requirement of paragraph 5/108A-3 entirely useless and meaningless. In effect, by concentrating solely on the original purposes of the criminalization of this activity, which emphasize privacy concerns, the Illinois Supreme Court ignored the legislature's intent that is at the heart of the later enactment of article 5/108A: unless all parties consent to the eavesdropping, the eavesdropper engaged in a surreptitious recording must have court-ordered authorization.

Equally as strange was the Court's suggestion in *dicta* that electronically transmitting to another person not present during a conversation, as opposed to mere recording, might be illegal.

---

[204] People v. Beardsley, 115 Ill. 2d 47, 55, 503 N.E.2d 346, 350 (1986).

[205] People v. Beardsley, 115 Ill. 2d 47, 62, 503 N.E.2d 346, 353 (1986) (Simon, J., concurring).

[206] People v. Beardsley, 115 Ill. 2d 47, 62, 503 N.E.2d 346, 352-55 (1986) (Simon, J., concurring).

[207] People v. Beardsley, 115 Ill. 2d 47, 64, 503 N.E.2d 346, 354-55 (1986) (Simon, J., concurring).

[208] People v. Beardsley, 115 Ill. 2d 47, 64, 503 N.E.2d 346, 354 (1986).

[209] This precise point is articulated in Scott O. Reed, *Eavesdropping Regulation in Illinois,* 21 J. MARSHALL L. REV. 251, 296 (1988).

We emphasize, however, that our holding in this case should not be construed as holding that the same result would necessarily prevail if the defendant here would have been equipped with a transmitter instead of a recorder and, therefore, the conversation by the officer, would by this means, have been overheard or intercepted by another."[210]

The distinction that the Illinois Supreme Court made here in *Beardsley* was considered to be irrelevant in federal constitution analysis conducted by the United States Supreme Court in *United States v. White*.[211] As was discussed above,[212] *White* involved a law enforcement official's warrantless transmission of his conversation with the defendant to other agents who then recorded the conversation, which the Court explicitly *approved*. If it is true, as *White* clearly states, that one has *no* reasonable expectation of privacy even with respect to eavesdropping in the form of a transmission of the conversation to a third party, then the Illinois enactment may not prohibit this type of eavesdropping, as well. The *Beardsley* dicta led subsequent Illinois appellate courts to conclude that its exact holding was that "eavesdropping occurs only when a party uses an electronic device 'to listen in on conversations it could not otherwise have heard.'"[213]

Following *Beardsley*, various appellate opinions assumed that warrantless consensual eavesdropping was legal even though the person recorded may not have realized he or she was being recorded.[214] For example, in *Smith v. Associated Bureaus, Inc.*,[215] the first district appellate court held that the eavesdropping statute did not prohibit a collection agency's recording of a conversation

---

[210] People v. Beardsley, 115 Ill. 2d 47, 59, 503 N.E.2d 346, 352 (1986).

[211] 401 U.S. 745, 751 (1971).

[212] *See* § 10.04 of this chapter.

[213] People v. O'Toole, 226 Ill. App. 3d 974, 983, 590 N.E.2d 950, 956 (4th Dist. 1992) (quoting People v. Beardsley, 115 Ill. 2d 47, 56, 503 N.E.2d 346, 351 (1986)).

[214] *See, e.g.,* Bender v. Board of Fire & Police Comm'rs of Village of Dolton, 183 Ill. App. 3d 562, 565-66, 539 N.E.2d 234, 236-37 (1st Dist. 1989) (a police officer did not violate the eavesdropping statute by using a pocket recorder to record a conversation he had with the chief of police since he was not intercepting a conversation he could not otherwise have heard nor was he invading any reasonable expectation of privacy of the chief of police); People v. Cole, 186 Ill. App. 3d 1002, 1006, 542 N.E.2d 1145, 1148 (5th Dist. 1989) (defendant could not complain about a police chief's recording of a telephone conversation between himself and the chief since his statements during the conversation were freely given and there was no indication that the chief had indicated that their telephone dialogue would remain confidential); People v. Regains, 187 Ill. App. 3d 713, 717, 543 N.E.2d 1090, 1093 (3rd Dist. 1989) (a police officer's recording of defendant's conversation during a telephone call to officer did not violate the eavesdropping statute since the defendant could not reasonably expect that his voluntary confession to a crime during the call would remain private if told to a police officer). *See also* People v. Jansen, 203 Ill. App. 3d 985, 987-89, 561 N.E.2d 312, 313-14 (5th Dist. 1990) (criminal information which simply alleged defendant recorded a conversation between himself and another person without the latter's consent properly dismissed for failure to allege an offense).

[215] 177 Ill. App. 3d 286, 532 N.E.2d 301 (1st Dist. 1988).

between a debtor's attorney and a collection agency employee, regardless of whether the attorney consented to or knew of the recording, since the agency employee "could have taken notes or transcribed the conversations, rather than taping them, and could have testified concerning the conversations."[216]

In *People v. Herrington*,[217] decided by the Illinois Supreme Court in 1994, the court made it clear that they were determined to uphold warrantless consensual eavesdropping even where the defendant was unaware that his conversation was being recorded. In that case, police tape recorded a telephone conversation between the defendant and a sixteen-year-old alleged victim of aggravated criminal sexual abuse.[218] The victim had placed a call to defendant from a police station, after the victim consented to the recording, but the defendant was unaware of the fact that his conversation with the victim was being monitored by police and being recorded.[219] The appellate court upheld the suppression of the statement on grounds that the statutory prohibition was breached while distinguishing *Beardsley*.[220] The appellate court reasoned that the police officers in *Beardsley* knew their conversations were being recorded and, thus, could not be private, while here it was fair for the defendant to assume his conversation with the victim was private.[221]

However, the Illinois Supreme Court later reversed the appellate court's decision.[222] The court followed *Beardsley* and held that the Illinois eavesdropping statute permitted "the [warrantless] recording of a conversation by a party to that conversation."[223] Relying on *Beardsley*, the court stated that "[t]he recording of a conversation by a party to that conversation was simply a means of preserving a more accurate account of what he had heard. Therefore, there can be no invasion of an 'expectation of privacy' when a party to a conversation makes a recording of that conversation."[224]

Significantly, the Illinois legislature in late 1994 amended the statute apparently to supersede the *Beardsley* and *Herrington* court's interpretation of the statute requiring an "expectation of privacy" in order for a conversation to be covered by the statute. The definition of "Conversation" was amended to include "any oral communication between 2 or more persons *regardless* of

---

[216] Smith v. Associated Bureaus, Inc., 177 Ill. App. 3d 286, 291, 532 N.E.2d 301, 304 (1st Dist. 1988).

[217] 163 Ill. 2d 507, 645 N.E.2d 957 (1994).

[218] People v. Herrington, 163 Ill. 2d 507, 508, 645 N.E.2d 957, 957-58 (1994).

[219] People v. Herrington, 163 Ill. 2d 507, 508, 645 N.E.2d 957, 958 (1994).

[220] People v. Herrington, 252 Ill. App. 3d 63, 69, 623 N.E.2d 760, 764 (4th Dist. 1993), *rev'd*, 163 Ill. 2d 507, 645 N.E.2d 957 (1994).

[221] People v. Herrington, 252 Ill. App. 3d 63, 69, 623 N.E.2d 760, 764 (4th Dist. 1993), *rev'd*, 163 Ill. 2d 507, 645 N.E.2d 957 (1994).

[222] People v. Herrington, 163 Ill. 2d 507, 511, 645 N.E.2d 957, 959 (1994).

[223] People v. Herrington, 163 Ill. 2d 507, 511, 645 N.E.2d 957, 959 (1994).

[224] People v. Herrington, 163 Ill. 2d 507, 510, 645 N.E.2d 957, 958 (1994).

whether one or more of the parties intended their communication to be of a private nature under circumstances justifying that expectation."[225] However, until a relevant case comes before it, it is still unclear whether the Illinois Supreme Court will follow the amendment or persist in following the *Beardsley/Herrington* approach, which requires an invasion of a person's reasonable "expectation of privacy" before the statute will apply.

An Illinois appellate court, in *In re Marriage of Almquist*,[226] did rely on the amended definition of "conversation" in an indirect criminal contempt adjudication arising out of a dispute over child visitation following a dissolution of marriage. In that case, the petitioner filed a petition for adjudication of indirect contempt, alleging that the mother of his child had interfered with his right to court-ordered telephone visitations with his daughter. Specifically, when the petitioner attempted to engage in telephone conversations with his daughter, the respondent-mother (ex-wife of petitioner) had argued with petitioner and, later, played a "suicide tape" while the petitioner was attempting to reach or converse with his daughter. The "suicide tape" was a recording of petitioner's voice made approximately one and one-half years earlier, wherein petitioner had apparently discussed committing suicide. Petitioner recorded his telephone efforts to reach his daughter, including his conversation with his daughter and the respondent's playing of the "suicide tape" in the background when he unsuccessfully attempted to talk to his daughter. The trial court admitted petitioner's recording and found respondent in contempt of court.

After a review of the *Beardsley* doctrine and the subsequent legislative redefinition of "conversation," the appellate court noted that "the amended statute prohibits the recording of any conversation without the consent of all parties regardless of any party's expectation of privacy."[227] Applying the law to the facts, the court concluded that the petitioner's conversations with his daughter qualified as "conversations" within the meaning of the statute and, as such, should have been suppressed in the trial court.[228] However, those portions of the petitioner's recording of his calls, which reflected no more than someone answering the phone during his various efforts to call his daughter and playing the "suicide tape" was not a recording of a "conversation," but instead a "criminal" effort by respondent carried out "for the purpose of interfering with his telephone visitation."[229] The court concluded that "the broad remedial purpose and coverage of the eavesdropping statute prohibits the recording of conversations without the consent of all parties thereto, but not the recording of a mere tele-

---

[225] 720 ILCS 5/14-1(d) (1999) (emphasis added).

[226] 299 Ill. App. 3d 732, 704 N.E.2d 68 (3d Dist. 1998).

[227] In re Marriage of Almquist, 299 Ill. App. 3d 732, 736, 704 N.E.2d 68, 71 (3d Dist. 1998).

[228] In re Marriage of Almquist, 299 Ill. App. 3d 732, 736-37, 704 N.E.2d 68, 71 (3d Dist. 1998).

[229] In re Marriage of Almquist, 299 Ill. App. 3d 732, 737, 704 N.E.2d 68, 71 (3d Dist. 1998).

phone connection."[230] Thus, the latter portion of petitioner's recording was admissible in the contempt proceeding to establish respondent's willful criminal contempt.[231]

Beyond the possible scope of criminal eavesdropping in regard to the *type of conversation* that cannot be recorded without a court order are the issues regarding the appropriate *means* used in that recording. In various cases, the courts have faced government claims that the device they used to monitor conversations was not an *eavesdropping device* as that term is defined in paragraph 5/14-1. For example, Illinois courts have, in addressing this issue, agreed that a telephone itself does not constitute an eavesdropping device.[232] Thus, where an informant dialed a defendant bookie to place a bet and then held the telephone in such a way as to allow a police officer to overhear their conversation, this was not eavesdropping under the statute.[233] Similarly, listening in on an extension telephone does not fall within the prohibition's purview.[234] However, the Illinois Supreme Court ruled in *People v. Gervasi*[235] that the removal of the transmitter or speaking element from the mouthpiece of an extension telephone, which made it incapable of transmitting sound thereby allowing a court reporter to record the defendant's incriminating statements on a court reporter shorthand machine, transformed the phone into an eavesdropping device within the meaning of the eavesdropping statute.[236] The *Gervasi* court based its decision on the reasoning that the statute is directed against the use of devices that are designed for eavesdropping, and not against normal telephone equipment, such as the extension telephone, assuming that the latter has not been functionally altered.[237] The court noted, however, that the removal of a transmitter or speaking element from an extension telephone alters it in such a way as to prevent it from performing its normal function and thereby transforms it into a mere listening or eavesdropping device.[238] Meanwhile, in *People v. Shinkle*,[239] the Illinois Supreme Court distinguished *Gervasi*, in a case where a police officer merely placed his hand

---

[230] In re Marriage of Almquist, 299 Ill. App. 3d 732, 738, 704 N.E.2d 68, 72 (3d Dist. 1998).

[231] In re Marriage of Almquist, 299 Ill. App. 3d 732, 738, 704 N.E.2d 68, 72 (3d Dist. 1998). The appellate court affirmed the trial court's finding of indirect criminal contempt against respondent because the evidence as a whole was sufficient to convict and the evidence wrongly admitted in the trial court was harmless error.

[232] People v. Petrus, 98 Ill. App. 3d 514, 517, 424 N.E.2d 755, 757 (1st. Dist. 1981).

[233] People v. Petrus, 98 Ill. App. 3d 514, 517, 424 N.E.2d 755, 757 (1st. Dist. 1981).

[234] People v. Gaines, 88 Ill. 2d 342, 362, 430 N.E.2d 1046, 1056 (1981) (where police overheard defendant's call to his mother and brother on extension phone with mother's permission, "extension telephone is not an eavesdropping device."), *cert. denied*, 456 U.S. 1001 (1982).

[235] 89 Ill. 2d 522, 434 N.E.2d 1112 (1982).

[236] People v. Gervasi, 89 Ill. 2d 522, 526-27, 434 N.E.2d 1112, 1114 (1982).

[237] People v. Gervasi, 89 Ill. 2d 522, 526-27, 434 N.E.2d 1112, 1114 (1982).

[238] People v. Gervasi, 89 Ill. 2d 522, 526-27, 434 N.E.2d 1112, 1114 (1982).

[239] 128 Ill. 2d 480, 539 N.E.2d 1238 (1989).

over the mouthpiece of an extension phone and listened to a conversation between the defendant and a cooperating witness. The court reasoned that since the officer had not mechanically altered the telephone as in *Gervasi*, the extension phone was not an eavesdropping device.[240]

Beyond the cases above, it has been held that the police use of a radio scanner to overhear the defendant's mobile telephone conversation did not involve the use of an "eavesdropping device" within the meaning of the Illinois statute not only because of the "common knowledge that conversations transmitted by radio waves may be easily intercepted . . .," but also because "the user's guide accompanying the particular mobile telephone at issue here informed the user of this fact."[241] Illinois courts have also recognized that a camera is not an eavesdropping device, because it in not capable of being used to hear or record conversation,[242] and that a telephone company's disclosure of long distance numbers that have been allegedly illegally dialed by the defendant does not violate the eavesdropping statute where no conversations have been actually monitored.[243] But an apparatus placed on the earphone of a telephone that has an extension permitting anyone other than the telephone user to hear conversations is an eavesdropping device.[244] Furthermore, recording equipment installed on a police telephone line for the licit purpose of ensuring the recording of all emergency calls pursuant to the ordinary course of police duties was held not to be an "eavesdropping device" despite the fact that some non-emergency, "personal" calls were recorded.[245] Finally, the use of a monitoring system installed for the health and safety of persons incarcerated in a county jail does not violate the eavesdropping statute where the use of the system is open, apparent, and disclosed to the inmates; where the system is rationally related to the security needs of the jail; and where the system is used in a manner not unduly restrictive of the inmates rights.[246]

---

[240] People v. Shinkle, 128 Ill. 2d 480, 489, 539 N.E.2d 1238, 1242 (1989). *See also* People v. Gray, 209 Ill. App. 3d 407, 414, n.1, 568 N.E.2d 219, 224, n.1 (1st Dist. 1991).

[241] People v. Wilson, 196 Ill. App. 3d 997, 1009, 554 N.E.2d 545, 551 (1st Dist. 1990).

[242] Cassidy v. American Broadcasting Companies, Inc., 60 Ill. App. 3d 831, 835, 377 N.E.2d 126, 129 (1st Dist. 1978). *See also* People v. Klingenberg, 34 Ill. App. 3d 705, 708, 339 N.E.2d 456, 459 (2d Dist. 1975) (audio-visual recording of defendant arrested for drunk driving not violative of eavesdropping statute).

[243] People v. Smith, 31 Ill. App. 3d 423, 429, 333 N.E.2d 241, 245 (1st Dist. 1975), *cert. denied*, 425 U.S. 940 (1976) (defendant, who was alleged to have illegally used a device on his phone designed to place long distance phone calls and bypass telephone company's billing procedure, not protected by eavesdropping legislation).

[244] People v. Perez, 92 Ill. App. 2d 366, 373, 235 N.E.2d 335, 338-39 (1st Dist. 1968).

[245] People v. Pitzman, 293 Ill. App. 3d 282, 291-92, 687 N.E.2d 1135, 1140-41 (2d Dist. 1998) (involving monitoring of conversations of personnel within police department).

[246] Ill. Op. Att'y Gen. S-736 (1942).

§ 10.16.   Federal-State or Sister State Collusion.

When a matter is litigated in a federal or state court situated in Illinois and there is evidence obtained from eavesdropping by federal officials or officials of another state, there must be a determination of whether the Illinois eavesdropping statute will govern the admissibility of the evidence. If the eavesdropping was legally conducted under federal law and was conducted solely by federal officials for purposes of investigation of violations of federal law, then Article 5/14 of the Illinois Criminal Code does not govern the federal agent's conduct.[247] This is because of the operation of the federal supremacy clause.[248] Thus, in *United States v. Infelice*,[249] the admission in federal court of evidence gathered in Illinois by federal agents through electronic eavesdropping was not barred by the Illinois statute.[250]

However, if Illinois state officials (1) are involved in a general investigation of a defendant being carried out jointly by Illinois authorities and law enforcement authorities of the federal government or a sister state, where the latter is involved in eavesdropping of the defendant to be used later in Illinois state court, (2) are directly involved in the eavesdropping itself to be used in state court, or (3) pursue the prosecution of the defendant in state court, while relying on evidence of eavesdropping, a court will have to determine whether the Illinois state involvement or prosecution necessitates the application of Illinois law. To make this determination, the court will have to determine whether Illinois had "jurisdiction" over the government eavesdropping[251] and, if so, whether there existed a collusive attempt to evade Illinois law.[252]

In *People v. Barrow*,[253] Illinois and Maryland police conducted consensual eavesdropping of a defendant within the state of Maryland that was legal under the terms of Maryland law, which evidence led to a successful murder prosecution of defendant in Illinois. The Illinois Supreme Court ruled that the Illinois trial court had no jurisdiction over the eavesdropping that occurred entirely within the borders of Maryland, rejected the argument that the admissibility of the eavesdropping evidence was "controlled by the laws of the forum or trial state," noted that Maryland, unlike Illinois, permits warrantless consensual

---

[247] United States v. Teller, 412 F.2d 374, 377 (7th Cir. 1969), *cert. denied,* 402 U.S. 949 (1971).

[248] United States v. Teller, 412 F.2d 374, 377 (7th Cir. 1969), *cert. denied,* 402 U.S. 949 (1971).

[249] 506 F.2d 1358 (7th Cir. 1974).

[250] United States v. Infelice, 506 F.2d 1358, 1365 (7th Cir. 1974).

[251] People v. Barrow, 133 Ill. 2d 226, 258, 549 N.E.2d 240, 254 (1989) ("[E]vidence legally obtained through eavesdropping which occurs within the borders of another state is not inadmissible under section 14-5.")

[252] People v. Accardo, 195 Ill. App. 3d 180, 189, 551 N.E.2d 1349, 1354 (2d Dist. 1990); People v. Manna, 96 Ill. App. 3d 506, 516, 421 N.E.2d 542, 549 (2d Dist. 1981); People v. Fiddler, 72 Ill. App. 3d 924, 926, 391 N.E.2d 210, 211 (2d Dist. 1979).

[253] 133 Ill. 2d 226, 549 N.E.2d 240 (1989).

eavesdropping, and upheld the admissibility of the fruits of the consensual eavesdropping even though it was not pursuant to a court order.[254]

If the eavesdropping occurred in whole or in part on Illinois soil, the trial court must examine whether there is anything "in the record which suggests a collusive attempt to evade the Illinois Eavesdropping Statute" before admitting the evidence.[255] Thus, where a United States postal inspector placed a wiretap on an informant's phone with the authorization of the Chief Postal Inspector of the federal government, recorded conversations between the informant and defendant indicating that stolen postal money orders were in defendant's home and a subsequent federal official search of defendant's home pursuant to a federal warrant led to the discovery of illicit drugs in defendant's home, defendant could not suppress the drugs in a prosecution of state charges brought by Illinois authorities since the warrantless eavesdropping and later search pursuant to the warrant carried out by federal authorities were in conformity with federal law and there was "no hint of collusion between federal and state authorities seeking to evade the limitations of the Illinois Eavesdropping Statute."[256] Where federal officials were carrying out warrantless consensual eavesdropping with Illinois officers present while investing a possible violation of federal narcotics law, which led to state charges against defendant for sale of cocaine to an undercover federal agent, the eavesdropping evidence was admissible in state court because the state officers "were present only to protect the federal officers" and there was nothing suggestive of improper collusion.[257] Where federal and state officials were carrying out a joint "sting" operation on investing theft, which included warrantless consensual eavesdropping that was conducted in accordance with federal requirements but failed to conform with the terms of the Illinois eavesdropping statute, the fruits of the eavesdropping effort was ruled admissible "because the record [was] devoid of any collusion to avoid the Illinois requirements. . . ."[258] Where a joint federal/state investigation of illicit drug activity involved compliance with federal law but "ignored Illinois directives," the existence of an appropriate basis for the federal investigation of possible federal violations undermined defendant's claim of improper collusion.[259]

---

[254] People v. Barrow, 133 Ill. 2d 226, 258, 549 N.E.2d 240, 253-54 (1989).

[255] People v. Manna, 96 Ill. App. 3d 506, 516, 421 N.E.2d 542, 549 (2d Dist. 1981).

[256] People v. Fiddler, 72 Ill. App. 3d 924, 926, 391 N.E.2d 210, 211 (2d Dist. 1979).

[257] People v. Manna, 96 Ill. App. 3d 506, 516, 421 N.E.2d 542, 549 (2d Dist. 1981).

[258] People v. Winchell, 140 Ill. App. 3d 244, 247, 488 N.E.2d 620, 622 (5th Dist. 1986).

[259] People v. Mays, 188 Ill. App. 3d 974, 979-80, 544 N.E.2d 1264, 1268 (5th Dist. 1989) ("[w]hen Federal and State agents are engaged in a joint investigatory enterprise, noncompliance with the Illinois eavesdropping statute does not require the suppression of electronically obtained evidence so long as Federal directives are followed and there is no collusion among the authorities to evade State law.").

Two additional cases are illustrative of the difficulties of establishing collusion. In *People v. Hodge,*[260] the United States Bureau of Alcohol, Tobacco and Firearms (ATF) began an investigation of defendant for illegal sale of firearms. On the basis of information obtained from an informant, ATF granted an eavesdropping request and a recording was obtained of defendant selling a .38 caliber revolver to the informant.[261] Since the manufacturing date of the revolver could not be determined and, therefore, the weapon could not qualify as a "firearm" under federal law, the United States Attorney's Office declined federal prosecution of the defendant.[262] The ATF agent in charge of the investigation turned his reports over to the Illinois State's Attorney for prosecution under state law.[263] This ATF agent denied making any Illinois police agency aware of the specifics of his investigation in the beginning stages although he acknowledged that he may have contacted such agencies to request defendant's photograph or "rap sheet."[264]

The appellate court adopted the Webster's Third New International Dictionary definition of the words "collude" and "collusion" which are "to connive with one another; conspire; plot . . . [a] secret agreement, secret cooperation for a fraudulent or deceitful purpose."[265] In concluding that there was no collusion, the court emphasized that "[t]here is merely evidence that the two agencies cooperated with each other toward the end of determining whether [the defendant] violated State or Federal gun laws."[266]

In *People v. Barnes,*[267] a federal felon informant named White agreed to aid the Federal Drug Enforcement Administration (DEA) and the Federal Bureau of Investigation (FBI) in a narcotics-related investigation of the defendant.[268] Telephone conversations between the informant and defendant, which set up a drug sale, were recorded with the consent of the informant and with permission of the United States Attorney, but without any involvement of state officials.[269] However, before the drug sale occurred, federal prosecution was declined and the investigation was turned over to local authorities.[270] A municipal police officer in Illinois subsequently posed as the informant's financier during the drug

---

[260] 220 Ill. App. 3d 886, 581 N.E.2d 334 (1st Dist. 1991).

[261] People v. Hodge, 220 Ill. App. 3d 886, 887, 581 N.E.2d 334, 334 (1st Dist. 1991).

[262] People v. Hodge, 220 Ill. App. 3d 886, 887, 581 N.E.2d 334, 334-35 (1st Dist. 1991).

[263] People v. Hodge, 220 Ill. App. 3d 886, 887, 581 N.E.2d 334, 335 (1st Dist. 1991).

[264] People v. Hodge, 220 Ill. App. 3d 886, 887-88, 581 N.E.2d 334, 335 (1st Dist. 1991).

[265] People v. Hodge, 220 Ill. App. 3d 886, 889, 581 N.E.2d 334, 336 (1st Dist. 1991).

[266] People v. Hodge, 220 Ill. App. 3d 886, 889, 581 N.E.2d 334, 336 (1st Dist. 1991).

[267] 230 Ill. App. 3d 272, 595 N.E.2d 40 (1st Dist. 1992).

[268] People v. Barnes, 230 Ill. App. 3d 272, 274, 595 N.E.2d 40, 42 (1st Dist. 1992).

[269] People v. Barnes, 230 Ill. App. 3d 272, 275, 595 N.E.2d 40, 42 (1st Dist. 1992). Since the informant had consented to the recording, this situation did not appear to constitute eavesdropping under the *Beardsley* holding; however, the court here did not address that issue.

[270] People v. Barnes, 230 Ill. App. 3d 272, 275, 595 N.E.2d 40, 42 (1st Dist. 1992).

sale.[271] An FBI agent, who remained involved in the investigation, continued to record the conversations between White and defendant Barnes even though the FBI agent's "role was limited to surveillance and to protecting White . . . to insure that [the FBI] had complete control of him while he was out of [prison and in federal custody]."[272] The Illinois appellate court approved the trial court's admission into evidence of the telephone recordings since the federal/state involvement here "did not constitute the type of collusion which should operate to bar the use of the recordings. . . ."[273]

In a situation involving use of an eavesdropping device outside the state by a state law enforcement official in another state, which was designed to intercept an incriminating statement made by a person in Illinois, no violation of the Illinois eavesdropping statute was established. In *People v. Accardo*,[274] an informant who had been arrested in Oklahoma for unlawful distribution of cocaine agreed to a recording of his various telephone calls to a defendant in Illinois made from the office of an agent in the Oklahoma Bureau of Narcotics and Dangerous Drugs. An agreement was reached where defendant agreed to deliver fifty-five pounds of marijuana to the informant and the Oklahoma agent, posing as an illicit drug purchaser, in Illinois. After defendant agreed to delivery in Illinois, local authorities were notified, whereupon they charged defendant with possession and delivery of cannabis in violation of Illinois law. Here, the Illinois appellate court concluded that the tape recording in Oklahoma was in conformity with Oklahoma and federal law and, as such, the "policy behind the exclusionary rule . . . is not forwarded by the suppression of evidence obtained by others in conformance with laws governing their conduct, regardless of whether it is the Federal government or a foreign state agency."[275] In the absence of collusion between the Oklahoma authorities and Illinois authorities to circumvent Illinois eavesdropping procedures requiring a warrant for consensual eavesdropping, the trial court properly admitted the evidence collected in Oklahoma.[276]

In *People v. Bell*,[277] the appellate court upheld a trial judge's ruling that warrantless consensual eavesdropping carried out by municipal police officers was *not* pursuant to federal directives and, consequently, was properly suppressed.[278] In that case, the state called as a witness an FBI agent who testified that the municipal officers were "Special Federal Officers" as part of a federal/state task force investigating gang and illicit drug activity. The municipal officers testified

[271] People v. Barnes, 230 Ill. App. 3d 272, 275, 595 N.E.2d 40, 42 (1st Dist. 1992).
[272] People v. Barnes, 230 Ill. App. 3d 272, 275, 595 N.E.2d 40, 42 (1st Dist. 1992).
[273] People v. Barnes, 230 Ill. App. 3d 272, 276, 595 N.E.2d 40, 43 (1st Dist. 1992).
[274] 195 Ill. App. 3d 180, 551 N.E.2d 1349 (2d Dist. 1990).
[275] People v. Accardo, 195 Ill. App. 3d 180, 190, 551 N.E.2d 1349, 1355 (2d Dist. 1990).
[276] People v. Accardo, 195 Ill. App. 3d 180, 189-90, 551 N.E.2d 1349, 1354-55 (2d Dist. 1990).
[277] 294 Ill. App. 3d 951, 691 N.E.2d 891 (5th Dist. 1998).
[278] People v. Bell, 294 Ill. App. 3d 951, 953-54, 691 N.E.2d 891, 893 (5th Dist. 1998).

that they had "special deputizations" to pursue federal criminality. However, the trial court was unconvinced that these municipal officers were acting in accordance with federal directives because a Special Agent of the FBI who had authority to issue such authorization had refused to testify on behalf of the state and the United States Attorney did not appear in court to verify that federal authorization had been given.[279] Although the appellate court stated "noncompliance with the Illinois eavesdropping statute does not require suppression of electronically obtained evidence so long as Federal directives are followed and there is no collusion among the authorities to evade State law," the court concluded that the state had failed to carry its burden that warrantless "overhears" were consistent with the necessary federal authorization.[280]

---

[279] People v. Bell, 294 Ill. App. 3d 951, 953-54, 691 N.E.2d 891, 893 (5th Dist. 1998).
[280] People v. Bell, 294 Ill. App. 3d 951, 952, 691 N.E.2d 891, 892-93 (5th Dist. 1998).

CHAPTER 11

THEFT AND RELATED OFFENSES

§ 11.01. Introduction.

The substantive law of theft in Illinois changed dramatically on January 1, 1962, when the Criminal Code of 1961 took effect. The revision committee describes the development of sections 5/16 — "Theft and Related Offenses"[1] — and 5/17 — "Deception"[2] — as "probably the most comprehensive codification of the law on any subject contained in the Code."[3] The earlier code was essentially a codification of the common law theft-related offenses — larceny, larceny by trick, embezzlement, false pretenses, confidence game, and the multitude of variations thereof — that were scattered throughout "seventy-four separate sections which dealt in one form or another with the obtaining of property of another with the intent to permanently deprive such other or the true owner of the property of its beneficial use."[4] In recognizing the critical need for a consolidated theft statute, which had been pointed out by commentators as early as 1931,[5] the drafters of sections 5/16 and 5/17 accordingly abrogated from the

---

[1] 720 ILCS 5/16 (1999).

[2] 720 ILCS 5/17 (1999).

[3] ILL. ANN. STAT. ch. 38, § 16-1 (Smith-Hurd 1977), 1961 Committee Comments, at 18 (revised 1970).

[4] ILL. ANN. STAT. ch. 38, § 16-1 (Smith-Hurd 1977), 1961 Committee Comments, at 18 (revised 1970).

[5] See JOINT REPORT OF THE JUDICIAL ADVISORY COUNCILS OF COOK COUNTY AND THE STATE OF ILLINOIS (1931). See also Grenville Beardsley, *Why Revision?* 24 ILL. B.J. 41 (Oct. 1935).

code the "labels and highly technical distinctions which had developed through centuries of caselaw and statutory amendments."[6]

The current criminal code in Illinois states theft crimes in terms of the general acts sought to be prohibited without enumerating specific instances that exemplify the general act. Such an amalgamation of the common law theft offenses avoids the two major failings of Illinois' prior codes: (1) duplication of certain offenses, yet insufficient coverage of all theft crimes, and (2) diverse penalties for substantially similar crimes.[7] The current criminal code of Illinois covers virtually all crimes involving theft or fraud within the confines of articles 5/15 through 5/17 of chapter 720.[8] However, insurance fraud, fraud on a governmental entity, and related offenses are covered in article 5/46.[9] It is necessary to read each section defining a theft crime or crime of fraud in connection with the definitions contained in article 5/15 unless the prohibition provides a more specific definition.[10]

§ 11.02. Theft: The General Provision.

Section 5/16-1 contains the principal theft section and defines the necessary elements of theft: a proscribed act and the requisite mental state of intent or knowledge. Specifically, it provides:

(a) A person commits theft when he knowingly:

(1) Obtains or exerts unauthorized control over property of the owner; or
(2) Obtains by deception control over property of the owner; or
(3) Obtains by threat control over property of the owner; or
(4) Obtains control over stolen property knowing the property to have been stolen or under such circumstances as would reasonably induce him to believe that the property was stolen, or
(5) Obtains or exerts control over property in the custody of any law enforcement agency which is explicitly represented to him by any law enforcement officer or any individual acting in behalf of a law enforcement agency as being stolen, and

---

[6] ILL. ANN. STAT. ch. 38, § 16-1 (Smith-Hurd 1977), 1961 Committee Comments, at 19 (revised 1970). For a short history of common law theft offenses, see JEROME HALL, THEFT, LAW AND SOCIETY 3-152 (2d ed. 1952).

[7] See generally PRESIDENT'S COMMISSION ON ADMINISTRATION OF JUSTICE, TASK FORCE REPORT: THE COURTS 15 (1967) (criticism of inconsistent sentencing structures).

[8] 720 ILCS 5/15-1 through 5/17B-30 (1999).

[9] 720 ILCS 5/46-1 through 5/46-5 (1999).

[10] 720 ILCS 5/15-1 through 5/15-9 (1999).

(A) Intends to deprive the owner permanently of the use or benefit of the property; or

(B) Knowingly uses, conceals or abandons the property in such manner as to deprive the owner of such benefit; or

(C) Uses, conceals, or abandons the property knowing such use, concealment or abandonment probably will deprive the owner permanently of such use or benefit. • • •

(b) Sentence. • • •

(c) When a charge of theft of property exceeding a specified value is brought, the value of the property involved is an element of the offense to be resolved by the trier of fact as either exceeding or not exceeding the specified value.[11]

Because of special considerations involved with the theft by a lessee;[12] financial exploitation of an elderly person or disabled person;[13] the theft of lost or mislaid property;[14] false report of theft or other losses;[15] the theft of labor, services, or use of property;[16] the theft from coin-operated machines;[17] the unlawful use of recorded sounds or images[18] and unidentified sound or audio visual recordings;[19] the theft of cable television service[20] and the unauthorized use of television interception or decoding device;[21] unlawful interference with public utility services;[22] unlawful use of theft detection shielding device;[23] retail theft;[24] library theft;[25] computer tampering;[26] computer fraud;[27] delivery container theft;[28] theft of wireless service;[29] deceptive practices;[30] forgery;[31] and various

---

[11] 720 ILCS 5/16-1 (1999).
[12] 720 ILCS 5/16-1.1 (1999).
[13] 720 ILCS 5/16-1.3 (1999).
[14] 720 ILCS 5/16-2 (1999).
[15] 720 ILCS 5/16-3.1 (1999).
[16] 720 ILCS 5/16-3 (1999).
[17] 720 ILCS 5/16-5 (1999).
[18] 720 ILCS 5/16-7 (1999).
[19] 720 ILCS 5/16-8 (1999).
[20] 720 ILCS 5/16-10 (1999).
[21] 720 ILCS 5/16-11 (1999).
[22] 720 ILCS 5/16-14 (1999).
[23] 720 ILCS 5/16-15 (1999).
[24] 720 ILCS 5/16A-3 (1999).
[25] 720 ILCS 5/16B-2 (1999).
[26] 720 ILCS 5/16D-3 (1999).
[27] 720 ILCS 5/16D-5 (1999).
[28] 720 ILCS 5/16E-3 (1999).
[29] 720 ILCS 5/17F-3 (1999).
[30] 720 ILCS 5/17-1 (1999).
[31] 720 ILCS 5/17-3 (1999).

other special theft situations, these offenses are dealt with separately outside section 5/16-1.[32] Thus, the general theft provision includes all forms of theft, unless more clearly covered by other more specific and appropriate provisions.[33]

§ 11.03.— Definitions.

An understanding of the terminology of the general theft provision, as well as of the other theft provisions, necessitates an examination of the various definitions offered in article 5/15. The word *property* is defined as

> anything of value. Property includes real estate, money, commercial instruments, admission or transportation tickets, written instruments representing or embodying rights concerning anything of value, labor, or services, or otherwise of value to the owner; things growing on, affixed to, or found on land, or part of or affixed to any building; electricity, gas and water, telecommunication services; birds, animals and fish, which ordinarily are kept in a state of confinement; food and drink; samples, cultures, microorganisms, specimens, records, recordings, documents, blueprints, drawings, maps, and whole or partial copies, descriptions, photographs, computer programs or data, prototypes or models thereof or any other articles, materials, devices, substances and whole or partial copies, descriptions, photographs, prototypes, or models thereof which constitute, represent, evidence, reflect or record a secret scientific, technical, merchandising, production or management information, design, process, procedure, formula, invention, or improvement.[34]

An *owner* means "a person, other than the offender, who has possession of or any other interest in the property involved, even though such interest or possession is unlawful, and without whose consent the offender has no authority to exert control over the property."[35] The language "deprive an owner permanently" appears in a significant number of instances[36] and, thus, the phrase *permanently deprive* is defined as any effort designed to:

> (a) Defeat all recovery of the property by the owner; or (b) Deprive the owner permanently of the beneficial use of the property; or (c) Retain the property with intent to restore it to the owner only if the owner purchases or leases it back; or pays a reward or other compensation for its return; or

---

[32] *See* ILL. ANN. STAT. ch. 38, para. 16-1 (Smith-Hurd 1977), Committee Comments, at 18 (revised 1970).

[33] ILL. ANN. STAT. ch. 38, para. 16-1 (Smith-Hurd 1977), Committee Comments, at 18-19 (revised 1970).

[34] 720 ILCS 5/15-1 (1999).

[35] 720 ILCS 5/15-2 (1999).

[36] *See, e.g.,* 720 ILCS 5/16-1(a) (1999).

(d) Sell, give, pledge, or otherwise transfer any interest in the property or subject it to the claim of a person other than the owner.[37]

The meaning of *deception* is also codified. It means knowingly to:

(a) Create or confirm another's impression which is false and which the offender does not believe to be true; or (b) Fail to correct a false impression which the offender previously has created or confirmed; or (c) Prevent another from acquiring information pertinent to the disposition of the property involved; or
(d) Sell or otherwise transfer or encumber property, failing to disclose a lien, adverse claim, or other legal impediment to the enjoyment of the property, whether such impediment is or is not valid, or is or is not a matter of official record; or (e) Promise performance which the offender does not intend to perform or knows will not be performed. Failure to perform standing alone is not evidence that the offender did not intend to perform.[38]

The term *threat* appears in article 5/15. It means a menace, however communicated, to:

(a) Inflict physical harm on the person threatened or any other person or on property; or (b) Subject any person to physical confinement or restraint; or (c) Commit any criminal offense; or (d) Accuse any person of a criminal offense; or (e) Expose any person to hatred, contempt or ridicule; or (f) Harm the credit or business repute of any person; or (g) Reveal any information sought to be concealed by the person threatened; or (h) Take action as an official against anyone or anything, or withhold official action, or cause such action or withholding; or (i) Bring about or continue a strike, boycott or other similar collective action if the property is not demanded or received for the benefit of the group which he purports to represent; or (j) Testify or provide information or withhold testimony or information with respect to another's legal claim or defense; or (k) Inflict any other harm which would not benefit the offender[39]

Stolen property means "property over which control has been obtained by theft."[40] *Obtain* is spelled out: "(a) In relation to property, to bring about a transfer of interest or possession, whether to the offender or to another, and (b) In relation to labor or services, to secure the performance thereof."[41] The phrase *obtains or exerts control* over property "includes but is not limited to the taking,

---

[37] 720 ILCS 5/15-3 (1999).
[38] 720 ILCS 5/15-4 (1999).
[39] 720 ILCS 5/15-5 (1999).
[40] 720 ILCS 5/15-6 (1999).
[41] 720 ILCS 5/15-7 (1999).

THEFT AND RELATED OFFENSES

carrying away, or the sale, conveyance, or transfer of title to, or interest in, or possession of property."[42] Since the term *value* appears later in a number of theft offenses, it appears in this section. As used in these offenses, the "value" of property:

> consisting of any commercial instrument or any written instrument representing or embodying rights concerning anything of value, labor, or services or otherwise of value to the owner shall be: (a) The "market value" of such instrument if such instrument is negotiable and has a market value; and (b) The "actual value" of such instrument if such instrument is not negotiable or is otherwise without a market value. For the purpose of establishing such "actual value," the interest of any owner or owners entitled to part or all of the property represented by such instrument, by reason of such instrument, may be shown, even if another "owner" may be named in the complaint, information or indictment.[43]

Understanding an item's value is also relevant to whether the theft of the item is a felony or a misdemeanor.

It is noteworthy that a number of defendants have claimed, notwithstanding these definitions, that some of the language contained in these various theft offenses is unconstitutionally vague. Whether these constitutional attacks have been directed at entire provisions[44] or at specific terms, such as *owner*,[45] or phrases, such as *unauthorized control*,[46] they have been unsuccessful.

§ 11.04.— Scope of General Theft Statute.

The section 5/16-1 "catch-all" provision has been held as broad enough to encompass all forms of theft including robbery,[47] purse snatching and pocket-picking,[48] embezzlement,[49] extortion,[50] and smashing another's eye glasses,[51] since even in the latter situation, the victim has been "permanently deprive[d]" of the beneficial use of his or her glasses.[52] The general theft provision will not

---

[42] 720 ILCS 5/15-8 (1999).

[43] 720 ILCS 5/15-9 (1999).

[44] People v. Cleveland, 104 Ill. App. 2d 415, 418-19, 244 N.E.2d 212, 213-14 (2d Dist.), *cert. denied*, 396 U.S. 986 (1969) (section 5/16-1 theft prohibition is not vague).

[45] People v. Kamsler, 78 Ill. App. 2d 349, 223 N.E.2d 237 (1st Dist. 1966) (abstract) (not vague).

[46] People v. Harden, 42 Ill. 2d 301, 303-04, 247 N.E.2d 404, 405-06 (1969) (not vague).

[47] People v. Henderson, 72 Ill. App. 2d 89, 94-95, 218 N.E.2d 795, 797 (1st Dist. 1966).

[48] People v. Jackson, 66 Ill. App. 2d 276, 279-80, 214 N.E.2d 316, 317-18 (1st Dist. 1966).

[49] People v. Curoe, 97 Ill. App. 3d 258, 273, 422 N.E.2d 931, 942 (1st Dist. 1981).

[50] United States v. Karigiannis, 430 F.2d 148, 150 (7th Cir.), *cert. denied*, 400 U.S. 904 (1970) (federal court interpretation of Illinois theft statute).

[51] People v. Bell, 9 Ill. App. 3d 465, 292 N.E.2d 219 (1st Dist. 1972) (abstract).

[52] People v. Bell, 9 Ill. App. 3d 465, 292 N.E.2d 219 (1st Dist. 1972) (abstract).

apply to a theft only where the other theft provisions are more appropriate. The mere fact that a particular type of stealing is not explicitly stated in section 5/16-1 in no way conflicts[53] with the state statute that provides that "[n]o conduct constitutes an offense unless it is described as an offense in this Code or in another statute of this State."[54]

§ 11.05.— Knowledge: Element of Theft.

The common elements of theft stated in the general theft provision require individual examination. The first element — that the defendant must have some *knowledge* of the criminal nature of his or her act — is based on the language of section 5/16-1, namely, "When the defendant knowingly obtains. . . ."[55] This mental state modifies the act committed by the accused so as to assure that he or she knowingly took unauthorized control over property of another. However, later in the theft statute there exists what should be viewed as the primary mens rea requirement of theft, the intent to deprive, which will be discussed subsequently.

Knowledge that the property in question was stolen constitutes an essential element of theft that the state must plead and prove.[56] For example, a jury instruction stating that a defendant's guilt may be inferred if (1) he or she had exclusive possession of an item that had been recently stolen and (2) no reasonable explanation existed for his or her possession was a reversible error without an additional instruction that the defendant must have known that the property was stolen.[57]

Furthermore, a defendant cannot be held liable for the mistaken notions of others unless he or she knowingly creates or confirms a false impression that he or she knows is untrue.[58] Knowledge was found lacking where a car rental company demanded the return of its leased car by mailing a notice through registered mail; knowledge here meant that the defendant must have received actual notice or service of the demand.[59]

---

[53] People v. Jackson, 66 Ill. App. 2d 276, 279-80, 214 N.E.2d 316, 317-18 (1st Dist. 1966).

[54] 720 ILCS 5/1-3 (1999).

[55] 720 ILCS 5/16-1 (1999) *See* ch. 2 of this treatise for a discussion of "knowledge."

[56] People v. Dell, 77 Ill. App. 2d 318, 324, 222 N.E.2d 357, 361 (2d Dist. 1966), *cert. denied*, 389 U.S. 826 (1967). *See also* People v. West, 60 Ill. App. 3d 570, 571, 377 N.E.2d 124, 125-26 (1st Dist. 1978) (an essential element of theft by possession is that receiver of property knew it was stolen at time of receiving it).

[57] People v. Moats, 89 Ill. App. 3d 194, 200-201, 411 N.E.2d 573, 578 (3d Dist. 1980). *See also* People v. Housby, 84 Ill. 2d 415, 419-24, 420 N.E.2d 151, 153-55, *cert. denied*, 454 U.S. 845 (1981) (exclusive and unexplained possession of recently stolen property is not sufficient, standing alone or without corroborating evidence of guilt, for conviction of burglary or theft).

[58] People v. Wurster, 83 Ill. App. 3d 399, 403, 403 N.E.2d 1306, 1310 (3d Dist. 1980) (theft by deception conviction affirmed where based on false workers' compensation claim).

[59] People v. Harris, 96 Ill. App. 3d 536, 538-39, 421 N.E.2d 574, 576 (2d Dist. 1981).

Knowledge for theft can be demonstrated by either direct or circumstantial evidence.[60] Guilty knowledge may be proved from all facts and circumstances that would include a belief in the reasonable person's mind that the property was stolen.[61] Furthermore, the person receiving the property need not have actual positive knowledge of the theft but only needs to obtain the property under circumstances that would make that person believe the property was stolen.[62]

The "reasonable doubt" test is currently applied by Illinois courts in cases where only circumstantial evidence exists to prove guilty knowledge: any rational trier of fact must have been able to find the defendant's guilt beyond a reasonable doubt.[63] This test replaced the "reasonable hypothesis of innocence" test which required that the circumstantial evidence relied upon "exclude every reasonable hypothesis other than that of guilt." [64]

The circumstantial evidence was sufficient to prove beyond a reasonable doubt the defendant's guilt of theft where the defendant was found in recent and exclusive possession of stolen coins in his lap, while sitting in a car, and where

---

[60] People v. Dabrowski, 162 Ill. App. 3d 684, 691, 515 N.E.2d 1345, 1350 (2d Dist. 1987); *see also* People v. Hansen, 28 Ill. 2d 322, 338, 192 N.E.2d 359, 368 (1963) (circumstantial evidence can be used to prove corpus delicti of crime of theft; connect defendant with crime; and establish goods received were stolen), *cert. denied*, 376 U.S. 908 (1964).

[61] People v. Philyaw, 34 Ill. App. 3d 616, 620, 339 N.E.2d 461, 465 (2d Dist. 1975). *See also* People v. Althide, 71 Ill. App. 3d 963, 967-68, 389 N.E.2d 240, 242-43 (3d Dist. 1979) (defendant's theft conviction based on obtaining control over stolen property affirmed where defendant purchased hogs at his residence at 2 A.M. at price about one-third of value without inquiry as to source of ownership).

[62] People v. Block, 184 Ill. App. 3d 135, 139-40, 540 N.E.2d 512, 515 (2d Dist. 1989); *see also* People v. Stewart, 20 Ill. 2d 387, 393, 169 N.E.2d 796, 799-80 (1960) (circumstances indicated defendant knew motor and tools were stolen where defendant met seller of goods at tavern, did not know seller well, accompanied seller to disreputable neighborhood at night and waited in his car while seller disappeared into alley to retrieve goods and where defendant purchased goods at much less than actual value without asking for a bill of sale).

[63] *See* People v. Collins, 106 Ill. 2d 237, 261, 478 N.E.2d 267, 277 (1985) (quoting Jackson v. Virginia, 443 U.S. 307, 319 (1979) ("the relevant question is whether, after viewing the evidence in light most favorable to the prosecution, *any* rational trier of fact could have found the essential elements of the crime beyond a reasonable doubt")), *cert. denied*, 474 U.S. 935, *reh'g denied*, 474 U.S. 1027 (1985). The Illinois Supreme Court in People v. Pintos, 133 Ill. 2d 286, 291, 549 N.E.2d 344, 346 (1989) adopted the *Collins* test for all criminal cases in reviewing the sufficiency of both direct and circumstantial evidence.

[64] People v. Berg, 91 Ill. App. 2d 166, 170, 234 N.E. 400, 402 (1st Dist. 1968). *Cf.* People v. Rubin, 361 Ill. 311, 328, 197 N.E. 862, 870 (1935) (defendant's conviction for receiving stolen property reversed in circumstances where purchase of goods was at fair price from regular dealer known to the trade; purchase was in ordinary course of business; goods were openly delivered to defendant's place of business during business hours in presence of employees and customers; and defendant permitted original price tags to remain on goods).

he had knowledge that the coins were stolen.[65] Additionally, a defendant's theft conviction was affirmed in circumstances where a defendant testified that she received a purse from a person named Joseph, whom she later called Kevin (a discrepancy she never explained when she testified), acknowledged in her testimony that she believed that the purse did not belong to this person, and had told the theft victim prior to her trial that her friend had the purse, that she knew what it was like to have her purse stolen, and that she talked the friend into letting her have the purse.[66]

Illinois court decisions indicate that guilty knowledge required to convict one of theft based on receiving stolen property is indicated, in part, by one's failure to inquire as to the property's source or title.[67] Where a defendant was prosecuted for theft under the provision that prohibits "obtain[ing] control over stolen property knowing the property to have been stolen or under such circumstances as would reasonably induce him to believe that the property was stolen,"[68] his conviction was affirmed where he purchased on the street two stolen jackets at a price well below their market value without asking the seller how he acquired the jackets and without asking the seller for a bill of sale or other proof of ownership.[69] Similarly, circumstances indicated defendant's guilty knowledge where defendant assisted in unloading a trailer of merchandise after dark at a business where such goods would not ordinarily be delivered and defendant failed to inquire about the source of the merchandise or the circumstances of delivery.[70]

---

[65] People v. Legear, 29 Ill. App. 3d 884, 888, 331 N.E.2d 659, 662-63 (2d Dist. 1975). *Compare* People v. Dickerson, 41 Ill. App. 3d 464, 474-75, 353 N.E.2d 427, 433-34, (2d Dist. 1976) (evidence did not exclude every reasonable hypothesis other than guilt of theft by receiving stolen goods in circumstances where defendant paid cash for five snowmobiles at price substantially less than retail; bought them without bill of sale, receipt, or warranties from friend not regularly in trade; and made false statement to police in attempt to protect identify of seller). *Dickerson's* precedential value remains questionable today, however, as the "reasonable hypothesis of innocence" standard employed in *Dickerson* has been replaced by the "reasonable doubt" test of People v. Collins, 106 Ill. 2d 237, 261, 478 N.E.2d 267, 277, *cert. denied*, 474 U.S. 935, *reh'g. denied*, 474 U.S. 1027 (1985).

[66] People v. Block, 184 Ill. App. 3d 135, 139-40, 540 N.E.2d 512, 515 (2d Dist. 1989).

[67] People v. Ems, 81 Ill. App. 3d 574, 578, 401 N.E.2d 1336, 1339 (3d Dist. 1980), (citing People v. Stewart, 20 Ill. 2d 387, 392, 169 N.E.2d 796, 799 (1960)).

[68] 720 ILCS 5/16-1(a)(4) (1999).

[69] People v. West, 60 Ill. App. 3d 570, 572, 377 N.E.2d 124, 126 (1st Dist. 1978).

[70] People v. Grodkiewicz, 16 Ill. 2d 192, 197, 157 N.E.2d 16, 19-20 (1959). *See also* People v. Ems, 81 Ill. App. 3d 574, 578, 401 N.E.2d 1336, 1339-40 (3d Dist. 1980) (where defendant allegedly purchased three shotguns, a rifle, a chainsaw and various tools for $300 to $400 from a seller with an extensive criminal record, including burglary, and defendant attempted to conceal the stolen property from police observation when the police arrived at defendant's premises to execute a search warrant, defendant properly convicted of theft).

§ 11.06.— Obtains or Exerts Unauthorized Control: Alternative Element of Theft — Actus Reus (1).

The next element of theft to be examined — "obtains or exerts unauthorized control"[71] — reflects one of the four *alternative* actus reus requirements for theft. That is to say, since a person can be convicted of theft under this language in subsection (a)(1), *or* where he or she "obtains by deception control" under subsection (a)(2),[72] *or* where he or she "obtains by threat control" under subsection (a)(3),[73] *or* where he or she "obtains control over stolen property" under subsection (a)(4),[74] or where he or she "obtains or exerts control over [stolen] property in the custody of any law enforcement agency" under subsection (a)(5),[75] it is not essential in each and every case to prove the element of "obtains or exerts unauthorized control." Sufficient proof of any of the five alternative options involving an unauthorized taking is appropriate.

The phrase *obtains or exerts control* involves the taking of an object, but should in no way be confused with the now replaced concept of larceny. Formerly, under both the common law and the pre-1961 Illinois law, essential elements of larceny were that the property in question must have been taken from the possession of the owner into that of the accused[76] and been carried away by him or her.[77] This type of taking and carry away was known as "asportation."[78] Today, the Illinois theft statute no longer requires the common law element of asportation, but merely the exertion of unauthorized control. This is reinforced by the definition of *obtains control*, which refers to "taking, carrying away *or* the sale, conveyance, or transfer of title to, or interest in, or possession of property."[79] Thus, where a defendant — an attorney and administrator of an estate — issued himself checks totaling almost $400,000 out of the estate without the knowledge or consent of either the probate court or the heirs, his conduct was outside his authority and the appellate court could properly find the defendant's guilt of theft beyond a reasonable doubt.[80] Also, a defendant exerted unauthor-

---

[71] 720 ILCS 5/16-1(a)(1) (1999).
[72] 720 ILCS 5/16-1(a)(2) (1999).
[73] 720 ILCS 5/16-1(a)(3) (1999).
[74] 720 ILCS 5/16-1(a)(4) (1999).
[75] 720 ILCS 5/16-1(a)(5) (1999).
[76] People v. Baker, 365 Ill. 328, 332, 6 N.E.2d 665, 668 (1936).
[77] People v. Walker, 361 Ill. 482, 487, 198 N.E. 353, 356 (1935).
[78] People v. Walker, 361 Ill. 482, 487, 198 N.E. 353, 356 (1935).
[79] 720 ILCS 5/15-8 (1999) (emphasis added).
[80] *See* People v. Curoe, 97 Ill. App. 3d 258, 273-75, 422 N.E.2d 931, 941-43 (1st Dist. 1981) (rev'd on other grounds). *Compare* People v. Davis, 189 Ill. App. 3d 815, 819-20, 545 N.E.2d 774, 777 (3d Dist. 1989) (where defendant, a licensed insurance producer who wrote credit life and/or disability insurance policies insuring bank loan customers, failed to procure insurance policies for customers after premium deposits were made to his escrow account, he could not be convicted of theft without evidence that he withdrew any of the premiums deposited).

ized control over property to commit theft where, in her capacity as the city accountant, she was authorized to receive only her biweekly paycheck; however, the evidence established that she manipulated the city's cash journal and appropriated cash and wrote herself checks for her personal use.[81] Where a dentist filed a claim and accepted payment from a city for city employees' dental work that he never completed, this constituted theft by unauthorized control over the city's money.[82]

The obtaining or exertion of control must be *unauthorized*.[83] Essentially, this means the defendant must have taken the property without the owner's consent.[84]

Finally, the defendant must assume *control* over the item in question. The taking of articles with intent to steal, however brief the taking, will constitute theft.[85] The fact that the owner recovers the property,[86] is recompensed for his or her loss,[87] or receives restitution from the accused[88] does not extinguish the theft.

Mere association with an item[89] or mere possession of the item[90] does not, without more, furnish proof of theft. However, evidence of recent, exclusive, and unexplained possession of stolen property — either singly or jointly with

[81] People v. Kinion, 105 Ill. App. 3d 1069, 1071-72, 435 N.E.2d 533, 535-36 (3d Dist. 1982), *cert. denied*, 460 U.S. 1014 (1983). *See also* People v. Ortiz, 170 Ill. App. 3d 1083, 1087-88, 524 N.E.2d 1050, 1053 (1st Dist. 1988) (state need not show defendant actually took video and stereo equipment stolen in a burglary but only that defendant knowingly exerted unauthorized control over the property).

[82] People v. Berke, 236 Ill. App 3d 322, 328-28, 603 N.E.2d 737, 742 (1st Dist. 1992).

[83] People v. Miller, 24 Ill. App. 3d 504, 508, 321 N.E.2d 109, 112 (5th Dist. 1974).

[84] People v. Curoe, 97 Ill. App. 3d 258, 273, 422 N.E.2d 931, 942 (1st Dist. 1981).

[85] People v. Graydon, 38 Ill. App. 3d 792, 794, 349 N.E.2d 127, 129 (4th Dist. 1976).

[86] People v. Gant, 121 Ill. App. 2d 222, 225, 257 N.E.2d 181, 183 (1st Dist. 1970).

[87] People v. Reans, 20 Ill. App. 3d 1005, 1008, 313 N.E.2d 184, 187 (3d Dist. 1974); *See also* People v. Davis, 169 Ill. App. 3d 1, 6, 523 N.E.2d 165, 167 (2d Dist. 1988) (defendant's conviction for theft affirmed where defendant made belated attempt to return stolen gun after having retained gun for ten months).

[88] People v. Campbell, 28 Ill. App. 3d 480, 491, 328 N.E.2d 608, 616 (5th Dist. 1975).

[89] People v. Davis, 69 Ill. App. 2d 120, 125, 216 N.E.2d 490, 493 (1st Dist. 1966); *See also* People v. Modlin, 74 Ill. App. 3d 387, 390-91, 393 N.E.2d 5, 7-8 (4th Dist. 1979) (instructing jury that if it found defendant had exclusive possession of recently stolen items, they could infer defendant's involvement in theft was an improper instruction where items in question were found in back seat of squad car 20 hours after defendant transported in squad car).

[90] People v. Ems, 81 Ill. App. 3d 574, 578, 401 N.E.2d 1336, 1339 (3d Dist. 1980).

others — may raise an inference[91] or a presumption[92] of involvement in the theft so long as there exists other corroborating evidence of guilt.[93] However, where there has been a theft of various items, the unexplained exclusive possession of part of the stolen items will not necessarily give rise to an inference that the accused stole all of the property in question.[94] A defendant's possession of stolen items may be too remote from the time of the commission of the theft to support the inference that he or she stole the goods at an earlier time.[95] In such a case, the trier of fact determines, without employing this inference, whether the defendant stole the items at an earlier time.

Where a defendant is found in exclusive possession of a stolen item and attempts to explain it in an exculpatory fashion, the courts say he or she must "tell a reasonable story," or have his or her explanation be "judged by its improbabilities."[96] Clearly, the jury does not have to accept the defendant's explanation.[97] On the other hand, because the government shoulders the burden of proving the defendant's guilt, the defendant's refusal to offer an explanation is not by itself *conclusive* evidence of guilt at his or her trial.[98]

One final point must be made regarding the element of control: the exertion of control over the stolen item must involve the objective of *permanent deprivation*

---

[91] Rugendorf v. United States, 376 U.S. 528, 536-37, *reh'g denied*, 377 U.S. 940 (1964); People v. Reynolds, 27 Ill. 2d 523, 525-26, 190 N.E.2d 301, 302 (1963). There are many cases that have used this inference. *See, e.g.,* People v. Johnson, 64 Ill. App. 3d 1018, 1020, 382 N.E.2d 85, 86 (1st Dist. 1978); People v. Tribett, 54 Ill. App. 3d 777, 780, 370 N.E.2d 115, 117 (1st Dist. 1978).

[92] People v. Baynes, 87 Ill. App. 3d 1000, 1009, 410 N.E.2d 894, 901 (5th Dist.), *rev'd on other grounds*, 88 Ill. 2d 225, 430 N.E.2d 1070 (1980).

[93] People v. Housby, 84 Ill. 2d 415, 421, 420 N.E.2d 151, 154, *cert. denied*, 454 U.S. 845 (1981) (upholding inference, but clarifying that guilt cannot be based solely on such inference; other facts and circumstances must exist which corroborate defendant's guilt).

[94] People v. Depper, 89 Ill. App. 3d 135, 137, 411 N.E.2d 543, 545 (4th Dist. 1980) (will support inference). *But see* People v. Johnson, 96 Ill. App. 3d 1123, 1125, 422 N.E.2d 19, 21-22 (2d Dist. 1981) (where only proof that defendant stole victim's property was his unexplained possession of part of it, to-wit, property having only a nominal value allegedly taken during a burglary involving $1200 of loss, conviction of only misdemeanor and not felony theft was proper on theory that possession of part of the property that had only a nominal value showed defendant stole only that part of the property).

[95] People v. Jones, 97 Ill. App. 3d 619, 623, 423 N.E.2d 235, 239 (1st Dist. 1981) (although not too remote in case at hand).

[96] People v. Ortiz, 170 Ill. App. 3d 1083, 1088, 524 N.E.2d 1050, 1053 (1st Dist. 1988); People v. Ward, 31 Ill. App. 3d 1022, 1025, 335 N.E.2d 57, 60 (2d Dist. 1975).

[97] People v. Burris, 116 Ill. App. 2d 79, 83, 253 N.E.2d 628, 630 (1st Dist. 1969), *cert. denied*, 400 U.S. 835 (1970). *See also* People v. Brown, 163 Ill. App. 3d 976, 978-79, 516 N.E.2d 1349, 1351-52 (4th Dist. 1987) (where state's evidence is uncontradicted because defendant offers no evidence, inference of theft based on defendant's conduct proper).

[98] People v. Boulahanis, 50 Ill. App. 2d 440, 441, 200 N.E.2d 372, 373 (1st Dist. 1964).

from the owner. It does not include the taking of property with the intent to use it temporarily where it is thereafter returned to the owner.[99]

§ 11.07.— Obtains Control by Deception: Alternative Element of Theft — Actus Reus (2).

The second method of obtaining control over an item for purposes of theft involves the use of deception. The previous discussion of the terms *obtain* and *control* provides guidance concerning the appropriate use of these terms. Where the theft is by *deception*, the primary inquiry will involve determining what constitutes "deception."

Generally, the courts state there exist three critical elements in theft by deception: (1) the theft victim owned or possessed the property, (2) the accused knowingly obtained by deception control over the owner's property, and (3) the accused acted with intent to permanently deprive the owner of the use and benefit of his or her property.[100] *Deception* within the meaning of the "theft by deception" proscription is defined as knowingly creating or confirming an impression that is false and that the offender does not believe to be true.[101] Thus, where a contractor, with limited experience at building homes, agreed to build a home for $100,000, when in reality it would cost considerably more to do so, he lacked the intent to defraud necessary for theft by deception because the problem was in fact a product of his ineptitude.[102] One who accomplishes theft by deception clearly obtains "unauthorized control" over the stolen object even though the statutory subsection on theft by deception merely refers to obtaining "by deception control" without including the word *unauthorized*.[103]

In *People v. Ballard*,[104] the defendants set up a fraudulent scheme involving the sale of tool distributorships to purchasers, who the defendants referred to as "investors." Here, there was sufficient evidence of theft by deception inasmuch as the evidence showed that the defendants never intended to fulfill their promises to the so-called investors to (1) furnish locations in high-volume retail outlets to sell tools and other merchandise, and (2) furnish tools and other merchandise of the same high quality that they had demonstrated to the purchasers initially.[105] Also, the defendants had failed to refund the investment within one

---

[99] People v. Fragale, 2 Ill. App. 3d 992, 276 N.E.2d 139 (3d Dist. 1971) (abstract).

[100] People v. Gunn, 112 Ill. App. 3d 1011, 1013, 446 N.E.2d 281, 283 (3d Dist. 1983); People v. Puleo, 96 Ill. App. 3d 457, 460-61, 421 N.E.2d 367, 369-70 (1st Dist. 1981).

[101] People v. Wurster, 83 Ill. App. 3d 399, 403, 403 N.E.2d 1306, 1310 (3d Dist. 1980).

[102] People v. Reich, 241 Ill. App. 3d 666, 671-72, 610 N.E.2d 124, 127-28 (3d Dist. 1993).

[103] People v. Fowler, 72 Ill. App. 3d 491, 492-95, 390 N.E.2d 1377, 1378-80 (4th Dist. 1979); People v. Muskgrave, 60 Ill. App. 3d 742, 744, 377 N.E.2d 595, 597 (4th Dist. 1978).

[104] 65 Ill. App. 3d 831, 382 N.E.2d 800 (2d Dist. 1978), *cert. denied*, 444 U.S. 925 (1979).

[105] People v. Ballard, 65 Ill. App. 3d 831, 836, 382 N.E.2d 800, 805 (2d Dist. 1978), *cert. denied*, 444 U.S. 925 (1979).

year of the time the investors decided to cancel their involvement.[106] Finally, the defendants' effort to infer that the theft victims' losses came about from their own over-enthusiasm or business naivete was rejected by the court.[107] It thus appears that a defense based on caveat emptor will not prevail in the state of Illinois with respect to theft by deception.

The following situations constituted theft by deception: where a defendant filed a false workers' compensation claim,[108] where a defendant tendered a check knowing he had insufficient funds in his bank account;[109] where a defendant received a check from the owner in exchange for a television that he failed to deliver;[110] where a defendant under an assumed name bid an unduly high price on property at an auction and left with the property without paying for it;[111] and where certain victims gave a defendant money because of their confidence in his patently fraudulent statements that they would later receive much larger sums of money in return.[112] Thus, obtaining valuable consideration by means of a "confidence game,"[113] or what was previously referred to as "false pretenses,"[114] is now theft by deception.

Where the alleged victim of theft by deception is not actually deceived by the defendant, there is no theft.[115] In other words, where the alleged victim of a theft realizes the accused's representations are false, there is no deception. Thus, where a defendant advised a person, who was a friend and a manager of property of a prison inmate, as well as an undercover agent that he could gain an early release of the inmate for $5000 based on his connection with a federal judge and the governor, which the person and officer knew was false, there was no theft by deception when the agent handed marked money to the defendant.[116]

Where the defendant, a carpet store owner, filed for bankruptcy several days after accepting customers' payments on carpeting contracts, there was no theft

---

[106] People v. Ballard, 65 Ill. App. 3d 831, 836, 382 N.E.2d 800, 805 (2d Dist. 1978), cert. denied, 444 U.S. 925 (1979).

[107] People v. Ballard, 65 Ill. App. 3d 831, 836, 382 N.E.2d 800, 805 (2d Dist. 1978), cert. denied, 444 U.S. 925 (1979).

[108] People v. Wurster, 83 Ill. App. 3d 399, 403, 403 N.E.2d 1306, 1310 (3d Dist. 1980).

[109] People v. Reans, 20 Ill. App. 3d 1005, 1007-08, 313 N.E.2d 184, 186-87 (3d Dist. 1974).

[110] People v. Leonard, 18 Ill. App. 3d 527, 530, 310 N.E.2d 15, 18 (4th Dist. 1974).

[111] People v. Muskgrave, 60 Ill. App. 3d 742, 744-45, 377 N.E.2d 595, 597-98 (4th Dist. 1978).

[112] People v. Gipson, 29 Ill. 2d 336, 340, 194 N.E.2d 318, 321 (1963).

[113] People v. Gipson, 29 Ill. 2d 336, 340, 194 N.E.2d 318, 321 (1963).

[114] People v. Gruber, 362 Ill. 278, 285-86, 200 N.E. 483, 487 (1936) (relying on ILL. REV. STAT. ch. 38, § 253 (1935)).

[115] People v. Davis, 112 Ill. 2d 55, 62-3, 491 N.E.2d 1153, 1156-57 (1986). See also People v. Gordon, 45 Ill. App. 3d 282, 285-86, 359 N.E.2d 794, 795-96 (1st Dist. 1977) (defendant's conviction for theft by deception reversed where evidence showed party bought auto from defendant with knowledge of existence of lien on auto).

[116] People v. Davis, 112 Ill. 2d 55, 62-3, 491 N.E.2d 1153, 1156-57 (1986).

by deception.[117] Here, the appellate court found that the defendant at the time of the sale of the carpeting lacked the intent to obtain the customers' funds without supplying the carpeting, notwithstanding the fact that the customers never received the carpeting or a refund.[118]

It is noteworthy that some cases prosecuted as theft by deception would logically seem to fall into another category of theft. For instance, a defendant's placement of a stolen ham into a wife's purse while they were in a grocery store was considered theft by deception,[119] but it appears that this offense would have been more appropriately viewed as simple theft under subsection 5/16-1(a).

§ 11.08.— Obtains by Threat Control: Alternative Element of Theft — Actus Reus (3).

The third scenario that can give rise to theft occurs where the accused obtains control over property by means of a *threat*. This theft provision is perhaps the least employed because it closely parallels "robbery." Robbery exists where the defendant "takes property, except a motor vehicle . . ., from the person or presence of another by the use of force or by threatening the imminent use of force."[120] Robbery is normally used by the state instead of theft to prosecute a taking by threat because it is a more serious crime.[121] By definition, however, robbery requires a show of *force* or the *threat of an imminent use of force,* while theft does not, so the use of force or intimidation common to robbery represents one difference between it and theft.[122] Theft also differs from robbery because it requires a specific intent to steal or knowledge that what was received was stolen, which robbery does not.[123] A purse snatching could amount to a theft by threat.[124] Where a defendant removed the victim's wallet from his pocket and removed valuables from the wallet, this was theft by threat.[125] The statutory definition of the term *threat* suggests other possible situations in which theft by threat would exist — where the circumstances could not amount to robbery —

---

[117] People v. Glidewell, 251 Ill. App. 3d 312, 317-20, 621 N.E.2d 924, 927-29 (4th Dist. 1993).

[118] People v. Glidewell, 251 Ill. App. 3d 312, 317-20, 621 N.E.2d 924, 927-29 (4th Dist. 1993).

[119] People v. Johnson, 59 Ill. App. 3d 115, 117-18, 376 N.E.2d 8, 10-11 (1st Dist. 1978).

[120] 720 ILCS 5/18-1(a) (1999). *See* ch. 12 of this treatise for a discussion of robbery.

[121] Theft of property from a person is a class 3 felony (720 ILCS 5/16-1(b)(4) (1999)) while robbery is a class 2 felony unless the victim is 60 years of age or older or a physically handicapped person, in which case it is a class 1 felony (720 ILCS 5/18-1(b) (1999)).

[122] People v. Carlton, 31 Ill. App. 3d 313, 315, 333 N.E.2d 596, 598 (1st Dist. 1975).

[123] People v. Yanders, 32 Ill. App. 3d 599, 602-03, 335 N.E.2d 801, 804 (4th Dist. 1975). *See also* People v. Jones, 149 Ill. 2d 288, 297, 595 N.E.2d 1071, 1075 (1992) ("either intent, knowledge or recklessness is an element of robbery. . . .").

[124] People v. Moore, 11 Ill. App. 3d 459, 297 N.E.2d 375 (1st Dist. 1973) (abstract).

[125] People v. Davis, 90 Ill. App. 2d 1, 3-4, 234 N.E.2d 367, 368 (1st Dist. 1967).

for example, where the defendant merely threatens the person's reputation, credit, or business in order to gain what does not belong to him or her.[126]

§ 11.09.— Obtains Control over Property Knowing It to Be Stolen: Alternative Element of Theft — Actus Reus (4).

The fourth option the state has to prove theft is to demonstrate that the accused obtained "control over stolen property knowing the property to have been stolen or under such circumstances as would reasonably induce him to believe that the property was stolen."[127] This subsection obviously covers what is commonly referred to as "receiving stolen property,"[128] but it is technically considered "theft,"[129] since the former is not a separate offense in Illinois. Thus, a wrongful *taking* and a wrongful *receipt* should be viewed as distinct ways of establishing theft.[130]

Under the earlier language of this statute, it was essential to prove that the property was in fact stolen "by another" other than the accused and that the accused knew it was stolen, but this is no longer the case.[131] It is not necessary for the state to establish exactly how the theft occurred, since the unexplained possession of recently stolen goods is sufficient to infer guilt.[132] Because of these considerations, one cannot be convicted of both theft and the receipt of that property once stolen.[133]

A person who innocently receives stolen property and thereafter learns it is stolen can still be convicted of theft if he or she decides to retain it knowing its true character.[134] Possession of recently stolen goods not satisfactorily explained ordinarily supports an inference that the person in possession knew they were stolen.[135]

---

[126] 720 ILCS 5/15-5 (1999).

[127] 720 ILCS 5/16-1(a)(4) (1999).

[128] People v. Fowler, 72 Ill. App. 3d 491, 494, 390 N.E.2d 1377, 1379-80 (4th Dist. 1979); People v. Gray, 61 Ill. App. 3d 243, 245, 377 N.E.2d 1311, 1313 (4th Dist. 1978).

[129] People v. Fowler, 72 Ill. App. 3d 491, 494, 390 N.E.2d 1377, 1379-80 (4th Dist. 1979).

[130] People v. Thompson, 35 Ill. App. 3d 105, 108, 340 N.E.2d 631, 632-33 (1st Dist. 1975).

[131] People v. Dabrowski, 162 Ill. App. 3d 684, 690-91, 515 N.E.2d 1345, 1349-50 (2d Dist. 1987) (referring to 1984 amendment which deleted words "by another").

[132] People v. Loveless, 93 Ill. App. 3d 293, 297, 417 N.E.2d 206, 210 (3d Dist. 1981).

[133] People v. Horton, 126 Ill. App. 2d 401, 406-07, 261 N.E.2d 693, 695 (1st Dist. 1970).

[134] People v. Dickerson, 21 Ill. App. 3d 977, 979-80, 316 N.E.2d 519, 522 (2d Dist. 1974), rev'd on other grounds, 61 Ill. 2d 580, 338 N.E.2d 184 (1975).

[135] People v. Johnson, 13 Ill. App. 3d 1020, 1024-25, 304 N.E.2d 681, 685 (4th Dist. 1973), cert. denied, 419 U.S. 865 (1974); Compare People v. Perkins, 115 Ill. App. 3d 423, 425, 450 N.E.2d 818, 819 (1st Dist. 1983) (defendant's conviction reversed where State did not show defendant received stolen clothing from another knowing or under conditions where she would have known clothing was stolen).

The possession of stolen goods that is the basis of a theft conviction can be either constructive or actual.[136] Where the contraband is found in an area under the defendant's exclusive control and dominion, the defendant can be convicted of this type of theft.[137] Where the possession is joint possession, the charge is not defeated.[138]

Conviction for theft based on receipt of stolen property can be demonstrated by circumstantial evidence.[139] Thus, the accused's guilty knowledge was shown where the circumstantial evidence revealed, among other things, a substantial differential in what the defendant paid for goods, $200, and what they were worth, $700.[140] Where the defendant bought items for $15.00 from a stranger and then tried to sell them for more than three times what he paid, this was sufficient for threat by receiving stolen property, since the defendant made no inquiry about whether the stranger was engaged in a legitimate business.[141] The failure on the part of a defendant to inquire into the source of an item or the seller's proof of title suggests guilty knowledge.[142]

§ 11.10.— Or Obtains or Exerts Control Over Property in Custody of Law Enforcement Agency Which Has Been Represented to be Stolen: Alternative Element of Theft — Actus Reus (5).

Where a person takes control over property in the custody of a law enforcement agency in circumstances where it was explicitly represented to him by an agent of the law enforcement establishment to be stolen, he or she commits theft.[143] Presumably, this code provision is designed to allow a conviction for theft in circumstances where stolen property has been retrieved by the police and the defendant knows that the property was previously stolen and would argue that is legally impossible to re-steal what has already been stolen from its true owner.

At one time, subsection (a)(5) stood alone in 5/16-1 without an accompanying mens rea. In *People v. Zaremba*,[144] the Illinois Supreme Court struck down sub-

---

[136] People v. Mertens, 77 Ill. App. 3d 791, 795, 396 N.E.2d 595, 600 (2d Dist. 1979). *See* ch. 2 of this treatise for a complete discussion of "constructive possession."

[137] People v. Mertens, 77 Ill. App. 3d 791, 795, 396 N.E.2d 595, 600 (2d Dist. 1979) (conviction based on (a)(1)).

[138] People v. Mertens, 77 Ill. App. 3d 791, 795, 396 N.E.2d 595, 600 (2d Dist. 1979).

[139] People v. Ems, 81 Ill. App. 3d 574, 578, 401 N.E.2d 1336, 1339 (3d Dist. 1980) (conviction based on (a)(1) but receipt of stolen property "cases are analagous").

[140] People v. McCormick, 92 Ill. App. 2d 6, 14, 235 N.E.2d 832, 836 (1st Dist. 1968).

[141] People v. West, 60 Ill. App. 3d 570, 571-72, 377 N.E.2d 124, 125-26 (1st Dist. 1978).

[142] People v. Ems, 81 Ill. App. 3d 574, 578, 401 N.E.2d 1336, 1339 (3d Dist. 1980).

[143] 720 ILCS 5/16-1(a)(5) (1999).

[144] 158 Ill. 2d 36, 630 N.E.2d 797 (1994).

section (a)(5) as unconstitutional.[145] Because this subsection provided for guilt without proof of a culpable mental state, the court held it was violative of the due process clauses of the state and federal constitutions.[146] Subsequently, the Illinois legislature revised the theft statute so that subsection (a)(5) would be read in conjunction with the alternate mens rea provisions; thus, the statutory infirmity addressed in *Zaremba* no longer exists.[147]

§ 11.11.— Control Over Property: Element of Theft.

Under the common law, any personal property capable of individual ownership with an intrinsic value and a corporeal existence could be the subject of larceny.[148] The current Illinois Criminal Code has dramatically expanded the scope of what is meant by *property* by simply stating that "'property' means anything of value."[149] This type of definition avoids the pitfall of having the theft of services,[150] such as hopping a rapid transit turnstile or the theft of cable television service,[151] for example, go unpunished. However, some Illinois decisions may insist, consistent with larceny, that while the test is "not whether the property is corporeal or incorporeal or intangible" but rather whether it is "capable of being taken and carried away by someone other than the owner,"[152] a conclusion that belies the obvious legislative effort to avoid the narrow larceny definition of property. In any event, these more marginal situations involving "property" are covered either by the statutory definition of property or by the other theft offenses yet to be explored; accordingly, they warrant no further discussion here.

§ 11.12.— Of the Owner: Element of Theft.

It is essential to prove that there was an unauthorized taking of property from "the owner."[153] Proof that one other than the accused owns or has a superior property interest in the property allegedly stolen is an essential element of the offense of theft.[154] This type of proof is generally made by having the owner testify about the fact of (1) ownership and (2) lack of consent to the taking. Not all crime victims can be expected to have positive proof of ownership — sales

---

[145] People v. Zaremba, 158 Ill. 2d 36, 43, 630 N.E.2d 797, 800 (1994).

[146] People v. Zaremba, 158 Ill. 2d 36, 630 N.E.2d 797 (1994).

[147] Pub. Act 89-377 (1995).

[148] 52A C.J.S. *Larceny* § 2(b) (1968).

[149] 720 ILCS 5/15-1 (1999).

[150] 720 ILCS 5/16-3(a) (1999).

[151] 720 ILCS 5/16-10 (1999).

[152] People v. Zakarian, 121 Ill. App. 3d 968, 972-73, 460 N.E.2d 422, 426 (1st Dist. 1984) (rights to sound recordings not property for purposes of 5/15-1 definition).

[153] People v. Brown, 56 Ill. App. 3d 348, 350-51, 371 N.E.2d 982, 984-85 (1st Dist. 1977).

[154] People v. Taylor, 207 Ill. App. 3d 206, 207, 565 N.E.2d 749, 750 (3d Dist. 1991).

slips and serial numbers — and thus, the owner's failure to identify his or her property in such a manner will not prove fatal to the state's case.[155]

Theft is an offense against possession, and not necessarily legal title.[156] This being the case, it would not be essential in an auto theft case, for instance, to have a bank official of a bank that has extended a car loan to the auto theft victim, who thereby retains actual title, testify because the purchaser of the car has legal possession. Similarly, evidence of an agency or bailment that demonstrates legal possession would allow the agent or bailee to testify on lack of consent to the taking.[157] Thus, an airline representative, as bailee, could testify that the defendant stole a suitcase from an airport luggage conveyer belt.[158]

The fact that a property owner is now deceased does not render it impossible to show lack of consent; his or her estate continues after death.[159] Where a defendant was convicted of murder, armed robbery, concealment of a homicidal death, and theft arising from one incident, the defendant was not be relieved of liability for theft from the victim, who may have been dead at the time of the theft, simply because the victim was no longer able to testify.[160] The relaxed rules regarding ownership reflected in the statutory definition belie a defendant's inventive arguments regarding a victim's alleged lack of ownership.[161]

Historically, prosecuting theft was more complicated when the victim of a theft was a corporation. Formerly, in order to prove ownership by a corporation, the state had to submit proof of the victim's corporate existence. This required introduction of the corporate charter and evidence of the exercise of corporate powers, or oral testimony regarding both.[162] Later, it was held that in the absence of evidence to the contrary, the existence of a corporation could be shown by the direct oral testimony of a person with the requisite knowledge.[163] Furthermore, judicial notice was taken of the corporate existence of major concerns, such as J.C. Penney.[164] Finally, in 1980, the Illinois Supreme Court held, in the case of *In re W.S.*,[165] that since *owner* is broadly defined in Illinois, proof of the

---

[155] People v. Mertens, 77 Ill. App. 3d 791, 797, 396 N.E.2d 595, 601-02 (2d Dist. 1979).

[156] People v. Woods, 15 Ill. App. 3d 221, 223, 303 N.E.2d 562, 564 (5th Dist. 1973).

[157] People v. Demos, 3 Ill. App. 3d 284, 286, 278 N.E.2d 89, 90 (1st Dist. 1971).

[158] People v. Demos, 3 Ill. App. 3d 284, 286, 278 N.E.2d 89, 90 (1st Dist. 1971).

[159] People v. Curoe, 97 Ill. App. 3d 258, 265-66, 422 N.E.2d 931, 936-37 (1st Dist. 1981) (indictment not fatally defective, where administrator of estate charged with theft by embezzlement, because it failed to identify "owners" of estate; ten living heirs were named which was all that was required; conviction reversed on other grounds).

[160] People v. Wright, 109 Ill. App. 3d 137, 138-39, 440 N.E.2d 385, 386-87 (3d Dist. 1982).

[161] *Cf.* People v. Wright, 109 Ill. App. 3d 137, 138-39, 440 N.E.2d 385, 388 (3d Dist. 1982).

[162] People v. Gordon, 5 Ill. 2d 91, 95, 125 N.E.2d 73, 76 (1955).

[163] People v. McGuire, 35 Ill. 2d 219, 230-32, 220 N.E.2d 447, 455-56 (1966), *appeal after remand*, 39 Ill. 2d 244, 234 N.E.2d 772, *cert. denied*, 393 U.S. 884 (1968).

[164] People v. Ferraro, 79 Ill. App. 3d 465, 469-71, 398 N.E.2d 1001, 1004-05 (2d Dist. 1979).

[165] 81 Ill. 2d 252, 408 N.E.2d 718 (1980).

corporate existence of a company is no longer an element of theft from that company.[166] Thus, the testimony of an assistant manager of a retail store[167] or a store security guard[168] that there was a theft from the store will now clearly be sufficient to prove theft from the corporation's store.

Although proof of ownership and lack of consent are essential elements to the crime of theft, ownership need not be alleged in an indictment. For example, where the defendant, administrator of an estate, was accused of the theft of the estate assets and where the interests of ten living heirs were specifically set forth in the indictment, the failure to identify the parties as "owners" did not render the indictment fatally defective.[169]

The reason for the courts' insistence on proof of ownership and lack of consent serves several purposes. First, it protects a defendant against the possibility of successive prosecutions and double jeopardy.[170] Second, it assures that the item was neither abandoned nor owned by the accused.[171] Third, it is essential to demonstrate that it was taken from the person who in fact owned it.[172] Fourth, it is necessary to prove that the item was taken from an entity capable of owning property.[173]

§ 11.13.— And Intends to Deprive the Owner Permanently of the Use or Benefit of the Property: Alternative Element of Theft — Mens Rea (1).

The general theft statute in section 5/16-1 not only sets out five alternative actus reus requirements, any one of which will satisfy the "act" requirement for theft, it also specifies three *alternative* mental state requirements, any one of which will make the workings of the theft offense operable. Specifically, the state must offer sufficient proof that the defendant knowingly obtained control over the property of the owner and

(A) [i]ntends to deprive the owner permanently of the use or benefit of the property; or

(B) [k]nowingly uses, conceals or abandons the property in such manner as to deprive the owner permanently of such use or benefit; or

---

[166] In re W.S., 81 Ill. 2d 252, 254-57, 408 N.E.2d 718, 720-22 (1980).

[167] People v. Watts, 76 Ill. App. 3d 791, 794, 395 N.E.2d 199, 201-02 (2d Dist. 1979).

[168] People v. Tate, 87 Ill. 2d 134, 150, 429 N.E.2d 470, 479 (1981). *See also* People v. McAllister, 31 Ill. App. 3d 825, 829-30, 334 N.E.2d 885, 889-90 (1st Dist. 1975) (testimony of security guard sufficient).

[169] People v. Curoe, 97 Ill. App. 3d 258, 265-66, 422 N.E.2d 931, 936-37 (1st Dist. 1981) (reversed on other grounds).

[170] People v. Irons, 39 Ill. App. 3d 993, 996, 350 N.E.2d 754, 757 (5th Dist. 1976).

[171] People v. McAllister, 31 Ill. App. 3d 825, 826, 334 N.E.2d 885, 887 (1st Dist. 1975).

[172] People v. McAllister, 31 Ill. App. 3d 825, 826, 334 N.E.2d 885, 887 (1st Dist. 1975).

[173] People v. Sims, 29 Ill. App. 3d 815, 817-18, 331 N.E.2d 178, 179 (1st Dist. 1975).

(C) [u]ses, conceals, or abandons the property knowing such use, concealment or abandonment probably will deprive the owner permanently of such
use or benefit;[174]

These alternative mens rea provisions are clearly interpreted by the Illinois
courts to apply to all forms of theft.[175] The "intent to deprive" requirement is
viewed as nothing less than a specific intent requirement.[176] As with specific
intent generally,[177] the intent to deprive can be shown by circumstantial evidence.[178] Because of this specific intent mandate, this offense lends itself to the
usual defenses that are available for crimes with such a mens rea — for instance,
voluntary intoxication.[179]

The intent to deprive should in no way be construed so as to require a specific
demand for money because such a demand is not an essential ingredient of theft
by threat.[180] The intent to exercise control and to permanently deprive must be
present at the time of the unauthorized control; but once there is this merger of
control and intent to deprive, the subsequent abandonment of intent will still
support a conviction.[181]

Reliance on the use of circumstantial evidence to infer the necessary intent for
theft is perhaps most evident where the theft is based on possession of stolen
property or on receipt of stolen property. The Illinois courts consider the totality
of circumstances: the recentness of the theft, the kind of explanation offered by
the defendant, and the salability of the particular stolen property.[182] To illustrate,
a gun is relatively simple to sell, and the intent to permanently deprive the
owner cannot be inferred from mere possession four months after the gun was
stolen.[183] The recentness of the theft constitutes the most important factor in the

---

[174] 720 ILCS 5/16-1 (1999).

[175] People v. Ballard, 65 Ill. App. 3d 831, 833-34, 382 N.E.2d 800, 803-04 (2d Dist. 1978), *cert.
denied*, 444 U.S. 925 (1979) (theft by deception); People v. Yanders, 32 Ill. App. 3d 599, 602-03,
335 N.E.2d 801, 804 (4th Dist. 1975) (intent to permanently deprive lacking for theft by threat).

[176] People v. Yanders, 32 Ill. App. 3d 599, 600, 335 N.E.2d 801, 803 (4th Dist. 1975).

[177] *See* ch. 2 of this treatise for an extensive discussion of "specific intent."

[178] People v. Soskims, 128 Ill. App. 3d 564, 571, 470 N.E.2d 643, 648 (2d Dist. 1984); People
v. Ballard, 65 Ill. App. 3d 831, 836, 382 N.E.2d 800, 805 (2d Dist. 1978), *cert. denied*, 444 U.S.
925 (1979).

[179] People v. Hayes, 173 Ill. App. 3d 1043, 1047-48, 527 N.E.2d 1342, 1346-47 (5th Dist.
1988); People v. Brabson, 54 Ill. App. 3d 134, 136, 369 N.E.2d 346, 347-48 (3d Dist. 1977).

[180] People v. Bonner, 43 Ill. App. 2d 42, 47, 192 N.E.2d 568, 570 (1st Dist. 1963).

[181] People v. Davis, 70 Ill. App. 3d 454, 456-57, 388 N.E.2d 887, 889-90 (1st Dist. 1979) (conviction for attempted theft affirmed where defendant opened cash register with criminal intent and
then closed it upon realization of being observed).

[182] *See* People v. Malin, 372 Ill. 422, 427-28, 24 N.E.2d 349, 351-52 (1939) (factors to consider
when determining recency of possession include time, circumstances and character of goods, salability, and whether goods are cumbersome or easily portable).

[183] People v. Taylor, 25 Ill. 2d 79, 81-2, 182 N.E.2d 654, 656 (1962) (burglary context).

totality of the circumstances test.[184] There exists no hard-and-fast rule about when possession ceases to be recent,[185] but if reasonably recent, it can be inferred that the possessor is either the thief or is aware of the nature of the property, and the defendant has the responsibility to rebut this inference.[186] It should be noted that while the remoteness of the possession weakens the inference of guilt, it does not prevent its operation.[187] On the other hand, it is important to keep in mind that the inference of intent to commit theft based on recent, unexplained possession of proceeds of a theft must be corroborated by other evidence.[188]

Not only must there be intent to deprive, there must be proof of the accused's ambition to deprive *permanently*.[189] In the case of *People v. Curoe*,[190] the defendant maintained that because he executed promissory notes to the estate from which he had misappropriated $400,000, he lacked the requisite intent *and* had not permanently deprived the estate of the money. However, the appellate court found that since he had transferred interests in the estate property to himself without the consent of the probate court or the heirs, and had subjected that property to the claims of others than the rightful owners, the defendant intended to permanently deprive the heirs of their property.[191] On the other hand, where a defendant took a motor vehicle without the intent to permanently deprive the owner of it, he could not be convicted of theft, although he could have been convicted of a motor vehicle code violation not involving an intent to permanently deprive.[192]

---

[184] People v. Taylor, 25 Ill. 2d 79, 81-2, 182 N.E.2d 654, 656 (1962).

[185] People v. Nixon, 414 Ill. 125, 131, 111 N.E.2d 116, 119 (1953).

[186] *See, e.g.*, People v. Heard, 80 Ill. App. 3d 701, 706-07, 400 N.E.2d 65, 68-9 (1st Dist. 1980) (within minutes of theft, defendant's unexplained possession of stolen items provided inference of defendant's guilt of theft); People v. Tribett, 54 Ill. App. 3d 777, 781-82, 370 N.E.2d 115, 118 (1st Dist. 1977) (defendant's apprehension with stolen typewriters one day after theft sufficiently recent); People v. Donald, 132 Ill. App. 2d 598, 600, 270 N.E.2d 85, 86 (1st Dist. 1971) (5 days sufficiently recent for theft of auto); People v. Pride, 16 Ill. 2d 82, 91-93, 156 N.E.2d 551, 556-57 (1959) (stating that "recent" possession may be as long as 25 days); People v. Litberg, 413 Ill. 132, 136-38, 108 N.E.2d 468, 470-71 (1952) (three days possession since theft sufficient to infer defendant's guilt); People v. Malin, 372 Ill. 422, 427, 24 N.E.2d 349, 351-52 (1939) (six weeks sufficiently recent).

[187] People v. Kilgore, 33 Ill. App. 3d 557, 560, 338 N.E.2d 124, 127 (2d Dist. 1975).

[188] People v. Housby, 84 Ill. 2d 415, 419-24, 420 N.E.2d 151, 153-55, *cert. denied*, 454 U.S. 845 (1981).

[189] People v. Matthews, 122 Ill. App. 2d 264, 271-72, 258 N.E.2d 378, 382 (2d Dist. 1970) (failure to allege intent to "permanently" deprive in indictment fatally defective).

[190] 97 Ill. App. 3d 258, 422 N.E.2d 931 (1st Dist. 1981).

[191] People v. Curoe, 97 Ill. App. 3d 258, 273-74, 422 N.E.2d 931, 942 (1st Dist. 1981) (reversed on other grounds).

[192] People v. Cramer, 81 Ill. App. 3d 525, 529-30, 401 N.E.2d 644, 648 (3d Dist. 1980), *rev'd on other grounds*, 85 Ill. 2d 92, 421 N.E.2d 189 (1981). *See* 625 ILCS 5/4-103(a) (1993) ("It is a

Finally, section 5/16-1.2 addresses the situation where a person receives payment in advance for a promise to perform services of $3,000 or more and "willfully without good cause fails to substantially perform pursuant to the agreement after taking a downpayment of ten percent or more of the agreed upon consideration."[193] Specifically, if the person, within 45 days after written demand from the promisee, fails to return the down payments, this failure is interpreted as "prima facie evidence of intent" to obtain by deception control of property of another.[194] If the promisee initiated suspension of the services or the promisor responds to the demand in timely fashion, this presumption does not apply.[195]

§ 11.14.— Or Knowingly Uses, Conceals, or Abandons the Property in Such Manner as to Deprive the Owner Permanently of Such Use or Benefit: Alternative Element of Theft — Mens Rea (2).

In some circumstances, a person by his or her one act (1) may intend to deprive the owner permanently of the use of his or her property, (2) may do so by knowingly using and concealing the property, or (3) may use and conceal the property knowing the owner will probably be deprived of its use or benefit.[196] Where it is established that the defendant had the intent to deprive, it follows he or she "knowingly" deprived as well.[197] On the other hand, if evidence supportive of the intent to deprive is lacking, it may be feasible to convict by showing that the defendant had knowledge that his or her taking would result in permanent deprivation.[198]

Normally, the state's charging instrument — the indictment or information — will charge the alleged thief on the theory that he or she had the specific intent to permanently deprive.[199] Why the state so rarely employs the lesser mental state of "knowingly permanently deprives" is unclear. Virtually all of the case-law discussions of the mens rea of "knowledge" for theft pertains to the "know-

---

violation . . . for (a) A person not entitled to the possession of a vehicle or essential part of vehicle to receive, possess, conceal, sell, dispose, or transfer it, knowing it to have been stolen or converted. . . .").

[193] 720 ILCS 5/16-1.2 (1999).

[194] 720 ILCS 5/16-1.2 (1999). *But see* People v. Watts, 181 Ill. 2d 315, 140-50, 692 N.E.2d 315, 319-24 (1998) where the Illinois Supreme Court found a provision in a statute criminalizing home repair fraud, 815 ILCS 515/3(c) (1997), that created a rebuttable presumption that home repair contractor did not intend to perform home repairs, based on a failure to take certain actions that would be indicative of intent to repair, was a violation the due process.

[195] 720 ILCS 5/16-1.2 (1999).

[196] People v. Spera, 10 Ill. App. 3d 305, 310, 293 N.E.2d 656, 659-60 (2d Dist. 1973).

[197] People v. Sherman, 110 Ill. App. 3d 854, 858, 441 N.E.2d 896, 900 (2d Dist. 1982).

[198] 720 ILCS 5/16-1(a)(4)(B) (1999).

[199] People v. Sherman, 110 Ill. App. 3d 854, 858, 441 N.E.2d 896, 900 (2d Dist. 1982).

ingly *obtains*"[200] element of theft that was discussed above.[201] The state's attorney should bear in mind that the theft statute does not necessarily require proof of specific intent to permanently deprive the owner of his or her property, when faced with a situation where evidence of knowledge exists but intent is lacking.

§ 11.15.— Or Uses, Conceals, or Abandons the Property Knowing Such Use, Concealment, or Abandonment Probably Will Deprive the Owner Permanently of Such Use of Benefit: Alternative Element of Theft — Mens Rea (3).

The third alternative mens rea regarding the matter of permanent deprivation involves knowing that the use, concealment, or abandonment will "probably" permanently deprive the owner of his or her property.[202] Like the preceding mental state, this mental state of knowing with a probability is seldom, if ever, employed. But it should not be overlooked in appropriate circumstances by the prosecutorial authority.

§ 11.16.— Lesser Included Offenses and Theft.

As with many other offenses in Illinois, one is forced to consider the problem of (1) lesser included offenses that cannot stand in light of a conviction (or acquittal) on a greater offense, and (2) whether several crimes arose out of the same physical act.[203] First, there are those situations in which theft may be viewed as a lesser included offense of another crime, such as burglary.[204] In *People v. Hamilton*,[205] the Illinois Supreme Court ruled that where (1) a burglary charge by implication describes theft as a possible lesser included offense and (2) the evidence presented at trial suggests that a theft may have occurred but not a burglary, then an instruction on theft should be given to the jury.[206] On this theory, an acquittal of a defendant on burglary would not collaterally estop a jury from finding the defendant guilty of theft.[207] In *Hamilton*, the court disavowed its earlier ruling that theft could not be a lesser included offense of resi-

---

[200] *See, e.g.*, People v. Beauchemin, 71 Ill. App. 3d 102, 105, 389 N.E.2d 580, 584 (3d Dist. 1979).

[201] *See* § 11.05 this chapter.

[202] 720 ILCS 5/16-1(a)(4)(C) (1999).

[203] *See* ch. 1 of this treatise for a discussion of lesser included offenses and the same physical act doctrine.

[204] People v. Hamilton, 179 Ill. 2d 319, 325-28, 688 N.E.2d 1166, 1168-70 (1997).

[205] 179 Ill. 2d 319, 688 N.E.2d 1166 (1997).

[206] People v. Hamilton, 179 Ill. 2d 319, 325-28, 688 N.E.2d 1166, 1168-70 (1997).

[207] People v. Hamilton, 179 Ill. 2d 319, 325-28, 688 N.E.2d 1166, 1168-70 (1997).

dential burglary.[208] Concerning robbery and theft, the Illinois Supreme Court held in another case that theft may be a lesser included offense of robbery.[209] The court reasoned it is imperative that one examine the language of the charging instrument and the evidence presented at trial, not the abstract differences in the definitions of the respective crimes, when one is attempting to assess whether an offense is a lesser included crime of another.[210]

It has been held that a defendant could be convicted for unlawful possession of a controlled substance and theft of a controlled substance,[211] but not for forgery and theft.[212] Theft is not a lesser included offense of attempted murder.[213]

In some cases, it will be argued that another crime is a lesser included offense of theft. While there is not much caselaw on this point, in one case it was held that criminal trespass was *not* a lesser included offense of theft.[214] Also, possession of a stolen motor vehicle has been held not to be a lesser included offense of theft.[215]

§ 11.17.— Single versus Multiple Counts.

Where a defendant by his act simultaneously exerts control over several items of stolen property, he or she is properly charged with only one theft.[216] If a defendant committed theft by threat on two separate victims during one continuous course of conduct, he can be convicted of two separate counts of theft only if the offenses are "distinct and independently motivated."[217] Where there occurs a single theft of an object jointly owned by more than one party, there is only one theft.[218] For example, a defendant could be convicted of only one count of theft despite stealing numerous different items from a residence occupied by separate owners and despite stealing these various items from two separate bedrooms.[219]

---

[208] *See* People v. Schmidt, 126 Ill. 2d 179, 183-84, 533 N.E.2d 898, 900-01 (1988) (defendant could not be convicted of theft, since (1) it was not charged and (2) it could not be considered lesser included offense of residential burglary).

[209] People v. Jones, 149 Ill. 2d 288, 292-301, 595 N.E.2d 1071, 1073-77 (1992).

[210] People v. Jones, 149 Ill. 2d 288, 292-301, 595 N.E.2d 1071, 1073-77 (1992).

[211] People v. Noascono, 80 Ill. App. 3d 921, 925, 400 N.E.2d 720, 723 (5th Dist. 1980).

[212] People v. Rose, 7 Ill. App. 3d 374, 379-80, 287 N.E.2d 195, 199 (2d Dist. 1972).

[213] People v. Weaver, 8 Ill. App. 3d 299, 307-08, 290 N.E.2d 691, 697-98 (1st Dist. 1972).

[214] People v. Rainbolt, 52 Ill. App. 3d 374, 376-77, 367 N.E.2d 293, 294-95 (5th Dist. 1977).

[215] People v. Bryant, 128 Ill. 2d 448, 456-58, 539 N.E.2d 1221, 1225-26 (1989); People v. Ferguson, 204 Ill. App. 3d 146, 153-54, 561 N.E.2d 1118, 1124 (1st Dist. 1990).

[216] People v. Timmons, 233 Ill. App. 3d 591, 595, 599 N.E.2d 162, 165 (2d Dist. 1992) (defendant could only be charged with one theft where he simultaneously exerted control over several different items of stolen property).

[217] People v. Vaini, 33 Ill. App. 3d 246, 248-49, 337 N.E.2d 234, 236 (3d Dist. 1975).

[218] People v. Vaini, 33 Ill. App. 3d 246, 248-49, 337 N.E.2d 234, 236 (3d Dist. 1975).

[219] People v. Fuentes, 172 Ill. App. 3d 874, 877-78, 527 N.E.2d 152, 154-55 (3d Dist. 1988).

The appellate court held that the defendant's actions were not separable with respect to time, place, or the dwellers' separately owned property.[220]

§ 11.18.— Value of Property and Felony Theft Versus Misdemeanor Theft.

Determining the value of stolen property is a material element of the offense of theft when the theft will be prosecuted as a felony.[221] Theft becomes a felony when the value of the property exceeds three hundred dollars.[222] A misdemeanor theft occurs where value does not exceed three hundred dollars, assuming that it is the defendant's first theft offense.[223] Subsequent theft convictions of an accused, regardless of the value of the taking, are felonies.[224] Any theft of property from a *person*, regardless of the property value, is also a felony.[225] Furthermore, a theft of a firearm constitutes a felony regardless of the firearm's value.[226] To sustain a felony conviction for a theft not involving theft from a person, theft of a firearm, *or* subsequent offender theft, the value of the property must be proved beyond a reasonable doubt to exceed the value of three hundred dollars.[227] With respect to felony theft, if the state fails to prove the requisite value of the item, the defendant will stand convicted of misdemeanor theft.[228] Where the theft victim testifies about the original purchase price of the stolen item but no evidence is offered about the item's value at the time and place of the theft, the state has

---

[220] People v. Fuentes, 172 Ill. App. 3d 874, 877-78, 527 N.E.2d 152, 154-55 (3d Dist. 1988).

[221] 720 ILCS 5/16-1(c) (1999). Before the enactment of subsection (c)of 5/16-1, value was not considered a material element. *See* People v. Jackson, 99 Ill. 2d 476, 479, 459 N.E.2d 1362, 1363 (1984).

[222] 720 ILCS 5/16-1(b)(4) (1999).

[223] 720 ILCS 5/16-1(b)(1) (1999).

[224] 720 ILCS 5/16-1(b)(2) (1999) *See also* People v. Hayes, 87 Ill. 2d 95, 98, 429 N.E.2d 490, 491 (1981) (defendant's contention that information regarding felony theft was defective because it failed to charge that offense was second or subsequent theft was rejected; trial court determination that theft was second or subsequent offense was sufficient).

[225] 720 ILCS 5/16-1(b)(4) (1999).

[226] 720 ILCS 5/16-1(b)(3) (1999).

[227] *See* People v. Foster, 199 Ill. App. 3d 372, 391-92, 556 N.E.2d 1289, 1302 (4th Dist. 1990). *Cf.* People v. Traylor, 139 Ill. App. 3d 443, 447, 487 N.E.2d 1040, 1042-43 (1st Dist. 1985) (defendant not prejudiced by instruction that State need only prove value of stolen car was $150 to sustain felony theft conviction, despite statutory requirement that value of property stolen exceed $300, where evidence was uncontradicted that car value exceeded $300).

[228] People v. Burnside, 133 Ill. App. 3d 453, 457-58, 478 N.E.2d 884, 887-88 (3d Dist. 1985) (evidence was sufficient to demonstrate only that defendant had stolen two, not four, car tires and, thus, evidence established guilt of misdemeanor theft). *See also* People v. Dell, 52 Ill. 2d 393, 398-99, 288 N.E.2d 459, 461-62 (1972) (felony theft reversed where minimum value of property not reflected in jury verdict); People v. Stark, 59 Ill. App. 3d 676, 681-84, 375 N.E.2d 826, 830-31 (5th Dist. 1978) (where general verdict form returned by jury reflected guilty of theft without reference to value of property or felony theft, only misdemeanor theft conviction could stand).

not proved a prerequisite for felony theft.[229] Meanwhile, if misdemeanor theft is charged but valuation of the property is not established at trial, it is proper for a court to take judicial notice and conclude on the basis of the evidence before it that the property had "some value."[230]

Value is determined by the fair cash market value of the article at the time and place of its taking.[231] Original cost or replacement cost is not the standard in determining fair cash market value of stolen property.[232] Although some earlier Illinois decisions allowed a court to take judicial notice of the value of allegedly stolen property,[233] an amendment to the theft statute explicitly states that when "theft of property exceeding a specific value" is charged, the value of the property is an element of the offense to be resolved by the trier of fact.[234] It has been held that proof that some of the victim's recently stolen property is in the defendant's possession is not proof that the defendant stole all the property and, thus, proof that the defendant actually had in his possession property valued at less than $300 that was taken in a theft that exceeded $300 will not activate a legal inference that he was involved in *felony* theft.[235]

As stated, Illinois has an enhancement provision that allows a felony conviction for a second or subsequent misdemeanor theft.[236] Where a prior theft conviction elevates an offense from a misdemeanor to a felony, the prior theft conviction is an element of the felony theft that must be alleged and proved at trial.[237]

---

[229] People v. Moore, 109 Ill. App. 3d 874, 877-78, 441 N.E.2d 409, 411 (3d Dist. 1982). *Compare* People v. Richardson, 169 Ill. App. 3d 781, 783-84, 523 N.E.2d 1128, 1129-30 (1st Dist. 1988) (where the aggregate value of various items stolen exceeded $300, a felony theft verdict was proper); People v. Davis, 132 Ill. App. 3d 199, 204, 476 N.E.2d 1311, 1314 (1st Dist. 1985) (insurer's testimony of theft concerning insurance settlement sufficient to establish value of stolen property exceeded $300 and defendant, thus, properly convicted of felony theft).

[230] People v. Sparks, 9 Ill. App. 3d 470, 473, 292 N.E.2d 447, 450 (1st Dist. 1972) (automobile).

[231] People v. Langston, 96 Ill. App. 3d 48, 54, 420 N.E.2d 1090, 1094 (5th Dist. 1981). *Langston* was decided under an earlier statutory structure that required a value of $150 for a felony conviction. *See also* People v. Cobetto, 66 Ill. 2d 488, 491, 363 N.E.2d 854, 855 (1977) (fair cash market value); People v. Harden, 42 Ill. 2d 301, 305-06, 247 N.E.2d 404, 406-07 (1969) (opinion testimony of one who has sufficient knowledge to give estimate of fair cash market value, received without objection, is sufficient in absence of contrary evidence).

[232] People v. Collins, 48 Ill. App. 3d 643, 649, 362 N.E.2d 1118, 1123 (3d Dist. 1977).

[233] *See* People v. Tassone, 41 Ill. 2d 7, 12, 241 N.E.2d 419, 422-23 (1968), *cert. denied*, 394 U.S. 965 (1969) (court took judicial notice of value of a new model truck); People v. Matthews, 205 Ill. App. 3d 371, 409-11, 562 N.E.2d 1113, 1136-37 (1st Dist. 1990) (court took judicial notice that gun, jewelry, cash and drugs taken were worth more than statutory minimum in circumstances where actual cash value of items was not proven).

[234] 720 ILCS 5/16-1(c) (1999).

[235] People v. Johnson, 96 Ill. App. 3d 1123, 1125, 422 N.E.2d 19, 21 (2d Dist. 1981).

[236] 720 ILCS 5/16-1(b)(2) (1999).

[237] People v. Hicks, 119 Ill. 2d 29, 31, 518 N.E.2d 148, 149 (1987).

§ 11.19. Specific Theft Provisions — An Introduction.

Although when enacted in 1961, the theft statutes represented a thorough and comprehensive statutory scheme and gave Illinois a modern criminal theft code, the startling advancements in technology and the concurrent sophistication of the criminal milieu during the past thirty-five years have necessitated updating of the Illinois theft statutes. When the need has arisen, the Illinois legislature has plugged any gaps in the law with very specific legislation. For example, the remarkable increase in the number of coin-operated machines in our society, from laundromats to video arcade games, gave rise to the enactment of section 5/16-5, which makes tampering with such a machine a theft offense. [238] Additionally, when the code was originally enacted in 1961, the General Assembly saw fit to make reference to specific theft situations, such as "theft of labor or services or use of property,"[239] which it apparently felt deserved special consideration given the general terms of the general theft provision. In the interest of clarity, these various provisions beyond section 5/16-1 will be addressed in the order in which they appear in the code.

§ 11.20. Theft by Lessee.

In 1967, the state legislature added a provision now contained in section 5/16-1.1 that can be viewed as a clarification of section 5/16-1. It states that prima facie evidence exists that an individual has knowingly obtained or exerted control over an owner's property wherever the individual has failed to return it to the owner within thirty days following the owner's written demand for the return of the property.[240] The statute further provides that where the owner, after expiration of the lease, gives the lessee written notice by registered mail addressed to the lessee at the address reflected on the lease, this demand is sufficient.[241]

§ 11.21. Financial Exploitation of an Elderly or Disabled Person.

The Illinois legislature has added an offense of "financial exploitation of an elderly or disabled person" to the criminal code.[242] A person commits this of-

---

[238] 720 ILCS 5/16-5 (1999).

[239] 720 ILCS 5/16-3 (1999).

[240] 720 ILCS 5/16-1.1 (1999). *But see* People v. Watts, 181 Ill. 2d 315, 140-50, 692 N.E.2d 315, 319-24 (1998) (provision of home repair fraud act violative of due process where statute created a rebuttable presumption that a home repair contractor had no intent to perform agreed-to home repairs where contractor failed to perform certain predicate acts indicative of an intent to repair). Whether *Watts* raises constitutional problems in other areas where statutes create inferences of criminal intent remains to be seen.

[241] 720 ILCS 5/16-1.1 (1999).

[242] 720 ILCS 5/16-1.3 (1999). *See* People v. Simpson, 268 Ill. App. 3d 305, 315, 643 N.E.2d 1262, 1270 (1st Dist. 1994) (statute not unconstitutionally vague as applied).

fense where he or she "stands in a position of trust and confidence" with an elderly or disabled person and he or she "knowingly and by deception or intimidation obtains control" over that person's property "with the intent to permanently deprive" that person "of the use, benefit, or possession" of his or her property.[243] A person who violates this section commits a felony.[244]

An "elderly person" is defined as someone at least sixty years of age who suffers from a disease or infirmity associated with advanced age and "manifested by physical, mental, or emotional dysfunctioning to the extent that such person is incapable of avoiding or preventing the commission of the offense."[245] A "disabled person" is defined as any person "who suffers from a permanent physical or mental impairment resulting from disease, injury, functional disorder, or congenital condition which renders such person incapable of avoiding or preventing the commission of the offense."[246] "Intimidation" is defined as a communication that threatens the deprivation of the elderly or disabled person's "food and nutrition, shelter, prescribed medication or medical care and treatment."[247] "Deception" is defined as, in addition to its meaning in section 5/15-4 of the code, a "misrepresentation or concealment of a material fact relating to the terms of a contract or agreement," or to an existing or pre-existing condition of the property included in the contract; or the use of any misrepresentation, false pretense, or promise employed by a person to induce an elderly or disabled person to enter into such a contract.[248] A person who can be found to stand in "a position of trust and confidence" with an elderly or disabled person is any relative by blood or marriage, a joint tenant or tenant in common, or anyone having a legal or fiduciary relationship to such a person.[249]

Criminal liability shall not be imposed on a person who made a "good faith effort" to assist the alleged victim "but through no fault of his own has been unable to provide such assistance."[250] On the other hand, it is *not* a defense that the accused reasonably believed that the victim was not an elderly or disabled person.[251]

---

[243] 720 ILCS 5/16-1.3(a) (1999).

[244] 720 ILCS 5/16-1.3(a) (1999).

[245] 720 ILCS 5/16-1.3(b)(1) (1999).

[246] 720 ILCS 5/16-1.3(b)(2) (1999).

[247] 720 ILCS 5/16-1.3(b)(3) (1999).

[248] 720 ILCS 5/16-1.3(b)(4) (1999).

[249] 720 ILCS 5/16-1.3(c) (1999). *See* People v. Layne, 286 Ill. App. 3d 981, 987-88, 677 N.E.2d 469, 474 (5th Dist. 1997) (discussing factors for determining whether fiduciary relationship, not a product of explicit law, exists for purposes of this offense; factors include degree of kinship, disparity in age, the subject's age, health, mental condition, education and business experience, and the degree of trust placed in the dominant party).

[250] 720 ILCS 5/16-1.3(e) (1999).

[251] 720 ILCS 5/16-1.3(f) (1999).

Thus, where the defendant, an insurance agent, financially exploited his client, who was confined to a wheelchair because of postpoliosclerosis and dependent on social security benefits, this crime was committed.[252]

§ 11.22. Theft of Lost or Mislaid Property.

Section 5/16-2, which deals with theft of "lost or mislaid property,"[253] was part of the original 1961 enactments. It states:

> A person who obtains control over lost or mislaid property commits theft when he: (a) Knows or learns the identity of the owner or knows, or is aware of, or learns of a reasonable method of identifying the owner, and (b) Fails to take reasonable measures to restore the property to the owner, and (c) Intends to deprive the owner permanently of the use or benefit of the property.
>
> (d) Sentence. Theft of lost or mislaid property is a petty offense.[254]

The Revision Committee that drafted this legislation stated that this statute addresses the situation where the defendant knows who owns the property in question or, in the alternative, has a "clue" about who owns the property.[255] Accordingly, if the defendant (1) knows who owns the property or has a clue about its ownership, (2) has not made a reasonable effort to return the property to the owner, and (3) intends to permanently deprive the owner of the property, he or she can be convicted of this offense. If any of these three elements is lacking, there is no crime. For instance, if the accused does not have a clue as to whom the property he or she found actually belongs, it will be impossible to convict the defendant under this provision.[256]

§ 11.23. Theft of Labor or Services or Use of Property.

This next section involving the "theft of labor or services or the use of property" was part of the original enactment as well. Section 5/16-3 provides:

> (a) A person commits theft when he obtains the temporary use of property, labor or services of another which are available only for hire, by means of threat or deception or knowing that such use is without the consent of the person providing the property, labor or services.

---

[252] People v. Simpson, 268 Ill. App. 3d 305, 312-14, 643 N.E.2d 1262, 1266-69 (1st Dist. 1994).

[253] 720 ILCS 5/16-2 (1999).

[254] 720 ILCS 5/16-2 (1999).

[255] ILL. ANN. STAT. ch. 38, para. 16-2 (Smith-Hurd 1977), Committee Comments, at 216 (revised 1970).

[256] See People v. Betts, 367 Ill. 499, 502-03, 11 N.E.2d 942, 943-44 (1937).

(b) A person commits theft when after renting or leasing a motor vehicle, obtaining a motor vehicle through a "driveaway" service mode of transportation or renting or leasing any other type of personal property exceeding $500 in value, under an agreement in writing which provides for the return of the vehicle or other personal property to a particular place at a particular time, he without good cause wilfully fails to return the vehicle or other personal property to that place within the time specified, and is thereafter served or sent a written demand mailed to the last known address, made by certified mail return receipt requested, to return such vehicle or other personal property within 3 days from the mailing of the written demand, and who without good cause wilfully fails to return the vehicle or any other personal property to any place of business of the lessor within such period.
(c) Sentence. A person convicted of theft under subsection (a) of this Section is guilty of a . . . misdemeanor. A person convicted of theft under subsection (b) of this Section is guilty of a . . . felony.[257]

Although the revision committee has little to say about this proscription, the courts assume the legislature intended, among other things, to protect businesses of all types from the unscrupulous practices of prospective customers.[258] Thus, where a defendant procured reupholstery work with no intent to pay for that work, his conviction was upheld under this section.[259]

§ 11.24. False Report of Theft and Other Losses.

Under section 5/16-3.1, a person will be found guilty of a misdemeanor called "false report of theft or other losses" if he or she "knowingly makes a false report of a theft, destruction, damage or conversion of any property to a law enforcement agency or other governmental agency with the intent to defraud an insurer."[260] A subsequent violation of this law will be a felony.[261]

§ 11.25. Offender's Interest in Property: No Defense.

At common law, it was held that one could not steal what was partly one's own.[262] Joint ownership is no longer a defense to a larceny-type taking in Illinois because of section 5/16-4. Specifically, this provision states (1) it is not a defense to a charge of theft of property that the "offender has an interest therein" in circumstances where "the owner also has an interest to which the offender is not entitled," although (2) it is a defense that the "property involved is that of

---

[257] 720 ILCS 5/16-3 (1999).
[258] People v. Dillon, 93 Ill. App. 2d 151, 158, 236 N.E.2d 411, 415 (1st Dist. 1968).
[259] People v. Dillon, 93 Ill. App. 2d 151, 160-61, 236 N.E.2d 411, 416 (1st Dist. 1968).
[260] 720 ILCS 5/16-3.1(a) (1999).
[261] 720 ILCS 5/16-3.1(b) (1999).
[262] ROLLIN M. PERKINS & RONALD N. BOYCE, CRIMINAL LAW 302 (3d ed. 1982).

the offender's spouse" unless the offender and his spouse no longer live together in the same abode "as man and wife."[263] This statute eliminates any barrier to the prosecution of a theft by a co-owner, such as a partner, joint tenant or tenant in common in circumstances where the co-owner exercises unauthorized control over another co-owner's interest in the property while having the wrongful intent to permanently deprive the latter co-owner of his or her respective interest.[264]

§ 11.26. Offenses Related to Theft from Coin-Operated Machines.

In 1971, the General Assembly added two offenses addressing theft from coin-operated machines. The first, "theft from coin operated machine," which is normally a misdemeanor, (1) states that this crime is committed whenever an individual, who has intent to commit a theft, knowingly and without authority "opens, breaks into, tampers with, or damages a coin-operated machine" and (2) defines a "coin-operated machine" as including any automatic vending machine, parking meter, coin telephone, coin laundry machine, coin dry-cleaning machine, amusement machine, music machine, vending machine dispensing goods or services, or money changer.[265] It is noteworthy that the section 5/16-5(b) definition of *coin-operated machine* is not all-inclusive in its terminology and, accordingly, will include any future theft from a coin-operated machine not yet invented.

The second offense, possession of a key or device designed to open a coin-operated machine,[266] prohibits the mere possession of a key or other device that is designed to gain access to or otherwise damage a coin-operated machine. Specifically, this offense is directed at the possession of any device, including explosives, "designed to open, break into, tamper with or damage a coin-operated machine," as well as any "drawing, print or mold" of such a device.[267]

§ 11.27. Unlawful Use of Recorded Sounds and Unidentified Sound Recordings.

The rise of criminal activity known as "record piracy" — the underground market sale of unauthorized musical recordings — prompted a legislative response in 1975 to address this kind of crime. Specifically, section 5/16-7 prohibits as a felony the "unlawful use of recorded sounds or images," which occurs when any person or entity intentionally, knowingly, or recklessly (1) transfers

---

[263] 720 ILCS 5/16-4 (1999).

[264] ILL. ANN. STAT. ch. 38, para. 16-4 (Smith-Hurd 1977), Committee Comments, at 220 (revised 1970).

[265] 720 ILCS 5/16-5 (1999).

[266] 720 ILCS 5/16-6 (1999).

[267] 720 ILCS 5/16-6 (1999).

any sound or any audio-visual recording, without authorization of the owner, with the purpose of selling or using for profit the article to which the sound recording has been transferred; (2) sells, offers for sale, or uses for profit the article to which the sound or audio-visual recording has been transferred without authorization; (3) for any form of compensation, makes available "any equipment or machinery" to another person for the purpose of allowing that person to reproduce or transfer a sound or audio-visual recording without authorization; or (4) transfers any live performance with the purpose of selling or using for profit any sound or audio-visual recording without authorization.[268] Meanwhile, section 5/16-8 punishes as a felony the "unlawful use of unidentified sound or audio visual recordings" (which are sound or audio-visual recordings that do not identify the name of the manufacturer and the performer of the recording on the outside cover, jacket, or label of the recording) whenever a person or entity intentionally, knowingly, recklessly, or negligently for profit manufactures, sells, distributes, performs, or "otherwise deals in" unidentified sound recordings without the authorization of the owner.[269] A *sound or audio visual recording* is defined in broad terms to include: "any sound or audio visual phonograph record, disc, pre-recorded tape, film, wire, magnetic tape or other object, device or medium, now known or hereafter invented, by which sounds or images may be reproduced with or without the use of any additional machine, equipment or device."[270] Finally, these offenses contain provisions that (1) exempt radio and television activity where the transfers of recorded sounds relate to normal broadcast transmissions; (2) clarify that each individual unauthorized transfer, sale, or the like constitutes a separate offense; and (3) provide an affirmative defense to an accused where the recorded sounds transferred are "public domain material."[271]

§ 11.28. Theft of Cable Television Services.

Three offenses designed to curtail theft of cable television services appear in the Illinois penal code. These offenses attempt to prevent the flagrant pirating of cable television services through the manufacture or use of unauthorized wire connectors, boxes, adapters, decoders, and other devices sold on the black market. Section 5/16-10 prohibits any person from (1) knowingly obtaining or using any cable television service without the authorization of, or paid compensation to, the operator of the service; (2) assisting or instructing another, with the intent

---

[268] 720 ILCS 5/16-7 (1999). *See* People v. Zakarian, 121 Ill. App. 3d 968, 972-73, 460 N.E.2d 422, 425-26 (1st Dist. 1984) (it was held that "record piracy" does not fall within reach of general theft statute because there was no taking or carrying away of tangible item).

[269] 720 ILCS 5/16-8 (1999).

[270] 720 ILCS 5/16-7(b)(3) (1999).

[271] 720 ILCS 5/16-7(e), (g), (i) (1999).

to defraud a cable television operator, in obtaining unauthorized cable television service; or (3) selling, renting, or offering to sell or rent to another, with the intent to defraud a cable television operator, any equipment or instructions for making equipment that the person knows the recipient thereof will use to gain access to unauthorized cable television service.[272] A *cable television service* is defined broadly to include "any cable television system," "closed circuit coaxial cable communication system," or "microwave or similar transmission service" used in conjunction with a cable or closed circuit system.[273]

Section 5/16-11 prohibits a person from engaging in the unauthorized use of a television interception or decoding device with the intent to intercept, decode or use a transmission of a subscription television service without the provider's authorization.[274] A subscription television service is a television broadcast on the airwaves with Federal Communication Commission approval that is sold to subscribers by the provider for a fee.[275] Section 5/16-12 prevents "contributing" to the illegal use of a television interception or decoding device by manufacturing or distributing such a device with the intent that it be used to further a section 5/16-11 violation.[276] The possession or distribution of any of these devices may be prima facie evidence of a violation of section 5/16-11 or 5/16-12.[277]

§ 11.29. Unlawful Interference with Public Utility Service.

The state legislature has enacted a crime aimed at the unauthorized interference with public utility operations. Specifically, section 5/16-14 prohibits any person from engaging in the "unlawful interference with public utility services," which occurs when the person knowingly, and without authority of the owner of a public utility service, (1) "impairs or interrupts" any public water, gas, power supply, telecommunications, "or other public services"; (2) diverts such a power supply or service; or (3) installs or removes any device "for the purpose of such diversion."[278] Where any instrument or device, used to obtain public utility service without paying the full charge therefor, is found on premises under the control of a public utility customer or another person who derives the benefits of public utility service, the instrument or device shall raise a rebuttable presumption of the commission of this offense by the customer or person in question.[279]

---

[272] 720 ILCS 5/16-10 (1999). This offense is a misdemeanor unless committed for remuneration, in which case it is a felony. 720 ILCS 5/16-10(b) (1999).

[273] 720 ILCS 5/16-10 (1999).

[274] 720 ILCS 5/16-11(a) (1999). This offense is a misdemeanor. 720 ILCS 5/16-11(e) (1999).

[275] 720 ILCS 5/16-11(b) (1999).

[276] 720 ILCS 5/16-12 (1999). This offense is a felony. 720 ILCS 5/16-12(e) (1999).

[277] 720 ILCS 5/16-11(d), 5/16-12(d) (1999).

[278] 720 ILCS 5/16-14(a) (1999). Violation of this enactment is a misdemeanor unless it is for remuneration or is a subsequent offense, in which case it is a felony. 720 ILCS 5/16-14(d) (1999).

[279] 720 ILCS 5/16-14(c) (1999).

§ 11.30. Unlawful Use of Theft Detection Shielding Device.

With the growing use of electronic or magnetic theft alarm sensors designed for use in retail merchandise stores to detect the theft of goods carrying "live merchandise tags," inventive thieves have developed various containers or devices that may shield stolen merchandise from the electronic or magnetic sensors. In order to address this problem, the Illinois Legislature has enacted the crime of "unlawful use of theft detection shielding device."[280] Subsection (a) of section 5/16-15 outlaws the manufacture, sale, offering for sale, or distribution of a theft detection shielding device where it is marketed and intended for shielding merchandise from a sensor device.[281] Subsection (b) of this enactment prohibits the possession of a theft detection shielding device where the defendant has the intent to commit theft or retail theft.[282] Subsection (c) of this legislation prohibits the possession of any device designed to remove the live merchandise tags where the defendant has the intent to use such theft detection device remover to remove live merchandise tags from merchandise without the authority of the merchant.[283]

§ 11.31. Retail Theft.

In order to combat the rising cost to companies and consumers caused by shoplifting, "retail theft" has been given particular attention in the penal code in section 5/16A.[284] Although the basic theft statute covers shoplifting, the Illinois legislature saw the need to define retail theft.

The definitions contained in article 5/16A apply to retail theft and have utility "unless a contrary meaning is clear from the context."[285] The terms and phrases are defined as follows. *Conceal*: "To 'conceal' merchandise means that, although there may be some notice of its presence, that merchandise is not visible through ordinary observation."[286] *Full retail value* means "the merchant's stated or advertised price of the merchandise."[287] *Merchandise* is defined as "any item of tangible personal property."[288] A *merchant* is "an owner or operator of any retail mercantile establishment or any agent, employee, lessee, consignee, officer, director, franchisee or independent contractor of such owner or operator."[289]

---

[280] 720 ILCS 5/16-15 (1999). Violation of this enactment is a misdemeanor unless this is a subsequent offense, in which case violation is a felony. 720 ILCS 5/16-15(d) (1999).

[281] 720 ILCS 5/16-15(a) (1999).

[282] 720 ILCS 5/16-15(b) (1999).

[283] 720 ILCS 5/16-15(c) (1999).

[284] 720 ILCS 5/16A-1 (1999) (legislative declaration).

[285] 720 ILCS 5/16A-2 (1999).

[286] 720 ILCS 5/16A-2.1 (1999).

[287] 720 ILCS 5/16A-2.2 (1999).

[288] 720 ILCS 5/16A-2.3 (1999).

[289] 720 ILCS 5/16A-2.4 (1999).

A *minor* is "a person who is less than 19 years of age, is unemancipated and resides with his parents or legal guardian."[290] A *person* "means any natural person or individual."[291] A *peace officer* is defined as "any person who by virtue of his office or public employment is vested by law with a duty to maintain public order or to make arrests for offenses, whether that duty extends to all offenses or is limited to specific offenses."[292] *Premises of a retail mercantile establishment* "includes, but is not limited to, the retail mercantile establishment; any common use areas in shopping centers and all parking areas set aside by a merchant or on behalf of a merchant for the parking of vehicles for the convenience of the patrons of such retail mercantile establishment."[293] A *retail mercantile establishment* is "any place where merchandise is displayed, held, stored or offered for sale to the public."[294] A *shopping cart* should be understood to be "those push carts of the type or types which are commonly provided by grocery stores, drug stores or other retail mercantile establishments for the use of the public in transporting commodities in stores and markets and, incidentally, from the stores to a place outside the store."[295] An *under-ring* means "to cause the cash register or other sales recording device to reflect less than the full retail value of the merchandise."[296] A *theft detection shielding device* is any "laminated or coated bag or device designed and intended to shield merchandise from detection by an electronic or magnetic theft alarm sensor."[297] A *theft detection device remover* is "any tool or device specifically designed and intended to be used to remove any theft detection device from any merchandise."[298]

§ 11.32.— Retail Theft Codified.

Section 5/16A-3 defines the offense of "retail theft" as follows:

> A person commits the offense of retail theft when he or she knowingly:
> (a) Takes possession of, carries away, transfers or causes to be carried away or transferred, any merchandise displayed, held, stored or offered for sale in a retail mercantile establishment with the intention of retaining such merchandise or with the intention of depriving the merchant permanently of the possession, use or benefit of such merchandise without paying the full retail value of such merchandise; or

---

[290] 720 ILCS 5/16A-2.5 (1999).

[291] 720 ILCS 5/16A-2.6 (1999).

[292] 720 ILCS 5/16A-2.7 (1999) (refers to 720 ILCS 5/2-13 (1999) and its definition of peace officer, which is reflected in language accompanying this footnote).

[293] 720 ILCS 5/16A-2.8 (1999).

[294] 720 ILCS 5/16A-2.9 (1999).

[295] 720 ILCS 5/16A-2.10 (1999).

[296] 720 ILCS 5/16A-2.11 (1999).

[297] 720 ILCS 5/16A-2.12 (1999).

[298] 720 ILCS 5/16A-2.13 (1999).

(b) Alters, transfers, or removes any label, price tag, marking, indicia of value or any other markings which aid in determining value affixed to any merchandise displayed, held, stored or offered for sale, in a retail mercantile establishment and attempts to purchase such merchandise personally or in consort with another at less than the full retail value with the intention of depriving the merchant of the full retail value of such merchandise; or

(c) Transfers any merchandise displayed, held, stored or offered for sale, in a retail mercantile establishment from the container in or on which such merchandise is displayed to any other container with the intention of depriving the merchant of the full retail value of such merchandise; or

(d) Under-rings with the intention of depriving the merchant of the full retail value of the merchandise; or

(e) Removes a shopping cart from the premises of a retail mercantile establishment without the consent of the merchant given at the time of such removal with the intention of depriving the merchant permanently of the possession, use or benefit of such cart; or

(f) Represents to a merchant that he or another is the lawful owner of property, knowing that such representation is false, and conveys or attempts to convey that property to a merchant who is the owner of the property in exchange for money, merchandise credit or other property of the merchant; or

(g) Uses or possesses any theft detection shielding device or theft detection device remover with the intention of using such device to deprive the merchant permanently of the possession, use or benefit of any merchandise displayed, held, stored or offered for sale in a retail mercantile establishment without paying the full retail value of such merchandise . . .; or

(h) Obtains or exerts unauthorized control over property of the owner and thereby intends to deprive the owner permanently of the use or benefit of the property when a lessee of the personal property of another fails to return it to the owner, or if the lessee fails to pay the full retail value of such property to the lessor in satisfaction of any contractual provision requiring such, within 30 days after written demand from the owner for its return. A notice in writing, given after expiration of the leasing agreement, by registered mail, to the lessee at the address given by the lessee and shown on the leasing agreement shall constitute proper demand.[299]

One of the key differences between ordinary theft and retail theft is that ownership and proof of ownership are necessary elements to theft, but *not* to retail theft.[300] The essential elements of retail theft are: (1) knowingly taking of possession, carrying away, transferring, or causing to be carried away or transferred

---

[299] 720 ILCS 5/16A-3 (1999).

[300] People v. Drake, 131 Ill. App. 3d 466, 473, 475 N.E.2d 1018, 1023 (2d Dist. 1985); People v. Wynn, 84 Ill. App. 3d 591, 593, 406 N.E.2d 35, 37 (1st Dist. 1980).

(2) merchandise held for sale in a retail mercantile establishment (3) with the intent to retain or deprive a merchant permanently of its use and benefit without paying its full retail value.[301]

Another important difference between the theft and retail theft statutes relates to the value of the property stolen. If the value of the merchandise stolen from a retail establishment exceeds $150, the crime becomes a felony,[302] whereas under the basic theft statute, the value of the property stolen must exceed $300 to elevate the crime to a felony.[303] This difference holds importance for a person accused of retail theft of property that exceeds $150 in value but is less than $300 retail value.[304] The Illinois caselaw has upheld the differing property value thresholds between ordinary theft and retail theft, which determine whether the theft is a felony.[305] One court reasoned that the increased vulnerability of retail merchandise victims justified the legislature's differentiation between ordinary theft and retail theft in this regard and that these classifications were not violative of equal protection considerations.[306]

The merchant's stated or advertised price is the "full retail value," and paying less than full retail value is prohibited. For example, since switching price tags in a store with intent to deprive the merchant of the full retail value of the item is specifically prohibited, where the defendant switched the price tag from a less expensive clothes item to a more expensive one, thereby paying less money for a better quality product, she was guilty under the statute.[307]

A business need not be exclusively involved in retailing to qualify as a retail business. Where a defendant was charged under the retail theft statute with theft from a meat company, the defendant claimed that because the establishment was a wholesale meat company, it didn't fit the statutory requirement of a *retail mercantile establishment*, which is defined as any place where merchandise is displayed, held, stored, or offered for sale to the public.[308] However, the appellate court ruled that because the meat company conducted sales to the general public from time to time, the fact that the meat company was also a wholesale outlet did not preclude it from being a retail mercantile establishment under the statute.[309] It was held that it is only necessary that some items (not any particular

---

[301] People v. Liner, 221 Ill. App. 3d 578, 580, 582 N.E.2d 271, 272 (3d Dist. 1991).

[302] 720 ILCS 5/16A-10(3) (1999).

[303] 720 ILCS 5/16-1(b)(1) (1999).

[304] *See* People v. Taylor, 147 Ill. App. 3d 129, 131, 497 N.E.2d 861, 862 (3d Dist. 1986) (legislature enacted retail theft statute to respond to specific nature of theft in retail establishments; thus, defendant not denied due process or equal protection when convicted of felony for retail theft of merchandise valued at under $300).

[305] People v. James, 148 Ill. App. 3d 536, 537-38, 499 N.E.2d 1036, 1038 (4th Dist. 1986).

[306] People v. James, 148 Ill. App. 3d 536, 537-38, 499 N.E.2d 1036, 1038 (4th Dist. 1986).

[307] People v. Ferraro, 79 Ill. App. 3d 465, 471-72, 398 N.E.2d 1001, 1006 (2d Dist. 1979).

[308] People v. Porzelius, 97 Ill. App. 3d 865, 867, 423 N.E.2d 985, 986 (4th Dist. 1981).

[309] People v. Porzelius, 97 Ill. App. 3d 865, 867, 423 N.E.2d 985, 986 (4th Dist. 1981).

one) be held for sale in the retail establishment and, accordingly, the defendant's theft amounted to retail theft.[310]

The common law element in larceny of asportation has been excluded from the retail theft statute in Illinois as well as from the basic theft statute.[311] Section 5/16A-4 states that the concealment of merchandise on the person or among the defendant's belongings and the removal of the merchandise past the last known station for payment creates a presumption that the defendant acted with the intent to not pay the full retail value.[312] However, when the appellate courts considered this presumption, they found that it created a mandatory presumption violative of due process.[313]

The defendant need not be outside the store to be arrested for retail theft,[314] merely beyond the last known checkout point.[315] Testimony on the items in the defendant's possession and on their approximate value is sufficient proof of the items stolen; the actual items need not be placed into evidence.[316]

The common law merchant's privilege that allowed a merchant to detain a suspected shoplifter for a reasonable length of time in a reasonable manner has been codified in section 5/16A-5 of the retail theft statute in Illinois.[317] The stat-

---

[310] People v. Porzelius, 97 Ill. App. 3d 865, 867, 423 N.E.2d 985, 986 (4th Dist. 1981).

[311] *See, e.g.,* 720 ILCS 5/16A-3(a) (1999) ("[t]akes possession of, carries away, transfers *or* causes to be carried away or transferred") (emphasis added).

[312] 720 ILCS 5/16A-4 (1999) ("If any person: (a) conceals upon his or her person or among his or her belongings, unpurchased merchandise displayed, held, stored or offered for sale in a retail mercantile establishment; and (b) removes that merchandise beyond the last known station for receiving payments for that merchandise in that retail mercantile establishment such person shall be presumed to have possessed, carried away or transferred such merchandise with the intention of retaining it or with the intention of depriving the merchant permanently of the possession, use or benefit of such merchandise without paying the full retail value of such merchandise").

[313] People v. Dodd, 173 Ill. App. 3d 460, 467-70, 527 N.E.2d 1079, 1084-86 (2d Dist. 1988) (statute creates unconstitutional mandatory presumption due to the inclusion of the language "shall be presumed") (due to the language "shall be presumed"); People v. Flowers, 134 Ill. App. 3d 324, 326, 480 N.E.2d 198, 199-201 (4th Dist. 1985) (same).

[314] *See* People v. Caplinger, 162 Ill. App. 3d 74, 77-78, 514 N.E.2d 1221, 1223-24 (3d Dist. 1987) (defendant convicted of retail theft on accountability theory where defendant gave accomplice two tapes and remained in store while accomplice left store without paying for items).

[315] People v. Steele, 156 Ill. App. 3d 508, 512, 509 N.E.2d 719, 722 (2d Dist. 1987); People v. Connell, 91 Ill. App. 3d 326, 335, 414 N.E.2d 796, 803 (5th Dist. 1980).

[316] People v. Connell, 91 Ill. App. 3d 326, 335, 414 N.E.2d 796, 803 (5th Dist. 1980).

[317] 720 ILCS 5/16A-5 (1999) ("Any merchant who has reasonable grounds to believe that a person has committed retail theft may detain such person, on or off the premises of a retain mercantile establishment, in a reasonable manner and for a reasonable length of time for all or any of the following purposes: (a) To request identification; (b) To verify such identification; (c) To make reasonable inquiry as to whether such person has in his possession unpurchased merchandise and, to make reasonable investigation of the ownership of such merchandise; (d) To inform a peace officer of the detention of the person and surrender that person to the custody of a peace officer; (e) In the case of a minor, to inform a peace officer, the parents, guardian or other private person interested

ute provides that such a detention is not an arrest,[318] nor a commission of the offense of unlawful restraint,[319] nor shall it render the merchant liable to the person so detained.[320] A security guard's search of the thief is justified as part of the detention.[321] If the security guard does not, on the other hand, have reasonable grounds to believe that a retail theft has occurred, a defendant would have legal justification in resisting the security guard.[322] Further, once the store security guard's investigation leads him or her to the conclusion that the store patron was not involved in a theft, a continued detention would not be protected.[323] Thus, where an individual was detained for one-half hour, fifteen minutes of which was after the detained shopper was cleared from suspicion of theft, the detention was considered unreasonable and a basis for civil liability.[324]

§ 11.33. Library Theft and Criminal Mutilation or Vandalism of Library Materials.

The general assembly enacted two offenses designed to curtail theft and destruction of library materials. In 1982, a theft offense entitled "library theft" became law.[325] Furthermore, in order to curtail the destruction of library materials, the offense of "criminal mutilation or vandalism of library materials" was created.[326]

As with the general theft statute and the retail theft provisions, these enactments found in article 5/16B set out certain definitions followed by the strictures themselves. The following definitions appear in section 5/16B-1. *Library facility* "includes any public library or museum, or any library or museum of an educa-

---

in the welfare of that minor of this detention and to surrender custody of such minor to such person. A merchant may make a detention as permitted herein off the premises of a retail mercantile establishment only if such detention is pursuant to an immediate pursuit of such person. A merchant shall be deemed to have reasonable grounds to make a detention for the purposes of this section if the merchant detains a person because such person has in his possession either a theft detection shielding device or a theft detection device remover").

[318] 720 ILCS 5/16A-6 (1999).

[319] 720 ILCS 5/16A-6 (1999) (referring to 720 ILCS 5/10-3 (1999)).

[320] 720 ILCS 5/16A-6 (1999). *See* Davis v. Carson Pirie Scott & Co., 530 F. Supp. 799, 802-03 (N.D. Ill. 1982) (no "state action" or, accordingly, no valid civil rights claim under 42 U.S.C. § 1983)). *Accord* Klimzak v. City of Chicago, 539 F. Supp. 221, 223-24 (N.D. Ill. 1982).

[321] People v. Ferraro, 79 Ill. App. 3d 465, 472-73, 398 N.E.2d 1001, 1006 (2d Dist. 1979).

[322] *See* People v. Rickman, 73 Ill. App. 3d 755, 760-61, 391 N.E.2d 1114, 1118 (3d Dist. 1979) (dictum).

[323] Adams v. Zayre Corp., 148 Ill. App. 3d 704, 712, 499 N.E.2d 678, 685 (2d Dist. 1986).

[324] Adams v. Zayre Corp., 148 Ill. App. 3d 704, 712-14, 499 N.E.2d 678, 685 (2d Dist. 1986).

[325] 720 ILCS 5/16B-2 (1999).

[326] 720 ILCS 5/16B-2.1 (1999).

tional, historical or eleemosynary institution, organization or society."[327] *Library material* is defined as

> any book, plate, picture, photograph, engraving, painting, sculpture, statute, artifact, drawing, map, newspaper, pamphlet, broadside, magazine, manuscript, document, letter, microfilm, sound recording, audiovisual material, magnetic or other tape, electronic data processing record or other documentary, written or printed material regardless of physical form or characteristics, or any part thereof, belonging to, or on loan to or otherwise in the custody of a library facility.[328]

The *premises of a library facility* means

> the interior of a building, structure or other enclosure in which a library facility is located and in which the library facility keeps, displays and makes available for inspection or borrowing library material, but for purposes of this Article, such premises do not include the exterior appurtenances to such building, structure or enclosure nor the land on which such building, structure or other enclosure is located.[329]

A *library card* is "a card or plate issued by a library facility for purposes of identifying the person to whom the library card was issued as authorized to borrow library material, subject to all limitations and conditions imposed on such borrowing by the library facility issuing such card."[330]

The obvious purpose of this statute outlawing "library theft" was to prevent the depletion of library materials by people who may or may not have the authority to remove the materials from a library and who, at some point, form the intent to keep the materials. *Library theft* is committed whenever a person (1) knowingly and intentionally removes library material from a library without authority; (2) knowingly and intentionally conceals from ordinary observation library material on his or her person and removes the material beyond the last point in the library facility where materials are normally borrowed from the library; (3) borrows or attempts to borrow library material, with the intent to deceive, by using another's library card without his or her authorization or by using a library card that is not valid; or (4) borrows from a library facility material having an aggregate value of $50 or more through normal library procedures and, thereafter, "wilfully without good cause" fails to return the material to the library within thirty days of the library's written demand for the return of the materials.[331] Each library facility must post a notice of this enactment at the li-

---

[327] 720 ILCS 5/16B-1(a) (1999).
[328] 720 ILCS 5/16B-1(b) (1999).
[329] 720 ILCS 5/16B-1(c) (1999).
[330] 720 ILCS 5/16B-1(d) (1999).
[331] 720 ILCS 5/16B-2 (1999).

brary entrance and at each point in the premises at which the borrowing of library materials occurs.[332]

The second offense of "criminal mutilation or vandalism of library materials" states that a person commits this crime when he or she "knowingly tears, marks on, maliciously renders imperfect or otherwise damages or destroys library materials."[333] These offenses are a misdemeanor unless the aggregate loss to the library exceeds $300, in which case it is designated a felony.[334]

§ 11.34. Unlawful Sale of Household Appliances.

In 1984, the General Assembly added section 5/16C-1 through 16C-3,[335] which creates the offense of "unlawful sale of household appliances." Section 5/16C-1 sets out the following definitions. *Commercial context* means "a continuing business enterprise conducted for profit by any person whose primary business is the wholesale or retail marketing of household appliances, or a significant portion of whose business or inventory consists of household appliances kept or sold on a wholesale or retail basis."[336] A *household appliance* is "any gas or electric device or machine marketed for use as home entertainment or for facilitating or expediting household tasks or chores."[337] A *manufacturer's identification number* is "any serial number or other similar numerical or alphabetical designation imprinted upon or attached to or placed, stamped, or otherwise imprinted upon or attached to a household appliance by the manufacturer for purposes of identifying a particular appliance individually or by lot number."[338]

Section 5/16C-2 sets out the terms of the offense of "unlawful sale of household appliances." It provides:

> (a) A person commits the offense of unlawful sale of household appliances when he or she knowingly, with the intent to defraud or deceive another, keeps for sale, within any commercial context, any household appliance with a missing, defaced, obliterated or otherwise altered manufacturer's identification number. (b) Violation of this Section is a . . . felony if the value of the appliance or appliances exceeds $1,000 and a . . . misdemeanor if the value of the appliance or appliances is $1,000 or less.[339]

---

[332] 720 ILCS 5/16B-3 (1999).

[333] 720 ILCS 5/16B-2.1 (1999).

[334] 720 ILCS 5/16B-5 (1999).

[335] 720 ILCS 5/16C-1 through 5/16C-3 (1999).

[336] 720 ILCS 5/16C-1(1) (1999).

[337] 720 ILCS 5/16C-1(2) (1999).

[338] 720 ILCS 5/16C-1(3) (1999).

[339] 720 ILCS 5/16C-2 (1999).

§ 11.35. Computer Crimes.

The General Assembly has enacted a series of prohibitions outlawing various forms of computer crime. These are "computer tampering,"[340] "aggravated computer tampering,"[341] and "computer fraud."[342] "Computer tampering," prohibited by section 5/16D-3, occurs where a person knowingly and without the authorization of the computer owner:

(1) Accesses or causes to be accessed a computer or any part thereof, or a program or data;

(2) Accesses or causes to be accessed a computer or any part thereof, or a program or data, and obtains data or services;

(3) Accesses or causes to be accessed a computer or any part thereof, or a program or data, and damages or destroys the computer or alters, deletes, or removes a computer program or data;

(4) Inserts or attempts to insert a "program" into a computer or a computer program knowing or having reason to believe that such a "program" contains information or commands that will or may damage or destroy that computer, or any other computer subsequently accessing or being accessed by that computer, or that will or may alter, delete or remove a computer program or data from that computer, or any other computer program or data in a computer subsequently accessing or being accessed by that computer, or that will or may cause loss to the users of a computer which accesses or which is accessed by such "program."[343]

Depending on the circumstances, this may constitute a misdemeanor or a felony.[344]

The second offense, "aggravated computer tampering" is committed whenever he or she commits computer tampering as defined in section 5/16D-3 and he or she knowingly:

(1) causes disruption or interference with vital services or operations of State or local government or a public utility; or

(2) creates a strong possibility of death or great bodily harm to one or more individuals.[345]

This offense constitutes a felony.[346]

The last offense contained in article 5/16D is "computer fraud." It reads:

---

[340] 720 ILCS 5/16D-3 (1999).
[341] 720 ILCS 5/16D-4 (1999).
[342] 720 ILCS 5/16D-5 (1999).
[343] 720 ILCS 5/16D-3(a) (1999).
[344] 720 ILCS 5/16D-3(b) (1999).
[345] 720 ILCS 5/16D-4(a) (1999).
[346] 720 ILCS 5/16D-4(b) (1999).

A person commits the offense of computer fraud when he knowingly:

(1) Accesses or causes to be accessed a computer or any part thereof, or a program or data, for the purpose of devising or executing any scheme, artifice to defraud, or as part of a deception;

(2) Obtains use of, damages, or destroys a computer or any part thereof, or alters, deletes, or removes any program or data contained therein, in connection with any scheme, artifice to defraud, or as part of a deception; or

(3) Accesses or causes to be accessed a computer or any part thereof, or a program or data, and obtains money or control over any such money, property, or services of another in connection with any scheme, artifice to defraud, or as part of a deception.[347]

Computer fraud is a felony.[348]

Article 5/16D contains various definitions of terms. These definitions include the word *computer*, which is a "device that accepts, possesses, stores, retrieves, or outputs data. . . ."[349] A *computer program* means a "series of coded instructions or statements in a form acceptable to a computer which causes the computer to process data and supply the results of the data processing."[350] *Data* means "a representation of information, knowledge, facts, concepts or instructions, including program documentation, which is prepared in a formalized manner and is stored or processed in, or transmitted by a computer."[351] *Property* is given an expansive definition, including the likes of anything from "electronic impulses" to "software."[352] *Access* means "to use, instruct, communicate with, store data in, or retrieve or intercept data from, or otherwise utilize any services of a computer."[353] *Services* includes computer time, data manipulation, or storage functions.[354] *Vital services or operations* means those services which utilize computer assistance necessary to protect public health, safety, or welfare, such as those provided to emergency service agencies.[355]

§ 11.36. Delivery Container Crime.

Article 5/16E reflects the misdemeanor offense of "delivery container crime."[356] This offense is designed to protect against the removal of a trademarked basket, case, dolly or cart used to store or transport bakery or diary

---

[347] 720 ILCS 5/16D-5(a) (1999).

[348] 720 ILCS 5/16D-5(b) (1999).

[349] 720 ILCS 5/16D-2(a) (1999).

[350] 720 ILCS 5/16D-2(b) (1999).

[351] 720 ILCS 5/16D-2(c) (1999) ("Data shall be considered property . . . .").

[352] 720 ILCS 5/16D-2(d) (1999).

[353] 720 ILCS 5/16D-2(e) (1999).

[354] 720 ILCS 5/16D-2(f) (1999).

[355] 720 ILCS 5/16D-2(g) (1999).

[356] 720 ILCS 5/16E-1 through 5/16E-4 (1999).

products within or from the premises of a food processor, distributor or re-tailer.[357] A person commits this offense when he *knowingly* uses such a container off premises, sells such a container, obliterates the trade name on such a container, or removes the container from the parking lot or premises of the owner without the owner's permission.[358]

§ 11.37. Wireless Service Theft.

Article 5/16F reflects the misdemeanor offense of "wireless service theft."[359] This provision makes it a crime to "intentionally obtain wireless service by the use of an unlawful wireless device or without the consent of the wireless service provider."[360] *Wireless service* encompasses telephone service including, but not limited to cellular phone service.[361] This article also makes it illegal to *facilitate the theft of wire service* by manufacturing, possessing, assembling, advertising or distributing devices for theft of wireless service or concealment of such theft; or any instructions, plans or parts intended to be used in assembling such devices.[362]

§ 11.38. Deception Offenses Generally.

The number of specific offenses contained in article 5/17 are essentially theft-related and all involve the use of "deception." While the definition of *deception* appears in article 5/15, the various offenses contained in article 5/17 include deceptive practices,[363] impersonating a veteran or member of a police, fraternal, veteran's or charitable organization,[364] forgery,[365] deceptive altering or sale of coins,[366] deceptive collection practices,[367] state benefits fraud,[368] promotion of pyramid sales scheme,[369] health care benefits fraud,[370] public aid wire fraud,[371] public aid mail fraud,[372] odometer fraud,[373] hour meter fraud,[374] fraudulent ad-

---

[357] 720 ILCS 5/16E-2, 5/16E-3 (1999).
[358] 720 ILCS 5/16E-3 (1999).
[359] 720 ILCS 5/16F-1 through 5/16F-4 (1999).
[360] 720 ILCS 5/16F-3(a) (1999).
[361] 720 ILCS 5/16F-2 (1999).
[362] 720 ILCS 5/16F-4 (1999).
[363] 720 ILCS 5/17-1 (1999).
[364] 720 ILCS 5/17-2 (1999).
[365] 720 ILCS 5/17-3 (1999).
[366] 720 ILCS 5/17-4 (1999).
[367] 720 ILCS 5/17-5 (1999).
[368] 720 ILCS 5/17-6 (1999).
[369] 720 ILCS 5/17-7 (1999).
[370] 720 ILCS 5/17-8 (1999).
[371] 720 ILCS 5/17-9 (1999).
[372] 720 ILCS 5/17-10 (1999).
[373] 720 ILCS 5/17-11 (1999).

vertisement of corporate name,[375] fraudulent land sales and conveyances,[376] fraudulent production of infant,[377] fraudulent issuance of stock,[378] obstructing gas, water, electric and service meters,[379] and WIC fraud.[380]

§ 11.39. Deceptive Practices.

The crime "deceptive practices" appeared originally in the 1961 code. As currently amended, section 5/17-1 contains three major subsections: (1) a definition of terms,[381] (2) a general "deceptive practices" prohibition,[382] and (3) a specific set of prohibitions involving deception on a bank or other financial institution.[383]

The following definitions appear in section 5/17-1. A *financial institution* is "any bank, savings and loan association, credit union, or other depository of money, or medium of savings and collective investment."[384] An *account holder* is "any person, having a checking account or savings account in a financial institution."[385] Acting with the *intent to defraud* means acting "wilfully, and with the specific intent to deceive or cheat, for the purpose of causing financial loss to another, or to bring some financial gain to oneself."[386] It need not be established that anyone has been actually defrauded or deceived.[387]

Any general deception for purposes of fraud amounting to "deceptive practices" is covered by section 5/17-1(B). It reads:

A person commits a deceptive practice when, with intent to defraud:
(a) He causes another, by deception or threat to execute a document disposing of property or a document by which a pecuniary obligation is incurred, or
(b) Being an officer, manager or other person participating in the direction of a financial institution, he knowingly receives or permits the receipt of a deposit or other investment, knowing that the institution is insolvent, or

---

[374] 720 ILCS 5/17-11.1 (1999).
[375] 720 ILCS 5/17-12 (1999).
[376] 720 ILCS 5/17-13 through 5/17-15 (1999).
[377] 720 ILCS 5/17-16 (1999).
[378] 720 ILCS 5/17-17, 5/17-18 (1999).
[379] 720 ILCS 5/17-20, 5/17-21 (1999).
[380] 720 ILCS 5/17B-1 through 5/17B-30 (1999).
[381] 720 ILCS 5/17-1(A) (1999).
[382] 720 ILCS 5/17-1(B) (1999).
[383] 720 ILCS 5/17-1(C) (1999).
[384] 720 ILCS 5/17-1(A)(i) (1999).
[385] 720 ILCS 5/17-1(A)(ii) (1999).
[386] 720 ILCS 5/17-1(A)(iii) (1999).
[387] 720 ILCS 5/17-1(A) (1999).

(c) He knowingly makes or directs another to make a false or deceptive statement addressed to the public for the purpose of promoting the sale of property or services, or

(d) With the intent to obtain control over property or to pay for property, labor or services of another, or in satisfaction of an obligation for payment of tax under the Retailers' Occupation Tax Act or any other tax due to the State of Illinois, he issues or delivers a check or other order upon a real or fictitious depository for the payment of money, knowing that it will not be paid by the depository. Failure to have sufficient funds or credit with the depository when the check or other order is issued or delivered, or when such check or other order is presented for payment and dishonored on each of 2 occasions at least 7 days apart, is prima facie evidence that the offender knows that it will not be paid by the depository, and that he has the intent to defraud; [or]

(e) He issues or delivers a check or other order upon a real or fictitious depository in an amount exceeding $150 in payment of an amount owed on any credit transaction for property, labor or services, or in payment of the entire amount owed on any credit transaction for property, labor or services, knowing that it will not be paid by the depository, and thereafter fails to provide funds or credit with the depository in the face amount of the check or order within seven days of receiving actual notice from the depository or payee of the dishonor of the check or order.

Sentence. . . .[388]

The revision committee's comments point out that (1) the crime of "general deception" is designed to cover those wrongs not covered by section 5/16-1(b), theft by deception, which carries a more serious penalty; (2) subsection (a) is directed at causing another, by "deception or threat," to execute a legal document; (3) subsection (b) is aimed at the official of a financial institution who knowingly receives a deposit from another while knowing the institution is insolvent, even though no deception or threat of deception is involved; (4) subsection (c) prohibits "untrue, misleading and deceptive advertising" directed at the public, but not the usual "puffing" between individual salespeople and private customers; and (5) subsection (d) proscribes "making bad checks to defraud."[389] All forms of general deception, as the statute clearly reflects, require a specific "intent to defraud" and some form of deceptive activity, such as the conduct

---

[388] 720 ILCS 5/17-1(B) (1999).

[389] ILL. ANN. STAT. Ch. 38, para. 17-1 (Smith-Hurd 1977), 1961 Committee Comments, at 232 (revised 1970).

previously known as "false pretenses," "confidence game," or "fraudulent conveyances."[390]

The most common application of this offense involves the issuance of "bad checks." The state has the burden of proving the following elements in such a deceptive practice prosecution: (1) that the defendant made, drew, issued, or delivered a check, draft, or other for payment; (2) that he or she obtained thereby from another money, personal property, or other valuable thing; (3) that defendant knew at that time that his or her account was without sufficient funds to pay the check, draft, or order; and (4) that defendant acted with the intent to defraud.[391] *Defraud* necessarily implies an advantage to the defrauding party and a corresponding damage to the party who is defrauded.[392] The technical elements of fraud include (1) the use of ordinary care in discovering the truth by the person claiming he or she was defrauded and (2) actual reliance on the deception.[393]

The specific intent to defraud[394] constitutes an essential element of deceptive practices and must be included in the indictment or information.[395] The failure of the trial court to instruct the jury on that element has been deemed a reversible error cognizable under the "plain error" doctrine, even without a defense objection.[396] Intent to defraud is a different mental state from the knowledge requirement of subsection 5/17-1(B)(d) and 5/17-1(B)(e), which involves the knowledge that the check will not be paid by the depository.[397] Satisfactory proof of both mental states is necessary to a legitimate prosecution under these subsections of deceptive practices.

The intent to defraud will not be measured by the defendant's inability to pay the amount owed at some later date, but rather by the defendant's inability to pay *at the time* he or she issued the check while knowing that the check would

---

[390] ILL. ANN. STAT. Ch. 38, para. 17-1 (Smith-Hurd 1977), 1961 Committee Comments, at 232 (revised 1970).

[391] People v. Bormet, 142 Ill. App. 3d 422, 424-25, 491 N.E.2d 1281, 1283 (1st Dist. 1986); People v. Cundiff, 16 Ill. App. 3d 267, 269, 305 N.E.2d 735, 737 (3d Dist. 1973).

[392] People v. Ogunsola, 91 Ill. App. 3d 26, 29, 414 N.E.2d 219, 223 (4th Dist. 1980), *aff'd in part, rev'd in part*, 87 Ill. 2d 216, 429 N.E.2d 861 (1981).

[393] City of Evanston v. Connelly, 73 Ill. App. 3d 890, 893, 392 N.E.2d 211, 214 (1st Dist. 1979) (involving offense of obtaining temporary driver's permit by fraud).

[394] People v. Sumner, 107 Ill. App. 3d 368, 370, 437 N.E.2d 786, 787-88 (1st Dist. 1982) ("a person who writes and delivers a check knowing the account balance is deficient or that the bank will not pay the check when presented is guilty of a deceptive practice only if the check is written with the specific intent to defraud the recipient").

[395] People v. Greene, 92 Ill. App. 2d 201, 206-07, 235 N.E.2d 295, 297-98 (1st Dist. 1968).

[396] People v. Ogunsola, 87 Ill. 2d 216, 221-24, 429 N.E.2d 861, 864-65 (1981).

[397] People v. Ogunsola, 87 Ill. 2d 216, 220-21, 429 N.E.2d 861, 863 (1981). *See also* People v. Mc Laughlin, 123 Ill. App. 3d 24, 25, 462 N.E.2d 875, 876 (5th Dist. 1984) (defendant's conviction reversed where his representations to party, to whom he issued checks, gave notice he had insufficient funds to cover all checks when issued).

not be paid by the bank.[398] Thus, the intent to defraud cannot be inferred from any subsequent acts by the defendant,[399] including whether payment or restitution was made.[400] For example, where a defendant claimed her filing of bankruptcy one month after she issued a check disproved her intent to defraud, the appellate court ruled it was proper for the trial court to exclude such evidence because her intent to defraud based on her inability to pay was to be measured at the point where she issued the check, not when she declared bankruptcy.[401]

The language of 5/17-1(B)(d) declares that failure to have sufficient funds in the depository when the checks are issued is prima facie evidence of intent to defraud.[402] Illinois courts have determined this language to mean that having insufficient funds may raise an inference of intent to defraud, assuming it is corroborated by other evidence,[403] but this presumption cannot be conclusive or rebuttable, thereby impermissibly shifting the ultimate burden of persuasion to the accused.[404]

---

[398] People v. Mitchell, 50 Ill. App. 3d 120, 123, 365 N.E.2d 185, 188 (5th Dist.), aff'd, 68 Ill. 2d 309, 370 N.E.2d 165 (1977). See also People v. Bormet, 142 Ill. App. 3d 422, 426, 491 N.E.2d 1281, 1284 (1st Dist. 1986) (intent to defraud "must be present at moment a check issued . . . ."); People v. Brenner, 135 Ill. App. 3d 877, 884, 482 N.E.2d 396, 401 (1st Dist. 1985) (failure to have sufficient funds at time of issuance of check constitutes prima facie evidence of intent to defraud).

[399] People v. Bormet, 142 Ill. App. 3d 422, 426, 491 N.E.2d 1281, 1284 (1st Dist. 1986). Compare People v. Sumner, 107 Ill. App. 3d 368, 371-72, 437 N.E.2d 786, 788 (1st Dist. 1982) (court construed fact that defendant traded in car and paid substantial amount of cash to car dealer as evidence tending to negate defendant's intent to defraud dealer when he issued dealer bad check).

[400] People v. Bormet, 142 Ill. App. 3d 422, 426, 491 N.E.2d 1281, 1284 (1st Dist. 1986); People v. Cundiff, 16 Ill. App. 3d 267, 272, 305 N.E.2d 735, 739 (3d Dist. 1973).

[401] People v. Mitchell, 50 Ill. App. 3d 120, 123, 365 N.E.2d 185, 188 (5th Dist.), aff'd, 68 Ill. 2d 309, 370 N.E.2d 165 (1977).

[402] People v. Boyd, 292 Ill. App. 3d 94, 98 –99, 685 N.E.2d 398, 401 (2d Dist. 1997) ("once a bad check is deposited it is evidence of an intent to defrauded to obtain control"); People v. Brenner, 135 Ill. App. 3d 877, 884, 482 N.E.2d 396, 401 (1st Dist. 1985) (failure to have sufficient funds constitutes prima facie evidence of intent to defraud). Compare People v. Dennis, 43 Ill. App. 3d 518, 520, 357 N.E.2d 563, 565 (1st Dist. 1976) (no intent to defraud proved where defendant did not know bank had closed out her account and where her husband failed to deposit money in account as promised).

[403] See People v. Bormet, 142 Ill. App. 3d 422, 426, 491 N.E.2d 1281, 1284 (1st Dist. 1986) (deceptive practices conviction reversed) for a discussion of how the deceptive practices statute may only allow an inference of intent to defraud to be drawn only when meeting the standards set out in People v. Housby, 84 Ill. 2d 415, 419-24, 420 N.E.2d 151, 153-55, cert. denied, 454 U.S. 845 (1981), that requires that the inference be supported by corroborating evidence, which it had not in Bormet.

[404] People v. Bormet, 142 Ill. App. 3d 422, 491 N.E.2d 1281, 1284 (1st Dist. 1986). See also People v. Gray, 99 Ill. App. 3d 851, 853-54, 426 N.E.2d 290, 292 (5th Dist. 1981) (failure to properly explain to jury what constitutes a prima facie case and its relationship to ultimate burden of persuasion reversible error).

Section 5/17-1(C) deals with "deception on a bank or other financial institution."[405] It provides:

> 1) Any person who, with the intent to defraud, makes or causes to be made, any false statement in writing in order to obtain an account with a bank or other financial institution, or to obtain credit from a bank or other financial institution, knowing such writing to be false, and with the intent that it be relied upon, is guilty of a . . . misdemeanor. For purposes of this subsection (C), a false statement shall mean any false statement representing identity, address, or employment, or the identity, address or employment of any person, firm or corporation. * * *
>
> 2) Any person who possesses, with the intent to defraud, any check or order for the payment of money, upon a real or fictitious account, without the consent of the account holder, or the issuing financial institution, is guilty of a . . . misdemeanor. Any person who, within any 12 month period, violates this Section with respect to 3 or more checks or orders for the payment of money at the same time or consecutively, each the property of a different account holder or financial institution, is guilty of a . . . felony. * * *
>
> 3) Any person who possesses, with the intent to defraud, and without the authority of the account holder or financial institution any check imprinter, signature imprinter, or "certified" stamp is guilty of a . . . misdemeanor. A person who within any 12 month period violates this subsection (C) as to possession of 3 or more such devices at the same time or consecutively, is guilty of a . . . felony. * * *
>
> 4) Any person, who with the intent to defraud, possesses any check guarantee card or key card or identification card for cash dispensing machines without the authority of the account holder or financial institution, is guilty of a . . . misdemeanor. A person who, within any 12 month period, violates this Section at the same time or consecutively with respect to 3 or more cards, each the property of different account holders, is guilty of a . . . felony. A person convicted under this Section, when the value of property so obtained, in a single transaction, or in separate transactions within any 90 day period, exceeds $150 shall be guilty of a . . . felony.[406]

As the statute's language indicates, intent to defraud is an integral element of the offense,[407] and the victim must be a bank or other financial institution.[408]

---

[405] 720 ILCS 5/17-1(C) (1999).

[406] 720 ILCS 5/17-1(C) (1999).

[407] 720 ILCS 5/17-1(C) (1999).

[408] 720 ILCS 5/17-1(C) (1999).

§ 11.40. Impersonating a Police Officer or Member of Fraternal, Veterans, or Charitable Organization.

The next major provision of article 5/17 involves the deceptive impersonation of a police officer or a member of a fraternal, veteran's, or charitable organization. Section 5/17-2 provides:

> (a) A person commits a false impersonation when he or she falsely represents himself or herself to be a member of any police, fraternal or veterans' organization, including the Illinois Police Association, or a representative of any charitable organization, or when any person exhibits or uses in any manner any decal, badge or insignia of any police organization when not authorized to do by such police organization.
>
> (a-5) A person commits false personation when he or she falsely represents himself or herself to be a veteran in seeking employment or public office. In this subsection, "veteran" means a person who has served in the Armed Services or Reserved Forces of the United States.
>
> (b) No person shall use the words "Chicago Police," "Chicago Police Department," "Chicago Patrolman," "Chicago Sergeant," "Chicago Lieutenant," "Chicago Peace Officer" or any other words to the same effect in the title of any organization, magazine, or other publication without the express approval of the Chicago Police Board.
>
> (c) No person may solicit advertisements to appear in any firefighters', law enforcement or police officers' magazine, journal or other publication without first having obtained a current certificate of qualification from the Illinois Attorney General. Upon the presentation of proof that the applicant does in fact represent a legitimate and bona fide firefighters', law enforcement or police officers' publication, the Attorney General may issue to the applicant a certificate of qualification to solicit advertisements on behalf of such publication. The Attorney General shall prescribe forms and promulgate rules governing the making of applications and the certification of persons under this subsection.[409]

Subsection (d) of this enactment states that false personification is a misdemeanor unless the conviction is a second or subsequent offense, whereupon it is classified as a felony.[410]

With respect to this crime, it is important to note that "false representation of membership in the organization is sufficient: obtaining pecuniary or other benefit is not required."[411] Where a defendant, on a certain date at a certain place,

---

[409] 720 ILCS 5/17–2 (1999).

[410] 720 ILCS 5/17-2(d) (1999).

[411] ILL. ANN. STAT. Ch. 38, para. 17-2 (Smith-Hurd 1977), 1961 Committee Comments, at 279 (revised 1970).

stated to named individuals that he was a police officer, this was prohibited.[412] Also, evidence that an accused, without authorization, displayed a military police badge to a police officer after he was involved in an automobile accident was sufficient to support a conviction for false impersonation.[413]

§ 11.41. Forgery.

The next principal offense contained in article 5/17 is "forgery." Section 5/17-3 sets forth this stricture.

> (a) A person commits forgery when, with intent to defraud, he knowingly: (1) Makes or alters any document apparently capable of defrauding another in such manner that it purports to have been made by another or at another time, or with different provisions, or by authority of one who did not give such authority; or (2) Issues or delivers such document knowing it to have been thus made or altered; or (3) Possesses, with intent to issue or deliver, any such document knowing it to have been thus made or altered; or (4) Unlawfully uses the digital signature, as defined in the Financial Instructions Digital Signature Act.
>
> (b) An intent to defraud means an intention to cause another to assume, create, transfer, alter or terminate any right, obligation or power with reference to any person or property. As used in the Section, "document" includes, but is not limited to, any document, representation, or image produced manually, electronically, or by computer.
>
> (c) A document apparently capable of defrauding another includes, but is not limited to, one by which any right, obligation or power with reference to any person or property may be created, transferred, altered or terminated.
>
> (d) Sentence. Forgery is a . . . felony. [414]

The revision committee clarifies that section 5/17-3 is a mere codification of prior enactments which outlawed various forms of forgery: currency, records, securities, bills, notes, and public records.[415] Also, it was determined that it was useful to clarify in section (b) the "intent to defraud" language because of "the fragmentary elements enunciated in the cases but not brought together in any one statement" and to offer some definitional illustrations of documents having

---

[412] People v. Vysther, 49 Ill. App. 2d 223, 224, 199 N.E.2d 668, 669 (1st Dist. 1964).

[413] People v. Bolling, 181 Ill. App. 3d 845, 849, 537 N.E.2d 1100, 1102 (2d Dist 1989).

[414] 720 ILCS 5/17-3 (1999).

[415] ILL. ANN. STAT. Ch. 38, para. 17-3 (Smith-Hurd 1977), 1961 Committee Comments, at 280-81 (revised 1970).

the capacity to defraud without in any way limiting the definition to those illustrations, "since the possible variations are innumerable."[416]

In proving forgery, the state must demonstrate the existence of two mental states: (1) intent to defraud and (2) knowledgeable performance of one of the four acts specified in the statute.[417] An element of forgery is that the document made or altered have the apparent capability of defrauding another.[418] A document does not have to be in "due legal form"[419] or so skillfully prepared that only an expert could detect the forgery.[420] The test to determine whether a document has the apparent ability to defraud another is "whether a reasonable and ordinary person might be deceived into accepting the document as true and genuine and whether it creates, transfers, alters or terminates any right, obligation or power with reference to any person or property."[421]

The crime of forgery does not require that anyone actually be defrauded of valuable consideration.[422] A person is guilty of forgery even where he or she unsuccessfully attempts to pass a forged document.[423] Furthermore, delivery of the forged instrument to another is not required; it is sufficient if the alteration

---

[416] ILL. ANN. STAT. Ch. 38, para. 17-3 (Smith-Hurd 1977), 1961 Committee Comments, at 281 (revised 1970).

[417] People v. Stout, 108 Ill. App. 3d 96, 100, 438 N.E.2d 952, 955 (2d Dist. 1982). *See also* People v. Hockaday, 93 Ill. 2d 279, 282, 443 N.E.2d 566, 567 (1982) (setting out the elements of forgery by delivery).

[418] People v. Turner, 179 Ill. App. 3d 510, 516, 534 N.E.2d 179, 183 (2d Dist. 1989); People v. Mattingly, 180 Ill. App. 3d 573, 574, 536 N.E.2d 257, 258 (4th Dist. 1989). *Compare* People v. Kelley, 129 Ill. App. 3d 920, 921-22, 473 N.E.2d 572, 573 (3d Dist. 1985) (defendant's signing of alias on probation certificate did not make document capable of defrauding another since certificate had no apparent legal efficacy and could not affect rights of another).

[419] People v. Turner, 179 Ill. App. 3d 510, 518, 534 N.E.2d 179, 184 (2d Dist. 1989); People v. Tarkowski, 106 Ill. App. 3d 597, 601, 435 N.E.2d 1339, 1343 (2d Dist. 1982).

[420] People v. Turner, 179 Ill. App. 3d 510, 518, 534 N.E.2d 179, 184 (2d Dist. 1989).

[421] People v. Rennels, 227 Ill. App. 3d 263, 265, 591 N.E.2d 130, 131 (5th Dist. 1992) *quoting* People v. Panagiotis, 162 Ill. App. 3d 866, 872-73, 516 N.E.2d 280, 284 (1st Dist. 1987).

[422] People v. Varellas, 138 Ill. App. 3d 820, 826, 486 N.E.2d 388, 393 (2d Dist. 1985); People v. Tarkowski, 106 Ill. App. 3d 597, 601, 435 N.E.2d 1339, 1343 (2d Dist. 1982).

[423] People v. Douglas, 86 Ill. App. 3d 668, 672-73, 408 N.E.2d 239, 243 (1st Dist. 1980); People v. Eston, 49 Ill. App. 3d 747, 749, 364 N.E.2d 609, 611 (4th Dist. 1977).

occurs with the concurrent intent to defraud.[424] Where a forged document is delivered to another, however, intent to defraud is presumed.[425]

The crime of forgery presupposes lack of authority to prepare the document in question. Thus, where a defendant, the executor of an estate, had the authority to draw checks on the estate account, he could not be convicted of forgery.[426]

The meaning of the term *makes* as it appears in the forgery statute includes "endorses."[427] To *issue* a document means to "utter" or "offer" it to another.[428]

The forgery prohibition has been used in a wide variety of circumstances. Examples of forgery include: delivering a false prescription to a pharmacist in order to procure a controlled substance;[429] presenting a credit card sales draft on a credit card not belonging to the defendant;[430] a bookkeeper's unauthorized adding of his name as a party to whom a credit card was to be issued;[431] endorsing and depositing another's check in one's personal account;[432] and also the more obvious forgery situation.

§ 11.42. Deceptive Altering or Sale of Coins.

Section 5/17-4 is aimed at the "deceptive altering or sale of coins." It reads:

(a) A person commits a deceptive altering of coins when he in any manner alters any coin to increase the value of the coin to coin collectors.
(b) A person commits a deceptive sale of coins when he sells or advertises for sale any coin he knows has been deceptively altered for a higher rate or value than is indicated by the denomination of the coin.

---

[424] People v. Passantino, 67 Ill. App. 3d 469, 472, 385 N.E.2d 141, 143 (2d Dist. 1979) (defendant convicted of forgery on accountability theory). For a factually interesting case holding defendant liable for forgery on an accountability theory, *see* People v. Kunce, 196 Ill. App. 3d 388, 390-91, 553 N.E.2d 799, 801 (3d Dist. 1990) (evidence showed defendant "witnessed" signature of man who had been dead for several years but whose wife kept the body in her home, thinking he was only in a coma, and defendant knew document would be used by decedent's wife to defraud bank to refinance house).
[425] People v. Eston, 49 Ill. App. 3d 747, 750, 364 N.E.2d 609, 611 (4th Dist. 1977).
[426] People v. Lindquist, 97 Ill. App. 3d 894, 895, 424 N.E.2d 66, 67 (3d Dist. 1981).
[427] People v. Connell, 91 Ill. App. 3d 326, 334, 414 N.E.2d 796, 802 (5th Dist. 1980) (defendant's conviction for forgery affirmed where court found that he "made" a check by endorsing it with the name of another person). *See also* People v. Stevens, 128 Ill. App. 3d 823, 825-26, 471 N.E.2d 581, 583 (4th Dist. 1984) ("the test of an endorsement in a forgery trial is whether the endorsement renders the instrument capable of defrauding and is made for that purpose").
[428] People v. Henderson, 71 Ill. 2d 53, 57, 373 N.E.2d 1338, 1340 (1978). *See* People v. Varellas, 138 Ill. App. 3d 820, 826, 486 N.E.2d 388, 393 (2d Dist. 1985) (intent to defraud is presumed where a forged instrument is uttered or offered).
[429] People v. Henderson, 71 Ill. 2d 53, 57, 373 N.E.2d 1338, 1340 (1978).
[430] People v. Reynolds, 85 Ill. App. 3d 549, 554, 407 N.E.2d 64, 68-9 (5th Dist. 1980).
[431] People v. Murrah, 255 Ill. App. 3d 742, 748, 627 N.E.2d 1138, 1142 (4th Dist. 1993).
[432] People v. Toellen, 66 Ill. App. 3d 967, 971, 384 N.E.2d 480, 483 (3d Dist. 1978).

(c) Sentence. Deceptive altering or sale of coins is a . . . misdemeanor.[433]

Because no caselaw exists on this matter, it is unclear whether the offense may be in the nature of strict liability. The judicial presumption against strict liability,[434] however, makes this proposition unlikely.

§ 11.43. Deceptive Collection Practices.

Section 5/17-5 of chapter 720 covers "deceptive collection practices"[435] and is designed to control the egregious tactics of some debt collection bureaus.

> A collection agency . . . or any employee of such collection agency commits a deceptive collection practice when, with the intent to collect a debt owed to a person, corporation, or other entity, he:
>
> > (a) represents falsely that he is an attorney, a policeman, a sheriff or deputy sheriff, a bailiff, a county clerk or employee of a county clerk's office, or any other person who by statute is authorized to enforce the law or any order of a court; or
> >
> > (b) while attempting to collect an alleged debt, misrepresents to the alleged debtor or to his immediate family the corporate, partnership or proprietary name or other trade or business name under which the debt collector is engaging in debt collections and which he is legally authorized to use; or
> >
> > (c) while attempting to collect an alleged debt, adds to the debt any service charge, interest or penalty which he is not entitled by law to add; or
> >
> > (d) threatens to ruin, destroy, or otherwise adversely affect an alleged debtor's credit rating unless, at the same time, a disclosure is made in accordance with federal law that the alleged debtor has a right to inspect his credit rating; or
> >
> > (e) accepts from an alleged debtor a payment which he knows is not owed.
>
> The commission of a deceptive collection practice is a Business Offense punishable by a fine. . . .[436]

A mens rea of intent to collect a debt is an essential element of this offense.

---

[433] 720 ILCS 5/17-4 (1993).

[434] *See* ch. 2 of this treatise.

[435] 720 ILCS 5/17-5 (1999).

[436] 720 ILCS 5/17-5 (1999).

§ 11.44. State Benefits Fraud.

Because of the proliferation of false applications for various types of public aid and welfare benefits, the General Assembly included in the code a prohibition against "[s]tate benefit fraud."[437] Section 5/17-6 provides that this crime is committed whenever a person obtains or attempts to obtain money or benefits from the State of Illinois, any political subdivision in Illinois, or any program funded or administered, completely or partially, by the state or its political subdivisions, through the knowing (1) use of false identification documents, or (2) misrepresentation of age, residence, number of dependents, marital or family status, employment status, financial status, "or any other material fact" on which a recipient's eligibility for benefits or level of benefits "might be based."[438] Thus, a defendant who was actually employed during the four years she received over $19,000.00 in excess benefits from Aid to Dependent Children and received such aid due to her alleged unemployment was properly convicted of this offense.[439] Where a state benefits recipient failed to disclose that he was self-employed in a business selling used automobiles and had a bank account through which more than $35,000 flowed, he was convicted of state benefits fraud.[440] Also, it should be noted that a defendant cannot be convicted of both theft and state benefits fraud where the offenses arise from the same physical act.[441]

§ 11.45. Promotion of Pyramid Sales Schemes.

Section 5/17-7 took effect in 1984 and sets out the offense of "promotion of pyramid sales schemes." It provides:

(a) The term "pyramid sales scheme" means any plan or operation whereby a person, in exchange for money or other thing of value, acquires the opportunity to receive a benefit or thing of value, which is primarily based upon the inducement of additional persons, by himself or others, regardless of number, to participate in the same plan or operation and is not primarily contingent on the volume or quantity of goods, services, or other property sold or distributed or to be sold or distributed to persons for purposes of resale to consumers. For purposes of this subsection, "money or other thing of value" shall not include payments made for sales demonstration equipment and materials furnished on a nonprofit basis for use in making sales and not for resale.

---

[437] 720 ILCS 5/17-6 (1999).

[438] 720 ILCS 5/17-6 (1999).

[439] People v. Streit, 193 Ill. App. 3d 443, 444-45, 550 N.E.2d 244, 245-46 (3d Dist. 1990).

[440] People v. Brown, 295 Ill. App. 3d 128, 129-31, 691 N.E.2d 879, 880-81 (3d Dist 1998).

[441] People v. Powell, 199 Ill. App. 3d 291, 293, 556 N.E.2d 896, 897 (4th Dist. 1990).

(b) Any person who knowingly sells, offers to sell, or attempts to sell the right to participate in a pyramid sales scheme commits a . . . misdemeanor.[442]

§ 11.46. Health Care Benefits and Public Aid Fraud.

The Illinois legislature has created three offenses involving fraud upon a health care or public aid provider. The first is the offense of "health care benefits fraud."[443] Section 5/17-8 provides:

(a) A person commits health care benefits fraud if he or she with the intent to defraud or deceive any provider, other than a governmental unit or agency, obtains or attempts to obtain health care benefits.
(b) Health care benefits fraud is a . . . misdemeanor.[444]

The second offense is "public aid wire fraud."[445] Contained in section 5/17-9, this stricture prohibits anyone from knowingly engaging in any communication by telephone, wire, radio, or television, the transmission of which is made or received in Illinois, that is intended to further any scheme to unlawfully receive any benefit or payment under the Illinois Public Aid Code.[446] It also prohibits anyone from knowingly directing or causing another to communicate by wire for the same purpose.[447] This conduct is a felony.[448]

A companion prohibition is "public aid mail fraud."[449] Section 5/17-10 outlaws any person from knowingly communicating by mail or any other public or private delivery carrier system, whether the communication is placed or received in Illinois, where the communication to be delivered is intended to further any scheme designed to obtain illegal Illinois public aid benefits.[450] This crime is also committed where a person knowingly directs or causes another to communicate in the same way for the same purpose.[451] Violation of this law is a felony.[452]

---

[442] 720 ILCS 5/17-7 (1999).
[443] 720 ILCS 5/17-8 (1999).
[444] 720 ILCS 5/17-8 (1999).
[445] 720 ILCS 5/17-9 (1999).
[446] 720 ILCS 5/17-9(a) (1999).
[447] 720 ILCS 5/17-9(b) (1999).
[448] 720 ILCS 5/17-9(c) (1999).
[449] 720 ILCS 5/17-10 (1999).
[450] 720 ILCS 5/17-10(a) (1999).
[451] 720 ILCS 5/17-10(b) (1999).
[452] 720 ILCS 5/17-10(c) (1999).

§ 11.47. Odometer and Hour Meter Fraud.

The legislature has outlawed odometer and hour meter fraud in two separate prohibitions. "Odometer fraud," contained in section 5/17, makes it illegal for any person who, with the intent to defraud another, disconnects, resets, alters or causes another to disconnect, reset, or alter the odometer of any used motor vehicle for the purpose of concealing the vehicle's true mileage.[453] This offense does not apply to legitimate practices of automotive parts recyclers who recycle used odometers for resale.[454] Odometer fraud is a misdemeanor but is designated as a felony when it is a subsequent offense.[455]

Section 5/17-11.1 reflects the misdemeanor offense of "hour meter fraud."[456] This provision makes it a crime for a person who, "with intent to defraud another, disconnects, resets, or alters, or causes to be disconnected, reset, or altered, the hour meter of any used farm implement, . . . with intent to conceal or change the actual hours of operation . . . ."[457] This offense is also a misdemeanor unless it is a subsequent conviction, whereupon it is a felony.[458]

§ 11.48. Fraudulent Advertisement of Corporate Name.

Section 5/17-12 contains a provision called "fraudulent advertisement of a corporate name."[459] It reads: "If a company, association, or person puts forth a sign or advertisement and assumes, for the purpose of soliciting business, a corporate name, not being incorporated, the company, association, or person commits a petty offense and is guilty of an additional petty offense for each day he, she, or it continues to so offend."[460]

§ 11.49. Fraudulent Land Sales and Fraudulent Conveyances of Property.

A person who sells, barters, or disposes of a tract of land, and who then attempts to sell that same tract of land to another, is guilty of the felony offense of "fraudulent land sales."[461] Additionally, a person who is a party to a fraudulent conveyance of land, contract, or other interest, takes action with intent to deceive and defraud others, or to defeat or delay creditors or others of their just

---

[453] 720 ILCS 5/17-11 (1999). *See* 625 ILCS 5/3-112.1 (1999) for odometer certification, certificates of title and registration of vehicles.

[454] 720 ILCS 5/17-11 (1999).

[455] 720 ILCS 5/17-11 (1999).

[456] 720 ILCS 5/17-11.1 (1999).

[457] 720 ILCS 5/17-11.1 (1999).

[458] 720 ILCS 5/17-11.1 (1999).

[459] 720 ILCS 5/17-12 (1999).

[460] 720 ILCS 5/17-12 (1999).

[461] 720 ILCS 5/17-13 (1999).

debts, commits the business offense of "party to fraudulent land conveyance."[462] Where an officer authorized to take proof or acknowledgement of a conveyance of real or personal property willfully certifies a conveyance as having been made that was not in fact made, or made at a different time, with the intent to injure or defraud, or to enable another to injure or defraud, the officer commits the felony called "acknowledgment of fraudulent conveyance."[463]

§ 11.50. Fraudulent Production of an Infant.

Another type of fraudulent scheme was addressed when the legislature created the offense of "fraudulent production of an infant."[464] Section 5/17-16 provides:

> A person who fraudulently produces an infant, falsely pretending it to have been born of parents whose child would be entitled to a share of a personal estate, or to inherit real estate, with the intent of intercepting the inheritance of the real estate, or the distribution of the personal property from a person lawfully entitled to the property . . . is guilty of a felony.[465]

§ 11.51. Fraudulent Issuance of Stock.

The Illinois Criminal Code provides for the offense of "fraudulent issuance of stock,"[466] which provides that every officer, agent, attorney, or employee of a bank, railroad, or manufacturing or other corporation, and "every other person who, knowingly and . . . with intent to defraud . . .," issues, sells, transfers, assigns, or pledges . . . any false, fraudulent, or simulated certificate or . . . shares of the capital stock of a bank, railroad, or manufacturing or other corporation, is guilty of a . . . felony."[467] Additionally, anyone who signs a fraudulent certificate or other evidence of stock with intent to issue or sell, or cause to be sold, that stock is guilty of a felony called "officer signing fraudulent stock."[468]

§ 11.52. Use of Name "Pawner's Society."

There exists an offense of "use of name of pawner's society."[469] It provides that no person, firm, or corporation may use the name "Pawner's Society" in its

---

[462] 720 ILCS 5/17-14 (1999).
[463] 720 ILCS 5/17-15 (1999).
[464] 720 ILCS 5/17-16 (1999).
[465] 720 ILCS 5/17-16 (1999).
[466] 720 ILCS 5/17-17 (1999).
[467] 720 ILCS 5/17-17 (1999).
[468] 720 ILCS 5/17-18 (1999).
[469] 720 ILCS 5/17-19 (1999).

business name unless authorized under the Pawner's Society Act.[470] Anyone violating this statue shall be guilty of a petty offense.[471]

§ 11.53. Obstructing Gas, Water, Electric Current and Service Meters.

Section 5/17-20 creates the offense of "obstructing gas, water, and electric current meters," which makes it a misdemeanor for a person who, without authority and with intent to defraud a company or an individual, "injures, alters, obstructs, or prevents the action of a meter provided for the purpose of measuring and registering the quantity of gas, water, or electric current consumed by or at a burner, orifice, or place, or supplied to a lamp, motor, machine, or appliance," aids in the injuring or altering of any such meter, or the prevention of its action, or makes a connection to intercept gas, water or electric current without being registered by such meter.[472]

Meanwhile, section 5/17-21 contains the offense called "obstructing service meters."[473] It provides that a person who, with intent to defraud, and without the consent of the owner of the meter, tampers with, or otherwise alters a meter, register, or other counting or measuring device is guilty of a misdemeanor.[474]

§ 11.54. False Information on an Application for Employment with Certain Public or Private Agencies.

Section 5/17-22 outlaws false information on certain employment applications.[475] This misdemeanor stricture provides:

> It is unlawful for an applicant for employment with a public or private agency that provides State funded services to persons with mental illness or developmental disabilities to willfully furnish false information regarding professional certification, licensing, criminal background, or employment history for the 5 years immediately preceeding the date of application on an application for employment with the agency if the position of employment requires or provides opportunity for contact with persons with mental illness or developmental disabilities.[476]

---

[470] 720 ILCS 5/17-19 (1999) (referring to 205 ILCS 505/0.01 *et. seq.* (1999)).
[471] 720 ILCS 5/17-19 (1999).
[472] 720 ILCS 5/17-20 (1999).
[473] 720 ILCS 5/17-21 (1999).
[474] 720 ILCS 5/17-21 (1999).
[475] 720 ILCS 5/17-22 (1999).
[476] 720 ILCS 5/17-22 (1999).

§ 11.55. WIC Fraud.

The legislature enacted the "WIC Fraud" statute in response to the pervasive nature of fraud in the Special Supplemental Food Program for Women, Infants, and Children, known as WIC.[477] Any person who knowingly (1) "uses, acquires, possesses, or transfers . . . WIC Food Instruments" in any way not authorized by law, or (2) alters, possesses or uses such altered WIC food instruments is guilty of a violation of this article.[478] Anyone who misappropriates or converts to his own or another's use any public funds made available to subsidize WIC food programs also commits WIC fraud.[479] Any person who "possesses for an unlawful purpose another person's identification document" which entitles the second person to WIC benefits commits a violation.[480] This offense is a felony if the total amount of money involved is over $150.[481]

§ 11.56. Insurance Fraud and Fraud on a Governmental Entity.

In article 5/46 appears the offenses of "insurance fraud,"[482] "fraud on a governmental entity,"[483] "aggravated fraud,"[484] "conspiracy to commit to fraud,"[485] and "organizer of an aggravated fraud conspiracy."[486]

Section 5/46-1 of the Criminal Code defines "insurance fraud" as occurring whenever a person who "knowingly obtains, attempts to obtain, or causes to be obtained, by deception, control over property of an insurance company or self-insured entity by the making of a false claim on any policy of insurance" issued by such insurance company or entity, "intending to deprive an insurance company or self-insured entity permanently of the use and benefit of that property."[487] Insurance fraud is a misdemeanor where the claim or attempted claim involves $300 or less; otherwise, it is a felony.[488]

The offense of "fraud on a governmental entity," outlawed by section 5/46-1.1, occurs where a person "knowingly obtains, attempts to obtain, or causes to be obtained, by deception, control over the property of any governmental entity by the making of a false claim of bodily injury or of damage to or loss or theft of property against the governmental entity, intending to deprive the governmental

---

[477] 720 ILCS 5/17B-1 (1999) (statement of legislative intent).
[478] 720 ILCS 5/17B-5 (1999).
[479] 720 ILCS 5/17B-10 (1999).
[480] 720 ILCS 5/17B-15 (1999).
[481] 720 ILCS 5/17B-20 (1999).
[482] 720 ILCS 5/46-1 (1999).
[483] 720 ILCS 5/46-1.1 (1999).
[484] 720 ILCS 5/46-2 (1999).
[485] 720 ILCS 5/46-3 (1999).
[486] 720 ILCS 5/46-4 (1999).
[487] 720 ILCS 5/46-1(a) (1999).
[488] 720 ILCS 5/46-1(b) (1999).

entity permanently of the use and benefit of that property."[489] If the claim of loss is $300 or less, the offense is a misdemeanor; otherwise, it is a felony.[490]

Section 5/46-2 of the Criminal Code provides that a person commits "aggravated fraud" when, within an eighteen-month period, the person makes three or more false claims arising out of separate incidents or transactions,[491] each of which standing alone would constitute an act of insurance fraud or fraud on a governmental entity.[492] Aggravated fraud is a felony.[493]

Section 5/46-3 of the Criminal Code prohibits the offense of "conspiracy to commit fraud."[494] A person commits this conspiracy when, with the intent that a violation of insurance fraud, fraud on a governmental entity or aggravated fraud be committed, he or she agrees with another to violate either one or more of these offenses.[495] No person may be convicted of conspiracy to commit fraud unless an overt act or acts in furtherance of the agreement is alleged and proved to have been committed by this person or by a co-conspirator and this person is a part of a common scheme or plan to engage in the unlawful activity.[496] Where the offense intended to be committed is a violation of aggravated fraud, the person or persons with whom the accused is alleged to have agreed to commit the three or more violations of insurance fraud or fraud on a governmental entity need not be the same person or persons for each violation, as long as the accused was a part of the common scheme or plan to engage in each of the three or more alleged violations.[497]

Pursuant to this conspiracy law, the section provides that it is not a defense that the person or persons with whom the accused is alleged to have conspired have not been prosecuted or convicted, have been convicted of a different offense, are not amenable to justice, have been acquitted, or lacked the capacity to commit an offense.[498] The section also provides that, "notwithstanding Section [5/]8-5 of the Code, a person may be convicted and sentenced both for the offense of conspiracy to commit fraud and for any other crime that is the object of the conspiracy."[499]

Another crime directed at insurance fraud is the offense of "organizer of an aggravated fraud conspiracy."[500] This section provides that a person commits the

---

[489] 720 ILCS 5/46-1.1(a) (1999).

[490] 720 ILCS 5/46-1.1(b) (1999).

[491] 720 ILCS 5/46-2(a) (1999).

[492] 720 ILCS 5/46-2(a) (1999).

[493] 720 ILCS 5/46-2(b) (1999).

[494] 720 ILCS 5/46-3 (1999).

[495] 720 ILCS 5/46-3(a) (1999).

[496] 720 ILCS 5/46-3(a) (1999).

[497] 720 ILCS 5/46-3(a) (1999).

[498] 720 ILCS 5/46-3(b) (1999).

[499] 720 ILCS 5/46-3(c) (1999).

[500] 720 ILCS 5/46-4 (1999).

offense of organizer of an aggravated fraud conspiracy when this person, with the intent that a violation of aggravated fraud be committed, agrees with another to the commission of that offense, and "with respect to other persons within the conspiracy, occupies a position of organizer, supervisor, financier, or other position of management."[501] The offense further provides that no person may be convicted of this offense "unless an overt act or acts in furtherance of the agreement is alleged and proved to have been committed by him or a co-conspirator and the accused is part of a common scheme or plan to engage in the unlawful activity."[502] The person or persons with whom the accused is alleged to have agreed to commit three or more violations of insurance fraud or fraud on a governmental entity need not be the same person or persons for each violation, provided that the accused occupied a position as organizer, supervisor, financier, or other position of management in each of the three or more alleged violations.[503]

The defendant lacks the same defenses as for aggravated insurance fraud conspiracy.[504] Notwithstanding Section 5/8-5, the defendant may be convicted and sentenced for the offense of organizer of an aggravated insurance fraud conspiracy and for any other offense that is the object of the conspiracy.[505] This offense is a felony.[506]

---

[501] 720 ILCS 5/46-4(a) (1999).
[502] 720 ILCS 5/46-4(a) (1999).
[503] 720 ILCS 5/46-4(a) (1999).
[504] 720 ILCS 5/46-4(b) (1999).
[505] 720 ILCS 5/46-4(c) (1999).
[506] 720 ILCS 5/46-4(d) (1999).

CHAPTER 12

ROBBERY, ARMED ROBBERY AND RELATED OFFENSES

§ 12.01. Introduction.

The offenses of robbery and armed robbery are codified in article 5/18 of the Illinois Criminal Code. These offenses are identical with one exception: a robbery committed by an individual armed with a dangerous weapon is an armed robbery. Both offenses require the victim's property to be taken from his or her person or presence by force or threat of imminent use of force. Neither robbery nor armed robbery require a specific intent to permanently deprive the victim of the use or benefit of the property taken. Hence, the discussion of robbery which appears below is equally applicable to the subsequent analysis of armed robbery. In addition to robbery and armed robbery, article 5/18 contains the offense of aggravated robbery, which arises where the defendant claims to have a weapon during a robbery but in actuality is unarmed. Finally, article 5/18 reflects the crimes of vehicular hijacking, which is essentially robbery of a motor vehicle, and aggravated vehicular hijacking, which is basically vehicular hijacking involving circumstances of aggravation.

§ 12.02. Robbery.

The next sections deal in detail with the codification and elements of robbery.

§ 12.03.   — Robbery Codified.

The current Illinois robbery statute provides: "A person commits robbery when he or she takes property, except a motor vehicle covered by Section 18-3 or 18-4, from the person or presence of another by the use of force or by threatening the imminent use of force."[1] In enacting this legislation, it was the intent of the legislature to (1) incorporate into the statute the meaning of *property* as defined in section 5/15-1 and (2) not include a mental state requirement within the language of the prohibition, since "taking by force or threat of force is the gist of the offense and no intent need be charged."[2]

§ 12.04.   — Elements of Robbery.

The essential elements of robbery are (1) the taking from a person, or his presence, a thing of value other than a motor vehicle and (2) the use of either force or threat of imminent force.[3] Many courts have used the term "intimidation" to indicate a threat of the imminent use of force. Although "intimidation" does not appear in the definition of robbery, there is no difference between "intimidation" and the threat of imminent use of force.[4]

There are three major distinctions between robbery and theft. First, unlike theft, robbery requires the use of force or the threat of the imminent use of force.[5] Second, while some theft charges require the specific intent to permanently deprive a person of the use or benefit of the property taken, robbery only requires a showing of general intent.[6] Third, also unlike theft, the value of the property taken in a robbery is "immaterial as long as it is shown to have some value."[7] Thus, robbery is not a type of theft.[8] However, the Illinois Supreme

---

[1] 720 ILCS 5/18-1(1999). Robbery is a Class 2 felony. However, if the victim is 60 years of age or older or is physical handicapped, robbery is a Class 1 felony.

[2] ILL. ANN. STAT. ch. 38, para. 18-1 (Smith-Hurd Supp. 1992), 1961 Committee Comments, at 113 (revised 1970).

[3] People v. Robinson, 206 Ill. App. 3d 1046, 1053, 565 N.E.2d 206, 210 (1st Dist. 1990); People v. Cox, 197 Ill. App. 3d 1028, 1038, 557 N.E.2d 288, 296 (1st Dist. 1990).

[4] *See* People v. Gauwitz, 80 Ill. App. 3d 362, 368, 400 N.E.2d 92, 97 (4th Dist. 1980) ("The element of intimidation has been incorporated in the Criminal Code of 1961 by use of the language, 'by threatening the imminent use of force'").

[5] People v. Brooks, 202 Ill. App. 3d 164, 169, 559 N.E.2d 859, 862 (1st Dist. 1990); People v. Jackson, 158 Ill. App. 3d 394, 397, 511 N.E.2d 923, 925 (5th Dist. 1987).

[6] People v. Rivers, 194 Ill. App. 3d 193, 195, 550 N.E.2d 1179, 1180 (1st Dist. 1990); People v. Talley, 177 Ill. App. 3d 170, 173, 531 N.E.2d 1139, 1141 (4th Dist. 1988).

[7] People v. Caldwell, 62 Ill. App. 2d 279, 286, 210 N.E.2d 556, 559 (2d Dist. 1965).

[8] People v. McCarty, 94 Ill. 2d 28, 33, 445 N.E.2d 298, 302 (1983). In *McCarty*, the Illinois Supreme Court reversed, in relevant part, a decision by the Third Appellate District that held that robbery was an "aggravated form of theft." People v. McCarty, 101 Ill. App. 3d 355, 357, 427 N.E.2d 1382, 1384 (3d Dist. 1981), *aff'd in part, rev'd in part*, 94 Ill. 2d 28, 445 N.E.2d 298 (1983). The court noted that "while theft and robbery have the common element of a wrongful taking of property and may be viewed by laymen as different forms of the same crime, 'robbery' as

Court has declared that theft may be considered a lesser included offense of robbery.[9]

§ 12.05.   — A Taking of Property.

A critical element of robbery is that the victim must "be deprived of some property through the actions of the perpetrator."[10] Consequently, where no property is taken from an alleged victim, no robbery exists.[11] The duration of the deprivation is not pertinent to the offense of robbery.[12] Furthermore it is not necessary to establish the value of the property taken,[13] provided the property has "some value"[14] or "a value."[15] Where a victim's gun, wallet, and some small change were taken, there was a sufficient "taking" even though the value of the property taken was *de minimis*.[16] Similarly, the taking of one dollar was sufficient to sustain an armed robbery conviction.[17] In addition to the value of the property being immaterial, a precise identification of the property is unnecessary if its character is such that exact identification is difficult, which is particularly true of money.[18]

For purposes of the robbery statute, proof of the victim's actual ownership is not necessary where care, custody or control by the victim is shown.[19] Therefore, a sufficient taking occurs where the property taken belongs to the victim's family member,[20] employer,[21] partnership,[22] or corporation.[23] The taking requirement was met when a defendant forcibly re-took his gambling losses from a pool hustler since "the victim had an interest which was superior to that of the defendant."[24]

---

defined by the legislature is not a 'type of theft,' but a separate crime against property." People v. McCarty, 94 Ill. 2d 28, 34, 445 N.E.2d 298, 302 (1983).

[9] People v. Jones, 149 Ill. 2d 288, 298, 595 N.E.2d 1071, 1076 (1992).

[10] People v. Robinson, 92 Ill. App. 3d 397, 398, 416 N.E.2d 65, 66 (1st Dist. 1981).

[11] People v. Triplett, 138 Ill. App. 3d 1070, 1073, 487 N.E.2d 39, 41-42 (1st. Dist. 1985).

[12] People v. Banks, 75 Ill. 2d 383, 387, 388 N.E.2d 1244, 1246-47 (1979).

[13] People v. Crespo, 118 Ill. App. 3d 815, 822, 455 N.E.2d 854, 860 (1st Dist. 1983).

[14] People v. Smith, 66 Ill. App. 2d 257, 262, 213 N.E.2d 135, 137 (2d Dist. 1966).

[15] People v. Was, 22 Ill. App. 3d 859, 863, 318 N.E.2d 309, 313 (1st Dist. 1974).

[16] People v. Ford, 34 Ill. App. 3d 79, 83, 339 N.E.2d 293, 297 (1st Dist. 1975).

[17] *See* People v. Clemons, 179 Ill. App. 3d 667, 534 N.E.2d 676 (2d Dist. 1989).

[18] People v. Cookson, 108 Ill. App. 3d 861, 865, 439 N.E.2d 1033, 1036 (4th Dist. 1982).

[19] People v. Steenbergen, 31 Ill. 2d 615, 619, 203 N.E.2d 404, 407 (1964), *cert. denied*, 382 U.S. 853 (1965); People v. Ortiz, 156 Ill. App. 3d 170, 175, 509 N.E.2d 633, 637 (1st Dist. 1987).

[20] *See* People v. Ortiz, 156 Ill. App. 3d 170, 509 N.E.2d 633 (1st Dist. 1987).

[21] *See* People v. Aughinbaugh, 131 Ill. App. 2d 581, 583, 266 N.E.2d 530, 531-32 (1st Dist. 1970).

[22] *See* People v. Wooley, 127 Ill. App. 2d 249, 256-57, 262 N.E.2d 237, 240 (1st Dist. 1970).

[23] *See* People v. Steenbergen, 31 Ill. 2d 615, 619, 203 N.E.2d 404, 407 (1964), *cert. denied*, 382 U.S. 853 (1965).

[24] *See* People v. Robinson, 68 Ill. App. 3d 687, 689, 386 N.E.2d 165, 167 (4th Dist. 1979).

The taking element is satisfied where the robber takes either actual or constructive possession of the victim's property.[25] Where a robber pointed a pistol at his victim and said, "This is a stick-up," and where the victim dropped his money on the floor, the taking was complete even if the robber failed to pick up and carry away any of the victim's money.[26] Similarly, a taking occurred where a defendant forcefully removed his victim's watch after beating him, even though the defendant never took actual possession of the watch after laying it on the floor next to the victim.[27]

Obviously, the taking requirement is met when a victim relinquishes possession of property in an attempt to escape his or her robber.[28] For instance, the taking element was satisfied for the taking of a van where a victim, after being robbed of her van and while being kidnapped in her van, jumped out of that van in order to escape her attackers.[29] However, a taking did not occur despite the denial of a "large measure of control" of the victim's car where the defendant entered his victim's car and forced the victim to drive him out of town.[30] A taking is also complete when property is moved from its customary location with intent to deprive the owner of its possession, even though the attempt to escape with the property is thwarted.[31] Hence, there was a sufficient taking of property where the defendants placed an antique lamp, located in the victim's bedroom, in a pillowcase that was later found in the victim's kitchen near the door through which the defendants escaped.[32]

The Illinois Supreme Court has held that "[t]he property taken must have been taken from the victim of the robbery."[33] According to this rule, if a robber takes property from A (the victim) while B is also present, B has not been robbed unless property was also taken from him;[34] this remains true even if B was threatened with the imminent use of force.[35] Thus, a defendant may only be convicted for one count of robbery unless he has committed "multiple takings from

---

[25] People v. Smith, 78 Ill. 2d 298, 302-03, 399 N.E.2d 1289, 1292 (1980).

[26] People v. Gaines, 88 Ill. 2d 342, 367, 430 N.E.2d 1046, 1058-59 (1981).

[27] People v. Stout, 122 Ill. App. 3d 254, 258, 460 N.E.2d 1205, 1208 (4th Dist. 1984).

[28] See People v. Thomas, 163 Ill. App. 3d 670, 681, 516 N.E.2d 901, 908 (1st Dist. 1987).

[29] People v. Thomas, 163 Ill. App. 3d 670, 681, 516 N.E.2d 901, 908 (1st Dist. 1987). Today, this conduct would be considered vehicular hijacking. See § 12-17 of this chapter.

[30] People v. Strickland, 254 Ill. App. 3d 798, 627 N.E.2d 218 (1st Dist. 1993).

[31] People v. Hovenec, 232 Ill. App. 3d 57, 60, 596 N.E.2d 749, 751-52 (1st Dist. 1992); People v. Ortiz, 156 Ill. App. 3d 170, 174, 509 N.E.2d 633, 636 (1st Dist. 1987); People v. Ditto, 98 Ill. App. 3d 36, 38, 424 N.E.2d 3, 5 (1st Dist. 1981).

[32] People v. Withers, 69 Ill. App. 3d 568, 571, 387 N.E.2d 1007, 1009-10 (1st Dist. 1979).

[33] People v. Gaines, 88 Ill. 2d 342, 368, 430 N.E.2d 1046, 1059 (1981), cert. denied, 456 U.S. 1001 (1982).

[34] See People v. Gaines, 88 Ill. 2d 342, 368, 430 N.E.2d 1046, 1059 (1981), cert. denied, 456 U.S. 1001 (1982).

[35] People v. Tyllas, 96 Ill. App. 3d 1, 6, 420 N.E.2d 625, 629 (1st Dist. 1981).

multiple victims."[36] In contrast, two counts of robbery were sustained where a defendant ordered a gas station employee to empty the money from a cash register, whereupon the defendant took the money, shot that employee, and then demanded and received more money from another employee.[37] Where a defendant, while armed with a shotgun, obtained money from one clerk in the presence of a second clerk and then took an additional amount from the first clerk, which had been handed to her by the second clerk, the defendant committed a robbery of both clerks.[38] When two persons work together as a team in committing a robbery, it is immaterial under accountability principles which of the two actually took property from the victim; they have both committed a robbery.[39]

§ 12.06.   — From the Person or Presence of Another.

A taking of property by force or threat of the imminent use of force is not a robbery unless the property is taken "from the person or presence of another." The Illinois Supreme Court declared that the test for presence under both the robbery and armed robbery statutes is satisfied "if the property taken was sufficiently within the possession or control of the person so that it can be said that violence or the threat of violence was the means by which the taking was effected."[40] Thus, the element of presence may be shown even though the property taken was not on the victim's person or within the victim's immediate control.[41] The presence requirement "relates to the property taken; it must have been in the presence or control of the victim."[42] Accordingly, this requirement was satisfied where store managers were compelled by a defendant's bomb threats over the telephone to give up control of money at certain drop-off points.[43]

A taking occurs in the *presence* of a victim "if the owner, possessor, or custodian of the property is on the premises at the time of the occurrence."[44] Where two women were held at gunpoint in a second floor bedroom while property was being taken from the first floor, the property taken was found to be in the control, custody and, thus, presence of the women at the time of the occurrence.[45] Similarly, property taken from another room was found to be in the presence of a victim who had been raped by defendants and left in the bathroom of her

---

[36] People v. Mack, 105 Ill. 2d 103, 135, 473 N.E.2d 880, 897, *cert. denied*, 493 U.S. 1093, *reh. denied*, 494 U.S. 1092 (1990).

[37] People v. Waldron, 219 Ill. App. 3d 1017, 1042-44, 580 N.E.2d 549, 566-67 (2d Dist. 1991).

[38] People v. Kelly, 25 Ill. App. 3d 753, 759-60, 324 N.E.2d 82, 86-87 (1st Dist. 1975).

[39] *See* People v. Johnson, 220 Ill. App. 3d 550, 555-56, 581 N.E.2d 118, 122-23 (1st Dist. 1991).

[40] People v. Blake, 144 Ill. 2d 314, 320, 579 N.E.2d 861, 864 (1991).

[41] People v. Blake, 144 Ill. 2d 314, 320, 579 N.E.2d 861, 864 (1991).

[42] People v. Smith, 78 Ill. 2d 298, 302, 399 N.E.2d 1289, 1292 (1980).

[43] People v. Smith, 78 Ill. 2d 298, 303, 399 N.E.2d 1289, 1292-93 (1980).

[44] People v. Blake, 144 Ill. 2d 314, 320, 579 N.E.2d 861, 864 (1991).

[45] People v. Blake, 144 Ill. 2d 314, 318-21, 579 N.E.2d 861, 863-64 (1991).

apartment with her hands and ankles tied.[46] Property was also taken from the victim's presence when the victim locked himself in another room to escape from the robber.[47] A robbery conviction was sustained where a defendant took a van from his victim, a car salesman, after tying him up and placing him in the back of another van.[48] One court appeared to extend *presence* to encompass an area which is within walking distance.[49] Where a victim locked a purse in a drawer within her office and later had her keys forcibly taken from her by the defendant in another room, which was within walking distance to the office, the purse taken by the defendant from the office using those keys was found to be in the presence of the victim.[50] Finally, a taking may occur in the presence of a victim even if that victim is dead at the time of the taking.[51]

§ 12.07.   — By Use of Force.

An essential element of the crime of robbery is the use of force or the threat of imminent force.[52] This element has been characterized as the "crux"[53] or "gist"[54] of robbery and distinguishes robbery from theft.[55] A robbery conviction is only proper where the defendant has used "violence or fear of violence as the means to take property in the control of the victim."[56]

The Illinois courts have used two similar standards to determine whether the force or threat requirement is satisfied. Under the first standard, the requirement

> is satisfied if the fear of the alleged victim was of such nature as in reason and common experience is likely to induce a person to part with property for the sake of her person.[57]

Under the second standard,

---

[46] People v. Gibson, 137 Ill. App. 3d 330, 338-40, 484 N.E.2d 858, 864-65 (1st Dist. 1985).

[47] People v. Carpenter, 95 Ill. App. 3d 722, 726-27, 420 N.E.2d 640, 644 (1st Dist. 1981).

[48] People v. Rosa, 111 Ill. App. 3d 384, 390, 444 N.E.2d 233, 238 (2d Dist. 1982). Today, this would be considered vehicular hijacking. *See* § 12-17 of this chapter.

[49] *See* People v. Lee, 222 Ill. App. 3d 436, 442-43, 584 N.E.2d 185, 188 (1st Dist. 1991).

[50] People v. Lee, 222 Ill. App. 3d 436, 442-43, 584 N.E.2d 185, 188 (1st Dist. 1991).

[51] People v. Carreon, 225 Ill. App. 3d 133, 146-47, 587 N.E.2d 532, 541-42 (1st Dist. 1992).

[52] People v. Williams, 118 Ill. 2d 407, 415, 515 N.E.2d 1230, 1234 (1987).

[53] *See, e.g.*, People v. Carlton, 31 Ill. App. 3d 313, 315, 333 N.E.2d 596, 598 (1st Dist. 1975).

[54] *See, e.g.*, People v. Taylor, 129 Ill. 2d 80, 83, 541 N.E.2d 677, 679 (1989); People v. Downey, 162 Ill. App. 3d 322, 331, 515 N.E.2d 362, 367 (2d Dist. 1987).

[55] People v. Taylor, 129 Ill. 2d 80, 83, 541 N.E.2d 677, 679 (1989); People v. Jackson, 158 Ill. App. 3d 394, 397, 511 N.E.2d 923, 925 (5th Dist. 1987).

[56] People v. Tiller, 94 Ill. 2d 303, 316, 447 N.E.2d 174, 181 (1982), *cert. denied*, 461 U.S. 944 (1983).

[57] People v. Cox, 197 Ill. App. 3d 1028, 1038, 557 N.E.2d 288, 296 (1st Dist. 1990). *See also* People v. Generally, 170 Ill. App. 3d 668, 525 N.E.2d 106, 108 (5th Dist. 1988); People v. Downey, 162 Ill. App. 3d 322, 331, 515 N.E.2d 362, 368 (2d Dist. 1987).

the degree of force necessary to constitute robbery must be such that the power of the owner to retain his property is overcome either by actual violence physically applied, or by putting him in such fear as to overpower his will.[58]

The "fear" contained within either standard must be objective; sufficient force does not exist where the victim encounters an unreasonable subjective feeling of fear.[59] Some courts have emphasized that the force or threat must cause the victim to part with property against his or her will;[60] other courts have stressed that the force or threat must temporarily suspend the victim's power to exercise his or her will.[61]

The required force or threat of force must either *precede or be contemporaneous with* the taking of the victim's property.[62] However, the force or threatened force need not transpire before or during the time the property is taken; sufficient force exists where the force used is part of a series of events which constitute a *single incident*[63] or *occurrence*.[64] In other words, as long as there is *some concurrence* between the defendant's threat of force and the taking of the victim's property, there exists a robbery.[65] Thus, a robbery occurs where the taking is without force but the departure is accomplished by force.[66] The force requirement was satisfied where a defendant took a wallet from a woman who, upon noticing the taking, demanded the return of the wallet and was pushed in the shoulder by the defendant as he made his escape.[67] On the other hand, the requisite element of force was not fulfilled where a defendant pushed, kicked, and threatened his victim just before leaving the scene of the crime because the defendant's actions "did not immediately follow the taking or constitute part of

---

[58] People v. Bowel, 111 Ill. 2d 58, 63, 488 N.E.2d 995, 997 (1986); *See also* People v. Harris, 195 Ill. App. 3d 421, 423, 552 N.E.2d 392, 393 (4th Dist. 1990).

[59] People v. Simpson, 178 Ill. App. 3d 1091, 1095, 534 N.E.2d 217, 219 (3d Dist. 1989); People v. Hollingsworth, 120 Ill. App. 3d 177, 179, 457 N.E.2d 1062, 1064 (5th Dist. 1983).

[60] *See, e.g.,* People v. Generally, 170 Ill. App. 3d 668, 673, 525 N.E.2d 106, 108 (5th Dist. 1988); People v. Robinson, 92 Ill. App. 3d 397, 398, 416 N.E.2d 65, 66 (1st Dist. 1981).

[61] *See, e.g.,* People v. Thomas, 189 Ill. App. 3d 365, 370, 545 N.E.2d 289, 293 (1st Dist. 1989); People v. Romo, 85 Ill. App. 3d 886, 892, 407 N.E.2d 661, 666 (1st Dist. 1980).

[62] People v. Foster, 198 Ill. App. 3d 986, 994, 556 N.E.2d 1214, 1220 (1st Dist. 1990); People v. Cox, 197 Ill. App. 3d 1028, 1038-39, 557 N.E.2d 288, 296 (1st Dist. 1990).

[63] People v. Robinson, 206 Ill. App. 3d 1046, 1053-54, 565 N.E.2d 206, 210 (1st Dist. 1990); People v. Brooks, 202 Ill. App. 3d 164, 170, 559 N.E.2d 859, 863 (1st Dist. 1990).

[64] People v. Foster, 198 Ill. App. 3d 986, 995, 556 N.E.2d 1214, 1220 (1st Dist. 1990).

[65] People v. Cortes, 181 Ill. 2d 249, 281, 692 N.E.2d 1129, 1143 (1998); People v. Lewis, 165 Ill. 2d 305, 338, 651 N.E.2d 72, 88 (1995); People v. Hill, 294 Ill. App. 3d 962, 971-72, 691 N.E.2d 797, 804 (1st Dist. 1998).

[66] People v. Brooks, 202 Ill. App. 3d 164, 170, 559 N.E.2d 859, 863 (1st Dist. 1990); People v Foster, 198 Ill. App. 3d 986, 995, 556 N.E.2d 1214, 1220 (1st Dist. 1990); People v. Simpson, 178 Ill. App. 3d 1091, 1095, 534 N.E.2d 217, 219 (3d Dist. 1989).

[67] People v. Brooks, 202 Ill. App. 3d 164, 170, 559 N.E.2d 859, 863 (1st Dist. 1990).

the *res gestae* of the robbery."[68] The fact that the use of force against the victim has rendered the victim incapable of resistance at the time of the taking is not a defense to robbery.[69] Thus, even where no robbery was intended until after the victims were shot does not compel a finding that the force used in the shooting was "unrelated" to the robbery.[70]

The use of a dangerous weapon during a robbery will almost always satisfy the force or threat requirement. For example, property was obviously taken by force or intimidation where a defendant pointed a knife at a store clerk and ordered her to give him all the money.[71] The force requirement was satisfied where the defendant held a gun to the victim's head and robbed him of his money and keys.[72]

The use of a dangerous weapon is not essential to satisfy the force or threat requirement.[73] For instance, there was sufficient force where the defendant broke the car window of the victim and reached into her car and took her purse.[74] However, Illinois courts have made it clear that not all force is sufficient to satisfy a robbery conviction. The force incident to a "snatching" offense, for example, is not in and of itself sufficient to satisfy a robbery conviction.[75]

Historically, Illinois courts have split over how much of a connection must exist between the force and the taking of the property. Some courts have held that the necessary force or threat of imminent force must be used as the *means* of taking the property from the victim.[76] However, the recent trend is to look towards whether the force "facilitated the taking" and "remained in effect until after the defendants fled the scene."[77] The Illinois Supreme Court used the former test in *People v. Tiller*,[78] holding that where a defendant killed a postal carrier and later returned to the scene to take the carrier's postal truck, apparently as an afterthought, the force used in the killing was not for the purpose of obtaining the victim's property and, accordingly, did not satisfy the force element

---

[68] People v. Romo, 85 Ill. App. 3d 886, 892, 407 N.E.2d 661, 666 (1st Dist. 1980).

[69] People v. Foster, 198 Ill. App. 3d 986, 995, 556 N.E.2d 1214, 1220 (1st Dist. 1990).

[70] People v. Washington, 127 Ill. App. 3d 365, 377, 468 N.E.2d 1285, 1294 (1st Dist. 1984).

[71] *See* People v. Westefer, 169 Ill. App. 3d 59, 60-61, 522 N.E.2d 1381, 1383-84 (2d Dist. 1988).

[72] *See* People v. Fitzgerald, 171 Ill. App. 3d 218, 223, 524 N.E.2d 1190, 1193 (1st Dist. 1988).

[73] People v. Frazier, 63 Ill. App. 2d 226, 231, 211 N.E.2d 415, 417 (1st Dist. 1965).

[74] *See* People v. Ware, 168 Ill. App. 3d 845, 846, 523 N.E.2d 46, 47 (1st Dist. 1988).

[75] People v. Patton, 60 Ill. App. 3d 456, 459, 376 N.E.2d 1099, 1101 (3d Dist. 1978), *aff'd*, 76 Ill. 2d 45, 389 N.E.2d 1174 (1979).

[76] People v. Tiller, 94 Ill. 2d 303, 316, 447 N.E.2d 174, 181 (1982), *cert. denied*, 461 U.S. 944 (1983). The First Appellate District has interpreted the requirement that "the force or threat of force must be the means of taking the property" to be synonymous with "the force must precede or be contemporaneous with the taking." People v. Foster, 198 Ill. App. 3d 986, 994, 556 N.E.2d 1214, 1220 (1st Dist. 1990).

[77] People v. Gibson, 137 Ill. App. 3d 330, 339, 484 N.E.2d 858, 865 (1st Dist. 1985).

[78] 94 Ill. 2d 303, 447 N.E.2d 174 (1982), *cert. denied*, 461 U.S. 944 (1983).

of robbery.[79] However, the Illinois Supreme Court in *People v. Lewis*[80] later rejected this analysis and reinstated the standard that if one party gains upper hand as a result of force and that party, without having the intention before the incident, takes property of the vanquished, the offender has committed robbery.[81]

If the force and taking are "continuous acts"[82] or there exists "some concurrence" between the force and the taking,[83] robbery has occurred. The Illinois Supreme Court, in *People v. Williams*,[84] held that the force element was met where a defendant obtained possession of a victim's gold necklace during the commission or immediately following the rape of the victim.[85] The force requirement is also satisfied if there is a "necessary concurrence between the defendant's use or threat of force and his taking" of the property.[86] A robbery conviction has been sustained where a defendant took money and food stamps from another room after he had raped his victim and tied her hands and ankles while in her bathroom.[87] Similarly, where a defendant knocked his victim to the ground, threatened her life, and then, while attempting to rape her, removed her watch and placed it in his pocket, the court found a robbery had occurred because the defendant's physical force and threats caused the victim to part with possession of her property against her will.[88] A robbery also occurred where a defendant removed a coin purse from his victim's bra during the course of raping her and later, while the victim was in the washroom, placed the coin purse in his pocket.[89] Finally, where a defendant demanded money from his victim before choking and raping her in her bedroom, and then went into her living room and took money from her purse, the appellate court held that the force was not limited to the sexual assault; rather, it remained in effect and therefore satisfied robbery's force requirement.[90]

---

[79] People v. Tiller, 94 Ill. 2d 303, 316, 447 N.E.2d 174, 181 (1982), *cert. denied*, 461 U.S. 944 (1983); *See also* People v. Pack, 34 Ill. App. 3d 894, 899, 341 N.E.2d 4, 8 (5th Dist. 1976) (no robbery existed where as an afterthought to choking his victim, the defendant took money from her purse lying on a chair); *See also* People v. King, 67 Ill. App. 3d 754, 759, 384 N.E.2d 1013, 1016-17 (4th Dist. 1979) (no robbery occurred where defendant took victim's purse without force from another room after raping her).

[80] 165 Ill. 2d 305, 651 N.E.2d 72 (1995).

[81] People v. Lewis, 165 Ill. 2d 305, 337-338, 651 N.E.2d 72, 87 (1995), citing People v. Jordan, 303 Ill. 316, 135 N.E. 729 (1922).

[82] People v. Lewis, 165 Ill. 2d 305, 337-338, 651 N.E.2d 72, 87 (1995).

[83] People v. Cortes, 181 Ill. 2d 249, 281, 692 N.E.2d 1129, 1143 (1998).

[84] 118 Ill. 2d 407, 515 N.E.2d 1230 (1987).

[85] People v. Williams, 118 Ill. 2d 407, 416, 515 N.E.2d 1230, 1235 (1987).

[86] People v. Williams, 118 Ill. 2d 407, 416, 515 N.E.2d 1230, 1235 (1987).

[87] People v. Gibson, 137 Ill. App. 3d 330, 338-40, 484 N.E.2d 858, 864-65 (1st Dist. 1985).

[88] People v. Kleba, 110 Ill. App. 3d 345, 356, 442 N.E.2d 605, 613 (1st Dist. 1982).

[89] People v. Talley, 97 Ill. App. 3d 439, 444, 422 N.E.2d 1084, 1088 (1st Dist. 1981).

[90] People v. Pavic, 104 Ill. App. 3d 436, 446, 432 N.E.2d 1074, 1082 (1st Dist. 1982), *overruled in part on other grounds*, People v. Pettit, 101 Ill. 2d 309, 461 N.E.2d 991 (1984).

In *People v. Clemons*,[91] the Illinois appellate court utilized the language of the *Williams* court when it held that the necessary concurrence between the use of force and the taking was sufficient to sustain an armed robbery conviction.[92] In *Clemons*, it was unclear whether the defendant murdered his father and took a dollar from him immediately after the attack or whether he later returned from a bar and took the dollar after his father had already been dead for some time.[93] The court observed that the necessary concurrence between the use of force and the taking existed even if the defendant did not take the dollar until he returned from the bar "since the taking of the dollar resulted from the use of force from the first attack."[94]

The force required for a robbery "is not related to the force used on the object taken but to the force or intimidation directed at the person or the victim."[95] As the Third Appellate District has observed:

> if any force no matter how slight fulfills the requirement contemplated by the robbery statute then even the force necessary to overcome the resistance of friction or gravity which connects property to a person would be sufficient to elevate the offense to that of robbery. Such force would be present even in those cases where the offender does or seeks to exert such force and remove the property without the victim being aware of it. Force or intimidation which is directed at overcoming the will or resistance of the victim is substantially different in quality from that employed in the overcoming of the force which connects the property to the victim. In the usual purse snatching case the only force employed counters the force used to grasp the purse, which is of a different dimension than that contemplated by the robbery statute.[96]

Consequently, where "the article was taken without any sensible or material violence to the person, as snatching a hat from the head or a cane or umbrella from the hand," the offense will be held to be theft from the person rather than robbery.[97] A simple snatching or sudden taking of property from an unsuspecting person will generally yield insufficient force to constitute robbery.[98] Hence, there was insufficient force to sustain a robbery conviction where a defendant removed a purse from the arm of his victim who, failing to realize what was

---

[91] 179 Ill. App. 3d 667, 534 N.E.2d 676 (2d Dist. 1989).

[92] People v. Clemons, 179 Ill. App. 3d 667, 671-72, 534 N.E.2d 676 (2d Dist. 1989) (quoting People v. Williams, 118 Ill. 2d 407, 416, 515 N.E.2d 1230, 1235 (1987)).

[93] People v. Clemons, 179 Ill. App. 3d 667, 672-73, 534 N.E.2d 676, 679 (2d Dist. 1989).

[94] People v. Clemons, 179 Ill. App. 3d 667, 673, 534 N.E.2d 676, 679 (2d Dist. 1989).

[95] People v. Thomas, 119 Ill. App. 3d 464, 466, 456 N.E.2d 684, 685 (2d Dist. 1983).

[96] People v. Patton, 60 Ill. App. 3d 456, 458, 376 N.E.2d 1099, 1101 (3d Dist. 1978), *aff'd*, 76 Ill. 2d 45, 389 N.E.2d 1174 (1978).

[97] People v. Patton, 76 Ill. 2d 45, 52, 389 N.E.2d 1174, 1177 (1979) (quoting Hall v. People, 171 Ill. 540, 542-43, 49 N.E. 495, 496 (1898)).

[98] People v. Patton, 76 Ill. 2d 45, 49, 389 N.E.2d 1174, 1175-76 (1979).

happening until the defendant had fled, did not resist and was not injured in any manner.[99] Nor was there sufficient force where a woman carrying a purse in her fingertips had the purse "swiftly grabbed," throwing her arm back "a little bit."[100] Where a purse snatching left a "red streak" about an inch wide and five inches long on the victim's inner arm, the court held that the severity of the injury was insufficient to support a finding of force necessary to sustain a robbery conviction.[101]

Where property has been "snatched" and (1) a struggle ensues,[102] (2) the victim is injured[103] or (3) the property is so attached to the victim's person or clothing as to offer resistance to a taking,[104] the taking may constitute robbery.[105] If the amount of force exceeds the "mere physical effort" necessary to transfer the object from the owner to the taker a robbery is committed.[106] A robbery was found to exist where a defendant walked towards the victim, took her left hand with his left hand and "touched" her fingertips as he pulled the purse away with his right hand, leaving her fingertips "a little red."[107] A robbery was also committed where a woman's purse was torn from her grasp with force sufficient to spin her entire body around and cause her to lose her balance.[108] Where the victim grabbed the defendant's hand as the defendant snatched the victim's change from a store turnstile, which allowed the defendant's retention of some money while some other money was scattered on the floor, and the victim then grabbed the defendant and fell over the defendant in their physical encounter, the defendant had used force sufficient for robbery.[109]

---

[99] People v. Gray, 80 Ill. App. 3d 817, 819, 400 N.E.2d 473, 474-75 (5th Dist. 1980).

[100] People v. Patton, 76 Ill. 2d 45, 47, 389 N.E.2d 1174, 1175-76 (1979).

[101] People v. Thomas, 119 Ill. App. 3d 464, 467, 456 N.E.2d 684, 685-86 (2d Dist. 1983). *But see* People v. Taylor, 129 Ill. 2d 80, 84, 541 N.E.2d 677, 679 (1989) (where the Illinois Supreme Court held that a robbery occurs where the force used exceeds the "mere physical effort" necessary to transfer the property from the owner to the perpetrator).

[102] People v. Brooks, 202 Ill. App. 3d 164, 170, 559 N.E.2d 859, 862 (1st Dist. 1990); People v. Houston, 151 Ill. App. 3d 718, 721, 502 N.E.2d 1174, 1176 (5th Dist. 1986) (a snatch which is accomplished without force may become robbery where the perpetrator defends against a challenge immediately upon the taking or the perpetrator's departure is accomplished by force).

[103] *See* People v. Patton, 60 Ill. App. 3d 456, 459, 376 N.E.2d 1099, 1100 (3d Dist. 1978), *aff'd*, 76 Ill. 2d 45, 389 N.E.2d 1174 (1979) (a robbery occurs where the victim is substantially injured); People v. Chambliss, 69 Ill. App. 2d 459, 466, 217 N.E.2d 422, 426 (1st Dist. 1966) (a robbery exists where a snatch knocks the victim down).

[104] People v. Taylor, 129 Ill. 2d 80, 84, 541 N.E.2d 677, 679 (1989); People v. Brooks, 202 Ill. App. 3d 164, 169, 559 N.E.2d 859, 862 (1st Dist. 1990).

[105] People v. Brooks, 202 Ill. App. 3d 164, 169, 559 N.E.2d 859, 862 (1st Dist. 1990); People v. Houston, 151 Ill. App. 3d 718, 721, 502 N.E.2d 1174, 1176 (5th Dist. 1986).

[106] People v. Taylor, 129 Ill. 2d 80, 84, 541 N.E.2d 677, 679 (1989).

[107] People v. Bowel, 111 Ill. 2d 58, 61, 488 N.E.2d 995, 997 (1986).

[108] People v. Huntington, 115 Ill. App. 3d 943, 945, 451 N.E.2d 923, 924 (5th Dist. 1983).

[109] People v. Lewis, 285 Ill. App. 3d 653, 656, 673 N.E.2d 1105, 1107 (1st Dist. 1996).

A robbery occurs where property is taken which is "so attached to the person or clothes as to create resistance, however slight."[110] The force required to overcome the physical resistance created by the attachment of an item is distinguished from the "mere physical effort" which occurs when any item *not attached* to the person or clothing of the victim is transferred from the owner to another person.[111] Thus, where a snatch has occurred, the initial inquiry is whether an item is so attached as to create *resistance*.[112] If an item is attached offering resistance to a taking, a robbery occurs when that item is taken.[113] If the item is not so attached as to create resistance to the taking, the offender must use more than "the mere physical effort" of transferring the item from the owner to himself in order to constitute robbery.[114] Thus, the snatching of a necklace was a robbery where the taking by the defendant overcame the resistance created by the attachment.[115] A wallet located in a purse which was on the victim's arm was not found to be so attached as to offer resistance to a taking.[116] In the case of the wallet, something more than the "mere physical effort" to transfer the wallet from the owner to the defendant was needed to constitute a robbery.[117]

An individual may not consent to be robbed, even if the person expecting to be robbed is a police decoy pretending to be intoxicated.[118] A robbery also occurs where a defendant takes property from a victim who offered that property in order to avoid a physical assault from the defendant.[119] Thus, the force element of robbery was satisfied where a defendant after raping his victim informed her that he would now "knock" her unconscious, whereupon the victim offered anything to avoid another physical attack, handed over her money, and the defendant took the money that was offered.[120]

---

[110] People v. Taylor, 129 Ill. 2d 80, 84, 541 N.E.2d 677, 679 (1989).

[111] People v. Taylor, 129 Ill. 2d 80, 84, 541 N.E.2d 677, 679 (1989); People v, Robinson, 206 Ill. App. 3d 1046, 1053, 565 N.E.2d 206, 210 (1st Dist. 1990).

[112] *See* People v. Taylor, 129 Ill. 2d 80, 87-88, 541 N.E.2d 677, 681 (1989) (where the court distinguished earlier decisions where items taken were not so attached as to create resistance upon being taken); People v. Brooks, 202 Ill. App. 3d 164, 169-70, 559 N.E.2d 859, 862-63 (1st Dist. 1990).

[113] People v. Taylor, 129 Ill. 2d 80, 84, 541 N.E.2d 677, 679 (1989).

[114] People v. Brooks, 202 Ill. App. 3d 164, 169-70, 559 N.E.2d 859, 862-63 (1st Dist. 1990).

[115] People v. Taylor, 129 Ill. 2d 80, 85, 541 N.E.2d 677, 680 (1989).

[116] People v. Brooks, 202 Ill. App. 3d 164, 169, 559 N.E.2d 859, 862-63 (1st Dist. 1990).

[117] People v. Brooks, 202 Ill. App. 3d 164, 169, 559 N.E.2d 859, 862-63 (1st Dist. 1990).

[118] People v. Lewis, 80 Ill. App. 2d 101, 103, 224 N.E.2d 647, 649 (1st Dist. 1967).

[119] *See* People v. Holland, 121 Ill. 2d 136, 160-61, 520 N.E.2d 270, 281 (1987), *aff'd*, 493 U.S. 474 (1989), *reh. denied*, 494 U.S. 1050 (1989).

[120] People v. Holland, 121 Ill. 2d 136, 160-61, 520 N.E.2d 270, 281 (1987), *aff'd*, 493 U.S. 474 (1989), *reh. denied*, 494 U.S. 1050 (1989).

§ 12.08.   — By Threat of the Imminent Use of Force.

Actual force is not required to satisfy the force element of robbery; threats of the imminent use of force will suffice.[121] Generally, where a victim observes a weapon, a sufficient threat of force exists.[122] The threat requirement was satisfied where a victim observed the handle of a gun tucked in the front of the defendant's jeans and the defendant, without saying anything to her victim, took money off her victim's desk.[123] Obviously, a sufficient amount of force exists where defendant placed a gun to a victim's head and demanded money.[124] A person does not escape legal culpability for robbery by ordering another person under the threat of force to commit the actual taking of property from the person or presence of the robbery victim who is also under threat of force.[125]

Illinois courts find that a sufficient threat of force exists if there are facts from which a victim may have reasonably concluded that the defendant was armed with a deadly weapon.[126] Such facts include "menacing gestures," such as "reaching into a place where a weapon could be kept or a display of all or part of a weapon."[127] Accordingly, the element of threat of force was satisfied where a cashier, looking up from the defendant's note that instructed her to place money in a bag, saw the defendant move his entire right hand into a camera bag that hung from his shoulder.[128] A sufficient threat of force was also found where a service station attendant, who had been told by a passenger in an automobile to give him his money, saw the driver's right hand pointed toward him, even though the attendant could not see what was in the driver's hand because it was covered with either cloth or paper.[129] Similarly, where the defendant approached the victim with "something orange in his hands," which the victim believed to be a concealed can of mace or a gun, the element of force was met.[130] In addition, the victim need not feel personally threatened for her own personal

---

[121] People v. Taylor, 129 Ill. 2d 80, 84, 541 N.E.2d 677, 679 (1989).

[122] In People v. Hollingsworth, 120 Ill. App. 3d 177, 180, 457 N.E.2d 1062, 1065 (5th Dist. 1983), the court observed: "it is difficult to overestimate the coercive power of a deadly weapon; once its presence is indicated to the victim, nothing more need be communicated to the victim in order to generate a sense of terror."

[123] *See* People v. Hollingsworth, 120 Ill. App. 3d 177, 180, 457 N.E.2d 1062, 1064-65 (5th Dist. 1983).

[124] People v. Fitzgerald, 171 Ill. App. 3d 218, 223, 524 N.E.2d 1190, 1193 (1st Dist. 1988).

[125] People v. Parker, 192 Ill. App. 3d 779, 787, 549 N.E.2d 626, 631 (1st Dist. 1989).

[126] *See, e.g.*, People v. Hollingsworth, 120 Ill. App. 3d 177, 179-80, 457 N.E.2d 1062, 1064 (5th Dist. 1983).

[127] People v. Hollingsworth, 120 Ill. App. 3d 177, 179-80, 457 N.E.2d 1062, 1064 (5th Dist. 1983).

[128] People v. Bradford, 78 Ill. App. 3d 869, 874, 397 N.E.2d 863, 866-67 (1st Dist. 1979).

[129] People v. Arnold, 48 Ill. App. 3d 250, 251-53, 362 N.E.2d 461, 462-64 (3d Dist. 1977).

[130] People v. Coleman, 128 Ill. App. 3d 538, 544-46, 470 N.E.2d 1277, 1282-83 (5th Dist. 1984).

safety.[131] One court held that the force element was satisfied where a mother's "free exercise of will had been suspended" because she feared for the safety of her children.[132]

An Illinois court has observed that a reasonable person would feel threatened by defendants who demand money while concealing their hands in their pockets.[133] Thus, there was a sufficient threat of force where a defendant kept his right hand in his pocket while approaching his victim from behind and ordered him to face a wall.[134] The threat element was also satisfied where a defendant told his victim to put money in a bag while the defendant's hand remained in his pocket.[135] Where the defendant made an uninvited entry into the victim's car, made a statement indicating that he had a gun, and demanded money from the victim, this constituted a threat for purposes of robbery.[136] It must be noted, however, that absent a menacing gesture or other threat, mere verbal demands for money do not constitute sufficient threats of force.[137] The element of threat of force was not satisfied where a defendant, with his hands in his coat pockets, one of which appeared to be in the form of a fist, told his victim to put money into a paper bag.[138]

Although courts generally find a sufficient threat of force where a weapon is present, the use of a weapon is not essential to satisfy the threat element.[139] Sufficient threat of force existed where a defendant broke the victim's car window

---

[131] *See* People v. Thomas, 189 Ill. App. 3d 365, 370-71, 545 N.E.2d 289, 293 (1st Dist. 1989).

[132] People v. Thomas, 189 Ill. App. 3d 365, 370-71, 545 N.E.2d 289, 293 (1st Dist. 1989).

[133] People v. Dates, 100 Ill. App. 3d 365, 372-73, 426 N.E.2d 1033, 1038 (1st Dist. 1981).

[134] People v. Malone, 126 Ill. App. 2d 265, 269, 261 N.E.2d 776, 778 (1st Dist. 1970).

[135] People v. Carpenter, 71 Ill. App. 2d 137, 143-44, 217 N.E.2d 337, 340 (1st Dist. 1966).

[136] People v. Lovings, 275 Ill. App. 3d 19, 23, 655 N.E.2d 1152, 1155 (2d Dist. 1995). Today, this conduct would be considered vehicular hijacking. *See* § 12-17 of this chapter.

[137] The Fifth Appellate District has stated:

> When the word 'robbery' is mentioned, one normally envisions a defendant taking some action which would indicate that he is armed, combined with words spoken to the victim, either announcing the robbery or warning the victim that he will be harmed if he does not cooperate. If . . . such action was taken and such words were spoken, a defendant will be guilty of robbery even if he was not actually armed. On the other hand, if the defendant does not take any action which would reasonably allow the victim to conclude that he was armed, and only gives instructions such as "put the money in the bag," which do not, of themselves, threaten force, then no robbery is committed.

People v. Hollingsworth, 120 Ill. App. 3d 177, 179, 457 N.E.2d 1062, 1064 (5th Dist. 1983) (citations omitted).

[138] *See* People v. Williams, 42 Ill. App. 3d 134, 138, 355 N.E.2d 597, 601 (1st Dist. 1976) (noting that defendant made neither verbal threats nor menacing gestures with his hand and did nothing to create reasonable inference that he had a gun in his pocket).

[139] People v. Frazier, 63 Ill. App. 2d 226, 231, 211 N.E.2d 415, 417 (1st Dist. 1965).

with a metal object, reached in and took the victim's purse.[140] The threat element was satisfied where defendants, who had already removed a portion of the door to their victim's apartment, told their victim to open his door or they would break it down.[141] A sufficient threat of force also existed where the defendant followed the victim, demanded his eyeglasses, and said "don't run cause I'll get you."[142]

Like the use of a weapon, face-to-face confrontation between the defendant and his or her victim is not required to satisfy robbery's threat element.[143] One court has observed that a sufficient threat of force "can occur from afar off."[144] Thus, the threat element was satisfied where a defendant telephoned his victim, a service station attendant, and told her that a man across the street was aiming a gun, with a scope on it, at her and that unless she followed instructions, she would be shot.[145] A defendant's threats over the telephone to store managers, indicating that bombs located in the store would be detonated within minutes if money was not delivered to designated locations, were similarly held to be sufficient threats of force for robbery.[146]

It is imperative that the threat be *imminent* for purposes of robbery.[147] As was discussed in the previous chapter, the crime of theft may be accomplished by means of a threat; however, theft by threat does not require proof that the threat was imminent, as is the case with robbery.[148] Indeed, the Illinois courts have held that the threat that is an element of theft may be "less serious conduct both in quantity and quality" than the threat of force required for a robbery conviction.[149] Consistent with this, the Illinois Supreme Court has held that robbery carries a more severe penalty than theft precisely because there is a greater danger that the threat in robbery will actually result in death or serious bodily injury; accordingly, it uses this premise as a basis for insisting on clear evidence

---

[140] People v. Ware, 168 Ill. App. 3d 845, 846, 523 N.E.2d 46, 47 (1st Dist. 1988) ("[I]nherent in the defendant's conduct . . . [was] the imminent use of more force if she tried to stop him from taking the purse from her presence").

[141] People v. Whitley, 18 Ill. App. 3d 995, 999, 311 N.E.2d 282, 286 (1st Dist. 1974).

[142] People v. Mitchell, 37 Ill. App. 3d 372, 375, 346 N.E.2d 63, 66 (4th Dist. 1976).

[143] People v. Gauwitz, 80 Ill. App. 3d 362, 368, 400 N.E.2d 92, 97 (4th Dist. 1980).

[144] People v. Gauwitz, 80 Ill. App. 3d 362, 368, 400 N.E.2d 92, 97 (4th Dist. 1980). The court noted: "In an earlier, and perhaps simpler, day confrontation may have been necessary to establish a present ability to do violence, but the advent of electronic communications has vastly expanded the ability of one bent on savagery to overcome the psyche of another." *Id.*

[145] People v. Gauwitz, 80 Ill. App. 3d 362, 368, 400 N.E.2d 92, 93-94 (4th Dist. 1980).

[146] People v. Smith, 66 Ill. App. 3d 957, 961-62, 384 N.E.2d 473, 476 (3d Dist. 1978), *aff'd in relevant part*, 78 Ill. 2d 298, 399 N.E.2d 1289 (1980).

[147] People v. Taylor, 129 Ill. 2d 80, 84, 541 N.E.2d 677, 679 (1989).

[148] *See* ch. 11 this volume for a discussion of theft.

[149] People v. Arnold, 48 Ill. App. 3d 250, 252, 362 N.E.2d 461, 463-64 (3d Dist. 1977) (dicta).

in a robbery case that the defendant actually forced his or her victim by means of such an imminent threat to release control of the property.[150]

The existence of a time span between the threat of force and the actual taking of the victim's property may not be sufficient to preclude the threat from satisfying robbery's threat element.[151] For example, a sufficient threat of force was found to exist where a victim was subjected to violent threats for approximately 15 minutes, during which time the defendants held guns and acid to his head and ordered him to give them $1,000 within three hours, and the victim subsequently delivered the money at the designated time and location.[152]

Illinois courts have consistently rejected defendant's claims that the use or threatened use of force was justified under the circumstances. For example, a court held the forcible retaking of gambling losses from a pool hustler was not a justifiable use of force to defend one's property.[153] Furthermore, the appellate courts have recognized that neither force nor the threat of force may be lawfully used to collect a debt.[154]

§ 12.09.   — Mental State.

Robbery is a general intent crime.[155] Early confusion existed as to whether robbery was a general intent or specific intent offense under the current robbery statute.[156] In 1977 the Illinois Supreme Court held that the current robbery statute requires a showing of specific intent.[157] But, only two years later, in *People*

---

[150] *See* People v. Tiller, 94 Ill. 2d 303, 316, 447 N.E.2d 174, 181 (1982), *cert. denied*, 461 U.S. 944 (1983).

[151] People v. Stewart, 54 Ill. App. 3d 76, 80, 369 N.E.2d 131, 134 (1st Dist. 1977).

[152] People v. Stewart, 54 Ill. App. 3d 76, 80, 369 N.E.2d 131, 134 (1st Dist. 1977) (noting that time span between threats of force and actual taking "was not so long, given the imminent nature of the threats, as to preclude these events from constituting a single, uninterrupted and inseparable incident of terror to satisfy a conviction").

[153] People v. Robinson, 68 Ill. App. 3d 687, 692, 386 N.E.2d 165, 169 (4th Dist. 1979).

[154] People v. English, 32 Ill. App. 3d 691, 693, 336 N.E.2d 199, 201 (5th Dist. 1975) (noting that "a creditor may not employ violence, threats, or weapons to collect the [valid] debt but should pursue his remedies in the normal channels of peaceful and legal redress"); People v. Uselding, 107 Ill. App. 2d 305, 309-310, 247 N.E.2d 35, 37 (1st Dist. 1969).

[155] People v. Lewis, 165 Ill. 2d 305, 337, 651 N.E.2d 72, 87 (1995) (robbery); *see also* People v. Lee, 294 Ill. App. 3d 738, 743, 691 N.E.2d 117, 121 (3d Dist. 1998) ("Given that the crime charged is a general intent crime and the statute does not include a mental state as an element, an indictment charging armed robbery need not allege a mental state to be sufficient").

[156] One Illinois appellate court concluded that robbery required an intent to permanently deprive another of the possession of his property; therefore, robbery was a specific intent crime. *See* People v. Howell, 11 Ill. App. 3d 391, 394, 296 N.E.2d 760, 762 (4th Dist. 1973). Another appellate court, however, repeatedly rejected the contention that robbery required a specific intent. *See, e.g.*, People v. Berlin, 132 Ill. App. 2d 697, 699, 270 N.E.2d 461, 463 (1st Dist. 1971).

[157] People v. White, 67 Ill. 2d 107, 117, 365 N.E.2d 337, 342 (1977), *overruled by* People v. Banks, 75 Ill. 2d 383, 388 N.E.2d 1244 (1979).

v. Banks,[158] the Illinois Supreme Court overruled its prior decision and held that robbery under the current statute is a general intent crime. The *Banks* court observed that a literal reading of the current robbery statute indicates that the intent to permanently deprive another of his property is not an essential element of robbery, even though it was at common law.[159] Consequently, voluntary intoxication is not a defense to robbery.[160]

§ 12.10. Armed Robbery.

§ 12.11. — Armed Robbery Codified.

The current Illinois armed robbery statute provides the following: "A person commits armed robbery when he or she violates Section 5/18-1 while he or she carries on or about his or her person, or is otherwise armed with a dangerous weapon."[161] The comments of the committee that drafted this legislation pointed out that the current law differs very little from the prior armed robbery statute.[162] It is important to note that no effort was made to define the meaning of *carries . . . about his or her person* or *armed with a dangerous weapon*, thereby leaving the meaning to judicial interpretation.

§ 12.12. — Elements of Armed Robbery.

The Illinois Supreme Court has recognized that the impact of armed robbery "is focused more directly upon an individual victim than upon society generally. Danger to the person, as well as the taking of property, is the essence of the crime."[163] Armed robbery, like simple robbery, requires the taking of property from the person or presence of another by either the use of force or the threat of the imminent use of force; yet, unlike simple robbery, armed robbery also requires the taking to occur while the defendant is carrying, or armed with, a dangerous weapon.[164]

The sole difference between armed robbery and simple robbery is that the person committing the robbery must be carrying a dangerous weapon.[165] To prove armed robbery, the state must establish all of the elements of simple rob-

---

[158] 75 Ill. 2d 383, 388 N.E.2d 1244 (1979).

[159] People v. Banks, 75 Ill. 2d 383, 391-92, 388 N.E.2d 1244, 1246-48 (1979).

[160] People v. Rosas, 102 Ill. App. 3d 113, 116, 429 N.E.2d 898, 899-900 (3d Dist. 1981).

[161] 720 ILCS 5/18-2 (1999). Armed robbery is a Class X felony.

[162] ILL. ANN. STAT. ch. 38, para. 18-2 (Smith-Hurd 1977), 1961 Committee Comments, at 402 (revised 1970).

[163] People v. Jones, 53 Ill. 2d 460, 463, 292 N.E.2d 361, 363 (1973).

[164] People v. Thomas, 189 Ill. App. 3d 365, 369, 545 N.E.2d 289, 292 (1st Dist. 1989).

[165] People v. DeLeon, 40 Ill. App. 3d 308, 312, 352 N.E.2d 234, 238 (1st Dist. 1976). *See also* People v. Thomas, 189 Ill. App. 3d 365, 369, 545 N.E.2d 289, 292 (1st Dist. 1989); People v. Downey, 162 Ill. App. 3d 322, 331, 515 N.E.2d 362, 367 (2d Dist. 1987).

bery and must show that the defendant was either carrying, or armed with, a dangerous weapon.[166] It is important to note that the armed robbery statute makes the mere carrying, on or about one's person, of a dangerous weapon during the commission of a robbery, a basis for an armed robbery conviction even without displaying the weapon to, or use of the weapon against, the victims.[167]

§ 12.13.   — The Meaning of "Carrying . . . or Armed."

To commit armed robbery under the current statutory provision, the defendant must actually possess a dangerous weapon at the time of the offense.[168] It is not necessary to prove that the weapon caused injury or physical harm to the victim,[169] was aimed at the victim,[170] or was used in some other way or even displayed to the victim.[171] However, where a victim is led to believe, by the defendant, that the defendant possessed a dangerous weapon when in fact he does not, the defendant has not committed armed robbery.[172] It should be noted that if a defendant's companion threatens the victim with a dangerous weapon, the defendant can be convicted of armed robbery based on his or her actual participation in the offense, not merely on an accountability theory.[173] It should also be noted that if the defendant is armed with a dangerous weapon, the particular type of weapon used is not a material element of the offense.[174]

The use of a dangerous weapon may be inferred from circumstantial evidence.[175] An armed robbery conviction was sustained where a victim saw an

---

[166] See People v. Thomas, 189 Ill. App. 3d 365, 369, 545 N.E.2d 289, 292 (1st Dist. 1989); People v. Downey, 162 Ill. App. 3d 322, 331, 515 N.E.2d 362, 367 (2d Dist. 1987).

[167] People v. Thomas, 189 Ill. App. 3d 365, 369, 545 N.E.2d 289, 293 (1st Dist. 1989); People v. Downey, 162 Ill. App. 3d 322, 332, 515 N.E.2d 362, 368-69 (2d Dist. 1987). Prior to 1988, the statute referred only to "armed with a dangerous weapon" and did not include the "carries on or about his or her person" language. People v. Downey, 162 Ill. App. 3d 322, 332, 515 N.E.2d 362, 368 (2d Dist. 1987).

[168] People v. Bias, 131 Ill. App. 3d 98, 106, 475 N.E.2d 253, 259 (4th Dist. 1985); People v. Fiala, 85 Ill. App. 3d 397, 400, 406 N.E.2d 931, 933 (3d Dist. 1980).

[169] People v. Ratliff, 22 Ill. App. 3d 106, 108, 317 N.E.2d 63, 64 (4th Dist. 1974).

[170] People v. Simpson, 178 Ill. App. 3d 1091, 1095, 534 N.E.2d 217, 218 (3d Dist. 1989) ("There is no requirement that the victim wait until that weapon is aimed to strike a vital organ before" armed robbery is established).

[171] See People v. Thomas, 189 Ill. App. 3d 365, 370, 545 N.E.2d 289, 292 (1st Dist. 1989); People v. Downey, 162 Ill. App. 3d 322, 333, 515 N.E.2d 362, 369 (2d Dist. 1987).

[172] People v. Bias, 131 Ill. App. 3d 98, 106, 475 N.E.2d 253, 259 (4th Dist. 1985); People v. Fiala, 85 Ill. App. 3d 397, 400, 406 N.E.2d 931, 933 (3d Dist. 1980).

[173] See People v. Surges, 101 Ill. App. 3d 962, 973-74, 428 N.E.2d 1012, 1018 (1st Dist. 1981).

[174] People v. Ford, 34 Ill. App. 3d 79, 83, 339 N.E.2d 293, 297 (1st Dist. 1975); People v. Wyatt, 23 Ill. App. 3d 587, 590, 319 N.E.2d 575, 577 (3d Dist. 1974).

[175] People v. Partee, 157 Ill. App. 3d 231, 266, 511 N.E.2d 1165, 1188 (1st Dist. 1987), *cert. denied,* 484 U.S. 1072 (1987); *See also* People v. Meadows, 92 Ill. App. 3d 1028, 1031, 416 N.E.2d 404, 406-07 (3d Dist. 1981) ("the State may . . . prove the existence of a dangerous weapon circumstantially . . . [through] evidence of objective observations that lead to the reason-

object wrapped in a white handkerchief in the defendant's hand and believed it to be a gun because she "saw the barrel part."[176] The existence of a dangerous weapon was inferred where a victim saw only what appeared to be the barrel of a pistol, which was hidden at the defendant's side, and the defendant said, "give me the money before I put a hole in your head."[177] The existence of a dangerous weapon was also inferred where a victim saw part of a metallic object, which she believed to be the butt of a gun, and felt it when the defendant shoved it into her ribs.[178] An armed robbery conviction was sustained where the victim was confronted by the defendant with an orange object that the defendant held in both hands, the object was pointed at the victim and police later recovered from the defendant's automobile an orange and white towel wrapped around a 12-gauge sawed-off shotgun.[179] An armed robbery conviction was also upheld where a victim saw a shiny object in the defendant's hand, which she believed to be either a gun or a knife and which the defendant pushed into her side.[180] Another armed robbery conviction was upheld where a defendant put his hand in his pocket in such a way as to form a point, demanded that his victim give him money, and was subsequently apprehended in possession of a knife.[181] Finally, the existence of a dangerous weapon was inferred where a victim's throat was seriously cut by the defendant during a struggle to take the victim's money and a bystander shouted, "Look out. He has got a razor," as the defendant was running away from the victim.[182]

The use of a dangerous weapon may be found even if the victim, or a bystander, never sees the defendant's weapon or what appears to be a weapon under concealment.[183] In *People v. Elam*,[184] a defendant pushed a hard object into his victim's back, told him it was a small gun and demanded his money.[185] The defendant was apprehended less than ten minutes later approximately two blocks from the scene and found to be in possession of a knife; subsequently the defendant was convicted of armed robbery even though the victim never saw the weapon.[186] Sustaining the armed robbery conviction, the Illinois Supreme Court recognized that "the actual existence of a dangerous weapon in the possession of

---

able inference by the trier of fact that a dangerous weapon was used in the commission of a robbery").

[176] People v. DuPree, 69 Ill. App. 3d 260, 264, 387 N.E.2d 391, 394 (2d Dist. 1979).

[177] People v. Thompson, 35 Ill. App. 3d 773, 776, 342 N.E.2d 445, 448 (2d Dist. 1976).

[178] People v. Myatt, 66 Ill. App. 3d 642, 646, 384 N.E.2d 85, 88 (1st Dist. 1978).

[179] People v. Coleman, 128 Ill. App. 3d 538, 545-46, 470 N.E.2d 1277, 1283 (5th Dist. 1984).

[180] People v. Moore, 14 Ill. App. 3d 361, 363, 302 N.E.2d 425, 427 (1st Dist. 1973).

[181] People v. Fultz, 96 Ill. App. 2d 220, 222, 238 N.E.2d 222, 224 (1st Dist. 1968).

[182] People v. Rice, 109 Ill. App. 2d 391, 394-95, 248 N.E.2d 745, 746-47 (1st Dist. 1969).

[183] People v. Elam, 50 Ill. 2d 214, 219, 278 N.E.2d 76, 79 (1972); People v. Partee, 157 Ill. App. 3d 231, 266, 511 N.E.2d 1165, 1188 (1st Dist. 1987).

[184] 50 Ill. 2d 214, 278 N.E.2d 76 (1972).

[185] People v. Elam, 50 Ill. 2d 214, 216, 278 N.E.2d 76, 79 (1972).

[186] People v. Elam, 50 Ill. 2d 214, 216, 278 N.E.2d 76, 79 (1972).

the accused at the time of the robbery was sufficient to fulfill the requirements of the Code even though the weapon itself was neither seen nor accurately described by the victim."[187] Consistent with *Elam*, one appellate court held that lacerations and a puncture wound suffered by the victim provided sufficient evidence to find the defendant had used a dangerous weapon, even when no weapon was visible at the scene or ever recovered.[188]

As the Illinois appellate court observed in *People v. Dunivant*,[189] "some physical manifestation of a weapon is required . . . or some other evidence is necessary to establish the presence of the weapon at the scene."[190] In *Dunivant*, the court reversed an armed robbery conviction where "no weapon, part of a weapon, outline of a weapon or gesture indicating possession of a weapon was seen at the time of the robbery" and no weapon was recovered from any of the defendants observed at the scene.[191] Similarly, where no weapon was visible at the scene and no evidence was introduced that the defendant appeared to be concealing a weapon, insufficient circumstantial evidence existed for a finding that the defendant was armed during the commission of the robbery even though a gun was later recovered.[192]

It is clear that the use of a dangerous weapon at any point of a robbery, provided it can reasonably be said to be part of a single occurrence or incident, will constitute armed robbery.[193] Where a defendant threatens his or her victim with a dangerous weapon before taking his or her property, it is immaterial that the defendant does not display the weapon during the actual taking of the property.[194] For example, an armed robbery conviction was sustained where a defendant threatened his victim with a dangerous weapon before sexually assaulting her, and then robbed her approximately 45 minutes to an hour after threatening her with the weapon, because there was no evidence that the weapon had been discarded or otherwise made inaccessible after the sexual assault.[195] An armed robbery was also found to exist where a defendant forced his victim into her bedroom at gunpoint, put the gun in a closet and, while raping her, took a coin

---

[187] People v. Elam, 50 Ill. 2d 214, 220, 278 N.E.2d 76, 81 (1972).

[188] People v. Partee, 157 Ill. App. 3d 231, 266, 511 N.E.2d 1165, 1188 (1st Dist. 1987), *cert. denied*, 484 U.S. 1072 (1987).

[189] 96 Ill. App. 3d 62, 420 N.E.2d 1110 (2d Dist. 1981).

[190] People v. Dunivant, 96 Ill. App. 3d 62, 64, 420 N.E.2d 1110, 1112-13 (2d Dist. 1981); *See also* People v. Coleman, 128 Ill. App. 3d 538, 545, 470 N.E.2d 1277, 1282 (5th Dist. 1984) (recognizing the necessity for some physical manifestation of a weapon or some other evidence from which presence of a weapon may be inferred).

[191] People v. Dunivant, 96 Ill. App. 3d 62, 64-65, 420 N.E.2d 1110, 1113 (2d Dist. 1981).

[192] People v. Fiala, 85 Ill. App. 3d 397, 401, 406 N.E.2d 931, 933-34 (3d Dist. 1980).

[193] People v. Foster, 198 Ill. App. 3d 986, 994-95, 556 N.E.2d 1214, 1220 (1st Dist. 1990); People v. Ortiz, 156 Ill. App. 3d 170, 175, 509 N.E.2d 633, 636 (1st Dist. 1987).

[194] People v. Thomas, 189 Ill. App. 3d 365, 370, 545 N.E.2d 289, 292 (1st Dist. 1989); People v. Downey, 162 Ill. App. 3d 322, 333, 515 N.E.2d 362, 369 (2d Dist. 1987).

[195] People v. Robinson, 73 Ill. 2d 192, 202, 383 N.E.2d 164, 170 (1978).

purse from the victim; it is "immaterial that the defendant did not have the gun in hand at the time of the taking . . . [because] the weapon had been displayed to the victim, and thereafter remained accessible to the perpetrator."[196]

An armed robbery may also be found to exist where a defendant uses a dangerous weapon after he or she has taken the victim's property if the use is part of a continuous act.[197] For instance, where a victim attempted to retrieve his wallet immediately after the defendant had taken it and the defendant prevented the recovery of the wallet by firing a gun at the victim, an armed robbery occurred because the weapon was used as part of a single incident or occurrence.[198] Where a defendant took his victim's suitcase and then, in an attempt to escape, struck him in the face and back with a screwdriver, an armed robbery was found to exist because the defendant committed one continuous act.[199] Nevertheless, where the acts that constituted a robbery of the victim's property were completed before any weapon was used and where the defendant neither used nor threatened to use any weapon until after he had possession of the victim's property, and then used his gun solely in connection with a subsequent aggravated battery of the victim, no armed robbery was held to have occurred.[200]

§ 12.14.   — The Meaning of "Dangerous Weapon."

As result of the armed robbery statute's failure to define the term *dangerous weapon*,[201] the parameters of what constitutes such a weapon "have been left primarily to judicial construction. . . ."[202] It should be noted that, for purposes of the armed robbery statute, dangerous weapons are not limited to those specified under the separate armed violence statute.[203] A *deadly weapon* has been defined as any "weapon with which death may be easily and readily produced. . . ."[204]

---

[196] People v. Talley, 97 Ill. App. 3d 439, 444-45, 422 N.E.2d 1084, 1089 (1st Dist. 1981).

[197] People v. Olmos, 67 Ill. App. 3d 281, 290, 384 N.E.2d 853, 861 (1st Dist. 1978).

[198] People v. Olmos, 67 Ill. App. 3d 281, 290, 384 N.E.2d 853, 861 (1st Dist. 1978).

[199] People v. Ditto, 98 Ill. App. 3d 36, 39, 424 N.E.2d 3, 5 (1st Dist. 1981).

[200] People v. Simmons, 34 Ill. App. 3d 970, 972, 342 N.E.2d 322, 323-24 (2d Dist. 1975).

[201] People v. Watkins, 94 Ill. App. 3d 749, 752, 419 N.E.2d 54, 56 (3d Dist. 1981) ("Nowhere in the armed robbery statute is a dangerous weapon defined").

[202] People v. Partee, 157 Ill. App. 3d 231, 266, 511 N.E.2d 1165, 1188 (1st Dist. 1987), *cert. denied*, 484 U.S. 1072 (1988); People v. Meadows, 92 Ill. App. 3d 1028, 1031, 416 N.E.2d 404, 406 (3d Dist. 1981).

[203] People v. Myers, 101 Ill. App. 3d 1073, 1075, 428 N.E.2d 1156, 1157 (3d Dist. 1981); People v. Watkins, 94 Ill. App. 3d 749, 753, 419 N.E.2d 54, 56 (3d Dist. 1981); See 720 ILCS 5/33A-2 (1998) (definition of armed violence); 720 ILCS 5/33A-1 (definition of dangerous weapon used in connection with armed violence prohibition).

[204] People v. Greer, 53 Ill. App. 3d 675, 678, 368 N.E.2d 996, 998 (5th Dist. 1977) (quoting People v. Dwyer, 324 Ill. 363, 365, 155 N.E. 316, 317 (1927)). *See also* People v. Dwyer, 324 Ill. 363, 365, 155 N.E. 316, 317 (1927) ("anything made for the purpose of destroying life or for another purpose, or not made by man at all, if it is a thing with which death can be easily and readily produced, the law recognized as a deadly weapon"); People v. De La Fuente, 92 Ill. App. 3d 525,

In determining whether a particular weapon is dangerous, it is the weapon's potential for inflicting deadly or serious injury which must be determined, not whether the weapon was, in fact, used or threatened to be used in a harmful or deadly manner.[205] Thus, the question of whether a particular object is a dangerous weapon depends upon the object's character.[206] Generally, whether a weapon is dangerous is a question for the trier of fact.[207] However, where "the character of a weapon is such as to leave only one conclusion, the question becomes one of law for the court."[208]

In an attempt to determine which weapons are dangerous, the courts have noted the existence of four categories of objects.[209] One category consists of weapons which are dangerous per se, for example, a loaded gun capable of firing bullets.[210] Another category contains weapons that are not dangerous per se, but that are capable of inflicting serious injury, such as an unloaded gun that can be used as a bludgeon.[211] Weapons that are not dangerous as a matter of law comprise a third category, for example, a toy gun made entirely of plastic.[212] A final category consists of weapons that become dangerous per se because of the manner in which they are *actually used*, such as a starter pistol used as a bludgeon.[213]

In addition to this elaborate categorization, there is a significant body of precedent that attempts to designate which weapons are dangerous. Knives[214]

535, 414 N.E.2d 1355, 1363 (3d Dist. 1981) (discussion of weapons that are (1) dangerous per se and (2) not dangerous per se but which are capable of inflicting serious injury and, also, items that are as a matter of law not dangerous).

[205] People v. Thompson, 125 Ill. App. 3d 665, 678, 466 N.E.2d 380, 390 (2d Dist. 1984); *See also* People v. Skelton, 83 Ill. 2d 58, 66, 414 N.E.2d 455, 458 (1980).

[206] People v. Westefer, 169 Ill. App. 3d 59, 61, 522 N.E.2d 1381, 1383 (2d Dist. 1988).

[207] People v. Skelton, 83 Ill. 2d 58, 66, 414 N.E.2d 455, 458 (1980); People v. Westefer, 169 Ill. App. 3d 59, 61, 522 N.E.2d 1381, 1383 (2d Dist. 1988).

[208] People v. Skelton, 83 Ill. 2d 58, 66, 414 N.E.2d 455, 458 (1980); People v. Westefer, 169 Ill. App. 3d 59, 61-62, 522 N.E.2d 1381, 1383 (2d Dist. 1988).

[209] People v. De La Fuente, 92 Ill. App. 3d 525, 535-36, 414 N.E.2d 1355, 1363-64 (3d Dist. 1981).

[210] People v. De La Fuente, 92 Ill. App. 3d 525, 535-36, 414 N.E.2d 1355, 1363-64 (3d Dist. 1981).

[211] People v. De La Fuente, 92 Ill. App. 3d 525, 535-36, 414 N.E.2d 1355, 1363-64 (3d Dist. 1981).

[212] People v. De La Fuente, 92 Ill. App. 3d 525, 535-36, 414 N.E.2d 1355, 1363-64 (3d Dist. 1981).

[213] People v. De La Fuente, 92 Ill. App. 3d 525, 535-36, 414 N.E.2d 1355, 1363-64 (3d Dist. 1981).

[214] People v. Westefer, 169 Ill. App. 3d 59, 62, 522 N.E.2d 1381, 1383-84 (2d Dist. 1988) (where utility knife with a one inch blade was held to be dangerous per se); People v. Downey, 162 Ill. App. 3d 322, 333, 515 N.E.2d 362, 369 (2d Dist. 1987); People v. De La Fuente, 92 Ill. App. 3d 525, 535, 414 N.E.2d 1355, 1363 (3d Dist. 1981).

and loaded guns[215] have been held dangerous per se. One appellate court has held that a firearm, even if unloaded or inoperable, is dangerous per se.[216] However, another appellate court has declared that "if the weapon used was not actually capable of inflicting death or grievous bodily injury, then its use was nothing more than a threat of the imminent use of force, an element of simple robbery."[217] Thus, that appellate court determined that whether an unloaded gun was a deadly weapon was a question for the jury.[218] The same court also found that the jury should decide whether an inoperable sawed-off rifle was a dangerous weapon where it had not been used to injure the victim.[219]

The most significant guidance from the Illinois Supreme Court as to what constitutes a dangerous weapon for purposes of armed robbery appeared in *People v. Skelton*,[220] which will be discussed in greater detail later in this section. In *Skelton* the defendant displayed a small, light-weight, toy plastic revolver during a robbery. The court indicated that where the character of the weapon is such as to admit of only one conclusion, the question becomes one of law for the court.[221] Here, the toy gun not only had no capacity to fire real bullets but also was not designed in a manner that it could be used as a bludgeon and, accordingly, held the toy gun was not dangerous as a matter of law.[222] However, the court went on to observe that beyond weapons that are deadly *per se* and, thus, as a matter of law satisfy the statutory requirement for armed robbery, there are (1) objects designed for a different purpose that are dangerous because of the manner in which they are *actually used*, for example, "a handgun . . . used as a bludgeon is equally dangerous whether loaded or unloaded,"[223] and (2) items that are considered dangerous because of their *potential for such use*, for example, "unloaded real guns and many toy guns, because of their size and weight could be used in a deadly fashion as bludgeons.[224]

Weapons not dangerous *per se* but found to be dangerous because of their potential to inflict death or serious injury include guns which are unloaded or inoperable,[225] air and pellet guns,[226] starter pistols,[227] a toy cap gun,[228] and hard

---

[215] People v. Myers, 101 Ill. App. 3d 1073, 1076, 428 N.E.2d 1156, 1158 (3d Dist. 1981); People v. De La Fuente, 92 Ill. App. 3d 525, 536, 414 N.E.2d 1355, 1363 (3d Dist. 1981).

[216] *See* People v. Ellis, 94 Ill. App. 3d 777, 779, 419 N.E.2d 727, 728 (3d Dist. 1981).

[217] People v. Greer, 53 Ill. App. 3d 675, 682-83, 368 N.E.2d 996, 1001 (5th Dist. 1977).

[218] People v. Greer, 53 Ill. App. 3d 675, 683, 368 N.E.2d 996, 1002 (5th Dist. 1977).

[219] People v. Richards, 28 Ill. App. 3d 505, 510, 328 N.E.2d 692, 695-96 (5th Dist. 1975).

[220] 83 Ill. 2d 58, 414 N.E.2d 455 (1980).

[221] People v. Skelton, 83 Ill. 2d 58, 66, 414 N.E.2d 455, 458 (1980).

[222] People v. Skelton, 83 Ill. 2d 58, 66, 414 N.E.2d 455, 458 (1980).

[223] People v. Skelton, 83 Ill. 2d 58, 64, 414 N.E.2d 455, 457 (1980).

[224] People v. Skelton, 83 Ill. 2d 58, 66, 414 N.E.2d 455, 458 (1980); *see also* People v. Bell, 264 Ill. App. 3d 753, 756, 636 N.E.2d 614, 616 (1st Dist. 1993) (inoperable replica of gun constituted a "dangerous weapon").

[225] *See, e.g.,* People v. Myers, 101 Ill. App. 3d 1073, 1076, 428 N.E.2d 1156, 1158 (3d Dist. 1981) (unloaded 6.35 millimeter, semiautomatic handgun, weighing little less than 13 ounces made of heavy metal, and having "metal corners which could cause serious injury if the weapon

objects appearing to be guns.[229] Items or substances considered to be dangerous because of the manner in which they were actually used include a screwdriver,[230] a fingernail clipper,[231] firecrackers,[232] acid held to a victim's head,[233] a nine-inch metal conduit with a jagged edge,[234] a tree branch approximately three feet in length and three inches in diameter,[235] and pepper spray.[236] Finally, a sharp fingernail has been found not to be a dangerous weapon as a matter of law.[237]

---

were used as a bludgeon"); People v. Ellis, 94 Ill. App. 3d 777, 779, 419 N.E.2d 727, 728 (3d Dist. 1981) (incorrectly loaded revolver with lodged shell in its barrel); People v. Chapman, 73 Ill. App. 3d 546, 549, 392 N.E.2d 391, 394 (3d Dist. 1979) (unloaded .38 caliber revolver).

[226] See, e.g., People v. Martinico, 101 Ill. App. 3d 250, 252, 427 N.E.2d 1340, 1341-42 (4th Dist. 1981) (unloaded and inoperable pellet gun); People v. Johnson, 100 Ill. App. 3d 251, 253, 426 N.E.2d 1041, 1043 (1st Dist. 1981) (.22 caliber air gun with sawed-off stock and barrel); People v. Greer, 53 Ill. App. 3d 675, 683, 368 N.E.2d 996, 1002 (5th Dist. 1977) (.22 caliber gas-operated pellet piston, even if it was unloaded); People v. Hill, 47 Ill. App. 3d 976, 977-78, 362 N.E.2d 470, 470 (3d Dist. 1977) (unloaded, uncocked air pistol that was made of metal and had appearance similar to .45 caliber automatic pistol).

[227] See, e.g., People v. De La Fuente, 92 Ill. App. 3d 525, 536, 414 N.E.2d 1355, 1364 (3d Dist. 1981) (starter pistol, incapable of firing bullets, used to strike victim in head); People v. Ratliff, 22 Ill. App. 3d 106, 107, 317 N.E.2d 63, 64 (4th Dist. 1974) (.22 caliber pistol designed to fire blanks could have been used as bludgeon because it was made of metal); People v. Trice, 127 Ill. App. 2d 310, 321, 262 N.E.2d 276, 282 (1st Dist. 1970) (because charge of its shell creates "high flash," starter pistol can cause considerable damage when held close to victim's head).

[228] See People v. Bayless, 99 Ill. App. 3d 532, 537, 425 N.E.2d 1192, 1195-96 (3d Dist. 1981) (noting that toy gun could have been used as a bludgeon to inflict serious harm because it weighed 5.88 ounces, was approximately five inches long, had metal sight and metal hammer, and appeared similar to snub nosed .38 caliber pistol). See also People v. Skelton, 79 Ill. App. 3d 569, 577, 399 N.E.2d 157, 160 (5th Dist. 1979) (if made of metal, toy gun can be dangerous weapon if it is "used or threatened to be used as a bludgeon"), aff'd, 83 Ill. 2d 58, 414 N.E.2d 455 (1980).

[229] See, e.g., People v. Meadows, 92 Ill. App. 3d 1028, 1032, 416 N.E.2d 404, 408 (3d Dist. 1981) (object with 18-inch metal barrel and wooden stock that made sound similar to cocking of gun's firing mechanism); People v. Agee, 85 Ill. App. 3d 74, 85, 405 N.E.2d 1245, 1254-55 (1st Dist. 1980) (hard, cold metal object that was placed to victim's neck).

[230] People v. Ditto, 98 Ill. App. 3d 36, 39, 424 N.E.2d 3, 5 (1st Dist. 1981) (victim was struck in face and back with screwdriver).

[231] People v. Robinson, 73 Ill. 2d 192, 202, 383 N.E.2d 164, 169 (1978) (fingernail clipper containing sharp, pointed fingernail file that caused slight cut when held to victim's throat). See also People v. Robinson, 52 Ill. App. 3d 658, 663, 367 N.E.2d 1034, 1037 (4th Dist. 1977) (noting that if "sufficient pressure had been applied, an artery or vein in the victim's neck could have been gouged"), aff'd, 73 Ill. 2d 192, 383 N.E.2d 164 (1978).

[232] See People v. Larson, 82 Ill. App. 3d 129, 144-45, 402 N.E.2d 732, 742 (2d Dist. 1980) ("M-80" firecrackers thrown at victims during course of robbery).

[233] People v. Stewart, 54 Ill. App. 3d 76, 80, 369 N.E.2d 131, 134 (1st Dist. 1977).

[234] People v. Lindsay, 263 Ill. App. 3d 523, 528, 635 N.E.2d 551, 555 (1st Dist. 1994).

[235] People v. Guzman, 276 Ill. App. 3d 750, 757, 658 N.E.2d 1268, 1273 (1st. Dist. 1995).

[236] People v. Elliott, 299 Ill. App. 3d 766, 773, 702 N.E.2d 643, 648 (4th Dist. 1998).

[237] People v. Bias, 131 Ill. App. 3d 98, 106-07, 475 N.E.2d 253, 259 (4th Dist. 1985).

Two approaches to determining whether an object is dangerous underlie all attempts to categorize weapons as dangerous or not dangerous; one approach is subjective,[238] the other is objective.[239] An armed robbery has occurred under the subjective approach where the defendant "intends to create in the victim the belief . . . [he] had a dangerous weapon and the victim in fact so believed."[240] Under this approach, "the objective dangerousness of the weapon is immaterial."[241] By contrast, the objective approach "requires that the weapon employed in the robbery be actually dangerous in the setting it is used."[242] Although the Illinois Supreme Court has rejected a purely subjective approach for determining whether a weapon is dangerous,[243] a discussion of both the subjective and objective approaches is essential to a thorough understanding of what weapons are considered dangerous under Illinois law.

A subjective standard regards the issue of whether a weapon is dangerous to be resolved by "standing (or quavering) in the shoes" of the victim.[244] Under such a standard, "an unloaded pistol, or a toy pistol, may be a dangerous weapon if the victim believes the weapon to be a loaded, operable weapon."[245] The great appeal of the subjective approach is that a "victim may be placed in terror and fear by a toy gun as readily as by an operable weapon. . . ."[246]

A comprehensive judicial opinion in favor of the subjective approach in Illinois is found in Justice Jones's concurring opinion in *People v. Greer*,[247] an Illinois appellate court decision. Contending the existing precedent had consistently employed a subjective standard, Justice Jones unsuccessfully attempted to persuade the court to adopt the subjective approach.[248] Justice Jones argued that in

---

[238] *See* People v. Chapman, 73 Ill. App. 3d 546, 550, 392 N.E.2d 391, 394 (3d Dist. 1977); People v. Greer, 53 Ill. App. 3d 675, 685, 368 N.E.2d 996, 1003 (5th Dist. 1977) (Jones, J., concurring).

[239] *See* People v. Skelton, 83 Ill. 2d 58, 63-64, 414 N.E.2d 455, 456-57 (1980); People v. Watkins, 94 Ill. App. 3d 749, 752, 419 N.E.2d 54, 56 (3d Dist. 1981); People v. Greer, 53 Ill. App. 3d 675, 680-83, 368 N.E.2d 996, 1001-02 (5th Dist. 1977).

[240] People v. Watkins, 94 Ill. App. 3d 749, 752, 419 N.E.2d 54, 56 (3d Dist. 1981).

[241] People v. Watkins, 94 Ill. App. 3d 749, 752, 419 N.E.2d 54, 56 (3d Dist. 1981).

[242] People v. Watkins, 94 Ill. App. 3d 749, 752, 419 N.E.2d 54, 56 (3d Dist. 1981).

[243] *See* People v. Skelton, 83 Ill. 2d 58, 63, 414 N.E.2d 455, 456-57 (1980); People v. Meadows, 92 Ill. App. 3d 1028, 1032, 416 N.E.2d 404, 406-07 (3d Dist. 1981).

[244] People v. Greer, 53 Ill. App. 3d 675, 682, 368 N.E.2d 996, 1001 (5th Dist. 1977).

[245] People v. Skelton, 79 Ill. App. 3d 569, 572, 399 N.E.2d 157, 160 (5th Dist. 1979), *aff'd*, 83 Ill. 2d 58, 414 N.E.2d 455 (1980).

[246] People v. Skelton, 79 Ill. App. 3d 569, 572, 399 N.E.2d 157, 160 (5th Dist. 1979), *aff'd*, 83 Ill. 2d 58, 414 N.E.2d 455 (1980); *See also* People v. Greer, 53 Ill. App. 3d 675, 682, 368 N.E.2d 996, 1001 (5th Dist. 1977) ("a robbery victim's belief that his assailant is armed with a dangerous weapon has great coercive effect").

[247] 53 Ill. App. 3d 675, 685-90, 368 N.E.2d 996, 1003-1007 (5th Dist. 1977) (Jones, J., concurring).

[248] *See* People v. Greer, 53 Ill. App. 3d 675, 685-90, 368 N.E.2d 996, 1003-1007 (5th Dist. 1977) (Jones, J., concurring).

determining whether a weapon is dangerous, the focus should be on the defendant's intent in using the weapon and on the belief that the use of the weapon could have reasonably instilled in the victim, rather than on the weapon itself.[249] Noting that a defendant, by pointing an object that appears to be a gun at his or her victim, represents that object to be an operable firearm, Justice Jones recognized: "One looking into the barrel of a gun will be strongly inclined to accept it for what it appears to be."[250] Justice Jones further recognized that it is the fear instilled in the victim, rather than the actual dangerousness of the weapon, that brings the victim into subjection.[251] Justice Jones concluded that the question of whether a weapon is dangerous should be resolved "by looking to the effect the weapon had on the victim."[252]

Nevertheless, in *People v. Skelton*,[253] in a unanimous opinion, that was briefly discussed above, the Illinois Supreme Court adopted an objective approach to determine which weapons are dangerous.[254] The *Skelton* case involved an armed robbery conviction of a defendant who had used a toy gun in committing a robbery. The four-and-one-half inch gun, which had an appearance similar to a small-caliber revolver, was made entirely of hard plastic. It fired neither pellets nor blank shells, gave out no flash, and was too small and light to be effectively used as a bludgeon. The only conceivable danger presented by the toy gun was that it could be used to poke the victim in the eye, in the same way that a finger

---

[249] People v. Greer, 53 Ill. App. 3d 675, 686, 368 N.E.2d 996, 1004 (5th Dist. 1977) (Jones, J., concurring). *See also* People v. Chapman, 73 Ill. App. 3d 546, 550, 392 N.E.2d 391, 394 (3d Dist. 1979) (adopting this focus for determining whether weapon is dangerous).

[250] People v. Greer, 53 Ill. App. 3d 675, 686, 368 N.E.2d 996, 1004 (5th Dist. 1977) (Jones, J., concurring).

[251] Justice Jones contended:

> We are essentially dealing with intent, motivation and effect. Whether the firearm used is operable or not would have no bearing on those motifs. When we consider the effect of the use of an objective standard upon the evil sought to be corrected (the use of weapons in a robbery) we find that the evil result remains (a terrorized victim) and the deterrence factor is eliminated.

People v. Greer, 53 Ill. App. 3d 675, 686, 368 N.E.2d 996, 1004 (5th Dist. 1977) (Jones, J., concurring).

[252] Justice Jones concluded his concurring opinion by suggesting the following standard:

> If the victim subjectively and reasonably determines that the assailant is possessed of a dangerous weapon and is subdued to the will of the assailant and suffers his property to be taken, then the weapon is, as a matter of law, dangerous within the purview of the armed robber statute.

People v. Greer, 53 Ill. App. 3d 675, 689, 368 N.E.2d 996, 1006 (5th Dist. 1977) (Jones, J., concurring).

[253] 83 Ill. 2d 58, 414 N.E.2d 455 (1980).

[254] People v. Skelton, 83 Ill. 2d 58, 64, 414 N.E.2d 455, 457 (1980).

could.[255] The issue before the Illinois Supreme Court was whether this toy gun constituted a dangerous weapon under the armed robbery statute.

The *Skelton* court initially noted that the intent underlying the enhanced penalty for armed, as opposed to simple, robbery is "to deter the use of dangerous weapons and prevent the kind of violence that often attends the use of a deadly weapon in the perpetration of a robbery."[256] The court then observed that although it is clear that a simple robbery may be committed by a defendant using a toy gun, there is confusion over whether that defendant would be considered armed with a dangerous weapon.[257] Suggesting that this confusion arose as the result of the competing objective and subjective approaches to determining what weapons are dangerous, the court stated that neither standard "is completely free of logical and practical difficulties in its application."[258]

The *Skelton* court then quoted extensively from a criminal law treatise:

> The great weight of authority holds that an unloaded pistol, not used as a bludgeon, is nevertheless a dangerous weapon for armed-robbery purposes. (Some jurisdictions even hold that a toy pistol is such a weapon.) The majority view seems wrong, however: intimidation by some means is a necessary ingredient of simple robbery without violence; something additional in the way of dangerousness is needed for aggravated robbery; but the rob-

---

[255] People v. Skelton, 83 Ill. 2d 58, 66, 414 N.E.2d 455, 458 (1980).

[256] People v. Skelton, 83 Ill. 2d 58, 62, 414 N.E.2d 455, 456 (1980).

[257] People v. Skelton, 83 Ill. 2d 58, 62, 414 N.E.2d 455, 456 (1980).

[258] People v. Skelton, 83 Ill. 2d 58, 62, 414 N.E.2d 455, 456 (1980). Addressing the difficulties of the subjective approach, Justice Underwood declared:

> The problem with the subjective test when carried to its logical extreme is that the victim may very well believe, and the robber may very well intend that the victim believe, that a dangerous weapon is being used in a robbery when in fact the robber has a finger or some innocuous object in his pocket. . . . A fair reading of [the current Illinois armed robbery statute] seems to require something more than a finger in the pocket, and to this extent, at least, it would appear that the legislature has rejected the subjective test.

Yet Justice Underwood also noted that there were problems with the objective test:

> That test requires that there be literal compliance with the statute, and asks whether the instrumentality was actually dangerous in the circumstances in which it was used. This standard, however, seems to run afoul of logical and common sense in the cases where the intended victim is behind bulletproof glass. Presumably, an armed robbery has occurred if property is actually taken, although even a loaded gun would not be dangerous in such circumstances. Too, the weight of authority permits application of the armed robbery statute to unloaded guns, a result which has been criticized.

Id. at 63-64, 414 N.E.2d at 457.

ber's use of an unloaded (or toy) gun adds nothing extra to the bare fact that he intimidated the victim.[259]

Agreeing that something additional in the way of dangerousness is needed for armed robbery, the court concluded that the Illinois armed robbery statute "requires that 'something' to be a dangerous weapon."[260] Nevertheless, despite the opinion expressed in the quoted material, the Illinois Supreme Court declared that:

> a weapon can be dangerous, even though used in a manner for which it was not designed or intended. Thus, a rifle or a shotgun, whether loaded or not, may be used as a club with devastating effect. Similarly, a handgun, when gripped by the barrel and used as a bludgeon, is equally dangerous whether loaded or unloaded.[261]

After discussing competing policy considerations,[262] the *Skelton* court announced that:

---

[259] People v. Skelton, 83 Ill. 2d 58, 64, 414 N.E.2d 455, 457 (1980). (quoting WAYNE LAFAVE & AUSTIN SCOTT, HANDBOOK ON CRIMINAL LAW 703 (1973)) (footnotes omitted). Further quoting that treatise, the supreme court explained:

> Perhaps another way to express the matter is this: the greater punishment is awarded for armed robbery so as to deter the dangerous person who is actually capable of inflicting death or serious bodily harm. The robber with the unloaded or toy gun is not nice — is guilty in fact of (simple) robbery — but his is not the dangerous type for who the greater penalty is reserved.

Id. (quoting WAYNE LAFAVE & AUSTIN SCOTT, HANDBOOK ON CRIMINAL LAW 703, n.67 (1972)).

[260] People v. Skelton, 83 Ill. 2d 58, 64, 414 N.E.2d 455, 457 (1980).

[261] People v. Skelton, 83 Ill. 2d 58, 64, 414 N.E.2d 455, 457 (1980). Justice Underwood noted:

> [S]ome weapons are deadly *per se* and thus as a matter of law satisfy the statutory requirement for armed robbery. An object not deadly *per se* may still be a dangerous weapon because of its capacity to inflict serious harm even though not designed for that purpose, as in the case of a baseball bat.

People v. Skelton, 83 Ill. 2d 58, 64, 414 N.E.2d 455, 457 (1980).

[262] In weighing these policy considerations, the *Skelton* court observed:

> On the one hand, to require the State to prove a firearm used to commit a robbery was loaded and operable would greatly restrict the applicability of the armed robbery statute. Under such a requirement, a defendant could be convicted of armed robbery only if he were apprehended at the scene of the crime or immediately thereafter with the loaded and operable gun in his possession, or if the gun itself were discovered, identified and found to be loaded and operable, or if the defendant actually fired the weapon. On the other hand, it would be illogical and, perhaps, unfair to convict a person of robbery "while armed with a dangerous weapon" in the face of evidence that his weapon was, in fact, not dangerous.

People v. Skelton, 83 Ill. 2d 58, 65-66, 414 N.E.2d 455, 458 (1980) (quoting People v. Greer, 53 Ill. App. 3d 675, 682, 368 N.E.2d 996, 1001 (5th Dist. 1977)).

many objects, including guns, can be dangerous and cause serious injury, even when used in a fashion for which they were not intended. Most, if not all unloaded real guns and many toy guns, because of their size and weight, could be used in a deadly fashion as a bludgeons. Since the robbery victim could be quite badly hurt or even killed by such weapon if used in that fashion, it seems to us they can properly be classified as dangerous weapons although they were not in fact used in that manner during the commission of the particular offense. It suffices that the potential for such uses is present; the victim need not provoke its actual use in such manner.[263]

Finally, while noting that in most cases, the trier of fact must determine whether the particular object used was sufficiently capable of causing serious injury and could therefore be classified as a dangerous weapon, the *Skelton* court recognized that where "the character of a weapon is such as to admit of only one conclusion, the question becomes one of law for the court."[264] Accordingly, the court affirmed the appellate court's decision, reversing the armed robbery conviction, because it found that the toy gun involved in *Skelton* was not "the type of weapon which can be used to cause the additional violence and harm to which the greater penalty attached to armed robbery was designed to deter."[265]

§ 12.15.   — Mental State.

Like simple robbery, armed robbery is a general intent offense; it does not require a specific intent to permanently deprive another of his or her property.[266] Consequently, a voluntarily drugged condition is not a defense to armed robbery.[267]

The requisite mental state for armed robbery can be demonstrated by circumstantial evidence. For example, it was held that a defendant's intent to commit armed robbery could be inferred from his otherwise unexplained presence in his victim's store while armed with a sawed-off shotgun.[268]

---

[263] People v. Skelton, 83 Ill. 2d 58, 65-66, 414 N.E.2d 455, 458 (1980). *See also* People v. Meadows, 92 Ill. App. 3d 1028, 1031, 416 N.E.2d 404, 406 (3d Dist. 1981) (quoting this passage of Skelton opinion).

[264] People v. Skelton, 83 Ill. 2d 58, 66, 414 N.E.2d 455, 458 (1980).

[265] People v. Skelton, 83 Ill. 2d 58, 66, 414 N.E.2d 455, 458 (1980).

[266] People v. Talley, 177 Ill. App. 3d 170, 173, 531 N.E.2d 1139, 1141 (4th Dist. 1988).

[267] People v. Burks, 29 Ill. App. 3d 74, 79, 331 N.E.2d 581, 586 (2d Dist. 1975).

[268] People v. Sullivan, 48 Ill. App. 3d 555, 562, 362 N.E.2d 1313, 1318 (1977).

§ 12.16. Aggravated Robbery.

In 1994, the legislature created the offense of "aggravated robbery,"[269] Section 5/18-5 of the Criminal Code defines aggravated robbery as follows:

A person commits aggravated robbery when he or she takes property from the person or presence of another by the use of force or by threatening the imminent use of force while indicating verbally or by his or her actions to the victim that he or she is presently armed with a firearm or other dangerous weapon, including a knife, club, ax, or bludgeon. This offense shall be applicable even though it is later determined that he or she had no firearm or other dangerous weapon . . . in his or her possession when he or she committed the robbery.[270]

§ 12.17. Vehicular Hijacking.

In 1993, the legislature created the offense of "vehicular hijacking."[271] Section 5/18-3 defines the offense of vehicular hijacking as the taking of "a motor vehicle from the person or the immediate presence of another by the use of force or by threatening the imminent use of force."[272]

In *People v. Aguilar*,[273] the court rule that since the robbery statute "contains language virtually identical to that at issue in the vehicular hijacking statute," issues regarding the reach of this offense "can be resolved with reference to cases under the robbery statute."[274] Thus, where the defendant's physical attack caused the victim to abandon his vehicle, which was then taken by the defendant, this amounted to vehicular hijacking.[275]

§ 12.18. Aggravated Vehicular Hijacking.

In 1993, the legislature also created the offense of "aggravated vehicular hijacking."[276] This elevates the offense of vehicular hijacking to this more serious crime in the following instances: (1) where "the person from whose immediate presence the motor vehicle is taken is a physically handicapped person or a person 60 years of age or over; (2) a person under 16 years of age is a passenger in the motor vehicle at the time of the offense; (3) or he or she carries on or about

---

[269] 720 ILCS 5/18-5(1999); People v. Brackett, 288 Ill. App. 3d 12, 18-19, 679 N.E.2d 1285, 1289 (2d Dist. 1997) (offense of aggravated robbery not unconstitutionally vague).

[270] 720 ILCS 5/18-5(1999). Aggravated robbery is a Class 1 felony.

[271] 720 ILCS 5/18-3(c) (1999).

[272] 720 ILCS 5/18-3(c) (1999).

[273] 286 Ill. App. 3d 493, 676 N.E.2d 324 (1st Dist. 1997).

[274] People v. Aguilar, 286 Ill. App. 3d 493, 497-98, 676 N.E.2d 324, 327 (1st Dist. 1997).

[275] People v. Aguilar, 286 Ill. App. 3d 493, 497-498, 676 N.E.2d 324, 327 (1st Dist. 1997).

[276] 720 ILCS 5/18-4 (1999).

his person, or is otherwise armed with a dangerous weapon."[277] Aggravated vehicular hijacking is a felony.[278]

§ 12.19.   Lesser Included Offenses.

For a complete discussion on lesser included offenses, see chapter 1. The Illinois Supreme Court has declared that theft may be considered a lesser included offense of robbery.[279] Robbery is clearly a lesser included offense of armed robbery.[280] However, aggravated robbery is not necessarily a lesser included offense of armed robbery.[281]

---

[277] 720 ILCS 5/18-4(a) (1999).

[278] 720 ILCS 5/18-4(b) (1999).

[279] People v. Jones, 149 Ill. 2d 288, 296, 595 N.E.2d 1071, 1076 (1992).

[280] People v. Burg, 207 Ill. App. 3d 67, 70, 565 N.E.2d 306, 308 (4th Dist. 1990).

[281] People v. Jones, 293 Ill. App. 3d 119, 128-29, 687 N.E.2d 1128, 1134 (1st Dist. 1997).

CHAPTER 13

BURGLARY, ARSON, AND OTHER
OFFENSES AGAINST PROPERTY

645

§ 13.01.　Introduction.

There are a number of Illinois crimes that affect property interests — private and governmental. While a number of these offenses were explored in Chapter 11 (theft-related crimes) and Chapter 12 (robbery and armed robbery),[1] there are a number of other offenses that impact property interests that will be examined in this chapter. They include burglary[2] and the related offenses of possession of burglary tools[3] and residential burglary[4] (contained in article 5/19); arson[5] and the related crimes of aggravated arson,[6] residential arson,[7] and possession of explosives or incendiary devices[8] (found in article 5/20); various offenses involving criminal damage or trespass to property[9] (located in article 5/21); and several additional crimes, such as causing a catastrophe[10] and looting,[11] that also involve the protection of property.

§ 13.02.　Burglary.

The first, and perhaps most significant, crime to be examined in this chapter is the crime of burglary.[12] At common law, *burglary* was defined as "the breaking and entering of the dwelling of another in the nighttime with the intent to

---

[1] As one author has noted, it "is incongruous that robbery and armed robbery . . . are considered as 'Offenses Directed Against Property,' particularly in view of the fact that robbery is listed as a forcible felony in section [5/]2-8 and the fact that a forcible felony is defined as involving 'the use or threat of physical force or violence against any individual.'" Howard N. Morse, *The Criminal Code of Illinois of 1961*, 15 DEPAUL L. REV. 27, 44 (1965). In any event, it is so characterized.

[2] 720 ILCS 5/19-1 (1999).

[3] 720 ILCS 5/19-2 (1999).

[4] 720 ILCS 5/19-3 (1999).

[5] 720 ILCS 5/20-1 (1999).

[6] 720 ILCS 5/20-1.1 (1999).

[7] 720 ILCS 5/20-1.2 (1999).

[8] 720 ILCS 5/20-2 (1999).

[9] *See, e.g.,* 720 ILCS 5/21 (1999) (criminal damage to property).

[10] 720 ILCS 5/20.5-5 (1999).

[11] 720 ILCS 5/42-1 (1999).

[12] 720 ILCS 5/19-1 (1999).

commit a felony."[13] However, the crime of burglary has evolved in Illinois in such a way that it no longer requires (1) a breaking, (2) a dwelling house, or (3) the nighttime.[14] In addition to the intent to commit a felony, proof of intent to commit a theft (including petty theft) is sufficient.[15] The present code provision, then, has an impact on a broader range of behavior than the common law stricture.

§ 13.03.   — Burglary Codified.

Section 5/19-1 of the Criminal Code defines burglary as follows:

> (a) A person commits burglary when without authority he knowingly enters or without authority remains within a building, housetrailer, watercraft, aircraft, motor vehicle as defined in the Illinois Vehicle Code, railroad car, or any part thereof, with intent to commit therein a felony or theft . . . (b) Sentence. Burglary is a . . . felony.[16]

This same statutory provision provides that "[t]his offense shall not include the offenses set out in Section 5/4-102 [of chapter 625] of the Illinois Vehicle Code, nor the offense of residential burglary as defined in Section 5/19-3 hereof."[17] Section 5/4-102 of the Illinois Vehicle Code states:

> It is a violation of this Chapter for: (a) A person, without authority to do so, to damage a vehicle or to damage or remove any part of a vehicle . . . (b) A person, without authority to do so, to tamper with a vehicle or go in it, on it, or work or attempt to work any of its parts, or set or attempt to set it in motion.[18]

Also, according to section 5/19-3, any burglary of a "dwelling" is "residential burglary," which carries more severe penalties than other burglaries.[19]

§ 13.04.   — Elements of Burglary.

The crime of nonresidential burglary exists where a person (1) knowingly (2) enters or without authority remains (3) within a building, housetrailer, water-

---

[13] ROLLIN M. PERKINS & RONALD N. BOYCE, CRIMINAL LAW 246 (3d ed. 1982). *See also* ILL. ANN. STAT. ch. 38, para. 19-1 (Smith-Hurd 1977), 1961 Committee Comments, at 569 (revised 1970).

[14] ILL. ANN. STAT. ch. 38, para. 19-1 (Smith-Hurd 1977), 1961 Committee Comments, at 569 (revised 1970).

[15] People v. Grigsby, 75 Ill. App. 2d 184, 194, 220 N.E.2d 498, 504 (4th Dist. 1966).

[16] 720 ILCS 5/19-1 (1999).

[17] 720 ILCS 5/19-1 (1999).

[18] 625 ILCS 5/4-102 (1999).

[19] 720 ILCS 5/19-3(b) (1999) (residential burglary is Class 1 felony); *see id.* 5/19-1(b) (burglary is Class 2 felony).

craft, aircraft, motor vehicle, railroad car, or any part thereof (4) with intent to commit therein a felony or theft.[20]

§ 13.05. —— "Knowingly."

Proof that the defendant "knowingly" made an unauthorized entry is a key element of burglary that must be proved at trial.[21] This mental state should be alleged in the charging instrument, although if it is not, and the charging instrument alleges intent to steal or intent to commit a felony, then the mens rea requirement is alleged by implication.[22] Thus, if a defendant unwittingly opened a door in the darkness thinking that the door merely led to an open courtyard but instead the defendant actually entered a building without the owner's permission, he or she could not be convicted of burglary of the building. This assumes that he did not knowingly remain there without authority.

§ 13.06. —— "Enters or Without Authority Remains."

If the defendant enters the protected area with the requisite felonious intent, this is sufficient for burglary.[23] A common law "breaking" is not required.[24] The entry does not have to be with force.[25] It is no defense that the entryway was open and that the entry was made without overcoming some type of impediment.[26]

It is not required, although it is usually the case, that the entire body of the defendant entered into the premises. So long as there is an entry "by any portion of [defendant's] person or by an instrument inserted [by him or her] for the purpose of committing the contemplated theft," this is sufficient.[27] Thus, if a defendant argues on appeal that the point of entry was too small to allow for the entry of his or her person, this is not a defense, for "it is not the size of the hole that is determinative but rather . . . it is whether a hand or instrument was actually in-

---

[20] 720 ILCS 5/19-1 (1999).

[21] People v. Dandridge, 98 Ill. App. 3d 1021, 1026-27, 424 N.E.2d 1262, 1266 (5th Dist. 1981).

[22] People v. Gregory, 59 Ill. 2d 111, 113-14, 319 N.E.2d 483, 485 (1974).

[23] People v. Woolsey, 24 Ill. App. 3d 1079, 1082, 322 N.E.2d 614, 616-17 (5th Dist. 1975).

[24] People v. Weaver, 41 Ill. 2d 434, 438, 243 N.E.2d 245, 248 (1968), *cert. denied*, 395 U.S. 959 (1969).

[25] People v. Blair, 1 Ill. App. 3d 6, 8, 272 N.E.2d 404, 406 (5th Dist. 1971), *aff'd,* 52 Ill. 2d 371, 288 N.E.2d 443 (1972).

[26] People v. Blair, 1 Ill. App. 3d 6, 8, 272 N.E.2d 404, 406 (5th Dist. 1971), *aff'd,* 52 Ill. 2d 371, 288 N.E.2d 443 (1972).

[27] People v. Davis, 3 Ill. App. 3d 738, 740, 279 N.E.2d 179, 181 (5th Dist. 1972) (burglary reduced to attempted burglary because evidence was insufficient to prove that some type of entry occurred).

serted into the hole for the purpose of committing the felony."[28] For example, a defendant's physical act of kicking his foot through a store window constituted an unlawful entry into a premises where the store was subsequently looted by a cheering crowd.[29] On the other hand, throwing a brick through a store window is not an "entry" into a building.[30] Apparently, the instrument that makes the entry must be under the physical control of the accused. In one case, where blood spots of the defendant's blood type were found immediately inside a building, this was considered sufficient evidence of entry even though the defendant claimed that he never entered or intended to enter the building, and the blood that was discovered was only found just inside and below the broken window.[31] In such circumstances, where the defendant claims, for example, that the blood could have spurted into the building from his hand, which was outside the building, this can be contradicted by the presence of fingerprints on glass fragments found on both the interior and exterior of window.[32]

The time of day the entry occurs is immaterial. That is, the unlawful entry does not have to be in the nighttime to constitute a burglary,[33] as was the case at common law.[34]

Although the statute reads that the defendant must either "enter or without authority remain" in the protected area, suggesting that the "without authority" requirement applies only to one who "remains," and not to one who "enters," this is obviously not the case. Where a church had an open-door policy for members and non-members, such policy gave authority to the defendant to enter the church and, as such, the defendant could not be convicted of burglary since there was no *unauthorized* entry.[35] If the protected area is a private place, the courts state that "the element of entry without authority must be established apart from the element of entry to commit a felony or theft. . . ."[36] However, if the protected area is open to the public, the element of entry without authority

---

[28] People v. Davis, 3 Ill. App. 3d 738, 739, 279 N.E.2d 179, 180 (5th Dist. 1972). *See also* People v. Palmer, 83 Ill. App. 3d 732, 735-36, 404 N.E.2d 853, 856 (4th Dist. 1980) (entry by part of defendant's body sufficient for burglary).

[29] People v. Roldan, 100 Ill. App. 2d 81, 85-86, 241 N.E.2d 591, 593 (1st Dist. 1968).

[30] People v. Williams, 28 Ill. App. 3d 402, 403-04, 328 N.E.2d 682, 683 (5th Dist. 1975).

[31] People v. Roberts, 189 Ill. App. 3d 66, 70, 544 N.E.2d 1340, 1343 (4th Dist. 1989).

[32] People v. Roberts, 189 Ill. App. 3d 66, 71, 544 N.E.2d 1340, 1344 (4th Dist. 1989).

[33] People v. Glickman, 377 Ill. 360, 367, 36 N.E.2d 720, 723 (1941).

[34] *See* § 13.02 of this chapter.

[35] People v. Meeker, 86 Ill. App. 3d 162, 172-73, 407 N.E.2d 1058, 1066-67 (5th Dist. 1980).

[36] People v. Baker, 59 Ill. App. 3d 100, 102-03, 375 N.E.2d 176, 179 (2d Dist. 1978) (private parking garage); *see also* People v. Hepler, 132 Ill. App. 3d 705, 711, 477 N.E.2d 768, 773 (2d Dist. 1985) (finding insufficient evidence that defendant entered private home without authority and stating that "the fact of an unauthorized entry must be proved separately from the fact of an entry with a wrongful intent").

need not be proven apart from the element of entry with wrongful intent because such an entry with criminal intent is "without authority."[37]

If a defendant has "unlimited consent" to enter a building, he or she cannot be convicted for a burglary of that structure; however, "concerning the right of an employee to enter premises of the employer, consent, either stated or implied, but limited to the place, time or purpose, is not a defense where entry occurs outside the limitation."[38] Thus, where a defendant received a key to a store from an assistant manager who was not authorized to allow the defendant's entry, the defendant could not defend his entry as authorized by the assistant manager's actions.[39]

A more difficult problem arises when a defendant enters an establishment open to the public with the intent to commit a felony or theft in the establishment. The courts hold that if the defendant enters the establishment with a felonious intent, his or her entry is beyond his or her "limited authority" to enter and, accordingly, is "without authority."[40] The courts insist that the "essence" of the crime of burglary is the entry of premises with the intent to commit a felony or theft in the premises.[41] The authority to enter a building open to the public "extends only to those who enter with a purpose consistent with the reason the building is open."[42] In *People v. Blair*,[43] the defendants drove a car into an open-ended building housing a car wash, washed their car, and then forced open a coin box. Since the defendants admitted that they had the intent to commit a theft on their entry into the car wash, the Illinois Supreme Court upheld their convictions for burglary.[44] Similarly, the authority that clothes an invitee who enters a museum is not unlimited and does not include authority to enter for a purpose different than viewing exhibits.[45] Thus, where a defendant was found in the Chicago Historical Society after closing hours, he was convicted of burglary, given the trial court's finding that he had made his original entry with a felonious intent.[46]

---

[37] People v. Bailey, 188 Ill. App. 3d 278, 285, 543 N.E.2d 1338, 1342 (5th Dist. 1989).

[38] People v. Hart, 132 Ill. App. 2d 558, 561, 270 N.E.2d 102, 104 (1st Dist. 1971).

[39] People v. Castile, 34 Ill. App. 3d 220, 226, 339 N.E.2d 366, 370 (5th Dist. 1975).

[40] People v. Bailey, 188 Ill. App. 3d 278, 285-86, 543 N.E.2d 1338, 1342-43 (5th Dist. 1989); People v. Schneller, 69 Ill. App. 2d 50, 54, 216 N.E.2d 510, 512 (1st Dist. 1966).

[41] *See, e.g.,* People v. Rand, 29 Ill. App. 3d 873, 875, 331 N.E.2d 15, 18 (2d Dist. 1975).

[42] People v. Blair, 52 Ill. 2d 371, 374, 288 N.E.2d 443, 445 (1972) (quoting People v. Weaver, 41 Ill. 2d 434, 439, 243 N.E.2d 245, 248 (1968), *cert. denied,* 395 U.S. 959 (1969)); People v. Drake, 172 Ill. App. 3d 1026, 1028-29, 527 N.E.2d 519, 520 (4th Dist. 1988) (defendant who entered grocery store with intent to commit forgery was properly convicted of both forgery and burglary).

[43] 52 Ill. 2d 371, 288 N.E.2d 443 (1972).

[44] People v. Blair, 52 Ill. 2d 371, 374, 288 N.E.2d 443, 445 (1972).

[45] People v. Schneller, 69 Ill. App. 2d 50, 54, 216 N.E.2d 510, 512 (1st Dist. 1966).

[46] People v. Schneller, 69 Ill. App. 2d 50, 54, 216 N.E.2d 510, 512 (1st Dist. 1966).

The "limited authority" doctrine has been extended to entries other than into public buildings.[47] In *People v. Fisher,*[48] the defendants entered a particular private residence to attend a party. On their arrival in the residence, the two defendants pulled guns on the victims and demanded their money. In upholding the defendants' convictions for burglary (which would now be called residential burglary), the appellate court concluded that the defendants had carried out their thefts pursuant to a preconceived plan hatched before their entry.[49] "Because defendants were given authority to enter the apartment for the purpose of a social visit only, the criminal actions they planned were inconsistent with this limited authority, and served to vitiate the consent given for the entry."[50] Parenthetically, had the defendants in these cases not formulated the requisite intent until *after* they made their entry, the evidence would not have supported a burglary.[51]

By similar reasoning, a person who has limited authority to enter a building can be convicted of burglary if he or she enters at a time and in a manner inconsistent with that authority.[52] In *People v. Woolsey,*[53] a defendant used his employee key to enter his workplace after hours, in order to commit a theft.[54] The defendant's employer testified that the defendant had permission to use his key only during the "normal course of business hours."[55] The appellate court held that the entry exceeded the defendant's authority in terms of both "time and purpose" and, as a result, the defendant's burglary conviction was affirmed.[56]

The obvious implication of these cases is that a defendant can never defend his or her illegal entry merely because the building he or she enters happens to

---

[47] People v. Bailey, 188 Ill. App. 3d 278, 285-86, 543 N.E.2d 1338, 1342-43 (5th Dist. 1989) (automobile). *See also* People v. Hudson, 113 Ill. App. 3d 1041, 1045, 448 N.E.2d 178, 181 (5th Dist. 1983) ("without authority" language in burglary and home invasion carries the same meaning) and People v. Bush, 157 Ill. 2d 248, 253-54, 623 N.E.2d 1361, 1364 (1993) (in home invasion, limited authority doctrine does apply where defendant enters premises with criminal purpose but does not apply if defendant enters with innocent purpose and later formulates criminal intent).

[48] 83 Ill. App. 3d 619, 404 N.E.2d 859 (1st Dist. 1980).

[49] People v. Fisher, 83 Ill. App. 3d 619, 622, 404 N.E.2d 859, 862 (1st Dist. 1980).

[50] People v. Fisher, 83 Ill. App. 3d 619, 623, 404 N.E.2d 859, 862-63 (1st Dist. 1980).

[51] People v. Bailey, 188 Ill. App. 3d 278, 284, 543 N.E.2d 1338, 1341 (5th Dist. 1989); People v. Fisher, 83 Ill. App. 3d 619, 622, 404 N.E.2d 859, 862 (1st Dist. 1980).

[52] People v. Woolsey, 24 Ill. App. 3d 1079, 1082, 322 N.E.2d 614, 617 (5th Dist. 1975).

[53] People v. Woolsey, 24 Ill. App. 3d 1079, 1082, 322 N.E.2d 614, 617 (5th Dist. 1975).

[54] People v. Woolsey, 24 Ill. App. 3d 1079, 1082, 322 N.E.2d 614, 616-17 (5th Dist. 1975).

[55] People v. Woolsey, 24 Ill. App. 3d 1079, 1082, 322 N.E.2d 614, 615 (5th Dist. 1975).

[56] People v. Woolsey, 24 Ill. App. 3d 1079, 1082, 322 N.E.2d 614, 617 (5th Dist. 1975). *Compare* People v. Meeker, 86 Ill. App. 3d 162, 172-73, 407 N.E.2d 1058, 1066-67 (5th Dist. 1980) (rejecting application of "limited purpose" doctrine because there was no evidence presented suggesting church congregation member had limited access to church that had open-door policy).

be open at least some of the time to the public.[57] It would be contrary to reason and ordinary human understanding to deduce that the business invitation extended by the owners to the public generally includes entry for an unlawful purpose.[58]

Concerning the entry itself, the state is not obligated to prove the particular manner by which the entry was made.[59] Assuming it is unclear whether the defendant picked a lock to enter through a door or, instead, entered through an unlocked window, evidence demonstrating the defendant's illegal presence in the premises in which he or she committed a felony or theft is sufficient to convict the defendant of burglary.[60]

Aside from prohibiting unauthorized entry, the burglary statute also allows for a conviction of burglary where the defendant "without authority remains" in a protected place.[61] For example, burglary convictions were sustained for three defendants where one of them apparently hid himself in a pharmacy as it closed for the day (unlawfully remained) and then opened a door that could be unlocked only from the inside, to allow his companions to enter (unlawful entry).[62] Since this code paragraph provides two alternative ways to commit burglary — (1) by unlawful entry and (2) by unlawfully remaining following lawful entry[63] — the charging instrument should specify which method was involved.[64]

Although there are few reported cases that rest solely on the theory that the accused "without authority remained" in certain premises, this is somewhat understandable, since the Illinois courts hold that even one who has general author-

---

[57] *See* People ex rel. McLain v. Housewright, 9 Ill. App. 3d 803, 805-06, 293 N.E.2d 911, 913 (5th Dist. 1973) (supermarket). *See also* People v. Glover, 276 Ill. App. 3d 934, 938, 659 N.E.2d 78, 81 (2d Dist. 1995) (where defendant was instructed to remain in doorway of church instead entered church and stole vacuum cleaners, he had exceeded the limited scope of authority to be in the church; burglary conviction affirmed).

[58] People ex rel. McLain v. Housewright, 9 Ill. App. 3d 803, 806, 293 N.E.2d 911, 913 (5th Dist. 1973).

[59] People v. Stanton, 16 Ill. 2d 459, 468, 158 N.E.2d 47, 52 (1959).

[60] *See* People v. Stanton, 16 Ill. 2d 459, 468, 158 N.E.2d 47, 52 (1959). *See also* People v. Davis, 54 Ill. App. 3d 517, 520, 369 N.E.2d 1376, 1381-82 (4th Dist. 1977) (key to crime of burglary is entry into prohibited space, not whether entry was made by turning a handle, cracking a lock or walking through an open portal).

[61] 720 ILCS 5/19-1(a) (1999).

[62] *See* People v. Castile, 34 Ill. App. 3d 220, 225, 339 N.E.2d 366, 369-70 (5th Dist. 1975).

[63] 720 ILCS 5/19-1 (1999).

[64] People v. Boone, 217 Ill. App. 3d 532, 533, 577 N.E.2d 788, 789 (3d Dist. 1991) (holding that the defendant could not be convicted of burglary by unlawfully remaining where evidence showed that the defendant unlawfully entered the building); People v. Green, 83 Ill. App. 3d 982, 986, 404 N.E.2d 930, 932 (3d Dist. 1980) (overturning conviction for armed violence based on burglary since indictment alleged "burglary-by-remaining" when, in fact, evidence established "unauthorized entry;" variance in indictment was fatal since it denied defendant ability to prepare for trial).

ity to enter an area can lose this authority if his or her original entry was for an unlawful purpose.[65] Thus, by finding that the *entry* was illegal, the courts essentially avoid an analysis revolving around the "remains without authority" approach.

As with other elements of burglary, proof of illegal entry or remaining without legal authority is not dependent on direct evidence but can be established by circumstantial evidence.[66] Thus, where there was a forced entry of a business after hours and defendant's fingerprints were found inside, he was properly convicted of burglary.[67]

§ 13.07.   —— "Within a Building."

Most of the cases involving non-residential burglary arise where there has been an entry into a "building."[68] Since the statute offers no definition of this term, the judiciary determines its meaning. A review of the cases reflects a lenient interpretation of what constitutes a building, for even a telephone booth has been so viewed.[69] Other structures that have been treated as buildings for burglary purposes include an open-ended car wash,[70] a private club,[71] a laundromat,[72] a museum,[73] a stockroom,[74] a toolshed,[75] a chicken house,[76] a stable,[77] an office,[78] and a tent.[79] On the other hand, a fenced-in lot where vehicles were parked was not considered a building.[80] Although a dwelling is clearly a building, entry into a dwelling is considered "residential burglary."[81]

---

[65] *See, e.g.,* People v. Bailey, 188 Ill. App. 3d 278, 285-86, 543 N.E.2d 1338, 1342-43 (5th Dist. 1989).

[66] *See, e.g.,* People v. Roberts, 189 Ill. App. 3d 66, 69-70, 544 N.E.2d 1340, 1343 (4th Dist. 1989) (burglary established by circumstantial evidence).

[67] *See, e.g.,* People v. Roberts, 189 Ill. App. 3d 66, 69-70, 544 N.E.2d 1340, 1343 (4th Dist. 1989).

[68] 720 ILCS 5/19-1(a) (1999).

[69] People v. Embry, 12 Ill. App. 3d 332, 336, 297 N.E.2d 604, 607 (5th Dist. 1973); People v. Borneman, 66 Ill. App. 2d 251, 255, 213 N.E.2d 52, 53 (2d Dist. 1966).

[70] People v. Blair, 52 Ill. 2d 371, 374, 288 N.E.2d 443, 445 (1972).

[71] People v. Richardson, 104 Ill. 2d 8, 13-14, 470 N.E.2d 1024, 1027 (1984).

[72] *See* People v. Weaver, 41 Ill. 2d 434, 438-39, 243 N.E.2d 245, 248 (1968), *cert. denied*, 395 U.S. 959 (1969).

[73] *See* People v. Schneller, 69 Ill. App. 2d 50, 54, 216 N.E.2d 510, 512 (1st Dist. 1966).

[74] *See* People v. Songer, 28 Ill. 2d 433, 437-38, 192 N.E.2d 861, 864 (1963).

[75] People v. Gillespie, 344 Ill. 290, 294, 176 N.E. 316, 319 (1931).

[76] Gillock v. People, 171 Ill. 307, 312, 49 N.E. 712 (1898).

[77] Orrell v. People, 94 Ill. 456, 458 (1880).

[78] People v. Roberts, 189 Ill. App. 3d 66, 69-70, 544 N.E.2d 1340, 1343 (4th Dist. 1989).

[79] People v. Netznik, 66 Ill. App. 3d 72, 75, 383 N.E.2d 640, 643 (5th Dist. 1978).

[80] In re E.S., 93 Ill. App. 3d 171, 174, 416 N.E.2d 1233, 1235 (2d Dist. 1981).

[81] 720 ILCS 5/19-3 (1999). *See also* People v. Childress, 158 Ill. 2d 275, 302, 633 N.E.2d 635, 647 (1994) (a dwelling is not a building for purposes of ordinary burglary); People v. Johnson,

§ 13.08.   ── ── Housetrailer, Watercraft, Aircraft, Motor Vehicle, Railroad Car or Any Part Thereof.

Section 5/19-1 allows for a finding of burglary where the defendant knowingly enters, or without authority remains in, a "housetrailer, watercraft, aircraft, motor vehicle as defined in the Illinois Motor Vehicle Code, railroad car, or any part thereof," assuming the person has the requisite felonious intent for this offense.[82] This statutory language has a long history in Illinois. For instance, the Illinois Supreme Court ruled in 1873 that breaking into a railroad freight car constituted burglary.[83] Most of the cases involving burglary of areas that are not buildings deal with automobiles.[84] As stated, the burglary statute provides that if a person were to "damage a vehicle," "remove any part of a vehicle," or "tamper" with it in violation of the motor vehicle code,[85] this is not burglary.[86] Courts have judicially construed this Motor Vehicle Code exception to burglary in relatively narrow terms:

> [W]e hold that "remove" for the purpose of section 4-102(a) [of the Illinois Motor Vehicle Code] means to take or move a part or component from its proper place in relation to a motor vehicle without damage to either, and without intent to commit a theft within the meaning of . . . [burglary]. We further hold that the clear legislative intent of section 4-102(a) is to prevent the commission of malicious mischief upon a motor vehicle. Since such malicious mischief may be performed by the damaging of a vehicle or its parts, or by the complete or partial disassembly of a vehicle without "damage" *per se,* the inclusion of the term "remove" as we have defined it is a necessary element of this . . . provision.[87]

Thus, entering a motor vehicle with the intent to steal a CB radio is burglary.[88] However, if the purpose of the entry is "malicious mischief" or "tampering,"

---

305 Ill. App. 3d 102, 103, 711 N.E.2d 787, 788 (3d Dist. 1999) (residential burglary can only occur in a dwelling and burglary can only occur in a building that is not a dwelling).

[82] 720 ILCS 5/19-1(a) (1999).

[83] Lyons v. People, 68 Ill. 271, 276 (1873).

[84] *See, e.g.,* People v. Cole, 256 Ill. App. 3d 1, 628 N.E.2d 713 (1st Dist. 1993); People v. Bournes, 55 Ill. App. 3d 237, 370 N.E.2d 1230 (2d Dist. 1977).

[85] *See* 625 ILCS 5/4-102 (1999).

[86] 720 ILCS 5/19-1 (1999).

[87] People v. Bournes, 55 Ill. App. 3d 237, 241, 370 N.E.2d 1230, 1233 (2d Dist. 1977).

[88] People v. Bournes, 55 Ill. App. 3d 237, 241, 370 N.E.2d 1230, 1233 (2d Dist. 1977). *See also* People v. Joyner, 57 Ill. App. 3d 948, 952, 373 N.E.2d 778, 781 (2d Dist. 1978) (removal of CB radio could be burglary, citing *Bournes*). Opening hood of a car and stealing a battery has been deemed a burglary. People v. Dail, 139 Ill. App. 3d 941, 943, 488 N.E.2d 286, 287 (3d Dist. 1985). So too, removing a sledgehammer from the open end of a parked pickup truck was a burglary. People v. Frey, 126 Ill. App. 3d 484, 485-88, 467 N.E.2d 302, 303-04 (5th Dist. 1984).

there is no burglary.[89] "Tampering," as stated, is prohibited by section 5/4-102(b) of the Motor Vehicle Code.[90] In addition, knowingly entering a motor vehicle to steal the vehicle itself can be burglary.[91]

§ 13.09.   —— "With Intent to Commit Therein a Felony or Theft."

The courts state that the essence,[92] gist,[93] or gravamen[94] of burglary is the unlawful entry with the intent to commit a felony or theft. The mental state required is nothing less than specific intent,[95] and it must exist at the time of the unauthorized entry.[96] If this criminal intent is formulated after a lawful entry, it is insufficient.[97] Thus, where defendants stole money from a store clerk's purse and a cash drawer, absent proof that defendants harbored the specific intent to steal before their entry into the store, they could not be convicted of burglary.[98] Consequently, the offense of burglary "is complete" on entering with the requisite criminal intent.[99] This is true even if the defendant's entry was motivated in part by a legitimate objective.[100] For example, where a defendant entered a store with the intent to purchase some goods and also with the intent to steal other goods, this constituted an unlawful entry without authority.[101]

Furthermore, the actual commission of the intended offense is irrelevant.[102] It is not necessary, for instance, to prove that anything was taken to support a burglary conviction.[103] Thus, where the defendant entered a grocery store with the intent to commit a forgery, burglary existed even though the defendant failed to get any money.[104] In that same vein, where the crime charged was burglary with

---

[89] *See* People v. Bournes, 55 Ill. App. 3d 237, 241, 370 N.E.2d 1230, 1233 (2d Dist. 1977).

[90] 625 ILCS 5/4-102 (1999).

[91] People v. Pitsonbarger, 142 Ill. 2d 353, 370-71, 568 N.E.2d 783, 789 (1990); People v. Steppan, 105 Ill. 2d 310, 317, 473 N.E.2d 1300, 1305-06 (1985).

[92] *See, e.g.,* People v. Rand, 29 Ill. App. 3d 873, 875, 331 N.E.2d 15, 18 (2d Dist. 1979).

[93] *See, e.g.,* People v. Martin, 77 Ill. App. 2d 183, 185, 222 N.E.2d 180, 181 (1st Dist. 1966).

[94] *See, e.g.,* People v. Craig, 117 Ill. App. 2d 411, 415, 254 N.E.2d 581, 584 (1st Dist. 1969).

[95] People v. Loden, 27 Ill. App. 3d 761, 762, 327 N.E.2d 58, 60 (2d Dist. 1975).

[96] People v. Loden, 27 Ill. App. 3d 761, 762, 327 N.E.2d 58, 60 (2d Dist. 1975). *See also* People v. Bryant, 79 Ill. App. 3d 501, 504-05, 398 N.E.2d 941, 944 (3d Dist. 1979) (quoting People v. Rossi, 112 Ill. App. 2d 208, 211-12, 250 N.E.2d 528, 529-30 (2d Dist. 1969)).

[97] People v. Fisher, 83 Ill. App. 3d 619, 622, 404 N.E.2d 859, 862 (1st Dist. 1980).

[98] People v. Perruquet, 173 Ill. App. 3d 1054, 1060, 527 N.E.2d 1334, 1338 (5th Dist. 1988).

[99] People v. Palmer, 83 Ill. App. 3d 732, 734, 404 N.E.2d 853, 855 (4th Dist. 1980).

[100] People v. Stager, 168 Ill. App. 3d 457, 460, 522 N.E.2d 812, 813-14 (2d Dist 1988).

[101] People v. Stager, 168 Ill. App. 3d 457, 460, 522 N.E.2d 812, 813-14 (2d Dist 1988).

[102] People v. Palmer, 83 Ill. App. 3d 732, 734, 404 N.E.2d 853, 855 (4th Dist. 1980).

[103] People v. Clark, 30 Ill. 2d 216, 219, 195 N.E.2d 631, 633 (1964); People v. Hancock, 65 Ill. App. 3d 694, 699, 382 N.E.2d 677, 681 (4th Dist. 1978); People v. Jefferson, 64 Ill. App. 3d 200, 205, 380 N.E.2d 1070, 1074 (1st Dist. 1978).

[104] People v. Drake, 172 Ill. App. 3d 1026, 1028, 527 N.E.2d 519, 520 (4th Dist. 1988) (affirming conviction for forgery and burglary).

intent to commit rape, it was not necessary to prove the existence of a rape.[105] Since the element of intent is an essential part of the crime of burglary, it must be alleged in the charging instrument and proved at trial.[106]

One who illegally enters another's premises to commit petty theft is as guilty of burglary as one who makes the same entry to murder or kidnap.[107] The fact that certain types of theft may only amount to a misdemeanor is immaterial.[108]

There is an assumption that the entry of the premises of another without his or her permission was not purposeless and that, in the absence of proof, theft was a likely purpose.[109] The unexplained possession of recently stolen property may support an inference of guilt of the crime of burglary where (1) there is a rational connection between the possession and participation in the burglary, (2) the guilt of burglary is more likely than not to flow from possession of the burglary proceeds, and (3) there is corroborating evidence of guilt.[110] This presumption of guilt from recent, unexplained possession of stolen property is not unconstitutional on the theory that it makes a person guilty until proven innocent or causes the person to be a witness against himself or herself.[111] There is, however, no similar legal presumption of involvement in a burglary where a defendant is merely found in the vicinity of the burglarized premises.[112]

A conviction for burglary may be sustained by circumstantial evidence as well as by direct evidence.[113] Proof of the requisite intent for burglary can be based on such evidence.[114] For example, where a defendant was found prying an apartment door off its hinges, this clearly supported his intent to commit a theft in the apartment.[115] So too, completely breaking the hinges on a door supports this intent as well, provided there are no circumstances inconsistent with this conclusion.[116] A defendant's statements to another in advance of a burglary that he intended to "score" the night of the burglary was relevant circumstantial evi-

---

[105] People v. Clerk, 68 Ill. App. 3d 1021, 1027-28, 386 N.E.2d 630, 635-36 (1st Dist. 1979), *cert. denied*, 444 U.S. 981 (1979).

[106] *See* People v. Kerestes, 38 Ill. App. 3d 681, 683, 348 N.E.2d 274, 276 (3d Dist. 1976).

[107] People v. Grigsby, 75 Ill. App. 2d 184, 194, 220 N.E.2d 498, 505 (4th Dist. 1966).

[108] *See* 720 ILCS 5/16-1(b)(1) (1999).

[109] People v. King, 2 Ill. App. 3d 870, 873, 275 N.E.2d 918, 920 (4th Dist. 1971).

[110] People v. Housby, 84 Ill. 2d 415, 424, 420 N.E.2d 151, 155 (1981); People v. Felters, 105 Ill. App. 3d 1066, 1067, 433 N.E.2d 368, 368-69 (2d Dist. 1982).

[111] People v. Harris, 131 Ill. App. 2d 824, 830, 268 N.E.2d 724, 729 (3d Dist. 1971), *aff'd*, 53 Ill. 2d 83, 288 N.E.2d 873 (1972).

[112] *Cf.* People v. Bean, 121 Ill. App. 2d 290, 296, 257 N.E.2d 558, 561 (1st Dist. 1970), *cert. denied*, 402 U.S. 1009 (1971).

[113] People v. Stevenson, 107 Ill. App. 2d 441, 447, 246 N.E.2d 309, 313 (2d Dist. 1969).

[114] People v. Kerestes, 38 Ill. App. 3d 681, 683, 348 N.E.2d 274, 276 (3d Dist. 1976).

[115] People v. Bryant, 79 Ill. App. 3d 501, 505, 398 N.E.2d 941, 944 (3d Dist. 1979).

[116] People v. Moody, 75 Ill. App. 3d 674, 678-79, 394 N.E.2d 643, 647-48 (1st Dist. 1979).

dence.[117] The presence of the defendant's automobile, which was observed outside the burglarized premises, might prove to be of some evidentiary value.[118] Likewise, the defendant's presence in the vicinity, while not raising an evidentiary presumption, might be useful circumstantial evidence.[119]

Discovery of the defendant's unexplained fingerprints[120] or shoeprints[121] at the scene will usually be very damning evidence. The defendant's flight from the burglary scene after hearing the police arrive shows the defendant's consciousness of guilt,[122] as does a defendant's effort to hide from the police after their arrival.[123] Discovery of burglary tools in the defendant's car is also valuable circumstantial evidence.[124]

Although burglary may be proved by circumstantial evidence and inferences drawn therefrom, proof of circumstances must be of a conclusive nature and tendency, leading on the whole to a satisfactory conclusion and producing a reasonable and moral certainty that the accused, and no one else, committed the crime.[125] However, the fact finder need not seek out a series of potential explanations compatible with innocence and raise them to the status of reasonable doubt; rather, the evidence will be deemed sufficient unless it is "so improbable as to raise a reasonable doubt of defendant's guilt."[126]

§ 13.10.   — Adequacy of Charging Instrument and Proof.

With respect to the adequacy of the information or indictment, the elements of "unauthorized entry"[127] and "intent"[128] must be alleged to avoid dismissal of the charge. In addition, the charging instrument should specify whether the defendant had the intent to commit a theft *or* intent to commit a felony.[129] However,

---

[117] People v. Sorice, 182 Ill. App. 3d 949, 958-59, 538 N.E.2d 834, 840-41 (1st Dist. 1989).

[118] People v. Ring, 89 Ill. App. 2d 161, 168, 232 N.E.2d 23, 27 (5th Dist. 1967).

[119] People v. Ring, 89 Ill. App. 2d 161, 168, 232 N.E.2d 23, 27 (5th Dist. 1967).

[120] People v. King, 88 Ill. App. 3d 548, 553, 410 N.E.2d 1070, 1074-75 (3d Dist. 1980).

[121] People v. Harris, 162 Ill. App. 3d 618, 623, 515 N.E.2d 1272, 1275 (4th Dist. 1987), *cert. denied*, 488 U.S. 842 (1988).

[122] People v. Moody, 75 Ill. App. 3d 674, 681, 394 N.E.2d 643, 648 (1st Dist. 1979).

[123] *See* People v. Songer, 28 Ill. 2d 433, 435, 192 N.E.2d 861, 864 (1963).

[124] People v. Ruberto, 81 Ill. App. 3d 636, 640, 401 N.E.2d 1302, 1309 (2d Dist. 1980).

[125] People v. Rhodes, 81 Ill. App. 3d 339, 344, 401 N.E.2d 237, 240 (5th Dist. 1980), *aff'd*, 85 Ill. 2d 241, 422 N.E.2d 605 (1981).

[126] People v. Harris, 162 Ill. App. 3d 618, 622, 515 N.E.2d 1272, 1274 (4th Dist. 1987), *cert. denied*, 488 U.S. 842 (1988).

[127] People v. Walker, 61 Ill. App. 3d 891, 896, 378 N.E.2d 607, 611 (2d Dist. 1978) (holding that the indictment lacked specificity regarding entry and, accordingly, was fatally defective).

[128] People v. Kerestes, 38 Ill. App. 3d 681, 684, 348 N.E.2d 274, 276 (3d Dist. 1976) (indictment sufficient).

[129] People v. Walker, 61 Ill. App. 3d 891, 896, 378 N.E.2d 607, 611 (2d Dist. 1978) (where burglary indictment did not specify and evidence at trial showed defendant made two distinct en-

in one case where a burglary indictment recited that the defendant knowingly entered a building of a named individual with intent to commit a felony or theft in the building, the indictment was deemed valid even though the words "without authority" were not included in the charge,[130] because the element of "without authority" is implicit in such a charge.[131]

Beyond this, a burglary charge need not allege the ownership of the building concerned.[132] The fact that the charging instrument does not specify the street address of the burglarized premises does not render it defective.[133] Similarly, where the exact date of the burglary is unknown, the indictment will not be deficient if it alleges a reasonable time span during which the defendant obtained control over the property.[134] The general rule regarding alleged shortcomings in the charging instrument is that the allegations must be set out with such particularity as to inform the defendant of the offense with which he or she is charged, enable the defendant to prepare his or her defense, and protect him or her against later prosecution for the same crime.[135]

Regarding proof at trial, the courts are understandably more demanding. The elements of "knowingly,"[136] "unauthorized entry"[137] and "specific intent"[138] must be demonstrated. Moreover, that the entry was "without authority" must also be supported by evidence.[139]

A defendant's motive need not be proved.[140] As stated, proof of intent to commit a crime within the burglarized premises does not require proof of the commission of the intended crime as well.[141] Likewise, the particular manner in which the entry occurred need not be supported by the evidence.[142]

---

tries into burglarized home, one with intent to commit theft and another to commit rape, it was unclear which entry was basis of burglary count; reversible error).

[130] People v. Alequin, 12 Ill. App. 3d 837, 837, 298 N.E.2d 723, 724 (2d Dist. 1973).

[131] People ex rel. McLain v. Housewright, 9 Ill. App. 3d 803, 805, 293 N.E.2d 911, 913 (5th Dist. 1973).

[132] People v. Gregory, 59 Ill. 2d 111, 114, 319 N.E.2d 483, 485 (1974).

[133] People v. Campbell, 40 Ill. 2d 463, 464, 240 N.E.2d 635, 637 (1968).

[134] People v. Collins, 51 Ill. App. 3d 993, 996, 367 N.E.2d 504, 506 (3d Dist. 1977).

[135] People v. Zuniga, 99 Ill. App. 3d 396, 399, 425 N.E.2d 1094, 1097 (1st Dist. 1981).

[136] People v. Dandridge, 98 Ill. App. 3d 1021, 1027, 424 N.E.2d 1262, 1266 (5th Dist. 1981) (evidence sufficient).

[137] People v. Harris, 33 Ill. App. 3d 600, 601, 338 N.E.2d 129, 130 (3d Dist. 1977) (evidence sufficient).

[138] People v. Polansky, 6 Ill. App. 3d 773, 776, 287 N.E.2d 747, 749 (3d Dist. 1972) (evidence sufficient).

[139] People v. Blakeney, 59 Ill. App. 3d 119, 123-24, 375 N.E.2d 1309, 1313 (1st Dist. 1978), cert. denied, 440 U.S. 915 (1979) (evidence sufficient).

[140] People v. Parks, 133 Ill. App. 2d 348, 351, 273 N.E.2d 162, 164 (1st Dist. 1971).

[141] See § 13.09 of this chapter.

[142] People v. Davis, 54 Ill. App. 3d 517, 520, 369 N.E.2d 1376, 1381-82 (4th Dist. 1977).

A precise identification of the property taken is immaterial if the character of the property is such that exact identification of it is impossible.[143] In that same vein, courts have held that proof of the specific items taken is not essential since the gist of the offense is the entry with a felonious purpose.[144] Proof of technical legal ownership of the burglarized premises is likewise unnecessary to obtain a conviction for burglary;[145] proof of lawful occupancy and possession by the complainant is sufficient.[146] Lastly, the state is not required to prove the exact time the burglary occurred.[147]

Regarding defenses, consent by the owner to the defendant's entry is most important and effective.[148] Since burglary is a specific intent offense, the defense of intoxication can be raised.[149]

§ 13.11. Possession of Burglary Tools.

"Possession of burglary tools" is a separate offense from burglary in Illinois.[150] This statute reads:

> (a) A person commits the offense of possession of burglary tools when he possesses any key, tool, instrument, device, or any explosive, suitable for use in breaking into a building, housetrailer, watercraft, aircraft, motor vehicle as defined in The Illinois Vehicle Code, railroad car, or any depository designed for the safekeeping of property, or any part thereof, with intent to enter any such place and with intent to commit therein a felony or theft. (b) Sentence. Possession of burglary tools . . . is a . . . felony.[151]

An accused can be convicted of this offense only if (1) the tools are adapted and designed for breaking and entering, (2) they are possessed by a defendant with

---

[143] People v. Tolefree, 9 Ill. App. 3d 475, 480, 292 N.E.2d 452, 456 (1st Dist. 1972).

[144] People v. Palmer, 26 Ill. 2d 464, 472, 187 N.E.2d 236, 241 (1962), *cert. denied*, 373 U.S. 951 (1963).

[145] People v. Rothermel, 88 Ill. 2d 541, 545, 431 N.E.2d 378, 380 (1982) (holding that the state need only prove someone other than defendant had a "superior" interest in the premises).

[146] People v. Foster, 30 Ill. 2d 106, 108, 195 N.E.2d 700, 701 (1964).

[147] People v. Van Dyke, 414 Ill. 251, 256, 111 N.E.2d 165, 168 (1952), *cert. denied*, 345 U.S. 978 (1953).

[148] *See* People v. Hart, 132 Ill. App. 2d 558, 270 N.E.2d 102 (1st Dist. 1971) (employee who entered employer's warehouse through hole in the wall at 5:40 a.m. when all doors were locked did not have authority to enter premises).

[149] People v. Boose, 139 Ill. App. 3d 471, 473-74, 487 N.E.2d 1088, 1091 (1st Dist. 1985).

[150] People v. Cox, 71 Ill. App. 3d 850, 862, 389 N.E.2d 1238, 1247 (1st Dist. 1979).

[151] 720 ILCS 5/19-2 (1999).

knowledge of their character, and (3) the defendant intended to use them for breaking and entering.[152]

The tools themselves may be those generally associated with criminality, like a lock puller,[153] or they may be those which could easily be used for an innocent purpose.[154] For example, it makes no difference that a screwdriver was originally designed for a legal purpose, since it can be adapted and used as a burglary tool.[155] However, in cases such as this where the tool was originally designed and intended for innocent purposes, the defendant's intent then becomes the controlling factor in the charge.[156]

In addition to screwdrivers[157] and pliers,[158] a crowbar,[159] cable cutters modified for removing and cutting locks,[160] a general assortment of mechanic's tools usable to remove an automobile transmission,[161] a key usable to open a vending machine,[162] a lug wrench,[163] and a knife[164] have also been viewed as possible burglary tools. It appears that a sense-enhancing device, such as a flashlight, can be viewed as a burglary tool.[165] Similarly, a radio scanner, gloves, stocking caps and taped penlights were found "peculiarly suitable for use in a burglary."[166]

As to the mental state requirement for possession of burglary tools, the statutory language is a bit misleading. For example, although the statute requires proof of possession of burglary tools "with intent to enter" a protected area *and* "intent to commit therein a felony or theft,"[167] an Illinois appellate court has in-

---

[152] People v. Faginkrantz, 21 Ill. 2d 75, 79, 171 N.E.2d 5, 7 (1960); People v. Waln, 169 Ill. App. 3d 264, 270, 523 N.E.2d 1318, 1323 (5th Dist. 1988); People v. Budzynski, 31 Ill. App. 3d 604, 607, 334 N.E.2d 341, 343 (2d Dist. 1975).

[153] *See* People v. Moore, 10 Ill. App. 3d 998, 295 N.E.2d 588 (1st Dist. 1973) (abstract).

[154] People v. Whitfield, 214 Ill. App. 3d 446, 456, 573 N.E.2d 1267, 1273 (1st Dist. 1991).

[155] People v. Taylor, 410 Ill. 469, 473-74, 102 N.E.2d 529, 532 (1951).

[156] People v. Whitfield, 214 Ill. App. 3d 446, 456, 573 N.E.2d 1267, 1273 (1st Dist. 1991).

[157] People v. Waln, 169 Ill. App. 3d 264, 270-71, 523 N.E.2d 1318, 1323 (5th Dist. 1988).

[158] People v. Guthrie, 60 Ill. App. 3d 293, 297-98, 376 N.E.2d 425, 429 (4th Dist. 1978).

[159] *See* People v. Bryan, 27 Ill. 2d 191, 194-95, 188 N.E.2d 692, 693 (1963); People v. Johnson, 88 Ill. App. 2d 265, 272-73, 280-81, 232 N.E.2d 554, 558-59, 563-64 (1st Dist. 1967).

[160] People v. Johnson, 88 Ill. App. 2d 265, 280-81, 232 N.E.2d 554, 562 (1st Dist. 1967).

[161] People v. Matthews, 122 Ill. App. 2d 264, 268-70, 258 N.E.2d 378, 380-81 (2d Dist. 1970).

[162] People v. Weaver, 41 Ill. 2d 434, 439-40, 243 N.E.2d 245, 249 (1968), *cert. denied*, 395 U.S. 959 (1969); People v. Oliver, 129 Ill. App. 2d 83, 90, 262 N.E.2d 597, 600 (4th Dist. 1970).

[163] People v. Ruberto, 81 Ill. App. 3d 636, 640, 401 N.E.2d 1306, 1309 (2d Dist. 1980).

[164] People v. Clerk, 68 Ill. App. 3d 1021, 1029-30, 386 N.E.2d 630, 635-36 (1st Dist. 1979), *cert. denied*, 444 U.S. 981 (1979).

[165] People v. Clerk, 68 Ill. App. 3d 1021, 1029-30, 386 N.E.2d 630, 635-36 (1st Dist. 1979), *cert. denied*, 444 U.S. 981 (1979) (flashlight, along with knife and screwdriver, found to be a burglary tool). *But see* People v. Taylor, 410 Ill. 469, 474, 102 N.E.2d 529, 532 (1951) (possession of flashlight alone is not possession of burglary tool, but evidence of its possession with other tools admissible for issue of intent).

[166] People v. Waln, 169 Ill. App. 3d 264, 271-72, 523 N.E.2d 1318, 1324 (5th Dist. 1988).

[167] 720 ILCS 5/19-2 (1999).

sisted that possession of burglary tools is not a specific intent offense.[168] Rather, a general intent to commit a burglary of *some* place or vehicle is deemed sufficient to sustain a conviction.[169] That is, the state need not establish an intent to break in and enter a *particular* place with the burglary tools.[170] Indeed, no burglary need occur to convict a defendant of possession of burglary tools.[171]

The requisite intent for possession of burglary tools can be demonstrated by circumstantial evidence.[172] For example, where items stolen during a burglary were discovered in the defendant's automobile along with a pliers, a pry bar, rolls of nylon tape, and two pairs of gloves that were apparently used to advance a burglary, the defendant's conviction for burglary, possession of burglary tools and theft was upheld.[173] However, if there is no evidence of the accused's intent to commit burglary, then the conviction for possession of burglary tools cannot be sustained.[174]

§ 13.12.   Residential Burglary.

Although burglary was originally a crime against habitation, it was eventually broadened in Illinois to include the unlawful entering of a substantial number of protected places besides "dwellings."[175] Later, the legislature concluded that there was an apparent need to differentiate between nonresidential burglaries, and illegal entries of a home where there is a substantial likelihood that people will be present.[176] Since these illegal entries of homes presumably involve greater threats to personal safety,[177] the General Assembly created a separate felony offense of "residential burglary" which carries a more serious penalty than ordinary burglary.[178]

---

[168] People v. Ray, 3 Ill. App. 3d 517, 521-22, 278 N.E.2d 170, 173 (3d Dist. 1972), *rev'd on other grounds*, 54 Ill. 2d 377, 297 N.E.2d 168 (1973).

[169] People v. Ray, 3 Ill. App. 3d 517, 521-22, 278 N.E.2d 170, 173 (3d Dist. 1972), *rev'd on other grounds*, 54 Ill. 2d 377, 297 N.E.2d 168 (1973).

[170] People v. Ray, 3 Ill. App. 3d 517, 521-22, 278 N.E.2d 170, 173 (3d Dist. 1972), *rev'd on other grounds*, 54 Ill. 2d 377, 297 N.E.2d 168 (1973); People v. Matthews, 122 Ill. App. 2d 264, 270-71, 258 N.E.2d 378, 381 (2d Dist. 1970).

[171] People v. Watson, 24 Ill. App. 3d 237, 239, 321 N.E.2d 187, 189 (2d Dist. 1974).

[172] *See* People v. Budzysnki, 31 Ill. App. 3d 604, 607, 334 N.E.2d 341, 343 (2d Dist. 1975).

[173] People v. Ricketson, 129 Ill. App. 2d 365, 264 N.E.2d 220 (2d Dist. 1970).

[174] People v. Polenisiak, 26 Ill. 2d 317, 320, 186 N.E.2d 271, 273 (1962); People v. Bibbs, 60 Ill. App. 3d 878, 881, 377 N.E.2d 559, 562 (2d Dist. 1978).

[175] People v. Powell, 9 Ill. App. 3d 54, 55-56, 291 N.E.2d 669, 671 (4th Dist. 1972).

[176] People v. Walker, 212 Ill. App. 3d 410, 413, 570 N.E.2d 1268, 1270 (5th Dist. 1991).

[177] People v. Gomez, 120 Ill. App. 3d 545, 549, 458 N.E.2d 565, 568 (3d Dist. 1983).

[178] 720 ILCS 5/19-3(b) (1999) (residential burglary is a class 1 felony); 720 ILCS 5/19-1(b) (1999) (burglary is a class 2 felony).

§ 13.13.   — Residential Burglary Codified.

The residential burglary stricture reads as follows: "A person commits residential burglary who knowingly and without authority enters the dwelling place of another with the intent to commit therein a felony or theft."[179] The Illinois penal code contains a special definition of "dwelling," designed specifically for the residential burglary prohibition, which states that a "dwelling" means a "house, apartment, mobile home, trailer, or other living quarters in which at the time of the alleged offense the owners or occupants actually reside or in their absence intend within a reasonable period of time to reside."[180] As the Illinois appellate court has stated:

> [T]here is a rational basis for distinguishing between residential burglary and nonresidential burglary . . . . The basis is the emphasis and value placed upon the privacy and sanctity of the home. The special treatment afforded a person's right to be free from intrusion into the home was a basic freedom guaranteed in our Constitution, and has continued to receive high protection from intrusion of all natures (citations omitted). Furthermore, the State correctly notes other considerations that justify a difference in treatment for those violating the sanctity of a residence, as opposed to a non-residence. It notes the propriety of a legislative determination that residential burglary contains more possibility for danger and serious harm than that of places not used as dwellings. There is a considerably greater chance of injury and danger to persons in the home context than in the burglary of a place of business. We can note that most businesses are closed at night often with few or no persons present, or with those hired to act as guards only; while most homes at night contain people unprepared for criminal intrusion. Furthermore, the legislature may well have been concerned with protection for the elderly and the handicapped, or the young and others unable to protect themselves, when it enacted more stiff penalties for residential burglary. These people are clearly more often the victims in their own homes than in the non-residential burglary context.[181]

---

[179] 720 ILCS 5/19-3 (1999).

[180] 720 ILCS 5/2-6(b) (1999).

[181] People v. Gomez, 120 Ill. App. 3d 545, 549, 458 N.E.2d 565, 568 (3d Dist. 1983). In *Gomez*, the court held that this "rational basis" allowed for different sentencing as between the residential burglary and the ordinary burglar. Accordingly, the court rejected the defendant's claim that this was a violation of equal protection of the laws. *Id.* at 548-49, 458 N.E.2d at 567-68. Also, the court rejected the notion that the mandatory four-year imprisonment term constituted a violation of the cruel-and-unusual-punishment clauses of the state and federal constitutions. *Id* at 548, 458 N.E.2d at 567.

§ 13.14.   — Elements of Residential Burglary.

A comparison of the ordinary burglary statute[182] and the residential burglary statute reveals that they are identical in all respects except two: (1) with residential burglary, the entry must be into the dwelling place of another; and (2) ordinary burglary covers the defendant who *enters without authority* or *without authority remains* in the protected place, while the residential burglary statute reaches only the defendant who enters.[183] However, the exclusion of the "without authority remains" language from the residential burglary statute is of little consequence. First, as was pointed out above in connection with non-residential burglary, the Illinois courts hold that one who has general authority to make an entry into a facility can lose that authority if the entry is for an unlawful purpose.[184] Thus, one who was an invitee to a social gathering in a residence and who remained there to follow through on his purpose of robbing some of the guests could be convicted of burglary since his entry was wrongful.[185] Similarly, where defendant was invited into a dwelling by his aunt to assist her in moving out of the dwelling she had shared with another, the defendant's apparent intent to commit theft in the dwelling vitiated his legal authority to enter and, as such, the appellate court's reliance on the "limited authority" doctrine sustained defendant's conviction for residential burglary.[186] Consequently, because of this broad interpretation of the word "enters," there is little need for the additional language of "or without authority remains." Second, almost every defendant who has been convicted of ordinary burglary under section 5/19-1 has been convicted for his illegal entry and few have been convicted under the "without authority remains" language.[187]

Because the basic elements of residential burglary are essentially the same as those of nonresidential burglary (except that the entry must be into the "dwelling of another"), the opinions dealing with nonresidential burglary address, for the most part, those concerns relating to residential burglary. First, it must be established that defendant *knowingly* entered a dwelling.[188] Thus, where the defendant claimed that he believed he was entering a church or museum, but there were no signs or other indication that the premises were anything other than a dwelling, the defendant was convicted of residential burglary.[189] Second, the

---

[182] *See* § 13.02 of this chapter.

[183] 720 ILCS 5/19-3 (1999).

[184] *See* § 13.06 of this chapter.

[185] People v. Fisher, 83 Ill. App. 3d 619, 623, 404 N.E.2d 859, 862-63 (1st Dist. 1980) (convicted of burglary).

[186] People v. Wilson, 155 Ill. 2d 374, 376-78, 614 N.E.2d 1227, 1228-29 (1993).

[187] *See* § 13.06 of this chapter.

[188] People v. Quiver, 205 Ill. App. 3d 1067, 1071-72, 563 N.E.2d 991, 994 (1st Dist. 1990).

[189] People v. Quiver, 205 Ill. App. 3d 1067, 1071-72, 563 N.E.2d 991, 994 (1st Dist. 1990).

state must prove that an *entry* into a dwelling was made *without authority.*[190] The common law "breaking" is no longer required.[191] Third, the state must demonstrate that the defendant unlawfully entered the home with an *intent* to commit theft[192] or a felony.[193] This "necessary" element[194] of intent as required for residential burglary can be established by circumstantial evidence.[195] The defendant must have possessed the intent at the time of the unauthorized entry.[196] For example, the unlawful breaking and entering into a dwelling is sufficient to infer an intent to commit theft in the dwelling.[197] However, it is important to note that such an entry does not give rise to a legal inference of intent to commit other offenses.[198] In *People v. Toolate,*[199] a defendant entered a woman's apartment, touched the woman while she was asleep in bed, thereby awakening her, and then ran out of the apartment after she screamed, "you get out of here."[200] Although there was "no evidence whatever that he used force against or that he intended to have sexual intercourse"[201] with the woman, the lower court convicted the defendant of residential burglary with intent to commit rape, based on, in part, an inference that he must have had that intent because of his illegal entry. The Supreme Court of Illinois reversed the conviction, stating:

> [B]reaking and entering cannot be used to infer any other felony [than theft]. If it could, the requirement of specific intent to commit that other felony would be meaningless. There would be no need to prove any specific intent at all, since all types of intent would be inferred from the unauthorized entry.[202]

---

[190] People v. Snow, 124 Ill. App. 3d 955, 960, 464 N.E.2d 1262, 1266 (2d Dist. 1984).

[191] People v. Wilson, 155 Ill. 2d 374, 376-77, 614 N.E.2d 1227, 1228 (1993).

[192] People v. Snow, 124 Ill. App. 3d 955, 961, 464 N.E.2d 1262, 1266 (2d Dist. 1984) (conviction based on intent to commit theft).

[193] People v. Williams, 222 Ill. App. 3d 129, 133-36, 582 N.E.2d 1158, 1161-62 (1st Dist. 1991) (conviction based on intent to commit unlawful restraint).

[194] In re L.F., 119 Ill. App. 3d 406, 410, 456 N.E.2d 646, 649 (2d Dist. 1984).

[195] People v. Williams, 222 Ill. App. 3d 129, 135, 582 N.E.2d 1158, 1162 (1st Dist. 1991).

[196] People v. Morrison, 114 Ill. App. 3d 828, 830, 449 N.E.2d 859, 860 (3d Dist. 1983).

[197] People v. Lobdell, 172 Ill. App. 3d 26, 29, 525 N.E.2d 963, 965 (3d Dist. 1988).

[198] People v. Toolate, 101 Ill. 2d 301, 308, 461 N.E.2d 987, 990 (1984); People v. Payne, 194 Ill. App. 3d 238, 243, 550 N.E.2d 1214, 1217 (1st Dist. 1990).

[199] 101 Ill. 2d 301, 461 N.E.2d 987 (1984).

[200] People v. Toolate, 101 Ill. 2d 301, 303-05, 461 N.E.2d 987, 989 (1984).

[201] People v. Toolate, 101 Ill. 2d 301, 303-05, 461 N.E.2d 987, 989 (1984).

[202] People v. Toolate, 101 Ill. 2d 301, 308, 461 N.E.2d 987, 990 (1984). *Compare* People v. Cunningham, 265 Ill. App. 3d 3, 7, 637 N.E.2d 1247, 1251 (2d Dist. 1994) (upholding a residential burglary with intent to commit criminal sexual assault where the defendant was found in the victim's doorway at 5:00 a.m., one year after the defendant was charged and convicted of making harassing calls of a sexual nature to the victim).

With respect to residential burglary, the prohibition has been applied to structures intended for use as residences, regardless of whether the residence was being actively used as a dwelling at the time of the burglary.[203] Thus, where the defendant burglarized a house that was vacated by the full-time occupants, but nonetheless was periodically checked and occupied by the owner, this was residential burglary.[204] The court noted that *dwelling,* as then defined in the Illinois penal code, included "a building . . . which is *used* or *intended for use* as a human habitation, home or residence."[205]

In any event, a "dwelling," for purposes of this enactment, has been redefined and now requires that the dwelling must be actually used as a residence or is intended for such use "within a reasonable period of time."[206] However, in spite of this somewhat narrower definition, the courts are still willing to broadly interpret the statute. For example, a vacation home, which was used only in the summer and as weather permitted, was still considered a "dwelling" under the revised definition of residential burglary.[207] However, a house which was left vacant for over seven years and which was not expected to be occupied in the near future did not meet the qualifications of a "dwelling."[208] Where a building that originally had been a six-unit motel or hotel was undergoing a substantial rehab effort, the premises were not a dwelling for purposes of residential burglary but rather a building for purposes of burglary.[209]

Moreover, it is important to note that the "dwelling place" goes beyond that portion of the residence that is used for domestic purposes. For example, a furnished, screened porch attached to a house that was used both in winter and summer was part of "living quarters" and, thus, constituted a "dwelling" for

---

[203] People v. Sexton, 118 Ill. App. 3d 998, 1000, 455 N.E.2d 884, 886 (4th Dist. 1983).

[204] People v. Sexton, 118 Ill. App. 3d 998, 999, 455 N.E.2d 884, 885-86 (4th Dist. 1983).

[205] People v. Sexton, 118 Ill. App. 3d 998, 999-1000, 455 N.E.2d 884, 886 (4th Dist. 1983) (citing Ill. Rev. Stat. ch. 38, para. 2-6 (1981) (emphasis added). It is important to note that the "intended for use" language in the prior definition was without limitation in regards to *when,* in the future, it might be used.

[206] 720 ILCS 5/19.2-6(b) (1999); People v. Flynn, 291 Ill. App. 3d 512, 523-24, 685 N.E.2d 376, 383-84 (2d Dist. 1997).

[207] People v. Smith, 209 Ill. App. 3d 1091, 1095, 568 N.E.2d 417, 419-20 (4th Dist. 1991). *See also* People v. Walker, 212 Ill. App. 3d 410, 412-13, 570 N.E.2d 1268, 1269-70 (5th Dist. 1991) (holding that a house which was unoccupied for nearly a year qualified as a"dwelling" where owner was in a nursing home but planned to return as soon as his health permitted); People v. Moore, 206 Ill. App. 3d 769, 773-74, 565 N.E.2d 154, 156-57 (1st Dist. 1990) (owner's intention to sell the house after returning from month-long absence did not alter house's character as "dwelling"); People v. Benge, 196 Ill. App. 3d 56, 58, 552 N.E.2d 1264, 1265 (4th Dist. 1990) (cabin that was used by owner primarily on weekends was a "dwelling" for purposes of residential burglary offense).

[208] People v. Bonner, 221 Ill. App. 3d 887, 889, 583 N.E.2d 56, 58 (1st Dist. 1991).

[209] People v. Willard, 303 Ill. App. 3d 231, 232-35, 707 N.E.2d 1249, 1250-52 (2d Dist. 1999).

purposes of the offense of residential burglary.[210] On the other hand, an attached garage may or may not be considered a dwelling depending upon the circumstances[211]

§ 13.15.   — Lesser Included Offenses and Burglary.

Theft may or may not be a lesser included offense of burglary[212] or residential burglary, depending on the circumstances.[213] The offenses of armed violence,[214] possession of burglary tools,[215] and criminal damage to property are not necessarily lesser included offenses.[216]

Where another crime, such as unlawful restraint, is committed during the course of a residential burglary, one is not a lesser included offense of the other.[217] Similarly, a conviction for a burglary and an armed robbery occurring in the burglarized premises will both be upheld.[218] Where defendant entered the victim's premises with the intent to beat her with a hammer and, then, in a cover up effort, took a stereo to make it appear that the entry was a burglary, he could be convicted of residential burglary and attempted murder.[219]

---

[210] People v. McIntyre, 218 Ill. App. 3d 479, 485, 578 N.E.2d 314, 315-16 (4th Dist. 1991).

[211] *See* People v. Thomas, 137 Ill. 2d 500, 519, 561 N.E.2d 57, 64 (1990), *cert. denied*, 498 U.S. 1127 (1991) (not a dwelling, although not creating a per se rule that an attached garage can never be considered a dwelling for purposes of residential burglary); People v. Borgen, 282 Ill. App. 3d 116, 120-22, 688 N.E.2d 234, 238-39 (2d Dist. 1996) (attached garage can be considered a dwelling for purposes of residential burglary); People v. Cunningham, 265 Ill. App. 3d 3, 9, 637 N.E.2d 1247, 1252 (2d Dist. 1994) (attached garage was a dwelling for purposes of residential burglary).

[212] People v. Monroe, 294 Ill. App. 3d 697, 699-702, 691 N.E.2d 1171, 1172-73 (2d Dist. 1996) (where there existed evidence that defendant's unauthorized entry into a school was not accompanied by the criminal intent required for burglary, a theft instruction was required); *see also* People v. Bussan, 306 Ill. App. 3d 836, 839, 715 N.E.2d 820, 822 (2d Dist. 1999) (theft was lesser included offense of burglary as charged); People v. Buress, 274 Ill. App. 3d 164, 166-67, 653 N.E.2d 841, 842-43 (1st Dist. 1995) (defendant entitled to theft instruction, relying on pleadings approach to lesser included offense determination). *Compare* People v. Chandler, 278 Ill. App. 3d 213, 216-17, 662 N.E.2d 508, 511-12 (1st Dist. 1996) (where theft occurred after burglary was committed, lesser included offense instruction on theft was required).

[213] People v. Hamilton, 179 Ill. 2d 319, 328, 688 N.E.2d 1166, 1168-70 (1997) (where there was evidence the defendant's unauthorized entry into a residence was not accompanied by the criminal intent required for residential burglary, a theft instruction was required).

[214] People v. Payne, 102 Ill. App. 3d 950, 963, 429 N.E.2d 1344, 1354 (1st Dist. 1981), *cert. denied*, 465 U.S. 1036 (1982).

[215] People v. Cox, 71 Ill. App. 3d 850, 862, 389 N.E.2d 1238, 1247 (1st Dist. 1979).

[216] People v. Vasquez, 97 Ill. App. 3d 1142, 1143, 424 N.E.2d 42, 43 (3d Dist. 1981) (criminal damage to property is not a lesser included offense of burglary).

[217] People v. Williams, 222 Ill. App. 3d 129, 136-37, 582 N.E.2d 1158, 1163 (1st Dist. 1991).

[218] People v. Graves, 54 Ill. App. 3d 1027, 1033-34, 370 N.E.2d 1219, 1224 (3d Dist. 1977).

[219] People v. Ranstrom, 304 Ill. App. 3d 664, 679, 710 N.E.2d 61, 72 (1st Dist. 1999).

Where a burglary and a residential burglary arise out of the same physical act, the former is clearly a lesser included offense of the latter.[220] Residential burglary, however, will not necessarily be viewed as a lesser included offense of home invasion because of their different elemental compositions.[221] That is, residential burglary is complete once the unlawful entry is made with the requisite intent to commit a felony or theft. Home invasion is not complete until, after the unlawful entry, the defendant either uses force, threatens the use of force on a person in the home while armed with a dangerous weapon or intentionally causes injury to a person in the home.[222] Therefore, it cannot be said that residential burglary is necessarily a lesser included offense of home invasion.[223] In addition, a defendant's convictions for both home invasion and residential burglary may or may not be upheld against a challenge that they were contrary to the same physical act doctrine depending on whether or not they arose out of the same exact act.[224] Lastly, the offense of criminal trespass to residence is not necessarily a lesser included offense of residential burglary.[225]

§ 13.16.   Criminal Trespass to Residence.

Where a person without authority enters the dwelling of an absent owner merely to watch television or to take a swim in the owner's indoor swimming pool, he or she cannot be convicted of residential burglary or burglary, since he or she did not harbor an intent to commit a theft or felony on the premises.[226] In order to deter such unauthorized entries where there is no felonious intent to engage in criminality within the dwelling, the General Assembly enacted a proscription covering such conduct and labeled it "criminal trespass to residence."[227] It reads:

---

[220] People v. Thomas, 137 Ill. 2d 500, 519, 561 N.E.2d 57, 64 (1990), *cert. denied*, 498 U.S. 1127 (1991).

[221] People v. Hawkins, 125 Ill. App. 3d 520, 521-22, 466 N.E.2d 299, 300 (5th Dist. 1984).

[222] People v. Jones, 148 Ill. App. 3d 133, 145, 498 N.E.2d 772, 779 (1st Dist. 1986).

[223] People v. Snow, 124 Ill. App. 3d 995, 963, 464 N.E.2d 1262, 1267 (2d Dist. 1984).

[224] People v. McLaurin, 184 Ill. 2d 58, 106, 703 N.E.2d 11, 34 (1998) (where residential burglary carved out of same physical act as home invasion, residential burglary conviction vacated); People v. Newbern, 276 Ill. App. 3d 623, 629-30, 659 N.E.2d 6, 11 (1st Dist. 1995) (where residential burglary arose out of same physical act of entry as home invasion, conviction for residential burglary vacated). *Compare* People v. Stokes, 281 Ill. App. 3d 972, 980-81, 667 N.E.2d 600, 606-07 (1st Dist. 1996) (convictions for both residential burglary and home invasion upheld where offenses did not arise out of same physical act).

[225] People v. Alksnis, 291 Ill. App. 3d 347, 354, 682 N.E.2d 1112, 1117 (1st Dist. 1997) (was not); People v. Austin, 216 Ill. App. 3d 913, 916, 576 N.E.2d 505, 507 (2d Dist. 1991) (was).

[226] *See* 720 ILCS 5/19-1(a) (1999) (burglary); *id.* 5/19-3(a) (residential burglary).

[227] 720 ILCS 5/19-4 (1999).

(a) A person commits the offense of criminal trespass to residence when, without authority, he knowingly enters or remains within any residence, including a house trailer. For purposes of this Section, in the case of a multi-unit residential building or complex, "residence" shall only include the portion of the building or complex which is the actual dwelling place of any person and shall not include such places as common recreational areas or lobbies.

(b) Sentence. Criminal trespass to residence is a . . . . misdemeanor.[228]

This offense is distinguishable from residential burglary not only because of the absence of a felonious intent requirement, but also because it specifically provides that the illegal intrusion involved must be into the "*actual* dwelling place" of another.[229] Therefore, where the entry was into a detached garage that was not actively used as a residence, it was not "criminal trespass to a residence."[230]

Where the owner of a residence had made clear to certain minor defendants that they were not permitted in the owner's residence, the defendant's subsequent presence in the residence amounted to criminal trespass to residence even though the child of the owner, a friend of the defendants, had invited the defendants into the residence in the owner's absence.[231]

§ 13.17.   Criminal Fortification of a Residence or Building.

It is now a crime for a person to fortify a residence for the purpose of concealing his or her illegal drug activity. This stricture called "criminal fortification of residence or a building" reads as follows:

(a) A person commits the offense of criminal fortification of a residence or building, when with the intent to prevent the lawful entry of a law enforcement officer or another, he maintains a residence or building in a fortified condition, knowing that such residence or building is used for the manufacture, storage, delivery or trafficking of cannabis, or controlled substances as defined in the Cannabis Control Act or Illinois Controlled Substances Act. (b) "Fortified Condition" means preventing or impeding entry through the use of steel doors, wooden planking, crossbars, alarm systems, dogs, or other similar means. (c) Criminal fortification of a residence or a building is a . . . felony.[232]

---

[228] 720 ILCS 5/19-4 (1999).

[229] 720 ILCS 5/19-4 (1999) (emphasis added).

[230] In re A.C., 215 Ill. App. 3d 611, 614, 575 N.E.2d 584, 586 (2d Dist. 1991).

[231] People v. Long, 283 Ill. App. 3d 224, 226, 669 N.E.2d 1237, 1238 (2d Dist. 1996); People v. Banks, 281 Ill. App. 3d 417, 421-22, 667 N.E.2d 118, 120-21 (2d Dist. 1996).

[232] 720 ILCS 5/19-5 (1999).

The criminal fortification of residence statute has withstood constitutional vagueness attacks.[233]

§ 13.18.   Arson.

Article 5/20 covers arson and related offenses.[234] At common law, arson was defined as the willful and malicious burning of the dwelling house of another.[235] However, most jurisdictions, including Illinois, have broadened by statute the definition of arson to include the burning of nonresidential buildings, vehicles, watercraft, and other types of personal property.[236]

§ 13.19.   — Arson Codified.

This current version of arson is now codified in section 5/20-1, which states:

> A person commits arson when, by means of fire or explosive, he knowingly: (a) Damages any real property, or any personal property having a value of $150 or more, of another without his consent; or (b) With intent to defraud an insurer, damages any property or any person's property having a value of $150 or more. Property "of another" means a building or other property, whether real or personal, in which a person other than the offender has an interest which the offender has no authority to defeat or impair, even though the offender may also have an interest in the building or property. (c) Sentence. Arson is a . . . felony.[237]

In enacting this statute, the legislature was determined to expand the definition of arson to: (1) include injury to all forms of real property and most forms of personal property; (2) include arson by fire or through the use of explosives; and (3) leave the less serious burnings of property to be covered by "criminal damage to property."[238]

§ 13.20.   — Elements of Arson.

The basic elements of arson exist where a person (1) knowingly (2) by means of fire or explosive either (3) damages any real property regardless of value, or

---

[233] People v. Rasmussen, 233 Ill. App. 3d 352, 359-62, 598 N.E.2d 1368, 1373-75 (2d Dist. 1992).

[234] 720 ILCS 5/20-1 through 20-2 (1999).

[235] ILL. ANN. STAT. ch. 38, para. 20-1 (Smith-Hurd 1977), 1961 Committee Comments, at 9 (revised 1970).

[236] *See* JOHN DECKER & BRUCE OTTLEY, THE INVESTIGATION AND PROSECUTION OF ARSON § 6-3 (1999).

[237] 720 ILCS 5/20-1 (1999).

[238] ILL. ANN. STAT. ch. 38, § 20-1 (Smith-Hurd 1977), 1961 Committee Comments, at 10 (revised 1970).

any person property having a value of $150 or more, belonging to another with-out that person's consent, or (4) damages any property having a value of $150 or more with the intent to defraud an insurer.

§ 13.21.   ——"Knowingly."

The crime of arson can only exist where an accused "knowingly" causes a fire or explosion.[239] If the fire or explosion is caused by a defendant's conduct that is accidental, negligent, or reckless in nature, this would not be arson.[240] On the other hand, a specific intent to destroy is not required where the statute is cast in terms of knowledge.[241] Thus, the defendant simply needs to be "consciously aware" that the defendant's conduct is of such a nature that it may result in a fire or explosion.[242]

§ 13.22.   —— "By Means of Fire or Explosion."

Essential to arson in Illinois is a "fire or explosion" that involves some "dam-age."[243] A fire is any burning that destroys, for instance, wood fiber in a resi-dence.[244] It is not clear whether mere blackening by smoke or discoloration by heat would constitute a burning.[245] In one case, it was ruled that a wood door frame that was apparently charred and scorched was sufficient evidence of ar-son.[246] Obviously, a destruction by means of a deliberate explosion, such as might be caused by a bomb[247] or a gasoline conflagration,[248] can amount to arson if the other elements of this offense are proved.

---

[239] 720 ILCS 5/20-1(a) (1999).

[240] *Cf.* ROLLIN M. PERKINS & RONALD N. BOYCE, CRIMINAL LAW 276 (3d ed. 1982) (pointing out that negligent conduct is insufficient to constitute arson).

[241] ROLLIN M. PERKINS & RONALD N. BOYCE, CRIMINAL LAW 277 (3d ed. 1982) (discussing the tendency to eliminate the "intent to destroy" clause from statutes).

[242] People v. Pearson, 74 Ill. App. 2d 400, 403, 220 N.E.2d 876, 878 (1st Dist. 1966). *See* ch. 2 of this treatise for a discussion of the mens rea of "knowledge."

[243] 720 ILCS 5/20-1 (1999).

[244] People v. Oliff, 361 Ill. 237, 244, 197 N.E. 777, 780 (1935).

[245] ROLLIN M. PERKINS & RONALD N. BOYCE, CRIMINAL LAW 278 (2d ed. 1982) (arguing that blackening by smoke or discoloration by heat are insufficient to constitute a "burning").

[246] People v. Lockwood, 240 Ill. App. 3d 137, 144, 608 N.E.2d 132, 137 (1st Dist. 1992).

[247] ILL. ANN. STAT. ch. 38, para. 20-1 (Smith-Hurd 1977), 1961 Committee Comments, at 10 (revised 1970).

[248] People v. Grayle, 2 Ill. App. 3d 4, 6, 276 N.E.2d 98, 100 (1st Dist. 1971).

§ 13.23. —— **"Damages Any Real Property, or Any Personal Property Having a Value of $150 or More."**

Where a residence is involved, a fire sufficient to cause some damage, no matter how small in extent, will suffice for arson.[249] Thus, a fire which merely caused the wasting of wood fibers in a residence would be sufficient to constitute "damage."[250] Charring and scorching wood in a residence amounts to damage.[251] This is the case because the statute provides that *any* damage to real property is sufficient; proof that the value of the property destroyed exceeds $150 only applies to personal property.[252]

Since the property damaged can be any real property or any personal property, a broad range of real estate and chattel qualify as property for arson purposes. For example, a home,[253] an automobile,[254] a bank,[255] a savings and loan facility,[256] a restaurant,[257] an oil storage tank,[258] a currency exchange,[259] a unit within an apartment building,[260] and a school-house[261] have been held to be property for purposes of arson in Illinois.

§ 13.24. —— **"Of Another Without His Consent."**

Subsection (a) of the arson statute requires the government to prove that the damaged property belonged to "another" and that the damage occurred "without his consent."[262] If the damage is done to the defendant's own property for the purpose of defrauding an insurer in violation of subsection (b), there is no similar requirement.[263] The arson statute clarifies that property "of another" includes personal or real property in which the defendant may have an interest, but in which another individual also has an interest that the defendant has "no authority to defeat or impair."[264] Hence, if a defendant were to burn down a building of which the defendant was a part owner, this conduct would amount to arson, in-

---

[249] 720 ILCS 5/20-1(a) (1999).

[250] People v. Oliff, 361 Ill. 237, 244, 197 N.E. 777, 780 (1935).

[251] People v. Lockwood, 240 Ill. App. 3d 137, 144, 608 N.E.2d 132, 136-37 (1st Dist. 1992).

[252] People v. Helm, 9 Ill. App. 3d 143, 148, 291 N.E.2d 680, 683-84 (4th Dist. 1973).

[253] People v. Taylor, 58 Ill. 2d 69, 78, 317 N.E.2d 97, 102 (1974).

[254] People v. Watts, 36 Ill. App. 3d 1011, 1012, 344 N.E.2d 606, 607 (4th Dist. 1976).

[255] People v. Feinberg, 2 Ill. App. 3d 83, 84, 276 N.E.2d 95, 96 (1st Dist. 1971).

[256] People v. Ross, 41 Ill. 2d 445, 447, 244 N.E.2d 608, 611-12, *cert. denied*, 395 U.S. 920 (1969).

[257] People v. Abruscato, 77 Ill. App. 2d 75, 82-83, 222 N.E.2d 263, 266 (1st Dist. 1966).

[258] People v. Johnson, 23 Ill. App. 3d 886, 894, 321 N.E.2d 38, 44 (1st Dist. 1974).

[259] People v. Shorter, 59 Ill. App. 3d 468, 471, 375 N.E.2d 513, 516 (1st Dist. 1978).

[260] People v. Rawls, 57 Ill. App. 3d 702, 705, 373 N.E.2d 742, 744 (1st Dist. 1978).

[261] People v. Reed, 333 Ill. 397, 400, 164 N.E. 847, 857 (1928).

[262] 720 ILCS 5/20-1(a) (1999).

[263] 720 ILCS 5/20-1(b) (1999).

[264] 720 ILCS 5/20-1 (1999).

asmuch as he or she has no right to impair the co-owner's interest in the building.

Regarding the property interests of another, a broad range of interests are protected. They include the rights of an owner,[265] co-owners,[266] a leaseholder,[267] a mortgagee,[268] and a contract purchaser.[269] Accordingly, the state need not prove the identity of the owner whose property was damaged; however, the state must show that someone other than the defendant owned or had some type of legal interest in the damaged property.[270]

Consent is an affirmative defense to arson.[271] This consent must have been given by everyone who can claim a legal interest in the damaged property. It is extremely important to note that there is a legal presumption that no consent was given to an accused to damage another's premises.[272] Thus, the state is under no obligation to prove that the owner of the damaged premises did not consent,[273] unless the defendant offers some evidence in support of this affirmative defense.[274]

§ 13.25.   —— "Or, with Intent to Defraud an Insurer, Damages Any Property or Any Personal Property Having a Value of $150 or More."

The statute further states that arson exists where a defendant who intends to defraud an insurer, damages any real property, regardless of value, or any personal property with a value of $150 or more, regardless of who owns it.[275] Thus, where a defendant burned his own grocery store to defraud his insurer, his conviction for arson was upheld.[276] Although the crime of arson is not per se a specific intent crime under subsection (a), proof of specific intent to defraud is necessary where the accused is charged under subsection (b).[277]

---

[265] People v. Feinberg, 2 Ill. App. 3d 83, 85, 276 N.E.2d 95, 96 (1st Dist. 1971).

[266] People v. Smith, 258 Ill. App. 3d 633, 637-39, 629 N.E.2d 598, 601-02 (1st Dist. 1994) (holding co-owners and other tenants in building were included although Housing and Urban Development (HUD) was not, since HUD only had contingent interest, which could be defeated by defendant's redemption rights).

[267] People v. Feinberg, 2 Ill. App. 3d 83, 85, 276 N.E.2d 95, 96 (1st Dist. 1971).

[268] People v. Ross, 41 Ill. 2d 445, 449, 244 N.E.2d 608, 612, *cert. denied*, 395 U.S. 920 (1969).

[269] People v. Tisley, 20 Ill. App. 3d 145, 148, 313 N.E.2d 204, 206-07 (1st Dist. 1974).

[270] People v. Knowles, 92 Ill. App. 3d 537, 540, 414 N.E.2d 1322, 1325 (4th Dist. 1980).

[271] People v. White, 22 Ill. App. 3d 206, 208, 317 N.E.2d 273, 274 (5th Dist. 1974).

[272] People v. Abruscato, 77 Ill. App. 2d 75, 80-81, 222 N.E.2d 263, 265 (1st Dist. 1966).

[273] People v. Abruscato, 77 Ill. App. 2d 75, 80-81, 222 N.E.2d 263, 265 (1st Dist. 1966).

[274] *See* 720 ILCS 5/3-2(a) (1999).

[275] 720 ILCS 5/20-1(b) (1999).

[276] *See* People v. Musitief, 201 Ill. App. 3d 872, 559 N.E.2d 520 (2d Dist. 1990).

[277] *See* ch. 2 for a discussion of "specific intent."

§ 13.26. — Adequacy of Charging Instrument and Proof.

A significant number of the Illinois cases dealing with arson involve the adequacy of the indictment or information. Where the charge failed to allege that the defendant "knowingly" started a fire with a gasoline bomb, this did not void the information.[278] The charge did state that the defendant made the gasoline bomb and set it aflame in a certain building on a certain street; accordingly, the defendant could not properly claim that he was not informed of the nature of the crime and thus unable to prepare a defense.[279] The fact than an indictment failed to allege the means by which the arson was achieved did not invalidate the charge.[280] Likewise, the failure to specify the street address where the arson occurred does not per se invalidate a charge involving the destruction of another's property.[281] Finally, where the defendant was charged under subsection (b) with the destruction of his own property with the intent to defraud an insurer, the charge was sufficient even though the state failed to allege that the personal property destroyed had a value of $150 or more.[282]

Regarding the adequacy of the proof at trial, it is clear that the state is not obligated to show that the arson involved the destruction of a "dwelling,"[283] as it was at common law.[284] With respect to motive, although it is not necessary to establish motive in an arson case, evidence of the defendant's motives will be admissible.[285]

Furthermore, circumstantial evidence can be relied on to support an inference of a defendant's involvement in arson.[286] For example, the fact that the defendant suffered burns at the time of the fire was significant.[287] Likewise, evidence that established the defendant's presence on the premises immediately before a fire started, his prior threat to burn down an apartment, and his violent encounter with an occupant of the damaged building were adequate proof of his criminal intent and actions.[288] Where a defendant had threatened to burn down his own store to deprive his creditors of their financial interest in it, the court found this

---

[278] People v. Shelton, 42 Ill. 2d 490, 494-95, 248 N.E.2d 65, 68 (1969).

[279] People v. Shelton, 42 Ill. 2d 490, 495, 248 N.E.2d 65, 69 (1969).

[280] People v. McDavid, 3 Ill. App. 3d 169, 171, 278 N.E.2d 182, 184 (1st Dist. 1971).

[281] People v. Pearson, 74 Ill. App. 2d 400, 402, 220 N.E.2d 876, 877 (1st Dist. 1966).

[282] People v. O'Dell, 84 Ill. App. 3d 359, 368-69, 405 N.E.2d 809, 817 (5th Dist. 1980).

[283] People v. Abruscato, 77 Ill. App. 2d 75, 81, 222 N.E.2d 263, 266-67 (1st Dist. 1966).

[284] ILL. ANN. STAT. ch. 38, para. 20-1 (Smith-Hurd 1977), 1961 Committee Comments, at 9 (revised 1970).

[285] People v. Martin, 59 Ill. App. 3d 785, 788, 376 N.E.2d 65, 68 (2d Dist. 1978).

[286] People v. McKinney, 193 Ill. App. 3d 1012, 1017, 550 N.E.2d 604, 607 (4th Dist. 1990).

[287] People v. Russ, 31 Ill. App. 3d 385, 393-94, 334 N.E.2d 108, 115 (1st Dist. 1975); People v. Schabatka, 18 Ill. App. 3d 635, 644-45, 310 N.E.2d 192, 199 (3d Dist. 1974), cert. denied, 420 U.S. 928 (1975).

[288] People v. Alexander, 77 Ill. App. 2d 151, 155, 222 N.E.2d 172, 174 (1st Dist. 1966).

to be important circumstantial evidence of arson.[289] Similarly, where a defendant was observed standing in an apartment building with matches in her hand immediately before the fire, this too was relevant circumstantial evidence.[290] Lastly, a pipe bomb discovered in the trunk of an accused's automobile that was very similar to the one found under a damaged oil tanker was significant circumstantial evidence.[291]

In prosecuting a defendant for burning his own house with the intent to defraud an insurer, the defendant's prior threats to burn down the house to collect insurance, firefighters' testimony that the defendant offered to pay them if they allowed his house to continue to burn and the discovery of a container of gasoline in the bathroom closet of a defendant's home were considered to be ample evidence to show that he had set fire to his own house.[292] Similarly, where a defendant's grocery store had been destroyed in a fire, defendant's other financial misdeeds before the fire as well as his poor financial status were important pieces of evidence implicating him in arson for fraud.[293]

§ 13.27. Aggravated Arson.

The crime of "aggravated arson"[294] in Illinois is a class X felony.[295] It provides:

> A person commits aggravated arson when in the course of committing arson he knowingly damages, partially or totally, any building or structure, including any adjacent building or structure and (1) he knows or reasonably should know that one or more persons are present therein or (2) any person suffers great bodily harm, or permanent disability or disfigurement as a result of the fire or explosion or (3) a fireman or policeman who is present at the scene acting in the line of duty, is injured as a result of the fire or explosion.[296]

---

[289] People v. Brown, 104 Ill. App. 3d 1110, 1117, 433 N.E.2d 1081, 1087 (1st Dist. 1982).

[290] People v. Rawls, 57 Ill. App. 3d 702, 704, 373 N.E.2d 742, 743-44 (1st Dist. 1978).

[291] People v. Green, 14 Ill. App. 3d 972, 986, 304 N.E.2d 32, 43 (1st Dist. 1973), *cert. denied,* 417 U.S. 972 (1974).

[292] People v. McAleer, 34 Ill. App. 3d 821, 826-27, 341 N.E.2d 72, 76-77 (5th Dist. 1975).

[293] People v. Musitief, 201 Ill. App. 3d 872, 877, 559 N.E.2d 520, 524 (2d Dist. 1990).

[294] 720 ILCS 5/20-1.1 (1999). The predecessor to the existing statute, ILL. REV. STAT. ch. 38, para. 20-1.1 (1983), was ruled unconstitutional in that it was directed in part at innocent conduct. People v. Wick, 107 Ill. 2d 62, 481 N.E.2d 676 (1985) (section (a)(3) of prior statute invalid); People v. Johnson, 114 Ill. 2d 69, 499 N.E.2d 470 (1986) (section (a)(1) of prior statute invalid). The statute was amended in 1985 to overcome the prior constitutional objections. *See* P.A. 84-1100 (1985).

[295] 720 ILCS 5/20-1.1(b) (1999).

[296] 720 ILCS 5/20-1.1(a) (1999).

This legislation is meant to deter those arsons that may involve an incidental threat to a person, whether that be to a victim within the arsoned premises, or to a firefighter who is injured in the line of duty. Where a defendant committed an arson, and the evidence supported the conclusion that defendant knew a person or persons were present, the crime becomes aggravated arson.[297] Indeed, the Illinois Supreme Court has stated where the defendant had attacked a victim and then set fire to her residence, defendant's "guilt of aggravated arson should not depend on the happenstance of whether the decedent expired before or after the defendant struck the match ... considering the victim's death and the arson were part of a closely related criminal episode."[298] Regarding subsection (a)(3) of the prohibition, it has been held that smoke inhalation and wrist pain to a firefighter, suffered as a consequence of fighting a fire set by a defendant, were sufficiently traumatic injuries to justify a finding of aggravated arson.[299] While "injury" is not defined in the statute for purposes of aggravated arson, a jury finding that an injury was suffered by a fireman is a sufficient basis to satisfy the statute.[300]

Regarding the adequacy of proof at trial, elements of aggravated arson may be shown by circumstantial evidence.[301] Thus, issues such as motive, opportunity or knowledge can be inferred from the surrounding facts of each case.[302] For example, in a case involving a racially motivated firebombing in the middle of the night where one bomb was placed at the front entrance of the house and one at the back, the appellate court held there was sufficient evidence for purposes of aggravated arson to show that the defendant knew or should have known that the house was occupied at the time of the firebombing, given the residential character of the building and surrounding area, occupation of the house by the victim's family in excess of four months, and the method of attack which was designed to deliver some kind of message to the victims.[303]

§ 13.28.   Residential Arson.

In 1999, the offense of "residential arson"[304] was enacted by the Illinois legislature. The statute provides: "A person commits the offense of residential arson when, in the course of committing an arson, he or she knowingly damages, partially or totally, any building or structure that is the dwelling place of an-

---

[297] People v. Thomas, 137 Ill. 2d 500, 529-33, 561 N.E.2d 57, 69-70 (1990).

[298] People v. Thomas, 137 Ill. 2d 500, 531-33, 561 N.E.2d 57, 70 (1990).

[299] People v. Hanks, 174 Ill. App. 3d 555, 559, 528 N.E.2d 1044, 1048 (4th Dist. 1988).

[300] People v. Hanks, 174 Ill. App. 3d 555, 559, 528 N.E.2d 1044, 1048 (4th Dist. 1988).

[301] People v. Burrett, 216 Ill. App. 3d 185, 190, 576 N.E.2d 293, 296 (1st Dist. 1991).

[302] People v. Burrett, 216 Ill. App. 3d 185, 190, 576 N.E.2d 293, 296-97 (1st Dist. 1991).

[303] People v. Burrett, 216 Ill. App. 3d 185, 190, 576 N.E.2d 293, 296 (1st Dist. 1991).

[304] 720 ILCS 5/20-1.2 (1999).

other."[305] This felony[306] carries more serious sanctions than ordinary arson but less serious penalties than aggravated arson.[307]

§ 13.29. — Lesser Included Offenses and Arson.

There seems to be a split in the courts as to whether both arson and murder convictions arising out of the same act of arson may stand.[308] However, where the arson caused damage to several residences, multiple convictions for arson could lie even though the fires were started by the same act.[309] Where defendant's arson caused the injury to more than one victim, multiple convictions for aggravated arson could stand.[310]

Although the crime of arson can be committed in two distinct ways — by destroying someone else's interest in property *or* by destroying one's own property for the purpose of collecting insurance — one cannot be convicted of two counts of arson where the same act involved both concerns. For example, where a defendant started a fire in his own residence with the intent to defraud an insurer and thereby impaired a mortgagee's interest in the residence, this was one crime, not two.[311]

§ 13.30. Possession of Explosives or Incendiary Devices.

The final section of article 5/20 covers the crime of "possession of explosives or explosive or incendiary devices."[312] It reads as follows:

> A person commits the offense of possession of explosives or explosive or incendiary devices in violation of this Section when he possesses, manufactures or transports any explosive compound, timing or detonating device for use with an explosive compound or incendiary device and either in-

---

[305] 720 ILCS 5/20-1.2(a) (1999).

[306] 720 ILCS 5/20-1.2(b) (1999) (class 1 felony).

[307] 720 ILCS 5/20-1 (1999) (arson: class 2 felony); 5/20-1.1 (aggravated arson: class X felony).

[308] *Compare* People v. Brent, 175 Ill. App. 3d 459, 465, 530 N.E.2d 43, 47 (1st Dist. 1988) (holding both arson and murder convictions arose out of the same act and could not stand), *with* People v. Britt, 265 Ill. App 3d 129, 148-51, 638 N.E.2d 282, 296-98 (4th Dist. 1994) (holding aggravated arson and first degree murder convictions not barred by the same physical act doctrine because aggravated arson is not a lesser included offense of first degree murder). *See also* People v. Washington, 272 Ill. App. 3d 913, 919-20, 651 N.E.2d 625, 630 (1st Dist. 1995) (using the charging instrument approach, the court held that aggravated arson was a lesser included offense of felony-murder and thus had to be vacated).

[309] People v. Orr, 149 Ill. App. 3d 348, 365-66, 500 N.E.2d 665, 678 (1st Dist. 1986).

[310] People v. Hanks, 174 Ill. App. 3d 555, 560-61, 528 N.E.2d 1044, 1047-48 (4th Dist. 1988).

[311] People v. Bostick, 60 Ill. App. 3d 581, 585-86, 377 N.E.2d 146, 150 (1st Dist. 1978).

[312] 720 ILCS 5/20-2 (1999).

tends to use such explosive or device to commit any offense or knows that another intends to use such explosive or device to commit a felony.[313]

It is important to note that this felony[314] crime of possession[315] only arises where the explosive is possessed with the intent to commit an offense or with knowledge that another intends to use it to commit a felony.[316]

Various items have been considered explosive or incendiary devices for purposes of this stricture. For example, defendants have been convicted for possession of such a device where they have been found in possession of a Molotov cocktail (a bottle containing an explosive substance such as gasoline),[317] dynamite,[318] or a pipe bomb.[319] It is important to note that the statute is violated when either the defendant himself or herself has been apprehended in possession of such a device,[320] or when the defendant has supplied another with such a device.[321] If a defendant "possesses, manufactures or transports" such a device, this will constitute the requisite actus reus.[322]

As stated, the required mental state is satisfied if the state can prove that the defendant *intended* to use such explosives to commit an offense or *knew* someone else would use them to commit a crime.[323] Circumstantial evidence of the requisite mens rea will be sufficient.[324] For example, where the evidence revealed that the defendant possessed a large quantity of dynamite and a number of bombs, that he had no legitimate need for such devices, and that he had threatened to kill certain individuals by throwing bombs at them, this was sufficient to prove his intent to use the devices for an illegal purpose.[325] Likewise, where a defendant supplied an undercover police officer with explosives and told the officer how powerful the explosives were and how they could blow off the front of a tavern if they were taped to the tavern wall, the appellate court found that this evidence was sufficient to indicate that the defendant "knew" that another was planning to use the explosives for an illegal purpose.[326] Even

---

[313] 720 ILCS 5/20-2(a) (1999).

[314] 720 ILCS 5/20-2(b) (1999).

[315] *See* ch. 2 for a discussion of the elements of criminal possession.

[316] ILL. ANN. STAT. ch. 38, para. 20-2 (Smith-Hurd 1977), 1961 Committee Comments, at 33 (revised 1970).

[317] People v. Gee, 121 Ill. App. 2d 22, 23, 257 N.E.2d 212, 213 (1st Dist. 1970).

[318] People v. Koba, 58 Ill. App. 3d 713, 715, 374 N.E.2d 713, 715 (1st Dist. 1978).

[319] People v. Johnson, 23 Ill. App. 3d 886, 890, 321 N.E.2d 38, 42 (1st Dist. 1974).

[320] People v. Johnson, 23 Ill. App. 3d 886, 890, 321 N.E.2d 38, 42 (1st Dist. 1974).

[321] People v. Thomas, 3 Ill. App. 3d 1079, 1081-82, 279 N.E.2d 784, 786 (3d Dist. 1972).

[322] 720 ILCS 5/20-2(a) (1999).

[323] 720 ILCS 5/20-2(a) (1999).

[324] People v. Beacham, 358 Ill. 373, 376-77, 193 N.E. 205, 206 (1934).

[325] Hroneck v. People, 134 Ill. 139, 153-54, 24 N.E. 861, 865-66 (1890).

[326] People v. Thomas, 3 Ill. App. 3d 1079, 1081-82, 279 N.E.2d 784, 786 (3d Dist. 1972).

where a person makes an otherwise legal sale of explosives to another, the sale is criminal if the person knows they are intended for unlawful use.[327]

§ 13.31.　Causing a Catastrophe.

With the heightened concern regarding the possible terrorist deployment of bombs, radioactive materials, biological substances or other weapons of mass destruction, the Illinois General Assembly created the offense called "causing a catastrophe."[328] This class X measure[329] reads:

> A person commits the offense of causing a catastrophe if he or she knowingly causes a catastrophe by explosion, fire, flood, collapse of a building, release of poison, radioactive material, bacteria, virus, or other dangerous and difficult to confine force or substance.[330]

A "catastrophe" is defined as (1) "serious physical injury to 5 or more persons;" (2) "substantial damage to 5 or more buildings or inhabitable structures;" or (3) "substantial damage to a vital public facility that seriously impairs its usefulness or operation."[331] A "vital public facility" is any facility which "is necessary to ensure the public health, safety or welfare, including but not limited to, a hospital, law enforcement agency, fire department, private or public utility company, national defense contractor, a facility of the armed forces, or emergency services agency."[332]

§ 13.32.　Criminal Damage to Property.

The next collection of offenses to be examined is found in article 5/21. These offenses include "criminal damage to property,"[333] "criminal damage of fire fighting apparatus, hydrants or equipment,"[334] "institutional vandalism,"[335] "criminal defacement of property,"[336] "jackrocks,"[337] "criminal trespass to vehicles,"[338] "criminal trespass to real property,"[339] "criminal damage to government

---

[327] People v. Ficke, 343 Ill. 367, 384, 175 N.E. 543, 550 (1931).
[328] 720 ILCS 5/20.5-5 (1999).
[329] 720 ILCS 5/20.5-5(c) (1999).
[330] 720 ILCS 5/20.5-5(a) (1999).
[331] 720 ILCS 5/20.5-5(b) (1999).
[332] 720 ILCS 5/20.5-5(b) (1999).
[333] 720 ILCS 5/21-1 (1999).
[334] 720 ILCS 5/21-1.1 (1999).
[335] 720 ILCS 5/21-1.2 (1999).
[336] 720 ILCS 5/21-1.3 (1999).
[337] 720 ILCS 5/21-1.4 (1999).
[338] 720 ILCS 5/21-2 (1999).
[339] 720 ILCS 5/21-3 (1999).

supported property,"[340] "criminal trespass to state supported land,"[341] "unauthorized possession or storage of weapons,"[342] and "criminal trespass to restricted areas and restricted landing areas at airports."[343] These offenses "comprise a catch-all of relatively minor offenses against property" and are designed to complement the more serious offenses against property, such as arson.[344] These offenses cover behavior that includes, but is not limited to, "malicious mischief" activities that were scattered throughout the prior code.[345]

§ 13.33. — Criminal Damage to Property Codified.

The statute that prohibits "criminal damage to property" provides:

> A person commits an illegal act when he: (a) knowingly damages any property of another without his consent; or (b) recklessly by means of fire or explosive damages property of another; or (c) knowingly starts a fire on the land of another without his consent; or (d) knowingly injures a domestic animal of another without his consent; or (e) knowingly deposits on the land or in the building of another, without his consent, any stink bomb or any offensive smelling compound and thereby intends to interfere with the use of another of the land or building; or (f) damages any property, other than that described in [arson], with intent to defraud an insurer; or (g) knowingly shoots a firearm at any portion of a railroad train.[346]

This crime may be a felony or misdemeanor, depending upon the amount of damages involved.[347]

§ 13.34. — Elements of Criminal Damage to Property.

The state must prove that the defendant "knowingly" damaged the property of another[348] except where (1) the damage was by means of a fire or explosion (not covered by arson), whereupon only "recklessness" need be proved;[349] (2) the

---

[340] 720 ILCS 5/21-4 (1999).

[341] 720 ILCS 5/21-5 (1999).

[342] 720 ILCS 5/21-6 (1999).

[343] 720 ILCS 5/21-7 (1999).

[344] ILL. ANN. STAT. ch. 38, para. 21-1 (Smith-Hurd 1977), 1961 Committee Comments, at 38 (revised 1970).

[345] ILL. ANN. STAT. ch. 38, para. 21-1 (Smith-Hurd 1977), 1961 Committee Comments, at 38 (revised 1970).

[346] 720 ILCS 5/21-1(a) (1999).

[347] 720 ILCS 5/21-1(2) (1999).

[348] People v. Smith, 133 Ill. App. 3d 613, 616, 479 N.E.2d 328, 330-31 (5th Dist. 1985) (even though defendant intoxicated, he harbored sufficient self-awareness and volition from which requisite element of knowledge could be inferred).

[349] 720 ILCS 5/21-1(b) (1999).

damage was done "with the intent to defraud an insurer" (and the conduct does not constitute arson);[350] or (3) the damage was caused by a stink bomb, where-upon the "intent to interfere" with another's use of property must be proved.[351] Regarding proof of knowledge, such was not established where the accused, while driving an automobile in excess of the speed limit, struck another automobile with the car he was driving but had made a clear effort to avoid a collision between the two vehicles.[352] On the other hand, knowledge was demonstrated where defendant, angered by an argument with his estranged wife, drove his car into her car, totaling it.[353]

Both real[354] and personal[355] property are included within the ambit of this criminal damage enactment. The statute encompasses any property that is capable of being damaged. Probably the largest single class of property damage reflected in the Illinois caselaw involves the breaking of windows.[356] Breaking windows of a house,[357] a store,[358] or an automobile[359] without justification will constitute criminal damage to property. Breaking a door off its hinges,[360] vandalizing a fraternity house,[361] wrecking a beauty shop,[362] damaging an American flag,[363] felling an electric power pole,[364] crashing a car into a building,[365] destroying a shotgun,[366] damaging a police department Breathalyzer machine,[367] breaking an automobile's ignition switch,[368] and pouring molasses in the engine of a van and destroying the motor[369] are all acts that have been deemed criminal damage to property.

---

[350] 720 ILCS 5/21-1(f) (1999).

[351] 720 ILCS 5/21-1(e) (1999).

[352] In re T.A.B., 181 Ill. App. 3d 581, 585, 537 N.E.2d 419, 420-21 (2d Dist. 1989).

[353] People v. Jones, 145 Ill. App. 3d 835, 836-38, 495 N.E.2d 1371, 1372-73 (3d Dist. 1986).

[354] People v. Cleaves, 169 Ill. App. 3d 252, 258-61, 523 N.E.2d 720, 724-25 (5th Dist. 1988) (holding that a glass on door of store building is covered by the statute).

[355] People v. Vesley, 86 Ill. App. 2d 283, 287, 229 N.E.2d 886, 888 (1st Dist. 1967) (holding that a car window is covered by the statute).

[356] See, e.g., People v. Vesley, 86 Ill. App. 2d 283, 287, 229 N.E.2d 886, 888 (1st Dist. 1967).

[357] People v. McGath, 11 Ill. App. 3d 855, 298 N.E.2d 14 (1st Dist. 1973) (abstract).

[358] People v. Cleaves, 169 Ill. App. 3d 252, 258-61, 523 N.E.2d 720, 724-25 (5th Dist. 1988).

[359] People v. Vesley, 86 Ill. App. 2d 283, 287, 229 N.E.2d 886, 888 (1st Dist. 1967).

[360] People v. Ludke, 15 Ill. App. 3d 960, 962, 305 N.E.2d 557, 559 (1st Dist. 1973).

[361] People v. Bristow, 8 Ill. App. 3d 805, 809-10, 291 N.E.2d 189, 192-93 (1st Dist. 1972).

[362] People v. Crouch, 77 Ill. App. 2d 290, 293-94, 222 N.E.2d 46, 47 (4th Dist. 1966).

[363] People v. McKirdie, 45 Ill. 2d 300, 303, 259 N.E.2d 16, 19 (1970), cert. denied, 400 U.S. 1010 (1971).

[364] People v. Elam, 39 Ill. App. 3d 705, 709, 350 N.E.2d 832, 835 (5th Dist. 1976).

[365] People v. Robie, 92 Ill. App. 3d 1059, 1061, 416 N.E.2d 754, 755 (5th Dist. 1981).

[366] People v. Masini, 65 Ill. App. 3d 1011, 1013-14, 383 N.E.2d 1, 2 (2d Dist. 1978), aff'd, 78 Ill. 2d 17, 397 N.E.2d 1368 (1979).

[367] People v. Oswald, 69 Ill. App. 3d 524, 526-27, 387 N.E.2d 886, 887 (1st Dist. 1979).

[368] People v. Fender, 91 Ill. App. 3d 844, 844, 415 N.E.2d 22, 23 (1st Dist. 1980).

[369] People v. Berry, 75 Ill. App. 3d 925, 926, 394 N.E.2d 731, 732 (2d Dist. 1979).

Knowingly injuring a domestic animal constitutes criminal damage to property as well.[370] For example, shooting a dog,[371] castrating a bull,[372] and poisoning a horse[373] are all acts that violate this statute. Starting a fire in a building is also criminal damage to property if done recklessly,[374] although it will be considered arson if done knowingly.[375]

Proof of the exact value of the damages is not an element that must be proved at trial where the defendant is convicted of misdemeanor criminal damage to property.[376] However, since felony criminal damage is predicated on a finding of a particular amount of damage, proof of the amount of damages is required in this context.[377] Since criminal damage to property involves damage to the property "of another," the victim's legal interest — ownership[378] or some other legal interest in the property[379] — must be proved. Although the state must show that the property belongs "to another," it is not incumbent that the titleholder testify.[380] Thus, the state could rely on the testimony of a security guard of a store in which the damage occurred.[381] Finally, where a defendant damages property of which he is part owner, he or she can still be convicted of this offense.[382] Thus, where defendant destroyed his estranged wife's automobile, he could be convicted even though he shared with her a legal interest in the vehicle.[383]

While consent is an affirmative defense to criminal damage to property, there is a legal presumption that the owner of the damaged property did not consent to the damage of the owner's property.[384] Only where the defendant comes forward with some evidence of consent is the state under an obligation to prove lack of consent.[385]

---

[370] People v. Pope, 66 Ill. App. 3d 303, 304-06, 383 N.E.2d 278, 279 (4th Dist. 1978).

[371] People v. Pope, 66 Ill. App. 3d 303, 304-06, 383 N.E.2d 278, 279 (4th Dist. 1978).

[372] People v. Jones, 241 Ill. 482, 491-92, 89 N.E. 752, 753 (1909).

[373] Swartzbaugh v. People, 85 Ill. 457, 459 (1877).

[374] 720 ILCS 5/21-1(b) (1999).

[375] People v. Ryan, 97 Ill. App. 3d 1071, 1074, 424 N.E.2d 20, 22 (1st Dist. 1981).

[376] People v. Masini, 65 Ill. App. 3d 1011, 1014, 383 N.E.2d 1, 2 (2d Dist. 1978), aff'd, 78 Ill. 2d 17, 397 N.E.2d 1368 (1979).

[377] People v. Roby, 202 Ill. App. 3d 143, 146-47, 559 N.E.2d 840, 842-43 (1st Dist. 1990).

[378] People v. Smith, 18 Ill. App. 3d 851, 852, 310 N.E.2d 796, 797 (1st Dist. 1974).

[379] People v. Tate, 87 Ill. 2d 134, 149, 429 N.E.2d 470, 478-79 (1981).

[380] People v. Tate, 87 Ill. 2d 134, 149, 429 N.E.2d 470, 478-79 (1981).

[381] People v. Tate, 87 Ill. 2d 134, 149, 429 N.E.2d 470, 478-79 (1981).

[382] People v. Jones, 145 Ill. App. 3d 835, 837, 495 N.E.2d 1371, 1372 (3d Dist. 1986).

[383] People v. Jones, 145 Ill. App. 3d 835, 837, 495 N.E.2d 1371, 1372 (3d Dist. 1986).

[384] People v. Masini, 65 Ill. App. 3d 1011, 1014, 383 N.E.2d 1, 2 (2d Dist. 1978), aff'd, 78 Ill. 2d 17, 397 N.E.2d 1368 (1979).

[385] People v. Masini, 65 Ill. App. 3d 1011, 1014, 383 N.E.2d 1, 2 (2d Dist. 1978), aff'd, 78 Ill. 2d 17, 397 N.E.2d 1368 (1979). See also 720 ILCS 5/3-2 (1999).

§ 13.35.   — Lesser Included Offenses and Criminal Damage to Property.

Where a defendant engages in conduct that results in injury to both property and a person, he or she can be convicted of both criminal damage to property and, for example, aggravated battery since the former is clearly not a lesser included offense of the latter.[386] Where a defendant destroys property while engaged in a theft, he or she can be convicted for both the criminal damage and the theft.[387] For example, a defendant who felled a power pole and destroyed lightning arresters on the pole in order to steal copper wire on the pole was properly convicted of both criminal damage and attempted theft.[388] Similarly, criminal damage to property is not a lesser included offense of either burglary[389] or attempted burglary[390] since it contains an element of damage to property, which is not an element of either burglary or attempted burglary.[391] On the other hand, criminal damage to property may be a lesser included offense of aggravated arson.[392] Lastly, where convictions for criminal damage to property and reckless conduct rested on the same physical act — namely, the breaking of a tavern door — the criminal damage to property charge was vacated.[393]

§ 13.36.   Criminal Damage of Fire Fighting Apparatus, Hydrants, or Equipment.

Beyond the general prohibition against criminally damaging property, the General Assembly has enacted the offense of "criminal damage of fire fighting apparatus, hydrants or equipment."[394] The statute provides:

> Whoever wilfully and maliciously cuts, injures, damages, tampers with or destroys or defaces any fire hydrant or any fire hose or any fire engine, or other public or private fire fighting equipment, or any apparatus appertaining to such equipment, or intentionally opens any fire hydrant without proper authorization, is guilty of a . . . misdemeanor.[395]

Although the behavior covered by this proscription is rather obvious, what is curious about this law is the appearance of the mens rea of *maliciously*, a rarity in the Criminal Code of 1961. In any event, the term generally denotes a mental

---

[386] People v. Quinn, 23 Ill. App. 3d 476, 478, 319 N.E.2d 538, 540 (4th Dist. 1974).
[387] People v. Elam, 39 Ill. App. 3d 705, 709, 350 N.E.2d 832, 835 (5th Dist. 1976).
[388] People v. Elam, 39 Ill. App. 3d 705, 709, 350 N.E.2d 832, 835 (5th Dist. 1976).
[389] People v. Booker, 214 Ill. App. 3d 286, 288-89, 573 N.E.2d 385, 387 (2d Dist. 1991).
[390] People v. Roberts, 189 Ill. App. 3d 66, 74, 544 N.E.2d 1340, 1346 (4th Dist. 1989).
[391] People v. Roberts, 189 Ill. App. 3d 66, 74, 544 N.E.2d 1340, 1346 (4th Dist. 1989).
[392] People v. Bradley, 256 Ill. App. 3d 514, 515-17, 628 N.E.2d 257, 259-60 (1st Dist. 1993).
[393] People v. Pearson, 108 Ill. App. 3d 241, 244, 439 N.E.2d 31, 33 (4th Dist. 1982).
[394] 720 ILCS 5/21-1.1 (1999).
[395] 720 ILCS 5/21-1.1 (1999).

state that encompasses what is normally understood as intent, knowledge, *or* recklessness.[396]

It is unclear why the General Assembly did not treat this criminal conduct as merely another form of "criminal damage to property." An appropriate amendment to the general prohibition would have better served the state's interest in maintaining a unified penal code.

§ 13.37.   Institutional Vandalism.

Another article 5/21 crime is the offense of "institutional vandalism."[397] It reads:

> (a) A person commits institutional vandalism when, by reason of the actual or perceived race, color, creed, religion or national origin of another individual or group of individuals, he knowingly and without consent inflicts damage to any of the following properties: (1) A church, synagogue or other building, structure or place used for religious worship or other religious purpose; (2) A cemetery, mortuary, or other facility used for the purpose of burial or memorializing the dead; (3) A school, educational facility or community center; (4) The grounds adjacent to, and owned and rented by, any institution, facility, building, structure of place described in paragraphs (1), (2) or (3) of this subsection (a); or (5) Any personal property contained in any institution, facility, structure or place described in paragraphs (1), (2) or (3) of this subsection (a).
>
> (b) Institutional vandalism is a . . . felony.[398]

Although this stricture is aimed at the damage of certain types of property — damage motivated by certain egregious purposes — that is viewed as sufficiently serious to warrant felony sanctions, it seems the General Assembly could have achieved this same objective by simply labeling this conduct "aggravated criminal damage to property." This would have maintained continuity in the code and avoided the patchwork tendency that article 5/21 has taken on in recent years.

§ 13.38.   Criminal Defacement of Property.

In 1993, the legislature created the offense of "criminal defacement of property."[399] The Criminal Code defines criminal defacement of property as follows:

---

[396] A TREATISE ON THE LAW OF CRIMES (CLARK & MARSHALL) § 5.05 (Marian Quinn Barnes, 7th ed. 1967).

[397] 720 ILCS 5/21-1.2 (1999).

[398] 720 ILCS 5/21-1.2 (1999).

[399] 720 ILCS 5/21-1.3 (1999).

(a) A person commits criminal defacement of property when the person knowingly damages the property of another without his or her consent by defacing, deforming, or otherwise damaging the property by the use of paint or any other similar substance, or by the use of a writing instrument, etching tool or any other similar device. (b) Sentence. Criminal defacement of property is a . . . misdemeanor for a first offense if the damage to the property does not exceed $300. Criminal defacement of property is a . . . felony for a second or subsequent conviction or if the damage to the property exceeds $300.[400]

§ 13.39.   Jackrocks.

In 1995, a prohibition against "jackrocks" was added to the Criminal Code.[401] This misdemeanor offense is committed by any person, except a law enforcement officer in the course of his or her official duties, who knowingly (1) sells, gives away, manufactures, purchases, or possesses a jackrock or (2) throws a jackrock on public or private property.[402] A "jackrock" is defined as a "caltrop or other object manufactured with one or more rounded or sharpened points, which when placed or thrown present at least at one point at such an angle that it is peculiar to and designed for use in puncturing or damaging vehicle tires."[403]

§ 13.40.   Criminal Trespass to Vehicles.

Section 5/21-2 sets out the offense of "criminal trespass to vehicles."[404] It reads: "[w]hoever knowingly and without authority enters any part of or operates any vehicle, aircraft, watercraft or snowmobile commits a . . . misdemeanor."[405] This statute is presumably designed to cover intrusions on a vehicle that are *not* covered by burglary[406] or by the various forms of malicious mischief — "damage," "removal of components," and "tampering" — on motor vehicles covered by the motor vehicle code.[407] On the other hand, if the trespass to the vehicle also involves *damage* to the vehicle, the legislature's clear intent is to allow the defendant to be convicted of both criminal damage to property (under section 5/21-1) and criminal trespass to vehicles (under section 5/21-2).[408]

---

[400] 720 ILCS 5/21-1.3 (1999).

[401] 720 ILCS 5/21-1.4 (1999).

[402] 720 ILCS 5/21-1.4 (1999).

[403] 720 ILCS 5/21-1.4(b) (1999).

[404] 720 ILCS 5/21-2 (1999).

[405] 720 ILCS 5/21-2 (1999).

[406] 720 ILCS 5/19-1 (1999).

[407] 625 ILCS 5/4-102 (1999).

[408] ILL. ANN. STAT. ch. 38, para. 21-2 (Smith-Hurd 1977), 1961 Committee Comments, at 55 (revised 1970).

§ 13.41.   — Elements of Criminal Trespass to Vehicles.

This offense requires only (1) a knowing entry (2) without authority (3) of a vehicle.[409] Thus, knowledge is an essential element of criminal trespass to a vehicle.[410] This means the state must prove that the defendant knew that the vehicle he or she entered belonged to another and that the owner had not authorized the entry.[411] Thus, where the defendants entered an automobile at the request of its occupants, not knowing at the time of their entry that the automobile had been stolen, they could not be convicted of criminal trespass to vehicle.[412]

The entry must be "without authority." In other words, it must be without the consent of the owner.[413] In one case, the defendant rented a truck pursuant to a rental agreement that clearly stated that the lessor had the right to terminate the agreement at any time and to take possession of the truck.[414] When the defendant was informed by the lessor that he had to return the truck, the defendant agreed to do so, but instead of complying, he tried to move the truck to another location. For this, he was convicted of criminal trespass to the truck.[415]

The third essential element of the offense is that the trespass be on a vehicle, aircraft, watercraft, or snowmobile. The identity of the vehicle is a material element of this type of criminal trespass.[416] Testimony of an automobile owner concerning the make, year, license number, and motor serial number of the vehicle that has been illegally entered would be sufficient in this regard.[417]

§ 13.42.   — Adequacy of Charging Instrument and Proof.

Although the elements of "knowingly," "entry," and "vehicle" — with the latter being described with some specificity — must presumably be averred in the charging instrument, the indictment or information need not allege that the entry was "without authority" if it otherwise implies that it was without the consent of the owner.[418] On the other hand, the name of the owner (or the person who has rightful possession) should appear.[419]

Regarding proof at trial supportive of criminal trespass to a vehicle, an accused's knowledge that a vehicle does not belong to him or her and that he or she was not authorized to enter it may be established by the accused's own ad-

---

[409] 720 ILCS 5/21-2 (1999).

[410] People v. Canamore, 88 Ill. App. 3d 639, 642-43, 411 N.E.2d 292, 295 (3d Dist. 1980).

[411] People v. Owes, 5 Ill. App. 3d 936, 939, 284 N.E.2d 465, 467-68 (1st Dist. 1972).

[412] People v. Owes, 5 Ill. App. 3d 936, 939, 284 N.E.2d 465, 467-68 (1st Dist. 1972).

[413] People v. Pettis, 104 Ill. App. 3d 275, 277, 432 N.E.2d 935, 936 (1st Dist. 1982).

[414] People v. Slaughter, 87 Ill. App. 3d 1066, 1068, 409 N.E.2d 508, 509-10 (2d Dist. 1980).

[415] People v. Slaughter, 87 Ill. App. 3d 1066, 1069, 409 N.E.2d 508, 510 (2d Dist. 1980).

[416] People v. Bunch, 36 Ill. App. 3d 235, 237, 343 N.E.2d 575, 576 (1st Dist. 1976).

[417] People v. Bunch, 36 Ill. App. 3d 235, 237, 343 N.E.2d 575, 576 (1st Dist. 1976).

[418] People v. Harvey, 132 Ill. App. 2d 761, 764-65, 270 N.E.2d 80, 83 (1st Dist. 1971).

[419] People v. Harvey, 132 Ill. App. 2d 761, 764-65, 270 N.E.2d 80, 83 (1st Dist. 1971).

missions[420] or by circumstantial evidence.[421] For example, evidence of a defendant's recent, unexplained possession of a stolen automobile, coupled with evidence that the automobile in which he was a passenger was in fact stolen, supported his conviction for criminal trespass.[422]

In some cases, there may be a tension between the law of theft and the law of criminal trespass to vehicles. It is important to understand that theft requires an intentional or knowledgeable *permanent* deprivation of the owner's use or benefit of property.[423] Accordingly, a joyriding escapade not involving intent to permanently deprive will not be treated as theft, but as criminal trespass to the vehicle.[424] Also, intent to commit theft is the element that distinguishes burglary from criminal trespass to a vehicle.[425]

The offense of criminal trespass to a vehicle is not necessarily a lesser included offense of theft of such vehicle since a theft could be accomplished without an entry, although an entry is an essential element of criminal trespass.[426] A person could, for example, tow away a vehicle, and thus engage in a theft of the vehicle without entry.[427] Likewise, there could be a trespass within a vehicle without a theft of it.[428] In contrast, since criminal trespass to a vehicle and burglary both have in common an entry without authority, the former may be a lesser included offense of the latter.[429] In addition, a criminal trespass to a vehicle has been held to be a lesser included offense of possession of a stolen motor vehicle.[430] Finally, an appellate court has ruled that criminal trespass to a vehicle and criminal possession of a stolen vehicle convictions cannot both stand where the trespass and possession arose out of the same continuous act.[431]

---

[420] People v. Chandler, 84 Ill. App. 2d 231, 236, 228 N.E.2d 588, 591 (1st Dist. 1967).

[421] People v. Harvey, 132 Ill. App. 2d 761, 764-65, 270 N.E.2d 80, 83 (1st Dist. 1971).

[422] People v. Harvey, 132 Ill. App. 2d 761, 764-65, 270 N.E.2d 80, 83 (1st Dist. 1971).

[423] 720 ILCS 5/16-1 (1999).

[424] People v. Woods, 17 Ill. App. 3d 835, 838, 308 N.E.2d 856, 858-59 (5th Dist. 1974).

[425] People v. Cole, 256 Ill. App. 3d 1, 4, 628 N.E.2d 713, 715 (1st Dist. 1993) (burglary conviction affirmed).

[426] People v. Rainbolt, 52 Ill. App. 3d 374, 376-78, 367 N.E.2d 293, 294-95 (5th Dist. 1977).

[427] People v. Rainbolt, 52 Ill. App. 3d 374, 378, 367 N.E.2d 293, 295 (5th Dist. 1977).

[428] *Cf.* People v. Rainbolt, 52 Ill. App. 3d 374, 378, 367 N.E.2d 293, 295 (5th Dist. 1977).

[429] People v. Dandridge, 98 Ill. App. 3d 1021, 1027, 424 N.E.2d 1262, 1266 (5th Dist. 1981). *But see* People v. Cole, 256 Ill. App. 3d 1, 4, 628 N.E.2d 713, 715 (1st Dist. 1993) (holding trial court properly refused to instruct jury on criminal trespass to vehicles as lesser included offense to burglary).

[430] People v. Cook, 279 Ill. App. 3d 718, 722, 665 N.E.2d 299, 301 (1st Dist. 1995).

[431] People v. Owens, 205 Ill. App. 3d 43, 46, 563 N.E.2d 75, 77 (3d Dist. 1990).

§ 13.43.   Criminal Trespass to Real Property.

The next section of this article contains a prohibition against "criminal trespass to real property," which was previously called "criminal trespass to land." It states:

> (a) Whoever: (1) knowingly and without lawful authority enters or remains within a building; or (2) enters upon the land of another, after receiving, prior to such entry, notice from the owner or occupant that such entry is forbidden; or (3) remains upon the land of another; or (4) enters upon one of the following areas in or on a motor vehicle (including an off-road vehicle . . .), after receiving prior to that entry, notice from owner or occupant that the entry is forbidden or remains upon or in the area after receiving notice from the owner or occupant to depart: (A) any field that is used for growing crops or which is capable of being used for growing crops; or (B) an enclosed area containing livestock; or (C) an orchard; or (D) a barn or other agriculture building containing livestock; commits a . . . misdemeanor. * * * (b) A person has received notice from the owner or occupant within the meaning of Subsection (a) if he has been notified personally, either orally or in writing, including a valid court order . . ., or if a printed or written notice forbidding such entry has been conspicuously posted or exhibited at the main entrance to such land or forbidden part thereof.[432]

There are three exemptions built into this statutory framework. First, subsection (c) provides that anyone visiting a migrant worker at the worker's living quarters is exempt from charges of criminal trespass lodged by, presumably, the owner of the land on which the migrant worker works and resides.[433] Second, subsection (d) provides that anyone who beautifies unoccupied and abandoned properties in a municipal area is exempt.[434] Third, subsection (f) provides that any person who enters another's building or land for emergency purposes is exempt.[435]

The revision committee responsible for drafting this statute amplified the importance of the notice requirement in their Committee Comments:

> Note that it is criminal trespass to land . . . only if, immediately prior to entry, the offender receives oral or written notice that such entry is forbidden, or he remains upon the land after being notified to leave. . . . Note particularly that notice posted at the *main entrance* to the land is all that is required. This puts the burden on the trespasser to ascertain at his peril when he leaves his own or public land and goes upon the land of another whether

---

[432] 720 ILCS 5/21-3 (1999).
[433] 720 ILCS 5/21-3(c) (1999).
[434] 720 ILCS 5/21-3(d) (1999).
[435] 720 ILCS 5/21-3(f) (1999).

such is permitted. The expansive requirement that farmers and other land-owners post their entire acreage is eliminated.[436]

The courts state that this statute creates two distinct offenses: the first precludes entry on another's land after being warned that such entry is forbidden; the second precludes remaining on another's land, after being notified to depart, without regard to the lawfulness of the initial entry.[437] It is critical that the defendant had notice that his or her entry or presence on the land was without permission.[438] Where the defendant does not have notice regarding entry but is thereafter notified that his or her presence on certain property is forbidden, he or she must be given a reasonable opportunity to leave the property before his or her presence will be considered criminal.[439] In other words, if a person knows he or she is on the real property of another, knows he or she has been directed to leave by the owner or occupant and refuses to leave, this constitutes a breach of the second type of trespass.[440] For example, where a defendant entered certain school property with no notice that his entry was without permission and was arrested immediately after authorities informed him that he was not to be on the premises, he could not be convicted since he was not given an opportunity to depart.[441] However, where an employer gave notice of dismissal to a defendant and directed him to leave the employment premises, the defendant's failure to leave promptly constituted criminal trespass to land.[442] Where a disruptive movie-goer was asked to leave a movie theatre and subsequently refused, he committed criminal trespass to land.[443]

It is important to note that this form of criminal trespass protects all properties that constitute real property. Trespass on school property,[444] an enclosed mall,[445] a government business office not open to the general public,[446] a department store during non-business hours,[447] or a medical center[448] is considered a crimi-

---

[436] ILL. ANN. STAT. ch. 38, para. 21-3 (Smith-Hurd 1977), 1961 Committee Comments, at 61 (revised 1970).

[437] People v. Yutt, 231 Ill. App. 3d 718, 721-22, 597 N.E.2d 208, 211 (3d Dist. 1992); People v. Morgan, 33 Ill. App. 3d 41, 43, 337 N.E.2d 400, 401 (1st Dist. 1975); People v. Spencer, 131 Ill. App. 2d 551, 553-54, 268 N.E.2d 192, 194 (1st Dist. 1971).

[438] People v. Gregorich, 71 Ill. App. 3d 251, 256, 389 N.E.2d 619, 622 (5th Dist. 1979).

[439] People v. Mims, 8 Ill. App. 3d 32, 35, 288 N.E.2d 891, 893 (1st Dist. 1972).

[440] People v. Yutt, 231 Ill. App. 3d 718, 721-22, 597 N.E.2d 208, 211 (3d Dist. 1992).

[441] People v. Mims, 8 Ill. App. 3d 32, 35, 288 N.E.2d 891, 893 (1st Dist. 1972).

[442] People v. Spencer, 131 Ill. App. 2d 551, 556, 268 N.E.2d 192, 194 (1st Dist. 1971).

[443] People v. Mortensen, 178 Ill. App. 3d 871, 872-76, 533 N.E.2d 1134, 1135-37 (2d Dist. 1989).

[444] People v. Thompson, 56 Ill. App. 3d 557, 564-65, 372 N.E.2d 117, 120-21 (3d Dist. 1978).

[445] People v. Sterling, 52 Ill. 2d 287, 292-93, 287 N.E.2d 711, 712 (1972).

[446] People v. Vasquez, 132 Ill. App. 2d 291, 292-93, 270 N.E.2d 229, 229-30 (1st Dist. 1971) (sit-down demonstration in the business office of a board of election commissioner).

[447] People v. Morgan, 33 Ill. App. 3d 41, 43, 337 N.E.2d 400, 402 (1st Dist. 1975).

[448] People v. Krizka, 92 Ill. App. 3d 288, 289, 416 N.E.2d 36, 37-38 (1st Dist. 1980).

nal act. Where an abortion clinic "owned" the sidewalk in front of the facility, the presence of defendants on the sidewalk along with others who refused to leave amounted to a criminal trespass to real property.[449] Any trespass to a dwelling is a separate, more serious offense called "criminal trespass to residence."[450] If property has been abandoned, criminal trespass on that property is essentially a legal impossibility.[451]

One of the recurring claims in cases of criminal trespass to real property is the argument that somehow the trespass is justified by certain circumstances.[452] In one case, the defendants claimed their trespass in an abortion facility of a medical center was justified by the defense of necessity.[453] These defendants, who were pro-life proponents, felt their interest in protecting the lives of the fetuses destroyed in the facility outweighed the property interests involved in the criminal trespass.[454] However, the trial and appellate courts agreed that with the legalization of abortion, the "injury" prevented by the acts of criminal trespass was not protected by principles of necessity or due process.[455] Whether a trespass arises from a quiet protest in front of an abortion clinic[456] or from the defendants' refusal to leave a school board meeting because they believed they have not had an opportunity to air their grievances,[457] it will still be criminal, regardless of the motivation of those accused.

A person who has a legal interest in real property may use non-deadly force when and to the extent such "is necessary to prevent or terminate" another's trespass on such property.[458] Such person cannot resort to deadly force in defense of property unless he or she is in addition attempting to prevent the trespasser's commission of a forcible felony against the interest-holder or another.[459] Thus, if a trespasser attempted to kill a landowner who was objecting to the trespasser's presence on his or her land, the landowner could use deadly force since personal life and limb, rather than mere property, are at stake.

---

[449] People v. Yutt, 231 Ill. App. 3d 718, 721-23, 597 N.E.2d 208, 211-12 (3d Dist. 1992).

[450] See § 13.16 of this chapter.

[451] People v. Miller, 344 Ill. App. 574, 580-81, 101 N.E.2d 874, 877 (3d Dist. 1951).

[452] See, e.g., People v. Krizka, 92 Ill. App. 3d 288, 416 N.E.2d 36 (1st Dist. 1980).

[453] People v. Krizka, 92 Ill. App. 3d 288, 289-90, 416 N.E.2d 36, 37 (1st Dist. 1980).

[454] People v. Krizka, 92 Ill. App. 3d 288, 289-90, 416 N.E.2d 36, 37 (1st Dist. 1980).

[455] People v. Krizka, 92 Ill. App. 3d 288, 290, 416 N.E.2d 36, 37-38 (1st Dist. 1980).

[456] People v. Yutt, 231 Ill. App. 3d 718, 723-25, 597 N.E.2d 208, 212-13 (3d Dist. 1992) (no violation of federal or state constitutional right to free speech).

[457] People v. Thompson, 56 Ill. App. 3d 557, 560, 372 N.E.2d 117, 119-20 (3d Dist. 1978) (trespass not justified by first amendment right to free speech). See also People v. Diguida, 152 Ill. 2d 104, 118-32, 604 N.E.2d 336, 342-49 (1992) (holding private store's invocation of criminal trespass statute, in order to exclude circulator of political nominating petition from its premises, was not violation of free speech or free election provisions of Illinois Constitution).

[458] 720 ILCS 5/7-3 (1999).

[459] 720 ILCS 5/7-3 (1999).

Beyond the issue regarding the use of force *against a trespasser*, there exists a question concerning the amount of force that the trespasser may employ *against a landowner* when the trespasser is faced with a landowner who uses excessive force to remove the trespasser from his or her land. In *People v. Connelly*,[460] the defendants entered Hall's property and refused to leave. Hall then went into his house, returned to his porch with a loaded shotgun, and fired a shot over the defendants' heads. At this point, the defendants jumped Hall, disarmed him, and took turns beating him until he lost consciousness. The defendants raised the defense of self-defense, but the jury convicted them of criminal trespass to property and aggravated battery. In affirming the defendants' convictions, the court made the following statement:

> In the case of a trespasser, the use of force against a property owner may, in certain cases, be justified on the basis of self-defense if the owner uses excessive force in attempting to remove the trespasser from the owner's property. However, *no amount of force by a trespasser can be justified* unless the trespasser believes that force is necessary to alleviate the imminent danger posed by the landowner. A defendant may not continue to use force against an antagonist who has been disarmed or disabled.[461]

Here, the court determined that the evidence supported the jury's decision that the defendants' actions were unjustified.[462] Thus, while it appears the landowner may use an appropriate degree of non-deadly force to prevent or terminate a trespass, and deadly force to prevent a forcible felony directed against himself or another, the trespasser can employ no degree of force unless his life or limb is threatened by the landowner's illegal show of force.

§ 13.44.   Criminal Damage to Government Supported Property.

Section 5/21-4 presents the felony offense of "criminal damage to government supported property." It punishes as a felony the following acts: where a person knowingly (1) damages any property supported in whole or in part with state or federal funds administered by the state; (2) by means of fire or explosive, damages such property; (3) starts a fire on such property; or (4) deposits on such land or in such a building any stink bomb or any offensive smelling compound with the intent to interfere with the use by another of the land or building.[463] This enactment was primarily in response to the unlawful disruption of aca-

---

[460] 57 Ill. App. 3d 955, 373 N.E.2d 823 (3d Dist. 1978).

[461] People v. Connelly, 57 Ill. App. 3d 955, 957, 373 N.E.2d 823, 825 (3d Dist. 1978) (emphasis added) (citations omitted).

[462] People v. Connelly, 57 Ill. App. 3d 955, 957, 373 N.E.2d 823, 825 (3d Dist. 1978).

[463] 720 ILCS 5/21-4(a) (1999).

demic communities and the willful and malicious destruction of academic property.[464]

§ 13.45.   Criminal Trespass to State Supported Land.

The next proscription appearing in article 5/21 is the offense of "criminal trespass to state supported land." It provides:

> Whoever enters upon land supported in whole or in part with State funds, or Federal funds . . . or any building on such land, after receiving, prior to such entry, notice from the State or its representatives that such entry is forbidden, or remains upon such land or in such building after receiving notice from the State or its representatives to depart, and who thereby interferes with another person's lawful use or enjoyment of such building or land, commits a . . . misdemeanor.[465]

It is important to note that this offense requires not only a trespass but also a trespass that "interferes with another person's lawful use or enjoyment" of a state supported building or land.[466] *Interferes* has been judicially interpreted to mean hinder, disrupt, or obstruct orderly functions of an official enterprise being carried on in such a building or on such land.[467] For example, in one case a defendant was soliciting signatures for a petition in a university snack bar, and when campus police requested that he leave or cease solicitations, he refused and was thereafter arrested.[468] However, since there was no evidence that the defendant-student had interfered with the use or enjoyment of the premises by any other person, he could not be convicted of this form of criminal trespass.[469]

§ 13.46.   Unauthorized Possession or Storage of Weapons.

Section 5/21-6 prohibits the "unauthorized possession or storage of weapons" in any building or on land supported in whole or in part with public funds without the prior written permission from the chief security officer for the land or building.[470] This misdemeanor offense was also designed primarily to deal with disorderly activities in state educational facilities.[471]

---

[464] ILL. ANN. STAT. ch. 38, para. 21-4 (Smith-Hurd 1977), Historical Note, at 65.

[465] 720 ILCS 5/21-5 (1999).

[466] 720 ILCS 5/21-5 (1999).

[467] People v. Holtzman, 10 Ill. App. 3d 528, 529-30, 294 N.E.2d 708, 709 (4th Dist. 1973).

[468] People v. Holtzman, 10 Ill. App. 3d 528, 530, 294 N.E.2d 708, 709 (4th Dist. 1973).

[469] People v. Holtzman, 10 Ill. App. 3d 528, 530, 294 N.E.2d 708, 709 (4th Dist. 1973).

[470] 720 ILCS 5/21-6 (1999).

[471] ILL. ANN. STAT. ch. 38, para. 21-4 (Smith-Hurd 1977), Historical Note, at 65.

§ 13.47.   Criminal Trespass to Restricted Areas at Airports.

In section 5/21-7 there appears the crime of "criminal trespass to restricted areas and restricted landing areas at airports." It provides:

> Whoever enters upon, or remains in, any restricted area or restricted landing area used in connection with an airport facility . . . in this State, after such person has received notice from the airport authority that such entry is forbidden commits a . . . misdemeanor.[472]

§ 13.48.   Residential Picketing.

To maintain and preserve the right of persons to quiet enjoyment of their homes in residential areas, as well as to privacy, security and peace in their homes — interests that nurture stability of community and family life — the General Assembly decided to prohibit "residential picketing."[473] This law, which carries misdemeanor sanctions,[474] provides:

> It is unlawful to picket before or about the residence or dwelling of any person, except when the residence or dwelling is used as a place of business. However, this Article does not apply to a person peacefully picketing his own residence or dwelling and does not prohibit the peaceful picketing of the place of holding a meeting or assembly on premises commonly used to discuss subjects of general public interest.[475]

§ 13.49.   Written Solicitation on School Property.

In 1993, the legislature created the offense of "distributing or delivering written or printed solicitation on school property"[476] This section provides:

> (a) Distributing or delivering written or printed solicitation on school property or within 1,000 feet of school property, for the purpose of inviting students to any event when a significant purpose of the event is to commit illegal acts or to solicit attendees to commit illegal acts, or to be held in or around abandoned buildings, is prohibited. (b) A violation is a . . . misdemeanor.[477]

---

[472] 720 ILCS 5/21-7 (1999).

[473] 720 ILCS 5/21.1-1 (1999) (Legislative finding and declaration).

[474] 720 ILCS 5/21.1-3 (1999).

[475] 720 ILCS 5/21.1-2 (1999). Previously, this enactment provided another exemption, namely, "picketing of a place of employment involved in a labor dispute." However, this provision was deemed unconstitutional on equal protection grounds. *See* Carey v. Brown, 447 U.S. 455 (1980). In that case, the United States Supreme Court ruled that allowing picketing in places of employment in a labor dispute, but not at the home of the mayor of Chicago, was discriminatory. *Id.*

[476] 720 ILCS 5/21.3-5 (1999).

[477] 720 ILCS 5/21.3-5 (1999).

§ 13.50.   Looting.

Another offense that can be described as an offense against property interests is the crime of "looting," which is found in article 5/42. It states:

> A person commits looting when he knowingly without authority of law or the owner enters any home or dwelling, or upon any premises of another, or enters any commercial, mercantile, business or industrial building, plant or establishment, in which normal security of property is not present by virtue of a hurricane, fire or vis major of any kind or by virtue of a riot, mob, or other human agency and obtains or exerts control over property of the owner.[478]

This offense is a felony.[479] Although this is a crime that addresses a significant social problem and, accordingly, serves a legitimate function in the state penal code, it is a further example of a misplaced stricture. That is, it is curious that it was not placed in article 5/19 (burglary-related crimes), since it concerns the taking of illegal control of another's property.

For the most part, this offense is analogous to burglary. Most of the reported cases dealing with this offense involve defense claims that illegal entries during the course of a civil disturbance should have been prosecuted as looting, not burglary.[480] However, this is a matter of prosecutorial discretion.[481] In enacting this section, it was not the legislature's intent to frustrate and impede prosecutions for burglary perpetrated during the course of a civil disturbance.[482]

---

[478] 720 ILCS 5/42-1 (1999).

[479] 720 ILCS 5/42-2 (1999).

[480] *See, e.g.,* People v. Parks, 133 Ill. App. 2d 348, 350-51, 273 N.E.2d 162, 163-64 (1st Dist. 1971).

[481] *See, e.g.,* People v. Parks, 133 Ill. App. 2d 348, 350-51, 273 N.E.2d 162, 163-64 (1st Dist. 1971).

[482] People v. Long, 126 Ill. App. 2d 103, 105-06, 261 N.E.2d 437, 439 (1st Dist. 1970).

CHAPTER 14

OFFENSES AFFECTING GOVERNMENTAL FUNCTIONS

§ 14.01. Introduction.

In part E of the Criminal Code of 1961, there appears the various "offenses affecting governmental functions."[1] They include treason,[2] misprision of treason,[3] advocating overthrow of the government,[4] resisting or obstructing a peace officer or correctional institution employee,[5] disarming a police officer,[6] obstructing service of process,[7] obstructing justice,[8] concealing or aiding a fugitive,[9] escape,[10] aiding escape,[11] refusing to aid an officer,[12] bringing contraband into a penal institution,[13] compounding a crime,[14] perjury,[15] subornation of perjury,[16] communicating with jurors or witnesses,[17] excusing a person from jury duty through bribery,[18] harassment of jurors, witnesses and their family members,[19] false personation of attorney, judicial or governmental officials,[20] false

---

[1] 720 ILCS 5/30-5/33 (1999).
[2] 720 ILCS 5/30-1 (1999).
[3] 720 ILCS 5/30-2 (1999).
[4] 720 ILCS 5/30-3 (1999).
[5] 720 ILCS 5/31-1 (1999).
[6] 720 ILCS 5/31-1a (1999).
[7] 720 ILCS 5/31-3 (1999).
[8] 720 ILCS 5/31-4 (1999).
[9] 720 ILCS 5/31-5 (1999).
[10] 720 ILCS 5/31-6 (1999).
[11] 720 ILCS 5/31-7 (1999).
[12] 720 ILCS 5/31-8 (1999).
[13] 720 ILCS 5/31A-1.1; 5/31A-1.2 (1999).
[14] 720 ILCS 5/32-1 (1999).
[15] 720 ILCS 5/32-2 (1999).
[16] 720 ILCS 5/32-3 (1999).
[17] 720 ILCS 5/32-4 (1999).
[18] 720 ILCS 5/32-4b (1999).
[19] 720 ILCS 5/32-4a (1999).
[20] 720 ILCS 5/32-5 (1999).

personation of a peace officer,[21] performance of unauthorized acts,[22] simulating legal process,[23] tampering with public records,[24] tampering with public notice,[25] violation of a bail bond,[26] bribery,[27] failure to report a bribe,[28] and official misconduct.[29] In a few instances, criminality involving governmental operations is addressed outside of part E. For instance, violation of an order of protection appears in article 5/12.[30] Interference with a public institution of higher learning appears in article 5/21.2.[31] Those offenses that have bearing on governmental functions will be examined in this chapter.

§ 14.02.   Treason.

In Illinois, treasonous activity against the state is a class X felony that carries the death penalty as a possible sanction.[32] *Treason* is defined in section 5/30-1 as follows:

> (a) A person owing allegiance to this State commits treason when he or she knowingly: Levies war against this State; or (2) Adheres to the enemies of this State, giving them aid or comfort.
> (b) No person may be convicted of treason except on the testimony of 2 witnesses to the same overt act, or on his confession in open court.[33]

Although a variation of this stricture has been law in Illinois since 1819,[34] not a single reported case has been prosecuted using this restriction.

§ 14.03.   Misprision of Treason.

Related to treason is "misprision of treason," found in section 5/30-2. It provides: "(a) A person owing allegiance to this State commits misprision of treason when he conceals or withholds his knowledge that another has committed

---

[21] 720 ILCS 5/32-5.1; 5/32-5.2 (1999).

[22] 720 ILCS 5/32-6 (1999).

[23] 720 ILCS 5/32-7 (1999).

[24] 720 ILCS 5/32-8 (1999).

[25] 720 ILCS 5/32-9 (1999).

[26] 720 ILCS 5/32-10 (1999).

[27] 720 ILCS 5/33-1 (1999).

[28] 720 ILCS 5/33-2 (1999).

[29] 720 ILCS 5/33-3 (1999).

[30] 720 ILCS 5/12-30 (1999).

[31] 720 ILCS 5/21.2-2 (1999).

[32] 720 ILCS 5/30-1(c) (1999).

[33] 720 ILCS 5/30-1 (1999).

[34] ILL. ANN. STAT. ch. 38, para. 30-1 (Smith-Hurd 1977), 1961 Committee Comments, at 301 (revised 1970).

treason against this State. (b) Sentence. Misprision of treason is a . . . felony."[35] Similar to treason, misprision is essentially a "dead letter" in the code.

§ 14.04.   Advocating Overthrow of Government.

"Advocating overthrow of government" is the final article 5/30 ("Treason and Related Offenses") stricture. It reads: "A person who advocates, or with knowledge of its contents knowingly publishes, sells or distributes any document which advocates or with knowledge of its purpose, knowingly becomes a member of any organization which advocates the overthrow or reformation of the existing form of government of this State by violence or unlawful means commits a . . . felony."[36]

The predecessor to the current statutory provision was prosecuted over seventy-five years ago against a number of individuals in connection with their advocacy of mass strikes and an overthrow of the government, as well as their participation with the Communist Labor Party.[37] The Illinois statute is comparable in its language to the federal Smith Act,[38] which was upheld as constitutional by the United States Supreme Court.[39] However, advocacy of violent overthrow of the government is protected by the First Amendment if it does not urge that anything be done, but only that it be believed.[40] Active membership in an organization that aims to overthrow the government by violent means can be successfully prosecuted without encountering "guilt by association" problems outlawed by the Fifth Amendment or freedom of speech or association restrictions barred by the First Amendment.[41]

§ 14.05.   Resisting or Obstructing a Peace Officer or Correctional Institution Employee.

The offense of "resisting or obstructing a peace officer or correction institution employee" is the first of the article 5/31 ("Interference With Public Officers") crimes. It provides: "A person who knowingly resists or obstructs the performance by one known to the person to be a peace officer or correctional institution employee of any authorized act within his official capacity commits a . . . misdemeanor."[42] "Correctional institution employee" is defined as, "any person employed to supervise and control inmates incarcerated in a penitentiary, State

---

[35] 720 ILCS 5/30-2 (1999).

[36] 720 ILCS 5/30-3 (1999).

[37] People v. Lloyd, 304 Ill. 23, 136 N.E. 505 (1922).

[38] 18 U.S.C.A. § 2385 (1999).

[39] Dennis v. United States, 341 U.S. 494, 500 (1951).

[40] Yates v. United States, 354 U.S. 298, 324 (1957).

[41] Scales v. United States, 367 U.S. 203, 228 (1961).

[42] 720 ILCS 5/31-1 (1999).

farm, reformatory, prison, jail, house of correction, police detention area, half-way house, or other institution or place for the incarceration or custody of persons under sentence for offenses or awaiting trial or sentence for offenses, under arrest for an offense, a violation of probation, a violation of parole, or a violation of mandatory supervised release, or awaiting a bail setting hearing or preliminary hearing."[43]

§ 14.06. — Elements of Resisting or Obstructing a Peace Officer.

The basic elements of this offense are satisfied where a person (1) knowingly (2) resists or obstructs (3) the performance by one known to be a peace officer (4) of any authorized act within his or her official capacity.

First, the defendant must engage in the resistance or obstruction "knowingly."[44] Thus, to sustain a charge of resisting arrest, the state has to show, among other things, that the defendant knowingly resisted the arrest in question.[45]

Second, the defendant must "resist" or "obstruct" an officer engaged in his or her official duties. This element requires a physical act.[46] Therefore, the accused, by his or her actions, must have imposed an obstacle that may impede, hinder, interrupt, prevent, or delay performance of an officer's legitimate responsibilities.[47] This usually arises in circumstances in which the defendant forcefully resists an arrest or aids a third party in avoiding an arrest.[48] A citizen's resistance to or obstruction of a police officer in the performance of the officer's duties may be passive as well as active conduct.[49] However, the difference between passive conduct and inaction, which does not satisfy the actus reus element of the crime, is often a fine line. While courts from a generation ago found passive conduct on many occasions,[50] the trend has been to find that the same instances constitute "inaction."[51] Recent cases that have found inaction include an occasion where the defendants failed to open their door to allow a

---

[43] 720 ILCS 5/31-1(b) (1999).

[44] People v. Williams, 267 Ill. App. 3d 82, 93, 640 N.E.2d 981, 989 (2d Dist. 1994).

[45] People v. Royer, 101 Ill. App. 2d 44, 48, 242 N.E.2d 288, 290 (5th Dist. 1968).

[46] People v. Stoudt, 198 Ill. App. 3d 124, 126, 555 N.E.2d 825, 827 (2d Dist. 1990).

[47] People v. Raby, 40 Ill. 2d 392, 399, 240 N.E.2d 595, 599 (1968), cert. denied, 393 U.S. 1083 (1969).

[48] See, e.g., People v. Raby, 40 Ill. 2d 392, 399, 240 N.E.2d 595, 599 (1968), cert. denied, 393 U.S. 1083 (1969).

[49] See, e.g., People v. Schehr, 88 Ill. App. 2d 287, 289, 232 N.E.2d 566, 569 (1st Dist. 1967).

[50] See, e.g., People v. Gibbs, 115 Ill. App. 2d 113, 117, 253 N.E.2d 117, 119 (1st Dist. 1969) (defendant continued to speak after the police ordered a crowd to disperse when the debate was degenerating into a physical battle); United States ex. rel. Raby v. Woods, 440 F.2d 478, 482 (7th Cir. 1971) (defendant convicted when he failed to vacate a street intersection).

[51] See, e.g., People v. Hilgenberg, 223 Ill. App. 3d 286, 290, 585 N.E.2d 180, 184 (2d Dist. 1991); People v. Stoudt, 198 Ill. App. 3d 124, 127, 555 N.E.2d 825, 827 (2d Dist. 1990).

sheriff to make an unauthorized entrance[52] and an instance where defendants refused to remove themselves from a highway at an officer's request.[53]

A defendant can be charged with resisting arrest for actions he takes after the arrest. If a defendant runs away,[54] struggles with the police,[55] or punches and kicks an officer,[56] this will constitute resisting an arrest. On the other hand, where the police attempted to handcuff a defendant's hands behind his back and the defendant pulled his hands down and in front of him because of the severe pain he experienced, this was not sufficient for resisting an arrest.[57]

Although a defendant cannot physically resist an arrest, he or she may inquire about the reason for the arrest, point out the officer's mistakes and verbally protest the arrest.[58] Merely arguing with a police officer about the alleged illegitimacy of the arrest is not grounds for arresting the defendant for resisting arrest.[59] Nor is it resisting arrest if the defendant's language becomes abusive and disrespectful toward the police.[60] The Illinois Supreme Court ruled that where an antagonistic and belligerent defendant refused, following his arrest, to answer police questions that were pursuant to normal police booking procedures, this was neither resisting nor obstructing a police officer.[61]

If a defendant obstructs proper police action with respect to a third party, this is a violation of section 5/31-1.[62] Where police were attempting to arrest a relative of the defendant, whereupon the defendant jumped an arresting officer from behind and desisted from his interventionist activities only after he was struck with an officer's flashlight, the defendant was properly convicted of obstructing a police officer.[63]

Obstruction of a police officer can arise in circumstances other than arrest situations. For example, where police, under the authority of the Illinois Domes-

---

[52] People v. Hilgenberg, 223 Ill. App. 3d 286, 290, 585 N.E.2d 180, 184 (2d Dist. 1991).

[53] People v. Stoudt, 198 Ill. App. 3d 124, 127, 555 N.E.2d 825, 827 (2d Dist. 1990).

[54] People v. Holdman, 73 Ill. 2d 213, 218-19, 383 N.E.2d 155, 158-59 (1978), cert. denied, 440 U.S. 938 (1979); People v. Carroll, 133 Ill. App. 2d 78, 80, 272 N.E.2d 822, 824 (1st Dist. 1971).

[55] People v. McKinney, 62 Ill. App. 3d 61, 66-67, 378 N.E.2d 1125, 1129-30 (1st Dist. 1978); People v. Fort, 91 Ill. App. 2d 212, 214, 234 N.E.2d 384, 386 (1st Dist. 1968), cert. denied, 393 U.S. 1014, reh'g denied, 393 U.S. 1112 (1969).

[56] People v. Pickett, 34 Ill. App. 3d 590, 593, 340 N.E.2d 259, 261 (1st Dist. 1975).

[57] City of Pekin v. Ross, 81 Ill. App. 3d 127, 130, 400 N.E.2d 992, 994 (3d Dist. 1980).

[58] City of Joliet v. Schmidt, 35 Ill. App. 3d 978, 980, 343 N.E.2d 40, 42 (3d Dist. 1976); People v. Raby, 40 Ill. 2d 392, 398, 240 N.E.2d 595, 599 (1968), cert. denied, 393 U.S. 1083 (1969).

[59] Landry v. Daley, 280 F. Supp. 938, 959 (N.D. Ill. 1968); City of Joliet v. Schmidt, 35 Ill. App. 3d 978, 980, 343 N.E.2d 40, 42 (3d Dist. 1976).

[60] People v. Flannigan, 131 Ill. App. 2d 1059, 1062, 267 N.E.2d 739, 742 (5th Dist. 1971); but see People v. Crawford 152 Ill. App. 3d 992, 995, 505 N.E.2d 394, 396 (4th Dist. 1987) (finding under similar circumstances that defendant did resist arrest).

[61] People v. Weathington, 82 Ill. 2d 183, 187, 411 N.E.2d 862, 863-64 (1980).

[62] People v. Joseph, 46 Ill. App. 3d 747, 749, 361 N.E.2d 365, 366-67 (3d Dist. 1977).

[63] People v. Joseph, 46 Ill. App. 3d 747, 749, 361 N.E.2d 365, 366-67 (3d Dist. 1977).

tic Violence Act,[64] attempted to retrieve from a defendant the keys of a home and car belonging to a domestic abuse victim, whereupon the defendant physically resisted the police removal of the keys from his pocket, he was convicted of obstructing a police officer.[65] Regardless of whether resisting or obstructing a police officer is charged, a charging instrument that merely recites the statutory language of section 5/31-1 is insufficient; it must describe the facts that give rise to the resistance or obstruction charge.[66]

The third essential component of obstructing or resisting a police officer is that the defendant knew the officer to be a peace officer. Where a defendant intervened with physical force between a plainclothes police officer and an arrestee in circumstances in which the defendant did not realize the arrestee was illegally resisting the arresting officer, the defendant could not be convicted of any crime, since he did not know the officer was a peace officer, and also because he was acting pursuant to the legal defense of "defense of another."[67]

The final element of this crime requires the prosecution to demonstrate that the officer was carrying out an "authorized act within his official capacity."[68] Although the enactment covers only resistance or obstruction to "authorized" acts of the officer, the clear intent of the legislature was to *disallow* forcible resistance or obstruction by a private person to an arrest "even though he knows the arrest is unlawful."[69] In other words, this offense must be interpreted consistent with section 5/7-7 of the Criminal Code, which states that a person cannot "resist an arrest which he knows is being made . . . by a peace officer . . . even if he believes that the arrest is unlawful and the arrest in fact is unlawful."[70] The policy behind this concept emanates from a recognition that "arrests are frequently made under hazardous conditions and that the peace is best preserved when the citizen submits to arrest without regard to the merits of the case."[71] Section 5/31-1 is designed to deter interference with acts of law enforcement officials on the basis of a person's own conclusion about the impropriety of the act,[72] regardless of whether the person is right or wrong in his or her assess-

---

[64] 750 ILCS 60/102 (1999).

[65] People v. Hetzel, 176 Ill. App. 3d 630, 635-36, 531 N.E.2d 436, 438-39 (2d Dist. 1988).

[66] People v. Leach, 3 Ill. App. 3d 389, 393, 279 N.E.2d 450, 452 (1st Dist. 1972).

[67] People v. Smith, 19 Ill. App. 3d 704, 707, 312 N.E.2d 355, 358 (1st Dist. 1974).

[68] 720 ILCS 5/31-1 (1999).

[69] ILL. ANN. STAT. ch. 38, para. 31-1 (Smith-Hurd 1977), 1961 Committee Comments, at 307 (revised 1970).

[70] 720 ILCS 5/7-7 (1998). *See also* People v. Gilman, 17 Ill. App. 3d 827, 830, 308 N.E.2d 666, 668 (4th Dist. 1974); People v. Carroll, 133 Ill. App. 2d 78, 81, 272 N.E.2d 822, 824 (1st Dist. 1971).

[71] People v. Fort, 91 Ill. App. 2d 212, 214, 234 N.E.2d 384, 386 (1st Dist. 1968), *cert. denied*, 393 U.S. 1014, *reh'g denied*, 393 U.S. 1112 (1969).

[72] Landry v. Daley, 280 F. Supp. 938, 959 (N.D. Ill. 1968).

ment.[73] Thus, *authorized* as used in this section means endowed with authority;[74] it does not go to the correctness of the exercise of that authority when making an arrest.[75] If the probable cause to make an arrest is lacking this does not justify avoidance of the arrest.[76]

However, where a police officer is carrying out an investigatory stop, often referred to as a "Terry stop,"[77] which is not supported by the "reasonable suspicion" required for such a detention of a suspect, the suspect's failure to submit to the police order to stop is not committing the offense of resisting or obstructing a peace officer.[78] Thus, where a police officer, lacking a basis for an investigatory stop, ordered the defendant to stop, whereupon the defendant fled, this offense was not committed.[79]

Notwithstanding the inability to resist or obstruct a legal arrest, a defendant can resist or obstruct a police officer's use of excessive force.[80] In a case where the defendant testified that he was clubbed from behind by an individual who possibly was an officer, the court ruled that the jury should have been provided with instructions on self-defense.[81]

§ 14.07.   — Lesser Included Offenses.

A defendant may not claim that resisting or obstructing a police officer is a lesser included offense of other more serious crimes against the officer. For instance, convictions for aggravated battery and obstruction could be upheld even though they arose from the same act, namely, striking an officer.[82]

§ 14.08.   Disarming a Peace Officer.

The legislature has created the offense of "disarming a peace officer."[83] Section 5/31-1a provides:

---

[73] People v. Villarreal, 152 Ill. 2d 368, 374, 604 N.E.2d 923, 926 (1992); People v. Shinn, 5 Ill. App. 3d 468, 472, 283 N.E.2d 502, 505 (3d Dist. 1972).

[74] People v. Villarreal, 152 Ill. 2d 368, 374, 604 N.E.2d 923, 926 (1992); People v. Shinn, 5 Ill. App. 3d 468, 472, 283 N.E.2d 502, 505 (3d Dist. 1972).

[75] People v. Locken, 59 Ill. 2d 459, 464, 322 N.E.2d 51, 53-54 (1974); People v. Shinn, 5 Ill. App. 3d 468, 472, 283 N.E.2d 502, 505 (3d Dist. 1972).

[76] People v. Locken, 59 Ill. 2d 459, 464, 322 N.E.2d 51, 53-54 (1974); People v. Suriwka, 2 Ill. App. 3d 384, 391, 276 N.E.2d 490, 496 (1st Dist. 1971).

[77] Terry v. Ohio, 392 U.S. 1 (1968) (stop and frisk of suspect that police reasonably suspect to be armed and dangerous comports with Fourth Amendment).

[78] People v. Moore, 286 Ill. App. 3d 649, 652-55, 676 N.E.2d 700, 703-04 (3d Dist. 1997).

[79] People v. Moore, 286 Ill. App. 3d 649, 652-55, 676 N.E.2d 700, 703-04 (3d Dist. 1997).

[80] People v. Bailey, 108 Ill. App. 3d 392, 398, 439 N.E.2d 4, 9 (2d Dist. 1982).

[81] People v. Willey, 85 Ill. App. 3d 734, 735, 407 N.E.2d 1119, 1120 (3d Dist. 1980).

[82] People v. Rinks, 80 Ill. App. 2d 152, 156, 224 N.E.2d 29, 31 (2d Dist. 1967). *See* ch. 1 of this treatise for a discussion of lesser included offenses.

[83] 720 ILCS 5/31-1a (1999).

A person who knowingly disarms a person known to him to be a peace officer, while the peace officer is engaged in the performance of his official duties by taking a firearm from the person of the peace officer or from an area within the peace officer's immediate presence without the peace officer's consent shall be guilty of a . . . felony.[84]

§ 14.09.   Obstructing Service of Process.

Section 5/31-3 prohibits "obstructing service of process." It states: "Whoever knowingly resists or obstructs the authorized service or execution of any civil or criminal process or order of any court commits a . . . misdemeanor."[85] This crime is directed at flouting the authority of the judiciary represented by its judicial process.[86] It normally arises where a defendant engages in a physical act that "may impede, hinder, interrupt, prevent, or delay performance" of the duties of a law enforcement official who is acting on behalf of a court.[87] Where an accused knowingly thwarts an officer's attempt to execute an arrest warrant[88] or to serve a summons,[89] this constitutes obstructing service of process. Where a defendant misleads the authorities, this offense is committed even though the defendant committed no "physical act" of obstruction and failed to create an obstacle the police were unable to overcome in their effort to serve process.[90] In contrast, merely arguing with an official about the service in question does not amount to a crime.[91]

§ 14.10.   Obstructing Justice.

Another crime prohibiting interference with official endeavors is "obstructing justice":

A person obstructs justice when, with intent to prevent the apprehension or obstruct the prosecution or defense of any person, he knowingly commits any of the following acts: (a) Destroys, alters, conceals or disguises physical evidence, plants false evidence, furnishes false information; or (b) Induces a witness having knowledge material to the subject at issue to leave

---

[84] 720 ILCS 5/31-1a (1999).

[85] 720 ILCS 5/31-3 (1999).

[86] ILL. ANN. STAT. ch. 38, para. 31-3 (Smith-Hurd 1977), 1961 Committee Comments, at 318 (revised 1970).

[87] Silverman v. Ballantine, 694 F.2d 1091, 1095 (7th Cir. 1982).

[88] People v. Koester, 31 Ill. App. 3d 28, 32-33, 332 N.E.2d 755, 757-58 (1st Dist. 1975).

[89] People v. Rauschenberg, 29 Ill. App. 2d 293, 298-99, 173 N.E.2d 6, 10 (2d Dist. 1961).

[90] People v. Meister, 289 Ill. App. 3d 337, 340-43, 682 N.E.2d 306, 307-10 (4th Dist. 1997).

[91] Silverman v. Ballantine, 694 F.2d 1091, 1095 (7th Cir. 1982).

the State or conceal himself; or (c) Possessing knowledge material to the subject at issue, he leaves the State or conceals himself.[92]

This felony[93] is obviously a specific intent offense.[94] The state is required to prove that the accused engaged in the proscribed acts "with intent to prevent the apprehension or obstruct the prosecution or defense of any person."[95] Thus, where the defendant allegedly gave police false names after his arrest, he could not have had the intent to avoid apprehension as alleged in the complaint since he already had been apprehended.[96] As for the acts proscribed, the language of the statute is rather clear.

The outcome of a trial for obstruction of justice is not dependent on the outcome of the prosecution alleged to have been obstructed.[97] For example, where a dead body was found on a defendant's farm, the defendant was convicted of conspiring to obstruct justice, and his acquittal on murder charges did not invalidate the conspiracy conviction.[98]

If a defendant conceals physical evidence of a crime, this may amount to obstructing justice.[99] Thus, where a defendant took records subject to a subpoena and concealed them in various rest areas to prevent the prosecution of him and others for obscenity, this amounted to obstructing justice.[100]

Although the statute does not facially reflect an exemption for a defendant's denials to police regarding his or her own guilt as to a crime, Illinois caselaw has judicially construed section 5/31-4 to reflect such an exemption.[101] Where defendants were charged with attempted murder and were clearly among the targets of an investigation, their exculpatory denials falsely made to the police while responding to police questioning did not constitute obstructing justice since their truthful answers would have amounted to a confession of guilt.[102]

---

[92] 720 ILCS 5/31-4(a) (1999).

[93] 720 ILCS 5/31-4(b) (1999).

[94] See ch. 2 for a discussion of specific intent.

[95] 720 ILCS 5/31-4(a) (1999).

[96] People v. Miller, 253 Ill. App. 3d 1032, 1035, 628 N.E.2d 893, 896 (2d Dist. 1993) ("the complaint charged the defendant with the intent to prevent his own 'apprehension' and did not charge him with intent to obstruct his prosecution").

[97] People v. Saiken, 49 Ill. 2d 504, 514, 275 N.E.2d 381, 387 (1971), cert. denied, 405 U.S. 1066 (1972).

[98] People v. Saiken, 49 Ill. 2d 504, 514, 275 N.E.2d 381, 387 (1971), cert. denied, 405 U.S. 1066 (1972).

[99] People v. Morgan, 169 Ill. App. 3d 368, 371, 523 N.E.2d 560, 561-62 (4th Dist. 1988).

[100] People v. Morgan, 169 Ill. App. 3d 368, 371, 523 N.E.2d 560, 561-62 (4th Dist. 1988).

[101] People v. Brooks, 51 Ill. App. 3d 800, 803-05, 367 N.E.2d 236, 239 (2d Dist. 1977); but see Brogan v. United States, 522 U.S. 398 (1998) (Fifth Amendment privilege against self-incrimination does not entitle a person to utter a false statement consisting of a mere denial of wrong doing; "exculpatory no" doctrine rejected).

[102] People v. Brooks, 51 Ill. App. 3d 800, 803-05, 367 N.E.2d 236, 239 (2d Dist. 1977).

Additionally, where underage smokers provided false birth dates to the police, the inaccurate statements fell under the exculpatory doctrine.[103]

If a defendant's false statements to police go beyond the limits of his or her own involvement and, therefore, beyond his or her own denial of wrongdoing, the defendant has no privilege to intentionally mislead police or to withhold information as to the crimes of others which are not inextricably connected with charges against himself or herself.[104] This is because there may be Fifth Amendment self-incrimination problems in the former situation, but there are none in the latter.[105] In *People v. Childs*,[106] the court acknowledged that a defendant's false statement made to the police for the purpose of preventing police apprehension of another suspect had to be voluntary to sustain an obstruction of justice conviction.[107] In *Childs*, the court rejected the defendant's claim that his false statements about the suspect's whereabouts were involuntary where the police officer ordered the defendant to kneel and questioned him in a loud assertive tone while pointing a gun at him.[108]

Another problem arising in connection with an obstructing justice charge not addressed by the language of the statute concerns whether, for instance, concealment of evidence is a continuing offense for purposes of the statute of limitations. Apparently, concealment of evidence is not a continuing offense. In one case, the appellate court ruled that the defendant's failure to dig up a body he had concealed or to indicate to the authorities that he had concealed the body did not prevent the eighteen-month statute of limitations period from running.[109] In that case, the court rejected the state's argument that the concealment was a continuing series of acts and that the statute of limitations did not begin to run until the defendant disclosed his concealment to the authorities.[110]

Finally, this statute clearly applies to the concealment of evidence by the authorities themselves. Where federal agents sent an informer-witness, whose testimony was crucial on the issue of the defendant's entrapment defense, beyond the jurisdiction of the state court, this along with the trial court's denial of the

---

[103] People v. Alvarado, 301 Ill. App. 3d 1017, 1023, 704 N.E.2d 937, 941 (2d Dist. 1998).

[104] People v. Brooks, 51 Ill. App. 3d 800, 803, 367 N.E.2d 236, 239 (2d Dist. 1977).

[105] *See* People v. Remias, 169 Ill. App. 3d 309, 311, 523 N.E.2d 1106, 1108 (3d Dist. 1988) (giving police false names when stopped for traffic offense amounted to obstructing justice, since providing true names would not have amounted to admission of guilt); People v. Jackiewicz, 163 Ill. App. 3d 1062, 1064-65, 517 N.E.2d 316, 318 (4th Dist. 1987) (defendant's false statement that brother did not possess gun on night of several incidents amounted to obstructing justice, since defendant was not charged with brother's crimes and defendant had been told he would not be prosecuted).

[106] 271 Ill. App. 3d 787, 651 N.E.2d 252 (4th Dist. 1995).

[107] People v. Childs, 272 Ill. App. 3d 787, 790, 651 N.E.2d 252, 254 (4th Dist. 1995).

[108] People v. Childs, 272 Ill. App. 3d 787, 791, 651 N.E.2d 252, 254-55 (4th Dist. 1995).

[109] People v. Criswell, 12 Ill. App. 3d 102, 107, 298 N.E.2d 391, 393 (1st Dist. 1973).

[110] People v. Criswell, 12 Ill. App. 3d 102, 107, 298 N.E.2d 391, 393 (1st Dist. 1973).

defendants' motion to compel the production of the witness, deprived the defendants of their right to a fair trial and caused a reversal of their convictions.[111] In other words, the federal agent's de facto violation of section 5/31-4 vitiated the conviction of those defendants whose constitutional rights were also violated because of this wrongdoing.[112]

§ 14.11. Concealing or Aiding a Fugitive.

The next article 5/31 stricture is "concealing or aiding a fugitive." Section 5/31-5 provides: "Every person not standing in the relation of husband, wife, parent, child, brother or sister to the offender, who, with intent to prevent the apprehension of the offender, conceals his knowledge that an offense has been committed or harbors, aids or conceals the offender, commits a . . . felony."[113]

This crime was designed by the General Assembly to punish those who were previously understood to be "accessories after the fact" to another's commission of criminality.[114] The mere failure to reveal knowledge that another person has committed a crime, standing alone, does not constitute "concealing or aiding a fugitive."[115] "Concealed," as used in this statute, has been interpreted to mean something more than failing to come forward with information; some *affirmative act* on the part of the defendant is essential.[116] Thus, where a burglar told the defendant about his involvement in a particular burglary and, thereafter, the defendant took no steps to inform the authorities about the information he had about the burglary, this did not amount to concealment for purposes of this offense.[117] Similarly, in another case, the appellate court held that where a defendant gave police the physical description of a murderer but withheld knowledge of the murderer's specific identity, the defendant had not committed the affirmative act necessary for concealment.[118] "Offender," as used in this felony stricture, includes misdemeanant fugitives as well as felons.[119]

---

[111] People v. Wilson, 24 Ill. 2d 425, 432, 182 N.E.2d 203, 205-06 (1962).

[112] People v. Wilson, 24 Ill. 2d 425, 432, 182 N.E.2d 203, 205-06 (1962).

[113] 720 ILCS 5/31-5 (1999).

[114] ILL. ANN. STAT. ch. 38, para. 31-5 (Smith-Hurd 1977), 1961 Committee Comments, at 322 (revised 1970).

[115] People v. Donelson, 45 Ill. App. 3d 609, 611, 359 N.E.2d 1225, 1227 (4th Dist. 1977).

[116] People v. Donelson, 45 Ill. App. 3d 609, 611, 359 N.E.2d 1225, 1227 (4th Dist. 1977).

[117] People v. Donelson, 45 Ill. App. 3d 609, 611, 359 N.E.2d 1225, 1227 (4th Dist. 1977).

[118] People v. Thomas, 198 Ill. App. 3d 1035, 1038, 556 N.E.2d 721, 723 (1st Dist. 1990).

[119] People v. Miller, 171 Ill. 2d 330, 333-37, 664 N.E.2d 1021, 1022-24 (1996) (application of felony concealment statute to defendant who concealed misdemeanant did not violate due process or proportionate penalties clause of Illinois Constitution).

§ 14.12. Escape.

The crime of "escape" is prohibited in the Illinois penal code. A person convicted of or charged with a felony who (1) intentionally escapes from any penal institution or from the custody of an employee of that institution or (2) knowingly fails to return for periodic imprisonment or from a furlough or from work and day release is guilty of a felony.[120] A person convicted of or charged with a misdemeanor who (1) intentionally escapes from any penal institution or from the custody of an employee of that institution or (2) knowingly fails to return to periodic imprisonment or from a furlough or from work and day release is guilty of a misdemeanor,[121] unless this person does so while armed with a dangerous weapon, in which case it is a felony.[122] A person civilly committed under the Sexually Violent Persons Commitment Act who escapes commits a felony.[123] A person in the lawful custody of a police officer for the alleged commission of a felony who intentionally escapes from that custody commits a felony.[124] A person in lawful custody of a police officer for the alleged commission of a misdemeanor, who intentionally escapes from that custody, commits a misdemeanor,[125] unless the person does so while armed with a dangerous weapon, in which case it is a felony.[126] A person in lawful custody for an alleged violation of probation, conditional discharge, parole or mandatory supervised release for a felony commits felony escape,[127] unless the release was for a misdemeanor, in which case the escape is a misdemeanor.[128] Because of the rather clear intent of the legislature, as reflected in the section 5/2-14 definition of *penal institution*,[129] the law provides that escape from a county jail can give rise to a conviction for escape, notwithstanding the statutory language in section 5/31-6 that makes reference to escape from a "penal institution."[130] Also, a defendant can be convicted of escape arising from his or her escape from a facility while another charge is pending even though eventually either the defendant is acquitted of the charge that was pending or the charge is dismissed.[131]

---

[120] 720 ILCS 5/31-6(a) (1999).

[121] 720 ILCS 5/31-6(b) (1999).

[122] 720 ILCS 5/31-6(d) (1999).

[123] 720 ILCS 5/31-6(b-1) (1999) (referring to 725 ILCS 207/1 *et. seq.* (1999)).

[124] 720 ILCS 5/31-6(c) (1999).

[125] 720 ILCS 5/31-6(c) (1999).

[126] 720 ILCS 5/31-6(d) (1999).

[127] 720 ILCS 5/31-6(c-5) (1999).

[128] 720 ILCS 5/31-6(c-6) (1999).

[129] 720 ILCS 5/2-14 (1999). *See also* ILL. ANN. STAT. ch. 38, para. 31-6 (Smith-Hurd 1977), 1961 Committee Comments, at 324 (revised 1970).

[130] *See, e.g.,* People v. Newbolds, 194 Ill. App. 3d 539, 551 N.E.2d 813 (5th Dist. 1990) (escape from county jail; conviction affirmed).

[131] People v. Boucher, 75 Ill. App. 3d 322, 324, 394 N.E.2d 60, 62 (3d Dist. 1979).

§ 14.13. Aiding Escape.

"Aiding escape" by another is a companion to the crime of escape. Any person, having the "intent to aid any prisoner in escaping from any penal institution," who "conveys into the institution or transfers to the prisoner anything for use in escaping" commits the misdemeanor of aiding escape,[132] regardless of whether the aided person actually escapes.[133] Furthermore, whoever "knowingly aids a person" already convicted of or charged with a felony in escaping from a penal institution, in escaping from the custody of an employee of that institution, or in failing to return from a furlough or from work and day release commits the felony of aiding escape.[134] However, if the accused knowingly aids a person convicted of or charged with a misdemeanor in escaping from a penal institution or failing to return to custody from a furlough or work and day release, the accused commits the misdemeanor of aiding escape,[135] unless the accused does so while armed with a dangerous weapon, in which case it is a felony.[136]

The statute is not limited to escapes from penal institutions, furloughs, and work programs. One who "knowingly aids a person in escaping from any public institution, other than a penal institution, in which he is lawfully detained, or from the custody of an employee of that institution," commits the misdemeanor of aiding escape,[137] unless the accused does so while armed with a dangerous weapon, in which case it is the felony of aiding escape.[138] This would arise, for instance, where the defendant aided the escape of a person from a mental institution in which the person was confined pursuant to a court order.

Beyond the above circumstances, the felony crime of aiding escape is also committed where an accused knowingly aids a person's escape from the "lawful custody of a peace officer" for an alleged felony, while misdemeanor escape is committed where the accused aids a person's escape from the lawful custody of an officer for an alleged misdemeanor,[139] unless the accused does so while armed with a dangerous weapon, in which case the latter crime is elevated to a felony.[140] This type of aiding escape would occur, for example, where the defendant lent support to the escape of an arrestee from a police squad car immediately following his arrest.

---

[132] 720 ILCS 5/31-7(a) (1999).

[133] ILL. ANN. STAT. ch. 38, para. 31-7 (Smith-Hurd 1977), 1961 Committee Comments, at 331 (revised 1970).

[134] 720 ILCS 5/31-7(b) (1999).

[135] 720 ILCS 5/31-7(c) (1999).

[136] 720 ILCS 5/31-7(g) (1999).

[137] 720 ILCS 5/31-7(d) (1999).

[138] 720 ILCS 5/31-7(g) (1999).

[139] 720 ILCS 5/31-7(e) (1999).

[140] 720 ILCS 5/31-7(g) (1999).

Finally, an "officer or employee of any penal institution who recklessly permits any prisoner in his custody to escape" commits a misdemeanor.[141] However, an official who aids the likes of a felony probationer or parolee in custody for violation of the terms of their release commits a felony, while whoever aids the likes of a misdemeanor probationer or parolee in custody for violation of the terms of their release commits a misdemeanor.[142] If an official negligently permits a prisoner's escape, this would not be criminal.[143]

§ 14.14. Refusing to Aid an Officer.

Another article 5/31 stricture is "refusing to aid an officer." It provides: "Whoever upon command refuses or knowingly fails reasonably to aid a person known by him to be a peace officer in: (a) Apprehending a person whom the officer is authorized to apprehend; or (b) Preventing the commission by another of any offense, commits a petty offense."[144] This infraction creates a duty to aid an officer on the officer's command or in circumstances that reasonably warrant such aid where the officer is apprehending a criminal wrongdoer or is preventing a criminal wrongdoing. It does not impose a duty on citizens generally to apprehend criminals or to prevent crimes. While § 14.06 discussed the need for an "action" to satisfy the crime of obstruction of justice, here "passive refusal" to aid an officer is enough to convict a person of this offense.[145]

§ 14.15. Bringing Contraband into Penal Institutions.

Both section 5/31A-1.1[146] and section 5/31A-1.2[147] prohibit "bringing contraband into a penal institution" and "possessing contraband in a penal institution." These two felony offenses are delineated according to whether the person bringing the contraband into a penal institution is a nonemployee[148] or an employee[149] of the penal institution. Both of the offenses prohibit either (1) the bringing of an item of contraband into the penal institution in question,[150] (2) causing another to bring an item of contraband into such a facility,[151] or (3) possessing con-

---

[141] 720 ILCS 5/31-7(f) (1999).

[142] 720 ILCS 5/31-7(f-5) & (f-6) (1999).

[143] ILL. ANN. STAT. ch. 38, para. 31-7 (Smith-Hurd 1977), 1961 Committee Comments, at 331 (revised 1970).

[144] 720 ILCS 5/31-8 (1999).

[145] See People v. Cope, 299 Ill. App. 3d 184, 191, 701 N.E.2d 165, 170 (2d Dist. 1998).

[146] 720 ILCS 5/31A-1.1 (1999).

[147] 720 ILCS 5/31A-1.2 (1999).

[148] 720 ILCS 5/31A-1.1 (1999).

[149] 720 ILCS 5/31A-1.2 (1999).

[150] 720 ILCS 5/31A-1.1(a)(1) (1999) (nonemployees); 5/31A-1.2(a)(1) (1999) (employees).

[151] 720 ILCS 5/31A-1.1(a)(2) (1999) (nonemployees); 5/31A-1.2(a)(2) (1999) (employees).

traband in such a facility.[152] For nonemployees, placing an item of contraband in such proximity to a penal institution as to give an inmate access is also prohibited.[153] For employees, delivery, possession with intent to deliver, conspiracy to deliver, soliciting the delivery or permitting the delivery of contraband to inmates is outlawed.[154]

For purposes of these offenses, *contraband* includes alcoholic liquor,[155] cannabis,[156] a controlled substance,[157] a hypodermic syringe,[158] a weapon,[159] firearms,[160] ammunition,[161] explosives,[162] tools to defeat security mechanisms,[163] cutting tools,[164] and electronic contraband.[165] A "penal institution" is broadly defined by statute[166] and has been interpreted as including any place near to where a convict is sentenced to electronic home detention.[167]

§ 14.16. Compounding a Crime.

The next grouping of crimes appearing in the Illinois Criminal Code are the article 5/32 offenses that reflect strictures aimed at "interference with judicial

---

[152] 720 ILCS 5/31A-1.1(b) (1999) (nonemployees); 5/31A-1.2(b) (1999) (employees).

[153] 720 ILCS 5/31A-1.1(a)(3) (1999).

[154] 720 ILCS 5/31A-1.2(c) (1999).

[155] 720 ILCS 5/31A-1.1(c)(2)(i) (1999) (nonemployees); 5/31A-1.2(d)(4)(i) (1999) (employees).

[156] 720 ILCS 5/31A-1.1(c)(2)(ii) (1999) (nonemployees); 5/31A-1.1(d)(4)(ii) (1999) (employees).

[157] 720 ILCS 5/31A-1.1(c)(2)(iii) (1999) (nonemployees); 5/31A-1.2(d)(4)(iii) (1999) (employees).

[158] 720 ILCS 5/31A-1.1(c)(2)(iv) (1999) (nonemployees); 5/31A-1.2(d)(4)(iv) (1999) (employees).

[159] 720 ILCS 5/31A-1.1(c)(2)(v) (1999) (nonemployees); 5/31A-1.1(d)(4)(v) (1999) (employees); *see* People v. Dal Collo, 294 Ill. App. 3d 893, 896, 691 N.E.2d 894, 895-97 (3d Dist. 1998) (2 to 2½ inch file clip with sharpened outer edges constituted weapon for purposes of possession of contraband in a penal institution).

[160] 720 ILCS 5/31A-1.1(c)(2)(vi) (1999) (nonemployees); 5/31A-1.2(d)(4)(vi) (1999) (employees).

[161] 720 ILCS 5/31A-1.1(c)(2)(vii) (1999) (nonemployees); 5/31A-1.2(d)(4)(vii) (1999) (employees).

[162] 720 ILCS 5/31A-1.1(c)(2)(viii) (1999) (nonemployees); 5/31A-1.2(d)(4)(viii) (1999) (employees).

[163] 720 ILCS 5/31A-1.1(c)(2)(ix) (1999) (nonemployees); 5/31A-1.2(d)(4)(ix) (1999) (employees).

[164] 720 ILCS 5/31A-1.1(c)(2)(x) (1999) (nonemployees); 5/31A-1.2(d)(4)(x) (1999) (employees).

[165] 720 ILCS 5/31A-1.1(c)(2)(xi)(1999) (nonemployees); 5/31A-1.2(d)(4)(xi) (1999) (employees).

[166] 720 ILCS 5/31A-1.1(c)(1) (1999).

[167] People v. Moss, 274 Ill. App. 3d 77, 80, 654 N.E.2d 248, 250 (5th Dist. 1995) (defendant was distributing cocaine on neighbor's driveway adjacent to defendant's residence).

procedure."[168] The first of these offenses is "compounding a crime," which reads: "A person compounds a crime when he receives or offers to another any consideration for a promise not to prosecute or aid in the prosecution of an offender."[169] An offender of this crime is guilty of a petty offense.[170] It is contrary to public policy to condition forbearance from filing criminal charges against someone on that person's making restitution, and an agreement of this nature constitutes compounding a crime.[171] However, there is no legislative "intent to prohibit a victim of theft or other property offense [from] taking steps to recover his property, so long as such action does not involve, as consideration for such recovery, a promise not to prosecute or aid in the prosecution."[172]

Where a defendant offered to pay a complaining witness, contingent on the witness's agreement to ask the state's attorney to drop charges against the defendant's nephews, the defendant's acts evinced intent to cause the witness not to aid in the prosecution of the nephews and could have amounted to compounding a crime.[173] Similarly, where a defendant offered money to a sexual assault complainant to not appear in court, this could have amounted to compounding a crime, had that offense been charged, even though it did not amount to illegal communication with a witness.[174]

§ 14.17. Perjury.

The most serious article 5/32 ("interference with judicial procedure") crime is perjury,[175] which is a felony.[176] Subsection (a) of section 5/32-2 provides: "A person commits perjury when, under oath or affirmation, in a proceeding or in any other matter where by law such oath or affirmation is required, he makes a false statement, material to the issue or point in question, which he does not believe to be true."[177] Subsection (b) states that a charging instrument alleging perjury because of "contradictory statements" made under oath "need not specify which statement is false" and that at trial, "the prosecution need not establish which [contradictory] statement is false."[178] Subsection (c) provides that

---

[168] 720 ILCS 5/32 (1999).

[169] 720 ILCS 5/32-1(a) (1999).

[170] 720 ILCS 5/32-1(b) (1999).

[171] Falco, Inc. v. Bates, 30 Ill. App. 3d 570, 571, 334 N.E.2d 169, 170 (4th Dist. 1975).

[172] ILL. ANN. STAT. ch. 38, para. 32-1 (Smith-Hurd 1977), 1961 Committee Comments, at 335-36 (revised 1970).

[173] People v. Scribner, 108 Ill. App. 3d 1138, 1143-44, 440 N.E.2d 160, 164-65 (5th Dist. 1982) (communication with witness conviction reversed although conduct might have amounted to compounding a crime if it had been charged).

[174] People v. Robinson, 186 Ill. App. 3d 1, 3, 541 N.E.2d 1336, 1338 (1st Dist. 1989).

[175] 720 ILCS 5/32-2(a) (1999).

[176] 720 ILCS 5/32-2(e) (1999).

[177] 720 ILCS 5/32-2(a) (1999).

[178] 720 ILCS 5/32-2(b) (1999).

"[w]here the contradictory statements are made in the same continuous trial, an admission by the offender in that same continuous trial of the falsity of a contradictory statement shall bar prosecution therefor."[179]

§ 14.18. — Elements of Perjury.

The purpose of this crime is, in part, to ensure validity of the judicial fact-finding process.[180] This objective helps define the proper scope of what constitutes perjury. The basic elements of perjury are that a person (1) while under oath or affirmation, (2) in a proceeding or other matter in which an oath or affirmation is required, (3) makes a statement, with knowledge of its falsity at the time of the utterance, (4) that is material to the issue or point in question.[181]

§ 14.19. —— Oath or Affirmation.

First, the statement must be made under oath or affirmation in any type of matter where the law requires an oath or affirmation.[182] The alleged false statements need not occur before a trier of fact or anyone else.[183] Where a defendant signed an application for aid to dependent children that contained a statement that the application was made under the penalties of perjury, this met the oath or affirmation requirement.[184] Where a defendant answered "no" to a question regarding whether his driver's license had ever been revoked on a verified driver's license application form, he was convicted for perjury where his driver's privileges had been revoked earlier.[185]

§ 14.20. —— In a Proceeding or Matter Where an Oath or Affirmation is Required.

The second major element of perjury is that a false statement be willfully uttered "in a proceeding or in any other matter where by law such oath or affirmation is required."[186] A voluntary oath neither required nor authorized — that is, not provided for by law — cannot provide a basis for perjury.[187] Thus, where there was no "clear legislative base" for requiring a tax preparer's oath under the

---

[179] 720 ILCS 5/32-2(c) (1999).

[180] People v. Mason, 60 Ill. App. 3d 463, 466, 376 N.E.2d 1059, 1061-62 (4th Dist. 1978).

[181] 720 ILCS 5/32-2(a).

[182] People v. Davis, 164 Ill. 2d 309, 310, 647 N.E.2d 977, 979 (1995).

[183] People v. Davis, 164 Ill. 2d 309, 310, 647 N.E.2d 977, 979 (1995) (false statement in deposition amounted to perjury).

[184] People v. Coleson, 25 Ill. App. 3d 43, 45, 322 N.E.2d 600, 602 (5th Dist. 1975).

[185] People v. Barrios, 114 Ill. 2d 265, 273-75, 500 N.E.2d 415, 418-19 (1986).

[186] 720 ILCS 5/32-2(a) (1999); People v. House, 202 Ill. App. 3d 893, 907, 560 N.E.2d 1224, 1234 (4th Dist. 1990).

[187] People v. Watson, 85 Ill. App. 3d 649, 652, 406 N.E.2d 1148, 1151 (4th Dist. 1980).

State Income Tax Act, there was no basis supportive of a perjury conviction of an attorney tax preparer.[188] On the other hand, where a defendant testified falsely at a bail hearing while under oath, this amounted to perjury since his taking the oath was not voluntary inasmuch as it was mandated by the inherent power of the court to require witnesses in matters pending before it be sworn to tell the truth.[189]

Regarding the "proceeding or other matter" in which the oath or affirmation is mandated, the false statement necessary for a perjury conviction can arise in a variety of situations. It can occur or appear in a trial,[190] before a grand jury,[191] in a probation hearing,[192] in a bail hearing,[193] in an attorney disciplinary commission hearing,[194] in a certificate of voter identity form used in an election,[195] in a deposition,[196] or in an income tax return.[197]

§ 14.21. —— Makes a Statement with Knowledge of Its Falsity.

The third essential element of perjury is proof of knowledge of the falsity of the statement at the time of the utterance.[198] Thus, a statement may constitute perjury when, as a matter of fact, the witness knew the statement was untrue.[199] However, a defendant cannot be convicted of perjury for a truthful answer to a question subject to various interpretations.[200] The questions preceding the allegedly perjurious response must be stated in such a precise way as not to require an interpretation or a construction by those required to answer them.[201] The questions and answers at issue must be interpreted in the context of what immediately preceded and succeeded them.[202] A charge of perjury may not be sustained by the device of lifting an isolated answer out of its immediate context,

---

[188] People v. Doss, 99 Ill. App. 3d 1026, 1029, 426 N.E.2d 324, 326 (4th Dist. 1981).

[189] People v. House, 202 Ill. App. 3d 893, 907-08, 560 N.E.2d 1224, 1234 (4th Dist. 1990).

[190] People v. Boyd, 81 Ill. App. 3d 259, 260-61, 401 N.E.2d 304, 306 (3d Dist. 1980).

[191] People v. Ricker, 45 Ill. 2d 562, 563, 262 N.E.2d 456, 457 (1970).

[192] People v. Spears, 83 Ill. App. 2d 18, 20, 226 N.E.2d 67, 68 (4th Dist. 1967).

[193] People v. House, 202 Ill. App. 3d 893, 908, 560 N.E.2d 1224, 1234 (4th Dist. 1990).

[194] People v. Harrod, 140 Ill. App. 3d 96, 97, 488 N.E.2d 316, 317 (4th Dist. 1986).

[195] People v. Thomas, 76 Ill. App. 3d 969, 970, 395 N.E.2d 601 (5th Dist. 1979).

[196] People v. Davis, 164 Ill. 2d 309, 310, 647 N.E.2d 977, 979 (1995).

[197] Werdell v. Twrzynski, 128 Ill. App. 2d 139, 154, 262 N.E.2d 833, 840 (1st Dist. 1970).

[198] People v. Boyd, 81 Ill. App. 3d 259, 261, 401 N.E.2d 304, 306 (3d Dist. 1980).

[199] People v. Watson, 85 Ill. App. 3d 649, 652, 406 N.E.2d 1148, 1151 (4th Dist. 1980).

[200] People v. Watson, 85 Ill. App. 3d 649, 651, 406 N.E.2d 1148, 1150 (4th Dist. 1980).

[201] People v. Watson, 85 Ill. App. 3d 649, 651, 406 N.E.2d 1148, 1150 (4th Dist. 1980) (citing People v. White, 59 Ill. 2d 416, 322 N.E.2d 1 (1974)).

[202] People v. Watson, 85 Ill. App. 3d 649, 651, 406 N.E.2d 1148, 1150 (4th Dist. 1980).

thus giving it a meaning entirely different than that which its context clearly represents.[203]

A conviction for perjury cannot be predicated on a "belief,"[204] "conclusion,"[205] "opinion,"[206] or "deduction,"[207] drawn from given facts, even if it does prove to be erroneous.[208] This rule is subject to the qualification that such a statement of belief, conclusion, opinion, or deduction may constitute perjury when, as a matter of fact, the utterer had no such belief or opinion.[209]

Where a police sergeant testified that he did not remember any of the circumstances to which he had positively attested on three prior occasions, he was properly convicted of perjury.[210] Where a defendant testified as an alibi witness in a murder trial that the alleged murderer had been positively seen by him at a particular time and place that was contradicted by other evidence that indicated the defendant himself was nowhere near the place in question at the time in question, he was convicted of perjury.[211] Where a defendant charged with drunk-driving denied that he was driving the automobile in question and testified that his female companion was the driver while the car plunged into a ditch, he was convicted of perjury given the testimony of a state trooper who saw the defendant behind the steering wheel and the female in the right front seat immediately after the car went into the ditch.[212] Conversely, where a defendant police officer, when questioned before a grand jury about whether he had taken money from an attendant at a parking lot, stated, "Unless there is someone was repaying some money, I loaned them or something like that," his answer was considered too equivocal to support a perjury conviction, notwithstanding the fact that the attendant testified that he had given the defendant money on several occasions, but not in repayment on any loan.[213]

---

[203] People v. Chancy, 91 Ill. App. 3d 817, 820, 414 N.E.2d 1239, 1241 (1st Dist. 1980); People v. Watson, 85 Ill. App. 3d 649, 651, 406 N.E.2d 1148, 1150 (4th Dist. 1980).

[204] People v. Drake, 63 Ill. App. 3d 633, 635, 380 N.E.2d 522, 524 (4th Dist. 1978).

[205] People v. White, 59 Ill. 2d 416, 420, 322 N.E.2d 1, 3 (1974).

[206] People v. White, 59 Ill. 2d 416, 420, 322 N.E.2d 1, 3 (1974).

[207] People v. White, 59 Ill. 2d 416, 420, 322 N.E.2d 1, 3 (1974).

[208] People v. White, 59 Ill. 2d 416, 420, 322 N.E.2d 1, 3 (1974). *See also* People v. Toner, 55 Ill. App. 3d 688, 694, 371 N.E.2d 270, 274 (1st Dist. 1977).

[209] People v. Drake, 63 Ill. App. 3d 633, 635, 380 N.E.2d 522, 524 (4th Dist. 1978).

[210] People v. Prokop, 2 Ill. App. 3d 109, 112, 276 N.E.2d 136, 138 (1st Dist. 1971).

[211] People v. Boyd, 81 Ill. App. 3d 259, 261, 401 N.E.2d 304, 306-07 (3d Dist. 1980).

[212] People v. Goff, 57 Ill. App. 3d 384, 386, 373 N.E.2d 71, 73 (4th Dist. 1978).

[213] People v. Toner, 55 Ill. App. 3d 688, 694, 371 N.E.2d 270, 275 (1st Dist. 1977).

§ 14.22. —— Material to the Issue or Point in Question.

Fourth, to convict one of perjury, the state must prove not only the false statement but also that it was "material to the issue or point in question."[214] "Materiality" looks to the relationship between the propositions for which evidence is offered and the issues in the case.[215] Whether the statement is material in a question of law is for the trial court to determine.[216]

Where a defendant was subpoenaed before a grand jury that was investigating a complaint that he had unlawfully shot another person, his testimony before the grand jury that he lawfully shot the person in self-defense was material to the grand jury's investigation for purposes of a subsequent perjury prosecution.[217] In a criminal jury trial, where defendant denied during his testimony as a witness that he made certain statements to the police, those denials were material to the issues in the criminal trial because the defendant's denials tended to disprove the criminal involvement of the person on trial.[218] In a deposition in a civil suit, defendant's false statement under oath amounted to perjury even though the case was settled without any trial court reliance on the false statements in its later rulings during the course of the litigation.[219] In a bail hearing, where a person testified as a surety that he owned four hundred tons of hay worth a certain amount of money situated in a particular village when, in fact, the hay was located outside the village, this did not amount to perjury if he did in fact own the hay and if it was worth about the value he had ascribed to it; the precise location of the hay was immaterial to the court's concern regarding whether he was fully able to discharge the obligation he proposed to assume.[220] Where the defendant during a suppression hearing denied he possessed cocaine, this could not amount to perjury since his statement was not material to the issue in question at the hearing, namely, whether his Fourth Amendment rights had been violated by the police during an earlier search.[221]

---

[214] 720 ILCS 5/32-2(a) (1999); People v. Cantrell, 79 Ill. App. 3d 626, 630, 398 N.E.2d 864, 867 (1st Dist. 1979).

[215] People v. Mason, 60 Ill. App. 3d 463, 465, 376 N.E.2d 1059, 1061 (4th Dist. 1978) (quoting People v. Harris, 102 Ill. App. 2d 335, 337, 242 N.E.2d 782, 784 (5th Dist. 1968)).

[216] People v. Briddle, 84 Ill. App. 3d 523, 527, 405 N.E.2d 1357, 1360 (2d Dist. 1980), cert. denied, 450 U.S. 986 (1981).

[217] People v. Beacham, 50 Ill. App. 3d 695, 701-02, 365 N.E.2d 737, 742 (1st Dist. 1977).

[218] People v. Acevedo, 275 Ill. App. 3d 420, 424, 656 N.E.2d 118, 121 (2d Dist. 1995).

[219] People v. Davis, 164 Ill. 2d 309, 311, 647 N.E.2d 977, 979 (1995).

[220] Pollard v. People, 69 Ill. 148, 154 (1873).

[221] People v. Rutledge, 257 Ill. App. 3d 769, 629 N.E.2d 233 (3d Dist. 1994) (issue at suppression hearing was not whether defendant was lying about his possession of cocaine but rather whether his Fourth Amendment rights were violated).

§ 14.23.   — Contradictory Statements.

As pointed out above, perjury can arise where a defendant makes contradictory statements under oath[222] unless they are made in the same continuous trial and the defendant admits to the falsity of one of the contradictory statements.[223] The government is not obligated to prove which of the contradictory statements are in fact false.[224]

Mere conflicts in the testimony of a witness with his or her prior statements do not ipso facto establish that the witness has committed perjury.[225] Where the discrepancies of a witness's testimony reflect the usual conflicts that occur when a witness is asked to repeat the same story on various occasions over an extended period of time, this is not perjury.[226] However, where the statements are patently inconsistent and the conflicts clearly are not attributable to a failure to vividly recollect facts or to an inability to consistently articulate facts in a scriptlike manner, then perjury may exist.[227]

Where a defendant makes inconsistent statements in the same continuous proceeding, but thereafter acknowledges one of the statements to be error, this is not perjury. Where a witness made an inadvertent response to a question that was inconsistent with an earlier statement but quickly corrected that latter response, this could not amount to perjury.[228] Also, courts usually view inconsistencies in testimony as a matter that merely goes to the weight and credibility of the testimony, not as a matter that is the basis of perjury.[229]

Where the admission to the falsity occurs in a separate proceeding, no exemption from perjury exists.[230] For example, where a defendant testified at a criminal trial that she fired a shot and, after a verdict was returned, testified in a post-trial hearing that a codefendant had actually fired the shot, this was not part of the same continuous trial and, as such, she was responsible for perjury.[231]

---

[222] *See* People v. Prokop, 2 Ill. App. 3d 109, 276 N.E.2d 136 (1st Dist. 1971).

[223] 720 ILCS 5/32-2(c) (1993). *Compare* People v. Jarrett, 263 Ill. App. 3d 364, 366, 636 N.E.2d 62, 64 (4th Dist. 1994) (statements made at the pretrial bond hearing which defendant later recanted at trial were not part of the same continuous trial and thus amounted to perjury).

[224] 720 ILCS 5/32-3(b) (1993).

[225] People v. Burnett, 35 Ill. App. 3d 109, 122, 341 N.E.2d 86, 96 (1st Dist. 1975).

[226] People v. Henderson, 36 Ill. App. 3d 355, 384, 344 N.E.2d 239, 261 (1st Dist. 1976).

[227] *See* People v. Prokop, 2 Ill. App. 3d 109, 276 N.E.2d 136 (1st Dist. 1971).

[228] People v. Hamby, 6 Ill. 2d 559, 562, 129 N.E.2d 746, 748 (1955).

[229] People v. Tyner, 40 Ill. 2d 1, 3, 238 N.E.2d 377, 378 (1968).

[230] People v. Jarrett, 263 Ill. App. 3d 364, 366, 636 N.E.2d 62, 64 (4th Dist. 1994) (statements made at the pretrial bond hearing which he later recanted at trial were not part of the same continuous trial and thus amounted to perjury).

[231] People v. Roberts, 54 Ill. App. 3d 506, 508-09, 369 N.E.2d 356, 357-58 (4th Dist. 1977).

§ 14.24.   Subornation of Perjury.

A companion offense of perjury is "subornation of perjury." It provides: "A person commits subornation of perjury when he procures or induces another to make a statement in violation of Section 5/32-2 which the person knows to be false."[232] Subornation of perjury is a felony.[233] Thus, where a defendant knowingly induced a witness against him to lie under oath, this was subornation of perjury.[234] A prerequisite to a conviction for subornation of perjury is the actual commission of perjury by someone other than the defendant.[235]

§ 14.25.   Communicating with Jurors and Witnesses.

Section 5/32-4, which prohibits "communicating with jurors and witnesses," combines into one package several different wrongs that interfere with judicial procedure. Subsection (a) states that any "person who with intent to influence any person whom he believes has been summoned as a juror, regarding any matter which is or may be brought before such juror, *communicates*, directly or indirectly, with such juror otherwise than as authorized by law" commits a felony.[236] Subsection (b) provides that any "person who, with intent to deter any party or witness from testifying freely, fully and truthfully" in any type of judicial or administrative proceeding, (1) *"forcibly detains* such party or witness," (2) *"communicates*, directly or indirectly, to such party or witness any knowingly false information or a threat of injury or damage" to the person or property of the party or witness, or (3) *"offers or delivers money or threatens to withhold money or anything of value"* to the party or witness commits a felony.[237]

§ 14.26.   Harassment of Representatives for a Child, Jurors, Witnesses and Their Family Members.

Another article 5/32 crime is "harassment of representatives for a child, jurors, witnesses and family members of representatives for a child, jurors and witnesses." It states:

> A person, who with intent to harass or annoy one who has served or is serving or who is a family member of a person who has served or is serving (1) as a juror because of the verdict returned by the jury in a pending

---

[232] 720 ILCS 5/32-3 (1999).

[233] 720 ILCS 5/32-3 (1999).

[234] ROLLIN M. PERKINS & RONALD N. BOYCE, CRIMINAL LAW 524-26 (3d ed. 1982).

[235] ROLLIN M. PERKINS & RONALD N. BOYCE, CRIMINAL LAW 524, 525 (3d ed. 1982). *Cf.* People v. Beaston, 55 Ill. App. 3d 203, 371 N.E.2d 131 (2d Dist. 1977) (where not clear witness committed perjury during earlier forgery trial, defendant could not be convicted of subornation of perjury).

[236] 720 ILCS 5/32-4(a) (1999) (emphasis added).

[237] 720 ILCS 5/32-4(b) (1999) (emphasis added).

legal proceeding or the participation of the juror in the verdict or (2) as a witness, or who may be expected to serve as a witness in a pending legal proceeding, because of the testimony or potential testimony or potential testimony of the witness, communicates directly or indirectly with the juror, witness, or family member of a juror or witness in such manner as to produce mental anguish or emotional distress or who conveys a threat of injury or damage to the property or person of any juror, witness, or family member of the juror or witness commits a . . . felony.[238]

Likewise, where a person who, with intent to harass or annoy any individual, or a family member of such individual, where the individual has served or will serve in a representative capacity for a child pursuant to a court order, because of their representative capacity, communicates to such individual or family member in such manner as to produce mental anguish or emotional distress, or who communicates a threat of injury or damage to property to such individual or family member also commits a felony.[239]

Although there is some obvious overlap between this crime and "communicating with jurors and witnesses" in regard to the actus reus of communicating threats to a juror or witness, this offense is distinguishable because of the mens rea and actus reus which address a defendant's deliberate efforts to "harass or annoy." In other words, it is one thing to attempt to influence a juror or witness; it is another to harass or annoy the person. Thus, where the defendant, a deputy sheriff, screamed threats and spit at a city police officer because of her testimony in another case in which she had disclosed the defendant's affair with a third party, the defendant was found to have the requisite specific intent to harass and annoy in a manner sufficient to produce mental anguish and emotional distress.[240]

§ 14.27. Witnesses Accepting Payments Before Judgment or Verdict.

Effective since 1997, a statute prohibits witnesses and potential witnesses from accepting payments before judgment of verdict.[241] The statute provides:

(a) A person who, after the commencement of a criminal prosecution, has been identified in the criminal discovery process as a person who may be called as a witness in a criminal proceeding shall not accept or receive, directly or indirectly, any payment or benefit in consideration for providing information obtained as a result of witnessing an event or occurrence or

---

[238] 720 ILCS 5/32-4a(a) (1999).
[239] 720 ILCS 5/32-4a(b) (1999).
[240] People v. Calvert, 258 Ill. App. 3d 504, 508, 629 N.E.2d 1154, 1157 (5th Dist. 1994).
[241] 720 ILCS 5/32-4c (1999).

having personal knowledge of certain facts in relation to the criminal proceeding.

(b) A violation of this Section is a . . . misdemeanor.[242]

This prohibition does not apply to the lawful compensation of those who are traditionally compensated for their testimony and information, including expert witnesses, investigators, employees, informants, the media, or agents of a prosecutor, law enforcement agency, or an attorney employed to represent a person in a criminal matter.[243]

§ 14.28. Jury Commissioner Bribery.

In Illinois, it is illegal for a jury commissioner to solicit or receive any valuable consideration in exchange for excusing a prospective juror from jury service.[244] Specifically, the statute prohibits a jury commissioner, or anyone acting on his or her behalf, from requesting, soliciting, suggesting, or accepting financial compensation or any other form of consideration for a promise to excuse, or for excusing any person from jury duty.[245] This offense is a felony.[246]

§ 14.29. False Personation of Attorney, Judicial or Governmental Officials.

Section 5/32-5 outlaws the "false personation of attorney, judicial or governmental officials." This offense states: "A person who falsely represents himself or herself to be an attorney authorized to practice law for purposes of compensation or consideration commits a . . . felony."[247] Also, it provides: "A person who falsely represents himself or herself to be a public officer or public employee commits a . . . misdemeanor."[248] The false representation itself constitutes the offense; it is not necessary that it be done for the purpose of gain or benefit or that there be proof that anything of value was received.[249] Thus, if a person were to falsely hold himself or herself out to be an attorney, those acts could be a violation of this law.[250]

---

[242] 720 ILCS 5/32-4c (1999).

[243] 720 ILCS 5/32-4c(d) (1999).

[244] 720 ILCS 5/32-4b (1999).

[245] 720 ILCS 5/32-4b (1999).

[246] 720 ILCS 5/32-4b (1999).

[247] 720 ILCS 5/32-5(a) (1999).

[248] 720 ILCS 5/32-5(b) (1999).

[249] ILL. ANN. STAT. ch. 38, para. 32-5 (Smith-Hurd 1977), 1961 Committee Comments, at 357 (revised 1970).

[250] *See* People v. Peters, 10 Ill. 2d 577, 581, 141 N.E.2d 9, 11 (1957) (a person "holding himself out" as or "representing" himself to be an attorney at law violates statute).

§ 14.30.   False Personation of a Peace Officer.

Section 5/32-5.1 prohibits the "false personation of a peace officer."[251] It reads: "A person who knowingly and falsely represents himself to be a peace officer of any jurisdiction commits a . . . felony.[252] This offense occurs where defendant represents himself to be a peace officer of a fictitious or an actual legally existing jurisdiction.[253]

§ 14.31.   Aggravated False Personation of a Peace Officer.

Section 5/32-5.2 creates the offense of "aggravated false personation of a peace officer."[254] It provides: "A person who knowingly and falsely represents himself to be a peace officer of any jurisdiction in attempting or committing a felony commits a . . . felony.[255]

§ 14.32.   False Personation of a Parent or Legal Guardian.

Section 5/32-5.3 creates the offense of "false personation of a parent or legal guardian."[256] It provides: "A person who falsely represent himself or herself to be the parent, legal guardian, or other relation of a minor child to any public official, public employee, or elementary or secondary school employee or administrator commits a . . . misdemeanor."[257]

§ 14.33.   Performance of Unauthorized Acts.

Whenever any person, "knowing that his performance is not authorized by law," either (1) conducts a marriage ceremony, (2) acknowledges the execution of any document that by law may be recorded, or (3) becomes a surety for any party in any civil or criminal proceeding before any court or public officer authorized to accept the surety commits a felony.[258] This crime is called, rather simplistically, "performance of unauthorized acts."[259]

---

[251] 720 ILCS 5/32-5.1 (1999).

[252] 720 ILCS 5/32-5.1 (1999).

[253] People v. Ellis, 296 Ill. App. 3d 862, 846-66, 696 N.E.2d 1, 2-3 (1st Dist. 1998) (defendant represented he was a member of the "Beta Christian University Territorial Security Police," a fictitious organization).

[254] 720 ILCS 5/32-5.2 (1999).

[255] 720 ILCS 5/32-5.2 (1999).

[256] 720 ILCS 5/32-5.3 (1999).

[257] 720 ILCS 5/32-5.3 (1999).

[258] 720 ILCS 5/32-6 (1999).

[259] 720 ILCS 5/32-6 (1999).

§ 14.34. Simulating Legal Process.

Another offense that interferes with judicial procedures is "simulating legal process." This statute provides that "a person who issues or delivers any document which he knows falsely purports to be or simulates any civil or criminal process commits a . . . misdemeanor."[260]

§ 14.35. Tampering with Public Records.

Section 5/32-8 outlaws as a felony "tampering with public records." This proscription covers "[a] person who knowingly and without lawful authority alters, destroys, defaces, removes or conceals any public record. . . ."[261] It is noteworthy to mention that stealing public records would constitute "theft."[262] Also, if the tampered records belonged to, for instance, a municipality, this could still be the basis of a conviction under this section,[263] notwithstanding its inclusion in the article that is denoted "interference with judicial procedure."

§ 14.36. Tampering with Public Notice.

"Tampering with public notice" is also illegal in Illinois. Section 5/32-9 defines this proscription as follows: "A person who knowingly and without lawful authority alters, destroys, defaces, removes or conceals any public notice, posted according to law, during the time for which the notice was to remain posted, commits a petty offense."[264] Under this statute, it would be a violation of law, for instance, to tear down a notice of a tax sale before the date of the sale.[265]

§ 14.37. Violation of Bail Bond.

Section 5/32-10 covers the important crime of "violation of bail bond." It reads:

> (a) Whoever, having been admitted to bail for appearance before any court of this State, incurs a forfeiture of the bail and willfully fails to surrender himself within 30 days following the date of such forfeiture, commits, if the bail was given in connection with a charge of felony or pending appeal or certiorari after conviction of any offense, a felony of the next lower Class or a Class A misdemeanor if the underlying offense was a Class 4 felony; or, if the bail was given in connection with a charge of committing

---

[260] 720 ILCS 5/32-7 (1999).

[261] 720 ILCS 5/32-8 (1999).

[262] ILL. ANN. STAT. ch. 38, para. 32-8 (Smith-Hurd 1977), 1961 Committee Comments, at 362 (revised 1970).

[263] Ill. Op. Att'y Gen. 82-054 (1982).

[264] 720 ILCS 5/32-9 (1999).

[265] Faulds v. People, 66 Ill. 210 (1872).

a misdemeanor, or for appearance as a witness, commits a misdemeanor of the next lower Class, but not less than a Class C misdemeanor.

(a-5) Any person who violates a condition of bail bond by possessing a firearm in violation of his or her conditions of bail commits a . . . felony.

(b) Whoever, having been admitted to bail for appearance before any court of this State, while charged with a criminal offense in which the victim is a family or household member . . . knowingly violates a condition of that release as set forth in [725 ILCS 5/110-10(d)] . . ., commits a . . . misdemeanor.

(c) Whoever, having been admitted to bail for appearance before any court of this State for a felony, Class A misdemeanor or a criminal offense in which the victim is a family or household member . . . is charged with any other felony, Class A misdemeanor, or a criminal offense in which the victim is a family or household member . . . while on such release, must appear before the court before bail is statutorily set.

(d) Nothing in this section shall interfere with or prevent the exercise by any court of its power to punishment for contempt. Any sentence imposed for violation of this Section shall be served consecutive to the sentence imposed for the charge for which bail had been granted and with respect to which the defendant has been convicted.[266]

This enactment conditions a finding of criminal liability on a finding that the defendant (1) incurred a forfeiture of bail and (2) willfully failed to surrender himself or herself to a court within 30 days of the date of the forfeiture.[267] It should also be understood to apply to defendants who are released on their own recognizance and who willfully fail to appear in court in contravention of a court's directive.[268] However, the forfeiture of a bail bond or failure to appear following release on personal recognizance does not alone constitute a violation of this paragraph[269] unless there later occurs the willful failure to surrender to the court within 30 days. However, a defendant's failure to comply with a condition of his or her release on bail or personal recognizance will provide a basis for an immediate issuance of a warrant to arrest the defendant,[270] the incarceration of the defendant pending a hearing in the alleged breach of the condition of his or her release,[271] a hearing to determine if the conditions of the defendant's

---

[266] 720 ILCS 5/32-10 (1999).

[267] People v. Ratliff, 65 Ill. 2d 314, 317-18, 357 N.E.2d 1172, 1175 (1976); People v. Albarran, 40 Ill. App. 3d 344, 346, 352 N.E.2d 379, 381 (1st Dist. 1976).

[268] 725 ILCS 5/110-2 (1999).

[269] People v. Turner, 57 Ill. App. 3d 62, 65-66, 372 N.E.2d 1089, 1092 (1st Dist. 1978) (bail bond).

[270] 725 ILCS 5/110-3 (1999).

[271] 725 ILCS 5/110-6(f)(1) (1999) (assuming the alleged violation was a felony).

release shall be modified,[272] and, if circumstances warrant, a revocation of the court's original order to release the defendant from custody.[273] In other words, these *procedural* possibilities that follow a breach of conditions of release on bail or recognizance are separate and distinct from the offense described here.

Although violation of any of the conditions of bail bond release, such as leaving the state without the court's permission[274] or violating the criminal statutes of any jurisdiction,[275] may constitute grounds for returning the defendant to custody, the *criminal sanctions* of section 5/32-10 arise only when the defendant intentionally avoids his or her *required appearance* at trial or sentence.[276] If the defendant fails to appear, for instance, at a hearing on a motion for a new trial in circumstances where the defendant's appearance has not been compelled by a court order, then there is no basis for convicting the defendant under this statute.[277]

In enacting this crime, which is often referred to as "bail jumping,"[278] the legislature "intended to create a separate offense for violation of conditions of bail bond apart from the initial offense for which the bond was issued."[279] Thus, where the underlying charge is later determined to be invalid[280] or declared unconstitutional,[281] the willful failure to surrender within thirty days and face the charge is still a criminal act.[282]

Where a defendant is simultaneously charged with two separate offenses and released on bail, the defendant's failure to appear in violation of a court order will constitute two counts of bail jumping.[283] Accordingly, where the defendant was charged with unlawful use of weapons and unlawful possession of a firearm, his willful failure to surrender himself to the authorities constituted two separate bail jumping charges even though both were based on a single course of conduct.[284]

Finally, an innocent or excusable failure to surrender is not punishable.[285] Thus, a defendant's inability to be in court because he or she is in custody else-

---

[272] 725 ILCS 5/110-6(a) (1999).

[273] 725 ILCS 5/110-6(b); 5/110-6(f)(3) (1999).

[274] 725 ILCS 5/110-10(a)(3) (1999).

[275] 725 ILCS 5/110-10(a)(4) (1999).

[276] ILL. ANN. STAT. ch. 38, para. 32-10 (Smith-Hurd 1977), 1961 Committee Comments, at 365 (revised 1970); People v. Arron, 15 Ill. App. 3d 645, 648, 305 N.E.2d 1, 4 (1st Dist. 1973).

[277] People v. Cox, 74 Ill. App. 2d 348, 351, 220 N.E.2d 10, 12 (4th Dist. 1966).

[278] People v. Albarran, 40 Ill. App. 3d 344, 345, 352 N.E.2d 379, 382 (1st Dist. 1976).

[279] People v. Minefee, 14 Ill. App. 3d 796, 797, 303 N.E.2d 591, 592 (1st Dist. 1973).

[280] People v. Tompkins, 26 Ill. App. 3d 322, 324, 325 N.E.2d 83, 84 (4th Dist. 1975).

[281] People v. Arnone, 15 Ill. App. 3d 278, 279, 304 N.E.2d 95, 96 (2d Dist. 1973).

[282] People v. Arnone, 15 Ill. App. 3d 278, 279, 304 N.E.2d 95, 96 (2d Dist. 1973).

[283] People v. Albarran, 40 Ill. App. 3d 344, 347, 352 N.E.2d 379, 382 (1st Dist. 1976).

[284] People v. Albarran, 40 Ill. App. 3d 344, 347, 352 N.E.2d 379, 382 (1st Dist. 1976).

[285] People v. Lynn, 89 Ill. App. 3d 712, 714, 412 N.E.2d 15, 18 (2d Dist. 1980).

where obviously cannot amount to bail jumping.[286] However, a defendant's failure to appear is willful and not excused where the defendant claims that he or she feared he or she would be harmed if incarcerated.[287]

§ 14.38.   Barratry.

A person commits "barratry" when he or she "wickedly and willfully excites and stirs up actions or quarrels between the people of this State with a view to promote strife and contention."[288] This offense is considered a petty offense.[289] If the offender is an attorney, he or she shall be suspended for a period not exceeding 6 months.[290]

§ 14.39.   Maintenance.

A person commits "maintenance" if he or she "officiously intermeddles" in an action not pertaining to that person by maintaining or assisting either party to such action, with money, to prosecute or defend the action, with a view toward promoting litigation.[291] This offense is considered a petty offense.[292] However, it is not considered maintenance for a person to assist a relative, servant or a poor person out of charity.[293]

§ 14.40.   Unlawful Clouding of Title.

A person who "intentionally records or files or causes to be recorded or filed any document in the office of the recorder or registrar of titles of any county in this State that is a cloud on title of land in this State," who knows that the theory of clouding is not legitimate, is guilty of "unlawful clouding of title."[294] This is punishable as a misdemeanor.[295] In addition to the sentence imposed, the court shall order the person convicted to execute a release of the purported cloud of title.[296] This section does not apply to attorneys who in good faith file a lien on behalf of a client and believe that the lien is valid according to statutory law, a decision of a court of law, or by a good faith argument for an extension, modifi-

---

[286] People v. Ratliff, 65 Ill. 2d 314, 319-20, 357 N.E.2d 1172, 1175-76 (1976).

[287] People v. Turner, 57 Ill. App. 3d 62, 66, 372 N.E.2d 1089, 1092 (1st Dist. 1978).

[288] 720 ILCS 5/32-11 (1999).

[289] 720 ILCS 5/32-11 (1999).

[290] 720 ILCS 5/32-11 (1999).

[291] 720 ILCS 5/32-11 (1999).

[292] 720 ILCS 5/32-12 (1999).

[293] 720 ILCS 5/32-12 (1999).

[294] 720 ILCS 5/32-13(a) (1999).

[295] 720 ILCS 5/32-13(b) (1999).

[296] 720 ILCS 5/32-13(c) (1999).

cation, or reversal of existing court decision that relates to the lien and its validity.[297]

§ 14.41.   Bribery.

Article 5/33 is directed at various forms of "official misconduct."[298] The first of these offenses appearing in the Criminal Code is the crime of "bribery."[299] Section 5/33-1 provides:

> A person commits bribery when: (a) With intent to influence the performance of any act related to the employment or function of any public officer, public employee, juror or witness, he promises or tenders to that person any property or personal advantage which he is not authorized by law to accept; or
>
> (b) With intent to influence the performance of any act related to the employment or function of any public officer, public employee, juror or witness, he promises or tenders to one whom he believes to be a public officer, public employee, juror or witness, any property or personal advantage which a public officer, public employee, juror or witness would not be authorized by law to accept; or
>
> (c) With intent to cause any person to influence the performance of any act related to the employment or function of any public officer, public employee, juror or witness, he promises or tenders to that person any property or personal advantage which he is not authorized by law to accept; or
>
> (d) He receives, retains or agrees to accept any property or personal advantage which he is not authorized by law to accept knowing that such property or personal advantage was promised or tendered with intent to cause him to influence the performance of any act related to the employment or function of any public officer, public employee, juror or witness; or
>
> (e) He solicits, receives, retains, or agrees to accept any property or personal advantage pursuant to an understanding that he shall improperly influence or attempt to influence the performance of any act related to the employment or function of any public officer, public employee, juror or witness.
>
> (f) Sentence. Bribery is a . . . felony.[300]

The revision committee's comments clarify that (1) subsection (a) was intended to proscribe the promise or tender directed to the person sought to be influenced; (2) subsection (b) was designed to cover the situation where the

---

[297] 720 ILCS 5/32-13(c-5) (1999).

[298] 720 ILCS 5/33 (1999).

[299] 720 ILCS 5/33-1 (1999).

[300] 720 ILCS 5/33-1 (1999).

promise or tender was directed toward an individual *believed* to have some official capacity; (3) subsection (c) is aimed at the tender or promise to the individual who has no official capacity but where it is intended that that individual attempt to influence a third party who has such a capacity; (4) subsection (d) prohibits the acceptance of a bribe offer by *anyone*, whether in fact a public official or the like, a person who pretends to be such an official, or a person who admits to having no official capacity but who suggests he or she will influence a third party who has such capacity; and (5) subsection (e) punishes the solicitation of a bribe.[301] Thus, it is apparent that subsections (a), (b), and (c) were created to penalize the briber, while subsections (d) and (e) were directed at the person who receives or solicits a bribe.

§ 14.42.   — Intent to Influence the Performance of an Official Act.

The Illinois bribery statute requires that the accused had the intent to influence the performance of an act related to the employment of a public officer, public employee, or the like.[302] The mere offer or acceptance of a gratuity, fee, or award without more is not criminal.[303] Thus, where a defendant police officer received money from an ambulance driver, but where there was no evidence that the defendant accepted it in his official capacity or accepted it for the performance of any act, such as causing the driver's ambulance to be summoned, there was no bribery.[304] On the other hand, the courts will infer an "intent to influence" from a defendant's conduct[305] or statements.[306] Thus, where a defendant-arrestee pushed money toward an officer following his arrest for possession of a controlled substance, this supported his intent to bribe.[307] Similarly, where a defendant-arrestee, while being booked at a police station for disorderly conduct and unlawful use of a weapon said, "I'm married. I have a baby. I'll give you one hundred dollars. You let me go. You keep the gun and give me a chance," this was clear evidence of his intent to influence the officers in question.[308]

Under this section, no particular act need be contemplated by the offerer or offeree.[309] "There is bribery if the offer is made [to a public official] with intent that the offeree act favorably to the offerer when necessary."[310]

---

[301] ILL. ANN. STAT. ch. 38, para. 33-1 (Smith-Hurd 1977), 1961 Committee Comments, at 370 (revised 1970) (emphasis added).

[302] People v. Gokey, 57 Ill. 2d 433, 438, 312 N.E.2d 637, 640 (1974).

[303] People v. Jordan, 15 Ill. App. 3d 672, 675, 304 N.E.2d 713, 716 (1st Dist. 1973) (receipt of property alone does not constitute bribery).

[304] People v. Jordan, 15 Ill. App. 3d 672, 675, 304 N.E.2d 713, 716 (1st Dist. 1973).

[305] People v. Evans, 80 Ill. App. 3d 87, 92-93, 398 N.E.2d 1219, 1223-24 (1st Dist. 1979).

[306] People v. Lugo, 39 Ill. App. 3d 472, 474, 349 N.E.2d 697, 699 (1st Dist. 1976).

[307] People v. Evans, 80 Ill. App. 3d 87, 92-93, 398 N.E.2d 1219, 1223-24 (1st Dist. 1979).

[308] People v. Lugo, 39 Ill. App. 3d 472, 473, 349 N.E.2d 697, 698-99 (1st Dist. 1976).

[309] United States v. Isaacs, 493 F.2d 1124, 1145 (7th Cir.), *cert. denied*, 417 U.S. 976 (1974).

If either the offerer or offeree harbors the wrongful intent, there is bribery; mutual illegal intent is not required.[311] Where a payment was made to a defendant-police officer pursuant to a previous arrangement with police authorities for the sole purpose of apprehending the defendant-officer in an illegal act, the defendant-officer was properly convicted of accepting a bribe notwithstanding the offerer's legal motive.[312]

§ 14.43. — Promises or Tenders.

In order to satisfy the "promise or tender" language of section 5/22-1, a mere offer or promise with the requisite intent is all that is required to convict a person of making a bribe.[313] It is not required that the offeree actually accept the bribe offer[314] or actually perform some unauthorized act.[315] Also, the legislature intended the word *tender* to be interpreted in a sense much broader than its usage in contractual law and to include offers made even though the offerer does not have in his or her possession the money offered.[316]

§ 14.44. — Property or Personal Advantage Not Authorized by Law.

The crime of bribery requires that the consideration offered to, or solicited or accepted by, the public official, juror, or witness by unauthorized by law.[317] In *People v. Brandstetter*,[318] the "not authorized by law" language was at issue where the defendant, a proponent of the Equal Rights Amendment (ERA) to the federal Constitution, handed an Illinois state representative a note on which was handwritten: "Mr. Swanstrom the offer for help in your election and $1000 for your campaign for Pro ERA vote." After being convicted of bribery, the defendant appealed. The appellate court stated that a public official is "authorized by law" to receive campaign contributions from those who might seek to influence his or her performance as long as no promise for or performance of a specific official act is given in exchange.[319] The court also stated that the bribery statute does not prohibit a prospective campaign worker from offering a candidate for

---

[310] United States v. Isaacs, 493 F.2d 1124, 1145 (7th Cir.), *cert. denied*, 417 U.S. 976 (1974).

[311] People v. Lyons, 4 Ill. 2d 396, 399, 122 N.E.2d 809, 812 (1954).

[312] People v. Lyons, 4 Ill. 2d 396, 399, 122 N.E.2d 809, 812 (1954).

[313] People v. Wallace, 57 Ill. 2d 285, 290, 312 N.E.2d 263, 266 (1974).

[314] *See, e.g.,* People v. Evans, 80 Ill. App. 3d 87, 92, 398 N.E.2d 1219, 1223 (1st Dist. 1979).

[315] People v. Herron, 76 Ill. App. 3d 437, 440-41, 395 N.E.2d 169, 171 (1st Dist. 1979).

[316] People v. Brandstetter, 103 Ill. App. 3d 259, 269, 430 N.E.2d 731, 739 (4th Dist.), *cert. denied*, 459 U.S. 988 (1982).

[317] People v. Thoms, 30 Ill. App. 3d 229, 232-33, 332 N.E.2d 538, 541-42 (1st Dist. 1975), *cert. denied*, 424 U.S. 968 (1976).

[318] 103 Ill. App. 3d 259, 430 N.E.2d 731 (4th Dist.), *cert. denied*, 459 U.S. 988 (1982).

[319] People v. Brandstetter, 103 Ill. App. 3d 259, 266, 430 N.E.2d 731, 736 (4th Dist.), *cert. denied*, 459 U.S. 988 (1982).

election or reelection certain campaign services even if the worker intends to influence the candidate's performance of his or her duties as long as the candidate neither promises to perform nor performs a specific official act in consideration of the offer.[320] However, the court stated that the offer or acceptance of property to influence a representative or candidate to vote a particular way on a particular issue in consideration for the property is *not* authorized by law.[321] Since the defendant admitted that the offer of the $1,000 was contingent on the representative's vote in favor of ERA, she had made a "tender" in violation of the state bribery statute.[322]

§ 14.45.   — Offering or Tendering a Bribe.

The caselaw has upheld the making of a bribe offer in a variety of circumstances. Where a defendant, a salvage yard employee, said to police that he would consider providing them with information regarding other "chop shops" in the area, as well as with money payments, in exchange for having the police leave his yard alone, this amounted to bribery of the police.[323] Where defendants who had been arrested offered money to officers who were transporting the defendants to the police station in return for their release, this could amount to bribery.[324] Where a defendant offered a police officer five dollars to forget about towing the defendant's automobile, which had been parked illegally, this was bribery.[325] Where a defendant offer to pay $25 to a witness if the witness dropped charges against defendant's wife, this amounted to bribery.[326]

§ 14.46.   — Soliciting or Accepting a Bribe.

Just as the making of a bribe *to* a public official, juror, or witness is prohibited by section 5/33-1, the solicitation or receipt of a bribe *by* a public official, juror, or witness is proscribed thereby. Where the defendant, a court clerk, solicited $20 for advancement of a case on the court's calendar, this was bribery.[327] Where a defendant-juror made a proposal to a party to an action in which he was a juror that involved an exchange of money for his influence in the jury's delib-

---

[320] People v. Brandstetter, 103 Ill. App. 3d 259, 266, 430 N.E.2d 731, 736 (4th Dist.), *cert. denied*, 459 U.S. 988 (1982).

[321] People v. Brandstetter, 103 Ill. App. 3d 259, 266-269, 430 N.E.2d 731, 736-738 (4th Dist.), *cert. denied*, 459 U.S. 988 (1982).

[322] People v. Brandstetter, 103 Ill. App. 3d 259, 268-269, 430 N.E.2d 731, 738-739 (4th Dist.), *cert. denied*, 459 U.S. 988 (1982).

[323] People v. Senez, 80 Ill. App. 3d 1021, 1023, 400 N.E.2d 928, 930 (2d Dist. 1980).

[324] People v. Wallace, 57 Ill. 2d 285, 290, 312 N.E.2d 263, 266 (1974) (attempted bribery conviction affirmed).

[325] People v. Davis, 130 Ill. App. 2d 1047, 1050, 268 N.E.2d 179, 181 (1st Dist. 1971).

[326] People v. Jackson, 231 Ill. App. 3d 801, 805, 596 N.E.2d 1251, 1253 (4th Dist. 1993).

[327] People v. Herron, 76 Ill. App. 3d 437, 440, 395 N.E.2d 169, 171 (1st Dist. 1979).

erations, there was bribery.[328] Where the defendants, who were deputy sheriffs, questioned some persons and told them they could not "let them go for nothing" and, thereafter, one of the persons gave the defendants $20, this amounted to bribery.[329] Where a defendant, a parole officer, took money from a parolee to refrain from reporting the parolee's violation of the conditions of his parole, this constituted bribery.[330] Where a defendant, a member of a city planning commission agreed to recommend to other members of the zoning commission that a particular area be rezoned for the benefit of certain developers in exchange for $5,000, this was bribery.[331] Where a defendant-police officer solicited and received a bribe in consideration for not filing a complaint charging a physician with unlawfully prescribing a dangerous drug, this was violative of section 5/33-1.[332] Where a defendant, a member of a board of education, accepted a bribe from an applicant for a position as a schoolteacher, he was properly convicted.[333] Finally, where a township supervisor accepted money that was tendered in order to influence his official acts as liquor commissioner, this was bribery.[334]

A defense often used to challenge a charge of soliciting or aiding a bribe is entrapment.[335] For a discussion of this defense, *see* Chapter 19.

§ 14.47. Failure to Report a Bribe.

Section 5/33-2 imposes a "positive duty" on public officers, employees, and jurors to report a bribe offer.[336] A breach of that duty amounts to a crime called "failure to report a bribe."[337] It reads: "Any public officer, public employee or juror who fails to report forthwith to the local State's Attorney, or in the case of a State employee to the Department of State Police, any offer made to him in violation of Section [5/33-1] commits a . . . misdemeanor."[338] In addition to this

---

[328] People v. Harris, 66 Ill. App. 2d 46, 51-52, 213 N.E.2d 588, 591 (5th Dist. 1966).

[329] People v. Clemons, 26 Ill. 2d 481, 483, 187 N.E.2d 260, 261 (1962).

[330] People v. Patillo, 386 Ill. 566, 575-76, 54 N.E.2d 548, 553 (1944).

[331] People v. Drish, 24 Ill. App. 3d 225, 227, 321 N.E.2d 179, 181 (4th Dist. 1974).

[332] People v. Fleming, 50 Ill. 2d 141, 142, 277 N.E.2d 872, 873-74 (1971). *See also* People v. Muersch, 4 Ill. App. 3d 1003, 1007, 282 N.E.2d 767, 770 (1st Dist. 1972) (bribery was found where police solicited and accepted money from person in return for police refraining from notifying person's father that person was speeding); People v. Gralewski, 132 Ill. App. 2d 755, 757, 270 N.E.2d 566, 567 (1st Dist. 1971) (officer took money from person to whom he had issued traffic ticket under agreement to influence disposition of case).

[333] People v. Holub, 382 Ill. 571, 573, 48 N.E.2d 379, 380 (1943).

[334] People ex rel. Ryan v. Coles, 64 Ill. App. 3d 807, 813, 381 N.E.2d 990, 995 (2d Dist. 1978).

[335] *See, e.g.,* People v. Gillespie, 136 Ill. 2d 496, 557 N.E.2d 894 (1990).

[336] ILL. ANN. STAT. ch. 38, para. 33-2 (Smith-Hurd 1977), 1961 Committee Comments, at 380 (revised 1970).

[337] 720 ILCS 5/33-2 (1999).

[338] 720 ILCS 5/33-2 (1999).

language, this section states that a copy of any such report made to the Department of State Police shall be forwarded to the appropriate State's Attorney.[339]

§ 14.48. Official Misconduct.

Another article 5/33 crime is "official misconduct." It provides:

> A public officer or employee commits misconduct when, in his official capacity, he commits any of the following acts: (a) Intentionally or recklessly fails to perform any mandatory duty as required by law; or (b) Knowingly performs an act which he knows he is forbidden by law to perform; or (c) With intent to obtain a personal advantage for himself or another, he performs an act in excess of his lawful authority; or (d) Solicits or knowingly accepts for the performance of any act a fee or reward which he knows is not authorized by law. A public officer or employee convicted of violating any provision in this Section forfeits his office or employment. In addition, he commits a . . . felony."[340]

A person only commits this offense if he or she engaged in the proscribed acts in his or her "official capacity." Thus, where a janitor in a veteran's home engaged in financial transactions with a resident in the home contrary to the terms of his employment, there was no official misconduct because defendant had no official capacity in his position as a janitor.[341] "Official capacity," within the meaning of the official misconduct statute, exists only if a government employee had some official position that could be exploited in some fashion to the detriment of the public good.[342] As the face of this enactment reflects, there are four different types of wrongdoing that fall within the ambits of this statute. These four bases for criminal liability will be explored individually.

§ 14.49. — Intentionally or Recklessly Fails to Perform Any Mandatory Duty.

Subsection (a) is couched in terms of a legal duty, the breach of which constitutes a crime. It outlaws the intentional or reckless failure by a public official or public employee in his or her official capacity to perform any mandatory duty as required by law. Possible examples of violations of this subsection are the following: a court clerk's failure to report to the secretary of state the drunk-driving conviction of a particular person as required by law,[343] a city commissioner's

---

[339] 720 ILCS 5/33-2 (1999).

[340] 720 ILCS 5/33-3 (1999).

[341] People v. Gray, 221 Ill. App. 3d 677, 681-85, 583 N.E.2d 109, 111-14 (4th Dist. 1991).

[342] People v. Gray, 221 Ill. App. 3d 677, 681-85, 583 N.E.2d 109, 111-14 (4th Dist. 1991).

[343] People v. Gill, 30 Ill. App. 2d 32, 50-51, 173 N.E.2d 568, 577 (1st Dist. 1961) (indictment reinstated). *Accord* People v. Reiner, 6 Ill. 2d 337, 345, 129 N.E.2d 159, 163 (1955) (magistrate's

failure to deposit a check belonging to the city in the city treasury as required by law,[344] and the failure of a sheriff to turn over to the county treasurer certain funds that had been appropriated but not used by the sheriff.[345]

§ 14.50. — Knowingly Performing an Act Forbidden by Law.

Subsection (b) prohibits the knowing performance by a public official or employee of an act that is "forbidden by law." Since this subsection does not delineate any specific criminal conduct, it is essential to consult other provisions of the law to determine what is forbidden by law.[346] Obviously, any charging instrument alleging that a public official or employee has knowingly engaged in activity forbidden by law must spell out which statute, rule, or regulation has in fact been breached.[347]

The rulings dealing with this offense reflect various wrongs that might fall into this category. They include a city planning commissioner's acceptance of a bribe,[348] a police chief's release of an offender without bond where he had no legal authority to do so,[349] a county hospital employee's acceptance of compensation for overtime work that he did not perform,[350] a city building inspector's false report that certain code violations in a particular building had been corrected,[351] and a township highway commissioner's directions to a township employee to perform maintenance work on his personal automobile.[352]

§ 14.51. — Performs an Act in Excess of Lawful Authority with Intent to Obtain Personal Advantage.

Subsection (c) of the official misconduct law prohibits the performance of any act by a public official or employee in excess of lawful authority with intent to obtain a personal advantage for himself or herself or another. The offense of official misconduct was designed to reach those situations in which a public of-

---

failure to report drunk-driving conviction to state could have amounted to violation of law; indictments reinstated).

[344] People v. Hughey, 382 Ill. 136, 138, 47 N.E.2d 77, 79 (1943) (conviction of omission of duty reversed on other grounds).

[345] People v. Cornille, 136 Ill. App. 3d 1011, 1016-17, 484 N.E.2d 301, 306 (5th Dist. 1985).

[346] People v. Adams, 64 Ill. App. 3d 547, 549, 381 N.E.2d 738, 740 (5th Dist. 1978).

[347] People v. Adams, 64 Ill. App. 3d 547, 549, 381 N.E.2d 738, 740 (5th Dist. 1978).

[348] People v. Drish, 24 Ill. App. 3d 225, 227, 321 N.E.2d 179, 182-83 (4th Dist. 1974).

[349] People v. Thoms, 50 Ill. App. 3d 398, 403, 365 N.E.2d 717, 720 (1st Dist. 1977).

[350] People v. Nickson, 58 Ill. App. 3d 470, 476, 374 N.E.2d 804, 808-10 (1st Dist. 1978) (official misconduct conviction vacated since it arose out of same physical act as conspiracy to commit theft).

[351] People v. McGreal, 4 Ill. App. 3d 312, 317-18, 278 N.E.2d 504, 508-09 (1st Dist. 1971) (reinstatement of indictment).

[352] People v. Mehelic, 152 Ill. App. 3d 843, 848-49, 504 N.E.2d 1310, 1314-15 (5th Dist. 1987).

ficial or employee has in some fashion exploited his or her official position to the detriment of the public good.[353] It must be proved that the public official or employee's conduct that was in excess of his or her lawful authority was carried out with the objective of serving his or her personal advantage, as opposed to the advantage of the public he or she is supposed to serve.[354] Thus, where a mayor purchased a confiscated weapon from the city police department, which gun was supposed to be kept or destroyed by the governmental body that seized it, this amounted to official misconduct.[355] Where a police officer accepted money from a tow truck owner in exchange for refraining from issuing a traffic ticket to the driver of the tow truck, this was official misconduct.[356] Where certain driver's license examiners took money from unqualified applicants for a license and thereafter gave these applicants a license, this amounted to official misconduct.[357] Where a police officer solicited a fee to have certain charges lodged against another dismissed when they came up for hearing, this was official misconduct.[358] Where a township tax collector withheld tax funds from the taxing body and appropriated these funds to his own use, this constituted official misconduct.[359] Where a deputy patrol sergeant used a police computer information system to determine whether potential prostitution clients were undercover police officers in order to facilitate the prostitution in which he intended to engage, this was official misconduct.[360] Where a probation officer engaged in sexual activity with probationers he was monitoring, this constituted official misconduct.[361]

§ 14.52.   — Solicits or Knowingly Accepts a Fee or Reward.

A public official or employee's solicitation or acceptance of a fee or reward for acts done in his or her official capacity is at odds with the public policy of the state. Where a sheriff accepted a reward for the arrest and conviction of a criminal, this was a violation of the law.[362] Where a state driver's license facility employee accepted a gratuity, this was official misconduct.[363]

---

[353] People v. Steinmann, 57 Ill. App. 3d 887, 897, 373 N.E.2d 757, 764 (5th Dist. 1978).

[354] People v. Kleffman, 90 Ill. App. 3d 1, 4, 412 N.E.2d 1057, 1061 (3d Dist. 1980).

[355] People v. Kleffman, 90 Ill. App. 3d 1, 6, 412 N.E.2d 1057, 1061-1062 (3d Dist. 1980) (reinstatement of indictment).

[356] People v. Bouse, 46 Ill. App. 3d 465, 471-72, 360 N.E.2d 1340, 1344-45 (1st Dist. 1977).

[357] People v. Hunt, 3 Ill. App. 3d 1074, 1076-77, 280 N.E.2d 46, 47-48 (2d Dist. 1972).

[358] People v. Smith, 57 Ill. App. 2d 74, 77, 206 N.E.2d 463, 467 (1st Dist. 1965), cert. denied, 383 U.S. 910 (1966).

[359] People v. Haycraft, 3 Ill. App. 3d 974, 981, 278 N.E.2d 877, 882 (5th Dist. 1972).

[360] People v. Krause, 241 Ill. App. 3d 394, 397, 609 N.E.2d 980, 982 (2d Dist. 1993).

[361] People v. Lewis, 269 Ill. App. 3d 523, 528, 646 N.E.2d 305, 309 (4th Dist. 1994).

[362] Hogan v. Stophlet, 179 Ill. 150, 156, 53 N.E. 604, 606 (1899).

[363] People v. Wright, 105 Ill. App. 3d 187, 192, 434 N.E.2d 26, 29 (2d Dist. 1982).

§ 14.53.   Peace Officer or Correctional Officer Acting in Furtherance of Gang-Related Activity.

A statute, added in 1998, provides that "[i]t is unlawful for a peace officer or correctional officer to knowingly commit any act in furtherance of gang-related activities, except when acting in furtherance of an undercover law enforcement investigation."[364] Violation of this statute is a felony.[365] The State's Streetgang Terrorism Omnibus Prevention Act defines "gang-related activity" as:

> any criminal activity . . . directed by, ordered by, authorized by, consented to, agreed to, requested by, acquiesced in, or ratified by any gang leader . . . (1) with the intent to increase the gang's size, membership, prestige, dominance, or control in any geographical area; or (2) with the intent to provide the gang with any advantage in, or any control or dominance over any criminal market sector . . . or (3) with the intent to exact revenge or retribution for the gang or any member of the gang; or (4) with the intent to obstruct justice, or intimidate or eliminate any witness against the gang or any member of the gang; or (5) with the intent to otherwise directly or indirectly cause any benefit, aggrandizement, gain, profit or other advantage whatsoever to or for the gang, its reputation, influence, or membership.[366]

§ 14.54.   Interference with Public Contracting.

Article 5/33E outlaws various forms of "interference with public contracting."[367] Section 5/33E-3 outlaws "bid rigging," which arises where a defendant enters into an agreement or collusion with a competitor for a public contract that is designed to take advantage of the government.[368] Section 5/33E-4 prohibits "bid rotating," which occurs where a person and a possible competitor enter into a scheme where they rotate bids between each other in order to avoid a truly competitive bidding arrangement on government contracts.[369] Section 5/33E-5 proscribes as illegal a public official's irregular disclosure of the contents of a sealed bid in order to provide a bidder an advantage in the bidding on public contracts.[370] Section 5/33E-6 forbids a public official from interfering with contract submissions and awards in a fashion that would be detrimental to the contracting and awarding process.[371] Section 5/33E-7 is directed against "kick-

---

[364] 720 ILCS 5/33-4(a) (1999).
[365] 720 ILCS 5/33-4(b) (1999).
[366] 740 ILCS 147/10 (1999).
[367] 720 ILCS 5/33E-1 (1999).
[368] 720 ILCS 5/33E-3 (1999).
[369] 720 ILCS 5/33E-4 (1999).
[370] 720 ILCS 5/33E-5 (1999).
[371] 720 ILCS 5/33E-6 (1999).

backs" of any type in the arena of public contracting.[372] Section 5/33E-8 prohibits the bribery of an inspector employed by a contractor involved in any public project.[373] Finally, section 5/33E-9 outlaws a government employee from making any irregular changes in a government contract without proper authority.[374] Each of these offenses are felonies.[375]

§ 14.55.   Legislative Misconduct.

Notwithstanding the consolidation of all of the various crimes discussed above in part E of the Criminal Code of 1961 as amended, which are designated "offenses affecting governmental functions," there are several other crimes that impact on governmental operations that appear outside part E, but which seemingly should have been placed therein. A notable example of a misplaced code provision is that of "legislative misconduct," which appears in article 645 of chapter 720 of the code.[376] It provides: "No member of the General Assembly shall accept or receive, directly or indirectly, any money or other valuable thing, from any corporation, company or person, for any vote or influence he may give or withhold on any bill, resolution or appropriation, or for any other official act."[377] This offense is punishable as a felony.[378]

§ 14.56.   Interference with Public Institution of Higher Education.

Another crime that impacts on governmental functions and that appears outside part E of the code is "interference with public institution of higher education," which appears in article 5/21.2. It reads:

A person commits interference with a public institution of higher education when, on the campus of a public institution of higher education, or at or in any building or other facility owned, operated or controlled by the institution, without authority from the institution he, through force or violence, actual or threatened:
(a) willfully denies to a trustee, employee, student or invitee of the institution: (1) Freedom of movement at such place; or (2) Use of property or facilities of the institution; or (3) The right of ingress or egress to the property or facilities of the institution; or
(b) willfully impedes, obstructs, interferes with or disrupts: (1) the performance of institutional duties by a trustee or employee of the institution;

---

[372] 720 ILCS 5/33E-7 (1999).
[373] 720 ILCS 5/33E-8 (1999).
[374] 720 ILCS 5/33E-9 (1999).
[375] 720 ILCS 5/33E-1 through 5/33F-9 (1999).
[376] 720 ILCS 645/0.01 (1999).
[377] 720 ILCS 645/1 (1999).
[378] 720 ILCS 645/2 (1999).

or (2) the pursuit of educational activities, as determined or prescribed by the institution, by a trustee, employee, student or invitee of the institution; or

(c) knowingly occupies or remains in or at any building, property or other facility owned, operated or controlled by the institution after due notice to depart.[379]

This article, which punishes such interference as a misdemeanor,[380] limits the reach of this offense in two ways. First, it defines a *public institution of higher education* to include only "post-high school education program[s] . . . supported in whole or in part by [the state]."[381] Second, it exempts "lawful assembly of the trustees, employees, students or invitees" of such institutions and their "petition for redress of grievances."[382]

This law took effect in 1969 in response to "unlawful campus disorders across the nation."[383] It has been prosecuted, for instance, where a defendant impeded access or movement of others within the Illinois Union Building, which is on the campus of the University of Illinois, after having been given notice by a peace officer to depart.[384] This statute has been upheld as not violative of individual freedom of expression.[385]

§ 14.57. Violation of Order of Protection.

In 1986, the offense of "violation of an order of protection" was created.[386] Whenever a court issues an order of protection under the Illinois Domestic Violence Act of 1986,[387] the person who violates such an order of protection commits a misdemeanor unless the defendant has a prior conviction for this offense or domestic battery in which case the sanction is a felony.[388] Where the defendant placed between six and twelve calls to his estranged wife on one evening, with defendant claiming he was merely attempting to speak to his children but the wife repeatedly hung up, this did not amount to criminal violation of an order of protection because the defendant did not have a malicious purpose.[389] On

---

[379] 720 ILCS 5/21.2-2 (1999).

[380] 720 ILCS 5/21.2-4 (1999).

[381] 720 ILCS 5/21.2-5 (1999).

[382] 720 ILCS 5/21.2-3 (1999).

[383] 720 ILCS 5/21.2-1 (1999) ("Legislative declaration — Construction").

[384] People v. Witzkowski, 53 Ill. 2d 216, 217, 290 N.E.2d 236, 237 (1972), *appeal dismissed,* 411 U.S. 961 (1973).

[385] People v. Barnett, 7 Ill. App. 3d 185, 190, 287 N.E.2d 247, 250 (1st Dist. 1972).

[386] 720 ILCS 5/12-30 (1999).

[387] 720 ILCS 5/12-30(a) (1999) (referring to 750 ILCS 60/101 *et. seq.* (1999)).

[388] 720 ILCS 5/12-30(d) (1999). Domestic battery appears at 720 ILCS 5/12-3.2 (1999). Domestic battery is discussed in ch. 9 of this treatise.

[389] People v. Karich, 293 Ill. App. 3d 135, 137-39, 687 N.E.2d 1169, 1170-71 (2d Dist. 1997).

the other hand, where a defendant made an unauthorized entry into the home of his ex-wife and battered her, he was convicted of violation of an order of protection, domestic battery and home invasion.[390]

---

[390] People v. Priest, 297 Ill. App. 3d 797, 807, 698 N.E.2d 223, 229 (4th Dist. 1998).

CHAPTER 15

OFFENSES AFFECTING THE PUBLIC HEALTH, SAFETY, AND DECENCY

§ 15.01. Introduction.

Part D of the Criminal Code of 1961 contains a category of proscriptions known as "offenses affecting public health, safety and decency."[1] Included in

---

[1] 720 ILCS 5/24 through 5/29C (1999).

this category are strictures dealing with the unlawful use of weapons[2] and armor piercing bullets,[3] mob action,[4] and disorderly conduct,[5] which were designed to protect public health and safety. Other strictures, such as the statutes dealing with gambling,[6] bribery in athletic contests,[7] commercial bribery,[8] and money laundering[9] were enacted to protect public decency. This chapter will explore the crimes described above, with few exceptions, in the same order in which they appear in the Code.

§ 15.02.   Unlawful Use of Weapons.

The first group of offenses affecting public health, safety and decency are those dealing with "deadly weapons."[10] "Unlawful use of weapons"[11] arises where a person knowingly: (1) sells, manufactures, purchases, possesses or carries any bludgeon, black-jack, slung-shot, sand-club, sand-bag, metal knuckles, throwing star, or any switchblade knife, or ballistic knife;[12] (2) possesses with intent to use the same unlawfully against another, a dagger, dirk, billy, dangerous knife, razor, stiletto, broken bottle or other piece of glass, stun gun or taser or any other dangerous or deadly weapon or instrument of like character;[13] (3) carries on or about his or her person or in any vehicle a tear gas gun projector or bomb or any object containing noxious liquid gas or substance, other than non-lethal noxious gas designed for personal defense carried by a person 18 years of age or older;[14] (4) possesses in any vehicle or concealed on or about his or her person, except when on his or her own land or in his or her own abode or fixed place of business, any pistol, revolver, stun gun or taser or other firearm;[15] (5) sets a spring gun;[16] (6) possesses any device for silencing the report of any fire-

---

[2] 720 ILCS 5/24-1 (1999).

[3] 720 ILCS 5/24-2.1 (1999).

[4] 720 ILCS 5/25-1 (1999).

[5] 720 ILCS 5/26-1 (1999).

[6] 720 ILCS 5/28-1 (1999).

[7] 720 ILCS 5/29-1 through 5/29-3 (1999).

[8] 720 ILCS 5/29A-1 through 5/29A-3 (1999).

[9] 720 ILCS 5/29B-1 (1999).

[10] 720 ILCS 5/24-1 through 5/24-8 (1999).

[11] 720 ILCS 5/24-1 (1999).

[12] 720 ILCS 5/24-1(a)(1) (1999).

[13] 720 ILCS 5/24-1(a)(2) (1999).

[14] 720 ILCS 5/24-1(a)(3) (1999).

[15] 720 ILCS 5/24-1(a)(4) (1999). *See* People v. Laubscher, 183 Ill. 2d 330, 335, 701 N.E.2d 489, 491 (1998) (state bears the burden of establishing beyond a reasonable doubt that the "on his land" exception is inapplicable); People v. Wilson, 29 Ill. App. 3d 1033, 1036, 332 N.E.2d 6, 9 (1st Dist. 1975) (the "on his land or in his abode" exception does not apply to public areas of an apartment building).

[16] 720 ILCS 5/24-1(a)(5) (1999).

arm;[17] (7) sells, manufactures, purchases, possesses or carries a machine gun (a weapon that fires more than one shot without manually reloading by a single function of the trigger), parts designed to convert any weapon into a machine gun, or a sawed-off shotgun (a rifle having one or more barrels less than 16 inches in length, a shotgun having one or more barrels less than 18 inches in length, or a rifle with an entire measure less than 26 inches in length), or any bomb, grenade, or like device (containing over one-quarter ounce of an explosive substance) such as black powder bombs, Molotov cocktails or artillery projectiles;[18] (8) possesses a firearm, stun gun, or taser or other deadly weapon in any place which is licensed to sell intoxicating beverages, or at any public gathering held pursuant to a license issued by a government body or where attendance is charged;[19] (9) possesses in a vehicle or on or about his or her person any pistol, revolver, stun gun, taser, firearm or ballistic knife, when masked in such manner to conceal his or her identity;[20] (10) possesses any stun gun or taser (defined as an electrically charged device capable of firing electric current rendering its victim incapable of normal functioning), pistol, revolver, or other firearm upon any public street or public lands within the limits of a city, village or town, except for the lawful display or commerce in weapons or except when in his or her own abode or fixed place of business;[21] or (11) sells, manufactures or purchases any explosive bullet.[22]

The sentences for each of the unlawful use of weapons violations are outlined in subparagraph (b) of paragraph 5/24-1 of the statute,[23] with additional sentencing variations in subparagraph (c) where such violations occur in a school, college, or university or on the institution's property, in a public park, in a courthouse, on residential property owned, operated or managed by a public housing agency, or on a public road within 1,000 feet of a school, college, or university or the institution's property, a public park, a courthouse,[24] or residential property owned, operated or managed by a public housing agency.[25]

---

[17] 720 ILCS 5/24-1(a)(6) (1999).

[18] 720 ILCS 5/24-1(a)(7) (1999).

[19] 720 ILCS 5/24-1(a)(8) (1999).

[20] 720 ILCS 5/24-1(a)(9) (1999). *See* People v. Martin, 121 Ill. App. 3d 196, 212, 459 N.E.2d 279, 291 (2d Dist. 1984) (where defendant wore tinted glasses and ski hat, this did not satisfy 5/24-1(a)(9)).

[21] 720 ILCS 5/24-1(a)(10) (1999).

[22] 720 ILCS 5/24-1(a)(11) (1999) (defined as the projectile portion of an ammunition cartridge which contains or carries an explosive charge which will explode upon contact with human or animal flesh).

[23] 720 ILCS 5/24-1(b) (1999).

[24] 720 ILCS 5/24-1(c)(2) (1999) (courthouse means any building that is used by the circuit, appellate, or Supreme Court of this state for the conduct of official business).

[25] 720 ILCS 5/24-1(c)(1), (1.5), (2) (1999).

Subparagraph (d) creates a presumption that the presence of any weapon described in subparagraph (a)(7) by one person in an automobile, other than a public bus, is prima facie evidence that all persons in the automobile have possession of the weapon.[26] The presumption has exceptions where (1) the weapon is found on the person of an occupant of the automobile,[27] or (2) where the driver is licensed to operate the automobile for hire in the lawful pursuit of his or her trade, such as a limousine or taxi driver.[28]

Subparagraph (e) exempts from the definition of a ballistic knife,[29] as prohibited in subparagraph (a)(1), crossbows, common or compound bows and underwater spearguns.[30]

§ 15.03.   — Exemptions.

Paragraph 5/24-2 sets out various exemptions from the preceding unlawful use of weapons statute for specific groups of persons.[31] First, the prohibitions dealing with possession of a tear gas gun or bomb,[32] concealment of a firearm in a vehicle or on a person[33] and possession of a weapon in a city, village or town[34] do not apply to (1) peace officers;[35] (2) prison, jail or other detention officials;[36] (3) military officers, while in performance of their official duty;[37] (4) public transportation and utility guards;[38] (5) licensed private security contractors and private detectives;[39] (6) registered security guards;[40] (7) Illinois Legislative Investigating Commission personnel authorized by the Commission to carry weapons;[41] (8) licensed bank guards and the like;[42] (9) armored car guards;[43] (10) fire department investigatory peace officers;[44] (11) investigators of the Office of the State's Attorneys Appellate Prosecutor authorized by the board of

---

[26] 720 ILCS 5/24-1(d) (1999). *See* People v. Hood, 49 Ill. 2d 526, 529, 276 N.E.2d 310, 312 (1971) (statutory presumption not unconstitutional).

[27] 720 ILCS 5/24-1(d)(i) (1999).

[28] 720 ILCS 5/24-1(d)(ii) (1999).

[29] *See* 720 ILCS 5/24-1(a)(1) (1999).

[30] 720 ILCS 5/24-1(e) (1999).

[31] 720 ILCS 5/24-2 (1999).

[32] *See* 720 ILCS 5/24-1(a)(3) (1999).

[33] *See* 720 ILCS 5/24-1(a)(4) (1999).

[34] *See* 720 ILCS 5/24-1(a)(10) (1999).

[35] 720 ILCS 5/24-2(a)(1) (1999).

[36] 720 ILCS 5/24-2(a)(2) (1999).

[37] 720 ILCS 5/24-2(a)(3) (1999).

[38] 720 ILCS 5/24-2(a)(4) (1999).

[39] 720 ILCS 5/24-2(a)(5) (1999).

[40] 720 ILCS 5/24-2(a)(6) (1999).

[41] 720 ILCS 5/24-2(a)(7) (1999).

[42] 720 ILCS 5/24-2(a)(8) (1999).

[43] 720 ILCS 5/24-2(a)(9) (1999).

[44] 720 ILCS 5/24-2(a)(10) (1999).

governors of the Office to carry weapons;[45] (12) investigators appointed by a State's Attorney;[46] (13) court security officers;[47] and (14) those who manufacture, transport or sell weapons to those authorized to possess such weaponry.[48] Second, none of the prohibitions in paragraph 5/24-1 aimed at possession of firearms[49] apply to (1) members of organizations assembled for the purpose of shooting at targets on a shooting range while using their firearms on such ranges,[50] (2) members of authorized military or civil organizations while participating in a parade,[51] (3) licensed hunters,[52] or (4) persons transporting weapons that are broken down in a non-functioning state or that are not immediately accessible.[53] Third, the prohibition against machine guns, sawed-off shotguns and bombs[54] does not apply to peace officers,[55] prison guards,[56] and military personnel[57] acting within their official duties, and those authorized to manufacture, transport and sell such weapons to such officials.[58] Fourth, the prohibition against black jacks or slung-shots[59] does not apply to peace officers.[60] Fifth, the prohibition of the possession of firearms or deadly weapons at places where alcoholic beverages are sold and licensed public gatherings[61] does not apply to owners, managers, or authorized employees or law enforcement officers.[62] Sixth, the prohibition against explosive bullets[63] does not apply to military reserve officers or Illinois National Guard officers while in the performance of their official duty,[64] bona fide collectors of antique or surplus military ordinance,[65] laboratories specializing in forensic ballistics or development of ammunition or ex-

---

[45] 720 ILCS 5/24-2(a)(11) (1999).

[46] 720 ILCS 5/24-2(a)(12) (1999).

[47] 720 ILCS 5/24-2(a)(13) (1999).

[48] 720 ILCS 5/24-2(a)(14) (1999).

[49] *See* 720 ILCS 5/24-1(a)(4), (a)(10) (1999).

[50] 720 ILCS 5/24-2(b)(1) (1999).

[51] 720 ILCS 5/24-2(b)(2) (1999).

[52] 720 ILCS 5/24-2(b)(3) (1999).

[53] 720 ILCS 5/24-2(b)(4) (1999).

[54] *See* 720 ILCS 5/24-1(a)(7) (1999).

[55] 720 ILCS 5/24-2(c)(1) (1999).

[56] 720 ILCS 5/24-2(c)(2) (1999).

[57] 720 ILCS 5/24-2(c)(3) (1999).

[58] 720 ILCS 5/24-2(c)(4) through (c)(6) (1999).

[59] *See* 720 ILCS 5/24-1(a)(1) (1999).

[60] 720 ILCS 5/24-2(d) (1999).

[61] *See* 720 ILCS 5/24-1(a)(8) (1999).

[62] 720 ILCS 5/24-2(e) (1999).

[63] 720 ILCS 5/24-1(a)(11) (1999) (prohibits sale, manufacture or purchase of explosive bullets). *See also* 720 ILCS 5/24-3.1(a)(6) (1999) (prohibits possession of explosive bullets).

[64] 720 ILCS 5/24-2(g)(1) (1999).

[65] 720 ILCS 5/24-2(g)(2) (1999).

plosives[66] and commerce, preparation, assembly, or possession of explosive bullets by manufacturers or transporters exempted by law.[67] Seventh, the prohibition of the possession of firearms or deadly weapons in any school, public housing property, public parks or any real property comprising thereof, and any conveyance transporting students[68] does not apply to law enforcement officers or
security officers of such school, college, or university or to students carrying or
possessing firearms for use in training courses, parades, hunting, target shooting
on school ranges, or otherwise with the consent of school authorities and which
firearms are transported, unloaded or enclosed, in a suitable package.[69] Lastly,
exempted from the prohibition against possessing firearms in a vehicle or concealed on a person[70] are common carriers licensed by the State of Illinois or the
federal government acting incident to lawful transportation in which the common carrier is engaged, and possessors of Firearm Owners Identification Cards
when the firearms are unloaded and enclosed in containers.[71]

§ 15.04. — Knowledge.

An essential element of the crime of unlawful use of weapons is the requirement that the defendant acted "knowingly" when he or she engaged in the conduct proscribed in paragraph 5/24-1.[72] For instance, before a defendant can be
convicted for such unlawful use arising from the possession or concealment of a
weapon, it must be proved that he or she knowingly possessed[73] or concealed[74]
the instrument. This mental state can be demonstrated through circumstantial
evidence.[75]

§ 15.05. — Intent to Use Weapon Unlawfully Against Another.

Ordinarily, the mere knowledgeable possession of one of the weapons described in paragraph 5/24-1, such as a switchblade, is sufficient to establish
criminal liability.[76] This is because such a weapon is considered dangerous or

---

[66] 720 ILCS 5/24-2(g)(3) (1999).

[67] 720 ILCS 5/24-2(g)(4) (1999).

[68] 720 ILCS 5/24-1(c) (1999).

[69] 720 ILCS 5/24-1(c)(3) (1999).

[70] See 720 ILCS 5/24-1(a)(4) (1999).

[71] 720 ILCS 5/24-2(i) (1999).

[72] People v. Nunez, 24 Ill. App. 3d 163, 168, 320 N.E.2d 462, 465 (1st Dist. 1974) (citing People v. McKnight, 39 Ill. 2d 577, 237 N.E.2d 488 (1968), cert. denied, 394 U.S. 993 (1969)).

[73] People v. Perez, 97 Ill. App. 3d 278, 280, 422 N.E.2d 945, 947 (1st Dist. 1981).

[74] People v. Williams, 39 Ill. App. 3d 129, 130-31, 350 N.E.2d 81, 82-83 (1st Dist. 1976).

[75] People v. Seibech, 141 Ill. App. 3d 45, 49-50, 489 N.E.2d 1138, 1141 (3d Dist. 1986)
(knowledge not established by circumstantial evidence); People v. Janis, 56 Ill. App. 3d 160, 165,
371 N.E.2d 1063, 1067 (1st Dist. 1977) (knowledge established by circumstantial evidence).

[76] See 720 ILCS 5/24-1(a)(1) (1999).

deadly per se.[77] On the other hand, certain other instruments, such as a stone or bottle, are not dangerous or deadly weapons per se but may become so by the manner in which they are used.[78] Accordingly, subparagraph (a)(2) of 5/24-1 provides that possession of "a dagger, dirk, billy, dangerous knife, razor, stiletto, broken bottle or other piece of glass, stun gun or taser or any other dangerous or deadly weapon or instrument of like character" becomes criminal only if it is carried or possessed "with intent to use the same unlawfully against another."[79] Hence, proof of intent to use a hunting knife unlawfully against another is essential to a conviction for unlawful use of weapons.[80]

§ 15.06. — Weapons.

For the most part, the unlawful use of weapons statutes specifically delineate which instruments are "weapons" for purposes of a prosecution. Notwithstanding, the language of subparagraph (a)(2), quoted in relevant part in the proceeding section, makes reference to "dangerous or deadly weapons." A *deadly weapon* has been defined as an instrument that can be used for the purpose of offense or defense and is capable of producing death.[81] Striking a person with a sizable stone or throwing a bottle at another could amount to the use of a deadly weapon.[82] What amounts to a dangerous weapon for purposes of the paragraph 5/24 is not entirely clear, but presumably the definition of *dangerous weapon*[83] used in connection with the crime of armed violence[84] provides a useful reference point. The statute does not require that a gun be operational in order to satisfy an unlawful use of a weapon charge.[85]

---

[77] "A deadly weapon has been defined as 'an instrument that is used or may be used for the purpose of offense or defense and capable of producing death.'" People v. Fort, 119 Ill. App. 2d 350, 354, 256 N.E.2d 63, 66 (1st Dist. 1970) (citing People v. Dwyer, 324 Ill. 363, 155 N.E. 316 (1927)). Any weapons listed in 720 ILCS 5/33A-1 (1999) (armed violence statute) is dangerous per se. People v. Charles, 217 Ill. App. 3d 509, 512, 577 N.E.2d 534, 536 (2d Dist. 1991); People v. Weger, 154 Ill. App. 3d 706, 712, 506 N.E.2d 1072, 1076 (4th Dist. 1987).

[78] *See* People v. Fort, 119 Ill. App. 2d 350, 354, 256 N.E.2d 63, 66 (1st Dist. 1970).

[79] 720 ILCS 5/24-1(a)(2) (1999).

[80] People v. Sullivan, 46 Ill. 2d 399, 403, 263 N.E.2d 38, 39 (1970).

[81] People v. Fort, 119 Ill. App. 2d 350, 354, 256 N.E.2d 63, 66 (1st Dist. 1970).

[82] People v. Fort, 119 Ill. App. 2d 350, 354, 256 N.E.2d 63, 66 (1st Dist. 1970). *See also* People v. Villalobos, 53 Ill. App. 3d 234, 240, 368 N.E.2d 556, 560 (1st Dist. 1977) (unbroken bottle found to be deadly weapon).

[83] 720 ILCS 5/33A-1 (1999) (handgun, rifle, shotgun, spring gun, or any other firearm, sawed-off shotgun, stun gun, taser, knife with a blade of at least 3 inches in length, dagger, dirk, switchblade knife, stiletto, axe, hatchet, bludgeon, blackjack, slungshot, sand-bag, sand-club, metal knuckles, billy or other dangerous weapon).

[84] *See* 720 ILCS 5/33A-1 (1999).

[85] People v. Martinez, 285 Ill. App. 3d 881, 884, 674 N.E.2d 944, 946-47 (1st Dist. 1996) (stun gun need not be operational).

§ 15.07. — Possession.

The ordinary rules of criminal possession discussed in an earlier chapter,[86] which create liability for either actual or constructive possession, are obviously relevant where the unlawful weapons charge rests on the defendant's possession of contraband weaponry, such as a sawed-off shotgun.[87] The possession of *components* that could be used in the manufacture of contraband black powder bombs or Molotov cocktails could amount to "unlawful use of a weapon."[88] However, where the unlawful use of weapon charge is based on possession of a non-contraband weapon, then possession may be interpreted as requiring immediate possession rather than constructive possession.[89] Thus, the "carries or possesses" a weapon in a vehicle language in 5/24-1(a)(4) is designed to outlaw only the possession of a weapon that is "immediately accessible" to the defendant.[90]

§ 15.08. — Concealed.

Subparagraph (a)(4) prohibits a person from carrying a firearm that is "concealed on or about his person."[91] A weapon is concealed where it is hidden from "ordinary observation."[92] That is to say, even if there is "some notice of its presence," it could be considered concealed[93] as long as it is covered in a way "to make its recognition as a weapon at least difficult."[94] Where a gun was situated in a defendant's coat pocket with the butt apparently protruding from the pocket but covered by the defendant's hand, it was considered concealed for purposes of this section.[95]

A weapon must not only be hidden from ordinary observation to be considered concealed, it must also be within "such proximity to the accused as to lie

---

[86] *See* ch. 2 for a discussion of criminal possession.

[87] People v. Williams, 98 Ill. App. 3d 844, 847-48, 424 N.E.2d 1234, 1236 (3d Dist. 1981) (construing 5/24-1(a)(7)).

[88] ILL. OP. ATT'Y GEN. S-329 (1971). *See* 720 ILCS 5/24-1(a)(7)(iii) (1999).

[89] People v. Martin, 1 Ill. App. 3d 798, 799, 274 N.E.2d 593, 594 (3d Dist. 1971) (it was error to rely on a constructive possession theory in convicting a defendant of unlawful use of a weapon in a vehicle; there must be immediate access to the weapon under 5/24-1(a)(4)).

[90] People v. Bean, 65 Ill. App. 3d 104, 106, 382 N.E.2d 475, 477 (1st Dist. 1978).

[91] 720 ILCS 5/24-1(a)(4) (1999).

[92] People v. Williams, 39 Ill. App. 3d 129, 131, 350 N.E.2d 81, 83 (1st Dist. 1976).

[93] People v. Taylor, 31 Ill. App. 3d 20, 24, 332 N.E.2d 735, 737 (1st Dist. 1975).

[94] People v. Schuford, 50 Ill. App. 3d 408, 410, 365 N.E.2d 731, 733 (1st Dist. 1977).

[95] People v. Colson, 14 Ill. App. 3d 375, 376, 302 N.E.2d 409, 410 (1st Dist. 1973). *Accord* People v. Williams, 39 Ill. App. 3d 129, 131, 350 N.E.2d 81, 83 (1st Dist. 1976) (conviction upheld where gun lying on floor of back seat and observable to officer only after officer within one foot of vehicle).

within [his] easy reach. . . ."[96] In other words, it must be "immediately accessible"[97] or "readily available for use."[98] Where a defendant was within four feet of a coat in which a snub-nosed .38 caliber pistol was situated in the pocket, the pistol "could have easily been reached if defendant had been prompted by a violent motive;" accordingly, his conviction for unlawful use of weapon was affirmed.[99] Where a fully loaded .22 caliber revolver was located within a locked glove compartment in an automobile the defendant owned and was about to enter, the jury's finding that the weapon was accessible was affirmed by the Illinois Supreme Court.[100] In addition, even an unloaded weapon which is arguably accessible to the defendant is sufficient to support a conviction.[101] In conclusion, a concealed weapon, for purposes of paragraph 5/24-1, is one that is both (1) hidden and (2) accessible.

§ 15.09. Unlawful Use or Possession of Weapons by Felons or Persons in the Custody of the Department of Corrections Facilities.

Although the possession of a firearm on one's own land or in one's abode or fixed place of business is not normally criminal,[102] the General Assembly enacted a crime that makes it unlawful for a person to "knowingly possess on or about his person or on his land or in his own abode or fixed place of business any weapon prohibited under [Paragraph] 24 of this Act or any firearm or firearm ammunition *if the person has been convicted of a felony* under the laws of this State or any other jurisdiction."[103] The General Assembly also made it unlawful for "any person confined in a penal institution, which is a facility of the Illinois Department of Corrections, to possess any weapon prohibited under Section 5/24-1 of this Code or any other firearm or firearm ammunition, regardless of the intent with which he possesses it."[104] These prohibitions fall under

---

[96] People v. Thompson, 215 Ill. App. 3d 514, 519, 575 N.E.2d 256, 259 (4th Dist. 1991). *See also* People v. Akis, 63 Ill. 2d 296, 299, 347 N.E.2d 733, 735 (1976) (where officer observed defendant in automobile remove "something" from his pocket and hand it to passenger, who then dropped revolver to ground, defendant properly convicted of unlawful use of weapon).

[97] People v. Bean, 65 Ill. App. 3d 104, 106, 382 N.E.2d 475, 477 (1st Dist. 1978).

[98] People v. Smith, 71 Ill. 2d 95, 102, 374 N.E.2d 472, 474 (1978).

[99] People v. Bean, 65 Ill. App. 3d 104, 106, 382 N.E.2d 475, 477 (1st Dist. 1978).

[100] People v. Smith, 71 Ill. 2d 95, 102, 374 N.E.2d 472, 474 (1978). *Compare* People v. Staples, 88 Ill. App. 3d 400, 403, 410 N.E.2d 592, 594 (3d Dist. 1980) (revolver in storage box of pickup truck not immediately accessible).

[101] People v. Williams, 266 Ill. App. 3d 752, 757, 640 N.E.2d 1275, 1279 (1st Dist. 1994).

[102] *See* 720 ILCS 5/24-1(a)(4) (1999).

[103] 720 ILCS 5/24-1.1(a) (1999) (emphasis added).

[104] 720 ILCS 5/24-1.1(b) (1999). Note that unlawful intent regarding use of the weapon is irrelevant, thus making possession by confined persons a strict liability offense. *See* People v. Ryan, 117 Ill. 2d 28, 37, 509 N.E.2d 1001, 1002 ("the apparent purpose of the statute is to prohibit even

the heading of "unlawful use or possession of weapons by felons or persons in the custody of the Department of Corrections facilities,"[105] which is punishable as a felony, with penalties that depend upon the type of weapon and whether the offender is incarcerated.[106]

A convicted felon can be convicted of unlawful use of a weapon by felon even if the weapon is *not* immediately accessible, such as where a gun was found under the hood of the defendant's automobile.[107] Even if a felon is in possession of an inoperable firearm, this amounts to a violation of this crime.[108] Since this law is designed in part to prevent convicted felons from engaging in any show of force, real or apparent, it is sufficient if the object possessed the outward appearance and characteristics of a firearm.[109] The statute does, however, provide an exemption for a felon who has been given permission by the Department of Corrections to use a weapon otherwise prohibited.[110] On the other hand, an incarcerated convict can never claim the defense of necessity if found in possession of a weapon in a penal institution.[111]

§ 15.10.   Aggravated Discharge of a Firearm.

"Aggravated discharge of a firearm" arises where a defendant intentionally or knowingly discharges a firearm and does so knowing that the discharge is in the direction of a person or an occupied building or vehicle.[112] Specifically, paragraph 5/24-1.2 criminalized the intentional or knowing discharge of a firearm either: (1) at or into a building when he knows the building to be occupied and the firearm is discharged from a place or position outside that building,[113] (2) in the direction of another person or a vehicle known to be occupied,[114] (3) in the direction of a person he knows to be a peace officer, a community policing volunteer, a correctional institution employee, or a firefighter, while engaged in the execution of their official duties, to prevent execution of their official duties, or in retaliation for performing their official duties,[115] (4) in the direction of a vehi-

---

the innocent possession of items that are likely to be hazardous in a penal setting"), *cert. denied*, 484 U.S. 865 (1987).

[105] 720 ILCS 5/24-1.1 (1999).

[106] 720 ILCS 5/24-1.1(e) (1999).

[107] People v. Jastrzemski, 196 Ill. App. 3d 1037, 1039-40, 554 N.E.2d 583, 584-85 (1st Dist. 1990).

[108] People v. White, 253 Ill. App. 3d 1097, 1098, 627 N.E.2d 383, 384 (4th Dist. 1993).

[109] People v. White, 253 Ill. App. 3d 1097, 1098, 627 N.E.2d 383, 384 (4th Dist. 1993).

[110] 720 ILCS 5/24-1.1(c) (1999).

[111] 720 ILCS 5/24-1.1(d) (1999). *See* ch. 19 for a discussion of the defense of necessity.

[112] 720 ILCS 5/24-1.2(a) (1999); People v. Vich, 302 Ill. App. 3d 214, 219, 705 N.E.2d 115, 118 (2d Dist. 1998).

[113] 720 ILCS 5/24-1.2(a)(1) (1999).

[114] 720 ILCS 5/24-1.2(a)(2) (1999).

[115] 720 ILCS 5/24-1.2(a)(3) (1999).

cle known to be occupied by a peace officer, a correctional institution employee, or a firefighter, while engaged in the execution of their official duties, to prevent execution of their official duties or in retaliation for performing their official duties,[116] (5) in the direction of a person known to be a paramedic, ambulance driver, or other medical assistance or first aid personnel, employed by a municipality or other governmental unit while engaged in the execution of their official duties, to prevent execution of their official duties, or in retaliation for performing their official duties,[117] or (6) in the direction of a vehicle known to be occupied by a paramedic, ambulance driver, or other medical assistance or first aid personnel, employed by a municipality or other governmental unit while engaged in the execution of their official duties, to prevent execution of their official duties, or in retaliation for performing their official duties.[118] This offense is a felony with harsher penalties for violations involving municipal officers and medical personnel.[119]

§ 15.11. Reckless Discharge of a Firearm.

The Illinois penal code contains the offense of "reckless discharge of a firearm."[120] Section 5/24-1.5 of the Criminal Code defines reckless discharge of a firearm as follows:

> (a) A person commits reckless discharge of a firearm by discharging a firearm in a reckless manner which endangers the bodily safety of an individual. (b) If the conduct described in subsection (a) is committed by a passenger of a moving motor vehicle with the knowledge and consent of the driver of the motor vehicle the driver is accountable for such conduct. (c) Sentence. Reckless discharge of a firearm is a . . . felony. (d) This section does not apply to a peace officer while in the performance of his or her official duties.[121]

§ 15.12. Unlawful Use of Armor Piercing Bullets.

Illinois law forbids the "unlawful use of any armor piercing bullets,"[122] which is a felony.[123] The statute reads in relevant part:

---

[116] 720 ILCS 5/24-1.2(a)(4) (1999).

[117] 720 ILCS 5/24-1.2(a)(5) (1999).

[118] 720 ILCS 5/24-1.2(a)(6) (1999). *See* People v. Townsend, 275 Ill. App. 3d 413, 654 N.E.2d 1096 (2d Dist. 1995) (upholding aggravated discharge of a firearm statute against unconstitutional vagueness and disproportionality challenges).

[119] 720 ILCS 5/24-1.2(b) (1999).

[120] 720 ILCS 5/24-1.5 (1999).

[121] 720 ILCS 5/24-1.5 (1999).

[122] 720 ILCS 5/24-2.1(a) (1999).

[123] 720 ILCS 5/24-2.1(d) (1999).

A person commits the offense of unlawful use of armor piercing bullets when he knowingly manufactures, sells, purchases, possesses, or carries any metal piercing bullet.

The statute contains a definition of "armor piercing bullet,"[124] and also creates an exemption for peace officers;[125] prison and jail guards;[126] military personnel;[127] federal officials required to carry firearms;[128] U.S. Marshals;[129] persons licensed under federal law to manufacture, import or sell armor piercing bullets;[130] laboratories involved in forensic ballistics or the development of ammunition;[131] and those who manufacture, transport or sell such ammunition to those authorized to possess it,[132] all of whom must be acting within the lawful scope of their official duties or legitimate business activities.

§ 15.13.   Manufacture, Sale or Transfer of Bullets Represented to be Armor Piercing Bullets.

A companion stricture to the one immediately above is "manufacture, sale or transfer of bullets represented to be armor piercing bullets."[133] It makes it "unlawful for any person to knowingly manufacture, sell, offer to sell, or transfer any bullet which is represented to be armor piercing."[134] This offense is a felony.[135] The same parties as in the preceding companion section have an exemption "with respect to activities which are within the lawful scope of the exemption therein granted."[136]

§ 15.14.   Unlawful Sale of Firearms.

Illinois law imposes felony sanctions[137] for the "unlawful sale of firearms."[138] A person commits this crime when he or she knowingly sells or gives any fire-

---

[124] *See* 720 ILCS 5/24-2.1(a) (1999) ("armor piercing bullet" defined as any handgun ammunition with projectiles or projectile cores constructed of a variety of hard-metal materials, and designed for purposes other than sport or industrial use).

[125] 720 ILCS 5/24-2.1(b)(1) (1999).

[126] 720 ILCS 5/24-2.1(b)(2) (1999).

[127] 720 ILCS 5/24-2.1(b)(3) (1999).

[128] 720 ILCS 5/24-2.1(b)(4) (1999).

[129] 720 ILCS 5/24-2.1(b)(5) (1999).

[130] 720 ILCS 5/24-2.1(b)(6) (1999).

[131] 720 ILCS 5/24-2.1(b)(7) (1999).

[132] 720 ILCS 5/24-2.1(b)(8) (1999).

[133] 720 ILCS 5/24-2.2 (1999).

[134] 720 ILCS 5/24-2.2(a) (1999).

[135] 720 ILCS 5/24-2.2(d) (1999).

[136] 720 ILCS 5/24-2.2(b) (1999).

[137] 720 ILCS 5/24-3(k) (1999).

[138] 720 ILCS 5/24-3 (1999).

arm (1) that may be concealed on a person to any person under 18 years of age;[139] (2) to a person under 21 years of age who has been convicted of a misdemeanor, other than a traffic offense, or adjudged delinquent;[140] (3) to any narcotic addict;[141] (4) to any person convicted of a felony under the laws of any jurisdiction;[142] (5) to any person who has been a patient in a mental hospital in the past five years;[143] (6) to any person who is mentally retarded;[144] or (7) to any person under 18 years of age who does not possess a valid Firearm Owner's Identification Card.[145] In addition, this offense forbids (1) the delivery of a concealable firearm, incidental to a sale, without withholding delivery for at least 72 hours after application for a purchase has been made, or (2) delivery of any rifle, shotgun, or other long gun, incidental to a sale, without withholding delivery for at least 24 hours after application for purchase has been made.[146] However, this withholding delivery requirement does not apply to (1) purchases by law enforcement officers, bank guards, armed truck guards, and those having similar employment;[147] (2) mail order sales of firearms to nonresidents of Illinois that will be mailed to a point outside Illinois;[148] (3) sales at recognized firearm showings or displays within Illinois to nonresidents of Illinois;[149] or (4) sales to federally licensed dealers.[150] Finally, this section prohibits federally licensed dealers, manufacturers, importers, or pawnbrokers from delivering or selling to any unlicensed person a handgun having a barrel, slide, frame, or receiver of zinc alloy or other nonhomogeneous metal that will melt or deform at a temperature of less than 800 degrees Fahrenheit.[151] This subparagraph is obviously designed to rid the streets of those cheap, dangerous handguns known as "Saturday night specials."[152]

§ 15.15.   Unlawful Possession of Firearms and Firearm Ammunition.

Paragraph 5/24-3.1 makes punishable the "unlawful possession of firearms or firearm ammunition."[153] A person commits this crime if he or she (1) has pos-

---

[139] 720 ILCS 5/24-3(a) (1999).

[140] 720 ILCS 5/24-3(b) (1999).

[141] 720 ILCS 5/24-3(c) (1999).

[142] 720 ILCS 5/24-3(d) (1999).

[143] 720 ILCS 5/24-3(e) (1999).

[144] 720 ILCS 5/24-3(f) (1999).

[145] 720 ILCS 5/24-3(i) (1999). *See also* 430 ILCS 65/0.01 through 65/16-3 (1999) ("Firearm Owners Identification Card Act").

[146] 720 ILCS 5/24-3(g) (1999).

[147] 720 ILCS 5/24-3(g)(1) (1999).

[148] 720 ILCS 5/24-3(g)(2) (1999).

[149] 720 ILCS 5/24-3(g)(3) (1999).

[150] 720 ILCS 5/24-3(g)(4) (1999).

[151] 720 ILCS 5/24-3(h) (1999).

[152] *See generally* ROBERT SHERRILL, THE SATURDAY NIGHT SPECIAL 97-117 (1983).

[153] 720 ILCS 5/24-3.1 (1999) (unlawful possession of a "handgun" is a felony; unlawful possession of other firearms or firearm ammunition is a misdemeanor).

session of a firearm of a size which may be concealed and is a person under 18 years of age;[154] (2) has possession of any firearm or firearm ammunition, is under 21 years of age *and* has previously been convicted of a non-traffic misdemeanor or adjudged delinquent;[155] (3) is a narcotic addict and has any firearms or firearm ammunition in his or her possession;[156] (4) has been a patient in a mental hospital within the past five years and has any firearms or firearm ammunition in his or her possession;[157] (5) is mentally retarded and has any firearms or firearm ammunition in his or her possession;[158] or (6) has possession of any explosive bullet.[159] Since this is a crime of possession, the usual rules of criminal possession apply.[160]

§ 15.16.   Unlawful Discharge of Armor Piercing Bullets.

Paragraph 5/24-3.2 prohibits the "unlawful discharge of armor piercing bullets."[161] First, whenever any person, knowing a firearm is loaded with an armor piercing bullet, intentionally or recklessly discharges the firearm and the bullet strikes another person, the offender commits a class X felony.[162] Second, any person who possesses or conceals on his or her person an armor piercing bullet and a firearm suitable for the discharge thereof commits a different (although less serious) felony.[163] Again, peace officers,[164] jail and prison guards and officials,[165] military personnel,[166] federal officials[167] and U.S. Marshals[168] required to carry such weaponry during the ordinary scope of their profession are exempted.

§ 15.17.   Unlawful Sale or Delivery of Firearms on the Premises of Any School.

Paragraph 5/24-3.3 makes it a felony for any person, aged 18 years or older, to sell, give or deliver any firearm to any person under 18 years of age in any

---

[154] 720 ILCS 5/24-3.1(a)(1) (1999).

[155] 720 ILCS 5/24-3.1(a)(2) (1999).

[156] 720 ILCS 5/24-3.1(a)(3) (1999).

[157] 720 ILCS 5/24-3.1(a)(4) (1999).

[158] 720 ILCS 5/24-3.1(a)(5) (1999).

[159] 720 ILCS 5/24-3.1(a)(6) (1999).

[160] *See, e.g.*, People v. Zentz, 26 Ill. App. 3d 265, 266, 325 N.E.2d 40, 41 (3d Dist. 1975). *See generally* ch. 2 for a complete discussion of the requirements of criminal possession.

[161] 720 ILCS 5/24-3.2 (1999). The definition of "armor piercing bullet" appearing in this section (*id.* 5/24-3.2(a)) is the same as that used in the "unlawful use of armor piercing bullets" section. *See* § 15.12 of this chapter for a discussion of "unlawful use of armor piercing bullets."

[162] 720 ILCS 5/24-3.2(b) (1999).

[163] 720 ILCS 5/24-3.2(c) (1999).

[164] 720 ILCS 5/24-3.2(d)(1) (1999).

[165] 720 ILCS 5/24-3.2(d)(2) (1999).

[166] 720 ILCS 5/24-3.2(d)(3) (1999).

[167] 720 ILCS 5/24-3.2(d)(4) (1999).

[168] 720 ILCS 5/24-3.2(d)(5) (1999).

school or on any school premises.[169] This provision does not apply to peace officers or students involved in training courses, parades, target shooting or other activities with the consent of school authorities where the firearms are transported unloaded and enclosed in suitable containers.[170]

§ 15.18. Unlawful Sale of Firearms by Liquor Licensee.

Paragraph 5/24-3.4 criminalizes the sale or delivery of any firearm by a person licensed to sell alcoholic liquor or their agents to any person on the real property of the licensed establishment, unless the sale or delivery is otherwise legal under the Code.[171] Such a violation is a felony.[172]

§ 15.19. Gunrunning.

Paragraph 5/24-3A punishes as "gunrunning"[173] a person's transfer of three or more firearms contrary to the "unlawful sale of firearms" statute.[174] Such an offense is punishable as a felony.[175]

§ 15.20. Register of Sales by Dealer.

Paragraph 5/24-4 requires any seller of firearms that may be concealed on the person to keep a register of all such firearms sold or given away.[176] The register must contain the date of the sale or gift; the receiver's name, address, age and occupation; the price of the weapon; a precise description of the firearm; and the purpose for which it was purchased or obtained.[177] The statute also requires sellers on demand to allow peace officers to inspect the register and stock.[178] The law does not apply to manufacturers who sell to bona fide wholesalers or wholesalers who sell to bona fide retailers.[179] Violation of the law requiring "register of sales by dealer" is a misdemeanor.[180]

---

[169] 720 ILCS 5/24-3.3 (1999).
[170] 720 ILCS 5/24-3.3 (1999).
[171] 720 ILCS 5/24-3.4(a) (1999).
[172] 720 ILCS 5/24-3.4(b) (1999).
[173] 720 ILCS 5/24-3A(a) (1999).
[174] *See* 720 ILCS 5/24-3 (1999). *See* § 15.14 of this chapter for a discussion of "unlawful sale of firearms."
[175] 720 ILCS 5/24-3A(b) (1999).
[176] 720 ILCS 5/24-4(a) (1999).
[177] 720 ILCS 5/24-4(b) (1999).
[178] 720 ILCS 5/24-4(c) (1999).
[179] 720 ILCS 5/24-4(a) (1999).
[180] 720 ILCS 5/24-4(d) (1999).

§ 15.21. Defacing Identification Marks of Firearms.

Illinois law criminalizes "defacing identification marks of firearms,"[181] which is a felony.[182] Defacing identification marks of firearms is committed when any person alters or obliterates the name of the maker, model, manufacturer's number or other mark of identification of any firearm.[183] This enactment also states that possession of a firearm with a defaced identifying mark is prima facie evidence that the possessor defaced the particular firearm.[184]

§ 15.22. Unlawful Possession or Distribution of Nitrous Oxide.

Paragraph 5/24.5 makes it a misdemeanor for any person to possess nitrous oxide or any substance containing nitrous oxide with intent to breathe, inhale, or ingest for the purpose of causing a condition of intoxication.[185] In addition, it is illegal to sell or distribute this substance to another where it will be used for purposes of intoxication.[186] Legitimate medical use is exempted.[187]

§ 15.23. Mob Action.

The second group of strictures dealing with public health, safety and decency are the proscriptions of mob action and related offenses.[188] The statute of mob action criminalizes:

(1) The use of force or violence disturbing the public peace by 2 or more persons acting together and without authority of law;
(2) The assembly of 2 or more persons to do an unlawful act; or
(3) the assembly of 2 or more persons, without authority of law, for the purpose of doing violence to the person or property of one supposed to have been guilty of a violation of the law, or for the purpose of exercising correctional powers or regulative powers over any person by violence.[189]

Mob action is punishable as a misdemeanor if contrary to subparagraph (2) or (3),[190] unless either force or violence is used contrary to subparagraph (1)[191] or the perpetrator's violence inflicts injury on the person or property of another,[192]

---

[181] 720 ILCS 5/24-5 (1999).
[182] 720 ILCS 5/24-5(a) (1999).
[183] 720 ILCS 5/24-5(a) (1999).
[184] 720 ILCS 5/24-5(b) (1999).
[185] 720 ILCS 5/24.5-5 (1999).
[186] 720 ILCS 5/24.5-10 (1999).
[187] 720 ILCS 5/24.5-5 (1999).
[188] 720 ILCS 5/25-1 (1999).
[189] 720 ILCS 5/25-1(a) (1999).
[190] 720 ILCS 5/25-1(c) (1999).
[191] 720 ILCS 5/25-1(b) (1999).
[192] 720 ILCS 5/25-1(d) (1999).

in which case it is a felony. This statute also punishes as a misdemeanor the failure of any participant in a mob action to withdraw from the action on the demand of a peace officer.[193]

Notwithstanding the facial absence of a mens rea element in the mob action statute, this enactment has been judicially interpreted to require proof of intent, knowledge or recklessness,[194] or, possibly, even negligence.[195] Regarding the actus reus for mob action, there are three different bases for finding mob action. First, if two or more persons acting together use force or violence, thereby disturbing the public peace without authority of law, this is sufficient for mob action under subparagraph (a)(1). Thus, where there was a violent altercation between several inmates in a county jail during which the defendant and at least one codefendant repeatedly beat another inmate and approximately a dozen other persons congregated nearby, this was mob action.[196] In this case, the Illinois Supreme Court explicitly said that a breach of the "public peace" under subparagraph (a)(1) did not have to occur in a public area and could occur in a county jail, as had been charged.[197] In addition, criminal acts constituting mob action need not occur in public view.[198] The second basis for a finding of mob action states that if two or more persons assembled together engage in an unlawful act, this is mob action under subparagraph (a)(2). Thus, if two or more persons assembled and destroyed another's property deliberately and without justification, this could amount to mob action. Lastly, if two or more persons assembled for the purpose of doing violence to the person or property of another believed to have committed a crime, this is mob action under subparagraph (a)(3). For example, if a group of vigilantes gathered to inflict injury on the person or residence of a person suspected of having engaged in some heinous crime, this act of "taking the law into their own hands" would constitute mob action.

In *People v. Montgomery*,[199] the defendant was convicted of mob action where she incited a large group of persons to interfere with a police arrest of two individuals.[200] The court held that the defendant's exhortations were not protected by the First Amendment.[201]

---

[193] 720 ILCS 5/25-1(e) (1999).

[194] Landry v. Daley, 280 F. Supp. 938, 957-58 (N.D. Ill. 1968), *rev'd on other grounds*, 401 U.S. 77 (1971).

[195] People v. Leach, 3 Ill. App. 3d 389, 392-93, 279 N.E.2d 450, 452 (1st Dist. 1972).

[196] People v. Dixon, 91 Ill. 2d 346, 349, 438 N.E.2d 180, 182 (1982).

[197] People v. Dixon, 91 Ill. 2d 346, 354-55, 438 N.E.2d 180, 184-85 (1982).

[198] People v. Garza, 298 Ill. App. 3d 452, 460, 699 N.E.2d 181, 187 (2d Dist. 1998) (where no witnesses to defendant's commission of aggravated battery and armed robbery could be found, conviction for mob action upheld because "acts constituting mob action need not occur in public view").

[199] 179 Ill. App. 3d 330, 534 N.E.2d 651 (1st Dist. 1989).

[200] People v. Montgomery, 179 Ill. App. 3d 330, 332-33, 534 N.E.2d 651, 653 (1st Dist. 1989).

[201] People v. Montgomery, 179 Ill. App. 3d 330, 335, 534 N.E.2d 651, 654 (1st Dist. 1989).

§ 15.24. Disorderly Conduct.

Although generally a misdemeanor,[202] "disorderly conduct" is a noteworthy crime in Illinois. The Code provides that a person commits disorderly conduct when he knowingly:

(1) Does any act in such unreasonable manner as to alarm or disturb another and to provoke a breach of the peace; or

(2) Transmits or causes to be transmitted in any manner to the fire department of any city, town, village or fire protection district a false alarm of fire, knowing at the time of such transmission that there is no reasonable ground for believing that such fire exists; or

(3) Transmits or causes to be transmitted in any manner to another a false alarm to the effect that a bomb or other explosive of any nature is concealed in such place that its explosion would endanger human life, knowing at the time of such transmission that there is no reasonable ground for believing that such bomb or explosive is concealed in such place; or

(4) Transmits or causes to be transmitted in any manner to any peace officer, public officer or public employee a report to the effect that an offense will be committed, is being committed, or has been committed, knowing at the time of such transmission that there is no reasonable ground for believing that such an offense will be committed, is being committed, or has been committed; or

(5) Enters upon the property of another and for a lewd or unlawful purpose deliberately looks into the dwelling on the property through any window or opening in it; or

(6) While acting as a collection agency as defined in the "Collection Agency Act" or as an employee of such collection agency, and while attempting to collect an alleged debt, makes a telephone call to the alleged debtor which is designed to harass, annoy or intimidate the alleged debtor; or

(7) Transmits or causes to be transmitted a false report to the Department of Children and Family Services under Section 4 of the "Abused and Neglected Child Reporting Act"; or

(8) Transmits or causes to be transmitted a false report to the Department of Public Health under the Nursing Home Care Act; or

---

[202] 720 ILCS 5/26-1(a) (1999). A violation of subparagraph (a)(6) is a "business offense" punishable by a fine only. *See id.* 5/26-1(a)(6). However, violations of subparagraphs (a)(2) (making false fire report), (a)(3) (making false bomb threat), (a)(4) (making false report of crime) and (a)(9) (making false report ambulance is needed) are felonies. *See id.* 5/26-1(b)(1). Violations of all other subparagraphs are misdemeanors. *See id.* 5/26-1(b)(1). In all cases not involving incarceration, community service shall be imposed for not less than 30 and not more than 120 hours in addition to any other sentence imposed. *See id.* 5/26-1(c).

(9) Transmits or causes to be transmitted in any manner to the police department or fire department of any municipality or fire protection district, or any privately owned and operated ambulance service, a false request for an ambulance, emergency medical technician-ambulance or emergency medical technician-paramedic knowing at the time there is no reasonable ground for believing that such assistance is required;

(10) Transmits or causes to be transmitted a false report under Article II of "An Act in relation to victims of violence and abuse," . . .; or

(11) Transmits or causes to be transmitted a false report to any public safety agency without the reasonable grounds necessary to believe that transmitting such a report is necessary for the safety and welfare of the public; or

(12) Calls the number "911" for the purpose of making or transmitting a false alarm or complaint and reporting information when, at the time the call or transmission is made, the person knows there is no reasonable ground for making the call or transmission and further knows that the call or transmission could result in the emergency response of any public safety agency.[203]

The Committee comments reveal the General Assembly's intentions regarding the appropriate scope of this article's stricture:

Section 26-1(a) is a general provision intended to encompass all of the usual types of "disorderly conduct" and "disturbing the peace." Activity of this sort is so varied and contingent upon surrounding circumstances as to almost defy definition. Some of the general classes of conduct which have traditionally been regarded as disorderly conduct are listed here as examples: the creation or maintenance of loud or raucous noises of all sorts; unseemly, boisterous or foolish behavior induced by drunkenness; threatening damage to property or indirectly threatening bodily harm (which may not amount to assault); carelessly or recklessly displaying firearms or other dangerous instruments; preparation for engaging in violence or fighting; and fighting of all sorts. In addition, the task of defining disorderly conduct is further complicated by the fact that the type of conduct alone is not determinative, but rather culpability is equally dependent upon the surrounding circumstances. Thus, the discharge of a pistol on the desert by a lone marksman is harmless, whereas the discharge of the same pistol in a library or church is blameworthy. Similarly, shouting waving and drinking beer may be permissible at the ball park, but not at a funeral. . . . As defined by the Code, the gist of the offense is not so much that a certain overt type of behavior was accomplished, as it is the offended knowingly engaged in

---

[203] 720 ILCS 5/26-1(a) (1999).

some activity in an unreasonable manner which he knew or should have known would tend to disturb, alarm or provoke others. The emphasis is on the unreasonableness of his conduct and its tendency to disturb.[204]

An examination of the language of the statute, the intent of the legislature, and the caselaw suggests that there are three essential elements of disorderly conduct. There must be (1) some activity or language (2) engaged in knowingly (3) that actually provokes a significant breach of the peace. Regarding the caselaw, the courts have found disorderly conduct where a spectator commenced to shout at a public meeting, which prevented an orderly continuation of the meeting;[205] where a defendant made loud and raucous noise in the middle of the night prior to a workday in a residential neighborhood;[206] where a defendant tailgated and later deliberately blocked another person's automobile's forward movements;[207] where a defendant threatened a minor schoolmate by threatening to "kick his butt" if he did not pay $5.00 owed to him;[208] where an intoxicated defendant urinated in public while standing approximately 30 feet from a female patron seated at an outdoor eating area of a restaurant;[209] where a 47-year-old male defendant made crude, sexual remarks to teenage boys using provocative language and threatened to start rumors that the boys were "queer" and destroy their reputations, which threats and language were "a form of mental and sexual harassment" and caused the boys to avoid appearing in public;[210] where a defendant interfered with the arrest of a third party and pushed the officer;[211] and where a defendant shouted profane language toward a police officer while disobeying the officer's order to move his automobile, with a result that a crowd converged on the scene.[212] On the other hand, the courts have held the public use of vulgar language toward the police, however distasteful or offensive to one's sensibilities, does not amount to disorderly conduct even if it causes people to stop, look and listen.[213] Similarly, a quarrel or the use of threatening or insulting words is not, without more, disorderly conduct.[214] Language or words give rise to disorderly conduct only where, by their very utterance, they tend to incite an

---

[204] ILL. ANN. STAT. ch. 38, para. 26-1 (Smith-Hurd 1977), 1961 Committee Comments, at 149 (revised 1970).

[205] United States v. Woodward, 376 F.2d 136, 139-40 (7th Cir. 1967).

[206] People v. Albert, 243 Ill. App. 3d 23, 26-28, 611 N.E.2d 567, 569-70 (2d Dist. 1993).

[207] People v. Davis, 291 Ill. App. 3d 552, 556, 683 N.E.2d 1260, 1263-64 (3d Dist. 1997).

[208] In re D.W., 150 Ill. App. 3d 729, 730, 502 N.E.2d 419, 420 (4th Dist. 1986).

[209] People v. Duncan, 259 Ill. App. 3d 308, 310, 631 N.E.2d 803, 804 (4th Dist. 1994).

[210] People v. Allen, 288 Ill. App. 3d 502, 506-10, 680 N.E.2d 795, 798-800 (4th Dist. 1997).

[211] People v. Jackson, 131 Ill. App. 2d 57, 59, 266 N.E.2d 475, 476-77 (1st Dist. 1970).

[212] People ex rel. Village of Melrose Park v. Scheck, 42 Ill. App. 2d 117, 119, 191 N.E.2d 645, 646-47 (1st Dist. 1963).

[213] People v. Douglas, 29 Ill. App. 3d 738, 742-43, 331 N.E.2d 359, 363 (1st Dist. 1975).

[214] People v. Cooper, 32 Ill. App. 3d 516, 518, 336 N.E.2d 247, 249 (1st Dist. 1975).

immediate breach of the peace.[215] Accordingly, only what courts call "fighting words" will be punishable.[216]

The charges in caselaw involving arguments with, or insulting words directed at, police officers almost invariably will not amount to disorderly conduct because the impact on the public order (1) is usually tenuous and (2) is not of a nature to evoke a violent response, since a police officer is presumably trained to preserve the public order and not to over react to the provocation.[217]

The vital importance of proof of a breach of peace as an element of disorderly conduct is reflected in two cases. In *People v. Klick*,[218] the Illinois Supreme Court reviewed a subparagraph which no longer appears in the state disorderly conduct statute. Specifically, it stated that disorderly conduct occurred where a person knowingly made a telephone call "with the intent to annoy another."[219] The Illinois Supreme Court ruled that this provision was unconstitutionally overbroad in that it made criminal conduct that was protected by the First and Fourteenth Amendments to the United States Constitution.[220] The court stated that this subparagraph could be construed to "apply to conduct other than that which might provoke a breach of the peace" and that conduct of words that were merely annoying or disturbing did not meet the breach of the peace test.[221] A second opinion, *People v. Trester*,[222] makes an additional important point. In *Trester*, a defendant, while speaking in a normal tone of voice, swore at a police officer and challenged him to remove his badge and guns and fight.[223] The court held there was no disorderly conduct as a matter of law, since there was, at best, evidence that the defendant's conduct had the *tendency* to bring about a breach of the peace, whereas it must be proved that the conduct *actually* brought about a breach of the peace.[224] In contrast, then, where the defendant made a false report to the police alleging he had just been victimized by an armed robber, this amounted to disorderly conduct because, as an *actual* result of the defendant's conduct, the building manager was attracted to the scene and believed it necessary to call the police, at least three police officers were taken from other duties and sent to the apartment building where the robbery was claimed to have occurred, one officer was required to enter the apartment in which the armed rob-

---

[215] People v. Kellstedt, 29 Ill. App. 3d 83, 85, 329 N.E.2d 830, 831 (3d Dist. 1975) (quoting Lewis v. City of New Orleans, 415 U.S. 130 (1974)).

[216] People v. Slaton, 24 Ill. App. 3d 1062, 1063, 322 N.E.2d 553, 554 (5th Dist. 1974).

[217] *See, e.g,* People v. Slaton, 24 Ill. App. 3d 1062, 1063, 322 N.E.2d 553, 554 (5th Dist. 1974).

[218] 66 Ill. 2d 269, 362 N.E.2d 329 (1977).

[219] People v. Klick, 66 Ill. 2d 269, 271, 362 N.E.2d 329, 330 (1977).

[220] People v. Klick, 66 Ill. 2d 269, 275, 362 N.E.2d 329, 332 (1977).

[221] People v. Klick, 66 Ill. 2d 269, 273-74, 362 N.E.2d 329, 331 (1977).

[222] 96 Ill. App. 3d 553, 421 N.E.2d 959 (4th Dist. 1981).

[223] People v. Trester, 96 Ill. App. 3d 553, 554, 421 N.E.2d 959, 960 (4th Dist. 1981).

[224] People v. Trester, 96 Ill. App. 3d 553, 555, 421 N.E.2d 959, 960 (4th Dist. 1981).

ber was alleged to be situated, and a man was wrongfully arrested and finger-printed.[225]

Finally, although a breach of the public peace must flow from the defendant's conduct, the courts do not require that the disorderly conduct actually occur in a *public* place.[226] Thus, where a defendant entered the home of an eighty-one-year-old invalid woman, waved a sheet of paper at her, and in effect told her that if a charge against his brother was prosecuted, some undefined threat would be carried out, this was disorderly conduct.[227]

§ 15.25. Interference with Emergency Communication.

Illinois law punishes as a misdemeanor[228] the "interference with emergency communication."[229] This crime arises where a person "knowingly, intentionally or without lawful justification interrupts, disrupts, impedes or otherwise interferes with the transmission of a communication over a citizens band radio channel, the purpose of which communication is to inform or inquire about an emergency."[230] For purposes of this crime, an *emergency* means any condition or circumstance in which the person making the transmission reasonably believes an individual is in imminent danger of serious bodily injury or an individual's property is in imminent danger of damage or destruction.[231]

§ 15.26. Use of a Facsimile Machine in Unsolicited Advertising or Fund-Raising.

The Illinois legislature has proscribed the "use of a facsimile machine in unsolicited advertising or fundraising."[232] It defines both "facsimile machine"[233] and "person"[234] for use in the statute and further reads:

> No person shall knowingly use a facsimile machine to send or cause to be sent to another person a facsimile of a document containing unsolicited advertising or fund-raising material, except to a person which the sender

---

[225] People v. Stevens, 40 Ill. App. 3d 303, 307-08, 352 N.E.2d 352, 356 (1st Dist. 1976).
[226] People v. Davis, 82 Ill. 2d 534, 538, 413 N.E.2d 413, 415 (1980).
[227] People v. Davis, 82 Ill. 2d 534, 537-38, 413 N.E.2d 413, 415 (1980).
[228] 720 ILCS 5/26-2(c) (1999).
[229] 720 ILCS 5/26-2 (1999).
[230] 720 ILCS 5/26-2(a) (1999).
[231] 720 ILCS 5/26-2(b) (1999).
[232] 720 ILCS 5/26-3 (1999).
[233] 720 ILCS 5/26-3(a)(1) (1999) ("a device which is capable of sending or receiving facsimiles of documents through connection with a telecommunication network").
[234] 720 ILCS 5/26-3(a)(2) (1999) (individual, corporation, government unit, partnership or unincorporated association).

knows or under all of the circumstances reasonably believes has given the sender permission . . . for the sending of such material.[235]

Use of a facsimile machine in unsolicited advertising or fundraising is punishable as a petty offense.[236]

§ 15.27.   Unauthorized Videotaping.

The Illinois legislature has criminalized the videotaping, photographing or filming of "another person without that person's consent in a restroom, tanning bed, or tanning salon."[237] The crime, known as "unauthorized videotaping," is a misdemeanor.[238] Exempted from the statute are the videotaping, photographing and filming by (1) law enforcement officers pursuant to a lawful criminal investigation,[239] and (2) correctional officers for security reasons and for investigation of alleged misconduct on the part of Department of Corrections inmates.[240] The statute does not criminalize audio recording of an oral conversation as a result of unlawful videotaping or filming.[241] Eavesdropping strictures cover this activity.[242]

§ 15.28.   Gambling.

Another major portion of the "offenses affecting public health, safety and decency" section of the Criminal Code of 1961 covers the strictures regarding "gambling and related offenses."[243] A person commits illegal gambling when he or she (1) plays a game of chance or skill for money or other thing of value;[244] (2) makes a wager;[245] (3) operates, keeps, owns, uses, purchases, exhibits, rents, sells, bargains for the sale or lease of, manufactures or distributes a gambling device;[246] (4) enters into a contract to buy or sell what are commonly known as grain, commodity, stock, or securities futures except as allowed for by law under the Illinois securities law;[247] (5) knowingly possesses any book, instrument, or

---

[235] 720 ILCS 5/26-3(b) (1999).
[236] 720 ILCS 5/26-3(c) (1999).
[237] 720 ILCS 5/26-4(a) (1999).
[238] 720 ILCS 5/26-4(d) (1999).
[239] 720 ILCS 5/26-4(b)(1) (1999).
[240] 720 ILCS 5/26-4(b)(2) (1999).
[241] 720 ILCS 5/26-4(c) (1999).
[242] See 720 ILCS 5/14-1 through 5/14-9 (1999). See ch. 10 of this treatise for a discussion of the prohibitions against electronic eavesdropping.
[243] 720 ILCS 5/28-1 through 5/28-9 (1999).
[244] 720 ILCS 5/28-1(a)(1) (1999).
[245] 720 ILCS 5/28-1(a)(2) (1999).
[246] 720 ILCS 5/28-1(a)(3) (1999).
[247] 720 ILCS 5/28-1(a)(4) (1999).

apparatus used to record wagers or any money received in a wager;[248] (6) sells chances on wagering pools;[249] (7) sets up or promotes any lottery;[250] (8) sets up or promotes a policy game or possesses policy slips or the like;[251] (9) knowingly drafts, prints or publishes any lottery ticket, policy slip, record or other similar device;[252] (10) knowingly advertises any lottery or policy game;[253] or (11) transmits information on wagers or betting odds by telephone, radio, and so on unless the information is transmitted in connection with news reporting of sporting events.[254] This state gambling law specifically exempts (1) insurance contracts,[255] (2) prizes awarded to contestants in games of skill, speed, strength, or endurance,[256] (3) pari-mutuel betting as authorized by state law,[257] (4) the manufacture of gambling devices to be transported and allowed by law outside the state,[258] (5) bingo games sponsored by nonprofit organizations licensed to do so,[259] (6) the Illinois State Lottery,[260] (7) the possession of antique slot machines not used or intended for use in connection with illicit gambling activity,[261] (8) raffles as authorized by state law,[262] (9) charitable games as authorized by state law,[263] (10) pull tabs and jar games,[264] and (11) riverboat gambling as authorized under state law.[265]

Paragraph 5/28-2 defines a *gambling device* as "any clock, tape machine, slot machine or other machines or device for the reception of money or other thing of value on chance or skill or upon the action of which money or other thing of value is staked, hazarded, bet, won, or lost;" as well as other equipment, including furniture, designed primarily for use in a gambling place.[266] This statute specifically states that (1) a "coin-in-the-slot" device such as a pinball machine, video game or similar device that rewards players with the right to replay with-

---

[248] 720 ILCS 5/28-1(a)(5) (1999).

[249] 720 ILCS 5/28-1(a)(6) (1999).

[250] 720 ILCS 5/28-1(a)(7) (1999).

[251] 720 ILCS 5/28-1(a)(8) (1999). *See* § 15.29 of this chapter and accompanying text for an explanation of "policy."

[252] 720 ILCS 5/28-1(a)(9) (1999).

[253] 720 ILCS 5/28-1(a)(10) (1999).

[254] 720 ILCS 5/28-1(a)(11) (1999).

[255] 720 ILCS 5/28-1(b)(1) (1999).

[256] 720 ILCS 5/28-1(b)(2) (1999).

[257] 720 ILCS 5/28-1(b)(3) (1999).

[258] 720 ILCS 5/28-1(b)(4) (1999).

[259] 720 ILCS 5/28-1(b)(5) (1999).

[260] 720 ILCS 5/28-1(b)(6) (1999).

[261] 720 ILCS 5/28-1(b)(7) (1999).

[262] 720 ILCS 5/28-1(b)(8) (1999).

[263] 720 ILCS 5/28-1(b)(9) (1999).

[264] 720 ILCS 5/28-1(b)(10) (1999).

[265] 720 ILCS 5/28-1(b)(11) (1999).

[266] 720 ILCS 5/28-2(a) (1999).

out returning money,[267] (2) normal vending machines,[268] (3) "crane games" which offer toys and novelties as prizes valued at no more than the lesser of either seven times the amount of one play or five dollars,[269] and (4) certain "redemption machines" or games, such as what is commonly known as "skee ball," that reward a player's skill with tokens which can be redeemed for inexpensive prizes,[270] are *not* gambling devices. The courts have ruled that the term *gambling devices* includes punch boards, poker games, and tickets, not just machines or mechanical devices.[271] Paragraph 5/28-1 punishes gambling as a misdemeanor.[272]

§ 15.29. Syndicated Gambling.

In response to the recognized relationship between professional gambling and other organized crime, and in the interest of deterring persons from engaging in the business of gambling for profit,[273] the legislature enacted the offense of "syndicated gambling," which is a felony.[274] The statute states: "A person engages in syndicated gambling when he [or she] operates a 'policy game' or engages in the business of bookmaking."[275] *Policy* is the name given a lottery type gambling system where a combination of numbers, such as 3-13-33, is selected by a player who marks his or her "numbers" or "guesses" on a slip or ticket, for which he pays a particular sum, and thereafter a lottery drawing occurs that results in winnings by the person or persons who selected the correct combination of numbers.[276] A person operates a *policy game* for the purposes of the syndicated gambling statute when he or she knowingly uses certain premises for the purpose of receiving money or policy game records from a person other than a better or player whose bets or plays are represented by the money or records.[277] A person engages in *bookmaking* when he or she receives more than five bets or wagers, "which bets or wagers shall be of such size that the total amounts paid

---

[267] 720 ILCS 5/28-2(a)(1) (1999).

[268] 720 ILCS 5/28-2(a)(2) (1999).

[269] 720 ILCS 5/28-2(a)(3) (1999).

[270] 720 ILCS 5/28-2(a)(4) (1999).

[271] People v. McDonald, 26 Ill. 2d 325, 329-30, 186 N.E.2d 303, 306 (1962).

[272] 720 ILCS 5/28-1(c) (1999) (although certain subsequent convictions may constitute a felony).

[273] 720 ILCS 5/28-1.1(a) (1999).

[274] 720 ILCS 5/28-1.1(f) (1999).

[275] 720 ILCS 5/28-1.1(b) (1999).

[276] 22 ENCYCLOPEDIA BRITANNICA 303 (1955). *See also* 720 ILCS 5/28-2(c) (1999) (a policy game is any scheme or procedure whereby a person promises by any instrument, bill, or token that any ticket or certificate shall in the event of any contingency in the nature of a lottery entitle the purchaser or holder to receive money, property or evidence of debt).

[277] 720 ILCS 5/28-1.1(c) (1999).

to such bookmaker on account thereof shall exceed $2,000."[278] Essentially the same activities that are exempt under the ordinary gambling statutes (raffles, etc.) are exempt from the reach of the syndicated gambling statute as well.[279]

§ 15.30.   Keeping a Gambling Place.

Paragraph 5/28-3 is designed to eradicate "keeping a gambling place," which is ordinarily a misdemeanor.[280] The crime is committed whenever "[a]ny person . . . knowingly permits any premises or property owned or occupied by him or under his control to be used as a gambling place. . . ."[281] A gambling place can be "any real estate, vehicle, boat or other property whatsoever used for the purposes of gambling."[282] Thus, tavern owners or operators could be convicted of this crime as long as they knew the establishment was being used for gambling purposes even though they were not otherwise participants in the gambling activities.[283]

§ 15.31.   Bribery in Contests.

The Criminal Code of 1961 addresses "bribery in contests" and sets out three separate offenses: "offering a bribe,"[284] "accepting a bribe,"[285] and the "failure to report offer of bribe."[286] With this legislative package, the legislature intended "to protect the moral character of participants and officials" from corrupt influences as well to avoid the "economic and psychological ill effects" of "fixed" contests.[287] Regarding the scope of this legislation, these crimes are merely an extension of common law bribery strictures into the field of sports; as such, the rules that apply to the bribery of public officials (as discussed in the previous chapter) are generally applicable.[288]

Paragraph 5/29-1 outlaws "offering a bribe" in contests:

---

[278] 720 ILCS 5/28-1.1(d) (1999). In addition, "bookmaking" does not require that the wagers be recorded. People v. Dugan, 109 Ill. 2d 8, 11-13, 485 N.E.2d 315, 317-318 (1985); People v. Scheidt, 142 Ill. App. 3d 844, 846, 492 N.E.2d 248, 250 (3d Dist. 1986).

[279] 720 ILCS 5/28-1.1(e) (1999).

[280] 720 ILCS 5/28-3 (1993) (second or successive conviction is punishable as a felony).

[281] 720 ILCS 5/28-3 (1999).

[282] 720 ILCS 5/28-3 (1999).

[283] People v. Katsigiannis, 171 Ill. App. 3d 1090, 1096, 526 N.E.2d 508, 513 (2d Dist. 1988).

[284] 720 ILCS 5/29-1 (1999).

[285] 720 ILCS 5/29-2 (1999).

[286] 720 ILCS 5/29-3 (1999).

[287] ILL. ANN. STAT. ch. 38, art. 29 (Smith-Hurd 1977), 1961 Committee Comments, at 296 (revised 1972).

[288] ILL. ANN. STAT. ch. 38, art. 29 (Smith-Hurd 1977), 1961 Committee Comments, at 296 (revised 1972). See ch. 14 of this treatise for a discussion of bribery of public officials.

Any person who, with intent to influence any person participating in, officiating or connected with any professional or amateur athletic contest, sporting event or exhibition gives, offers or promises any money, bribe or other thing of value or advantage to induce such participant, official or other person not to use his [or her] best efforts in connection with such contest, event or exhibition commits a . . . felony.[289]

In addition, where a person, with the intent to influence the decision of any individual, offers anything of value to another person to induce that person to (1) attend, (2) refrain from attending, or (3) continue attending any educational institution, for the purpose of participating or not participating in interscholastic athletic competition, that person commits a misdemeanor.[290] Legitimate scholarship inducements or the like are not contemplated by this statute.[291] Finally, where a person gives anything of value to an athlete enrolled in an institution of higher learning and represents or attempts to represent such athlete in future negotiations for employment with a professional sports team, that person commits a misdemeanor.[292]

The companion of the previous paragraph forbids "accepting a bribe," which appears in paragraph 5/29-2:

Any person participating in, officiating or connected with any professional or amateur athletic contest, sporting event or exhibition gives, who accepts or agrees to accept any money, bribe or other thing of value or advantage with the intent, understanding or agreement that he will not use his [or her] best efforts in connection with such contest, event or exhibition commits a . . . felony.[293]

The final proscription in the "bribery in contests" trilogy is the "failure to report offer of bribe."[294] It requires any participant, official or other person connected with an athletic contest or similar contest who receives a bribe offer made by another in violation of paragraph 5/29-1 "to report forthwith to his [or her] employer, the promoter of such contest, event or exhibition, a peace officer or the local State's Attorney" and makes a failure to report the bribe offer a misdemeanor.[295]

---

[289] 720 ILCS 5/29-1(a) (1999).

[290] 720 ILCS 5/29-1(b) (1999).

[291] 720 ILCS 5/29-1(b) (1999).

[292] 720 ILCS 5/29-1(c) (1999).

[293] 720 ILCS 5/29-2 (1999).

[294] 720 ILCS 5/29-3 (1999).

[295] 720 ILCS 5/29-3 (1999).

§ 15.32. Commercial Bribery.

Another form of bribery prohibited in Illinois is "commercial bribery," which includes two proscriptions relating to commercial affairs: offering a bribe[296] and accepting a bribe.[297] Paragraph 5/29A-1 reads: "A person commits commercial bribery when he confers, or offers or agrees to confer, any benefit upon any employee, agent or fiduciary without the consent of the latter's employer or principal, with intent to influence his [or her] conduct in relation to his [or her] employer's or principal's affairs."[298] Paragraph 5/29A-2 states: "An employee, agent or fiduciary commits commercial bribe receiving when, without consent of his [or her] employer or principal, he [or she] solicits, accepts or agrees to accept any benefit from another person upon an agreement or understanding that such benefit will influence his [or her] conduct in relation to the employer's or principal's affairs."[299] Both of these violations are "business offenses" punishable by a fine.[300]

§ 15.33. Money Laundering.

In an attempt to curtail the "laundering" of money accumulated from illegal endeavors, the General Assembly created the offense of "money laundering."[301] It provides:

> A person commits the offense of money laundering when he [or she] knowingly engages or attempts to engage in a financial transaction in criminally derived property with either the intent to promote the carrying on of the unlawful activity from which the criminally derived property was obtained or where he [or she] knows or reasonably should know the financial transaction is designed in whole or in part to conceal or disguise the nature, the location, the source, the ownership or the control of the criminally derived property.[302]

A "financial transaction" is defined as "a purchase, sale, loan, pledge, gift, transfer, delivery or other disposition utilizing criminally derived property, and with respect to financial institutions, includes a deposit, withdrawal, transfer between accounts, exchange of currency, loan, extension of credit, purchase or sale of any stock, bond, certificate of deposit or other monetary instrument or any other

---

[296] 720 ILCS 5/29A-1 (1999).
[297] 720 ILCS 5/29A-2 (1999).
[298] 720 ILCS 5/29A-1 (1999).
[299] 720 ILCS 5/29A-2 (1999).
[300] 720 ILCS 5/29A-3 (1999).
[301] 720 ILCS 5/29B-1(a) (1999).
[302] 720 ILCS 5/29B-1(a) (1999).

payment, transfer or delivery by, through, or to a financial institution."[303] A "financial institution" is given an expansive definition, including the likes of pawnbrokers, dealers in precious metals, or brokers in securities or commodities.[304] "Monetary instrument" is likewise given a broad meaning, including such things as certificates of stock.[305] "Criminally derived property" means anything gained through a violation of Illinois laws."[306] Money laundering is punishable as a felony.[307]

§ 15.34.   International Terrorism.

In 1997, the Illinois General Assembly enacted legislation which included the "solicitation of material support or resources in support of international terrorism"[308] and "providing material support or resources for international terrorism"[309] among the group of crimes which affect the public health, safety, and decency. First, paragraph 5/29C-5 defines "international terrorism" as activities that:

> (i) involve a violent act or acts, perpetrated by a private person or non-governmental entity, dangerous to human life that would be a felony under the laws of the State of Illinois if committed within the jurisdiction of the State of Illinois; and
> (ii) occur outside the United States; and
> (iii) are intended to intimidate or coerce a civilian population, influence the policy of a government by intimidation or coercion, or affect the conduct of government by assassination or kidnapping.[310]

A person commits the offense of "solicitation of material support or resources in support of international terrorism" when that person, charitable organization, professional fund raiser or solicitor raises, solicits, or collects material support or resources intending that the support or resources will be used to plan, prepare, carry out, or escape from an act of international terrorism.[311] To constitute a violation, therefore, an accused must have both solicited material support or resources for an international terrorist and intended that the material support or resources be used in furtherance of an act of terrorism.[312] In addition, a person

---

[303] 720 ILCS 5/29B-1(b)(1) (1999).
[304] 720 ILCS 5/29B-1(b)(2) (1999).
[305] 720 ILCS 5/29B-1(b)(3) (1999).
[306] 720 ILCS 5/29B-1(b)(4) (1999).
[307] 720 ILCS 5/29B-1(c) (1999).
[308] 720 ILCS 5/29C-10 (1999).
[309] 720 ILCS 5/29C-15 (1999).
[310] 720 ILCS 5/29C-5 (1999).
[311] 720 ILCS 5/29C-10(a) (1999).
[312] 720 ILCS 5/29C-10(a) (1999).

commits the offense of "providing material support or resources for international terrorism" when he or she provides material support or resources to any
person or organization intending that the support or resources will be used to
plan, prepare, carry out, or escape from an act of international terrorism.[313]
Again, the commission of this crime requires both the criminal act of providing
material support or resources and the mens rea requirement of intent to provide
material support or resources.[314]

"Material support or resources" is defined as any currency, securities, financial services, lodging, training, safe houses, false documentation or identification, communications equipment, facilities, weapons, lethal substances, explosives, personnel, transportation, and other physical assets.[315] Both soliciting[316]
and providing[317] any of the aforementioned resources in support of international
terrorism is punishable as a felony.

It should be noted that the legislature provides an explicit statutory bar against
investigating persons or groups for soliciting or providing material support or
resources for international terrorism simply because those persons or groups
provide non-violent support to other persons or groups who share their religious,
political, or philosophical ideologies.[318] The statute prohibits the initiation or
continuation of an investigation which focuses on activities protected by the
First Amendment to the United States Constitution.[319] Rather, the statute permits
an investigation under this section *only* when the facts reasonably indicate that a
person or group of persons knowingly and intentionally engages or has engaged
in a violation of this act or any other criminal law of this state.[320]

---

[313] 720 ILCS 5/29C-15(a) (1999).
[314] 720 ILCS 5/29C-15(a) (1999).
[315] 720 ILCS 5/29C-5 (1999).
[316] 720 ILCS 5/29C-10(b) (1999).
[317] 720 ILCS 5/29C-15(c) (1999).
[318] 720 ILCS 5/29C-15(b)(2) (1999).
[319] 720 ILCS 5/29C-15(b)(2) (1999).
[320] 720 ILCS 5/29C-15(b)(1)(A) through 720 ILCS 5/29C-15(b)(1)(B) (1999).

CHAPTER 16

DRUG CONTROL LAWS

§ 16.01.   Introduction.

Drug-related offenses became part of the Criminal Code of Illinois in 1935 under the Uniform Narcotic Drug Act.[1] The Act was substantially revised in 1957[2] and incorporated into the Criminal Code of 1961.[3] The Uniform Narcotic

---

[1] Act of July 8, 1935, Ill. Laws 723-33.

[2] Act of July 11, 1957, Ill. Laws 2569-86.

[3] ILL. REV. STAT. ch. 38, paras. 22-1 to 22-49.1 (repealed 1971).

Drug Act was removed from the criminal code in 1971,[4] with drug-related strictures being integrated into the food and drug laws of chapter 56½.[5] Legal scholars criticized the change, arguing that the criminal code had become fragmented and incomplete.[6] In 1992, the General Assembly, perhaps in response to such commentary and with the advent of the Illinois Compiled Statutes,[7] reinstated the prosecution for drug-related crimes under the chapter 720 prohibition of criminal offenses.[8]

Drug-related crimes appear[9] in the Cannabis Control Act,[10] the Controlled Substances Act[11] and the Drug Paraphernalia Control Act.[12] The latter enactment is directed at devices used for the consumption of drugs.[13] Further, many Illinois municipalities and other home-rule units have enacted drug control ordinances,[14] pursuant to their constitutional home-rule powers.[15]

The practitioner should note that certain drug-related conduct falls within the scope of federal law,[16] although prosecution under the federal system (or a similar law of any state) may be a bar to prosecution for the same conduct under Illinois law.[17] The scope of Illinois provisions will be examined in this chapter.

---

[4] P.A. 77-757 (1971).

[5] *See, e.g.*, ILL. REV. STAT. Ch. 56½, §§ 701-19 (1971) (Cannabis Control Act); ILL. REV. STAT. Ch. 56½, §§ 1100-1660 (1971) (Controlled Substances Act); ILL. REV. STAT. Ch. 56½, §§ 2101-07 (1971) (Drug Paraphernalia Control Act).

[6] Harry G. Fins, *Criminal Code of Law and Procedure for Illinois*, 71 ILL. B.J. 294 (1983).

[7] P.A. 87-1005 (1992).

[8] 720 ILCS 550/1 through 550/19 (1999) (Cannabis Control Act), 570/100 through 570/603 (Controlled Substances Act), 600/1 through 600/7 (Drug Paraphernalia Control Act). In addition to placing the Cannabis Control Act, the Controlled Substances Act and the Drug Paraphernalia Control Act under chapter 720 of criminal offenses, the compiled statutes removed the Narcotics Profit Forfeiture Act and the Drug Asset Forfeiture Procedure Act from chapter 56½ of food and drugs and placed such acts in chapter 725 relating to Criminal Procedure, 725 ILCS 175/1 through 175/9, 150/1 through 150/14 (1999), and the Intergovernmental Drug Laws Enforcement Act was included in chapter 30 of Finance, 30 ILCS 715/1 through 715/6 (1999).

[9] The only exception is the Hypodermic Syringes and Needles Act. *See* 720 ILCS 635/1 through 635/6 (1999).

[10] 720 ILCS 550/1 through 550/19 (1999).

[11] 720 ILCS 570/100 through 570/603 (1999).

[12] 720 ILCS 600/1 through 600/7 (1999).

[13] 720 ILCS 600/1 through 600/7 (1999).

[14] *See, e.g.*, CHICAGO, ILL., MUNICIPAL CODE ch. 7-24 (1990) (confiscation and fines for possession of certain substances); JOLIET, ILL., MUNICIPAL CODE § 21-14 (Supp. 1992) (drug regulations).

[15] ILL. CONST. art. VII, § 6(a).

[16] *See, e.g.*, Controlled Substances Act, 21 U.S.C. § 801 (1970).

[17] 720 ILCS 550/13(b), 570/409 (1999).

§ 16.02. Cannabis Control Act.

The Cannabis Control Act[18] (CCA) is a regulatory system for the production, distribution and possession of marijuana.[19] It was enacted notwithstanding (1) major national studies minimizing the hazards associated with marijuana use[20] and recommendations that offenses relating to personal-use possession or small amounts for non-profitable distribution be eliminated;[21] (2) that most marijuana strictures are widely criticized;[22] (3) the de-criminalization of possession of marijuana to various degrees by some states;[23] (4) the Illinois Supreme Court's finding that marijuana is not a narcotic;[24] and (5) the Illinois General Assembly's determination that marijuana use is pervasive and widely used among Illinois citizens and that previous legislation has been unsuccessful.[25] Still, the state legislature continues to insist that the harmful effect of cannabis[26] makes it necessary to prohibit the possession of even a minuscule amount of the substance.[27] Furthermore, courts have upheld such laws in the face of constitutional challenges.[28]

---

[18] 720 ILCS 550/1 through 550/19 (1999).

[19] 720 ILCS 550/1 through 550/19 (1999).

[20] *See* FIRST REPORT OF THE NATIONAL COMMISSION ON MARIHUANA AND DRUG ABUSE, MARIHUANA: A SIGNAL OF MISUNDERSTANDING 90 (1972) ("From what is now known about the effects of marihuana, its use at the present level does not constitute a major threat to public health"). *Accord* GOVERNMENT OF CANADA, CANNABIS, A REPORT OF THE COMMISSION OF INQUIRY INTO THE NON-MEDICAL USE OF DRUGS 101-30 (1972); SECOND REPORT OF THE NATIONAL COMMISSION ON MARIHUANA AND DRUG ABUSE, DRUG ABUSE IN AMERICA: A PROBLEM IN PERSPECTIVE 224 (1973) (affirming findings of the FIRST REPORT stating that when compared to other drugs, including alcohol, the use of marijuana required minimal social concern).

[21] *See, e.g.,* FIRST REPORT OF THE NATIONAL COMMISSION ON MARIHUANA AND DRUG ABUSE, MARIHUANA: SIGNAL OF MISUNDERSTANDING 152 (1972).

[22] *See, e.g.,* John F. Decker, *The Official Report of the National Commission Studying Marihuana: More Misunderstanding,* 8 U.S.F. L. REV. 1 (1973).

[23] Some states have eliminated incarceration as a penalty for possession. *See* CAL. HEALTH & SAFETY CODE § 11357(b) (Supp. 1992, supplemented 1999) (possession of 28.5 grams or less of marijuana is misdemeanor punishable by fine of not more than $100); *see also* MINN STAT. ANN. § 152.027 (4) (1998) (possession or selling of "small amount" of marijuana for no remuneration is petty misdemeanor punishable by fine up to $200); MISS. CODE ANN. § 41-29-139(c)(2) (1999) (one ounce or less punishable by fine not less than $100; not more than $250); NEB. REV. STAT. § 28-416(13)(a) (1995) (one ounce or less is "infraction," will receive citation, fine of $100, and attend course); N.Y. PENAL LAW § 221.05 (McKinney 1989, supplemented 1999) (possession punishable only by fine of not more than $100).

[24] People v. McCabe, 49 Ill. 2d 338, 349, 275 N.E.2d 407, 413 (1971).

[25] 720 ILCS 550/1 (1999).

[26] 720 ILCS 550/1 (1999).

[27] 720 ILCS 550/4(a) (1999) (possession of 2.5 grams or less punishable as a misdemeanor).

[28] *See, e.g.,* Illinois NORML v. Scott, 66 Ill. App. 3d 633, 636, 383 N.E.2d 1330, 1333 (1st Dist. 1978) (prohibition against private possession and use of cannabis was not protected by right

Although the primary concern of the CCA is directed "toward the commercial traffickers and large-scale purveyors of cannabis,"[29] the possession[30] or delivery[31] of even a small amount[32] is prohibited. Furthermore, the CCA applies to marijuana in many forms, including the "seeds thereof."[33]

The CCA contains several paragraphs comprised of a number of important proscriptions. The meaning of *cannabis* is delineated in paragraph 550/3.[34] Paragraph 550/4 addresses the problem of simple possession[35] and paragraph 550/5 sets out the strictures aimed at the manufacturing, delivery, and possession with intent to deliver cannabis.[36] Paragraph 550/5.1 outlaws "cannabis trafficking"[37] while 550/5.2 criminalizes delivery of cannabis on school grounds.[38] Paragraph 550/6 punishes the "casual delivery" of marijuana[39] and paragraph 550/8 forbids the "production . . . of the cannabis sativa plant."[40] Paragraph 550/9 outlaws a "calculated criminal cannabis conspiracy"[41] and the remaining sections deal with penalties,[42] directives for continued research on the substance,[43] and property forfeiture.[44] At this juncture, an examination and interpretation of this legislative package is in order.

§ 16.03.   — Cannabis Defined.

The CCA defines *marijuana* as any part of, or derivative from, the cannabis sativa plant.[45] While the drug is usually administered after the plants are dried or processed,[46] even immature plants are prohibited.[47] The parts of the cannabis

---

to privacy and sanctions were not cruel and unusual punishment); People v. McCaffrey, 29 Ill. App. 3d 1088, 1091, 332 N.E.2d 28, 31 (2d Dist. 1975) (not violation of equal protection).

[29] 720 ILCS 550/1 (1999) (legislative policy statement).

[30] 720 ILCS 550/4 (1999).

[31] 720 ILCS 550/5 (1999).

[32] 720 ILCS 550/4(a) (1999) (possession of not more than 2.5 grams); 720 ILCS 550/5(a) (1999) (delivery of more than 2.5 grams).

[33] 720 ILCS 550/3(a) (1999).

[34] 720 ILCS 550/3(a) (1999).

[35] 720 ILCS 550/4 (1999).

[36] 720 ILCS 550/5 (1999).

[37] 720 ILCS 550/5.1 (1999).

[38] 720 ILCS 550/5.2 (1999).

[39] 720 ILCS 550/6 (1999).

[40] 720 ILCS 550/8 (1999).

[41] 720 ILCS 550/9 (1999).

[42] 720 ILCS 550/7 (1999) (enhanced penalty for delivery to minor); 720 ILCS 550/10 (1999) (first offender probation); 720 ILCS 550/10.1 (1999) (fines); 720 ILCS 550/10.3 (1999) (assessments).

[43] 720 ILCS 550/11, 550/15 (1999).

[44] 720 ILCS 550/12 (1999).

[45] 720 ILCS 550/3(a) (1999).

[46] LESTER GRINSPOON, MARIHUANA RECONSIDERED 30-41 (1971).

[47] 720 ILCS 550/3(a) (1999); *see also* 1972 Ill. Op. Att'y Gen. S-390 (possession of marijuana is unlawful, regardless of whether it is growing or processed); People v. Wells, 241 Ill. App. 3d

plant that have a drug value[48] are considered "cannabis,"[49] while those that do not, such as "mature stalks" and "sterilized seeds," are explicitly excluded from the definition.[50] The statute is not clear as to what conditions constitute a "mature stalk" or "sterilized seed" and is, therefore, open to judicial interpretation. In *People v. Newell*,[51] expert witness testimony established that mature cannabis plants measure from eight to twelve feet in height.[52] The plants at issue in that case had measured one to two feet and, as such, were arguably not mature and prohibited by law.[53] A federal court upheld the defendant's conviction on habeas corpus appeal, defining a "mature stalk" as one that has "fully grown."[54] The court reasoned that while the exact age of the plants could not be determined, the fact that the plants were six to eleven feet short of mature growth suggested that they were "immature" and, therefore, fell within the definition of cannabis.[55]

The issue, however, seems moot in most situations because non-cannabinoid matter (such as roots, seeds, stalks, soil and moisture) may be included[56] in the

---

141, 147, 608 N.E.2d 578, 583-84 (3d Dist. 1993) (holding defendant could be convicted of criminal possession of cannabis even though cannabis is not in processed form, i.e., dried out and removed from stem of plant).

[48] The active drug in cannabis is delta-9 tetrahydrocannabinol (THC). Normal content ranges from 0.02 to 2.50%. Dwight S. Fullerton & Marc G. Kurzman, *The Chemistry and Botany of Marijuana-An Update*, 2 NAT'L J. CRIM. DEF. 145 (1976); *see also* LESTER GRINSPOON, MARIJUANA RECONSIDERED 42-54 (1971) (discussing the chemistry and pharmacology of cannabis). Many cannabis plants and plant parts contain less than 0.01% THC. Marc G. Kurzman, Dwight S. Fullerton & Michael O. McGuire, *Winning Strategies for Defense of Marijuana Cases: Chemical and Botanical Issues*, 1 NAT'L J. CRIM. DEF. 487, 510 (1975).

[49] 720 ILCS 550/3(a) (1999).

[50] 720 ILCS 550/3(a) (1999) ("'Cannabis' . . . shall not include the mature stalks of such plant, fiber produced from such stalks, oil or cake made from the seeds of such plant . . . or the sterilized seed of such plant which is incapable of germination").

[51] 77 Ill. App. 3d 577, 396 N.E.2d 291 (4th Dist. 1979), *habeas corpus granted sub nom.* United States ex rel. Newell v. Mizell, 497 F. Supp. 442 (C.D. Ill. 1980), *rev'd*, 667 F.2d 1247 (7th Cir.) (conviction reinstated), *cert. denied*, 459 U.S. 868 (1982).

[52] United States ex rel. Newell v. Mizell, 667 F.2d 1247, 1250 (7th Cir.), *cert. denied*, 459 U.S. 868 (1982).

[53] United States ex rel. Newell v. Mizell, 667 F.2d 1247, 1250 (7th Cir.), *cert. denied*, 459 U.S. 868 (1982). *But see* LESTER GRINSPOON, MARIJUANA RECONSIDERED 32 (1971) ("the plant may reach a height of 16 to 20 feet, or reach maturity at 1 foot, depending on varying conditions").

[54] United States ex rel. Newell v. Mizell, 667 F.2d 1247, 1250 (7th Cir.), *cert. denied*, 459 U.S. 868 (1982).

[55] United States ex rel. Newell v. Mizell, 667 F.2d 1247, 1251 (7th Cir.), *cert. denied*, 459 U.S. 868 (1982).

[56] *See* People v. Newell, 77 Ill. App. 3d 577, 579, 396 N.E.2d 291, 293 (4th Dist. 1979) (citing People v. Calhoun, 46 Ill. App. 3d 691, 696, 361 N.E.2d 55, 59 (3d Dist. 1977) (cannabis contained paper and bits of soil)).

weight of "any substance containing cannabis."[57] For example, in *Newell*,[58] the live plants that were seized — including stalks, moisture, roots and soil — weighed more than six hundred grams.[59] The defendant was convicted of possession of more than five hundred grams (giving rise to graduated penalties) even though the dried weight of the marijuana, with root and seeds removed, weighed only eighty-seven grams.[60] Further, Illinois courts have ruled that a person can be convicted on the basis of the weight of the substance at the time it is seized.[61] Thus, it is fair to conclude, that for all practical purposes, the only "mature stalks" or "sterilized seeds" that can be discounted or not included in the weight of the confiscated substance are those stalks and seeds that have been cleansed of all traces of cannabis.

It is well established that the positive identification of cannabis requires the aid of both chemical and microscopic analysis.[62] The Illinois Supreme Court has ruled that to determine accurately that a particular substance contains cannabis, it is necessary to perform a microscopic examination combined with the Duquenois-Levine test, which is a chemical analysis that is easy to perform.[63] In combination, the two tests are highly reliable.[64]

The state is not required to prove by chemical and microscopic analysis that every cannabis plant or gram of cannabis seized contains cannabis.[65] "The fact that only a portion is positively identified as containing the contraband goes only to the weight to be given the [expert] testimony, not to its admissibility."[66] In other words, the expert is permitted to give an opinion on the entire amount seized, based on the random selection and analysis of only a small amount of the substance.[67] If various lots or containers of cannabis are combined before the

---

[57] 720 ILCS 550/4 (1999) (possession); 720 ILCS 550/5 (1999) (manufacture or delivery).

[58] People v. Newell, 77 Ill. App. 3d 577, 396 N.E.2d 291 (4th Dist. 1979).

[59] People v. Newell, 77 Ill. App. 3d 577, 578, 396 N.E.2d 291, 292 (4th Dist. 1979).

[60] People v. Newell, 77 Ill. App. 3d 577, 579, 396 N.E.2d 291, 293 (4th Dist. 1979).

[61] People v. Newell, 77 Ill. App. 3d 577, 579, 396 N.E.2d 291, 293 (4th Dist. 1979); *see also* People v. Rhoades, 74 Ill. App. 2d 247, 253, 392 N.E.2d 923, 927 (4th Dist. 1979) (although sterile seeds are expressly excluded from statutory definition of cannabis, they can be included in weight of "substance containing cannabis").

[62] People v. Jackson, 134 Ill. App. 3d 785, 787, 481 N.E.2d 1222, 1224 (3d Dist. 1985).

[63] People v. Park, 72 Ill. 2d 203, 213, 380 N.E.2d 795, 800 (1978).

[64] People v. Park, 72 Ill. 2d 203, 213, 380 N.E.2d 795, 800 (1978).

[65] People v. Jackson, 134 Ill. App. 3d 785, 787, 481 N.E.2d 1222, 1224 (3d Dist. 1985) (where 20 envelopes of cannabis combined and then tested, sufficient); *see also* People v. Little, 140 Ill. App. 3d 682, 684, 489 N.E.2d 322, 324 (3d Dist. 1986) (not necessary to test each envelope where contents were combined before testing).

[66] People v. Newell, 77 Ill. App. 3d 577, 579, 396 N.E.2d 291, 293 (4th Dist. 1979).

[67] People v. Kline, 41 Ill. App. 3d 261, 267, 354 N.E.2d 46, 51 (2d Dist. 1976) (opinion regarding the whole of the substance based on small amount analyzed must be from substances after they are combined). *Compare* People v. Games, 94 Ill. App. 3d 130, 131, 418 N.E.2d 520, 521 (3d Dist. 1981) (expert opinion as to content of one bag based on chemical analysis did not permit inference as to second bag of cannabis).

random testing, this is acceptable; otherwise, each container must be tested individually.[68] Attacks on the sufficiency of the identification itself are rarely successful,[69] although one older study showed that preliminary identifications indicating marijuana may prove to be incorrect in perhaps as many as twenty percent of the samples analyzed by forensic laboratories.[70] Notwithstanding the suggestions on the part of defense attorneys and scientists that cannabis is polytypic and that certain varieties are of little or no value as a drug source,[71] Illinois courts have rejected attempts to distinguish other varieties, such as cannabis indica or cannabis roderalis, from cannabis sativa.[72] Moreover, the mere fact that the substance contains matter other than cannabis is irrelevant, as long as, the substance contains *any* cannabis.[73]

§ 16.04. — Amount of Cannabis.

The penalty structure of the Cannabis Control Act is directly related to the amount of cannabis seized.[74] Whether the offense is simple possession,[75] manu-

---

[68] People v. Jackson, 134 Ill. App. 3d 785, 787, 481 N.E.2d 1222, 1224 (3d Dist. 1985).

[69] *See, e.g.*, People v. Brisco, 78 Ill. App. 3d 282, 284-87, 397 N.E.2d 160, 162-64 (1st Dist. 1979).

[70] Marc G. Kurzman, Dwight S. Fullerton & Michael O. McGuire, *Winning Strategies for Defense of Marijuana Cases: Chemical and Botanical Issues*, 1 NAT'L J. CRIM. DEF. 487 (1975); *see also* Marc G. Kurzman, *Challenging "Scientific Evidence": Using the Results of the Laboratory Proficiency Testing Research Program*, in RESULTS OF THE LABORATORY TESTING PROGRAM ix, xii (National College for Criminal Defense 1979) (18% of controlled substances misidentified or otherwise subjected to unacceptable response). *But see* People v. Brisco, 78 Ill. App. 3d 282, 284-87, 397 N.E.2d 160, 162-64 (1st Dist. 1979) (conviction affirmed notwithstanding expert testimony of Professor Kurzman).

These critical studies have prompted this author to call for greater defense access to independent expert witnesses. *See* John F. Decker, *Expert Services in the Defense of Criminal Cases: The Constitutional and Statutory Rights of Indigents*, 51 U. CINN. L. REV. 574 (1982); *reprinted in* 6 CRIM. L. REV. 267 (1984); John F. Decker, *Access to Expertise*, 101 F.R.D. 599 (1983).

[71] *See* Marc G. Kurzman, Dwight S. Fullerton & Michael O. McGuire, *Winning Strategies for Defense of Marijuana Cases: Chemical and Botanical Issues*, 1 NAT'L J. CRIM DEF. 487, 500-08 (1975). *But see* People v. Brisco, 78 Ill. App. 3d 282, 284-87, 397 N.E.2d 160, 162-64 (1st Dist. 1979) (conviction affirmed notwithstanding defense expert testimony from Professor Kurzman).

[72] People v. Rege, 30 Ill. App. 3d 127, 131, 332 N.E.2d 154, 157, *aff'd in part, rev'd in part on other grounds*, 64 Ill. 2d 473, 356 N.E.2d 537 (1976) (legislative intent was that possession of all types of cannabis is prohibited by act, whether all is of species cannabis sativa or there is more than one species); People v. Krall, 29 Ill. App. 3d 86, 87, 329 N.E.2d 441, 442 (4th Dist. 1975) (noting that it is generally accepted that marihuana is monotypic); People v. Binkley, 25 Ill. App. 3d 27, 33, 322 N.E.2d 514, 518 (5th Dist. 1975) (studies regarding existence of three varieties are "preliminary and speculative").

[73] *See* People v. Newell, 77 Ill. App. 3d 577, 579, 396 N.E.2d 291, 293 (4th Dist. 1979) (citing People v. Calhoun, 46 Ill. App. 3d 691, 361 N.E.2d 55 (3d Dist. 1977)); *see also* 720 ILCS 550/4, 550/5 (1999).

[74] 720 ILCS 550/4, 550/5 (1999).

[75] 720 ILCS 550/4 (1999).

facturing, delivery, or possession with intent to deliver marijuana,[76] the most severe punishment attaches when more than 5000 grams of the substance is involved.[77] The next lower gradation relates to offenses involving more than 2000 grams but not more than 5000 grams of marijuana.[78] A lesser penalty attaches when the amount of cannabis seized is more than 500 grams, but not more than 2000 grams.[79] The next lower gradation occurs when the amount of cannabis seized is more than 30 grams, but less than 500 grams.[80] A lesser penalty attaches if the amount seized is more than ten grams but not more than thirty grams of cannabis.[81] A lighter penalty arises if the amount in question is more than two and one-half grams but not more than ten grams.[82] And finally, the least significant sanctions apply if no more than two and one-half grams of the substance are involved.[83]

A necessary consequence of the graduated penalty scheme is that proof of the weight of the cannabis is an essential element of the offense that must be alleged and proven, if an elevated penalty is sought.[84] It is not improper for the state to aggregate the weight of the various lots of seized contraband.[85] However, it is obviously not possible to aggregate the weight of cannabis and another type of illegal drug.[86]

---

[76] 720 ILCS 550/5 (1999).

[77] 720 ILCS 550/4(g) (1999) (possession: class 1 felony), 550/5(g) (manufacture, delivery, or intent to deliver: class X felony).

[78] 720 ILCS 550/4(f) (1999) (possession: class 2 felony), 550/5(f) (manufacture, delivery, or intent to deliver: class 1 felony).

[79] 720 ILCS 550/4(e) (1999) (possession: class 3 felony), 550/5(e) (manufacture, delivery, or intent to deliver: class 2 felony).

[80] 720 ILCS 550/4(d) (1999) (possession: class 4 felony, subsequent offenses are a class 3 felony), 550/5(d) (manufacture, delivery, or intent to deliver: class 3 felony).

[81] 720 ILCS 550/4(c) (1999) (possession: class A misdemeanor, subsequent offenses are a class 4 felony), 550/5(c) (manufacture, delivery, or intent to deliver: class 4 felony).

[82] 720 ILCS 550/4(b) (1999) (possession: class B misdemeanor), 550/5(b) (manufacture, delivery, or intent to deliver: class A misdemeanor).

[83] 720 ILCS 550/4(a) (1999) (possession: class C misdemeanor), 550/5(a) (manufacture, delivery, or intent to deliver: class B misdemeanor).

[84] People v. Calhoun, 46 Ill. App. 3d 691, 696, 361 N.E.2d 55, 58 (3d Dist. 1977).

[85] People v. Calhoun, 46 Ill. App. 3d 691, 696, 361 N.E.2d 55, 58 (3d Dist. 1977).

[86] People v. Tovar, 169 Ill. App. 3d 986, 995, 523 N.E.2d 1178, 1184 (1st Dist. 1988) (possession of marijuana and possession of controlled substance are two separate offenses even though acts closely related because offenses are under two different statutes).
The only instance where different "types" of marijuana must be segregated is where one type, obviously for personal use, is intermingled with other marijuana that is possessed with intent to deliver. Thus, where a partially burned marijuana cigarette was used as evidence of possession with intent to deliver it was inadmissible because the cigarette was not likely to be delivered. People v. Pates, 80 Ill. App. 3d 1062, 1068, 400 N.E.2d 553, 558 (3d Dist. 1980), aff'd, 84 Ill. 2d 82, 417 N.E.2d 618 (1981).

In addition to the penalty scheme for simple possession and manufacture, delivery and possession with intent to deliver, the quantity of marijuana seized may affect other criminal prohibitions as well. A calculated criminal drug conspiracy arises where, among other things, the amounts involved are thirty grams or more.[87] On the other end of the spectrum, the minor sanctions associated with "casual delivery" may only be applied if the amount is less than ten grams.[88] And, if a defendant possesses a large amount of the substance that is not likely to be consumed for personal use, it will give rise to the inference that the defendant possessed the cannabis with intent to deliver.[89]

§ 16.05. — Possession of Cannabis.

Paragraph 550/4 of the CCA is directed at what is often described as the *simple* possession of marijuana.[90] The penalty for possession of thirty grams or less is a misdemeanor,[91] while possession in excess of thirty grams constitutes a felony.[92] A defendant may be convicted for possession if the amount involved exceeds the applicable weight classification of the penalty charged and the substance contains "*any quantity of cannabis.*"[93] However, if no graduated penalties are sought, then it appears that any measurable quantity possessed activates the CCA.[94]

As with other criminal offenses, the normal rules of possession apply to cannabis.[95] That is, possession arises where the defendant (1) had knowledge of the

---

[87] 720 ILCS 550/9(b)(1) (1999).

[88] 720 ILCS 550/3(b), 550/6 (1999).

[89] People v. Cordle, 210 Ill. App. 3d 740, 741, 569 N.E.2d 209, 210 (4th Dist. 1991) (amount of cannabis alone, over 500 grams, without additional evidence is sufficient to support intent to deliver); People v. Kline, 41 Ill. App. 3d 261, 264, 354 N.E.2d 46, 49 (2d Dist. 1976) (6,433 grams); *see also* People v. Friend, 177 Ill. App. 3d 1002, 1021, 533 N.E.2d 409, 421-22 (2d Dist. 1988) (amount possessed may be less substantial than other cases but inference of delivery still enhanced by the manner in which drugs are kept: three separate packages of 92.9, 107.6, 101.6 grams).

[90] 720 ILCS 550/4 (1999).

[91] 720 ILCS 550/4(a)-(c) (1999) (unless between 10 and 30 grams involved and conviction is subsequent offense, whereupon sanction is a felony).

[92] 720 ILCS 550/4(d)-(g) (1999).

[93] People v. Rhoades, 74 Ill. App. 3d 247, 253, 392 N.E.2d 923, 927 (4th Dist. 1979) (emphasis original).

[94] *See* People v. Pates, 80 Ill. App. 3d 1062, 1068, 400 N.E.2d 553, 558 (3d Dist. 1980), *aff'd*, 84 Ill. 2d 82, 417 N.E.2d 618 (1981) (partially burned marijuana cigarette would be probative of simple possession but not possession with intent to deliver); People v. Hartfield, 94 Ill. App. 2d 421, 431, 237 N.E.2d 193, 198 (5th Dist. 1968) (prior statute; no minimum amount required; 0.995 grams amounts to possession).

[95] *See* ch. 2 of this treatise for a discussion of criminal possession.

presence of the contraband and (2) the contraband was in the defendant's "immediate and exclusive control."[96]

Possession of cannabis may be established by evidence of actual physical possession or constructive possession.[97] Actual possession occurs where the defendant exercised physical dominion over the cannabis while constructive possession exists where the defendant does not have personal present dominion over the drugs but there is intent and a capacity to maintain control of the cannabis.[98] The cannabis may have been found on the defendant's person or while the defendant is in the process of trying to conceal it or throw it away.[99] Mere proximity to the drug, however, is insufficient to establish actual possession.[100] On the other hand, constructive possession can be inferred where the defendant had control over the area in which the cannabis was found.[101] While a defendant's mere presence in the vicinity of the contraband does not create an inference that he controlled it,[102] both his knowledge and control over the substance may be inferred where he had control over the residence,[103] containers,[104] or

---

[96] People v. Nettles, 23 Ill. 2d 306, 307, 178 N.E.2d 361, 362 (1961) (possession of narcotics conviction affirmed), *cert. denied,* 369 U.S. 853 (1962); People v. Flores, 231 Ill. App. 3d 813, 817-18, 596 N.E.2d 1204, 1207 (4th Dist. 1992). It is important to remember that "exclusive" possession for purposes of constructive possession does not mean sole possession. In other words, the rule that possession must be exclusive does not mean that possession may not be joint. People v. Wells, 241 Ill. App. 3d 141, 146-47, 608 N.E.2d 578, 583 (3d Dist. 1993); People v. Lawrence, 46 Ill. App. 3d 305, 308, 360 N.E.2d 990, 992 (4th Dist. 1977).

[97] People v. Flores, 231 Ill. App. 3d 813, 817-18, 596 N.E.2d 1204, 1207 (4th Dist. 1992).

[98] People v. Wells, 241 Ill. App. 3d 141, 146-47, 608 N.E.2d 578, 582-83 (3d Dist. 1993) (possession of cannabis conviction affirmed); People v. Flores, 231 Ill. App. 3d 813, 817-18, 596 N.E.2d 1204, 1207 (4th Dist. 1992) (possession of cannabis conviction affirmed); People v. Howard, 29 Ill. App. 3d 387, 389, 330 N.E.2d 262, 264 (4th Dist. 1975) (possession of cannabis conviction reversed).

[99] People v. Lawrence, 46 Ill. App. 3d 305, 308, 360 N.E.2d 990, 992 (4th Dist. 1977) (evidence sufficient); People v. Howard, 29 Ill. App. 3d 387, 389, 330 N.E.2d 262, 264 (4th Dist. 1975) (evidence insufficient).

[100] People v. Howard, 29 Ill. App. 3d 387, 389, 330 N.E.2d 262, 264 (4th Dist. 1975).

[101] *See* People v. Nettles, 23 Ill. 2d 306, 309, 178 N.E.2d 361, 363 (1961), *cert. denied,* 369 U.S. 853 (1962); People v. Flores, 231 Ill. App. 3d 813, 817-18, 596 N.E.2d 1204, 1207 (4th Dist. 1992).

[102] People v. Kissinger, 26 Ill. App. 3d 260, 263, 325 N.E.2d 28, 31 (3d Dist. 1975); *see also* People v. Mosley, 131 Ill. App. 2d 722, 724, 265 N.E.2d 889, 890 (3d Dist. 1971) (marijuana found in trunk of car in which accused was passenger was insufficient to establish control); People v. Archie, 105 Ill. App. 2d 211, 214, 245 N.E.2d 59, 60 (1st Dist. 1969) (marijuana found on floor near student's desk not sufficient).

[103] People v. Galloway, 28 Ill. 2d 355, 359, 192 N.E.2d 370, 373 (possession of narcotics conviction upheld where premises in defendant's control and where his mail, other personal papers and men's clothing were found), *cert. denied,* 376 U.S. 910 (1963); People v. Miller, 97 Ill. App. 3d 970, 972-73, 423 N.E.2d 1152, 1154 (1st Dist. 1981) (possession of cannabis conviction affirmed).

[104] People v. Flores, 231 Ill. App. 3d 813, 819, 596 N.E.2d 1204, 1208 (4th Dist. 1992) (control found where cannabis was in containers in front wheel well of auto owned by defendant).

automobile[105] in which the marijuana is found. And this is true whether others were also present at the time of the seizure.[106]

Title to drugs is irrelevant in a prosecution for their possession.[107] Where an invitee brought marijuana to a party which was held in the defendant's apartment, evidence that the substance found on the defendant was given to him by the invitee was sufficient to show his possession.[108]

The possession of various "types" of marijuana is aggregated and deemed to be one offense.[109] Additionally, where multiple counts exist, possession is usually considered a lesser-included offense in charges of intent to deliver,[110] delivery,[111] manufacture,[112] and calculated criminal cannabis conspiracy.[113] However, where the defendant's alleged possession of cannabis was complete before any overt act of delivery occurred, sentences for both possession and calculated criminal cannabis conspiracy have been upheld.[114] On the other hand, possession of cannabis will not be viewed as a lesser-included offense of crimes under the Controlled Substances Act.[115]

§ 16.06. — Manufacture, Delivery, or Possession to Deliver or Manufacture Cannabis.

Paragraph 550/5 of the CCA makes it "unlawful for any person knowingly to manufacture, deliver, or possess with intent to deliver, or manufacture, canna-

---

[105] It is control of vehicle, not ownership, which is pertinent to proving control of area. People v. Whalen, 145 Ill. App. 3d 125, 131, 495 N.E.2d 122, 126 (4th Dist. 1986) (sufficient that defendant was driver of auto since he could refuse to transport passenger if passenger had cannabis).

[106] People v. Mack, 12 Ill. 2d 151, 161, 145 N.E.2d 609, 613 (1957) (control of heroin established where defendant paid rent, even though others had access to apartment; possession of heroin conviction affirmed); People v. Turnbeaugh, 116 Ill. App. 3d 199, 204-05, 451 N.E.2d 1016, 1020-21 (5th Dist. 1983) (presence of passenger in automobile did not defeat defendant's cannabis possession conviction).

[107] People v. Kane, 31 Ill. App. 3d 500, 509-10, 333 N.E.2d 247, 254 (1st Dist. 1975) (possession of cannabis and heroin convictions affirmed).

[108] People v. Fabing, 42 Ill. App. 3d 379, 383, 355 N.E.2d 719, 723 (1st Dist. 1976).

[109] People v. Calhoun, 46 Ill. App. 3d 691, 695-97, 361 N.E.2d 55, 58-59 (3d Dist. 1977) (where defendant in possession of various packets of cannabis, state properly aggregated together).

[110] People v. Anderson, 74 Ill. App. 3d 363, 372, 392 N.E.2d 938, 945 (4th Dist. 1979).

[111] People v. Austin, 23 Ill. App. 3d 520, 524, 319 N.E.2d 306, 310 (2d Dist. 1974).

[112] People v. Mills, 239 Ill. App. 3d 997, 998-99, 607 N.E.2d 608, 609 (3d Dist. 1993). Compare People v. Elam, 39 Ill. App. 3d 705, 709, 350 N.E.2d 832, 835-36 (5th Dist. 1976) (production of cannabis vacated as lesser-included offense of possession of cannabis).

[113] People v. Jones, 75 Ill. App. 3d 214, 229, 393 N.E.2d 1132, 1143 (5th Dist. 1979) (affirming calculated cannabis conspiracy while vacating delivery and simple possession convictions), cert. denied, 445 U.S. 968 (1980).

[114] People v. Binkley, 25 Ill. App. 3d 27, 34, 322 N.E.2d 514, 519 (5th Dist. 1975).

[115] See People v. Tovar, 169 Ill. App. 3d 986, 995, 523 N.E.2d 1178, 1184 (1st Dist. 1988) (possession of marijuana and possession of a controlled substance deemed two separate offenses even though acts closely related, because offenses under two different statutes).

bis."[116] With respect to the element of knowledge,[117] the state need only prove that the defendant knowingly delivered or manufactured any amount of cannabis;[118] it is not necessary to prove that the defendant had knowledge of the quantity delivered.[119] The particular amount of the substance relates only to the penalty which may be imposed.[120]

The mens rea of specific intent[121] is mandated where possession with intent to deliver is charged. To support a conviction of intent to deliver, it must be proved that the (1) accused had knowledge of the presence of cannabis, (2) that it was in his or her immediate control, and (3) that the quantity was in excess of the amount which might be viewed as possessed for personal use.[122] There is a legal inference that the defendant harbored intent whenever the amount is in excess of likely personal use.[123] Thus, where a defendant possessed 6,443 grams of marijuana, sufficient for 3,200 potential "joints" (marijuana cigarettes), he was properly convicted for possession with intent to deliver.[124] On the other hand, possession of one burnt marijuana cigarette will not give rise to such a presumption.[125] While evidence of a small amount could suggest simple possession, it would not support a charge of possession with intent to deliver.[126]

Specific intent is also required to prove a marijuana delivery charge on an accomplice theory.[127] For example, a conviction of aiding and abetting was upheld where the defendant was present during the sale of the marijuana and vouched that it was of good quality and worth the selling price.[128]

---

[116] 720 ILCS 550/5 (1999).

[117] *See* ch. 2 for a discussion of the mens rea of "knowledge."

[118] People v. Atchley, 97 Ill. App. 3d 85, 86-87, 422 N.E.2d 266, 268 (3d Dist. 1981) (where defendant acknowledged substance he delivered was cannabis, conviction for delivery of cannabis affirmed); People v. Jaffe, 64 Ill. App. 3d 831, 834-35, 381 N.E.2d 1018, 1021 (2d Dist. 1978) (where defendant was active and willing participant in drug transaction, delivery of cannabis conviction affirmed).

[119] *Cf.* People v. Ziehm, 120 Ill. App. 3d 777, 784, 458 N.E.2d 588, 593 (2d Dist. 1983) (delivery of controlled substances conviction affirmed).

[120] People v. Atchley, 97 Ill. App. 3d 85, 90-91, 422 N.E.2d 266, 271 (3d Dist. 1981) (weight is an element to be proved when defendant charged with delivery of more than 10 grams).

[121] *See* ch. 2 for a discussion of the mens rea of "specific intent."

[122] People v. Witherspoon, 216 Ill. App. 3d 323, 333, 576 N.E.2d 1030, 1037 (1st Dist. 1991).

[123] People v. Kline, 41 Ill. App. 3d 261, 266, 354 N.E.2d 46, 51 (2d Dist. 1976).

[124] People v. Kline, 41 Ill. App. 3d 261, 264, 354 N.E.2d 46, 49 (2d Dist. 1976).

[125] People v. Pates, 80 Ill. App. 3d 1062, 1068, 400 N.E.2d 553, 558 (3d Dist. 1980), *aff'd*, 84 Ill. 2d 82, 417 N.E.2d 618 (1981).

[126] People v. Pates, 80 Ill. App. 3d 1062, 1068, 400 N.E.2d 553, 558 (3d Dist. 1980), *aff'd*, 84 Ill. 2d 82, 417 N.E.2d 618 (1981).

[127] *See* ch. 3 for a discussion of accomplice theory.

[128] People v. Van Riper, 127 Ill. App. 2d 394, 397-398, 262 N.E.2d 141, 143 (2d Dist. 1970), *cert. denied*, 403 U.S. 918 (1971).

The *delivery* of cannabis requires an affirmative act. It is defined as "the actual, constructive or attempted transfer of possession of cannabis, with or without consideration, whether or not there is an agency relationship."[129] For instance, a conviction was upheld where the defendant told an informant that the marijuana was "more or less his roommates," took the marijuana off a shelf, and handed it to his roommate who then handed it to the informant.[130] Further, if a defendant willingly makes a delivery to an undercover government agent, he cannot claim the defense of entrapment if he had the intent or predisposition to sell the drug in question.[131]

The *manufacturing* of cannabis arises where an accused is involved in the "production, preparation, propagation, compounding, conversion or processing of cannabis, either directly or indirectly . . . and includes any packaging or repackaging of cannabis or labeling of its container."[132] In one case, defendants were convicted of manufacturing the drug where they were observed turning or stirring the marijuana under a heat lamp and packaging it.[133] A conviction for manufacturing was also upheld where the accused was at a friend's residence where the substance was found drying in the oven and raw marijuana was found in the basement.[134]

Simple possession and possession with intent to deliver are lesser-included offenses[135] of the delivery of cannabis.[136] So too, simple possession of cannabis is a lesser-included offense of manufacturing.[137] Delivery of cannabis is a lesser-included offense of a calculated cannabis conspiracy.[138] Possession of cannabis with intent to deliver is a lesser-included offense of cannabis trafficking.[139]

---

[129] 720 ILCS 550/3(d) (1999).

[130] People v. Hanson, 44 Ill. App. 3d 977, 985, 359 N.E.2d 188, 195 (3d Dist. 1977).

[131] Hampton v. United States, 425 U.S. 484, 488-489 (1976); *see also* People v. Cross, 77 Ill. 2d 396, 404, 396 N.E.2d 812, 816 (1979) (government supplying defendant with controlled substance is merely "providing the opportunity" for delivery and is not entrapment), *cert. denied sub nom.* Thomas v. Illinois, 445 U.S. 929 (1980).

[132] 720 ILCS 550/3(h) (1999).

[133] People v. Calhoun, 46 Ill. App. 3d 691, 693, 361 N.E.2d 55, 56 (3d Dist. 1977); *see also* People v. Aldridge, 58 Ill. App. 3d 260, 262, 374 N.E.2d 236, 237 (4th Dist. 1978) (cannabis manufactured where it was growing on land owned by defendant and which he paid to have plowed).

[134] People v. Spear, 24 Ill. App. 3d 818, 821, 321 N.E.2d 705, 707 (4th Dist. 1974).

[135] *See* ch. 1 of this treatise for a discussion of lesser-included offenses.

[136] People v. Lewis, 83 Ill. 2d 296, 302, 415 N.E.2d 319, 321 (1980) (possession of cannabis with intent to deliver is an included offense of delivery of cannabis); People v. Austin, 23 Ill. App. 3d 520, 524, 319 N.E.2d 306, 310 (2d Dist. 1974) (delivery of cannabis upheld, possession of cannabis vacated).

[137] People v. Freeman, 121 Ill. App. 3d 1023, 1032, 460 N.E.2d 125, 131 (2d Dist. 1984).

[138] People v. Jones, 75 Ill. App. 3d 214, 229, 393 N.E.2d 1132, 1143 (5th Dist. 1979), *cert. denied*, 445 U.S. 968 (1980).

[139] People v. Olivarez, 279 Ill. App. 3d 90, 100-01, 664 N.E.2d 156, 163 (1st Dist. 1996).

However, no CCA violations may be viewed as lesser-included offenses of the same type of breaches under the Controlled Substances Act.[140]

Violations that arose out of the same act may be barred by the same physical act doctrine;[141] however, offenses that are not lesser-included offenses are not barred by the doctrine where more than one offense arises from "incidental or closely related acts."[142] For instance, a defendant who delivered separate packets of cannabis to two different individuals was convicted of two separate counts of delivery.[143] Similarly, two counts of delivery were upheld where a defendant delivered cannabis to an undercover officer on two separate dates.[144]

§ 16.07.   — Cannabis Trafficking.

The prohibition of "cannabis trafficking" is defined in paragraph 550/5.1 of the CCA.[145] The offense of "cannabis trafficking" occurs when a person "knowingly brings or causes to be brought into [the] State for the purpose of manufacture or delivery or with the intent to manufacture or deliver 2,500 grams or more of cannabis in [the] State or any other state or country . . . ."[146] The penalty for the offense will depend on the amount of cannabis involved, however, the sanction imposed must be at least twice the minimum sentence and not more than twice the maximum term authorized by paragraph 550/5 for manufacture or delivery.[147] The obvious import of this legislation is entirely consistent with the legislative intent to treat major traffickers more severely than those involved to a lesser extent.[148]

"Knowledge" is the requisite mental state and is applicable to the provision as a whole. It is therefore necessary to prove that the accused had both knowledge of "bringing" the substance into the state, and knowledge of the "aim of that activity."[149] Further, the question of whether inclusion of the phrase "for the purpose of" invariably requires proof of "specific intent" to deliver was apparently answered by the Illinois Supreme Court in *People v. Frieberg*,[150] a case which

---

[140] People v. Edwards, 47 Ill. App. 3d 780, 782, 362 N.E.2d 439, 440 (4th Dist. 1977) (delivery of cannabis not lesser-included offense of delivery of LSD).

[141] *See* ch. 1 of this treatise for a discussion of this doctrine.

[142] People v. King, 66 Ill. 2d 551, 566, 363 N.E.2d 838, 845, *cert. denied*, 434 U.S. 894 (1977).

[143] People v. Hill, 56 Ill. App. 3d 510, 515, 371 N.E.2d 1257, 1260 (4th Dist. 1978).

[144] People v. Binkley, 25 Ill. App. 3d 27, 33, 322 N.E.2d 514, 518 (5th Dist. 1975).

[145] 720 ILCS 550/5.1 (1999).

[146] 720 ILCS 550/5.1(a) (1999).

[147] 720 ILCS 550/5.1(b) (1999).

[148] 720 ILCS 550/1 (1999) (intent of General Assembly is to direct "the greatest efforts of law enforcement agencies toward the commercial traffickers and large-scale purveyors of cannabis").

[149] *See* People v. Frieberg, 147 Ill. 2d 326, 347, 589 N.E.2d 508, 518 (1992) (addressing requirements of controlled substances trafficking prohibition).

[150] 147 Ill. 2d 326, 589 N.E.2d 508 (1992); *see* § 2.25 of this treatise for a more detailed discussion of this case.

addresses the *controlled substances trafficking* prohibition. The court reasoned that the legislative history of the offense of controlled substances trafficking, which contains language virtually identical to that of the cannabis trafficking stricture, reveals that the statute is to be broadly construed to encompass those "operating at the outer reaches of the network."[151] To require that the trafficker's intent to *personally* deliver a drug be proved would "eviscerate the intended breadth of [the] enactment" inasmuch as the offense of unlawful delivery and possession with intent to deliver already cover the same conduct.[152] In other words, a conviction for trafficking would be appropriate when there was proof that the defendant (1) *knowingly* brought drugs into the state, and (2) did so *knowing* of someone's (his or another person's) purpose to deliver.[153] Thus, intent to deliver or manufacture is an element that is an "alternative to, rather than synonymous with the element 'for purpose of * * * delivery.'"[154]

Thus, where a defendant boarded a train in Texas and exited the train in Chicago carrying large, padlocked bags containing an excess of 2,500 grams of cannabis, he was properly convicted of cannabis trafficking.[155] Where another defendant was apprehended bringing fifteen pounds of cannabis into Illinois from Missouri in his van, he was convicted of cannabis trafficking based on the circumstantial evidence that defendant had this substantial amount of the substance in his vehicle and because the planned delivery of the substance to informants was arranged by his wife.[156] Where a defendant, who was a passenger in a vehicle driven from Texas by a man with whom she had a relationship, had knowledge of the presence of cannabis in the vehicle, she was convicted of cannabis trafficking where 17,995 grams of cannabis were found in the vehicle and $1000 and a gun were found in her purse.[157] Where defendant was apprehended bringing 5400 grams of cannabis into Illinois from Texas, he was convicted of *conspiracy* to commit cannabis trafficking and his claim that Wharton's Rule barred his conviction was rejected inasmuch as it is not impossible to commit the substantive offense of cannabis trafficking alone and without the cooperative action or agreement of another.[158]

§ 16.08. — Delivery of Cannabis to Minor or on School Grounds.

Any person over the age of eighteen years who delivers cannabis to a person under the age of eighteen years, who is at least three years the offender's junior,

---

[151] People v. Frieberg, 147 Ill. 2d 326, 350, 589 N.E.2d 508, 519 (1992).

[152] People v. Frieberg, 147 Ill. 2d 326, 350, 589 N.E.2d 508, 519 (1992).

[153] People v. Frieberg, 147 Ill. 2d 326, 347-52, 589 N.E.2d 508, 518-20 (1992).

[154] People v. Frieberg, 147 Ill. 2d 326, 351, 589 N.E.2d 508, 520 (1992).

[155] People v. Lynch, 241 Ill. App. 3d 986, 991-92, 609 N.E.2d 889, 893 (1st Dist. 1993).

[156] People v. Hampton, 246 Ill. App. 3d 667, 674-75, 616 N.E.2d 641, 646 (5th Dist. 1993).

[157] People v. Roberts, 263 Ill. App. 3d 348, 351-53, 636 N.E.2d 86, 89-90 (4th Dist. 1994).

[158] People v. Cooper, 239 Ill. App. 3d 336, 353-54, 606 N.E.2d 705, 718 (5th Dist. 1992). *See* ch. 4 for a discussion of Wharton's Rule.

may receive a sanction under an "enhancement of penalty" provision that doubles the ordinary sentence attached to the violation.[159] Further, any person who
delivers cannabis in any school, on school grounds, on a conveyance used to
transport students, or on any public way within 1,000 feet of any school or conveyance may be convicted of "delivery of cannabis on school grounds," making
him or her subject to more serious sanctions than otherwise would be prescribed
for such action.[160] The term "school" is not defined in the prohibition but the
Illinois appellate court has held in the context of the Controlled Substances Act
that, in addition to elementary and secondary institutions, state college and university premises fall within the definition of the term.[161]

§ 16.09.   — Casual Delivery of Cannabis as Possession.

Casual delivery of cannabis is defined in the CCA as "the delivery of not
more than 10 grams of any substance containing cannabis *without consideration*."[162] Paragraph 550/6 allows the "casual delivery" of marijuana to be
"treated in all respects as possession of cannabis for purposes of penalties."[163]
The aim of this provision is to punish less severely the delivery of a small quantity of cannabis not for gain, than a similar delivery for profit.[164] However, it
appears that the state does not generally prosecute a delivery of cannabis as a
casual delivery since there have been no reported cases as of the date of this
writing.

§ 16.10.   — Production or Possession of Cannabis Sativa Plant.

By virtue of paragraph 550/8, "[i]t is unlawful for any person knowingly to
produce the cannabis sativa plant or to possess such plants."[165] Under the terms
of the "unauthorized production or possession of cannabis sativa plant" stricture,

---

[159] 720 ILCS 550/7(a) (1999); *see also* People v. Barnes, 16 Ill. App. 3d 837, 839, 306 N.E.2d
892, 893 (3d Dist. 1974) (imposition of maximum term of 360 days in penitentiary for sale of three
marijuana cigarettes by 23-year-old to teenager was not abuse of discretion).

[160] 720 ILCS 550/5.2 (1999). For example, delivery of between 2.5 and 10 grams of cannabis on
school grounds is a class 4 felony, *id.*, 550/5-2(d), while ordinary delivery of the same amount is a
class A misdemeanor. *Id.*, 550/5(b).

[161] *See* People v. Goldstein, 204 Ill. App. 3d 1041, 1048, 562 N.E.2d 1183, 1187 (5th Dist.
1990) (interpreting ILL. REV. STAT. ch. 56½, para. 1407(b)(2) (1989)), *cert. denied*, 502 U.S. 810
(1991). Delivering a controlled substance in a school is now addressed in 720 ILCS 570/407(b)(2)
(1999).

[162] 720 ILCS 550/3(b) (1999) (emphasis added).

[163] 720 ILCS 550/6 (1999).

[164] Normally, delivery of not more than ten grams of cannabis is at most a class A misdemeanor.
720 ILCS 550/5(b) (1999). However, a casual delivery of not more than ten grams, which is
treated as simple possession, would amount at most to a class B misdemeanor. 720 ILCS 550/4(b)
(1999).

[165] 720 ILCS 550/8 (1999).

while the production or possession of not more than five plants is a misdemeanor,[166] growing more than five plants is a felony.[167] In order to invoke the greater penalty, the state is not obligated to prove that a minimum amount of plants individually tested positive for cannabis.[168] In one case, chemical tests performed on plant material confiscated at the site where cannabis plants were found were considered sufficient.[169]

The more lenient penalty structure of production should be of little solace to those involved in the growing of such plants. This is because a defendant may be prosecuted, for example, under either paragraph 550/4 for possession of cannabis or paragraph 550/8 for production or possession of cannabis plants, or both.[170] Where defendant is prosecuted and convicted of both, a conviction and sentence for the greater is appropriate although the conviction and sentence on the lesser must be vacated.[171] Since a prosecutor has unlimited discretion in selecting the most appropriate charge, it is likely that a defendant found growing cannabis will be prosecuted for a more serious offense than production in order to avoid the lesser penalties of paragraph 550/8 for production.[172] In one case, the defendant was charged with unlawful possession of more than 500 grams of cannabis, a felony, and later charged with unlawful production of cannabis sativa plants, a misdemeanor. The defendant argued that she should be able to elect the misdemeanor production charge rather than the felony possession charge.[173] The appellate court held that the state, not the defendant, has the power to elect which of the two sentence provisions will be imposed.[174] Meanwhile, in another case, where defendants were growing marijuana plants outside a residence and additional plants hanging out to dry were found in a garage, they could be convicted of the production of the plants being grown *and* manufacture of cannabis based on the separate activity in the garage.[175]

---

[166] 720 ILCS 550/8(a) (1999).

[167] 720 ILCS 550/8(b) (1999).

[168] People v. Kramer, 204 Ill. App. 3d 1011, 1018, 562 N.E.2d 654, 658 (2d Dist. 1990) (conviction reversed on other grounds).

[169] People v. Kramer, 204 Ill. App. 3d 1011, 1018, 562 N.E.2d 654, 658 (2d Dist. 1990) (proof sufficient beyond reasonable doubt where plants were counted and thought to be within the 20 to 50 range and plant material gathered from defendant's apartment tested positive for cannabis; however, conviction reversed on other grounds).

[170] People v. Wells, 241 Ill. App. 3d 141, 147-48, 608 N.E.2d 578, 584 (3d Dist. 1993).

[171] People v. Elam, 39 Ill. App. 3d 705, 709, 350 N.E.2d 832, 835 (5th Dist. 1976) (because accused cannot be convicted and sentenced for both a greater and lesser offense arising out of the same act, the lesser offense of production must be vacated).

[172] People v. Wells, 241 Ill. App. 3d 141, 147-48, 608 N.E.2d 578, 584 (3d Dist. 1993).

[173] People v. O'Mahoney, 169 Ill. App. 3d 194, 197, 523 N.E.2d 635, 637 (5th Dist. 1988).

[174] People v. O'Mahoney, 169 Ill. App. 3d 194, 198, 523 N.E.2d 635, 638 (5th Dist. 1988) (reversing trial court's granting of defendant's motion for advisement and election).

[175] People v. Wagers, 255 Ill. App. 3d 497, 502-03, 627 N.E.2d 738, 741-42 (3d Dist. 1994).

§ 16.11.   — Calculated Criminal Cannabis Conspiracy.

The final stricture of the CCA is "calculated criminal cannabis conspiracy," which is a felony.[176] Paragraph 550/9 states this offense occurs where a person (1) violates the CCA laws against possession, or manufacture, delivery or possession with the intent to deliver, or the production of cannabis where the transaction involves more than 30 grams of a substance containing cannabis or the production or possession of more than 20 marijuana plants; (2) the violation is part of a conspiracy involving two or more *other* persons; and (3) the defendant either obtains something of value greater than $500 from the conspiracy, or he organizes, directs, or finances it.[177]

A calculated criminal cannabis conspiracy differs from a simple, or ordinary, conspiracy under paragraph 5/8-2 of the Code in several respects. First, while a normal conspiracy may be constituted by only two people,[178] a calculated conspiracy requires at least three.[179] Second, a simple conspiracy may be found on the basis of an illicit agreement and an overt act, not necessarily itself a crime, in furtherance of the agreement;[180] whereas a calculated conspiracy requires a violation of specific CCA provisions.[181] Third, a simple conspiracy involving cannabis does not necessitate that there be a certain amount of cannabis,[182] while a calculated conspiracy does.[183] Fourth, unlike a simple conspiracy,[184] a calculated conspiracy is possible only where the defendant obtained $500 or more from the conspiracy, or organized, financed, or directed it.[185]

The interrelationship between a simple conspiracy and a calculated cannabis conspiracy is not entirely clear. In 1974, the Appellate Court of the Fourth District found that the CCA conspiracy stricture was "intended to excise" cannabis

---

[176] 720 ILCS 550/9(a) (1999).

[177] 720 ILCS 550/9(b) (1999).

[178] 720 ILCS 5/8-2(a) (1999). *See* ch. 4 of this treatise for a discussion of ordinary conspiracy.

[179] People v. Robinson, 245 Ill. App. 3d 410, 411-12, 614 N.E.2d 531, 532 (3d Dist. 1993) (although there were two or more co-conspirators, other aspects of CCA conspiracy did not exist; conspiracy to manufacture cannabis conviction under general conspiracy law upheld).

[180] 720 ILCS 5/8-2(a) (1999).

[181] 720 ILCS 550/9(b)(1) (1999) (simple possession or manufacture, delivery or possession with intent to deliver 30 grams or more of cannabis or production of 20 or more cannabis sativa plants).

[182] People v. Caryl, 54 Ill. App. 3d 537, 538, 369 N.E.2d 926, 927 (2d Dist. 1977) (a conspiracy involving less than 30 grams of cannabis could be prosecuted under the general conspiracy provisions; trial court dismissal of simple conspiracy charge reversed).

[183] *See* 720 ILCS 550/9(b)(1), 550/4(d), (e), 550/5(d), (e), 550/8(c), (d) (1999) (more than 30 grams of marijuana or more than 20 cannabis sativa plants).

[184] People v. Robinson, 245 Ill. App. 3d 410, 411-12, 614 N.E.2d 531, 532-33 (3d Dist. 1993) (conviction for simple conspiracy to manufacture cannabis conviction affirmed, while CCA conviction impossible where no evidence defendant obtained $500 or more from the conspiracy or organized, directed or financed it).

[185] 720 ILCS 550/9(b)(3) (1999).

from the general conspiracy provision.[186] Thus, in their view, the CCA entirely "preempted" the subject, barring application of the general provision even where the more specific requirements of the CCA could not be established.[187] Conversely, in 1977, the Appellate Court of the Second District ruled that where the CCA was silent as to certain quantities, those under 30 grams, the general conspiracy provision should apply.[188] The Second District agreed, however, that where the terms of the CCA conspiracy should apply, the CCA would preempt the more general conspiracy statute.[189] In 1993, the Third District Appellate Court made clear that it agreed that the CCA conspiracy enactment, which requires that defendant profited $500 or more or assumed a role of organizer, director, or financier, did not preempt the general conspiracy provision with regard to a conspiracy involving cannabis, where the defendant did not profit $500 or more or assume the necessary central role.[190] Like the Second District, the Third District stated the CCA only preempts prosecution under the general provision when the more specific CCA is applicable.[191]

In any event, once the applicability of the statute is determined, the sufficiency of the evidence is essential. The defendant's CCA conviction was upheld where it was established that he directed the conspiracy by setting the price of the drug, deciding who would be allowed to buy the marijuana and where he assisted in making the actual sales.[192] Similarly, a CCA conspiracy conviction was upheld where the accused was centrally involved in a scheme with two other persons to sell thirty pounds of marijuana for $240 and the cannabis had been purchased for $170, with three-fourths of the price being paid by the defendant.[193]

§ 16.12. Controlled Substances Act.

The most comprehensive act of the Illinois drug laws is the Controlled Substances Act (CSA).[194] It is a complex and highly specialized statute and is mod-

---

[186] People v. Taylor, 18 Ill. App. 3d 480, 482, 309 N.E.2d 595, 596-97 (4th Dist. 1974).

[187] People v. Taylor, 18 Ill. App. 3d 480, 481, 309 N.E.2d 595, 596-97 (4th Dist. 1974). When *Taylor* was decided, the CCA addressed only cannabis in amounts between 30 and 500 grams, an obvious legislative oversight, while the amount at issue in *Taylor* was in excess of 500 grams. The statute was later amended.

[188] People v. Caryl, 54 Ill. App. 3d 537, 538, 369 N.E.2d 926, 927 (2d Dist. 1977) (general conspiracy statute applied since quantity involved was less than 30 grams).

[189] People v. Caryl, 54 Ill. App. 3d 537, 538, 369 N.E.2d 926, 927 (2d Dist. 1977) (CCA did not preempt general conspiracy provision in case at hand).

[190] People v. Robinson, 245 Ill. App. 3d 410, 411-12, 614 N.E.2d 531, 532 (3d Dist. 1993) (conviction for simple conspiracy to manufacture cannabis affirmed).

[191] People v. Robinson, 245 Ill. App. 3d 410, 412, 614 N.E.2d 531, 532 (3d Dist. 1993).

[192] People v. Jones, 75 Ill. App. 3d 214, 225, 393 N.E.2d 1132, 1141 (5th Dist. 1979), *cert. denied*, 445 U.S. 968 (1980).

[193] People v. Binkley, 25 Ill. App. 3d 27, 29, 322 N.E.2d 514, 515 (5th Dist. 1975).

[194] 720 ILCS 570/100 through 570/602 (1999).

eled after the Uniform Controlled Substances Act. The CSA is aimed at regulating the distribution and use of drugs, except marijuana, in Illinois.[195] This Act not only defines illicit drug trade,[196] but also regulates legitimate drug business and use.[197]

The Controlled Substances Act consists of six articles. Article I sets out the legislative intent that underlies the Act[198] and an extensive catalogue of definitions.[199] Article II contains exhaustive lists, called "schedules," of the substances that are regulated by the CSA.[200] Article III sets out the requirements for the lawful manufacture, distribution, and dispensing of controlled substances.[201] Violations and penalties for the unauthorized manufacture, delivery, and possession of controlled substances are proscribed in Article IV.[202] Article V authorizes the enforcement and administration of the CSA by government agencies[203] and Article VI consists of two short provisions regarding the application and validity of the Act.[204] Since the principle focus of this study is an examination of those controls directed at trafficking, possession, and the use of illegal drugs, most of the attention in this chapter will be placed on legislation of that nature, the schedules of controlled substances, and the crimes of possession, manufacturing, delivery, and trafficking of controlled substances.

§ 16.13.   — Article I: Legislative Intent.

In Article I of the CSA, the General Assembly expressed its recognition of "the rising incidence in the abuse of drugs and other dangerous substances and its resultant damage to the peace, health, and welfare of the citizens of Illinois" and its intent to provide a more effective system of control over the distribution and use of controlled substances, particularly to limit access of such substances to persons who have a lawful and legitimate reason to possess them, and to deter the unlawful abuse of the substances.[205] Furthermore, the Act is intended to pe-

---

[195] It should be noted that not all "controlled substances" are "drugs." *See* 720 ILCS 570/102(f) (1999) (definition of "controlled substances"). *Compare* 720 ILCS 570/102(t) (1999) (definition of "drug"). However, these terms will be used interchangeably in their broader meaning throughout this chapter.

[196] *See, e.g.,* 720 ILCS 570/401 (1999) (controlled substances manufacture or delivery); 570/401.1 (controlled substances trafficking).

[197] 720 ILCS 570/301 through 570/315 (1999) (registration and control of manufacture, distribution, and dispensing).

[198] 720 ILCS 570/100 (1999).

[199] 720 ILCS 570/102 (1999).

[200] 720 ILCS 570/201 through 570/216 (1999).

[201] 720 ILCS 570/301 through 570/315 (1999).

[202] 720 ILCS 570/401 through 570/413 (1999).

[203] 720 ILCS 570/501 through 570/509 (1999).

[204] 720 ILCS 570/601 through 570/602 (1999).

[205] 720 ILCS 570/100 (1999).

nalize most severely illicit traffickers and profiteers of controlled substances, and to acknowledge the functional and consequential differences between the various types of controlled substances.[206] Moreover, the CSA was passed to help unify state efforts to control illegal substances with the efforts of the federal government and other states, and to provide law enforcement authorities with the necessary resources to make the system of control effective.[207]

The General Assembly noted that it did not intend to treat the unlawful user or occasional petty distributor as harshly as the large-scale purveyor or trafficker.[208] To that end, the Act contains guidelines, along with a large degree of sentencing discretion, to enable courts to order penalties that can best effectuate the purposes of the CSA.[209]

§ 16.14.   — Article II: Schedules of Controlled Substances.

Article II of the CSA divides controlled substances into five schedules based on the degree of perceived harm that particular substances may cause.[210] The Illinois Department of Human Services has the responsibility of adding, rescheduling, and deleting substances within the schedules based upon: (1) their actual or relative potential for abuse; (2) scientific evidence of their pharmacological effects; (3) scientific knowledge regarding the substances; (4) their history and current pattern of abuse; (5) their scope, duration and significance of abuse; (6) risk to the public health; (7) potential to produce psychological or physiological dependence; (8) whether they are an immediate precursor of a substance already controlled by the Act; (9) potential to cause a fatal overdose; and (10) the long-range effects on health.[211] Currently, there are approximately two hundred controlled substances listed in the combined schedules.

Substances determined by the department to have the greatest potential for abuse and lack accepted medical use are listed in Schedule I.[212] This schedule involves certain opiates and opium derivatives, including heroin; various hallucinogenic substances, such as LSD; and a number of other highly dangerous drugs.[213]

Schedule II reflects the next most serious category of drugs. These are substances that have a high potential for abuse, are currently accepted for medical

---

[206] 720 ILCS 570/100 (1999).

[207] 720 ILCS 570/100 (1999).

[208] 720 ILCS 570/100 (1999).

[209] 720 ILCS 570/100 (1999).

[210] 720 ILCS 570/201 through 570/215 (1999).

[211] 720 ILCS 570/201(a) (1999).

[212] 720 ILCS 570/203 (1999).

[213] 720 ILCS 570/204 (1999).

use, and may lead to severe dependence.[214] Included in this schedule are opium, morphine, cocaine, methadone, amphetamines, and secobarbital.[215]

Schedule III substances have a potential for abuse less than those in schedules I and II, are currently accepted for medical use, and may lead to moderate or low psychological dependence.[216] The substances referred to in this category are certain dosages of codeine, compounds or mixtures of opium and morphine and anabolic steroids.[217]

Schedule IV substances have a low potential for abuse relative to those in Schedule III, are accepted for medical use, and may lead to limited physiological dependence or psychological dependence relative to the drugs listed in Schedule III.[218] This section includes phenobarbital and other substances that have a potential for abuse associated with a depressant effect on the central nervous system.[219]

Finally, Schedule V lists those substances that have the lowest potential for abuse, are accepted for medical use, and are least likely to lead to any dependence.[220] Among these substances are compounds that contain limited quantities of narcotic drugs such as codeine or opium.[221]

Upon its enactment, Article II was challenged by some defendants on the ground that it was improper for the legislature to delegate to an administrative agency the authority to decide which substances are to be placed in which schedule.[222] It was argued, among other things, that the scheme of this article failed to give ample notice to the citizenry as to what substances were controlled and that it breached the first article of the state criminal code, which states that "[n]o conduct constitutes an offense unless it is described as an offense in the Code" by the legislature.[223]

In response to these arguments, one commentator pointed out that:

> [T]he agency does not define what constitutes a crime — the legislature makes that determination when it adopts the statute by deciding that the use of certain substances with defined effects should be illegal. Therefore, lacking the expertise to determine which substances have the defined ef-

---

[214] 720 ILCS 570/205 (1999).
[215] 720 ILCS 570/206 (1999).
[216] 720 ILCS 570/207 (1999).
[217] 720 ILCS 570/208 (1999).
[218] 720 ILCS 570/209 (1999).
[219] 720 ILCS 570/210 (1999).
[220] 720 ILCS 570/211 (1999).
[221] 720 ILCS 570/212 (1999).
[222] See People v. Avery, 67 Ill. 2d 182, 367 N.E.2d 79 (1977).
[223] 720 ILCS 5/1-3 (1999).

fects, the legislature acts properly when it authorizes a panel of experts to make that determination.[224]

In *People v. Avery*,[225] the Illinois Supreme Court ruled that the delegation of authority was proper given the clear language and intent of the legislature.[226] Since Article II contained "intelligible standards to delimit (the administrative) authority," including the right of the legislature to negate any agency scheduling decision, the improper delegation theory was rejected.[227]

§ 16.15.   — Article III: Registration and Control of Manufacture, Distribution and Dispensing of Controlled Substances.

Article III of the Controlled Substances Act provides the necessary regulatory framework for the lawful manufacture and sale of controlled substances.[228] Just as the management of Article II is delegated to the Illinois Department of Human Services, the administration of Article III is to be performed under the direction of the Illinois Department of Professional Regulation.[229] "Every person who manufactures, distributes, or dispenses any controlled substances," or who "engages in chemical analysis, and instructional activities which utilize controlled substances" must be registered with the department.[230] The department retains the right to inspect any "controlled premises" of registrants.[231]

Under this Article, registrants are required to maintain records and inventories regarding their dealings with controlled substances.[232] Any distribution of controlled substances between registrants can only occur pursuant to a written order.[233] Prescriptions issued by practitioners for certain controlled substances, including all Schedule II "narcotics,"[234] must be issued on certain "official prescription blanks," each in triplicate, furnished by the governing agency.[235] One

---

[224] Note, *Administrative Law — The Uniform Controlled Substance Act*, 5 WM. MITCHELL L. REV. 229, 233-34 (1979).

[225] 67 Ill. 2d 182, 367 N.E.2d 79 (1977).

[226] People v. Avery, 67 Ill. 2d 182, 187, 367 N.E.2d 79, 81 (1977).

[227] People v. Avery, 67 Ill. 2d 182, 186, 367 N.E.2d 79, 80 (1977).

[228] 720 ILCS 570/301 through 570/315 (1999).

[229] 720 ILCS 570/301 (1999).

[230] 720 ILCS 570/302(a) (1999). Exempt from this registration requirement are (1) employees of such registered persons, (2) common carriers or warehousers, (3) ultimate users or persons in possession of such substances pursuant to a prescription, (4) officials of the state or federal government whose official duties require such possession, and (5) properly licensed pharmacists. 720 ILCS 570/302(c) (1999). *See also* 720 ILCS 570/313 (1999) (licensed treatment programs, hospitals and other licensed institutions exempt from Article III).

[231] 720 ILCS 570/302(e) (1999).

[232] 720 ILCS 570/306 (1999).

[233] 720 ILCS 570/307 (1999).

[234] 720 ILCS 570/102(aa) (1999) (definition of "narcotic drug").

[235] 720 ILCS 570/308 (1999).

of the triplicate forms must be preserved by the prescriber for agency inspection.[236] The person receiving the prescription must be given the original and remaining duplicate form from the prescriber.[237] That person then delivers both
copies of the prescription to whomever fills the prescription in order to receive
the controlled substance medication.[238] The person filling the prescription must
retain the original copy for his or her records and forward the duplicate copy to
the governing agency.[239]

By definition, Schedule I drugs cannot be dispensed since there is no accepted
medical use for such substances.[240] Most Schedule II drugs are considered "designated products"[241] that may only be dispensed pursuant to an official prescription blank.[242] However, Schedule III, IV and V prescription regulations are
somewhat more relaxed.[243]

The law relating to legitimate distribution also states that the practitioner may
only dispense controlled substances "in good faith," regardless of how they are
scheduled.[244] It should be mentioned that the good faith provision has been upheld as constitutional when challenged on the grounds of vagueness.[245]

The term "practitioners" refers to individuals or corporations, and a corporate
practitioner may allow a non-pharmacist employee to dispense a Schedule III or
IV drug to a recipient with a written, but not oral prescription.[246] Of course,
there are other concerns the practitioner must adhere to, such as ensuring that
dispensed controlled substances are properly labeled with cautionary instructions.[247] Failure to comply with these requirements may result in revocation of
registration[248] as well as criminal charges.[249]

Practitioners may be subject to severe criminal penalties for authorizing delivery of controlled substances "not in the regular course of professional treatment."[250] Specifically, paragraph 570/312(h) states that where a practitioner

---

[236] 720 ILCS 570/310 (1999).

[237] 720 ILCS 570/311 (1999).

[238] 720 ILCS 570/311 (1999).

[239] 720 ILCS 570/311 (1999).

[240] 720 ILCS 570/203 (1999).

[241] 720 ILCS 570/102(n) (1999).

[242] 720 ILCS 570/102(n), 570/308 (1999).

[243] See 720 ILCS 570/312 (1999).

[244] 720 ILCS 570/312(a) (1999).

[245] Ballin Drugs, Inc. v. Ill. Dept. Reg. & Educ., 166 Ill. App. 3d 520, 525, 519 N.E.2d 1151,
1155 (1st Dist. 1988).

[246] People v. Osco Drug, Inc., 12 Ill. App. 3d 603, 605, 298 N.E.2d 753, 755 (3d Dist. 1973).

[247] 720 ILCS 570/312(f) (1999).

[248] 720 ILCS 570/304(a) (1999).

[249] 720 ILCS 570/406(a) (1999) (first conviction: misdemeanor; subsequent convictions: felony
sanctions).

[250] 720 ILCS 570/312(h) (1999).

makes "[a]n order purporting to be a prescription" outside the scope of normal treatment practice, which is intended to provide an individual with controlled substances sufficient to maintain that person's or any other person's "physical or psychological addiction, habitual or customary use, dependence, or diversion of that controlled substance," that order "is not a prescription within the meaning and intent of [the] Act; and the person issuing it, shall be subject to the penalties provided for violations of the law relating to controlled substances."[251] Thus, although a technical breach of Article III will normally give rise to Article III misdemeanor sanctions,[252] a violation of paragraph 570/312(h) may be punishable under Article IV felony sanctions directed at completely illicit drug transactions.[253] Courts construing this and similar statutes have concluded that "[t]here is nothing in the statutory scheme to prohibit a physician who may be prosecuted for the relatively technical violation of [paragraph 570/312] from being prosecuted under [paragraph 570/401 (unauthorized manufacture or delivery)] for the significantly greater offense of acting as a 'drug pusher.'"[254]

§ 16.16. — Article IV: Unauthorized Manufacture, Delivery, Trafficking and Possession of Controlled or Counterfeit Substances, Controlled Substance Analog and Look-Alike Substances.

The strictures aimed at the illicit manufacture, delivery, trafficking, and possession of controlled substances are found in Article IV of the Controlled Substances Act.[255] Any manufacture, delivery, or possession with intent to manufacture or deliver such a controlled or counterfeit substance is subject to penalty

---

[251] 720 ILCS 570/312(h) (1999).

[252] 720 ILCS 570/406(a) (1999). Breaches include (1) a registrant dispensing drugs not allowed by his or her registration, (2) failure to comply with record or order-form requirements, (3) a refusal to allow authorized inspectors to enter registered premises, and (4) the keeping or maintaining of any place that is resorted to by a person unlawfully possessing controlled substances or any place where controlled substances are possessed, manufactured, or distributed in violation of the CSA. *Id.*

[253] *See* § 16.16 of this chapter. *See, e.g.*, People v. Cliche, 111 Ill. App. 3d 593, 598, 444 N.E.2d 649, 652 (1st Dist. 1982) (licensed medical doctor convicted of unlawful delivery of controlled substances under § 401).

[254] People v. Cliche, 111 Ill. App. 3d 593, 598, 444 N.E.2d 649, 652 (1st Dist. 1982) (placing physician on 30 months probation and assessing $1,185 in costs and fees because purported "prescriptions" issued without accompanying examination "were outside the regular course of professional treatment"). *Compare* People v. Albano, 216 Ill. App. 3d 247, 265, 576 N.E.2d 998, 1109 (1st Dist. 1991) (conviction reversed where physician prescribed dosages within range, fees charged not unreasonable, charts were kept on patients and some sort of examination conducted); People v. Chua, 156 Ill. App. 3d 187, 193, 509 N.E.2d 533, 537 (1st Dist. 1987) (conviction reversed where patient's complaint documented, physician refused cash offer or to prescribe for patient's wife and would not recommend pharmacy).

[255] 720 ILCS 570/401 through 570/413 (1999).

under paragraph 570/401,[256] unless authorized elsewhere in the Act.[257] Further, in the interest of controlling so-called "designer drugs," paragraph 570/401 prohibits the illegal manufacture, delivery, or possession with intent to deliver a "controlled substance analog."[258] A controlled substance analog is defined in this paragraph as "a substance which is intended for human consumption, other than a controlled substance, that has a chemical structure substantially similar to that of a controlled substance in Schedule I or II, or that was specifically designed to produce an effect substantially similar to that of a controlled substance listed in Schedule I or II."[259] Paragraph 570/401.1 outlaws "controlled substances trafficking," which arises where a defendant knowingly brings into this state a controlled substance for the purpose of manufacture or delivery.[260] Paragraph 570/401.5 prohibits the "chemical breakdown of illicit controlled substances," which arises where a person manufactures a controlled substance by chemically deriving the substance from another controlled substance or possesses a substance with the intent to manufacture from it another illicit substance.[261] Paragraph 570/402 prohibits any unauthorized ordinary possession of a controlled substance, except as covered by paragraph 570/401.[262] Paragraph 570/404 makes it an offense to manufacture, distribute, advertise, or possess uncontrolled substances intended to look like a controlled substance, which is referred to as a "look-alike substance."[263] A "calculated criminal drug conspiracy," which carries severe penalties,[264] is covered under paragraph 570/405 and paragraph 570/405.1 reflects the offense of "criminal drug conspiracy."[265] In addition, the Illinois legislature has added an offense entitled "streetgang criminal drug conspiracy," punished as a class X felony, which is detailed in 570/405.2.[266] Paragraph 570/406.1 prohibits "permitting unlawful use of a building," where a person knowingly permits a building under his or her control to be used for illicit delivery or manufacture.[267] Paragraph 570/406 sets out "miscellaneous violations" of this Article.[268] Paragraph 570/407 sets out "enhanced penal-

---

[256] 720 ILCS 570/401 (1999).

[257] 720 ILCS 570/401 (1999) ("Except as authorized by this Act," deliveries and the like of controlled substances prohibited); see, e.g., 720 ILCS 570/312 (1999) (authorized dispensing of controlled substances by practitioners).

[258] 720 ILCS 570/401 (1999).

[259] 720 ILCS 570/401 (1999).

[260] 720 ILCS 570/401.1 (1999).

[261] 720 ILCS 570/401.5 (1999).

[262] 720 ILCS 570/402 (1999).

[263] 720 ILCS 570/404 (1999).

[264] 720 ILCS 570/405 (1999).

[265] 720 ILCS 570/405.1 (1999).

[266] 720 ILCS 570/405.2 (1999).

[267] 720 ILCS 570/406.1 (1999).

[268] 720 ILCS 570/406 (1999).

ties" for delivery of a controlled substance to a person under eighteen years of age, delivery at a truck stop or rest area, delivery on school or public housing property, and delivery at or near a place of worship.[269] Paragraph 570/407.1 imposes enhanced penalties where a person aged eighteen or over employs a person under the age of eighteen to deliver a controlled substance.[270] Finally, paragraph 570/407.2 punishes delivery of a controlled substance to a pregnant woman.[271]

The penalties outlined in Article IV vary with the type of offense, the type of substance involved, and the amount of that substance. For example, the manufacture, delivery, or possession with intent to manufacture or deliver is treated more harshly than simple possession of the same amount of the same substance.[272] Offenses involving the most dangerous and least medically useful substances (especially those listed in Schedules I and II) are more serious than those involving less hazardous drugs.[273] The amount of the controlled substances involved in the crime is especially important in determining the proper penalty.[274] The graduated penalty scheme of Article IV has been challenged and found to have a rational basis and upheld as constitutional.[275]

§ 16.17. — Type of Controlled Substance.

A perusal of Article III reveals that the most serious penalties are reserved for offenses involving Schedule I and II substances, while the least serious punishment applies to Schedule V substances. Accordingly, the harshest sanctions are directed at drugs such as heroin, cocaine, morphine, peyote, derivatives of barbituric acid, amphetamines, LSD, pentazocine, methaqualone, and PCP, all of which are Schedule I and II substances.[276] Furthermore, "counterfeit substances,"[277] which are copycat controlled substances bearing a trademark or like-

---

[269] 720 ILCS 570/407 (1999).

[270] 720 ILCS 570/407.1 (1999).

[271] 720 ILCS 570/407.2 (1999).

[272] See, e.g., 720 ILCS 570/401(a)(1)(A) (1999) (manufacture or delivery, 15-100 grams heroin: 6 to 30 years). Compare 720 ILCS 570/402(a)(1)(A) (1999) (possession, 15-100 grams heroin: 4 to 15 years).

[273] See, e.g., 720 ILCS 570/401(d) (1999) (manufacture or delivery of narcotic drug: class 2 felony). Compare 720 ILCS 570/401(e) (1999) (manufacture or delivery of non-narcotic drug: class 3 felony).

[274] See, e.g., 720 ILCS 570/401(a)(2)(A) (1999) (manufacture or delivery of cocaine, 15-100 grams: 6 to 30 years). Compare 720 ILCS 570/401(a)(2)(B) (1999) (same offense but 100-400 grams: 9 to 40 years).

[275] People v. Hermann, 180 Ill. App. 3d 939, 948, 536 N.E.2d 706, 712 (1st Dist. 1988).

[276] See 720 ILCS 570/401(a), (b) (1999) (manufacture or delivery), 570/402(a) (possession), 570/405(b)(1) (calculated criminal drug conspiracy involving paragraph 570/401(a), (b) or paragraph 570/402(a)).

[277] See 720 ILCS 570/102(g) (1999) (definition of "counterfeit substances").

ness to a more well-known or recognizable drug — whether manufactured,[278] delivered,[279] or simply possessed,[280] — are prohibited in virtually the same way as true controlled substances.[281] The manufacture, delivery, or possession with intent to deliver a controlled substance analog is treated in the same manner as a scheduled controlled substance.[282]

Unless otherwise provided, an offense involving a Schedule I or II substance that is a "narcotic drug" is considered more serious[283] than one involving a scheduled substance that is "not a narcotic."[284] A drug offense, such as manufacture or delivery of a Schedule III substance, is the subject of a less serious sanction[285] than an offense involving a Schedule I or II drug that is not a narcotic.[286] Similarly, a delivery of a Schedule IV substance[287] is less of a concern than a Schedule III delivery.[288] And, a Schedule V crime is subject to the least harsh of penalties.[289]

§ 16.18.   — Amount of Controlled Substance.

Penalties under the CSA are graduated on the basis of the amount of the substance involved. Since large quantities of a dangerous substance are, logically, more dangerous than smaller quantities, sanctions relating to classifications on the basis of quantity are considered reasonable by the courts.[290] For example, a delivery of 15 or more grams but less than 100 grams of heroin is punished as a class X felony.[291] Delivery of more than 10 grams and less than 15 grams of the same matter is considered a less serious felony.[292] And, delivery of 10 or fewer grams of heroin amounts to an even lesser offense, albeit a felony.[293]

---

[278] 720 ILCS 570/401 (1999).

[279] 720 ILCS 570/401 (1999).

[280] 720 ILCS 570/402 (1999).

[281] Throughout Article III, the statutes routinely read "a controlled or counterfeit substance" without further distinction in terms of penalty or the like. *See, e.g.*, 720 ILCS 570/401 (1999) (manufacture, delivery or possession with intent to deliver).

[282] 720 ILCS 570/401(a) (1999) ("For purposes of this Act, a controlled substance analog shall be treated in the same manner as the controlled substance to which it is substantially similar").

[283] *See* 720 ILCS 570/401(d) (1999) (manufacture, delivery or possession with intent to deliver narcotic: class 2 felony).

[284] *See* 720 ILCS 570/401(e) (1999) (manufacture, delivery or possession with intent to deliver non-narcotic: class 3 felony).

[285] 720 ILCS 570/401(f) (1999) (Schedule III: class 3 felony, $125,000 fine).

[286] 720 ILCS 570/401(e) (1999) (Schedule I or II: class 3 felony, $150,000 fine).

[287] 720 ILCS 570/401(g) (1999) (Schedule IV: class 3 felony, $100,000 fine).

[288] *See* 720 ILCS 570/401(f) (1999) (Schedule III: class 3 felony, $125,000 fine).

[289] 720 ILCS 570/401(h) (1999) (Schedule V: class 3 felony, $75,000).

[290] People v. Hampton, 14 Ill. App. 3d 427, 433, 302 N.E.2d 691, 696 (1st Dist. 1973).

[291] 720 ILCS 570/401(a)(1)(A) (1999).

[292] 720 ILCS 570/401(c)(1) (1999) (class 1 felony).

[293] 720 ILCS 570/401(d) (1999) (class 2 felony).

The line of demarcation between various offenses that are dependent on the amount of substance involved varies from drug to drug. For instance, delivery of 200 or more grams of a barbiturate would be a class X felony,[294] delivery of more than 50 grams and less than 200 grams of a barbituate would be a lesser felony,[295] and delivery of smaller amounts of barbituate would involve still less severe penalty.[296] Constitutional challenges resting on arguments that the CSA punishes possession of certain amounts of certain substances, such as cocaine, more than possession of the same amounts of other substances, such as heroin, have not succeeded.[297] The Illinois appellate court explained that broad penalties to protect society from particular drugs, including cocaine, were "reasonably designed to remedy the evils the legislature has determined to be a threat to public health, safety and general welfare."[298]

The statutes measure quantity on the basis of "any substance containing" a controlled substance.[299] It is irrelevant whether the substance was pure or "cut" with an uncontrolled substance.[300] The Illinois Supreme Court has determined that it is reasonable to base the penalty schemes on the total amount of the substance containing the contraband, rather than on the amount of pure substance in the mixture.[301] This leads to the somewhat anomalous result that a person selling 15 grams of a substance containing a minute amount of cocaine commits a class X felony,[302] while one who sells fourteen grams of pure cocaine (which could be cut to yield several times that amount at the consumer level) commits a lesser felony.[303] Notwithstanding this anomaly, it has been ruled that this sentencing scheme is rational and does not violate due process or the equal protection

---

[294] 720 ILCS 570/401(a)(5) (1999).

[295] 720 ILCS 570/401(c)(5) (1999) (class 1 felony).

[296] 720 ILCS 570/401(d) (1999) (class 2 felony).

[297] People v. Pehrson, 190 Ill. App. 3d 928, 930, 547 N.E.2d 613, 614 (2d Dist. 1989).

[298] People v. Pehrson, 190 Ill. App. 3d 928, 932, 547 N.E.2d 613, 615 (2d Dist. 1989).

[299] See, e.g., 720 ILCS 570/401(a)(1)(A) (1999) (class X felony, delivery of heroin: "15 grams or more . . . of a substance containing heroin, or analog thereof").

[300] See People v. Mayberry, 63 Ill. 2d 1, 7, 345 N.E.2d 97, 100, cert. denied sub nom. Hurley v. Illinois, 429 U.S. 828 (1976).

[301] People v. Mayberry, 63 Ill. 2d 1, 9, 345 N.E.2d 97, 101, cert. denied sub nom. Hurley v. Illinois, 429 U.S. 828 (1976). See also People v. Kimbrough, 163 Ill. 2d 231, 237-43, 644 N.E.2d 1137, 1141-44 (1994) (upholding against equal protection and due process challenges the LSD provisions in the CSA which punish more severely LSD in object/carrier form than in pure form).

[302] 720 ILCS 570/401(a)(2)(A) (1999).

[303] 720 ILCS 570/401(c)(2) (1999) (class 1 felony). See People v. Yettke, 95 Ill. App. 3d 365, 372, 420 N.E.2d 194, 199 (4th Dist. 1981) (Craven, J., dissenting) ("Clearly, if a defendant has the intent of delivery, or for that matter manufacture, possession of 29 grams of cocaine is potentially more harmful to society than the possession of 29 grams of sugar mixed with one gram of cocaine"), cert. denied, 455 U.S. 1000 (1982). At the time Yettke was decided, the quantity for a class X felony was 30 grams of cocaine versus the present quantity requirement of 15 grams.

clause.[304] One appellate court explained that the legislature may have believed that a given amount of a drug may be distributed to a greater number of people and thus have a greater potential to be harmful if it is mixed with another substance.[305] And, while the soundness of that belief may be questionable, the court noted that the determination is one for the legislature to make and is not so unreasonable as to be unconstitutional.[306] Furthermore, the potential for unfair penalties can be diminished by the broad sentencing discretion provided to judges under the CSA.[307] As long as penalties are imposed within the statutory limits, the equal protection clause is not offended by similarly situated defendants receiving different penalties for the same offense.[308]

Similar to the way courts determine how much controlled substance is involved by weighing the whole substance, including the uncontrolled filler substances, courts are free to determine the value of the recovered substance based on the average street value per traditional street unit.[309] For example, where defendant was found guilty of unlawful delivery of cocaine, the lower court correctly calculated the mandatory fine, which is found by multiplying the number of grams by the average street price.[310] In that case, 82.9 grams were seized and the defendant was fined $8,290 based on reliable testimony that the street value was $100 per gram.[311]

The involvement of large quantities of drugs may jeopardize the defendant in another way. Possession of a particularly large quantity may justify prosecution for possession with intent to deliver, rather than for simple possession.[312] Where the quantity involved is large enough to distribute and is more than would likely be held for personal use, it is reasonable for the trier of fact to infer that the drug was possessed with intent to deliver.[313] That is, the quantity alone may be suffi-

---

[304] People v. Behnke, 41 Ill. App.3d 276, 280, 353 N.E.2d 684, 687 (5th Dist. 1976).

[305] People v. Behnke, 41 Ill. App.3d 276, 279, 353 N.E.2d 684, 686 (5th Dist. 1976).

[306] People v. Behnke, 41 Ill. App.3d 276, 280, 353 N.E.2d 684, 687 (5th Dist. 1976).

[307] See 720 ILCS 570/100 (1999) (legislative intent is to grant "wide latitude in sentencing discretion").

[308] People v. Hampton, 14 Ill. App. 3d 427, 433, 302 N.E.2d 691, 696 (1st Dist. 1973).

[309] People v. Lusietto, 131 Ill. 2d 51, 55, 544 N.E.2d 785, 787 (1989).

[310] People v. Lusietto, 131 Ill. 2d 51, 53-54, 544 N.E.2d 785, 786 (1989).

[311] People v. Lusietto, 131 Ill. 2d 51, 52-53, 544 N.E.2d 785, 785-86 (1989).

[312] See, e.g., People v. Munoz, 103 Ill. App. 3d 1080, 1082, 432 N.E.2d 370, 372 (3d Dist. 1982) (intent to deliver inferred from 250 grams of cocaine).

[313] See, e.g., People v. Munoz, 103 Ill. App. 3d 1080, 1082, 432 N.E.2d 370, 372 (3d Dist. 1982); see also People v. Taylor, 171 Ill. App. 3d 261, 265, 524 N.E.2d 1216, 1218 (1st Dist. 1988) (intent to deliver inferred from possession of 46 grams of powder containing pentazocine and codeine); People v. Carrasquilla, 167 Ill. App. 3d 1069, 1079, 522 N.E.2d 139, 145 (1st Dist. 1988) (intent to deliver inferred since 3,888.61 grams of cocaine was more than amount reasonably intended for personal use); People v. Tovar, 169 Ill. App. 3d 986, 994, 523 N.E.2d 1178, 1183 (1st Dist. 1988) (intent to deliver inferred from possession of 31.9 grams of cocaine and 5.2 grams of heroin).

cient to raise a presumption that the accused committed a more serious offense. For example, where the accused was found to be in possession of four plastic bags containing a white powdered substance, two of which contained a total of 1,953 grams of cocaine, the defendant's conviction for possession with intent to deliver cocaine was upheld.[314]

Inasmuch as the prohibitions against manufacture, delivery, possession with intent to deliver,[315] and simple possession of controlled substances,[316] counterfeit substances,[317] or look-alike substances[318] can be demonstrated by evidence of "any . . . amount" of such a substance,[319] there is no need to allege or prove that a particular weight was involved to gain a conviction.[320] On the other hand, if an increased penalty is sought because of the significant amount involved, then the weight is "an essential element going to the substance of the charge" that must be alleged and proved.[321] If the charging instrument fails to allege the minimum amount necessary for the increased penalty, the increased penalty is unavailable even if the facts presented at trial establish conclusively that the minimum weight was satisfied.[322] Also, if the prosecution proves that the offense has been committed but fails to prove the amount alleged necessary to justify the increased sanction, the conviction will stand, but the minimum penalty range will be applicable.[323] Thus, weight must be viewed as an essential element of the offenses carrying the increased penalties,[324] but it is not an element of the lesser-included offense involving "any other amount" of controlled substance.[325]

---

[314] People v. Atencia, 113 Ill. App. 3d 247, 250, 446 N.E.2d 1243, 1245 (1st Dist. 1983), cert. denied, 464 U.S. 917 (1983).

[315] 720 ILCS 570/401(d)-(h) (1999).

[316] 720 ILCS 570/402(c) (1999).

[317] 720 ILCS 570/401(d)-(h) (1999) (manslaughter, delivery and possession with intent to deliver); 570/402(c) (simple possession).

[318] 720 ILCS 570/404(b) (1999) (manufacture, delivery and possession with intent to deliver); 570/404(c) (simple possession).

[319] See, e.g., 720 ILCS 570/401(d)-(h) (1999).

[320] See, e.g., People v. Kadlec, 21 Ill. App. 3d 289, 296, 313 N.E.2d 522, 528 (3d Dist. 1974) ("The crime is committed by the delivery of a controlled substance regardless of the amount thereof. The particular amount of the controlled substance relates only to the extent of the penalty which may properly be imposed"). Accord People v. Cortez, 77 Ill. App. 3d 448, 451, 395 N.E.2d 1177, 1180 (1st Dist. 1979).

[321] People v. Kadlec, 21 Ill. App. 3d 289, 295, 313 N.E.2d 522, 527 (3d Dist. 1974).

[322] People v. Clutts, 43 Ill. App. 3d 366, 368, 356 N.E.2d 1367, 1370 (5th Dist. 1976) (where indictment charged defendants with sale of 50,000 tablets of amphetamines without specifying gram amount, defendant could only be convicted of a lesser offense involving "any other amount").

[323] People v. Clutts, 43 Ill. App. 3d 366, 371, 356 N.E.2d 1367, 1371 (5th Dist. 1976). Accord People v. Wolff, 75 Ill. App. 3d 966, 969, 394 N.E.2d 755, 758 (3d Dist. 1979).

[324] People v. Jones, 174 Ill. 2d 427, 428-29, 675 N.E.2d 99, 100 (1996). See also People v. Hill, 169 Ill. App. 3d 901, 911, 524 N.E.2d 604, 611 (1st Dist. 1988) (where there exists a lesser-included offense for possessing a smaller amount of controlled substance, weight of controlled

Although weight is an essential element to be proved where there exists a lesser-included offense of possession of a smaller amount, it is not necessary to test every sample seized in order to establish the makeup of the substance as a whole.[326] Random testing is permissible when the samples seized are sufficiently homogenous so that one may conclude the untested samples contain the same substances as those that are conclusively tested.[327] However, when such samples are not sufficiently homogenous, a portion of *each* container or sample must be tested.[328] Thus, where the likes of tablets or capsules have identical markings, lettering characteristics, beveling and scoring, it would be unnecessary to test each tablet; however, where five packets, each containing a loose, white rocky substance, were seized together, each packet must be tested.[329] It is important to note, however, that a field test alone is insufficient to prove the nature of a substance.[330]

§ 16.19.   — Counterfeit Substances.

The General Assembly gave added strength to the CSA by including within the reach of the Act, the simple possession, possession with intent to deliver, delivery, manufacture, and trafficking of so-called *counterfeit* substances.[331] The CSA defines a counterfeit substance as any controlled substance or accompanying packaging material "which, without authorization bears [any identification mark] of a manufacturer, distributor, or dispenser other than the person who in fact manufactured, distributed, or dispensed the substance."[332]

Since 1982, counterfeit substances have been treated exactly the same as other controlled substances.[333] The delivery or possession of a counterfeit substance is punishable in the same way as the delivery or possession of a controlled substance.[334]

---

substance is essential element of greater charge of possession of controlled substance and must be proved beyond a reasonable doubt).

[325] People v. Clutts, 43 Ill. App. 3d 366, 368, 356 N.E.2d 1367, 1370 (5th Dist. 1976).

[326] People v. Jones, 174 Ill. 2d 427, 428-29, 675 N.E.2d 99, 100 (1996).

[327] People v. Jones, 174 Ill. 2d 427, 428-29, 675 N.E.2d 99, 100 (1996).

[328] People v. Jones, 174 Ill. 2d 427, 428-29, 675 N.E.2d 99, 101 (1996); People v. Hall, 306 Ill. App. 3d 848, 849, 715 N.E.2d 300, 302 (3d Dist. 1999).

[329] People v. Jones, 174 Ill. 2d 427, 428-29, 675 N.E.2d 99, 100-01 (1996).

[330] People v. Hagberg, 301 Ill. App. 3d 491, 494-96, 703 N.E.2d 973, 975-76 (2d Dist. 1998) (field test insufficient to identify a controlled substance). *Hagberg* suggests a lab test by a trained chemist is required.

[331] *See, e.g.,* 720 ILCS 570/401.1(a) (1999) (prohibiting controlled substance trafficking in controlled or counterfeit substances).

[332] 720 ILCS 570/102(g) (1999).

[333] *See, e.g.,* 720 ILCS 570/401 (1999) (prohibits, manufacture, delivery or possession with intent to deliver "a controlled or counterfeit substance").

[334] *See, e.g.,* 720 ILCS 570/401 (1999).

It is important to recognize that a counterfeit substance is not the same as a look-alike substance. A counterfeit substance is a *controlled* substance that was manufactured in a manner to bear a likeness to another perhaps more well known or recognizable drug.[335] Presumably, if an illicit manufacturer unlawfully produced valium tablets bearing a legitimate manufacturer's imprint and packaged them in containers bearing the trade name of the legitimate manufacturer who had not authorized the production in question, this would be considered a counterfeit substance.[336] In contrast, a look-alike substance is an *uncontrolled* substance that appears or purports to be or is represented to be a controlled substance.[337] In most instances, penalties for conduct involving counterfeit substances are more severe than those for conduct involving look-alike substances.[338]

§ 16.20. — Look-Alike Substances.

Paragraph 570/404 states that "[i]t is unlawful for any person knowingly to manufacture, distribute, advertise or possess with intent to manufacture or distribute a look-alike substance."[339] The CSA forbids even the simple possession of a look-alike substance.[340] These laws are primarily directed at drug pushers who attempt to avoid the reach of the criminal law by profiting from the drug trade without actually distributing drugs that are true controlled substances.[341] The Illinois Supreme Court has considered and rejected arguments that paragraph 570/404 is at odds with the due process clause and has held that the statute is not unconstitutionally vague.[342]

---

[335] *See* 720 ILCS 570/102(g) (1999).

[336] *See* 720 ILCS 570/102(g) (1999).

[337] 720 ILCS 570/102(y) (1999).

[338] *See, e.g.,* 720 ILCS 570/404(b) (1999) (delivery of look-alike substance, for instance, a substance purported to be heroin, is a class 3 felony regardless of quantity and type). *Compare* 720 ILCS 570/401(e) (1999) (delivery of 15 grams or more of a counterfeit substance containing heroin is class X felony).

[339] 720 ILCS 570/404(b) (1999). *See also* 720 ILCS 570/102(y) (1999) (definition of "look-alike substance").

[340] 720 ILCS 570/404(c) (1999). Exempt from the reach of this paragraph's strictures, among other persons, are "persons acting in the course and legitimate scope of their employment as law enforcement officers." 720 ILCS 570/404(e)(2) (1999).

[341] *See generally* Comment, *Look-Alike Drugs: Eliminating a Profitable Loophole in Existing Drug Laws,* 87 DICK. L. REV. 155 (1982) (discussing justifications for outlawing look-alike substances).

[342] People v. Upton, 114 Ill. 2d 362, 366-76, 500 N.E.2d 943, 945-50 (1986) (penalty structure that penalizes some look-alike substances more than bona-fide controlled substances upheld); People v. Matkovick, 101 Ill. 2d 268, 276, 461 N.E.2d 964, 968 (prohibition not unconstitutionally vague or overbroad), *appeal dismissed,* 469 U.S. 806 (1984).

Look-alike drugs are the only substances governed by the CSA that do not appear in one of the Article II schedules. These "pseudo narcotics"[343] are usually made from substances that are readily available without a prescription and are made or marketed in such a way as to suggest that they are controlled substances.[344] For example, where an accused claimed to a purchaser that certain tablets were either methaquaglone or amphetamine, the caffeine tablets were considered look-alike substances.[345] If the substance contains any amount of a controlled substance, then by definition it is not a look-alike substance since look-alike substances are substances "other than a controlled substance."[346] Thus, if an illicit drug trafficker delivered L.S.D. that was represented to be mescaline, the trafficker would be punished for delivery of a controlled substance, not a look-alike substance.[347]

In order to convict a person of a paragraph 570/404 infraction, the state must prove that the defendant knew that the substance was a look-alike[348] or "believed the look-alike substance actually to be a controlled substance."[349] In order to qualify as a look-alike substance, it must bear a likeness to a controlled substance or be purported to be a controlled substance.[350] This means that the substance's "overall . . . appearance . . . would lead a reasonable person to believe that the substance is a controlled substance," or that it is "expressly or impliedly represented to be a controlled substance or is distributed under circumstances which would lead a reasonable person to believe that the substance is a controlled substance."[351] In making this determination, the court may consider (1) statements made by the owner of the substance "concerning its nature, use or effect;" (2) statements made to the buyer of the substance "that the substance may be resold for profit;" (3) the packaging of the substance in a manner suggesting it is a controlled substance; and (4) whether there was consideration involved and if the amount of the consideration "was substantially greater than the reasonable retail market value of the substance."[352]

The Illinois appellate court has held that simultaneous possession of a controlled substance and a look-alike substance is sufficient to support two separate

---

[343] People v. Jones, 174 Ill. 2d 427, 430, 675 N.E.2d 99, 101 (1996).

[344] See 720 ILCS 570/102(y) (1999).

[345] See People v. Upton, 114 Ill. 2d 362, 366-76, 500 N.E.2d 943, 945-50 (1986) (convictions for delivery of look-alike substances upheld).

[346] 720 ILCS 570/102(y) (1999).

[347] People v. James, 38 Ill. App. 3d 594, 595-97, 348 N.E.2d 295, 297-98 (2d Dist. 1976), appeal dismissed, 429 U.S. 1082, reh'g denied, 430 U.S. 976 (1977).

[348] 720 ILCS 570/404(b), (c) (1999).

[349] 720 ILCS 570/404(d) (1999) (belief that look-alike is controlled substance is not a defense).

[350] 720 ILCS 570/102(y) (1999).

[351] 720 ILCS 570/102(y) (1999).

[352] 720 ILCS 570/102(y) (1999).

charges.[353] Because the CSA contains "separate and distinct" paragraphs regulating possession of controlled and look-alike substances, the simultaneous possession of both substances is considered to constitute two separate offenses.[354] An intriguing question about the current look-alike enactment revolves around its penalty structure. Usually, the sanctions attached to delivery of a controlled or counterfeit substance exceed the penalties attached to a look-alike substance,[355] and possession of a controlled substance is invariably treated as a more serious crime than possession of a look-alike substance.[356] However, while delivery of a Schedule III, IV, or V substance and delivery of a look-alike substance are both felonies of the same class,[357] the maximum fines for delivery of a Schedule III, IV, or V substance are less severe than for delivery of a look-alike substance.[358] In other words, the potential penalty for delivery of a look-alike substance represented to be either a Schedule III, IV or V drug exceeds the potential penalty that would be available had the delivery actually been the controlled substance that it was claimed to be.

In 1982, the Illinois Supreme Court held that the penalty provisions of the statute were unconstitutional where the defendant had in fact received a potentially greater penalty for delivering 0.4 grams of a "harmless" substance than an offender might have faced for delivering any amount of real controlled substances classified in the lower schedules.[359] The court found that "[j]ust as delivery of a controlled substance represents a greater threat to the public under the Illinois Controlled Substances Act than the possession of a controlled substance, the delivery of a controlled substance represented a greater threat to the public than the delivery of a non-controlled harmless substance.[360] After concluding that paragraph 570/404 (as it is now designated) was "not reasonably designed to remedy the evil which the legislature determined to be a greater

---

[353] People v. Watkins, 172 Ill. App. 3d 168, 171, 526 N.E.2d 448, 449 (1st Dist. 1988).

[354] People v. Watkins, 172 Ill. App. 3d 168, 171, 526 N.E.2d 448, 449 (1st Dist. 1988).

[355] See § 16.19 of this chapter.

[356] See 720 ILCS 570/402(c) (1999) (class 4 felony is least serious penalty for possession of controlled or counterfeit substance). Compare 720 ILCS 570/404(c) (1999) (possession of look-alike substance is petty offense unless subsequent conviction, whereupon misdemeanor).

[357] See 720 ILCS 570/401(f) (1999) (delivery Schedule III substance: class 3 felony), 570/401(g) (delivery Schedule IV substance: class 3 felony), 570/401(h) (delivery Schedule V substance: class 3 felony), 570/404(b) (delivery look-alike substance: class 3 felony).

[358] See 720 ILCS 570/401(f) (1999) (delivery Schedule III substance: fine $125,000), 570/401(g) (delivery Schedule IV substance: $100,000), 570/401(h) (delivery Schedule V substance: fine $75,000). Compare 720 ILCS 570/404(b) (1999) (delivery of look-alike substance is subject to fine of $150,000).

[359] People v. Wagner, 89 Ill. 2d 308, 313, 433 N.E.2d 267, 270 (1982).

[360] People v. Wagner, 89 Ill. 2d 308, 313, 433 N.E.2d 267, 270 (1982).

threat to the public," the court held this paragraph to be violative of the due process clause of the state constitution.[361]

However, the issue was revisited in 1986 by the Illinois Supreme Court in *People v. Upton,*[362] where the court held that the fact that look-alike substances are treated more severely than some controlled substances was not violative of due process.[363] The Illinois Supreme Court explained that the legislature included a preamble to justify its determination that the look-alike substances were warranted:[364]

> Some of the other justifications for the harsher penalties . . . are rationally related to the purposes of the Act. It is not inconceivable that look-alike drugs may cause overdoses, either because they contain impurities, or because they mislead users as to the potency and dosages of actual controlled substances. It is also plausible that dealers in look-alike drugs are able to reap a greater profit from their sale, and therefore will only be deterred by fines set higher than those levied upon dealers in Schedule III, IV and V controlled substance. Since these asserted, and plausible, hypotheses support a substantial relationship between harsher penalties for sale of look-alike drugs and the greater goal of reducing actual drug abuse . . . [the penalty structure] as amended, does not violate due process.[365]

§ 16.21.   — Possession of a Controlled Substance.

To convict a person of possession of a controlled or counterfeit substance[366] or possession with intent to deliver,[367] the normal requirements for criminal possession of contraband apply:[368] knowledge and control.[369] Proof of ownership or title is not required.[370] However, criminal possession of a controlled substance cannot be based on positive test results that a defendant has a controlled substance in her bloodstream.[371]

---

[361] People v. Wagner, 89 Ill. 2d 308, 312, 433 N.E.2d 267, 269 (1982).

[362] 114 Ill. 2d 362, 500 N.E.2d 943 (1986).

[363] People v. Upton, 114 Ill. 2d 362, 366, 500 N.E.2d 943, 945 (1986).

[364] People v. Upton, 114 Ill. 2d 362, 370-71, 500 N.E.2d 943, 947 (1986).

[365] People v. Upton, 114 Ill. 2d 362, 375, 500 N.E.2d 943, 949 (1986).

[366] 720 ILCS 570/402 (1999).

[367] 720 ILCS 570/401 (1999).

[368] *See* ch. 2 of this treatise for a discussion of criminal possession.

[369] People v. Nettles, 23 Ill. 2d 306, 307, 178 N.E.2d 361, 362 (1961), *cert. denied,* 369 U.S. 853 (1962); People v. Knight, 133 Ill. App. 3d 248, 258-59, 478 N.E.2d 1082, 1091 (1st Dist. 1985).

[370] People v. Agyei, 231 Ill. App. 3d 546, 556, 597 N.E.2d 697, 703 (1st Dist. 1992) (conviction for possession of heroin affirmed).

[371] People v. Chatman, 297 Ill. App. 3d 57, 61-62, 696 N.E.2d1159, 1162 (2d Dist. 1998).

Proof of possession can be actual, where a person has actual personal present dominion over the substance, or constructive, where the individual is not in physical control but has the intent and capability to maintain control and dominion over the contraband.[372] Possession can be established by circumstantial evidence such that where a package of cocaine was found in a trash can in an airplane restroom, which airplane contained approximately 65 passengers, plus five crew members, the Illinois Supreme Court upheld the defendant's conviction for possession of cocaine since the defendant's fingerprints were found on the package.[373] In contrast, where an officer testified that he observed defendant in an apartment with lights on where drugs were later removed, the defendant's conviction was reversed because there was no evidence that the officer saw the defendant in the bedroom where the drugs were located.[374]

It is not essential that the accused knew exactly what type of controlled substance he or she possessed,[375] since the statute simply requires that the accused knowingly . . . possess a controlled or counterfeit substance."[376] Nor is it essential that the accused knew exactly the amount of the controlled substance possessed, even if the amount involved is important from the standpoint of the elevated penalties.[377] Regarding the possession of a look-alike substance, it is required that the accused knew the substance was a look-alike substance[378] or believed it to be a controlled substance.[379]

One critical issue relating to possession of controlled substances arises where a defendant is in possession of more than one controlled substance. This situation has the potential for becoming very complex where the defendant is in possession of a particular substance that is a mixture of various controlled substances, such as heroin and cocaine. In *People v. Manning*,[380] the Illinois Supreme Court stated in 1978 that "in the absence of a statutory provision to the contrary, the simultaneous possession of more than one type of controlled sub-

---

[372] People v. Adams, 161 Ill. 2d 333, 344-45, 641 N.E.2d 514, 519-20 (1994); People v. McCias, 299 Ill. App. 3d 480, 484, 701 N.E.2d 212, 216 (1st Dist. 1998).

[373] People v. Adams, 161 Ill. 2d 333, 344-45, 641 N.E.2d 514, 519-20 (1994).

[374] People v. Macias, 299 Ill. App. 3d 480, 486-87, 701 N.E.2d 212, 217 (1st Dist. 1998) (evidence insufficient to establish defendant had either knowledge or possession of controlled substance or immediate and exclusive control of contraband, as was required to sustain conviction).

[375] *Cf.* People v. James, 38 Ill. App. 3d 594, 596, 348 N.E.2d 295, 297 (2d Dist. 1976) (delivery of LSD conviction upheld although defendant thought he was delivering mescaline), *appeal dismissed*, 429 U.S. 1082, *reh'g denied*, 430 U.S. 976 (1977).

[376] 720 ILCS 570/402 (1999).

[377] *Cf.* People v. Cortez, 77 Ill. App. 3d 448, 451, 395 N.E.2d 1177, 1179-80 (1st Dist. 1979) (conviction for delivery of more than 30 grams of controlled substance did not require that defendant knew exact amount he was delivering).

[378] 720 ILCS 570/404(c) (1999).

[379] 720 ILCS 570/404(d) (1999).

[380] 71 Ill. 2d 132, 374 N.E.2d 200 (1978).

stance, under the circumstances shown on this record, constituted a single offense, and only one sentence should have been imposed."[381] In post-*Manning*
cases, where the court found that the simultaneous possession of more than one
type of controlled substance constituted one act, the defendant was convicted
with only one count of possession.[382] In contrast, when a court concluded that
the possession of more than one type of controlled substance constituted two
separated acts, the defendant was charged with multiple counts of possession.[383]
However, in 1995 the Illinois legislature enacted legislation that eliminated the
need for courts to distinguish between one act and multiple acts of possession of
different controlled substances. Under this Public Act, a defendant can face multiple convictions for possessing more than one type of controlled substance, regardless of whether the possession was deemed to be the result of one act.[384]

The appellate courts have had no difficulty upholding multiple convictions
where the defendant has in his or her possession both a controlled substance and
cannabis.[385] In such instance, two separate charges are permissible because each
substance is regulated under a separate and distinct statute: the CSA and the
CCA.[386] This reasoning applied even where the controlled substance and the
cannabis were both contained in a single plastic bag concealed in the accused's
shirt-sleeve.[387]

The simultaneous possession of two substances, such as cocaine and a look-
alike substance that are regulated under separate prohibitions of the CSA, will
allow two separate offenses to stand.[388] As one appellate court noted, by placing

---

[381] People v. Manning, 71 Ill. 2d 132, 137, 374 N.E.2d 200, 202 (1978).

[382] *See, e.g.,* People v. Tonaldi, 98 Ill. App. 3d 528, 533, 424 N.E.2d 1200, 1204 (1st Dist.
1981) (possession of cocaine and phenobarbital one crime); People v. Dunlap, 59 Ill. App. 3d 615,
621, 375 N.E.2d 989, 993 (2d Dist. 1978) (possession of LSD and amphetamine one crime).

[383] *See, e.g.,* People v. Brownstein, 105 Ill. App. 3d 459, 460, 434 N.E.2d 505, 506-07 (1st Dist.
1982) (possession of cocaine, diazepam and codeine in different locations constituted separate
offenses), *cert. denied,* 459 U.S. 1176 (1983).

[384] Public Act 89-404 (1995); 720 ILCS 570/100 (1995). It was the intent of the legislature to
recognize "that persons who violate this Act with respect to the manufacture, delivery, possession
with intent to deliver, or possession of more than one type of controlled substance listed herein
may . . . receive multiple convictions and sentences under each Section of this Act." The Illinois
Appellate Court subsequently ruled Public Act 89-404 unconstitutional as violative of the Illinois
Constitution's single-subject rule in People v. Reedy, 295 Ill. App. 3d 34, 43-44, 692 N.E.2d 376,
384 (2d Dist. 1998). However, this provision was re-enacted in 1998 by the legislature in a manner
designed to avoid this constitutional impediment. Public Act 90-593 (1998); 720 ILCS 570/100
(1999).

[385] People v. Kline, 41 Ill. App. 3d 261, 269, 354 N.E.2d 46, 53 (2d Dist. 1976) (possession of
cocaine and LSD separate from possession of cannabis); People v. Downing, 37 Ill. App. 3d 297,
303, 347 N.E.2d 848, 853 (2d Dist. 1976) (possession of cannabis separate from possession of
LSD).

[386] People v. Tovar, 169 Ill. App. 3d 986, 996, 523 N.E.2d 1178, 1184 (1st Dist. 1988).

[387] People v. Downing, 37 Ill. App. 3d 279, 303, 347 N.E.2d 848, 853 (2d Dist. 1976).

[388] People v. Watkins, 172 Ill. App. 3d 168, 171, 526 N.E.2d 448, 449 (1st Dist. 1988).

the regulation of different substances in separate and distinct paragraphs, the legislature set forth distinct penalties for each substance based upon different types of harm.[389] Thus, "the legislature sufficiently enunciated its intent to make each offense a separate unit of prosecution."[390]

Possession under the CSA is a lesser-included offense of possession with intent to deliver the same substance.[391] Where the offenses charged are possession and delivery of the same substance, the possession is generally viewed as a lesser-included offense of the delivery.[392] Where an accused was convicted of possession ar ˙ 'ᵊlivery of the same heroin, the possession charge had to be vacated.[393] On ˙ ˍ ˍ other hand, where two separate "batches" of heroin were involved, delivery of the first and possession of the second were considered independent and separable acts, and convictions for both were upheld.[394]

§ 16.22. — Manufacture, Delivery and Possession with Intent to Deliver a Controlled Substance or Controlled Substance Analog.

Paragraph 570/401 makes it "unlawful for any person knowingly to manufacture or deliver, or possess with intent to manufacture or deliver, a controlled or counterfeit substance or controlled substance analog."[395] The mens rea for this infraction is normally *knowing* that the substance in question is a controlled substance.[396] For example, where officers testified that they saw defendant arrive at the location of an undercover officer's controlled drug buy from a codefendant, defendant carried a box that he retrieved from his vehicle into a codefendant's office, he left office minutes later without the box which was later found to contain drugs, defendant attempted to flee when an officer stopped him after the drug transaction, an officer found $32,000 in defendant's vehicle, and defendant told police that cash found in his pocket was drug money, the evidence warranted the conclusion that defendant knew that which he had delivered was a controlled substance.[397]

---

[389] People v. Watkins, 172 Ill. App. 3d 168, 171, 526 N.E.2d 448, 449-50 (1st Dist. 1988).

[390] People v. Watkins, 172 Ill. App. 3d 168, 171, 526 N.E.2d 448, 450 (1st Dist. 1988).

[391] People v. Crenshaw, 202 Ill. App. 3d 432, 436, 559 N.E.2d 1051, 1053-54 (1st Dist. 1990) (evidence warranted reduction of conviction to simple possession of controlled substance).

[392] *See, e.g.*, People v. Holliman, 22 Ill. App. 3d 95, 103, 316 N.E.2d 812, 818 (2d Dist. 1974) and cases cited therein.

[393] People v. Lilly, 56 Ill. 2d 493, 495, 309 N.E.2d 1, 2 (1974); People v. Holliman, 22 Ill. App. 3d 95, 103, 316 N.E.2d 812, 818 (2d Dist. 1974).

[394] People v. Brownfield, 52 Ill. App. 3d 829, 831, 366 N.E.2d 308, 309 (3d Dist. 1976).

[395] 720 ILCS 570/401 (1999).

[396] People v. James, 38 Ill. App. 3d 594, 596, 348 N.E.2d 295, 297 (2d Dist. 1976), *appeal dismissed*, 429 U.S. 1082, *reh'g denied*, 430 U.S. 976 (1977).

[397] People v. Rivas, 302 Ill. 2d 421, 430, 707 N.E.2d 159, 167 (1st Dist. 1998) (delivery of a controlled substance conviction upheld).

Like possession of a controlled substance, it is not essential that the accused knew precisely what type of controlled substance he or she was delivering.[398] For instance, the conviction was upheld where the accused delivered what he believed to be mescaline, when in fact it was LSD.[399] And it is not necessary that the defendant knew the exact amount he or she was delivering, even for a conviction involving delivery of a specific quantity that elevates the penalty.[400] For example, the state did not have to prove that the defendant knew the exact amount involved when he delivered more than thirty grams of heroin.[401]

There are two exceptions to the general rule that knowledge[402] is sufficient to secure a conviction under paragraph 570/401. First, if the defendant is charged with possession with intent to deliver or manufacture, a specific intent must be proved.[403] Second, if a physician makes an unauthorized paragraph 570/401 delivery, it must be demonstrated that the defendant's dispensing of the controlled substance in question was not in good faith and was intended to maintain a person's dependent or illicit use.[404]

Regardless of whether proof of intent or knowledge is involved, both mental states can be demonstrated by circumstantial evidence.[405] With respect to the requisite knowledge for a delivery based on sale, the very nature of a delivery for a sale creates a reasonable inference that the defendant knew the nature of the substance he or she was selling.[406]

The actus reus of *delivery* under paragraph 570/401 crimes is defined as "the actual, constructive or attempted transfer of possession of a controlled substance, with or without consideration, whether or not there is an agency relationship."[407] Further, a delivery need not be part of a sale or for profit.[408] And although delivery involves a transfer of possession to a recipient, the courts in Illinois have always construed this term very liberally. The deliverer need not be

---

[398] People v. James, 38 Ill. App. 3d 594, 596, 348 N.E.2d 295, 297 (2d Dist. 1976), *appeal dismissed*, 429 U.S. 1082, *reh'g denied*, 430 U.S. 976 (1977).

[399] People v. James, 38 Ill. App. 3d 594, 596, 348 N.E.2d 295, 297 (2d Dist. 1976), *appeal dismissed*, 429 U.S. 1082, *reh'g denied*, 430 U.S. 976 (1977).

[400] People v. Cortez, 77 Ill. App. 3d 448, 451, 395 N.E.2d 1177, 1179-80 (1st Dist. 1979).

[401] People v. Cortez, 77 Ill. App. 3d 448, 451, 395 N.E.2d 1177, 1179-80 (1st Dist. 1979).

[402] *See generally* ch. 2 for discussion of the mental state of "knowledge."

[403] *See generally* ch. 2 for discussion of the mental state of "specific intent."

[404] 720 ILCS 570/312(h) (1999). *See* § 16.15 of this chapter.

[405] People v. Munoz, 103 Ill. App. 3d 1080, 1082, 432 N.E.2d 370, 372 (3d Dist. 1982) (circumstantial evidence established proof of possession with intent to deliver); People v. Chicon, 55 Ill. App. 3d 100, 105, 370 N.E.2d 605, 609 (5th Dist. 1977) (circumstantial evidence established proof that the defendant knowingly delivered controlled substance).

[406] People v. Castro, 10 Ill. App. 3d 1078, 1085, 295 N.E.2d 538, 544 (1st Dist. 1973).

[407] 720 ILCS 570/102(h) (1999).

[408] *See* People v. Collins, 25 Ill. 2d 302, 304, 185 N.E.2d 147, 149 (1962) (prior statute, now repealed). The current code does not even use the term sale.

the owner of the substance delivered;[409] the delivery can be made by an agent;[410] and the state need not allege in its charging instrument the identity of the recipient (although it is imperative to identify him or her at trial).[411] In addition, a conviction under this article can also be obtained on an accountability theory. For instance, a conviction was upheld even though the defendant was never found handling the drugs but merely verbally encouraged the transaction so that he could collect a debt from the dealer.[412] As already noted, delivery of a controlled substance can be in any amount.[413] Only if the state seeks an increased penalty due to large quantity, is the state obligated to allege and prove a delivery of that particular quantity.[414] Also, it is not incumbent that the state prove that the amount in question was a "usable quantity" or would have a particular desired effect.[415]

Possession of a controlled substance is normally viewed as a lesser-included offense of delivery of the same substance.[416] It is significant that if the state fails to prove delivery but proves possession, the trier of fact may convict on the uncharged offense of possession, but only if the jury is given instructions regarding the lesser offense.[417] And, although possession is by definition an element of delivery, the trial court is not required to instruct the jury on the meaning of the term possession for purposes of their understanding of what constitutes a delivery.[418] Further, it is not invariably necessary to instruct the jury regarding possession as a lesser-included offense.[419]

---

[409] Cf. People v. Agyei, 231 Ill. App. 3d 546, 556, 597 N.E.2d 697, 703 (1st Dist. 1992) (title is unnecessary to prove possession).

[410] People v. Shannon, 15 Ill. 2d 494, 496, 155 N.E.2d 578, 580 (1959).

[411] People v. Copeland, 92 Ill. App. 3d 475, 481, 415 N.E.2d 1173, 1179 (1st Dist. 1980) (charging instrument does not need identity of recipient since statute does not make reference to it). Compare Roviaro v. United States, 353 U.S. 53 (1957) (normally, disclosure of identity of recipient must be made at trial).

[412] People v. Tinoco, 185 Ill. App. 3d 816, 823, 541 N.E.2d 1198, 1203 (1st Dist. 1989).

[413] People v. Cortez, 77 Ill. App. 3d 448, 451, 395 N.E.2d 1177, 1180 (1st Dist. 1979).

[414] See § 16.18 of this chapter.

[415] People v. Bolden, 62 Ill. App. 3d 1009, 1011, 379 N.E.2d 912, 915 (4th Dist. 1978). Cf. Note, Criminal Liability for Possession of Non-usable Amounts of Controlled Substances, 77 COLUM. L. REV. 596, 605 (1977).

[416] People v. Holliman, 22 Ill. App. 3d 95, 103, 316 N.E.2d 812, 818 (2d Dist. 1974).

[417] People v. Lewis, 83 Ill. 2d 296, 302, 415 N.E.2d 319, 321 (1980) (although defendant was only charged with delivery of cannabis, where trial court instructed jury as to delivery and possession with intent to deliver, jury's verdict finding of lesser-included offense of possession with intent to deliver upheld).

[418] People v. Monroe, 32 Ill. App. 482, 488, 335 N.E.2d 783, 788 (3d Dist. 1975) ("The term 'deliver' is commonly used and understood by laymen"), aff'd, 66 Ill. 2d 317, 362 N.E.2d 295 (1977).

[419] People v. Dunn, 49 Ill. App. 3d 1002, 1010, 365 N.E.2d 164, 170 (5th Dist. 1977) (where there was no evidence of possession, refusal to instruct on possession upheld).

Generally, a separate offense of delivery occurs with each act of delivery; thus, separate counts of delivery may lie in appropriate circumstances.[420] The deliveries of various substances to different individuals constitute separate offenses even though the deliveries occur at the same time.[421] Thus, where the defendant delivered MDA to one person, and MDA and PCP to another person, the defendant was properly convicted of three counts of delivery.[422] Meanwhile, in another case, the appellate court upheld one conviction but reversed a second conviction for delivery where one officer negotiated the sale, inspected the drugs, provided the money, and handed the second officer money to give to the defendant for another purchase.[423] The court held that the second officer played no active role in the transaction and, consequently, there was no constructive delivery to the second officer.[424]

Under paragraph 570/401, *manufacture* "means the production, preparation, propagation, compounding, conversion or processing of a controlled substance, either directly or indirectly, by extraction from substances of natural origin, or independently by means of chemical synthesis, or by a combination of extraction and chemical synthesis, . . . and includes any packaging or repackaging of the substance or labeling of its container . . . ."[425] As with delivery of a controlled substance, the prohibition against manufacture covers the production of any amount of the substance.[426]

To obtain a conviction of possession with intent to deliver, the state must prove three elements: (1) that the defendant had knowledge of the presence of the narcotics, (2) the narcotics were in the immediate possession or control of the defendant, and (3) the defendant intended to deliver the narcotics.[427] A precondition, then, of possession with intent to deliver is proof of *possession* of the controlled substance. Thus, where the evidence was insufficient to establish defendant's possession was knowing, his conviction for possession with intent to deliver was reversed.[428] Similarly, where the evidence neither supported the conclusion that defendant had knowledge of the possession of the narcotics nor

---

[420] *See, e.g.*, People v. Meeks, 81 Ill. 2d 524, 529-36, 411 N.E.2d 9, 12-15 (1980) (concurrent sentences for each of three counts of delivery of phencyclidine upheld); People v. Miller, 115 Ill. App. 3d 592, 601-04, 450 N.E.2d 767, 774-76 (concurrent sentences for two different counts of delivery of heroin upheld), *cert. denied*, 465 U.S. 1033 (1984).

[421] People v. Hill, 56 Ill. App. 3d 510, 515, 371 N.E.2d 1257, 1260 (4th Dist. 1978).

[422] People v. Hill, 56 Ill. App. 3d 510, 515, 371 N.E.2d 1257, 1260 (4th Dist. 1978).

[423] People v. Reed, 255 Ill. App. 3d 949, 951, 627 N.E.2d 729, 731 (2d Dist. 1994).

[424] People v. Reed, 255 Ill. App. 3d 949, 951, 627 N.E.2d 729, 731 (2d Dist. 1994).

[425] 720 ILCS 570/102(z) (1999); *see also* People v. Cruz, 129 Ill. App. 3d 278, 287, 472 N.E.2d 175, 180 (1st Dist. 1984) (manufacture of methaqualone conviction upheld).

[426] 720 ILCS 570/401(d)-(h) (1999).

[427] People v. Robinson, 167 Ill. 2d 397, 407, 657 N.E.2d 1020, 1026 (1995); People v. Pintos, 133 Ill. 2d 286, 291-92, 549 N.E.2d 344, 346 (1989).

[428] People v. Hodogbey, 306 Ill. App. 3d 555, 561, 714 N.E.2d 1072, 1077 (1st Dist. 1999).

immediate and exclusive control over them, his conviction for possession with intent to deliver had to be reversed.[429]

With respect to the third element, the quantity of a controlled substance alone, such that it could not reasonably be viewed as designed for personal consumption, can be sufficient evidence to prove intent to deliver.[430] However, Illinois courts have considered other factors as probative of intent to deliver such as (1) the high purity of the drug confiscated, (2) the possession of weapons, (3) the possession of large amounts of cash, (4) the possession of police scanners, beepers or cellular telephones, (5) the possession of drug paraphernalia, and (6) the manner in which the substance is packaged.[431] Thus, even where a defendant possesses only a small quantity of a controlled substances, such circumstantial evidence may support a conviction of intent to deliver. For example, in *People v. Robinson*,[432] the Illinois Supreme Court upheld a possession with intent to deliver conviction where the defendant possessed only 1.47 grams of cocaine and 1.1 grams of PCP.[433] The court found that several phone calls to police by citizens complaining of drug sales at the defendant's apartment, the police officer's observation of a dozen people coming in and out of defendant's apartment over a twenty minute time period, and the fact that the drugs were contained in 40 small packages constituted sufficient evidence to infer intent to deliver.[434] Indeed, the court stated that, in appropriate circumstances, packaging alone might be sufficient evidence of intent to deliver.[435]

In addition, in one case, circumstantial evidence was considered sufficient to affirm a conviction for possession with intent to deliver a controlled substance where the appellate court found the defendant was apprehended with 3.9 grams of cocaine, over $3,100 in cash, and an "underwear cachet" used to carry cocaine.[436] Similarly, evidence of 3.15 grams of cocaine packaged in seven or eight baggies found on defendant's person was sufficient independent evidence to corroborate his confession that he possessed with intent to deliver.[437] However, in another case, no intent to deliver was found where the defendant was found in possession of 11.2 grams of cocaine divided into 22 packets, since it was not clear whether the defendant had himself packaged the cocaine or whether he had received the cocaine already packaged.[438] Similarly, in yet another case, no in-

---

[429] People Macias, 299 Ill. App. 3d 480, 488, 701 N.E.2d 212, 218 (1st Dist. 1998).

[430] People v. Robinson, 167 Ill. 2d 397, 410-11, 657 N.E.2d 1020, 1028 (1995).

[431] People v. Robinson, 167 Ill. 2d 397, 408, 657 N.E.2d 1020, 1026-27 (1995); People v. Rivera, 293 Ill. App. 3d 574, 575-76, 688 N.E.2d 752, 753 (1st Dist. 1997).

[432] 167 Ill. 2d 397, 657 N.E.2d 1020 (1995).

[433] People v. Robinson, 167 Ill. 2d 397, 409, 657 N.E.2d 1020, 1027 (1995).

[434] People v. Robinson, 167 Ill. 2d 397, 413-14, 657 N.E.2d 1020, 1029 (1995).

[435] People v. Robinson, 167 Ill. 2d 397, 413-14, 657 N.E.2d 1020, 1029 (1995).

[436] People v. Berry, 198 Ill. App. 3d 24, 28-29, 555 N.E.2d 434, 438 (2d Dist. 1990).

[437] People v. Parich, 256 Ill. App. 3d 247, 250, 627 N.E.2d 1289, 1292 (2d Dist. 1994).

[438] People v. Crenshaw, 202 Ill. App. 3d 432, 434, 559 N.E.2d 1051, 1053 (1st Dist. 1990).

tent to deliver was established where defendant possessed 6.6 grams of cocaine contained in four small packets.[439]

§ 16.23.   — Controlled Substance Trafficking.

The prohibition of "controlled substance trafficking" is contained in paragraph 570/401.1 of the CSA.[440] The felony crime of trafficking occurs when a person "knowingly brings or causes to be brought into [the] State for the purpose of manufacture or delivery or with the intent to manufacture or deliver a controlled or counterfeit substance."[441] Further, it is a felony for a person to "knowingly use a cellular radio telecommunication device in the furtherance of controlled substance trafficking" and such penalty is to be *in addition* to any other penalties attached to the trafficking.[442] As with cannabis trafficking, the penalty for controlled substance trafficking is to be determined by the amount of controlled substance "brought or caused to be brought" into the state.[443] The penalty imposed, though, must "not be less than twice the minimum . . . and not more than twice the maximum term" authorized by paragraph 570/401 for manufacture, delivery or possession with intent to deliver unauthorized substances.[444]

Proof of knowledge is the requisite mental state for controlled substances trafficking.[445] Specifically, it is necessary to prove that the defendant had knowledge of bringing an unauthorized substance into the state as well as knowledge of the aim of that activity.[446] However, in *People v. Frieberg*,[447] the court held that the paragraph does not require proof of defendant's specific intent to *personally* deliver or manufacture an unauthorized substance.[448] Rather, so long as the defendant knowingly brings a controlled substance into the state and is consciously aware that someone, himself or another whose purpose he serves, will deliver or manufacture the controlled substance, this is sufficient.[449] The scope of the trafficking provision was intended to be broad enough to snare not only the individuals responsible for the actual delivery of controlled substances, but also those operating at the outer reaches of the drug network who know they are

---

[439] People v. Nixon, 278 Ill. App. 3d 453, 458-59, 663 N.E.2d 66, 69-70 (3d Dist. 1996).

[440] 720 ILCS 570/401.1 (1999). *See also* People v. Govin, 213 Ill. App. 3d 928, 935, 572 N.E.2d 450, 455 (4th Dist. 1991) (statute not unconstitutionally vague).

[441] 720 ILCS 570/401.1(a), (b) (1999).

[442] 720 ILCS 570/401.1(c) (1999).

[443] 720 ILCS 570/401.1(b) (1999).

[444] 720 ILCS 570/401.1(b) (1999).

[445] 720 ILCS 570/401.1(a), (c) (1999).

[446] People v. Frieberg, 147 Ill. 2d 326, 347, 589 N.E.2d 508, 518 (1992). *See* § 2.25 of this treatise for a more detailed discussion of this case.

[447] 147 Ill. 2d 326, 589 N.E.2d 508 (1992).

[448] People v. Frieberg, 147 Ill. 2d 326, 350-51, 589 N.E.2d 508, 519-20 (1992).

[449] People v. Frieberg, 147 Ill. 2d 326, 349-51, 589 N.E.2d 508, 518-20 (1992).

bringing substances into the state with an awareness that delivery of them likely will occur.[450] To require proof of a defendant's specific intent to personally deliver would eviscerate the intended scope of the trafficking provision.[451]

In order to convict a defendant of the offense of controlled substance trafficking, the state must establish that the defendant: (1) knowingly brought or caused to be brought into Illinois; (2) aware of the purpose of delivery or manufacture by someone; (3) or with the intent to deliver or manufacture; (4) a controlled substance.[452] Where state police found large black garbage bags filled with bricks of cocaine located throughout a motor home, which defendant had rented in Florida and in which defendant was riding as passenger, and the driver acknowledged that the cocaine had been loaded into the motor home in California to be delivered in Chicago, the circumstantial evidence supported defendant's conviction for trafficking.[453] Where cocaine was located in a suitcase which had been shipped to defendant from Nigeria and undercover police officers, who delivered the container, returned twenty minutes later to find the suitcase in defendant's bedroom with a false bottom torn open and cocaine exposed, defendant was convicted of controlled substances trafficking for having knowingly caused the importation of the cocaine into Illinois with the intent to deliver it.[454] A defendant was convicted of this offense on an accountability theory where an informant telephoned defendant requesting to purchase cocaine and defendant gave the informant a telephone number of a friend who later shipped cocaine from Florida to the informant in Illinois.[455]

§ 16.24.   — Calculated Criminal Drug Conspiracy.

Paragraph 570/405 proscribes a "calculated criminal drug conspiracy" which is punishable as a class X felony.[456] A person engages in such a conspiracy when (1) he or she violates either of the provisions of subsection (a) or (c) or paragraph 570/401 (manufacture, delivery, or possession with intent to deliver certain Schedule I or II narcotic drugs involving certain significant amounts) or subsection (a) of paragraph 570/402 (simple possession of certain Schedule I or II narcotic drugs in certain significant amounts); (2) that violation is part of a conspiracy carried out with two or more other persons; or (3) he or she obtains anything of value greater than five hundred dollars from the conspiracy or organizes, directs or finances the violation or conspiracy.[457]

---

[450] People v. Frieberg, 147 Ill. 2d 326, 350, 589 N.E.2d 508, 519 (1992).

[451] People v. Frieberg, 147 Ill. 2d 326, 350, 589 N.E.2d 508, 519 (1992).

[452] People v. Frieberg, 147 Ill. 2d 326, 345-46, 589 N.E.2d 508, 517 (1992).

[453] People v. Sanchez, 292 Ill. App. 3d 763, 771, 686 N.E.2d 367, 373 (5th Dist. 1997).

[454] People v. Nwosu, 289 Ill. App. 3d 487, 494-95, 683 N.E.2d 148, 154 (1st Dist. 1997).

[455] People v. Govin, 213 Ill. App. 3d 928, 930-32, 572 N.E.2d 450, 452-53 (4th Dist. 1991).

[456] 720 ILCS 570/405(a) (1999).

[457] 720 ILCS 570/405(b) (1999).

As mentioned in the previous section on cannabis, just as a calculated criminal cannabis conspiracy is distinguishable from a simple conspiracy, a calculated criminal drug conspiracy is different in the same respect from a simple conspiracy.[458] A CSA conspiracy requires an agreement to commit the requisite offenses with two or more *other* individuals.[459] The CSA conspiracy statute, like its general conspiracy counterpart, encompasses a bilateral theory such that if there is no true criminal purpose on the part of one of the two other alleged co-conspirators, there is no CSA conspiracy.[460] Thus, where one of the other two individuals necessary to a CSA conspiracy was actually a police informant feigning criminal complicity, the CSA conspiracy was not established.[461]

A CSA conspiracy requires that defendant receive more than $500 in value from the conspiracy *or* organize, direct or finance the conspiracy.[462] Thus, where defendant and three others were charged with a CSA conspiracy, it was insufficient that any one of the alleged co-conspirators received more than $500 because *each* defendant convicted of a CSA conspiracy must have obtained more than $500 in value from the conspiracy, unless the defendant assumed a central organizational role.[463] If the defendant has not obtained more than $500 in value, then evidence of his or her organization, direction or financing of the CSA conspiracy must exist or, at best, there was an ordinary conspiracy.[464] In making this determination, one appellate court stated the evidence must show "that the defendant either had sufficient influence over his co-conspirators to be in a position to systemize their activities or to give orders or instructions that would be to some extent binding" and, as such, the statute "implicitly requires" that "the extent of his involvement must be measured against that of his co-conspirators."[465]

If the proof is insufficient to satisfy a calculated criminal drug conspiracy, the normal conspiracy stricture of paragraph 5/8-2 is available.[466] If convictions are

---

[458] *See* § 16.11 of this chapter.

[459] People v. Harmison, 108 Ill. 2d 197, 200-03, 483 N.E.2d 508, 510-11 (1985).

[460] People v. Harmison, 108 Ill. 2d 197, 203-04, 483 N.E.2d 508, 511 (1985).

[461] People v. Harmison, 108 Ill. 2d 197, 203-04, 483 N.E.2d 508, 511 (1985) (CSA conspiracy conviction reversed); People v. Caballero, 237 Ill. App. 3d 797, 804-06, 604 N.E.2d 1028, 1034-35 (3d Dist. 1992) (same).

[462] 720 ILCS 570/405(a)(3) (1999).

[463] People v. Biers, 41 Ill. App. 3d 576, 579-81, 353 N.E.2d 389, 392-93 (3d Dist. 1976) (CSA conspiracy conviction reversed).

[464] People v. Lucas, 33 Ill. App. 3d 309, 312-15, 337 N.E.2d 103, 106-08 (3d Dist. 1975) (CSA conspiracy conviction reversed).

[465] People v. Lucas, 33 Ill. App. 3d 309, 315, 337 N.E.2d 103, 107 (3d Dist. 1995).

[466] People v. Caballero, 237 Ill. App. 3d 797, 807-09, 604 N.E.2d 1028, 1036-37 (3d Dist. 1992) (calculated criminal drug conspiracy conviction reversed while conspiracy to deliver controlled substances affirmed); People v. Simon, 101 Ill. App. 3d 89, 101, 427 N.E.2d 843, 852 (1st Dist. 1981) (where evidence is insufficient for calculated criminal drug conspiracy a simple conspiracy may exist). *See* 720 ILCS 5/8-2 (1999) (general conspiracy prohibition). *See generally* ch. 4 regarding paragraph 5/8-2 conspiracies.

entered at the trial court for both a calculated criminal drug conspiracy and a simple conspiracy to deliver a controlled substance, the calculated criminal drug conspiracy will be set aside if the evidence does not support that conviction, and the defendant will be sentenced on the simple conspiracy.[467] On the other hand, if the defendant is convicted of both types of conspiracy involving a delivery of a controlled substance, and the evidence is sufficient for both, the defendant can only be convicted and sentenced on the calculated drug conspiracy.[468] If there are two different conspiracies involving two separate deliveries, where one delivery satisfies the elements of a calculated criminal drug conspiracy and the other satisfies only an ordinary conspiracy, the defendant may be convicted and sentenced for both.[469] Finally, if a defendant is convicted for both a calculated criminal drug conspiracy and delivery of a controlled substance arising out of the same incident, the delivery count will merge into the conspiracy count.[470] However, if the evidence is insufficient on the CSA conspiracy charge, but sufficient for ordinary conspiracy and the underlying delivery, judgment of conviction can be entered on either simple conspiracy *or* the delivery, but not both.[471]

Consistent with ordinary conspiracy law in Illinois,[472] the fact that a defendant's two alleged co-conspirators are acquitted of a CSA conspiracy in a separate trial does not prevent a defendant from being convicted of a CSA conspiracy.[473] On the other hand, Wharton's Rule, which holds that an agreement by multiple persons to commit a crime cannot be prosecuted for conspiracy where the underlying crime necessarily requires the complicity of persons, does not apply to a CSA conspiracy.[474]

§ 16.25. — Criminal Drug Conspiracy.

In an effort to create a conspiracy prohibition less complex than the "calculated criminal drug conspiracy," the legislature created the offense of "criminal

---

[467] People v. Caballero, 237 Ill. App. 3d 797, 807-09, 604 N.E.2d 1028, 1036-37 (3d Dist. 1992); People v. Simon, 101 Ill. App. 3d 89, 101, 427 N.E.2d 843, 852 (1st Dist. 1981).

[468] People v. Vincent, 92 Ill. App. 3d 446, 459, 415 N.E.2d 1147, 1157 (1st Dist. 1980) (simple conspiracy vacated).

[469] People v. Simon, 101 Ill. App. 3d 89, 100, 427 N.E.2d 843, 851-52 (1st Dist. 1981) (CSA conspiracy conviction affirmed while second separate CSA conspiracy reversed and reduced to ordinary conspiracy to deliver).

[470] People v. Shimkus, 135 Ill. App. 3d 981, 990, 482 N.E.2d 194, 200 (2d Dist. 1985) (delivery is considered the lesser-included offense).

[471] People v. Simon, 101 Ill. App. 3d 89, 100-02, 427 N.E.2d 843, 852-53 (1st Dist. 1981) (on remand, trial court instructed to enter judgment on either substantive offense of delivery or conspiracy). Such choice is dictated by 720 ILCS 5/8-5 (1999) ("no person shall be convicted of both the inchoate and the principal offense").

[472] 720 ILCS 5/8-2(b) (1999).

[473] People v. Lane, 133 Ill. App. 3d 215, 218-19, 478 N.E.2d 1160, 1163-64 (1st Dist. 1985).

[474] People v. Caballero, 237 Ill. App. 3d 797, 805-07, 604 N.E.2d 1028, 1035-36 (3d Dist. 1992).

drug conspiracy."[475] This enactment parallels the general conspiracy statute of Illinois.[476]

A person commits a criminal drug conspiracy when he or she intentionally agrees with another to manufacture, deliver, or possess an unauthorized substance.[477] A person may not be convicted of criminal drug conspiracy unless some act in furtherance of the conspiracy is proven to have been committed by the person or by a co-conspirator.[478] In addition, consistent with the general conspiracy statute, a defendant cannot be convicted of both criminal drug conspiracy and an underlying principal drug offense, such as possession with intent to deliver or unlawful delivery.[479] The statute expressly states that it is not a defense to a conspiracy that a co-conspirator: (1) has not been prosecuted or convicted; (2) has been convicted of a different offense; (3) is not amenable to justice; (4) has been acquitted; or (5) lacked the capacity to commit an offense.[480] A criminal drug conspiracy is punishable by a fine, imprisonment, or both not to exceed the maximum penalty for the crime which is the object of the conspiracy.[481]

§ 16.26.   — Streetgang Criminal Drug Conspiracy.

Paragraph 405.2 sets out the prohibition of "streetgang criminal drug conspiracy."[482] This class X felony arises where (1) a person commits delivery, manufacture or possession with intent to deliver a sizeable amount of controlled substances as specified in subsection (a) or (c) of paragraph 570/401; (2) the violation is part of a conspiracy with two or more other individuals; (3) the conspiracy is in furtherance of the activities of an organized streetgang; and (4) the person occupies a position of organizer, supervisor, or manager with the other parties to the conspiracy.[483] An organized streetgang carries the meaning ascribed by the Illinois Streetgang Terrorism Omnibus Prevention Act.[484] If three or more persons are part of an alliance with an established hierarchy that participates in a pattern of criminal activity, they constitute a streetgang.[485] A "pattern of crimi-

---

[475] 720 ILCS 570/405.1 (1999). *See* People v. Hickman, 163 Ill. 2d 250, 256-60, 644 N.E.2d 1147, 1150-52 (1994) (upholding the criminal drug conspiracy statute against vagueness and proportionate penalties clause challenges).

[476] 720 ILCS 5/8-2 (1999).

[477] 720 ILCS 570/405.1(a) (1999).

[478] 720 ILCS 570/405.1(a) (1999).

[479] People v. Castenada, 299 Ill. App. 3d 779, 781, 701 N.E.2d 1190, 1191 (4th Dist. 1998).

[480] 720 ILCS 570/405.1(b) (1999).

[481] 720 ILCS 570/405.1(c) (1999).

[482] 720 ILCS 570/405.2 (1999).

[483] 720 ILCS 570/405.2(a) (1999).

[484] 740 ILCS 147/1-135 (1999).

[485] 740 ILCS 147/10 (1999).

nal activity" means two or more gang-related offenses within five years of each other that are felonies.[486]

§ 16.27. — Enhanced Penalties for Delivery of Controlled Substance to Minor or Pregnant Woman, on School or Public Housing Property or Engaging Minor to Deliver Controlled Substances.

Under certain circumstances, paragraph 570/407 of the CSA enhances the penalties for manufacture, delivery, or intent to deliver any controlled, counterfeit, or look-alike substance.[487] Any person, eighteen years of age or older, who delivers an illegal substance to a person under the age of eighteen[488] or engages or employs a minor to deliver an illegal substance[489] may be subject to a penalty that doubles the sanction ordinarily applied to the crime of delivery.[490] A double penalty may also be imposed upon any person who delivers a controlled substance to a woman knowing that she is pregnant.[491] Further, any person who manufactures, delivers, or intends to deliver a controlled, counterfeit, or look-alike substance at the following places: (1) a school or a school vehicle used to transport students; (2) residential property owned, operated and managed by a public housing agency or public park; (3) a place of worship; (4) nursing homes or places used primarily to house or provide activities for senior citizens; or (5) a public way within 1,000 feet of the real property comprising a school, public housing, public park, place of worship or place for senior citizens will be subject to enhanced penalties.[492] Likewise, enhanced penalties attach to such illicit drug activity in a roadside safety rest area, truck stop or within 1000 feet of either.[493]

Where a sergeant was a ten-year-veteran of the police department, and was familiar with the nature of the local park and had made over 100 arrests there, his testimony was sufficient to establish the park's status as public.[494] The statute does not define the term "school," however; it has been held that schools include "any public or private, elementary or secondary school, community college, college or university,"[495] whether urban or rural.[496] The legislative history

---

[486] 740 ILCS 147/10 (1999).

[487] 720 ILCS 570/407 through 570/407.2 (1999).

[488] 720 ILCS 570/407(a)(1) (1999).

[489] 720 ILCS 570/407.1 (1999).

[490] 720 ILCS 570/407(a)(1), 570/407.1 (1999).

[491] 720 ILCS 570/407.2 (1999).

[492] 720 ILCS 570/407(b) (1999).

[493] 720 ILCS 570/407(a)(2) (1999).

[494] 720 ILCS 570/407(b) (1999); People v. Morgan, 301 Ill. App. 3d 1026, 1031, 704 N.E.2d 928, 932 (2d Dist. 1998) (whether a particular place has the status of a park could be established by mere testimony of a police officer).

[495] People v. Goldstein, 204 Ill. App. 3d 1041, 1048, 562 N.E.2d 1183, 1187 (5th Dist. 1990), cert. denied, 502 U.S. 810 (1991).

[496] People v. Owens, 240 Ill. App. 3d 168, 172, 608 N.E.2d 159, 162 (1st Dist. 1992).

of the CSA shows that paragraph 570/407 was one of several provisions aimed at gang activities[497] and that the statute was intended to protect young persons by creating "safe school zones around schools in addition to protecting the actual school grounds."[498]

Although it is an essential element to be proved that the defendant was "on a public way" within 1,000 feet of a school or public housing,[499] it is not necessary for the state to establish that the defendant had knowledge of the existence of a school or public housing within 1,000 feet of his illegal delivery.[500] In addition, although the statute does not define "housing," the Illinois appellate court has held that housing need not be contiguous or occupied.[501] This enhanced penalty provision as it applies to "public housing" has survived an equal protection challenge.[502]

§ 16.28.   — Miscellaneous Violations of the Controlled Substances Act.

There are several additional "miscellaneous violations" of the CSA. Paragraph 570/406 prohibits any person from knowingly (1) distributing, as a registrant, a controlled substance classified in Schedule I or II without the appropriate prescription forms; (2) using a fictitious, revoked, or suspended registration number or a number that is issued to another in the course of the manufacture or distribution of a controlled substance; (3) obtaining a controlled substance through some type of deception; (4) furnishing false or fraudulent information, or omitting material information, from any type of document required under the CSA; (5) making, distributing, or possessing anything designed to reproduce a trademark on any controlled substance or its container so as to render a drug a counterfeit substance; (6) possessing without authorization official blank prescription forms or counterfeit prescription forms; or (7) issuing or filling a prescription without lawful prescription forms except in emergencies.[503] These infractions constitute a felony.[504]

Paragraph 570/406.1 outlaws "permitting unlawful use of a building" which arises where a person, who controls a building, knowingly makes a building

---

[497] People v. Goldstein, 204 Ill. App. 3d 1041, 1047, 562 N.E.2d 1183, 1187 (5th Dist. 1990), *cert. denied*, 502 U.S. 810 (1991).

[498] People v. Owens, 240 Ill. App. 3d 168, 172, 608 N.E.2d 159, 161 (1st Dist. 1992).

[499] People v. Jones, 288 Ill. App. 3d 293, 296-97, 681 N.E.2d 537, 539-40 (1st Dist. 1997).

[500] People v. Brooks, 271 Ill. App. 3d 570, 571, 648 N.E.2d 626, 627 (4th Dist. 1995) (public housing); People v. Pacheco, 281 Ill. App. 3d 179, 187-88, 666 N.E.2d 370, 376 (2d Dist. 1996) (school).

[501] People v. Dorris, 265 Ill. App. 3d 156, 158, 638 N.E.2d 279, 281 (4th Dist. 1994).

[502] People v. Sheppard, 152 Ill. 2d 489, 498, 605 N.E.2d 518, 523 (1992).

[503] 720 ILCS 570/406(b) (1999).

[504] 720 ILCS 570/406(b) (1999).

available to another for the purpose of unlawful manufacture or delivery of a controlled substance.[505] This crime is a felony.[506]

§ 16.29. Drug Paraphernalia Control Act.

In 1983, the General Assembly passed the Drug Paraphernalia Control Act (DPCA), which was designed to prohibit the possession, delivery, and sale of paraphernalia associated with the production or use of drugs.[507] The DPCA contains an extensive definition of drug paraphernalia that includes:

> all equipment, products and materials of any kind which are peculiar to and marketed for use in planting, propagating, cultivating, growing, harvesting, manufacturing, compounding, concerting, producing, processing, preparing, testing, analyzing, packing, repackaging, storing, containing, concealing, injecting, ingesting, inhaling or otherwise introducing into the human body, cannabis or a controlled substance . . . .[508]

However, a number of items that have legitimate uses, such as tobacco pipes, are specifically exempted from the definition of drug paraphernalia.[509]

Under the DPCA, any person who keeps for sale, offers for sale, sells, or delivers for commercial consideration any item of drug paraphernalia is guilty of a felony for which a minimum fine of $1000 per item shall be imposed.[510] It is a more serious felony for a person eighteen years of age or older to sell or deliver for commercial consideration drug paraphernalia to a person under the age of eighteen,[511] and it is an even more serious felony for a person to sell or deliver for commercial consideration drug paraphernalia to a pregnant woman.[512] Possession of paraphernalia with the intent to use it for illicit drug activity is a misdemeanor.[513] Any place where drug paraphernalia is exchanged will be considered a public nuisance.[514]

As originally written, the DPCA was found to be unconstitutionally vague by the Illinois Supreme Court in *People v. Monroe*.[515] Under the penalty section of the Act then in existence, which referred to any item that a person "knows, or

---

[505] 720 ILCS 570/406.1(a) (1999). *See* People v. Parker, 277 Ill. App. 3d 585, 588-90, 600 N.E.2d 1296, 1298-1300 (4th Dist. 1996) (offense not unconstitutionally vague or overbroad; sentence not unconstitutionally disproportionate).

[506] 720 ILCS 570/406.1(b) (1999).

[507] 720 ILCS 600/1 through 600/7 (1999).

[508] 720 ILCS 600/2(d) (1999).

[509] 720 ILCS 600/4 (1999).

[510] 720 ILCS 600/3(a) (1999) (class 4 felony).

[511] 720 ILCS 600/3(a) (1999) (class 3 felony).

[512] 720 ILCS 600/3(b) (1999) (class 2 felony).

[513] 720 ILCS 600/3.5 (1999).

[514] 720 ILCS 600/3 (1999).

[515] 118 Ill. 2d 298, 515 N.E.2d 42 (1987).

under all the circumstances reasonably should have known" is used for drugs, only constructive knowledge that an item is used in connection with drugs was required.[516] As a result of this flaw that could predicate criminal liability on a defendant's unwitting negligence, the DPCA did not afford fair notice of what conduct was prohibited and law enforcement officials were not provided clear standards in applying the law, thus creating the danger of arbitrary and discriminatory enforcement.[517] Thus, the court concluded that the Act was unconstitutionally vague.[518] Subsequent to this decision, the legislature deleted the "reasonably should have known" language from the statute to avoid constitutional problems.[519]

Other vagueness challenges to the DPCA have been rebuffed by the courts in several decisions. In one case, the court held that the Act's definition of "drug paraphernalia" was reasonably clear and provided sufficient notice to individuals.[520] In several other cases, courts have ruled that the description of drug paraphernalia as that which is "peculiar" to the use of drugs does provide sufficient notice of what is prohibited by the DPCA.[521]

According to the definition section of the DPCA, violations of the Act occur only when someone deals with an item that is "peculiar to and marketed for use" with drugs.[522] "Marketed for use" has been interpreted as requiring a showing that an accused intended to market the "product for use with illicit drugs."[523]

---

[516] People v. Monroe, 118 Ill. 2d 298, 301-05, 515 N.E.2d 42, 43-45 (1987).

[517] People v. Monroe, 118 Ill. 2d 298, 305, 515 N.E.2d 42, 45 (1987).

[518] People v. Monroe, 118 Ill. 2d 298, 303, 515 N.E.2d 42, 44 (1987).

[519] P.A. 86-1459 (1991).

[520] Adams Apple Distributing Co. v. Zagel, 152 Ill. App. 3d 157, 159-60, 501 N.E.2d 302, 303-05 (1st Dist. 1986) (upholding against vagueness challenge definition of drug paraphernalia); Accord People v. Feld, 267 Ill. App. 3d 56, 60, 641 N.E.2d 924, 928 (2d Dist. 1994).

[521] People v. Crow's Nest, Inc., 137 Ill. App. 3d 461, 462-64, 484 N.E.2d 907, 908 (3d Dist. 1985); Accord People v. Ziegler, 139 Ill. App. 3d 1088, 1091, 488 N.E.2d 310, 310-12 (3d Dist. 1986).

[522] 720 ILCS 600/2(d) (1999).

[523] People v. Feld, 267 Ill. App. 3d 56, 60-61, 641 N.E.2d 924, 928-29 (2d Dist. 1994).

PART 3

AFFIRMATIVE DEFENSES

The final part of this book analyzes the various defenses, generally referred to as affirmative defenses, that are recognized in Illinois. Chapter 17 (Defense of Person and Property) examines the justification of self-defense, defense of another, defense of dwelling, and defense of other property. Chapter 18 (Defenses: Lack of Criminal Responsibility Due to Insanity, Intoxication, and Infancy) reviews the various defenses that arise because of one's incapacity. In this connection, one gains an understanding of how and why a person is excused from conduct otherwise considered criminal because of his or her mental disease or defect, intoxication or drugged condition, or immaturity due to age considerations. Finally, chapter 19 (Defenses: Mistake, Compulsion, Necessity, Entrapment, Public Authority, and Other Justifications or Excuses) considers the remaining defenses that an accused might interpose when criminal charges are lodged against him or her. Some of the defenses are justifications (for example, necessity); some are excuses (for example, compulsion); some can be placed in either category (for example, entrapment); and some (for example, statute of limitations), which might be described as nonexculpatory[1] in nature, can be placed in neither category. Collectively, these defenses are derived from article 5/1 (for example, former prosecution),[2] article 5/4 (for example, ignorance or mistake of fact or law),[3] article 5/7 (for example, public authority),[4] other provisions outside of the major defense articles (for example, consent to criminal sexual assault),[5] and caselaw.

In differentiating between "justifications" and "excuses" the following observation can be made:

> Justified conduct is correct behavior that is encouraged or at least tolerated. In determining whether conduct is justified, the focus in on the *act*, not the actor. An excuse represents a legal conclusion that the conduct is wrong, undesirable, but the criminal liability is inappropriate because some characteristic of the actor vitiates society's desire to punish him. Excuses do not destroy blame . . . rather, they shift it from the actor to the excusing

---

[1] *See* 2 PAUL ROBINSON, CRIMINAL LAW DEFENSES § 202 (1984).

[2] *See, e.g.,* 720 ILCS 5/3-4 (1999).

[3] *See, e.g.,* 720 ILCS 5/4-8 (1999).

[4] *See, e.g.,* 720 ILCS 5/7-5 (1999) (peace officer's use of force in making arrest).

[5] *See, e.g.,* 720 ILCS 5/12-17 (1999).

conditions. The focus in excuses is on the *actor*. Acts are justified; actors are excused.[6]

Here, then, the *act* of self-defense is justified. The *insane* defendant is excused.

Nonexculpatory defenses neither justify nor excuse. These "arise where important public policy other than that of convicting culpable offenders, is protected or furthered by foregoing trial or conviction and punishment."[7] Thus, the statute of limitations is a defense not because the defendant is excused or because his or her conduct is justified. Rather, it protects the defendant from charges long after the alleged crime has been committed because it "further[s] society's need to avoid preoccupation with the past when it no longer serves a significant present purpose."

---

[6] *See* 2 PAUL ROBINSON, CRIMINAL LAW DEFENSES § 25(d) (1984).
[7] *See* 2 PAUL ROBINSON, CRIMINAL LAW DEFENSES § 201(a) (1984).

CHAPTER 17

DEFENSE OF PERSON AND PROPERTY

§ 17.01.　Introduction.

Article 5/7 covers affirmative defenses[8] that justify the use of force in "defense of person"[9] and in "defense of property."[10] The purpose of this chapter is to explore the basic elements and scope of these defenses.

§ 17.02.　Defense of Person: Codification and Legislative Intent.

Section 5/7-1 ("Use of force in defense of person") covers the concepts of both "self-defense"[11] and "defense of another,"[12] which have roots in natural law,[13] the common law,[14] and "model" codifications.[15] Many jurisdictions distinguish between "self-defense" and "defense of another" in one important respect.[16] For instance, self-defense will be available where one *reasonably believes* that one is in immediate danger of unlawful bodily harm from one's adversary,[17] whereas in some jurisdictions, defense of another may only be a defense in situations in which the person defended is *actually* faced with an immediate danger of unlawful bodily harm from his or her assailant.[18] In other words, in the later situation, an accused will not have a defense if he or she reasonably believed another deserved protection from a third-party assailant.[19] Illinois, however, makes no such distinction and provides for self-defense and defense of another in the same statutory provision. It reads:

---

[8] 720 ILCS 5/3-2 (1999):

> Affirmative Defense: (a) "Affirmative defense" means that unless the State's evidence raises the issue involving the alleged defense, the defendant, to raise the issue, must present some evidence thereon; (b) If the issue involved in an affirmative defense . . . is raised then the State must sustain the burden of proving the defendant guilty beyond a reasonable doubt as to that issue together with all the other elements of the crime.

[9] 720 ILCS 5/7-1 (1999) ("Use of force in defense of person").

[10] 720 ILCS 5/7-2 (1999) ("Use of force in defense of dwelling") and 5/7-3 ("Use of force in defense of other property").

[11] WAYNE LAFAVE & AUSTIN SCOTT, CRIMINAL LAW § 5.7 (2d ed. 1986).

[12] WAYNE LAFAVE & AUSTIN SCOTT, CRIMINAL LAW § 5.8 (2d ed. 1986).

[13] *See* M. CHERIF BASSIOUNI, CRIMINAL LAW AND ITS PROCESSES 462 (1969) (discussing self-defense).

[14] *See* WAYNE LAFAVE & AUSTIN SCOTT, CRIMINAL LAW § 5.8(a) (2d ed. 1986) (discussing defense of another).

[15] *See* MODEL PENAL CODE §§ 3.04, 3.05 (1962) (self-defense and defense of another).

[16] WAYNE LAFAVE & AUSTIN SCOTT, CRIMINAL LAW §§ 5.7-5.8 (2d ed. 1986).

[17] WAYNE LAFAVE & AUSTIN SCOTT, CRIMINAL LAW § 5.7(c) (2d ed. 1986).

[18] WAYNE LAFAVE & AUSTIN SCOTT, CRIMINAL LAW § 5.8(b) (2d ed. 1986).

[19] *See, e.g.,* People v. Young, 11 N.Y.2d 274, 183 N.E.2d 319, 229 N.Y.S.2d 1 (1962) (defendant guilty of battery on plainclothes police officer whom defendant reasonably believed was unlawfully attacking arrestee when in fact arrest of subject by officer was valid).

A person is justified in the use of force against another when and to the extent that he reasonably believes that such conduct is necessary to defend himself or another against such other's imminent use of unlawful force. However, he is justified in the use of force which is intended or likely to cause death or great bodily harm only if he reasonably believes that such force is necessary to prevent imminent death or great bodily harm to himself or another, or the commission of a forcible felony.[20]

The Revision Committee responsible for drafting section 5/7-1 stated that the Illinois "defense of person" provision was intended to reflect several propositions: (1) the person claiming defense of person cannot be the aggressor; (2) the danger of harm must be present, as opposed to harm threatened in the future; (3) the danger of harm must appear to be real, as distinguished from the situation where the aggressor lacks the present ability of carrying out the threatened harm; (4) the force threatened must be unlawful, which includes both "criminal and tortious" harm; (5) the person asserting the defense must *actually* believe that the danger of harm existed and that the type and amount of force employed against the aggressor was necessary to thwart the attack; (6) the person's belief, in each of the aspects described above, must be reasonable, even if mistaken; (7) the "defense of person" privilege extends not only to the person threatened but also to third parties who make an effort to protect the person or persons threatened; (8) the privilege of using deadly force in defense of person is available only where the person in danger is faced with deadly force or a forcible felony; and (9) the person using deadly force in defense of person is not obliged to retreat to an avenue of safety before resorting to such force.[21] As will become apparent during the discussion of the Illinois caselaw dealing with defense of person, the judiciary has continuously looked to, and been guided by, these principles described above.

Notwithstanding the consolidation of the principles of self-defense and defense of another, it is best to consider these defenses individually for purposes of clarity. Accordingly, this study will now focus on the concept of self-defense.

§ 17.03. Self-Defense Generally.

The inherent right to prevent bodily harm to oneself and one's property originates in the natural law of self-preservation.[22] There are six major points with respect to the concept of self-defense which should be remembered throughout this section. First, in Illinois, self-defense is a defense that may justify the use of

---

[20] 720 ILCS 5/7-1 (1999).

[21] ILL. ANN. STAT. ch. 38, para. 7-1 (Smith-Hurd 1989), 1961 Committee Comments, at 351-54 (revised 1972).

[22] M. CHERIF BASSIOUNI, SUBSTANTIVE CRIMINAL LAW 462 (1978).

force against an assailant, even to the extent of killing the assailant.[23] The Illinois Criminal Code exonerates a person who defends himself or herself in circumstances in which he or she reasonably believes he or she is faced with an imminent and unlawful use of force by an aggressor.[24] The defendant is then freed from criminal responsibility even for the mistaken infliction of harm on another through acts arising out of justifiable self-defense.[25] In addition, criminal decisions and statutes pertaining to self-defense are persuasive authority in civil cases where a wrongful death is alleged.[26]

Second, some earlier decisions held that self-defense could not apply where the accused claimed that death or injury to the alleged aggressor was an accident.[27] These courts reasoned that "[b]y its very nature [self-defense] relates to knowingly and intentionally using force to deter another and not to an accidental shooting."[28] It was thought that if a person injures or kills another in self-defense, the act is necessarily intentional. However, the Illinois Supreme Court later held that defendants are entitled to have the jury receive self-defense instructions even if the defendant also claims that the act in question was accidental, so long as the defendant presented some evidence that he acted in self-defense.[29]

A third point to be made is that when a defendant asserts the right of self-defense, there is a presupposition that he committed the act.[30] "Raising the issue of self-defense requires as its *sine qua non* that defendant had admitted . . . [the act] . . . as the basis for a belief that the exertion of such force was necessary."[31] On the other hand, the denial of the commission of the act that results in injury to another entirely precludes the issue of self-defense.[32] The only exception to this would be where the defendant raises as alternative defenses both accident

---

[23] People v. Rodriguez, 187 Ill. App. 3d 484, 489, 543 N.E.2d 324, 327 (1st Dist. 1989).

[24] 720 ILCS 5/7-1 (1999).

[25] People v. Rodriguez, 187 Ill. App. 3d 484, 489, 543 N.E.2d 324, 327 (1st Dist. 1989).

[26] First Midwest Bank of Waukegan v. Denson, 205 Ill. App. 3d 124, 130, 562 N.E.2d 1256, 1260 (2d Dist. 1990) (in civil wrongful death action, defendant acted in self-defense and was not liable to estate of deceased).

[27] People v. Chatman, 110 Ill. App. 3d 19, 22, 441 N.E.2d 1292, 1295 (1st Dist. 1982); People v. Purrazzo, 95 Ill. App. 3d 886, 893, 420 N.E.2d 461, 467 (1st Dist. 1981), *cert. denied,* 455 U.S. 948 (1982); People v. Dzambazovic, 61 Ill. App. 3d 703, 717, 377 N.E.2d 1077, 1087 (1st Dist. 1978).

[28] People v. Joyner, 50 Ill. 2d 302, 309, 278 N.E.2d 756, 760 (1972).

[29] People v. Everette, 141 Ill. 2d 147, 156-57, 565 N.E.2d 1295, 1299 (1990). *Accord* People v. Bedoya, 288 Ill. App. 3d 226, 237, 681 N.E.2d 19, 27 (1st Dist. 1997).

[30] People v. Hawkins, 88 Ill. App. 3d 178, 182, 410 N.E.2d 309, 313 (1st Dist. 1980).

[31] People v. Diaz, 101 Ill. App. 3d 903, 915, 428 N.E.2d 953, 962 (1st Dist. 1981) (quoting People v. Lahori, 13 Ill. App. 3d 572, 577, 300 N.E.2d 761, 764-65 (1st Dist. 1973)).

[32] People v. Diaz, 101 Ill. App. 3d 903, 915, 428 N.E.2d 953, 962-63 (1st Dist. 1981).

and self-defense.[33] In addition, since various cases state "a claim of self-defense negatives an inference of sudden and intense passion,"[34] a defendant *may* encounter difficulty in a given case arguing simultaneously for outright acquittal by reason of self-defense *and* reduction of a first degree murder charge to sudden and intense passion second degree murder.[35]

Fourth, a defendant's flight after a violent incident tends to refute the theory of the victim's fear that resulted in the act of self-defense.[36] Concealment[37] or disposal[38] of a weapon that may have been used is clear evidence of a defendant's consciousness of guilt.[39]

Fifth, the privilege of self-defense is not available to a forcible felon who wrongfully causes death or great bodily harm to another.[40] Illinois courts have emphatically refused to recognize a right of self-defense for a felony-murderer,[41] an accomplice to an armed robbery,[42] or an aggressor who wrongfully stabs another.[43] An individual who attempts a forcible felony[44] is likewise precluded from invoking self-defense.[45]

---

[33] People v. Everette, 141 Ill. 2d 147, 156-57, 565 N.E.2d 1295, 1299 (1990); People v. Bedoya, 288 Ill. App. 3d 226, 238, 681 N.E.2d 19, 27-28 (1st Dist. 1997).

[34] *See, e.g.,* People v. Yates, 65 Ill. App. 3d 319, 324, 382 N.E.2d 505, 509 (1st Dist. 1978).

[35] *See, e.g.,* People v. Bailey, 141 Ill. App. 3d 1090, 1104, 490 N.E.2d 1334, 1344 (1st Dist. 1986) (discussing voluntary manslaughter). More recently, voluntary manslaughter has been replaced by second degree murder in Illinois. *See* 720 ILCS 5/9-2 (1999). *But see* People v. Johnson, 215 Ill. App. 3d 713, 727-29, 575 N.E.2d 1247, 1255-57 (1st Dist. 1991) (failure to instruct jury on "sudden and intense passion" second-degree murder where self-defense instruction given was error; first degree murder conviction reversed).

[36] People v. Ferguson, 102 Ill. App. 3d 702, 715, 429 N.E.2d 1321, 1331 (1st Dist. 1981), *cert. denied,* 459 U.S. 872 (1982); People v. Aguero, 87 Ill. App. 3d 358, 363, 408 N.E.2d 1092, 1096 (1st Dist. 1980).

[37] People v. Lynch, 43 Ill. App. 3d 1039, 1043, 358 N.E.2d 17, 19 (1st Dist. 1976).

[38] People v. Cox, 121 Ill. App. 3d 118, 123, 459 N.E.2d 269, 272 (3d Dist.), *cert. denied,* 469 U.S. 963 (1984).

[39] People v. Cox, 121 Ill. App. 3d 118, 123, 459 N.E.2d 269, 272 (3d Dist.), *cert. denied,* 469 U.S. 963 (1984).

[40] People v. Gates, 47 Ill. App. 3d 109, 115, 361 N.E.2d 809, 813 (1st Dist. 1977).

[41] People v. Baker, 57 Ill. App. 3d 401, 402-03, 372 N.E.2d 438, 440 (4th Dist. 1978).

[42] People v. Gates, 47 Ill. App. 3d 109, 115, 361 N.E.2d 809, 813 (1st Dist. 1977).

[43] People v. Oliver, 11 Ill. App. 3d 152, 156, 296 N.E.2d 70, 73 (3d Dist. 1973).

[44] Forcible felony is defined as "treason, first degree murder, second degree murder, predatory criminal sexual assault of a child, aggravated criminal sexual assault, criminal sexual assault, robbery, burglary, residential burglary, aggravated arson, arson, kidnapping, aggravated kidnapping, aggravated battery resulting in great bodily harm or permanent disability or disfigurement and any other felony which involves the use or threat of physical force or violence against an individual." 720 ILCS 5/2-8 (1999).

[45] 720 ILCS 5/7-4 (1999) provides that self-defense "is not available to a person who ... [is] attempting to commit, committing, or escaping after the commission of, a forcible felony." *See also* People v. Baker, 57 Ill. App. 3d 401, 403, 372 N.E.2d 438, 440 (4th Dist. 1978).

The sixth point to keep in mind is that one can resort to deadly force not only where one is faced with an assailant's deadly force but also where one is confronted by an assailant's efforts to cause great bodily harm. The criminal code mentions the phrase *great bodily harm* in the sections pertaining to various offenses including first degree murder,[46] aggravated kidnapping,[47] aggravated battery,[48] and aggravated arson,[49] and the defense of person limiting use of force by an aggressor.[50] The General Assembly concluded that this language required no further definition or explanation.[51] The courts state in other contexts that what constitutes great bodily harm is a question of fact.[52] Similarly, what constitutes great bodily harm for purposes of self-defense is also an issue for the trier of fact.[53] The use of deadly force in self-defense is justified only where there is a reasonable belief that the force is necessary to prevent imminent death or great bodily harm.[54] Such a threat must be apparent, although it need not be real if the belief is reasonable.[55]

§ 17.04.   Elements of Self-Defense.

Once the accused has asserted self-defense, the state has the burden to prove that one or more elements of self-defense has not been satisfied and that burden is met if the state has negated *any one of the elements* beyond a reasonable doubt.[56] The elements of self-defense are: (1) force is threatened against a person; (2) the person threatened is not the aggressor; (3) the danger of harm is imminent; (4) the force threatened is unlawful — either criminal or tortious; (5) the person threatened actually believes that (a) danger exists, (b) the use of force

---

[46] 720 ILCS 5/9-1(a) (1999).

[47] 720 ILCS 5/10-2(a)(3) (1999).

[48] 720 ILCS 5/12-4 (1999).

[49] 720 ILCS 5/20-1.1 (1999).

[50] 720 ILCS 5/7-4 (1999).

[51] ILL. ANN. STAT. ch. 38, para. 7-1 (Smith-Hurd 1989), 1961 Committee Comments, at 353.

[52] People v. Dowdy, 21 Ill. App. 3d 821, 825, 316 N.E.2d 33, 35-36 (1st Dist. 1974) (discussing aggravated battery). *See generally* 1 BISHOP ON CRIMINAL LAW §§ 865-66 (9th ed. 1923).

[53] People v. Dowdy, 21 Ill. App. 3d 821, 825, 316 N.E.2d 33, 36 (1st Dist. 1974).

[54] 720 ILCS 5/7-1 (1999); *see* People v. Chavez, 228 Ill. App. 3d 54, 71, 592 N.E.2d 69, 82 (1st Dist. 1992).

[55] People v. Polk, 70 Ill. App. 3d 903, 904, 388 N.E.2d 864, 867 (1st Dist. 1979).

[56] People v. Chavez, 228 Ill. App. 3d 54, 70-71, 592 N.E.2d 69, 81 (1st Dist. 1992); People v. De Oca, 238 Ill. App. 3d 362, 368, 606 N.E.2d 332, 336 (1st Dist. 1992); People v. Brown, 218 Ill. App. 3d 890, 898, 578 N.E.2d 1168, 1174 (1st Dist. 1991); People v. Belpedio, 212 Ill. App. 3d 155, 161, 569 N.E.2d 1372, 1375 (2d Dist. 1991); People v. Ellis, 187 Ill. App. 3d 295, 302, 543 N.E.2d 196, 200 (1st Dist. 1989), *cert. denied*, 498 U.S. 942 (1990); People v. Hoffer, 122 Ill. App. 3d 13, 21, 460 N.E.2d 824, 830 (2d Dist. 1984), *cert. denied*, 474 U.S. 847 (1985).

is necessary to avert the imminent danger, and (c) the kind and amount of force used is necessary; and (6) the above beliefs are reasonable, even if mistaken.[57]

§ 17.05.   — Force Threatened Against a Person.

The force threatened against the person asserting self-defense must be substantial in nature. Mere verbal threats,[58] movement toward a pocket,[59] or provocation[60] are not enough, standing alone, to satisfy this element. Disparity in size of parties, by itself, does not justify use of force in self-defense.[61]

The accused's perception of danger is sufficient to raise the issue of self-defense.[62] Perception of danger includes the defendant's knowledge of prior violent acts by the victim.[63]

§ 17.06.   — Person Threatened Generally Cannot be Aggressor.

Generally, the right of self-defense arises only where the person asserting the defense was not the aggressor.[64] However, there are two exceptions to the general rule. First, an aggressor met with deadly force, after using only nondeadly force, may defend himself or herself in like manner.[65] Second, the right of self-

---

[57] People v. Williams, 56 Ill. App. 2d 159, 165, 205 N.E.2d 749, 752 (1st Dist. 1965) (*Williams* court was first to spell out the elements of self-defense after adoption of Criminal Code of 1961; these elements are now generally accepted). *See, e.g.,* People v. Shields, 298 Ill. App. 3d 943, 947, 700 N.E.2d 168, 172 (1st Dist. 1998); People v. De Oca, 238 Ill. App. 3d 362, 368, 606 N.E.2d 332, 336 (1st Dist. 1992); People v. Chavez, 228 Ill. App. 3d 54, 70, 592 N.E.2d 69, 81 (1st Dist. 1992); People v. Belpedio, 212 Ill. App. 3d 155, 160, 569 N.E.2d 1372, 1375 (2d Dist. 1991); People v. Brown, 218 Ill. App. 3d 890, 898, 578 N.E.2d 1168, 1173-74 (1st Dist. 1991); People v. Parker, 194 Ill. App. 3d 1048, 1055, 551 N.E.2d 1012, 1017 (1st Dist. 1990); People v. Ellis, 187 Ill. App. 3d 295, 302, 543 N.E.2d 196, 200 (1st Dist. 1989), *cert. denied,* 498 U.S. 942 (1990); People v. Ross, 100 Ill. App. 3d 1033, 1038, 427 N.E.2d 955, 959 (1st Dist. 1981); People v. Kyles, 91 Ill. App. 3d 1019, 1021-22, 415 N.E.2d 499, 501 (1st Dist. 1980); People v. Seiber, 76 Ill. App. 3d 9, 13, 394 N.E.2d 1044, 1048 (3d Dist. 1979).

[58] People v. Strohl, 118 Ill. App. 3d 1084, 1089, 456 N.E.2d 276, 279 (4th Dist. 1983) (verbal threat to kill). *See also* People v. Everette, 141 Ill. 2d 147, 161, 565 N.E.2d 1295, 1301 (1990) (threats alone will not justify use of deadly force); People v. Chatman, 102 Ill. App. 3d 692, 699, 430 N.E.2d 257, 263 (1st Dist. 1981) (threat to harm); People v. Carbajal, 67 Ill. App. 3d 236, 241, 384 N.E.2d 824, 828 (1st Dist. 1978) (threat to kill).

[59] People v. Pietrzyk, 54 Ill. App. 3d 738, 745, 369 N.E.2d 1299, 1303 (1st Dist. 1977).

[60] People v. Coleman, 85 Ill. App. 3d 1020, 1026, 407 N.E.2d 832, 837 (1st Dist. 1980).

[61] People v. Smith, 58 Ill. App. 3d 784, 790, 374 N.E.2d 1285, 1289 (1st Dist. 1978), *cert. denied,* 440 U.S. 973 (1979).

[62] People v. Shipp, 52 Ill. App. 3d 470, 476, 367 N.E.2d 966, 970 (2d Dist. 1977).

[63] People v. Adams, 71 Ill. App. 3d 70, 75, 388 N.E.2d 1326, 1329-30 (2d Dist. 1979).

[64] People v. Hines, 31 Ill. App. 3d 295, 301, 334 N.E.2d 233, 238 (1st Dist. 1975) (articulating general rule). *See also* People v. Woods, 81 Ill. 2d 537, 543, 410 N.E.2d 866, 869 (1980) (no self-defense where defendant took a "very aggressive, intimidating role in confronting" victim).

[65] *See* People v. Hudson, 71 Ill. App. 3d 504, 390 N.E.2d 5 (1st Dist. 1979). *See also* WAYNE LAFAVE & AUSTIN SCOTT, CRIMINAL LAW § 5.7(e) (2d ed. 1986).

defense is restored when the initial aggressor withdraws from the confrontation and clearly announces his or her withdrawal.[66] Section 5/7-4 states that self-defense is not available to a person who:

> (c) Otherwise initially provokes the use of force against himself, unless:
> (1) Such force is so great that he reasonably believes that he is in imminent danger of death or great bodily harm, and that he has exhausted every reasonable means to escape such danger other than the use of force which is likely to cause death or great bodily harm to the assailant; or
> (2) In good faith, he withdraws from physical contact with the assailant and indicates clearly to the assailant that he desires to withdraw and terminate the use of force, but the assailant continues or resumes the use of force.[67]

Where a dangerous situation arises out of a person's own making, that person cannot claim a right of self-defense.[68] Section 5/7-4 provides that self-defense "is not available to a person who: ... [i]nitially provokes the use of force against himself, with the intent to use such force as an excuse to inflict bodily harm upon the assailant ...."[69] Also, section 7-4 provides that a person who is committing or is about to commit a forcible felony cannot claim justifiable use of force.[70] In essence, "[a person] may not seek out a perilous situation, then assert that he acted in self-defense."[71]

§ 17.07.   — Danger of Harm is Imminent.

In order to justify use of force against another, the danger of harm must be imminent. *Imminent* is defined as "immediate."[72] In other words, the danger of harm must be a present danger, not one sometime in the future. Also, the adver-

---

[66] 720 ILCS 5/7-4(c)(2) (1999). *See also* WAYNE LAFAVE & AUSTIN SCOTT, CRIMINAL LAW § 5.7(e) (2d ed. 1986).

[67] 720 ILCS 5/7-4(c) (1999).

[68] People v. Andersch, 107 Ill. App. 3d 810, 819, 438 N.E.2d 482, 488 (1st Dist. 1982).

[69] 720 ILCS 5/7-4(b) (1999).

[70] 720 ILCS 5/7-4(a) (1999). *See also* People v. Mills, 252 Ill. App. 3d 792, 799, 624 N.E.2d 384, 389 (2d Dist. 1993) (defendant who engaged in attempted armed robbery not entitled to use self-defense); People v. Freeman, 234 Ill. App. 3d 380, 386, 600 N.E.2d 862, 866 (3d Dist. 1992) (defendant who committed home invasion not entitled to instruction on justifiable use of force).

[71] People v. Zolidis, 115 Ill. App. 3d 669, 675, 450 N.E.2d 1290, 1295 (1st Dist. 1983). *See also* People v. Love, 83 Ill. App. 3d 948, 950, 404 N.E.2d 1085, 1087 (3d Dist. 1980) ("defendant provoked the use of force against himself by seeking out the victim ... and thereby placing himself in a volatile situation"); People v. Echoles, 36 Ill. App. 3d 845, 856, 344 N.E.2d 620, 628 (1st Dist. 1976) ("An accused will not be heard to complain or assert self-defense when the situation with which he is confronted arose out his own aggressive conduct in seeking the difficulty").

[72] WAYNE LAFAVE & AUSTIN SCOTT, CRIMINAL LAW § 5.7(d) (2d ed. 1986).

sary must appear to be capable of carrying out the threats.[73] Although imminent danger is a vital element of self-defense, Illinois courts have not elaborated on its meaning, but instead assume that the term *imminent* is universally understood.[74]

In *People v. Chatman*,[75] the issue of imminence arose where a defendant was convicted of aggravated battery after he stabbed another man. The unarmed victim was the first to use force in an argument with the armed defendant. After hitting the defendant over the head with a rotten board, the victim turned away. The court found that the defendant's belief that he would suffer imminent death or great bodily harm when he subsequently stabbed the victim was not justified.[76]

The apparent danger need not be real,[77] as long as the defendant's perception of imminent peril is reasonable.[78] On the other hand, belief of imminent danger has been found unreasonable under certain circumstances.[79] Such was the case where the defendant sought out and shot an unarmed victim after an earlier fight, believing the victim to be armed and positioned to shoot the defendant.[80] Where a defendant shot and killed two armed friends of his female roommate and, thereafter, a third unarmed friend of the roommate when she appeared following the first two shootings, the shooting of the third individual was considered unreasonable, where the actual state of affairs surrounding the incident belied the necessity of resorting to deadly force against the third individual.[81] The surrounding facts and circumstances of each case determine the accused's subjective belief of imminent danger and his or her consequent right to self-defense.[82]

---

[73] ILL. ANN. STAT. ch. 38, para. 7-1 (Smith-Hurd 1989), 1961 Committee Comments, at 351; People v. Brown, 218 Ill. App. 3d 890, 899, 578 N.E.2d 1168, 1174 (1st Dist. 1991).

[74] *See, e.g.,* People v. Ross, 100 Ill. App. 3d 1033, 1038, 427 N.E.2d 955, 959 (1st Dist. 1981) (referring to imminence requirement without further explanation); People v. Christiansen, 96 Ill. App. 3d 540, 542-43, 421 N.E.2d 570, 572 (2d Dist. 1981) (referring to imminence requirement without further explanation); People v. Seiber, 76 Ill. App. 3d 9, 13, 394 N.E.2d 1044, 1048 (3d Dist. 1979) (referring to imminence requirement without further explanation).

[75] 102 Ill. App. 3d 692, 430 N.E.2d 257 (1st Dist. 1981).

[76] People v. Chatman, 102 Ill. App. 3d 692, 699, 430 N.E.2d 257, 263 (1st Dist. 1981).

[77] People v. Polk, 70 Ill. App. 3d 903, 905, 388 N.E.2d 864, 867 (1st Dist. 1979).

[78] People v. Tirrell, 87 Ill. App. 3d 511, 518, 408 N.E.2d 1202, 1207 (3d Dist. 1980) (rejecting defense claim that defendant's subjective belief in the necessity of self-defense is sufficient to satisfy self-defense claim even though belief is unreasonable).

[79] People v. Tirrell, 87 Ill. App. 3d 511, 518, 408 N.E.2d 1202, 1207 (3d Dist. 1980).

[80] People v. Polk, 70 Ill. App. 3d 903, 905, 388 N.E.2d 864, 867 (1st Dist. 1979).

[81] People v. Brown, 19 Ill. App. 3d 757, 763, 312 N.E.2d 789, 794 (1st Dist. 1974); *see also* People v. Willis, 210 Ill. App. 3d 379, 385, 569 N.E.2d 113, 116-17 (1st Dist. 1991) (even if defendant acted in self-defense in stabbing victim first time, he acted unreasonably in stabbing him ten more times after victim was injured, unarmed and turning away from defendant).

[82] People v. Chavez, 228 Ill. App. 3d 54, 70, 592 N.E.2d 69, 81 (1st Dist. 1992).

Although the reasonableness of the defendant's perception of the danger, not the actual peril, is the test applied to belief of imminent danger, "infallible judgment" is not required.[83]

> The law does not charge an individual, when he has reasonable grounds to believe himself in apparent danger of losing his life or suffering great bodily injury, to use infallible judgment. It would be unreasonable to require such an exercise of careful judgment in the space of a few seconds while one under great stress and excitement was being pursued by another, apparently bent on doing him great bodily harm.[84]

Thus, in *People v. Shipp*,[85] a woman's fear of imminent danger was found to be reasonable when she shot her unarmed former husband during an argument. The couple's relationship had been riddled with violence directed by the decedent against the defendant, and the defendant knew that the decedent had killed his first wife. The appellate court recognized that under the circumstances, the defendant could not be expected to have "perfect judgment."[86]

Even after the victim has been wounded and has fallen, there may not be sufficient time for the defendant to realize that he or she is no longer in danger.[87] For example, a fourteen-year-old's decision to shoot four teenagers who were pursuing him in a menacing fashion in a school parking lot was deemed reasonable under the circumstances.[88] Here, the court determined that the interval between the initial shot and subsequent shots was not "sufficient to allow the accused, acting as a reasonable person, to realize that no further shooting was necessary."[89]

§ 17.08.   — Force Threatened Is Unlawful.

For one to be entitled to use force in self-defense or defense of another, the adversary's force must be unlawful or believed to be unlawful.[90] Generally, the assailant's unlawful force must amount to an assault or battery,[91] whether crimi-

---

[83] People v. Tirrell, 87 Ill. App. 3d 511, 518, 408 N.E.2d 1202, 1207 (3d Dist. 1980).

[84] People v. Motuzas, 352 Ill. 340, 346, 185 N.E. 614, 617 (1933). *See also* People v. Harling, 29 Ill. App. 3d 1053, 1060, 331 N.E.2d 653, 658 (1st Dist. 1975).

[85] 52 Ill. App. 3d 470, 367 N.E.2d 966 (2d Dist. 1977).

[86] People v. Shipp, 52 Ill. App. 3d 470, 477, 367 N.E.2d 966, 971 (2d Dist. 1977).

[87] People v. Bailey, 27 Ill. App. 3d 128, 136, 326 N.E.2d 550, 556 (1st Dist. 1975).

[88] In re S.M., 93 Ill. App. 3d 105, 110-111, 416 N.E.2d 1212, 1216 (1st Dist. 1981).

[89] In re S.M., 93 Ill. App. 3d 105, 110-111, 416 N.E.2d 1212, 1216 (1st Dist. 1981).

[90] People v. Daily, 79 Ill. App. 3d 928, 936, 398 N.E.2d 923, 929 (1st Dist. 1979) (attempt to take life of police officer that reasonable person would know was properly performing law enforcement duties not justified by self-defense).

[91] People v. Perry, 27 Ill. App. 3d 230, 232-33, 327 N.E.2d 167, 169-70 (1st Dist. 1975) (private security guards' attempt to handcuff defendant was a battery and defendant's resistance justified by self-defense; defendant's battery conviction reversed).

nal or tortious.[92] Consequently, a person has no right of self-defense or defense of others when the force used against him or her is lawful.[93]

Lawful force includes the right of a peace officer to make an arrest.[94] This is true even if the arrestee believes that the arrest is unlawful and it is in fact unlawful.[95] An Illinois statute provides:

> A person is not authorized to use force to resist an arrest which he knows is being made either by a peace officer or by a private person summoned and directed by a peace officer to make the arrest, even if he believes that the arrest is unlawful, and arrest in fact is unlawful.[96]

Nevertheless, the right of self-defense against a peace officer may be invoked where the officer uses excessive force in making the arrest, since "[t]he use of excessive force invokes the right of self-defense."[97]

The defendant's response to unlawful force was of central importance in *People v. Christiansen*,[98] where the defendant provoked an argument with a woman at her home and repeatedly slapped her.[99] The woman's father attempted to intervene but the defendant kicked and punched him, later alleging he had been in fear of imminent harm. The court determined that since the defendant had responded to *lawful* force — the father's defense of his daughter — he had no right of self-defense.[100] In addition, the defendant had been the initial aggressor, and although he claimed fear of imminent harm, this fear was found to be unreasonable.[101] Consequently, his conviction of battery was affirmed.[102]

§ 17.09. — Actual Belief.

The person threatened must actually believe that (a) danger exists, (b) the use of force is necessary to avert the imminent danger, and (c) the kind and amount of force is necessary.

§ 17.10. — — Belief That Danger Exists.

An individual must *subjectively*, as well as objectively, believe that imminent danger exists in order to be justified in defending himself or herself with force

---

[92] ILL. ANN. STAT. ch. 38, para. 7-1 (Smith-Hurd 1989), 1961 Committee Comments, at 352.

[93] People v. Daily, 79 Ill. App. 3d 928, 936, 398 N.E.2d 923, 929 (1st Dist. 1979) (attempt to take life of police officer that reasonable person would know was properly performing law enforcement duties not justified by self-defense).

[94] *See* 725 ILCS 5/107-2 (1999) (authorization for arrest by peace officer).

[95] People v. Bailey, 108 Ill. App. 3d 392, 398, 439 N.E.2d 4, 9 (2d Dist. 1982).

[96] 720 ILCS 5/7-7 (1993) (formerly ILL. REV. STAT. ch. 38, para. 7-7 (1991)).

[97] People v. Bailey, 108 Ill. App. 3d 392, 398, 439 N.E.2d 4, 9 (2d Dist. 1982).

[98] 96 Ill. App. 3d 540, 421 N.E.2d 570 (2d Dist. 1981).

[99] People v. Christiansen, 96 Ill. App. 3d 540, 544, 421 N.E.2d 570, 574 (2d Dist. 1981).

[100] People v. Christiansen, 96 Ill. App. 3d 540, 543, 421 N.E.2d 570, 573 (2d Dist. 1981).

[101] People v. Christiansen, 96 Ill. App. 3d 540, 543, 421 N.E.2d 570, 573 (2d Dist. 1981).

[102] People v. Christiansen, 96 Ill. App. 3d 540, 544, 421 N.E.2d 570, 574 (2d Dist. 1981).

directed against another.[103] In *People v. Goodman*,[104] a woman shot her estranged husband, a police officer, during a quarrel in which the victim had pistol whipped her. The defendant was able to grab the decedent's weapon and, fearing for her life, shot him. Even though it was not clear whether the decedent would actually have caused the defendant great bodily harm, the court found her belief of imminent danger to be both subjective and reasonable.[105]

In contrast, in *People v. Andersche*,[106] the defendant's lack of subjective belief in the need to resort to force was one reason his self-defense claim failed. In that case, the defendant shot two noisy and intoxicated men in the corridor of a residential YMCA, in circumstances where "an angry bluff precipitate[d] a deadly confrontation . . . ."[107] Specifically, the defendant was awakened by a raucous group outside his room. He left the room, armed with a rifle, and told the group to be quiet lest he shoot. Apparently, one of the group confronted the defendant, whereupon the defendant fired two shots in rapid succession, fatally striking two victims.

In reviewing this incident, the appellate court determined that the defendant had not subjectively or reasonably entertained the fear necessary to resort to deadly force. First, the defendant's own testimony revealed that the group member who prompted the defendant's actions "would not have been a match for [him]."[108] In addition, the defendant testified that during this confrontation, he "felt somewhat threatened. But not really that I thought I was."[109] These statements prompted the court to question whether the defendant's fears were genuine.[110]

Second, the court did not believe that the defendant could have reasonably believed he was in imminent danger. The court noted, among other things, that the first victim had been shot in the back and that the second victim had been struck while standing behind the first victim, thereby eroding the defendant's claim that he was threatened by an "on-rushing horde."[111]

Third, the court stated that the defendant could not claim self-defense where the situation he encountered was of his own making.[112] Here, the court inferred

---

[103] People v. Ellis, 187 Ill. App. 3d 295, 302, 543 N.E.2d 196, 200 (1st Dist. 1989), *cert. denied*, 498 U.S. 942 (1990); People v. Andersch, 107 Ill. App. 3d 810, 819, 438 N.E.2d 482, 488 (1st Dist. 1982); People v. Goodman, 77 Ill. App. 3d 569, 575, 396 N.E.2d 274, 278 (4th Dist. 1979).

[104] 77 Ill. App. 3d 569, 396 N.E.2d 274 (4th Dist. 1979).

[105] People v. Goodman, 77 Ill. App. 3d 569, 575, 396 N.E.2d 274, 278 (4th Dist. 1979).

[106] 107 Ill. App. 3d 810, 438 N.E.2d 482 (1st Dist. 1982).

[107] People v. Andersch, 107 Ill. App. 3d 810, 818, 438 N.E.2d 482, 488 (1st Dist. 1982).

[108] People v. Andersch, 107 Ill. App. 3d 810, 819, 438 N.E.2d 482, 488 (1st Dist. 1982).

[109] People v. Andersch, 107 Ill. App. 3d 810, 819, 438 N.E.2d 482, 488 (1st Dist. 1982).

[110] People v. Andersch, 107 Ill. App. 3d 810, 819, 438 N.E.2d 482, 488-89 (1st Dist. 1982).

[111] People v. Andersch, 107 Ill. App. 3d 810, 819, 438 N.E.2d 482, 488-89 (1st Dist. 1982).

[112] People v. Andersch, 107 Ill. App. 3d 810, 819, 438 N.E.2d 482, 488-89 (1st Dist. 1982).

from the defendant's own testimony that before the shooting, he had an opportunity to retreat into his room and close the door behind him, assuming he was in
fact confronted by this "unfriendly" group.[113] In conclusion, since the defendant
had no right of self-defense, his conduct was deemed reckless, and his convictions for involuntary manslaughter were upheld.[114]

Perception of danger includes the defendant's knowledge of specific facts regarding the victim.[115] In *People v. Brumbeloe*,[116] a defendant perceived the existence of imminent danger and stabbed the victim to death during a street fight. In
finding his actions justified, the appellate court considered that (1) the deceased,
armed with a knife, had twice assaulted the defendant the day before the killing
and the defendant had managed to escape; (2) the deceased had threatened to kill
the defendant on the previous day; and (3) the defendant had learned on the day
of the killing that the deceased was looking for him.[117]

In contrast, where a defendant is not subjectively aware of certain facts about
the violent proclivities of his or her victim, he or she cannot use these facts to
advance his or her self-defense claim. For example, in a manslaughter prosecution where there was no showing that the defendant was actually aware of the
victim's violent tendencies when he slew the victim, the appellate court held that
the trial court properly refused to admit evidence of the victim's reputation for
violent behavior.[118]

In addition to the subjective requirement, use of force in self-defense is justified only where the defendant acts in accordance with a *reasonable* belief that
he or she is confronted with a threat of force.[119] Further, deadly force is only
permissible where the defendant harbors a *reasonable* belief that he or she faces
the "danger of imminent death or great bodily harm" as a consequence of the
aggressor's conduct.[120] In *People v. Davis*,[121] the defendant's use of deadly force
was found to be unreasonable. In that case, a woman, after an argument with the
father of three of her children, went home, changed clothes, and returned to the
decedent. The two continued to argue, and when the unarmed decedent physi-

---

[113] People v. Andersche, 107 Ill. App. 3d 810, 819, 438 N.E.2d 482, 488-89 (1st Dist. 1982).

[114] People v. Andersche, 107 Ill. App. 3d 810, 819, 438 N.E.2d 482, 488-89 (1st Dist. 1982).

[115] People v. Evans, 104 Ill. App. 3d 598, 602, 432 N.E.2d 1285, 1289 (1st Dist. 1982).

[116] 97 Ill. App. 2d 370, 240 N.E.2d 150 (1st Dist. 1968).

[117] People v. Brumbeloe, 97 Ill. App. 2d 370, 376-77, 240 N.E.2d 150, 154 (1st Dist. 1968).

[118] People v. Johnson, 172 Ill. App. 3d 371, 377-78, 526 N.E.2d 611, 615 (1st Dist. 1988).

[119] In Interest of D.N., 178 Ill. App. 3d 470, 474-75, 533 N.E.2d 84, 87-88 (1st Dist. 1988) (evidence of self-defense was insufficient where elementary school student could reasonably have
judged teacher down on her knees was not in position to take offensive action against student following struggle between student and teacher; adjudication of delinquency against student for
commission of aggravated battery against teacher upheld).

[120] People v. Parker, 194 Ill. App. 3d 1048, 1055, 551 N.E.2d 1012, 1017 (1st Dist. 1990); People v. Rodriguez, 187 Ill. App. 3d 484, 489, 543 N.E.2d 324, 327 (1st Dist. 1989).

[121] 33 Ill. App. 3d 105, 337 N.E.2d 256 (1st Dist. 1975).

cally attacked the defendant, she shot him. The appellate court found that the defendant's belief that an unarmed man would immediately kill or greatly injure her was not reasonable.[122]

In another case, a "mentally and physically abused young woman who suffered greatly at the hands of a brutal man for whom she bore three children"[123] shot and killed her intoxicated husband after he pistol whipped her and ordered her to handcuff herself to the bed. Based on past experience, the defendant knew that a severe beating would follow the handcuffing. Instead of following her husband's orders, the defendant became fearful for her life and shot him with the gun that he had required her to keep nearby. The appellate court reversed and remanded the defendant's conviction of murder, holding that the jury was entitled to instructions on self-defense.[124] The court stated if the defendant was reasonable in her subjective belief that she was in danger of imminent death or great bodily harm, she should have been exonerated.[125]

In determining whether a defendant reasonably apprehends danger, the victim's prior specific acts of violence that are known to the defendant are factors to be considered.[126] This knowledge may affect the defendant's state of mind at the time of the incident.[127] In *People v. Adams*,[128] the defendant and the victim had lived together for five and one-half years, during which time the victim had frequently beaten her. During an argument, the victim advanced menacingly toward her, possibly carrying a tire iron. After verbally warning the victim and firing a warning shot, the defendant shot him. The appellate court stated it was error for the trial court to exclude evidence during the defendant's murder trial regarding her knowledge that the victim, on at least one previous occasion, had killed a man.[129]

However, a defendant's awareness of his or her victim's propensity for violence does not per se render the defendant's perception of imminent harm reasonable. In a case where the defendant testified that he was in danger when the victim, who had a reputation for violence and for carrying a gun, made threatening gestures as if to reach for a pocketed gun while standing on the street out-

---

[122] People v. Davis, 33 Ill. App. 3d 105, 109-10, 337 N.E.2d 256, 259-60 (1st Dist. 1975).

[123] People v. Scott, 97 Ill. App. 3d 899, 901, 424 N.E.2d 70, 71 (3d Dist. 1981).

[124] People v. Scott, 97 Ill. App. 3d 899, 903, 424 N.E.2d 70, 72 (3d Dist. 1981).

[125] People v. Scott, 97 Ill. App. 3d 899, 903, 424 N.E.2d 70, 72-73 (3d Dist. 1981).

[126] People v. Adams, 71 Ill. App. 3d 70, 75, 388 N.E.2d 1326, 1329-30 (2d Dist. 1979).

[127] People v. Stombaugh, 52 Ill. 2d 130, 139, 284 N.E.2d 640, 645 (1972) (evidence concerning the violent temper and disposition of the deceased and his prior threats toward defendant should have been admitted; murder conviction reversed); People v. Moore, 89 Ill. App. 3d 202, 210, 411 N.E.2d 579, 585-86 (3d Dist. 1980) (evidence of victim's prior murder conviction and violent behavior should have been admitted; harmless error, voluntary manslaughter conviction affirmed).

[128] 71 Ill. App. 3d 70, 388 N.E.2d 1326 (2d Dist. 1979).

[129] People v. Adams, 71 Ill. App. 3d 70, 75, 388 N.E.2d 1326, 1329-30 (2d Dist. 1979) (harmless error; murder conviction affirmed).

side, the appellate court upheld defendant's aggravated battery conviction where the jury had sufficient evidence from which it could conclude that the defendant did not reasonably apprehend imminent harm under circumstances where the defendant shot from a second-floor apartment window and wounded the victim, to whom he owed twelve dollars.[130]

§ 17.11.   —— Belief That Use of Force is Necessary.

The second prong of the element of belief is that the defendant must actually believe that the *use of force is necessary*. In the context of using deadly force in self-defense, the defendant must have thought it necessary to avert imminent death or great bodily harm.[131] For instance, there is no defense where an enemy is killed or injured by an individual who is totally ignorant of his or her enemy's imminent attack.[132] The right remains, however, in spite of any ulterior motivation the claimant may have that is beyond mere defense of self, provided the individual is justified in his or her act of self-defense.[133] The difference between a justified killing under self-defense and one not justified, amounting to second degree murder, is that in the former instance the belief that the use of force is necessary is reasonable under the circumstances, and in the latter, the subjective belief is unreasonable.[134] Thus, in determining whether the use of force is justified, courts will examine the reasonableness of the defendant's subjective belief that the use of force is necessary.[135] If the belief is unreasonable, the defendant may be convicted of second degree murder.[136] Indeed, this type of homicide may be referred to as "imperfect defense" second degree murder.[137] For example, where the defendant subjectively believed his shooting was justified as self-defense, he was properly convicted of second degree murder where an unarmed victim, who defendant had previously fought without serious injury to either, approached defendant and defendant shot the victim three times.[138] Meanwhile, if the defendant was clearly the aggressor and had not subjectively harbored

---

[130] People v. Evans, 104 Ill. App. 3d 598, 601, 432 N.E.2d 1285, 1288-89 (1st Dist. 1982).

[131] People v. Parker, 194 Ill. App. 3d 1048, 1055-56, 551 N.E.2d 1012, 1017-18 (1st Dist. 1990) (defendant "did not act with a belief, reasonable or unreasonable, in the need for self-defense"; murder conviction affirmed).

[132] WAYNE LAFAVE & AUSTIN SCOTT, CRIMINAL LAW § 5.7(c) (2d ed. 1986).

[133] WAYNE LAFAVE & AUSTIN SCOTT, CRIMINAL LAW § 5.7(c) (2d ed. 1986).

[134] People v. Bosek, 210 Ill. App. 3d 573, 597, 569 N.E.2d 551, 566-67 (2d Dist. 1991), *cert. denied*, 502 U.S. 1098 (1992).

[135] *See, e.g.,* People v. Bosek, 210 Ill. App. 3d 573, 597, 569 N.E.2d 551, 566-67 (2d Dist. 1991), *cert. denied*, 502 U.S. 1098 (1992).

[136] People v. Chavez, 228 Ill. App. 3d 54, 70-71, 592 N.E.2d 69, 81 (1st Dist. 1992).

[137] *See* ch. 6 of this treatise for a discussion of imperfect defense second degree murder.

[138] People v. Brown, 218 Ill. App. 3d 890, 898, 578 N.E.2d 1168, 1174-75 (1st Dist. 1991).

even an unreasonable belief in the need to kill in self-defense, he is liable for first degree murder.[139]

A defendant's own opinion about his or her state of mind during an occurrence, as well as the defendant's belief regarding the number of potential adversaries, may be useful evidence in determining the reasonableness of his or her belief regarding the need to use deadly force in self-defense. For example, where a defendant, a nervous police informant, shot three men during a drug transaction, and during his subsequent trial the defendant was not allowed to explain why he had brought a gun to the scene of a planned drug transaction where a number of potential adversaries were present before he fired the shots, the appellate court reversed defendant's convictions and the case was remanded for retrial for a more thorough consideration of the defendant's claim of self-defense.[140]

Because a defendant need only offer "some evidence"[141] supportive of the need to resort to self-defense, the trial court will normally be obligated to issue self-defense instructions to the jury if the defendant offers his or her own testimony in support of his or her belief in the necessity of acting in self-defense . For example, one trial court judge erred by failing to instruct the jury on self-defense where the defendant presented evidence suggesting that he was sufficiently threatened when the victim approached him in an intoxicated condition and made threatening statements, while knowing of the victim's propensity for violence and the victim's habit of carrying a knife, prior to his stabbing of the victim, whom defendant did not realize was actually unarmed.[142] Accordingly, the appellate court reversed the defendant's murder conviction and ordered a retrial so that the issue of self-defense could be considered by the jury.[143]

§ 17.12. — — Belief that Kind and Amount of Force is Necessary.

As a matter of law, the amount of force must be no more than appears reasonably necessary to avoid or end the assailant's aggression.[144] For example, where a woman shot and killed the man with whom she was living, in circumstances where the couple was in the process of separating when the victim woke the defendant and commenced beating her, as he had done frequently in the past, the appellate court, in denying the defendant's claim of self-defense, noted that there was no reason to believe that the last beating would have been any more

---

[139] People v. Mayoral, 299 Ill. App. 3d 899, 912, 702 N.E.2d 238, 247-48 (1st Dist. 1998).

[140] People v. Kline, 90 Ill. App. 3d 1008, 1014-15, 414 N.E.2d 141, 146-47 (1st Dist. 1980).

[141] People v. Lockett, 82 Ill. 2d 546, 552, 413 N.E.2d 378, 381 (1980).

[142] People v. Foster, 81 Ill. App. 3d 915, 921-22, 401 N.E.2d 1221, 1225-26 (1st Dist. 1980).

[143] People v. Foster, 81 Ill. App. 3d 915, 926, 401 N.E.2d 1221, 1229 (1st Dist. 1980).

[144] People v. Nunn, 184 Ill. App. 3d 253, 269, 541 N.E.2d 182, 193 (1st Dist. 1989), *cert. denied*, 497 U.S. 1027 (1990); People v. Christiansen, 96 Ill. App. 3d 540, 544, 421 N.E.2d 570, 573 (2d Dist. 1981).

serious than the previous beatings, which had always involved nondeadly force.[145] Similarly, a defendant's conviction of second degree murder was upheld after he thrice shot the unarmed victim whom he had previously fought in fistfights without serious injury to either.[146]

Where evidence shows that the defendant used more force than was reasonably necessary for his own self-defense, the defense will fail. Thus, where the defendant was over one foot taller and twenty-seven pounds heavier than his female victim, who was four feet, eleven inches tall and weighed 145 pounds, it was held that excessive force was used, negating a self-defense claim, when he used such force that he fractured her neck bone when he strangled her to death.[147] Similarly, where the decedent was harassing the defendant's family, the defendant's action of shooting the unarmed victim three times, once in the back, was deemed excessive even though defendant claimed he believed the victim was about to stab him with a knife.[148]

An actual subjective belief that force is needed to avert danger is crucial to a self-defense theory. However, the defendant's determination of the "precise amount of force" that is necessary to avert the assailant's attack is not required.[149] Thus, where a robust young man followed and prevented a small, elderly man from closing the door to his room in a boarding house, the older man was justified in shooting the victim, since he reasonably anticipated violence and could not have physically repelled the younger man.[150]

§ 17.13. — Reasonable Belief, Even if Mistaken.

As the cases discussed above indicate, a defendant who claims self-defense must reasonably believe, even if his or her perception is actually mistaken, that: (1) he or she is faced with force or a threat of force; (2) the victim, not the defendant, is the aggressor; (3) the danger the defendant faces at the hands of the assailant is imminent; (4) the force or threat of force confronting the defendant is unlawful; (5) his or her use of force is necessary to avert the assailant's attack; and (6) the degree of force he or she employs in self-defense is necessary.

"'Reasonable belief' or 'reasonably believes' means that the person concerned, acting as a reasonable man, believes that the described facts exist."[151] Reasonableness is a crucial factor of self-defense, and this concern pervades the

---

[145] People v. Chapman, 49 Ill. App. 3d 553, 557-58, 364 N.E.2d 577, 580-81 (1st Dist. 1977). *But see* § 17.13 of this chapter for a discussion of battered woman syndrome.

[146] People v. Brown, 218 Ill. App. 3d 890, 898, 578 N.E.2d 1168, 1174-75 (1st Dist. 1991).

[147] People v. Kirkman, 170 Ill. App. 3d 106, 111-12, 522 N.E.2d 588, 592 (1st Dist. 1988).

[148] People v. Diaz, 38 Ill. App. 3d 447, 454, 348 N.E.2d 199, 205 (1st Dist. 1976).

[149] People v. Givens, 26 Ill. 2d 371, 376, 186 N.E.2d 225, 227 (1962).

[150] People v. Givens, 26 Ill. 2d 371, 376, 186 N.E.2d 225, 227-28 (1962) (murder conviction reversed).

[151] 720 ILCS 5/2-19 (1999).

self-defense cases.[152] "The perceptions that form the basis of a reasonable belief need not be limited to the instant circumstances."[153] The trier of fact can consider the surrounding facts and circumstances in determining whether an otherwise criminal act is justified under the law of self-defense.[154]

For example, a defendant's altercation in a lounge did not constitute self-defense because he could not have reasonably believed the amount of deadly force actually used against one of several rowdy patrons was necessary to prevent imminent death or great bodily harm.[155] In this case, the court determined that the two-hundred-pound male defendant, who it described as "very capable of handling himself in a fight," was not reasonable in his infliction of multiple blows with his fists that caused the death of the one-hundred-and-thirty-pound male victim.[156] Another defendant's use of deadly force against a victim who had made a homosexual advance but had not threatened him was unreasonable because the defendant was not in danger of imminent, life-threatening harm at the time he hit the victim over the head with a liquor bottle.[157] A defendant's killing was unreasonable where, at the point in time immediately prior to defendant's shooting of the victim, defendant was not being physically attacked, was not outnumbered, and was not cornered by the victim when he entered the vestibule of his building and remained on the interior staircase, standing ready to

---

[152] *See, e.g.,* People v. Belpedio, 212 Ill. App. 3d 155, 161, 569 N.E.2d 1372, 1375-77 (2d Dist. 1991) (defendant did not reasonably believe use of force was necessary to prevent great bodily harm to himself; aggravated battery conviction affirmed); People v. Woods, 81 Ill. 2d 537, 542, 410 N.E.2d 866, 869 (1980) (defendant did not reasonably believe force he executed was necessary to prevent imminent death or great bodily injury to himself; involuntary manslaughter conviction affirmed); People v. Aguero, 87 Ill. App. 3d 358, 364, 408 N.E.2d 1092, 1096 (1st Dist. 1980) (defendant did not reasonably believe resort to deadly force was necessary to prevent death or great bodily injury to himself or another; involuntary manslaughter upheld); People v. Mosley, 68 Ill. App. 3d 721, 726, 386 N.E.2d 545, 549 (1st Dist. 1979) (defendant's belief that victim might kill or injure her was unreasonable; aggravated battery affirmed); People v. Davis, 33 Ill. App. 3d 105, 109, 337 N.E.2d 256, 260 (1st Dist. 1975) (defendant's belief that victim might kill or gravely injure her was unreasonable; voluntary manslaughter affirmed).

[153] Edward Ronkowski, *Uses and Misuses of Deadly Force,* 28 DEPAUL L. REV. 701, 708 (1980).

[154] People v. Woods, 81 Ill. 2d 537, 542, 410 N.E.2d 866, 868-69 (1980). *See also* People v. Chavez, 228 Ill. App. 3d 54, 70, 592 N.E.2d 69, 81 (1st Dist. 1992); People v. Brown, 218 Ill. App. 3d 890, 899, 578 N.E.2d 1168, 1175 (1st Dist. 1991); People v. Martin, 98 Ill. App. 3d 649, 652, 424 N.E.2d 949, 951-52 (3d Dist. 1981); People v. Henry, 86 Ill. App. 3d 602, 604, 408 N.E.2d 228, 230 (1st Dist. 1980).

[155] People v. Woods, 81 Ill. 2d 537, 542, 410 N.E.2d 866, 869 (1980).

[156] People v. Woods, 81 Ill. 2d 537, 542, 410 N.E.2d 866, 869 (1980).

[157] People v. Gaurige, 168 Ill. App. 3d 855, 522 N.E.2d 1306 (1st Dist. 1988) (where defendant went willingly to victim's apartment, was seen with victim on previous occasions, and did not attempt to leave after being shown homosexual films; and where victim was unarmed and did not threaten defendant, it was held that defendant's use of a bottle to strike victim on head was unreasonable use of force).

shoot the victim as soon as the victim pushed the outside door open.[158] Where another defendant believed the victim was procuring a gun from his car, it was unreasonable for him to shoot the victim from the back door of his apartment because there was no evidence of a threat to the defendant or another and no evidence that the victim intended to enter defendant's apartment.[159]

Of course, these cases do not suggest that the courts will ignore the defendant's knowledge as it contributes to the reasonableness of his or her belief of the need to resort to deadly force in self-defense. If the defendant is aware of the victim's proclivities toward violence[160] or believes that he or she may be faced with multiple adversaries,[161] this information is relevant in assessing the reasonableness of the defendant's use of force. In *People v. McGrath,*[162] two defendants were aware that they were being pursued in a threatening manner by a group of six men who were prone toward violence.[163] The events took place in a dark parking lot in early morning hours, the defendants knew that they were outnumbered, and did not know if the assailants were armed.[164] The appellate court held that where the defendants had not been the initial aggressors, the fact they had a few minutes to arm themselves and prepare for the group of "angry men" did not transform the defendants into the aggressors and, as such, their belief in the necessity of firing warning shots in the air and toward the ground near the attackers, which ricocheted and struck two of their assailants, was reasonable in light of the circumstances.[165]

In certain circumstances, the defendant's resort to deadly force in self-defense may not be justified even though reliance on nondeadly force would have been reasonable. For example, in one case, the defendant used deadly force against an assailant based on an unreasonable belief that the force was appropriate.[166] The defendant shot his houseguest of five days. The houseguest had refused to leave the defendant's home, and the defendant felt threatened when the victim lunged at him. The appellate court recognized that the defendant was entitled to use some force against his assailant, but not deadly force, since the unarmed victim had apparently not threatened the defendant with death or great bodily injury.[167]

---

[158] People v. Alcazar, 173 Ill. App. 3d 344, 349-53, 527 N.E.2d 325, 328-31 (1st Dist. 1988).

[159] People v. Collins, 187 Ill. App. 3d 531, 535, 543 N.E.2d 572, 575 (4th Dist. 1989).

[160] *See* People v. Strombaugh, 52 Ill. 2d 130, 139, 284 N.E.2d 640, 645 (1972) (error for trial court to exclude this evidence).

[161] *See* People v. Kline, 90 Ill. App. 3d 1008, 1014-15, 414 N.E.2d 141, 146-47 (1st Dist. 1980) (error for trial court to exclude this evidence).

[162] 193 Ill. App. 3d 12, 549 N.E.2d 843 (1st Dist. 1989).

[163] People v. McGrath, 193 Ill. App. 3d 12, 28-29, 549 N.E.2d 843, 853-54 (1st Dist. 1989).

[164] People v. McGrath, 193 Ill. App. 3d 12, 28-29, 549 N.E.2d 843, 853-54 (1st Dist. 1989).

[165] People v. McGrath. 193 Ill. App. 3d 12, 28-29, 549 N.E.2d 843, 853-54 (1st Dist. 1989) (armed violence and aggravated battery convictions reversed).

[166] People v. Ellis, 107 Ill. App. 3d 603, 437 N.E.2d 409 (2d Dist. 1982).

[167] People v. Ellis, 107 Ill. App. 3d 603, 611, 437 N.E.2d 409, 416 (2d Dist. 1982) (voluntary manslaughter conviction affirmed).

Regarding the reasonableness of the use of deadly force, one would be entirely remiss if one failed to make reference to the growing concern over the "battered woman syndrome" as it relates to self-defense.[168] This syndrome is an "emerging concept" that is useful "for the purpose of explaining why the abuse a woman has suffered causes her to reasonably believe that her life is in danger and that she must use deadly force to escape her batterer."[169] This syndrome is of particular importance where the physically abused and emotionally distraught woman takes the life of her batterer-husband, or her long-time companion, where his attack does not clearly appear to be imminent or deadly but where she fears his repeated attacks are about to, and inevitably will, cross the homicide threshold.

The thrust of the battered woman syndrome defense usually revolves around the testimony of an expert witness, such as a psychologist, who attempts to educate the jury regarding the battered wife's typical fears and reactions that might cause her to take the life of her husband or long-time companion. Recognition of this syndrome helps debunk myths about domestic violence in society: (1) that domestic violence is rare when in fact it is prevalent; (2) that the woman had a means to escape her batterer when, in fact, she does not; and (3) that there was no reason to believe his threats were life-threatening now because they were not before, when, in fact, many batterer's attacks gradually escalate from non-life-threatening to life-threatening. However, the courts have not uniformly accepted evidence of this syndrome.[170] Courts that have rejected this defense have relied on various reasons: (1) the substance of the expert testimony is within the understanding and province of the jury; (2) the syndrome is not sufficiently developed as a matter of commonly accepted scientific knowledge to warrant testimony under the guise of expertise; and (3) the prejudicial impact of the evidence outweighs its probative value.[171]

A noteworthy Illinois case involving evidence of the battered woman syndrome is *People v. Minnis*,[172] where an abused wife killed her husband and dismembered his body. Although the defendant's testimony, if believed by the jury, would have been sufficient to warrant the conclusion that killing her husband was justified by self-defense, the state used the dismemberment of the body to prove her consciousness of guilt.[173] When the defense sought to introduce evi-

---

[168] *See* Loraine Eber, *The Battered Wife's Dilemma: To Kill or To Be Killed*, 32 HASTINGS L.J. 895 (1981); Annie E. Thar, *The Admissibility of Expert Testimony on Battered Wife Syndrome: An Evidentiary Analysis*, 77 N.W. U. L. REV. 348 (1982).

[169] People v. Minnis, 118 Ill. App. 3d 345, 356, 455 N.E.2d 209, 217 (4th Dist. 1983).

[170] People v. Minnis, 118 Ill. App. 3d 345, 356, 455 N.E.2d 209, 217 (4th Dist. 1983).

[171] State v. Thomas, 66 Ohio St. 2d 518, 521-22, 423 N.E.2d 137, 139-40 (1981), *overruled by* State v. Koss, 551 N.E.2d 970, 974 (Ohio 1990) (expert testimony concerning battered wife syndrome now admissible to support claim of self-defense).

[172] 118 Ill. App. 3d 345, 455 N.E.2d 209 (4th Dist. 1983).

[173] People v. Minnis, 118 Ill. App. 3d 345, 356-57, 455 N.E.2d 209, 217 (4th Dist. 1983).

dence of the "battered wife syndrome" to explain her motivation for the dismemberment, this evidence was excluded, and she was convicted of murder. The appellate court reversed and remanded the conviction, stating that "the trial court took too narrow a view of the matter" when it excluded the expert evidence on the syndrome.[174] The appellate court even went on to state that it was "greatly concerned that the defendant was deprived of her constitutional right to present a defense."[175]

In *People v. Evans*,[176] the defendant, whom the court described as a "victim of battered woman's syndrome," claimed she stabbed and killed her husband in self-defense during a beating.[177] The court applied ten factors to determine whether the deadly force used by the defendant was necessary and reasonable: (1) the attacker's apparent mental state and sobriety, (2) the woman's apparent mental state and sobriety, (3) the difference between the physical attributes and apparent strengths of the attacker and the woman, (4) whether the attacker has physically or verbally abused and threatened the woman on prior occasions and to what extent the threats were carried out, (5) whether the attacker was the apparent aggressor, (6) what recourse and what options were readily available to the woman during the course of the attack, (8) the weapon that was used by the woman to stop the attack, (9) the apparent escalation or diminishment of the attack at the time the woman resorted to deadly force, and (10) the reasonable apprehension of the woman at the time the deadly force was used, which encompasses the fact that she is a victim of battered wife's syndrome.[178] In conclusion, the court found it was clear that the defendant's use of deadly force was necessary and reasonable, especially in light of the escalation of the victim's attacks.[179]

However, in *People v. Beasley*,[180] the court rejected a claim of self-defense based on battered woman's syndrome where the defendant shot her intoxicated husband when he went to sleep immediately following a severe beating during which he threatened repeatedly to kill her.[181] Although evidence was presented and supported by witnesses that the defendant was continually abused during her eight-year marriage to the victim, a drug user and a heavy drinker, and as a result suffered from battered woman's syndrome, the court found the jury could have reasonably concluded that the defendant's use of deadly force was unreasonable.[182] In addition, the court noted that even though the defendant suffered

---

[174] People v. Minnis, 118 Ill. App. 3d 345, 357, 455 N.E.2d 209, 217 (4th Dist. 1983).

[175] People v. Minnis, 118 Ill. App. 3d 345, 355, 455 N.E.2d 209, 217 (4th Dist. 1983).

[176] 259 Ill. App. 3d 195, 631 N.E.2d 281 (1st Dist. 1994).

[177] People v. Evans, 259 Ill. App. 3d 195, 210-11, 631 N.E.2d 281, 291-92 (1st Dist. 1994).

[178] People v. Evans, 259 Ill. App. 3d 195, 210-11, 631 N.E.2d 281, 291 (1st Dist. 1994).

[179] People v. Evans, 259 Ill. App. 3d 195, 210-11, 631 N.E.2d 281, 291-92 (1st Dist. 1994).

[180] 251 Ill. App. 3d 872, 622 N.E.2d 1236 (5th Dist. 1993).

[181] People v. Beasley, 251 Ill. App. 3d 872, 883, 622 N.E.2d 1236, 1244 (5th Dist. 1993).

[182] People v. Beasley, 251 Ill. App. 3d 872, 883, 622 N.E.2d 1236, 1244 (5th Dist. 1993).

from this syndrome, the fact that she was pregnant with another man's child at the time of the killing suggests she may have killed him for that reason.[183]

While the appellate decisions focusing on reasonableness are most often addressing the reasonableness of taking a life in self-defense, it must be remembered that use of force in self-defense where the force does not prove deadly must also be reasonable in all respects. For example, in one case, three defendants beat and stabbed their victim at a service station during an apparently unprovoked fight.[184] In affirming one count of aggravated battery against each defendant, the court stated:

> [I]t is not reasonable to believe that a man is about to produce a weapon and inflict great bodily harm merely on the basis of seeing that man reach for his pocket, especially where, as here, no one had seen a weapon in the man's possession prior to the movement.[185]

§ 17.14. Scope of Self-Defense.

Beyond the basic elements of self-defense, a thorough understanding of this defense requires examination of various other concerns. First, it is necessary to appreciate the interplay between self-defense and retaliation, a defendant's provocation, and the assailant's withdrawal. Second, it is essential to determine the difference between deadly force and nondeadly force as it relates to the assailant's attack and the defendant's response. Third, it is important to consider the relevance of the doctrine of retreat in Illinois.

§ 17.15. — Retaliation.

Just as self-defense does not imply a right of initial aggression,[186] it also does not apply to situations where an individual lashes out at an adversary for reasons other than protection.[187] The Illinois Supreme Court has been very clear on this point: "The right of self-defense does not justify an act of retaliation or revenge . . . . The self-defense concept is to protect person, not pride."[188] If one responds

---

[183] People v. Beasley, 251 Ill. App. 3d 872, 883, 662 N.E.2d 1236, 1244 (5th Dist. 1993).

[184] People v. Pietrzyk, 54 Ill. App. 3d 738, 369 N.E.2d 1299 (1st Dist. 1977).

[185] People v. Pietrzyk, 54 Ill. App. 3d 738, 745, 369 N.E.2d 1299, 1303 (1st Dist. 1977).

[186] People v. White, 90 Ill. App. 3d 1067, 1070-71, 414 N.E.2d 196, 199 (1st Dist. 1980).

[187] As the appellate court stated in *White*: "[T]his court is duty bound to measure and evaluate the legal right of self-defense by the situation which existed when the malefactor was killed. Any other course would be pure anarchy and cannot be tolerated." People v. White, 90 Ill. App. 3d 1067, 1071, 414 N.E.2d 196, 200 (1st Dist. 1980).

[188] People v. Woods, 81 Ill. 2d 537, 543, 410 N.E.2d 866, 869 (1980) (citations omitted); *see also* People v. Everette, 141 Ill. 2d 147, 162, 565 N.E.2d 1295, 1301 (1990); People v. Belpedio, 212 Ill. App. 3d 155, 161, 569 N.E.2d 1372, 1376 (2d Dist. 1991); People v. Ellis, 187 Ill. App. 3d 295, 302, 543 N.E.2d 196, 200 (1st Dist. 1989), *cert. denied*, 498 U.S. 942 (1990); People v. Nunn, 184 Ill. App. 3d 253, 270, 541 N.E.2d 182, 193 (1st Dist. 1989), *cert. denied,* 497 U.S. 1027 (1990).

with such excessive force that he or she is no longer acting in self-defense but in retaliation, the excessive response renders he or she the protagonist.[189] Thus, in *People v. Woods*,[190] the defendant was wrongfully punched in the face by his assailant, although he later admitted that the assailant's blow did not hurt him. Immediately following the punch, the defendant struck the assailant with such force that the original assailant bounced off of a gate. Although the original aggressor did not attempt additional punches after his first, the defendant hit the aggressor in the head two more times. As the original assailant fell, the defendant "continued to deliver blows to [the assailant's] head," and these blows cumulatively caused the original assailant's death. The Illinois Supreme Court upheld the defendant's involuntary manslaughter conviction, stating: "These are not the actions of a person defending himself but those of one on the attack seeking revenge."[191]

§ 17.16.   — Provocation and Other Aggressive Conduct.

Illinois legislation clearly states that one who initially provokes another's use of force against himself or herself with the intent of using the force as an excuse to inflict bodily harm on the assailant cannot claim self-defense.[192] Thus, where the defendant decided to terminate the victim's lawful right to remain within the defendant's apartment, the appellate court upheld the trial court's submission of a jury instruction limiting the use of force in self-defense by one who is the initial aggressor, inasmuch as there was evidence that the defendant initially provoked the confrontation that led to a homicide.[193] Here, the defendant fired a revolver into the wall to frighten the victim, whereupon the victim lunged at the defendant, and the defendant responded by shooting the victim. The appellate court upheld the defendant's conviction and opined that the jury could have properly concluded that the defendant's actions provoked the victim's use of force.[194] Similarly, where a defendant initially provoked an ultimately deadly confrontation with his victim, he and seven codefendants' brutal attack upon the victim was in no way supported by reasonable or unreasonable defense principles, and his conviction for murder was upheld.[195] In effect, the provoking defendant is treated as the initial aggressor.

---

[189] People v. Nunn, 184 Ill. App. 3d 253, 270, 541 N.E.2d 182, 193 (1st Dist. 1989), *cert. denied*, 497 U.S. 1027 (1990).

[190] 81 Ill. 2d 537, 410 N.E.2d 866 (1980).

[191] People v. Woods, 81 Ill. 2d 537, 543-44, 410 N.E.2d 866, 869 (1980).

[192] *See* 720 ILCS 5/7-4(b) (1999).

[193] People v. Ellis, 107 Ill. App. 3d 603, 612, 437 N.E.2d 409, 418 (2d Dist. 1982) ("The instruction correctly stated that an initial aggressor must retreat before he regains the privilege to use force").

[194] People v. Ellis, 107 Ill. App. 3d 603, 612, 437 N.E.2d 409, 418 (2d Dist. 1982).

[195] People v. Nunn, 184 Ill. App. 3d 253, 270, 541 N.E.2d 182, 193-94 (1st Dist. 1989), *cert. denied*, 497 U.S. 1027 (1990). *Nunn* relied on the legislation denying self-defense to a provocateur. *See* 720 ILCS 5/7-4(b) (1999).

Illinois law explicitly states that one committing or attempting to commit a forcible felony is barred from claiming defense of person.[196] Thus, where defendant and his brother were engaged in the commission of robbery, whereupon the robbery victim produced a knife, the defendant could not claim self-defense when he stabbed the victim in response.[197]

Where an individual creates or seeks out a dangerous situation, he or she may not then assert self-defense.[198] In *People v. Echoles*,[199] the defendant was present at his wife's separate residence, which she had maintained for six years. While his wife was entertaining several dinner guests, the defendant insisted on talking with her about their marital difficulties, but she refused. The defendant then initiated physical contact by grabbing the wife's arm, an act that according to the court, could have been "construed as an act of physical aggression."[200] The wife's daughter (who was the defendant's stepdaughter) attempted to intervene at which point the defendant inflicted several stab wounds upon the wife and stabbed the daughter to death. Although the evidence was contradictory about who originally produced the knife used in the stabbings, the jury found the defendant guilty of attempted murder and voluntary manslaughter. In upholding the attempted murder conviction but vacating the voluntary manslaughter verdict, the court stated that a defendant cannot assert self-defense "when the perilous situation with which he was confronted arose out of his own aggressive conduct in seeking the difficulty."[201]

While the use of a weapon in self-defense may be a justifiable response to a physical attack, where a defendant introduces a weapon into an altercation where the introduction is clearly unnecessary to save a life or limb, the introduction of the weapon may render the defendant the aggressor.[202] For example, in *People v. Wickenhauser*,[203] the defendant's conviction of aggravated battery was affirmed after the court found the defendant to be the "aggressor" in the incident at issue. In that case, the defendant had unsuccessfully attempted to intervene in

---

[196] 720 ILCS 5/7-4(a) (1999).

[197] People v. Bell, 191 Ill. App. 3d 877, 884-85, 548 N.E.2d 397, 402 (1st Dist. 1989).

[198] People v. Zolidis, 115 Ill. App. 3d 699, 675, 450 N.E.2d 1290, 1295 (1st Dist. 1983).

[199] 36 Ill. App. 3d 845, 344 N.E.2d 620 (1st Dist. 1976).

[200] People v. Echoles, 36 Ill. App. 3d 845, 852, 344 N.E.2d 620, 625 (1st Dist. 1976).

[201] People v. Echoles, 36 Ill. App. 3d 845, 856, 344 N.E.2d 620, 628 (1st Dist. 1976). While the court's reasoning for vacating the voluntary manslaughter conviction was somewhat confusing given the finding that the daughter's "use of force was both justified and reasonable under the circumstances," the court apparently accepted the defendant's claim that the killing of the daughter presented a "murder-or-nothing" argument. *Id.* at 854-55, 344 N.E.2d at 627. Because the jury concluded that this killing did not amount to murder, the defendant was impliedly acquitted of the lesser included offense of manslaughter because there was insufficient evidence offered supporting a manslaughter theory. *Id.* at 855, 344 N.E.2d at 627-28.

[202] People v. Wickenhauser, 75 Ill. App. 3d 145, 147, 393 N.E.2d 1185, 1187 (5th Dist. 1979).

[203] 75 Ill. App. 3d 145, 393 N.E.2d 1185 (5th Dist. 1979).

an argument between his friend and the victim. When the defendant went to his car, returned with a gun and ordered the victim to leave the defendant's friend alone, the victim began pushing the defendant, whereupon the defendant shot the victim. The court found the defendant's armed force an unnecessary response to the victim's actions.[204]

§ 17.17. — Withdrawal by the Assailant.

Just as there is no justification for force where the accused is the aggressor,[205] once an aggressor flees a confrontation, the initial victim cannot pursue lest he or she becomes the aggressor.[206] Thus, shooting or stabbing a victim in the back will tend to undermine the self-defense claim.[207] Similarly, where a defendant became involved in a physical quarrel with several men inside a lounge, chased one of the men outside, and there engaged another man in a fistfight which resulted in death, the court upheld the defendant's involuntary manslaughter conviction, stating, "[t]he right to defend oneself does not permit the pursuit and injuring of an aggressor after the aggressor abandons the quarrel."[208] Hence, where the original assailant retreats from his or her attack, self-defense is no longer a viable justification for an attack on the assailant.[209]

In a similar vein, there is no justification for using force, particularly deadly force, against an antagonist who has already been disarmed or disabled.[210] "[S]elf-defense is no justification for the use of deadly force once the antagonist has been subdued or is lying helpless on the ground."[211] Thus, where three brothers beat their solitary victim to death after the victim was on the ground and unable to pose a serious threat, the defendants were convicted of murder since their conduct was viewed as retaliatory, even though they claimed the victim was the initial aggressor.[212] Where a defendant shot his alleged assailant at least three times after disabling his victim with the first bullet, the defendant could not claim the repeated shots were in self-defense.[213]

---

[204] People v. Wickenhauser, 75 Ill. App. 3d 145, 148, 393 N.E.2d 1185, 1188 (5th Dist. 1979).

[205] People v. Lockwood, 37 Ill. App. 3d 502, 505, 346 N.E.2d 404, 406 (5th Dist. 1976).

[206] People v. Easter, 102 Ill. App. 3d 974, 980, 430 N.E.2d 612, 617 (1st Dist. 1981); see also People v. De Oca, 238 Ill. App. 3d 362, 368, 606 N.E.2d 332, 336 (1st Dist. 1992); People v. Belpedio, 212 Ill. App. 3d 155, 161, 569 N.E.2d 1372, 1376 (2d Dist. 1991); People v. Ellis, 187 Ill. App. 3d 295, 302, 543 N.E.2d 196, 200 (1st Dist. 1989), cert. denied, 498 U.S. 942 (1990).

[207] People v. Zolidis, 115 Ill. App. 3d 669, 676, 450 N.E.2d 1290, 1296 (1st Dist. 1983) (stabbing victim in back); People v. Easter, 102 Ill. App. 3d 974, 980, 430 N.E.2d 612, 617 (1st Dist. 1981) (shooting victim in back).

[208] People v. Woods, 80 Ill. App. 3d 56, 60, 398 N.E.2d 1086, 1090 (1st Dist. 1979), aff'd, 81 Ill. 2d 537, 410 N.E.2d 866 (1980).

[209] People v. Yates, 65 Ill. App. 3d 319, 325, 382 N.E.2d 505, 511 (1st Dist. 1978).

[210] People v. Zolidis, 115 Ill. App. 3d 669, 676, 450 N.E.2d 1290, 1296 (1st Dist. 1983).

[211] People v. Chavez, 228 Ill. App. 3d 54, 71, 592 N.E.2d 69, 82 (1st Dist. 1992).

[212] People v. Tirrell, 87 Ill. App. 3d 511, 517-18, 408 N.E.2d 1202, 1206 (3d Dist. 1980).

[213] People v. Limas, 45 Ill. App. 3d 643, 652, 359 N.E.2d 1194, 1201 (2d Dist. 1977).

§ 17.18.   — Deadly and Nondeadly Force.

The only statutory justification for the use of deadly force arises where there is a reasonable belief "that such force is necessary to prevent imminent death or great bodily harm . . . or the commission of a forcible felony."[214] Since the degree of force used in self-defense must be (1) commensurate with the force encountered[215] and (2) no more than reasonably necessary to ward off the assailant's attack,[216] the amount of force that can be used in self-defense cannot exceed the degree of force employed by the assailant.[217] Thus, a defendant who was allegedly struck by his unarmed attacker's hands and feet was not justified in hitting his assailant with a dangerous weapon, thereby splitting open his scalp.[218]

Only nondeadly force is permitted in self-defense against unlawful nondeadly force.[219] On the other hand, when met with deadly force, a defendant may respond with deadly force, even to the extent of taking the assailant's life.[220] If the defendant reasonably believes that the danger is sufficiently urgent and pressing that resort to deadly force is necessary to save his or her own life or to prevent receiving great bodily harm, then the defendant may resort to such force.[221] There is no requirement that the use of deadly force in self-defense prove absolutely or actually necessary, for it is enough that the defendant reasonably believes that such force is necessary to accomplish this purpose even though he is mistaken as to the danger and the danger is only apparent.[222] The law of self-defense does not demand "inerrible judgement."[223]

Once the objective of self-defense has been accomplished, further use of deadly force is not justified;[224] but again, the accused is not expected to use perfect judgment in deciding when such force is no longer necessary.[225] Thus, a claim of self-defense may be negated where the state establishes that an interval existed between the defendant's initial response to the danger and the defendant's later use of force against the aggressor, provided the time frame was sufficient to allow the accused, acting as a reasonable person, to realize that no fur-

---

[214] 720 ILCS 5/7-1 (1999).

[215] People v. Wood, 24 Ill. App. 3d 15, 20, 320 N.E.2d 32, 35 (4th Dist. 1974).

[216] People v. Fort, 119 Ill. App. 2d 350, 357, 256 N.E.2d 63, 67 (1st Dist. 1970).

[217] People v. Fort, 119 Ill. App. 2d 350, 357, 256 N.E.2d 63, 67 (1st Dist. 1970).

[218] People v. Fort, 119 Ill. App. 2d 350, 357, 256 N.E.2d 63, 67 (1st Dist. 1970).

[219] *See, e.g.,* People v. Dillard, 5 Ill. App. 3d 896, 902, 284 N.E.2d 490, 494 (5th Dist. 1972) (nondeadly force but not deadly force could be used to prevent trespass to property).

[220] People v. Rodriguez, 187 Ill. App. 3d 484, 489, 543 N.E.2d 324, 327 (1st Dist. 1989).

[221] People v. Hubert, 251 Ill. 514, 522-23, 96 N.E. 294, 297 (1911).

[222] People v. White, 87 Ill. App. 3d 321, 323, 409 N.E.2d 73, 74 (1st Dist. 1980).

[223] People v. White, 87 Ill. App. 3d 321, 323, 409 N.E.2d 73, 75 (1st Dist. 1980).

[224] Edward Ronkowski, *Uses and Misuses of Deadly Force*, 28 DEPAUL L. REV. 701, 713 (1980) (citing People v. Limas, 45 Ill. App. 3d 643, 359 N.E.2d 1194 (2d Dist. 1977) for proposition that right to self-defense ceases when there is no longer fear of death or great bodily harm).

[225] People v. Chapman, 49 Ill. App. 3d 553, 557, 364 N.E.2d 577, 580 (1st Dist. 1977).

ther force was needed.[226] But if the interval between the accused's initial deadly response and his or her subsequent deadly responses was of insufficient duration for the accused to recognize that any shots beyond the first were unnecessary — such as where an accused fired a gun in rapid succession — then the subsequent responses will normally be protected as part of the accused's defense of self.[227] Where a defendant's actions involve "a brief period of time while under great stress and excitement," courts will not quibble over the defendant's failure to have exercised "infallible judgement."[228] While a person facing an attack "cannot take the law into his own hands, we must bear in mind that a person in such a position is not in a contest governed by established rules enforced by an on-the-scene umpire."[229]

What constitutes deadly force by an aggressor varies from situation to situation. Although this determination is a question of fact dependent on surrounding circumstances,[230] a perusal of the caselaw reveals certain patterns that are useful in gauging whether the force will be viewed as deadly. Use of a firearm is almost always considered deadly force.[231] Illinois prohibitions aimed at the illegal use[232] or possession[233] of dangerous weapons serve as a useful reference point in determining whether the weapon is deadly. A deadly weapon need not necessarily have been created for the purpose of killing nor be of any particular size or description.[234] Any instrumentality may become deadly by the manner in which it is used.[235]

---

[226] In re S.M., 93 Ill. App. 3d 105, 110-111, 416 N.E.2d 1212, 1216 (1st Dist. 1981).

[227] In re S.M., 93 Ill. App. 3d 105, 110-111, 416 N.E.2d 1212, 1216 (1st Dist. 1981).

[228] People v. Tirrell, 87 Ill. App. 3d 511, 518, 408 N.E.2d 1202, 1207 (3d Dist. 1980).

[229] People v. White, 87 Ill. App. 3d 321, 323, 409 N.E.2d 73, 75 (1st Dist. 1980).

[230] People v. Smith, 58 Ill. App. 3d 784, 789, 374 N.E.2d 1285, 1289 (1st Dist. 1978), cert. denied, 440 U.S. 973 (1979).

[231] People v. Daily, 79 Ill. App. 3d 928, 936, 398 N.E.2d 923, 929 (1st Dist. 1979) (shotgun deadly per se); Edward Ronkowski, Uses and Misuses of Deadly Force, 28 DEPAUL L. REV. 701, 706 (1980) (firearms almost categorically construed as deadly per se).

[232] See 720 ILCS 5/33A-1 (1999) (definition of "armed with a dangerous weapon" for purpose of crime of armed violence includes a handgun, shotgun, rifle, machine gun, spring gun, stun gun or taser, knife with a blade of at least three inches in length, dagger, dirk, switchblade knife, stiletto, axe, hatchet, bludgeon, blackjack, slungshot, sand-bag, metal knuckles, billy or any "other dangerous weapon of like character"). See ch. 9 of this treatise for discussion of crime of "armed violence."

[233] See 720 ILCS 5/24-1(a) (1999) (unlawful use of weapons); 720 ILCS 5/24-3.1 (1999) (unlawful possession of firearms and firearms amunition). See ch. 15 of this treatise for a discussion of these crimes.

[234] People v. Carter, 410 Ill. 462, 465, 102 N.E.2d 312, 313 (1951) (pocketknife considered deadly weapon).

[235] People v. Fort, 119 Ill. App. 2d 350, 354, 256 N.E.2d 63, 66 (1st Dist. 1970). See also People v. Skelton, 83 Ill. 2d 58, 66, 414 N.E.2d 455, 458 (1980) (discussion of how manner of use of item may make it a dangerous weapon for purposes of armed robbery).

The use of bare fists[236] or the infliction of a physical beating[237] on another may constitute deadly force under certain circumstances. The use of a bottle, whether broken[238] or unbroken,[239] whether thrown[240] or used as a club,[241] may amount to deadly force. Throwing a brick[242] or repeatedly kicking[243] another individual may be construed as deadly force.

Of course, merely because a deadly weapon was used does not mean deadly force was employed by the assailant. For instance, shooting a pistol into the ground or air has been viewed as not necessarily likely to cause death or bodily harm to a person some distance away.[244]

It is extremely important to recognize that "there is no requirement that the alleged attacker actually possess a weapon before self-defense can be asserted."[245] Although a victim need not possess a weapon to justify killing, the absence of a weapon is a factor that may be considered by the court.[246] Regardless, the presence *or* absence of a weapon is not dispositive of the question of whether actual or apparent danger existed.[247] The law does not require the aggressor to be armed before the use of deadly force or a deadly weapon is justified; rather, it must appear that the aggressor is capable of inflicting serious bodily harm with or without a weapon and also is intending to do so.[248] In *People v. Reeves*,[249] the defendant argued with her husband, who had beaten her in the past. Hours after the altercation, the victim sought out his wife, who had armed herself with a pistol in the meantime. When he dragged her down the street, concurrently choking her and beating her about the head, the defendant shot him once. Because the court maintained serious doubt about her guilt, they reversed her murder conviction, stating, "It is a firmly established rule that the aggressor need not have a weapon to justify one's use of deadly force in self-defense."[250]

Another case that makes the same point is *People v. Woodward*.[251] It involved a defendant who was fifteen and a victim who was sixteen at the time of the in-

---

[236] People v. Drumheller, 15 Ill. App. 3d 418, 421, 304 N.E.2d 455, 458 (2d Dist. 1973).

[237] People v. Reeves, 47 Ill. App. 3d 406, 411, 362 N.E.2d 9, 13 (5th Dist. 1977); People v. Baker, 31 Ill. App. 3d 51, 55, 334 N.E.2d 249, 252 (2d Dist. 1975).

[238] People v. Villalobos, 53 Ill. App. 3d 234, 240, 368 N.E.2d 556, 560 (1st Dist. 1977).

[239] People v. Fort, 119 Ill. App. 2d 350, 354, 256 N.E.2d 63, 66 (1st Dist. 1970).

[240] People v. Fort, 119 Ill. App. 2d 350, 354, 256 N.E.2d 63, 66 (1st Dist. 1970).

[241] People v. Villalobos, 53 Ill. App. 3d 234, 240, 368 N.E.2d 556, 560 (1st Dist. 1977).

[242] People v. Williams, 56 Ill. App. 2d 159, 169, 205 N.E.2d 749, 754 (1st Dist. 1965).

[243] People v. Driver, 62 Ill. App. 3d 847, 851, 379 N.E.2d 840, 844 (4th Dist. 1978).

[244] People v. Post, 39 Ill. 2d 101, 105, 233 N.E.2d 565, 567 (1968).

[245] People v. Foster, 81 Ill. App. 3d 915, 922, 401 N.E.2d 1221, 1226 (1st Dist. 1980).

[246] People v. Easter, 102 Ill. App. 3d 974, 980, 430 N.E.2d 612, 617 (1st Dist. 1981).

[247] People v. Kelly, 24 Ill. App. 3d 1018, 1026, 322 N.E.2d 527, 534 (2d Dist. 1975).

[248] People v. Brown, 218 Ill. App. 3d 890, 899, 578 N.E.2d 1168, 1174 (1st Dist. 1991).

[249] 47 Ill. App. 3d 406, 362 N.E.2d 9 (5th Dist. 1977).

[250] People v. Reeves, 47 Ill. App. 3d 406, 411, 362 N.E.2d 9, 13 (5th Dist. 1977).

[251] 77 Ill. App. 3d 352, 395 N.E.2d 1203 (2d Dist. 1979).

cident. The victim had encouraged his dog to behave offensively near the defendant and the defendant's father. When an argument between the father and the victim ensued, the victim said that he would go home but would come back with his gun. The victim returned with his hands in his jacket, accompanied by two dogs. The defendant took a gun from his house and fired two warning shots. He subsequently shot the victim, who was taunting him. Even though the victim did not display a weapon during the confrontation and may in fact have been carrying only a pellet gun, if he was armed at all, the appellate court concluded that the defendant's actions may still have been justified as self-defense and, accordingly, the trial court's refusal to instruct the jury on self-defense was ruled reversible error.[252]

Although an owner or an owner's agent may use reasonable nondeadly force against a simple trespasser to accomplish a cessation of the trespass, if the trespasser is confronted with deadly force, even the trespasser may kill his or her assailant in defense of his or her life.[253] This situation arose where three friends stopped their car behind a closed, dark gas station to urinate. Suddenly and unexpectedly, one of the three was shot by a station attendant. During an ensuing scuffle, the uninjured trespassers shot and killed the attendant. Ultimately, the appellate court reversed their murder convictions. The court reasoned that no person may, in defense of mere land, "assault the invaders with a dangerous weapon for the law forbids such a menacing of human life for so trivial a cause."[254] Here, the degree of force used by the station attendant had been excessive.[255] Accordingly, the subsequent use of deadly force by the defendants was justified by self-defense.[256]

Neither an alleged assailant's verbal threats[257] nor his or her ominous physical stature will justify, without more, the taking of his or her life.[258] For example, the use of deadly force was not justified against the estranged husband of a defendant's girlfriend, despite the defendant's knowledge that the victim, an extremely large man, had threatened to kill the defendant, who was small in stature.[259] Here, the victim's mere threats and the fear induced by his physical stature did not justify the defendant's use of deadly force against the unarmed, stationary victim.[260]

In *People v. Adams*,[261] a case of first impression in Illinois, the appellate court adopted the generally accepted rule that a person who justifiably defends him-

---

[252] People v. Woodward, 77 Ill. App. 3d 352, 357-58, 395 N.E.2d 1203, 1208 (2d Dist. 1979).

[253] People v. Dillard, 5 Ill. App. 3d 896, 901, 284 N.E.2d 490, 494 (5th Dist. 1972).

[254] People v. Dillard, 5 Ill. App. 3d 896, 902, 284 N.E.2d 490, 494 (5th Dist. 1972).

[255] People v. Dillard, 5 Ill. App. 3d 896, 902-903, 284 N.E.2d 490, 494-95 (5th Dist. 1972).

[256] People v. Dillard, 5 Ill. App. 3d 896, 903, 284 N.E.2d 490, 495 (5th Dist. 1972).

[257] People v. Everette, 141 Ill. 2d 147, 162, 565 N.E.2d 1295, 1301 (1990).

[258] People v. Pearson, 40 Ill. App. 3d 315, 318, 352 N.E.2d 240, 242-43 (1st Dist. 1976).

[259] People v. Pearson, 40 Ill. App. 3d 315, 318, 352 N.E.2d 240, 242-43 (1st Dist. 1976).

[260] People v. Pearson, 40 Ill. App. 3d 315, 318, 352 N.E.2d 240, 242-43 (1st Dist. 1976).

[261] 9 Ill. App. 3d 61, 291 N.E.2d 54 (5th Dist. 1972).

self or herself from an aggressor commits no crime if he or she inadvertently kills a third party other than the aggressor, unless the defender's conduct is reckless with regard to the third party.[262] In *Adams*, the defendant was fired on by an assailant who was seated in an automobile along with three other persons. The defendant immediately shot the assailant several times, killing him. However, one of the defendant's bullets passed through the body of the assailant and inflicted a mortal wound on a woman seated next to the assailant. Although the defendant was acquitted of the alleged murder of the assailant on self-defense grounds, the state argued that the defendant's killing of the innocent woman passenger arose out of the defendant's reckless disregard for the life of the woman; accordingly, he was guilty of involuntary manslaughter. Although the jury agreed, the appellate court did not accept the argument under these circumstances and therefore reversed the manslaughter conviction. Since (1) the defendant was fired on by the assailant at close range, (2) he had very little time to assess the situation, (3) it was dark, (4) he had to act quickly in order to protect himself, and (5) he did not shoot wildly or carelessly, the court concluded that the defendant's actions constituted no crime.[263]

The *Adams* court was quick to point out that had the defendant's acts in response to the assailant's attack not been justified, then the defendant would have been guilty of the same degree of homicide for the killing of the innocent third party as for the killing of the assailant.[264] The court also cautiously proclaimed that the general rule that there is no crime where one unintentionally kills a third party while acting in self-defense "is not absolute and . . . may be subject to modification" in appropriate circumstances.[265]

Finally, a defender can resort to deadly force in self-defense *before* any injury occurs to him or her.[266] As the Illinois appellate court stated, "The defense of justifiable use of deadly force against an attacker would be meaningless if, as a prerequisite to such defense, the defendant would be required to exhibit mortal wounds to himself as well. The force used is justified if 'necessary to *prevent* imminent death or great bodily harm.'"[267] For instance, a defendant was exonerated for shooting an angry and violent neighbor who had previously cut the defendant with a knife after it was determined that the defendant had acted under a reasonable belief of imminent danger.[268] The appellate court stated that this de-

---

[262] People v. Adams, 9 Ill. App. 3d 61, 63-64, 291 N.E.2d 54, 55-56 (5th Dist. 1972).

[263] People v. Adams, 9 Ill. App. 3d 61, 64, 291 N.E.2d 54, 56 (5th Dist. 1972).

[264] People v. Adams, 9 Ill. App. 3d 61, 63, 291 N.E.2d 54, 55-56 (5th Dist. 1972).

[265] People v. Adams, 9 Ill. App. 3d 61, 64, 291 N.E.2d 54, 56 (5th Dist. 1972).

[266] People v. Woods, 81 Ill. 2d 537, 543, 410 N.E.2d 866, 869 (1980); People v. Speed, 52 Ill. 2d 141, 146, 284 N.E.2d 636, 639, *cert. denied,* 409 U.S. 983 (1972).

[267] People v. Gossett, 115 Ill. App. 3d 655, 665, 451 N.E.2d 280, 287 (2d Dist. 1983) (emphasis in original while quoting in part ILL. REV. STAT. ch. 38, para. 7-1 (1981)).

[268] People v. White, 87 Ill. App. 3d 321, 323, 409 N.E.2d 73, 75 (1st Dist. 1980) (voluntary manslaughter conviction reversed).

fendant's judgment was not required to be flawless; and his right to protect himself arose "before the first blood [was] drawn."[269]

§ 17.19. — Retreat from Aggression.

Distinct from the concept of "withdrawal" — which arises where the initial aggressor removes himself or herself from a confrontation, thereby eliminating the original victim's justification for using force against the aggressor[270] — there is the doctrine of "retreat." Under this doctrine, a *victim* of an attack must elect an obviously safe avenue of escape, if available, before resorting to deadly force in self-defense.[271] Although this is the law in a substantial number of states,[272] Illinois follows the majority of jurisdictions and does *not* require the victim of aggression to exhaust every effort to escape before using deadly force in self-defense:[273]

> The common-law doctrine that one must exhaust every effort to escape before he can avail himself of the right of self-defense does not prevail in this State. It has been held that if a person is in a place where he has a lawful right to be and is unlawfully assaulted and put in apparent danger of his life, or great bodily harm, he need not attempt to escape but may lawfully stand his ground and meet force with force, even to the taking of his assailant's life if necessary.[274]

An Illinois trial court's jury instruction that the defendant was under a duty to retreat will almost invariably result in reversal where the accused claims self-defense.[275] This occurred in a case where a defendant was convicted of the voluntary manslaughter of her husband. Apparently, her husband had kicked and beaten her for no apparent reason before she shot him. Later, she gave a statement to the authorities that after the beating, she had confronted her seated husband and had shot him "in the heat of the moment." At her trial, she repudiated this statement and claimed that she shot him while he followed her and threat-

---

[269] People v. White, 87 Ill. App. 3d 321, 323, 409 N.E.2d 73, 75 (1st Dist. 1980).

[270] *See* § 17.17 of this chapter.

[271] ROLLIN M. PERKINS & RONALD N. BOYCE, CRIMINAL LAW 1133 (3d ed. 1982) (there are several exceptions to retreat doctrine, including exception that no retreat is required in one's own home or by police officer attempting to make arrest).

[272] ROLLIN M. PERKINS & RONALD N. BOYCE, CRIMINAL LAW 1133 (3d ed. 1982).

[273] People v. Underwood, 50 Ill. App. 3d 908, 912, 365 N.E.2d 1370, 1374 (4th Dist. 1977), *aff'd in part, rev'd on other grounds,* 72 Ill. 2d 124, 378 N.E.2d 513 (1978). *See also* People v. Williams, 57 Ill. 2d 239, 243, 311 N.E.2d 681, 684, *cert. denied,* 419 U.S. 1026 (1974); People v. Willis, 210 Ill. App. 3d 379, 382, 569 N.E.2d 113, 115 (1st Dist. 1991); People v. Rodriguez, 187 Ill. App. 3d 484, 489, 543 N.E.2d 324, 328 (1st Dist. 1989).

[274] People v. Horton, 4 Ill. 2d 176, 183, 122 N.E.2d 214, 217 (1954). *See also* People v. Harling, 29 Ill. App. 3d 1053, 1057, 331 N.E.2d 653, 657 (1st Dist. 1975) (Illinois self-defense law does not require retreat).

[275] People v. Bailey, 15 Ill. App. 3d 558, 560-61, 304 N.E.2d 668, 669-70 (1st Dist. 1973).

ened her with his own gun. In any event, the trial court told the jury that one is not allowed to use deadly force unless one "has exhausted every reasonable means to escape the danger." The appellate court concluded it was obliged to reverse defendant's conviction because the erroneous instruction regarding the duty to retreat might have prejudiced the defendant's trial.[276]

There is one situation, however, where retreat is an important consideration in Illinois, namely, where the accused was the initial aggressor. Illinois law explicitly states that one who initially provokes the use of force against himself or herself cannot claim self-defense unless he or she reasonably believes he or she is faced with imminent danger of death or grievous bodily injury *and* he or she "has exhausted every reasonable means to escape such danger other than the use of force which is likely to cause death or great bodily harm to the assailant."[277] This issue was raised in *People v. Barnett*,[278] where an automobile collision evolved into a homicide situation. After the defendant's car was bumped from behind by another car driven by the victim, the defendant got out of his car and shot the victim. Although the defendant claimed at his trial that he had feared severe injury or death by the victim's deliberate and dangerous misuse of a car, the state asserted that the defendant's conduct in exiting his own car while armed with a gun had actually precipitated the deadly confrontation, inasmuch as the defendant could not have reasonably feared for his life while within his automobile. The trial court instructed the jury consistent with the state statute regarding the aggressor's duty to escape the danger, and the jury thereafter found the defendant guilty of murder. The appellate court determined that the jury was properly instructed on the law[279] and that the evidence warranted the conclusion that the defendant was never actually faced with deadly force when he commenced his deadly attack on the victim.[280] The court questioned why the defendant would fear for his life on a busy road where so many others were present to observe any wrongdoing, why anyone who was fearful would have gotten out of his car, and why the defendant admitted to another person several hours after the killing that he did not know why he had shot the victim.[281]

Similarly, in *People v. Nunn*,[282] where the defendant provoked an assault on the victim, the defendant and his confederates' use of deadly force against the victim was not justified. Here, the court held that even if the defendant's life was in jeopardy when he was fighting with the victim, the defendants were required to use every available means to escape the deadly confrontation because

---

[276] People v. Bailey, 15 Ill. App. 3d 558, 560-61, 304 N.E.2d 668, 669-70 (1st Dist. 1973).

[277] 720 ILCS 5/7-4(c)(1) (1999).

[278] 48 Ill. App. 3d 121, 362 N.E.2d 420 (4th Dist. 1977).

[279] People v. Barnett, 48 Ill. App. 3d 121, 125, 362 N.E.2d 420, 423 (4th Dist. 1977).

[280] People v. Barnett, 48 Ill. App. 3d 121, 126, 362 N.E.2d 420, 424 (4th Dist. 1977).

[281] People v. Barnett, 48 Ill. App. 3d 121, 126, 362 N.E.2d 420, 424 (4th Dist. 1977).

[282] 184 Ill. App. 3d 253, 541 N.E.2d 182 (1st Dist. 1989), *cert. denied*, 497 U.S. 1027 (1990).

it was the defendant who had precipitated the situation.[283] Thus, these cases support a statement often recited in Illinois opinions: "A non-aggressor has no duty to retreat, but he does have a duty not to become the aggressor."[284]

§ 17.20. Defense of Another Generally.

Defense of another overlaps the defense of crime prevention[285] and, in Illinois, encompasses all the rules of law governing self-defense.[286] Section 5/7-1 requires the person asserting defense of another to reasonably believe that the action is necessary to prevent imminent unlawful force.[287] To justify deadly force in the protection of another, the protector must reasonably believe that the person defended is in imminent danger of death or great bodily harm and that deadly force is necessary to prevent that harm.[288]

The theory behind the principle of exonerating otherwise unlawful acts based on defense of another is the encouragement of citizens to aid others. As one Illinois court said: "[P]ublic policy forbids us to say a person must leave the victim of a brutal beating lie on the street when called upon to render aid. A citizen must feel free to help the victim of an assault."[289]

§ 17.21. Elements of Defense of Another.

As previously stated, the elements of defense of another are identical in all respects to those of self-defense except this defense justifies a defendant's acts that are designed to protect others. It is incumbent to show that the defendant (1) reasonably believed (2) another, who was not the aggressor, (3) was faced with an imminent, (4) unlawful (5) danger (6) that had to be averted (7) through force that was commensurate with the exigencies of the situation.

It is not necessary to demonstrate in Illinois, contrary to some jurisdictions, that the person protected was *actually* in need of aid.[290] As long as the defendant reasonably believes another warrants defense,[291] even if he or she is mistaken, the defendant's action taken against the person he or she believes to be a wrongful assailant will be justified.[292] Thus, where the defendant may have reasonably

---

[283] People v. Nunn, 184 Ill. App. 3d 253, 271, 541 N.E.2d 182, 195 (1st Dist. 1989), *cert. denied*, 497 U.S. 1027 (1990).

[284] In Interest of D.N., 178 Ill. App. 3d 470, 475, 533 N.E.2d 84, 88 (1st Dist. 1988).

[285] WAYNE LAFAVE & AUSTIN SCOTT, CRIMINAL LAW § 5.8(b) (2d ed. 1986). *See* § 19.49 of this treatise for a discussion of this defense.

[286] ILL. ANN. STAT. ch. 38, para. 7-1 (Smith-Hurd 1989), 1961 Committee Comments, at 352.

[287] 720 ILCS 5/7-1 (1999). *See* § 17.02 of this chapter for text of statute.

[288] 720 ILCS 5/7-1 (1999).

[289] People v. Williams, 56 Ill. App. 2d 159, 167, 205 N.E.2d 749, 753 (1st Dist. 1965).

[290] *See* § 17.02 of this chapter for a discussion on this point.

[291] ILL. ANN. STAT. ch. 38, para. 7-1 (Smith-Hurd 1989), 1961 Committee Comments, at 352.

[292] People v. Smith, 19 Ill. App. 3d 704, 707, 312 N.E.2d 355, 357 (1st Dist. 1974).

believed police were using excessive force against her husband, she was entitled to defense of another instructions in her trial on charges of resisting a police officer.[293] Similarly, where the defendant tried to intervene when uniformed police officers choked, "hog-tied," and violently handled the defendant's brother during an arrest, the Illinois appellate court held that the instructions on defense of another should have been given to the jury requiring them to find that the defendant's conduct was justified so long as the defendant had "a reasonable belief on his part that his conduct was necessary to protect his brother from the [officers'] use of excessive force."[294]

Where a defendant came to the aid of a stranger who was scuffling with a plainclothes police officer, the court found that the defendant's belief of the necessity of protecting the stranger from unlawful force and the amount of force used was reasonable.[295] Here, the defendant's conviction for battery was reversed on grounds of defense of another even though the person defended had in actuality been unlawfully resisting arrest and had no personal right of defense.[296] Thus, if the defendant does not realize that the party he or she is protecting is actually the aggressor or that the force used by the perceived assailant is actually lawful, then the defendant still has a defense if he or she harbored a reasonable belief that such was not the case.

In addition, a defendant who relies on principles of defense of another is not required to prove, as was the case at common law,[297] that he or she had some personal relationship with the person defended.[298] The language of section 5/7-1, which refers to the defense of "another" without further limitation, is broad enough to cover the defense of total strangers.[299] Furthermore, the caselaw, albeit sparse on this point, suggests that no relationship is required.[300]

Just as in self-defense, there is no defense of another where unlawful force is used in aid of another. If a defendant uses deadly force based on an unreasonable belief in the need to defend another and kills an individual in the process, he or she may be guilty of second-degree murder.[301] For example, in one case, a defendant and a companion went to the victim's apartment to complain about some "bad narcotics," a venture apparently thought dangerous enough to prompt

---

[293] People v. Veatch, 145 Ill. App. 3d 23, 29, 495 N.E.2d 674, 678 (2d Dist. 1986).

[294] People v. Lyda, 190 Ill. App. 3d 540, 545-46, 546 N.E.2d 29, 33 (2d Dist. 1989).

[295] People v. Smith, 19 Ill. App. 3d 704, 707, 312 N.E.2d 355, 357 (1st Dist. 1974).

[296] People v. Smith, 19 Ill. App. 3d 704, 707-709, 312 N.E.2d 355, 357-58 (1st Dist. 1974).

[297] ROLLIN M. PERKINS & RONALD N. BOYCE, CRIMINAL LAW 1144-45 (3d ed. 1982). Interestingly, these authors point out that the genesis of this concept was based on protection of property principles (for example, protection of a servant).

[298] WAYNE LAFAVE & AUSTIN SCOTT, CRIMINAL LAW § 5.8(a) (2d ed. 1986).

[299] WAYNE LAFAVE & AUSTIN SCOTT, CRIMINAL LAW § 5.8(a) (2d ed. 1986).

[300] See, e.g., People v. Smith, 19 Ill. App. 3d 704, 312 N.E.2d 355 (1st Dist. 1974) (stranger); People v. Williams, 56 Ill. App. 2d 159, 205 N.E.2d 749 (1st Dist. 1965) (stranger).

[301] 720 ILCS 5/9-2 (1999).

one of the two to carry a gun.[302] There, the defendant engaged in an altercation with the victim, who was armed, during which the victim was killed by the companion's gunfire. The defendant appealed his voluntary manslaughter — which now would be referred to as second degree murder — conviction, that was based on an accomplice theory, on the grounds that the companion's shooting of the victim was justified because of the companion's interest in protecting the defendant. The court affirmed the conviction, stating: "In a proper case, a third person may be justified in using force against another to defend a friend . . . . However, where a person uses unlawful force [as here] in aid of a friend and death results, his acts [constituted] voluntary manslaughter."[303]

Similarly, a pregnant woman who killed her husband by shooting him in the back, an act that she failed to justify on self-defense principles, could not claim as an alternative that her taking his life was authorized by her interest in protecting the life of her unborn child.[304] Where a defendant shot and killed a man in circumstances in which the victim was hitting the defendant's husband in a manner that did not cause serious injury to the husband, her conviction was affirmed because the jury apparently concluded that her use of deadly force was not commensurate with the force necessary under the circumstances.[305] Where a defendant provoked a fight with his victim, whereupon seven other defendants intervened with deadly force against the victim because they believed that the first defendant was "losing the fight" and that his life was in jeopardy, they could not claim defense of another.[306] In that case, these multiple defendants were not entitled to defense of another because they had not exhausted every reasonable means to escape the situation which is required where the original defendant provoked the victim.[307]

Lawful use of force, including deadly force, exonerates the defendant where the defendant's acts in defending another originate out of an effort to aid a police officer upon the officer's request.[308] For example, a defendant's conviction

---

[302] People v. Hill, 53 Ill. App. 3d 280, 368 N.E.2d 714 (1st Dist. 1977).

[303] People v. Hill, 53 Ill. App. 3d 280, 285, 368 N.E.2d 714, 718 (1st Dist. 1977).

[304] People v. Gaines, 9 Ill. App. 3d 589, 593, 292 N.E.2d 500, 503 (3d Dist. 1973) (voluntary manslaughter conviction affirmed).

[305] People v. Williams, 15 Ill. App. 3d 303, 307, 304 N.E.2d 178, 181 (4th Dist. 1973) (voluntary manslaughter conviction affirmed).

[306] People v. Nunn, 184 Ill. App. 3d 253, 270-71, 541 N.E.2d 182, 194 (1st Dist. 1989) (murder conviction affirmed), cert. denied, 497 U.S. 1027 (1990).

[307] People v. Nunn, 184 Ill. App. 3d 253, 271, 541 N.E.2d 182, 195 (1st Dist. 1989) (citing ILL. REV. STAT. ch. 38, para. 7-4(c)(1) (1983)), cert. denied, 497 U.S. 1027 (1990). See 720 ILCS 5/7-4(c)(1) (1999) (provocateurs are required to retreat). See also § 17.16 of this chapter.

[308] See 720 ILCS 5/7-5 (1999) (a peace officer or anyone he has summoned may use whatever force is necessary to effectuate an arrest, including deadly force "when he reasonably believes that such force is necessary to prevent death or great bodily harm to himself or such other person . . . .").

was reversed where the appellate court accepted his two affirmative defense claims of self-defense and assisting a police officer.[309] In that case, the defendant, a tavern owner, had attempted to evict several loud and abusive patrons. Another patron, a police officer, came to the defendant's aid and ordered the offensive people to leave or they would be arrested. The patrons defied the police officer, broke beer bottles, and threatened the defendant with the broken bottles. The defendant fired a warning shot into a post and soon thereafter was forced to shoot the victim when the victim attacked the defendant with a broken bottle. Although the affirmative defense of defense of another was not successful in the trial court, the appellate court stated: "If the defendant reasonably believed that he was aiding a police officer, he was entitled to use such force as he reasonably believed necessary to protect himself or another, including deadly force in the appropriate case."[310]

§ 17.22. Defense of Dwelling and Other Property Generally.

In addition to self-defense[311] and defense of another,[312] article 5/7 presents the affirmative defenses[313] of "defense of dwelling", codified in section 5/7-2,[314] and "defense of other property," codified in section 5/7-3.[315] The defenses of person, of dwelling, and of other property are stated separately in the code to simplify what would otherwise result in a complicated statute.[316] Section 5/7-2 (use of force in defense of dwelling) reads:

> A person is justified in the use of force against another when and to the extent that he reasonably believes that such conduct is necessary to prevent or terminate such other's unlawful entry into or attack upon a dwelling. However, he is justified in the use of force which is intended or likely to cause death or great bodily harm only if:
> (a) The entry is made or attempted in a violent, riotous, or tumultuous manner, and he reasonably believes that such force is necessary to prevent an assault upon, or offer of personal violence to, him or another then in the dwelling, or

---

[309] People v. Lenzi, 41 Ill. App. 3d 825, 836, 355 N.E.2d 153, 163 (1st Dist. 1976).

[310] People v. Lenzi, 41 Ill. App. 3d 825, 836, 355 N.E.2d 153, 163 (1st Dist. 1976) (voluntary manslaughter and aggravated battery convictions reversed).

[311] 720 ILCS 5/7-1 (1999).

[312] 720 ILCS 5/7-1 (1999).

[313] See § 17.38 of this chapter.

[314] 720 ILCS 5/7-2 (1999).

[315] 720 ILCS 5/7-3 (1999).

[316] ILL. ANN. STAT. ch. 38, para. 7-2 (Smith-Hurd 1989), 1961 Committee Comments, at 389.

(b) He reasonably believes that such force is necessary to prevent the commission of a forcible felony in the dwelling.[317]

Section 5/7-3 (use of force in defense of other property) reads:

A person is justified in the use of force against another when and to the extent that he reasonably believes that such conduct is necessary to prevent or terminate such other's trespass on or other tortious or criminal interference with either real property (other than a dwelling) or personal property, lawfully in his possession or in the possession of another who is a member of his immediate family or household or of a person whose property he had a legal duty to protect. However, he is justified in the use of force which is intended or likely to cause death or great bodily harm only if he reasonably believes that such force is necessary to prevent the commission of a forcible felony.[318]

§ 17.23.   Use of Force in Defense of Dwelling Codified.

While nondeadly force may be employed to defend against both attacks on dwellings and attacks directed at other property, the code clearly distinguishes between these two types of property when one resorts to deadly force. First, the terms of paragraph 5/7-2 state that the use of deadly force[319] is permitted in defense of a dwelling to prevent or terminate *any* felony therein.[320] In contrast, paragraph 5/7-3 states that deadly force is permitted in defense of other property only to prevent or terminate the commission of a *forcible* felony.[321] In addition, paragraph 5/7-2 permits the use of deadly force against unlawful entry into a dwelling where the entry is violent and the defender believes "that such force is necessary to prevent an assault upon . . . him or another then in the dwelling."[322] On the other hand, paragraph 5/7-3 (defense of other property) sets out no equivalent alternative justification beyond the forcible felony situation. It would appear, then, that the language of 5/7-2, standing alone, would permit the defender of a dwelling to use deadly force to prevent a felony that is not deemed forcible in the dwelling even if there is no actual threat against the resident or

---

[317] 720 ILCS 5/7-2 (1999).

[318] 720 ILCS 5/7-3 (1999).

[319] *See* § 17.18 of this chapter for a discussion of the distinction between deadly and nondeadly force in the context of defense of person.

[320] 720 ILCS 5/7-2 (1999). However, the legislature's intent, as reflected in the Committee Comments, is essentially silent on this point.

[321] 720 ILCS 5/7-3 (1999). *See also* People v. Dillard, 5 Ill. App. 3d 896, 901, 284 N.E.2d 490, 494 (5th Dist. 1972) (property owner can only use deadly force to prevent "forcible felony" on property).

[322] 720 ILCS 5/7-2 (1999). *See also* People v. Suerth, 97 Ill. App. 3d 1005, 1012, 423 N.E.2d 1185, 1191 (1st Dist. 1981) (referring to jury instruction with approval).

other occupant of the dwelling. However, paragraph 5/7-2 must be interpreted in conjunction with the revision committee comments that make clear deadly force is only justifiable where such force is used in the *context* of defense of dwelling *and* there is a serious threat to life or limb.

> This aspect of justification seems to be rather well-settled: a person may prevent or repel with force another's unlawful entry into a dwelling, whether the dwelling is occupied by the person using such force or by someone else, and whether the trespasser uses force or enters without force; but the use of deadly force is limited to the situations of the violent or forcible felony, and the violent entry with apparent threat of personal violence to someone in the dwelling.[323]

Furthermore, even if it were proper to read the language of section 5/7-2 as literally allowing deadly force to prevent a felony not involving threat to life or limb, then the legitimacy of this statute would be in question in light of the United States Supreme Court's ruling in *Tennessee v. Garner*,[324] where it was held impermissible for even a police officer to kill an unarmed felon who posed no significant threat of death or serious bodily injury to anyone. In any event, as long as the property is a dwelling, it need not be the defender's own.[325] The dwelling may be an apartment or portion of a building,[326] but it must be used for habitation purposes.[327]

The reasonable belief requirement under paragraph 5/7-2 is to be interpreted in the same manner as for cases arising under paragraph 5/7-1,[328] except that deadly force *may* be justified even where the defender does not face imminent death or great bodily harm.[329] A dwelling may be defended with deadly force by a person who reasonably anticipates assault or violence against himself or herself or another within the dwelling.[330]

---

[323] ILL. ANN. STAT. ch. 38, para. 7-2 (Smith-Hurd 1989), 1961 Committee Comments, at 388.

[324] 471 U.S. 1 (1985).

[325] People v. Stombaugh, 52 Ill. 2d 130, 135, 284 N.E.2d 640, 643 (1972).

[326] People v. Eatman, 405 Ill. 491, 496-97, 91 N.E.2d 387, 389-90 (1950).

[327] 720 ILCS 5/2-6 (1999) (dwelling defined as an enclosure used or intended for use as a human habitation). *See also* People v. Smith, 404 Ill. 125, 132, 88 N.E.2d 444, 449 (1949) (manslaughter affirmed where killing of mine employee by coal mine official occurred in open public mine office, which could not be considered a dwelling for purposes of defense of habitation).

[328] ILL. ANN. STAT. ch. 38, para. 7-2 (Smith-Hurd 1989), 1961 Committee Comments, at 389. *See also* § 17.13 of this chapter for a discussion of the "reasonable belief" requirement.

[329] People v. Eatman, 405 Ill. 491, 497-98, 91 N.E.2d 387, 390-91 (1950).

[330] People v. Eatman, 405 Ill. 491, 497, 91 N.E.2d 387, 390 (1950) (defense of habitation warranted reversal of murder conviction). *See also* People v. Lavac, 357 Ill. 554, 558-59, 192 N.E. 568, 569-70 (1934) (defense of habitation and self-defense warranted reversal of murder conviction).

§ 17.24. Elements of Defense of Dwelling.

As with other affirmative defenses, once the accused has raised the issue in the pleadings or has presented some evidence of defense of dwelling,[331] the state must prove that one or more elements of defense of dwelling have not been satisfied in order to establish the offense charged.[332] The jury need not be instructed on this defense unless it has been properly raised.[333] The elements of defense of dwelling are (1) an entry or attack upon a dwelling exists; (2) the entry or attack is unlawful; (3) the force used is necessary to prevent or terminate the entry or attack; (4) deadly force can only be used to prevent an assault against a person or the commission of a felony that involves a threat to life or limb; (5) the defender actually believes in the necessity of defending the dwelling or person therein; (6) the defender reasonably believes in the necessity of defending the dwelling or person therein, even if mistaken; and (7) the defender is not the aggressor.[334] As with all article 5/7 defenses, the state has the burden of negating justification for the use of force in defense of dwelling, as well as the burden of proving each and every element of the offense charged.[335]

§ 17.25. — Entry or Attack Upon Dwelling.

If there was no entry or attack upon a dwelling, then the defense of dwelling cannot be an issue. Thus, where the defense evidence was to the effect that the victim stepped from an automobile and immediately shot at the defendant and no evidence was presented that the victim threatened the defendant's dwelling or other property, the trial court's refusal in an attempted murder case to instruct the jury on defense of dwelling (in addition to a self-defense instruction which it had provided the jury) was considered proper.[336] A "dwelling" is defined in the criminal code as a "building or portion thereof, a tent, a vehicle, or any other enclosed space which is used or intended for use as a human habitation, home or residence."[337]

---

[331] People v. Williams, 96 Ill. App. 3d 8, 16-17, 420 N.E.2d 710, 717 (1st Dist. 1981).

[332] *See, e.g.,* People v. Miles, 188 Ill. App. 3d 471, 479-80, 544 N.E.2d 986, 992 (1st Dist. 1989) (no evidence in record to support defense of dwelling claim).

[333] People v. Sedlacko, 65 Ill. App. 3d 659, 665, 382 N.E.2d 363, 369 (1st Dist. 1978) (trial court properly refused defense of dwelling instruction).

[334] 720 ILCS 5/7-2 (1999).

[335] People v. Muldrow, 30 Ill. App. 3d 209, 218-21, 332 N.E.2d 664, 670-72 (1st Dist. 1975) ("defense of habitation" claim rejected).

[336] People v. Smalley, 10 Ill. App. 3d 416, 426, 294 N.E.2d 305, 312 (2d Dist. 1973).

[337] 720 ILCS 5/2-6 (1999).

§ 17.26.   — Unlawful Entry or Attack.

The affirmative defense of defense of dwelling presupposes that there existed at least a threat of *unlawful* entry or attack. For example, where the occupants of a dwelling welcomed the victim into their apartment and the victim did not physically or verbally threaten anyone in the apartment while he was there, the defendant's attack upon the victim that resulted in a conviction for attempted murder could not be justified by reason of the defense of dwelling.[338] Where three homicide victims had entered an apartment at the request of the woman with whom the defendant lived, their lawful entry precluded a defense of habitation claim.[339] Similarly, a defendant's conviction of aggravated assault against two police officers was affirmed when his claim of defense of dwelling was found to be "at best, tenuous."[340] In that case, the defendant's common law wife of sixteen years had summoned the two officers to her apartment, wherein the defendant pointed a revolver at the officers. Here, the defendant's own testimony indicated that he knew the strangers to be police officers, although they were not in uniform.[341] Also, where police officers in full uniform arrived at the scene of a disturbance, knocked on an apartment door which appeared to have a bullet hole in it, announced, "This is the police," entered the apartment after the door was opened by a woman, and encountered the defendant who took aim at the police with a handgun, the defendant's actions directed at the officers while they were engaged in legitimate police activity were not in defense of dwelling and his conviction for aggravated assault was affirmed.[342]

Once a person has lawfully entered a residence, defense of dwelling is not available as justification for use of force even after the person has been asked by the occupant to leave.[343] Such is the case even where the defendant is threatened or actually injured by the victim in the defendant's dwelling.[344] For example, a defendant could not claim she was defending her dwelling when she shot the victim after the victim had allegedly beaten her as she slept because the victim shared the dwelling with her and was therefore not an intruder.[345] Additionally, she was not justified in shooting the victim because of self-defense, since the evidence revealed that the victim had been attempting to escape and had been shot in the back.[346]

---

[338] People v. Miles, 188 Ill. App. 3d 471, 480, 544 N.E.2d 986, 992 (1st Dist. 1989).

[339] People v. Brown, 19 Ill. App. 3d 757, 763, 312 N.E.2d 789, 794-95 (1st Dist. 1974).

[340] People v. Garmon, 19 Ill. App. 3d 192, 196, 311 N.E.2d 299, 302 (1st Dist. 1974).

[341] People v. Garmon, 19 Ill. App. 3d 192, 196, 311 N.E.2d 299, 302 (1st Dist. 1974).

[342] People v. Sedlacko, 65 Ill. App. 3d 659, 664-65, 382 N.E.2d 363, 368-69 (1st Dist. 1978).

[343] People v. Barnard, 208 Ill. App. 3d 342, 351, 567 N.E.2d 60, 66-67 (5th Dist. 1991); People v. Ellis, 107 Ill. App. 3d 603, 613, 437 N.E.2d 409, 417 (2d Dist. 1982).

[344] People v. Chapman, 49 Ill. App. 3d 553, 556, 364 N.E.2d 577, 580 (1st Dist. 1977).

[345] People v. Chapman, 49 Ill. App. 3d 553, 553, 364 N.E.2d 577, 577 (1st Dist. 1977).

[346] People v. Chapman, 49 Ill. App. 3d 553, 557-58, 364 N.E.2d 577, 580-81 (1st Dist. 1977).

Where the victim's entry is unlawful, defense of dwelling may be available. Thus, where a defendant was a guest in the apartment of the victim's estranged wife and the victim allegedly forced entry into the apartment and proceeded to attack the defendant, the defendant was entitled to have the jury instructed on defense of dwelling.[347]

§ 17.27.   — Force was Necessary.

Defense of dwelling insists the use of force was necessary to prevent an unlawful entry or attack upon a dwelling.[348] Virtually all of the cases that explore the *necessary* element involve the necessity of using deadly force. In this regard, it is important to determine if deadly force can be used to prevent or terminate an unlawful entry where the entry may not involve a serious threat to a person. Some earlier cases suggested *any* degree of force would be permissible:

> The law of this state dictates that a man's habitation is one place where he may rest secure in the knowledge he will not be disturbed by persons coming within, without proper invitation or warrant, and that he may use all of the force apparently necessary to repel any invasion of his home.[349]

However, in *People v. Sawyer*,[350] the Illinois Supreme Court held a defendant is entitled to the defense of dwelling "only when two factors are present."[351] First, the victim's entry must be in a violent, riotous or tumultuous manner and, second, the defendant must subjectively and reasonably believe deadly force is necessary to "prevent an assault, or an offer of personal violence to, him or another in the dwelling. . . ."[352] Here, while the victim had minutes earlier slapped his former girlfriend in the dwelling, had shouted profanity at her, had left the house and then ignored her request not to reenter the house as he peaceably reentered, the defendant's stabbing of the victim was not justified.[353] First, the victim's reentry was not violent, riotous or tumultuous in that he simply opened the

---

[347] People v. Stombaugh, 52 Ill. 2d 130, 135-36, 284 N.E.2d 640, 643 (1972) (murder conviction reversed).

[348] 720 ILCS 5/7-2 (1999).

[349] People v. Suerth, 97 Ill. App. 3d 1005, 1012, 423 N.E.2d 1185, 1192 (1st Dist. 1981); People v. Stombaugh, 52 Ill. 2d 130, 137-38, 284 N.E.2d 640, 644 (1972); People v. Eatman, 405 Ill. 491, 498, 91 N.E.2d 387, 390 (1950).

[350] 115 Ill. 2d 184, 503 N.E.2d 331 (1986), *cert. denied,* 482 U.S. 930, *reh'g denied,* 483 U.S. 1044 (1987).

[351] People v. Sawyer, 115 Ill. 2d 184, 192, 503 N.E.2d 331, 335 (1986), *cert. denied,* 482 U.S. 930, *reh'g denied,* 483 U.S. 1044 (1987).

[352] People v. Sawyer, 115 Ill. 2d 184, 192, 503 N.E.2d 331, 335 (1986), *cert. denied,* 482 U.S. 930, *reh'g denied,* 483 U.S. 1044 (1987).

[353] People v. Sawyer, 115 Ill. 2d 184, 192-93, 503 N.E.2d 331, 335 (1986), *cert. denied,* 482 U.S. 930, *reh'g denied,* 483 U.S. 1044 (1987).

screen door of the dwelling and stepped inside.[354] Second, there was no threat of assault or personal violence in that the victim did not attempt to strike his former girlfriend again after he reentered or threaten anyone else, the defendant expressed no fear the victim was armed, the defendant had known the victim for eight or nine years, and the defendant and victim were of roughly the same size and age.[355]

§ 17.28.   — Deadly Force Used to Prevent Assault or Felony.

If the defendant had a reasonable belief that force was necessary to prevent an assault on himself or another, then resort to deadly force is permitted.[356] Thus, where the victim entered defendant's building firing a gun, deadly force in response would be permissible.[357] Similarly, where the victim, a "well-developed" thirty-five-year-old man weighing 170 pounds, followed the defendant, a nearly blind fifty-nine-year-old man weighing approximately 130 pounds, to his room in a boarding house, then prevented the defendant from closing the door to his room and, thereafter, advanced toward the defendant, the defendant's shooting of the victim, who was a stranger to the defendant, was justified by defense of dwelling.[358]

On the other hand, where the defendant's entry into a dwelling is not violent, riotous or tumultuous nor one which involves a threat of assault or violence to a person, defense of dwelling does not permit the use of deadly force.[359] "The theory of using deadly force to protect one's dwelling is not for the protection of the physical dwelling itself; rather, it is for the protection of the individuals therein."[360] Finally, if the victim's entry or presence in the dwelling is lawful, the victim's subsequent commission of a forcible felony, such as aggravated battery, against the defendant while in the dwelling does not permit deadly force in "defense of dwelling" since the victim was not an intruder.[361]

---

[354] People v. Sawyer, 115 Ill. 2d 184, 192-93, 503 N.E.2d 331, 335 (1986), *cert. denied*, 482 U.S. 930, *reh'g denied*, 483 U.S. 1044 (1987).

[355] People v. Sawyer, 115 Ill. 2d 184, 192-97, 503 N.E.2d 331, 335-37 (1986) (voluntary manslaughter conviction affirmed), *cert. denied*, 482 U.S. 930, *reh'g denied*, 483 U.S. 1044 (1987). *See also* ILL. ANN. STAT. ch. 38, para. 7-2 (Smith-Hurd 1989), 1961 Committee Comments, at 388.

[356] People v. Morris, 162 Ill. App. 3d 1046, 1055, 516 N.E.2d 412, 418 (1st Dist. 1987).

[357] People v. Morris, 162 Ill. App. 3d 1046, 1055, 516 N.E.2d 412, 418 (1st Dist. 1987).

[358] People v. Givens, 26 Ill. 2d 371, 372-76, 186 N.E.2d 225, 226-28 (1962).

[359] People v. Sawyer, 115 Ill. 2d 184, 193-97, 503 N.E.2d 331, 335-37 (1986) (voluntary manslaughter conviction affirmed), *cert. denied*, 482 U.S. 930, *reh'g denied*, 483 U.S. 1044 (1987).

[360] People v. Morris, 162 Ill. App. 3d 1046, 1054-55, 516 N.E.2d 412, 418 (1st Dist. 1987) (failure to instruct on defense of dwelling requires reversal of voluntary manslaughter conviction).

[361] People v. Chapman, 49 Ill. App. 3d 553, 556, 364 N.E.2d 577, 580 (1st Dist. 1977) (although it may raise self-defense).

§ 17.29. — Actual Belief.

To claim justifiable defense of dwelling, the defender must actually or subjectively believe that an unlawful entry has been or is about to be made. Where the evidence is contrary to the conclusion that the defendant actually believed there had been an illegal entry into a dwelling, a defense of dwelling claim will not succeed.[362] Regarding deadly force, there must also be actual belief that the use of such force is necessary to avert either a violent entry or a felony within the dwelling.[363] Thus, where there was no evidence that two shooting victims' entry into the defendant's residence was in a violent, riotous or tumultuous manner and both victims were shot in the back of the head, the defendant's claim that he had an actual belief in the need to kill was dismissed as having no basis.[364] Where an individual commits a mere criminal trespass on real property, the defendant cannot justify killing the trespasser absent a belief that force is necessary to protect the dwelling or an occupant therein from serious danger.[365] Thus, a conviction of manslaughter was affirmed where the defendant, without belief that force was necessary, hit the victim over the head with a bat after the victim had committed a trespass on the defendant's property while looking into the defendant's window from the outside.[366]

§ 17.30. — Reasonable Belief, Even if Mistaken.

As in defense of person,[367] the actual beliefs of a defendant claiming defense of dwelling must be reasonable.[368] "Reasonable belief" or "reasonably believes" requires that the defendant, acting as a reasonable person, believed that the described facts existed.[369] For example, the battery and resisting arrest convictions of a defendant, who was pregnant at the time of the occurrence, were reversed after the appellate court found reasonable her belief that her conduct was neces-

---

[362] *See, e.g.,* People v. Sedlacko, 65 Ill. App. 3d 659, 382 N.E.2d 363 (1st Dist. 1978); People v. Garmon, 19 Ill. App. 3d 192, 311 N.E.2d 299 (1st Dist. 1974). In both cases, the defendants knew their victims were police officers, and such knowledge belied the conclusion that the defendants were actually faced with an unlawful entry.

[363] People v. Sawyer, 115 Ill. 2d 184, 193-97, 503 N.E.2d 331, 335-37 (1986), *cert. denied,* 482 U.S. 930, *reh'g denied,* 483 U.S. 1044 (1987).

[364] People v. Rogers, 263 Ill. App. 3d 120, 127, 635 N.E.2d 889, 894 (1st Dist. 1994) (first degree murder and second degree murder convictions affirmed).

[365] People v. Hubert, 251 Ill. 514, 520, 96 N.E. 294, 296 (1911) (manslaughter conviction affirmed).

[366] People v. Hubert, 251 Ill. 514, 520, 96 N.E. 294, 296 (1911).

[367] *See* § 17.13 of this chapter.

[368] Hayner v. People, 213 Ill. 142, 149-50, 72 N.E. 792, 795 (1904) (defense of habitation was reasonable, requiring reversal of manslaughter conviction); ILL. ANN. STAT. ch. 38, para. 7-2 (Smith-Hurd 1989), 1961 Committee Comments, at 389.

[369] 720 ILCS 5/2-19 (1999).

sary to protect her apartment against the unlawful entry of three police officers who were attempting an illegal search.[370]

A bare subjective fear of violence on a dwelling or on a person therein is not sufficient to justify a homicide allegedly committed to prevent that violence.[371] "It must appear that the circumstances were sufficient to excite the fears of a reasonable person, and that the party killing really acted under the influence of those fears, and not in a spirit of revenge."[372]

The jury must determine the reasonableness of the defendant's subjective belief of the need to employ deadly force against an intruder.[373] In the case of *People v. Epps*,[374] the court determined that the jury could have properly concluded that the defendant's belief of the necessity for shooting the victim, who defendant claimed was a possible burglar, was unreasonable. Analyzing the circumstances surrounding the homicide, including the fact that defendant conceded that the victim had just run out the door as he shot him, the court agreed with the state that the "defendant's argument that his decision to shoot an unarmed man in the back of the head through a closed door was not a reasonable belief."[375]

Although a subjective, but unreasonable, fear of offense against a dwelling is not sufficient to justify use of force against another in defense of dwelling,[376] a mistaken belief, if reasonable, will preclude a defendant's criminal liability for the victim's death.[377] This remains true even where subsequent examination of the facts reveals that no felony was intended and that the victim's actions were merely in jest or meant to frighten the inhabitants of the dwelling.[378]

§ 17.31. — The Defender is Not the Aggressor.

As with a claim of self-defense,[379] the individual claiming justifiable use of force in defense of dwelling cannot be the initial aggressor.[380] For example, in

---

[370] People v. Young, 100 Ill. App. 2d 20, 25-26, 241 N.E.2d 587, 590 (1st Dist. 1968).

[371] Hayner v. People, 213 Ill. 142, 150, 72 N.E. 792, 795 (1904) (defense of habitation requires reversal of manslaughter conviction).

[372] Hayner v. People, 213 Ill. 142, 150, 72 N.E. 792, 795 (1904) (quoting ILL. ANN. STAT. ch. 38, para. 149 (1899)).

[373] People v. Epps, 117 Ill. App. 3d 507, 511, 453 N.E.2d 816, 819 (1st Dist. 1983).

[374] 117 Ill. App. 3d 507, 453 N.E.2d 816 (1st Dist. 1983).

[375] People v. Epps, 117 Ill. App. 3d 507, 510, 453 N.E.2d 816, 819 (1st Dist. 1983) (voluntary manslaughter conviction affirmed). Here, the defendant argued defense of dwelling while raising para. 5/7-3 (defense of property) rather than 5/7-2 (defense of dwelling).

[376] Hayner v. People, 213 Ill. 142, 150, 72 N.E. 792, 795 (1904).

[377] Foster v. Shepherd, 258 Ill. 164, 175, 101 N.E. 411, 416-17 (1913) (wrongful death action).

[378] Foster v. Shepherd, 258 Ill. 164, 176, 101 N.E. 411, 416-17 (1913).

[379] *See* § 17.06 of this chapter.

[380] People v. Epps, 117 Ill. App. 3d 507, 510, 453 N.E.2d 816, 818 (1st Dist. 1983) (voluntary manslaughter conviction affirmed over defendant's claim that victim was possible burglar where victim was shot in the back of the head after he had exited premises).

Greschia v. People,[381] the victim lawfully entered the defendant's room where he had previously resided to retrieve his clothing, whereupon a heated argument ensued between the defendant and the victim. After the victim had left the room, the defendant provoked the victim into returning to the room where he repeatedly struck the deceased with a rolling pin. In upholding the defendant's murder conviction, the Illinois Supreme Court noted that the unarmed victim had not sought forcible entry into the defendant's room. Furthermore, the defendant had taunted his victim to "come on." Accordingly, the court held that there was no justification for the defendant's actions in fracturing the victim's skull.[382]

§ 17.32. Use of Force in Defense of Other Property Codified.

While recognizing the superior right to defend a dwelling, the revision committee responsible for drafting the Criminal Code of 1961 nevertheless acknowledged that a person has certain limited rights to use force in defense of his or her "other" property.[383] "[H]e may use force which he reasonably believes . . . necessary to protect the property, but he may not use deadly force except to prevent the commission of a forcible felony."[384] The committee alluded to the availability of civil remedies for trespass to real property,[385] citing *Davison v. People*[386] as precedent. The *Davison* court had earlier declared:

> The law affords ample redress for trespasses committed on a man's land, but does not sanction the taking of life to prevent it. The owner may, no doubt, oppose force with force to protect his property from injury or destruction, but not to the extent of taking life, or in excess of the necessity of the case. When he carries resistance to excess and uses more force than is reasonably necessary, he becomes a wrongdoer.[387]

Beyond concern over real property, several other cases have limited the right to defend against trespass to personal property,[388] but the "factual situation of each case must be analyzed to determine whether . . . defense of the person is [also] involved" where substantial force is directed at the trespasser.[389] In other

---

[381] 53 Ill. 295 (1870).

[382] Greschia v. People, 53 Ill. 295, 30 (1870).

[383] ILL. ANN. STAT. ch. 38, para. 7-3 (Smith-Hurd 1989), 1961 Committee Comments, at 395.

[384] ILL. ANN. STAT. ch. 38, para. 7-3 (Smith-Hurd 1989), 1961 Committee Comments, at 395 (citing 1 BISHOP ON CRIMINAL LAW §§ 857, 861, 862, 875 (9th ed. 1923)).

[385] ILL. ANN. STAT. ch. 38, para. 7-3 (Smith-Hurd 1989), 1961 Committee Comments, at 396.

[386] 90 Ill. 221 (1878).

[387] Davison v. People, 90 Ill. 221, 229-30 (1878).

[388] *See, e.g.,* People v. Capello, 282 Ill. 542, 118 N.E. 927 (1918) (defendant not justified in killing victim who trespassed on wagon but intended no personal violence against defendant). *Compare* Wentworth v. People, 5 Ill. 550 (1843) (defendant justified in resisting officer's unlawful seizure of goods with nondeadly force).

[389] ILL. ANN. STAT. ch. 38, para. 7-3 (Smith-Hurd 1989), 1961 Committee Comments, at 396.

words, the use of significant force against a trespasser will be justified only where the trespass or confiscation of property somehow evolves into a situation in which the sanctity of the *person* is threatened as well.

Paragraph 5/7-3, which codifies "defense of other property,"[390] contains an important restriction that does not apply to defense of dwelling. Specifically, the right of a person to use force in preventing a trespass on or interference with another person's property is limited to circumstances in which the interference is to property lawfully in the possession of a family or household member or a person the defender has a legal duty to protect.[391] Although there was no prior Illinois caselaw pertaining to this requirement, the revision committee expressly recognized the requirement as reasonable "in the interest of limiting the use of force in minor and non-violent offenses involving a third person's property."[392] In addition, deadly force is only permitted in the context of one's defense of property where the defender is preventing a forcible felony.[393]

§ 17.33.   Elements of Defense of Other Property.

Paragraph 5/7-3 delineates the elements of "defense of other property."[394] The elements of this defense are (1) trespass or other tortious or criminal interference is threatened; (2) the property threatened is real (but not a dwelling) or personal; (3) the property is lawfully in the possession of the defender, a member of his or her immediate family or household, or a person whose property the defender has a legal duty to protect; (4) the defender must actually believe that (a) an unlawful trespass or tortious or criminal interference has been or is about to be committed, (b) the use of force is necessary to prevent or terminate the trespass or tortious or criminal interference, (c) the kind and amount of force used is necessary; and (5) the above beliefs are reasonable, even if mistaken.[395]

§ 17.34.   — Trespass or Other Tortious or Criminal Interference.

In order to defend one's property, there must be unlawful trespass to or interference with that property.[396] The trespass or interference may be to real[397] or

---

[390] 720 ILCS 5/7-3 (1999).

[391] 720 ILCS 5/7-3 (1999).

[392] ILL. ANN. STAT. ch. 38, para. 7-3 (Smith-Hurd 1989), 1961 Committee Comments, at 397.

[393] 720 ILCS 5/7-3 (1999).

[394] 720 ILCS 5/7-3 (1999).

[395] 720 ILCS 5/7-3 (1999).

[396] People v. Vaughn, 116 Ill. App. 3d 193, 198, 451 N.E.2d 898, 902 (5th Dist. 1983) (evidence did not warrant defense of property instructions; aggravated battery conviction affirmed).

[397] People v. Raber, 130 Ill. App. 2d 813, 264 N.E.2d 274 (5th Dist. 1970) (trespass to land and removal of personal property).

personal property.[398] The "interference" need not constitute a crime but may be merely tortious in nature.[399]

In regards to the trespass situation, in one case it was held that a tavern owner had a right to use reasonable force to eject an angry trespasser; thus, the defendant-trespasser's infliction of a battery on the tavern owner was not justified by self-defense.[400] The tavern owner had calmly placed his hand on the defendant's arm in order to remove the defendant from a private party in the tavern, to which the defendant responded by illegally striking the owner.[401] In contrast, where an assault victim was on a landlord's property at the express invitation of a tenant, there was no trespass and, consequently, no justification for forcible defense of property.[402]

In regard to the "interference" situation, where a passenger in defendant's automobile grabbed the keys from the ignition of defendant's automobile and began to exit the automobile, the defendant may have been justified in grabbing the victim by the hair in order to protect his personal property.[403] Here, the trial judge's refusal to instruct the jury in defendant's battery trial that the defendant's actions may have been permissible in order to prevent the passenger's "wrongful interference" with his property was considered reversible error.[404] Meanwhile, where defendant forcibly entered another's residence to retrieve what he claimed was a stolen necklace, he was not entitled to defense of property instructions inasmuch as there was no evidence that he was taking action "*necessary* to prevent or terminate another's criminal interference with property"; rather, the defendant should have contacted the police instead of "resorting to self-help tactics."[405]

§ 17.35. — Real or Personal Property is Threatened.

Use of force in defense of real property (other than a dwelling) may be justified under section 5/7-3.[406] Thus, where certain individuals entered upon defendant's farm property and commenced to bale straw which they intended to re-

---

[398] People v. Swartz, 186 Ill. App. 3d 399, 401-02, 542 N.E.2d 515, 517 (4th Dist. 1989) (removal of keys from automobile).

[399] 720 ILCS 5/7-3 (1999).

[400] People v. Bradshaw, 100 Ill. App. 3d 45, 46, 426 N.E.2d 345, 346 (4th Dist. 1981).

[401] People v. Bradshaw, 100 Ill. App. 3d 45, 46, 426 N.E.2d 345, 346 (4th Dist. 1981).

[402] People v. Rynberk, 92 Ill. App. 3d 112, 115-16, 415 N.E.2d 1087, 1090-91 (1st Dist. 1980) (assault conviction affirmed).

[403] People v. Swartz, 186 Ill. App. 3d 399, 401-02, 542 N.E.2d 515, 517 (4th Dist. 1989).

[404] People v. Swartz, 186 Ill. App. 3d 399, 401-02, 542 N.E.2d 515, 517 (4th Dist. 1989).

[405] People v. Hicks, 286 Ill. App. 3d 588, 595, 676 N.E.2d 725, 729 (2d Dist. 1997) (emphasis added) (home invasion conviction affirmed), *aff'd in pertinent part, rev'd in part,* 181 Ill. 2d 541, 693 N.E.2d 373 (1998).

[406] 720 ILCS 5/7-3 (1999).

move, the appellate court found that the defendant's act of pointing an unloaded shotgun at these individuals did not support a conviction of criminal assault given the fact that these individuals were trespassing on defendant's farm property and baling straw which she claimed belonged to her and her bedridden husband.[407] However, where a park superintendent parked his vehicle on a public road and confronted defendant "on or about" the road, which was immediately adjacent to defendant's property, whereupon the defendant pushed the official toward his vehicle while claiming the official had trespassed on his property, there was no evidence of substantial encroachment on defendant's property justifying a defense of property claim.[408]

Personal property may also be protected, either by the absolute owner or by the person in lawful possession.[409] Thus, a defendant could use reasonable force to prevent a passenger in his automobile from removing from his automobile keys she had taken from the ignition without his permission.[410]

§ 17.36.   — In Lawful Possession.

The individual with no lawful right to possession of property may not claim defense of property as justification for the use of force, although exclusive right to possession is not necessary.[411] Thus, a defendant could not advance a claim of protection of property where the several rows of beans that had allegedly been damaged by a road commission were actually planted in a township roadway.[412] Similarly, a defendant could not claim justifiable use of force in defense of property where he had forcibly reclaimed illegal gambling losses from a pool hustler.[413] Here, "the *victim* was in possession" of the gambling proceeds and, thus, defense of property was simply inapplicable.[414]

§ 17.37.   — Actual and Reasonable Belief.

As with other article 5/7 defenses, both actual and reasonable belief are necessary elements of justifiable use of force in defense of other property.[415] Thus,

---

[407] People v. Raber, 130 Ill. App. 2d 813, 814-15, 264 N.E.2d 274, 275 (5th Dist. 1970).

[408] People v. Lowe, 202 Ill. App. 3d 648, 654-55, 560 N.E.2d 438, 442-43 (4th Dist. 1990) (aggravated battery conviction affirmed).

[409] Wentworth v. People, 5 Ill. 550 (1843).

[410] People v. Swartz, 186 Ill. App. 3d 399, 401-02, 542 N.E.2d 515, 517 (4th Dist. 1989) (battery conviction reversed).

[411] Roach v. People, 77 Ill. 25, 31 (1875) (manslaughter conviction reversed).

[412] People v. Vaughn, 116 Ill. App. 3d 193, 197-98, 451 N.E.2d 898, 902 (5th Dist. 1983) (aggravated battery conviction affirmed).

[413] People v. Robinson, 68 Ill. App. 3d 687, 692, 386 N.E.2d 165, 169 (4th Dist. 1979) (armed robbery conviction affirmed).

[414] People v. Robinson, 68 Ill. App. 3d 687, 692, 386 N.E.2d 165, 169 (4th Dist. 1979) (emphasis added).

[415] 720 ILCS 5/7-3 (1999).

where defense evidence was to the effect that the defendant shot at the victim in self-defense and the defense offered no evidence that the defendant's actions were somehow motivated by protection of this dwelling or other property, no instruction on defense of property was warranted.[416]

Not only must there be an actual belief in the necessity for use of force in defense of property, but also the belief must be reasonable. Thus, a landlord's assault on a tenant's visitor could not be justified as an action in defense of property, since the defendant's belief that the handicapped victim would harm his property was unreasonable.[417] Another defendant's claim that defense of his bean crop justified beating up a road commissioner performing official duties was not reasonable.[418]

In the absence of prevention of a forcible felony, use of deadly force is never reasonable against a trespasser.[419] This point was made in a case where two defendants' murder convictions were ultimately reversed by reason of self-defense for fatally shooting a service station attendant.[420] The victim had wrongfully shot at the defendants, apparently believing the defendants to be trespassing on private property. The defendants returned gunfire and struck the victim. The victim, however, did not have any right to protect his employer's property by use of deadly force under circumstances that indicated no intent by the defendants to commit a forcible felony.[421]

Finally, "[t]he phrase 'reasonable belief' applies not only to the existence of the trespass or other interference, the necessity of using force, and the proper amount of force to be used, but also to the lawfulness of the possession which is being protected . . . and the duty to protect the property of a third person."[422]

§ 17.38. Affirmative Defense.

Defense of person and defense of property are affirmative defenses.[423] An *affirmative defense* means that unless the state's evidence raises the defense issue, the defendant has the burden of coming forward with "some evidence."[424] At this point, the burden shifts to the state to prove the defendant guilty beyond a reasonable doubt concerning the defense issue together with all other elements

---

[416] People v. Smalley, 10 Ill. App. 3d 416, 426, 294 N.E.2d 305, 312 (2d Dist. 1973) (attempted murder and aggravated assault convictions affirmed).

[417] People v. Rynberk, 92 Ill. App. 3d 112, 116, 415 N.E.2d 1087, 1091 (1st Dist. 1980) (assault conviction affirmed).

[418] People v. Vaughn, 116 Ill. App. 3d 193, 197-98, 451 N.E.2d 898, 902 (5th Dist. 1983) (aggravated battery conviction affirmed).

[419] People v. Dillard, 5 Ill. App. 3d 896, 901, 284 N.E.2d 490, 494 (5th Dist. 1972).

[420] People v. Dillard, 5 Ill. App. 3d 896, 901, 284 N.E.2d 490, 494 (5th Dist. 1972).

[421] People v. Dillard, 5 Ill. App. 3d 896, 901, 284 N.E.2d 490, 494 (5th Dist. 1972).

[422] ILL. ANN. STAT. ch. 38, para. 7-3 (Smith-Hurd 1989), 1961 Committee Comments, at 397.

[423] 720 ILCS 5/7-14 (1999).

[424] 720 ILCS 5/3-2(a) (1999).

of the offense.[425] In other words, the ultimate burden is then shouldered by the government to disprove the defense claim. In addition, once the defendant offers some evidence supportive of the defense, the trial court is obligated to give defense instructions to the jury.[426]

Although the meaning of the "some evidence" standard seems rather straightforward at first glance, this is not necessarily the case because of the differential interpretations given this language. The Illinois courts have variously stated that raising an affirmative defense requires "very slight evidence,"[427] "slight evidence,"[428] "some evidence,"[429] "when any evidence is presented showing the defendant's subjective belief that use of force was necessary,"[430] "some evidence of a reasonable belief in the necessity for the use of deadly force,"[431] and "some minimum amount of evidence."[432]

While the cases that reflect the "very slight evidence" or "slight evidence" standards seem to open the door to requiring instructions even if the evidence does not address each of the elements of the defense, the cases that explicitly address this issue state that the affirmative defense is raised only "if defendant presents some evidence regarding each element."[433] Also, when the state raises the issue by its own evidence,[434] the affirmative defense has been raised even though the defendant denies committing the act.[435] On the other hand, the state's offer of evidence that there was no justification for the act is not tantamount to raising the affirmative defense.[436] Thus, where the state offers evidence in a bat-

---

[425] 720 ILCS 5/3-2(b); *see* People v. Belpedio, 212 Ill. App. 3d 155, 162, 569 N.E.2d 1372, 1375 (2d Dist. 1991); People v. Ellis, 187 Ill. App. 3d 295, 302, 543 N.E.2d 196, 200 (1st Dist. 1989), *cert. denied*, 498 U.S. 942 (1990).

[426] People v. Woodward, 77 Ill. App. 3d 352, 357, 395 N.E.2d 1203, 1207 (2d Dist. 1979) (self-defense instruction required).

[427] People v. Bratcher, 63 Ill. 2d 534, 539, 349 N.E.2d 31, 34 (1976) (self-defense instructions not required).

[428] People v. Sunquist, 55 Ill. App. 3d 263, 267, 370 N.E.2d 864, 867 (3d Dist. 1977) (self-defense instruction required).

[429] People v. Lockett, 82 Ill. 2d 546, 551, 413 N.E.2d 378, 381 (1980) (self-defense instruction required).

[430] People v. Lockett, 82 Ill. 2d 546, 552, 413 N.E.2d 378, 381 (1980).

[431] People v. Woodward, 77 Ill. App. 3d 352, 357, 395 N.E.2d 1203, 1207 (2d Dist. 1979) (self-defense instruction required).

[432] People v. Warren, 52 Ill. App. 2d 374, 380, 202 N.E.2d 131, 134 (1st Dist. 1964), *aff'd,* 33 Ill. 2d 168, 210 N.E.2d 507 (1965) (self-defense instructions not required).

[433] People v. Kyles, 91 Ill. App. 3d 1019, 1022, 415 N.E.2d 499, 501 (1st Dist. 1980) (self-defense).

[434] People v. Rorer, 44 Ill. App. 3d 553, 557-58, 358 N.E.2d 681, 684 (5th Dist. 1976) (self-defense and defense of another).

[435] People v. Bailey, 108 Ill. App. 3d 392, 399, 439 N.E.2d 4, 9 (2d Dist. 1982) (defense of another instruction required).

[436] People v. Meeks, 75 Ill. App. 3d 357, 361, 393 N.E.2d 1190, 1194 (5th Dist. 1979) (discussing exemptions in controlled substances prohibition), *rev'd on other grounds,* 81 Ill. 2d 524, 411 N.E.2d 9 (1980).

tery case that the defendant caused bodily harm "without legal justification," a statutory element of the crime,[437] this by no means automatically raises the defense of self or another.

The purpose of affirmative defenses "is to relieve the State of the time-consuming and wasteful task of alleging and proving many negative propositions which, if proven in the affirmative, would provide a good defense to the charges."[438] An affirmative defense cannot be developed by an accused on cross-examination.[439]

Where a defendant's defense claim is that he or she intentionally or knowingly used force against another with justification, an instruction on self-defense will be appropriate. A defendant's claim that he or she cannot remember whether he or she shot the victim because he or she blacked out before the victim was shot precludes the giving of a self-defense instruction,[440] for this claim goes to whether the defendant consciously and voluntarily committed any actus reus. If the defendant offers no evidence that his or her actions were a product of, for instance, defense of dwelling or defense of other property, then no instructions are warranted on these defense theories.[441]

If the evidence is such that a jury could infer the accused's acts were in defense of a person, the defendant will then be entitled to the instructions.[442] Even if the trial court believes the jury is very likely to reject the defendant's testimony because of his or her apparent lack of credibility, it is still obligated to offer the instructions, assuming the testimony raises the defense issue, since the credibility of the defendant is a factual issue for the jury.[443] Even the defendant's denial of the commission of an act in self-defense does not eliminate the need for instructions if other evidence advanced at trial raises the issue.[444] And even if the accused fails to tender appropriate defense instructions to the trial court, if the evidence raises an article 5/7 defense, the court is obligated to give the jury appropriate instructions.[445]

Once the defendant or the state has effectively raised the affirmative defense, not only is it necessary that the trial court instruct the jury on that defense, but it is also imperative that the state disprove this defense while proving the elements of the crime charged beyond a reasonable doubt.[446] Any evidence produced at trial that negates the existence of any one of the elements of the defense beyond

---

[437] 720 ILCS 5/12-3(a) (1999).

[438] People v. Williams, 80 Ill. App. 3d 963, 968, 400 N.E.2d 532, 536 (5th Dist. 1980).

[439] People v. Greene, 102 Ill. App. 3d 933, 936, 430 N.E.2d 23, 26 (1st Dist. 1981).

[440] People v. Lahori, 13 Ill. App. 3d 572, 578, 300 N.E.2d 761, 765 (1st Dist. 1973).

[441] People v. Smalley, 10 Ill. App. 3d 416, 426, 294 N.E.2d 305, 312 (2d Dist. 1973).

[442] People v. Cruz, 66 Ill. App. 3d 760, 764, 384 N.E.2d 137, 140 (1st Dist. 1978).

[443] People v. Dowdy, 21 Ill. App. 3d 821, 826, 316 N.E.2d 33, 36 (1st Dist. 1974).

[444] People v. Bailey, 108 Ill. App. 3d 392, 399, 439 N.E.2d 4, 9 (2d Dist. 1982).

[445] People v. Graves, 61 Ill. App. 3d 732, 742, 378 N.E.2d 293, 301 (1st Dist. 1978).

[446] People v. Rice, 108 Ill. App. 3d 344, 355, 438 N.E.2d 1333, 1340-41 (1st Dist. 1982).

a reasonable doubt defeats the defense claim, and the state's burden of proof is satisfied.[447]

Where the evidence suggests that the defendant may have been the initial aggressor in a case where defense of person is raised, it is not error to give the jury an instruction stating: "A person is not justified in the use of force if he initially provokes the use of force against himself with the intent to use that force as an excuse to inflict bodily harm upon the other person."[448] In addition, it is proper to inform the jury that the provoking defendant, faced with the response of deadly force, is duty bound to "exhaust every reasonable means to escape the danger" before resorting to deadly force.[449] Instructing the jury regarding the use of force in self-defense by the first aggressor does not erroneously assume that the defendant was in fact the initial aggressor. As long as the jury is given an additional instruction concerning self-defense generally, the jury is deemed able to resolve the issues on either hypothesis.[450]

---

[447] People v. De Oca, 238 Ill. App. 3d 362, 367, 606 N.E.2d 332, 336 (1st Dist. 1992); People v. Chavez, 228 Ill. App. 3d 54, 70, 592 N.E.2d 69, 81 (1st Dist. 1992); People v. Belpedio, 212 Ill. App. 3d 155, 162, 569 N.E.2d 1372, 1376 (2d Dist. 1991); People v. Brown, 218 Ill. App. 3d 890, 898, 578 N.E.2d 1168, 1174 (1st Dist. 1991); People v. Ross, 100 Ill. App. 3d 1033, 1038, 427 N.E.2d 955, 959 (1st Dist. 1981).

[448] People v. Munguia, 33 Ill. App. 3d 880, 883, 338 N.E.2d 574, 577 (2d Dist. 1975).

[449] People v. Nunn, 184 Ill. App. 3d 253, 271, 541 N.E.2d 182, 195 (1st Dist. 1989), *cert. denied*, 497 U.S. 1027 (1990); People v. Barnett, 48 Ill. App. 3d 121, 125, 362 N.E.2d 420, 422-23 (4th Dist. 1977).

[450] People v. Ellis, 107 Ill. App. 3d 603, 614, 437 N.E.2d 409, 418 (2d Dist. 1982).

CHAPTER 18

DEFENSES: LACK OF CRIMINAL RESPONSIBILITY DUE TO INSANITY, INTOXICATION, AND INFANCY

§ 18.01.   Introduction.

Article 5/6 of the Criminal Code of Illinois contains three affirmative defenses under the general heading of "responsibility."[1] Specifically, this article deals with excuses that relate to the accused's criminal capacity, or lack thereof, as affected by his or her (1) insanity, (2) infancy, or (3) intoxication. The defense of incapacity because of age is addressed in section 5/6-1;[2] the defense of insanity is considered in section 5/6-2;[3] and the defense of intoxication is covered in section 5/6-3.[4] Because of the relative importance of the insanity defense, it will be reviewed first.

---

[1] 720 ILCS 5/6-4 (1999): "A defense based upon any of the provisions of Article 6 is an affirmative defense. . . ."

[2] 720 ILCS 5/6-1 (1999).

[3] 720 ILCS 5/6-2 (1999).

[4] 720 ILCS 5/6-3 (1999).

§ 18.02.   Defense of Insanity: Background of Current Law.

Few issues have engendered as much tumultuous discussion in the area of criminal liability as has the insanity defense.[5] Before the adoption of the General Assembly's codification of the insanity defense in 1961, Illinois had no statutory law that contained a formulation for determining criminal responsibility in the face of a defendant's claim of insanity.[6] Rather, by way of caselaw, the test for determination of criminal responsibility was a combination of the widely used *M'Naghten* rule,[7] known as the "right-wrong" test,[8] and the "irresistible impulse" test.[9]

In 1961, the Illinois legislature adopted the American Law Institute's ("A.L.I.") version of the insanity defense.[10] This version concentrated on both the defendant's cognitive and volitional capacity. Although this two-prong test was not formally adopted by statute until 1961, cases ranging as far back as 1920 required examination of both the defendant's cognitive and volitional capacity: "The mere ability to distinguish right from wrong is not the correct test

---

[5] ILL. ANN. STAT. ch. 38, § 6-2 (Smith-Hurd 1989), 1961 Committee Comments, at 300 (revised 1972); People v. Haun, 71 Ill. App. 2d 262, 267, 217 N.E.2d 470, 473 (4th Dist. 1966) ("The concept of legal insanity is probably one of the most controversial areas in the law").

[6] ILL. ANN. STAT. ch. 38, § 6-2 (Smith-Hurd 1989), 1961 Committee Comments, at 300 (revised 1972).

[7] M'Naghten's Case, 10 Clark & F. 200, 210, 8 Eng. Rep. 718, 722 (1843):

> [T]o establish a defence on the ground of insanity, it must be clearly proved that, at the time of the committing of the act, the party accused was labouring under such a defect of reason, from disease of the mind, as not to know the nature and quality of the act he was doing; or, if he did know it, that he did not know he was doing what was wrong.

[8] M. CHERIF BASSIOUNI, SUBSTANTIVE CRIMINAL LAW 489 (1978).

[9] *See* People v. Carpenter, 11 Ill. 2d 60, 66, 142 N.E.2d 11, 12 (1957). The following jury instruction was approved:

> [T]he unsoundness of mind, or affliction of insanity, must be of such a degree as to create an uncontrollable impulse to do the act charged by overriding the reason and judgment and obliterating the sense of right or wrong as to the particular act done or depriving the accused of the power of choosing between right and wrong.

See generally DONALD H.J. HERMANN, THE INSANITY DEFENSE: PHILOSOPHICAL, HISTORICAL AND LEGAL PERSPECTIVES 5-6, 34-58 (1983) (discussion of these and other tests accepted by courts over the years).

One significant test, which has never been the law in Illinois, is the "product" test or *Durham* rule. It provided: "An accused is not criminally responsible if his unlawful act was the product of mental disease or defect." Durham v. United States, 214 F.2d 862, 874-75 (D.C. Cir. 1954), *overruled*, United States v. Brawner, 471 F.2d 969 (D.C. Cir. 1972). The *Durham* "product" test was never generally accepted throughout the American courts. *See also* M. CHERIF BASSIOUNI, SUBSTANTIVE CRIMINAL LAW 491 (1978).

[10] ILL. ANN. STAT. ch. 38, para. 6-2 (Smith-Hurd 1989), 1961 Committee Comments, at 304 (revised 1972).

... the accused must also be mentally capable of choosing either to do or not to do the act in accordance with such a choice."[11] Thus, even though the legislature adopted a more modern statutory provision in preference to the *M'Naghten* "right-wrong" formula,[12] the statute was in actuality similar in scope to the combination of the *M'Naghten* rule and the "irresistible impulse" test used in the past in Illinois in that it had both a cognitive and volitional control aspect.

There were two noteworthy distinctions between the *M'Naghten* rule and the 1961 law that need to be highlighted. Under the old *M'Naghten* rule, in order for a defendant to successfully plead an insanity defense, the defendant had to lack the ability to "know" right from wrong with respect to his or her criminal act. Use of the term *know* in the *M'Naghten* rule stimulated much criticism, particularly from the psychiatric community. For instance, "two psychiatrists may be in basic agreement as to the diagnosis of the defendant but be in sharp conflict on the issue whether the defendant could distinguish between right and wrong."[13] Moreover, although the defendant may have an *intellectual* understanding of the difference between right and wrong, he or she may lack a comprehension of the kind that involves "the emotional or affective parts of his or her personality. In fact, it is said this separation between intellectual and affective aspects of his or her personality may be the primary symptom of the person suffering some types of serious mental afflictions."[14] In order to rectify the problems that arose with the term *know* in the *M'Naghten* test, the Illinois legislative drafting committee adopted the American Law Institute's Model Penal Code test, which concentrated on the defendant's capacity to "appreciate" the criminality of his or her

---

[11] People v. Lowhone, 292 Ill. 32, 48, 126 N.E. 620, 626 (1920).

[12] ILL. ANN. STAT. ch. 38, para. 6-2 (Smith-Hurd 1989), 1961 Committee Comments, at 302 (revised 1972).

[13] ILL. ANN. STAT. ch. 38, para. 6-2 (Smith-Hurd 1989), 1961 Committee Comments, at 302 (revised 1972).

[14] ILL. ANN. STAT. ch. 38, para. 6-2 (Smith-Hurd 1989), 1961 Committee Comments, at 302 (revised 1972). Additional criticism of the *M'Naghten* test was summarized by the drafting committee as follows:

> Second, it is sometimes said that framing the test in terms of right and wrong poses an unfair question to the expert witness. Thus, it is said that psychiatrists are men of science and *qua* psychiatrists know nothing about right and wrong. . . . Third, some psychiatrists candidly assert that it is impossible to determine with accuracy, whether, in many cases of the most advanced mental disorder, the defendant does have the capacity to distinguish between right and wrong. The point also contains the implication that in some instances persons very severely afflicted, and who would therefore be appealing cases for exculpation, may possess at least rudimentary powers of identifying right and wrong. . . . Fourth, it is often asserted that the right-wrong test narrows too severely the scope of expert . . . testimony useful for the evaluation of the defendant . . . .

conduct.[15] The term *appreciate* incorporates both the defendant's intellectual understanding and his or her affective understanding.

The second difference between *M'Naghten* standing alone and the A.L.I. test was that the latter contained a volitional prong, which addressed the person who had an understanding of the wrongfulness of his behavior but was unable to control or contain his criminal proclivities.[16] Although Illinois had adopted the "irresistible impulse" test prior to 1961, which reflected concern over a defendant's volitional capacity, the A.L.I. language made clear that a defendant's volitional powers were of equal concern as his or her cognitive abilities.[17]

The third difference between the *M'Naghten* rule and the 1961 A.L.I. law centered on the quantitative aspect of incapacity required to plead a successful insanity defense. Under both the *M'Naghten* rule and "irresistible impulse" test, *total* incapacity was required. In other words, the defendant had to be totally incapable of knowing right from wrong or totally incapable of controlling his or her criminal conduct.[18] The 1961 law provided that a person was not criminally responsible for his or her conduct if he or she lacked *substantial* capacity to either appreciate or conform.[19] It is also important to point out that the revision committee incorporated into the Illinois law the Model Penal Code decision to exclude from the insanity defense those persons classified as "psychopathic."[20] Often referred to as a "personality disorder," the psychopathic personality is characterized by emotional instability, lack of responsible judgment, and amoral and asocial feelings. The psychopathic personality often manifests itself in "repeated criminal or otherwise antisocial conduct."[21] The psychopathic defendant was expressly excluded from the insanity defense by the legislative drafting committee because his or her abnormality distinguishes him or her from the normal person only in a quantitative, not a qualitative, way.[22] Normal, healthy persons all harbor some sort of anti-social feelings; the psychopathic defendant,

---

[15] ILL. ANN. STAT. ch. 38, para. 6-2 (Smith-Hurd 1989), 1961 Committee Comments, at 304 (revised 1972).

[16] ILL. ANN. STAT. ch. 38, para. 6-2 (Smith-Hurd 1989), 1961 Committee Comments, at 304 (revised 1972).

[17] ILL. ANN. STAT. ch. 38, para. 6-2 (Smith-Hurd 1989), 1961 Committee Comments, at 304 (revised 1972).

[18] ILL. REV. STAT. ch. 38, para. 6-2 (Smith-Hurd 1989), 1961 Committee Comments, at 303 (revised 1972).

[19] ILL. ANN. STAT. ch. 38, para. 6-2 (Smith-Hurd 1989), 1961 Committee Comments, at 304 (revised 1972).

[20] ILL. ANN. STAT. ch. 38, para. 6-2 (Smith-Hurd 1989), 1961 Committee Comments, at 304 (revised 1972).

[21] *See* 720 ILCS 5/6-2(b) (1999) (mental disease or defect does "not include an abnormality manifested only by repeated or otherwise antisocial conduct").

[22] ILL. REV. STAT. ch. 38, para. 6-2 (Smith-Hurd 1989), 1961 Committee Comments, at 304 (revised 1972).

simply has *more* asocial feelings and *acts* on those feelings when he or she performs a criminal act. Since the psychopathic personality is not one that lacks substantial capacity either to appreciate or conform, it was excluded from the insanity plea enacted in 1961.[23] In other words, it was recognized that a defendant who lacks the substantial capacity either to appreciate or conform might *also* be psychopathic, but it would be the lack of ability to appreciate or conform that would make for a successful insanity defense — not the "psychopathic" classification.

Legislative skepticism about the integrity of the insanity defense has been the basis of significant departures from the insanity defense enacted in 1961. One such change arose from the 1981 codification of the concept of "guilty but mentally ill," which will be discussed later.[24] In 1984, the Illinois General Assembly raised the burden of proof necessary for a successful insanity defense[25] to a "preponderance of the evidence."[26] This 1984 change was very significant. Under pre-1984 caselaw, where the evidence raised a reasonable doubt of the defendant's sanity, which rebutted the legal presumption that the defendant was sane, the state was thereafter required to introduce evidence which established beyond a reasonable doubt that the defendant was sane.[27] The 1984 law stated that government bore the burden of *initially* establishing a defendant's guilt beyond a reasonable doubt and *thereafter* the *defendant* bears the burden of proving defendant's insanity, leaving "no corresponding requirement that the prosecution disprove that claim, by any quantum of proof."[28]

In 1995, the Illinois legislature again amended the insanity statute and raised the accused's proof necessary to be acquitted by reason of insanity to "clear and convincing" evidence.[29] However, in 1998, the Public Act containing the 1995 amendment was found to be unconstitutional because it violated the single subject rule of the Illinois Constitution.[30] Later that same year, a new Public Act

---

[23] ILL. ANN. STAT. ch. 38, para. 6-2 (Smith-Hurd 1989), 1961 Committee Comments, at 304 (revised 1972).

[24] *See* ILL. REV. STAT. ch. 38, para. 6-2(c) (1981) (a person who is not insane may nevertheless be "guilty but mentally ill").

[25] However, the defense of insanity was not treated like any other "affirmative defense," (*e.g.*, defense of person) namely, that only "some evidence" had to be offered to raise such defense. *See generally* 720 ILCS 5/6 (1999). Rather, the defendant had to present evidence which raised a reasonable doubt about his or her sanity. People v. Redmond, 59 Ill. 2d 328, 337, 320 N.E.2d 321, 326 (1974) (rejecting defense argument that defendant only required to offer "some evidence" of insanity). After the defendant offered such evidence, the State had the burden of proving sanity beyond a reasonable doubt. People v. Smothers, 55 Ill. 2d 172, 174, 302 N.E.2d 324, 326 (1973).

[26] 720 ILCS 5/6-2(e) (1993).

[27] People v. Redmond, 59 Ill. 2d 328, 336, 320 N.E.2d 321, 326 (1974).

[28] People v. Seuffer, 144 Ill. 2d 482, 518, 582 N.E.2d 71, 86 (1991).

[29] Pub. Act 89-404 (1995). *See* 720 ILCS 5/6-2(e) (1995).

[30] People v. Reedy, 295 Ill. App. 3d 34, 41, 692 N.E.2d 376, 383 (2d Dist. 1998) (citing Ill. Const. 1970, art. IV, § 8(d)) (permits no more than one subject matter per legislative enactment), *aff'd*, 186 Ill. 2d 1, 708 N.E.2d 1114 (1999).

was approved by the legislature that reenacted the "clear and convincing evidence" standard of the insanity defense consistent with the 1995 statute but in a legislative manner that would avoid single subject rule problems.[31]

The most critical development regarding the insanity defense came in 1995 when the Illinois legislature amended the Illinois insanity defense in an effort to abolish the volitional prong of the defense. Specifically, they removed the portion of the defense which referred to an accused's inability "to conform his conduct to the requirements of law."[32] However, in 1998 this provision was found unconstitutional in that it too violated the single subject rule of the Illinois Constitution.[33] However, the Illinois legislature in 1998 reenacted the statute designed to abolish the volitional prong of the insanity defense.[34] Thus, while the insanity defense has undergone a tremendous amount of turmoil in the past decade, the current law as codified in the code does not allow an insanity defense to be brought from evidence that a defendant cannot conform his conduct to the requirements of the law. A valid defense must rest solely upon the cognitive prong of the statute, where an accused must prove that due to mental disease he did not appreciate the criminality of his conduct.

In the meantime, another significant aspect of the Illinois insanity legislation was placed in question. The "guilty but mentally ill" provisions in the code were found unconstitutional in 1997 on the theory that they encourage "compromise verdicts in violation of due process."[35] However, the Illinois Supreme Court reversed the appellate opinion in 1999 and found that a "guilty but mentally ill" verdict was constitutional.[36]

§ 18.03. Defense of Insanity Codified.

The Illinois insanity defense is codified in section 5/6-2 of the Criminal Code. It reads:

> (a) A person is not criminally responsible for conduct if at the time of such conduct, as a result of mental disease or mental defect, he lacks substantial capacity to appreciate the criminality of his conduct.

---

[31] Pub. Act 90-593 (1998). *See* 720 ILCS 5/6-2(e) (1999). It should be noted that a defendant who committed an offense before the burden of proof standard was raised from the "preponderance" test to the "clear and convincing" test must be tried under the earlier test. People v. Gill, 304 Ill. App. 3d 23, 28-36, 713 N.E.2d 124, 127-28 (1st Dist. 1999) (application of amended statute retroactively violated ex post facto clause of federal and state constitutions).

[32] Pub. Act 89-404 (1995).

[33] People v. Reedy, 295 Ill. App. 3d 34, 41, 692 N.E.2d 376, 383 (2d Dist. 1998) (citing Ill. Const. 1970, art. IV, § 8(d) permits no more than one subject matter per legislative enactment), *aff'd*, 186 Ill. 2d 1, 708 N.E.2d 1114 (1999)).

[34] Pub. Act 90-593 (1998). *See* 720 ILCS 5/6-2(a) (1999).

[35] People v. Robles, 288 Ill. App. 3d 935, 952, 682 N.E.2d 194, 205 (2d Dist. 1997), *rev'd sub. nom.* People v. Lantz, 186 Ill. 2d 243, 712 N.E.2d 314 (1999).

[36] People v. Lantz, 186 Ill. 2d 243, 254-59, 712 N.E.2d 314, 320-22 (1999).

(b) The terms "mental disease or mental defect" do not include an abnormality manifested only by repeated criminal or otherwise antisocial conduct.

(c) A person who, at the time of the commission of a criminal offense, was not insane but was suffering from a mental illness, is not relieved of criminal responsibility for his conduct and may be found guilty but mentally ill.

(d) For purposes of this Section, "mental illness" or "mentally ill" means a substantial disorder of thought, mood or behavior which afflicted a person at the time of the commission of the offense and which impaired that person's judgment, but not to the extent that he is unable to appreciate the wrongfulness of his behavior.

(e) When the defense of insanity has been presented during the trial, the burden of proof is on the defendant to prove by clear and convincing evidence that the defendant is not guilty by reason of insanity. However, the burden of proof remains on the State to prove beyond a reasonable doubt each of the elements of each of the offenses charged, and, in a jury trial where the insanity defense has been presented, the jury must be instructed that it may not consider whether the defendant has met his burden of proving that he is not guilty by reason of insanity until and unless it has first determined that the State has proven the defendant guilty beyond a reasonable doubt of the offense with which he is charged.[37]

An examination of the respective subsections reveals that subsection (a) sets out the basic requirements of the insanity defense; subsection (b) specifically deletes psychopathic disorders from the reach of this defense; subsection (c) states that a verdict of "guilty but mentally ill," which will be discussed in detail below, can be imposed in certain circumstances; subsection (d) defines the type of mental disorder that can be the basis of a "guilty but mentally ill" verdict; and subsection (e) addresses the burden of proof problems associated with this defense.

§ 18.04. Elements of Insanity Defense.

The defense of insanity involves various essential elements. An accused will be exonerated if (1) at the time of the alleged criminal conduct, (2) as a result of mental disease or mental defect, (3) the accused lacks substantial capacity (4) to appreciate the criminality of his or her conduct. As previously mentioned, the current law reshaped the insanity defense by eliminating a possible avenue of the defense, namely, a defendant can no longer provide evidence that he could not conform his conduct to the requirements of the law at the time of the offense. Because this change is very recent, the law surrounding the now extinct

---

[37] 720 ILCS 5/6-2 (1999).

volitional arm of the insanity defense will still be explored. In order to examine these elements in a coherent manner, each of them will be studied in the order in which they appear in the statute. Since the courts use the terms *mental disease* and *mental defect* interchangeably, the discussion that follows will do so as well, unless otherwise noted.

§ 18.05.   — At Time of Criminal Conduct.

The insanity defense is available only to exculpate a defendant of criminal responsibility *if at the time of his or her criminal conduct*, he or she lacked the substantial capacity to appreciate his or her criminality. In *People v. Dunigan*,[38] the court definitively stated that "[t]he insanity of a person either before or after the commission of a crime cannot excuse the crime; only insanity existing at the very time of the crime can excuse the same."[39] Accordingly, where the defense counsel at trial directed questions to the accused concerning what conduct the accused thought is wrong for people to do, what the accused saw himself doing in the future, how much is nine times eight, and similar questions, prosecutorial objections to these questions were sustained as irrelevant, since they raised questions about the accused's mental condition at the time of the trial, not at the time of the criminal occurrence.[40]

Although only the insanity existing at the time of the commission of the crime will serve to relieve the defendant of criminal responsibility, the court may allow testimony on the defendant's post-arrest mental condition. The rationale for allowing this type of testimony is that "post-arrest symptoms . . . are relevant in evaluating defendant's mental condition at the time of the offense."[41] It is noteworthy, however, that the appellate court that made the statement quoted above never embellished this statement with any explanation of how post-arrest symptoms are relevant in determining the defendant's mental condition at the time of the crime. One can only conjecture that the court was assuming that if the defendant is, for instance, psychotic immediately after his or her arrest, he or she was also psychotic at the time of the commission of the crime, or if he or she was not psychotic after arrest, he or she was not psychotic at the time of the offense. This is, to say the least, a tenuous proposition, since the course of the most common psychosis, schizophrenia, is extremely variable. On the other hand, since there may not have been any witnesses to the alleged criminal con-

---

[38] 96 Ill. App. 3d 799, 421 N.E.2d 1319 (1st Dist. 1981).

[39] People v. Dunigan, 96 Ill. App. 3d 799, 820, 421 N.E.2d 1319, 1335 (1st Dist. 1981). *See also* People v. Count, 106 Ill. App. 2d 258, 264, 246 N.E.2d 91, 94 (1st Dist. 1969) (upholding jury instruction which read that only insanity existing at "very time of the crime can excuse the same").

[40] People v. Ward, 19 Ill. App. 3d 833, 839-40, 313 N.E.2d 314, 319-20 (1st Dist. 1974), *aff'd*, 61 Ill. 2d 559, 338 N.E.2d 171 (1975).

[41] People v. Taylor, 110 Ill. App. 3d 112, 119, 441 N.E.2d 1231, 1235 (1st Dist. 1982).

duct, much less a psychiatrist studying the defendant at the time of the occurrence in question, the courts are generally willing to extrapolate from the post-arrest observation of the accused about his or her condition at the time of the offense.[42]

Of course, the reliability of post-arrest symptoms as a useful tool to shed light on the defendant's mental condition at the time of the crime, which may be somewhat questionable in any event, progressively diminishes as the time between the commission of the crime and the symptoms under scrutiny increases. For example, the defendant's observed state of hysteria immediately after the commission of the crime would be a more reliable gauge of his or her mental condition at the time of the crime than would be an observed state of hysteria one year after the crime.

Since the insanity defense focuses on the mental condition of the defendant at the time of the crime, a finding of not guilty by reason of insanity regarding offenses that transpired at one point will not be dispositive concerning the defendant's state of mind when other crimes were committed by him or her at another point. Thus, where a defendant was acquitted on May 15, 1969, for certain offenses perpetrated on May 21, 1967, this did not mean he was insane at the time of his attempted escape from custody on January 15, 1968.[43] Likewise, where the defendant was charged with a series of sex crimes arising out of his incestuous relations with his son and daughter, merely because he was acquitted by reason of insanity on charges allegedly occurring on December 31, 1983; January 1, 1984; and January 22, 1984, did not necessarily mean he was insane on December 2, 1983; February 6, 1984; or February 7, 1984.[44]

Where a defendant is determined by a jury to be incompetent to stand trial because he was unable to cooperate with counsel and conduct his defense in a rational and reasonable manner, this does not mean per se that he was also insane on the date of his or her alleged criminality and should therefore be excused of criminal responsibility for it.[45] Thus, where a defendant committed an attempted murder on October 10, 1966, was found unfit to stand trial on February 27,

---

[42] *See, e.g.,* People v. Williams, 265 Ill. App. 3d 283, 289, 638 N.E.2d 345, 349-50 (1st Dist. 1994) (defendant did not establish insanity beyond a preponderance of the evidence where a 911 call taped immediately after defendant shot victim indicated that he was fully aware of the act he just committed); People v. Bradley, 220 Ill. App. 3d 890, 904, 581 N.E.2d 310, 319 (1st Dist. 1991) (testimony of police officers that the "defendant appeared normal shortly after the crime" was determinative evidence of sanity);

[43] People v. Hinton, 11 Ill. App. 3d 907, 908, 297 N.E.2d 681, 681-82 (1st Dist. 1973). *See also* People v. Seawright, 73 Ill. App. 2d 426, 429, 220 N.E.2d 101, 102 (1st Dist. 1966) (although a jury found defendant insane for a crime committed in September, this did not preclude a different jury from finding defendant guilty and sane for a crime committed two months prior, in July).

[44] People v. Fosdick, 166 Ill. App. 3d 491, 497, 519 N.E.2d 1102, 1107 (1st Dist. 1988) (convictions for rape, deviant sexual assault, and child pornography affirmed).

[45] People v. Britton, 119 Ill. App. 2d 110, 113, 255 N.E.2d 211, 213 (4th Dist. 1970).

1967, was institutionalized and then discharged the following July, the incompetence finding in February did not necessarily mean defendant was insane the preceding October.[46] Conversely, a finding of competence to stand trial does not stop the defendant from asserting that he or she was insane at the time of the crime.[47] Indeed, fitness to stand trial, to enter a plea, or to be sentenced[48] are concerns separate and apart from the accused's mental state at the time of the commission of the crime.[49]

The Illinois Supreme Court has held that the insanity defense is not available to a probationer in a probation revocation proceeding.[50] Where a probationer violated the terms of her probation and claimed the defense of insanity in a probation revocation proceeding on the theory that she was unable to control her behavior, the trial judge received into the record psychiatric testimony indicative of insanity at the time of the violation of probation but then ruled insanity could not be raised in such a proceeding.[51] The Illinois Supreme Court in defendant's appeal examined the Illinois statutes as written at the time which discussed the defense of insanity,[52] the required proceedings after acquittal by reason of insanity[53] and the required procedures for revocation of probation,[54] and concluded that the legislature did not intend that the insanity defense apply in proceedings where guilt, innocence, or criminal responsibility were not at issue.[55] Since a probationer in a probation revocating hearing has already been convicted and the issue in such a proceeding is whether the probationer's continued presence in society poses a threat to the public, the court concluded the use of the insanity defense in such proceeding would be against the implied intent of the legislature.[56]

---

[46] People v. Britton, 119 Ill. App. 2d 110, 113, 255 N.E.2d 211, 213 (4th Dist. 1970).

[47] People v. Carter, 84 Ill. App. 2d 135, 141 n.4, 228 N.E.2d 522, 525 n.4 (1st Dist. 1967).

[48] 725 ILCS 5/104-10 (1999) ("A defendant is unfit if, because of his mental . . . condition, he is unable to understand the nature and purpose of the proceedings against him or assist in his defense").

[49] See People v. Foster, 56 Ill. App. 3d 22, 37-38, 371 N.E.2d 961, 974 (1st Dist. 1977) (trial, adjudication of guilt, sentence, or execution of incompetent person violates due process); rev'd on other grounds, 76 Ill. 2d 365, 392 N.E.2d 6 (1979). Compare People v. Allegri, 109 Ill. 2d 309, 313, 487 N.E.2d 606, 607-08 (1985) (insanity can not be raised as defense in probation revocation proceeding since non-culpable conduct can form basis of revocation of probation).

[50] People v. Allegri, 109 Ill. 2d 309, 314-17, 487 N.E.2d 606, 608-09 (1985).

[51] People v. Allegri, 109 Ill. 2d 309, 313, 487 N.E.2d 606, 606-07 (1985).

[52] ILL. REV. STAT. ch. 38, para. 5/6-2(a) (1984) (insanity can arise where defendant unable to conform his conduct as required by law). The insanity statute has since been modified. See 720 ILCS 5/6-2 (1999) (defendant's inability to "appreciate" criminality of his conduct is only basis for finding insanity).

[53] ILL. REV. STAT. ch. 38, para. 5/5-2-4 (1984) (procedures for treating defendants found insane).

[54] ILL. REV. STAT. ch. 38, para. 5/5-6-2(c) (1984) (procedures for revoking probation).

[55] People v. Allegri, 109 Ill. 2d 309, 312-15, 487 N.E.2d 606, 607-08 (1985).

[56] People v. Allegri, 109 Ill. 2d 309, 315-16, 487 N.E.2d 606, 608-09 (1985).

§ 18.06. — As Result of Mental Disease or Defect.

Neither the statute nor the Committee Comments define what constitutes a *mental disease* or *mental defect*.[57] The statute does, however, narrow the scope of possible definitions by way of exclusion. Subsection (b) of the statute and the Committee Comments specifically exclude psychopathic personality disorders from the purview of mental disease and mental defect.[58]

The courts have not only refrained from developing a viable legal concept of what constitutes a mental disease or mental defect but have also demonstrated reluctance in defining these concepts even in medical terms.[59] The courts fear that expert testimony will replace the role of the jury in determining the issue of insanity.[60] One appellate opinion observed: "'[T]his reluctance may also come from the apprehension that strictly medical nomenclature may in fact be anchored upon shifting sands.'"[61] As a result, "courts have held that classifications of mental disease or defect developed by psychiatrists for the purpose of treatment need not control the legal definition used for assessing criminal responsibility."[62]

This reluctance to defer to medical expertise and medical definitions has carried over to evidentiary questions as well. Thus, where the defense presented two psychiatrists who stated that the defendant was insane, and the state's evidence on sanity rested on the lay opinion of a police officer, the defendant's conviction was nonetheless upheld.[63] Clearly, the trier of fact is not obligated to

---

[57] People v. Kapsalis, 186 Ill. App. 3d 96, 105-06, 541 N.E.2d 1323, 1328 (1st Dist. 1989) (insanity statute not violative of due process for failing to define "mental disease or mental defect").

[58] 720 ILCS 5/6-2 (1999); ILL. ANN. STAT. ch. 38, § 6-2 (Smith-Hurd 1989), 1961 Committee Comments, at 304 (revised 1972).

[59] People v. Uppole, 97 Ill. App. 3d 72, 78, 422 N.E.2d 245, 249 (3d Dist. 1981).

[60] People v. Uppole, 97 Ill. App. 3d 72, 78, 422 N.E.2d 245, 249 (3d Dist. 1981).

[61] People v. Uppole, 97 Ill. App. 3d 72, 78, 422 N.E.2d 245, 249 (3d Dist. 1981). It is interesting to note, for instance, that for years homosexuality was designated by the American Psychiatric Association (APA) as a type of personality disorder. *See* AMERICAN PSYCHIATRIC ASSOCIATION, DSM-II: DIAGNOSTIC AND STATISTICAL MANUAL OF MENTAL DISORDERS 23 (2d ed. 1968). However, in 1973 homosexuality was removed from this list by the American Psychiatric Association. *See* Editorial Note: *Changes in Nomenclature with Regard to Homosexuality* in READINGS IN LAW AND PSYCHIATRY 71 (Richard C. Allen *et al.* eds., rev. ed. 1975).

Similarly, there is considerable difference of opinion as to whether persons who engage in the profession of prostitution are generally attracted to such business because they suffer from some type of mental disorder. *See* JOHN F. DECKER, PROSTITUTION: REGULATION AND CONTROL 307-16 (1979).

As one author stated: "We have . . . come to regard phobias, delinquencies, divorce, homicide, addiction and so on almost without limit as psychiatric illnesses. This is a colossal and costly mistake." THOMAS SZASZ, THE MYTH OF MENTAL ILLNESS 43 (paperback ed. 1961).

[62] People v. Uppole, 97 Ill. App. 3d 72, 78, 422 N.E.2d 245, 249 (3d Dist. 1981).

[63] People v. Banks, 17 Ill. App. 3d 746, 753-55, 308 N.E.2d 261, 267-69 (1st Dist. 1974).

accept the ultimate opinion of experts.[64] As stated in *People v. Meeker*,[65] legal and medical concepts of insanity will not always correspond: "We find the evidence amply supported the jury's conclusion that defendant was [legally] sane at the time of the instant offense . . . [although] [d]efendant was certainly insane in a medical sense when he set the church fire."[66] Significantly, the Illinois appellate court, in *People v. Bradley*,[67] found that if the testimony of expert witnesses on the issue of insanity is directly contradictory, courts will allow the jury to "reject *all* expert testimony. . . ."[68] The court held that in such cases lay observations, if they are based on events that occurred shortly before or after the crime was committed, are "especially relevant . . . ."[69]

One authority has stated that a mental disease or defect *may* suffice for purposes of legal insanity if three conditions are satisfied: (1) the offender must have suffered from a medically recognized disorder at the time of the crime; (2) the symptoms of the disorder must have included manifestations apart from the conduct designated criminal; and (3) the condition must have been "severe enough to distinguish the actor as abnormal in the eyes of the community."[70] Although these factors have not been adopted by a court of law as determinative of whether legal insanity has been proven, they provide a useful reference point in evaluating the Illinois law dealing with the insanity defense.

§ 18.07.   —— Medically Accepted Mental Illness.

Concerning the first of these requirements, the legal community relies on the medical terminology of the psychiatrist to assess whether a medically accepted mental illness rendered a defendant legally insane.[71] Illness or impairment of the

---

[64] People v. Banks, 17 Ill. App. 3d 746, 755, 308 N.E.2d 261, 268 (1st Dist. 1974). *See also* People v. Ware, 88 Ill. App. 3d 115, 119, 410 N.E.2d 357, 360 (1st Dist. 1980) (trial court's reliance on lay testimony over defense psychiatrist testimony proper); People v. Dominique, 86 Ill. App. 3d 794, 808, 408 N.E.2d 280, 291 (1st Dist. 1980) (jury properly rejected opinion of defense psychiatrist); People v. Romaine, 79 Ill. App. 3d 1089, 1096, 399 N.E.2d 319, 325 (3d Dist. 1979) (jury is not required to accept psychiatrists' conclusion and may accept lay testimony over defense expert testimony).

[65] 86 Ill. App. 3d 162, 407 N.E.2d 1058 (5th Dist. 1980).

[66] People v. Meeker, 86 Ill. App. 3d 162, 168, 407 N.E.2d 1058, 1064 (5th Dist. 1980). *See also* People v. Hood, 203 Ill. App. 3d 289, 299, 560 N.E.2d 1187, 1194 (1st Dist. 1990) (jury's verdict of guilty but mentally ill, rather than not guilty by reason of insanity, was upheld despite the fact that only one out of five testifying doctors found defendant sane).

[67] 220 Ill. App. 3d 890, 581 N.E.2d 310 (1st Dist. 1991).

[68] People v. Bradley, 220 Ill. App. 3d 890, 904, 581 N.E.2d 310, 319 (1st Dist. 1991) (emphasis added). *See also* People v. Gacy, 103 Ill. 2d 1, 68-69, 468 N.E.2d 1171, 1199 (1984) (fact that all defense experts arrived at consistent diagnosis while the state's experts did not did not undermine the jury's finding of sanity), *cert. denied*, 470 U.S. 1037 (1985).

[69] People v. Bradley, 220 Ill. App. 3d 890, 904, 581 N.E.2d 310, 319 (1st Dist. 1991).

[70] 2 PAUL ROBINSON, CRIMINAL LAW DEFENSES § 173(b)(1) (1984).

[71] ANDRE MOENSSENS ET AL., SCIENTIFIC EVIDENCE IN CIVIL AND CRIMINAL CASES 1083 (4th ed. 1995).

mind is medically defined by constantly changing diagnostic labels.[72] The American Psychiatric Association classifies mental disorders and publishes a Diagnostic and Statistical Manual of Mental Disorders, the current version of which is DSM-IV.[73] The DSM is one of the most comprehensive and thorough listing of medically accepted mental illnesses. A wide range of mental disorders are categorized in DSM-IV, such as cognitive disorders, substance-related disorders, mood disorders, anxiety disorders, personality disorders, and psychotic disorders.[74] In the instance of psychotic disorders, DSM-IV characterizes the symptoms as hallucinations and schizophrenic actions (i.e. disorganized speech, grossly disorganized or catatonic behavior).[75] It is not surprising, then, that Illinois caselaw contains the statement that "psychosis would qualify as a mental disease or defect. . . ."[76]

Potentially broadening the term *psychosis* to reflect recent developments in the medical community, the court in *People v. Wilhoite*[77] recognized that such a mental illness may be of short duration.[78] In *Wilhoite*, the court held that psychosis may be determined by specific reference to scholarly authority, such as the DSM-III-R (which was replaced by DSM-IV).[79] The DSM-III-R manual provided that "brief reactive psychosis" may occur in response to events which are markedly stressful,[80] and that such psychosis may only last "a few hours."[81]

At the other end of the spectrum of medically recognized disorders are "personality disorders."[82] These include disorders such as the "paranoid," "borderline," "obsessive-compulsive," and "antisocial" personalities.[83] A personality

---

[72] ANDRE MOENSSENS ET AL., SCIENTIFIC EVIDENCE IN CIVIL AND CRIMINAL CASES 1083 (4th ed. 1995).

[73] DIAGNOSTIC AND STATISTICAL MANUAL OF MENTAL DISORDERS (4th ed. 1994) (hereinafter DSM-IV). DSM-IV was published as part of an ongoing process to maintain consistent, clear and conceptually accurate diagnostic criteria for mental disorders. DSM-IV at xviii.

[74] *See generally* DSM-IV.

[75] DSM-IV at 273.

[76] People v. Kuhn, 68 Ill. App. 3d 59, 64, 385 N.E.2d 388, 391 (3d Dist. 1979) (although this was not defendant's diagnosis; insanity claim rejected).

[77] 228 Ill. App. 3d 12, 592 N.E.2d 48 (1st Dist. 1991).

[78] People v. Wilhoite, 228 Ill. App. 3d 12, 24, 592 N.E.2d 48, 56 (1st Dist. 1991).

[79] People v. Wilhoite, 228 Ill. App. 3d 12, 23, 592 N.E.2d 48, 55 (1st Dist. 1991) (citing DIAGNOSTIC AND STATISTICAL MANUAL OF MENTAL DISORDERS (3d ed., rev. 1987) (hereinafter DSM-III-R)). The American Psychiatric Association has since updated its Manual in DSM-IV. Appendix D of DSM-IV provides an annotated listing of DSM-III-R and corresponding DSM-IV categories, noting changes in mental disorder classification and criteria between the two manuals. *See* DSM-IV at 773.

[80] People v. Wilhoite, 228 Ill. App. 3d 12, 24, 592 N.E.2d 48, 56 (1st Dist. 1991) (citing DSM-III-R at 205).

[81] People v. Wilhoite, 228 Ill. App. 3d 12, 24, 592 N.E.2d 48, 56 (1st Dist. 1991) (citing DSM-III-R at 205).

[82] 2 PAUL ROBINSON, CRIMINAL LAW DEFENSES § 173(b)(2) (1984) (citing AMERICAN PSYCHIATRIC ASSOCIATION DSM-III: STATISTICAL MANUAL OF MENTAL DISORDERS (3d ed. 1980) (hereinafter referred to as DSM-III).

[83] DSM-IV at 629.

disorder can be evidenced by an inability of the person to adjust to the world around and to conform to prevailing social norms.[84] Although recognized by the psychiatric community, this disorder is the least likely to be accepted in the legal community as a basis for a finding of insanity.[85] The 5/6-2(b) exclusion of the "abnormality manifested only by repeated criminal or otherwise antisocial conduct"[86] is the most obvious example of a medically recognized disorder that is rejected in legal circles.[87] Consistent therewith, Illinois caselaw has ignored the problems of the "psychopath,"[88] the "sociopath,"[89] the "anti-social personality,"[90] and those suffering from "personality disorders" generally.[91]

More difficult to assess from a legal perspective of insanity are those mental diseases and mental defects that are recognized by the medical community and are not explicitly excluded from the insanity defense. These include what have been described as "affective disorders,"[92] "organic mental disorders,"[93] and "anxiety disorders."[94]

---

[84] DSM-IV at 630.

[85] *See* 2 PAUL ROBINSON, CRIMINAL LAW DEFENSES § 173(b)(2) (1984) for a discussion of this point and legal psychiatric criticisms of the MODEL PENAL CODE's exclusion of these personalities from the reach of the insanity defense.

[86] 720 ILCS 5/6-2(b) (1999).

[87] *See* 2 PAUL ROBINSON, CRIMINAL LAW DEFENSES § 173(b)(2) (1984).

[88] *See, e.g.*, People v. Uppole, 97 Ill. App. 3d 72, 78, 422 N.E.2d 245, 249 (3d Dist. 1981) (psychopathic behavior excluded from Illinois definition of insanity). *See also* MODEL PENAL CODE § 4.01, comment at 160 (Tentative Draft No. 4., 1955) ("the diagnosis of psychopathic personality does not carry with it any explanation of the causes of the abnormality").

[89] *See, e.g.*, People v. Smothers, 2 Ill. App. 3d 513, 521, 276 N.E.2d 427, 432 (4th Dist. 1971) ("A sociopath is defined as one whose antisocial behavior is undertaken with an awareness of reality and understanding of the significance of his acts"), *aff'd*, 55 Ill. 2d 172, 302 N.E.2d 324 (1973). *Compare* People v. Fierer, 124 Ill. 2d 176, 192, 529 N.E.2d 972, 978 (1988) ("sociopath" jury instruction, which directs jury to dismiss "sociopath" condition as basis for insanity, should only be given where the defendant has a history of "repeated" criminal or other antisocial conduct; instruction in instant case was error).

[90] *See, e.g.*, People v. McClellan, 46 Ill. App. 3d 584, 586, 360 N.E.2d 1225, 1227 (4th Dist. 1977).

[91] People v. Williams, 38 Ill. 2d 115, 123, 230 N.E.2d 224, 229 (1967) (personality disorders are not mental disease within meaning of statute concerned); People v. Lono, 11 Ill. App. 3d 443, 449, 297 N.E.2d 349, 354 (1st Dist. 1993) (same).

[92] DSM-III at 101. This diagnostic class in now called "mood disorders." DSM-IV at 317.

[93] DSM-III at 305; DSM-III-R at 97. DSM-IV states:

> The term *organic mental disorder* is no longer used in DSM-IV because it incorrectly implies that "nonorganic" mental disorders do not have a biological basis. In DSM-IV, disorders formerly called "organic mental disorders" have been grouped into three sections: 1) Delirium, Dementia, and Amnestic and Other Cognitive Disorders; 2) Mental Disorders Due to a General Medical Condition; and 3) Substance-Related Disorders.

DSM-IV at 123.

[94] DSM-IV at 393.

Patients with organic mental disorders or affective disorders suffer severe impairment of mental functions. Hallucinations, delusions, and severe alterations of mood are characteristic symptoms. Patients with anxiety disorders, in contrast, are aware of the impairment of their mental functioning. Hallucinations may accompany conversion disorders, which are induced in anxiety disorders, but anxiety remains the chief characteristic of this class.[95]

The most demonstrable disorders, of course, are those of organic origin. Mental retardation, which can range from borderline to profound, is often congenital in that it results from arrested development of the brain.[96] Organic brain syndromes can be associated with psychosis traceable to senility where there is hardening of the blood vessels supplying the brain with oxygen.[97] Syphilis of the nervous system is also an organic brain disorder that involves the degeneration of the nerve cells of the brain and spinal cord, with a resultant loss of mental power.[98] Epilepsy and encephalitis (sleeping sickness) are also considered organic brain disorders.[99]

There are also psychosis problems that are apparently not traceable to any identifiable physical defect or chemical change in the brain that are considered "functional" mental diseases.[100] The functional mental illness "is considered the result of a complex interplay of instinctual, acquired and environmental forces which intersect with the adaptive and defensive forces of the subconscious mind."[101] For instance, the schizophrenic functional psychosis involves an "inability to conceive reality, to build relationships or to fashion concepts."[102] Delusions, hallucinations, and a loss of interest in human relations are common. A second major subcategory of the functional psychoses is the "affective" psychosis, which includes the manic-depressive state of mind, which is evidenced by mood swings, illusions, delusions, and hallucinations.[103] A third subcategory of the functional psychosis is the paranoid state.[104]

Another major category of mental illness is the "neuroses," the chief symptom of which is anxiety that is "the result of the individual's attempt to resolve unconscious emotional conflicts in a manner which handicaps the achievement of

---

[95] 2 PAUL ROBINSON, CRIMINAL LAW DEFENSES § 173(b)(3) (1984).

[96] ANDRE MOENSSENS ET AL., SCIENTIFIC EVIDENCE IN CRIMINAL CASES 1088 (4th ed. 1995).

[97] ANDRE MOENSSENS ET AL., SCIENTIFIC EVIDENCE IN CRIMINAL CASES 1088 (4th ed. 1995).

[98] ANDRE MOENSSENS ET AL., SCIENTIFIC EVIDENCE IN CRIMINAL CASES 1088 (4th ed. 1995).

[99] ANDRE MOENSSENS ET AL., SCIENTIFIC EVIDENCE IN CRIMINAL CASES 1089 (4th ed. 1995).

[100] ANDRE MOENSSENS ET AL., SCIENTIFIC EVIDENCE IN CRIMINAL CASES 1089 (4th ed. 1995).

[101] ANDRE MOENSSENS ET AL., SCIENTIFIC EVIDENCE IN CRIMINAL CASES 1089 (4th ed. 1995).

[102] ANDRE MOENSSENS ET AL., SCIENTIFIC EVIDENCE IN CRIMINAL CASES 1089 (4th ed. 1995).

[103] ANDRE MOENSSENS ET AL., SCIENTIFIC EVIDENCE IN CRIMINAL CASES 1089 (4th ed. 1995).

[104] ANDRE MOENSSENS ET AL., SCIENTIFIC EVIDENCE IN CRIMINAL CASES 1089 (4th ed. 1995).

normal living patterns."[105] Unlike the normal person who may periodically exhibit feelings of anxiety, the neurotic person displays a constant or recurrent maladjustment in this regard.[106]

A determination that the accused suffers from "organic" mental illness is of no value unless the mental illness undermines the defendant's capacity to appreciate the criminality of his or her conduct. For instance, in a number of cases, it has been held that evidence of mental retardation is not necessarily sufficient to establish legal insanity.[107] Evidence that the defendant suffered from syphilis was held insufficient in an early case.[108] Evidence that a defendant suffered from an epileptic condition at the time of the crime was ruled insufficient to acquit by reason of insanity.[109] Evidence of mental impairment caused by alcoholism does not necessarily mean the defendant was insane.[110] Where the evidence revealed that a defendant suffered brain damage in a prior accident, this did not necessarily mean he was less than sane at the time of the crime.[111]

Concerning evidence of functional mental illness claims, these claims are even less likely to lead to a finding of insanity. For instance, where there was evidence that a defendant suffered from paranoid schizophrenia on the day of the crime, this did not preclude a conviction.[112] The lack of organic deficiency poses a problem, for it may prompt the fact finder to state, as did one judge in a bench trial where a psychiatrist had testified about the accused's apparent schizophrenia, that the psychiatric opinion is "conjectural, a theoretical, abstract conclusion based upon certain facts which the person being examined provides the examiner."[113] Thus, merely because there was evidence that the defendant

---

[105] ANDRE MOENSSENS ET AL., SCIENTIFIC EVIDENCE IN CRIMINAL CASES 1089 (4th ed. 1995).

[106] ANDRE MOENSSENS ET AL., SCIENTIFIC EVIDENCE IN CRIMINAL CASES 1089 (4th ed. 1995).

[107] See, e.g., People v. Rockamann, 79 Ill. App. 3d 575, 582-83, 399 N.E.2d 162, 167-68 (5th Dist. 1979) (defendant suffered "borderline" retardation).

[108] People v. Geary, 297 Ill. 608, 615, 131 N.E. 97, 100 (1921) (alcoholism and syphilis).

[109] People v. Felton, 26 Ill. App. 3d 395, 398, 325 N.E.2d 400, 402 (3d Dist. 1975) (although the occurrence of an epileptic seizure would raise a serious doubt regarding the defendant's ability to form a criminal state).

[110] See, e.g., People v. Mask, 34 Ill. App. 3d 668, 674-75, 339 N.E.2d 417, 422 (5th Dist. 1975). See also People v. Free, 94 Ill. 2d 378, 408, 447 N.E.2d 218, 232 (toxic psychosis induced by voluntary consumption of alcohol, drugs, or both, is not a mental disease within definition of insanity), cert. denied, 464 U.S. 865 (1983). Compare People v. Wheeler, 194 Ill. App. 3d 178, 182, 550 N.E.2d 1170, 1173 (1st Dist. 1990) (insanity defense not precluded if habitual or chronic use of drugs or alcohol has resulted in a "permanent type of insanity").

[111] See People v. Jackson, 42 Ill. App. 3d 919, 920-22, 356 N.E.2d 979, 980-82 (1st Dist. 1976). See also People v. Bacon, 293 Ill. 210, 216, 127 N.E. 386, 388 (1920) (evidence of amnesia and blackouts insufficient).

[112] People v. Muskgrove, 44 Ill. App. 3d 381, 386, 358 N.E.2d 336, 340 (3d Dist. 1976). See also People v. DePompeis, 410 Ill. 587, 592, 102 N.E.2d 813, 816 (1951) (the adjudication of mental illness of defendant on a specific date did not place defendant in the status of a legally insane person over two years later), cert. denied, 346 U.S. 904 (1953).

[113] People v. Banks, 17 Ill. App. 3d 746, 756, 308 N.E.2d 261, 269 (1st Dist. 1974).

was hearing "spirits and voices," this was inconclusive of his alleged insanity.[114] The fact that another accused formed unrealistic judgments and was unable to evaluate situations was also found to be insufficient.[115]

A psychiatrist's opinion that the defendant suffered from a paranoid condition is not alone a basis for finding insanity.[116] Where evidence was offered that a defendant had been previously hospitalized for mental problems, that he experienced feelings of depression and loss of memory, that he thought he did not belong to the world, that he felt people were out to get him, and that there was an unusual and offensive odor about his body, the appellate court agreed with the trial court that there was insufficient evidence to *instruct the jury* on insanity.[117]

A "depressive neurosis" had been characterized by one Illinois court as "more closely associated with a personalty disorder than with a mental disease or defect contemplated in section 6-2."[118] Psychiatric evidence of suicidal tendencies was held to have been properly rejected by the trial court as having no bearing on the defendant's insanity claim.[119] Neither "idiosyncratic behavior,"[120] "depravity of character,"[121] nor "abandoned habits"[122] are sufficient to raise the insanity issue.

In conclusion, it is imperative that the insanity claim be based on a mental disease or defect recognized by the medical community, but this recognition is no guarantee that the illness will be accepted as a basis for a finding of legal insanity by a court of law.

§ 18.08.　— — Mental Illness Symptoms Apart From Criminality.

The mental illness not only must be recognized by the medical community if it is to serve as a foundation for an insanity finding in a criminal court, but also it must also satisfy (as a practical matter if not a legal matter) other conditions

---

[114] People v. Redmond, 59 Ill. 2d 328, 338, 320 N.E.2d 321, 327 (1974). *See also* People v. Williams, 201 Ill. App. 3d 207, 216, 558 N.E.2d 1258, 1264 (1st Dist. 1990) (evidence that defendant heard voices prior to killing two 76-year-old women was insufficient to establish insanity). *But see* People v. Garcia, 156 Ill. App. 3d 417, 424, 509 N.E.2d 600, 604 (1st Dist. 1987) (defendant found not guilty by reason of insanity based on his inability to ignore voices commanding him to harm his brother). However, since the *Garcia* court in its reversal relied on defendant's lack of volitional control, no longer a basis for finding insanity, this case may lack precedential value.

[115] People v. Miller, 33 Ill. 2d 439, 443, 211 N.E.2d 708, 711 (1965).

[116] People v. Robinson, 102 Ill. App. 3d 884, 893, 429 N.E.2d 1356, 1363 (1st Dist. 1981).

[117] People v. Rivera, 7 Ill. App. 3d 983, 987, 289 N.E.2d 36, 39 (1st Dist. 1972), *cert. denied*, 412 U.S. 907 (1973).

[118] People v. Uppole, 97 Ill. App. 3d 72, 79-80, 422 N.E.2d 245, 250 (3d Dist. 1981).

[119] People v. Muir, 67 Ill. 2d 86, 95-96, 365 N.E.2d 332, 337 (1977), *cert. denied*, 434 U.S. 986 (1978).

[120] People v. Lono, 11 Ill. App. 3d 443, 449, 297 N.E.2d 349, 354 (1st Dist. 1973); People v. McBride, 130 Ill. App. 2d 201, 207, 264 N.E.2d 446, 450 (1st Dist. 1970).

[121] People v. Lono, 11 Ill. App. 3d 443, 449, 297 N.E.2d 349, 354 (1st Dist. 1973).

[122] People v. Lono, 11 Ill. App. 3d 443, 449, 297 N.E.2d 349, 354 (1st Dist. 1973).

— for example, the illness must include "manifestations apart from" the commission of the crime itself.[123] The Illinois caselaw is replete with statements that the commission of an "atrocious"[124] or even "bizarre"[125] crime is insufficient, without more, to prove the existence of a mental disease or defect required of the insanity defense. This is a mere corollary of the proposition that even repeated criminality is not necessarily evidence of insanity.[126]

In *People v. Ureste*,[127] a defendant was convicted of voluntary manslaughter and attempted murder after a shooting exchange incident in a nightclub. The defendant asserted on appeal that the "irrationality" of the shooting spree in which he was involved demonstrated that there was insufficient evidence about his sanity at the time of the occurrence.[128] However, there were several concerns that prompted the appellate court to affirm defendant's convictions. First, according to a hospital physician who treated the defendant for a gunshot wound sustained in the exchange, he did not exhibit any unusual symptoms.[129] Second, the defendant's employer had testified that the defendant had never "complained of any odd feelings or experiences" and that he "had acted quite normally" before the crime.[130] Finally, a psychiatrist testified that the "hallucinations, voices and other symptoms of disorientation" of which the accused later complained "were subjective" and "*not verifiable* by defendant's previous conduct or history."[131] Quite simply, there existed no documented "*prior history* of mental illness."[132]

However, even where the defense is able to point to such symptoms independent of the crime charged, this is not necessarily a basis for an acquittal. In *People v. Lono*,[133] the defendant was charged with murder after shooting a person on the street for no apparent motive or reason. No expert witness testified at the defendant's bench trial, and no lay witnesses were asked to offer an opinion about the accused's insanity. However, there was *uncontradicted* testimony, almost all of which was offered by various witnesses, with the balance offered by the accused himself, of the defendant's unusual:

---

[123] 2 PAUL ROBINSON, CRIMINAL LAW DEFENSES § 173(b)(1) (1984).

[124] *See, e.g.*, People v. Martinez, 86 Ill. App. 3d 486, 491, 408 N.E.2d 358, 362 (2d Dist. 1980).

[125] *See, e.g.*, People v. Horton, 29 Ill. App. 3d 704, 711, 331 N.E.2d 104, 110 (1st Dist. 1975).

[126] *See, e.g.*, People v. Ward, 61 Ill. 2d 559, 566, 338 N.E.2d 171, 175 (1975).

[127] 7 Ill. App. 3d 545, 288 N.E.2d 45 (3d Dist. 1972).

[128] People v. Ureste, 7 Ill. App. 3d 545, 549, 288 N.E.2d 45, 48 (3d Dist. 1972).

[129] People v. Ureste, 7 Ill. App. 3d 545, 549-50, 288 N.E.2d 45, 49 (3d Dist. 1972).

[130] People v. Ureste, 7 Ill. App. 3d 545, 550, 288 N.E.2d 45, 49 (3d Dist. 1972).

[131] People v. Ureste, 7 Ill. App. 3d 545, 550, 288 N.E.2d 45, 48 (3d Dist. 1972) (emphasis added).

[132] People v. Ureste, 7 Ill. App. 3d 545, 550, 288 N.E.2d 45, 48 (3d Dist. 1972) (emphasis added).

[133] 11 Ill. App. 3d 443, 297 N.E.2d 349 (1st Dist. 1973).

behavior prior to the day of the crime and to his conduct on that day: his head injuries [including an earlier concussion for which he was hospitalized two weeks], talking to himself, periods of depression and frustration, memory loss, irrational ideas about flying out a window and grandiose schemes of becoming an astronaut and a world traveller; his kicking his feet and waving his arms, his incoherent mumblings, his killing a man without motive or reason, his returning to the scene of the offense [as a crowd gathered] and being chased by [small] children, his not remembering firing the gun, working, or the other things he did on the day of the crime.[134]

At the close of the evidence, the trial judge "said that he did not believe there had been a real attempt to raise the issue of insanity and that the presumption of sanity had not been overcome. He said there was no real evidence that the defendant had any mental disorder — there was just evidence of bizarre behavior."[135] Following defendant's conviction, the appellate court ruled that "[a]lthough we might disagree with the trial court's opinion that the defendant's evidence did not overcome the presumption of sanity, we cannot disagree with its finding that the defendant was sane at the time of the crime. . . . The evidence presented in his behalf fell far short of establishing a mental disease or mental defect within the statutory definition of insanity."[136]

Where the defendant produces no significant evidence regarding his or her prior psychiatric history, the appellate courts seem inclined to dismiss a defendant's insanity claim.[137] For example, in *People v. Quay*,[138] the defendant was indicted for aggravated battery and resisting a police officer, which allegedly occurred in 1986. Later that year, she was found unfit to stand trial.[139] In a discharge hearing conducted in 1988, the parties stipulated that a psychiatrist had examined the defendant approximately two months after the offenses and was prepared to testify that defendant was insane at the time of the offense.[140] At the discharge hearing, the trial court determined that the defendant was not entitled

---

[134] People v. Lono, 11 Ill. App. 3d 443, 447, 297 N.E.2d 349, 353 (1st Dist. 1973).

[135] People v. Lono, 11 Ill. App. 3d 443, 447, 297 N.E.2d 349, 353 (1st Dist. 1973).

[136] People v. Lono, 11 Ill. App. 3d 443, 448-49, 297 N.E.2d 349, 353-54 (1st Dist. 1973).

[137] People v. Smothers, 55 Ill. 2d 172, 175, 302 N.E.2d 324, 326 (1973) ("Although the evidence shows some irrational or bizarre conduct and some degree of confusion on the part of the defendant at the time of the occurrence . . ., there is no evidence of either prior mental treatment or prior irrational conduct"; insanity instructions properly denied).

[138] 175 Ill. App. 3d 965, 530 N.E.2d 644 (4th Dist. 1988).

[139] People v. Quay, 175 Ill. App. 3d 965, 966, 530 N.E.2d 644, 645 (4th Dist. 1988).

[140] People v. Quay, 175 Ill. App. 3d 965, 966, 530 N.E.2d 644, 645 (4th Dist. 1988). At a discharge hearing, the trial court may acquit the defendant by reason of insanity.

to an acquittal by reason of insanity at the time of the offense.[141] The appellate court affirmed the refusal to discharge, while pointing out that while the psychiatrist was "certain" that the defendant's present mental state made her unfit to stand trial, he indicated "less certainty" about her insanity at the time of the offense and, indeed, had recommended "research of the records of defendant's past mental health care" to bolster his opinion that she was insane at the time of the crimes.[142] Since the trial record did not reflect the "prior psychiatric history" of the defendant, the defendant had "failed to carry her burden of proof" that she was insane at the time of the offenses.[143]

In contrast, in *People v. Janecek*,[144] a defendant's convictions were reversed on grounds of insanity where the evidence revealed that the "medical history of defendant [included] numerous hospitalizations for mental problems in the previous ten years. . . ."[145] Here, the court determined that the trial judge's rejection, during a bench trial, of the defense psychiatrist's conclusions that defendant was insane was against the manifest weight of the evidence.[146] Of course, it is unclear as to whether *Janecek* would be decided the same way under the 1998 amendments and revisions to the insanity law.

§ 18.09.   —— Severe Mental Disease: Abnormal in Eyes of Community.

As stated above, to qualify as a mental illness for purposes of the insanity defense, it appears it must be a medically accepted mental disease or defect and that it was exhibited by symptoms apart from the commission of the crime itself. In addition, it must be sufficiently severe to "distinguish the [accused] as abnormal in the eyes of the community."[147] An analysis of this latter requirement involves two related conditions and contains both theoretical and practical considerations.

First, since the effect of the mental illness must be sufficient to undermine the defendant's capacity to appreciate his or her criminality, the more severe the illness, the more likely it is that it affected the defendant's cognition. Thus, the severity of the mental problem and its effect are indelibly intertwined. Not only will a more severe mental disease produce a more prominent effect, but more importantly, it will be more likely to produce a different type of effect — namely, the inability to appreciate one's criminality. Accordingly, the less se-

---

[141] People v. Quay, 175 Ill. App. 3d 965, 966, 530 N.E.2d 644, 645 (4th Dist. 1988). Accordingly, the defendant was remanded to the Department of Mental Health and Development Disabilities for an additional period.

[142] People v. Quay, 175 Ill. App. 3d 965, 969, 530 N.E.2d 644, 646 (4th Dist. 1988).

[143] People v. Quay, 175 Ill. App. 3d 965, 969, 530 N.E.2d 644, 646-47 (4th Dist. 1988).

[144] 185 Ill. App. 3d 89, 540 N.E.2d 1139 (4th Dist. 1989).

[145] People v. Janecek, 185 Ill. App. 3d 89, 92, 540 N.E.2d 1139, 1141 (4th Dist. 1989).

[146] People v. Janecek, 185 Ill. App. 3d 89, 95, 540 N.E.2d 1139, 1143 (4th Dist. 1989).

[147] 2 PAUL ROBINSON, CRIMINAL LAW DEFENSES § 173(b)(1) (1984).

vere psychopathic disorder is explicitly excluded from exculpation under the insanity defense because it is deemed to result in mere impaired judgment — and not in a loss of cognition.[148] In addition, the caselaw suggests that the more severe psychiatric disorder — psychosis — does in fact "qualify as a mental disease or defect" for purposes of section 5/6-2.[149] Thus, practically speaking, the caselaw and the statute, considered together, create areas where the insanity defense will and will not be entertained.

Second, it appears that the mental disease must distinguish the accused as abnormal in the eyes of the community — not just in the psychiatric community but also in the community at large. This point requires further analysis, for it raises a theoretical problem about the statutory language and a practical problem with successfully advancing an insanity claim.

The explicit language of the insanity statute requires that the defendant's lack of ability to appreciate must *result* from a mental disease or defect. And, as stated, this mental disease must be severe enough to distinguish the accused as abnormal in the eyes of the community. Complicating the analysis of determining which mental problems are deserving of recognition is the fact that, in psychiatry, there are two forms of mental disease: organic and functional. Since organic mental disease can be scientifically discovered by detection of physical abnormalities, such as chemical and hormonal imbalances, it poses no problem for this statute. But functional mental disease has no discoverable organic causes and, in this sense, is truly an abstraction.

Many, if not most, of the defendants that raise the insanity defense suffer from functional mental disorders. Since the functional mental disease is not physically detectable in a contained and demonstrable form, it proves difficult to establish the link between mental disease and lack of capacity to appreciate the criminality of any given conduct. Pragmatically, no such clear-cut link between the mental disease and the lack of ability to appreciate the criminality of any given conduct exists. In turn, it is difficult to establish that such disorders are severe enough to be seen as abnormal in the eyes of the community.

A second, more technical problem exists with functional illnesses as well. In psychiatry, in order to diagnose a mental disease, the psychiatrist is first presented with the symptoms. Depression, hysteria, lack of capacity to appreciate: these are all observable symptoms in the patient that allow the psychiatrist to conclude that there is in fact a mental disease. Granted, it is the mental disease in its abstract form that causes the symptoms, but it is, practically speaking, the symptoms that define the perimeters of the mental disease.

With this knowledge, one should realize that it is difficult to determine conclusively that it was a mental disease or defect that caused a defendant's lack of

---

[148] 720 ILCS 5/6-2(d) (1999).
[149] People v. Kuhn, 68 Ill. App. 3d 59, 64, 385 N.E.2d 388, 391 (3d Dist. 1979).

capacity to appreciate his or her criminality. In fact, as symptoms, one must view the defendant's lack of capacity to appreciate as an indicator in determining whether or not a mental disease even exists. The insanity defense statute requires that the mental disease *cause* the lack of capacity to appreciate, yet the existence of the mental disease itself is largely determined by the lack of capacity to appreciate. The tautology created by the statute seems inescapable.

The way out of this theoretical bind is the jury system. A jury is not bound by the dictates of logic; the jury is also "not required to accept the conclusions of a psychiatrist."[150] The law is clear on the point that a jury "may properly reach a finding of sanity by accepting lay testimony over expert testimony."[151] Thus, theoretical inconsistencies in the insanity statute will not prevent a jury from exculpating a defendant of criminal responsibility or, conversely, of holding a defendant criminally responsible when they deem it proper. The jury truly has tremendous discretion in determining whether a defendant will be exonerated under the insanity defense. This point echoed throughout the pre-1984 amendment caselaw on the insanity defense, where it is routinely stated that questions regarding the existence of mental illness are questions of fact to be resolved at the trial level, which findings will be disturbed only where the determination was "so improbable or unsatisfactory as to raise a reasonable doubt."[152] Since the enactment of the 1984 statutory amendment that placed the burden of persuasion on the defense, and the 1998 revision which requires a defense showing of "clear and convincing evidence" before a defendant is entitled to an acquittal, the jury's role remains immense. Rarely does one find an appellate reversal in this area of the law based on a factual determination that the defendant was insane following a finding of sanity in the trial court.

As a practical matter, as Professor Robinson has so aptly stated, the defendant must indeed *distinguish* himself as psychologically abnormal in the eyes of the community or, more specifically, the jury as the voice of the community.[153] Robinson has pointed out that a basic principle requires that their "recognition of the severity of the abnormality is essential if those who engage in prohibited conduct are to be excused without endangering the effectiveness of the general prohibition against that conduct."[154] For instance, when a novel theory of insanity,

---

[150] People v. Greenfield, 30 Ill. App. 3d 1044, 1048, 333 N.E.2d 36, 39 (4th Dist. 1975). *See also* People v. Harrington, 22 Ill. App. 3d 938, 944-45, 317 N.E.2d 161, 166 (2d Dist. 1974) (jury was not required to accept psychiatrists' conclusion that a psychotic episode by defendant was a mental disease or defect which would avoid criminal liability).

[151] People v. Uppole, 97 Ill. App. 3d 72, 78, 422 N.E.2d 245, 248-49 (3d Dist. 1981).

[152] *See, e.g.,* People v. Carlson, 79 Ill. 2d 564, 580, 404 N.E.2d 233, 240 (1980) (quoting People v. Ward, 61 Ill. 2d 559, 568, 338 N.E.2d 171, 177 (1975)).

[153] 2 PAUL ROBINSON, CRIMINAL LAW DEFENSES § 173(b)(1) n.10 (1984). *See, e.g.,* People v. Drummond, 87 Ill. App. 3d 890, 894, 409 N.E.2d 361, 364 (5th Dist. 1980) ("reactive depression" suffered by defendant after being dismissed from job is experienced by 20 per cent of population and is not sufficient to raise reasonable doubt as to his sanity).

[154] 2 PAUL ROBINSON, CRIMINAL LAW DEFENSES § 173(b)(1) (1984).

such as "compulsive gambling,"[155] is advanced — which may have an appeal at first glance — it must be asked, even if the psychiatric community is prepared to support such a defense, whether this disorder is so *unusual or distinctive* as to warrant a community finding of severe abnormality. Also, one must ask whether the average jury will not be concerned that if it excuses the compulsive gambler before it of crimes he or she committed as a result of the compulsive gambling, that it will be sending the wrong kind of signals to other compulsive gamblers who may be tempted to cross the criminal threshold.[156] The same might be said of the defendant who claimed the fatal shooting of his wife, who had been suffering from multiple sclerosis for many years, was excused by reason of his anxiety and depression over her illness.[157] The same might be said of other creative theories of insanity: "brainwashing,"[158] "premenstrual syndrome,"[159] "postwar syndrome,"[160] "homosexual panic,"[161] "postpartum depression,"[162] "black

---

[155] *See* Ann H. Rubin, Comment, *Beating the Odds: Compulsive Gambling as an Insanity Defense — State v. Lafferty*, 14 CONN. L. REV. 341 (1982) (examination of case where Connecticut trial judge held compulsive gambling was a defense).
But see People v. Lowitzki, 285 Ill. App. 3d 770, 776-80, 674 N.E.2d 859, 863-65 (1st Dist. 1996) (pathological gambling does not provide an insanity defense to the non-gambling offense of embezzlement-type theft); United States v. Gould, 741 F.2d 45, 52 (4th Cir. 1984) ("pathological gambling" no defense to bank robbery); United States v. Torniero, 735 F.2d 725, 732 (2d Cir. 1984) (compulsive gambling no defense to interstate transportation of stolen property), *cert. denied*, 469 U.S. 1110 (1985).

[156] *See* Sanford Kadish, *Excusing Crime*, 75 CAL. L. REV. 257, 285 (1987) (the threat to social control functions of the criminal law may justify departure from criminal blame).

[157] People v. Williams, 265 Ill. App. 3d 283, 289, 638 N.E.2d 345, 349-50 (1st Dist. 1994) (insanity claim rejected and second degree murder conviction affirmed).

[158] Donald T. Lunde & Thomas E. Wilson, *Brainwashing as a Defense to Criminal Liability: Patty Hearst Revisited*, 13 CRIM. L. BULL. 341 (1977) (critical review of defense). *See also* United States v. Hearst, 563 F.2d 1331 (9th Cir. 1977), *cert. denied*, 435 U.S. 1000 (1978) (guilty as charged notwithstanding brainwashing defense claim).

[159] *See* Robert Carney & Brian Williams, *Recent Decisions, Criminal Law — Premenstrual Syndrome: A Criminal Defense*, 59 NOTRE DAME L. REV. 253 (1983) (supportive of defense theory although not technically considered form of insanity). These authors conceded that no American court had approved of this defense theory. *See also* DSM-III-R at xxv (late luteal phase dysphoric disorder is a narrowly defined version of premenstrual syndrome and was not included in the DSM-III). This disorder was included in Appendix A of the DSM-III-R as a proposed diagnostic category needing further study. DSM-III-R at 367. This disorder is not included in DSM-IV.

[160] John R. Ford, *In Defense of the Defenders: The Vietnam Vet Syndrome*, 19 CRIM. L. BULL. 434 (1983) (advancing such defense claims). *But see* Brian Grant & David Coons, *Guilty Verdict in a Murder Committed by a Veteran with Post-Traumatic Stress Disorder*, 11 BULL. AM. ACAD. PSYCHIATRY L. 355 (1983) (actual case history). *See also* People v. Kapsalis, 186 Ill. App. 3d 96, 104, 541 N.E.2d 1323, 1327 (1st Dist. 1989) ("Although post-traumatic stress disorder has been recognized as a mental illness, the evidence in the case at bar does not support defendant's assertion that he experienced a flashback to combat in Vietnam at the time of the offense").

[161] *See, e.g.*, People v. Parisie, 5 Ill. App. 3d 1009, 1019, 287 N.E.2d 310, 315 (4th Dist. 1972) (not basis for insanity defense, although it may be a personality disorder). *Cf.* People v. Jones, 6 Ill. 2d 252, 256, 128 N.E.2d 739, 741 (1955) (homosexuality not defense to crime against nature).

rage,"[163] "post-traumatic stress disorder,"[164] "Holocaust syndrome,"[165] "urban psychosis,"[166] drug addiction,[167] and so on.[168] It is submitted that the general rejection of those theories[169] has to do with the criminal defense practitioner's failure to recognize these basic considerations and to *distinguish their client from others* who share the same problems, who have had the same experiences, and who have been confronted by the same stimuli without responding with criminal behavior.

---

[162] Christine Gardner, Note, *Postpartum Depression Defense: Are Mothers Getting Away with Murder?*, 24 New Eng. L. Rev. 953 (1990) (discussing defense with general disapproval, but citing some instances where defense has been successful).

[163] Patricia J. Falk, *Novel Theories of Criminal Defense Based Upon the Toxicity of the Social Environment: Urban Psychosis, Television Intoxication, and Black Rage,* 74 N.C. L. Rev. 731 (1996) (supporting broadening recognition of such defense claims); Deborah L. Goldklang, *Post-Traumatic Stress Disorder and Black Rage: Clinical Validity, Criminal Responsibility,* 5 Va. J. Soc. Pol'y & L. 213 (1997) (reflecting skepticism about recognition of such defense).

[164] Deborah L. Goldklang, *Post-Traumatic Stress Disorder and Black Rage: Clinical Validity, Criminal Responsibility,* 5 Va. J. Soc. Pol'y & L. 213 (1997).

[165] Werner v. State, 711 S.W.2d 639 (Tex. Crim. App. 1996) (defense evidence rejected by trial court and murder conviction upheld).

[166] Rogers Worthington, *"Urban psychosis" rejected as slaying defense,* Chi. Trib., Nov. 5, 1992 at A8; Junda Woo, *Urban Trauma Mitigates Guilt, Defenders Say,* Wall St. J., Apr. 27, 1993 at B1; Patricia J. Falk, *Novel Theories of Criminal Defense Based Upon the Toxicity of the Social Environment: Urban Psychosis, Television Intoxication, and Black Rage,* 74 N.C. L. Rev. 731 (1996).

[167] *See, e.g.,* Gary W. Lunter, *The Effect of Drug-Induced Intoxication on the Issue of Criminal Responsibility,* 8 Crim. L. Bull. 731 (1972). *But see* United States v. Lyons, 731 F.2d 243, 245 (5th Cir.) (narcotics addiction standing alone raises no issue of mental disease or defect within definition of insanity), *cert. denied,* 469 U.S. 930 (1984); *accord* United States v. Coffman, 567 F.2d 960, 963 (10th Cir. 1977); United States v. Moore, 486 F.2d 1139, 1154 (D.C. Cir.), *cert. denied,* 414 U.S. 980 (1973).
See also Powell v. Texas, 392 U.S. 514 (1968) (conviction of chronic alcoholic for public drunkenness upheld); People v. Downey, 162 Ill. App. 3d 322, 334, 515 N.E.2d 362, 369 (2d Dist. 1987) ("Drug addiction alone will not support an insanity defense unless there is a mental disease or defect traceable to the habitual or chronic use of drugs"); People v. Whitehead, 171 Ill. App. 3d 900, 906, 525 N.E.2d 1084, 1087 (1st Dist. 1988) (voluntary use of PCP producing intoxication cannot be equated with insanity).

[168] *See, e.g.,* Fred Cohen, *Old Age as a Criminal Defense,* 21 Crim. L. Bull. 5 (1985); Adrienne Drell, *Witchcraft Murder Defense Fails,* A.B.A. J., May 1993, at 40; Betty Jean Lifton, *Can the "adopted child syndrome" be used as a defense in criminal cases?,* Chi Daily Law Bulletin, Apr. 26, 1986, at 14; Zamora v. State, 361 So. 2d 776 (Fla. 3d Dist. 1978) (judge's refusal of evidence of involuntary subliminal television intoxication not reversible error); Gail Diane Cox, *Abuse Excuse: Success Grows,* The Nat'l L.J., May 9, 1994, at A1; Associated Press, *Killer blames sleep disorder,* Chi Daily Law Bulletin, November 16, 1994, at 1 (discussing sleep apnea defense claim); State v. MacDonald, 718 A.2d 195 (Maine 1998) (trial court did not err in refusing to permit defendant to offer expert testimony on a form of post-traumatic stress disorder the expert called "adult children of alcoholics syndrome").

[169] *See* cases cited in this section and accompanying text.

Where an insanity defense claim is supported by psychiatric testimony suggesting that the defendant suffered from a mental disorder at the time of the crime, this is often, at best, sufficient to merely raise the defense for jury consideration. It must be realized that "[t]he jury is not required to accept the conditions of *any* witness as to the issue of a defendant's sanity" and that "the weight of the psychiatrist's opinion is to be measured by the reasons given for the conclusion and the *factual details supporting it*."[170] Thus, some independent *verification* of the illness is almost invariably necessary.[171] For instance, the trier of fact may consider, as was the case in *Ureste*, the absence of evidence of a history of manifestations of prior mental illness.[172] They might consider, as was the case in *Lono*, that "[t]here was *no evidence* of prior psychiatric treatment or confinement in a mental institution."[173]

In addition, as a practical matter, the mental illness must be severe. The Illinois caselaw that describes a depressive neurosis as "more closely associated with a personality disorder" than legally recognized illnesses[174] illustrates the tendency on the part of the courts to play down the importance of the less severe psychiatric disorders in the context of insanity defense claims. More importantly, the plain language of the various judicial opinions in which an illness is rejected for purposes of insanity because it "falls far short of portraying a *serious* mental condition"[175] provides a clear indication that it is appropriate to attach importance to the *severity* of the disorder. Moreover, even if the mental problem is relatively serious, the fact that the defendant was taking medication to control his illness at the time of the offense will be viewed as yet another consideration militating against an insanity finding.[176]

§ 18.10. — Lacks Substantial Capacity.

The law offers little guidance on the meaning of the "lacks substantial capacity" language appearing in paragraph 5/6-2. The Committee Comments to some extent explain the quantitative aspect of substantial capacity: *total* lack of capac-

---

[170] People v. Martinez, 86 Ill. App. 3d 486, 491, 408 N.E.2d 358, 362 (2d Dist. 1980) (emphasis added).

[171] *See, e.g.*, People v. Ureste, 7 Ill. App. 3d 545, 550, 288 N.E.2d 45, 48 (3d Dist. 1972) (discussed above).

[172] People v. Ureste, 7 Ill. App. 3d 545, 550, 288 N.E.2d 451, 458-59 (3d Dist. 1972).

[173] People v. Lono, 11 Ill. App. 3d 443, 448, 297 N.E.2d 349, 354 (1st Dist. 1973) (emphasis added). *But see* People v. Davidson, 82 Ill. App. 2d 245, 249, 225 N.E.2d 727, 729 (2d Dist. 1967) (defendant convicted even though he had previously spent three years in a mental institution).

[174] People v. Uppole, 97 Ill. App. 3d 72, 79-80, 422 N.E.2d 245, 250 (3d Dist. 1981).

[175] *See, e.g.*, People v. Varnado, 66 Ill. App. 3d 413, 419, 384 N.E.2d 37, 40 (1st Dist. 1978) (emphasis added).

[176] People v. Martin, 166 Ill. App. 3d 428, 434, 519 N.E.2d 1085, 1089 (1st Dist. 1988) (defendant's condition was chronic paranoid schizophrenia).

ity to appreciate is not required to successfully plead the insanity defense.[177] Exactly what constitutes a lack of substantial capacity is rarely addressed by the courts. In one case, the appellate court stated that the mental illness in question must have "substantially impaired" behavioral controls.[178] In any event, these quantitative questions are factual in nature and are left to the jury.

Lack of substantial capacity should not be confused with "subnormal mentality," which is not a defense to a crime.[179] Where the defense seeks to introduce evidence of the defendant's low IQ, the trial court's rejection of that evidence will normally be upheld unless it raised serious question about his ability to form a judgment about the criminality of his conduct.[180]

Another concern revolving around the substantial capacity concern specifically, and insanity claims generally, is that there is a presumption that all persons are sane.[181] This presumption was overcome before the pre-1984 statutory revision *only* when the defendant presented evidence that raised a reasonable doubt of his or her sanity.[182] The 1984 statutory amendment, which places the burden of persuasion in proving insanity on the defendant, combined with the 1998 statutory amendment, which requires a defense showing of insanity by "clear and convincing evidence" to warrant an acquittal, has in no way undercut the legal presumption of sanity. Thus, it can be asserted that all persons are presumed to have the substantial capacity to appreciate until substantial evidence is presented that undermines the presumption.[183]

---

[177] ILL. ANN. STAT. ch. 38, § 6-2 (Smith-Hurd 1989), 1961 Committee Comments, at 303-04 (revised 1972). *See also* People v. Spears, 63 Ill. App. 3d 510, 516, 380 N.E.2d 423, 427-28 (5th Dist. 1978) (substantial incapacity rather that total incapacity is the standard).

[178] People v. Uppole, 97 Ill. App. 3d 72, 77, 422 N.E.2d 245, 248 (3d Dist. 1981).

[179] People v. McMullen, 88 Ill. App. 3d 611, 615, 410 N.E.2d 1174, 1177 (4th Dist. 1980) (exclusion of psychologist's testimony upheld; evidence need only be admitted if defendant's low IQ made him "unable to distinguish between right and wrong"). *See also* People v. Jenko, 410 Ill. 478, 483, 102 N.E.2d 783, 785-86 (1951) (sub-normal mentality not a defense to a charge of crime); People v. Marquis, 344 Ill. 261, 267, 176 N.E. 314, 316 (1931) (mental capacity similar to that of a 12-year-old not a defense to murder).

[180] People v. McMullen, 88 Ill. App. 3d 611, 614-15, 410 N.E.2d 1174, 1177 (4th Dist. 1980) ("It is well established that a subnormal mentality is not a defense to a crime unless a defendant is unable to distinguish right and wrong with respect to the act in question"). *See also* People v. Smothers, 55 Ill. 2d 172, 174, 302 N.E.2d 324, 326 (1973) (antisocial and bizarre conduct not sufficient evidence for defense of insanity).

[181] People v. Uppole, 97 Ill. App. 3d 72, 77, 422 N.E.2d 245, 250 (3d Dist. 1981).

[182] People v. Redmond, 59 Ill. 2d 328, 338, 320 N.E.2d 321, 326 (1974); People v. Smothers, 55 Ill. 2d 172, 174, 302 N.E.2d 324, 326 (1973).

[183] The pre-1984 amendment caselaw disallowed the presumption-of-sanity instruction where evidence of lack of sanity had been presented. *See* People v. Haun, 71 Ill. App. 2d 262, 271, 217 N.E.2d 470, 474 (4th Dist. 1966) (where there was evidence that defendant was insane, it was no longer proper to instruct the jury that all persons are presumed to be sane; "there is no reason to instruct as to a presumption where there is competent evidence to the contrary"). *Compare* People v. Robinson, 22 Ill. 2d 162, 169, 174 N.E.2d 820, 824 (evidence presented by defendant was in-

The term *capacity* as an isolated concept is rarely dealt with by the courts. The courts prefer to couple the term *capacity* with either the term *appreciate* or, if referring to cases before the 1998 change in the insanity law (which removed concern over volition), the term *conform* and thus examine the defendant's "capacity to appreciate" or "capacity to conform" as complete concepts. In any event, because the Illinois legislature's removal of the volitional arm of the insanity defense is so relatively recent, both the cognitive and volitional aspects of insanity will be addressed. The following two sections analyze the concepts of capacity to appreciate and capacity to conform.

§ 18.11.   —— Appreciate the Criminality of Conduct: Cognition.

"Lack of substantial capacity to appreciate" the criminality of one's conduct is the central component of the insanity defense since the 1998 legislative revision of the insanity defense statute removed the volitional prong. Before the change in the insanity law, the defense offered the defendant an either/or proposition for exculpation. The defendant could successfully plead the insanity defense if he or she lacked substantial capacity to appreciate his or her conduct *or* if he or she lacked substantial capacity to conform his or her conduct to the requirements of law.[184] It was not necessary for the defendant to demonstrate that he or she lacked substantial capacity to both appreciate and conform.[185] The current law, though, narrows the possibility of a successful defense by allowing only evidence that the defendant lacked substantial capacity to appreciate, not evidence that the defendant could not conform his conduct to the requirements of the law.[186]

Like so many of the other terms in the insanity defense, it is difficult to place a precise meaning on the term *appreciate*. The Committee Comments make an explicit distinction between *know* and *appreciate*.[187] As discussed above, the term *appreciate* is meant to include the defendant's affective or emotional personality.[188] Indeed, a defendant's intellectual knowledge of the criminality or

---

sufficient to overcome presumption of defendant's sanity and, accordingly, state was not required to affirmatively prove it), *cert. denied*, 368 U.S. 857 (1961). Both *Haun* and *Robinson* were pre-1984 statutory revision decisions.

[184] People v. Spears, 63 Ill. App. 3d 510, 516, 380 N.E.2d 423, 427 (5th Dist. 1978).

[185] People v. Teague, 108 Ill. App. 3d 891, 903, 439 N.E.2d 1066, 1074 (1st Dist. 1982) ("an accused who understood the nature of his conduct and appreciated its wrongfulness will still be excused from criminal liability if his ability to consciously refrain from that conduct was substantially impaired by a mental disease or defect"), *cert. denied*, 464 U.S. 867 (1983).

[186] 720 ILCS 5/6-2(a) (1999).

[187] ILL. ANN. STAT. ch. 38, para. 6-2 (Smith-Hurd 1989), 1961 Committee Comments, at 304 (revised 1972) ("[T]he term 'appreciate' is employed, instead of 'know'").

[188] ILL. ANN. STAT. ch. 38, para. 6-2 (Smith-Hurd 1989), 1961 Committee Comments, at 302-04 (revised 1972): ("[I]n many cases of advanced psychosis, cases which everyone would deem appropriate for exculpation, the defendant may have a kind of verbal knowledge of right and wrong.

wrongfulness of his or her conduct is not the primary question posed by the cognitive prong of the insanity defense.[189]

A defendant may indeed possess an intellectual understanding of the criminality of his or her act, yet if he or she lacks an emotional understanding, he or she may be exonerated by the insanity defense.[190] For example, a defendant may be able to tell the court verbally that killing is wrong and may not appreciate the immorality of killing someone. In this example, the defendant possesses an intellectual understanding of the criminality of the act but does not "appreciate" the criminality of his or her act. Whether a defendant has substantial capacity to appreciate the criminality of his or her conduct is answered by the question, "Is the defendant deprived, by virtue of mental disorder, of normal powers of ethical discrimination?'"[191]

In determining whether a defendant actually appreciated his or her criminality, the courts will often examine his or her reactions to certain stimuli as indicative of his or her cognition. The primary evidence the courts accept as demonstrative of the defendant's capacity to appreciate the criminality of his or her actions is (1) fleeing after the commission of a crime and (2) discontinuance of the criminal activity on the approach of a police officer.[192] Also, the existence of

---

What he lacks is understanding of the sort that involves the emotional or affective parts of his personality. * * * * The change [from 'know' to 'appreciate'] represents an effort to find a term more congenial to modern psychiatric notions of understanding"). It is noteworthy that some caselaw continues to address the concept of "appreciation" in terms of the former language (see, e.g., People v. Clark, 102 Ill. App. 3d 414, 418, 429 N.E.2d 1255, 1258 (1st Dist. 1981) (the insanity defense considers not simply whether the accused was "able to distinguish right from wrong but rather that he is able to . . . choose between them")) while others use the Committee's nomenclature (see, e.g., People v. Uppole, 97 Ill. App. 3d 72, 80, 422 N.E.2d 245, 250 (3d Dist. 1981) ("The defendant's affective system, which the neurosis allegedly affected, remained under control")).

[189] 2 PAUL ROBINSON, CRIMINAL LAW DEFENSES § 173(d)(3) n.47 (1984) (citing United States v. Freeman, 357 F.2d 606, 623 (2d Cir. 1966) ("mere intellectual awareness that the conduct is wrongful, when divorced from appreciation or understanding of the moral or legal import of behavior, can have little significance")).

[190] ILL. ANN. STAT. ch. 38, para. 6-2 (Smith-Hurd 1989), 1961 Committee Comments, at 302 (revised 1972). Accord 2 PAUL ROBINSON, CRIMINAL LAW DEFENSES § 173(d)(3) n.47 (1984).

[191] ILL. REV. STAT. ch. 38, para. 6-2 (Smith-Hurd 1989), 1961 Committee Comments, at 303 (revised 1972) (citing MODEL PENAL CODE, comment at 173 (Tentative Draft No. 4, 1955)).

[192] There is an abundance of caselaw recognizing the defendant's flight from the scene of a crime or the defendant's discontinuance of criminal activity on the approach of a police officer as constituting strong evidence of his or her capacity to appreciate the criminality of his or her conduct: People v. Romaine, 79 Ill. App. 3d 1089, 1097, 399 N.E.2d 319, 325 (3d Dist. 1979) ("Certainly, the fact that the defendant discontinued his criminal activity when the State trooper appeared supports the conclusion that he appreciated the criminality of his conduct. . . . In addition, the jury could have considered the defendant's attempt to flee after attacking . . . [his victim] as indicating the defendant appreciated the criminality of his conduct"); People v. Roberts, 71 Ill. App. 3d 124, 128, 389 N.E.2d 596, 600 (5th Dist. 1979) ("Especially with regard to the defen-

a plan or design to commit a crime is a relevant consideration in determining if a defendant's acts were rational in nature.[193]

One last point should be made on the issue of a defendant's capacity to appreciate the criminality of his or her conduct. One of the primary reasons Illinois adopted the American Law Institute's insanity defense was to make a clear distinction between the terms *know* and *appreciate*; yet, the courts often treat *knowledge* and *appreciation* as synonymous terms.[194] And despite the fact that both the Illinois legislative drafting Committee Comments and Model Penal Code comments make it explicitly clear that a defendant's intellectual understanding of the criminality of his or her conduct will not exclude him or her from successfully pleading a lack of capacity to "appreciate" the criminality of his or her conduct, the courts repeatedly and erroneously fail to recognize this point.[195] For instance, in *People v. Spears*,[196] the court stated, "In view of defendant's obvious *intelligence* and his awareness of his right to remain silent as evidenced by his repeated pointing at such right on a *Miranda* form while in the company of F.B.I. agent Bond, such silence may be as plausibly explained as a calculated tactic as of evidence of legal insanity."[197] Also, in *People v. Meeker*,[198] the court stated, "[Dr.] Sunderland's opinion that defendant was not capable of appreciating the criminality of his acts was undercut when Sunderland stated defendant *knew* burning a building was unlawful."[199] Equally disconcerting is the Illinois court's confusion regarding the significance of a defendant's lack of emotional understanding about the criminality of his actions. For example, in *People v. Tylkowski*,[200] the Illinois appellate court acknowledged that defendant had cited various authorities, articles and commentaries that sug-

---

dant's attempt to escape, [this] indicated that the defendant both appreciated the criminality of his conduct and could conform his conduct to the requirements of law"); People v. Varnado, 66 Ill. App. 3d 413, 418, 384 N.E.2d 37, 41 (1st Dist. 1978) (defense psychiatrist "acknowledged that defendant's flight from the murder scene could indicate defendant knew right from wrong").

[193] *See, e.g.,* People v. Clark, 102 Ill. App. 3d 414, 422, 429 N.E.2d 1255, 1261 (1st Dist. 1981).

[194] *See, e.g.,* People v. Varnado, 66 Ill. App. 3d 413, 418, 384 N.E.2d 37, 41 (1st Dist. 1978) (evidence existed that defendant "knew the murder was wrong").

[195] *See* § 18.02 of this chapter for a discussion of this point.

[196] 63 Ill. App. 3d 510, 380 N.E.2d 423 (5th Dist. 1978).

[197] People v. Spears, 63 Ill. App. 3d 510, 520, 380 N.E.2d 423, 430 (5th Dist. 1978) (emphasis added). *But see* Wainright v. Greenfield, 474 U.S. 284, 289-95 and n.13 (1986) (it is fundamentally unfair and a violation of due process to introduce defendant's post-arrest, post-*Miranda* silence or statements of his intent to remain silent as evidence of his sanity at time offense was committed).

[198] 86 Ill. App. 3d 162, 407 N.E.2d 1058 (5th Dist. 1980).

[199] People v. Meeker, 86 Ill. App. 3d 162, 169, 407 N.E.2d 1058, 1064 (5th Dist. 1980) (emphasis added).

[200] 171 Ill. App. 3d 93, 524 N.E.2d 1112 (1st Dist. 1988).

gested that "testimony concerning a defendant's emotional capacity is relevant in determining sanity."[201] Yet, the court responded:

> While we acknowledge that such testimony may be relevant, we again point out that there is no authority which indicates that the Illinois legislature intended to adopt a requirement that a defendant appreciate both emotionally and intellectually that his actions are criminal, or that it is an error for a trial court to reject testimony as to a defendant's emotional appreciation.[202]

§ 18.12.   — — Conform Conduct to Requirements of Law: Volition.

In 1995, the Illinois legislature amended the Illinois insanity defense in an effort to abolish the volitional prong of the defense. Specifically, the General Assembly removed the portion of the defense which referred to an accused's inability "to conform his conduct to the requirements of law."[203] Subsequently, this amendment was found unconstitutional because it violated the single subject rule of the Illinois constitution.[204] In 1998, the Illinois legislature reenacted the provision, designed to abolish the volitional prong of the insanity defense, but in a manner that should avoid constitutional attack.[205] Because this change in the law is relatively new, it is unknown how the paring down of the insanity defense will affect decisions. It is conceivable that Illinois courts will consider the defendant's volitional controls as they assess whether the defendant had the capacity to appreciate his or her criminality and, as such, a brief overview of the pre-revision caselaw that focuses on volition will be presented.

The volitional prong of the insanity defense reflected the "fundamental principle that a person is not criminally responsible for an involuntary act."[206] Thus, even though an accused understood the nature of his conduct and appreciated its wrongfulness, the volition prong "excused [the defendant] from criminal liability if his ability to consciously refrain from the conduct was substantially impaired by a mental defect."[207]

---

[201] People v. Tylkowski, 171 Ill. App. 3d 93, 103, 524 N.E.2d 1112, 1119 (1st Dist. 1988).

[202] People v. Tylkowski, 171 Ill. App. 3d 93, 103, 524 N.E.2d 1112, 1119 (1st Dist. 1988).

[203] Pub. Act 89-404 (1995).

[204] People v. Reedy, 295 Ill. App. 3d 34, 41, 692 N.E.2d 376, 379 (2d Dist. 1998) (citing Ill. Const. 1970, art. IV, § 8(d)) (permits no more than one subject matter per legislative enactment), aff'd, 186 Ill. 2d 1, 708 N.E.2d 1114 (1999).

[205] Pub. Act 90-593 (1998). See 720 ILCS 5/6-2(a) (1999).

[206] People v. Clark, 102 Ill. App. 3d 414, 417, 429 N.E.2d 1255, 1257 (1st Dist. 1981) (citing People v. Grant, 71 Ill. 2d 551, 377 N.E.2d 4 (1978)).

[207] People v. Spears, 63 Ill. App. 3d 510, 516, 380 N.E.2d 423, 428 (5th Dist. 1978) (citing People v. Bender, 20 Ill. 2d 45, 169 N.E.2d 328 (1960)). This same language appears in People v. Uppole, 97 Ill. App. 3d 72, 77, 422 N.E.2d 245, 248 (3d Dist. 1981), in People v. Meeker, 86 Ill. App. 3d 162, 168, 407 N.E.2d 1058, 1063 (5th Dist. 1980) and other cases.

The caselaw that attempted to establish whether the defendant possessed the capacity to conform often centered on two areas of concern: the existence of a plan or design that was used in committing the crime[208] and the discontinuance of criminal activity on the approach of a police officer.[209] Concerning a defendant's plan, it was said in one case:

> The evidence presented herein suggests a deliberate, rational approach to the offense, and it appears that defendant was capable of directing his actions in conformity with such plan, which thereby tends to dispel any reasonable doubt that at the time of the offense [that] defendant's mental disease or defect substantially impaired his capacity to control his conduct or conform it to the requirements of the law.[210]

With the narrowing in the law regarding the insanity defense, ostensibly Illinois courts will no longer discuss a defendant's volitional capacity as they did before the change in the law. While pre-1998 opinions where the defendant succeeded with his or her insanity claim seldom specified which prong of the insanity defense the defendant satisfied, those cases which did explicitly state that the defendant lacked the ability to conform his conduct to the requirements of the law are the cases whose precedential value is placed into considerable question in light of the new insanity law. For example, in *People v. Garcia*,[211] the appellate court reversed convictions of attempted murder, aggravated battery, and armed violence on the basis that, while the defendant was able to appreciate the criminality of his conduct, evidence and psychiatrists' testimony revealed that defendant was unable to conform his conduct to the requirements of the law.[212] Under the revised statute that abolishes the volitional prong of the insanity de-

---

[208] *See* People v. Meeker, 86 Ill. App. 3d 162, 168, 407 N.E.2d 1058, 1064 (5th Dist. 1980) ("It has been recognized that one fact of particular relevance to a defendant's sanity is the existence of a plan or design for the crime. * * * The evidence here sufficiently indicates defendant was able to choose between a lawful course of conduct and an unlawful one at the time in question. Significant in this regard is defendant's . . . extensive planning. . . . These [and other] facts substantially demonstrate that the offense at bar was the product of lengthy consideration, not what defendant characterized as an irresistible impulse"). *See also* People v. Fosdick, 166 Ill. App. 3d 491, 500, 519 N.E.2d 1102, 1109 (1st Dist. 1988) (where evidence of defendant's method of forced incestuous acts with his son and daughter demonstrated a manner to avoid detection, the fact finder had evidence upon which to determine that defendant appreciated his criminality and could have conformed his conduct to the law).

[209] *See* People v. Elliot, 32 Ill. App. 3d 654, 659, 336 N.E.2d 146, 149 (5th Dist. 1975) (fact that defendant terminated his activity when he saw approaching police was evidence "that he could control himself"). *See also* People v. Martin, 166 Ill. App. 3d 428, 434, 519 N.E.2d 1085, 1089 (1st Dist. 1988) (evidence showing that defendant fled from scene of arson fires that he set supports a finding against insanity).

[210] People v. Clark, 102 Ill. App. 3d 414, 422, 429 N.E.2d 1255, 1261 (1st Dist. 1981).

[211] 156 Ill. App. 3d 417, 509 N.E.2d 600 (1st Dist. 1987).

[212] People v. Garcia, 156 Ill. App. 3d 417, 424, 509 N.E.2d 600, 604 (1st Dist. 1987).

fense, the *Garcia* court might not have the basis to reverse the defendant's convictions and declare him insane. The revised law necessitates that appellate courts rely on a defendant's lack of ability to appreciate the criminality of his or her conduct.

§ 18.13. Guilty but Mentally Ill.

In 1981, the General Assembly adopted the concept of "guilty but mentally ill" (GBMI).[213] This law allows the fact finder to convict a defendant who "was not insane but was suffering from a mental illness." A "guilty but mentally ill" verdict *does not* by definition relieve the accused of criminal responsibility.[214] *Mental illness* for purposes of this statute means "a substantial disorder of thought, mood, or behavior which afflicted a person at the time of the commission of the offense and which impaired that person's judgment, but not to the extent" that the person could be considered legally insane because of his or her lack of cognition.[215] The upshot of this legislative change is to allow juries faced with insanity claims essentially three alternatives: (1) convict the defendant as charged; (2) find that the defendant is guilty but mentally ill; or (3) acquit the defendant by reason of insanity.[216]

A jury cannot find a defendant who pleads insanity guilty but mentally ill when the evidence supports a finding of insanity. In *People v. Palmer*,[217] the appellate court reversed the jury trial verdict that found the defendant guilty of murder but mentally ill.[218] The defendant presented a number of expert and lay witnesses to testify at trial as to his extensive history of mental disease and his irrational behavior at the time the crime was committed.[219] The court noted that the jury must weigh conflicting testimony, is not required to accept a particular psychiatric expert's testimony, and may rely on lay testimony and reject expert testimony.[220] In the instant case, the court found the defendant not guilty by reason of insanity because the lay testimony supported the defense experts' testimony that the defendant's mental disease resulted in mental incapacity rising to the level of insanity as defined by law, and the facts of the case rendered the state's expert's testimony not reliable or credible.[221]

---

[213] 720 ILCS 5/6-2(c), (d) (1999).

[214] 720 ILCS 5/6-2(c) (1999).

[215] 720 ILCS 5/6-2(d) (1999).

[216] 2 PAUL ROBINSON, CRIMINAL LAW DEFENSES § 173(h) (1984).

[217] 139 Ill. App. 3d 966, 487 N.E.2d 1154 (2d Dist. 1986).

[218] People v. Palmer, 139 Ill. App. 3d 966, 973-74, 487 N.E.2d 1154, 1159 (2d Dist. 1986).

[219] People v. Palmer, 139 Ill. App. 3d 966, 969-71, 487 N.E.2d 1154, 1155-57 (2d Dist. 1986).

[220] People v. Palmer, 139 Ill. App. 3d 966, 972-73, 487 N.E.2d 1154, 1158 (2d Dist. 1986).

[221] People v. Palmer, 139 Ill. App. 3d 966, 973-74, 487 N.E.2d 1154, 1159 (2d Dist. 1986) (describing state's expert testimony as "weak and self-contradictory").

The effect of the guilty but mentally ill verdict is to allow the court to "impose any sentence upon the defendant which could be imposed pursuant to law upon a defendant who had been convicted of the same offense without a finding of mental illness."[222] In *People v. Gozier*,[223] the Illinois Supreme Court held that this verdict allows trial courts to make an alternative finding of guilty but mentally ill when the defendant has unsuccessfully presented a defense of insanity.[224] If such a finding is made, the defendant is sentenced to the Department of Corrections, and it must make a "periodic inquiry and examination" of the defendant's mental illness.[225] The Department of Corrections must provide "such psychiatric, psychological, or other counseling and treatment for the defendant as it determines necessary."[226] It can have the defendant transferred to the Department of Human Services for treatment, with the provision that if ever that department determines that the defendant "no longer requires hospitalization for mental treatment, mental retardation, or addiction," the defendant must be returned to the Department of Corrections to serve the rest of his or her sentence.[227]

This concept of "guilty but mentally ill" has been praised[228] and condemned[229] by various criminal law authorities. The principal arguments in favor of the concept are that it holds those who are mentally ill but blameworthy accountable for their actions, provides for appropriate treatment alternatives beyond the prison walls, and extends to the jury an alternative to the all-or-nothing choice of guilty as charged or acquittal. The drawbacks of the concept are that it may only confuse juries, allow for compromise verdicts, and is really nothing less than an abolition of the insanity defense in disguise. Up to 1997, GBMI verdicts with-

---

[222] 730 ILCS 5/5-2-6(a) (1999). *See* People v. Gindorf, 159 Ill. App. 3d 647, 662-67, 512 N.E.2d 770, 779-83 (2d Dist. 1987) (imposition of mandatory natural life sentence, pursuant to 730 ILCS 5/5-8-1 (1999), for defendant found guilty of murdering more than one victim is not mitigated by finding of mental illness of defendant held guilty but mentally ill for murder of her two children), *cert. denied*, 486 U.S. 1011 (1988). *See also* People v. Crews, 122 Ill. 2d 266, 280-83, 522 N.E.2d 1167, 1173-75 (1988) (a plea of guilty but mentally ill does not preclude the imposition of the death penalty and is not cruel and unusual punishment under the Eighth and Fourteenth Amendments; furthermore, a finding of mental illness does not necessarily establish mitigating circumstances for purposes of avoidance of imposition of the death penalty), *cert. denied*, 492 U.S. 925 (1989).

[223] 145 Ill. 2d 127, 582 N.E.2d 89 (1991), *cert. denied*, 504 U.S. 987 (1992).

[224] People v. Gozier, 145 Ill. 2d 127, 141, 582 N.E.2d 89, 96 (1991), *cert. denied*, 504 U.S. 987 (1992).

[225] 730 ILCS 5/5-2-6(b) (1999).

[226] 730 ILCS 5/5-2-6(b) (1999).

[227] 730 ILCS 5/5-2-6(c), (d)(1) (1999).

[228] *See* ROLLIN M. PERKINS & RONALD N. BOYCE, CRIMINAL LAW 993 (3d ed. 1982).

[229] *See* 2 PAUL ROBINSON, CRIMINAL LAW DEFENSES § 173(h) (1984).

stood constitutional challenge.[230] In a 1997 Illinois appellate decision, the court
found that a GBMI verdict placed conflicting burdens of proof on the defense
and that the statute encouraged compromise verdicts.[231] However, in 1999 the
Illinois Supreme Court reinstated the GBMI verdict, overruling the Illinois appellate court's decision.[232] The Illinois Supreme Court concluded that although
the defense bears the burden of persuasion on the issue of mental illness, it does
not conflict with the defendant's burden of presenting evidence of insanity.[233]
The court reasoned that mental illness is not a completely different defense, it is
simply a less serious form of psychological functioning than insanity.[234] Also,
the jury does not consider mental illness and insanity simultaneously; only when
a jury has determined that a defendant is guilty and not insane may the jury consider a GBMI verdict.[235] The state supreme court also concluded that the GBMI
verdict was not a meaningless choice and thus not a compromise for the jury.[236]
The court found that a GBMI option helps to "clarify the distinction between
insanity and mental disorders that do not meet the definition of insanity."[237]

§ 18.14.   Waiver of Insanity Defense.

A defendant's decision to waive an insanity defense raises serious implications where the defendant continues to suffer from a mental problem following
his commission of an offense. This difficulty is aggravated where the defendant
chooses to exercise such waiver over competent defense counsel's objection. In
a case of first impression in Illinois, the appellate court in *People v. Gettings*[238]
addressed this type of situation. In that decision, the court articulated the issue
as follows: "[W]hen the court is advised by defendant's counsel that a competent defendant had decided to waive a viable insanity defense over defense
counsel's objection, must the court ascertain whether the waiver is voluntary

---

[230] *See, e.g.,* People v. Martin, 166 Ill. App. 3d 428, 435, 519 N.E.2d 1085, 1089 (1st Dist.
1988) (guilty but mentally ill does not violate due process or equal protection clauses of federal or
Illinois constitutions); People v. Smith, 124 Ill. App. 3d 805, 812, 465 N.E.2d 101, 106 (1st Dist.
1984) (verdict of guilty of murder but mentally ill entered by trial court for murder committed after
enactment of guilty-but-mentally-ill statute does not violate state and federal prohibitions on ex
post facto laws). *See also* United States ex rel. Weismiller v. Lane, 815 F.2d 1106, 1109-13 (7th
Cir. 1987) (in case of first impression within federal system, court upheld Illinois' guilty-but-
mentally-ill statute under the federal constitution).
[231] People v. Robles, 288 Ill. App. 3d 935, 952, 682 N.E.2d 194, 205 (2d Dist. 1997), *overruled
sub nom.* People v. Lantz, 186 Ill. 2d 243, 712 N.E.2d 314 (1999).
[232] People v. Lantz, 186 Ill. 2d 243, 260, 712 N.E.2d 314, 323 (1999).
[233] People v. Lantz, 186 Ill. 2d 243, 254-56, 712 N.E.2d 314, 320-21 (1999).
[234] People v. Lantz, 186 Ill. 2d 243, 253, 712 N.E.2d 314, 320 (1999).
[235] People v. Lantz, 186 Ill. 2d 243, 253-57, 712 N.E.2d 314, 320-21 (1999).
[236] People v. Lantz, 186 Ill. 2d 243, 256-59, 712 N.E.2d 314, 321-23 (1999).
[237] People v. Lantz, 186 Ill. 2d 243, 258, 712 N.E.2d 314, 322 (1999).
[238] 175 Ill. App. 3d 920, 530 N.E.2d 647 (4th Dist. 1988).

and intelligent before it is accepted or can the trial judge simply accept the waiver without conducting an inquiry with the defendant?"[239] The court indicated that the judge should make an inquiry before he accepts a waiver.[240]

> An inquiry would include a short discussion between the judge and the defendant, addressing such issues as: (1) whether the defendant has been advised of the availability of the defense; (2) what reason the defendant has for waiving the defense; (3) whether defendant understands the consequences of waiving an insanity defense; and (4) whether defendant understands the consequences of a successful insanity defense.[241]

In a case where the court determines that the defendant is capable of making a voluntary and intelligent waiver, the defendant's decision must be respected.[242]

§ 18.15.   Theoretical Basis for Insanity Defense.

An understanding of the theoretical foundation underlying the insanity defense is necessary both conceptually and practically for a variety of reasons. First, it is imperative to understand the operable effects of a successful insanity plea. The question might be posed as follows: Exactly why are an insane person's acts not culpable acts? Second, this discussion may shed some light on the propriety of total abolition of this defense — an issue that has been the subject of serious discussion in recent years.[243] Third, the implications of recent changes in burden of proof procedures in Illinois insanity claims — which will be discussed below — can only be understood by an examination of these questions.

The insanity defense focuses on the nature of the mental problems harbored by the accused at the time of the alleged crime and the impact of these problems on his or her capacity for commission of the various elements of the crime charged. At first glance, it may appear that the question of liability revolves around the interrelationship of the defendant's mental state at the time of the crime and the requisite mental state or mens rea required of the offense. But this might not be the case. Professor Donald H.J. Hermann addresses this problem in a passage from his treatise on the insanity defense. Professor Hermann first con-

---

[239] People v. Gettings, 175 Ill. App. 3d 920, 923, 530 N.E.2d 647, 649 (4th Dist. 1988).

[240] People v. Gettings, 175 Ill. App. 3d 920, 924-25, 530 N.E.2d 647, 650 (4th Dist. 1988).

[241] People v. Gettings, 175 Ill. App. 3d 920, 925, 530 N.E.2d 647, 650-51 (4th Dist. 1988).

[242] People v. Gettings, 175 Ill. App. 3d 920, 923, 530 N.E.2d 647, 650 (4th Dist. 1988).

[243] *See, e.g.,* NORVAL MORRIS, MADNESS AND THE CRIMINAL LAW 53-54, 129 (1982) (proposes abolition of special defense of insanity and substitution of diminished responsibility — reduction of charge — as well as mitigation of punishment). *See also* Peter Arenella, *Reflections on Current Proposals to Abolish or Reform the Insanity Defense*, 8 AM. J.L. & MED. 271 (1982). The abolitionist movement gained much support after the acquittal of John Hinckley, Jr., for the attempted assassination of President Ronald Reagan. JOHN KLOTTER, CRIMINAL LAW § 12.3, at 304 (2d ed. 1986).

siders the mens rea concept and then discusses conclusions about insanity claims that flow from one's understanding of the concept:

> [W]hen it comes to attaching a precise meaning to *mens rea*, courts and commentators are in hopeless disagreement. Some define it in the broadest and most general terms; others define it with greater precision, but with greatly varying meanings. Here, two paradigmatic approaches [can] be considered: the first regards *mens rea* in broad terms requiring an element of moral culpability; the second defines *mens rea* with particularization as to specified mental states and leaves the general issue of moral culpability as established by a presumed capacity for responsibility to be negated by the establishment of excusing conditions or circumstances. These alternative formulations have great significance for the insanity defense since the broad approach anticipates insanity as a general defense negating of *mens rea*, while the more particular approach limits the issue of mental disease to its effect on the ability to entertain specific mental states and remits the defense of insanity proper to the question of capacity and culpability in general.[244]

Accordingly, adoption of the "broad" approach to mens rea, which is dependent on a finding of moral blameworthiness, leads to the conclusion that insanity and mens rea cannot coexist; the former negates the latter.[245] An adherent of this thesis,[246] Professor Jerome Hall has stated: "If the defendant was insane at the time of the conduct in issue, the requisite mens rea was lacking and no crime was *committed*."[247] As Professors Perkins and Boyce reported: "Under the prevailing view insanity is a defense because it negatives an element of the offense charged."[248] This approach is obviously antithetical to abolitionist proposals.

On the other hand, some courts and authorities "consider that proof of insanity does not disprove any element of the offense charged, but establishes an excuse which entitles defendant to an acquittal."[249] Here, the "particularized" view of mens rea, which is "morally neutral in comparison to the traditional view," is

---

[244] DONALD H.J. HERMANN, THE INSANITY DEFENSE: PHILOSOPHICAL, HISTORICAL AND LEGAL PERSPECTIVES 109-10 (1983).

[245] DONALD H.J. HERMANN, THE INSANITY DEFENSE: PHILOSOPHICAL, HISTORICAL AND LEGAL PERSPECTIVES 111 (1983).

[246] JEROME HALL, GENERAL PRINCIPLES OF CRIMINAL LAW 146 (2d ed. 1960): "The principle of mens rea is the ultimate summation of the moral judgments expressed in the proscription of the voluntary (intentional or reckless) commission of . . . social harm. . . ."

[247] JEROME HALL, GENERAL PRINCIPLES OF CRIMINAL LAW 449 (2d ed. 1960).

[248] ROLLIN M. PERKINS & RONALD N. BOYCE, CRIMINAL LAW 985 (3d ed. 1982).

[249] ROLLIN M. PERKINS & RONALD N. BOYCE, CRIMINAL LAW 986 (3d ed. 1982). These authors suggest that this approach lends itself to the "guilty but insane" concept. ROLLIN M. PERKINS & RONALD N. BOYCE, CRIMINAL LAW 991 (3d ed. 1982).

operable.[250] This thesis denies that insanity negates mens rea; rather, it views insanity as an extenuating circumstance that provides exculpation from criminal liability. As determined in a previous chapter, intent can exist where an accused harbors a "conscious objective or purpose" to accomplish a particular result to engage in certain conduct that is criminal.[251] Under the "particularized" approach, a "conscious objective" to kill someone could conceivably exist in a defendant's mind even though, at the same time, he or she may lack substantial capacity to appreciate the criminality of his or her killing. The question is not whether the defendant committed the actus reus and had the requisite mens rea, but whether the lack of *capacity* should be an excuse.[252] Parenthetically then, if mens rea and *just punishment* are grounded in neutral, as opposed to moral, considerations, then abolition of the special insanity defense could occur by the simple expedient of a legislative determination that lack of substantial appreciation is no longer an excuse.

The abolitionist does not have the support of all of those who abide by the particularized approach, however. Professor Hermann insists:

> The proper approach requires the recognition of the element of capacity as a third criterion of responsibility, which can be defeated by certain excuses. The elements together — act, *mens rea*, and capacity — provide a unifying principle for criminal liability. . . . These three elements together provide a set of criteria for criminal liability that determines whether a person is properly said to be *blameworthy, a prerequisite for the imposition of just punishment*. The third element being argued for here satisfies a critically important principle of responsibility: the individual must have the capacity and a fair chance to conform.[253]

While clarifying that with the "particularized" approach to mens rea, the "requirement of moral culpability is not captured entirely in the elements of act and *mens rea*,"[254] Professor Hermann adds:

> The defense of insanity thus becomes a matter of negating the *capacity for culpable conduct*; it is an assertion that the insane person is *not morally responsible, not blameworthy*, and therefore incapable of being held criminally culpable. Since blameworthiness is essential for criminal liability and

---

[250] DONALD H.J. HERMANN, THE INSANITY DEFENSE: PHILOSOPHICAL, HISTORICAL AND LEGAL PERSPECTIVES 111 (1983). Professor Hermann notes that this is the approach adopted by the Model Penal Code, which in turn was adopted by the state of Illinois.

[251] 720 ILCS 5/4-4 (1999).

[252] ROLLIN M. PERKINS & RONALD N. BOYCE, CRIMINAL LAW 991 (3d ed. 1982).

[253] DONALD H.J. HERMANN, THE INSANITY DEFENSE: PHILOSOPHICAL, HISTORICAL AND LEGAL PERSPECTIVES 126 (1983) (emphasis added).

[254] DONALD H.J. HERMANN, THE INSANITY DEFENSE: PHILOSOPHICAL, HISTORICAL AND LEGAL PERSPECTIVES 126 (1983).

justified punishment, and since the insanity defense defines those who cannot be held blameworthy, then the defense of insanity must be viewed as addressed to an essential element of criminal liability, the requirement of capacity for conforming behavior.[255]

As Professor George Fletcher stated in a discussion of this point:

The formal attachment to the criminal trial, stripped of all issues of responsibility, blame and punishment, leaves one puzzled. If only an "act in violation of the law" must be proved, the question is why? What is the theory of political authority that justifies the state's intervention against someone who has committed a blameless act?[256]

The discussion below will reveal the Illinois stance on these issues.

§ 18.16.   Affirmative Defenses: Burden of Proof.

A basic premise of criminal liability is that all persons are presumed to be sane.[257] This presumption is overcome only where the defendant comes forward with evidence establishing insanity.[258]

The general provision regarding "affirmative defenses" in Illinois states the accused is obliged to offer only "some evidence" in support of his or her affirmative defense.[259] However, in *People v. Redmond*,[260] the Illinois Supreme Court in 1975 rejected this "some evidence" test in the context of an insanity claim and insisted the evidence be sufficient "to raise a reasonable doubt as to [defendant's] guilt of the offense charged."[261] In other words, only after the accused had raised a doubt about his or her sanity was the presumption no longer valid.[262]

Prior to the 1984 revisions of the insanity statute, once the defendant had raised the issue of insanity by presenting evidence that cast a reasonable doubt on his or her sanity, the *state* had the ultimate "burden of proving sanity at the

---

[255] DONALD H.J. HERMANN, THE INSANITY DEFENSE: PHILOSOPHICAL, HISTORICAL AND LEGAL PERSPECTIVES 127 (1983) (emphasis added).

[256] GEORGE FLETCHER, RETHINKING CRIMINAL LAW 844 (1978).

[257] People v. Clark, 102 Ill. App. 3d 414, 417, 429 N.E.2d 1255, 1257 (1st Dist. 1981).

[258] This is true "unless the State's evidence raises the issue involving the alleged defense. . . ." 720 ILCS 5/3-2(a) (1999). *See also* Ake v. Oklahoma, 470 U.S. 68, 76-83 (1985) (when indigent defendant's sanity at time of offense is to be significant factor at trial, he is entitled to state-supplied psychiatrist to assist in evaluating, preparing and presenting defense).

[259] 720 ILCS 5/3-2(a) (1999).

[260] 59 Ill. 2d 328, 320 N.E.2d 321 (1974).

[261] People v. Redmond, 59 Ill. 2d 328, 337-38, 320 N.E.2d 321, 326 (1974) (quoting ILL. ANN. STAT. ch. 38, para. 3-2 (Smith-Hurd 1989), 1961 Committee Comments, at 192-93 (revised 1972)).

[262] People v. Smothers, 55 Ill. 2d 172, 174, 302 N.E.2d 324, 326 (1973).

time of the offenses beyond a reasonable doubt."[263] Thus, once the insanity issue had been successfully raised, the state was required to "establish beyond a reasonable doubt that the defendant was sane at the time [of the offense] in order to secure a conviction."[264]

However, in 1984 the General Assembly placed the burden of persuasion regarding establishing insanity on the defendant and in 1998 made that burden "clear and convincing" evidence. Today, the "affirmative defense" statute reads "[i]f the affirmative defense of insanity is raised, the *defendant* bears the burden of proving by clear and convincing evidence his insanity at the time of the offense."[265] This "clear and convincing test" is reinforced by similar language in the revised insanity statute itself.[266] In *People v. Seuffer*,[267] the Illinois Supreme Court held the revised statutes make clear that "[w]hen the defense of insanity is raised, . . . there is no corresponding requirement that the prosecution disprove that claim, by any quantum of proof."[268] Moreover, in *People v. Scott*,[269] the Illinois Supreme Court held that placing the burden on the defendant to prove insanity was not unconstitutional[270] while rejecting the argument that sanity was an element of the crime charged to be proved by the state.[271] Thus, the state no longer must rebut defense evidence by establishing defendant was sane at the time of the offense.

The insanity statute states that in a jury trial where the insanity defense has been presented, the jury must be instructed that it may not consider whether the defendant has met his or her burden of proving that he or she is not guilty by reason of insanity *unless* it has *first* determined that the state has proved the defendant guilty beyond a reasonable doubt of the offense with which he or she is charged.[272] Procedurally then, the accused must be found guilty of the crime be-

---

[263] People v. Carlson, 79 Ill. 2d 564, 580, 404 N.E.2d 233, 240 (1980).

[264] People v. Marshall, 114 Ill. App. 3d 217, 226, 448 N.E.2d 969, 975 (4th Dist. 1983).

[265] 720 ILCS 5/3-2(b) (1999) (emphasis added).

[266] 720 ILCS 5/6-2(e) (1999). The burden of proof in previous statutes was previously a "preponderance of the evidence." *See* People v. Gill, 304 Ill. App. 3d 23, 29-30, 713 N.E.2d 124, 128 (1st Dist. 1999) (where amended insanity statute raising defendant's burden of proof was not in effect at the time of trial, application of the new statute to the defendant violated ex post facto clause of state and federal constitution and, as such, constituted reversible error).

[267] 144 Ill. 2d 482, 582 N.E.2d 71 (1991).

[268] People v. Seuffer, 144 Ill. 2d 482, 519, 582 N.E.2d 71, 86 (1991). *See also* People v. Wilhoite, 228 Ill. App. 3d 12, 20, 592 N.E.2d 48, 53 (1st Dist. 1991) ("The state bears no burden on the issue of insanity").

[269] 148 Ill. 2d 479, 594 N.E.2d 217 (1992), *cert. denied*, 507 U.S. 989 (1993).

[270] People v. Scott, 148 Ill. 2d 479, 540-41, 594 N.E.2d 217, 242-43 (1992) (not violative of due process), *cert. denied*, 507 U.S. 989 (1993). *See also* People v. Vernon, 276 Ill. App. 3d 386, 390, 657 N.E.2d 1117, 1121 (1st Dist. 1995) (not violative of equal protection).

[271] People v. Scott, 148 Ill. 2d 479, 541-43, 594 N.E.2d 217, 243 (1992), *cert. denied*, 507 U.S. 989 (1993).

[272] 720 ILCS 5/6-2(e) (1999).

fore the insanity issue can be addressed and a finding of not guilty returned.[273] This "now-you're-guilty, now-you're-not" procedure raises both conceptual and constitutional issues.

A number of considerations make it clear that the "broad" approach to mens rea generally, and the theory that insanity negates mens rea specifically, is not the law in Illinois. First, the Illinois mens rea provisions and insanity statutes are patterned after the Model Penal Code, which adopted the "particularized" theory. Second, it is difficult to reconcile the inclusion of absolute liability[274] (crimes requiring no mens rea) possibilities in the Illinois Criminal Code with the theory that insanity negates mens rea, since acceptance of such a theory would apparently mean insanity claims could never be advanced for crimes that have no mens rea requirement. This is a proposition that has no support in either the code, the legislative intent, or the caselaw. Third, and most important, the 1984 statutory amendments dealing with insanity plea procedures discussed above are completely at odds with the concept that insanity negates mens rea, since section 5/6-2(e) explicitly states "each of the elements of each of the offenses charged" must be proved *before* the insanity issue can be considered by the jury.[275]

More to the point than what the Illinois insanity defense is *not* is the question of whether it is, then, in tandem with the "excusing circumstance" concept. Again, reference to the section 5/6-2(e) language that insanity is not an issue "until and unless it has first [been] determined that the state has proven the defendant guilty" dictates the conclusion that the "excuse" theory is law in Illinois. In other words, not until the requisite act and mens rea is established can the question of the accused's culpability be addressed.[276] Clearly, the insanity question can only be disposed of by employing a three-factor analysis: (1) act; (2) mens rea; and (3) culpability.

A constitutional question may indeed arise by requiring a defendant to prove insanity by a preponderance of the evidence or clear and convincing evidence. It is elementary that "it is not within the province of a legislature to declare an individual guilty or presumptively guilty of a crime."[277] However, in *Patterson v. New York*,[278] the United States Supreme Court held that a New York law requiring the defendant, in a prosecution for second-degree murder, to prove the af-

---

[273] *See* People v. Wells, 294 Ill. App. 3d 405, 408, 690 N.E.2d 645, 647 (1st Dist. 1998) ("State must prove the defendant guilty beyond a reasonable doubt of each of the elements of each of the offenses charged before a defendant may be found NGRI [Not Guilty by Reason of Insanity]").

[274] 720 ILCS 5/4-9 (1999).

[275] 720 ILCS 5/6-2(e) (1999).

[276] People v. Scott, 148 Ill. 2d 479, 540-42, 594 N.E.2d 217, 242-43 (1992), *cert. denied,* 507 U.S. 989 (1993).

[277] McFarland v. American Sugar Ref. Co., 241 U.S. 79, 86 (1916).

[278] 432 U.S. 197 (1977).

firmative defense of extreme emotional disturbance in order to reduce the crime to manslaughter did not violate the Due Process Clause of the Fourteenth Amendment. The court stated that such an affirmative defense "does not serve to negative any facts of the crime which the State is to prove in order to convict of murder. It constitutes a separate issue on which the defendant is required to carry the burden of persuasion. . . ."[279] The same reasoning applies to a question of the constitutionality of an insanity defense that places the burden of proof on defendant.[280] In *Patterson*, the Court concluded:

> [I]f the State . . . chooses to recognize a factor that mitigates the degree of criminality or punishment, we think the State may assure itself that the fact has been established with reasonable certainty. To recognize at all a mitigating circumstance does not require the State to prove its non-existence in each case in which the fact is put in issue, if in its judgment this would be too cumbersome, too expensive, and too inaccurate.[281]

Hence, placing the burden on the defendant to prove insanity poses no constitutional problems.[282]

The problems associated with the differing burdens of proof for purposes of a guilty but mentally ill verdict were addressed in 1998 in *People v. Fierer*,[283] a case where the alleged criminality occurred after the 1984 burden of proof amendment. In that case, the court pointed out that the burden is on the defendant to show insanity, while "at the same time the state bears the burden of proof of noninsanity for purposes of the GBMI verdict."[284] The court criticized this statutory arrangement.

---

[279] Patterson v. New York, 432 U.S. 197, 206-07 (1977).

[280] Leland v. Oregon, 343 U.S. 790, 799 (1952) (state statute that required defendant to prove his insanity beyond reasonable doubt did not violate due process). *See also* Rivera v. Delaware, 429 U.S. 877 (1976) (appeal was dismissed for not presenting a substantial federal question where statute burdened defendant with proving his affirmative defense of insanity by preponderance of evidence); Mullaney v. Wilbur, 421 U.S. 684, 706 (1976) (Rehnquist, J., concurring) ("the existence or nonexistence of legal insanity bears no necessary relationship to the existence or nonexistence of the required mental elements of the crime").

[281] Patterson v. New York, 432 U.S. 197, 209 (1977).

[282] People v. Scott, 148 Ill. 2d 479, 540-41, 594 N.E.2d 217, 242-43 (1992) (requiring defendant to prove insanity by preponderance of evidence does not violate federal or state due process), *cert. denied*, 507 U.S. 989 (1993); People v. Vernon, 276 Ill. App. 3d 386, 390, 657 N.E.2d 1117, 1121 (1st Dist. 1995) (not violative of equal protection); People v. Martin, 166 Ill. App. 3d 428, 435, 519 N.E.2d 1085, 1089 (1st Dist. 1988) (requiring defendant to prove affirmative defense of insanity by preponderance of evidence does not violate federal or state due process or equal protection); People v. Hightower, 172 Ill. App. 3d 678, 682-87, 526 N.E.2d 1129, 1131-33 (5th Dist. 1988) (preponderance of evidence standard does not violate federal or state due process).

[283] 124 Ill. 2d 176, 529 N.E.2d 972 (1988).

[284] People v. Fierer, 124 Ill. 2d 176, 185, 529 N.E.2d 972, 975 (1988).

Under this scheme, a theoretical class of defendants exists who cannot be found insane and thus not guilty by reason of insanity, because they have not carried their preponderance burden, but who also may not be found GBMI because their noninsanity has not been proved by the State beyond a reasonable doubt. In other words, defendants whose sanity is a close question, the very group one would think should be covered by the GBMI verdict, may not be found GBMI because they fall into the gap between "preponderance" and "beyond a reasonable doubt."[285]

This court added that if the goal of the GBMI verdict was to identify those in need of psychiatric help, this statutory scheme undermines that goal.[286] While the court did not find the statutory arrangement unconstitutionally vague or the like, it counseled trial judges to attempt to fashion instructions that would avoid the vagaries of these "seemingly conflicting" statutes and the state legislature to review the "interplay between these unclear and confusing statutes."[287] In any event, in the case before it, the court found the trial judge's efforts to reconcile these provisions in his jury instructions a reversible error.[288]

In 1990, the legislature amended the procedural guidelines regarding instructing juries about GBMI, presumably in an effort to address the court's objections in *Fierer*. Specifically, the Code of Criminal Procedure was revised to require a jury considering a GBMI verdict to find that: (1) the state had proven the defendant guilty of the offense beyond a reasonable doubt; (2) the defendant had failed to prove his insanity as required under the insanity statute; and (3) the defendant has proved by a preponderance of the evidence that he was mentally ill.[289] In 1999, the Illinois Supreme Court in *People v. Lantz*[290] upheld the constitutionality of the GBMI statutory scheme against claims the defense is required to shoulder conflicting burdens and conflicting propositions in an attempt to prove insanity and avoid a GBMI verdict.[291] Because the issues of fact are bifurcated – "the jury does not consider mental illness until it has first decided the defendant's claim of insanity" – and not considered "simultaneously," the court rejected the argument that defendants' right to due process would be infringed by the burden of proof arrangement.[292]

---

[285] People v. Fierer, 124 Ill. 2d 176, 189, 529 N.E.2d 972, 977 (1988).

[286] People v. Fierer, 124 Ill. 2d 176, 190, 529 N.E.2d 972, 977 (1988).

[287] People v. Fierer, 124 Ill. 2d 176, 191, 529 N.E.2d 972, 978 (1988).

[288] *See* instructions given at People v. Fierer, 124 Ill. 2d 176, 186, 529 N.E.2d 972, 975 (1988).

[289] 725 ILCS 5/115-4(j) (1999).

[290] 186 Ill. 2d 243, 712 N.E.2d 314 (1999).

[291] People v. Lantz, 186 Ill. 2d 243, 253-58, 712 N.E.2d 314, 320-22 (1999).

[292] People v. Lantz, 186 Ill. 2d 243, 253-58, 712 N.E.2d 314, 320-22 (1999).

§ 18.17. Defense of Intoxication or Drugged Condition: Background of Current Law.

Before the Criminal Code of 1961 became law, voluntary intoxication was not a defense by statute, although involuntary intoxication was so.[293] Instead, the code at that time explicitly stated that voluntary drunkenness was not an excuse.[294] Notwithstanding this statutory mandate, the caselaw provided that when voluntary "drunkenness had proceeded so far as to render the defendant incapable of forming the particular mens rea required for the offense, the defendant was entitled to be acquitted on that charge."[295] However, the Illinois opinions were not very receptive to voluntary intoxication claims (which is a trend that continues today). Historically, most courts limited these defense arguments to specific-intent crimes only, others barred the defense altogether, and still others may have even viewed voluntary intoxication as a factor in aggravation.[296] In addition, few cases dealt with drug-induced intoxication before 1961 (a trend that obviously does not continue today).

In 1961, the legislature provided that a person in an "intoxicated or drugged condition" had a defense if such either (1) "negative[d] the existence of a mental state which is an element of the crime" or (2) was "involuntarily produced" depriving the person of the "substantial capacity either to appreciate the criminality of his conduct or to conform his conduct to the requirements of law."[297] Thus, this affirmative defense was extended to those (1) under the influence of drugs or narcotics as well as alcohol and (2) charged with a general intent as well as a specific intent crime.[298] Furthermore, if the defendant's intoxication was involuntary, he or she would have a defense if it affected his or her cognitive or volitional powers.

In 1988, the General Assembly amended the first prong of this defense. The revision provided an intoxicated or drugged condition defense only would be available if the voluntary intoxication was "so extreme as to suspend the power of reason and render him incapable of forming a specific intent which is an ele-

---

[293] See ILL. REV. STAT. ch. 38, para. 599 (1959) ("Drunkenness shall not be an excuse for any crime or misdemeanor, unless such drunkenness be occasioned by the fraud, contrivance or force of some other person . . .").

[294] See ILL. REV. STAT. ch. 38, para. 599 (1959).

[295] ILL. REV. STAT. ch. 38, para. 6-3 (Smith-Hurd 1989), 1961 Committee Comments, at 335 (revised 1972). See also People v. Freedman, 4 Ill. 2d 414, 420, 123 N.E.2d 317, 319 (1954) ("while voluntary intoxication affords no excuse for a crime, an offense which is by law made to depend upon the state or condition of the mind of the accused cannot be committed by one who is incapable of forming the specific intent").

[296] People v. Rosas, 102 Ill. App. 3d 113, 115-16, 429 N.E.2d 898, 900 (3d Dist. 1981).

[297] ILL. REV. STAT. ch. 38, para. 6-3 (1961).

[298] ILL. ANN. STAT. ch. 38, para. 6-3 (Smith-Hurd 1989), 1961 Committee Comments, at 335 (revised 1972).

ment of the crime."[299] Obviously, general intent crimes were excluded from the defense.

§ 18.18.   Defense of Intoxication or Drugged Condition Codified.

The defense of "intoxication or drugged condition"[300] as an affirmative defense[301] currently reads:

> A person who is in an intoxicated or drugged condition is criminally responsible for conduct unless such condition either:
> (a) Is so extreme as to suspend the power of reason and render him incapable of forming a specific intent which is an element of the crime; or
> (b) Is involuntarily produced and deprives him of substantial capacity either to appreciate the criminality of his conduct or to conform his conduct to the requirements of law.[302]

In codifying the defense of intoxication or drugged condition, the committee responsible for drafting the 1961 law intended to create a statute that essentially would be in conformity with the earlier caselaw.[303] The drafting committee (1) clearly recognized the defense of voluntary intoxication in circumstances in which the "defendant was incapable of forming the particular *mens rea* required for the offense," (2) maintained the defense of involuntary intoxication, and (3) clarified that the intoxication in question could be attributable to drugs as well as alcohol.[304] In addition, the language of the statute itself reflected that intoxication or a drugged condition was not per se a defense to a crime; accordingly, the intoxicated person normally remained "criminally responsible" for his or her illegal acts. The General Assembly which later enacted the 1988 amendment was bent on narrowing the defense by excluding all but "specific intent" crimes from the statute's reach.[305]

§ 18.19.   Elements of Defense of Intoxication or Drugged Condition.

The defense of intoxication or drugged condition (hereinafter referred to as "intoxication" unless otherwise noted for purposes of clarity) is divided into two

---

[299] P.A. 85-670 § 1 (1988). This statutory change was criticized in Timothy O'Neill, *Illinois' Latest Version of the Defense of Voluntary Intoxication: Is It Wise? Is It Constitutional?*, 39 DEPAUL L. REV. 15 (1989).

[300] 720 ILCS 5/6-3 (1999).

[301] 720 ILCS 5/6-4 (1999).

[302] 720 ILCS 5/6-3 (1999).

[303] *See* ILL. ANN. STAT. ch. 38, para. 6-3 (Smith-Hurd 1989), 1961 Committee Comments, at 335 (revised 1972).

[304] *See* ILL. ANN. STAT. ch. 38, para. 6-3 (Smith-Hurd 1989), 1961 Committee Comments, at 335 (revised 1972).

[305] *See* ch. 2 for a discussion of "specific intent" crimes.

components: one addressing voluntary intoxication, the other concerning itself with involuntary intoxication. *Voluntary* intoxication is a defense only where it negates the requisite mental state of specific intent. *Involuntary* intoxication is treated much like the prior Illinois statute addressing insanity — it exculpates only where it deprives the actor of his or her substantial capacity to appreciate the criminality of his or her conduct or to conform his or her conduct to the dictates of the law.[306] Because these are distinct concepts, they will be addressed individually.

§18.20. — Voluntary Intoxication Generally.

Section 5/6-3(a) sets forth the requirements for voluntary intoxication. The caselaw is replete with statements that voluntary drunkenness or intoxication is "ordinarily not a defense" to a crime.[307] Also, the decisions continually repeat that "[m]erely being drunk or intoxicated is insufficient to create a defense of intoxication."[308] In order to raise this defense, "the accused must show that his intoxication was so extreme as to suspend all reason."[309] Not unless the intoxicated state "*entirely*"[310] defeats the power of reason, thereby making "impossible the existence of a mental state which is an element of the crime," can the accused use voluntary intoxication as a defense.[311] In this regard, it should be mentioned that the concept of "diminished capacity,"[312] whereby a state of intoxication may act not as a complete defense, but rather to reduce the degree of an offense, for example, from murder to manslaughter, has been explicitly found *not* to be the law in Illinois.[313]

The fact that the intoxication may be attributable to alcoholism or drug addiction does not support a claim that the alcoholic's intoxication is somehow "involuntary" rather than voluntary.[314] "Involuntary" intoxication *only* refers to in-

---

[306] *See* § 18.02 of this chapter.

[307] *See, e.g.*, People v. Winters, 29 Ill. 2d 74, 80, 193 N.E.2d 809, 812 (1963).

[308] *See, e.g.*, People v. Moon, 107 Ill. App. 3d 568, 572, 437 N.E.2d 823, 825 (5th Dist. 1982).

[309] People v. Moon, 107 Ill. App. 3d 568, 572, 437 N.E.2d 823, 825 (5th Dist. 1982). *See also* People v. Roesler, 105 Ill. App. 3d 1007, 1013, 552 N.E.2d 1242, 1246 (5th Dist. 1990) (voluntary intoxication must entirely suspend power of reason; "When the record indicates that defendant acted with any purpose or rationality, the defense is unavailable").

[310] People v. Fuller, 91 Ill. App. 3d 922, 927, 415 N.E.2d 502, 506 (1st Dist. 1980) (emphasis added).

[311] People v. Walcher, 42 Ill. 2d 159, 163, 246 N.E.2d 256, 259 (1969).

[312] *See* ROLLIN M. PERKINS & RONALD N. BOYCE, CRIMINAL LAW 980-85 (3d ed. 1982).

[313] People v. Fuller, 91 Ill. App. 3d 922, 927, 415 N.E.2d 502, 506 (1st Dist. 1980). *See also* People v. Smith, 124 Ill. App. 3d 720, 723, 464 N.E.2d 824, 827 (4th Dist. 1984) (voluntary intoxication does not entitle an accused charged with murder jury instructions on manslaughter).

[314] People v. Rogers, 123 Ill. 2d 487, 508, 528 N.E.2d 667, 678 (1988), *cert. denied,* 488 U.S. 1046 (1989); People v. Walcher, 42 Ill. 2d 159, 163, 246 N.E.2d 256, 259 (1969); People v. Downey, 162 Ill. App. 3d 322, 335, 515 N.E.2d 362, 370 (2d Dist. 1987).

toxication resulting from some outside influence such as trick, artifice, or force.[315] Evidence of chronic alcoholism does not even have to be accepted by a trial court where the evidence otherwise indicates that the defendant possessed the requisite mental state.[316] Likewise, the fact that defendant may have been a narcotics addict does not mean his drug use was "involuntary," and, as with the chronic alcoholic, a trial court was not required to admit evidence offered by the defense that would have attempted to excuse defendant's criminality because of "chronic multiple drug dependency."[317] In addition, voluntary intoxication cannot be equated with temporary insanity.[318] Indeed, voluntary intoxication or a drugged condition "precludes the use of the insanity defense except where the mental disease or defect is traceable to the habitual or chronic use of drugs and alcohol and results in a permanent type of insanity."[319]

The defense of voluntary intoxication is further limited by the court's willingness to examine whether the defendant formulated the wrongful intent before becoming intoxicated. Thus, even if the intoxication suspended all reason at the time of the criminal act, the defendant will not be exonerated if he or she formed the requisite intent before becoming intoxicated.[320] For example, the accused who formulates the requisite mens rea for a crime and then becomes extremely intoxicated in order to deliberately cloud his or her faculties so as to relieve himself or herself of responsibility or to "work up the courage" to go through with the criminal plan cannot avail themselves of the intoxication defense. In conclusion, "an actor should not be insulated from criminal responsibility for

---

[315] People v. Rogers, 123 Ill. 2d 487, 508, 528 N.E.2d 667, 678 (1988), *cert. denied,* 488 U.S. 1046 (1989); People v. Downey, 162 Ill. App. 3d 322, 335, 515 N.E.2d 362, 370 (2d Dist. 1987).

[316] People v. Davis, 54 Ill. App. 3d 517, 525, 369 N.E.2d 1376, 1383 (4th Dist. 1977) ("Proof of chronic alcoholism, by itself, does not exempt a defendant from criminal liability"; exclusion of proof thereof upheld).

[317] People v. Rogers, 123 Ill. 2d 487, 508, 528 N.E.2d 667, 677 (1988), *cert. denied,* 488 U.S. 1046 (1989).

[318] People v. Kenzik, 22 Ill. 2d 567, 575, 177 N.E.2d 162, 166-67 (1961); *See also* People v. Whitehead, 171 Ill. App. 3d 900, 905-06, 525 N.E.2d 1084, 1087 (1st Dist. 1988) (defendant's voluntary use of PCP, leading to intoxication, could not insulate him from criminal responsibility based on insanity defense, despite claim that defendant also suffered major depressive episodes that combined with intoxication to make him lack capacity to appreciate criminality of his actions); People v. Downey, 162 Ill. App. 3d 322, 334, 515 N.E.2d 362, 369 (2d Dist. 1987) (drug addiction alone does not support finding of insanity).

[319] People v. Britz, 123 Ill. 2d 446, 463, 528 N.E.2d 703, 711 (1988), *cert. denied,* 489 U.S. 1044 (1989). *See also* People v. Free, 94 Ill. 2d 378, 406, 447 N.E.2d 218, 231-32 (toxic psychosis induced by voluntary intoxication of drugs, alcohol or both is not a "mental disease or defect" which amounts to legal insanity), *cert. denied,* 464 U.S. 865 (1983).

[320] People v. Bartz, 342 Ill. 56, 66-67, 173 N.E. 779, 783 (1930); People v. Cochran, 313 Ill. 508, 518, 145 N.E. 207, 211 (1924).

acts which result from a temporary mental state that is voluntarily self-induced."[321]

§ 18.21. — Intoxication Negating Intent.

As stated above, the accused's voluntary intoxication must render him or her wholly "incapable of forming a specific intent which is an element of the charge."[322] Most important (and most confusing) is the *type* of *mens rea* that voluntary intoxication is capable of negating.[323] If one reviews the caselaw before the 1988 statutory amendment, where the law provided intoxication had the capacity to negate any "mental state," it readily reveals how the post-amendment law, which limits the defense to "specific intent" crimes, will only continue the confusion. While some of the pre-amendment cases considered voluntary intoxication claims against both general intent and specific intent crimes,[324] many other Illinois decisions stated that "there is a distinction between general and specific intent offenses and voluntary intoxication may be a defense to the latter but not to the former."[325] Of the cases that recognized the defense for specific-intent crimes only, some of the cases referred to *specific intent* as any "mental state which is an *element* of the crime" and held that "a person who is voluntarily intoxicated is always criminally responsible for his conduct unless his condition negates the existence of a specific mental state which is an element of the offense."[326] Here, the courts were using a broad interpretation of *specific intent* that looks to whether the crime requires *any* particular mens rea.[327] Accordingly, courts employing this broad definition of specific intent would conclude, for instance, that battery is subject to this defense, inasmuch as "[b]attery by making physical contact of an insulting nature is a specific intent crime because it requires that the contact of an insulting nature be made intentionally or know-

---

[321] People v. Free, 94 Ill. 2d 378, 406, 447 N.E.2d 218, 231 (where defendant consumed beer, marijuana and PCP and then had no recollection of his actions, not entitled to defense of insanity instructions), *cert. denied*, 464 U.S. 865 (1983).

[322] 720 ILCS 5/6-3(a) (1999).

[323] *See* Timothy O'Neill, *Illinois' Latest Version of the Defense of Voluntary Intoxication: Is It Wise? Is It Constitutional?*, 39 DEPAUL L. REV. 15, 33 (1989).

[324] *See, e.g.,* People v. Green, 130 Ill. App. 2d 609, 612, 265 N.E.2d 184, 186 (1st Dist. 1970) (considering but rejecting claims against attempted rape, which is "specific intent" crime and battery, which is "general intent" offense).

[325] *See, e.g.,* People v. Rosas, 102 Ill. App. 3d 113, 116, 429 N.E.2d 898, 900-01 (3d Dist. 1981) (no defense to armed robbery because it is a general intent crime). *See also* People v. Arndt, 50 Ill. 2d 390, 394, 280 N.E.2d 230, 233 (1972) ("[V]oluntary intoxication is not a defense to the crime of involuntary manslaughter, since involuntary manslaughter is not a specific intent crime").

[326] *See, e.g.,* People v. Harkey, 69 Ill. App. 3d 94, 96, 386 N.E.2d 1151, 1153 (5th Dist. 1979).

[327] *See* ch. 2 of this treatise for a discussion of the different approaches to what constitutes "specific intent."

ingly."[328] Applying this approach to murder, some courts described murder as a "specific-intent" offense that was subject to this defense,[329] even though other courts consider murder a general intent stricture.[330] Consistent with this approach, these same courts concluded, for example, that voluntary intoxication was no defense to robbery since robbery "has no mental state which is an element of the offense."[331]

Other pre-amendment cases that stated voluntary intoxication is only a defense to specific intent crimes appeared to employ a narrower definition of specific intent that considers whether the crime requires proof that the accused harbored in his or her mind a criminal *purpose or objective*.[332] For instance, it was stated with respect to burglary that "[a]n essential element of that offense is that defendant entered the building with the specific intent to commit a *theft* therein" and that voluntary intoxication is a defense to such a crime.[333] Finally, some of the courts that limited the reach of this defense to specific intent offenses simply did not explain what they mean by *specific intent*.[334]

With the 1988 amendment which explicitly limits the reach of the voluntary intoxication defense to those crimes which require "a specific intent which is an element of the offense,"[335] inconsistency in application of this defense will continue to occur as it did before the amendment because of the judicial inconsistency in defining specific intent. For example, a 1994 Illinois appellate opinion

---

[328] *See, e.g.*, People v. Hayes, 37 Ill. App. 3d 772, 774, 347 N.E.2d 327, 329 (1st Dist. 1976). *See also* People v. Jones, 67 Ill. App. 3d 477, 478, 384 N.E.2d 523, 525 (3d Dist. 1978) ("Battery and resisting a peace officer are both specific intent crimes requiring proof that the defendant acted knowingly"); People v. Long, 30 Ill. App. 3d 815, 819, 333 N.E.2d 534, 538 (2d Dist. 1975) (voluntary intoxication may negate specific intent; "specific intent relevant to aggravated kidnapping is knowledge").

[329] *See, e.g.*, People v. Lenser, 102 Ill App. 3d 214, 217, 430 N.E.2d 495, 497 (3d Dist. 1981) (defense claim of voluntary intoxication considered but rejected).

[330] *See, e.g.*, People v. Calhoun, 4 Ill. App. 3d 683, 689, 281 N.E.2d 363, 367 (1st Dist. 1972) (explicitly stating proof of specific intent is not necessary for murder).

[331] *See, e.g.*, People v. Harkey, 69 Ill. App. 3d 94, 96-97, 386 N.E.2d 1151, 1153 (5th Dist. 1979). *See also* People v. Foster, 32 Ill. App. 2d 462, 468, 178 N.E.2d 402, 405 (4th Dist. 1961) (unlawful use of weapon is not specific intent crime because intent or knowledge is not required).

[332] This is the approach taken in most jurisdictions. Annot., 8 A.L.R.3d 1236. *See also* ch. 2 of this treatise.

[333] People v. Foster, 23 Ill. App. 3d 559, 560-61, 319 N.E.2d 522, 523 (4th Dist. 1974) (reversible error due to erroneous instructions regarding voluntary intoxication defense) (emphasis added). *See also* People v. Wirth, 77 Ill. App. 3d 253, 257, 395 N.E.2d 1106, 1109 (1st Dist. 1979) (burglary requires specific intent to commit felony or theft).

[334] *See, e.g.*, People v. Newlin, 31 Ill. App. 3d 735, 739, 334 N.E.2d 349, 352 (5th Dist. 1975) (burglary conviction affirmed; "[f]or voluntary intoxication to be a legal excuse and render the specific intent [for burglary] impossible, the condition must be so extreme as to suspend all reason. [citations omitted] The same test would apply if drugs were the agent that deprived a defendant of the capacity to form the necessary specific intent.").

[335] 720 ILCS 5/6-3(a) (1999).

interpreting the revised law (which again addresses only *specific intent* criminality) stated: "[w]hether a defendant's intoxication was so extreme as to render him incapable of committing a *knowing or intentional* act is a question for the trier of fact."[336]

§ 18.22.   — Evidence Supportive of Intent.

The courts consider a broad range of evidence offered by the state that tends to rebut this defense claim: "Where the evidence on the record indicates that defendant acted with any purpose or rationality or remembered the offense with clarity or detail, voluntary intoxication is not an available defense."[337] Thus, where there was evidence that the defendant was intoxicated because of the consumption of alcohol and fifty amphetamine pills, he was nonetheless convicted of murder over a claim of voluntary intoxication because he remembered his activities in killing the victim, remembered that the victim asked him to stop assaulting her, checked the body to see if the victim was still alive, and then attempted to conceal the dead body, which indicated the defendant acted with rationality and purpose.[338] Where evidence revealed the defendant remembered whom he had been drinking alcohol with, how much he had consumed, and where he had gone afterward, including all events up until the time he entered the house where he engaged in a shooting, he failed to demonstrate that he *entirely* lacked the power of reason and mental capacity and, as such, was properly convicted of murder and attempted murder.[339] In addition, this same court considered the perceptions of lay persons about the level of defendant's intoxication, finding that none of the persons who had seen him during his episode of criminality described him as intoxicated.[340] Where another defendant who had taken heroin was aware that he had left a bus he was riding before reaching his desired destination, had checked to see if he had enough money for bus fare,

---

[336] People v. Redmond, 265 Ill. App. 3d 292, 302, 637 N.E.2d 526, 534 (1st Dist. 1994) (first degree murder conviction affirmed after voluntary intoxication claim considered but rejected).

[337] People v. Nichols, 96 Ill. App. 3d 354, 359, 420 N.E.2d 1166, 1170 (2d Dist. 1981); *see* People v. Hurt, 175 Ill. App. 3d 970, 976-78, 530 N.E.2d 698, 703-04 (2d Dist. 1988) (where defendant was able to go to police station, thinking to carry a pistol, where he feigned injuries and fabricated a story about being beaten to get past a security guard, then pointed a gun at officer in apparent effort to provoke officer to shoot him so that he would not have to kill himself, and then complained afterward that he had not been killed by officer, this was evidence of "elaborate plan" suggestive of rationality sufficient to defeat claim of defense of voluntary intoxication); People v. Hayes, 173 Ill. App. 3d 1043, 1048-49, 527 N.E.2d 1342, 1347 (5th Dist. 1988) (defendant's attempt to avoid detection of criminality and elude police indicative of rationality sufficient to defeat claim of voluntary intoxication).

[338] People v. Nichols, 96 Ill. App. 3d 354, 359, 420 N.E.2d 1166, 1170 (2d Dist. 1981) (murder conviction affirmed).

[339] People v. Jones, 56 Ill. App. 3d 600, 605, 371 N.E.2d 1150, 1154 (5th Dist. 1977).

[340] People v. Jones, 56 Ill. App. 3d 600, 605, 371 N.E.2d 1150, 1154 (5th Dist. 1977).

knew the relative positions of himself and his victim before his attack, had attempted to borrow cab fare from his victim, and had hit the victim and tried to pull the victim to the ground, his recollections to these various events defeated his voluntary intoxication defense.[341] The mere fact that a defendant claimed he could not remember his crime was not a defense where the evidence revealed he was capable of driving an automobile, obeying traffic regulations, loading a rifle, accurately shooting his wife, and driving her to a hospital.[342]

Where a psychiatrist testifies that the accused was overcome by an "alcoholic blackout," the fact finder can still determine that the accused harbored the requisite mens rea from other evidence.[343] Not only can an expert offer his or her opinion regarding the defendant's level of intoxication,[344] but a trial court may also allow a lay person to express an opinion on the accused's intoxication without invading the province of the jury, assuming the opinion is based on personal observation and experience.[345]

An evaluation of the defendant's speech, demeanor, and activities at or near the commission of the crime are important considerations. For example, where the defendant apparently exhibited ordinary behavior and demeanor immediately before and after his stabbing of the decedent, this overcame evidence of intoxication consisting of a blood test showing .19% alcohol content; thus, his murder conviction was affirmed.[346] Where a defendant who had consumed 25 drinks of brandy and beer possessed normal speech, ability to walk, and coherency, this

---

[341] People v. Wicker, 4 Ill. App. 3d 990, 996, 282 N.E.2d 771, 775 (1st Dist. 1972) (specific intent to commit attempted murder established).

[342] People v. Gale, 132 Ill. App. 2d 986, 990, 271 N.E.2d 94, 96 (3d Dist. 1971); see People v. Madej, 106 Ill. 2d 201, 216-17, 478 N.E.2d 392, 398-99 (voluntary intoxication no defense to felony-murder when defendant was able to lead police on high-speed chase, flee on foot, jump a fence, and hide under a parked car), cert. denied, 474 U.S. 935 (1985); People v. Bradney, 170 Ill. App. 3d 839, 856, 525 N.E.2d 112, 123 (4th Dist. 1988) (voluntary intoxication no defense to residential burglary where defendant wore gloves to avoid fingerprints and quickly formulated explanation for presence at crime scene); People v. Hayes, 173 Ill. App. 3d 1043, 1048-49, 527 N.E.2d 1342, 1347 (5th Dist. 1988) (voluntary intoxication instruction in trial for burglary and theft properly refused where evidence showed that defendant drove an automobile, attempted to elude police, appeared to understand police instructions and refused a breathalyzer).

[343] People v. Jones, 56 Ill. App. 3d 600, 603-05, 371 N.E.2d 1150, 1153-54 (5th Dist. 1977) (murder and attempted murder convictions affirmed). See also People v. Winters, 29 Ill. 2d 74, 81, 193 N.E.2d 809, 813 (1963) (where defendant claimed "alcoholic amnesia," defendant's conviction for murder affirmed).

[344] See, e.g., People v. Olsen, 96 Ill. App. 3d 193, 197, 420 N.E.2d 1161, 1164 (2d Dist. 1981) (defense presented expert testimony from two medical experts).

[345] See, e.g., People v. Beller, 45 Ill. App. 3d 816, 818, 360 N.E.2d 130, 132 (2d Dist. 1977) (police officer responding to emergency call from victim of battery).

[346] People v. Hicks, 35 Ill. 2d 390, 397, 220 N.E.2d 461, 465 (1966), cert. denied, 386 U.S. 986 (1967).

defeated his defense claim to sexual assault charges.[347] Where the defendant presented evidence of a blood alcohol level of .356 (which an expert stated would cause a person to enter an "anesthesia stage"), this evidence was effectively overcome in a murder trial by (1) the state's demonstration that the defendant could understand and answer questions after the murder, did not need help in walking, and exhibited no unusual behavior; and (2) evidence that the blood test had been administered four hours after the killing, during which time the defendant had continued to drink.[348] Finally, the fact that an accused exhibited lucid behavior and speech near the time of the crime[349] or was able to give a detailed confession to the police soon thereafter may overcome such a defense claim.[350]

As with insanity claims, a defendant's effort to escape or cover up his crime will often be considered sufficient to overcome a claim of voluntary intoxication.[351] Thus, where there was evidence that the defendants were "stoned" on LSD, the fact that they knew enough to jump out of the automobile as police pursued, threw merchandise out of the vehicle as they fled, and were able to elude police after they abandoned their automobile was considered adequate proof that they had the intent necessary for burglary.[352]

It has been argued that intent is established per se when certain acts are committed and, therefore, the defense of voluntary intoxication should not be available in those cases. In a case where the defendant was charged with battery, the state argued that when a drunk hospital patient reached out of his emergency room bed and pinched a nurse's left buttock, intent to commit battery should be "inferred from the nature of the alleged criminal conduct."[353] However, the appellate court explicitly rejected this rule and held that the defendant was entitled

---

[347] People v. Green, 130 Ill. App. 2d 609, 612, 265 N.E.2d 184, 186 (2d Dist. 1970).

[348] People v. Johnson, 32 Ill. App. 3d 36, 43, 335 N.E.2d 144, 151 (3d Dist. 1975).

[349] People v. Long, 30 Ill. App. 3d 815, 817, 333 N.E.2d 534, 538 (2d Dist. 1975). *See also* People v. Redmond, 265 Ill. App. 3d 292, 303, 637 N.E.2d 526, 535 (1st Dist. 1994) (state presented sufficient evidence in first degree murder prosecution to rebut an intoxication defense where, after the shooting, defendant gave a coherent and consistent statement to police and was able to tell police the reason why he killed the victim).

[350] People v. Zynda, 53 Ill. App. 3d 794, 806, 368 N.E.2d 1079, 1090 (2d Dist. 1977).

[351] *See, e.g.*, People v. Jones, 5 Ill. App. 3d 926, 928, 284 N.E.2d 404, 405 (5th Dist. 1972).

[352] People v. Jones, 5 Ill. App. 3d 926, 928, 284 N.E.2d 404, 405 (5th Dist. 1972). *See also* People v. Bradney, 170 Ill. App. 3d 839, 856, 525 N.E.2d 112, 123 (4th Dist. 1988) (where the defendant wore gloves to avoid leaving fingerprints when committing a burglary and promptly fabricated a story when confronted by a neighbor, a finding that his voluntary intoxication was not so extreme so as to prevent him from forming the requisite intent was proper); People v. Hayes, 173 Ill. App. 3d 1043, 1048, 527 N.E.2d 1342, 1347 (5th Dist. 1988) (where defendant broke a window to enter a car dealership, searched an office, placed dealer plates on a stolen vehicle, fled from the police, was physically able to drive, and refused to take a breathalyzer test, these actions demonstrated requisite mental state for crimes charged).

[353] People v. Baczkowski, 180 Ill. App. 3d 17, 21-22, 535 N.E.2d 484, 488 (2d Dist. 1989).

to proper voluntary intoxication instructions because the defense had offered some evidence of intoxication and that this conduct could not be considered per se or inherently intentional.[354]

As stated previously, mere evidence of intoxication, even "extreme intoxication,"[355] will not per se satisfy the defense of voluntary intoxication. Thus, the fact that a defendant's blood alcohol level was .34% (and evidence was presented that .3% to .4% can cause death)[356] or that another defendant had smoked marijuana "all day" on the date of the offense[357] will not, standing alone, exonerate.

§ 18.23.   — Involuntary Intoxication.

Distinct from the defense of voluntary intoxication is involuntary intoxication, governed by section 6-3(b), which provides a defense if the intoxication (or drugged condition) deprives the accused of "substantial capacity either to appreciate the criminality of his conduct or to conform his conduct to the requirements of law."[358] Intoxication is considered involuntary if it is a product of *innocent* mistake, duress, or medical prescription.[359]

Early Illinois caselaw held that intoxication caused by the fraud or contrivance of some other person for the purpose of causing the accused to commit an crime was a defense.[360] Intoxication is only "involuntary" if it resulted "from some outside influence such as trick, artifice or force."[361] The language "involuntarily produced" in the statute refers to "the mechanical act of ingesting the drug, not to the willing and intelligent assumption of the possible harmful consequences of taking the drug."[362]

The intoxication must truly be a result of consumption of alcohol or drugs where the accused could not be considered blameworthy. Thus, where a defendant obtained some pills from his brother to alleviate a stomach ache and had

---

[354] People v. Baczkowski, 180 Ill. App. 3d 17, 25, 535 N.E.2d 484, 490 (2d Dist. 1989) (conviction reversed).

[355] *See* People v. Johnson, 32 Ill. App. 3d 36, 42-43, 335 N.E.2d 144, 149 (3d Dist. 1975) (defendant's blood alcohol level was .356 per cent following shooting of victim, which resulted in murder conviction).

[356] People v. Olsen, 96 Ill. App. 3d 193, 195, 420 N.E.2d 1161, 1163-64 (2d Dist. 1981) (intoxication did not negate mental state required for murder; conviction reversed on other grounds) (burglary and theft convictions upheld).

[357] People v. Newlin, 31 Ill. App. 3d 735, 739, 334 N.E.2d 349, 352 (5th Dist. 1975) (burglary and theft convictions upheld).

[358] 720 ILCS 5/6-3(b) (1999).

[359] ROLLIN M. PERKINS & RONALD N. BOYCE, CRIMINAL LAW 1002-05 (3d ed. 1982); WAYNE LAFAVE & AUSTIN SCOTT, CRIMINAL LAW § 4.10(f) (2d ed. 1986).

[360] Bartholomew v. People, 104 Ill. 601, 606 (1882).

[361] People v. Downey, 162 Ill. App. 3d 322, 335, 515 N.E.2d 362, 370 (2d Dist. 1987).

[362] People v. Downey, 162 Ill. App. 3d 322, 335, 515 N.E.2d 362, 370 (2d Dist. 1987).

consumed several of these pills, along with some beer and wine, before the commission of his criminal acts, he had no defense of involuntary intoxication even though he did not realize the pills were Seconal, a tranquilizing drug, which when mixed with alcohol can have the effect of intensifying intoxication and reducing control over impulses.[363] This is not the type of innocent mistake that might arise where, for instance, a person consumed a pill from a bottle of Valium thinking it to be a bottle of aspirin. Likewise, a person who claims his criminality should be excused on the theory that it was a byproduct of, for example, cocaine addiction[364] or alcohol dependence will not prevail because the defendant's condition is one that is self-imposed and over which the accused had the "power" to control.[365]

Unlike the defense of voluntary intoxication, involuntary intoxication as a defense is *not* limited to offenses requiring a particular mental state. For example, rape (now repealed and replaced with criminal sexual assault[366]) was considered a general intent crime, which most Illinois courts reasoned was not excusable by reason of voluntary intoxication.[367] However, involuntary intoxication was considered a defense to rape, inasmuch as "section 6-3(b) relieves an individual of criminal responsibility for the commission of *any* crime."[368]

§ 18.24.   — Burden of Proof, Instructions, and Trier of Fact's Verdict.

Voluntary and involuntary intoxication (or drugged condition) are both affirmative defenses.[369] Unless the state's evidence raises either or both of these claims, it is incumbent on the accused to offer some evidence in support of his or her defense.[370] If the accused offers no or insufficient evidence that his or her voluntary intoxication made him or her wholly incapable of forming the requi-

---

[363] People v. Walker, 33 Ill. App. 3d 681, 688, 338 N.E.2d 449, 454 (2d Dist. 1975).

[364] People v. Downey, 162 Ill. App. 3d 322, 335, 515 N.E.2d 362, 370 (2d Dist. 1987).

[365] People v. McKay, 208 Ill. App. 3d 242, 247-48, 566 N.E.2d 979, 982 (4th Dist. 1991).

[366] *See* ch. 8 of this treatise for a discussion of these offenses.

[367] *See, e.g.,* People v. Hunter, 14 Ill. App. 3d 879, 886, 303 N.E.2d 482, 486 (1st Dist. 1973).

[368] People v. Brumfield, 72 Ill. App. 3d 107, 111, 390 N.E.2d 589, 592 (5th Dist. 1979) (emphasis added). In *Brumfield,* the defendant's rape conviction was reversed and the case was remanded for a new trial because the trial court judge prior to trial incorrectly dismissed a defense offer of proof supporting an involuntary-intoxication claim. The defendant had contended that he smoked a marihuana cigarette that contained a powerful intoxicating drug, "angel dust." The appellate court's reversal centered on the trial court's consideration of this defense claim at a pretrial hearing on the state's motion in limine that successfully sought to exclude any evidence offered by the defense at trial regarding the defendant's intoxicated state at the time of the crime. The appellate court ruled: "The state and the trial court were without authority to question the propriety of that defense prior to trial." People v. Brumfield, 72 Ill. App. 3d 107, 112, 390 N.E.2d 589, 593 (5th Dist. 1979).

[369] 720 ILCS 5/6-4 (1999).

[370] 720 ILCS 5/3-2(a) (1999).

site intent for the crime charged, no jury instructions on that defense need be given.[371] Likewise, if the accused offers no or insufficient evidence that his or her involuntary intoxication undermined his or her ability to appreciate and conform, no instructions supportive of that claim need be offered.[372] If jury instructions are warranted and given, it is imperative that the state prove all of the various elements of the crime as well as disprove the defense claim.[373] The question of whether the defendant's voluntary intoxication made him or her incapable of forming the requisite intent, for instance, is a question of fact for the trier of fact, and the decision "will not be upset on review unless there is a question of whether or not the defendant was proven guilty beyond a reasonable doubt, an unjust decision was reached, or an error of prejudicial dimension occurred in the trial."[374]

§ 18.25.   Defense of Infancy: Background of Current Law.

A defense of infancy existed in common law.[375] This defense entirely shielded a child of less than seven years of age from criminal liability and created a rebuttable presumption of criminal incapacity for children who were less than fourteen years of age but who were seven years or older.[376] The children in this latter age group could be convicted of a crime only on "clear proof of such precocity as to establish a real appreciation of the wrong done."[377] Any person of age fourteen years and up had the same capacity as an adult and could be convicted of a crime.[378]

Before the enactment of the Illinois Criminal Code of 1961, the State of Illinois followed the common law approach to this defense, also known as "immaturity," with one exception: any child under the age of ten was irrebuttably presumed incapable of committing a crime.[379] Preferring the traditional "specific age cutoff" approach, rather than one that examines the actual maturity of the

---

[371] People v. Arnold, 104 Ill. 2d 209, 214-17, 470 N.E.2d 981, 984-85 (1984). *Compare* People v. Feagans, 118 Ill. App. 3d 991, 996-97, 455 N.E.2d 871, 875 (4th Dist. 1983) (evidence warranted voluntary manslaughter instruction; conviction reversed).

[372] People v. King, 58 Ill. App. 3d 199, 205, 373 N.E.2d 1045, 1050 (4th Dist. 1978).

[373] 720 ILCS 5/3-2 (1999).

[374] People v. Fields, 56 Ill. App. 3d 1068, 1069, 372 N.E.2d 980, 981 (1st Dist. 1978).

[375] ROLLIN M. PERKINS & RONALD N. BOYCE, CRIMINAL LAW 936 (3d ed. 1982).

[376] ROLLIN M. PERKINS & RONALD N. BOYCE, CRIMINAL LAW 936 (3d ed. 1982).

[377] ROLLIN M. PERKINS & RONALD N. BOYCE, CRIMINAL LAW 936 (3d ed. 1982).

[378] ROLLIN M. PERKINS & RONALD N. BOYCE, CRIMINAL LAW 936 (3d ed. 1982).

[379] ILL. ANN. STAT. ch. 38, para. 6-1 (Smith-Hurd 1989), 1961 Committee Comments, at 296 (revised 1972) (quoting ILL. REV. STAT. ch. 38, para. 591 (1959)): "An infant under the age of ten years shall not be found guilty of any crime or misdemeanor," and citing Angelo v. People, 96 Ill. 209 (1880)).

child on a case-by-case basis,[380] and in tandem with the tendency of many juris-dictions to raise the age for complete criminal incapacity,[381] the Illinois General Assembly changed the law in Illinois to create an absolute defense of infancy for persons twelve years of age and below.[382]

§ 18.26.   Defense of Infancy Codified.

720 ILCS 5/6-1 now provides: "No person shall be convicted of any offenses unless he attained his 13th birthday at the time the offense was committed."[383] This law contains no provision covering a rebuttable presumption of incapacity for certain age groups, as did the prior law. The revision committee responsible for drafting this statutory section explained its purpose as twofold: (1) to raise the minimum age of criminal capacity, and (2) to eliminate the presumption of incapacity, thereby freeing juries from the troublesome task of assessing the child's legal maturity.[384] Thus, any child below the age of thirteen is deemed incapable per se of committing an offense; accordingly, his or her wrongdoing is within the exclusive province of the juvenile court. Meanwhile, a person thirteen or above is conclusively presumed capable of criminality, although this does not mean that he will be necessarily tried in the criminal courts. In other words, this statute allows the legislature leeway, in accordance with the Juvenile Court Act, to prosecute certain minors (thirteen and above) in the "adult" criminal courts where appropriate and to handle other minors in juvenile delinquency actions. This legislative determination regarding a minor's legal capacity has been re-spected by the courts. As one court commented, "The State cannot seriously dispute the legislature's power to raise or lower the age of accountability. . . ."[385]

§ 18.27.   — Affirmative Defense.

The defense of infancy is an affirmative defense[386] that the accused normally has the burden of raising.[387] Where a defendant was convicted at trial for theft, he could not argue for reversal after failing to raise the defense at trial merely

---

[380] See 2 PAUL ROBINSON, CRIMINAL LAW DEFENSES § 175(b) (1984) (critical assessment of tra-ditional approach).

[381] See ROLLIN M. PERKINS & RONALD N. BOYCE, CRIMINAL LAW 939 (3d ed. 1982). These au-thors note that criminal incapacity by reason of age now ranges from below ten (e.g., Louisiana) to below sixteen (e.g., New York).

[382] ILL. ANN. STAT. ch. 38, para. 6-1 (Smith-Hurd 1989), 1961 Committee Comments, at 296 (revised 1972).

[383] 720 ILCS 5/6-1 (1999).

[384] ILL. ANN. STAT. ch. 38, para. 6-1 (Smith-Hurd 1989), 1961 Committee Comments, at 296 (revised 1972).

[385] People v. Boclaire, 33 Ill. App. 3d 534, 540, 337 N.E.2d 728, 734 (1st Dist. 1975).

[386] 720 ILCS 5/6-4 (1999).

[387] 720 ILCS 5/3-2(a) (1999).

because the state failed to prove his age and the jury verdict contained no finding on his age.[388] The court ruled that the state was under no obligation to offer proof of the defendant's age where no evidence in support of the defense was presented and where the crime in question contained no minimum age requirement.[389] Only if the defendant effectively raises the defense by offering some evidence in support of his or her claim will the state be obligated to disprove the defense.[390]

Defense efforts to resurrect the common law rebuttable presumption of immaturity for persons thirteen years of age or older have not been successful. In one case, for example, the appellate court ruled that it was unnecessary for the state to affirmatively prove the criminal capacity of a fourteen year-old and that the trial court properly refused to tender defendant's instructions regarding proof of criminal capacity.[391]

---

[388] People v. DeBartolo, 24 Ill. App. 3d 1000, 1008, 322 N.E.2d 251, 258 (2d Dist 1975).

[389] People v. DeBartolo, 24 Ill. App. 3d 1000, 1008, 322 N.E.2d 251, 258 (2d Dist 1975). *Compare* People v. Boston, 52 Ill. App. 3d 18, 19, 367 N.E.2d 383, 384 (2d Dist. 1977) (where defendant was charged with contributing to sexual delinquency of minor and where prohibition read that only persons 14 years of age and older could be convicted of that crime, state was required to prove that accused was of age required as element of crime).

[390] 720 ILCS 5/3-2 (1999).

[391] People v. Miller, 31 Ill. App. 3d 436, 443, 334 N.E.2d 421, 426-27 (1st Dist. 1975).

CHAPTER 19

DEFENSES: MISTAKE, COMPULSION, NECESSITY, ENTRAPMENT, PUBLIC AUTHORITY, AND OTHER JUSTIFICATIONS OR EXCUSES

§ 19.01.   Introduction.

Beyond the article 5/7 defensive force justifications[1] (defense of person and property) discussed in chapter 17 and the article 5/6 disability excuses[2] (insanity, intoxication, and infancy) examined in chapter 18, there are other excuses and justifications in the Illinois code that will be reviewed in this chapter. They include the excuses of "ignorance or mistake" of fact or law contained in article 5/4 of the Criminal Code of 1961[3] and the "compulsion" excuse[4] found in article 5/7 of the code. There also appears certain article 5/7 justifications such as "necessity"[5] and the "public authority"[6] defenses.[7] In addition, there are other affirmative defenses, such as "entrapment,"[8] that do not fit neatly under the umbrella of excuse or justification,[9] but nevertheless merit scrutiny. Finally, it is useful to study certain other miscellaneous defenses, such as the statute of limi-

---

[1] 2 PAUL ROBINSON, CRIMINAL LAW DEFENSES §§ 131-35 (1984).

[2] 2 PAUL ROBINSON, CRIMINAL LAW DEFENSES §§ 171-76 (1984).

[3] 720 ILCS 5/4-8 (1999).

[4] 720 ILCS 5/7-11 (1999).

[5] 720 ILCS 5/7-13 (1999).

[6] This language is borrowed from 2 PAUL ROBINSON, CRIMINAL LAW DEFENSES §§ 141-49 (1984).

[7] 720 ILCS 5/7-5 (1999) ("Peace Officer's Use of Force in Making Arrest"), 5/7-6 ("Private Person's Use of Force in Making Arrest"), 5/7-10 ("Execution of Death Sentence").

[8] 720 ILCS 5/7-12 (1999).

[9] See generally 1 PAUL ROBINSON, CRIMINAL LAW DEFENSES § 110-14 (1984) (discussion of "problematic classification of this defense").

tations bar,[10] that are codified outside of articles 5/4, 5/6 and 5/7 — where the bulk of the Illinois affirmative defenses appear — and other defenses, such as "consent," that may arise in certain circumstances, largely as a product of case-law. The article 5/4 defenses will be reviewed initially; the article 5/7 defenses not examined in a previous chapter will be analyzed thereafter; and the remainder, whatever their source, will be studied last.

§ 19.02. Defense of Ignorance or Mistake of Fact or Law: Background of Current Law.

Beyond the "incapacity" or "disability excuses"[11] discussed in the previous chapter, there is another general category of excuse defenses that might be called "mistake excuses."[12] These are "ignorance or mistake of fact"[13] and "ignorance or mistake of law."[14]

§ 19.03.   — Mistake of Fact.

The general rule at common law was that a mistake of fact was a defense (subject to certain significant exceptions) if three preconditions were met: (1) the defendant *subjectively* harbored a mistaken belief about a fact, (2) the defendant's mistaken belief was *reasonable*, and (3) the mistaken belief was of such a nature that the conduct would have been legal and morally proper had the facts been as the accused reasonably supposed them to be.[15] The essence of this defense revolved around the concern that the mistaken belief negated a material element of the crime, namely, the requirement of mental state.[16] Thus, if an accused carried off an umbrella as he or she was leaving a restaurant, honestly and reasonably believing the umbrella to be his or her own, the accused could not have been convicted of larceny, since his or her mistake of fact negated the requisite mens rea of intent to steal required for larceny.[17] On the other hand, if the defendant had *not honestly* entertained such a mistaken belief that the umbrella

---

[10] 720 ILCS 5/3-5 through 5/3-8 (1999).

[11] *See generally* 2 PAUL ROBINSON, CRIMINAL LAW DEFENSES §§ 171-77 (1984). Professor Robinson places the following defenses in his "disability excuse" category: involuntary act, impaired consciousness, insanity, subnormality, immaturity, intoxication, and duress. *Id.*

[12] *See* 2 PAUL ROBINSON, CRIMINAL LAW DEFENSES §§ 181-85 (1984). Professor Robinson places in this category ignorance because of unavailable law, reliance on official misstatement of law, mistake as to justification, and mistaken obedience to an unlawful military order.

[13] *See generally* ROLLIN M. PERKINS & RONALD N. BOYCE, CRIMINAL LAW 1044-54 (3d ed. 1982).

[14] *See generally* ROLLIN M. PERKINS & RONALD N. BOYCE, CRIMINAL LAW 1029-43 (3d ed 1982).

[15] ROLLIN M. PERKINS & RONALD N. BOYCE, CRIMINAL LAW 1045 (3d ed. 1982).

[16] WAYNE LAFAVE & AUSTIN SCOTT, CRIMINAL LAW § 5.1(a) (2d ed. 1986).

[17] *See* WAYNE LAFAVE & AUSTIN SCOTT, CRIMINAL LAW § 5.1(a) (2d ed. 1986).

was his or hers or had *not reasonably* believed this to be the case (that is, if the defendant only owned a small black umbrella but had taken a large red one from the restaurant), he or she could have been convicted of larceny under the general rule. Moreover, if the defendant had actually, but mistakenly, believed that his or her actions were wrong in any event (that is, if the defendant thought he or she had stolen a parachute, not an umbrella), the accused would have had no defense.[18]

In order to understand the parameters of this defense as it existed at common law, it is important to discuss two of the three requirements mentioned above in greater detail. First, many of the common law courts tended not to insist on the general rule that the mistaken belief be reasonable if the defendant was charged with an offense requiring a specific intent.[19] Returning to the umbrella example for a moment, assuming the defendant's mistaken belief had been due to his or her voluntarily intoxicated condition, it would likely have been argued that the voluntary intoxication, which clouded the accused's mental faculties, rendered his or her mistake unreasonable and his or her actions indefensible. Yet, if the thrust of the mistake of fact defense in theory centered on the question of whether the defendant's mistake had negated the mens rea required for larceny, what difference should it have made if the mistaken belief was unreasonable?

> Because of the requirement of a specific intent to steal, there is no such thing as larceny by negligence. One does not commit this offense by carry-ing away the chattel of another in a mistaken belief that it is his own, no matter how great may have been the fault leading to this belief, if the belief itself is genuine.[20]

For this reason, some of today's authorities make no reference to the reason-ableness requirement even as to general intent crimes as long as (1) the mistaken belief was genuine and (2) it negated the mens rea of the offense charged.[21] The

---

[18] WAYNE LAFAVE & AUSTIN SCOTT, CRIMINAL LAW § 5.1(b) (2d ed. 1986) (using example of where defendant received stolen television knowing it was stolen but believing it was radio).

[19] PAUL ROBINSON, CRIMINAL LAW § 4.4 at 263 (1997) (At common law, "an honest, albeit 'un-reasonable,' mistake provided a defense to a specific intent offense but only a 'reasonable' mistake provided a defense to a general intent crime").

[20] ROLLIN M. PERKINS & RONALD N. BOYCE, CRIMINAL LAW 1046 (3d ed. 1982).

[21] *See, e.g.*, 1 CHARLES TORCIA, WHARTON'S CRIMINAL LAW § 76 (14th ed. 1978):

> [A] defendant is not guilty of larceny for taking the property of another if he mistakenly be-lieved that the property was his own or was abandoned; a defendant is not guilty of perjury if he took the false oath under advise of counsel and mistakenly believed that the statement was true; and a defendant is not guilty of resisting an officer if he mistakenly believed that the officer was a private person.

See also 1 PAUL ROBINSON, CRIMINAL LAW DEFENSES § 62(c)(2) (1984) ("One suspects that some jurisdictions simply do not understand the implications of such a [reasonableness] provision. . . .").

remaining authorities now follow the more commonly accepted view developed at common law: if the crime does not require a specific intent or knowledge, the mistake must be based on reasonable grounds; however, if the crime does require such a mens rea, then even an unreasonable (but genuine) mistake will be a defense.[22] Consistent with this latter view, if a defendant charged with forcible rape mistakenly believed his rape victim had consented to his sexual advances, his mistake must be reasonable to afford him a defense, since rape does not require proof of intent or knowledge.[23] On the other hand, if a defendant was charged with assault with intent to rape or attempted rape, then his mistaken belief need not have been reasonable, since these crimes call for proof of the accused's specific intent to rape.[24] In this latter situation, one might feel little sympathy for the accused who had the mistaken opinion that his alleged victim had consented to his overtures where, for instance, his erroneous belief was attributable to his drunken stupor; yet, if he had not in actuality had the conscious objective of rape in mind, an essential element of the crime was lacking notwithstanding the unreasonableness of his belief.

At common law, the defendant's mistaken belief had to have emanated from a wholly innocent mind.[25] If the defendant has subjectively, but erroneously, believed he or she was committing some *crime or immoral act* other than that which he or she had actually committed, the defendant had no defense.[26] For instance, if a defendant was truly mistaken regarding the consent or age of a young girl with whom he had sexual relations, he had no defense to a charge of rape[27] because the facts, as the accused believed them to be, would have immersed him in at least a moral wrong, namely, extramarital fornication.[28] Because his blameworthy mental state left him with no defense, he would have stood convicted of the crime charged. Today's authorities have rejected this common law doctrine and have replaced it with a modified version: if the defendant thought he or she was committing another *crime*, then he or she will not

---

[22] *See, e.g.,* ROLLIN M. PERKINS & RONALD N. BOYCE, CRIMINAL LAW 1046 (3d ed. 1982). *But see* 1 PAUL ROBINSON, CRIMINAL LAW DEFENSES § 62(c)(2) (1984), where the author rejects the "reasonableness" requirement in any circumstances. In addition, he states that limiting the mistake defense in certain circumstances to "specific intent" crimes is "absurd" because it "in effect" imposes a "strict liability as to every circumstance element that does not require a 'specific intent.'" *Id.* § (c)(3).

[23] WAYNE LAFAVE & AUSTIN SCOTT, CRIMINAL LAW § 5.1(b) (2d ed. 1986).

[24] WAYNE LAFAVE & AUSTIN SCOTT, CRIMINAL LAW § 5.1(b) (2d ed. 1986).

[25] ROLLIN M. PERKINS & RONALD N. BOYCE, CRIMINAL LAW 1049 (3d ed. 1982).

[26] ROLLIN M. PERKINS & RONALD N. BOYCE, CRIMINAL LAW 1049 (3d ed. 1982); WAYNE LAFAVE & AUSTIN SCOTT, CRIMINAL LAW § 5.1(c) (2d ed. 1986).

[27] *See* ROLLIN M. PERKINS & RONALD N. BOYCE, CRIMINAL LAW 1049 (3d ed. 1982) (discussing mistake as to age problem).

[28] ROLLIN M. PERKINS & RONALD N. BOYCE, CRIMINAL LAW 1049 (3d ed. 1982).

have a complete defense.[29] What is not entirely clear today is whether the defendant will be convicted of the crime he or she subjectively believed he or she was committing (including greater crimes) or of the crime with which he or she was charged.[30]

Where the offense in question is in the nature of strict liability (that is, one not having a mental state), then a mistake of fact cannot be a defense since there is no mental state that is negated by the mistake. For instance, most bigamy statutes in this country are silent about a mens rea requirement; accordingly, even a reasonably mistaken belief that a prior marriage was terminated would not be a defense.[31]

§ 19.04. — Mistake of Law.

A familiar maxim of the common law was that ignorance of the law is no excuse from criminal liability.[32] A corollary of this rule was that "everyone is presumed to know the law," which, of course, is absurd.[33] "But the principle that ignorance of the law is no excuse is born not of logic but of necessity, since otherwise a premium would be placed upon ignorance and any defendant could free himself from the grasp of the law merely by pleading ignorance."[34] In any event, "[t]he ancient notion that ignorance of the law is no excuse was a stern and inflexible rule of law *without any exception*."[35]

Somewhat later a significant exception did develop: if an honestly entertained mistake of non-penal law negated the specific intent required for a crime, this could be a defense.[36] Some cases limited the mistake of law defense to only those mistakes that were reasonable.[37] Applying this exception to a common law larceny problem, one might consider the following occurrence: A handed B a document that purportedly represented a legal title to a horse that was situated in C's barn and that B was interested in purchasing. B examined the document and erroneously concluded that it conferred ownership of the horse on the holder of the document. After A disappeared with B's money, B entered C's barn and re-

---

[29] MODEL PENAL CODE § 2.04(2) (1962); WAYNE LAFAVE & AUSTIN SCOTT, CRIMINAL LAW § 5.1(c) (2d ed. 1986).

[30] *See* 1 PAUL ROBINSON, CRIMINAL LAW DEFENSES § 62(c)(5) (1984) for a discussion of the divergent approaches taken in various jurisdictions. *See* MODEL PENAL CODE § 2.04(2)(1962) (defendant guilty of crime he thought he was committing).

[31] WAYNE LAFAVE & AUSTIN SCOTT, CRIMINAL LAW § 5.1(b) (2d ed. 1986).

[32] JUSTIN MILLER, HANDBOOK OF CRIMINAL LAW 152-54 (1934).

[33] 1 CHARLES TORCIA, WHARTON'S CRIMINAL LAW § 77 (14th ed. 1978).

[34] 1 CHARLES TORCIA, WHARTON'S CRIMINAL LAW § 77 (14th ed. 1978).

[35] ROLLIN M. PERKINS & RONALD N. BOYCE, CRIMINAL LAW 1031 n.26 (3d ed. 1982) (emphasis added).

[36] JUSTIN MILLER, HANDBOOK OF CRIMINAL LAW 155 (1934); JOSHUA DRESSLER, UNDERSTANDING CRIMINAL LAW § 13.02(D) (2d ed. 1995).

[37] WAYNE LAFAVE & AUSTIN SCOTT, CRIMINAL LAW § 5.1(b) (2d ed. 1986).

moved the horse, much to the consternation of C, who was the true owner of the horse. B would have had a defense to larceny, since B had no intent to steal the horse from C, especially if B's mistaken belief of the legal authenticity of the document had been reasonable.

As stated, the mistake of law had to have been attributable to a mistake of *non-penal* law.[38] In the example above, since B's confusion about the ownership of the horse was a product of B's mistaken understanding of *property* law, B would have had a defense. Suppose, instead, that B had reexamined the document after A's departure and concluded that it was a bogus document. However, believing that this bogus document would free B from criminal liability under the prohibition against larceny, B decided to take the horse anyway. Since B's confusion now emanated from B's mistaken understanding of the *penal* law, he would have had no defense. Indeed, this same result would have followed even if B had consulted with an attorney about the scope of the larceny laws and the attorney had incorrectly stated that it would not be larceny if B removed the horse from C's barn under the circumstances.

The modern trend has been to broaden the scope of the ignorance or mistake of law defense. First, there is a tendency to no longer limit the defense to crimes requiring a specific intent (that is, intent to achieve a particular criminal result) and to mistakes regarding non-penal law.[39] Thus, ordinarily a mistake can now negate any mental state.[40] Second, the mistake sufficient to negate a mens rea apparently no longer needs to be reasonable.[41] Third, by statute or caselaw, a defense is provided if a penal enactment is not properly published, the accused reasonably relies on a statute or judicial decision later determined to be invalid, or the accused reasonably relies on an *official* interpretation of a law by an officer or body who is responsible for the law's interpretation, administration, or

---

[38] *See* ROLLIN M. PERKINS & RONALD N. BOYCE, CRIMINAL LAW 1031-36 (3d ed. 1982).

[39] *See, e.g.,* 1 CHARLES TORCIA, WHARTON'S CRIMINAL LAW § 77 (14th ed. 1978) ("[A] person who engages in penally prohibited conduct may be relieved of criminal liability therefor if, because of ignorance or mistake of law, he did not entertain the culpable mental state required for commission of the offense"). *Compare* JOHN KLOTTER, CRIMINAL LAW § 12-8 (2d ed. 1986), who states the mistake must negate a specific intent but suggests that mistake could be based on confusion about the penal law.

[40] ROLLIN M. PERKINS & RONALD N. BOYCE, CRIMINAL LAW 1031-32 (3d ed. 1982) ("[I]t came to be firmly established that defendant is not guilty if the offense charged requires any special mental element, such as that the prohibited act be committed knowingly, fraudulently, corruptly, maliciously or wilfully, and this element of the crime was lacking because of some mistake of non-penal law").

[41] ROLLIN M. PERKINS & RONALD N. BOYCE, CRIMINAL LAW 1036 (3d ed. 1982) (unless mental state requirement is negligence, in which case mistake must be reasonable).

enforcement.[42] Reliance on the advice of private counsel offers no similar protection because of potential problems of collusion.[43] Hence the reliance could be
characterized as *reliance on an authoritative statement*.[44] Analytically, reliance
on an authoritative statement is a concept that excuses not because the reliance
necessarily negates a requisite mental state; rather, it excuses inasmuch as the
defendant is able to state that he or she simply accepted as legally true what the
state had told him or her.[45] Here, the reliance on an authoritative statement could
seemingly be raised as a defense even for strict liability crimes. In contrast, the
theory that a mistake of law might negate the element of mens rea would not be
relevant to absolute-liability prohibitions, which contain no mental state requirement.

§ 19.05.   — Fact versus Law.

One of the most difficult tasks regarding mistake defenses is to properly identify the mistake as either one of "fact" or "law."[46] As long as the courts use the
same standards in defining the defenses of mistake of fact and mistake of law
(for example, any genuine mistake of fact or law, whether reasonable or unreasonable, can negate any mental state requirement of a crime), the differentiation
between fact and law will be of little consequence. However, an examination of
the common law approach to mistake of *law* problems, as discussed above, reveals a stiff opposition to any recognition of mistake law as a defense. At the
same time, there was a willingness to consider certain mistakes of *fact* as a defense. Thus, it was imperative to properly identify the type of mistake involved.
A variation of the example given above illustrates the difficulty in labeling the
mistake in certain cases. Assume A advised B that A owned a horse, situated in
C's barn, which horse B was interested in purchasing. If A produced a legal
document purporting to represent title, which B accepted without bothering to
read before "purchasing" and removing the horse from C's barn, was this a mistake of fact or mistake of law? If charged with larceny, B would have likely argued that he or she was mistaken about the *fact* of ownership, so as to take advantage of the broader protections of the mistake of fact defense. In other words,
B would have claimed that he or she honestly accepted A's factual statement
regarding ownership as true, negating the requisite intent to steal for larceny.
The prosecutor, however, might have claimed that B's mistake was attributable

---

[42] WAYNE LAFAVE & AUSTIN SCOTT, CRIMINAL LAW § 5.1(e) (2d ed. 1986); 2 PAUL ROBINSON,
CRIMINAL LAW DEFENSES § 182 (1984); 1 CHARLES TORCIA, WHARTON'S CRIMINAL LAW § 77
(14th ed. 1978).

[43] WAYNE LAFAVE & AUSTIN SCOTT, CRIMINAL LAW § 5.1(e) (2d ed. 1986).

[44] This is a slight variation from the "authorized reliance" language employed in ROLLIN M.
PERKINS & RONALD N. BOYCE, CRIMINAL LAW 1039 (3d ed. 1982).

[45] ROLLIN M. PERKINS & RONALD N. BOYCE, CRIMINAL LAW 1039 (3d ed. 1982).

[46] M. CHERIF BASSIOUNI, SUBSTANTIVE CRIMINAL LAW 451 (1978).

to B's reliance on the legal validity of the document received from A; accordingly, since B was presumed to know the law (that is, understand the legal integrity of the document), B had no defense. Thus, to the extent that certain jurisdictions continue to distinguish, at least to a degree, the requirements for a mistake of fact defense claim from mistake of law, these sticky problems of appropriate nomenclature need to be answered. Obviously, this problem of affixing appropriate labels to various mistakes is best alleviated by the simple expedient of applying the same rules to each type of mistake.[47]

§ 19.06.   — Ignorance versus Mistake.

For purposes of clarity, it is useful to distinguish between ignorance of fact or law and mistake of fact or law. *Ignorance* implies a total want of knowledge of the facts in question or law at issue.[48] *Mistake* suggests the presence of certain knowledge that is the basis of an erroneous conclusion.[49] While *ignorance* is often discussed under the rubric of *mistake*, there is an essential difference between the two that should not be entirely dismissed. Although the defenses of ignorance or mistake — whether of fact or law — are subject to the same excuse principles, modern jurisdictions wisely refer to both concerns in their statutory schemes.

§ 19.07.   Defense of Ignorance or Mistake of Fact or Law Codified.

Section 5/4-8 of chapter 720 provides:

> Ignorance or Mistake. (a) A person's ignorance or mistake as to a matter of either fact or law, except as provided in Section 4-3(c) above, is a defense if it negatives the existence of the mental state which the statute prescribes with respect to an element of the offense.
>
> (b) A person's reasonable belief that his conduct does not constitute an offense is a defense if:
>
> > (1) The offense is defined by an administrative regulation or order which is not known to him and has not been published or otherwise made reasonably available to him, and he could not have acquired such knowledge by the exercise of due diligence pursuant to facts known to him; or
> >
> > (2) He acts in reliance upon a statute which later is determined to be invalid; or

---

[47] 1 Paul Robinson, Criminal Law Defenses § 62(3) (1984); Jerome Hall, General Principles of Criminal Law 377 (2d ed. 1960).

[48] Rollin M. Perkins & Ronald N. Boyce, Criminal Law 1028 (3d ed. 1982).

[49] Rollin M. Perkins & Ronald N. Boyce, Criminal Law 1028 (3d ed. 1982).

(3) He acts in reliance upon an order or opinion of an Illinois Appellate or Supreme Court, or a United States appellate court later overruled or reversed; or

(4) He acts in reliance upon an official interpretation of the statute, regulation or order defining the offense, made by a public officer or agency legally authorized to interpret such statute.

(c) Although a person's ignorance or mistake of fact or law, or reasonable belief, described in this Section 4-8 is a defense to the offense charged, he may be convicted of an included offense of which he would be guilty if the fact or law were as he believed it to be.

(d) A defense based upon this Section 4-8 is an affirmative defense.[50]

Section 5/4-3(c), incorporated by reference into section 5/4-8, states: "Knowledge that certain conduct constitutes an offense, or knowledge of the existence, meaning, or application of the statute defining an offense, is not an element of the offense unless the statute clearly defines it as such."[51] Thus, where a defendant may have honestly believed, for example, that his severe beating of his wife resulting in her death was excusable by reason of his religious tenets, his failure to realize that his conduct was a crime in the eyes of the state was no defense.[52]

The Committee Comments, which reflect on the legislature's intent in the creation of this statutory scheme, state that (1) subsection (a) was designed to provide a defense to an accused where a mistake of fact or law "disproves the existence of the mental state which is an element of the offense charged" except that a mistake of law is not a defense where the mistake goes to "the existence or character of the offense with which the person is charged" (as provided for in subsection 5/4-3(c)); (2) subsection (b) is directed toward the situation where the accused, without his or her fault, has not been apprised of the promulgation of an administrative rule or order or has relied on a statute subsequently found invalid, a judicial opinion later determined to be invalid or erroneous, or an authoritative statutory interpretation later found to be incorrect; and (3) subsection (c) is set out to clarify that where the accused's mistake of fact or law precludes a conviction for the offense charged, he or she still can be convicted of a lesser included offense for which he or she would be liable if the fact or law he or she

---

[50] 720 ILCS 5/4-8 (1999).

[51] 720 ILCS 5/4-3(c) (1999).

[52] *See* People v. Jones, 297 Ill. App. 3d 688, 691, 697 N.E.2d 457, 460 (5th Dist. 1998) ("This society will not abide defendant's actions regardless of the religious beliefs that may have motivated them. If a religion sanctions conduct that can form the basis for murder, and a practitioner engages in such conduct and kills someone, that practitioner need be prepared to talk to God from prison").

erroneously believed existed did in reality exist.[53] It is important to note that subsection (c) does not allow for liability for a lesser crime where the accused assumed the existence of a fact or law that, if true, would involve (1) no criminality whatsoever or (2) a lesser crime that is not a "lesser included" offense.

§ 19.08. — Ignorance or Mistake Negating Intent.

If the ignorance or mistake of fact or law negates the requisite mental state required of a crime, subsection (a) provides a defense to the charge.[54] It is important to note that by the terms of the statute, the mistake need not be "reasonable." Also, it is clear that the mistake can negate any mental state that requires proof of a conscious awareness of a particular prohibited risk,[55] such as knowledge.[56] Thus, where a defendant mistakenly believed that a person was dead when he poured gasoline onto that person and burned him, the trial court committed reversible error when it failed to instruct the jury on the defense of mistake of fact where such a mistake could have negated the requisite mental state required for murder.[57] Similarly, where a defendant mistakenly thought he was simply helping a friend move some property, his mistake of fact could have been found by the trial court to negate the intent requirement for burglary.[58] However, to have an absolute defense here, the defendant must have harbored a wholly innocent state of mind. Where a defendant shot a person to death with a gun that he stated he thought was unloaded, he had no defense to involuntary manslaughter, since the court determined that the mere pointing of a gun, loaded or unloaded, at a person without justification was a reckless act.[59] Where a defendant mistakenly believed his eventual murder victim was already dead when he threw her body into an abandoned strip-mine pit, he had no defense to first degree murder or concealment of a homicidal death since his concealment effort was preceded by a brutal attack on the victim designed to murder the victim and

---

[53] ILL. ANN. STAT. ch. 38, para. 4-8 (Smith-Hurd 1989), 1961 Committee Comments, at 222-24 (revised).

[54] 720 ILCS 5/4-8(a) (1999).

[55] 720 ILCS 5/4-8(a) (1999).

[56] ILL. ANN. STAT. ch. 38, para. 4-8 (Smith-Hurd 1989), 1961 Committee Comments, at 224 (revised) (discussing how knowledge required for criminal possession of narcotics could be negated by lack of knowledge of nature of substance which in actuality is narcotic).

[57] People v. Crane, 196 Ill. App. 3d 264, 269, 554 N.E.2d 1117, 1120 (2d Dist. 1990), aff'd, 145 Ill. 2d 520, 585 N.E.2d 99 (1991), cert. denied, 504 U.S. 924 (1992).

[58] People v. Ellison, 126 Ill. App. 3d 985, 998, 466 N.E.2d 1024, 1032 (2d Dist. 1984). See also People v. Atherton, 261 Ill. App. 3d 1012, 633 N.E.2d 1288 (2d Dist. 1994) (defendant's testimony that he was helping another person move some belongings from a prior residence to his new home required instruction on mistake of fact in residential burglary prosecution).

[59] People v. Schwartz, 64 Ill. App. 3d 989, 994, 382 N.E.2d 59, 64 (1st Dist. 1978).

which did in fact kill the victim.[60] Where a defendant delivered matter that he incorrectly believed to be a certain controlled substance — namely, mescaline — but that in actuality was LSD, his defense theory that he did not know what type of controlled substance he was delivering was rejected.[61] As the Committee Comments point out, if the accused honestly believes he or she is committing a "lesser included" offense rather than the greater offense charged, the accused will have a defense to the latter but can be convicted of the former under subsection (c).

§ 19.09.   — Reliance on Authoritative Statement.

Subsection (b) and the Committee Comments discussed above address a defendant's reliance on an authoritative statement. Consistent therewith, where a defendant engaged in certain off-track gambling activity in reliance on an appellate court decision, later overruled by the Illinois Supreme Court, that held that the prohibition against off-track betting was unconstitutional, she had a defense to a gambling charge.[62] In contrast, where a defendant merely stated that someone, without identifying the person or calling him as a witness, at a driver's licensing station told him that he could legally drive his car in Illinois on a valid Texas license notwithstanding that his Illinois license had been revoked, there was insufficient evidence of reliance on an authoritative statement that would provide an excuse defense.[63] In another case, the defendant mistakenly believed that he could rely on a circuit court judge's opinion interpreting the law.[64] The appellate court held that section 5/4-8(b)(3),[65] declaring only appellate and supreme court opinions authoritative, would be meaningless if section 5/4-8(b)(4)[66] included circuit court judges in the definition of "public officers" on whose advice a person could rely.[67]

---

[60] People v. Rollins, 295 Ill. App. 3d 412, 418, 695 N.E.2d 61, 65 (5th Dist. 1998) ("While the mistake of fact defense applies to those who attempt to destroy or conceal a body believed dead as the result of potentially justified conduct or to those who attempt to destroy or conceal a body believed dead as the result of someone else's criminal conduct, it cannot apply to those who attempt to destroy or conceal a body believed dead as the result of the of their own criminal conduct." Convictions for first degree murder and concealment of a homicidal death affirmed).

[61] People v. James, 38 Ill. App. 3d 594, 596-97, 348 N.E.2d 295, 297-98 (2d Dist. 1976), *appeal dismissed*, 429 U.S. 1082, *reh'g denied*, 430 U.S. 976 (1977).

[62] People v. Dean, 73 Ill. App. 3d 501, 502, 392 N.E.2d 57, 59 (5th Dist. 1979).

[63] People v. Jones, 100 Ill. App. 3d 831, 838, 426 N.E.2d 1214, 1218 (4th Dist. 1981).

[64] People v. Knop, 199 Ill. App. 3d 944, 951, 557 N.E.2d 970, 974 (2d Dist. 1990).

[65] *See* 720 ILCS 5/4-8(b)(3) (1999).

[66] *See* 720 ILCS 5/4-8 (1999).

[67] People v. Knop, 199 Ill. App. 3d 944, 951, 557 N.E.2d 970, 974 (2d Dist. 1990).

§ 19.10.   — Affirmative Defense.

Ignorance or mistake of fact or law is an affirmative defense[68] that must be raised by the defendant with some evidence[69] sufficient to raise a reasonable doubt in order to shift the burden regarding the defense issue to the state.[70] Otherwise, the state need not rebut the claim.[71]

§ 19.11.   Defense of Compulsion: Background of Current Law.

At common law, the defense of "compulsion,"[72] also known as "duress"[73] or "coercion,"[74] was clearly recognized as an excuse to a criminal charge. A defendant had a defense to a crime if he or she was compelled to engage in the crime by another person's threat of immediate death or great bodily harm if he or she should refuse to commit the criminal act.[75] If the accused was threatened with future (as opposed to imminent) harm, the accused had no defense to the crime.[76] Similarly, if the accused engaged in the criminal act in question after the threat had ceased to exist, the accused had no defense.[77] If the defendant was merely acting in response to a threat not involving at least serious injury to his or her person (for example, a threat to his or her property), the defendant had no defense.[78] A corollary to this principle was the common law doctrine holding that where a woman committed a crime while in the presence of her husband, there was a rebuttable presumption that the woman had been coerced by him to do so.[79]

---

[68] 720 ILCS 5/4-8(d) (1999).

[69] 720 ILCS 5/3-2 (1999). *See* People v. Williams, 80 Ill. App. 3d 963, 969, 400 N.E.2d 532, 536 (5th Dist. 1980) (Illinois statute requires some evidence to raise affirmative defense).

[70] People v. Jones, 100 Ill. App. 3d 831, 838, 426 N.E.2d 1214, 1218 (4th Dist. 1981) (citing People v. Redmond, 59 Ill. 2d 328, 320 N.E.2d 321 (1974)).

[71] People v. Jones, 100 Ill. App. 3d 831, 838, 426 N.E.2d 1214, 1218 (4th Dist. 1981) (citing People v. Redmond, 59 Ill. 2d 328, 320 N.E.2d 321 (1974)).

[72] *See* A TREATISE ON THE LAW OF CRIMES (CLARK & MARSHALL) 364 (Marian Quinn Barnes, 7th ed. 1967).

[73] *See* Walter Hitchler, *Duress as a Defense in Criminal Cases,* 4 VA. L. REV. 419 (1917).

[74] *See* Rollin M. Perkins, *The Doctrine of Coercion,* 19 IOWA L. REV. 507 (1934).

[75] *See* A TREATISE ON THE LAW OF CRIMES (CLARK & MARSHALL) 364 (Marian Quinn Barnes, 7th ed. 1967).

[76] A TREATISE ON THE LAW OF CRIMES (CLARK & MARSHALL) 364 (Marian Quinn Barnes, 7th ed. 1967).

[77] A TREATISE ON THE LAW OF CRIMES (CLARK & MARSHALL) 364 (Marian Quinn Barnes, 7th ed. 1967).

[78] A TREATISE ON THE LAW OF CRIMES (CLARK & MARSHALL) 366 (Marian Quinn Barnes, 7th ed. 1967).

[79] A TREATISE ON THE LAW OF CRIMES (CLARK & MARSHALL) 366 (Marian Quinn Barnes, 7th ed. 1967).

A major limitation regarding the reach of the common law defense of compulsion was that fear of personal danger would not excuse the commission of a homicide.[80] This restriction could be best explained by reference to the general philosophy behind the defense: for reasons of social policy, it is better that the defendant engage in some crime not involving the intent to take a life than to refuse and perhaps lose his or her own life.[81] In other words, from a utilitarian perspective, where a defendant succumbed to another's deadly threat to commit a burglary, this was a "lesser evil" than death given the intrinsic value of life, albeit his or her own. Where, however, defendant killed to avoid being killed himself or herself, the defendant was weighing one life against another, and no "lesser harm" was involved. Disagreement existed at common law about the applicability of this principle in the context of the felony-murder situation.[82] Where A coerced B to assist A in robbing C, during which robbery A shot C to death, it was unclear about whether B could have claimed the defense of duress to the felony-murder, assuming B had no intent to kill C.

Today, most jurisdictions provide that compulsion is a defense to all crimes, except those involving the intentional taking of life, where the accused is faced with threatening conduct that causes him or her to reasonably fear imminent death or serious bodily harm.[83] The Illinois law is essentially consistent with this generally accepted view.

§ 19.12.   Defense of Compulsion Codified.

Currently, the defense of compulsion is codified in section 5/7-11, which provides:

> Compulsion. (a) A person is not guilty of an offense, other than an offense punishable with death, by reason of conduct which he performs under the compulsion of threat or menace of the imminent infliction of death or great bodily harm, if he reasonably believes death or great bodily harm will be inflicted upon him if he does not perform such conduct.
> (b) A married woman is not entitled, by reason of the presence of her husband, to any presumption of compulsion, or to any defense of compulsion except that stated in Subsection (a).[84]

The language of the statute itself, as well as the comments of the committee responsible for its drafting,[85] reveal the essential elements of this affirmative de-

---

[80] A TREATISE ON THE LAW OF CRIMES (CLARK & MARSHALL) 365 (Marian Quinn Barnes, 7th ed. 1967).

[81] Cf. WAYNE LAFAVE & AUSTIN SCOTT, CRIMINAL LAW § 5.3(a) (2d ed. 1986).

[82] ILL. ANN. STAT. ch. 38, para. 7-11 (Smith-Hurd 1989), 1961 Committee Comments, at 430 (revised).

[83] WAYNE LAFAVE & AUSTIN SCOTT, CRIMINAL LAW § 5.3(b) (2d ed. 1986).

[84] 720 ILCS 5/7-11 (1999).

[85] ILL. ANN. STAT. ch. 38, para. 7-11 (Smith-Hurd 1989), 1961 Committee Comments, at 429-31 (revised).

fense: a defendant has an excuse to a crime if he or she (1) performed an act otherwise criminal, (2) other than an offense punishable by death, (3) as a consequence of another's threat (4) of the imminent (5) infliction of death or great bodily harm, (6) which harm he or she reasonably believes will be inflicted (7) on himself or herself if he or she does not perform the criminal conduct. An examination of these basic elements follows.

§ 19.13.   — Performed an Act Otherwise Criminal.

The defense can only become an issue if the accused performed an act or conduct that is normally criminal. Since the defense of compulsion excuses one from criminality, satisfaction of the excusing conditions frees the activity in question from the label of "criminal" conduct.

§ 19.14.   — Other Than an Offense Punishable by Death.

In Illinois, the defense of compulsion is not available in capital cases, namely, those that are "punishable by death." For instance, treason[86] against the state is a class X felony for which the death penalty may be imposed.[87] However, no Illinois cases have been reported where the compulsion issue was raised in such a prosecution.[88]

The only other crime in Illinois punishable by death under certain circumstances is first-degree murder.[89] Accordingly, this limitation on the scope of the compulsion defense most frequently arises in situations in which a defendant contends that he or she was compelled to participate in a crime, that resulted in the taking of the life of an innocent third party, while under the threat of death or great bodily injury.[90]

Although most jurisdictions follow the common law rule with respect to compulsion in generally refusing to recognize this defense in murder prosecutions,[91] the Illinois courts exhibited for a time a reluctance to interpret section 5/7-11

---

[86] 720 ILCS 5/30-1 (1999).

[87] 720 ILCS 5/30-1(c) (1999).

[88] Indeed, there are no reported cases where treason against the state has been prosecuted in Illinois. *See* ch. 14 of this treatise for a discussion of treason.

[89] 720 ILCS 5/9-1 (1999). Only first degree murders committed consistent with certain aggravating circumstances, *id.* 5/9-1(b), qualify for death penalty treatment. *Id.* 5/9-1(g) through 5/9-1(h).

[90] *See, e.g.*, People v. Moon, 38 Ill. App. 3d 854, 864-65, 350 N.E.2d 179, 186 (1st Dist. 1976) (evidence supported defendant's conviction of murder committed during course of armed robbery despite contention that he was not triggerman, that he never drew his gun, and that he had been forced by companion to be present).

[91] ILL. ANN. STAT. ch. 38, para. 7-11 (Smith-Hurd 1989), 1961 Committee Comments, at 430 (revised).

and the accompanying legislative drafting Committee Comments[92] as unequivocally excluding the defense in such circumstances.[93]

Any ambiguities that may have existed regarding the vitality of a compulsion
defense claim in a murder case disappeared in *People v. Gleckler*.[94] In that case,
the defendant contended that he shot to death two teenage boys with a shotgun
during an armed robbery because a companion told him he would blow his "f—
ing head off" if he refused.[95] Following the defendant's conviction, he appealed,
contending that the trial court erred in (1) not instructing the jury on the compulsion defense and (2) refusing to instruct the jury on voluntary manslaughter
because of the evidence of compulsion.[96] As to the first point, the defendant
claimed compulsion was an available defense, since it was not clear that murder
was "punishable by death" because of the discretionary nature of the Illinois
death penalty.[97] However, the Illinois Supreme Court concluded "as a matter of
legislative intent" that the defense of compulsion was "unavailable to one
charged with murder."[98] The court determined that the "State, in enacting this
[compulsion] provision, intended to apply the common law rule that one ought
himself to die rather than escape through the murder of an innocent."[99] The court
held that the discretionary imposition of the death penalty did not vitiate that
legislative intent; thus, "[u]se of the phrase 'offense punishable with death' can
only be explained with reference to this purpose."[100] Additionally, the court
noted that compulsion is specifically mentioned as a mitigating factor that might
be "sufficient to preclude the imposition of the death sentence."[101] Thus, to also
employ it as a *defense* to murder would not comport with the legislative intent

---

[92] *See* ILL. ANN. STAT. ch. 38, para. 7-11 (Smith-Hurd 1989), 1961 Committee Comments, at
433 (revised) ("[T]he established, more restrictive formulation seems adequate as a practical recognition of the most serious type of pressure to commit crime, and in denying the justification as to
offenses so serious as to be punishable with death"). *See also* People v. Lee, 86 Ill. App. 3d 922,
408 N.E.2d 335 (1st Dist. 1980), *rev'd on other grounds*, 87 Ill. 2d 182, 429 N.E.2d 461 (1981)
(while refusing to categorically deny compulsion as defense to murder, court expressed "serious
doubt" as to the viability of such a defense); People v. Smith, 19 Ill. App. 3d 36, 39, 311 N.E.2d
164, 166 (1st Dist. 1974) (same).

[93] *See, e.g.,* People v. Lee, 86 Ill. App. 3d 922, 408 N.E.2d 335 (1st Dist. 1980), *rev'd on other
grounds*, 87 Ill. 2d 182, 429 N.E.2d 461 (1981).

[94] 82 Ill. 2d 145, 411 N.E.2d 849 (1980).

[95] Apparently, the companion had already shot each of the boys once, but allegedly ordered
Gleckler to finish them off.

[96] People v. Gleckler, 82 Ill. 2d 145, 154, 411 N.E.2d 849, 853 (1980).

[97] People v. Gleckler, 82 Ill. 2d 145, 154, 411 N.E.2d 849, 852 (1980).

[98] People v. Gleckler, 82 Ill. 2d 145, 156-57, 411 N.E.2d 849, 854 (1980).

[99] People v. Gleckler, 82 Ill. 2d 145, 156-57, 411 N.E.2d 849, 854 (1980) (citing Committee
Comments generally).

[100] People v. Gleckler, 82 Ill. 2d 145, 156-57, 411 N.E.2d 849, 854 (1980).

[101] People v. Gleckler, 82 Ill. 2d 145, 156-57, 411 N.E.2d 849, 854 (1980) (quoting ILL. REV.
STAT. ch. 38, paras. 9-1(c)(4), 9-1(g) (1979)).

that compulsion constitutes a *mitigating factor* in death penalty sentencing hearings.[102]

The *Gleckler* court further held that evidence of compulsion did not require voluntary manslaughter (now called second-degree murder) instructions.[103] Although the defendant claimed that an imperfect article 5/7 defense claim might have reduced the murder to voluntary manslaughter,[104] the court held that where the article 5/7 defenses are inapplicable "by their own terms, history and purpose," voluntary manslaughter could not be established.[105] Since policy considerations prompted the legislature to bar compulsion claims in murder trials, the court concluded those same principles preclude the use of evidence of compulsion to accomplish mitigation of the charge to manslaughter.[106] Though periodically challenged, the Illinois Supreme Court has unequivocally reaffirmed the principle that the defense of compulsion is not an affirmative defense available to a defendant charged with an offense punishable by death.[107]

Just as a defendant himself cannot take a life and claim the defense of compulsion, the same result follows where the accused is charged with murder on an accountability theory. In *People v. Calvillo*,[108] defendant identified the victim of a shooting that a codefendant desired to identify and kill, drove two codefendants to the building where they shot the victim to death, and waited outside while the killing was accomplished.[109] At trial, where defendant was tried for murder on an accountability theory, the defendant testified that one of the codefendants insisted he drive the codefendant to the building in question lest he "blow defendant's brains out."[110] However, the appellate court ruled that the defense of compulsion was unavailable to the defendant, relying on *Gleckler*.[111]

Notwithstanding the preceding caselaw, an Illinois appellate court ruled that in a felony-murder prosecution, the defense of compulsion may be available to

---

[102] People v. Gleckler, 82 Ill. 2d 145, 157, 411 N.E.2d 849, 854 (1980).

[103] People v. Gleckler, 82 Ill. 2d 145, 157, 411 N.E.2d 849, 854 (1980).

[104] At the time, ILL. REV. STAT. ch. 38, para. 9-2(b) (1979) (repealed) stated:

A person who intentionally or knowingly kills an individual commits voluntary manslaughter if at the time of the killing he believes the circumstances to be such that, if they existed, would justify or exonerate the killing under the principles stated in Article 7 of this Code, but his belief is unreasonable.

[105] People v. Gleckler, 82 Ill. 2d 145, 158, 411 N.E.2d 849, 855 (1980).

[106] People v. Gleckler, 82 Ill. 2d 145, 157-58, 411 N.E.2d 849, 855-56 (1980).

[107] People v. Ganus, 148 Ill. 2d 466, 470, 594 N.E.2d 211, 213 (1992), *cert. denied,* 506 U.S. 1083 (1993).

[108] 170 Ill. App. 3d 1070, 524 N.E.2d 1054 (1st Dist. 1988).

[109] People v. Calvillo, 170 Ill. App. 3d 1070, 1077-78, 524 N.E.2d 1054, 1059 (1st Dist. 1988).

[110] People v. Calvillo, 170 Ill. App. 3d 1070, 1075, 524 N.E.2d 1054, 1057 (1st Dist. 1988).

[111] People v. Calvillo, 170 Ill. App. 3d 1070, 1079, 524 N.E.2d 1054, 1060 (1st Dist. 1988).

an accused.[112] In that case, the court held compulsion is a defense to armed robbery and that a defendant could not be convicted of felony-murder if he was coerced to commit the underlying felony.[113] The court reasoned that the rule that compulsion is unavailable for murder emanates from the rationale that one cannot sacrifice another's life to save one's own but that this rationale is inapplicable where the one is attempting to escape being killed by merely robbing another.[114]

§ 19.15.   — As a Consequence of Another's Threat.

A basic ingredient of this defense is proof that the accused's conduct was performed "under the compulsion of threat or menace."[115] If no evidence exists that suggests that the accused was seriously threatened by another, he or she could not have been coerced.[116] For instance, where a defendant claimed his involvement in an armed robbery was coerced because he and his girlfriend feared a codefendant because he had a gun and was "high" on drugs or alcohol or both, the defense of compulsion was unavailable, because neither defendant nor his girlfriend testified that he or she had actually been threatened by the codefendant with death or great bodily harm.[117] Even if a defendant was "ordered" to engage in certain criminal conduct, if the conduct was not a consequence of a threat but, instead, a product of his or her own free will, the defendant could not claim the defense of compulsion.[118] Where the person making the threat departs the crime scene[119] or where the defendant successfully leaves the presence of the one making the threat sometime before the crime,[120] it will be virtually impossible for the defendant to avoid the state's contention that he or she had ample

---

[112] People v. Serrano, 286 Ill. App. 3d 485, 490-91, 676 N.E.2d 1011, 1015 (1st Dist. 1997).

[113] People v. Serrano, 286 Ill. App. 3d 485, 490-91, 676 N.E.2d 1011, 1015 (1st Dist. 1997).

[114] People v. Serrano, 286 Ill. App. 3d 485, 490-91, 676 N.E.2d 1011, 1015 (1st Dist. 1997).

[115] 720 ILCS 5/7-11 (1999); ILL. ANN. STAT. ch. 38, para. 7-11 (Smith-Hurd 1989), 1961 Committee Comments, at 429 (revised) (no defense "in the absence of such threats").

[116] People v. Moon, 38 Ill. App. 3d 854, 864, 350 N.E.2d 179, 186 (1st Dist. 1976) (because no evidence of overt threat to harm defendant, defendant's claim of compulsion not established).

[117] People v. Milton, 182 Ill. App. 3d 1082, 1092-93, 538 N.E.2d 1227, 1234 (2d Dist. 1989).

[118] People v. Lee, 86 Ill. App. 3d 922, 933, 408 N.E.2d 335, 344 (1st Dist. 1980), *rev'd on other grounds*, 87 Ill. 2d 182, 429 N.E.2d 461 (1981) (where person who "ordered" defendant to shoot never threatened to harm defendant if he did not shoot, defendant could not claim compulsion).

[119] *See, e.g.,* People v. Lee, 86 Ill. App. 3d 922, 408 N.E.2d 335 (1st Dist. 1980), *rev'd on other grounds,* 87 Ill. 2d 182, 429 N.E.2d 461 (1981) (noting that because "Lee testified that Trosclair [who had ordered Lee to shoot] had run before he fired the second shot," this constituted evidence of lack of compulsion).

[120] *See, e.g.,* People v. Lighting, 83 Ill. App. 2d 430, 434, 228 N.E.2d 104, 106 (1st Dist. 1967).

opportunity to withdraw.[121] Lacking in each of these situations described above is any notion that the defendant's criminal conduct was a *consequence* of a reasonable threat perception.

§ 19.16.   — Threat is Imminent.

The threatened harm must be imminent or immediate before it will be sufficient for purposes of compulsion.[122] Although "gun to the head immediacy" is not essential to establish compulsion,[123] threatened future injury will not suffice.[124] For example, the threat of future injury by gang members has been held insufficient to excuse criminal conduct.[125]

Under the same principle, threats that take place after the commission of a crime cannot support a valid claim of coercion.[126] In *People v. Gray,*[127] the defendant contended that she was compelled to be present during her companions' multiple rapes of one victim and the subsequent murders of the rape victim and the victim's male companion. However, it was not until *after* the crimes had been committed that the defendant was told she and her family would be killed if the incidents were reported.[128] The appellate court held that "this threat, taking place after the crimes," could not support the defendant's claim of compulsion.[129]

Although some authorities have suggested that the imminent danger requirement should be disregarded in favor of a more general inquiry into the deprivation of the person's free will,[130] the legislature's intent was to restrict the de-

---

[121] People v. Moon, 38 Ill. App. 3d 854, 864-65, 350 N.E.2d 179, 186 (1st Dist. 1976) (defendant's failure to avail himself of opportunity to withdraw from robbery defeated compulsion claim).

[122] ILL. ANN. STAT. ch. 38, para. 7-11 (Smith-Hurd 1989), 1961 Committee Comments, at 429 (revised); People v. Coogler, 35 Ill. App. 3d 176, 178, 340 N.E.2d 623, 624 (1st Dist. 1975).

[123] People v. Unger, 33 Ill. App. 3d 770, 775, 338 N.E.2d 442, 446 (3d Dist. 1975), *aff'd,* 66 Ill. 2d 333, 362 N.E.2d 319 (1977).

[124] People v. Colone, 56 Ill. App. 3d 1018, 1021, 372 N.E.2d 871, 873 (1st Dist. 1978); People v. Robinson, 41 Ill. App. 3d 526, 529, 354 N.E.2d 117, 120 (1st Dist. 1976).

[125] People v. Jackson, 100 Ill. App. 3d 1064, 1068-69, 427 N.E.2d 994, 997 (1st Dist. 1981).

[126] People v. Gray, 87 Ill. App. 3d 142, 149, 408 N.E.2d 1150, 1155 (1st Dist. 1980), *cert. denied,* 450 U.S. 1032 (1981).

[127] 87 Ill. App. 3d 142, 408 N.E.2d 1150 (1st Dist. 1980), *cert. denied,* 450 U.S. 1032 (1981).

[128] People v. Gray, 87 Ill. App. 3d 142, 149, 408 N.E.2d 1150, 1155 (1st Dist. 1980), *cert. denied,* 450 U.S. 1032 (1981).

[129] People v. Gray, 87 Ill. App. 3d 142, 149, 408 N.E.2d 1150, 1155 (1st Dist. 1980), *cert. denied,* 450 U.S. 1032 (1981).

[130] *See* ILL. ANN. STAT. ch. 38, para. 7-11 (Smith-Hurd 1989), 1961 Committee Comments, at 429-30 (revised) (citing Lawrence Newman & Lawrence Weitzer, *Duress, Free Will and the Criminal Law,* 30 S. CAL. L. REV. 313, 326-34 (1954) (proposes such modification of compulsion defense)).

fense to the "most serious type of pressure to commit crime."[131] As the cases discussed above reveal, the courts have honored this "impending, imminent threat" requirement.[132]

§ 19.17.   — Threat of Death or Great Bodily Harm.

The harm that the accused is attempting to avoid must be "death or great bodily harm."[133] Some authorities have suggested that "the kind of threat recognized should be broadened from the present threat of death or great bodily harm, to any threat which, under the circumstances, deprives the person of his free will"[134] or to any threat that "a person of reasonable firmness in his situation would not have been able to resist."[135] Notwithstanding, the intent of the Illinois legislature is clear.

> To broaden the defense to accord completely with the "free will" theory would be to invite routine contentions of some kind of pressure, such as "threats of harm to property, reputation, health, general safety, and to acts done under the orders," with accompanying assertion of individual personality weakness.[136]

While pointing out that a noted criminal law authority had stated that this expanded concept of duress "would be a most dangerous rule," the legislative drafting committee explicitly rejected such a broadening of this defense.[137] The Illinois courts have honored the legislature's intent in this regard. For instance, where a defendant was threatened with loss of a public position if he did not cooperate with the state's attorney's investigation of another and faced an alleged threat by the state's attorney that he would be indicted if he refused to cooperate, this did not excuse the defendant's commission of perjury.[138]

Some opinions have stated that unless a defendant believes "violence" will be inflicted on himself or herself if he or she does not comply with the compellor's

---

[131] ILL. ANN. STAT. ch. 38, para. 7-11 (Smith-Hurd 1989), 1961 Committee comments, at 429 (revised) (rejects elimination of "imminent" requirement).

[132] People v. Unger, 66 Ill. 2d 333, 339, 362 N.E.2d 319, 322 (1977).

[133] People v. Colone, 56 Ill. App. 3d 1018, 1021, 372 N.E.2d 871, 873 (1st Dist. 1978).

[134] See ILL. ANN. STAT. ch. 38, para. 7-11 (Smith-Hurd 1989), 1961 Committee Comments, at 429-30 (revised) (citing Lawrence Newman & Lawrence Weitzer, *Duress, Free Will and the Criminal Law*, 30 S. CAL. L. REV. 313, 326-34 (1954) (proposes such modification of compulsion defense)).

[135] MODEL PENAL CODE § 2.09(1) (1962).

[136] ILL. ANN. STAT. ch. 38, para. 7-11 (Smith-Hurd 1989), 1961 Committee Comments, at 431 (revised).

[137] ILL. ANN. STAT. ch. 38, para. 7-11 (Smith-Hurd 1989), 1961 Committee Comments, at 434 (revised) (quoting 1 WHARTONS' CRIMINAL LAW § 384 (12th ed.).

[138] People v. Ricker, 45 Ill. 2d 562, 569, 262 N.E.2d 456, 460 (1970).

orders, he or she has no valid defense claim.[139] Thus, in *People v. Gray*,[140] (discussed above),[141] the defendant was convicted of various crimes, including rape, on an accountability theory, since she had held a cigarette lighter to light a darkened room while her companions raped another woman. Although she alleged that one of her male companions forcibly took her by the hand and told her to follow him to the room where the multiple rapes occurred, the court noted that there was "nothing in the record indicating imminent infliction of death or great bodily harm"; accordingly, no instructions on the defense of compulsion were warranted.[142] However, in a case where there was evidence offered suggesting that the defendant had engaged in an armed robbery because of a death threat directed at the defendant by a companion carrying a loaded gun at the scene, compulsion instructions were required to allow the jury to determine if the defendant was actually compelled to assist his companion in the robbery.[143] Likewise, where masked robbers threatened to kill the defendant if he did not cooperate, held a pistol to his head, and ordered him to open the freezer, into which the tavern owner was pushed, and to locate the tavern owner's car, which was stolen, this should have raised the affirmative defense of compulsion at his trial for armed robbery.[144]

§ 19.18. — Harm Reasonably Believed to be Inflicted.

As long as the defendant "reasonably believes" death or great bodily harm will be inflicted on himself or herself if he or she refused to commit the crime as dictated by his or her compellor,[145] the legislature's intent is to afford the defendant the defense of compulsion, assuming the other elements of the defense are satisfied.[146] The caselaw has consistently followed this intent in holding that the

---

[139] *See, e.g.*, People v. Davis, 16 Ill. App. 3d 846, 848, 306 N.E.2d 897, 898 (3d Dist. 1974).

[140] 87 Ill. App. 3d 142, 408 N.E.2d 1150 (1st Dist. 1980), *cert. denied*, 450 U.S. 1032 (1981).

[141] *See* § 19.16 of this chapter.

[142] People v. Gray, 87 Ill. App. 3d 142, 150, 408 N.E.2d 1150, 1155-56 (1st Dist. 1980), *cert. denied*, 450 U.S. 1032 (1981). *See also* People v. Williams, 97 Ill. App. 3d 394, 403, 422 N.E.2d 1091, 1098 (1st Dist. 1981) (no evidence that codefendants had threatened defendant "with death or serious physical harm 'if she refused to drive getaway car'"; armed robbery conviction affirmed); People v. Robinson, 41 Ill. App. 3d 526, 529, 354 N.E.2d 117, 120 (1st Dist. 1976) (because "there was an absence of evidence of a threat of imminent infliction of physical harm to defendant," defendant's armed robbery conviction was affirmed).

[143] People v. Johnson, 42 Ill. App. 3d 194, 196-97, 355 N.E.2d 577, 580 (1st Dist. 1976) (although the jury rejected the defendant's version of the event and convicted him of the armed robbery).

[144] People v. Peagram, 124 Ill. 2d 166, 168, 529 N.E.2d 506, 509 (1988) (conviction reversed).

[145] 720 ILCS 5/7-11 (1999).

[146] ILL. ANN. STAT. ch. 38, para. 7-11 (Smith-Hurd 1989), 1961 Committee Comments, at 432 (revised) ("'Reasonably believes' is used as defined in section [5/]2-19, and would require an inquiry of the same type as that which is required for the self-defense and other issues raised under

threatened behavior must induce in the defendant a reasonable fear of the requisite repercussions of death or great bodily harm.[147]

Analytically, this reasonableness requirement both narrows and broadens the defense of compulsion. For instance, threats that produce in the defendant an "unreasonable" fear of harm will not suffice.[148] On the other hand, the danger that produces the fear need not be actual or real, for the defendant only needs to reasonably believe that it exists.[149] Hence, the defense of compulsion will be available even though the defendant might have been mistaken in his or her belief of imminent danger of death or great bodily harm.[150]

In *People v. Lee*,[151] the defendant's companion ordered the defendant to kill all the individuals present in an apartment during the course of a robbery. The defendant fired at two persons, killing one. In considering the compulsion defense claim, the appellate court took notice of the facts surrounding the incident including the fact that the defendant was in possession of the only weapon, and that the defendant's companion neither threatened to harm him if he refused to comply with the order nor appeared to have the apparent ability to injure him.[152] The court concluded on the basis of this evidence that "any fear . . . was unreasonable under the circumstances of this case."[153] In *People v. Adcock*,[154] the op-

---

... Article [5/]7"). The Code defines "reasonably believes" as meaning "that the person concerned, acting as a reasonable man, believes the described facts exist." 720 ILCS 5/2-19 (1999).

[147] *See, e.g.,* People v. Ricker, 45 Ill. 2d 562, 569, 262 N.E.2d 456, 460 (1970); People v. Quick, 236 Ill. App. 3d 446, 454-55, 605 N.E.2d 53, 59 (1st Dist. 1992) (trial court's failure to include "reasonably believes" language in jury instructions on compulsion constituted reversible error); People v. Parker, 113 Ill. App. 3d 321, 328-29, 447 N.E.2d 457, 462 (4th Dist. 1983) (defendant had no reasonable belief of death or great bodily harm if he failed to steal money from foundation and corporation); People v. Nugin, 99 Ill. App. 3d 693, 698, 425 N.E.2d 1163, 1167 (1st Dist. 1981) (belief must be reasonable); People v. Gray, 87 Ill. App. 3d 142, 149, 408 N.E.2d 1150, 1155 (1st Dist. 1980) (belief not reasonable), *cert. denied*, 450 U.S. 1032 (1981); People v. Robinson, 41 Ill. App. 3d 526, 529, 354 N.E.2d 117, 120 (1st Dist. 1976) (belief must be reasonable); People v. Moon, 38 Ill. App. 3d 854, 864, 350 N.E.2d 179, 186 (1st Dist. 1976) (same); People v. Coogler, 35 Ill. App. 3d 176, 178, 340 N.E.2d 623, 624 (1st Dist. 1975) (same).

[148] WAYNE LAFAVE & AUSTIN SCOTT, CRIMINAL LAW § 5.3(b) (2d ed. 1986). *See* People v. Williams, 97 Ill. App. 3d 394, 402, 422 N.E.2d 1091, 1098 (1st Dist. 1981) (no evidence that defendant had such reasonable fear); People v. Colone, 56 Ill. App. 3d 1018, 1021, 372 N.E.2d 871, 873 (1st Dist. 1978) (no reasonable belief of imminent danger).

[149] WAYNE LAFAVE & AUSTIN SCOTT, CRIMINAL LAW § 5.3(b) (2d ed. 1986).

[150] People v. Lee, 86 Ill. App. 3d 922, 932, 408 N.E.2d 335, 343 (1st Dist. 1980), *rev'd on other grounds*, 87 Ill. 2d 182, 429 N.E.2d 461 (1981).

[151] 86 Ill. App. 3d 922, 408 N.E.2d 335 (1st Dist. 1980), *rev'd on other grounds*, 87 Ill. 2d 182, 429 N.E.2d 461 (1981).

[152] People v. Lee, 86 Ill. App. 3d 922, 933, 408 N.E.2d 335, 343-44 (1st Dist. 1980), *rev'd on other grounds*, 87 Ill. 2d 182, 429 N.E.2d 461 (1981).

[153] People v. Lee, 86 Ill. App. 3d 922, 933, 408 N.E.2d 335, 343-44 (1st Dist. 1980), *rev'd on other grounds*, 87 Ill. 2d 182, 429 N.E.2d 461 (1981).

[154] 29 Ill. App. 3d 917, 331 N.E.2d 573 (3d Dist. 1975).

posite result was reached. The defendant contended that he participated in an armed robbery because he feared for his safety.[155] The defendant's companion was extremely intoxicated from liquor and other drugs and threatened to shoot the defendant if he did not comply with his commands. The appellate court held that the facts of this case were such that the defendant could have reasonably feared serious bodily harm; thus, the trial court's failure to instruct the jury on compulsion was error.[156] The *Adcock* court further stated that this defense would be available despite the defendant's mistaken belief that he might have faced death or serious bodily injury if his erroneous assessment of the facts was reasonable.[157]

§ 19.19. — Harm Inflicted on Defendant Himself or Herself if He or She Refused Demand to Engage in Criminal Conduct.

The final element that is necessary to a successful compulsion defense claim is that the defendant reasonably believed that the requisite harm would have "be[en] inflicted upon him[self] if he [had] not perform[ed] such conduct" as demanded by the person making the threat.[158] Since the statute states that the defendant must prove that the threatened harm was to be directed at himself or herself if he or she did not obey his or her compellor's orders, it appears that threats of harm directed at third parties might be insufficient. Beyond the language of the statute, neither the legislative intent reflected in the Committee Comments nor the caselaw interpretations of section 5/7-11 have explicitly considered whether threats of death or great bodily harm directed, for instance, at one's spouse or children would excuse the defendant's conduct. In *People v. Gray*,[159] the defendant was told *after* a rape and two murders that she and her children would be killed if she told anyone what had happened.[160] As discussed earlier,[161] the *Gray* court dismissed the defendant's compulsion claim, since the threat of harm occurred *after* the crimes, to which she lent aid, had been committed. In any event, this court offered some hint about its possible stance regarding threats to third parties when it said, "There being nothing in the record indicating imminent infliction of death or great bodily harm or the reasonable

---

[155] People v. Adcock, 29 Ill. App. 3d 917, 918, 331 N.E.2d 573, 574 (3d Dist. 1975).

[156] People v. Adcock, 29 Ill. App. 3d 917, 920, 331 N.E.2d 573, 576 (3d Dist. 1975).

[157] People v. Adcock, 29 Ill. App. 3d 917, 920, 331 N.E.2d 573, 576 (3d Dist. 1975).

[158] 720 ILCS 5/7-11(a) (1999).

[159] 87 Ill. App. 3d 142, 408 N.E.2d 1150 (1st Dist. 1980), *cert. denied*, 450 U.S. 1032 (1981).

[160] People v. Gray, 87 Ill. App. 3d 142, 149, 408 N.E.2d 1150, 1155 (1st Dist. 1980), *cert. denied*, 450 U.S. 1032 (1981).

[161] *See* § 19.16 of this chapter.

belief that such would be inflicted *upon defendant* if she did not participate, we find the statute to be inapplicable."[162]

Although the caselaw is not clear concerning to *whom* the threat of harm must be directed, the caselaw has clarified what *type of conduct* the defendant must have been forced to perform. In *People v. Unger*,[163] the defendant escaped from a state prison in order to avoid homosexual assaults on himself by other inmates and later claimed that his prison escape was excused because of compulsion. While pointing out that the escape charge might have been justified under the defense of "necessity" (which will be examined later in this chapter),[164] the Illinois Supreme Court ruled that "[i]t is readily discernible that prison escapes induced by fear of homosexual assaults and accompanying reprisals do not conveniently fit within the traditional ambits of . . . the compulsion . . . defense."[165] This is because "the defense of compulsion generally requires an impending, imminent threat of great bodily harm together with a demand that the person *perform the specific criminal act for which he is eventually charged*."[166] Here, the inmates had *not* threatened the defendant with harm if he refused to commit the crime of escape; thus, compulsion was unavailable concerning that charge.

§ 19.20.   — Compulsion Arose Without Negligence or Fault of Defendant.

There is another limitation on the reach of the compulsion defense that is not reflected in section 5/7-11 but is recognized by caselaw. Specifically, the defense of compulsion is available only where the coercion has arisen without the negligence or fault of the person who insists on it as a defense.[167] In *People v. Rodriguez*,[168] the defendant was charged with escape from a correctional facility based on his failure to return from a home furlough. He claimed that a prison

---

[162] People v. Gray, 87 Ill. App. 3d 142, 150, 408 N.E.2d 1150, 1155-56 (1st Dist. 1980), *cert. denied*, 450 U.S. 1032 (1981) (emphasis added).

[163] 66 Ill. 2d 333, 362 N.E.2d 319 (1977).

[164] People v. Unger, 66 Ill. 2d 333, 338-40, 362 N.E.2d 319, 322-24 (1977).

[165] People v. Unger, 66 Ill. 2d 333, 340, 362 N.E.2d 319, 322 (1977).

[166] People v. Unger, 66 Ill. 2d 333, 340, 362 N.E.2d 319, 322 (1977) (emphasis added). The effect of *Unger* was to disallow the defense in certain circumstances where it was previously recognized by the Illinois appellate courts. *See, e.g.*, People v. Clinkscales, 19 Ill. App. 3d 173, 174-75, 311 N.E.2d 253, 255 (1st Dist. 1974). In *Clinkscales*, the defendant was attacked by an arresting officer who used excessive force to arrest the defendant. The appellate court ruled that the trial court erred in not discussing the defendant's compulsion claim as against a charge of resisting arrest because of evidence that suggested that the defendant was faced with great bodily harm. Yet, this ruling seems to have been wrong because the arresting officer was not threatening the defendant with harm if he refused to resist the arrest, which was the basis of the crime charged. Thus, it seems that the defendant's justification for resisting the arrest was not duress, but rather self-defense.

[167] People v. Rodriguez, 30 Ill. App. 3d 118, 120, 332 N.E.2d 194, 196 (5th Dist. 1975).

[168] 30 Ill. App. 3d 118, 332 N.E.2d 194 (5th Dist. 1975).

official had given him $165 with which to purchase one pound of marijuana, which he had squandered while celebrating his furlough, and that he feared "what the officer might do" should he return without the marijuana requested by the officer and, thus, his commission of the offense of escape was excused by the defense of compulsion.[169] The appellate court affirmed the escape conviction not only because "the defense of compulsion is a defense only with respect to the conduct demanded by the compellor," but also because that defense "is available only where the compulsion has arisen without the negligence or fault of the person who insists upon it as a defense."[170] Here, the alleged compulsion "arose only from the defendant's appropriation for his own use of the funds given to him by the prison officer," which wrongful conduct could not be the basis of a successful duress claim.[171] Similarly, in *People v. Lee*,[172] discussed earlier,[173] the defendant's argument of compulsion was defeated in part on the same theory because the defendant had failed to avail himself of opportunities to withdraw from the criminal enterprise in which he alleged he was forced to participate.[174]

§ 19.21.   — No Presumption of Husband's Compulsion of Wife's Criminality.

The common law recognized as an excuse to a crime the "matrimonial subjection of the wife to her husband."[175] There was a legal presumption at common law that a married woman's criminality committed in her husband's presence was a product of his domination and coercion; in other words, it was assumed that it was not a result of the exercise of her free will.[176] With the increased recognition of women's rights generally, and married women's rights specifically, the modern courts have abandoned this theory.[177] The legislature also eliminated

---

[169] People v. Rodriguez, 30 Ill. App. 3d 118, 120, 332 N.E.2d 194, 196 (5th Dist. 1975).

[170] People v. Rodriguez, 30 Ill. App. 3d 118, 120, 332 N.E.2d 194, 196 (5th Dist. 1975).

[171] People v. Rodriguez, 30 Ill. App. 3d 118, 120, 332 N.E.2d 194, 196 (5th Dist. 1975).

[172] 86 Ill. App. 3d 922, 408 N.E.2d 335 (1st Dist. 1980), *rev'd on other grounds*, 87 Ill. 2d 182, 429 N.E.2d 461 (1981).

[173] *See* § 19.18 of this chapter.

[174] People v. Lee, 86 Ill. App. 3d 922, 932-33, 408 N.E.2d 335, 344 (1st Dist. 1980), *rev'd on other grounds*, 87 Ill. 2d 182, 429 N.E.2d 461 (1981).

[175] ILL. ANN. STAT. ch. 38, para. 7-11 (Smith-Hurd 1989), 1961 Committee Comments, at 432 (revised).

[176] ILL. ANN. STAT. ch. 38, para. 7-11 (Smith-Hurd 1989), 1961 Committee Comments, at 432 (revised).

[177] ILL. ANN. STAT. ch. 38, para. 7-11 (Smith-Hurd 1989), 1961 Committee Comments, at 432 (revised).

this presumption in section 5/7-11(b), leaving only the general rule of compulsion.[178]

§ 19.22. — Affirmative Defense.

The defense of compulsion is an affirmative defense.[179] Once this defense is raised, the state must prove the defendant guilty beyond a reasonable doubt, on that issue as well as all other elements of the crime charged.[180] The trier of fact makes the final determination of whether the state has met its burden.[181] "[U]nless the proof is so unreasonable, improbable or unsatisfactory as to create a reasonable doubt" about the defendant's guilt, the Illinois reviewing courts will not set aside the trier of fact's judgment.[182]

The state penal code states an affirmative defense is only at issue, thereby requiring (1) jury instructions on the defense claim and (2) refutation of the claimed defense by evidence offered by the state, if "some evidence" is offered supportive of the defense in question.[183] What is not entirely clear is the appropriate quantum of proof that is required to satisfy the "some evidence" standard.[184] Some of the appellate court decisions state that *some evidence* means evidence sufficient to raise a reasonable doubt and that this "reasonable doubt" test is applicable to both the effective raising of the issue and the need for jury instructions.[185] Others hold that only "some evidence" (without reference to the "reasonable doubt" standard) is required before the state is required to disprove the compulsion claim or before the trial court is required to give jury instructions.[186] And yet other courts hold that while the "some evidence" must be suffi-

---

[178] ILL. ANN. STAT. ch. 38, para. 7-11 (Smith-Hurd 1989), 1961 Committee Comments, at 435 (revised).

[179] 720 ILCS 5/7-14 (1999).

[180] 720 ILCS 5/3-2 (1999).

[181] *See* People v. Aldridge, 65 Ill. App. 3d 995, 1000, 383 N.E.2d 19, 23 (1st Dist. 1976); People v. Johnson, 42 Ill. App. 3d 194, 197, 355 N.E.2d 577, 580 (1st Dist. 1976); People v. Nurse, 34 Ill. App. 3d 42, 46, 339 N.E.2d 328, 332 (1st Dist. 1975).

[182] People v. Nurse, 34 Ill. App. 3d 42, 47, 339 N.E.2d 328, 332-33 (1st Dist. 1975).

[183] 720 ILCS 5/3-2(a) (1999). *See also* People v. Jackson, 100 Ill. App. 3d 1064, 1067, 427 N.E.2d 994, 996 (1st Dist. 1981) (after some evidence of compulsion is established, state must disprove compulsion defense claim); People v. Lee, 86 Ill. App. 3d 922, 932, 408 N.E.2d 335, 343 (1st Dist. 1981), *rev'd on other grounds*, 87 Ill. 2d 182, 429 N.E.2d 461 (1981) (after some evidence of compulsion is established, it is error to refuse to instruct jury as to that defense).

[184] People v. Creach, 69 Ill. App. 3d 874, 897, 387 N.E.2d 762, 778 (1st Dist. 1979), *aff'd in part, rev'd in part*, 79 Ill. 2d 96, 402 N.E.2d 228 (1980), *cert. denied*, 449 U.S. 1010 (1981).

[185] *See, e.g.*, People v. Gray, 87 Ill. App. 3d 142, 150, 408 N.E.2d 1150, 1156 (1st Dist. 1980) (citing People v. Redmond, 59 Ill. 2d 328, 320 N.E.2d 321 (1974) ("reasonable doubt" of sanity must exist before defense of insanity properly raised)), *cert. denied*, 450 U.S. 1032 (1981). *Accord* People v. Williams, 97 Ill. App. 3d 394, 403, 422 N.E.2d 1091, 1098-99 (1st Dist. 1981).

[186] *See, e.g.*, People v. Lee, 86 Ill. App. 3d 922, 932, 408 N.E.2d 335, 343 (1st Dist. 1980), *rev'd on other grounds*, 87 Ill. 2d 182, 429 N.E.2d 461 (1981).

cient to raise a "reasonable doubt" in order to *raise* the defense of compulsion, only "some evidence," without reference to the "reasonable doubt" standard, is required for instructions.[187]

§ 19.23.   Defense of Necessity: Background of Current Law.

It has been said that "[t]here is no stranger animal in the realm of criminal law than the defense of necessity."[188] Although "necessity" as a justification for crime was known to the common law,[189] the precise limits of this defense have never been entirely clear.[190] This concept has developed on an ad hoc basis in response to the exigencies of certain situations in which an accused was forced to choose between two evils: noncompliance with the criminal law or compliance that carries the potential of an even greater harm.[191]

> A man steals food from a grocery store to feed his family. A woman driving on a narrow road hits a hiker to avoid driving off a cliff. During time of war, a ship pulls into an enemy port to avoid a threatening storm at sea. In each case a harm is committed; the store loses revenue, the hiker is hurt and the war effort is hindered. But in each case a benefit also accrues: a family is fed, a life is saved and the lives on the ship are secured.[192]

These are the types of scenarios from which the defense of necessity has evolved.

The justification of necessity should not be confused with the defense of duress. "Necessity is more universal than duress: there is no requirement that the greater evil involve the actor personally, or that it involve a life-endangering situation. The only essential showing is that the criminal act is the lesser of two evils and some choice is unavoidable."[193] Beyond this basic consideration, the law is less clear. For example, it is sometimes stated that duress or compulsion exists where a person is coerced to engage in an otherwise criminal act as a consequence of human forces, whereas necessity is a by-product of "natural

---

[187] *See, e.g.*, People v. Adcock, 29 Ill. App. 3d 917, 919, 331 N.E.2d 573, 575-76 (3d Dist. 1975).

[188] Frank Berry, Jr., *The Mysterious Defense of Necessity*, 54 CAL. ST. B.J. 384 (1979).

[189] ILL. ANN. STAT. ch. 38, para. 7-13 (Smith-Hurd 1989), 1961 Committee Comments, at 459 (revised). *See generally* Edward Arnolds & Norman Garland, *The Defense of Necessity in Criminal Law: The Right to Choose the Lesser Evil*, 65 J. CRIM. L. & CRIMINOLOGY 289 (1974) for a discussion of the early caselaw.

[190] ILL. ANN. STAT. ch. 38, para. 7-13 (Smith-Hurd 1989), 1961 Committee Comments, at 459 (revised).

[191] Michelle Conde, *Comment, Necessity Defined: A New Role in the Criminal Defense System*, 29 UCLA L. REV. 409, 409-10 (1981).

[192] Michelle Conde, *Comment, Necessity Defined: A New Role in the Criminal Defense System*, 29 UCLA L. REV. 409, 409 (1981).

[193] Frank Berry, Jr., *The Mysterious Defense of Necessity*, 54 CAL. ST. B.J. 384 (1979).

forces."[194] Consistent with this view, if a person was compelled to steal a loaf of bread because another threatened to kill him, the person would have a defense of duress; whereas if an indigent person felt it necessary to steal the loaf of bread to avoid his or her own starvation, he or she would have a defense of necessity.

However, this distinction is not always followed by the courts[195] and has been rejected by some authorities.[196] For instance, if a law enforcement officer learned that a terrorist had hidden an atomic bomb in Chicago that was scheduled to detonate at noon on a given day, the officer's physical torture of the terrorist, designed to learn the location of the bomb so as to defuse it before its explosion, would surely be justified by the necessity of saving millions of lives in Chicago.[197] The choice of evils faced by the law enforcement officer did not arise as a result of forces of nature, but rather from the actions of the terrorist in planting the atomic bomb. If necessity justifies this torture, then conceptually it is incorrect to say that necessity as a defense must be based on "natural force" considerations. Yet, the continual reference to this aspect of necessity in the caselaw[198] and by criminal law authorities[199] suggests that some, but certainly not all, jurisdictions may limit the defense to those situations in which the coercive power arose from the forces of nature.

Another feature of necessity that might distinguish it from duress is that the lesser evil in necessity situations could conceivably involve the justified taking of life,[200] whereas with compulsion this is never permissible.[201] For instance,

---

[194] WAYNE LAFAVE & AUSTIN SCOTT, CRIMINAL LAW § 5.4(a) (2d ed. 1986); ROLLIN M. PERKINS & RONALD N. BOYCE, CRIMINAL LAW 1065 (3d ed. 1982).

[195] See, e.g., People v. Unger, 66 Ill. 2d 333, 341, 362 N.E.2d 319, 323 (1977) (where defendant, a prison inmate threatened with homosexual rape, was entitled to necessity instruction where charged with escape).

[196] 2 PAUL ROBINSON, CRIMINAL LAW DEFENSES § 124(e) (1984) ("The limitation probably results from the historical accident that most lesser evil cases have in fact involved the forces of nature, and most cases of duress have arisen from incidents of human coercion. But that fortunately does not reflect the conceptually significant distinction between the two defenses. To limit the necessity defense on that basis would generate improper results").

[197] A variation of this hypothetical situation was discussed in M. Levin, The Case for Torture, NEWSWEEK, June 7, 1982, at 13.

This problem would not lend itself to the defense of duress because no person is threatening to kill or inflict great bodily injury on the law enforcement officer should he fail to torture the terrorist.

[198] See, e.g., People v. Cater, 78 Ill. App. 3d 983, 989, 398 N.E.2d 28, 33 (3d Dist. 1979) ("The major distinction between the defenses of compulsion and necessity is that in the former the source of the coercive power is from a human being and in the latter the coercive power has traditionally arisen from the forces of nature"), appeal dismissed, 449 U.S. 802 (1980).

[199] See WAYNE LAFAVE & AUSTIN SCOTT, CRIMINAL LAW § 5.4(a) (2d ed. 1986); ROLLIN M. PERKINS & RONALD N. BOYCE, CRIMINAL LAW 1065 (3d ed. 1982).

[200] See ILL. ANN. STAT. ch. 38, para. 7-13 (Smith-Hurd 1977), 1961 Committee Comments, at 459 (revised) (most dramatic example is homicide); WAYNE LAFAVE & AUSTIN SCOTT, CRIMINAL LAW § 5.4(a) (2d ed. 1986) (taking a life to save several lives defensible under necessity).

[201] See § 19.14 of this chapter.

assume the brakes failed to function on a school bus filled with children while its operator was driving the bus down a road with a steep incline. If the operator of the bus chose to strike and kill an innocent pedestrian with the bus rather than drive the bus into a deep crevice to avoid the pedestrian, which would likely cause the deaths of a large number of the children in the bus, the bus operator's decision to sacrifice the life of the pedestrian in order to save the lives of the children could theoretically be justified by necessity. Two famous cases suggest, however, that the taking of life might never be a lesser evil. In the English case of *Regina v. Dudley and Stephens*,[202] three sailors and a cabin boy were adrift on a lifeboat following a shipwreck a thousand miles from land. After the passage of almost three weeks, having been without food for nine days and without water for seven days, two of the sailors put to death the cabin boy (who was in the weakest condition and who would probably have died before rescue anyway) in order to feed on his body and drink his blood. Following their rescue, the two sailors were prosecuted and convicted of murder. The reviewing court affirmed the convictions, stating in dictum that the taking of life in such circumstances would never have been justified even if the group had drawn lots to see who would be sacrificed and the lot had fallen on the cabin boy.[203]

In an early American case, *United States v. Holmes*,[204] the scene of the alleged crime was again a lifeboat at sea following a shipwreck. In this case, an overloaded lifeboat carried nine seamen and thirty-two passengers. After a storm developed threatening to sink the lifeboat, some of the seamen, including the defendant, threw fourteen male passengers overboard to their deaths in order to lighten the load and save, as they did, the remaining individuals on the lifeboat. Although the trial court instructed the jury on the defense of necessity, the jury found the defendant guilty of manslaughter as charged. Although there was some language in the opinion suggesting that a different decision *might* have been reached had the victims been selected on a more equitable basis, the appellate court nevertheless affirmed the conviction.[205]

Both cases seem to rest on the notion that the taking of life will never be justified by necessity because of the intrinsic value of human life. As might be expected, these pronouncements have not been accepted by proponents of a broad approach to the defense of necessity.[206] All that can be said, particularly given

---

[202] L.R. 14 Q.B.D. 273, 15 Cox C.C. 624 (1884).

[203] Regina v. Dudley, L.R. 14 Q.B.D. 273, 285, 15 Cox C.C. 624, 635 (1884).

[204] 26 F. Cas. 360 (C.C.E.D. Pa. 1842).

[205] Among other concerns was the sailors' possible duty to sacrifice themselves to save their passengers. On the other hand, the necessity of having sailors with the expertise necessary to operate the boat would have to be considered.

[206] MODEL PENAL CODE § 3.02, comment at 8 (Tentative Draft No. 8, 1958) ("the numerical preponderance in the lives saved compared to those sacrificed surely establishes an ethical and legal justification for the act"); WAYNE LAFAVE & AUSTIN SCOTT, CRIMINAL LAW § 5.4(a) (2d ed. 1986); ROLLIN M. PERKINS & RONALD N. BOYCE, CRIMINAL LAW 1068-69 (3d ed. 1982); GLANVILLE WIL-

the sparsity of caselaw on this point, is that it is possible a homicide may never be justified by necessity in some jurisdictions and, then again, it is conceivable that it might be in appropriate circumstances in others.

To the extent that a homicide might be justified by necessity, on one point there appears to be a consensus: a person cannot take *one* life to save his or her own.[207] Returning to the school bus example, if the school bus carried no children but only the operator, the operator could not run down the innocent pedestrian for the purpose of saving his or her own life. Nor are the authorities prepared to say that one life (for example, a noted heart surgeon, a leader of a nation, an Albert Einstein) has an intrinsic worth that exceeds the value of another life (for example, a person with terminal cancer, a degenerate "bum," a convicted murderer). The implications of making such choices are fraught with danger.

There are several features of the defense of necessity, aside from those already discussed, on which there appears to be general agreement. First, if the legislature in a particular jurisdiction has declared that a designated act can never qualify as a potential "lesser evil," then the courts will normally defer to the legislature's value judgment in that regard.[208] Thus, if a legislature ruled out the taking of life as a basis for necessity, that decision would be respected. Or if the legislature limited the defense to situations in which the defendant is faced with a life-threatening force (as with duress),[209] this legislative determination would be honored as preempting invocation of the necessity doctrine.

Second, the courts uniformly agree that the necessity defense must be based on society's collective value judgments, not on personal value considerations.[210] For example, where several persons' political or moral values justified in their own minds the destruction of Selective Service office records (an effort designed to undermine the drafting of persons into the war in Vietnam),[211] the physical barring of women seeking abortions from rooms in an abortion clinic

---

LIAMS, CRIMINAL LAW: THE GENERAL PART 740 (2d ed. 1961) ("Where the killing results in a net saving of life . . . [it] should be regarded . . . as legally justifying").

[207] MODEL PENAL CODE § 3.02, comment at 8 (Tentative Draft No. 8, 1958) ("The life of every individual must be assumed in such a case to be of equal value"); WAYNE LAFAVE & AUSTIN SCOTT, CRIMINAL LAW § 5.4(b) (2d ed. 1986) ("the law doubtless considers one person's life equal to that of another . . .,without regard to the age, character, health or good looks of the persons involved"); ROLLIN M. PERKINS & RONALD N. BOYCE, CRIMINAL LAW 1068 (3d ed. 1982) ("the law regards all alike for such a purpose as in the formula one person-one vote").

[208] WAYNE LAFAVE & AUSTIN SCOTT, CRIMINAL LAW § 5.4(a) (2d ed. 1986); 2 PAUL ROBINSON, CRIMINAL LAW DEFENSES § 124(d)(3) (1984). See, e.g., KY. REV. STAT. § 503.030(1) (1975) (necessity not available where homicide is intentional).

[209] See, e.g., WIS. STAT. ANN. § 939.47 (West 1982).

[210] 2 PAUL ROBINSON, CRIMINAL LAW DEFENSES § 124(d)(1) (1984).

[211] United States v. Kroncke, 459 F.2d 697 (8th Cir. 1972) (convictions affirmed).

(conduct aimed at the protection of the lives of fetuses),[212] and the refusal to terminate a protest in a nuclear power plant (trespass designed to bring a halt to the dangers of nuclear power),[213] the refusal to extend jury instructions regarding the defense of necessity was upheld in each case because these individuals' assessments of what constituted the "greater evil" was not in tandem with the values of the larger society.[214] Thus, political protests involving "civil disobedience" are not deserving of the defense of necessity.[215]

Third, there is agreement that there must be no other alternative courses of conduct available beyond the lesser evils.[216] Thus, if the person who was starving to death resorted to theft in a grocery store instead of frequenting an available free-food pantry, that person would have no defense to the theft.[217]

Beyond these basic concerns, it is difficult to generalize about this "choice of evils" defense. Some jurisdictions require the choice of evils to be imminent.[218] Some hold that the defendant must not have been at fault in occasioning the choice in question.[219] And some deny the defense in circumstances of "economic necessity" — where persons in want steal to satisfy their privation.[220]

§ 19.24. Defense of Necessity Codified.

With the adoption of the Criminal Code of 1961, the defense of necessity was codified in section 5/7-13. It states:

> Conduct which would otherwise be an offense is justifiable by reason of necessity if the accused was without blame in occasioning or developing the situation and reasonably believed such conduct was necessary to avoid a public or private injury greater than the injury which might reasonably result from his own conduct.[221]

Before this enactment, there was no necessity statute available in Illinois and apparently no caselaw supportive thereof.[222]

---

[212] People v. Stiso, 93 Ill. App. 3d 101, 416 N.E.2d 1209 (1st Dist. 1981) (disorderly conduct convictions affirmed).

[213] People v. Warshow, 138 Vt. 22, 410 A.2d 1000 (1979) (trespass convictions affirmed).

[214] United States v. Kroncke, 459 F.2d 697 (8th Cir. 1972); People v. Stiso, 93 Ill. App. 3d 101, 416 N.E.2d 1209 (1st Dist. 1981); People v. Warshow, 138 Vt. 22, 410 A.2d 1000 (1979).

[215] Brent Wride, Comment, *Political Protest and the Illinois Defense of Necessity*, 54 U. CHI. L. REV. 1070 (1987).

[216] WAYNE LAFAVE & AUSTIN SCOTT, CRIMINAL LAW § 5.4(d)(5) (2d ed. 1986).

[217] WAYNE LAFAVE & AUSTIN SCOTT, CRIMINAL LAW § 5.4(d)(5) (2d ed. 1986).

[218] 2 PAUL ROBINSON, CRIMINAL LAW DEFENSES § 124(f)(1) (1984).

[219] *See* WAYNE LAFAVE & AUSTIN SCOTT, CRIMINAL LAW § 5.4(d)(6) (2d ed. 1986).

[220] WAYNE LAFAVE & AUSTIN SCOTT, CRIMINAL LAW § 5.4(d)(6) (2d ed. 1986).

[221] 720 ILCS 5/7-13 (1999).

[222] It is interesting to note that while the legislative drafting committee reported "[n]ecessity as a justification for crime has long been known to the law," it cited to only the *Dudley and Stephens*

The intent of the legislature in drafting this provision was to provide a defense in a wide variety of situations, such as:

> destruction of property to prevent the spread of fire; violation of speed limit in pursuit of criminal; mountain climbers lost in a storm taking refuge in a house, and possibly appropriating provisions; jettisoning of cargo at sea to save vessel; [and] druggist dispensing a drug without the requisite prescription to alleviate distress in an emergency.[223]

In addition, the legislature stated its intent that "economic necessity" not be a basis for such a defense unless a true emergency exists.[224] After commenting that "its most dramatic application is, perhaps, in homicide,"[225] the legislature did not exclude the homicide possibility in the statute itself (as it did in the drafting of the compulsion statute), which by implication suggests that no such restriction was intended.[226] What is clear from the statute is that the legislature sought to rule out the defense in circumstances in which the defendant's blameworthy acts occasioned the choice-of-evils situation.

After the enactment of the general provision reflecting the necessity defense, the Illinois legislature categorically ruled out a defense claim that the defense is available to a person charged with the unlawful use or possession of a weapon while in the custody of the Illinois Department of Corrections. The offense that prohibits any person confined in an Illinois penal institution from having possession of a weapon contains a provision that bars such person from raising the defense of necessity to such a charge.[227]

---

and the *Holmes* cases where, in fact, the defense was not recognized. No Illinois cases were cited. *See* ILL. ANN. STAT. ch. 38, para. 7-13 (Smith-Hurd 1989), 1961 Committee Comments, at 459 (revised).

[223] ILL. ANN. STAT. ch. 38, para. 7-13 (Smith-Hurd 1989), 1961 Committee Comments, at 459 (revised).

[224] ILL. ANN. STAT. ch. 38, para. 7-13 (Smith-Hurd 1989), 1961 Committee Comments, at 459 (revised).

[225] ILL. ANN. STAT. ch. 38, para. 7-13 (Smith-Hurd 1989), 1961 Committee Comments, at 459 (revised).

[226] However, Illinois courts have yet to recognize a necessity claim in a homicide situation. *See* People v. Doss, 214 Ill. App. 3d 1051, 1055-57, 574 N.E.2d 806, 809-10 (1st Dist. 1991) (defense of necessity rejected where 15-year-old defendant, who did not know that she was pregnant, claimed it was necessary to kill her new-born baby in order to avoid disgrace of unwed pregnancy); People v. Gindorf 159 Ill. App. 3d 647, 660-61, 512 N.E.2d 770, 778-79 (2d Dist. 1987) (defense of necessity denied where suicidal mentally-ill mother claimed it was necessary to kill her two young children in order to avoid the pain and misery that the children would go through after her planned suicide), *cert. denied*, 486 U.S. 1011 (1988).

[227] 720 ILCS 5/24-1.1(d) (1999).

§ 19.25.   Elements of Necessity.

A defendant may enjoy the defense of necessity concerning conduct that is otherwise criminal if he or she (1) is without blame in occasioning the situation and (2) reasonably believes (3) that the conduct was necessary (4) to avoid a greater public or private injury.

§ 19.26.   — Without Blame in Occasioning the Situation.

In Illinois, the necessity statute clearly requires that the defendant be without fault in occasioning the situation giving rise to the choice of evils. In *People v. Perez*,[228] the defendant was convicted of the crime of unlawful use of weapons after having been involved in a gunfight with members of a street gang. The defendant had previously admitted that the confrontation in question grew out of a feud that had developed after gang members had tried to kill him following his shooting at "them before."[229] In these circumstances, the appellate court held that the defendant was not justified in carrying a loaded revolver by reason of necessity, since (1) this "ongoing feud" had "developed at least in part" because of the activities of the defendant, and (2) the evidence showed that he had been driving around looking for the opportunity to shoot at the gang members.[230] The record was devoid of "any indication that defendant was without blame in occasioning the situation which caused him to carry a loaded revolver in the City of Chicago."[231] Thus, the appellate court ruled that the defendant had not effectively raised the defense of necessity.

§ 19.27.   — Reasonably Believes.

As long as the defendant "reasonably believes" the conduct is necessary to avoid the greater evil, he or she will have a defense. In *Perez* (discussed immediately above), the fact that "[n]othing at trial demonstrates that defendant reasonably believed that carrying a weapon was 'necessary' to avoid a private injury which he feared" undermined the defendant's necessity claim.[232] The appellate court felt that the defendant could have easily avoided any need for a weapon by the simple expedient of staying away from the street gang's "territory."[233] As such, the evidence was deemed insufficient to require the state to disprove the defendant's contention that the defense of necessity existed.[234] The defense of necessity was also unavailable to a defendant charged with attempted

---

[228] 97 Ill. App. 3d 278, 422 N.E.2d 945 (1st Dist. 1981).

[229] People v. Perez, 97 Ill. App. 3d 278, 279, 422 N.E.2d 945, 947 (1st Dist. 1981).

[230] People v. Perez, 97 Ill. App. 3d 278, 281, 422 N.E.2d 945, 948 (1st Dist. 1981).

[231] People v. Perez, 97 Ill. App. 3d 278, 281, 422 N.E.2d 945, 948 (1st Dist. 1981).

[232] People v. Perez, 97 Ill. App. 3d 278, 281, 422 N.E.2d 945, 948 (1st Dist. 1981).

[233] People v. Perez, 97 Ill. App. 3d 278, 281, 422 N.E.2d 945, 948 (1st Dist. 1981).

[234] People v. Perez, 97 Ill. App. 3d 278, 281, 422 N.E.2d 945, 948 (1st Dist. 1981).

murder when he fired shots at police officers during a high-speed chase, even though the defendant's testimony established that he believed one of the officers to be a drug dealer who was trying to kill him.[235] In this case, the appellate court ruled that the defendant had no reasonable basis to conclude that his life was in jeopardy, since prior to the police chase, an officer had approached the defendant's automobile in police uniform from a car marked as a police car, the officers had never threatened the defendant nor displayed any weapons in any threatening manner, during the chase the police used their sirens and emergency lights, and there was no indication that defendant was fleeing to a position of safety, such as a police station.[236]

In contrast, in *People v. Unger*,[237] the Illinois Supreme Court ruled that the evidence offered by the accused did warrant instructions on necessity.[238] At a trial on charges of escape from a state penitentiary, the defendant testified that he had been subjected to threats of forced homosexual activity; that on one occasion, the threatened abuse was carried out; and that just before his escape, he was told he was going to be killed.[239] After conviction, the defendant contended on appeal that the trial court erred in its failure to instruct the jury that the defendant's escape might have been justified by reason of necessity.[240] The supreme court reversed the defendant's conviction and indicated that the jury should have been given an opportunity to examine "the reasonableness of defendant's assertion that such conduct was necessary. . . ."[241] More recently, in *People v. Kite*,[242] the Illinois Supreme Court ruled that a defendant was not enti-

---

[235] People v. Wright, 171 Ill. App. 3d 573, 582-83, 525 N.E.2d 1165, 1171 (5th Dist. 1988).

[236] People v. Wright, 171 Ill. App. 3d 573, 582-83, 525 N.E.2d 1165, 1171 (5th Dist. 1988).

[237] 66 Ill. 2d 333, 362 N.E.2d 319 (1977).

[238] People v. Unger, 66 Ill. 2d 333, 341, 362 N.E.2d 319, 323 (1977); *see also* People v. Ferree, 221 Ill. App. 3d 212, 216-18, 581 N.E.2d 699, 702-03 (5th Dist. 1991) (defendant was entitled to necessity instruction in prosecution for unlawful possession of weapon by person in custody where defendant had received a note which posed specific threat on his life, defendant had no time before he obtained knife to complain to authorities and defendant had been previously cut and hospitalized). However, the legislature later enacted a law stating that necessity is unavailable in such circumstances (720 ILCS 5/24-1.1(d) (1999)). *See also* § 19.24 of this chapter.

[239] People v. Unger, 66 Ill. 2d 333, 336-37, 362 N.E.2d 319, 322-23 (1977).

[240] People v. Unger, 66 Ill. 2d 333, 337, 362 N.E.2d 319, 321 (1977). He had also contended it was justified by reason of compulsion, which the Supreme Court rejected. A discussion of this part of the opinion appears in § 19.19 of this chapter.

[241] People v. Unger, 66 Ill. 2d 333, 341, 362 N.E.2d 319, 323 (1977). *Compare* People v. Tackett, 169 Ill. App. 3d 397, 402, 523 N.E.2d 647, 650-51 (4th Dist. 1988) (where evidence existed that a white male prisoner had previously been assaulted by members of a black prison gang, such was an insufficient basis to support a necessity defense to a weapons charge where there was no evidence of imminent future assaults, no report of prior threats to prison authorities, no evidence that such complaints would have been futile, and no evidence that defendant had no access to the courts).

[242] 153 Ill. 2d 40, 605 N.E.2d 563 (1992).

tled to necessity instructions in a prosecution for unlawful possession of a weapon by a person in prison absent showing that alleged threats against his life by other inmates were specific and immediate.[243] Parenthetically, the legislature later enacted a law explicitly ruling out the defense of necessity where a person is charged with the unlawful possession of a weapon by a person in the custody of a correctional facility.[244]

§ 19.28.   — Conduct was Necessary.

It is incumbent on the accused who raises the defense of necessity to offer evidence that the conduct was necessary to avoid the greater harm involved. For instance, in *People v. Taylor*,[245] a defendant was convicted of carrying a concealed weapon and unlawful use of a weapon within five years of release from prison. On appeal, he contended he had in his possession the weapon of another while in a hotel because he was fearful of certain men who were waiting for him outside the hotel. The appellate court affirmed, holding that the defendant had not demonstrated why it was necessary for him to *conceal* the weapon in question.[246]

A basic tenet of the law of necessity is that the otherwise illegal conduct was the "sole reasonable alternative" available to the actor under the circumstances."[247] In *Perez*[248] (discussed above), the defendant had been convicted of the unlawful use of weapons for bringing a weapon into the city of Chicago and engaging in a gang fight that was part of an ongoing feud with members of a street gang. His claim of necessity was rejected by the appellate court.

> Simple common sense conjoined with the record in this case prohibits the conclusion that the sole reasonable alternative available to defendant was to carry a loaded revolver within the City of Chicago in order to protect himself against threats allegedly made against him. Only the most obvious "more reasonable" alternative, that of avoiding contact with the threatening street gang members by avoiding their "territory," needs mention here. Defendant, however, rather than utilizing a less dangerous alternative, instead may have incited a gun battle by stopping and exiting his car upon sighting members of the gang which allegedly threatened him.[249]

---

[243] People v. Kite, 153 Ill. 2d 40, 45-47, 605 N.E.2d 563, 566-67 (1992).

[244] 720 ILCS 5/24-1.1(d) (1999).

[245] 31 Ill. App. 3d 20, 332 N.E.2d 735 (1st Dist. 1975).

[246] People v. Taylor, 31 Ill. App. 3d 20, 25, 332 N.E.2d 735, 738 (1st Dist. 1975).

[247] People v. Perez, 97 Ill. App. 3d 278, 281, 422 N.E.2d 945, 948 (1st Dist. 1981) (citing with approval Lawrence Tiffany & Carl Anderson, *Legislating the Necessity Defense in Criminal Law*, 52 DEN. L.J. 839, 845-46 (1975)).

[248] People v. Perez, 97 Ill. App. 3d 278, 422 N.E.2d 945 (1st Dist. 1981).

[249] People v. Perez, 97 Ill. App. 3d 278, 281, 422 N.E.2d 945, 948 (1st Dist. 1981).

Similarly, where a defendant was found to be in unlawful possession of a weapon in a prison, he could not assert the necessity defense on grounds that he feared assault from other prisoners, because he had not expressed his fears to prison authorities or pursued potential redress in the courts.[250]

Thus, where the defendant has not availed himself or herself of a reasonable legal option to avoid the choice of evils, he or she has no defense. In *People v. White*,[251] the defendant was convicted of escape from a correctional center, which he claimed was justified by necessity, because he had learned that his wife had been raped and his daughter beaten. In affirming the defendant's conviction, the appellate court stated:

> Necessity requires that there be an alternative to an evil course and that alternative be evil as well. Where there is yet another alternative — besides the two evil choices — and such alternative, if carried out, will cause less harm, then a person is not justified in breaking the law [citation omitted]. Defendant had a *legal option* available to him. The testimony from the supervisor at the correctional center related the procedure for emergency leave and that no such request was made by the defendant. It is clear that defendant had more than a choice between two evil courses.[252]

Similarly, a criminal trespass in a medical center in which abortions were performed was not justified by necessity given the defendants' interest in protecting the lives of fetuses, for, among other reasons, the "[d]efendants chose criminal conduct rather than available legal means of dramatizing their opposition to abortion. . . ."[253] In another case, it was held that the defense of necessity was not available to a defendant who drove his automobile while his license was revoked on the theory that it was incumbent that he make an immediate repair of a water heater where he was employed, on a Sunday afternoon, because he had not shown that other transportation alternatives were unavailable.[254] Similarly, the defense of necessity was not available to the defendant who drove his automobile, while intoxicated, from the scene of a three-car accident to a nearby

---

[250] People v. Tackett, 169 Ill. App. 3d 397, 402, 523 N.E.2d 647, 650-51 (4th Dist. 1988). A similar principle would likely govern a case such as People v. Davis, 165 Ill. App. 3d 648, 650-52, 519 N.E.2d 103, 105-06 (2d Dist. 1988), where a defendant advanced a necessity-type claim at sentencing. In that case, the court rejected defendant's alleged "civil-minded purpose" in possessing drugs in circumstances where the defendant claimed his possession was motivated by his interest in demonstrating how easy it was to purchase illicit drugs in the community. *Id.* Had the defendant raised this issue as an affirmative defense at trial, the state could have defeated the argument by pointing out that another course of action was available to the defendant, namely, informing police about the potential sources of drugs in the community.

[251] 78 Ill. App. 3d 979, 397 N.E.2d 1246 (4th Dist. 1979).

[252] People v. White, 78 Ill. App. 3d 979, 981, 397 N.E.2d 1246, 1247 (4th Dist. 1979).

[253] People v. Krizka, 92 Ill. App. 3d 288, 291, 416 N.E.2d 36, 38 (1st Dist. 1981).

[254] People v. Dalton, 7 Ill. App. 3d 442, 287 N.E.2d 548 (2d Dist. 1972).

parking lot claiming that the car posed a danger to oncoming traffic as it was night and a slight curve in the road was located 200 yards from the intersection at which the accident occurred, when other reasonable courses of action were available to him, such as allowing a sober driver to move the car or waiting until police arrived.[255] On the other hand, where an armed robbery defendant testified an individual had threatened her life if she did not participate in the armed robbery and stated that she only participated in order to save her life and the life of a cashier, she was entitled to necessity instructions.[256]

§ 19.29.   — Avoid a Greater Public or Private Injury.

Unless the otherwise criminal conduct was engaged in to avoid a greater public or private injury than that which would have occurred given compliance with the criminal law, necessity is not available. In *People v. Janik*,[257] the Illinois Supreme Court held that a drunken driver who killed a pedestrian and was charged with leaving the scene of an accident involving death was not entitled to jury instructions on the defense of necessity when during the trial the defendant alleged that he thought that some large object had been thrown at his moving car and, accordingly, he feared for his safety.[258] The court reasoned that defendant's apparent assessment of the situation suggested an act of vandalism, in which case the defendant would have "had no duty to stop."[259]

> Moreover, necessity requires a balancing of two evils. [citation omitted]. According to defendant he was unaware of an accident and therefore could not have been balancing between the two evils and making a choice which promoted some higher value than literal compliance with the law. His testimony simply does not reflect that he was confronted with and made such a choice.[260]

This case clearly stands for the proposition that necessity only arises where the defendant forgoes the terms of the criminal law for some good reason in circumstances where the defendant realizes his actions are forbidden in the absence of a good reason. Concerning the injury to be avoided, it appears from the caselaw that the threatened injury must be immediate or imminent.[261] Where a defendant escaped from a penitentiary allegedly, among other reasons, because of lack of proper medical care, his defense of necessity claim was rejected, since he had not maintained that he was faced with an "immediate or imminent threat of dan-

---

[255] People v. Cord, 258 Ill. App. 3d 188, 193, 630 N.E.2d 173, 177 (2d Dist. 1994).

[256] People v. Houser, 305 Ill. App. 3d 384, 389, 712 N.E.2d 355, 359 (4th Dist. 1999).

[257] 127 Ill. 2d 390, 537 N.E.2d 756 (1988).

[258] People v. Janik, 127 Ill. 2d 390, 400, 537 N.E.2d 756, 760 (1988).

[259] People v. Janik, 127 Ill. 2d 390, 400, 537 N.E.2d 756, 760 (1988).

[260] People v. Janik, 127 Ill. 2d 390, 400, 537 N.E.2d 756, 760-61 (1988).

[261] People v. Davis, 16 Ill. App. 3d 846, 848, 306 N.E.2d 897, 898 (3d Dist. 1974).

ger" to his person.[262] Similarly, a court properly rejected a defendant from presenting evidence of dangerous circumstances that may have provoked his escape from jail because he failed to turn himself into authorities after escaping and removing himself from the imminent threat in the jail.[263] However, the caselaw does not require "gun to the head immediacy" as a prerequisite to proving necessity.[264]

The injury to be avoided must be a "public or private injury" greater than the injury that might reasonably result from the defendant's own conduct.[265] In *Krizka*[266] (discussed above), the defendants had argued that their criminal trespass in an abortion clinic was defensible by reason of necessity, since their aim was "to prevent the deaths of fetuses, which they perceived as the greater injury."[267] However, the appellate court ruled that given the United States Supreme Court's determination in *Roe v. Wade*[268] that abortions are constitutionally protected during the first trimester of pregnancy, the so-called injury was "not a legally recognized injury"; accordingly, an integral element of necessity was lacking.[269] "We . . . conclude that defendants did not engage in illegal conduct because they were faced with a choice of evils. Rather, they intentionally trespassed on complainant's property in order to interfere with the rights of others."[270] This case also illustrates that the choice-of-evils concern must revolve around society's collective values, not an individual or group's personal values.

As stated, the injury to be avoided can be either private or public. In *People v. Unger*,[271] the defendant's escape from prison might have been justified by his interest in avoiding serious injury to his private person.[272] Also, in *Mayer v. City of Chicago*,[273] where a defendant, a third-year medical student, interfered with a police officer's action in attempting to move an injured person without a

---

[262] People v. Davis, 16 Ill. App. 3d 846, 848, 306 N.E.2d 897, 898 (3d Dist. 1974).

[263] People v. Scott, 194 Ill. App. 3d 634, 641, 551 N.E.2d 288, 293 (1st Dist. 1990).

[264] People v. Unger, 33 Ill. App. 3d 770, 775, 338 N.E.2d 442, 446 (3d Dist. 1975), *aff'd*, 66 Ill. 2d 333, 362 N.E.2d 319 (1977).

[265] People v. Krizka, 92 Ill. App. 3d 288, 289-90, 416 N.E.2d 36, 37 (1st Dist. 1981).

[266] 92 Ill. App. 3d 288, 416 N.E.2d 36 (1st Dist. 1981).

[267] People v. Krizka, 92 Ill. App. 3d 288, 290, 416 N.E.2d 36, 37 (1st Dist. 1981).

[268] 410 U.S. 113 (1973).

[269] People v. Krizka, 92 Ill. App. 3d 288, 416 N.E.2d 36, 37 (1st Dist. 1981).

[270] People v. Krizka, 92 Ill. App. 3d 288, 416 N.E.2d 36, 37 (1st Dist. 1981). *See also* People v. Belsan, 253 Ill. App. 3d 1093, 1094, 625 N.E.2d 913, 915 (2d Dist. 1993) (defense of necessity is not available to trespassers who interfere with constitutional rights to have abortion); People v. Berquist, 239 Ill. App. 3d 906, 908-13, 608 N.E.2d 1212, 1215-18 (2d Dist. 1993) (defense of necessity is not available to trespassers who interfere with constitutional rights to have abortion); People v. Smith, 237 Ill. App. 3d 901, 909, 605 N.E.2d 105, 110 (3d Dist. 1992) (defense of necessity is not a permissible defense to criminal trespass in the abortion clinic setting).

[271] 66 Ill. 2d 333, 362 N.E.2d 319 (1977).

[272] People v. Unger, 66 Ill. 2d 333, 341, 362 N.E.2d 319, 323 (1977).

[273] 56 Ill. 2d 366, 308 N.E.2d 601 (1977).

stretcher, it was held that the defendant was entitled to necessity instructions concerning a charge of disorderly conduct, since his interference may have been necessary to avoid another's private injury.[274] It has also been held that a defendant was entitled to defense of another and necessity instructions in her trial on charges of resisting a police officer where the evidence revealed that the defendant's husband was faced with excessive force from police officers.[275] In another case, the appellate court ruled that a trial court committed reversible error in a home invasion trial because it refused to instruct a jury on the defense of necessity where the defendant's testimony, if believed, would have permitted the jury to find defendant had engaged in the home invasion in order to prevent his companions from injuring or killing the residents in the home.[276] An example of avoidance of a public injury might be where a person is tortured by a law enforcement official into revealing the whereabouts of a bomb before it explodes and kills many people.

Finally, it should be mentioned that in Illinois, the recognizable injury does not have to flow from natural forces, as some authorities and cases suggest.[277] The Illinois Supreme Court approval of necessity instructions in *Unger*,[278] where the coercive force were prison inmates, and in *Mayer*,[279] where the threatening force was a police officer, illustrates this point.

§ 19.30.   Defense of Entrapment: Background of Current Law.

Although overt criminality may be relatively susceptible to identification and prosecution through normal law enforcement detective and investigative strategies, the so-called victimless crimes,[280] which are generally undertaken by consensual offenders for personal gain, usually retain a covert quality. Since the crime occurs privately with no complaining participant, detection is usually difficult. To attain enforcement of the law, consensual, covert crimes must be dealt with in a circumvented manner. Exposure is achieved through deceptive government involvement in the criminal design. Without direct governmental participation, these victimless crimes would flourish. Examples of such crimes are

---

[274] City of Chicago v. Mayer, 56 Ill. 2d 366, 368-72, 308 N.E.2d 601, 602-04 (1974).

[275] People v. Veatch, 145 Ill. App. 3d 23, 28-29, 495 N.E.2d 674, 678 (2d Dist. 1986).

[276] People v. Blake, 168 Ill. App. 3d 581, 586-87, 522 N.E.2d 822, 826 (3d Dist. 1988).

[277] *See* § 19.23 of this chapter.

[278] 66 Ill. 2d 333, 362 N.E.2d 319 (1977).

[279] 56 Ill. 2d 366, 308 N.E.2d 601 (1974).

[280] *See* Robert C. Boruchowitz, *Victimless Crimes: A Proposal to Free the Courts*, 57 JUDICATURE 69 (1973); John F. Decker, *The Case for Recognition of an Absolute Defense or Mitigation in Crimes Without Victims*, 5 ST. MARY'S L.J. 40 (1973); Evelyn Cheverie, Comment, *Victimless Crime Laws*, 6 N.C. CENT. L.J. 258 (1975).

offenses involving drugs,[281] liquor bootlegging,[282] gambling,[283] prostitution,[284] possession of pornography,[285] counterfeiting,[286] bribery,[287] and fireworks and explosives.[288]

The doctrine of entrapment becomes an issue when governmental undercover criminal involvement extends beyond a point of mere detection. It is within the province of law enforcement for a governmental agent, in attempting to detect latent crimes, to provide predisposed individuals the opportunity to carry out their premeditated criminal design.[289] But the basic premise is violated when an officer overzealously formulates a crime in his or her own mind and induces a non-predisposed victim into its commission.[290] Entrapment is shown where "it appears that officers of the law or their agents incited, induced, instigated or lured the accused into committing an offense which he otherwise would not have committed and had no intention of committing."[291] This defense acknowledges that without this overreaching or special inducement, the crime would never have occurred. It has been denounced as reprehensible and contrary to sound public policy to permit government efforts aimed at preventing crime to

---

[281] See, e.g., People v. D'Angelo, 223 Ill. App. 3d 754, 755, 585 N.E.2d 1239, 1240 (5th Dist. 1992).

[282] See, e.g., People v. Cash, 26 Ill. 2d 595, 597, 188 N.E.2d 20, 21 (1963); Roberts v. Illinois Liquor Control Comm'n, 58 Ill. App. 2d 171, 173, 206 N.E.2d 799, 800 (1st Dist. 1965).

[283] See, e.g., People v. Hornstein, 64 Ill. App. 2d 319, 211 N.E.2d 756 (4th Dist. 1965) (abstract).

[284] See, e.g., People ex rel. Difanis v. Boston, 92 Ill. App. 3d 962, 963, 416 N.E.2d 333, 335 (4th Dist. 1981); People v. McCall, 52 Ill. App. 3d 407, 408, 367 N.E.2d 588, 589 (3d Dist. 1977); People v. Darling, 46 Ill. App. 3d 698, 699, 361 N.E.2d 121, 122 (3d Dist. 1977).

[285] People v. Hirsch, 221 Ill. App. 3d 772, 774, 582 N.E.2d 1228, 1229 (1st Dist. 1991).

[286] People v. Moran, 378 Ill. 461, 462, 38 N.E.2d 760, 761 (1941), cert. denied, 316 U.S. 665 (1942); People v. Boalbey, 143 Ill. App. 3d 362, 363, 493 N.E.2d 369, 370 (3d Dist. 1986) (illegal use of food stamps).

[287] People v. Gillespie, 136 Ill. 2d 496, 497, 557 N.E.2d 894, 895 (1990); People v. Lyons, 4 Ill. 2d 396, 397, 122 N.E.2d 809, 810 (1954).

[288] See, e.g., People v. Larson, 17 Ill. App. 3d 683, 684, 308 N.E.2d 148, 149 (2d Dist. 1974).

[289] People v. Marshall, 101 Ill. App. 3d 244, 247, 427 N.E.2d 1333, 1335 (4th Dist. 1981) ("in light of the ever growing drug problem, government action in infiltrating drug rings should not be criticized so strongly, and . . . [a] court should not foreclose the possibility that a conviction of a predisposed individual could be sustained even though the government did furnish the controlled substance").

[290] See, e.g., People v. Jensen, 37 Ill. App. 3d 1010. 1015, 347 N.E.2d 371, 375 (1st Dist. 1976) (conviction for driving on highway with suspended license was reversed because defendant's conduct originated from officer's request that defendant drive his automobile from one point to another).

[291] People v. Cash, 26 Ill. 2d 595, 597, 188 N.E.2d 20, 21 (1963).

manufacture it.[292] In such a case, the defense of entrapment provides grounds for the acquittal of a person otherwise substantively guilty as charged.[293]

The defense of entrapment did not exist at early English common law, but rather is a by-product of American law.[294] Although the concept of entrapment was alluded to with credence through dicta as early as 1895,[295] the United States Supreme Court did not recognize entrapment as an affirmative defense in a criminal prosecution until the 1932 landmark case of *Sorrells v. United States*.[296] In *Sorrells*, a prohibition agent, posing as a tourist, visited the defendant's home with the intended purpose of catching the defendant selling bootleg liquor. Gaining the defendant's confidence and benevolence through exchanges of war stories, the agent repeatedly expressed his desire to purchase a quantity of liquor. After the agent made a number of requests, the defendant procured and sold to the agent a half-gallon of whiskey.[297]

Although the Supreme Court acknowledged that entrapment was a viable defense and thus held that the trial judge erred in not allowing the issue to go to the jury, it was split on its underlying rationale. Writing for the majority, Justice Hughes stated, "[Entrapment occurs] when the criminal design originates with the officials of the government, and they implant in the mind of an innocent person the disposition to commit the alleged offense and induce its commission in order that they may prosecute."[298] This formulation of the entrapment defense, now known as the "subjective" theory of entrapment,[299] focused on the state of mind of the accused. If the accused harbored a wholly innocent state of mind until it was corrupted by the police conduct, he or she would have a defense;

---

[292] People v. Outten, 13 Ill. 2d 21, 24, 147 N.E.2d 284, 286 (1958) ("The law frowns upon the seduction of an otherwise innocent person into a criminal career, but tolerates the use of decoys and various other artifices to catch the criminal").

[293] *See* People v. Cooper, 17 Ill. App. 3d 934, 938, 308 N.E.2d 815, 818 (2d Dist. 1974) ("By invoking the defense of entrapment, a defendant admits commission of the crime charged").

[294] For an in-depth analysis of historical development of the entrapment defense, *see* PAUL MARCUS, THE ENTRAPMENT DEFENSE (2d ed. 1995); N.L.A Barlow, *Entrapment and the Common Law: Is There a Place for the American Doctrine of Entrapment?*, 41 MOD. L. REV. 266 (1978); William Mikell, *The Doctrine of Entrapment in the Federal Courts*, 90 U. PA. L. REV. 245 (1942); Daniel Rotenberg, *The Police Detection Practice of Encouragement*, 49 VA. L. REV. 871 (1963).

[295] *See* the Decoy cases: Price v. United States, 165 U.S. 311, 315 (1897); Andrews v. United States, 162 U.S. 420, 423 (1896); Rosen v. United States, 161 U.S. 29, 42 (1896); Goode v. United States, 159 U.S. 663, 669 (1895); Grimm v. United States, 156 U.S. 604, 609 (1895). *See also* Woo Wai v. United States 223 F. 412, 414 (9th Cir. 1915) (entrapment was recognized as proper defense in federal court for first time).

[296] 287 U.S. 435 (1932). *See also* Casey v. United States, 276 U.S. 413, 418-23 (1928) (strong divergence in entrapment theory first appeared through dicta included in majority opinion and within Justice Brandeis's dissent).

[297] Sorrells v. United States, 287 U.S. 435, 439-40 (1932).

[298] Sorrells v. United States, 287 U.S. 435, 442 (1932).

[299] WAYNE LAFAVE & JEROME ISRAEL, CRIMINAL PROCEDURE § 5.2(b) (2d ed. 1992).

however, if the accused was already predisposed to commit the crime when approached by the police, he or she would have no defense.[300] After examining the subjective intent of the alleged violator, the *Sorrells* majority exonerated the defendant, since the fact that the defendant had a good reputation and no criminal record suggested a lack of criminal intent.[301]

Justice Robert's concurring minority opinion followed a second formulation of entrapment, now known as the "objective" test,[302] and argued that the doctrine of entrapment was a "fundamental rule of public policy."[303] The concurring minority focused on the conduct of the governmental agent and ignored the alleged offender's predisposition, rationalizing that one in violation could not be held liable if the actions of the officer fell below a certain objective standard.[304] In this case, the agent's conduct could not be countenanced from a reasonable, objective standard, and the concurring opinion found entrapment as a matter of

---

[300] WAYNE LAFAVE & JEROME ISRAEL, CRIMINAL PROCEDURE § 5.2(b) (2d ed. 1992).

[301] Sorrells v. United States, 287 U.S. 435, 441 (1932) ("the act for which [the] defendant was prosecuted was instigated by the prohibition agent . . ., [the] defendant had no previous disposition to commit [the crime] but was an industrious, law abiding citizen, and . . . the agent lured defendant, otherwise innocent, to its commission by repeated and persistent solicitation").

[302] WAYNE LAFAVE & JEROME ISRAEL, CRIMINAL PROCEDURE § 5.2(b) (2d ed. 1992).

[303] Sorrells v. United States, 287 U.S. 435, 457 (1932) (Roberts, J., concurring).

[304] Sorrells v. United States, 287 U.S. 435, 458 (1932) (Roberts, J., concurring). In a later case, Justice Frankfurter stated that the test was "whether the police conduct revealed in the particular case falls below standards, to which common feelings respond, for the proper use of governmental power." Sherman v. United States, 356 U.S. 369, 382 (1958) (Frankfurter, J., concurring). Here, one takes into account the response of the objective, reasonable person to the police conduct. "[I]n holding out inducements [the police] should act in such a manner as is likely to induce to the commission of crime only these persons and not others who would normally avoid crime and through self-struggle resist ordinary temptations." *Id.* at 384.

Stated another way, this test considers whether the conduct of police agents would have tempted a reasonably prudent person, in the same or similar circumstances, into the commission of the crime in question. Roger Park, *The Entrapment Controversy*, 60 MINN. L. REV. 163, 171-76 (1976).

The MODEL PENAL CODE has adopted the "objective" approach:

A public law enforcement official or a person acting in cooperation with such an official perpetrates an entrapment if for the purpose of obtaining evidence of the commission of an offense, he induces or encourages another person to engage in conduct constituting such offense by . . . employing methods of persuasion or inducement which create a substantial risk that such an offense will be committed by persons other than those who are ready to commit it.

MODEL PENAL CODE § 2.13 (1962).

The objective view is based on the premise that "the defense should be a tool of judicial procedure rather than of statutory construction . . . regarded . . . as a fundamental rule of public policy." Michelle F. Dahlen, *Note, People v. Dollen and United States v. Russell: New Developments in the Defense of Entrapment*, 23 DEPAUL L. REV. 570, 573 (1973).

law.[305] Here, then, the paramount concern revolved around deterring the police from engaging in conduct that is not the appropriate business of government officials.[306]

The majority and the concurring minority opinions set forth in the *Sorrells* case delineate the subjective and objective dichotomy that existed for several decades within the Court as it addressed the doctrine of entrapment. In the first three cases decided after *Sorrells* in which the Supreme Court has directly addressed the entrapment issue,[307] the court was divided on the rationale supporting this doctrine. The majority sided with the subjective view, focusing on the origin of criminal intent,[308] while the minority was supportive of the objective view and looked to police conduct, rather than origin of intent, as the determinative factor.[309] In 1992, in *Jacobson v. United States*,[310] the court appeared to have wholly departed from any semblance of objective analysis. While divided on the outcome of the case, the debate between the majority and minority centered on the appropriate application of the subjective approach rather than which approach to apply.[311]

In *Jacobson*, the defendant ordered two magazines containing sexually explicit pictures of boys from a California adult bookstore prior to a change in the federal child pornography laws.[312] When the new law came into effect, postal

---

[305] Sorrells v. United States, 287 U.S. 435, 459 (1932) (Roberts, J., concurring). It is important to note that the "objective" theory of entrapment is a legal issue to be resolved by the trial judge, whereas the subjective approach is a factual issue to be determined by the jury. WAYNE LAFAVE & AUSTIN SCOTT, CRIMINAL LAW §§ 5.2(b), (c) (2d ed. 1986).

[306] Sorrells v. United States, 287 U.S. 435 (1932).

[307] In Sherman v. United States, 356 U.S. 369 (1958), the Court found entrapment to exist where a government informer, who had knowledge of the defendant's drug rehabilitation efforts, played on the defendant's sympathy and after repeated attempts, provoked the defendant into supplying him with narcotics.

In United States v. Russell, 411 U.S. 423 (1973), the Court found that entrapment did not exist where government agents supplied the defendant with an ingredient used in making methamphetamines that was difficult to obtain but legal. The surrounding facts led to the inference that the defendant manufactured the drug both before and after this sale.

In Hampton v. United States, 425 U.S. 484 (1976), the Court found that entrapment did not exist where the defendant initiated a drug sale in which both the supplier and the purchaser were government agents.

[308] The majority would state the issue as "whether the informer had convinced an otherwise unwilling person to commit a criminal act or whether [the defendant] was already predisposed to commit the act. . . ." Sherman v. United States, 356 U.S. 369, 371 (1958).

[309] The minority would state the issue as "whether the police conduct revealed in the particular case falls below standards, to which common feelings respond, for the proper use of government power." Sherman v. United States, 356 U.S. 369, 382 (1958) (Frankfurter, J., concurring).

[310] 503 U.S. 540 (1992).

[311] 503 U.S. 540 (1992).

[312] Jacobson v. United States, 503 U.S. 540, 542-43 (1992).

inspectors found defendant's name on the mailing list of the bookstore.[313] According to the opinion, "There followed over the next 2½ years, repeated efforts by two Government agencies, through five fictitious organizations and a bogus pen pal to explore [defendant's] willingness to break the new law by ordering sexually explicit photographs of children through the mail."[314] In the correspondence, the government, "by waving the banner of individual rights and disparaging the legitimacy and constitutionality of efforts to restrict the availability of sexually explicit materials, . . . not only excited [defendant's] interest in sexually explicit materials banned by law but also exerted substantial pressure on [defendant] to obtain and read such material as part of a fight against censorship and the infringement of individual rights"[315] Finally, the defendant ordered a pornographic magazine depicting young boys engaged in various sexual activities through one of the fake organizations and was arrested.[316]

In a footnote, Justice White made it clear that the majority was only considering the subjective view when he said that "[t]he sole issue is whether the Government carried its burden of proving that [the defendant] was predisposed to violate the law before the Government intervened."[317] In evaluating whether the government met this burden, the majority said that the evidence of predisposition fell into two categories: evidence developed prior to the Postal Service's mail campaign, and that developed during the course of the investigation. The fact that the defendant had ordered the original two magazines was dismissed as having little probative value since "to do what once was lawful is not, by itself, sufficient to show predisposition to do what is now illegal."[318] The fact that the defendant had filled out questionnaires for the organizations, had requested more information, and had finally ordered the magazine "Boys Who Love Boys," failed to carry the Government's burden.[319] The majority held that "[r]ational jurors could not say beyond a reasonable doubt that [defendant] possessed the requisite predisposition *prior* to the Government's investigation and that it existed independent of the Government's many and varied approaches to [defendant]."[320] Therefore, entrapment existed as a matter of law.[321]

Justice O'Connor wrote for the four dissenters and voiced concern over the fact that the majority opinion "has the potential to be misread . . . as requiring that the Government must have sufficient evidence of a defendant's predisposi-

---

[313] Jacobson v. United States, 503 U.S. 540, 543 (1992).

[314] Jacobson v. United States, 503 U.S. 540, 543 (1992).

[315] Jacobson v. United States, 503 U.S. 540, 542 (1992).

[316] Jacobson v. United States, 503 U.S. 540, 547 (1992).

[317] Jacobson v. United States, 503 U.S. 540, 549 (1992).

[318] Jacobson v. United States, 503 U.S. 540, 551 (1992).

[319] Jacobson v. United States, 503 U.S. 540, 551 (1992).

[320] Jacobson v. United States, 503 U.S. 540, 553 (1992) (emphasis added).

[321] Jacobson v. United States, 503 U.S. 540, 554 (1992).

tion *before it ever seeks to contact him*," thereby requiring the government to have a "reasonable suspicion" of a defendant's criminal predisposition beforehand.[322] She then proceeded to question the appropriateness of the court's holding that entrapment existed as a matter of law, stating that "it was . . . the jury's task, as the conscience of the community, to decide whether or not Mr. Jacobson was a willing participant in the criminal activity."[323]

Although some debate still exists in this area,[324] the subjective rule has become the federal standard and has closed out any objective formulation focusing on police conduct, except where police conduct is so "outrageous" that a possible due process of law violation has occurred.[325] Also, today most observers do

---

[322] Jacobson v. United States, 503 U.S. 540, 557 (1992) (O'Connor, J., dissenting) (emphasis original). Yet, this appears to be exactly what the majority stated: "Petitioner's ready response to these solicitations cannot be enough to establish beyond a reasonable doubt that he was predisposed, *prior* to the Government acts intended to create predisposition, to commit the crime of receiving child pornography through the mails." 503 U.S. 540, 553 (1992) (emphasis added). *See* Fred Warren Bennett, *From Sorrells to Jacobson: Reflections on Six Decades of Entrapment Law, and Related Defenses, in Federal Court*, 27 WAKE FOREST L. REV. 829 (1992).

[323] Jacobson v. United States, 503 U.S. 540, 560-61 (1992) (O'Connor, J., dissenting). *See also* Elena Lisa Garella, *Reshaping the Federal Entrapment Defense: Jacobson v. United States*, 68 WASH. L. REV. 185, 185 (1993) (stating that by finding entrapment as a matter of law, "the *Jacobson* court departed from precedent. Previous Supreme Court cases provide that judges may find entrapment as a matter of law only when the absence of predisposition is patently clear, or government conduct is so egregious that it completely dominates the will of a person who is, at most, slightly predisposed to commit the criminal act").

[324] For an excellent discussion of the various approaches to determining predisposition, *see* Catherine A. Schultz, Comment, *Victim or the Crime? The Government's Burden in Proving Predisposition in Federal Entrapment Cases*, 48 DEPAUL L. REV. 949 (1999).

[325] In United States v. Russell, 411 U.S. 423, 431-32 (1973), the Court said, "While we may someday be presented with a situation in which the conduct of law enforcement agents is so outrageous that due process principles would absolutely bar the government from invoking judicial processes to obtain a conviction, . . . the instant case is distinctly not of that breed." *Cf.* Rochin v. California, 342 U.S. 165, 172 (1952) (constitutional violation occurs where conduct of law enforcement agents so "shocks the conscience" of the Court that due process principles would absolutely bar government from invoking judicial process to obtain conviction).

Although somewhat vague, Hampton v. United States, 425 U.S. 484 (1976), appears to have reinforced the subjective view as the general guide, subject to an overriding exception that a predisposed defendant cannot be convicted if police over-involvement in his crime reaches a demonstrable level of "outrageousness." One Justice did not participate. Three Justices would make predisposition the only issue, three Justices would eliminate predisposition entirely, and two concurring Justices indicated that predisposition will be dispositive in all but the rare cases where police over-involvement in the crime reaches a demonstrable level of "outrageousness." Such a case has never been brought before the Court, but it is clear that police conduct would have to be extremely overzealous before a due process violation would be found. *See, e.g.,* People ex rel. Difanis v. Boston, 92 Ill. App. 3d 962, 966, 416 N.E.2d 333, 337 (4th Dist. 1981), where entrapment was not found where the actions of government agents in engaging in sexual activity with female employees of a house of prostitution for the purpose of obtaining evidence for a conviction were held not to reach

not even view the due process "outrageousness" approach to controlling police misconduct as a theory of entrapment but rather as a possible separate defense.[326]

Virtually every state recognizes the entrapment defense in some form.[327] The overwhelming majority favor a formulation of the subjective rationale.[328] However, a growing minority,[329] along with most scholarly commentators,[330] support an objective formulation. The Model Penal Code has also adopted the objective approach to entrapment.[331]

§ 19.31.   Defense of Entrapment Codified.

Before the passage of the Criminal Code of 1961, Illinois had no statutory defense of entrapment,[332] although it was recognized by caselaw.[333] Currently, section 5/7-12 defines the defense in general terms:

> A person is not guilty of an offense if his or her conduct is incited or induced by a public officer or employer, or agent of either, for the purpose of obtaining evidence for the prosecution of such person. However, this Section is inapplicable if the person was predisposed to commit the offense and the public officer or employee, or agent of the either, merely affords to that person the opportunity or facility for committing an offense.[334]

The original statute enacted in 1961 did *not* contain the qualification that the person was not "predisposed" and, instead, was cast in very general terms.[335]

---

the demonstrable level of outrageousness necessary to bar the action or exclude the evidence under a due process claim. *Compare* United States v. Twigg, 588 F.2d 373, 381 (3d Cir. 1978), where a federal court found a Fifth Amendment due process of law violation based on outrageous police conduct.

[326] *See* ROLLIN M. PERKINS & RONALD N. BOYCE, CRIMINAL LAW 1168, n.41 (3d ed. 1982).

[327] For a discussion of the different formulations accepted by various states, *see* ROLLIN M. PERKINS & RONALD N. BOYCE, CRIMINAL LAW 1172 (3d ed. 1982) (some follow subjective approach, some follow objective approach, and few reject both approaches); Roger Park, *Entrapment Controversy*, 60 MINN. L. REV. 163, 164 n.1 (1976); Jeffrey N. Klar, Note, *The Need for a Dual Approach to Entrapment*, 59 WASH. U. L.Q. 199, 200 n.9 (1981).

[328] Jeffrey N. Klar, *The Need for a Dual Approach to Entrapment*, 59 WASH. U. L.Q. 199, 200 n.9 (1981) (subjective approach is prevailing view).

[329] WAYNE LAFAVE & JEROME ISRAEL, CRIMINAL PROCEDURE § 5.2(c) (2d ed. 1992).

[330] *See* Roger Park, *Entrapment Controversy*, 60 MINN. L. REV. 163, 167 n.13 (1976).

[331] MODEL PENAL CODE § 2.13 (1962).

[332] ILL. ANN. STAT. ch. 38, para. 7-12 (Smith-Hurd 1989), 1961 Committee Comments, at 439 (revised).

[333] *See, e.g.*, In re Horwitz, 360 Ill. 313, 326, 196 N.E. 208, 213 (1935) (entrapment established).

[334] 720 ILCS 5/7-12 (1999).

[335] Originally, the second sentence in the statute read: "However, this section is inapplicable if a public officer or employee, or agent of either, merely affords to such person the opportunity or

The legislative drafting committee pointed out that this generality was deliberate, since "the existing court opinions [did] not sufficiently outline [the] scope [of the defense] or settle various problems which would affect the expression of a detailed definition."[336] Because of its generality, this statute was found to vindicate both subjective[337] and objective[338] rationales supporting the defense of entrapment. In fact, the legislative drafting committee made clear that it was leaving it up to the courts to further delineate the scope of this defense.[339] Later, in 1996, the statute was amended to include the predisposition qualification.[340]

Presently, the Illinois caselaw interprets the entrapment statute as being supported by a narrow, subjective (focus on defendants' predisposition) rationale.[341] Before 1979, section 5/7-12 had been interpreted to include an objective (focus on police conduct) test in situations in which improper state conduct occurred in the encouragement of crime.[342] To illustrate, whenever a government informer supplied a controlled substance to an individual who was later prosecuted for the unlawful delivery of that substance, entrapment was objectively found as a matter of law, without considering the defendant's predisposition.[343] However, in *People v. Cross*,[344] the Illinois Supreme Court stated that the law was confused in this area.[345] The court further expressed concern over the ever-growing

---

facility for committing an offense in furtherance of a criminal purpose which such person had originated." 720 ILCS 5/7-12 (1995). It was amended in 1996. Pub. Act 89-332 (1996).

[336] ILL. ANN. STAT. ch. 38, para. 7-12 (Smith-Hurd 1989), 1961 Committee Comments, at 442 (revised).

[337] *See, e.g.*, People v. Andreano, 64 Ill. App. 3d 551, 557, 381 N.E.2d 787, 788 (5th Dist. 1978) (to establish entrapment, "lack of predisposition" of accused must be demonstrated).

[338] *See, e.g.*, People v. Spahr, 56 Ill. App. 3d 434, 438-39, 371 N.E.2d 1261, 1264 (4th Dist. 1978) (objective theory of entrapment relied on in part in reversal of conviction).

[339] ILL. ANN. STAT. ch. 38, para. 7-12 (Smith-Hurd 1989), 1961 Committee Comments, at 442 (revised) ("If in time the defense becomes more clearly delineated, this provision may be stated in a more comprehensive form").

[340] Pub. Act 89-332 (1996).

[341] People v. Placek, 184 Ill. 2d 370, 380-81, 704 N.E.2d 393, 398 (1998). *See also* People v. Hatch, 49 Ill. App. 2d 177, 183-84, 199 N.E.2d 81, 84-85 (1st Dist. 1964) ("Although the defense of entrapment is available in Illinois, it . . . is accorded perhaps the narrowest scope of any American jurisdiction where it is recognized. . . .").

[342] People v. Cross, 77 Ill. 2d 396, 404, 396 N.E.2d 812, 815, *cert. denied*, 445 U.S. 929 (1980).

[343] *See* People v. Strong, 21 Ill. 2d 320, 325, 172 N.E.2d 765, 768 (1961); People v. Walker, 61 Ill. App. 3d 4, 6, 377 N.E.2d 604, 605 (3d Dist. 1978); People v. Spahr, 56 Ill. App. 3d 434, 438-39, 371 N.E.2d 1261, 1264 (4th Dist. 1978); People v. Carmichael, 80 Ill. App. 2d 293, 297, 225 N.E.2d 458, 460 (1st Dist. 1967). *Compare* People v. Gonzales, 125 Ill. App. 2d 225, 232-33, 260 N.E.2d 234, 237-38 (2d Dist. 1970) (entrapment was not found as matter of law even though government agent supplied drugs in question). *See also* United States v. Cansler, 419 F.2d 952, 953 (7th Cir. 1969), *cert. denied*, 397 U.S. 1278 (1970).

[344] 77 Ill. 2d 396, 396 N.E.2d 812, *cert. denied*, 445 U.S. 929 (1980).

[345] People v. Cross, 77 Ill. 2d 396, 404, 396 N.E.2d 812, 815, *cert. denied*, 445 U.S. 929 (1980) ("This confusion [in the conflicting caselaw] has led us to consider the subject anew").

drug market and the problems associated with effective government detection and infiltration of drug rings.[346] It was observed that where a governmental agent furnished a controlled substance to a predisposed individual for future unlawful delivery, the appellate courts were often critical and would strike down the conviction on grounds of entrapment.[347] The court in *Cross*, therefore, did away with any objective rationale, which found entrapment as a matter of law based on the actions of the government agent,[348] and made it clear that the courts were to follow the subjective, predisposition approach.[349] Thereafter, the Illinois courts evaluated an entrapment claim based on, for instance, the claim that the governmental agent supplied drugs to the accused, strictly from a subjective the-

---

[346] "In our reconsideration of the subject and in light of the ever-growing drug problem, we are not so sure that the court should be so critical, as it was in *Strong*, of governmental action in infiltrating drug rings, and we do not believe that the courts should foreclose the possibility that a conviction of a predisposed individual could be sustained even though the government did furnish the controlled substance." People v. Cross, 77 Ill. 2d 396, 404, 396 N.E.2d 812, 815, *cert. denied*, 445 U.S. 929 (1980).

[347] People v. Cross, 77 Ill. 2d 396, 404, 396 N.E.2d 812, 815, *cert. denied*, 445 U.S. 929 (1980). The rationale behind these rulings, which appeared in an earlier Illinois Supreme Court decision, was that the supplying of narcotics by government agent was "more than mere inducement. In reality the government [was] supplying the sine qua non of the offense." People v. Strong, 21 Ill. 2d 320, 325, 172 N.E.2d 765, 768 (1961).

[348] The phrase *entrapment as a matter of law* is denotative of a situation in which the issue in question is so "patently clear," from undisputed evidence, that it should be resolved by the court and not submitted to the jury for a factual determination. *See* United States v. Saucedo, 346 F.2d 371, 372 (7th Cir. 1965); People v. Carpentier, 20 Ill. App. 3d 1024, 1027, 314 N.E.2d 647, 649 (3d Dist. 1974).

One important point must be clarified in light of *Cross*. Given the *Cross* court's rejection of the "objective" theory of entrapment, it is important to note that to the extent that post-*Cross* opinions make reference to entrapment as "a matter of law," they are addressing situations where the evidence as to the predisposition of the accused is so entirely lacking as a factual matter, that the issue of predisposition should not be given to the jury. *See, e.g.,* People v. Garcia, 95 Ill. App. 3d 377, 380, 420 N.E.2d 221, 223 (4th Dist. 1981) ("The question of whether entrapment exists is ordinarily reserved for the jury and should not be disturbed on appeal unless the reviewing court concludes that entrapment exists as a matter of law. Based on the evidence presented [here], the jury could have found that defendant was predisposed to commit this burglary."); People v. Myers, 92 Ill. App. 3d 229, 234, 415 N.E.2d 1108, 1112 (1st Dist. 1981) ("Entrapment as a matter of law is not established where there is any substantial evidence from which it may be inferred that the criminal intent to commit a particular offense originated in the mind of the accused."); People v. Tipton, 78 Ill. 2d 477, 487, 401 N.E.2d 528, 533 (1980) (entrapment as a matter of law did not exist where sufficient evidence of predisposition existed to send case to jury). Thus, the "matter of law" language as used in these cases does not implicitly refer to the existence of an "objective" theory of entrapment that focuses on police conduct.

[349] People v. Cross, 77 Ill. 2d 396, 404-05, 396 N.E.2d 812, 816, *cert. denied*, 445 U.S. 929 (1980) ("The language in *Dollen* which interprets *Strong* as eliminating the need to consider predisposition, likewise should no longer be followed. Consideration of an individual's predisposition is required. . . .").

ory.[350] The 1996 legislative amendment which explicitly excludes from the entrapment defense the person who was predisposed, reinforces the importance of the predisposition qualification.

§ 19.32. Elements of Entrapment.

To establish the affirmative, statutory defense of entrapment in Illinois, certain elements must be present. First, the offense committed must have been induced or incited by a government official. Second, the defendant must be an innocent person not predisposed to commit an offense, who would not have committed the crime had he not been induced. Third, the entrapper must be a public officer or employer, or agent of either. And fourth, the government's purpose must have been to create evidence for the prosecution of the innocent accused.[351]

Although the first and second elements appear to be the same requirement stated in a converse manner, each test has a slightly different meaning. Under the first element, governmental inducement must be present. Without such incitement, the defense of entrapment will not lie. If such inducement exists, then the second element must be considered. Even where there exists a high level of governmental inducement, an individual must still be otherwise innocent (not predisposed) under the second element or the defense will not lie.[352]

§ 19.33. — Active Inducement.

To fulfill the first element of governmental inducement, police must actively encourage the suspect to commit the crime; their action cannot be passive.[353] Of course, the mere fact that a government agent affords the defendant an opportunity to commit a crime or aids and encourages a defendant, does not establish the entrapment defense in and of itself.[354] In other words, the law of entrapment

---

[350] See, e.g., People v. Barnes, 230 Ill. App. 3d 272, 276, 595 N.E.2d 40, 43 (1st Dist. 1992) ("The relevant inquiry is whether defendant has a predisposition to commit crime."); People v. Marshall, 101 Ill. App. 3d 244, 247, 427 N.E.2d 1333, 1335 (4th Dist. 1981); People v. Husted, 97 Ill. App. 3d 160, 168-69, 422 N.E.2d 962, 969 (2d Dist. 1981), cert. denied, 456 U.S. 945 (1982); People v. Stallings, 83 Ill. App. 3d 533, 537, 404 N.E.2d 461, 464 (1st Dist. 1980).

[351] People v. Wielgos, 142 Ill. 2d 133, 137, 568 N.E.2d 861, 863 (1991) cert. denied on remand, 506 U.S. 844 (1992).

[352] However, when the governmental conduct reaches a level of outrageousness that is shocking to the conscience of the court, constitutional due process may conceivably be an issue. See § 19.30 of this chapter.

[353] People v. Jensen, 37 Ill. App. 3d 1010, 1014, 347 N.E.2d 371, 375 (1st Dist. 1976).

[354] People v. Arbogast, 41 Ill. App. 3d 187, 190, 353 N.E.2d 434, 437 (1976). In Arbogast, a government agent actively solicited the defendant into obtaining and delivering a controlled substance. See also People v. Gonzales, 125 Ill. App. 2d 225, 231-32, 260 N.E.2d 234, 237 (2d Dist. 1970) (no entrapment was found where police offered new car and house to factory worker, who was supporting wife and six children on $92 per week, to engage in marijuana sales).

distinguishes "between the trap for the unwary innocent and the trap for the unwary criminal."[355]

The major point at issue, then, is what type of police activity qualifies as a wrongful inducement. Prohibited police conduct may include "solicitation, coercion, deception, trickery, fraud, or appeals to friendship or sympathy."[356] However, no entrapment was found where a government informer begged and pleaded with a childhood friend to sell a controlled substance for him.[357] The informer told the defendant that he needed the money to support his wife and several children and that he could not personally sell it because he owed a large sum of money to the prospective purchasers.[358] Likewise, no entrapment was found where an addict (turned informer) induced a friend into purchasing heroin for him because of his sick condition.[359] Other situations that have been found not to qualify as entrapment include drug purchases induced by a lover-turned-informer,[360] burglaries in which the government agent planned the crime and selected the residence to be burglarized,[361] and robberies in which an undercover agent posing as a potential robbery victim feigned drunkenness and sickness in an alley at 3:00 A.M.[362]

Entrapment was found to lie where government agents both planted a box of morphine in the back seat of a taxicab and purchased the drugs from the driver after the cab driver was unsuccessful in finding the owner.[363] Similarly, entrapment was found as a matter of law where the defendant was induced by a government agent into committing a conversion of a semi-automatic weapon to an illegal fully automatic weapon in circumstances where the undercover agent over a several month period first failed to induce the defendant to illegally buy a gun for him, and then coaxed the defendant into making the conversion of the weapon after the defendant expressed reservations about doing the conversion while suggesting to the agent that he could perform the conversion himself.[364] This extensive inducement effort belied the state's assertion that the defendant

---

[355] Sherman v. United States, 356 U.S. 369, 372 (1958).

[356] Michelle F. Dahlen, *Note, People v. Dollen and United States v. Russell: New Developments in the Defense of Entrapment*, 23 DEPAUL L. REV. 570, 582 (1973).

[357] People v. Marshall, 101 Ill. App. 3d 244, 246, 427 N.E.2d 1333, 1334-35 (4th Dist. 1981).

[358] People v. Marshall, 101 Ill. App. 3d 244, 246, 427 N.E.2d 1333, 1334-35 (4th Dist. 1981).

[359] People v. Hall, 25 Ill. 2d 297, 299, 185 N.E.2d 143, 144-45 (1962), *cert. denied*, 374 U.S. 849 (1963).

[360] *See* United States v. Carreon, 626 F.2d 528, 535 (7th Cir. 1980).

[361] People v. Garcia, 95 Ill. App. 3d 377, 379, 420 N.E.2d 221, 223 (4th Dist. 1981).

[362] People v. Johnson, 66 Ill. App. 2d 465, 467, 214 N.E.2d 354, 357 (1st Dist. 1966).

[363] People v. Dollen, 53 Ill. 2d 280, 282, 290 N.E.2d 879, 882 (1972).

[364] People v. Karraker, 261 Ill. App. 3d 942, 953-55, 633 N.E.2d 1250, 1258-59 (3d Dist. 1994).

was predisposed to convert weapons *before* he met the undercover agent.[365] Where government agents had to approach defendants ten or more times before they agreed to participate in a drug transaction, told the defendants when they cancelled a meeting with an undercover police officer prepared to make a drug purchase that the officer posing as a drug purchaser was not one to "play with," and initiated the meeting between defendants and the undercover officers who made the purchase, the court found entrapment.[366] Also, entrapment was found where the unlawful delivery of a controlled substance for which the defendant was convicted initially originated in the mind of a paid government who, for no apparent reason, arbitrarily engaged in a social relationship with the defendant and purposely encouraged its growth, as an inducement to obtain drugs.[367] Obviously, these cases illustrate that the entrapment issue cannot be resolved by proof of active inducement alone.

§ 19.34. — Otherwise Innocent Defendant Not Predisposed Toward Criminality.

The second element that must be met in order to fulfill the Illinois statute is that the accused must be "otherwise innocent,"[368] or not subjectively predisposed to commit the crime.[369] In analyzing this question, the predisposition of the defendant as well as the government involvement must be considered.[370] There exists a criminal predisposition on the part of the accused, thereby defeating a claim of entrapment, whenever it is determined (1) that the suspect originated the idea of committing the offense and (2) that the suspect engaged in the course of conduct involving similar offenses.[371] Even if the answer to the first inquiry is negative, the accused will not be considered worthy of protection if the answer to the second inquiry is positive, since he or she is not an otherwise innocent person.[372] Although this decision can be determined as a matter of law,[373] in most cases, it is a factual determination reserved for the jury.[374] Factual differences will, therefore, have a bearing on the outcome.[375]

---

[365] People v. Karraker, 261 Ill. App. 3d 942, 953-55, 633 N.E.2d 1250, 1258-59 (3d Dist. 1994).

[366] People v. Salazar, 284 Ill. App. 3d 794, 799-803, 672 N.E.2d 803, 808-09 (1st Dist. 1996).

[367] People v. Day, 279 Ill. App. 3d 606, 612, 665 N.E.2d 867, 871 (3d Dist. 1996).

[368] People v. Gibbons, 17 Ill. App. 3d 687, 308 N.E.2d 51 (2d Dist. 1974) (abstract).

[369] People v. Jensen, 37 Ill. App. 3d 1010, 1014, 347 N.E.2d 371, 375 (1st Dist. 1976).

[370] People v. Cross, 77 Ill. 2d 396, 405, 396 N.E.2d 812, 817, *cert. denied*, 445 U.S. 929 (1980).

[371] People v. Fisher, 74 Ill. App. 3d 330, 333-34, 392 N.E.2d 975, 978 (3d Dist. 1979).

[372] People v. Fisher, 74 Ill. App. 3d 330, 333-34, 392 N.E.2d 975, 978 (3d Dist. 1979).

[373] *See, e.g.,* People v. Day, 279 Ill. App. 3d 606, 665 N.E.2d 867 (3d Dist. 1996).

[374] People v. Placek, 184 Ill. 2d 370, 383, 704 N.E.2d 393, 399 (1998); People v. Gresham, 96 Ill. App. 3d 581, 583-84, 421 N.E.2d 1053, 1056 (4th Dist. 1981).

[375] People v. Ball, 91 Ill. App. 3d 1041, 1045, 415 N.E.2d 471, 475 (1st Dist. 1981).

In *People v. Kulwin*,[376] the Illinois appellate court laid out factors to be considered when determining whether a defendant had the predisposition to commit a crime: "(1) the character or reputation of the defendant; (2) whether the suggested criminal activity was made by the government or its informants; (3) whether the defendant had previously been engaged in criminal activity for profit; (4) whether the defendant expressed reluctance to commit the offense, which was overcome only by repeated persuasion; (5) the nature of the inducement or persuasion applied by the government; (6) the defendant's ready access to a source or supply of drugs; and (7) the defendant's previous criminal record."[377] In *People v. Day*,[378] the appellate court set out eight factors to assess predisposition in an illicit drug case: (1) defendant's initial willingness or reluctance, (2) defendant's familiarity with drugs and willingness to accommodate the needs of drug users, (3) defendant's willingness to make a profit from the illegal act, (4) defendant's prior or current use of illegal drugs, (5) defendant's participation in testing or cutting drugs, (6) defendant's engagement in a course of conduct involving similar offenses, (7) defendant's ready access to a drug supply and (8) defendant's subsequent activities.[379]

§ 19.35.   — Government Official or Agent.

The third element within the Illinois entrapment statute is that the entrapper must be a public officer or employer, or an agent of either.[380] Since the primary purpose of the entrapment defense is to censure improper governmental criminal inducement, the element of implanting a criminal design into an innocent mind is no longer present if the entrapper is not a government agent.[381] Parentheti-

---

[376] 229 Ill. App. 3d 36, 593 N.E.2d 717 (1st Dist. 1992).

[377] People v. Kulwin, 229 Ill. App. 3d 36, 39, 593 N.E.2d 717, 719 (1st Dist. 1992). Notice that factor number five seems to incorporate the objective view of entrapment as a mere sub-issue of predisposition in general. People v. D'Angelo, 223 Ill. App. 3d 754, 776, 585 N.E.2d 1239, 1253 (5th Dist. 1992) (factors in narcotics cases: the defendant's initial reluctance or his ready willingness to commit the crime, the defendant's familiarity with drugs and his willingness to accommodate the needs of drug users, the defendant's willingness to make a profit from the illegal act, the defendant's prior or current use of illegal drugs, and the defendant's participation in testing or cutting the drugs. *See also* People v. Placek, 184 Ill. 2d 370, 381, 704 N.E.2d 393, 398 (1998) (discussing similar factors); People v. Singletary, 237 Ill. App. 3d 503, 507, 604 N.E.2d 1009, 1011 (3d Dist. 1992) (discussing similar factors); People v. Lambrecht, 231 Ill. App. 3d 426, 436, 595 N.E.2d 1358, 1364-65 (2d Dist. 1992) (discussing similar factors).

[378] 279 Ill. App. 3d 606, 665 N.E.2d 867 (3d Dist. 1996) (court found lack of predisposition and government entrapment).

[379] People v. Day, 279 Ill. App. 3d 606, 612, 665 N.E.2d 867, 871 (3d Dist. 1996) (entrapment existed as a matter of law). *See also* People v. Salazar, 284 Ill. App. 3d 794, 802, 672 N.E.2d 803, 809 (1st Dist. 1996) (relying on same eight factors, court found defendant entrapped).

[380] People v. Myers, 92 Ill. App. 3d 229, 233-34, 425 N.E.2d 1108, 1111 (1st Dist. 1980).

[381] WAYNE LAFAVE & AUSTIN SCOTT, CRIMINAL LAW § 5.2(a) (2d ed. 1986).

cally, before the enactment of the 1961 criminal code, entrapment had been recognized where the inducement came from a non-governmental officer or agent.[382] Since the enactment of the code however, "there are no Illinois cases holding purely private action sufficient to provide an entrapment defense."[383] But it should be noted that where the government has used an agent or informer to induce the accused to commit a criminal act, it cannot thereafter disown that agent or informer and insist that it was not responsible for his or her actions in order to avoid the defense of entrapment.[384] Knowledge of the public officer's true identity is not necessary for an agency relationship to exist.[385]

§ 19.36. — Government Purpose to Create Evidence.

Closely related to the requirement that there be a government official or agent is the fourth requirement that the purpose of the enticements must have been to create evidence for the prosecution of the innocent person.[386] By showing that the governmental actions were simply motivated by a desire to obtain evidence necessary to convict a person who is already predisposed to commit a crime, entrapment will not lie as a defense.[387]

This element will rarely be disputed. However, in *People v. Wielgos,*[388] this issue was dispositive. An undercover drug officer had an ongoing investigation of a man named Ruschinski. Ruschinski, not knowing who the officer was, requested the help of the defendant for a drug transaction. After the defendant delivered four ounces of cocaine to the officer and was arrested, the defendant argued that Ruschinski was an agent of the officer and that he was entrapped. The trial court omitted the words "and/or an agent of a public officer" from the tendered entrapment jury instruction.[389] The appellate court reversed the defendant's conviction on the ground that "it was possible for Ruschinski to be an

---

[382] *See* People v. Lewis, 365 Ill. 156, 6 N.E.2d 175 (1936); In re Horwitz, 360 Ill. 313, 196 N.E. 208 (1935); People v. Smith, 251 Ill. 185, 95 N.E. 1041 (1911).

[383] Michelle F. Dahlen, *Note, People v. Dollen and United States v. Russell: New Developments in the Defense of Entrapment,* 23 DePaul L. Rev. 570, 582 (1973).

[384] Sherman v. United States, 356 U.S. 369, 375 (1958) (government cannot make use of informer and then "claim disassociation through ignorance").

[385] People v. Wielgos, 142 Ill. 2d 133, 137-38, 568 N.E.2d 861, 863 (1991), *cert. denied on remand,* 506 U.S. 844 (1992).

[386] People v. Jensen, 37 Ill. App. 3d 1010, 1014, 347 N.E.2d 371, 375 (1st Dist. 1976).

[387] Michelle F. Dahlen, *Note, People v. Dollen and United States v. Russell: New Developments in the Defense of Entrapment,* 23 DePaul L. Rev. 570, 587 (1973).

[388] 142 Ill. 2d 133, 568 N.E.2d 861 (1991), *cert. denied on remand,* 506 U.S. 844 (1992).

[389] People v. Wielgos, 142 Ill. 2d 133, 136, 568 N.E.2d 861, 862 (1991), *cert. denied on remand,* 506 U.S. 844 (1992).

agent of the government for entrapment purposes, even though he did not know he was acting on behalf of a police officer."[390]

The Illinois Supreme Court reversed the appellate court's decision and held that the defendant was not entitled to the requested jury instruction because the defendant did not produce evidence that the inducements were made for the purpose of obtaining evidence for prosecution.[391] The *Wielgos* court stated that it could "find no evidence that Ruschinski actually contemplated that his acts would lead to prosecution of defendant . . . [nor evidence] which creates a reasonable inference that [his] acts were intended toward that end."[392] Also, there was no evidence that the officer was aware that Ruschinski induced the defendant to sell drugs.[393]

The defense of entrapment is not often established in Illinois because of the narrow reading given the entrapment defense. If a defendant presents "some evidence" to support the elements of the entrapment defense, the state bears the burden to rebut the defense beyond a reasonable doubt, in addition to proving all other elements of the crime.[394] In addition, there are many procedural barriers and requirements that relate to the affirmative defense of entrapment that will now be explored.

§ 19.37.   Procedural Aspects and Evidentiary Problems of the Entrapment Defense.

The procedural requirements involved with using the affirmative defense of entrapment, as a practical matter, may create more limitations than the actual substance of the doctrine of entrapment itself. These procedural and operational limitations range from the types of crimes in which the defense can be raised to the ability to appeal a ruling involving this defense.

---

[390] People v. Wielgos, 190 Ill. App. 3d 63, 70, 545 N.E.2d 1031, 1034 (1989), *rev'd,* 142 Ill. 2d 133, 568 N.E.2d 861 (1991), *cert. denied on remand,* 506 U.S. 844 (1992).

[391] People v. Wielgos, 142 Ill. 2d 133, 138, 568 N.E.2d 861, 863 (1991), *cert. denied on remand,* 506 U.S. 844 (1992).

[392] People v. Wielgos, 142 Ill. 2d 133, 138, 568 N.E.2d 861, 863 (1991) ("For example, there is no evidence that Ruschinski ever acted as a government informant; that he became aware that he was subject to arrest, and then led the police to defendant in exchange for leniency in his own case; that he was to receive money from [the officer] in exchange for information leading to defendant's arrest; that he had any relationship with the government which predated the drug investigation in this case; or that he attempted to contact other police officers regarding this drug transaction."), *cert. denied on remand,* 506 U.S. 844 (1992).

[393] People v. Wielgos, 142 Ill. 2d 133, 138, 568 N.E.2d 861, 863 (1991), *cert. denied on remand,* 506 U.S. 844 (1992).

[394] People v. Placek, 184 Ill. 2d 370, 381, 704 N.E.2d 393, 398 (1998).

§ 19.38.   — Raise at Trial.

Theoretically, the affirmative defense of entrapment should be specifically urged in the trial court lest the issue be waived.[395] However, the caselaw provides that entrapment need not be specially pleaded or relied on exclusively where it is clearly suggested in the trial court and where *facts* suggesting entrapment have been presented in detail.[396] It is clear that entrapment may not be raised for the first time on appeal.[397] Facts offered in support of the defense should be presented in detail, and the defendant's counsel must at least "suggest" the point during trial.[398] Indeed, it is probably accurate to say that a failure to raise the question in the trial court by a *specific* plea or by facts that strongly support such a defense will be regarded as a waiver of the defense.[399]

The question of whether entrapment was properly raised in the trial court in order to preserve the issue on appeal is usually answered very narrowly. A defendant's denial that he sold narcotics to a police informer negated the contention that entrapment was clearly suggested in the trial court.[400] Similarly, a defense counsel's argument to the jury that the defendants were innocent persons kept at the scene of a drug sale by threat did not constitute a presentation that was detailed enough to preserve the issue of entrapment for appeal.[401]

§ 19.39.   — Nature of Charge.

Because of the general wording of section 5/7-12, the defense of entrapment is apparently available, in a proper case, for any offense. In contrast, in various other American jurisdictions, the defense has been denied for serious, heinous offenses.[402] In cases of crimes causing serious bodily injury, it would appear that most of the policy issues supporting the defense fail, for these are not covert crimes without a complaining victim. A Model Penal Code commentary states: "It will not seem generally unfair to punish someone who has caused or threatened bodily injury to another although he was induced to his action by law enforcement officials. A person who can be persuaded to cause such injury presents a danger that the public cannot safely disregard."[403] However, in Illinois,

---

[395] People v. Morgan, 98 Ill. App. 2d 435, 439, 240 N.E.2d 286, 287 (1st Dist. 1968) (where defense is not urged in trial court, it is not available on appeal).

[396] People v. Strong, 21 Ill. 2d 320, 324, 172 N.E.2d 765, 767 (1961).

[397] People v. Bouse, 46 Ill. App. 3d 465, 473, 360 N.E.2d 1340, 1346 (1st Dist. 1977).

[398] People v. Van Scoyk, 20 Ill. 2d 232, 235, 170 N.E.2d 151, 152 (1960).

[399] *See* People v. Fleming, 50 Ill. 2d 141, 144, 277 N.E.2d 872, 874 (1971).

[400] People v. Smith, 70 Ill. App. 2d 289, 294-95, 217 N.E.2d 546, 548 (1st Dist.), *rev'd on other grounds*, 390 U.S. 129 (1966). *See* § 19.40 of this chapter.

[401] People v. Hesler, 39 Ill. App. 3d 843, 850, 350 N.E.2d 748, 750 (2d Dist. 1976), *cert. denied*, 429 U.S. 1097 (1977).

[402] 2 PAUL ROBINSON, CRIMINAL LAW DEFENSES § 209(f) (1984).

[403] MODEL PENAL CODE § 2.13, commentary at 23-24 (Tentative Draft No. 9, 1958).

no authoritative judicial distinction has been drawn for the use of entrapment between crimes mala in se and statutory offenses of lesser gravity. Thus, the defense has been considered in many serious offense situations, ranging up to solicitation to commit murder.[404] Since the defense has no limitations in its use, it has been raised in many unusual cases. Examples are cases involving blocking traffic,[405] criminal usury,[406] practicing chiropractic without a license,[407] and unlawfully selling a railroad ticket.[408]

§ 19.40.   — Admission of Commission of Crime.

A criminal defendant is entitled to rely on the defense only if he or she admits to the commission of the offense with which he or she is charged.[409] Although the defendant need not take the stand and formally admit the crime,[410] because this is an affirmative defense, "some evidence" of entrapment must be presented in order to raise the defense.[411] Furthermore, "[b]y invoking the defense of entrapment, a defendant admits commission of the crime charged."[412] As a practical matter, of course, it could prove difficult to avoid confessing to the crime in front of the jury; on the other hand, it may be difficult to point to evidence of entrapment without taking the stand.[413]

Occasionally, a dispute arises about whether a defendant has admitted committing all of the acts constituting the offense charged so as to raise the issue of entrapment. A defendant charged with driving under a suspended license was

---

[404] *See* People v. Pagliuca, 119 Ill. App. 3d 906, 914-16, 458 N.E.2d 908, 916 (1st Dist. 1983) (conspiracy and solicitation to commit murder convictions affirmed); People v. Swimley, 57 Ill. App. 3d 116, 129-30, 372 N.E.2d 887, 897 (1st Dist.) (solicitation to commit murder conviction affirmed), *cert. denied*, 439 U.S. 911 (1978).

[405] City of Chicago v. Hill, 40 Ill. 2d 130, 134-35, 238 N.E.2d 403, 405 (1968).

[406] People v. Gallo, 54 Ill. 2d 343, 356, 297 N.E.2d 569, 576 (1973).

[407] People v. O'Dell, 343 Ill. App. 395, 399, 99 N.E.2d 367, 368 (3d Dist. 1951).

[408] People v. Lewis, 285 Ill. App. 171, 177, 1 N.E.2d 696, 696-97 (1st Dist.), *aff'd*, 365 Ill. 156, 6 N.E.2d 175 (1936).

[409] *See* People v. Gillespie, 136 Ill. 2d 496, 502, 557 N.E.2d 894, 896-97 (1990); People v. Fleming, 50 Ill. 2d 141, 144, 277 N.E.2d 872, 874 (1971) ("one may not at once deny the commission of the offense and claim entrapment").

[410] People v. Cooper, 239 Ill. App. 3d 336, 606 N.E.2d 705 (5th Dist. 1992).

[411] *See* 720 ILCS 5/3-2(a) (1999); People v. Lindo, 169 Ill. App. 3d 877, 881-82, 523 N.E.2d 1341, 1343 (2d Dist. 1988) (where defendant presented "slight evidence" that he had knowledge that a package he possessed contained cannabis, court improperly denied him jury instructions on entrapment in circumstances where state had argued he had denied having requisite mental states for possession with intent to deliver and unlawful delivery and was not deserving of entrapment instructions); People v. Pagliuca, 119 Ill. App. 3d 906, 916, 458 N.E.2d 908, 916 (1st Dist. 1983).

[412] People v. Cooper, 17 Ill. App. 3d 934, 938, 308 N.E.2d 815, 818 (2d Dist. 1974). *See also* People v. Terry, 38 Ill. App. 3d 795, 796, 349 N.E.2d 129, 130 (4th Dist. 1976) ("An affirmative defense admits the acts incident to the offense alleged").

[413] People v. Pagliuca, 119 Ill. App. 3d 906, 916-17, 458 N.E.2d 908, 916 (1st Dist. 1983).

allowed to invoke the defense of entrapment despite his argument that the road on which he was driving was not a highway as defined in the applicable statute.[414] In another case, entrapment was properly raised where the defendant admitted possession and delivering drugs but claimed a lack of the requisite intent.[415] In both of these cases, the court reasoned that there was no factual dispute about whether the *acts* constituting the crime had been committed. In contrast, the defense of entrapment was dismissed where the defendant in a robbery prosecution denied the use of force or threat against the victim, which is a requisite element of the offense.[416] Meanwhile, the defense was found to be incompatible with the accused's denials that he had the requisite *intent* required for the charge in a solicitation to commit murder prosecution.[417] Thus, the denial of the commission of the actus reus or the mens rea may constitute a barrier to any entrapment claim in Illinois.

In spite of the United States Supreme Court's more liberal ruling in federal criminal cases,[418] the Illinois Supreme Court refused to extend to defendants the right to deny committing the crime while concurrently claiming entrapment.[419] In addition, because a defendant must admit to commission of all the elements of a charged offense to claim entrapment, a defendant is denied instructions on possible lesser included offenses.[420] In *People v. Landwer*,[421] the Illinois Supreme Court held that a defendant who was charged with solicitation to commit murder was not entitled to a lesser included offense instruction regarding solicitation to commit aggravated battery.[422]

§ 19.41.   — Acquittal of Codefendant.

When the same charges arising out of the same transaction are brought against two defendants, the acquittal of one of the defendants on the grounds of entrap-

---

[414] People v. Jensen, 37 Ill. App. 3d 1010, 1014, 347 N.E.2d 371, 375 (1st Dist. 1976).

[415] People v. Jones, 73 Ill. App. 2d 55, 60, 219 N.E.2d 12, 14 (1st Dist. 1966).

[416] People v. Bradley, 75 Ill. App. 3d 347, 349, 391 N.E.2d 1078, 1081 (3d Dist. 1979).

[417] People v. Swimley, 57 Ill. App. 3d 116, 129-30, 372 N.E.2d 887, 897 (1st Dist.) ("At trial, defendant denied that she possessed the intent to solicit Saladino to murder her husband. In view of this denial that she lacked the requisite mental state for the offense charged, the defense of entrapment was incompatible and therefore not available to her."), *cert. denied*, 439 U.S. 911 (1978).

[418] Mathews v. United States, 485 U.S. 58, 64-66 (1988) (defendant charged with federal crime is still entitled to have jury receive entrapment instructions even if defendant denies one or more elements of crime).

[419] People v. Gillespie, 136 Ill. 2d 496, 500-01, 557 N.E.2d 894, 896-97 (1990) (defendant may not simultaneously deny element of charged crime and assert entrapment, despite contrary rule in federal criminal cases).

[420] People v. Landwer, 166 Ill. 2d 475, 488, 655 N.E.2d 848, 855 (1995).

[421] 166 Ill. 2d 475, 655 N.E.2d 848 (1995).

[422] People v. Landwer, 166 Ill. 2d 475, 488, 655 N.E.2d 848, 855 (1995).

ment is not necessarily a bar to conviction of the other.[423] If the codefendant succeeds in proving entrapment, the defendant can still be convicted. The convictions of two defendants for violating an act designed to regulate the use of explosives were upheld even though a third codefendant was freed from the same charges after successfully proving entrapment.[424]

§ 19.42.   — Subjective Theory of Entrapment: Jury Issue.

Ordinarily, entrapment is a question for determination by the jury under proper instructions.[425] This rule pertains to those jurisdictions, including Illinois, that follow the subjective rationale of entrapment, whereas the objective theory of entrapment involves a legal issue to be determined solely by the trial judge.[426] In other words, whether the defendant had the predisposition to commit the offense is a question of fact while whether the conduct of the government amounted to outrageous government misconduct presents a question of law. Where the testimony of the accused, on its face, tends to support entrapment, or where evidence with respect to this defense is conflicting, the issue should go to the jury.[427] But where uncontradicted evidence discloses no entrapment, it is unnecessary to submit the matter to the jury.[428] Furthermore, in reviewing the entrapment defense, the court is to determine all of the evidence in the light most favorable to the posecution.[429]

It must be stressed that when an Illinois appellate opinion states that the issue of entrapment is to be resolved by the jury unless entrapment exists as a matter of law,[430] the appellate court statement is *not* making reference to the objective theory of entrapment as a possible alternative theory of entrapment in Illinois.[431] It is merely stating a familiar appellate court proposition that where the evidence is so one-sided or uncontradicted that reasonable minds could not differ on the outcome of the factual issue involved, the trial court judge may appropriately

---

[423] People v. Ficke, 343 Ill. 367, 376-77, 175 N.E. 543, 550 (1931).

[424] People v. Ficke, 343 Ill. 367, 376-77, 175 N.E. 543, 550 (1931).

[425] *See* People v. Ball, 91 Ill. App. 3d 1041, 1045, 415 N.E.2d 471, 475-76 (1st Dist. 1980).

[426] 2 PAUL ROBINSON, CRIMINAL LAW DEFENSES § 209(c)(2) (1984).

[427] *See* People v. Pates, 80 Ill. App. 3d 1062, 1067-68, 400 N.E.2d 553, 558 (3d Dist. 1980), *aff'd*, 84 Ill. 2d, 417 N.E.2d 618 (1981) (reversal because of conflicting testimony regarding entrapment and inaccurate jury instruction on entrapment).

[428] *See* People v. Kadlec, 21 Ill. App. 3d 289, 293-94, 313 N.E.2d 522, 526 (1974).

[429] People v. Lambrecht, 231 Ill. App. 3d 426, 433, 595 N.E.2d 1358, 1363 (2d Dist. 1992). *But see* People v. Husted, 97 Ill. App. 3d 160, 170, 422 N.E.2d 962, 970 (2d Dist. 1981), *cert. denied*, 456 U.S. 945 (1982) (court is to determine evidence in light most favorable to defendant), *cert. denied*, 456 U.S. 945 (1982). *Lambrecht* insisted *Husted* was wrongly decided.

[430] *See, e.g.*, People v. Tipton, 78 Ill. 2d 477, 487, 401 N.E.2d 528, 533 (1980).

[431] *See, e.g.*, People v. Day, 279 Ill. App. 3d 606, 613, 665 N.E.2d 867, 872 (3d Dist. 1996) (lack of predisposition established as a matter of law; conviction reversed on grounds of entrapment).

resolve the issue himself or herself without sending it to the jury. In the context of entrapment, the judge's ruling that entrapment existed as a matter of law simply means that the evidence of the accused's predisposition was lacking to such an extent as a *factual* matter that it can be said with legal certitude that entrapment existed.[432]

§ 19.43.   — Jury Instructions.

In any case where the defendant offers some evidence of the lack of predisposition to commit the crime, instructions on the affirmative defense of entrapment must be given to the jury.[433] In *People v. Lindo*,[434] the defendant alleged he was entrapped into committing possession with intent to deliver and unlawful delivery of illicit drugs, but a request for instructions on entrapment was denied in the trial court. In that case, defendant offered some evidence proving that an undercover informant contacted defendant, supplied the drugs, and merely asked the defendant to pose as a drug dealer and use his Jamaican ancestry to bolster the quality of drugs he was trying to sell to another individual.[435] While declining to comment on whether the informant's actions amounted to entrapment, the appellate court ruled that the failure of the trial court to extend to the jury the issue of whether, in fact, the defendant had the predisposition to engage in drug deliveries was reversible error.[436]

Any divergence in the wording of this instruction may be grounds for a reversible error. In *People v. Pates*,[437] the Illinois Supreme Court upheld the appellate court's decision in ruling that a change in the wording of the Illinois Pattern Jury Instruction regarding entrapment was enough to cause a retrial. The clause, "in furtherance of a criminal purpose which the defendant originated," was deleted and the clause, "which he was willing to commit," was added.[438] The court reasoned that this rewording could lead the jury to believe that the state could rebut the defendant's claim of entrapment without showing that he had been predisposed.[439]

§ 19.44.   — Burden of Proof.

In rebutting a claim of entrapment, the burden of proof is of major significance. In Illinois, the defendant must initially come forth with some evidence of

---

[432] *See, e.g.,* People v. Day, 279 Ill. App. 3d 606, 613, 665 N.E.2d 867, 872 (3d Dist. 1996).

[433] People v. Placek, 184 Ill. 2d 370, 381, 704 N.E.2d 393, 398 (1998).

[434] 169 Ill. App. 3d 877, 523 N.E.2d 1341 (2d Dist. 1988).

[435] People v. Lindo, 169 Ill. App. 3d 877, 879, 523 N.E.2d 1341, 1342 (2d Dist. 1988).

[436] People v. Lindo, 169 Ill. App. 3d 877, 882, 523 N.E.2d 1341, 1344 (2d Dist. 1988).

[437] 84 Ill. 2d 82, 417 N.E.2d 618 (3d Dist. 1980).

[438] People v. Pates, 84 Ill. 2d 82, 86-87, 417 N.E.2d 618, 619-20 (3d Dist. 1980).

[439] People v. Pates, 84 Ill. 2d 82, 87, 417 N.E.2d 618, 620 (3d Dist. 1980).

entrapment.[440] This evidence does not need to be substantial but merely needs to suggest some likelihood that entrapment may have occurred. Once this evidence has been raised by the accused, the burden then shifts to the state to rebut that evidence.[441] The state must prove beyond a reasonable doubt that the accused committed all the elements of the crime and was not entrapped.[442]

In *People v. Villanueva*,[443] the affirmative defense of entrapment was rebutted beyond a reasonable doubt by the state, so that the defense failed. Here, evidence that the defendant initially showed reluctance to purchase and supply drugs to an informer was overcome by the state's evidence that the accused kept in contact with the informer and later showed no reluctance to transact the illegal sale.[444] Similarly, in a prosecution for the delivery of a controlled substance, the state's evidence was sufficient to rebut the defense of entrapment beyond a reasonable doubt where, although the defendant claimed that he was coaxed into making a drug deal, he made three separate transactions several days apart.[445]

In contrast, in *People v. Fisher*,[446] the state's evidence was found to be insufficient to rebut the entrapment defense beyond a reasonable doubt. In *Fisher*, the state's only witness testified that only one drug sale was ever transacted between himself and the defendant and, on this occasion, the drugs in question were found not to be a controlled substance.[447] Meanwhile, the defendant offered testimony that she had an overwhelming desire to stop the informer from bothering her, which led her to sell him drugs that she thought to be illegal and, as such, entrapment was found to exist.[448]

---

[440] People v. Placek, 184 Ill. 2d 370, 381, 704 N.E.2d 393, 398 (1998). In jurisdictions following the objective approach to entrapment, the defendant carries the burden of establishing the defense by a preponderance of the evidence. *See* Coffey v. State, 585 P.2d 514, 521 (Alaska 1978).

[441] *See* 720 ILCS 5/3-2(b) (1999); People v. Placek, 184 Ill. 2d 370, 381, 704 N.E.2d 393, 398 (1998).

[442] People v. Placek, 184 Ill. 2d 370, 381, 704 N.E.2d 393, 398 (1998); People v. Tipton, 78 Ill. 2d 477, 487, 401 N.E.2d 528, 532-33 (1980); People v. Husted, 97 Ill. App. 3d 160, 172-73, 422 N.E.2d 962, 971 (2d Dist. 1981), *cert. denied,* 456 U.S. 945 (1982).

[443] 46 Ill. App. 3d 826, 361 N.E.2d 357 (3d Dist. 1977).

[444] People v. Villanueva, 46 Ill. App. 3d 826, 830-31, 361 N.E.2d 357, 361 (3d Dist. 1977); *see also* People v. Chanath, 184 Ill. App. 3d 521, 526, 540 N.E.2d 468, 471 (1st Dist 1989) (defendant's predisposition to deliver controlled substance proved beyond reasonable doubt where evidence showed defendant was familiar with drugs and was willing to participate in prearranged sale); People v. Schillaci, 171 Ill. App. 3d 510, 518, 526 N.E.2d 871, 876 (4th Dist. 1988) (defendant's predisposition to deliver cocaine proved beyond a reasonable doubt where evidence showed that defendant was familiar with drugs, he and his wife had an expensive cocaine habit, he purchased a half ounce of cocaine about once a week, and he had ample opportunity to withdraw from the delivery when he suspected the government's involvement).

[445] People v. Marshall, 101 Ill. App. 3d 244, 248, 427 N.E.2d 1333, 1335 (4th Dist. 1981).

[446] 74 Ill. App. 3d 330, 392 N.E.2d 975 (3d Dist. 1979).

[447] People v. Fisher, 74 Ill. App. 3d 330, 334-35, 392 N.E.2d 975, 979 (3d Dist. 1979).

[448] People v. Fisher, 74 Ill. App. 3d 330, 334-35, 392 N.E.2d 975, 979 (3d Dist. 1979).

§ 19.45.   — Prior Convictions Admissible.

As stated, in rebutting the accused's tender of some evidence of entrapment, the defendant's predisposition to commit the crime must be proved beyond a reasonable doubt.[449] Therefore, where the defendant's predisposition and criminal design become an issue, the state may introduce evidence relating to these concerns, including prior crimes and convictions that are relevant to these material issues.[450] The relevancy of other crimes evidence may be demonstrated by the similarity of the other crime to the crime with which the defendant is charged, and by the proximity in time of the commission of other crimes.[451] But unless entrapment is properly raised, any direct proof of prior violations by the defendant is inadmissible.[452]

The accused's predisposition can be proven by submitting otherwise inadmissible evidence concerning the defendant's actions both before and after the commission of the crime[453] and general character evidence.[454] Once the defendant raises this affirmative defense, he or she cannot object to a search through his or her relevant other crimes to determine his or her predisposition. Of course, where the other crimes evidence was deemed irrelevant, such as where a trial court admitted evidence that defendant dealt in stolen auto parts in a prosecution for delivery of a controlled substance, the admission of the evidence was reversible error.[455]

Any evidence offered to explain, repel, contradict, or disprove evidence given by the accused can be classified as admissible rebuttal evidence. Because of this legal consideration, taken in conjunction with the broad allowances given to the state to prove criminal predisposition, the accused can potentially suffer extreme prejudice as a *practical* matter by claiming entrapment. For example, conversations the accused had with the police on earlier occasions were ruled to be admissible in a drug prosecution where the conversations indicated that the defendant was previously engaged in the sale of a wide variety of drugs.[456] Similarly, an officer's testimony that the defendant used and sold drugs on many prior occasions was admitted in a drug case to rebut a claim of entrapment.[457]

---

[449] People v. Walker, 61 Ill. App. 3d 4, 6, 377 N.E.2d 604, 605 (3d Dist. 1978).

[450] People v. Placek, 184 Ill. 2d 370, 385, 704 N.E.2d 393, 400 (1998).

[451] People v. Placek, 184 Ill. 2d 370, 386, 704 N.E.2d 393, 400 (1998).

[452] *See* People v. Outten, 13 Ill. 2d 21, 25, 147 N.E.2d 284, 286 (1958).

[453] *See* United States v. Carreon, 626 F.2d 528, 535-36 (7th Cir. 1980); United States v. Townsend, 555 F.2d 152, 159 (7th Cir.), *cert. denied*, 434 U.S. 897 (1977); People v. Tipton, 78 Ill. 2d 477, 484-85, 401 N.E.2d 528, 531-32 (1980).

[454] People v. Perez, 209 Ill. App. 3d 457, 465, 568 N.E.2d 250, 255 (1st Dist. 1991).

[455] People v. Placek, 184 Ill. 2d 370, 386-88, 704 N.E.2d 393, 400-01 (1998).

[456] People v. Price, 17 Ill. App. 3d 911, 913, 309 N.E.2d 56, 57 (4th Dist. 1974).

[457] People v. Husted, 97 Ill. App. 3d 160, 169, 422 N.E.2d 962, 971-72 (2d Dist. 1981), *cert. denied*, 456 U.S. 945 (1982).

It is important to note the difference between the subjective and objective rationales to entrapment in this regard. Under the subjective view, the possible relevant evidence of the accused's past criminal conduct is admissible. Under the objective rationale, since the focus is on police conduct rather than on predisposition, evidence of past criminal conduct becomes immaterial and is, therefore, not admissible.

§ 19.46.   Defense of Public Authority: Background of Current Law.

Beneath the umbrella of "public authority"[458] justifications there exist a number of defenses that are designed to protect or further a public interest.[459] Unlike defensive force justifications (discussed in chapter 18), "the actor's authority is not limited to defensive action in protection of persons or property. He may act *affirmatively* to further or defend a public or private interest, even one that is entirely intangible."[460]

§ 19.47.   — Law Enforcement Justifications.

The first grouping of public authority defenses are those relating to law enforcement interests.[461] These include the right of a law enforcement official, a person aiding him or her or, in some cases, even a normal citizen not vested with law enforcement responsibility to (1) effect an arrest, (2) prevent the commission of a crime, or (3) prevent the escape of a criminal.[462] Although there is considerable overlap between these concerns,[463] it is useful to examine them individually.

§ 19.48.   — Arrest.

At common law, a police officer, his or her agent, and a private person had certain authority to effect an arrest.[464] A police officer or person specially au-

---

[458] *See* ROLLIN M. PERKINS & RONALD N. BOYCE, CRIMINAL LAW 1093-1104 (3d ed. 1982).

[459] *See* 2 PAUL ROBINSON, CRIMINAL LAW DEFENSES § 141(a) (1984) for an outline of the justifications and interests served by each.

[460] 2 PAUL ROBINSON, CRIMINAL LAW DEFENSES § 141(a) (1984).

[461] *See generally* WAYNE LAFAVE & AUSTIN SCOTT, CRIMINAL LAW § 5.10 (2d ed. 1986).

[462] *See generally* WAYNE LAFAVE & AUSTIN SCOTT, CRIMINAL LAW § 5.10 (2d ed. 1986).

[463] *See* ROLLIN M. PERKINS & RONALD N. BOYCE, CRIMINAL LAW 1108 (3d ed. 1982) for some discussion of this point.

[464] The scope of the common law authority to arrest outlined in this section is largely deduced from the following authorities: WAYNE LAFAVE & AUSTIN SCOTT, CRIMINAL LAW § 5.10 (2d ed. 1986); ROLLIN M. PERKINS & RONALD N. BOYCE, CRIMINAL LAW 1093-1104 (3d ed. 1982); and 2 PAUL ROBINSON, CRIMINAL LAW DEFENSES § 142 (1984). It is important to note that these authorities are not in exact agreement with each other as to each specific feature of this aspect of public authority and, accordingly, this author will attempt to clarify the true scope of this defense by reference to what appears to be the most commonly accepted view.

thorized by him or her could use *nondeadly force* to arrest a person for (1) any reasonably apparent felony (with or without a warrant), (2) any reasonably apparent misdemeanor involving a breach of the peace committed in his or her presence (with or without a warrant), and (3) any misdemeanor where the officer had a warrant. *Reasonably apparent* meant, at common law, that the actor had reasonable grounds or probable cause to believe that the crime had been committed.[465] It did not have to be proved that the crime had actually occurred. Meanwhile, a private citizen (without special authorization) had the authority to effect an arrest for a felony or for any other offense involving a breach of the peace committed in his or her presence if the crime in question had *actually* occurred.[466]

Concerning the use of *deadly force*, the police officer (or person deputized by the officer) could resort to such force only against a person he or she reasonably believed to be a fleeing felon regardless of the nature of the felony. The law enforcement official could not, however, use deadly force to prevent the escape of a fleeing misdemeanant arrestee. A private person could use deadly force to prevent the escape of a fleeing felon, but only if a felony had actually occurred. In addition, there was some authority that suggested that deadly force could be used by the private person only if the actual felony in question was a dangerous or forcible felony. A different situation arose where the arrestee, whether felon or misdemeanant, actively resisted the arrest in question. If the arrestee suddenly resorted to deadly force, then the actor, whether police officer or private person, could respond to the arrestee's show of force to the extent necessary to defend himself or herself. In other words, in this latter situation, the rules of self-defense (discussed in chapter 17) would become operable, and public authority concerns would no longer govern. For example, if a private shopkeeper attempted to effect a citizen's arrest[467] of a shoplifter in the shopkeeper's store by using reasonable, nondeadly force and, immediately thereafter, the shoplifter attacked the shopkeeper with a knife, with the intent to kill the shopkeeper, the shopkeeper's resort to deadly force to protect himself or herself would be justified by self-defense. However, if the shoplifter had merely escaped the grasp of the arresting shopkeeper and was running out of the shop, at which point the

---

[465] ROLLIN M. PERKINS & RONALD N. BOYCE, CRIMINAL LAW 1095 (3d ed. 1982). This standard is in general accordance with the Fourth Amendment standard of the United States Constitution. U.S. CONST. amend. IV. *See also* Illinois v. Gates, 462 U.S. 213 (1984) for a discussion of this standard, which is further defined as a "fair probability" that a crime exists. In any event, the language "reasonably apparent," as used throughout this chapter, should be understood as consistent with "probable cause."

[466] To this extent, the private person who had been deputized with law enforcement authority essentially acted at his or her peril. If no crime had occurred, he or she could have been prosecuted for using force against the innocent arrestee. ROLLIN M. PERKINS & RONALD N. BOYCE, CRIMINAL LAW 1100 (3d ed. 1982).

[467] *See generally* M. CHERIF BASSIOUNI, CITIZEN'S ARREST (1977).

shopkeeper shot the shoplifter in the back, the shopkeeper's actions would not be justified by self-defense, since the shoplifter had not attacked the shopkeeper and, in fact, was withdrawing from any possible confrontation. Nor could the shoplifter's actions be justified by public authority concerns, since shoplifting is not a dangerous felony.

Today, most jurisdictions have statutes that carefully delineate the type of force that can be used in making arrests and the persons authorized to make such arrests. In some cases, the authority has been broadened beyond the common law rules; in others, it has been narrowed. It has been broadened in two significant ways. First, there appears a tendency to not limit private citizens' arrests to situations in which the felony or misdemeanor actually occurred. In many jurisdictions, the private person, like the police officer, can now resort to nondeadly force (or deadly force in appropriate circumstances) where it is reasonably apparent a crime has been committed. Second, the police officer's authority has been expanded to allow for warrantless misdemeanor arrests that the officer believes to be reasonably justified even though the crime occurred outside his or her presence.[468]

Concerning the resort to deadly force, the law has been narrowed in at least one significant respect. Deadly force is now allowed to effect an arrest only in circumstances in which the arrestee was apparently involved in a forcible or dangerous felony. For example, a law enforcement officer cannot use deadly force to apprehend an embezzler who poses no threat to the officer. Moreover, the United States Supreme Court ruled in *Tennessee v. Garner*[469] that police use of deadly force against a fleeing felon could constitute a violation of the arrestee's Fourth Amendment rights. In *Garner*, a police officer shot a young, unarmed burglar in the back of the head, killing him while he was fleeing from the burglary of an unoccupied house. The father of the deceased burglar instituted an action for asserted violations of his son's civil rights, which the federal district court dismissed. The Supreme Court upheld a United States Court of Appeals reversal of the district court ruling, holding that the Fourth Amendment should not be construed in light of the common law rule allowing the use of whatever force is necessary to effect the arrest of a fleeing felon.[470] The Court ruled that the reasonableness requirement of the Fourth Amendment precluded the use of deadly force unless it was necessary to prevent the felon's escape and the officer had probable cause to believe that the suspect posed a significant threat of death or serious bodily injury to the officer or others.[471]

---

[468] United States v. Watson, 423 U.S. 411, 422 (1976) (police have authority to conduct a warrantless arrest of a person in an area open to the public for a crime occurring outside their presence).

[469] 471 U.S. 1 (1985).

[470] Tennessee v. Garner, 471 U.S. 1, 12-13 (1985).

[471] Tennessee v. Garner, 471 U.S. 1, 3 (1985).

The United States Supreme Court has also limited the power of the police to conduct a warrantless arrest in certain places. In *United States v. Watson,*[472] the court ruled that it is permissible to arrest a person in a public place without a warrant.[473] However, in *Payton v. New York,*[474] the court ruled that, absent exigent circumstances or consent, it is violative of the Fourth Amendment to arrest a person in the confines of his or her home without an arrest warrant.[475] Moreover, the Court ruled in *Steagald v. United States*[476] that, absent exigent circumstances or consent, the police needed not only an arrest warrant to arrest a defendant in third-party premises but also a search warrant to protect the integrity of the third party's residence.[477] Finally, in *Welsh v. Wisconsin,*[478] the Court ruled that the Fourth Amendment prohibited the warrantless entry into premises to arrest a person for a minor offense only punishable by a fine regardless of any state claim that the warrantless arrest was necessitated by exigent circumstances.[479]

§ 19.49.   — Prevention of a Crime.

Closely related to the public authority to arrest is the public authority justification of "prevention of a crime."[480] While the arrest contemplates that the commission of a crime has already transpired, the prevention concept is designed to vindicate, in certain situations, the officer or private citizen who attempts to stop an anticipated crime from reaching fruition or a crime already underway from progressing further.[481]

Where the actor uses force to prevent a physical attack on himself or herself, the defense of self-defense is operable, and the concept of prevention is given little attention. The same is true with respect to preventing an assault on another where defense of another is the paramount concern. And where there is a threat to a person's property, defense of property is the central focus. However, where

---

[472] 423 U.S. 411, 418 n.6 (1976).

[473] United States v. Watson, 423 U.S. 411 (1976).

[474] 445 U.S. 573, 590 (1980).

[475] Payton v. New York, 445 U.S. 573 (1980).

[476] 451 U.S. 204, 205-06 (1981).

[477] Steagald v. United States, 451 U.S. 204 (1981).

[478] 466 U.S. 740 (1984).

[479] Welsh v. Wisconsin, 466 U.S. 740, 753-54 (1984). In *Welsh,* the defendant was arrested for driving while under the influence of an intoxicant. The state argued that there were exigent circumstances that justified the warrantless entry, that is, the need to secure evidence of the high blood-alcohol level before it dissipated and the possible threat to the public safety that the defendant might pose should he not be swiftly apprehended and drive again. However, the opinion indicated that where the offense is "relatively minor," the "exigent circumstances" exception is never operable. *Id.*

[480] WAYNE LAFAVE & AUSTIN SCOTT, CRIMINAL LAW § 5.10(c) (2d ed. 1986).

[481] ROLLIN M. PERKINS & RONALD N. BOYCE, CRIMINAL LAW 1108 (3d ed. 1982).

there is no threat to personal security or property, prevention can become a concern. This might be the case where the actor has attempted to stop the commission of treason (thereby protecting the sovereign) or statutory rape (thereby protecting the morals of a young girl).[482]

Since this public authority justification for prevention is seldom advanced in comparison to the public authority to arrest concept, the parameters of this defense are far less clear. At common law, there was a privilege on the part of police and private citizens to prevent felonies and misdemeanors amounting to a breach of the peace through the use of reasonable force.[483] No such authority existed, however, with respect to misdemeanor transgressions not involving a breach of the peace.[484] Concerning the use of deadly force to prevent a crime, originally one could resort to deadly force to prevent *any* felony.[485] The crime prevented had to be, at a minimum, reasonably apparent[486] and imminent.[487]

Today, in the absence of statutory authority to the contrary, the justification of "prevention of a crime" is consistent with the common law except in one important respect. It is impermissible to resort to deadly force to prevent the commission of a felony unless it is a dangerous or forcible felony.[488] Thus, it would be impermissible to kill a person about to engage in the non-dangerous felonies of adultery, bigamy, theft, or electronic eavesdropping.

§ 19.50.   — Prevention of Escape.

Another law enforcement justification are the defense of "prevention of escape" of someone in lawful custody.[489] Since there is considerable overlap between this concept and the arrest justification, the rules governing arrest and prevention of escape are the same.[490]

§ 19.51.   — Miscellaneous Public Authority Concerns.

At common law and today, there are a variety of public authority concerns beyond law enforcement justifications. Under the general rubric of "public authority" fall (1) "parental authority," as where a parent (or a parental substitute

---

[482] ROLLIN M. PERKINS & RONALD N. BOYCE, CRIMINAL LAW 1108 (3d ed. 1982).
[483] ROLLIN M. PERKINS & RONALD N. BOYCE, CRIMINAL LAW 1109 (3d ed. 1982).
[484] ROLLIN M. PERKINS & RONALD N. BOYCE, CRIMINAL LAW 1108 (3d ed. 1982).
[485] WAYNE LAFAVE & AUSTIN SCOTT, CRIMINAL LAW § 5.10(c) (2d ed. 1986). As to preventing misdemeanors, there was no authority at common law to employ deadly force. *Id.*
[486] Consistent with the power of arrest by citizens at common law, it may have been necessary for the actor to prove that a crime was actually about to occur. WAYNE LAFAVE & AUSTIN SCOTT, CRIMINAL LAW § 5.10(a) (2d ed. 1986).Id.
[487] WAYNE LAFAVE & AUSTIN SCOTT, CRIMINAL LAW § 5.10(c) (2d ed. 1986).
[488] WAYNE LAFAVE & AUSTIN SCOTT, CRIMINAL LAW § 5.10(c) (2d ed. 1986).
[489] WAYNE LAFAVE & AUSTIN SCOTT, CRIMINAL LAW § 5.10(c) (2d ed. 1986).
[490] WAYNE LAFAVE & AUSTIN SCOTT, CRIMINAL LAW § 5.10(c) (2d ed. 1986).

such as a foster parent) physically disciplines a child,[491] (2) "in loco parentis authority," as where a teacher disciplines a student,[492] (3) "medical authority," as where a doctor orders a hospital quarantine of a person with a communicable disease that threatens the public health,[493] (4) "judicial authority," as where a judge orders the demolition of a building that poses a threat to the public safety,[494] and (5) "military authority," as where a member of the military takes the life of an enemy soldier in time of war.[495] Further examples that might be included under the general classification of public authority might arise where a firefighter breaks into a nonconsenting homeowner's residence to extinguish a fire[496] or where a doctor administers a court-ordered lethal injection into the body of a convicted murderer who has been sentenced to death.[497]

§ 19.52.   Defense of Public Authority Codified.

Article 5/7 addresses two aspects of public authority that were mentioned above: (1) law enforcement concerns, as reflected in section 5/7-5 ("Peace Officer's Use of Force in Making Arrest"), section 5/7-6 ("Private Person's Use of Force in Making Arrest") and section 5/7-9 ("Use of Force to Prevent Escape"), and (2) "execution of the death sentence," as appears in section 5/7-10. None of the other public authority concerns mentioned above (for example, "medical authority") appears in the Criminal Code of 1961; accordingly, they will not be discussed hereafter.

Of major importance here are those sections of article 5/7 that govern the right to arrest, prevent the commission of crime, and prevent the escape of a person from lawful custody. Since article 5/7 explicitly addresses only the arrest and escape justifications, it can be said that any prevention concept, to the extent it *might* be recognized in Illinois as an independent defense, is subsumed into the other two concerns. Thus, the discussion of the law enforcement justifications below will focus only on these two statutory concerns.

The Illinois code grants peace officers considerable latitude in determining whether or not to use force in making an arrest or preventing escape. Although a private person is similarly justified in using force in these situations, the nature of the circumstances may limit the private person's ability to use force compared to the discretion given the peace officer.

---

[491] *See* 2 PAUL ROBINSON, CRIMINAL LAW DEFENSES § 144 (1984).

[492] *See* 2 PAUL ROBINSON, CRIMINAL LAW DEFENSES § 143(b)(1) (1984).

[493] *See* 2 PAUL ROBINSON, CRIMINAL LAW DEFENSES § 145 (1984).

[494] *See* 2 PAUL ROBINSON, CRIMINAL LAW DEFENSES § 147 (1984).

[495] *See* 2 PAUL ROBINSON, CRIMINAL LAW DEFENSES § 148 (1984).

[496] *See* 2 PAUL ROBINSON, CRIMINAL LAW DEFENSES § 149 (1984).

[497] *See* 720 ILCS 5/7-10 (1999) ("Execution of death sentence").

§ 19.53.   — Arrest by Peace Officer.

As stated, a peace officer's use of force in making an arrest is governed by section 5/7-5. It provides:

(a) A peace officer, or any person whom he has summoned or directed to assist him, need not retreat or desist from efforts to make a lawful arrest because of resistance or threatened resistance to the arrest. He is justified in the use of any force which he reasonably believes to be necessary to effect the arrest and of any force which he reasonably believes to be necessary to defend himself or another from bodily harm while making the arrest. However, he is justified in using force likely to cause death or great bodily harm only when he reasonably believes that such force is necessary to prevent death or great bodily harm to himself or such other person, or when he reasonably believes both that:

(1) Such force is necessary to prevent the arrest from being defeated by resistance or escape; and
(2) The person to be arrested has committed or attempted a forcible felony which involves the infliction or threatened infliction of great bodily harm or is attempting to escape by use of a deadly weapon, or otherwise indicates that he will endanger human life or inflict great bodily harm unless arrested without delay.

(b) A peace officer making an arrest pursuant to an invalid warrant is justified in the use of any force which he would be justified in using if the warrant were valid, unless he knows that the warrant is invalid.[498]

Where a peace officer is making a lawful arrest, he or she may be met with resistance or with the threat of resistance to the arrest. Where the officer reasonably believes that force is necessary to effect the arrest or to defend himself or herself or another from bodily harm while making the arrest, the officer is justified in using any nondeadly force he or she reasonably believes to be necessary. The officer is not obliged to retreat from resistance before using force to effect the arrest or to protect himself or herself or others from bodily harm.

In determining the necessity for the use of nondeadly force and the amount of force deemed necessary, the courts look to the officer's reasonable belief of necessity, rather than what may have been the actual necessity.[499] Resistance to a

---

[498] 720 ILCS 5/7-5 (1999).

[499] *See, e.g.,* People v. Fort, 91 Ill. App. 2d 212, 214, 234 N.E.2d 384, 386 (1st Dist.), *cert. denied,* 393 U.S. 1014 (1968) (defendant-arrestee's abusive and defiant remarks aggravated already tense situation and gave police reasonable cause to believe that force was required to maintain custody of defendant; conviction for resisting or obstructing police officer affirmed); People v. Lees, 60 Ill. App. 2d 254, 264-65, 208 N.E.2d 656, 662 (1st Dist. 1965) (while discrepancy existed as to amount of force used to subdue complainant-arrestee, evidence showed that two officer-

particular arrest may come in many forms; it can be passive as well as active.[500] Although one might speculate after the fact about whether the amount of force employed by the arresting officer was actually required, the courts will evaluate the situation in accordance with whether the officer harbored a reasonable belief that the degree of force was necessary.[501] Where an officer, attempting to effect an arrest of a burglary suspect, encountered resistance from the arrestee and, in response, used such force that it was necessary to give the suspect twenty-nine stitches to close his wounds, the appellate court held that it was "certain" that the officer was within the limits of section 5/7-5.[502] Specific acts of an arrestee in resisting arrest will be considered in the determination of the reasonableness of an officer's use or threat of force in response.[503]

The right of a peace officer to use deadly force is obviously more limited. Section 5/7-5 delineates four specific situations in which an officer is justified in using "force likely to cause death or great bodily harm."[504] The officer is justified in using such force where he or she reasonably believes that (1) it is necessary to prevent the arrestee's resistance or escape, which in and of itself poses a danger of death or great bodily harm to the officer or another; (2) the arrestee,

---

defendants who struck him were doing what they reasonably thought was necessary to effectuate lawful arrest; conviction for aggravated battery reversed).

[500] Migliore v. County of Winnebago, 24 Ill. App. 3d 799, 802, 321 N.E.2d 476, 479 (2d Dist. 1974) (plaintiff's belligerent attitude in his continued refusal to state his name during service of process by officers justified officers' subsequent arrest and handcuffing of plaintiff for such refusal; refusal of trial court to grant plaintiff civil relief based on plaintiff's claim that officers used unreasonable force was affirmed).

[501] Moore v. Chicago Police Bd., 42 Ill. App. 3d 343, 348, 355 N.E.2d 745, 749 (1st Dist. 1976) (reversal of municipal police board dismissal of police officer for violation of police regulation).

[502] Moore v. Chicago Police Bd., 42 Ill. App. 3d 343, 348, 355 N.E.2d 745, 749 (1st Dist. 1976).

[503] See, e.g., People v. Reynolds, 32 Ill. App. 3d 604, 608, 335 N.E.2d 805, 809 (4th Dist. 1975), aff'd in part, rev'd in part, 63 Ill. 2d 561, 401 N.E.2d 1391 (1976) (act of defendant-arrestee in throwing officer against wall and each subsequent act of defendant was such resistance to arrest as to justify officer's kneeing of defendant in groin and each subsequent counteruse or threat of force by officer).

[504] 720 ILCS 5/7-5 (1999). See also 720 ILCS 5/7-8 (1999) ("Force Likely to Cause Death or Great Bodily Harm"):

(a) Force which is likely to cause death or great bodily harm within the meaning of Sections [5/]7-5 and [5/]7-6 includes:
(1) The firing of a firearm in the direction of the person to be arrested, even though no intent exists to kill or inflict great bodily harm; and
(2) The firing of a firearm at a vehicle in which the person to be arrested is riding.
(b) A peace officer's discharge of a firearm using ammunition designed to disable or control an individual without creating the likelihood of death or great bodily harm shall not be considered force likely to cause death or great bodily harm within the meaning of Sections [5/]7-5 and [5/]7-6.

who is resisting the arrest or is attempting escape, has committed or attempted to commit a forcible felony; (3) the arrestee, who is resisting the arrest, is attempting escape through the use of a deadly weapon; or (4) the arrestee, who is resisting the arrest or is attempting escape, will endanger human life or inflict great bodily harm if not swiftly apprehended.[505]

As in the case of nondeadly force needed to carry out an arrest, a peace officer is justified in using deadly force when making an arrest only if he or she reasonably believes that the employment of such force is necessary.[506] The perceived danger harbored in the mind of the arresting authority, rather than what might have been the actual danger, is the controlling factor. The reasonableness of the officer's belief is distilled by an examination of all of the circumstances preceding and immediately surrounding the deadly confrontation.[507] The question of whether the danger of great bodily harm is actual or apparent does not depend on an assailant's use of a deadly weapon or on the assailant's actually having one in his or her possession.[508] Moreover, the caselaw implicitly recognizes that in the heat of a potentially deadly confrontation, drawing a fine line between what may be a reasonable belief as compared to an unreasonable suspicion can be exceedingly difficult. For instance, the Illinois caselaw states that where self-defense is an issue, if a person is in reasonable fear of his or her life, the passage of a few seconds during which the cause of the fear abates is normally not enough to hold that person guilty of an unjustified homicide where he or she would have been justified in using deadly force only a few seconds earlier; the law does not charge an individual in such circumstances to use infallible judgment.[509]

In *Fornuto v. Police Board*,[510] an officer was chasing a fleeing suspect, whom the officer apparently believed had just committed a robbery, when the suspect turned and lunged at him with a knife. The officer was able to sidestep the suspect's lunge and subsequently shot the suspect in the back, thereby causing the suspect's death. Although it was clear from the evidence that the officer's life was in danger when the suspect lunged at him with a knife, there was a dispute about whether the victim was fleeing when shot or whether he was still close enough to the officer to present an imminent danger to him.[511] The *Fornuto*

---

[505] 720 ILCS 5/7-5 (1999).

[506] 720 ILCS 5/7-5 (1999).

[507] Schnepf v. Grubb, 125 Ill. App. 2d 432, 438, 261 N.E.2d 47, 51 (4th Dist. 1970) (verdict in favor of defendant-police in wrongful-death action affirmed).

[508] Schnepf v. Grubb, 125 Ill. App. 2d 432, 435, 261 N.E.2d 47, 49 (4th Dist. 1970); People v. Lockett, 85 Ill. App. 2d 410, 414, 229 N.E.2d 386, 388 (1st Dist. 1967).

[509] People v. Bailey, 27 Ill. App. 3d 128, 135-36, 326 N.E.2d 550, 555-56 (1st Dist. 1975).

[510] 38 Ill. App. 3d 950, 349 N.E.2d 521 (1st Dist. 1976) (affirmance of trial court's reversal of police board finding that police officer unnecessarily took life of individual, which finding had led to dismissal of officer).

[511] Fornuto v. Police Board, 38 Ill. App. 3d 950, 956, 349 N.E.2d 521, 526 (1st Dist. 1976).

court reasoned that while in hindsight one might find that the danger to the officer had abated one or two seconds before he shot the suspect, it would be unreasonable under the circumstances of the case to require the officer to exercise perfect judgment immediately after the suspect had lunged at him with a knife.[512] In addition, the court held that the shooting could be justified for two other reasons: (1) the officer's belief that it was necessary in order to stop the escape of a person who had committed a forcible felony, since the officer originally believed the suspect had been involved in a robbery (which apparently had not actually occurred), and (2) the officer's reasonable belief that the suspect was attempting an escape by employing a deadly weapon, namely, the knife.[513]

If a suspect were to merely make a motion toward a pocket or coat as if to reach for a weapon, this act alone would not justify the use of deadly force absent some knowledge or mention of a weapon.[514] However, the knowledge that forms the reasonable belief that use of deadly force is required need not be limited to the circumstances present at the time deadly force is used.[515] Prior altercations or encounters may justify an otherwise questionable use of deadly force.[516]

In evaluating the necessity of resorting to deadly force, the courts will consider other circumstances. Although a police officer has no duty to retreat,[517] the court reviewing a self-defense claim may consider whether the accused made

---

[512] Fornuto v. Police Board, 38 Ill. App. 3d 950, 956, 349 N.E.2d 521, 527 (1st Dist. 1976).

[513] Fornuto v. Police Board, 38 Ill. App. 3d 950, 956, 349 N.E.2d 521, 527 (1st Dist. 1976).

[514] Because the rules of self-defense are relevant in such a situation, the following caselaw involving the self-defense principle determines an officer's appropriate use of force (even though the cases cited in this note do not involve police arrest exercises). *See, e.g.,* People v. Pietrzyk, 54 Ill. App. 3d 738, 744-45, 369 N.E.2d 1299, 1303 (1st Dist. 1977) (it was not reasonable to believe that person was about to produce weapon and inflict great bodily harm merely on basis of seeing that person reach for pocket, especially where no one had seen weapon in man's possession before movement; aggravated battery affirmed); People v. Carter, 3 Ill. App. 3d 121, 123-25, 278 N.E.2d 209, 210-11 (1st Dist. 1971) (evidence supported aggravated-battery conviction of defendant, who fired at victim twice after having been struck by victim and who fired again after victim began to draw his hand from below level of bar into defendant's sight without knowing whether hand contained weapon capable of causing great bodily harm and without any other indication of menacing motion in his direction).

[515] Schnepf v. Grubb, 125 Ill. App. 2d 432, 435-38, 261 N.E.2d 47, 49-51 (4th Dist. 1970).

[516] *See* Schnepf v. Grubb, 125 Ill. App. 2d 432, 435-38, 261 N.E.2d 47, 49-51 (4th Dist. 1970) (evidence that on two recent occasions, decedent had used great force against officer was considered relevant in determination of officer's belief that he had to use major force to prevent great bodily harm to himself in incident in question). *See also* People v. Honey, 69 Ill. App. 2d 429, 217 N.E.2d 371 (1st Dist. 1966) (abstract) (prior antagonistic encounters with deceased, including fistfight five days earlier, threat by decedent with gun four days earlier, and another scuffle, were considered in determining whether defendant's use of deadly force was reasonable; decedent had threatened to kill defendant while rushing defendant with his hand in same pocket that had previously produced gun; voluntary manslaughter conviction reversed).

[517] 720 ILCS 5/7-5 (1999).

any attempt at avoiding the dangerous confrontation in question.[518] It will also evaluate the relative size, strength, and age of the parties.[519] It will consider the availability of, or lack of, other persons who might tend to protect the officer.[520] And it will examine whether there was evidence suggesting that the aggressor was abandoning his or her deadly attack.[521]

Although the arresting officer's conduct will be evaluated consistent with ordinary self-defense principles where the officer wards off an arrestee's attack on himself or herself, it must be understood that section 5/7-5 provides alternative justifications for the invocation of the use of deadly force.[522] For instance, a police officer can use this ultimate show of force when motivated by the interest in avoiding the escape of a person whom the officer reasonably believes committed a forcible felony.[523] In *Simmons v. City of Chicago*,[524] where a police officer shot in the back and killed a sixteen-year-old boy who was engaged in a robbery — a forcible felony — the officer's actions were considered justified.[525] This ruling was apparently not at odds with the United States Supreme Court ruling of *Tennessee v. Garner*,[526] inasmuch as the evidence revealed that the officer

---

[518] *See, e.g.*, People v. Adams, 113 Ill. App. 2d 205, 216, 252 N.E.2d 35, 40-41 (1st Dist. 1969) ("although there is no duty to retreat in face of wrongdoer, there is no showing that defendant attempted in any way to decline or avoid the peril before dealing the fatal blow").

[519] *See* Schnepf v. Grubb, 125 Ill. App. 2d 432, 438, 261 N.E.2d 47, 51 (4th Dist. 1970) (elderly officer was justified in using deadly force in part because of physical disparities; decedent was 19 years old, 6 feet tall, weighed 175 pounds, and was physically strong, while officer was 76 years old and in poor physical health; decedent had previously beaten officer badly). *See also* People v. Schwartz, 11 Ill. App. 3d 959, 971, 297 N.E.2d 671, 679 (1st Dist. 1973) (court considered sizes of defendant and decedent, among other concerns; voluntary manslaughter conviction reversed due to insufficient evidence), *rev'd*, 58 Ill. 2d 274, 319 N.E.2d 23 (1974) (conviction reinstated), *on remand*, 34 Ill. App. 3d 1043, 340 N.E.2d 583 (1st Dist 1975) (voluntary manslaughter conviction affirmed).

[520] *See* Schnepf v. Grubb, 125 Ill. App. 2d 432, 438, 261 N.E.2d 47, 51 (4th Dist. 1970) ("The presence of [two other officers] some 20 feet or more away could not prevent several quick, severe blows or kicks which might cause great bodily harm to an elderly [officer]").

[521] *See, e.g.*, People v. Johnson, 33 Ill. App. 3d 957, 961, 338 N.E.2d 895, 899 (5th Dist. 1975) ("When the person originally the aggressor has withdrawn from the confrontation, the defendant who pursues him and uses deadly force against him loses the benefit of any claim of self-defense").

[522] 720 ILCS 5/7-5 (1999).

[523] A "forcible felony" is defined as including treason, first degree murder, second degree murder, predatory criminal sexual assault of a child, aggravated criminal sexual assault, criminal sexual assault, robbery, burglary, residential burglary, aggravated arson, arson, aggravated kidnapping, kidnapping, aggravated battery resulting in great bodily harm or permanent disability or disfigurement "and any other felony which involves the use or threat of physical force or violence against any individual." 720 ILCS 5/2-8 (1999).

[524] 118 Ill. App. 3d 676, 455 N.E.2d 232 (1st Dist. 1983) (jury verdict in favor of city and police officer arising out of civil action affirmed).

[525] 118 Ill. App. 3d 676, 682, 455 N.E.2d 232, 236-37 (1st Dist. 1983).

[526] 471 U.S. 1 (1985).

reasonably believed that the boy in *Simmons* "might well use deadly force against another victim including the officer himself."[527] It is noteworthy that the Illinois statute, by limiting the officer's use of force to those who are engaged in forcible felonies, provides for a power more curtailed than that which existed at common law.[528]

As with the arresting authorities' resort to deadly force in self-defense, the officer who reasonably believes that he or she is preventing the escape of a forcible felon will be justified in the taking of that life. Thus, in *Fornuto*,[529] the officer was justified in taking the life of the arrestee, since he reasonably thought he was faced with a robbery suspect, and the fact that no robbery may have actually occurred was, according to the court, irrelevant.[530]

In the fleeing of the forcible felon situation, the courts appear to be inclined to consider whether the officer used reasonable efforts to apprehend the escaping suspect before using deadly force, as part of the courts' examination of the reasonableness of the officer's actions.[531] Typically, the Illinois courts suggest that a verbal command or warning by the officer will satisfy the reasonableness requirement.[532] According to this caselaw, warning shots are not necessarily required.[533] In *Onesto v. Police Board*,[534] the appellate court reversed a finding that a police officer used deadly force unreasonably in stopping a fleeing felon. Here, the police officer killed a man who was fleeing after burglarizing a garage. The officer called to the offender to stop and believed he would not be able to

---

[527] Simmons v. City of Chicago, 118 Ill. App. 3d 676, 682, 455 N.E.2d 232, 236 (1st Dist. 1983).

[528] Simmons v. City of Chicago, 118 Ill. App. 3d 676, 681, 455 N.E.2d 232, 235 (1st Dist. 1983). On the other hand, article [5/]7 justifications for the use of deadly force by police have been criticized as being too broad. *See* Edward Ronkowski, *Uses and Misuses of Deadly Force*, 28 DEPAUL L. REV. 701 (1979).

[529] Fornuto v. Police Bd., 38 Ill. App. 3d 950, 349 N.E.2d 521 (1st Dist. 1976).

[530] Fornuto v. Police Bd., 38 Ill. App. 3d 950, 956, 349 N.E.2d 521, 527 (1st Dist. 1976).

[531] Fornuto v. Police Bd., 38 Ill. App. 3d 950, 957, 349 N.E.2d 521, 527 (1st Dist. 1976) (court reasoned that when officer has pursued suspect and shouted "Halt, police," he had expended all reasonable alternatives to prevent suspect's escape by nonviolent means and, therefore, reasonably believed that it was essential to use deadly force to prevent escape of fleeing felon).

[532] *See, e.g.*, Lamonte v. City of Belleville, 41 Ill. App. 3d 697, 704, 355 N.E.2d 70, 77 (5th Dist. 1976) (in civil rights action, denial of relief for police shooting of armed robbery suspect was affirmed because deadly force was justified; court noted that suspect continued his efforts to escape despite orders to halt by officer); Simmons v. City of Chicago, 118 Ill. App. 3d 676, 683, 455 N.E.2d 232, 237 (1st Dist. 1983) (officer testified that he believed that decedent was armed, that he believed decedent would effect escape, and that he ordered decedent to halt and fired two shots before firing at decedent).

[533] Fornuto v. Police Bd., 38 Ill. App. 3d 950, 957, 349 N.E.2d 521, 527 (1st Dist. 1976) ("The [Police] Board suggests that Officer Fornuto should have fired a warning shot first. We do not agree").

[534] 92 Ill. App. 3d 183, 416 N.E.2d 13 (1st Dist. 1980).

apprehend the offender on foot. The court determined that the action of the officer in firing his weapon to stop the forcible felon was reasonable as a matter of law.[535]

Onesto and other Illinois opinions that justify the taking of the life of a fleeing felon in circumstances in which an unarmed fleeing felon poses no danger to the arresting officer or others may be of doubtful validity in light of *Tennessee v. Garner*.[536] In *Garner*, an officer shot an unarmed burglar fleeing from an unoccupied burglarized residence after the officer called out "police, halt." Here, the United States Supreme Court ruled that deadly force may not be used against a fleeing felon unless an officer has probable cause to believe that the suspect poses a significant threat of death or serious physical injury to himself or herself or another.[537] It stated that insofar as a Tennessee statute permitted the deadly shooting of an apparently unarmed, nondangerous fleeing suspect, it was unconstitutional in violation of the Fourth Amendment.[538] Furthermore, the Court held that merely because the unarmed suspect had broken into a dwelling at night did not automatically justify an assumption that he was dangerous.[539] *Garner*, then, raises serious implications about the constitutionality of section 5/7-5 insofar as it authorizes the shooting of unarmed fleeing felons who pose no real danger to anyone. Additionally, the fact that the Illinois legislature has chosen to designate burglaries, for instance, as forcible felonies may be of no consequence in terms of justification when the escaping burglar in question poses no significant danger to life or limb.

Another rationale for resorting to deadly force in an arrest situation exists where the arrestee is attempting an escape through the aid of a deadly weapon.[540] Although the caselaw is sparse in this area, the drafting committee comments to section 5/7-5 indicate that when an arrestee is armed with a deadly weapon, it is a clear indication of danger.[541] This legislative committee has stated that "the peace officer should be authorized to act even if the offender has not actually used or apparently threatened to use the weapon: the normal inference is that he intends to use it to thwart apprehension."[542] Clearly, the arrestee need not be carrying a firearm in order for his or her or action to constitute flee-

---

[535] Onesto v. Police Board, 92 Ill. App. 3d 183, 186, 416 N.E.2d 13, 16 (1st Dist. 1980).

[536] 471 U.S. 1 (1985).

[537] Tennessee v. Garner, 471 U.S. 1, 3 (1985).

[538] Tennessee v. Garner, 471 U.S. 1, 20-22 (1985).

[539] Tennessee v. Garner, 471 U.S. 1, 21 (1985).

[540] *See* 720 ILCS 5/7-5 (1999).

[541] ILL. ANN. STAT. ch. 38, para. 7-5 (Smith-Hurd 1989), 1961 Committee Comments, at 411 (revised).

[542] ILL. ANN. STAT. ch. 38, para. 7-5 (Smith-Hurd 1989), 1961 Committee Comments, at 411 (revised).

ing with a deadly weapon; a knife or other deadly weapon will suffice.[543] Here, *Garner* would not pose a problem because it involved an unarmed suspect.

Yet another theory justifying deadly force in an arrest situation exists where the arrestee will endanger life or inflict great bodily harm if not swiftly apprehended.[544] Where a suspect demonstrated by his actions in carrying out two armed robberies that he posed a serious threat to other potential robbery victims, as well as to the pursuing arresting officer, the officer's resort to deadly force was justified.[545] This rationale, like the previous, is consistent with the appropriate use of deadly force to prevent the escape of a fleeing felon as announced in *Garner*.[546]

In Illinois, a peace officer is statutorily authorized to summon or direct private citizens who are bystanders to assist the officer in efforts to make a lawful arrest.[547] Because the private citizen is generally required by law to respond to these requests, the citizen should be able to rely on the same authority to make the lawful arrest and, in fact, may be entitled to even broader protection.[548] Since a citizen summoned has little opportunity to inquire into the lawfulness of an arrest, which would delay effecting the arrest, the citizen is justified in using such force unless he or she has actual knowledge that the arrest is unlawful.[549]

Where a citizen reasonably believes he or she is aiding a police officer in the execution of the latter's official duties, the citizen is entitled to use such force as he or she reasonably believes necessary, including deadly force under the appropriate circumstances. In *People v. Lenzi*,[550] a citizen, who was the owner of a tavern, testified that an officer asked him for help in arresting a group of four men who were conducting themselves in a rowdy, boisterous, and threatening manner. Since the defendant knew that the person who summoned him was a police officer and believed that the officer needed help to arrest the man, he was entitled to use such force as he reasonably believed necessary.[551] In an ensuing scuffle, the citizen shot the decedent, who had obtained the police officer's gun and was aiming it at the citizen. The citizen-defendant's convictions were reversed, based on both self-defense and assisting a police officer.[552]

---

[543] *See* Fornuto v. Police Bd., 38 Ill. App. 3d 950, 956, 349 N.E.2d 521, 527 (1st Dist. 1976).

[544] 720 ILCS 5/7-5 (1999).

[545] Simmons v. City of Chicago, 118 Ill. App. 3d 676, 682, 455 N.E.2d 232, 236 (1st Dist. 1983).

[546] Tennessee v. Garner, 471 U.S. 1 (1985).

[547] 720 ILCS 5/7-5 (1999).

[548] WAYNE LAFAVE & AUSTIN SCOTT, CRIMINAL LAW § 5.10(a) (2d ed. 1986).

[549] ILL. ANN. STAT. ch. 38, para. 7-5 (Smith-Hurd 1989), 1961 Committee Comments, at 412 (revised).

[550] 41 Ill. App. 3d 825, 355 N.E.2d 153 (1st Dist. 1976) (convictions for voluntary manslaughter and aggravated battery reversed).

[551] People v. Lenzi, 41 Ill. App. 3d 825, 836, 355 N.E.2d 153, 163 (1st Dist. 1976).

[552] People v. Lenzi, 41 Ill. App. 3d 825, 836, 355 N.E.2d 153, 163 (1st Dist. 1976).

§ 19.54.   — Arrest by Private Citizen.

The private person's use of force in making an arrest is governed by section 5/7-6 of chapter 720. It reads:

(a) A private person who makes, or assists another private person in making a lawful arrest is justified in the use of any force which he would be justified in using if he were summoned or directed by a peace officer to make such arrest, except that he is justified in the use of force likely to cause death or great bodily harm only when he reasonably believes that such force is necessary to prevent death or great bodily harm to himself or another.

(b) A private person who is summoned or directed by a peace officer to assist in making an arrest which is unlawful, is justified in the use of any force which he would be justified in using if the arrest were lawful, unless he knows that the arrest is unlawful.[553]

Although caselaw is basically nonexistent in this area, the legislative drafting Committee Comments indicate that the section was designed to clearly define "the private person's more limited right to use deadly force, and, on the other hand, his somewhat greater protection than that of a peace officer in the case of an unlawful arrest."[554]

Where a private person attempts to make a lawful arrest, he or she is justified in using that force which he or she reasonably believes is necessary to effect the arrest, except that he or she is justified in using deadly force only when he or she reasonably believes it is necessary to prevent death or great bodily harm to himself or herself or another.[555] In other words, in making the arrest, a private citizen enjoys the right of self-defense and defense of another in responding to the arrestee's illegal show of force.[556] In *People v. Harmon*,[557] a Burger King security guard justifiably hit a vandal on the head with a nightstick to detain him until police could arrive.[558] In this case, the security guard had asked several boisterous people drinking beverages not purchased at Burger King to leave.

---

[553] 720 ILCS 5/7-6 (1999).

[554] ILL. ANN. STAT. ch. 38, para. 7-6 (Smith-Hurd 1989), 1961 Committee Comments, at 416 (revised).

[555] ILL. ANN. STAT. ch. 38, para. 7-6 (Smith-Hurd 1989), 1961 Committee Comments, at 416 (revised).

[556] ILL. ANN. STAT. ch. 38, para. 7-6 (Smith-Hurd 1989), 1961 Committee Comments, at 416 (revised). *See also* People v. Rickman, 73 Ill. App. 3d 755, 760-61, 391 N.E.2d 1114, 1118 (3d Dist. 1979) (where security officer sustained injuries in attempting to apprehend defendant for theft, defendant's resistance to officer's apprehension was not justified, but officer's use of force was justified).

[557] 200 Ill. App. 3d 411, 558 N.E.2d 173 (1st Dist. 1990).

[558] People v. Harmon, 200 Ill. App. 3d 411, 412, 558 N.E.2d 173, 175 (1st Dist. 1990).

One of these people then scattered some decorative flowers and dirt on the floor. An employee called the police and the guard asked the vandal to remain until the police could arrive. The man ignored the guard and tried to leave. The guard repeated his request for the man to remain and threatened to use his handcuffs if necessary. The man exacerbated the situation when he pushed the guard in the chest hard enough to throw him against a wall. The appellate court found that, after the man escalated the violence, the security guard's action in hitting the man over the head with a nightstick was reasonable in order to detain him until the police could arrive.[559]

It is apparent that the private citizen cannot, as is the case with a peace officer, use deadly force to prevent the defeat of the arrest itself; to prevent the escape of a forcible felon; to prevent the escape of an arrestee who is fleeing with a dangerous weapon; or to prevent the escape of an arrestee who he or she believes poses a future danger to the public at large (as the peace officer is authorized to do)[560] unless he or she reasonably believes he or she or another is threatened by the arrestee's escape methods. In effect, then, a private citizen can resist the arrestee's show of deadly force but cannot otherwise prevent the arrestee's escape.

> [I]n view of the ready means of summoning peace officers and the mobility of such officers, doubt exists that it is necessary to give a private person the right to use deadly force to make an arrest after an offense has been committed, when he is in no danger himself: The evaluation of the necessity to use deadly force should be limited to the professional law enforcement officer. Consequently, Subsection [5/]7-6(a) would limit to the personal-defense situation the private person's right to use deadly force in attempting an arrest.[561]

Concerning the use of nondeadly force to effect the arrest, the private citizen is in effect given the same, if not slightly broader, authority as a peace officer. In other words, where the citizen reasonably believes an arrest is authorized, he or she can resort to reasonable force in effecting his or her purpose. The assessment for the need to arrest will apparently be given the greatest protection where the private person is summoned by a police officer unless the private person summoned knows the arrest to be unlawful.[562] The citizen's good faith assistance is justified unless he or she knows the arrest is unlawful, even if it turns out that the peace officer was exceeding his or her authority.

---

[559] People v. Harmon, 200 Ill. App. 3d 411, 414, 558 N.E.2d 173, 175 (1st Dist. 1990).

[560] 720 ILCS 5/7-5 (1999).

[561] ILL. ANN. STAT. ch. 38, para. 7-6 (Smith-Hurd 1989), 1961 Committee Comments, at 416 (revised).

[562] 720 ILCS 5/7-6(b) (1999).

§ 19.55.   — Prevention of Escape.

Under section 5/7-9 of the Criminal Code of 1961, where a peace officer or citizen has an arrestee in his or her custody, he or she is justified in using the same force to prevent the escape of the arrestee as he or she would have used if he or she were arresting that person. Section 5/7-9 provides:

> (a) A peace officer or other person who has an arrested person in his custody is justified in the use of such force to prevent the escape of the arrested person from custody as he would be justified in using if he were arresting such person.
>
> (b) A guard or other peace officer is justified in the use of force, including force likely to cause death or great bodily harm, which he reasonably believes to be necessary to prevent the escape from a penal institution of a person whom the officer reasonably believes to be lawfully detained in such institution under sentence for an offense or awaiting trial or commitment for an offense.[563]

As with the previous section discussed herein, there is essentially no caselaw dealing with this provision. However, the legislative intent is to provide under subsection (a) of 5/7-9 the same range of authority to the peace officer and private person, respectively, which that person enjoys with respect to his or her power of arrest.[564] In other words, nondeadly force can be used where reasonably necessary by either the peace officer or the private citizen to ward off an escape. Deadly force can be used by either type of actor in the situation in which the arrestee's escape methods are reasonably believed to threaten the life of the actor or another. In other words, where the resistance is deadly, the actor's show of force can be deadly if reasonably necessary. Concerning the true escape situation, where there is no indication of imminent endangerment to person, only the peace officer (or someone in aid of the officer) can prevent the escape of the forcible felon (as limited by *Garner*),[565] the escape of the person who is employing a dangerous weapon, or the escape of the person who poses a substantial danger to others in the future.

Subsection (b) concerns the escape from a place of confinement, as distinguished from personal custody after arrest.[566] Again, a reasonable belief is all that is required to justify force designed to halt the escape. The Committee Comments state, for example, that a guard or other person in charge of prisoners

---

[563] 720 ILCS 5/7-9 (1999).

[564] ILL. ANN. STAT. ch. 38, para. 7-9 (Smith-Hurd 1989), 1961 Committee Comments, at 425-26 (revised).

[565] Tennessee v. Garner, 471 U.S. 1 (1985).

[566] ILL. ANN. STAT. ch. 38, para. 7-9 (Smith-Hurd 1989), 1961 Committee Comments, at 426 (revised).

cannot be expected to know the history of each prisoner.[567] In view of the often sudden, unexpected, and desperate nature of an escape, it is justifiable to assume that a prisoner may resort to using deadly force where available.[568] The terms of the statute do not contemplate a private citizen's use of force to prevent escape from a penal institution.

§ 19.56.   — Execution of Death Sentence.

The final public authority justification appearing in the Illinois penal code is "execution of death sentence." Section 5/7-10 provides:

> A public officer who, in the exercise of his official duty, puts a person to death pursuant to a sentence of a court of competent jurisdiction, is justified if he acts in accordance with the sentence pronounced and the law prescribing the procedure for execution of a death sentence.[569]

Thus, if a physician, as authorized by the Code of Criminal Procedure, administers to a person sentenced to death an intravenous lethal quantity of an ultra-short-acting barbiturate in combination with a chemical paralytic agent until death is pronounced,[570] he or she would be justified in doing so.

§ 19.57.   Defense of Consent.

Although there is no defense of consent included in articles 5/4, 5/6, or 5/7 (where virtually all of the Illinois affirmative defenses appear), "consent" is a defense in certain circumstances. For instance, consent is a defense to the article 5/12 Criminal Sexual Assault Act crimes in particular instances.[571] Section 5/12-17 of chapter 720 provides for such a defense to the offenses of aggravated criminal sexual assault, criminal sexual assault, predatory criminal sexual assault of a child, aggravated criminal sexual abuse, and criminal sexual abuse.[572]

For example, in *People v. Haywood*,[573] the Illinois Supreme Court stated that where force is proven in a criminal sexual assault prosecution, this implicitly

---

[567] ILL. ANN. STAT. ch. 38, para. 7-9 (Smith-Hurd 1989), 1961 Committee Comments, at 426 (revised).

[568] ILL. ANN. STAT. ch. 38, para. 7-9 (Smith-Hurd 1989), 1961 Committee Comments, at 426 (revised).

[569] 720 ILCS 5/7-10 (1999).

[570] 725 ILCS 5/119-5(a)(1) (1999). If this means of carrying out capital punishment is ruled unconstitutional, the death sentence will be carried out by electrocution. 725 ILCS 5/119-5(a)(2) (1999). This prospect is highly doubtful in light of Heckler v. Chaney, 470 U.S. 821 (1985) (federal Food and Drug Administration's failure to ensure that drugs used for lethal injections were effective was upheld).

[571] *See* ch. 8 of this treatise for a discussion of the Criminal Sexual Assault Act.

[572] *See* 720 ILCS 5/12-17(a) (1999).

[573] 118 Ill. 2d 263, 515 N.E.2d 45 (1987).

demonstrates lack of consent unless the defendant offers evidence supportive of consent which, if offered, the state must disprove beyond a reasonable doubt.[574] On the other hand, consent is not a defense to other sex crimes, such as prostitution, even though it is claimed that the sexual conduct occurred between consenting adults.[575]

In some situations, consent is recognized as a defense as a result of Illinois caselaw. For instance, consent has been recognized as a defense to certain crimes against the person, such as kidnapping.[576] So, too, the courts have held consent to be a defense to certain crimes against property, such as burglary[577] or theft.[578] In a few instances, the defense of consent appears within the definition of the crime itself — for example, arson[579] and criminal damage to property.[580]

Obviously, consent is not a defense to all crimes. Since criminality is considered an affront to the integrity of the state and the various interests it attempts to protect, as opposed to a mere affront to the individual victimized, a defendant cannot invariably succeed in advancing the defense of consent.[581] For instance, the crime of murder was conceived not only to protect potential murder victims but also to protect the sanctity of life within the state. Thus, a defendant who takes the life of a person and argues that the act is justified because the victim was desirous of such a result, such as in a so-called mercy killing situation where the victim was painfully enduring the agony of terminal cancer, there is no defense.[582] Also, where the victim of an aggravated battery based on injurious touching consented to engage in a fistfight, this did not constitute a defense.[583] But, there are no hard-and-fast rules against, for instance, the use of physical force against another. Since societal values accept some forms of infliction of physical attacks, most notably in legitimate athletic contests such as boxing and football, the willingness of the participants will prevail.[584]

---

[574] People v. Haywood, 118 Ill. 2d 263, 274, 515 N.E.2d 45, 50 (1987).

[575] *See* ch. 8 for a discussion of prostitution.

[576] *See* ch. 7 for a discussion of kidnapping.

[577] *See* ch. 13 for a discussion of burglary.

[578] *See* ch. 11 for a discussion of theft.

[579] 720 ILCS 5/20-1(a) (1999). *See* ch. 13 for a discussion of arson.

[580] 720 ILCS 5/21-1 (1999). *See* ch. 13 for a discussion of criminal damage to property.

[581] *See* M. CHERIF BASSIOUNI, SUBSTANTIVE CRIMINAL LAW 447 (1978).

[582] M. CHERIF BASSIOUNI, SUBSTANTIVE CRIMINAL LAW 448 (1978). *See also* People v. Williams, 265 Ill. App. 3d 283, 638 N.E.2d 345 (1st Dist. 1994) (defendant's fatal shooting of his wife, who had been suffering from multiple sclerosis for many years, was second degree murder).

[583] People v. Reckers, 251 Ill. App. 3d 790, 792-93, 623 N.E.2d 811, 814 (4th Dist 1993).

[584] Of course, if the participants in such a contest actually agreed to "fight to the death," this would not be condoned by the state as legitimate because of the intrinsic value of life. For similar reasons, a wholly illegitimate contest, such as a game of Russian roulette or a duel, would not be tolerated.

With respect to crimes against property, the consent defense is more likely to be viable, since society's paramount concern is the avoidance of wrongful appropriation of the goods of another.[585] Thus, if a homeowner had no objection and, indeed, encouraged others to enter his or her home at their whim and caprice and to carry off whatever chattel they saw fit, the homeowner's consent would exonerate these persons from charges of burglary or theft. Since these crimes are designed to protect the proprietary rights of property owners, there is no crime because of the nonexistence of an asserted breach of those rights.

It must be recognized that certain classes of persons may not have the capacity to consent to certain forms of activity, although others might have that capacity concerning the same activity. For example, a minor girl might not have the capacity to consent to sexual activity, although an adult woman might have that power. Traditionally, it has been held that the girl under age cannot consent to statutory rape even though an adult woman has the authority to engage in sexual activity not otherwise criminal.[586]

§ 19.58.   Defense of Statute of Limitations.

Article 5/3 contains another defense of major importance, namely, the statute of limitations, which is a defense to most, but not all, Illinois crimes. Normally, a felony must be prosecuted within three years of its commission, while a misdemeanor is to be prosecuted within one year and six months.[587] By "prosecution," the statute requires that the prosecution has "commenced" within this period, not that it has reached ultimate fruition within this time frame.[588]

This defense is subject to certain important exceptions. First, the crimes of first degree murder, second degree murder, involuntary manslaughter, reckless homicide, treason, arson, aggravated arson, and forgery are exempt from this rule and "may be prosecuted at any time."[589] Second, the period within which the prosecution of other crimes (not exempt from the statute of limitations) must be commenced does not include any period within which (1) "the defendant is not usually and publicly resident within the state," (2) the "defendant is a public officer and the offense charged is theft of public funds while in public office," or (3) a "prosecution is pending against the defendant for the same conduct, even if the indictment or information which commences the prosecution is quashed or the proceedings thereon are set aside, or are reversed on appeal."[590]

---

[585] *See* M. CHERIF BASSIOUNI, SUBSTANTIVE CRIMINAL LAW 447 (1978).

[586] *See* M. CHERIF BASSIOUNI, SUBSTANTIVE CRIMINAL LAW 447 (1978).

[587] 720 ILCS 5/3-5(b) (1999).

[588] 720 ILCS 5/3-5(b) (1999).

[589] 720 ILCS 5/3-5(a) (1999).

[590] 720 ILCS 5/3-7 (1999). *See also* People v. Laughlin, 293 Ill. App. 3d 194, 197-99, 687 N.E.2d 1162, 1165-66 (2d Dist. 1997) (tolling provision that distinguishes between residents and non-residents not violative of equal protection).

Third, there is a special provision dealing with prosecution for "theft involving a breach of a fiduciary obligation."[591] Specifically, the statute of limitations term does not begin to run where an "aggrieved person" victimized by such a theft (1) is a minor or a person under legal disability, in which case the term begins to run one year after the minority or legal disability terminates, or (2) is unaware of the theft, whereupon the term begins to run one year after the discovery of the theft.[592] Next, there is a special provision concerning "misconduct in public office by a public officer or employee."[593] Here, the term does not begin to run until one year following the discovery of the offense.[594]

Any prosecution for any offense involving sexual conduct or sexual penetration, as defined in article 5/12,[595] where the victim and the defendant are family members may be commenced within one year after the victim has attained the age of eighteen.[596] A prosecution for child pornography, indecent solicitation of a child, soliciting for a juvenile prostitute, juvenile pimping, or exploitation of a child must be initiated within one year after the victim has achieved the age of eighteen *or* within three years of the commission of the offense, whichever is later.[597]

Any prosecution of criminal sexual assault, aggravated criminal sexual assault, aggravated criminal sexual assault, predatory criminal sexual assault of a child, criminal sexual abuse, or aggravated criminal sexual abuse can proceed within one year after the victim has turned eighteen *or* within three years of the offense, whichever is later.[598] Also, any prosecution for a crime involving sexual conduct or sexual penetration, where the defendant was within a professional or fiduciary relationship, real or purported, with the victim can be prosecuted within one year after the discovery of the offense by the victim.[599]

A prosecution of violations of the Environmental Protection Act may be prosecuted within five years of their discovery.[600] A prosecution of attempted first degree murder may be prosecuted within seven years after commission.[601] A prosecution for criminal sexual assault or aggravated criminal sexual assault

---

[591] 720 ILCS 5/3-6(a) (1999).

[592] 720 ILCS 5/3-6(a) (1999). Where the aggrieved person is unaware of the theft, the period of limitation cannot be "extended more than 3 years beyond the expiration of the period otherwise applicable." *Id.*

[593] 720 ILCS 5/3-6(b) (1999).

[594] 720 ILCS 5/3-6(b) (1999). "However, in no such case is the period of limitation so extended more than 3 years beyond the expiration of the period otherwise applicable." *Id.*

[595] 720 ILCS 5/12-12(e), (f) (1999).

[596] 720 ILCS 5/3-6(c) (1999).

[597] 720 ILCS 5/3-6(d) (1999).

[598] 720 ILCS 5/3-6(d) (1999).

[599] 720 ILCS 5/3-6(e) (1999).

[600] 720 ILCS 5/3-6(f) (1999) (referring to 415 ILCS 5/44 (1999)).

[601] 720 ILCS 5/3-6(g) (1999).

can be commenced within five years of commission if reported to authorities within six months of commission.[602]

In some cases, a crime may be divisible into a sequence of acts spread over a period of time. The code addresses this possible problem by providing that "[w]hen an offense is based on a series of acts performed at different times, the period of limitations . . . starts at the time when the last such act is committed."[603] Exactly when conduct constitutes the last act sufficient to start the statute of limitations is determined by the nature of the offense. Thus, charges brought five years after the defendant violated a bail bond should have been barred, absent some reason for tolling the statute of limitations, because this was not a continuing offense.[604] An offense is considered to be a continuing offense when it "poses a continuing threat to society," as where a convict escapes from jail.[605] Also, when the criminal conduct "can be defined as a series of related acts constituting a single [offense] such as conspiracy or embezzlement," the statute of limitations will commence with the last act in the series.[606]

Technically, the statute of limitations defense is not an affirmative defense like the others discussed in this chapter. This non-exculpatory defense[607] must be raised before trial pursuant to a motion to dismiss.[608] If it is not so raised, the defense may be waived.[609]

§ 19.59. Defense of Failure to Simultaneously Commence All Prosecutions Arising out of Same Conduct.

Not only does article 5/3 require the state's attorney to prosecute certain offenses within a prescribed period, it also forces the prosecutor ordinarily to commence the prosecution of all crimes arising out of the "same act" simultaneously.[610] Subsection 5/3-3(a) of the code recognizes that "[w]hen the same conduct of a defendant may establish the commission of more than one offense, the defendant may be prosecuted for each such offense."[611] Also, prosecution of an accused for multiple crimes arising out of the same conduct is, of course, limited

---

[602] 720 ILCS 5/3-6(h) (1999).

[603] 720 ILCS 5/3-8 (1999).

[604] People v. Grogan, 197 Ill. App. 3d 18, 22, 554 N.E.2d 665, 667 (1st Dist. 1990).

[605] People v. Grogan, 197 Ill. App. 3d 18, 21, 554 N.E.2d 665, 667 (1st Dist. 1990).

[606] People v. Grogan, 197 Ill. App. 3d 18, 21-22, 554 N.E.2d 665, 667 (1st Dist. 1990).

[607] *See* 2 PAUL ROBINSON, CRIMINAL LAW DEFENSES § 202 (1984). A "nonexculpatory defense" arises "where an important public policy other than that of convicting culpable offenders, is protected or furthered by foregoing trial or conviction and punishment." *Id.* § 202(b).

[608] 725 ILCS 5/114-1(a)(2) (1999).

[609] 725 ILCS 5/114-1(b) (1999).

[610] 720 ILCS 5/3-3(b) (1999).

[611] 720 ILCS 5/3-3(a) (1999).

to some extent by the state and federal double jeopardy bar and by the Illinois "same physical act" doctrine, which was discussed at length in chapter 1.[612]

Neither double jeopardy nor the "same physical act" doctrine requires the prosecution of multiple crimes arising out of a single transaction in a single action. In *Ciucci v. Illinois*,[613] the defendant murdered his wife and three children. The state's attorney in that case initially prosecuted the defendant for the murder of his wife, gained a conviction, and asked the jury (responsible for sentencing) to impose the death penalty. Instead, they sentenced the defendant to a term of imprisonment. Thereafter, the state's attorney, bent on seeing the defendant die for his crimes, prosecuted the defendant for the death of one of his children, gained a conviction, and asked for the death penalty, but this second jury also fixed the sentence at imprisonment. Finally, the prosecutor prosecuted the defendant for murder a third time, now for the death of a second child, gained a conviction, and a jury determined that death should be the penalty.[614] In a 5-4 decision, the Supreme Court of the United States ruled that it was not fundamentally unfair or a violation of double jeopardy for the prosecutor to pursue these multiple charges individually instead of simultaneously.[615] Ciucci was ultimately put to death in the state's electric chair.[616]

Not impressed by the state's attorney's method or by the *Ciucci* majority holding, the Illinois legislature enacted the following law:

> (b) If the several offenses are known to the proper prosecuting officer at the time of commencing the prosecution and are within the jurisdiction of a single court, they must be prosecuted in a single prosecution, except as provided in Subsection (c), if they are based on the same act.
>
> (c) When two or more offenses are charged as required by Subsection (b), the court in the interest of justice may order that one or more of such charges shall be tried separately.[617]

Subsection (c) contemplates the situation where it is determined that the defendant might be prejudiced if the trial court fails to sever the charges in question for purpose of trial.[618] Ordinarily, this prejudice is most likely to arise where the jury is considering multiple charges in a single trial; where different evidence is relevant to some, but not all, of the charges (for example, evidence

---

[612] *See* ch. 1 for a discussion of the same physical act doctrine.

[613] 356 U.S. 571 (1958).

[614] *See* ILL. ANN. STAT. ch. 38, para. 3-3 (Smith-Hurd 1989), 1961 Committee Comments, at 98-99 (revised), for a discussion of this case.

[615] *See also* Hoag v. New Jersey, 356 U.S. 464 (1958) for a similar holding.

[616] Bowman, *The year the electric chair claimed its last victim in Illinois*, CHI. TRIB. MAG., October 10, 1982, at 12.

[617] 720 ILCS 5/3-3(b), 3-3(c) (1999).

[618] *See* 725 ILCS 5/114-8 (1999) (motion for severance to be granted where potential "prejudice" exists).

A is relevant only to count I, evidence B is relevant only to count II, and so on); and where the trial court fears the jury is incapable of compartmentalizing the evidence concerning each count, notwithstanding jury instructions to do so.[619]

In the absence of problems of prejudice caused by the joinder of offenses, the prosecutor is obliged under subsection (b) to pursue multiple counts arising from the same conduct in a single prosecution. Where the prosecutor fails to prosecute multiple charges arising out of the same act in an earlier prosecution and therefore institutes a prosecution of the remaining count or counts that were known to him or her in the earlier prosecution, the latter charge or charges must be dismissed on an appropriate pretrial motion.[620] Like the previous "defense," this barrier to conviction is not an exculpatory defense that justifies or excuses otherwise criminal conduct. Rather, it exonerates because of policy considerations — in this case, the unfairness of unnecessary, repetitive prosecutions.

The reach of section 5/3-3 was clarified in *People v. Mueller*,[621] where a defendant was successfully prosecuted for concealment of a homicidal death following his earlier acquittal on two related murder charges in another county.[622] The court noted that subsection (b) of section 5/3-3 requires simultaneous prosecution "*if they are based on the same act.*"[623] The fact that the shootings and later concealment of the shootings were related was considered irrelevant.[624]

> The purpose of this section as enacted was to preclude successive prosecutions where more than one person was injured by a single act of the accused, such as setting off an explosive.[625]

Because the murder and concealment charges were based on separate acts of the accused, the compulsory joinder statute did not apply.[626]

In *People v. Jackson*,[627] the Illinois Supreme Court ruled that the compulsory joinder statute did not require the simultaneous prosecution of a defendant for

---

[619] *See* 725 ILCS 5/111-4 (1999) (joinder of offenses and defendants), 725 ILCS 5/114-7 (1999) (joinder of related prosecutions), 725 ILCS 5/114-8 (1999) (severance required where prejudice exists). *Cf.* John F. Decker, *Joinder and Severance in Federal Criminal Cases: An Examination of Judicial Interpretation of the Federal Rules*, 53 NOTRE DAME L. REV. 147 (1977) for a thorough discussion of this and related misjoinder problems that arise under the Federal Rules of Criminal Procedure, which are quite similar to those in Illinois.

[620] 725 ILCS 5/114-1(a)(2) (1999).

[621] 109 Ill. 2d 378, 488 N.E.2d 523 (1985).

[622] People v. Mueller, 109 Ill. 2d 378, 381, 488 N.E.2d 523, 524 (1985).

[623] People v. Mueller, 109 Ill. 2d 378, 385, 488 N.E.2d 523, 526 (1985), quoting ILL. REV. STAT. ch. 38, para. 3-3 (1981) (emphasis in original).

[624] People v. Mueller, 109 Ill. 2d 378, 385, 488 N.E.2d 523, 526 (1985).

[625] People v. Mueller, 109 Ill. 2d 378, 385, 488 N.E.2d 523, 526 (1985).

[626] People v. Mueller, 109 Ill. 2d 378, 386, 488 N.E.2d 523, 527 (1985).

[627] 118 Ill. 2d 179, 514 N.E.2d 983 (1987).

reckless homicide and driving under the influence.[628] In this case, the defendant was operating an automobile while intoxicated and was involved in a mishap resulting in a fatality.[629] At his initial court appearance, he entered a plea of guilty to DUI and the illegal transportation of alcohol.[630] After the pleas were accepted, the state successfully moved to enter a nolle prosequi to both charges and then indicted the defendant for two counts of reckless homicide.[631]

Since the pleas to the DUI and illegal transportation of alcohol charges had been entered and accepted by the trial court, the court ruled that double jeopardy attached to these offenses.[632] However, the court held that double jeopardy did not preclude the reckless homicide prosecution, since these various offense involved different elements.[633] Reaching the compulsory joinder issue, the court stated that section 5/3-3 provisions "do not apply to offenses that have been charged by use of a uniform citation and complaint form provided for traffic offenses.[634] The court reasoned:

> We do not believe that the legislature intended that a driver could plead guilty to a traffic offense on a traffic ticket issued by a police officer and thereby avoid prosecution of a serious offense brought by the State's Attorney, such as reckless homicide. . . .[635]

In *People v. Quigley*,[636] the Illinois Supreme Court ruled that misdemeanor and felony charges of driving under the influence should have been brought in the same proceeding pursuant to the compulsory joinder statute.[637] In that case, the court ruled that the misdemeanor and felony charges arose out of the same act of the defendant and, consequently, the trial court's dismissal of the misdemeanor DUI charge because of non-compliance with the state's speedy trial statute required dismissal of the felony DUI charge.[638]

§ 19.60.   Defense of Former Prosecution.

The last significant barrier to a criminal prosecution appearing in article 5/3 will arise by reason of "former prosecution," which is specifically addressed in section 5/3-4. Most of what is contemplated within this section is governed by

---

[628] People v. Jackson, 118 Ill. 2d 179, 193-94, 514 N.E.2d 983, 988-89 (1987).
[629] People v. Jackson, 118 Ill. 2d 179, 183, 514 N.E.2d 983, 984 (1987).
[630] People v. Jackson, 118 Ill. 2d 179, 183, 514 N.E.2d 983, 984 (1987).
[631] People v. Jackson, 118 Ill. 2d 179, 183, 514 N.E.2d 983, 984 (1987).
[632] People v. Jackson, 118 Ill. 2d 179, 188-89, 514 N.E.2d 983, 987 (1987).
[633] People v. Jackson, 118 Ill. 2d 179, 189-90, 514 N.E.2d 983, 987 (1987).
[634] People v. Jackson, 118 Ill. 2d 179, 192, 514 N.E.2d 983, 988-89 (1987).
[635] People v. Jackson, 118 Ill. 2d 179, 193, 514 N.E.2d 983, 989 (1987).
[636] 183 Ill. 2d 1, 697 N.E.2d 735 (1998).
[637] People v. Quigley, 183 Ill. 2d 1, 7-11, 697 N.E.2d 735, 738-40 (1998).
[638] People v. Quigley, 183 Ill. 2d 1, 12-16, 697 N.E.2d 735, 741-42 (1998).

the state and federal bars against double jeopardy.[639] Thus, where the defendant was previously convicted or acquitted of a crime (or essentially the same crime), the double jeopardy clause of the Fifth Amendment and the Illinois Constitution will bar another prosecution of the crime.[640]

For example, where defendant had pled guilty to felony child abduction, an indirect criminal contempt proceeding arising out of his violation of a child custody order, based on the same act that prompted the child abduction charge, was violative of double jeopardy.[641] Where defendant pled guilty to possession of a stolen vehicle in one county, this barred his prosecution in another county for robbery and car-jacking arising out of the same incident.[642]

What double jeopardy does not prohibit, however, is a prosecution of an offender for a crime in a state after the offender has been previously convicted or acquitted of the same crime in another state or at the federal level. A major limitation on the reach of the bar against double jeopardy is the "dual sovereignty doctrine."[643] In *United States v. Lanza*,[644] the Supreme Court first announced this doctrine by stating "an act denounced as a crime by both national and state sovereignties is an offense against the peace and dignity of both and may be punished by each."[645] Later, the Supreme Court reaffirmed this doctrine in *Bartkus v. Illinois*,[646] where a state conviction of a defendant for robbing a bank in Illinois was approved after he had been earlier acquitted for essentially the same crime in federal court.[647]

In subsection (c) of section 5/3-4, the Illinois legislature has determined that a former prosecution for a crime in another state or at the federal level shall constitute a barrier to a prosecution for the same offense in Illinois.[648] This rule, which essentially renders the dual sovereignty principle meaningless in Illinois, applies both to former prosecutions resulting in conviction and to those resulting

---

[639] *See* ch. 1 of this treatise. *See also* CHARLES WHITEBREAD & CHRISTOPHER SLOBIGIN, CRIMINAL PROCEDURE §§ 30.01-30.07 (3d ed. 1993).

[640] U.S. CONST. amend. V; ILL. CONST. art. I, § 10.

[641] In re Marriage of D'Attomo, 211 Ill. App. 3d 914, 922-23, 570 N.E.2d 796, 801 (1st Dist. 1991).

[642] People v. Eggerman, 292 Ill. App. 3d 644, 649-51, 685 N.E.2d 948, 951-52 (1st Dist. 1997) (plea to lesser included offense bars prosecution for greater offense).

[643] WAYNE LAFAVE & JEROME ISRAEL, CRIMINAL PROCEDURE § 25.5 (3d ed. 1992).

[644] 260 U.S. 377 (1922).

[645] United States v. Lanza, 260 U.S. 377, 382 (1922).

[646] 359 U.S. 121 (1959).

[647] Bartkus v. Illinois, 359 U.S. 121, 138-39 (1959); *see also* Abbate v. United States, 359 U.S. 187, 195-96 (1959), where the Court approved a federal conviction after the defendant had been convicted for the same crime in a state court and Heath v. Alabama, 474 U.S. 82, 88-90 (1985), where a defendant was successfully prosecuted for the same murder in two states.

[648] 720 ILCS 5/3-4(c) (1999).

in acquittal.[649] Additionally, in determining whether the former prosecution in the sister state or federal court was for the "same" crime, the *Blockburger* standard from double jeopardy caselaw is followed: the crimes are the same "unless each prosecution requires proof of a fact not required in the other prosecution. . . ."[650] Thus, because of their different elements, double jeopardy barred neither a state prosecution for intimidation after a federal acquittal for Hobbs Act extortion nor a state prosecution for bribery after a federal acquittal for mail fraud.[651] Similarly, where defendant was previously acquitted of a federal RICO charge, where a predicate crime was a murder committed in Illinois, he could thereafter be prosecuted for that same murder at the state level inasmuch as the State of Illinois prosecution for murder would require proof of facts different than those required in the federal prosecution for RICO.[652]

Like the other article 5/3 defenses reviewed herein, this is not a defense that truly exonerates the accused. Rather, the legislature has determined that it is appropriate policy to posit that a trial of an offender for a crime is unfair where the offender has already suffered a former prosecution for the same crime. Additionally, as with the other article 5/3 barriers to a trial, this "defense" must be asserted before trial pursuant to a motion to dismiss.

---

[649] 720 ILCS 5/3-4(c) (1999).
[650] 720 ILCS 5/3-4(c) (1999). *See also* Blockburger v. United States, 284 U.S. 299 (1931).
[651] People v. Kaye, 154 Ill. App. 3d 562, 569-71, 507 N.E.2d 12, 18-19 (1st Dist. 1987).
[652] People v. Porter, 156 Ill. 2d 218, 219-24, 620 N.E.2d 381, 383-385 (1993).

APPENDIX

SENTENCES FOR ILLINOIS CRIMES

In Illinois, the Unified Code of Corrections sets out six classifications of felonies, three classifications of misdemeanors, one category of "petty offenses," and one category of "business offenses." *See* 730 ILCS 5/5-5-1 (1999). Each classification carries a different potential sanction. Although most Illinois crimes fall into only one classification, some fall into two or more where, for instance, the crime involved an element of aggravation or where the offender has been previously convicted of the same offense and an enhanced sentence is imposed. The outlines below provide (1) an indication of the potential sanction attached to each offense classification and (2) a listing of Illinois offenses followed by an indication of the class or classes into which each offense falls.

GENERAL OFFENSE CLASSIFICATIONS AND RELATED SANCTIONS

Felonies

FIRST-DEGREE MURDER (as a separate class of felony):
— Where elements of aggravation existed: death penalty or natural life
— Where there was no element of aggravation or prior conviction:
> Imprisonment minimum — 20 years
> Imprisonment maximum — 60 years
> Fine — not to exceed $25,000 for persons and $50,000 for corporations

CLASS X: Imprisonment minimum — 6 years
Imprisonment maximum — 30 years
Fine — not to exceed $25,000 unless specific offense designates otherwise

CLASS 1: Imprisonment minimum — 4 years
Imprisonment maximum — 15 years
Fine — not to exceed $25,000 unless specific offense designates otherwise

CLASS 2: Imprisonment minimum — 3 years
Imprisonment maximum — 7 years
Fine — not to exceed $25,000 unless specific offense designates otherwise

CLASS 3: Imprisonment minimum — 2 years
Imprisonment maximum — 5 years

Fine — not to exceed $25,000 unless specific offense designates otherwise

CLASS 4:   Imprisonment minimum — 1 year
Imprisonment maximum — 3 years
Fine — not to exceed $25,000 unless specific offense designates otherwise

See 730 ILCS 5/5-8-1 (1999) (imprisonment), *id.* 5/5-9-1 (fines).

In regard to felonies, where certain elements of aggravation appear, the court may sentence the defendant to an "extended term" beyond those noted above. *See id.* 5/5-5-3.2 (factors in aggravation), *id.* 5/5-8-2 (extended term).

Misdemeanors

CLASS A: Imprisonment minimum — none
Imprisonment maximum — 364 days
Fine — not to exceed $2,500 unless specific offense designates otherwise

CLASS B: Imprisonment minimum — none
Imprisonment maximum — 6 months
Fine — not to exceed $1,500

CLASS C: Imprisonment minimum — none
Imprisonment maximum — 30 days
Fine — not to exceed $1,500

Petty Offenses

Fine — not to exceed $1,000

Business Offense

Fine — as specified in the statute

See 730 ILCS 5/5-8-3 (1999) (imprisonment), *id.* 5/5-9-1 (fines).

Beyond the imprisonment and fine sanctions applicable to the various Illinois crimes, as an *alternative*, the sentencing court may impose a sentence of probation (*id.* 5/5-6-1), conditional discharge (*id.*), supervision (*id.*), or periodic imprisonment (*id.* 5/5-7-1) for certain crimes, but not for others of more serious nature (for example, first-degree murder, Class X felonies, and so on).

CRIMINAL CODE OF 1961 — OFFENSES

Inchoate Crimes

Solicitation (5/8-1): Imprisonment or fine, or both, not to exceed the maximum provided for the offense solicited; however, penalty shall not exceed corresponding maximum limit as set out for criminal attempt
— Exceptions:
— Solicitation of murder (5/8-1.1): Class X felony (15-30 years)
— Solicitation of murder for hire (5/8-1.2): Class X felony (20-40 years)
Conspiracy (5/8-2): Imprisonment or fine, or both, not to exceed the maximum provided for the offense that is the object of the conspiracy (subject to miscellaneous exceptions)
Attempt (5/8-4): Imprisonment or fine, or both, not to exceed the maximum provided for the offense attempted (except for an attempt to commit armed violence (5/33A-2)), although:
— Attempted first-degree murder: Class X felony
— Attempt to commit other Class X felonies: Class 1 felony
— Attempt to commit a Class 1 felony: Class 2 felony
— Attempt to commit a Class 2 felony: Class 3 felony
— Attempt to commit any other felony: Class A misdemeanor

Homicide

First Degree Murder (5/9-1): See above
Intentional Homicide of an Unborn Child (5/9-1.2): Same as for first degree murder except the death penalty may not be imposed
Second Degree Murder (5/9-2): Class 1 felony
Voluntary Manslaughter of an Unborn Child (5/9-2.1): Class 1 felony
Involuntary Manslaughter or Reckless Homicide (5/9-3):
— Class 3 felony
— Class 2 felony for cases of reckless homicide in which the offender was under the influence of drugs or alcohol (3-14 years, if sentenced to a term of imprisonment)
Concealment of Homicidal Death (5/9-3.1): Class 3 felony
Involuntary Manslaughter or Reckless Homicide of an Unborn Child (5/9-3.2): Class 3 felony
Drug Induced Homicide (5/9-3.3): Class X felony (15-30 years)

Kidnaping and Related Offenses

Kidnaping (5/10-1): Class 2 felony
Aggravated Kidnaping (5/10-2): Class X felony
Unlawful Restraint (5/10-3): Class 4 felony

Aggravated Unlawful Restraint (5/10-3.1): Class 3 felony

Forcible Detention (5/10-4): Class 2 felony

Child Abduction (5/10-5):
— First offense: Class 4 felony
— Subsequent offenses: Class 3 felony

Harboring a Runaway (5/10-6): Class A misdemeanor

Aiding and Abetting Child Abduction (5/10-7): Class 4 felony

Unlawful Sale of a Public Conveyance Travel Ticket to a Minor (5/10-8): Class C misdemeanor

Sex Offenses

Indecent Solicitation of a Child (5/11-6):
— When the act, if done, would be criminal sexual abuse: Class A misdemeanor
— When the act, if done, would be criminal sexual assault, aggravated criminal sexual assault, or aggravated criminal sexual abuse: Class 4 felony

Indecent Soliciation of an Adult (5/11-6.5):
— When the act involves sexual penetration, as defined in (5/12-12), with a person under the age of 13: Class X felony
— When the act involves sexual penetration, as defined in (5/12-12), with a person 13 years of age or over but under the age of 17 years: Class 1 felony
— When the act involves sexual conduct, as defined in (5/12-12), with a person under the age of 13 years: Class 2 felony
— When the act involves sexual conduct, as defined in (5/12-12), with a person 13 years of age or older but under the age of 17 years: Class A misdemeanor

Adultery (5/11-7): Class A misdemeanor

Fornication (5/11-8): Class B misdemeanor

Public Indecency (5/11-9): Class A misdemeanor

Sexual Exploitation of a Child (5/11-9.1):
— First offense: Class A misdemeanor
— Subsequent offense: Class 4 felony

Custodial Sexual Misconduct (5/11-9.2): Class 3 felony

Presence Within School Zone by Child Sex Offender (5/11-9.2): Class 4 felony

Sexual Relations Within Families (5/11-11): Class 3 felony

Bigamy (5/11-12): Class 4 felony

Marrying a Bigamist (5/11-13): Class A misdemeanor

Prostitution (5/11-14):
— First or second offense: Class A misdemeanor

— Third or subsequent violation of this section or of this section in any combination with soliciting for a prostitute (5/11-15), keeping a place of prostitution (5/11-17), patronizing a prostitute (5/11-18), patronizing a juvenile prostitute (5/11-18.1), and pimping (5/11-19): Class 4 felony

Solicitation of a Sexual Act (5/11-14.1): Class B misdemeanor

Soliciting for a Prostitute (5/11-15):

— First or second offense: Class A misdemeanor

— Third or subsequent violation of this section or of this section in any combination with prostitution (5/11-14), keeping a place of prostitution (5/11-17), patronizing a prostitute (5/11-18), patronizing a juvenile prostitute (5/11-18.1), and pimping (5/11-19): Class 4 felony

Soliciting for a Juvenile Prostitute (5/11-15.1): Class 1 felony

Pandering (5/11-16): Class 4 felony

Keeping a Place of Prostitution (5/11-17):

— First or second offense: Class A misdemeanor

— Third or subsequent violation of this section or of this section in any combination with prostitution (5/11-14), soliciting for a prostitute (5/11-15), patronizing a prostitute (5/11-18), patronizing a juvenile prostitute (5/11-18.1), and pimping (5/11-19): Class 4 felony

Keeping a Place of Juvenile Prostitution (5/11-17.1):

— First offense: Class 1 felony

— Second or subsequent offense: Class X felony

Patronizing a Prostitute (5/11-18):

— First or second offense: Class A misdemeanor

— Third or subsequent violation of this section or of this section in any combination with prostitution (5/11-14), soliciting for a prostitute (5/11-15), keeping a place of prostitution (5/11-17), patronizing a juvenile prostitute (5/11-18.1), and pimping (5/11-19): Class 4 felony

Patronizing a Juvenile Prostitute (5/11-18.1): Class 4 felony

Pimping (5/11-19):

— First or second offense: Class A misdemeanor

— Third or subsequent violation of this section or of this section in any combination with prostitution (5/11-14), soliciting for a prostitute (5/11-15), keeping a place of prostitution (5/11-17), patronizing a prostitute (5/11-18), and patronizing a juvenile prostitute (5/11-18.1): Class 4 felony

Juvenile Pimping (5/11-19.1): Class 1 felony

Exploitation of a Child (5/11-19.2): Class X felony

Obscenity (5/11-20):

— First offense: Class A misdemeanor

— Subsequent offenses: Class 4 felony

Child Pornography (5/11-20.1):

— Preparation of child pornography, soliciting a child under 18 or a mentally retarded person for pornography, or allowing one's child under 18 or mentally retarded to engage in child pornography: Class 1 felony and mandatory fine (minimum $2,000; maximum $100,000)

— Exhibition of child pornography: Class 1 felony and mandatory fine (minimum $1,500; maximum $100,000)

— Dissemination of child pornography: Class 1 felony and mandatory fine (minimum $1,000; maximum $100,000)

— Possession of child pornography: Class 3 felony and mandatory fine (minimum $1,000; maximum $100,000)

Commercial Film and Photographic Print Processor (5/11-20.2):

— Failure to report: Business offense ($1,000 fine)

Harmful Material (5/11-21):

— First offense: Class A misdemeanor

— Subsequent offense: Class 4 felony

Tie-In Sales of Obscene Publications to Distributions (5/11-22): Petty offense

Bodily Harm

Assault (5/12-1): Class C misdemeanor

Aggravated Assault (5/12-2): Class A misdemeanor

— Assaulting a correctional officer: Class 4 felony

— Involving discharge of a firearm: Class 4 felony

Vehicular Endangerment (5/12-2.5): Class 2 felony

— If death results: Class 1 felony

Battery (5/12-3): Class A misdemeanor

Battery of an Unborn Child (5/12-3.1): Class A misdemeanor

Domestic Battery (5/12-3.2):

— First offense: Class A misdemeanor

— Subsequent offense or prior conviction of violation of order of protection: Class 4 felony

Aggravated Battery (5/12-4): Class 3 felony

Heinous Battery (5/12-4.1): Class X felony

Aggravated Battery with a Firearm (5/12-4.2): Class X felony

Aggravated Battery of a Child (5/12-4.3): Class X felony

Aggravated Battery of an Unborn Child (5/12-4.4): Class 2 felony

Tampering with Foods, Drugs, or Cosmetics (5/12-4.5): Class 2 felony

Aggravated Battery of a Senior Citizen (5/12-4.6): Class 2 felony

Drug Induced Infliction of Great Bodily Harm (5/12-4.7): Class 1 felony

Drug Induced Infliction of Aggravated Battery to a Child Athlete (5/12-4.9):

— First offense: Class A misdemeanor

— Subsequent offense: Class 4 felony

Reckless Conduct (5/12-5): Class A misdemeanor

Criminal Housing Management (5/12-5.1):
  — First offense: Class A misdemeanor
  — Subsequent offense: Class 4 felony
Common Carriers; Gross Neglect (5/12-5.5): Class 4 felony
Intimidation (5/12-6): Class 3 felony
  (subject to imprisonment no less than 2 years and not more than 10 years)
Compelling Organization Membership of Persons (5/12-6.1): Class 1 or Class 2
  felony (depending on circumstances)
Aggravated Intimidation (5/12-6.2): Class 1 or Class 2 felony
Interfering with the Reporting of Domestic Violence (5/12-6.3): Class A misde-
  meanor
Compelling Confession or Information by Force or Threat (5/12-7): Class 4 fel-
  ony
Hate Crime (5/12-7.1):
  — First offense: Class 4 felony
  — Subsequent offense: Class 2 felony
Educational Intimidation (5/12-7.2):
  — First offense: Class C misdemeanor
  — Subsequent offense: Class A misdemeanor
Stalking (5/12-7.3):
  — First offense: Class 4 felony
  — Subsequent offense: Class 3 felony
Aggravated Stalking (5/12-7.4):
  — First offense: Class 3 felony
  — Subsequent offense: Class 2 felony
Threatening Public Officials (5/12-9): Class 4 felony
Tattooing Body of a Minor (5/12-10): Class C misdemeanor
Home Invasion (5/12-11): Class X felony
Vehicular Invasion (5/12-11.1): Class 1 felony
Criminal Sexual Assault (5/12-13):
  — First offense: Class 1 felony
  — Subsequent offense or prior conviction of any offense involving crimi-
    nal sexual assault that is substantially equivalent or more serious: Class
    X felony
Aggravated Criminal Sexual Assault (5/12-14): Class X felony
Predatory Criminal Sexual Assault of a Child (5/12-14.1): Class X felony
Criminal Sexual Abuse (5/12-15):
  — First offense: Class A misdemeanor
  — Subsequent offense or prior conviction of any offense involving sexual
    abuse or sexual assault that is substantially equivalent or more serious:
    Class 2 felony
Aggravated Criminal Sexual Abuse (5/12-16): Class 2 felony

Criminal Transmission of HIV (5/12-16.2): Class 2 felony
Abuse and Gross Neglect of a Long Term Care Facility Resident (5/12-19):
— Abuse: Class 3 felony
— Gross neglect: Class 4 felony; and a business offense with a fine not exceeding $10,000 for owner or licensee of the facility
— Neglect: Petty offense for owner or licensee of the facility
Sale of Body Parts (5/12-20):
— First offense: Class A misdemeanor
— Subsequent offense: Class 4 felony
Criminal Neglect of an Elderly or Disabled Person (5/12-21): Class 3 felony
Child Abandonment (5/12-21.5):
— First offense: Class 4 felony
— Subsequent offense: Class 3 felony
Endangering the Life or Health of a Child (5/12-21.6):
— First offense: Class A misdemeanor
— Subsequent offense: Class 3 felony
Violation of an Order of Protection (5/12-30):
— First offense: Class A misdemeanor
— Subsequent offense or prior conviction for domestic battery: Class 4 felony
Inducement to Commit Suicide (5/12-31):
— When person commits suicide as a direct result of the coercion: Class 2 felony
— When person commits suicide as a direct result of the assistance: Class 4 felony
— When person attempts to commit suicide as a direct result of the coercion: Class 3 felony
— When a person attempts to commit suicide as a direct result of the assistance: Class A misdemeanor
Ritual Mutilation (5/12-32): Class 2 felony
Ritualized Abuse of a Child (5/12-33):
— First offense: Class 1 felony
— Subsequent offense: Class X felony
Female Genital Mutilation (5/12-34): Class X felony

Eavesdropping

Eavesdropping (5/14-4):
— First offense: Class 4 felony
— Subsequent offense: Class 3 felony

Theft and Related Offenses

Theft (5/16-1):

— Of property, other than a firearm, not from the person and not exceeding $300 in value:
  — First offense: Class A misdemeanor
  — Prior conviction of any type theft, robbery, armed robbery, burglary, residential burglary, possession of burglary tools or home invasion: Class 4 felony
— Of a firearm not from the person regardless of value:
  — First offense: Class 4 felony
  — Subsequent offense: Class 3 felony
— Of property from the person not exceeding $300: Class 3 felony
  — Of property with value:
  — Exceeding $300, but not exceeding $10,000: Class 3 felony
  — Exceeding $10,000, but not exceeding $100,000: Class 2 felony
  — Exceeding $100,000: Class 1 felony
  — By deception, of property valued at $5,000 or more from a senior citizen: Class 2 felony

Financial Exploitation of an Elderly or Disabled Person (5/16-1.3):
  — Property not exceeding $300 in value: Class 4 felony
  — Property exceeding $300, but not exceeding $5,000 in value: Class 3 felony
  — Property exceeding $5,000, but not exceeding $100,000 in value: Class 2 felony
  — Property valued as exceeding $100,000 in value: Class 1 felony

Theft of Lost or Mislaid Property (5/16-2): Petty offense

Theft of Labor or Services or Use of Property (5/16-3):
  — Generally: Class A misdemeanor
  — Failing to return rented or leased property exceeding $500 in value when due: Class 4 felony

False Report of Theft and Other Losses (5/16-3.1):
  — First offense: Class A misdemeanor
  — Subsequent offense: Class 4 felony

Theft from Coin-Operated Machines (5/16-5):
  — First offense: Class A misdemeanor
  — Prior conviction of any type of theft, robbery, armed robbery, burglary, residential burglary, possession of burglary tools or home invasion: Class 4 felony

Possession of Key or Device Designed to Open Coin-Operated Machines (5/16-6):
  — Generally: Class A misdemeanor
  — Causing damage or loss of more than $300: Class 4 felony

Unlawful Use of Recorded Sounds or Images (5/16-7): Class 4 felony; with possible fines up to $250,000 (depending on circumstances)

Unlawful Use of Unidentified Sound or Audio Visual Recordings (5/16-8): Class 4 felony; with possible fines up to $250,000 (depending on circumstances)

Theft of Cable Television Services (5/16-10):
— Generally: Class A misdemeanor
— Offense committed for remuneration: Class 4 felony

Unauthorized Use of Television Interception or Decoding Device (5/16-11): Class A misdemeanor

Contributing to Unauthorized Use of Television Interception or Decoding Device (5/16-12): Class 4 felony

Unlawful Interference with Public Utility Services (5/16-14):
— First Offense: Class A misdemeanor
— Subsequent offense, or for remuneration: Class 4 felony

Unlawful Use of Theft Detection Shielding Device (5/16-15):
— First offense: Class A misdemeanor
— Subsequent offense: Class 4 felony

Retail Theft (5/16A-10):
— Of property not exceeding $150 in value:
— First offense: Class A misdemeanor
— Prior conviction of any type of theft, robbery, armed robbery, burglary, residential burglary, possession of burglary tools or home invasion: Class 4 felony
— Of property exceeding $150 in value: Class 3 felony

Library Theft (5/16B-5):
— Of property not exceeding $300 in value: Class A misdemeanor
— Of property exceeding $300 in value: Class 3 felony

Unlawful Sale of Household Appliances (5/16C-2):
— Not exceeding $1,000 in value: Class B misdemeanor
— Exceeding $1,000 in value: Class 4 felony

Computer Tampering (5/16D-3):
— Gaining access: Class B misdemeanor
— Obtaining data or services:
— First offense: Class A misdemeanor
— Subsequent offense: Class 4 felony
— Destroying or altering data:
— First offense: Class 4 felony
— Subsequent offense: Class 3 felony

Aggravated Computer Tampering (5/16D-4):
— Disrupting a government entity or public utility: Class 3 felony
— Creating a strong probability of death or great bodily harm: Class 2 felony

Computer Fraud (5/16D-5):

— Gaining access: Class 4 felony
— Destroying or altering data: Class 3 felony
— Obtaining access to money, property, or services:
　　— Not exceeding $1,000 in value: Class 4 felony
　　— Exceeding $1,000, but less than $50,000 in value: Class 3 felony
　　— Worth $50,000 or more: Class 2 felony
Delivery Container Theft (5/16E-4):
— First offense: Class B misdemeanor, with a possible fine of $150
— Subsequent offense: Class B misdemeanor, with a possible fine of $500
Theft of Wireless Service (5/16F-3):
—First offense:
　　— Value of services obtained less than $300: Class A misdemeanor
　　— Value of services obtained greater than $300: Class 4 felony
— Subsequent offense: Class 2 felony
Facilitating Theft of Wireless Service by Manufacture, Distribution, or Posses-
sion of Devices for Theft of Wireless Services (5/16F-4):
— First offense:
　　— Value of services obtained less than $300: Class A misdemeanor
　　— Value of services obtained greater than $300: Class 4 felony
— Subsequent offense: Class 2 felony
Deceptive Practices (5/17-1):
— Generally: Class 4 felony or Class A misdemeanor (depending on cir-
　cumstances)
— On a bank or other financial institution:
　　— False statements: Class A misdemeanor
　　— Possession of stolen or fraudulently obtained checks: Class A mis-
　　　demeanor or Class 4 felony (depending on circumstances)
　　— Possession of identification card: Class A misdemeanor or Class 4
　　　felony (depending on circumstances)
Impersonating Veteran, Member of Police, Fraternal or Veteran's Organization
　or Representative of Charitable Organization (5/17-2): Class C misdemeanor,
　Class A misdemeanor or Class 4 felony (depending on circumstances)
Forgery (5/17-3): Class 3 felony
Deceptive Altering or Sale of Coins (5/17-4): Class A misdemeanor
Deceptive Collection Practices (5/17-5): Business offense punishable by a fine
　not exceeding $3,000
State Benefits Fraud (5/17-6):
— Money or benefits not exceeding $300 in value: Class 4 felony
— Money or benefits exceeding $300 in value: Class 3 felony
Promotion of Pyramid Sales Scheme (5/17-7): Class A misdemeanor
Health Care Benefits Fraud (5/17-8): Class A misdemeanor
Public Aid Wire Fraud (5/17-9): Class 4 felony

Public Aid Mail Fraud (5/17-10): Class 4 felony
Odometer Fraud (5/17-11):
— First offense: Class A misdemeanor
— Subsequent offense: Class 4 felony
Hour Meter Fraud (5/17-11.1):
— First offense: Class A misdemeanor
— Subsequent offense: Class 4 felony
Fraudulent Advertisement of Corporate Name (5/17-12): Petty offense
Fraudulent Land Sales (5/17-13): Class 3 felony
Party to Fraudulent Land Conveyance (5/17-14): Business offense with a fine not to exceed $1,000.
Acknowledgment of Fraudulent Conveyance (5/17-15): Class 4 felony
Fraudulent Production of Infant (5/17-16): Class 3 felony
Fraudulent Issuance of Stock (5/17-17): Class 3 felony
Officer Signing Fraudulent Stock (5/17-18): Class 3 felony
Use of Name Pawners' Society (5/17-19): Petty offense
Obstructing Gas, Water, and Electric Current Meters (5/17-20): Class B misdemeanor
Obstructing Service Meters (5/17-21): Class B misdemeanor
False Information on Employment Applications (5/17-22): Class A misdemeanor
Disqualification for State Benefits (5/17A-3):
— Less than $150:
— First offense: Class A misdemeanor
— Subsequent offense: Class 4 felony
— Worth $150 or more but less than $1,000:
— First offense: Class 4 felony
— Subsequent offense: Class 3 felony
— Worth $1,000 or more but less than $5,000:
— First offense: Class 3 felony
— Subsequent offense: Class 2 felony
— Worth $5,000 or more but less than $10,000:
— First offense: Class 2 felony
— Subsequent offense: Class 1 felony
— Worth $10,000 or more: Class 1 felony
WIC Fraud (5/17B-20): Class 1, 2, 3, or 4 felony, or Class A misdemeanor (depending on circumstances)

Robbery

Robbery (5/18-1): Class 2 felony
— Victim is 60 years of age or older, or is physically handicapped: Class 1 felony

Armed Robbery (5/18-2): Class X felony
Vehicular Hijacking (5/18-3): Class 1 felony
Aggravated Vehicular Hijacking (5/18-4):
  — Victim is 60 years of age or older, or is physically handicapped: Class X
    felony
  — Victim is under 16 years of age and a passenger in the motor vehicle at
    the time of the offense: Class X felony
  — Carries on or about, or is otherwise armed with a dangerous weapon:
    Class X felony for which a term of imprisonment of not less than 7
    years shall be imposed
Aggravated Robbery (5/18-5): Class 1 felony

Burglary

Burglary (5/19-1): Class 2 felony
Possession of Burglary Tools (5/19-2): Class 4 felony
Residential Burglary (5/19-3): Class 1 felony
Criminal Trespass to Residence (5/19-4): Class A misdemeanor
Criminal Fortification of a Residence or Building (5/19-5): Class 3 felony

Arson

Arson (5/20-1): Class 2 felony
Aggravated Arson (5/20-1.1): Class X felony
Residential Arson (5/20-1.2): Class 1 felony
Possession of Explosives or Explosive or Incendiary Devices (5/20-2): Class 2
  felony
Causing a Catastrophe (5/20.5-5): Class X felony

Damage and Trespass to Property

Criminal Damage to Property (5/21-1):
  — Generally:
      — Damage not exceeding $300: Class A misdemeanor
      — Damage exceeding $300, but not exceeding $10,000: Class 4 fel-
        ony
      — Damage exceeding $10,000, but not exceeding $100,000: Class 3
        felony
      — Damage exceeding $100,000: Class 2 felony, plus a fine equal to
        the value of the damages
  — Knowingly discharging a firearm at any portion of a railroad train: Class
    4 felony
Criminal Damage of Fire Fighting Apparatus, Hydrants or Equipment (5/21-
  1.1): Class B misdemeanor
Institutional Vandalism (5/21-1.2):

— Damage not exceeding $300: Class 3 felony

— Damage exceeding $300: Class 2 felony

Criminal Defacement of Property (5/21-1.3):

— First offense: Damage not exceeding $300: Class A misdemeanor

— Subsequent offense or damage exceeding $300: Class 4 felony

— Damage exceeding $300 and property is a school building: Class 3 felony

— Persons convicted of criminal defacement of property shall perform not less than 30 and not more than 120 hours of community service, if available in the jurisdiction

Jackrocks (5/21-1.4): Class A misdemeanor

Criminal Trespass to Vehicles (5/21-2): Class A misdemeanor

Criminal Trespass to Real Property (5/21-3): Class B misdemeanor

Criminal Damage to Government Supported Property (5/21-4):

— Damage not exceeding $500: Class 4 felony

— Damage exceeding $500, but not exceeding $10,000: Class 3 felony

— Damage exceeding $10,000, but not exceeding $100,000: Class 2 felony, plus a fine equal to the amount of damage

— Damage exceeding $100,000: Class 1 felony, plus a fine equal to the amount of damage

Criminal Trespass to State Supported Land (5/21-5): Class A misdemeanor

Unauthorized Possession or Storage of Weapons (5/21-6): Class A misdemeanor

Criminal Trespass to Restricted Areas and Restricted Landing Areas at Airports (5/21-7): Class A misdemeanor

Residential Picketing (5/21.1-3): Class B misdemeanor

Interference with a Public Institution of Higher Education (5/21.2-4):

— First offense: Class C misdemeanor

— Subsequent offense: Class B misdemeanor

Solicitation on School Property (5/21.3-5): Class C misdemeanor

Offenses Affecting Public Health, Safety, and Decency

Unlawful Use of Weapons (5/24-1): Class 2, 3, 4, or X felony or Class A misdemeanor (depending on circumstances)

Unlawful Use or Possession of Weapons by Felons or Persons in the Custody of the Department of Corrections Facilities (5/24-1.1):

— While not confined in a penal institution: Class 3 felony

— While confined in a penal institution:

— Generally: Class 1 felony

— Possession of a firearm, firearm ammunition or explosive: Class X felony

Aggravated Discharge of a Firearm (5/24-1.2):

— At a person, or a vehicle or building known to be occupied: Class 1 felony

— At a peace officer, community policing volunteer, correctional institution employee, firefighter, medical assistant, or other such officers engaged in official duties, or at a vehicle known to be occupied by such officers engaged in official duties: Class X felony

Reckless Discharge of Firearm (5/24-1.5): Class 4 felony

Unlawful Use of Armor Piercing Bullets (5/24-2.1): Class 3 felony

Manufacture, Sale or Transfer of Bullets Represented to be Armor Piercing Bullets (5/24-2.2): Class 4 felony

Unlawful Sale of Firearms (5/24-3):

— Generally: Class 4 felony

— Sell or give any firearm of a size which may be concealed upon the person to any person under 18 years of age: Class 2 or 3 felony (depending on circumstances)

— Sell or give any firearm to any person under 18 years of age who does not possess a valid FOID card: Class 2 or 3 felony (depending on circumstances)

Unlawful Possession of Firearms and Firearm Ammunition (5/24-3.1):

— Generally: Class A misdemeanor

— Possession of handguns: Class 4 felony

Unlawful Discharge of Armor Piercing Bullets (5/24-3.2):

— That strikes a person: Class X felony

— Concealment of firearm and armor piercing bullet: Class 2 felony

Unlawful Sale or Delivery of Firearms on the Premises of any School (5/24-3.3): Class 3 felony

Unlawful Sale of Firearms by Liquor Licensee (5/24-3.4): Class 4 felony

Gunrunning (5/24-3A): Class 1 felony

Register of Sales by Dealer (5/24-4): Class B misdemeanor

Defacing Identification Marks of Firearms (5/24-5): Class 2 felony

Mob Action (5/25-1):

— Infliction of injury to person or property: Class 4 felony

— Use of force or violence by 2 or more persons acting together to disturb the public peace: Class 4 felony

— Assembly of 2 or more persons for the purpose of committing an unlawful act: Class C misdemeanor

— Failure to disperse: Class A misdemeanor

Unlawful Contact with Streetgang Members (5/25-1.1): Class A misdemeanor

Disorderly Conduct (5/26-1): Class 4 felony, Class A, B, or C misdemeanor, or business offense with a fine not to exceed $3,000 (depending on circumstances)

Interference with Emergency Communication (5/26-2):

— Generally: Class B misdemeanor

— Serious bodily injury or property loss in excess of $1,000: Class A misdemeanor

Use of a Facsimile Machine in Unsolicited Advertising or Fund-Raising (5/26-3): Petty offense with a fine not to exceed $500

Unauthorized Videotaping (5/26-4): Class A misdemeanor

Gambling (5/28-1):

— First offense: Class A misdemeanor

— Subsequent offense: Class 4 felony or Class A misdemeanor (depending on circumstances)

Syndicated Gambling (5/28-1.1): Class 3 felony

Keeping a Gambling Place (5/28-3):

— First offense: Class A misdemeanor

— Subsequent offense: Class 4 felony

Registration of Federal Gambling Stamps (5/28-4):

— First offense: Class B misdemeanor

— Subsequent offense: Class A misdemeanor

Offering a Bribe in a Contest (5/29-1): Class 4 felony or Class A misdemeanor (depending on circumstances)

Accepting a Bribe in a Contest (5/29-2): Class 4 felony

Failure to Report Offer of a Bribe in a Contest (5/29-3): Class A misdemeanor

Commercial Bribery (5/29A-3): Business offense with a fine not to exceed $5,000

Money Laundering (5/29B-1):

— Not exceeding $10,000 in value: Class 3 felony

— Exceeding $10,000, but not exceeding $100,000 in value: Class 2 felony

— Exceeding $100,000 in value: Class 1 felony

Solicitation of Material Support or Resources in Support of International Terrorism (5/29C-10): Class 1 felony

Providing Material Support or Resources for International Terrorism (5/29C-15): Class 1 felony

Offenses Affecting Governmental Functions

Treason (5/30-1): Class X felony

Misprision of Treason (5/30-2): Class 4 felony

Advocating Overthrow of Government (5/30-3): Class 3 felony

Resisting or Obstructing a Peace Officer or Correctional Institution Employee (5/31-1): Class A misdemeanor

Disarming a Peace Officer (5/31-1a): Class 2 felony

Obstructing Service of Process (5/31-3): Class B misdemeanor

Obstructing Justice (5/31-4):

— Generally: Class 4 felony

— In furtherance of gang-related activity: Class 3 felony

Concealing or Aiding a Fugitive (5/31-5): Class 4 felony

Escape (5/31-6):

    — Escape from a penal institution:

        –– If convicted or charged with a felony: Class 2 felony

        — If convicted or charged with a misdemeanor: Class A misdemeanor

    — Failure to report to a penal institution or for periodic imprisonment:

        — If convicted or charged with a felony: Class 3 felony

        — If convicted or charged with a misdemeanor: Class B misdemeanor

    — Escapes from the custody of a peace officer:

        — If allegedly commits a felony: Class 2 felony

        — If allegedly commits a misdemeanor: Class A misdemeanor

Aiding Escape (5/31-7): Class 2 or 3 felony, or Class A or B misdemeanor (depending on circumstances)

Refusing to Aid an Officer (5/31-8): Petty offense

Bringing or Possessing Contraband in a Penal Institution (5/31A-1.1): Class X, 1, 2, 3, or 4 felony (depending on circumstances)

Unauthorized Bringing, Possessing, or Delivering Contraband in a Penal Institution by an Employee (5/31A-1.2): Class X, 1, 2, 3, or 4 felony (depending on circumstances)

Compounding a crime (5/32-1): Petty offense

Perjury (5/32-2): Class 3 felony

Subornation of Perjury (5/32-3): Class 4 felony

Communicating with Jurors and Witnesses (5/32-4):

    — Jurors: Class 4 felony

    — Witnesses: Class 3 felony

Harassment of Jurors, Witnesses, or Representatives for the Child (5/32-4a): Class 2 felony or Class A misdemeanor (depending on circumstances)

Bribes to Excuse Persons from Jury Duty (5/32-4b): Class 3 felony

Witnesses Accepting Payment Before Judgment or Verdict (5/32-4c): Class B misdemeanor with possible fine not to exceed three times the amount of compensation

False Personation of Attorney, Judicial or Governmental Officials (5/32-5): Class B misdemeanor

False Personation of a Peace Officer (5/32-5.1): Class 4 felony

Aggravated False Personation of a Peace Officer (5/32-5.2): Class 3 felony

False Personation of a Parent or Legal Guardian (5/32-5.3): Class A misdemeanor

Performance of Unauthorized Acts (5/32-6): Class 4 felony

Simulating Legal Process (5/32-7): Class B misdemeanor

Tampering with Public Records (5/32-8): Class 4 felony

Tampering with Public Notice (5/32-9): Petty offense

Violation of Bail Bond (5/32-10): Offense of the next lower class than the underlying offense for which the defendant has been released on bail

Bribery (5/33-1): Class 2 felony

Failure to Report a Bribe (5/33-2): Class A misdemeanor

Official Misconduct (5/33-3): Class 3 felony

Gang-Related Activity by a Peace Officer or Correctional Officer (5/33-4): Class 3 felony

Certain Aggravated Offenses

Armed Violence (5/33A-3): Class X, 1, or 2 felony (depending on circumstances)

Deception Relating to Certification of Disadvantaged Business Enterprises (5/33C-1 to 5/33C-4):
- — Fraudulently obtaining or retaining certification: Class 2 felony
- — Willfully making a false statement: Class 2 felony
- — Willfully obstructing or impeding an official or employee of any agency in his investigation: Class 2 felony
- — Fraudulently obtaining public moneys reserved for disadvantaged business enterprises: Class 2 felony

Contributing to the Criminal Delinquency of a Juvenile (5/33D-1): Offense of the next higher class than the underlying offense, or Class X felony if offense committed is Class X felony

Bid-Rigging (5/33E-3): Class 3 felony

Bid-Rotating (5/33E-4): Class 2 felony

Acquisition or Disclosure of Bidding Information by a Public Official (5/33E-5):
- — Knowingly and illegally opens a sealed bid: Class 4 felony
- — Knowingly discloses information contained in the sealed bids: Class 3 felony

Interference with Contract Submission and Award by a Public Official (5/33E-6):
- — Conveys specifications outside of official public bid invitations: Class 4 felony
- — Recipient's failure to inform law enforcement of the communication: Class A misdemeanor
- — Knowingly and illegally informs bidder of acceptance only if specified individuals are included as subcontractors: Class 3 felony
- — Awarding a contract based on criteria not publicly announced, when required: Class 3 felony

Kickbacks (5/33E-7):
- — Provides, solicits, or attempts to provide a kickback for a public contract: Class 3 felony

— Recipient's failure to inform law enforcement of the kickback, solicitation, or attempt: Class 4 felony

Bribery of Inspector Employed by Contractor (5/33E-8):
— Offering a bribe to an inspector: Class 4 felony
— Accepting a bribe: Class 3 felony
— Inspector's failure to inform law enforcement of the bribe: Class 4 felony

Change Orders in a Public Contract (5/33E-9): Class 4 felony

False Statement Material to Certification (5/33E-11): Class 3 felony

Unlawful Use of Body Armor (5/33F-3):
— First offense: Class A misdemeanor
— Subsequent offense: Class 4 felony

Added Articles

Maintaining Public Nuisance (5/37-1):
— First offense: Class A misdemeanor
— Subsequent offense: Class 4 felony

Criminal Usury (5/39-2): Class 4 felony

Looting (5/42-2): Class 4 felony, plus at least 100 hours of community service

Unlawful Transfer of Telecommunications Device to a Minor (5/44-2): Class A misdemeanor

Disclosure of Location of Domestic Violence Victim (5/45-2): Class A misdemeanor

Insurance Fraud (5/46-1):
— Not exceeding $300 in value: Class A misdemeanor
— Exceeding $300, but not exceeding $10,000 in value: Class 3 felony
— Exceeding $10,000, but not exceeding $100,000 in value: Class 2 felony
— Exceeding $100,000 in value: Class 1 felony

Fraud on a Governmental Entity (5/46-1.1):
— Not exceeding $300 in value: Class A misdemeanor
— Exceeding $300, but not exceeding $10,000 in value: Class 3 felony
— Exceeding $10,000, but not exceeding $100,000 in value: Class 2 felony
— Exceeding $100,000 in value: Class 1 felony

Aggravated Insurance Fraud (5/46-2): Class 1 felony

Insurance Fraud Conspiracy (5/46-3): Class 2 felony

Aggravated Insurance Fraud Conspiracy (5/46-3): Class 1 felony

Organizer of an Aggravated Insurance Fraud Conspiracy (5/46-4): Class X felony

Legislative Misconduct (645/2): Class 3 felony

CANNABIS CONTROL ACT

Possession of Cannabis (550/4):

— Not exceeding 2.5 grams: Class C misdemeanor
— Exceeding 2.5 grams, but not exceeding 10 grams: Class B misdemeanor
— Exceeding 10 grams, but not exceeding 30 grams:
     — First offense: Class A misdemeanor
     — Subsequent offense: Class 4 felony
— Exceeding 30 grams, but not exceeding 500 grams:
     — First offense: Class 4 felony
     — Subsequent offense: Class 3 felony
— Exceeding 500 grams, but not exceeding 2,000 grams: Class 3 felony
— Exceeding 2,000 grams, but not exceeding 5,000 grams: Class 2 felony
— Exceeding 5,000 grams: Class 1 felony

Manufacture, Delivery, or Possession with Intent to Deliver Cannabis (550/5):
— Not exceeding 2.5 grams: Class B misdemeanor
— Exceeding 2.5 grams, but not exceeding 10 grams: Class A misdemeanor
— Exceeding 10 grams, but not exceeding 30 grams: Class 4 felony
— Exceeding 30 grams, but not exceeding 500 grams: Class 3 felony, with a fine not to exceed $50,000
— Exceeding 500 grams, but not exceeding 2,000 grams: Class 2 felony, with a fine not to exceed $100,000
— Exceeding 2,000 grams, but not exceeding 5,000 grams: Class 1 felony, with a fine not to exceed $150,000
— Exceeding 5,000 grams: Class X felony, with a fine not to exceed $200,000

Cannabis Trafficking (550/5.1): Not less than twice the sanction for manufacture and delivery

Delivery of Cannabis on School Grounds (550/5.2):
— Not exceeding 2.5 grams: Class A misdemeanor
— Exceeding 2.5 grams, but not exceeding 10 grams: Class 4 felony, with a fine not to exceed $25,000
— Exceeding 10 grams, but not exceeding 30 grams: Class 3 felony, with a fine not to exceed $50,000
— Exceeding 30 grams, but not exceeding 500 grams: Class 2 felony, with a fine not to exceed $100,000
— Exceeding 500 grams: Class 1 felony, with a fine not to exceed $200,000

Casual Delivery of Cannabis (550/6): Same penalties as possession (depending on amount)

Production or Possession of Cannabis Sativa Plant (550/8):
— Not exceeding 5 plants: Class A misdemeanor
— Exceeding 5 plants, but not exceeding 20 plants: Class 4 felony
— Exceeding 20 plants, but not exceeding 50 plants: Class 3 felony

— Exceeding 50 plants: Class 2 felony, with a fine not to exceed $100,000

Calculated Criminal Cannabis Conspiracy (550/9):

— First offense: Class 3 felony, with a fine not to exceed $200,000

— Subsequent offense: Class 1 felony

CONTROLLED SUBSTANCES ACT

Manufacture, Delivery, or Possession with Intent to Deliver a Controlled Substance (570/401): Class X, 1, 2, or 3 felony (depending on amount and type of controlled substance involved)

Controlled Substance Trafficking (570/401.1): No less than twice the sanction for manufacture and delivery

— Use of a cellular radio telecommunication device to further the trafficking: Class 2 felony, with a fine not to exceed $100,000

Chemical Breakdown of Illicit Controlled Substances (570/401.5): Class 4 felony

Possession of a Controlled Substance (570/402):

— Generally: Class 1 or 4 felony (depending on amount and type of controlled substance involved)

— Possession of anabolic steroid: Class B or C misdemeanor (depending on circumstances)

Manufacture, Delivery or Possession with Intent to Deliver a Look-Alike Substance (570/404):

— Manufacture or delivery: Class 3 felony, with a fine not to exceed $150,000

— Possession:

— First offense: petty offense

— Subsequent offense: Class C misdemeanor

Calculated Criminal Drug Conspiracy (570/405): Class X felony, with a fine not to exceed $500,000

Criminal Drug Conspiracy (570/405.1): Fine or imprisonment not to exceed maximum for the offense which is object of conspiracy

Street Gang Criminal Drug Conspiracy (570/405.2): Class X felony

Permitting Unlawful Use of a Building (570/406.1): Class 4 felony

Delivery of Controlled, Counterfeit or Look-Alike Substances to Persons Under the Age of 18 at Truck Stops or Rest Areas, or on School or Surrounding Property (570/407): Class X, 1, 2, or 3 (depending on amount and type of controlled substance involved)

DRUG PARAPHERNALIA CONTROL ACT

Sale or Delivery of Drug Paraphernalia (600/3):

— Generally: Class 4 felony, with a minimum fine of $1,000

— To a person under 18 years of age: Class 3 felony
— To a woman known to be pregnant: Class 2 felony

TABLE OF CASES

A

B

C

D

F

G

J

K

TABLE OF CASES

T

U

V

W

TABLE OF STATUTES

United States Constitution

U.S. Const. art. III, § 2 — § 1.05, nn. 125, 127
U.S. Const. art. XIII, § 1 — § 1.10, n. 171
U.S. Const. amend. I — § 1.03, n. 59; § 8.52, n. 625; § 9.42, n. 438; § 9.44, n. 450; § 14.04; § 15.24; § 15.34
U.S. Const. amend. IV — § 10.02, n. 7; § 10.03, n. 11; § 10.04; § 10.05; § 10.06, n. 60; § 14.06, n. 77; § 14.22, n. 221; § 19.48, n. 465
U.S. Const. amend. V — § 1.19, nn. 265, 278; § 5.14, n. 197; § 7.30, n. 274; § 8.21, n. 268; § 8.30, n. 384; § 14.04; § 14.10, n. 101; § 19.60, n. 640
U.S. Const. amend. VI — § 8.26, n. 350
U.S. Const. amend. VII — § 18.13, n. 222
U.S. Const. amend. VIII — § 1.03, n. 61; § 2.05, n. 34; § 6.14, n. 202
U.S. Const. amend. XIV — § 2.05, n. 43; § 15.24; § 18.13, n. 222

United States Code

18 U.S.C. § 2385 (1999) — § 14.04, n. 38
18 U.S.C. § 2510 et seq. — § 10.01, n. 5
18 U.S.C. § 2510(5)(a)(ii) — § 10.06, nn. 40, 41
18 U.S.C. § 2511(1) — § 10.06, n. 34; § 10.07, n. 64
18 U.S.C. § 2511(2) — § 10.05, n. 30
18 U.S.C. § 2511(2)(a)(i) — § 10.06, n. 35
18 U.S.C. § 2511(2)(a)(ii) — § 10.06, n. 36
18 U.S.C. § 2511(2)(c) — § 10.06, nn. 37, 41
18 U.S.C. § 2511(2)(d) — § 10.06, n. 37
18 U.S.C. § 2511(2)(e) — § 10.06, n. 36
18 U.S.C. § 2511(2)(f) — § 10.06, n. 36
18 U.S.C. § 2515 — § 10.06, n. 60
18 U.S.C. § 2516 — § § 10.06, n. 43
18 U.S.C. § 2516(1) — § 10.06, n. 43
18 U.S.C. §§ 2516(1)(a)-(p) — § 10.06, n. 44
18 U.S.C. § 2516(2) — § 10.07, n. 63
18 U.S.C. §§ 2516-18 — § 10.06, n. 38
18 U.S.C. § 2518(1)(a) — § 10.06, n. 45
18 U.S.C. § 2518(2) — § 10.06, n. 53
18 U.S.C. § 2518(3) — § 10.06, n. 54
18 U.S.C. § 2518(4) — § 10.06, n. 55
18 U.S.C. § 2518(5) — § 10.06, n. 56
18 U.S.C. § 2518(6) — § 10.06, n. 57
18 U.S.C. § 2518(7) — § 10.05, n. 30
18 U.S.C. § 2518(8)(a) — § 10.06, n. 58
18 U.S.C. § 2518(8)(d) — § 10.06, n. 59
18 U.S.C. § 2518(10) — § 10.06, n. 60
18 U.S.C. § 2518(b)(i) — § 10.06, n. 46
18 U.S.C. § 2518(b)(ii) — § 10.06, n. 47

Illinois Constitution

Illinois Annotated Statutes

1149

Illinois Revised Statutes

Illinois Code

Illinois Public Acts

Illinois Popular Named Acts

Illinois Model Penal Code

Index

A

ABDUCTION. (*See* KIDNAPPING).

ABSOLUTE LIABILITY, §2.39.

ABUSE AND GROSS NEGLECT OF LONG TERM CARE FACILITY RESIDENT, §9.52.

ACCESSORY AFTER THE FACT, §3.02.

ACCESSORY BEFORE THE FACT, §3.02.

ACCOMPLICE LIABILITY. (*See* ACCOUNTABILITY FOR CRIMINALITY OF OTHERS).

ACCOUNTABILITY FOR CRIMINALITY OF OTHERS. (*See also* CONSPIRACY; SOLICITATION).
Accountability for conduct of corporation, §3.27.
Active assistance, §3.07.
Activities subsequent to crime, §3.16.
Actus reus, §§3.06 to 3.18.
Agreement to aid, §3.10.
Association.
   Affiliation with principal, §3.12.
   Group bent on criminality, §3.11.
Attempt to aid, §3.08.
Common law, §3.02.
Corporate criminality, §§3.25 to 3.27.
Crimes beyond initial common design, §3.21.
Current state of law, §3.03.
Elements of accomplice liability, §3.05.
Encouragement/solicitation, §3.09.
Exceptions, §3.24.
Guilt by association, §3.11.
Incidental crimes, §§3.18, 3.20.
Intent, §3.19.
Introduction, §3.01.
Legal duty to intervene, §3.15.
Mens rea, §§3.19 to 3.22.
Participation in/assent to criminality, §3.14.
Possession of/share of proceeds, §3.17.
Presence at crime scene, §3.13.
Reluctant participants, §3.22.
Statutory provisions, §3.04.
Withdrawal from crime, §3.23.

B

DECEPTION OFFENSES—Cont'd
Party to fraudulent land conveyance, §11.49.
Promotion of pyramid sales scheme, §11.45.
Public aid.
    Mail fraud, §11.46.
    Wire fraud, §11.46.
State benefits fraud, §11.44.
Use of name of pawner's society, §11.52.
WIC fraud, §11.55.

DECEPTION ON BANK OR OTHER FINANCIAL INSTITUTION, §11.39.

DECEPTIVE ALTERING OR SALE OF COINS, §11.42.

DECEPTIVE COLLECTION PRACTICES, §11.43.

DECEPTIVE PRACTICES, §11.39.

DEFACING IDENTIFICATION MARKS OF FIREARMS, §15.21.

DEFENSE OF ANOTHER, §§17.20, 17.21.

DEFENSE OF DWELLING.
Actual belief, §17.29.
Deadly force, §§17.27, 17.28.
Elements, §17.24.
Entry or attack upon dwelling, §17.25.
Force, §§17.23, 17.27, 17.28.
Generally, §17.22.
Provocation/aggressive, §17.31.
Reasonable belief, even if mistaken, §17.30.
Unlawful entry or attack, §17.26.

DEFENSE OF OTHER PROPERTY.
Actual and reasonable belief, §17.37.
Elements, §17.33.
Force, §17.32.
Generally, §17.22.
In lawful possession, §17.36.
Real/personal property threatened, §17.35.
Unlawful trespass/interference with property, §17.34.

DEFENSES.
Affirmative, §17.38.
Burglary, §13.10.
Commence prosecution of crimes arising out of same act simultaneously, §19.59.
Consent, §19.57.
Defense of.
    Another, §§17.20, 17.21.
    Dwelling, §§17.22 to 17.31. (*See* DEFENSE OF DWELLING).

E

EAVESDROPPING. (*See* ELECTRONIC EAVESDROPPING).

EDUCATIONAL INTIMIDATION, §9.43.

ELECTRONIC EAVESDROPPING.
Assumption-of-risk doctrine, §10.04.
Challenges to court authorization, §10.13.
Consensual eavesdropping, §§10.04, 10.10.
Elements, §10.09.
Emergency eavesdropping, §10.12.
Exclusionary rule, §10.14.
Federal.
   Constitutional/statutory considerations, §§10.02 to 10.06.
   State/sister state collusion, §10.16.
Generally, §10.07.
Historical background, §10.07.
Introduction, §10.01.
Permissible.
   Consensual eavesdropping, §10.10.
   Emergency eavesdropping, §10.12.
   Nonconsensual eavesdropping, §10.11.
Scope of eavesdropping, §10.15.
Statutory provisions, §10.08.

ENDANGERING LIFE OR HEALTH OF CHILD, §9.55.

ENTRAPMENT.
Acquittal of codefendant, §19.41.
Active inducement, §19.33.
Admission of commission of crime, §19.40.
Burden of proof, §19.44.
Elements, §19.32.
Government.
   Official/agent, §19.35.
   Purpose to create evidence, §19.36.
Historical background, §19.30.
Jury instructions, §19.43.
Nature of charge, §19.39.
Objective test, §19.30.
Otherwise innocent defendant, §19.34.
Prior convictions, §19.45.
Procedural requirements, §19.37.
Question for determination by jury, §19.42.
Raise at trial, §19.38.
Statutory provision, §19.31.

ESCAPE, §§14.12, 14.13.

KIDNAPPING-RELATED OFFENSES—Cont'd
Unlawful.
    Restraint, §§7.21 to 7.23.
    Sale of public conveyance travel ticket to minor, §7.29.
    Visitation interference, §7.26.

KNOWLEDGE, §§2.33 to 2.35.

L

LAW ENFORCEMENT JUSTIFICATIONS, §19.47.

LEGISLATIVE MISCONDUCT, §14.55.

LESSER INCLUDED OFFENSES.
Armed violence, §9.66.
Arson, §13.29.
Assault/aggravated assault, §9.11.
Attempt, and, §5.11.
Battery/aggravated battery, §9.23.
Burglary, §13.15.
Criminal damage to property, §13.35.
Evidentiary approach, §1.22.
Generally, §§1.19, 1.20.
Homicide, §6.35.
Inherent relationship approach, §1.24.
Kidnapping-related offenses, §7.30.
Pleadings/charging instrument approach, §1.23.
Restricting or obstructing peace officer, §14.07.
Robbery, §12.19.
Solicitation, and, §5.17.
Statutory definition/abstract elemental composition approach, §1.21.
Theft, §11.16.

LEVY-LOMBARDI RULE, §7.30.

LIBRARY THEFT, §11.33.

LIMITATION PERIODS, §19.58.

LOOK-ALIKE SUBSTANCES, §16.20.

LOOTING, §13.50.

M

MAINTENANCE, §14.39.

MALA IN SE, §1.09.

MALA PROBIBITA, §1.09.

MANSLAUGHTER, §§6.07 to 6.11, 6.23 to 6.29. (*See* HOMICIDE).

P